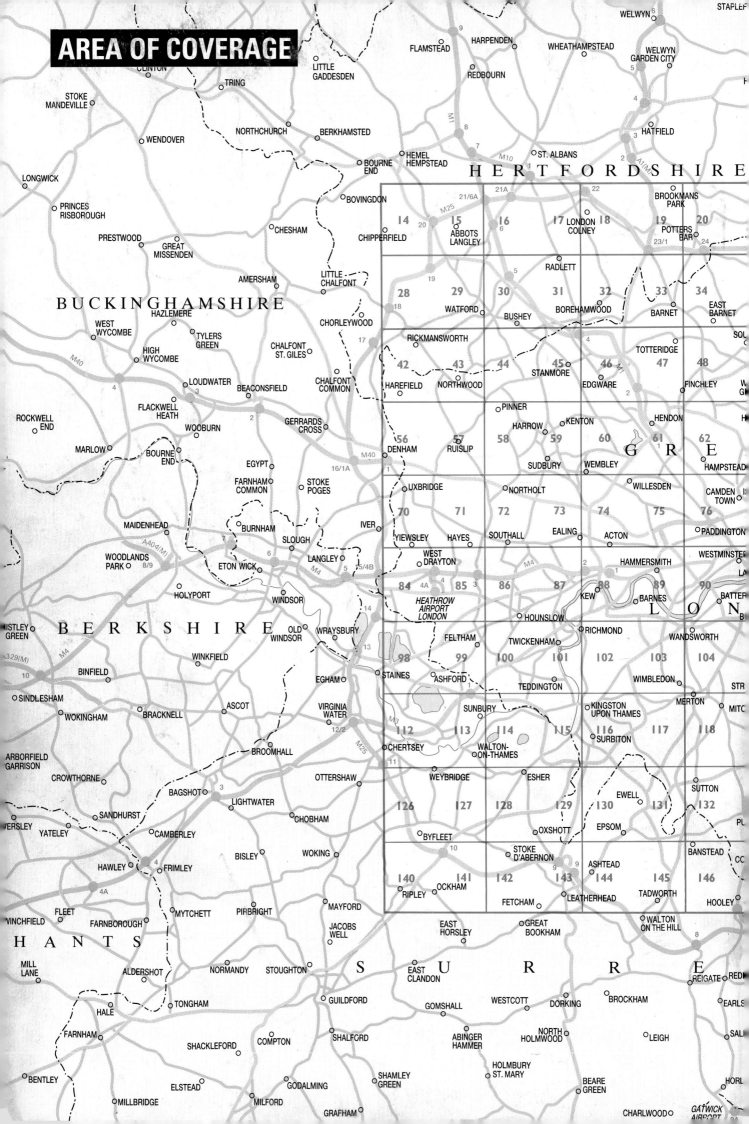

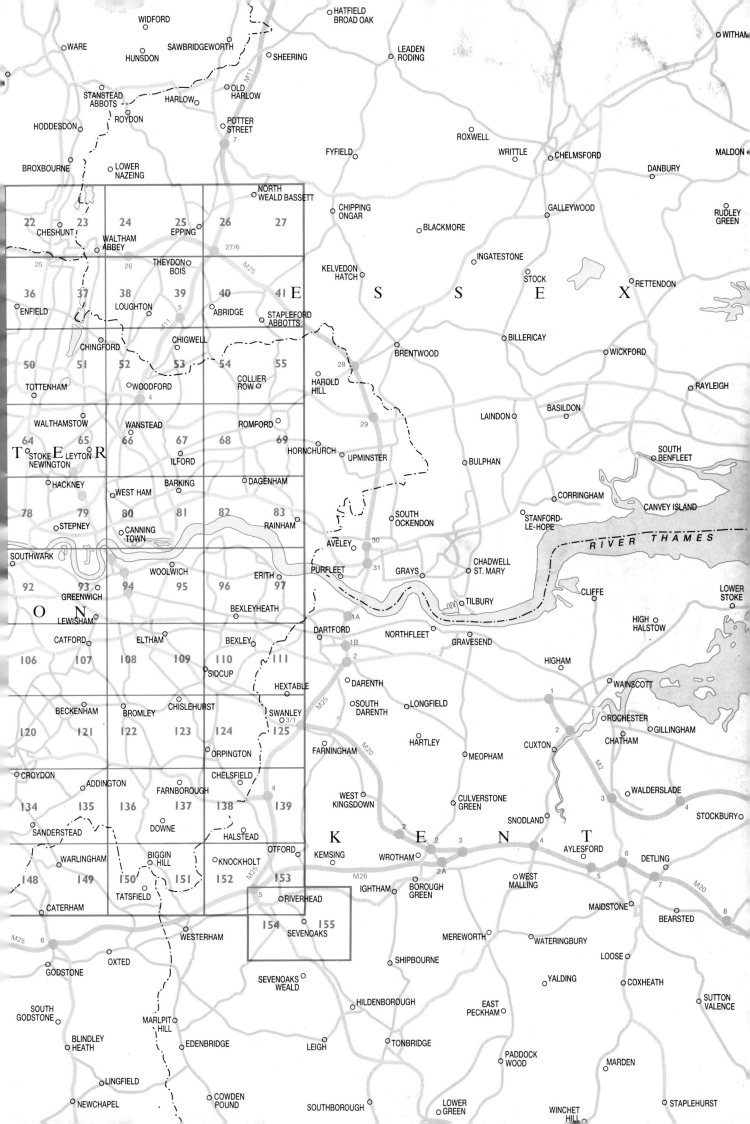

COLLINS
MASTER STREET ATLAS LONDON

CONTENTS

HarperCollins*Publishers*

Published by Collins
An imprint of HarperCollins*Publishers*
77-85 Fulham Palace Road, Hammersmith, London W6 8JB

Copyright © HarperCollins*Publishers* Ltd 1999
Mapping © Bartholomew Ltd 1995,1997,1998,1999

Mapping generated from Bartholomew digital databases

London Underground Map by permission of London Regional Transport
LRT Registered User No. 99/2818

The contents of this publication are believed correct at the time of printing. Nevertheless, the
publisher can accept no responsibility for errors or omissions, changes in the detail given, or
for any expense or loss thereby caused.

The representation of a road, track or footpath is no evidence of a right of way.

Printed in Italy

ISBN 0 00 448837 7 Paperback
     0 00 448838 5 Hardback   MM10142/MM10140   ANA

e-mail: roadcheck@harpercollins.co.uk   web site: www.bartholomewmaps.com

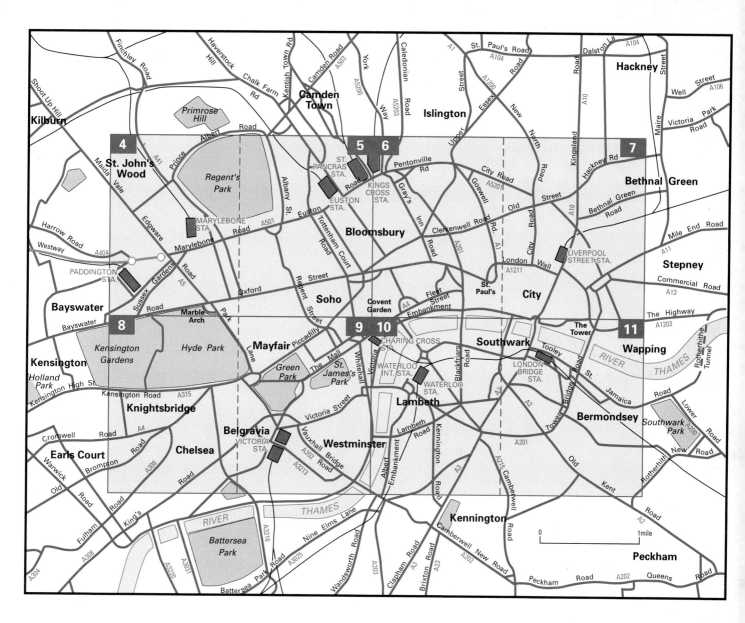

KEY TO MAP SYMBOLS

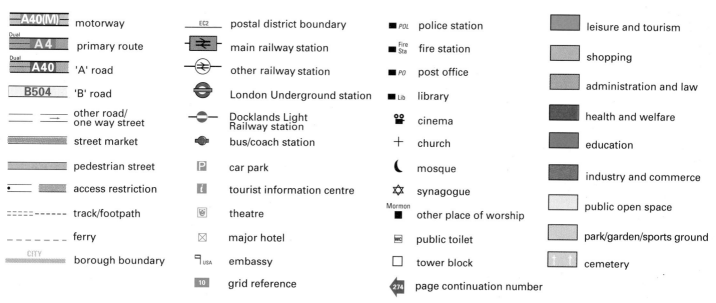

A40(M) motorway	EC2 postal district boundary	▪ POL police station	leisure and tourism
Dual **A 4** primary route	main railway station	▪ Fire Sta fire station	shopping
Dual **A40** 'A' road	other railway station	▪ PO post office	administration and law
B504 'B' road	London Underground station	▪ Lib library	health and welfare
other road/ one way street	Docklands Light Railway station	cinema	education
street market	bus/coach station	+ church	industry and commerce
pedestrian street	P car park	mosque	public open space
access restriction	i tourist information centre	synagogue	park/garden/sports ground
track/footpath	theatre	Mormon other place of worship	cemetery
ferry	major hotel	wc public toilet	
CITY borough boundary	USA embassy	tower block	
	10 grid reference	274 page continuation number	

Scale 1 : 10,000 (6.3 inches to 1 mile)

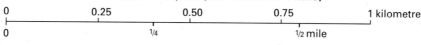

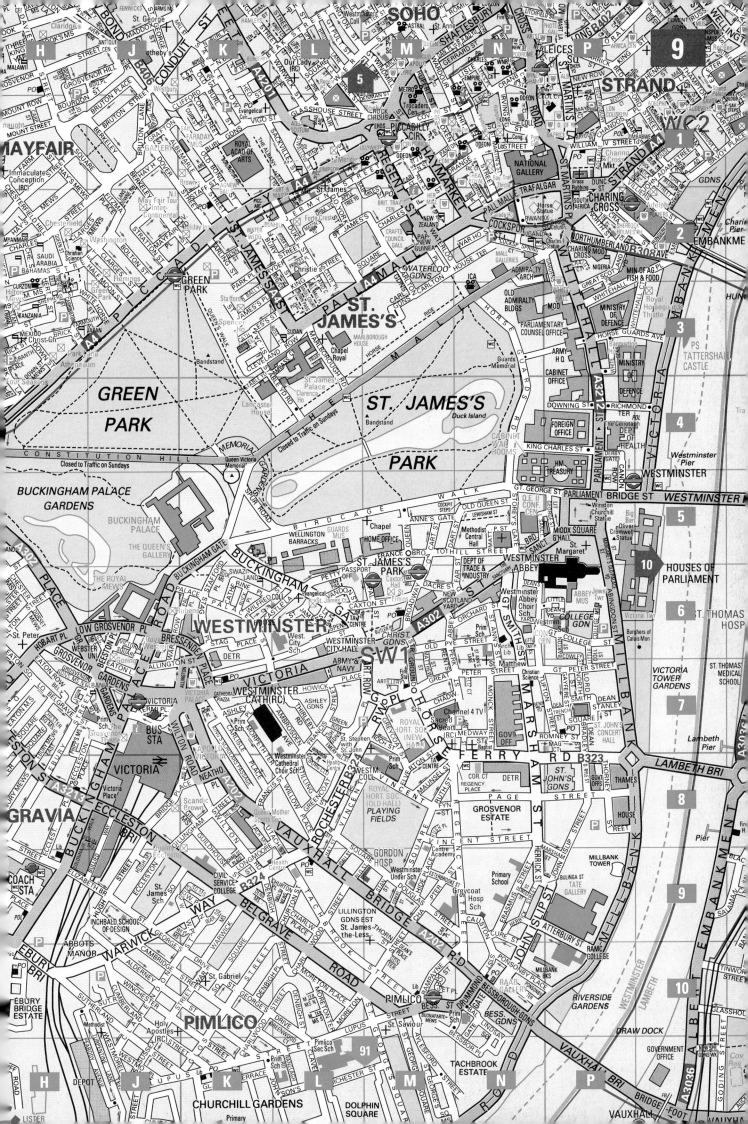

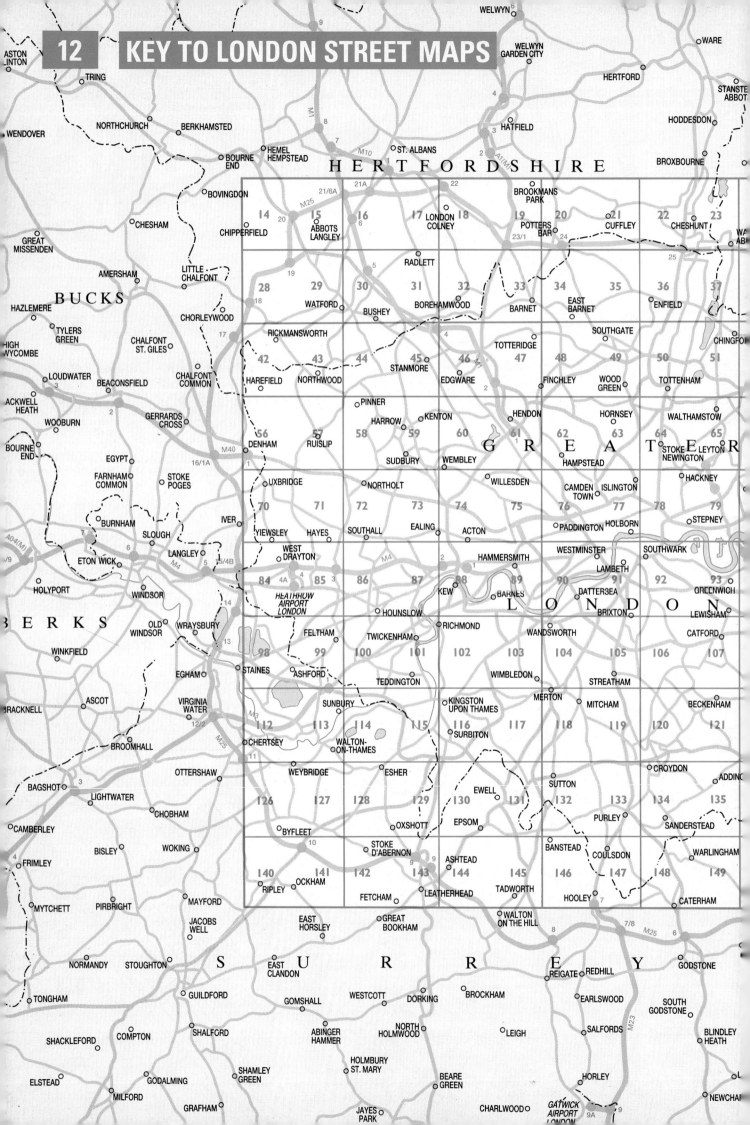

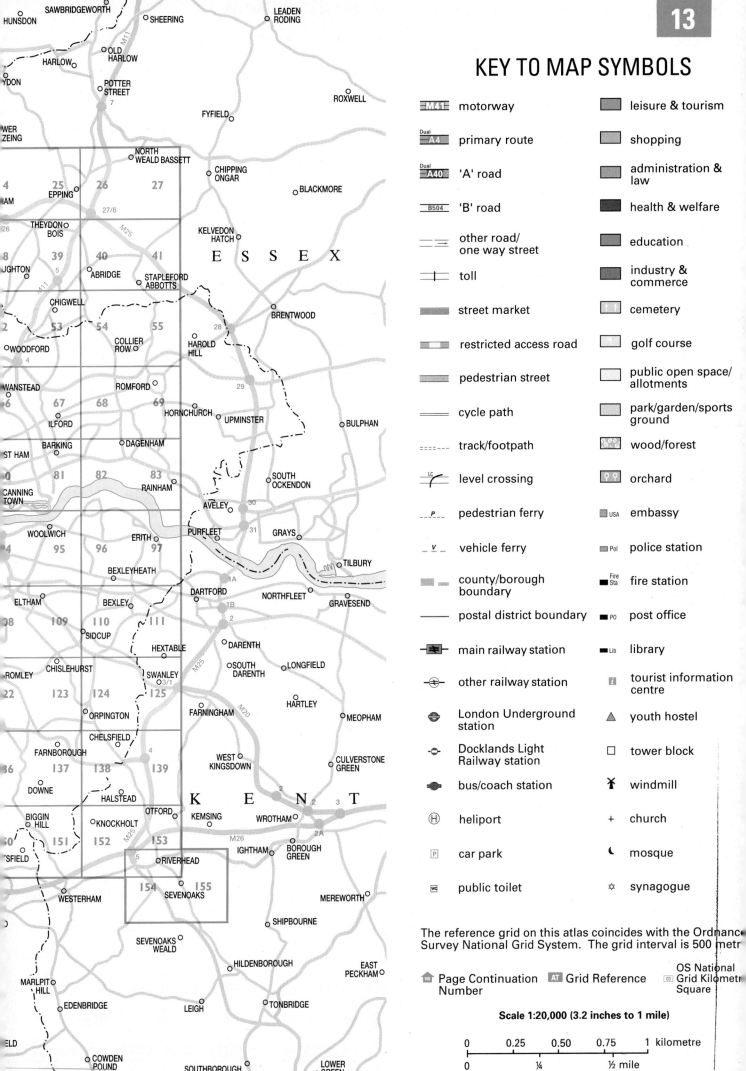

KEY TO MAP SYMBOLS

M41	motorway		leisure & tourism
Dual A4	primary route		shopping
Dual A40	'A' road		administration & law
B504	'B' road		health & welfare
	other road/ one way street		education
	toll		industry & commerce
	street market		cemetery
	restricted access road		golf course
	pedestrian street		public open space/ allotments
	cycle path		park/garden/sports ground
	track/footpath		wood/forest
LC	level crossing		orchard
P	pedestrian ferry	USA	embassy
V	vehicle ferry	Pol	police station
	county/borough boundary	Fire Sta	fire station
	postal district boundary	PO	post office
	main railway station	Lib	library
	other railway station	i	tourist information centre
	London Underground station	▲	youth hostel
	Docklands Light Railway station	□	tower block
	bus/coach station	✘	windmill
H	heliport	+	church
P	car park	☾	mosque
WC	public toilet	✡	synagogue

The reference grid on this atlas coincides with the Ordnance Survey National Grid System. The grid interval is 500 metres.

🔼 100 **Page Continuation Number**   AT **Grid Reference**   03 **OS National Grid Kilometre Square**

Scale 1:20,000 (3.2 inches to 1 mile)

0	0.25	0.50	0.75	1 kilometre

0	¼	½ mile

WIDFORD
HUNSDON
SAWBRIDGEWORTH
SHEERING
LEADEN RODING
YDON
HARLOW
OLD HARLOW
POTTER STREET
7
FYFIELD
ROXWELL
WER ZEING
NORTH WEALD BASSETT
CHIPPING ONGAR
BLACKMORE
4 25 26 27
EPPING
27/6
M25
KELVEDON HATCH
E S S E X
26
THEYDON BOIS
8 39 40 41
JGHTON
5
ABRIDGE
STAPLEFORD ABBOTTS
M11
CHIGWELL
BRENTWOOD
2 53 54 55
WOODFORD
COLLIER ROW
HAROLD HILL
28
4
WANSTEAD
ROMFORD
29
6 67 68 69
HORNCHURCH
UPMINSTER
ILFORD
BARKING
DAGENHAM
BULPHAN
ST HAM
0 81 82 83
CANNING TOWN
RAINHAM
SOUTH OCKENDON
WOOLWICH
ERITH
AVELEY
30
4 95 96 97
PURFLEET
31
GRAYS
BEXLEYHEATH
TILBURY
1A
DARTFORD
NORTHFLEET
GRAVESEND
ELTHAM
BEXLEY
1B
08 109 110 111
2
SIDCUP
DARENTH
HEXTABLE
SOUTH DARENTH
LONGFIELD
ROMLEY
CHISLEHURST
SWANLEY
M25
22 123 124 125
3/1
HARTLEY
ORPINGTON
FARNINGHAM
M20
CHELSFIELD
MEOPHAM
FARNBOROUGH
WEST KINGSDOWN
CULVERSTONE GREEN
36 137 138 139
DOWNE
K E N T
2
HALSTEAD
2
3
BIGGIN HILL
OTFORD
KEMSING
WROTHAM
KNOCKHOLT
2A
30 151 152 153
M25
M26
IGHTHAM
BOROUGH GREEN
SFIELD
5
RIVERHEAD
154 155
WESTERHAM
SEVENOAKS
MEREWORTH
SHIPBOURNE
SEVENOAKS WEALD
HILDENBOROUGH
EAST PECKHAM
MARLPIT HILL
EDENBRIDGE
LEIGH
TONBRIDGE
ELD
COWDEN POUND
SOUTHBOROUGH
LOWER GREEN

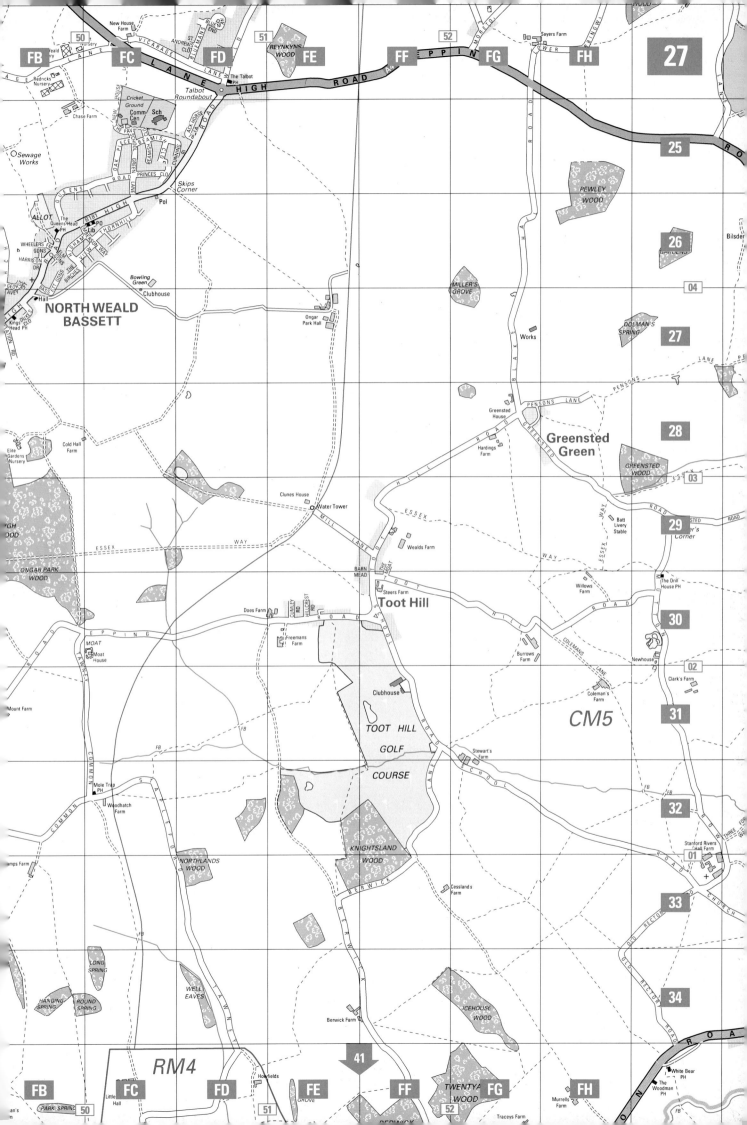

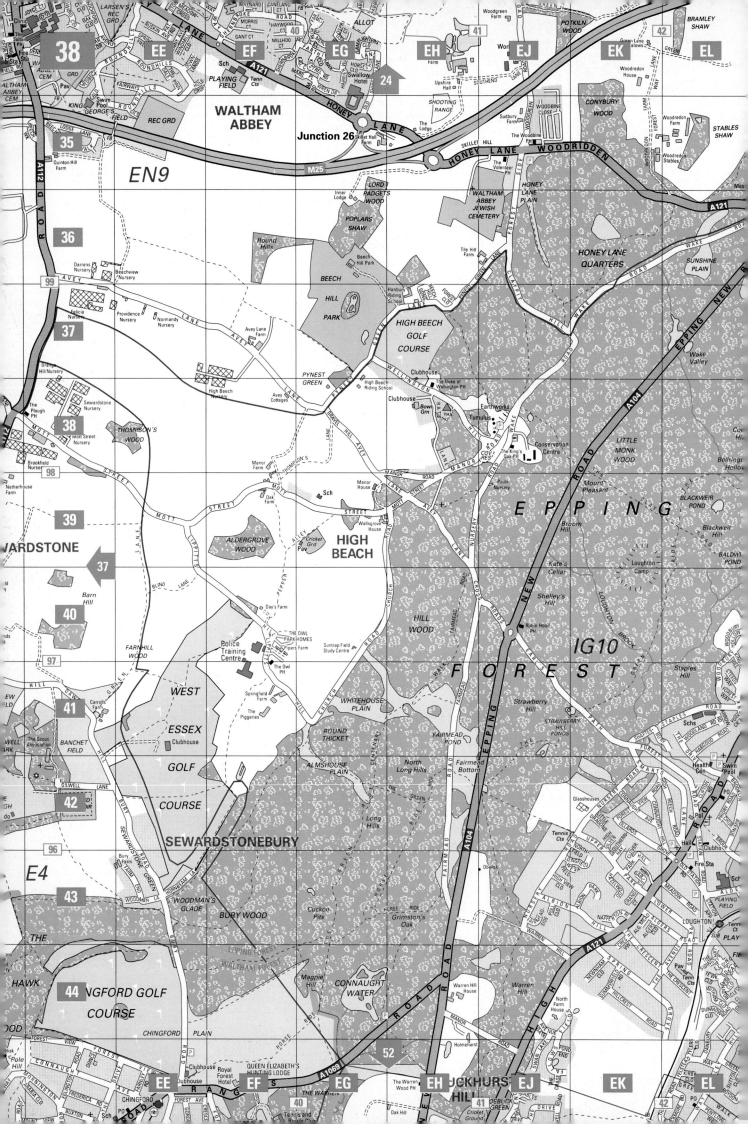

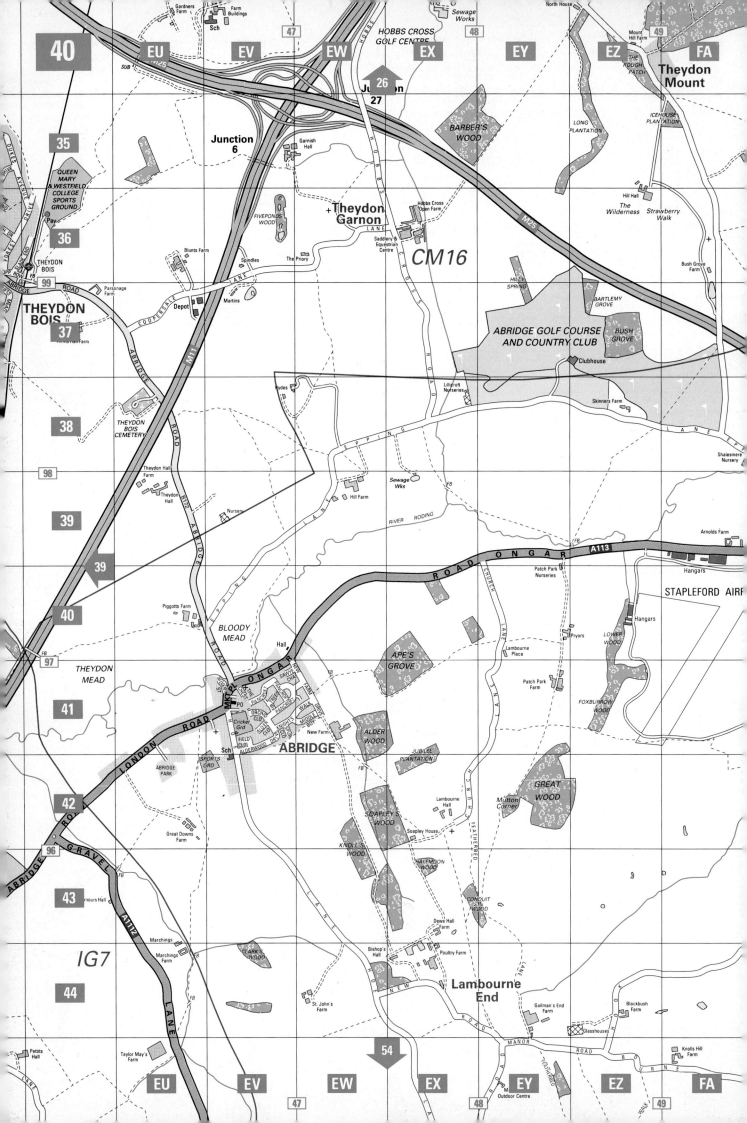

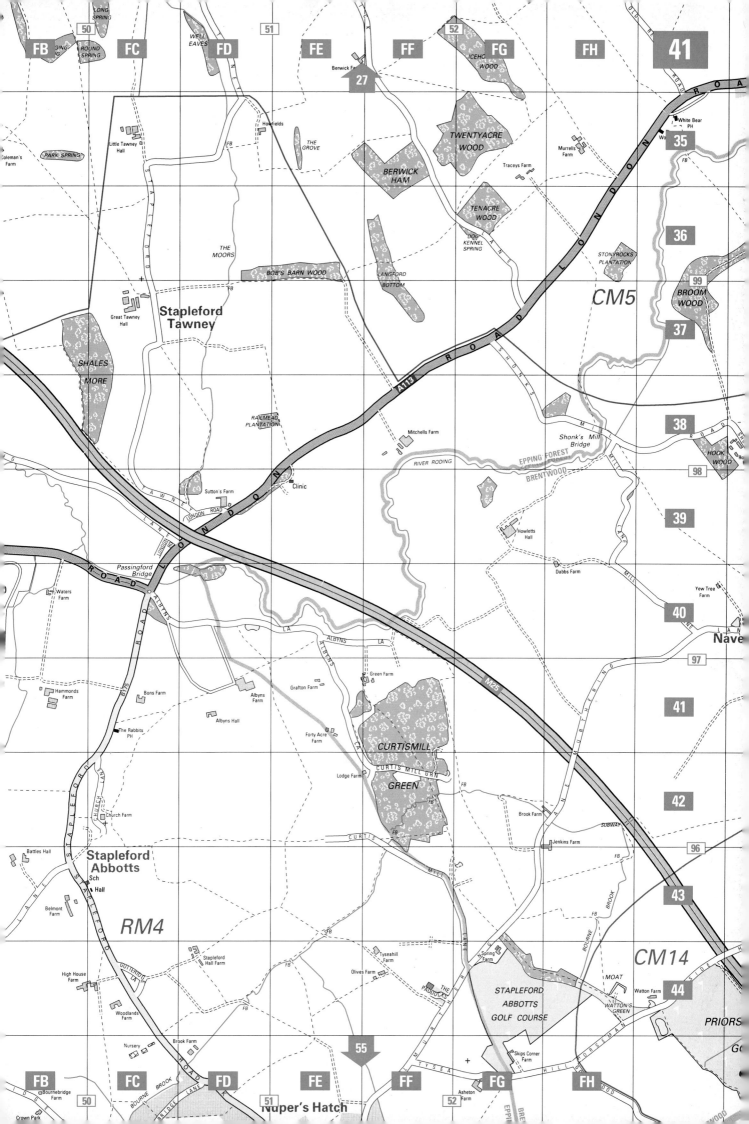

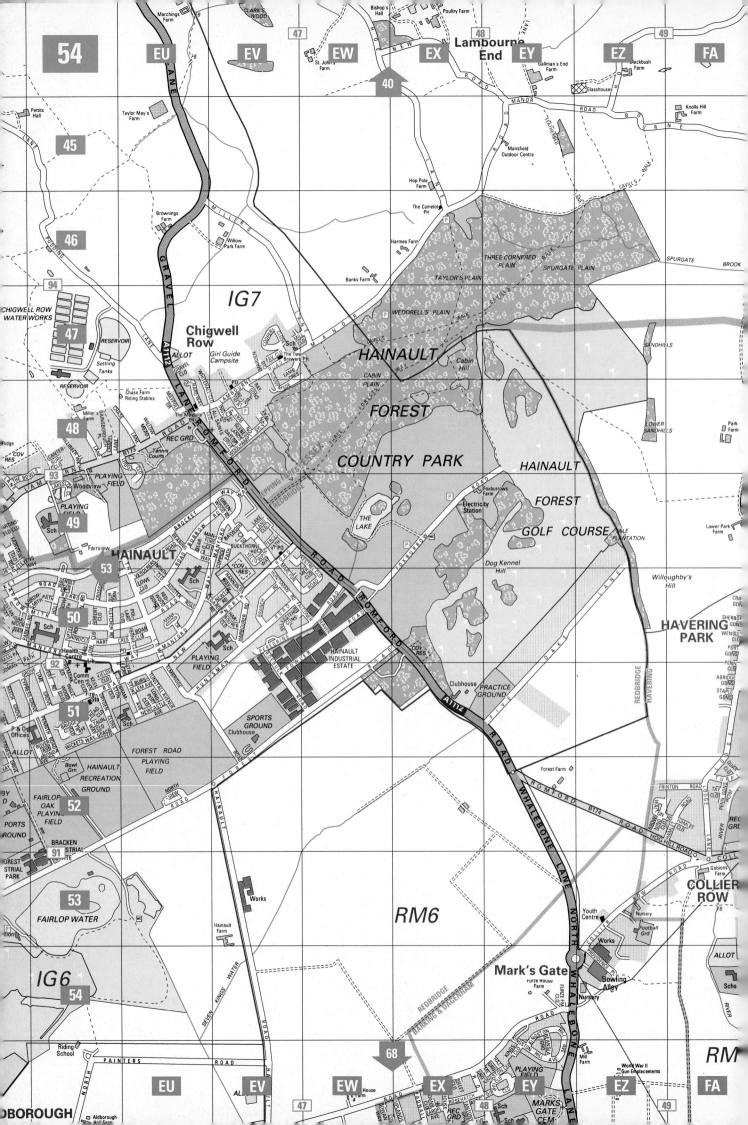

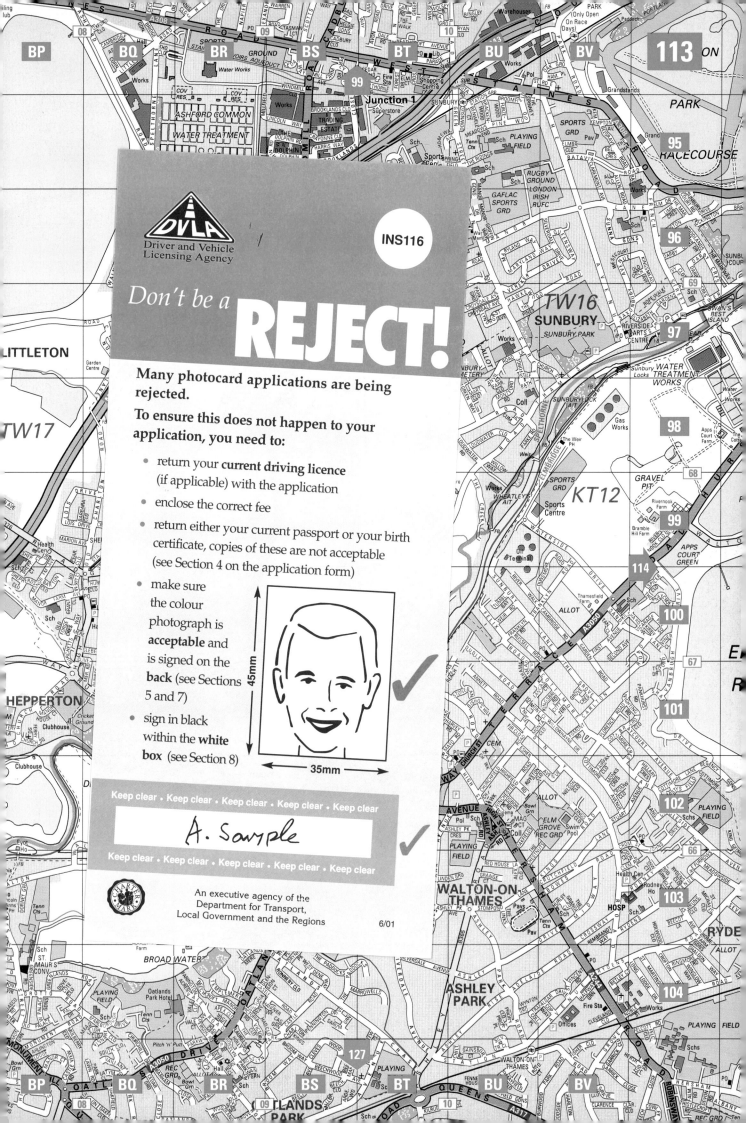

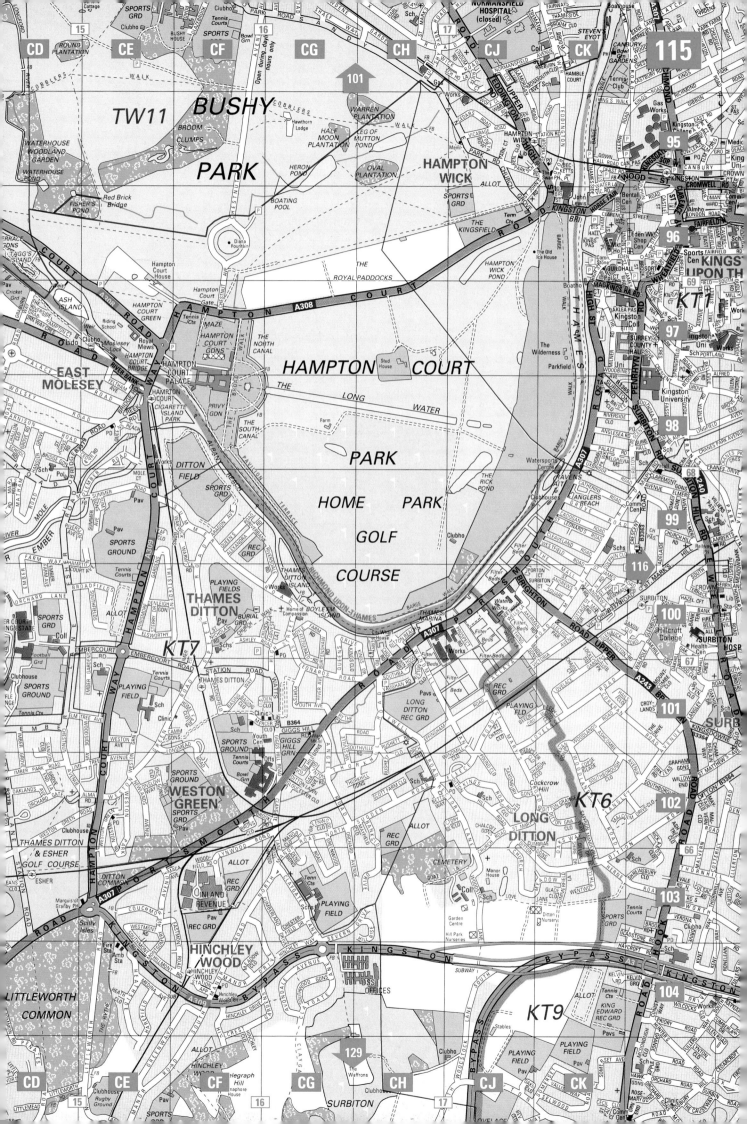

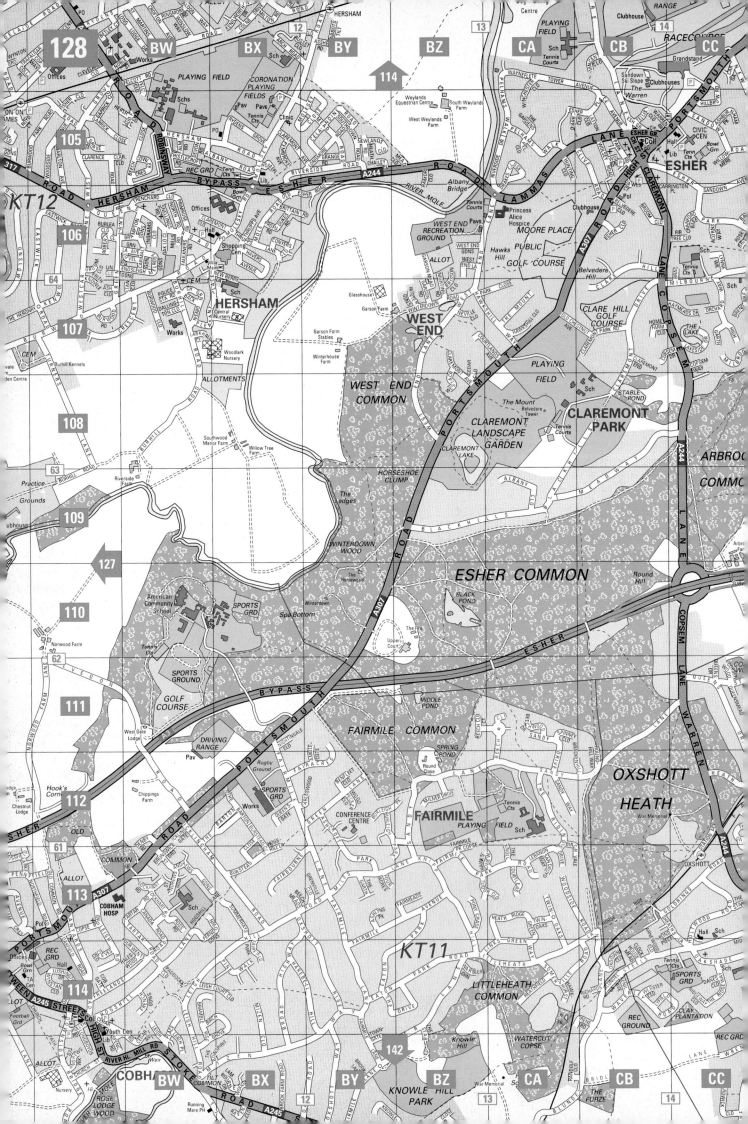

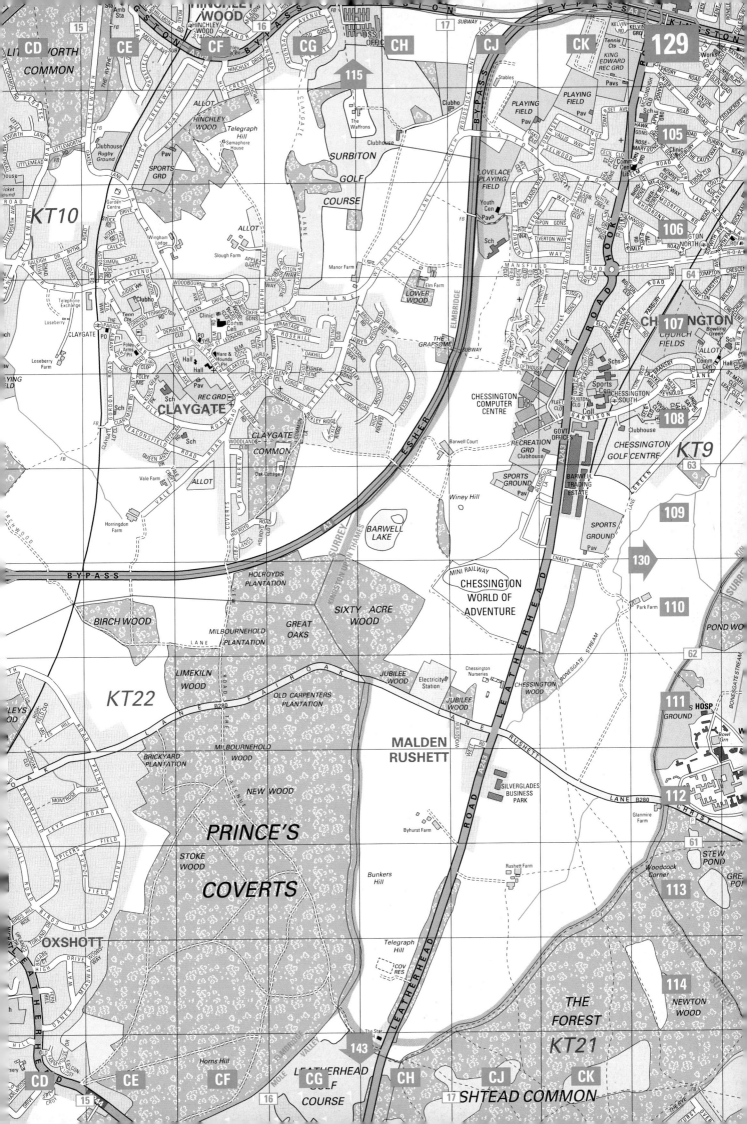

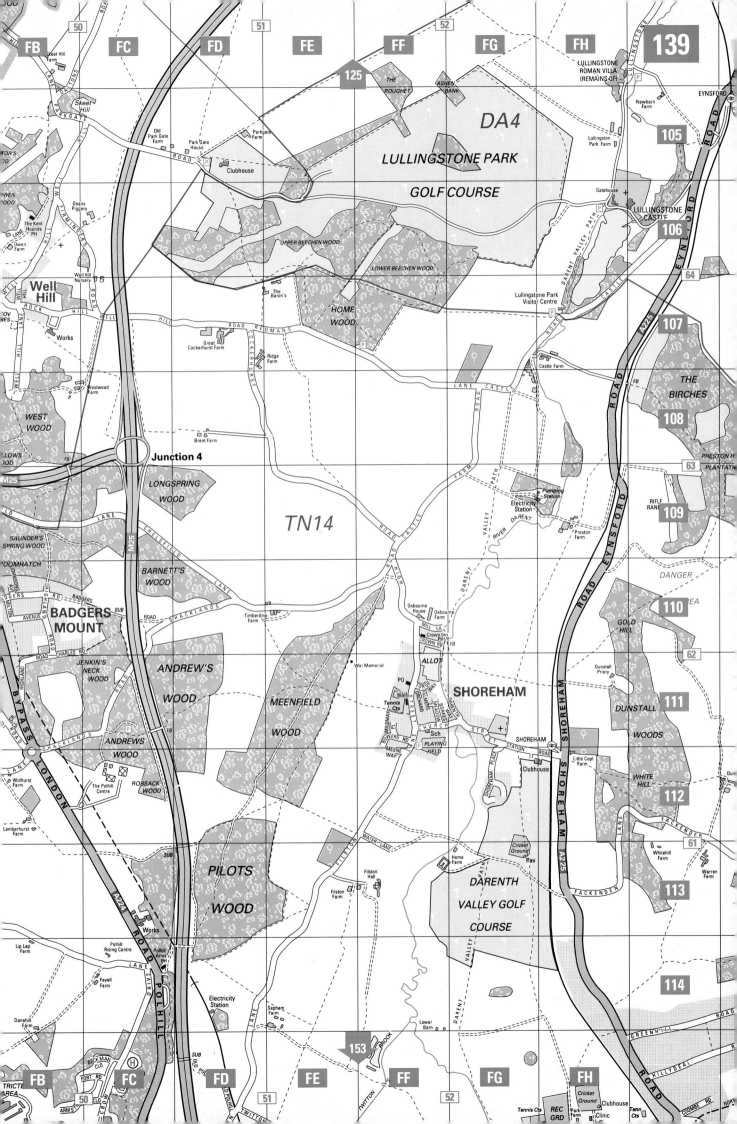

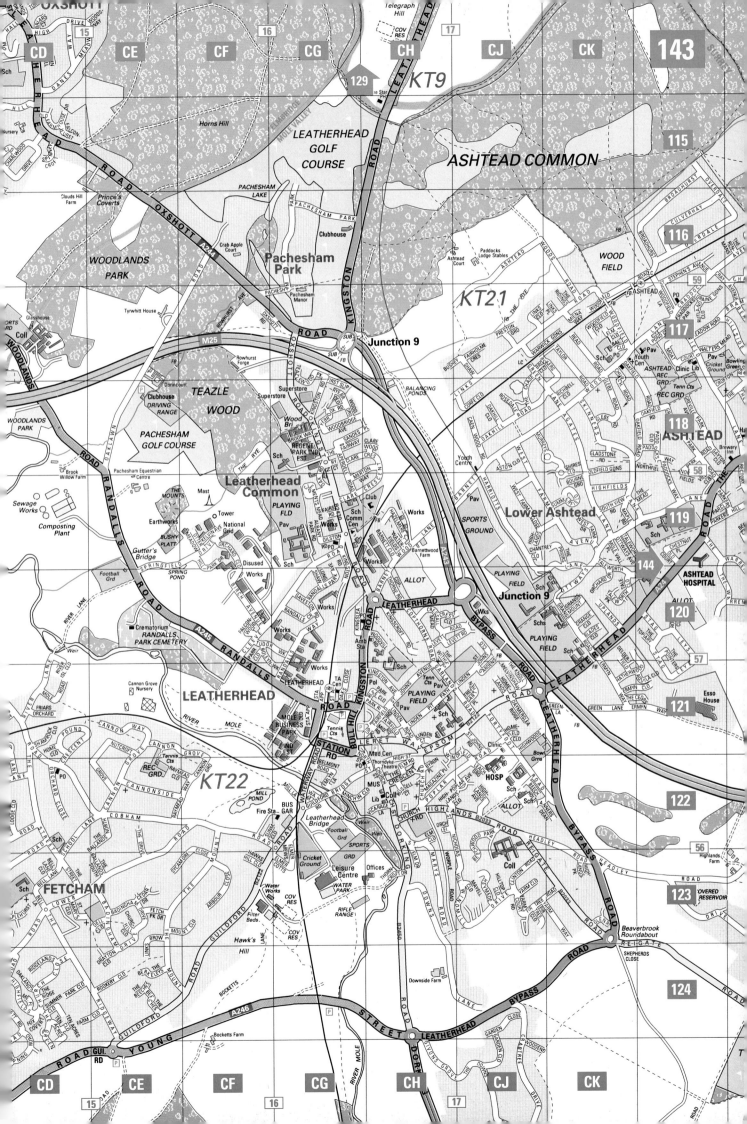

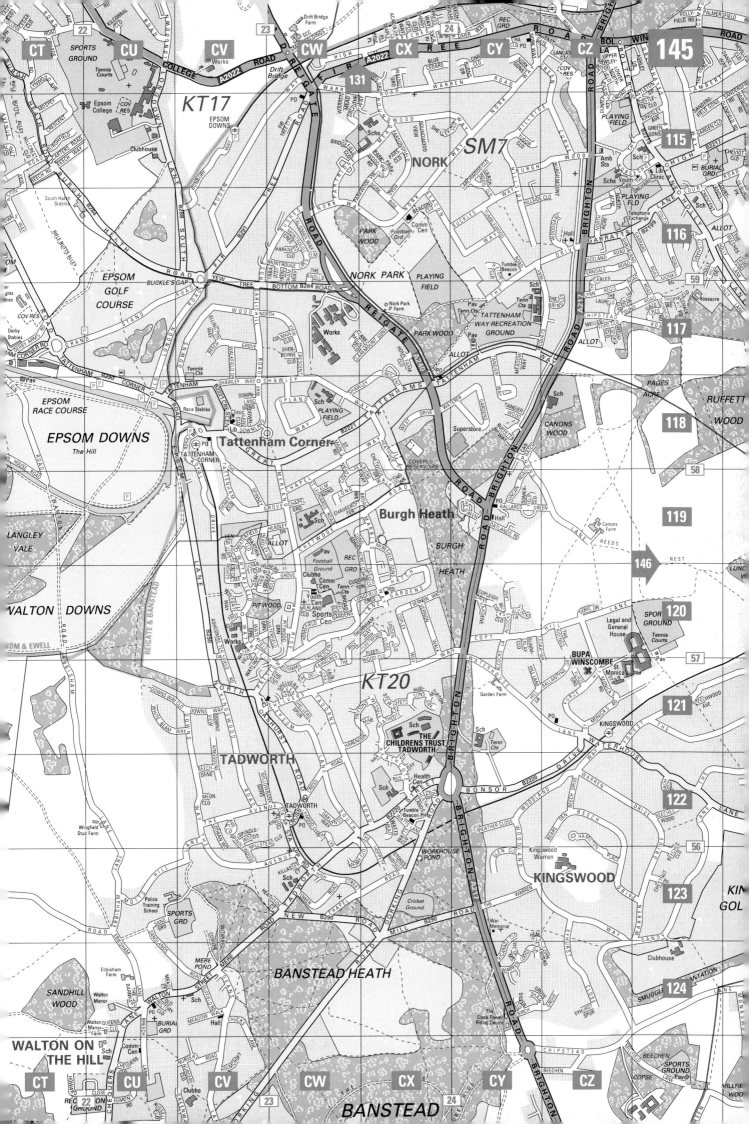

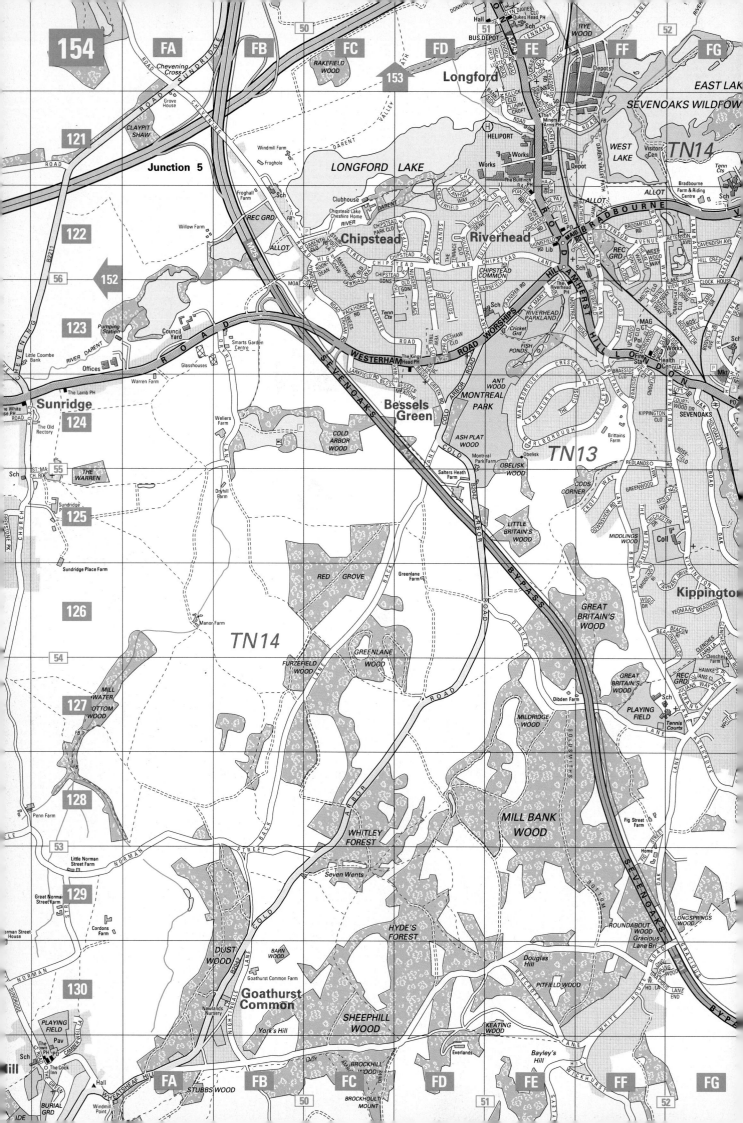

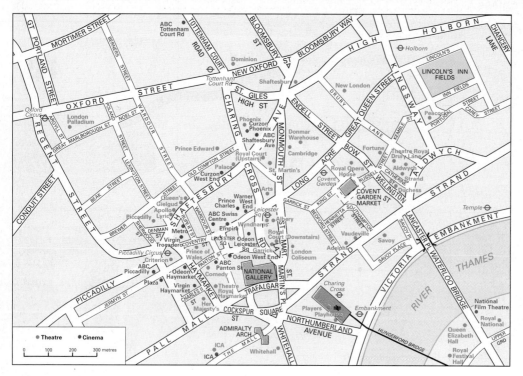

THEATRES

Adelphi *020 7344 0055*
Albery *020 7369 1730*
Aldwych *020 7416 6003*
Apollo *020 7416 6022*
Arts *020 7836 2132*
Cambridge *020 7494 5054*
Comedy *020 7369 1731*
Criterion *020 7369 1747*
Dominion *020 7656 1888*
Donmar Warehouse *020 7369 1732*
Duchess *020 7494 5075*
Fortune *020 7836 2238*
Garrick *020 7494 5085*
Gielgud *020 7494 5065*
Her Majesty's *020 7494 5400*
ICA *020 7930 3647*
London Coliseum *020 7632 8300*
London Palladium *020 7494 5020*
Lyric *020 7494 5045*
New London *020 7405 0072*
Palace *020 7434 0909*
Peacock *020 7314 8800*
Phoenix *020 7369 1733*
Piccadilly *020 7369 1734*
Players *020 7839 1134*
Playhouse *020 7839 4401*
Prince Edward *020 7734 8951*
Prince of Wales *020 7839 5987*
Queen Elizabeth Hall
020 7960 4242
Queen's *020 7494 5041*
Royal Court Theatre Downstairs
020 7565 5000
Royal Court Theatre Upstairs
020 7565 5000
Royal Festival Hall
020 7960 4242
Royal National *020 7452 3000*
Royal Opera House (CLOSED)
020 7304 4000
St. Martin's *020 7836 1443*
Savoy *020 7836 8888*
Shaftesbury *020 7379 5399*
Strand *020 7930 8800*
Theatre Royal, Drury Lane
020 7494 5550
Theatre Royal, Haymarket
020 7930 8800
Vaudeville *020 7836 9987*
Whitehall *020 7369 1735*
Wyndhams *020 7369 1736*

CINEMAS

ABC Panton St *020 7930 0631*
ABC Piccadilly *020 7437 3561*
ABC ShaftesburyAvenue
020 7836 6279
ABC Swiss Centre
020 7439 4470
ABC Tottenham Court Rd
020 7636 6148
Curzon Phoenix *020 7369 1721*

Curzon West End *020 7369 1722*
Empire *020 7437 1234*
ICA *020 7930 3647*
Metro *020 7437 0757*
National Film Theatre
020 7928 3232
Odeon Haymarket
0426 915353
Odeon Leicester Sq
020 8315 4215

Odeon Mezzanine
(Odeon Leicester Sq)
020 8315 4215
Odeon West End
020 8315 4221
Plaza *020 7437 1234*
Prince Charles *020 7437 8181*
Virgin Haymarket *0870 907 0712*
Virgin Trocadero *0870 907 0716*
Warner West End *020 7437 4347*

WEST END SHOPPING

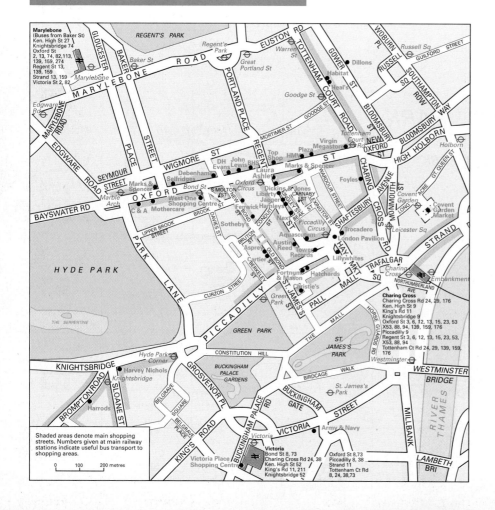

SHOPS

Aquascutum *020 7734 6090*
Army & Navy *020 7834 1234*
Asprey *020 7493 6767*
Austin Reed *020 7734 6789*
BHS (Oxford St) *020 7629 2011*
C & A *020 7629 7272*
Cartier *020 7493 6962*
Christie's *020 7839 9060*
Covent Garden Market *020 7836 9137*
DH Evans *020 7629 8800*
Debenhams *020 7580 3000*
Dickins & Jones *020 7734 7070*
Dillons *020 7636 1577*
Fenwick *020 7629 9161*
Fortnum & Mason *020 7734 8040*
Foyles *020 7437 5660*
Habitat (Tottenham Court Rd)
020 7631 3880
Hamleys *020 7734 3161*
Harrods *020 7730 1234*
Harvey Nichols *020 7235 5000*
Hatchards *020 7439 9921*
Heal's *020 7636 1666*
HMV *020 7631 3423*
Jaeger *020 7200 4000*
John Lewis *020 7629 7711*
Laura Ashley (Regent St) *020 7355 1363*
Liberty *020 7734 1234*
Lillywhites *020 7930 3181*
London Pavilion *020 7437 1838*
Marks & Spencer
(Marble Arch) *020 7935 7954*
Marks & Spencer (Oxford St)
020 7437 7722
Mothercare *020 7580 1688*
Next (Regent St) *020 7434 2515*
Plaza on Oxford St *020 7637 8811*
Selfridges *020 7629 1234*
Sotheby's *020 7493 8080*
Top Shop & Top Man *020 7636 7700*
Tower Records *020 7439 2500*
Trocadero *020 7439 1791*
Victoria Place Shopping Centre
020 7931 8811
Virgin Megastore *020 7580 5822*

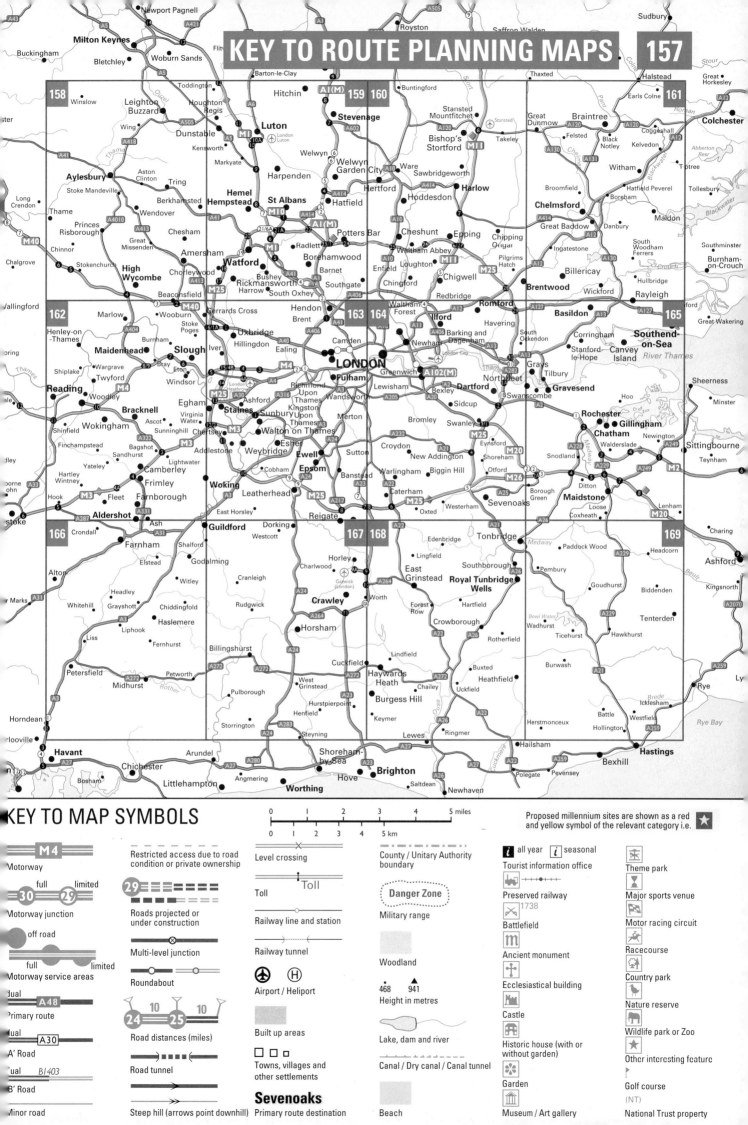

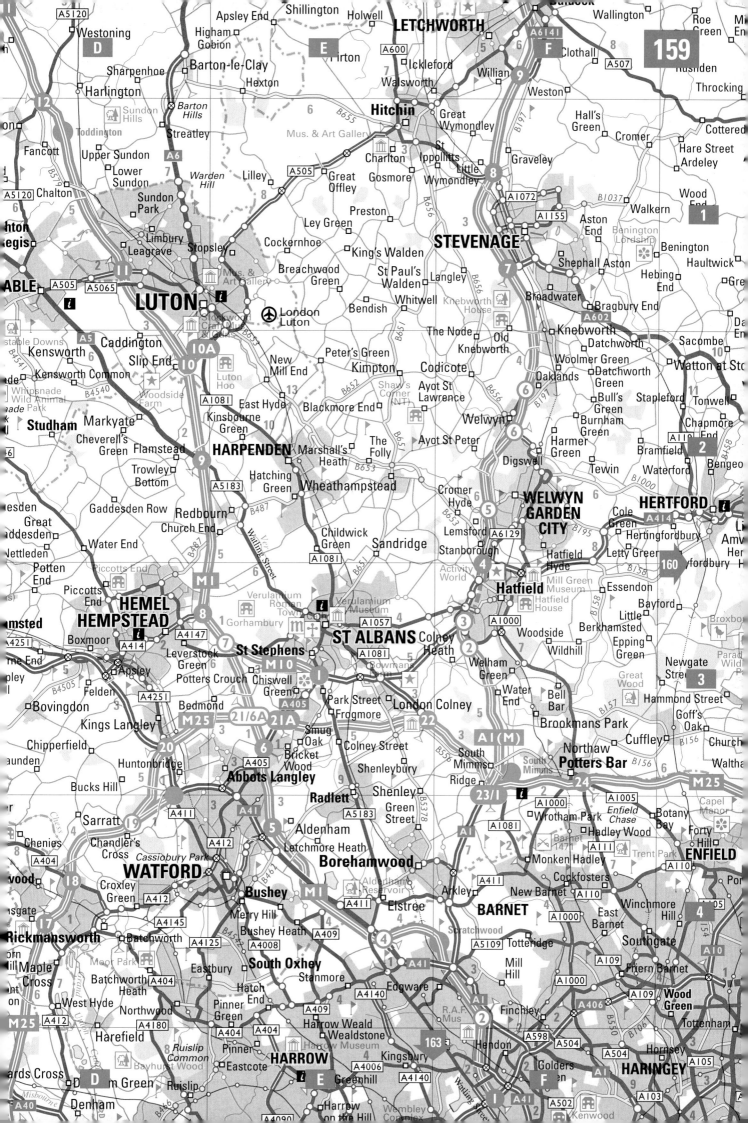

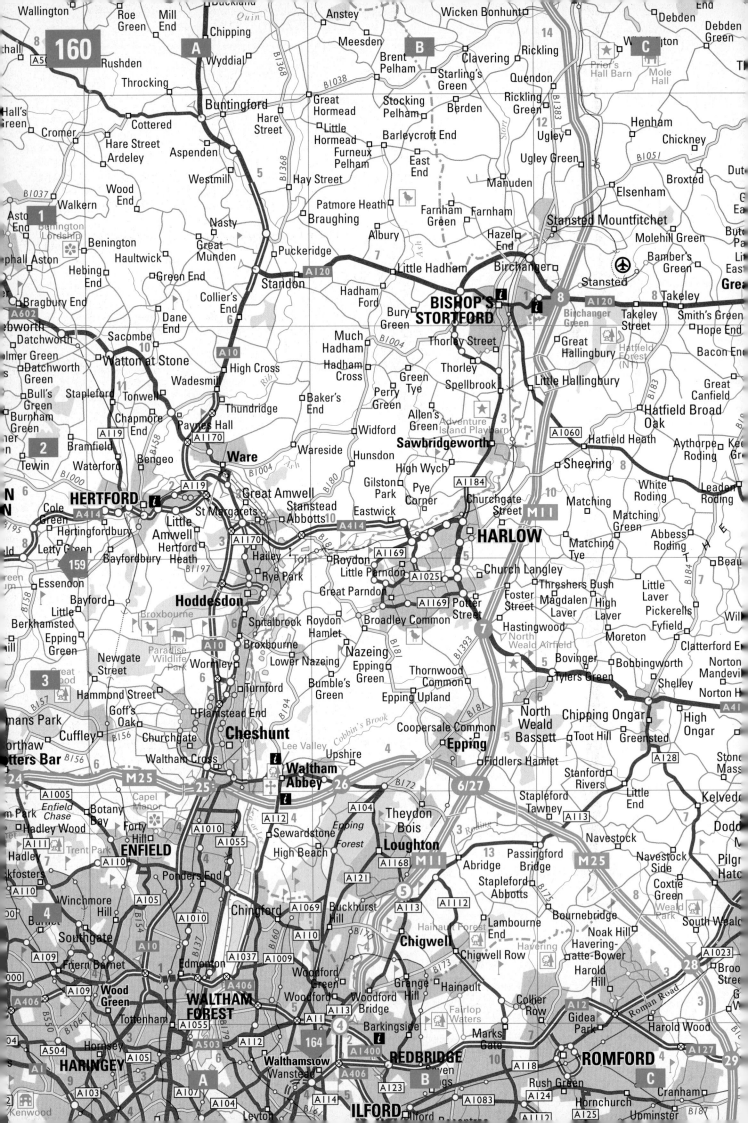

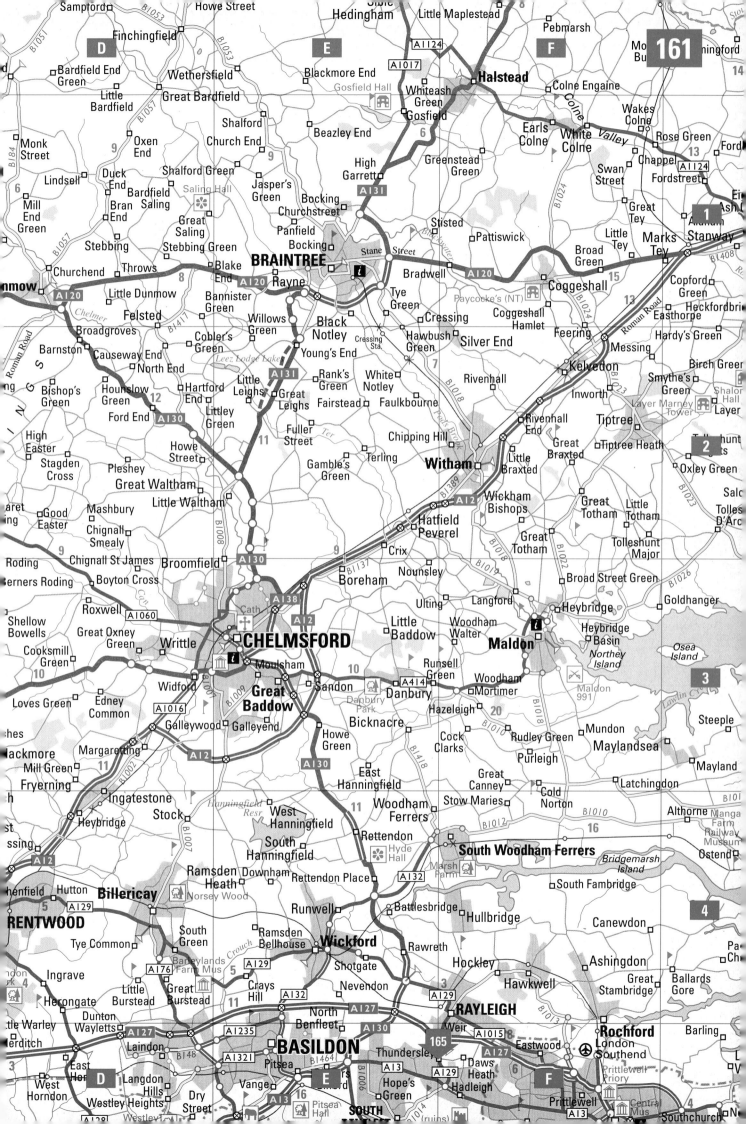

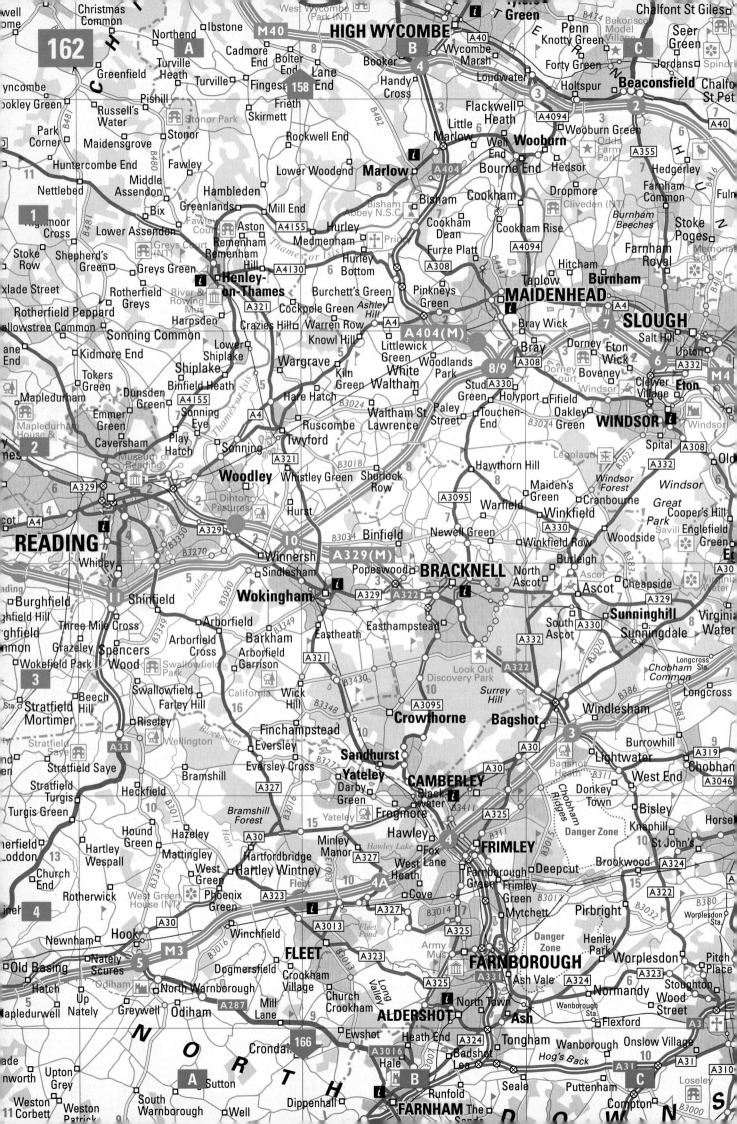

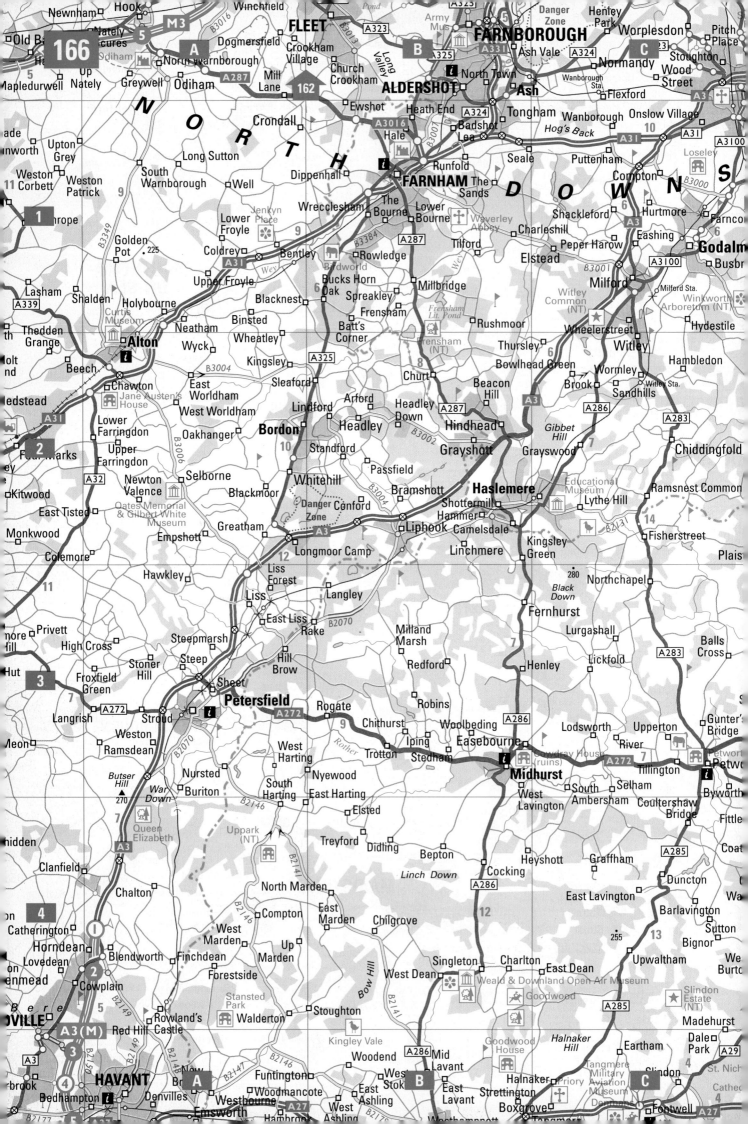

General Abbreviations

All	Alley	Conv	Convent	Gar	Garage	Ms	Mews	St.	Saint
Allot	Allotments	Cor	Corner	Gdn	Garden	Mt	Mount	Sta	Station
Amb	Ambulance	Cors	Corners	Gdns	Gardens	Mus	Museum	Sts	Streets
App	Approach	Coron	Coroners	Govt	Government	N	North	Sub	Subway
Arc	Arcade	Cotts	Cottages	Gra	Grange	PH	Public House	Swim	Swimming
Ave	Avenue	Cov	Covered	Grd	Ground	Par	Parade	TA	Territorial Army
Bdy	Broadway	Crem	Crematorium	Grds	Grounds	Pas	Passage	Tenn	Tennis
Bldgs	Buildings	Cres	Crescent	Grn	Green	Pav	Pavilion	Ter	Terrace
Boul	Boulevard	Ct	Court	Grns	Greens	Pk	Park	Thea	Theatre
Bowl	Bowling	Ctyd	Courtyard	Gro	Grove	Pl	Place	Trd	Trading
Bri	Bridge	Dep	Depot	Gros	Groves	Prec	Precinct	Twr	Tower
C of E	Church of England	Dr	Drive	Ho	House	Prom	Promenade	Twrs	Towers
Cath	Cathedral	Dws	Dwellings	Hos	Houses	Pt	Point	Vill	Villas
Cem	Cemetery	E	East	Hosp	Hospital	Quad	Quadrant	Vw	View
Cen	Central, Centre	Ed	Education	Ind	Industrial	RC	Roman Catholic	W	West
Cft	Croft	Elec	Electricity	Junct	Junction	Rd	Road	Wd	Wood
Cfts	Crofts	Embk	Embankment	La	Lane	Rds	Roads	Wds	Woods
Ch	Church	Est	Estate	Las	Lanes	Rec	Recreation	Wf	Wharf
Chyd	Churchyard	Ex	Exchange	Lo	Lodge	Res	Reservoir	Wk	Walk
Cin	Cinema	FB	Footbridge	Lwr	Lower	Ri	Rise	Wks	Walks
Circ	Circus	FC	Football Club	Mag	Magistrates	S	South	Yd	Yard
Clo	Close	Fld	Field	Mans	Mansions	Sch	School		
Co	County	Flds	Fields	Meml	Memorial	Shop	Shopping		
Coll	College	Fm	Farm	Mkt	Market	Sq	Square		
Comm	Community	Gall	Gallery	Mkts	Markets	St	Street		

Post Town Abbreviations

Abb.L.	Abbots Langley	Dag.	Dagenham	Nthlt.	Northolt	Sutt.	Sutton
Add.	Addlestone	Dart.	Dartford	Nthwd.	Northwood	Swan.	Swanley
Ash.	Ashtead	E.Mol.	East Molesey	Ong.	Ongar	T.Ditt.	Thames Ditton
Ashf.	Ashford	Edg.	Edgware	Orp.	Orpington	Tad.	Tadworth
Bans.	Banstead	Enf.	Enfield	Oxt.	Oxted	Tedd.	Teddington
Bark.	Barking	Epp.	Epping	Pnr.	Pinner	Th.Hth.	Thornton Heath
Barn.	Barnet	Felt.	Feltham	Pot.B.	Potters Bar	Twick.	Twickenham
Beck.	Beckenham	Grnf.	Greenford	Pur.	Purley	Uxb.	Uxbridge
Belv.	Belvedere	Har.	Harrow	Rad.	Radlett	W.Byf.	West Byfleet
Bex.	Bexley	Hat.	Hatfield	Rain.	Rainham	W.Mol.	West Molesey
Bexh.	Bexleyheath	Hem.H.	Hemel Hempstead	Red.	Redhill	W.Wick.	West Wickham
Borwd.	Borehamwood	Hert.	Hertford	Rich.	Richmond	Wal.Abb.	Waltham Abbey
Brent.	Brentford	Hmptn.	Hampton	Rick.	Rickmansworth	Wal.Cr.	Waltham Cross
Brom.	Bromley	Horn.	Hornchurch	Rom.	Romford	Wall.	Wallington
Brox.	Broxbourne	Houns.	Hounslow	Ruis.	Ruislip	Walt.	Walton-on-Thames
Brwd.	Brentwood	Ilf.	Ilford	S.Croy.	South Croydon	Warl.	Warlingham
Buck.H.	Buckhurst Hill	Islw.	Isleworth	Sev.	Sevenoaks	Wat.	Watford
Cars.	Carshalton	Ken.	Kenley	Shep.	Shepperton	Wdf.Grn.	Woodford Green
Cat.	Caterham	Kes.	Keston	Sid.	Sidcup	Well.	Welling
Cher.	Chertsey	Kings L.	Kings Langley	Slou.	Slough	Wem.	Wembley
Chess.	Chessington	Kings.T.	Kingston upon Thames	St.Alb.	St. Albans	West Dr.	West Drayton
Chig.	Chigwell	Loug.	Loughton	Stai.	Staines	West.	Westerham
Chis.	Chislehurst	Lthd.	Leatherhead	Stan.	Stanmore	Wey.	Weybridge
Cob.	Cobham	Mitch.	Mitcham	Sthl.	Southall	Whyt.	Whyteleafe
Couls.	Coulsdon	Mord.	Morden	Sun.	Sunbury-on-Thames	Wok.	Woking
Croy.	Croydon	N.Mal.	New Malden	Surb.	Surbiton	Wor.Pk.	Worcester Park

Notes

A strict word-by-word alphabetical order is followed in the index whereby generic terms such as Avenue, Close, Gardens etc., although abbreviated, are ordered in their expanded form. So, for example, Abbot St. comes before Abbots Ave., and Abbots Ri. comes before Abbots Rd.

Street names preceded by a definite article (i.e. The) are indexed from their second word onwards with the article being placed at the end of the name,
e.g. Avenue, The, or Long Walk, The

The alphabetical order extends to include postal information so that where two or more streets have exactly the same name, London post town references are given first in alpha-numeric order and are followed by non-London post town references in alphabetic order,
e.g. Abbey Rd. SE2 is followed by Abbey Rd. SW19 and then Abbey Rd., Barking.

In some cases there are two or more streets of the same name in the same postal area. In order to aid correct location, extra information will be given in brackets,
e.g. High St., Epsom and High St. (Ewell), Epsom.

The street name and postal district or post town of an entry is followed by the page number and grid reference on which the name will be found, e.g. Abbey Road SW19 will be found on page 104 and in square DC94. Likewise, Norfolk Crescent, Sidcup will be found on page 109 and in square ES87 (within postal district DA15).

All streets within the Central London enlarged-scale section (pages 4-11) are shown in **bold type** when named in the index, e.g. **Abbey St. SE1** will be found on page **11** and in square **N6**. Certain streets may also be duplicated on parts of pages 76-78 and 90-92. In these cases the Central London section reference is always given first in bold type, followed by the same name in standard type, e.g.

Abbey Orchard St. SW1 **9** **M6**
Abbey Orchard St. SW1 91 DK76

The index also contains some roads for which there is insufficient space to name on the map. The adjoining, or nearest named thoroughfare to such roads is shown in *italics*, and the reference indicates where the unnamed road is located off the named thoroughfare,
e.g. Oyster Catchers Close E16 is off *Freemasons Road* and is located off this road on page 80 in square EH72.

Agnes Ave., Ilf. 67 EP63
Agnes Clo. E6 81 EN73
Agnes Gdns., Dag. 68 EX63
Agnes Rd. W3 75 CT74
Agnes Scott Ct., Wey. 113 BP104
Palace Dr.
Agnes St. E14 79 DZ72
Agnesfield Clo. N12 48 DE51
Agnew Rd. SE23 107 DX87
Agricola Pl., Enf. 36 DT43
Aidan Clo., Dag. 68 EY63
Aileen Wk. E15 80 EF66
Devenay Rd.
Ailsa Ave., Twick. 101 CG85
Ailsa Rd., Twick. 101 CH85
Ailsa St. E14 79 EC71
Ainger Ms. NW3 76 DF66
Ainger Rd.
Ainger Rd. NW3 76 DF66
Ainsdale Clo., Orp. 123 ER102
Ainsdale Cres., Pnr. 58 CA55
Ainsdale Rd. W5 73 CK70
Ainsdale Rd., Wat. 44 BW48
Ainsley Ave., Rom. 69 FB58
Ainsley Clo. N9 50 DS46
Ainsley St. E2 78 DV69
Ainslie Wk. SW12 105 DH87
Balham Gro.
Ainslie Wd. Cres. E4 51 EB50
Ainslie Wd. Gdns. E4 51 EB50
Ainslie Wd. Rd. E4 51 EA50
Ainsty Est. SE16 93 DX75
Needleman St.
Ainsworth Clo. NW2 61 CU62
Ainsworth Rd. E9 78 DW66
Ainsworth Rd., Croy. 119 DP103
Ainsworth Way NW8 76 DC67
Albert Rd.
Aintree Ave. E6 80 EL67
Aintree Clo., Uxb. 71 BP72
Craig Dr.
Aintree Cres., Ilf. 53 EQ54
Aintree Est. SW6 89 CY80
Dawes Rd.
Aintree Rd., Grnf. 73 CH68
Aintree St. SW6 89 CY80
Air St. W1 9 L1
Air St. W1 77 DJ73
Airdrie Clo. N1 77 DM66
Airdrie Clo., Hayes 72 BY71
Glencoe Rd.
Airedale Ave. W4 89 CT77
Airedale Ave. S. W4 89 CT78
Netheravon Rd. S.
Airedale Rd. SW12 104 DF87
Airedale Rd. W5 87 CJ76
Airfield Way, Horn. 83 FH65
Airlie Gdns. W8 76 DA74
Campden Hill Rd.
Airlie Gdns., Ilf. 67 EP60
Airlinks Est., Houns. 86 BW78
Airport Ind. Est., West. 150 EK115
Airport Roundabout E16 80 EK74
Connaught Bri.
Airthrie Rd., Ilf. 68 EV61
Aisgill Ave. W14 89 CZ78
Aisher Rd. SE28 82 EW73
Aisher Way, Sev. 153 FD119
London Rd.
Aislibie Rd. SE12 94 EE84
Aitken Clo. E8 78 DU67
Pownall Rd.
Aitken Clo., Mitch. 118 DF101
Aitken Rd. SE6 107 EB89
Aitken Rd., Barn. 33 CW43
Ajax Ave. NW9 60 CS55
Ajax Rd. NW6 61 CZ64
Akabusi Clo., Croy. 120 DU100
Akehurst La., Sev. 155 FJ125
Akehurst St. SW15 103 CU86
Akenside Rd. NW3 62 DD64
Akerman Rd. SW9 91 DP82
Akerman Rd., Surb. 115 CJ100
Alabama St. SE18 95 ER80
Alacross Rd. W5 87 CJ75
Alan Dr., Barn. 33 CY44
Alan Gdns., Rom. 68 FA59
Alan Hocken Way E15 80 EE68
Alan Rd. SW19 103 CY92
Alandale Dr., Pnr. 43 BV54
Alanthus Clo. SE12 108 EF85
Alaska St. SE1 10 D3
Alba Clo., Hayes 72 BX70
Ramulis Dr.
Alba Gdns. NW11 61 CY58
Alba Pl. W11 75 CZ72
Portobello Rd.
Albacore Cres. SE13 107 EB86
Albain Cres., Ashf. 98 BL89
Alban Cres., Borwd. 32 CN39
Alban Highwalk EC2 78 DQ71
London Wall
Albans Vw., Wat. 15 BV33
Albany, The W1 9 K1
Albany, The, Wdf.Grn. 52 EF49
Albany Clo. N15 63 DP56
Albany Clo. SW14 88 CP84
Albany Clo., Bex. 110 EW87
Albany Clo., Esher 128 CA109
Albany Clo., Uxb. 56 BN64
Albany Clo. (Bushey), Wat. 31 CD44
Albany Ct. E4 37 EB44
Chelwood Clo.
Albany Ct., Epp. 25 ET30
Albany Ctyd. W1 9 L1
Albany Cres., Edg. 46 CN52
Albany Cres., Esher 129 CE107
Albany Mans. SW11 90 DE80
Albert Bri. Rd.
Albany Ms. N1 77 DN66
Barnsbury Pk.
Albany Ms. SE5 92 DQ79
Albany Rd.
Albany Ms., Brom. 108 EG93
Avondale Rd.
Albany Ms., Kings.T. 101 CK93
Albany Ms., St.Alb. 16 CA27
North Orbital Rd.
Albany Ms., Sutt. 132 DB106
Camden Rd.
Albany Pk. Ave., Enf. 36 DW39
Albany Pk. Rd., Kings.T. 101 CK93
Albany Pk. Rd., Lthd. 143 CG119
Albany Pas., Rich. 102 CM85
Albany Pl. N7 63 DN63
Benwell Rd.
Albany Pl., Brent. 88 CL79
Albany Rd. E10 65 EA59
Albany Rd. E12 66 EK63
Albany Rd. E17 65 DY58
Albany Rd. N4 63 DM58
Albany Rd. N18 50 DV50
Albany Rd. SE5 92 DR79
Albany Rd. SW19 104 DB92
Albany Rd. W13 73 CH73
Albany Rd., Belv. 96 EZ79
Albany Rd., Bex. 110 EW87
Albany Rd., Brent. 87 CK79
Albany Rd., Chis. 109 EP92
Albany Rd., Enf. 37 DX37
Albany Rd., Horn. 69 FG60
Albany Rd., N.Mal. 116 CR98
Albany Rd., Rich. 102 CM85
Albert Rd.
Albany Rd., Rom. 68 EZ58
Albany Rd., Walt. 128 BW105
Albany St. NW1 77 DH68
Albany Ter. NW1 77 DH70
Marylebone Rd.
Albany Vw., Buck.H. 52 EG46
Albatross Gdns., S.Croy. 135 DX111
Albatross St. SE18 95 ES80
Albatross Way SE16 93 DX75
Needleman St.
Albemarle SW19 103 CX89
Albemarle App., Ilf. 67 EP58
Albemarle Ave., Pot.B. 20 DB33
Albemarle Ave., Twick. 100 BZ88
Albemarle Ave. (Cheshunt), Wal.Cr. 22 DW28
Albemarle Gdns., Ilf. 67 EP58
Albemarle Gdns., N.Mal. 116 CR98
Albemarle Pk., Stan. 45 CJ50
Albemarle Rd., Barn. 48 DE45
Albemarle Rd., Beck. 121 EB95
Albemarle St. W1 9 J1
Albemarle St. W1 77 DH73
Albemarle Way EC1 6 F5
Alberon Gdns. NW11 61 CZ56
Albert Ave. E4 51 EA49
Albert Ave. SW8 91 DM80
Albert Ave., Cher. 112 BG97
Albert Bri. SW3 90 DE79
Albert Bri. SW11 90 DE80
Albert Bri. Rd. SW11 90 DE80
Albert Carr Gdns. SW16 105 DL92
Albert Clo. E9 78 DV67
Northiam St.
Albert Clo. N22 49 DK53
Albert Ct. SW7 90 DD75
Albert Cres. E4 51 EA49
Albert Dr. SW19 103 CY89
Albert Embk. SE1 91 DL78
Albert Gdns. E1 79 DX72
Albert Gate SW1 8 E4
Albert Gate SW1 90 DF75
Albert Gro. SW20 117 CX95
Albert Hall Mans. SW7 90 DD75
Kensington Gore
Albert Mans. SW11 90 DF81
Albert Bri. Rd.
Albert Ms. E14 79 DY73
Narrow St.
Albert Ms. W8 90 DC76
Victoria Gro.
Albert Pl. N3 48 DA53
Albert Pl. N17 64 DT55
High Rd.
Albert Pl. W8 90 DB75
Albert Rd. E10 65 EC61
Albert Rd. E16 80 EL74
Albert Rd. E17 65 EA57
Albert Rd. E18 66 EH55
Albert Rd. N4 63 DM60
Albert Rd. N15 64 DS58
Albert Rd. N22 49 DJ53
Albert Rd. NW4 61 CX56
Albert Rd. NW6 75 CZ68
Albert Rd. NW7 47 CT50
Albert Rd. SE9 108 EL90
Albert Rd. SE20 107 DX93
Albert Rd. SE25 120 DU98
Albert Rd. W5 73 CH70
Albert Rd., Add. 112 BK104
Albert Rd., Ashf. 98 BM92
Albert Rd., Ash. 144 CM118
Albert Rd., Barn. 34 DD42
Albert Rd., Belv. 96 EZ78
Albert Rd., Bex. 110 FA86
Albert Rd., Brom. 122 EK99
Albert Rd., Buck.H. 52 EK47
Albert Rd., Dag. 68 FA60
Albert Rd., Epsom 131 CT113
Albert Rd., Hmptn. 100 CC92
Albert Rd., Har. 58 CC55
Albert Rd., Hayes 85 BS76
Albert Rd., Houns. 86 CA84
Albert Rd., Ilf. 67 EP62
Albert Rd., Kings.T. 116 CM96
Albert Rd., Mitch. 118 DF97
Albert Rd., N.Mal. 117 CT98
Albert Rd., Orp. 138 EU106
Albert Rd. (St. Mary Cray), Orp. 124 EV100
Albert Rd., Rich. 102 CL85
Albert Rd., Rom. 69 FF57
Albert Rd., Sthl. 86 BX76
Albert Rd., Sutt. 132 DD106
Albert Rd., Tedd. 101 CF93
Albert Rd., Twick. 101 CF88
Albert Rd., Warl. 149 DZ117
Albert Rd., West Dr. 70 BL74
Albert Rd. Est., Belv. 96 EZ78
Albert Rd. N., Wat. 29 BV41
Albert Rd. S., Wat. 29 BV41
Albert Sq. E15 66 EE64
Albert Sq. SW8 91 DM80
Albert St. N12 48 DC50
Albert St. NW1 77 DH67
Albert Ter. NW1 76 DG67
Albert Ter. NW10 74 CR67
Albert Ter., Buck.H. 52 EK47
Albert Ter. Ms. NW1 76 DG67
Regents Pk. Rd.
Albert Wk. E16 95 EN75
Pier Rd.
Alberta Ave., Sutt. 131 CY105
Alberta Est. SE17 10 G10
Alberta Est. SE17 91 DP78
Alberta Rd., Enf. 36 DT44
Alberta Rd., Erith 97 FC81
Alberta St. SE17 10 F10
Alberta St. SE17 91 DP78
Albertine Clo., Epsom 145 CV116
Rose Bushes
Albion Ave. N10 48 DG53
Albion Ave. SW8 91 DK82
Albion Bldgs. EC1 78 DQ71
Bartholomew Clo.
Albion Clo. W2 4 C10
Albion Clo., Rom. 69 FD58
Albion Dr. E8 78 DT66
Albion Est. SE16 92 DW75
Albion Gdns. W6 89 CV77
Albion Gro. N16 64 DS63
Albion Hill SE13 93 EB82
Albion Hill, Loug. 38 EJ43
Albion Ms. N1 77 DN66
Albion Ms. NW6 75 CZ66
Kilburn High Rd.
Albion Ms. W2 4 C10
Albion Ms. W2 76 DE72
Albion Par. N16 64 DR63
Albion Rd.
Albion Pk., Loug. 38 EK43
Albion Pl. EC1 6 F6
Albion Pl. EC1 77 DP71
Albion Pl. SE25 120 DU97
High St.
Albion Pl. W6 89 CV77
Albion Rd. E17 65 EC55
Albion Rd. N16 64 DR63
Albion Rd. N17 50 DU54
Albion Rd., Bexh. 96 EZ84
Albion Rd., Hayes 71 BS72
Albion Rd., Houns. 86 CA84
Albion Rd., Kings.T. 116 CQ95
Albion Rd., Sutt. 132 DD107
Albion Rd., Twick. 101 CE88
Albion Sq. E8 78 DT66
Albion St. SE16 92 DW75
Albion St. W2 4 C9
Albion St. W2 76 DE72
Albion St., Croy. 119 DP102
Albion Ter. E8 78 DT66
Albion Vill. Rd. SE26 106 DW90
Albion Way EC1 7 H7
Albion Way SE13 93 EC84
Albion Way, Wem. 60 CP62
North End Rd.
Albion Yd. E1 78 DV71
Albright Ind. Est., Rain. 83 FF71
Albrighton Rd. SE22 92 DS83
Albuhera Clo., Enf. 35 DN39
Albury Ave., Bexh. 96 EY82
Albury Ave., Islw. 87 CF80
Albury Ave., Sutt. 131 CW109
Albury Clo., Hmptn. 100 CA93
Albury Dr., Pnr. 44 BW53
Albury Gro. Rd. (Cheshunt), Wal.Cr. 23 DX30
Albury Ms. E12 66 EJ60
Albury Ride (Cheshunt), Wal.Cr. 23 DX31
Albury Rd., Chess. 130 CL106
Albury Rd., Walt. 127 BS107
Albury St. SE8 93 EA79
Albury Wk. (Cheshunt), Wal.Cr. 22 DW30
Albyfield, Brom. 123 EM97
Albyn Rd. SE8 93 EA81
Albyns Clo., Rain. 83 FG66
South End Rd.
Albyns La., Rom. 41 FC40
Alcester Cres. E5 64 DV61
Alcester Rd., Wall. 133 DH105
Alcock Clo., Wall. 133 DK108
Alcock Rd., Houns. 86 BX80
Alcocks Clo., Tad. 145 CY120
Alcocks La., Tad. 145 CY121
Alconbury Rd. E5 64 DU61
Alcorn Clo., Sutt. 118 DA103
Alcott Clo. W7 73 CF71
Westcott Cres.
Alcuin Ct., Stan. 45 CJ51
Aldborough Rd., Dag. 83 FC65
Aldborough Rd. N., Ilf. 67 ET57
Aldborough Rd. S., Ilf. 67 ES60
Aldbourne Rd. W12 75 CT74
Aldbridge St. SE17 11 N10
Aldbridge St. SE17 92 DS78
Aldburgh Ms. W1 4 G8
Aldbury Ave., Wem. 74 CP66
Aldbury Clo., Wat. 30 BX36
Aldbury Ms. N9 50 DR45
Aldebert Ter. SW8 91 DL80
Aldeburgh Clo. E5 64 DV61
Southwold Rd.
Aldeburgh Pl., Wdf.Grn. 52 EG49
Aldeburgh St. SE10 94 EG78
Alden Ave. E15 80 EF70
Aldenham Ave., Rad. 31 CG36
Aldenham Dr., Uxb. 71 BP70
Aldenham Gro., Rad. 17 CG34
Aldenham Rd., Borwd. 31 CG41
Aldenham Rd., Rad. 31 CG35
Aldenham Rd., Wat. 30 BX44
Aldenham Rd. (Bushey), Wat. 30 BY44
Aldenham Rd. (Letchmore Heath), Wat. 31 CE39
Aldenham St. NW1 5 L1
Aldenham St. NW1 77 DJ68
Aldenholme, Wey. 127 BS107
Aldensley Rd. W6 89 CV76
Alder Clo. SE15 92 DT79
Alder Clo., St.Alb. 16 CB28
Alder Cft., Couls. 147 DM116
Alder Gro. NW2 61 CU61
Alder Ind. Est., Hayes 85 BR75
Alder Ms. N19 63 DJ61
Bredgar Rd.
Alder Rd. SW14 88 CR83
Alder Rd., Sid. 109 ET90
Alder Rd., Uxb. 70 BJ65
Alder Wk., Ilf. 67 EQ64
Loxford La.
Alder Wk., Wat. 29 BV35
Aspen Pk. Dr.
Alder Way, Swan. 125 FD96
Alderbrook Rd. SW12 105 DH86
Alderbury Rd. SW13 89 CU79
Aldercroft, Couls. 147 DM116
Aldergrove Gdns., Houns. 86 BY82
Bath Rd.
Alderholt Way SE15 92 DT80
Daniel Gdns.
Alderman Ave., Bark. 82 EU69
Alderman Judge Mall, Kings.T. 116 CL96
Eden St.
Aldermanbury EC2 7 J8
Aldermanbury EC2 78 DQ72
Aldermanbury Sq. EC2 7 J7
Aldermans Hill N13 49 DL49
Alderman's Wk. EC2 7 M7
Aldermary Rd., Brom. 122 EG95
Aldermoor Rd. SE6 107 DZ90
Alderney Ave., Houns. 86 CB80
Alderney Gdns., Nthlt. 72 BZ66
Alderney Rd. E1 79 DX70
Alderney Rd., Erith 97 FG80
Alderney St. SW1 9 J10
Alderney St. SW1 91 DH77
Alders, The N21 35 DN44
Alders, The, Felt. 100 BY91
Alders, The, Houns. 86 BZ79
Alders, The, W.Byf. 126 BJ112
Alders, The, W.Wick. 121 EB102
Alders Ave., Wdf.Grn. 52 EE51
Alders Clo. E11 66 EH61
Aldersbrook Rd.
Alders Clo. W5 87 CK76
Alders Clo., Edg. 46 CQ50
Alders Gro., E.Mol. 115 CD99
Esher Rd.
Alders Rd., Edg. 46 CQ50
Aldersbrook Ave., Enf. 36 DS40
Aldersbrook Dr., Kings.T. 102 CM93
Aldersbrook La. E12 67 EM62
Aldersbrook Rd. E11 66 EH61
Aldersbrook Rd. E12 66 EH61
Aldersey Gdns., Bark. 81 ER65
Aldersford Clo. SE4 107 DX85
Aldersgate St. EC1 7 H6
Aldersgate St. EC1 78 DQ71
Aldersgrove, Wal.Abb. 24 EE34
Roundhills
Aldersgrove Ave. SE9 108 EJ90
Aldershot Rd. NW6 75 CZ67
Aldersmead Ave., Croy. 121 DX100
Aldersmead Rd., Beck. 107 DY94
Alderson Pl., Sthl. 72 CC74
Alderson St. W10 75 CY70
Kensal Rd.
Alderstead Heath, Red. 147 DK124
Alderton Clo. NW10 60 CR62
Alderton Clo., Loug. 39 EN42
Alderton Cres. NW4 61 CV57
Alderton Hall La., Loug. 39 EN42
Alderton Hill, Loug. 38 EL43
Alderton Ri., Loug. 39 EN42
Alderton Rd. SE24 92 DQ83
Alderton Rd., Croy. 120 DT101
Alderton Way NW4 61 CV57
Alderton Way, Loug. 39 EM43
Alderville Rd. SW6 89 CZ82
Alderwick Dr., Houns. 87 CD83
Alderwood Clo., Rom. 40 EV41
Alderwood Dr., Rom. 40 EV41
Alderwood Rd. SE9 109 ER86
Alford St. W1 8 F2
Alford St. W1 76 DG74
Aldgate EC3 7 N9
Aldgate EC3 78 DS72
Aldgate Ave. E1 7 P8
Aldgate High St. EC3 7 P9
Aldgate High St. EC3 78 DT72
Aldine Ct. W12 75 CW74
Aldine St.
Aldine Pl. W12 75 CW74
Uxbridge Rd.
Aldine St. W12 75 CW74
Aldingham Ct., Horn. 69 FG64
Easedale Dr.
Aldingham Gdns., Horn. 69 FG64
Aldington Clo., Dag. 68 EW59
Aldington Rd. SE18 94 EK76
Aldis Ms. SW17 104 DE92
Aldis St.
Aldis St. SW17 104 DE92
Aldred Rd. NW6 62 DA64
Aldren Rd. SW17 104 DC90
Aldrich Cres., Croy. 135 EC109
Aldrich Gdns., Sutt. 117 CZ104
Aldrich Ter. SW18 104 DC89
Lidiard Rd.
Aldriche Way E4 51 EC51
Aldridge Ave., Edg. 46 CP48
Aldridge Ave., Enf. 37 EA38
Aldridge Ave., Ruis. 58 BX61
Aldridge Ave., Stan. 46 CL53
Aldridge Ri., N.Mal. 116 CS101
Aldridge Rd. Vill. W11 75 CZ71
Aldridge Wk. N14 49 DL45
Aldrington Rd. SW16 105 DJ91
Aldsworth Clo. W9 76 DB70
Aldwick Clo. SE9 109 ER90
Aldwick Rd., Croy. 119 DM104
Aldworth Gro. SE13 107 EC86
Aldworth Rd. E15 80 EE66
Aldwych WC2 6 B10
Aldwych WC2 77 DM73
Aldwych Ave., Ilf. 67 EQ56
Aldwych Clo., Horn. 69 FG61
Alers Rd., Bexh. 110 EX85
Aleston Beck Rd. E16 80 EK72
Fulmer Rd.
Alexa Ct. W8 90 DA77
Lexham Gdns.
Alexander Ave. NW10 75 CV66
Alexander Clo., Barn. 34 DD42
Alexander Clo., Brom. 122 EG102
Alexander Clo., Sid. 109 ES86
Alexander Clo., Sthl. 72 CC74
Alexander Clo., Twick. 101 CF89
Alexander Ct., Wal.Cr. 23 DX30
Alexander Evans Ms. SE23 107 DX88
Sunderland Rd.
Alexander Godley Clo., Ash. 144 CM119
Alexander Ms. W2 76 DB72
Alexander St.
Alexander Pl. SW7 8 B8
Alexander Pl. SW7 90 DE77
Alexander Rd. N19 63 DL62
Alexander Rd., Bexh. 96 EX82
Alexander Rd., Chis. 109 EP92
Alexander Rd., Couls. 147 DH115
Alexander Rd., St.Alb. 17 CJ25
Alexander Sq. SW3 8 B8
Alexander Sq. SW3 90 DE77
Alexander St. W2 76 DA72
Alexandra Ave. N22 49 DK53
Alexandra Ave. SW11 90 DG81
Alexandra Ave. W4 88 CR80
Alexandra Ave., Har. 58 BZ60
Alexandra Ave., Sthl. 72 BZ73
Alexandra Ave., Sutt. 118 DA104
Alexandra Ave., Warl. 149 DZ117
Alexandra Clo., Ashf. 99 BR94
Alexandra Rd.
Alexandra Clo., Har. 58 CA62
Alexandra Ave.
Alexandra Clo., Stai. 98 BK93
Alexandra Clo., Swan. 125 FE96
Alexandra Clo., Walt. 113 BU103
Alexandra Cotts. SE14 93 DZ81
Alexandra Ct. N14 35 DJ43
Alexandra Ct., Ashf. 99 BR93
Alexandra Rd.
Alexandra Ct., Wem. 60 CM63
Alexandra Cres., Brom. 108 EF93
Alexandra Dr. SE19 106 DS92
Alexandra Dr., Surb. 116 CN101
Alexandra Est. NW8 76 DB67
Alexandra Gdns. N10 63 DH56
Alexandra Gdns. W4 88 CS80
Alexandra Gdns., Cars. 132 DG109
Alexandra Gdns., Houns. 86 CB82
Alexandra Gro. N4 63 DP60
Alexandra Gro. N12 48 DB50
Alexandra Ms. N2 62 DF55
Fortis Grn.
Alexandra Ms. SW19 104 DA93
Alexandra Rd.
Alexandra Palace N22 63 DK55
Alexandra Palace Way N22 63 DJ56
Alexandra Pk. Rd. N10 49 DH54
Alexandra Pk. Rd. N22 49 DJ53
Alexandra Pl. NW8 76 DC67
Alexandra Pl. SE25 120 DR99

Alexandra Pl., Croy. 120 DS102
Alexandra Rd.
Alexandra Rd. E6 81 EN69
Alexandra Rd. E10 65 EC62
Alexandra Rd. E17 65 DZ58
Alexandra Rd. E18 66 EH55
Alexandra Rd. N8 63 DN55
Alexandra Rd. N9 50 DV45
Alexandra Rd. N10 49 DH53
Alexandra Rd. N15 64 DR57
Alexandra Rd. NW4 61 CX56
Alexandra Rd. NW8 76 DC66
Alexandra Rd. SE26 107 DX93
Alexandra Rd. SW14 88 CR83
Alexandra Rd. SW19 103 CZ93
Alexandra Rd. W4 88 CR75
Alexandra Rd., Add. 126 BK105
Alexandra Rd., Ashf. 99 BR94
Alexandra Rd., Borwd. 32 CR38
Alexandra Rd., Brent. 87 CK79
Alexandra Rd., Croy. 120 DS102
Alexandra Rd., Enf. 37 DX42
Alexandra Rd., Epsom 131 CT113
Alexandra Rd., Erith 97 FF79
Alexandra Rd., Houns. 86 CB82
Alexandra Rd., Kings L. 14 BN29
Alexandra Rd. (Chipperfield), Kings L. 14 BG30
Alexandra Rd., Kings.T. 102 CN94
Alexandra Rd., Mitch. 104 DE94
Alexandra Rd., Rain. 83 FF67
Alexandra Rd., Rich. 88 CM82
Alexandra Rd., Rick. 28 BG36
Alexandra Rd., Rom. 69 FF58
Alexandra Rd. (Chadwell Heath), Rom. 68 EX58
Alexandra Rd., T.Ditt. 115 CF99
Alexandra Rd., Twick. 101 CJ86
Alexandra Rd., Uxb. 70 BK68
Alexandra Rd., Warl. 149 DY117
Alexandra Rd., Wat. 29 BU40
Alexandra Rd., West. 150 EH119
Alexandra Sq., Mord. 118 DA99
Alexandra St. E16 80 EG71
Alexandra St. SE14 93 DY80
Alexandra Wk. SE19 106 DS92
Alexandra Way, Wal.Cr. 23 DZ34
Alexandria Rd. W13 73 CG73
Alexis St. SE16 92 DU77
Alfan La., Dart. 111 FD92
Alfearn Rd. E5 64 DW63
Alford Grn., Croy. 135 ED107
Alford Pl. N1 7 J1
Alford Rd. SW8 91 DK81
Alford Rd., Erith 97 FC78
Alfoxton Ave. N15 63 DP56
Alfred Gdns., Sthl. 72 BY73
Alfred Ms. W1 5 M6
Alfred Ms. W1 77 DK71
Alfred Pl. WC1 5 M6
Alfred Pl. WC1 77 DK71
Alfred Prior Ho. E12 67 EN63
Alfred Rd. E15 66 EF64
Alfred Rd. SE25 120 DU99
Alfred Rd. W2 76 DA71
Alfred Rd. W3 74 CQ74
Alfred Rd., Belv. 96 EZ78
Alfred Rd., Buck.H. 52 EK47
Alfred Rd., Felt. 100 BW89
Alfred Rd., Kings.T. 116 CL97
Alfred Rd., Sutt. 132 DC106
Alfred St. E3 79 DZ69
Alfred St. E16 80 EF73
Alfreda St. SW11 91 DH81
Alfred's Gdns., Bark. 81 ES68
Alfreds Way, Bark. 81 EQ69
Alfreds Way Ind. Est., Bark. 82 EU67
Alfreton Clo. SW19 103 CX90
Alfriston Ave., Croy. 119 DL101
Alfriston Ave., Har. 58 CA58
Alfriston Clo., Surb. 116 CM99
Alfriston Rd. SW11 104 DF85
Algar Clo., Islw. 87 CG83
Algar Rd.
Algar Clo., Stan. 45 CF50
Algar Rd., Islw. 87 CG83
Algarve Rd. SW18 104 DB88
Algernon Rd. NW4 61 CU58
Algernon Rd. NW6 76 DA67
Algernon Rd. SE13 93 EB83
Algers Clo., Loug. 38 EK43
Algers Mead, Loug. 38 EK43
Algers Rd., Loug. 38 EK43
Algiers Rd. SE13 93 EA84
Alibon Gdns., Dag. 68 FA64
Alibon Rd., Dag. 68 EZ64
Alice Gilliatt Ct. W14 89 CZ78
Alice La. E3 79 DZ67
Alice Ms., Tedd. 101 CF92
Luther Rd.
Alice St. SE1 11 M7
Alice St. SE1 92 DS76
Alice Thompson Clo. SE12 108 EJ89
Alice Walker Clo. SE24 91 DP84
Shakespeare Rd.
Alice Way, Houns. 86 CB84
Alicia Ave., Har. 59 CH56
Alicia Clo., Har. 59 CJ56
Alicia Gdns., Har. 59 CH56
Alie St. E1 78 DT72
Alington Cres. NW9 60 CQ60
Alington Gro., Wall. 133 DJ109
Alison Clo. E6 81 EN72
Alison Clo., Croy. 121 DX102
Shirley Oaks Rd.
Aliwal Rd. SW11 90 DE84
Alkerden Rd. W4 88 CS78
Alkham Rd. N16 64 DT60
All Hallows Rd. N17 50 DS53
All Saints Clo. N9 50 DU47
All Saints Clo., Chig. 54 EV48
All Saints Cres., Wat. 16 BX33
All Saints Dr. SE3 94 EE82
All Saints Dr., S.Croy. 134 DT112
All Saints La., Rick. 28 BN44
All Saints Ms., Har. 45 CE51
All Saints Pas. SW18 104 DB85
Wandsworth High St.
All Saints Rd. SW19 104 DC94
All Saints Rd. W3 88 CQ76
All Saints Rd. W11 75 CZ72
All Saints Rd., Sutt. 118 DB104
All Saints St. N1 77 DM68
All Saints Twr. E10 65 EB59
All Souls Ave. NW10 75 CV68
All Souls Pl. W1 5 J7
Allan Barclay Clo. N15 64 DT58
High Rd.
Allan Clo., N.Mal. 116 CR99
Allan Way W3 74 CQ71
Allandale Ave. N3 61 CY55
Allandale Cres., Pot.B. 19 CZ32
Allandale Pl., Orp. 124 EX104
Allandale Rd., Enf. 37 DX36
Allandale Rd., Horn. 69 FF59
Allard Clo., Orp. 124 EW101
Allard Clo. (Cheshunt), Wal.Cr. 22 DT27
Allard Cres. (Bushey), Wat. 44 CC46
Allard Gdns. SW4 105 DK85
Allardyce St. SW4 91 DM84
Allbrook Clo., Tedd. 101 CE92
Allcot Clo., Felt. 99 BT88
Allcroft Rd. NW5 62 DG64
Allen Clo., Mitch. 119 DH95
Allen Clo., Rad. 18 CL32
Russet Dr.
Allen Clo., Sun. 113 BV95
Allen Ct., Grnf. 59 CF64
Allen Edwards Dr. SW8 91 DL81
Allen Pl., Twick. 101 CG88
Church St.
Allen Rd. E3 79 DZ68
Allen Rd. N16 64 DS63
Allen Rd., Beck. 121 DX96
Allen Rd., Croy. 119 DM102
Allen Rd., Sun. 113 BV95
Allen St. W8 90 DA76
Allenby Ave., S.Croy. 134 DQ109
Allenby Clo., Grnf. 72 CA69
Allenby Rd. SE23 107 DY90
Allenby Rd., Sthl. 72 CA69
Allenby Rd., West. 150 EL117
Allendale Ave., Sthl. 72 CA72
Allendale Clo. SE5 92 DR81
Daneville Rd.
Allendale Clo. SE26 107 DX92
Allendale Rd., Grnf. 73 CH65
Allens Rd., Enf. 36 DW43
Allensbury Pl. NW1 77 DK66
Allenswood Rd. SE9 94 EL83
Allerford Ct., Har. 58 CB57
Allerford Rd. SE6 107 EB90
Allerton Clo., Borwd. 32 CM38
Allerton Rd. N16 64 DQ61
Allerton Rd., Borwd. 32 CL38
Allerton Wk. N7 63 DM61
Durham Rd.
Allestree Rd. SW6 89 CY80
Alleyn Cres. SE21 106 DR89
Alleyn Pk. SE21 106 DR89
Alleyn Pk., Sthl. 86 CA78
Alleyn Rd. SE21 106 DR90
Alleyndale Rd., Dag. 68 EW61
Allfarthing La. SW18 104 DB86
Allgood Clo., Mord. 117 CX100
Allgood St. E2 78 DT68
Allhallows La. EC4 11 K1
Allhallows Rd. E6 80 EL71
Alliance Clo., Wem. 59 CK63
Milford Gdns.
Alliance Rd. E13 80 EJ70
Alliance Rd. SE18 96 EU79
Alliance Rd. W3 74 CP70
Allied Ind. Est. W3 88 CS75
Allied Way W3 88 CS75
Larden Rd.
Allingham Clo. W7 73 CF73
Allingham St. N1 78 DQ68
Allington Ave. N17 50 DS51
Allington Clo. SW19 103 CX92
High St. Wimbledon
Allington Clo., Grnf. 72 CC66
Allington Ct. SW19 103 CX92
High St. Wimbledon
Allington Ct., Enf. 37 DX43
Allington Rd. NW4 61 CV57
Allington Rd. W10 75 CY68
Allington Rd., Har. 58 CC57
Allington Rd., Orp. 123 ER103
Allington St. SW1 9 J7
Allington St. SW1 91 DH76
Allison Clo. SE10 93 EC81
Dartmouth Hill
Allison Clo., Wal.Abb. 24 EG33
Allison Gro. SE21 106 DS88
Allison Rd. N8 63 DN57
Allison Rd. W3 74 CQ72
Allitsen Rd. NW8 4 B1
Allitsen Rd. NW8 76 DE68
Allmains Clo., Wal.Abb. 24 EH25
Allnutt Way SW4 105 DK85
Allnutts Rd., Epp. 26 EU33
Alloa Rd. SE8 93 DY78
Alloa Rd., Ilf. 68 EU61
Allonby Dr., Ruis. 57 BP59
Allonby Gdns., Wem. 59 CJ60
Allotment La., Sev. 155 FJ122
Alloway Rd. E3 79 DY69
Allsop Pl. NW1 4 E5
Allsop Pl. NW1 76 DF70
Allum Clo., Borwd. 32 CL42
Allum Gro., Tad. 145 CV121
Preston La.
Allum La., Borwd. 31 CK43
Allum Way N20 48 DC46
Allwood Clo. SE26 107 DX91
Allwood Rd., Wal.Cr. 22 DT27
Alma Ave. E4 51 EC52
Alma Cres., Sutt. 131 CY106
Alma Gro. SE1 92 DT77
Alma Pl. NW10 75 CV69
Harrow Rd.
Alma Pl. SE19 106 DT94
Alma Pl., Th.Hth. 119 DN99
Alma Rd. N10 49 DH52
Alma Rd. SW18 90 DC84
Alma Rd., Cars. 132 DE106
Alma Rd., Enf. 37 DY41
Alma Rd., Esher 115 CE102
Alma Rd., Orp. 124 EX103
Alma Rd., Sid. 110 EU90
Alma Rd., Sthl. 72 BY73
Alma Row, Har. 45 CD53
Alma Sq. NW8 76 DC69
Alma St. E15 79 ED65
Alma St. NW5 77 DH65
Alma Ter. SW18 104 DD87
Almack Rd. E5 64 DW63
Almeida St. N1 77 DP66
Almer Rd. SW20 103 CU94
Almeric Rd. SW11 90 DF84
Almington St. N4 63 DL60
Almond Ave. W5 88 CL76
Almond Ave., Cars. 118 DF103
Almond Ave., Uxb. 57 BP62
Almond Ave., West Dr. 84 BN76
Almond Clo. SE15 92 DU82
Almond Clo., Brom. 123 EN101
Almond Clo., Hayes 71 BS73
Almond Clo., Ruis. 57 BT62
The Roundways
Almond Clo., Shep. 113 BQ96
Almond Dr., Swan. 125 FD96
Almond Gro., Brent. 87 CH80
Almond Rd. N17 50 DU52
Almond Rd. SE16 92 DV77
Almond Rd., Epsom 130 CR111
Almond Way, Borwd. 32 CP42
Almond Way, Brom. 123 EN101
Almond Way, Har. 44 CB54
Almond Way, Mitch. 119 DK99
Almonds Ave., Buck.H. 52 EG47
Almorah Rd. N1 78 DR66
Almorah Rd., Houns. 86 BX81
Alms Heath, Wok. 141 BP121
Almshouse La., Chess. 129 CJ109
Almshouse La., Enf. 36 DV37
Alnwick Gro., Mord. 118 DB98
Bordesley Rd.
Alnwick Rd. E16 80 EJ72
Alnwick Rd. SE12 108 EH87
Alperton La., Grnf. 73 CK68
Alperton La., Wem. 73 CK68
Alperton St. W10 75 CY70
Alpha Clo. NW1 4 C3
Alpha Ct., Whyt. 148 DU118
Alpha Gro. E14 93 EA75
Alpha Pl. NW6 76 DA68
Alpha Pl. SW3 90 DE79
Alpha Rd. E4 51 EA48
Alpha Rd. N18 50 DU51
Alpha Rd. SE14 93 DZ81
Alpha Rd., Croy. 120 DS102
Alpha Rd., Enf. 37 DY42
Alpha Rd., Surb. 116 CM100
Alpha Rd., Tedd. 101 CD92
Alpha Rd., Uxb. 71 BP70
Alpha St. SE15 92 DU82
Alphabet Gdns., Cars. 118 DD100
Alphabet Sq. E3 79 EA71
Hawgood St.
Alphea Clo. SW19 104 DE94
Courtney Rd.
Alpine Ave., Surb. 116 CQ103
Alpine Clo., Croy. 120 DS104
Alpine Copse, Brom. 123 EN96
Alpine Rd. SE16 92 DW77
Alpine Rd., Walt. 113 BU101
Alpine Vw., Cars. 132 DE106
Alpine Wk., Stan. 45 CE47
Alpine Way E6 81 EN71
Alric Ave. NW10 74 CR66
Alric Ave., N.Mal. 116 CS97
Alroy Rd. N4 63 DN59
Alsace Rd. SE17 11 M10
Alsace Rd. SE17 92 DS78
Alscot Rd. SE1 92 DT77
Alscot Way SE1 11 P8
Alscot Way SE1 92 DT77
Alsike Rd. SE2 96 EX76
Alsike Rd., Erith 96 EY76
Alsom Ave., Wor.Pk. 131 CT105
Alston Clo., Surb. 115 CH101
Alston Rd. N18 50 DV50
Alston Rd. SW17 104 DD91
Alston Rd., Barn. 33 CY41
Alt Gro. SW19 103 CZ94
St. George's Rd.
Altair Clo. N17 50 DT51
Altair Way, Nthwd. 43 BT50
Altash Way SE9 109 EM89
Altenburg Ave. W13 87 CH76
Altenburg Gdns. SW11 90 DF84
Altham Rd., Pnr. 44 BY52
Althea St. SW6 90 DB82
Althorne Gdns. E18 66 EF56
Althorne Way, Dag. 68 FA61
Althorp Rd. SW17 104 DF88
Althorpe Gro. SW11 90 DD81
Westbridge Rd.
Althorpe Ms. SW11 90 DD81
Westbridge Rd.
Althorpe Rd., Har. 58 CC57
Altmore Ave. E6 81 EM66
Alton Ave., Stan. 45 CF52
Alton Clo., Bex. 110 EY88
Alton Clo., Islw. 87 CF82
Alton Gdns., Beck. 107 EA94
Alton Gdns., Twick. 101 CD86
Alton Rd. N17 64 DR55
Alton Rd. SW15 103 CU88
Alton Rd., Croy. 119 DN104
Alton Rd., Rich. 88 CL84
Alton St. E14 79 EB71
Altyre Clo., Beck. 121 DZ99
Altyre Rd., Croy. 120 DR103
Altyre Way, Beck. 121 DZ100
Alva Way, Wat. 44 BX47
Alvanley Gdns. NW6 62 DB64
Alverston Gdns. SE25 120 DS99
Alverstone Ave. SW19 104 DA89
Alverstone Ave., Barn. 48 DE45
Alverstone Gdns. SE9 109 EQ88
Alverstone Rd. E12 67 EN63
Alverstone Rd. NW2 75 CW66
Alverstone Rd., N.Mal. 117 CT98
Alverstone Rd., Wem. 60 CM60
Alverton St. SE8 93 DZ78
Alveston Ave., Har. 59 CH55
Alvey Est. SE17 11 M9
Alvey St. SE17 11 M10
Alvey St. SE17 92 DS78
Alvia Gdns., Sutt. 132 DC105
Alvington Cres. E8 64 DT64
Alway Ave., Epsom 130 CQ106
Alwold Cres. SE12 108 EH86
Alwyn Ave. W4 88 CR78
Alwyn Clo., Borwd. 32 CM44
Alwyn Clo., Croy. 135 EB108
Alwyn Gdns. NW4 61 CU56
Alwyn Gdns. W3 74 CP72
Alwyne La. N1 77 DP66
Alwyne Vill.
Alwyne Pl. N1 78 DQ65
Alwyne Rd. N1 78 DQ66
Alwyne Rd. SW19 103 CZ93
Alwyne Rd. W7 73 CE73
Alwyne Sq. N1 78 DQ65
Alwyne Vill. N1 77 DP66
Alyth Gdns. NW11 62 DA58
Alzette Ho. E2 79 DX68
Mace St.
Amalgamated Dr., Brent. 87 CG79
Amanda Clo., Chig. 53 ER51
Amazon St. E1 78 DV72
Hessel St.
Ambassador Clo., Houns. 86 BY82
Ambassador Gdns. E6 81 EM71
Ambassador Sq. E14 93 EB77
Ambassador's Ct. SW1 9 L3
Amber Ave. E17 51 DY53
Amber Gro. NW2 61 CX60
Prayle Gro.
Amber St. E15 79 ED65
Salway Rd.
Ambercroft Way, Couls. 147 DP119
Amberden Ave. N3 62 DA55
Ambergate St. SE17 10 G10
Ambergate St. SE17 91 DP78
Amberley Clo., Orp. 137 ET106
Warnford Rd.
Amberley Clo., Pnr. 58 BZ55
Amberley Ct., Sid. 110 EW92
Amberley Gdns., Enf. 50 DS45
Amberley Gdns., Epsom 131 CT105
Amberley Gro. SE26 106 DV92
Amberley Gro., Croy. 120 DT101
Amberley Rd. E10 65 EA59
Amberley Rd. N13 49 DM47
Amberley Rd. SE2 96 EX79
Amberley Rd. W9 76 DA71
Amberley Rd., Buck.H. 52 EJ46
Amberley Rd., Enf. 50 DT45
Amberley Way, Houns. 100 BW85
Amberley Way, Mord. 117 CZ101
Amberley Way, Rom. 69 FB56
Amberley Way, Uxb. 70 BL69
Amberside Clo., Islw. 101 CD86
Amberwood Ri., N.Mal. 116 CS100
Amblecote, Cob. 128 BY112
Amblecote Clo. SE12 108 EH90
Amblecote Meadows SE12 108 EH90
Amblecote Rd. SE12 108 EH90
Ambler Rd. N4 63 DP62
Ambleside, Brom. 107 ED93
Ambleside, Epp. 26 EU31
Ambleside Ave. SW16 105 DK91
Ambleside Ave., Beck. 121 DY99
Ambleside Ave., Horn. 69 FH64
Ambleside Ave., Walt. 114 BW102
Ambleside Clo. E9 64 DW64
Churchill Wk.
Ambleside Clo. E10 65 EB59
Ambleside Cres., Enf. 37 DX41
Ambleside Dr., Felt. 99 BT88
Ambleside Gdns., Ilf. 66 EL56
Ambleside Gdns., S.Croy. 135 DX109
Ambleside Gdns., Sutt. 132 DC107
Ambleside Gdns., Wem. 59 CK60
Ambleside Rd. NW10 75 CT66
Ambleside Rd., Bexh. 96 FA82
Ambrey Way, Wall. 133 DK109
Ambrooke Rd., Belv. 96 FA76
Ambrosden Ave. SW1 9 L7
Ambrosden Ave. SW1 91 DJ76
Ambrose Ave. NW11 61 CY59
Ambrose Clo. E6 80 EL71
Lovage App.
Ambrose Clo., Dart. 97 FF84
Ambrose Clo., Orp. 123 ET104
Stapleton Rd.
Ambrose Ms. SW11 90 DF82
Abercrombie St.
Ambrose St. SE16 92 DV77
Ambrose Wk. E3 79 EA68
Malmesbury Rd.
Amelia St. SE17 11 H10
Amelia St. SE17 91 DP78
Amen Cor. EC4 6 G9
Amen Cor. SW17 104 DF93
Amen Ct. EC4 6 G8
Amenity Way, Mord. 117 CW101
America Sq. EC3 7 P10
America St. SE1 11 H3
Amerland Rd. SW18 103 CZ85
Amersham Ave. N18 50 DR51
Amersham Gro. SE14 93 DZ80
Amersham Rd. SE14 93 DZ81
Amersham Rd., Croy. 120 DQ100
Amersham Vale SE14 93 DZ80
Amery Gdns. NW10 75 CV67
Amery Rd., Har. 59 CG61
Amesbury, Wal.Abb. 24 EG32
Amesbury Ave. SW2 105 DL89
Amesbury Clo., Epp. 25 ET31
Amesbury Rd.
Amesbury Clo., Wor.Pk. 117 CW102
Amesbury Dr. E4 37 EB44
Amesbury Rd., Brom. 122 EK97
Amesbury Rd., Dag. 82 EX66
Amesbury Rd., Epp. 25 ET31
Amesbury Rd., Felt. 100 BX89
Amethyst Rd. E15 65 ED63
Amey Dr., Lthd. 142 CC124
Amherst Ave. W13 73 CJ72
Amherst Clo., Orp. 124 EU98
Amherst Dr., Orp. 123 ET98
Amherst Hill, Sev. 154 FE122
Amherst Rd. W13 73 CJ72
Amherst Rd., Sev. 155 FH122
Amhurst Gdns., Islw. 87 CF81
Amhurst Par. N16 64 DT59
Amhurst Pk.
Amhurst Pk. N16 64 DR59
Amhurst Pas. E8 64 DU64
Amhurst Rd. E8 64 DV64
Amhurst Rd. N16 64 DT63
Amhurst Ter. E8 64 DU63
Amhurst Wk. SE28 82 EU74
Pitfield Cres.
Amidas Gdns., Dag. 68 EV63
Amiel St. E1 78 DW70
Amies St. SW11 90 DF83
Amina Way SE16 92 DU76
Yalding Rd.
Amis Ave., Add. 126 BG110
Amis Ave., Epsom 130 CN107
Amity Gro. SW20 117 CW95
Amity Rd. E15 80 EF67
Ammanford Gdn. NW9 60 CS58
Ruthin Clo.
Amner Rd. SW11 104 DG86
Amoco Ho. W5 74 CL69
Amor Rd. W6 89 CW76
Amott Rd. SE15 92 DU83
Amoy Pl. E14 79 EA72
Ampere Way, Croy. 119 DL101
Ampleforth Rd. SE2 96 EV75
Ampthill Sq. Est. NW1 5 L1
Ampton Pl. WC1 6 B3
Ampton Pl. WC1 77 DM69
Ampton St. WC1 6 B3
Ampton St. WC1 77 DM69
Amroth Clo. SE23 106 DV88
Amsterdam Rd. E14 93 EC76
Amwell Clo., Enf. 36 DR43
Amwell Clo., Wat. 30 BY35
Phillipers
Amwell Ct., Wal.Abb. 24 EE33
Amwell Ct. Est. N4 64 DQ60
Amwell St. EC1 6 D2
Amwell St. EC1 77 DN69
Amy Warne Clo. E6 80 EL70
Evelyn Denington Rd.
Amyand Cotts., Twick. 101 CH86
Amyand Pk. Rd.
Amyand La., Twick. 101 CH87
Marble Hill Gdns.
Amyand Pk. Gdns., Twick. 101 CH87
Amyand Pk. Rd.
Amyand Pk. Rd., Twick. 101 CG87
Amyruth Rd. SE4 107 EA85
Anatola Rd. N19 63 DH61
Dartmouth Pk. Hill
Ancaster Cres., N.Mal. 117 CU100
Ancaster Ms., Beck. 121 DX97
Ancaster Rd.

Ancaster Rd., Beck. 121 DX97
Ancaster St. SE18 95 ES80
Anchor & Hope La. SE7 94 EJ77
Anchor Clo. (Cheshunt), Wal.Cr. 23 DX28
Anchor Dr., Rain. 83 FH69
Anchor Ms. SW12 105 DH86
Hazelbourne Rd.
Anchor St. SE16 92 DV77
Anchor Wf. E3 79 EB71
Watts Gro.
Anchor Yd. EC1 7 J4
Anchorage Clo. SW19 104 DA92
Ancill Clo. W6 89 CY79
Ancona Rd. NW10 75 CU68
Ancona Rd. SE18 95 ER78
Andace Pk. Gdns., Brom. 122 EJ95
Andalus Rd. SW9 91 DL83
Ander Clo., Wem. 59 CK63
Anderson Clo. N21 35 DM43
Worlds End La.
Anderson Clo. W3 74 CR72
Anderson Clo., Epsom 130 CP112
Anderson Clo., Uxb. 42 BG53
Anderson Dr., Ashf. 99 BQ91
Anderson Ho., Bark. 81 ER68
The Coverdales
Anderson Pl., Houns. 86 CB84
Anderson Rd. E9 79 DX65
Anderson Rd., Rad. 18 CN33
Anderson Rd., Wey. 113 BR104
Anderson Rd., Wdf.Grn. 66 EK55
Anderson St. SW3 8 D10
Anderson St. SW3 90 DF78
Anderson Way, Belv. 97 FB75
Anderton Clo. SE5 92 DR83
Andover Ave. E16 80 EK72
King George Ave.
Andover Clo., Epsom 130 CR111
Andover Clo., Felt. 99 BT88
Andover Clo., Grnf. 72 CB70
Ruislip Rd.
Andover Clo., Uxb. 70 BH68
Andover Pl. NW6 76 DB68
Andover Rd. N7 63 DM61
Andover Rd., Orp. 123 ES103
Andover Rd., Twick. 101 CD88
Andre St. E8 64 DU64
Andrew Borde St. WC2 5 N8
Andrew Clo., Bex. 111 FD85
Andrew Clo., Dart. 111 FD85
Andrew Clo., Ilf. 53 ER51
Andrew Pl. SW8 91 DK81
Cowthorpe Rd.
Andrew St. E14 79 EC72
Andrewes Gdns. E6 80 EL72
Andrewes Ho. EC2 78 DQ71
Fore St.
Andrews Clo. E6 80 EL72
Linton Gdns.
Andrews Clo., Buck.H. 52 EJ47
Andrews Clo., Epsom 131 CT114
Andrews Clo., Har. 59 CD59
Bessborough Rd.
Andrews Clo., Orp. 124 EX97
Andrews Clo., Wor.Pk. 117 CW103
Andrews Crosse WC2 6 D9
Andrews La. (Cheshunt), Wal.Cr. 22 DS28
Andrews Pl. SE9 109 EP86
Andrew's Rd. E8 78 DV67
Andrews Wk. SE17 91 DP79
Dale Rd.
Andwell Clo. SE2 96 EV75
Anerley Gro. SE19 106 DT94
Anerley Hill SE19 106 DT93
Anerley Pk. SE20 106 DU94
Anerley Pk. Rd. SE20 106 DV94
Anerley Rd. SE19 106 DU94
Anerley Rd. SE20 106 DU94
Anerley Sta. Rd. SE20 120 DV95
Anerley St. SW11 90 DF82
Anerley Vale SE19 106 DT94
Anfield Clo. SW12 105 DJ87
Belthorn Cres.
Angas Ct., Wey. 127 BQ106
Angel All. E1 78 DU72
Whitechapel Rd.
Angel Clo. N18 50 DT50
Angel Ct. EC2 7 L8
Angel Ct. SW1 9 L3
Angel Ct. SW17 104 DF91
Angel Hill, Sutt. 118 DB104
Sutton Common Rd.
Angel Hill Dr., Sutt. 118 DB104
Angel La. E15 79 ED65
Angel La., Hayes 71 BR71
Angel Ms. N1 6 E1
Angel Ms. N1 77 DN68
Angel Pas. EC4 11 K1
Angel Pl. N18 50 DU50
Angel Clo.
Angel Pl. SE1 11 K4
Angel Rd. N18 50 DU50
Angel Rd., Har. 59 CE58
Angel Rd., T.Ditt. 115 CG101
Angel Rd. Wks. N18 50 DW50
Angel Sq. EC1 77 DN68
Islington High St.
Angel St. EC1 7 H8
Angel St. EC1 78 DQ72
Angel Wk. W6 89 CW78
Angel Way, Rom. 69 FE57
Angelfield, Houns. 86 CB84
Angelica Dr. E6 81 EN71
Angelica Gdns., Croy. 121 DX102
Angell Pk. Gdns. SW9 91 DN83
Angell Rd. SW9 91 DN83
Angerstein La. SE3 94 EF81
Angle Clo., Uxb. 70 BN67
Angle Grn., Dag. 68 EW60
Burnside Rd.
Anglers Clo., Rich. 101 CJ91
Locksmeade Rd.
Angler's La. NW5 77 DH65
Angles Rd. SW16 105 DL91
Anglesea Ave. SE18 95 EP77
Anglesea Rd. SE18 95 EP77
Anglesea Rd., Kings.T. 115 CK98
Anglesea Rd., Orp. 124 EW100
Anglesea Ter. W6 89 CV76
Wellesley Ave.
Anglesey Clo., Ashf. 98 BN91
Anglesey Ct. Rd., Cars. 132 DG107
Anglesey Dr., Rain. 83 FG70
Anglesey Gdns., Cars. 132 DG107
Anglesey Rd., Enf. 36 DV42
Anglesey Rd., Wat. 44 BW50
Anglesmede Cres., Pnr. 58 BY55
Anglesmede Way, Pnr. 58 BY55
Anglia Clo. N17 50 DV52
Park La.
Anglia Ho. E14 79 DY72
Anglia Wk. E6 81 EM67
Napier Rd.
Anglian Clo., Wat. 30 BW40
Anglian Ind. Est., Bark. 82 EU71
Anglian Rd. E11 65 ED62
Anglo Rd. E3 79 DZ68
Angrave Ct. E8 78 DT67
Angrave Pas. E8 78 DT67
Haggerston Rd.
Angus Clo., Chess. 130 CN106
Angus Dr., Ruis. 58 BW63
Angus Gdns. NW9 46 CR53
Angus Rd. E13 80 EJ69
Angus St. SE14 93 DY80
Anhalt Rd. SW11 90 DE80
Ankerdine Cres. SE18 95 EP81
Anlaby Rd., Tedd. 101 CE92
Anley Rd. W14 89 CX75
Anmersh Gro., Stan. 45 CK53
Ann La. SW10 90 DD80
Ann Moss Way SE16 92 DW76
Ann St. SE18 95 EQ78
Anna Clo. E8 78 DT67
Anna Neagle Clo. E7 66 EG63
Dames Rd.
Annabel Clo. E14 79 EB72
Annan Way, Rom. 55 FD53
Annandale Gro., Uxb. 57 BQ62
Thorpland Ave.
Annandale Rd. SE10 94 EF78
Annandale Rd. W4 88 CS78
Annandale Rd., Croy. 120 DU103
Annandale Rd., Sid. 109 ES87
Anne Boleyn's Wk., Kings.T. 102 CL92
Anne Boleyn's Wk., Sutt. 131 CX108
Anne Case Ms., N.Mal. 116 CR97
Sycamore Gro.
Anne St. E13 80 EG70
Anne Way, Ilf. 53 EQ51
Anne Way, W.Mol. 114 CB98
Anne's Wk., Cat. 148 DS120
Annesley Ave. NW9 60 CR55
Annesley Clo. NW10 60 CS62
Annesley Dr., Croy. 135 DZ105
Annesley Rd. SE3 94 EH81
Annesley Wk. N19 63 DJ61
Macdonald Rd.
Annett Clo., Shep. 113 BS98
Annett Rd., Walt. 113 BU101
Annette Clo., Har. 45 CE54
Spencer Rd.
Annette Cres. N1 78 DQ66
Essex Rd.
Annette Rd. N7 63 DM62
Annie Besant Clo. E3 79 DZ67
Anning St. EC2 7 N4
Annington Rd. N2 62 DF55
Annis Rd. E9 79 DY65
Ann's Clo. SW1 8 E5
Ann's Pl. E1 7 P7
Annsworthy Ave., Th.Hth. 120 DR97
Grange Pk. Rd.
Annsworthy Cres. SE25 120 DR96
Grange Rd.
Ansdell Rd. SE15 92 DW82
Ansdell St. W8 90 DB76
Ansdell Ter. W8 90 DB76
Ansdell St.
Ansell Gro., Cars. 118 DG102
Ansell Rd. SW17 104 DE90
Anselm Clo., Croy. 120 DT104
Park Hill Ri.
Anselm Rd. SW6 90 DA79
Anselm Rd., Pnr. 44 BZ52
Ansford Rd., Brom. 107 EC92
Ansleigh Pl. W11 75 CX73
Ansley Clo., S.Croy. 134 DV114
Anson Clo., Ken. 148 DR120
Anson Clo., Rom. 55 FB54
Anson Rd. N7 63 DJ63
Anson Rd. NW2 61 CV64
Anson Ter., Nthlt. 72 CB65
Anson Wk., Nthwd. 43 BP49
Anstead Dr., Rain. 83 FG68
Anstey Rd. SE15 92 DU83
Anstey Wk. N15 63 DP56
Anstice Clo. W4 88 CS80
Anstridge Path SE9 109 ER86
Anstridge Rd.
Anstridge Rd. SE9 109 ER86
Antelope Rd. SE18 95 EM76
Anthony Clo. NW7 46 CS49
Anthony Clo., Sev. 154 FE121
Anthony Clo., Wat. 44 BW46
Anthony La., Swan. 125 FG95
Anthony Rd. SE25 120 DU100
Anthony Rd., Borwd. 32 CM40
Anthony Rd., Grnf. 73 CE68
Anthony Rd., Well. 96 EU81
Anthony St. E1 78 DV72
Commercial Rd.
Anthorne Clo., Pot.B. 20 DB31
Anthus Ms., Nthwd. 43 BS52
Antigua Clo. SE19 106 DR92
Salters Hill
Antigua Wk. SE19 106 DR92
Salters Hill
Antill Rd. E3 79 DY69
Antill Rd. N15 64 DU56
Antill Ter. E1 79 DX72
Antlers Hill E4 37 EB42
Antoinette Ct., Abb.L. 15 BT29
Anton Cres., Sutt. 118 DA104
Anton St. E8 64 DU64
Antoneys Clo., Pnr. 44 BX54
Antrim Gro. NW3 76 DF65
Antrim Mans. NW3 76 DF65
Antrim Rd.
Antrim Rd. NW3 76 DF65
Antrobus Clo., Sutt. 131 CZ106
Antrobus Rd. W4 88 CQ77
Anvil La., Cob. 127 BU114
Anvil Rd., Sun. 113 BU98
Anworth Clo., Wdf.Grn. 52 EH51
Anyards Rd., Cob. 127 BV113
Apeldoorn Dr., Wall. 133 DL109
Aperdele Rd., Lthd. 143 CG118
Aperfield Rd., Erith 97 FF79
Aperfield Rd., West. 150 EL117
Apex Clo., Beck. 121 EB95
Apex Clo., Wey. 113 BR104
Apex Cor. NW7 46 CR49
Apex Twr., N.Mal. 116 CS97
Aplin Way, Islw. 87 CE81
Apollo Ave., Brom. 122 EH95
Rodway Rd.
Apollo Ave., Nthwd. 43 BU50
Apollo Clo., Horn. 69 FH61
Apollo Pl. E11 66 EE62
Apollo Pl. SW10 90 DD80
Riley St.
Apollo Way SE28 95 ER76
Broadwater Rd.
Apostle Way, Th.Hth. 119 DP96
Apothecary St. EC4 6 F9
Appach Rd. SW2 105 DN85
Apple Garth, Brent. 87 CK77
Apple Gro., Chess. 130 CL105
Apple Gro., Enf. 36 DS41
Apple Mkt., Kings.T. 115 CK96
Eden St.
Apple Orchard, Swan. 125 FD98
Apple Rd. E11 66 EE62
Apple Tree Ave., Uxb. 70 BM72
Apple Tree Ave., West Dr. 70 BM72
Apple Tree Yd. SW1 9 L2
Appleby Clo. E4 51 EB51
Appleby Clo. N15 64 DR57
Appleby Clo., Twick. 101 CD89
Appleby Gdns., Felt. 99 BT88
Appleby Rd. E8 78 DU66
Appleby Rd. E16 80 EF72
Appleby St. E2 7 P1
Appleby St. E2 78 DT68
Appleby St. (Cheshunt), Wal.Cr. 22 DR25
Applecroft, St.Alb. 16 CB28
Appledore Ave., Bexh. 97 FC81
Appledore Ave., Ruis. 58 BW62
Appledore Clo. SW17 104 DF89
Appledore Clo., Brom. 122 EF99
Appledore Clo., Edg. 46 CN53
Appledore Cres., Sid. 109 ES90
Appledown Ri., Couls. 147 DJ115
Appleford Rd. W10 75 CY70
Applegarth, Croy. 135 EB108
Applegarth, Esher 129 CF106
Applegarth Dr., Ilf. 67 ET56
Applegarth Rd. SE28 82 EV74
Applegarth Rd. W14 89 CX76
Appleton Gdns., N.Mal. 117 CU100
Appleton Rd. SE9 94 EL83
Appleton Rd., Loug. 39 EP41
Appleton Sq., Mitch. 118 DE95
Appletree Clo. SE20 120 DV95
Jasmine Gro.
Appletree Clo., Lthd. 142 CC122
Kennel La.
Appletree Gdns., Barn. 34 DE42
Appletree Wk., Wat. 15 BV34
Applewood Clo. N20 48 DE46
Applewood Clo. NW2 61 CV62
Appold St. EC2 7 M6
Appold St. EC2 78 DS71
Appold St., Erith 97 FF79
Apprentice Way E5 64 DV63
Clarence Rd.
Approach, The NW4 61 CX57
Approach, The W3 74 CR72
Approach, The, Enf. 36 DV40
Approach, The, Lthd. 142 BY123
Maddox La.
Approach, The, Orp. 123 ET103
Approach, The, Pot.B. 19 CZ32
Approach Clo. N16 64 DS64
Cowper Rd.
Approach Rd. E2 78 DW68
Approach Rd. SW20 117 CW96
Approach Rd., Ashf. 99 BQ93
Approach Rd., Barn. 34 DC42
Approach Rd., Pur. 133 DP112
Approach Rd., W.Mol. 114 CA99
Aprey Gdns. NW4 61 CW56
April Clo. W7 73 CE73
April Clo., Ash. 144 CM117
April Clo., Felt. 99 BU90
April Clo., Orp. 137 ET106
Briarswood Way
April Glen SE23 107 DX90
April St. E8 64 DT63
Apsley Clo., Har. 58 CC57
Apsley Rd. SE25 120 DV98
Apsley Rd., N.Mal. 116 CQ97
Apsley Way NW2 61 CU61
Apsley Way W1 8 G4
Aquarius Way, Nthwd. 43 BU50
Aquila Clo., Lthd. 144 CL121
Aquila St. NW8 76 DD68
Aquinas St. SE1 10 E3
Arabella Dr. SW15 88 CS84
Arabia Clo. E4 51 EC45
Arabin Rd. SE4 93 DY84
Aragon Ave., Epsom 131 CV109
Aragon Ave., T.Ditt. 115 CF99
Aragon Clo., Brom. 123 EM102
Seymour Dr.
Aragon Clo., Croy. 136 EE110
Aragon Clo., Enf. 35 DM38
Aragon Clo., Loug. 38 EL44
Aragon Clo., Rom. 55 FB51
Aragon Clo., Sun. 99 BT94
Aragon Dr., Ilf. 53 EQ52
Aragon Dr., Ruis. 58 BX60
Aragon Ms. E1 78 DU74
Thomas More St.
Aragon Rd., Kings.T. 102 CL92
Aragon Rd., Mord. 117 CX100
Aragon Wk., W.Byf. 126 BM113
Aran Ct., Wey. 113 BR103
Mallards Reach
Aran Dr., Stan. 45 CJ49
Arandora Cres., Rom. 68 EV59
Arbery Rd. E3 79 DY69
Arbor Clo., Beck. 121 EB96
Arbor Ct. N16 64 DR61
Lordship Rd.
Arbor Rd. E4 51 ED48
Arbour Clo., Lthd. 143 CF123
Arbour Rd., Enf. 37 DX42
Arbour Sq. E1 79 DX72
Arbour Way, Horn. 69 FH64
Arbroath Grn., Wat. 43 BU48
Arbroath Rd. SE9 94 EL83
Arbrook Clo., Orp. 124 EU97
Arbrook La., Esher 128 CC107
Arbury Ter. SE26 106 DV90
Oaksford Ave.
Arbuthnot La., Bex. 110 EY86
Arbuthnot Rd. SE14 93 DX82
Arbutus St. E8 78 DT67
Arcade, The EC2 7 M7
Arcade Pl., Rom. 69 FE57
Arcadia Ave. N3 48 DA53
Arcadia Clo., Cars. 132 DG105
Arcadia St. E14 79 EA72
Arcadian Ave., Bex. 110 EY86
Arcadian Clo., Bex. 110 EY86
Arcadian Gdns. N22 49 DM52
Arcadian Rd., Bex. 110 EY86
Arch Rd., Walt. 114 BX104
Arch St. SE1 11 H7
Arch St. SE1 92 DQ76
Archangel St. SE16 93 DX75
Archbishops Pl. SW2 105 DM86
Archdale Pl., N.Mal. 116 CP97
Archdale Rd. SE22 106 DT85
Archel Rd. W14 89 CZ79
Archer Clo., Kings L. 14 BM29
Archer Clo., Kings.T. 102 CL94
Archer Ho. SW11 90 DD81
Vicarage Cres.
Archer Ms., Hmptn. 100 CC93
Windmill Rd.
Archer Rd. SE25 120 DV98
Archer Rd., Orp. 124 EU99
Archer St. W1 5 M10
Archer Ter., West Dr. 70 BL73
Yew Ave.
Archer Way, Swan. 125 FF96
Archers Dr., Enf. 36 DW40
Archers Wk. SE15 92 DT81
Exeter Rd.
Archery Clo. W2 4 C9
Archery Clo. W2 76 DE72
Archery Clo., Har. 59 CF55
Archery Rd. SE9 109 EM85
Arches, The SW6 89 CZ82
Munster Rd.
Arches, The WC2 10 A2
Arches, The, Har. 58 CB61
Archibald Ms. W1 9 H1
Archibald Ms. W1 76 DG73
Archibald Rd. N7 63 DK63
Archibald St. E3 79 EA70
Archie Clo., West Dr. 84 BN75
Archway, Rom. 55 FH51
Archway Clo. N19 63 DJ61
St. Johns Way
Archway Clo. SW19 104 DB91
Archway Clo., Wall. 119 DK104
Archway Mall N19 63 DJ61
Magdala Ave.
Archway Rd. N6 62 DF57
Archway Rd. N19 63 DJ60
Archway St. SW13 88 CS83
Arcola St. E8 64 DT64
Arctic St. NW5 62 DG64
Gillies St.
Arcus Rd., Brom. 108 EE93
Ardbeg Rd. SE24 106 DR85
Arden Clo., Har. 59 CD62
Arden Clo. (Bushey), Wat. 45 CF45
Arden Ct. Gdns. N2 62 DD58
Arden Cres. E14 93 EA77
Arden Cres., Dag. 82 EW66
Arden Est. N1 7 M1
Arden Est. N1 78 DS68
Arden Gro., Orp. 137 EP105
Arden Ms. E17 65 EB57
Arden Mhor, Pnr. 57 BV56
Arden Rd. N3 61 CY55
Arden Rd. W13 73 CJ73
Ardent Clo. SE25 120 DS97
Ardesley Wd., Wey. 127 BS105
Ardfern Ave. SW16 119 DN97
Ardfillan Rd. SE6 107 ED88
Ardgowan Rd. SE6 108 EE87
Ardilaun Rd. N5 64 DQ63
Ardingly Clo., Croy. 121 DX104
Ardleigh Gdns., Sutt. 118 DA101
Ardleigh Ho., Bark. 81 EQ67
St. Ann's
Ardleigh Ms., Ilf. 67 EP62
Bengal Rd.
Ardleigh Rd. E17 51 DZ53
Ardleigh Rd. N1 78 DS65
Ardleigh Ter. E17 51 DZ53
Ardley Clo. NW10 60 CS62
Ardley Clo. SE6 107 DY90
Ardley Clo., Ruis. 57 BQ59
Ardlui Rd. SE27 106 DQ89
Ardmay Gdns., Surb. 116 CL99
Ardmere Rd. SE13 107 ED86
Ardmore La., Buck.H. 52 EH45
Ardmore Pl., Buck.H. 52 EH45
Ardoch Rd. SE6 107 ED89
Ardra Rd. N9 51 DX48
Ardross Ave., Nthwd. 43 BS50
Ardrossan Gdns., Wor.Pk. 117 CU104
Ardshiel Clo. SW15 89 CX83
Bemish Rd.
Ardwell Ave., Ilf. 67 EQ57
Ardwell Rd. SW2 105 DL89
Ardwick Rd. NW2 62 DA63
Arena Ind. Est., Enf. 37 DZ38
Argall Ave. E10 65 DX59
Argent St. SE1 10 G4
Argenta Way NW10 74 CP66
Argon Ms. SW6 90 DA80
Argon Rd. N18 51 DX50
Harbet Rd.
Argosy La., Stai. 98 BK87
Argus Clo., Rom. 55 FB53
Argus Way W3 88 CP76
Argus Way, Nthlt. 72 BY69
Argyle Ave., Houns. 100 CA86
Argyle Clo. W13 73 CG70
Argyle Pas. N17 50 DT53
Argyle Rd.
Argyle Pl. W6 89 CV77
Argyle Rd. E1 79 DX70
Argyle Rd. E15 66 EE64
Argyle Rd. E16 80 EH72
Argyle Rd. N12 48 DA50
Argyle Rd. N17 50 DU53
Argyle Rd. N18 50 DU49
Argyle Rd. W13 73 CG71
Argyle Rd., Barn. 33 CW42
Argyle Rd., Grnf. 73 CF69
Argyle Rd., Har. 58 CB58
Argyle Rd., Houns. 100 CB85
Argyle Rd., Ilf. 67 EN61
Argyle Rd., Sev. 155 FH125
Argyle Rd., Tedd. 101 CE92
Argyle Sq. WC1 6 A2
Argyle Sq. WC1 77 DL69
Argyle St. WC1 5 P2
Argyle St. WC1 77 DL69
Argyle Wk. WC1 5 P3
Argyle Way SE16 92 DU78
Argyll Ave., Sthl. 72 CB74
Argyll Clo. SW9 91 DM83
Dalyell Rd.
Argyll Gdns., Edg. 46 CP54
Argyll Rd. W8 90 DA75
Argyll St. W1 5 K9
Argyll St. W1 77 DJ72
Arica Rd. SE4 93 DY84
Ariel Rd. NW6 76 DA65
Ariel Way W12 75 CW74
Ariel Way, Houns. 85 BV83
Aristotle Rd. SW4 91 DK83
Arkell Gro. SE19 105 DP94
Arkindale Rd. SE6 107 EC90
Arkley Cres. E17 65 DZ57
Arkley Dr., Barn. 33 CU42
Arkley La., Barn. 33 CU41
Arkley Rd. E17 65 DZ57
Arkley Vw., Barn. 33 CV42
Arklow Ms., Surb. 116 CL103
Vale Rd. S.
Arklow Rd. SE14 93 DZ79
Arkwright Rd. NW3 62 DC64
Arkwright Rd., S.Croy. 134 DT110
Arlesey Clo. SW15 103 CY86
Lytton Gro.
Arlesford Rd. SW9 91 DL83
Arlingford Rd. SW2 105 DN85
Arlington N12 48 DA48

Ashton Rd., Enf. 37 DY36
Ashton St. E14 79 EC73
Ashtree Ave., Mitch. 118 DD96
Ashtree Clo., Orp. 137 EP105
Broadwater Gdns.
Ashurst Clo. SE20 120 DV95
Ashurst Clo., Dart. 97 FF83
Ashurst Clo., Ken. 148 DR115
Ashurst Clo., Nthwd. 43 BS52
Ashurst Dr., Ilf. 67 EP58
Ashurst Dr., Shep. 112 BL99
Ashurst Rd. N12 48 DE50
Ashurst Rd., Barn. 34 DF43
Ashurst Rd., Tad. 145 CV121
Ashurst Wk., Croy. 120 DV103
Ashvale Gdns., Rom. 55 FD50
Ashvale Rd. SW17 104 DF92
Ashville Rd. E11 65 ED61
Ashwater Rd. SE12 108 EG88
Ashwell Clo. E6 80 EL72
Northumberland Rd.
Ashwin St. E8 78 DT65
Ashwood, Warl. 148 DW120
Ashwood Ave., Rain. 83 FH69
Ashwood Ave., Uxb. 70 BN72
Ashwood Gdns., Croy. 135 EB107
Ashwood Gdns., Hayes 85 BT77
Cranford Dr.
Ashwood Pk., Lthd. 142 CC123
Ashwood Rd. E4 51 ED48
Ashwood Rd., Pot.B. 20 DB33
Ashworth Clo. SE5 92 DR82
Denmark Hill
Ashworth Rd. W9 76 DB69
Aske St. N1 7 M2
Askern Clo., Bexh. 96 EX84
Askew Cres. W12 89 CT75
Askew Rd. W12 75 CT74
Askew Rd., Nthwd. 43 BR47
Askham Ct. W12 75 CU74
Askham Rd. W12 75 CU74
Askill Dr. SW15 103 CY85
Keswick Rd.
Askwith Rd., Rain. 83 FD69
Asland Rd. E15 79 ED67
Aslett St. SW18 104 DB87
Asmar Clo., Couls. 147 DL115
Asmara Rd. NW2 61 CY64
Asmuns Hill NW11 62 DA57
Asmuns Pl. NW11 61 CZ57
Aspen Clo. N19 63 DJ61
Hargrave Pk.
Aspen Clo. W5 88 CM75
Aspen Clo., Cob. 142 BY116
Aspen Clo., Orp. 138 EU106
Aspen Clo., St.Alb. 16 BY30
Aspen Clo., Swan. 125 FD95
Aspen Clo., West Dr. 70 BM74
Aspen Copse, Brom. 123 EM96
Aspen Ct., Hayes 85 BS77
Clement Gdns.
Aspen Dr., Wem. 59 CG63
Aspen Gdns. W6 89 CV78
Aspen Gdns., Mitch. 118 DG99
Aspen Grn., Erith 96 EZ76
Aspen La., Nthlt. 72 BY69
Aspen Pk. Dr., Wat. 29 BV35
Aspen Sq., Wey. 113 BR104
Oatlands Dr.
Aspen Way E14 79 ED73
Aspen Way, Bans. 131 CX114
Aspen Way, Enf. 37 DX35
Aspen Way, Felt. 99 BV90
Aspenlea Rd. W6 89 CX79
Aspern Gro. NW3 62 DE64
Aspinall Rd. SE4 93 DX83
Aspinden Rd. SE16 92 DV77
Aspley Rd. SW18 104 DB85
Aspley Way NW2 61 CU61
Asplins Rd. N17 50 DU53
Asquith Clo., Dag. 68 EW60
Crystal Way
Ass Ho. La., Har. 44 CB49
Assam St. E1 78 DU72
White Ch. La.
Assata Ms. N1 77 DP65
St. Paul's Rd.
Assembly Pas. E1 78 DW71
Assembly Wk., Cars. 118 DE101
Assher Rd., Walt. 114 BY104
Assurance Cotts., Belv. 96 EZ78
Heron Hill
Astall Clo., Har. 45 CE53
Sefton Ave.
Astbury Rd. SE15 92 DW81
Aste St. E14 93 EC75
Astell St. SW3 8 C10
Astell St. SW3 90 DE78
Asteys Row N1 77 DP66
River Pl.
Asthall Gdns., Ilf. 67 EQ56
Astle St. SW11 90 DG82
Astleham Rd., Shep. 112 BL97
Astley Ave. NW2 61 CW64
Aston Ave., Har. 59 CJ59
Aston Clo., Ash. 143 CJ118
Aston Clo., Sid. 110 EU90
Aston Clo., Wat. 30 BW40
Aston Clo. (Bushey), Wat. 30 CC44
Aston Grn., Houns. 86 BW82
Aston Ms., Rom. 68 EW59
Reynolds Ave.
Aston Rd. SW20 117 CW96
Aston Rd. W5 73 CK72
Aston Rd., Esher 129 CE106
Aston St. E14 79 DY72
Aston Way, Epsom 145 CT116
Aston Way, Pot.B. 20 DD32
Astons Rd., Nthwd. 43 BQ48
Astonville St. SW18 104 DA88
Astor Ave., Rom. 69 FC58
Astor Clo., Add. 126 BK105
Astor Clo., Kings.T. 102 CP93
Astoria Wk. SW9 91 DN83
Astra Clo., Horn. 83 FH65
Astrop Ms. W6 89 CW76
Astrop Ter. W6 89 CW75
Astwood Ms. SW7 90 DB77
Asylum Rd. SE15 92 DV80
Atalanta Clo., Pur. 133 DN110
Atalanta St. SW6 89 CX81
Atbara Ct., Tedd. 101 CH93
Atbara Rd., Tedd. 101 CH93
Atcham Rd., Houns. 86 CC84
Atcost Rd., Bark. 82 EU71
Atheldene Rd. SW18 104 DC87
Athelney St. SE6 107 EA90
Athelstan Rd., Kings.T. 116 CM98
Athelstan Way, Orp. 124 EU95
Athelstane Gro. E3 79 DZ68
Athelstane Ms. N4 63 DN60
Stroud Grn. Rd.
Athelstone Rd., Har. 45 CD54
Athena Clo., Har. 59 CE61
Byron Hill Rd.
Athena Clo., Kings.T. 116 CM97
Athena Pl., Nthwd. 43 BT53
The Dr.
Athenaeum Pl. N10 63 DH55
Fortis Grn. Rd.
Athenaeum Rd. N20 48 DC46
Athenlay Rd. SE15 107 DX85
Athens Gdns. W9 76 DA70
Elgin Ave.
Atherden Rd. E5 64 DW63
Atherfold Rd. SW9 91 DL83
Atherley Way, Houns. 100 BZ87
Atherstone Ms. SW7 90 DC77
Atherton Clo., Stai. 98 BK86
Atherton Dr. SW19 103 CX91
Atherton Heights, Wem. 73 CJ65
Atherton Ms. E7 80 EF65
Atherton Pl., Har. 59 CD55
Atherton Pl., Sthl. 72 CB73
Longford Ave.
Atherton Rd. E7 80 EF65
Atherton Rd. SW13 89 CU80
Atherton Rd., Ilf. 52 EL54
Atherton St. SW11 90 DE82
Athlon Rd., Wem. 73 CK68
Athlone, Esher 129 CE107
Athlone Clo. E5 64 DV63
Goulton Rd.
Athlone Clo., Rad. 31 CG36
Athlone Rd. SW2 105 DM87
Athlone St. NW5 76 DG65
Athol Clo., Pnr. 43 BV53
Athol Gdns., Pnr. 43 BV53
Athol Rd., Erith 97 FC78
Athol Sq. E14 79 EC72
Athol Way, Uxb. 70 BN69
Athole Gdns., Enf. 36 DS43
Atholl Rd., Ilf. 68 EU59
Atkins Dr., W.Wick. 121 ED103
Atkins Rd. E10 65 EB58
Atkins Rd. SW12 105 DK87
Atkinson Clo., Orp. 138 EU106
Martindale Ave.
Atkinson Rd. E16 80 EJ71
Atlanta Boul., Rom. 69 FE58
Atlantic Rd. SW9 91 DN84
Atlas Gdns. SE7 94 EJ77
Atlas Ms. E8 78 DT65
Tyssen St.
Atlas Ms. N7 77 DM65
Atlas Rd. E13 80 EG68
Atlas Rd. NW10 74 CS69
Atlas Rd., Wem. 60 CQ63
Atley Rd. E3 79 EA67
Atlip Rd., Wem. 74 CL67
Atney Rd. SW15 89 CY84
Atria Rd., Nthwd. 43 BU50
Attenborough Clo., Wat. 44 BY48
Harrow Way
Atterbury Rd. N4 63 DN58
Atterbury St. SW1 9 P9
Atterbury St. SW1 91 DL77
Attewood Ave. NW10 60 CS62
Attewood Rd., Nthlt. 72 BY65
Attfield Clo. N20 48 DD47
Attle Clo., Uxb. 70 BN68
Attlee Clo., Hayes 71 BV69
Attlee Clo., Th.Hth. 120 DQ100
Attlee Rd. SE28 82 EV73
Attlee Rd., Hayes 71 BU69
Attlee Ter. E17 65 EB56
Attneave St. WC1 6 D3
Attwood Clo., S.Croy. 134 DV114
Atwater Clo. SW2 105 DN88
Atwell Clo. E10 65 EB58
Belmont Pk. Rd.
Atwell Rd. SE15 92 DU82
Rye La.
Atwood, Lthd. 142 BY124
Atwood Ave., Rich. 88 CN82
Atwood Rd. W6 89 CV77
Aubert Pk. N5 63 DN63
Aubert Rd. N5 63 DP63
Aubrey Ave., St.Alb. 17 CJ26
Aubrey Pl. NW8 76 DC68
Violet Hill
Aubrey Rd. E17 65 EA55
Aubrey Rd. N8 63 DL57
Aubrey Rd. W8 75 CZ74
Aubrey Wk. W8 75 CZ74
Aubyn Hill SE27 106 DQ91
Aubyn Sq. SW15 89 CU84
Auckland Ave., Rain. 83 FF69
Auckland Clo. SE19 120 DT95
Auckland Clo., Enf. 36 DV37
Auckland Gdns. SE19 120 DS95
Auckland Hill SE27 106 DQ91
Auckland Ri. SE19 120 DS95
Auckland Rd. E10 65 EB62
Auckland Rd. SE19 120 DT95
Auckland Rd. SW11 90 DE84
Auckland Rd., Cat. 148 DS122
Auckland Rd., Ilf. 67 EP60
Auckland Rd., Kings.T. 116 CM98
Auckland Rd., Pot.B. 19 CX32
Auckland St. SE11 91 DM78
Kennington La.
Auden Pl. NW1 76 DG67
Manley St.
Audleigh Pl., Chig. 53 EN51
Audley Clo. N10 49 DH52
Audley Clo. SW11 90 DG83
Audley Clo., Add. 126 BH106
Audley Clo., Borwd. 32 CN41
Audley Ct. E18 66 EF56
Audley Ct., Pnr. 44 BW54
Audley Dr., Warl. 148 DW115
Audley Firs, Walt. 128 BW105
Audley Gdns., Ilf. 67 ET61
Audley Gdns., Loug. 39 EQ40
Audley Gdns., Wal.Abb. 23 EC34
Audley Pl., Sutt. 132 DB108
Audley Rd. NW4 61 CU58
Audley Rd. W5 74 CM71
Audley Rd., Enf. 35 DP40
Audley Rd., Rich. 102 CM85
Audley Sq. W1 8 G2
Audley Wk., Orp. 124 EW100
Audrey Clo., Beck. 121 EB100
Audrey Gdns., Wem. 59 CH61
Audrey Rd., Ilf. 67 EP62
Audrey St. E2 78 DU68
Audric Clo., Kings.T. 116 CN95
Audwick Clo. (Cheshunt), Wal.Cr. 23 DY28
Augurs La. E13 80 EH69
Augusta Clo., W.Mol. 114 BZ97
Freeman Dr.
Augusta Rd., Twick. 100 CC89
Augusta St. E14 79 EB72
Augustine Rd. W14 89 CX76
Augustine Rd., Har. 44 CB53
Augustine Rd., Orp. 124 EX97
Augustus Clo., Brent. 87 CK80
Augustus La., Orp. 124 EU103
Augustus Rd. SW19 103 CX88
Augustus St. NW1 5 J1
Augustus St. NW1 77 DH68
Aulton Pl. SE11 91 DN78
Milverton St.
Aultone Way, Cars. 118 DF104
Aultone Way, Sutt. 118 DB103
Aurelia Gdns., Croy. 119 DM99
Aurelia Rd., Croy. 119 DL100
Auriel Ave., Dag. 83 FD65
Auriga Ms. N16 64 DR64
Auriol Clo., Wor.Pk. 116 CS104
Auriol Pk. Rd.
Auriol Dr., Grnf. 73 CD66
Auriol Dr., Uxb. 71 BP65
Auriol Pk. Rd., Wor.Pk. 116 CS104
Auriol Rd. W14 89 CY77
Austell Gdns. NW7 46 CS48
Austen Clo. SE28 82 EV74
Austen Clo., Loug. 39 ER41
Austen Ho. NW6 76 DA69
Austen Rd., Erith 97 FB81
Belmont Rd.
Austen Rd., Har. 58 CB61
Austin Ave., Brom. 122 EL99
Austin Clo. SE23 107 DZ87
Austin Clo., Couls. 147 DP118
Austin Clo., Twick. 101 CJ85
Austin Ct. E6 80 EJ67
Kings Rd.
Austin Friars EC2 7 L8
Austin Friars EC2 78 DR72
Austin Friars Pas. EC2 7 L8
Austin Friars Sq. EC2 7 L8
Austin Rd. SW11 90 DG81
Austin Rd., Hayes 85 BT75
Austin Rd., Orp. 124 EU100
Austin St. E2 7 P3
Austin St. E2 78 DT69
Austin Waye, Uxb. 70 BJ67
Austin's La., Uxb. 57 BQ62
Austral Clo., Sid. 109 ET90
Austral St. SE11 10 F8
Austral St. SE11 91 DP77
Australia Rd. W12 75 CV73
Austyn Gdns., Surb. 116 CP102
Autumn Clo., Enf. 36 DU39
Autumn Dr., Sutt. 132 DB109
Autumn St. E3 79 EA67
Avalon Clo. SW20 117 CY96
Avalon Clo. W13 73 CG71
Avalon Clo., Enf. 35 DN40
Avalon Clo., Orp. 124 EX104
Avalon Clo., Wat. 16 BY32
Avalon Rd. SW6 90 DB81
Avalon Rd. W13 73 CG70
Avalon Rd., Orp. 124 EV103
Avard Gdns., Orp. 137 EQ105
Isabella Dr.
Avarn Rd. SW17 104 DF93
Ave Maria La. EC4 6 G9
Ave Maria La. EC4 77 DP72
Avebury Ct. N1 78 DR67
Poole St.
Avebury Pk., Surb. 115 CK101
Avebury Rd. E11 65 ED60
Southwest Rd.
Avebury Rd. SW19 117 CZ95
Avebury Rd., Orp. 123 ER104
Avebury St. N1 78 DR67
Poole St.
Aveley Clo., Erith 97 FF79
Aveley Rd., Rom. 69 FD56
Aveline St. SE11 91 DN78
Aveling Clo., Pur. 133 DM113
Aveling Pk. Rd. E17 51 EA54
Avelon Rd., Rain. 83 FG67
Avelon Rd., Rom. 55 FD51
Avenell Rd. N5 63 DP62
Avening Rd. SW18 104 DA87
Brathway Rd.
Avening Ter. SW18 104 DA86
Avenons Rd. E13 80 EG70
Avenue, The E4 51 ED51
Avenue, The (Leytonstone) E11 66 EF61
Avenue, The (Wanstead) E11 66 EH58
Avenue, The N3 48 DA54
Sylvan Ave.
Avenue, The N8 63 DN55
Avenue, The N10 49 DJ54
Avenue, The N11 49 DH50
Avenue, The N17 50 DS54
Avenue, The NW6 75 CX67
Avenue, The SE7 94 EJ80
Avenue, The SE10 93 ED80
Avenue, The SW4 104 DG85
Avenue, The SW11 104 DF87
Bellevue Rd.
Avenue, The SW18 104 DE87
Avenue, The W4 88 CS76
Avenue, The W13 73 CH73
Avenue, The, Add. 126 BG110
Avenue, The, Barn. 33 CY41
Avenue, The, Beck. 121 EB95
Avenue, The, Bex. 110 EX86
Avenue, The, Brom. 122 EK97
Avenue, The, Cars. 132 DG108
Avenue, The, Couls. 147 DK115
Avenue, The, Croy. 120 DS104
Avenue, The, Epsom 131 CV108
Avenue, The, Esher 129 CE107
Avenue, The, Hmptn. 100 BZ93
Avenue, The, Har. 45 CF53
Avenue, The, Houns. 100 CB85
Avenue, The (Cranford), Houns. 85 BU81
Avenue, The, Islw. 87 CD80
Jersey Rd.
Avenue, The, Kes. 122 EK104
Avenue, The, Lthd. 129 CF112
Avenue, The, Loug. 38 EK44
Avenue, The, Nthwd. 43 BQ51
Avenue, The, Orp. 123 ET103
Avenue, The (St. Paul's Cray), Orp. 110 EV94
Avenue, The, Pnr. 58 BZ58
Avenue, The (Hatch End), Pnr. 44 BZ51
Avenue, The, Pot.B. 19 CZ30
Avenue, The, Rad. 17 CG33
Avenue, The, Rich. 88 CM82
Avenue, The, Rom. 69 FD56
Avenue, The, Stai. 112 BH95
Avenue, The, Sun. 113 BV95
Avenue, The, Surb. 116 CM100
Avenue, The, Sutt. 131 CY109
Avenue, The (Cheam), Sutt. 131 CV108
Avenue, The, Tad. 145 CV122
Avenue, The, Twick. 101 CH85
Avenue, The (Cowley), Uxb. 70 BK70
Avenue, The (Ickenham), Uxb. 56 BN63
Avenue, The, Wal.Abb. 24 EJ25
Avenue, The, Wat. 29 BU40
Avenue, The (Bushey), Wat. 30 BZ42
Avenue, The, Wem. 60 CL60
Avenue, The, West Dr. 84 BL76
Avenue, The, W.Wick. 121 EC101
Avenue, The, West. 151 EM122
Avenue, The, Whyt. 148 DU119
Avenue, The, Wor.Pk. 117 CT103
Avenue App., Kings L. 14 BN30
Avenue Clo. N14 35 DJ44
Avenue Clo. NW8 76 DE67
Avenue Clo., Houns. 85 BU81
The Ave.
Avenue Clo., Tad. 145 CV122
Avenue Clo., West Dr. 84 BK76
Avenue Cres. W3 88 CP75
Avenue Cres., Houns. 85 BV80
Avenue Elmers, Surb. 116 CL99
Avenue Gdns. SE25 120 DU97
Avenue Gdns. SW14 88 CS83
Avenue Gdns. W3 88 CP75
Avenue Gdns., Houns. 85 BU80
The Ave.
Avenue Gdns., Tedd. 101 CF94
Avenue Gate, Loug. 38 EJ44
Avenue Ind. Est. E4 51 DZ51
Avenue Ms. N10 63 DH55
Avenue Pk. Rd. SE27 105 DP89
Avenue Ri. (Bushey), Wat. 30 CA43
Avenue Rd. E7 66 EH63
Avenue Rd. N6 63 DJ59
Avenue Rd. N12 48 DC49
Avenue Rd. N14 49 DH45
Avenue Rd. N15 64 DR57
Avenue Rd. NW3 76 DD66
Avenue Rd. NW8 76 DD66
Avenue Rd. NW10 75 CT68
Avenue Rd. SE20 120 DW95
Avenue Rd. SE25 120 DT96
Avenue Rd. SW16 119 DK96
Avenue Rd. SW20 117 CV96
Avenue Rd. W3 88 CP75
Avenue Rd., Bans. 146 DB115
Avenue Rd., Beck. 121 DX95
Avenue Rd., Belv. 97 FC77
Avenue Rd., Bexh. 96 EY84
Avenue Rd., Brent. 87 CJ78
Avenue Rd., Cat. 148 DR122
Avenue Rd., Cob. 142 BX116
Avenue Rd., Epp. 39 ER36
Avenue Rd., Epsom 130 CR114
Avenue Rd., Erith 97 FC80
Avenue Rd., Felt. 99 BT90
Avenue Rd., Hmptn. 114 CB95
Avenue Rd., Islw. 87 CF81
Avenue Rd., Kings.T. 116 CL97
Avenue Rd., N.Mal. 116 CS98
Avenue Rd., Pnr. 58 BY55
Avenue Rd. (Chadwell Heath), Rom. 68 EV60
Avenue Rd., Sev. 155 FJ124
Avenue Rd., Sthl. 86 BZ75
Avenue Rd., Sutt. 132 DA110
Avenue Rd., Tedd. 101 CG94
Avenue Rd., Wall. 133 DJ108
Avenue Rd., West. 150 EL120
Avenue Rd., Wdf.Grn. 52 EJ51
Avenue S., Surb. 116 CM101
Avenue Ter., N.Mal. 116 CQ97
Kingston Rd.
Avenue Ter., Wat. 30 BY44
Averil Gro. SW16 105 DP93
Averill St. W6 89 CX79
Avern Gdns., W.Mol. 114 CB98
Avern Rd., W.Mol. 114 CB98
Avery Fm. Row SW1 9 H9
Avery Gdns., Ilf. 67 EM57
Avery Hill Rd. SE9 109 ER86
Avery Row W1 5 J10
Avery Row W1 77 DH73
Avey La., Loug. 38 EH39
Avey La., Wal.Abb. 37 ED36
Aviary Clo. E16 80 EF71
Aviary Rd., Wok. 140 BG116
Aviemore Clo., Beck. 121 DZ99
Aviemore Way, Beck. 121 DY99
Avignon Rd. SE4 93 DX83
Avington Ct. SE1 92 DS77
Old Kent Rd.
Avington Gro. SE20 106 DW94
Avington Way SE15 92 DT80
Daniel Gdns.
Avior Dr., Nthwd. 43 BT49
Avis Gro., Croy. 135 DY111
Avis Sq. E1 79 DX72
Avoca Rd. SW17 104 DG91
Avocet Ms. SE28 95 ER76
Avon Clo., Add. 126 BG107
Avon Clo., Hayes 72 BW70
Avon Clo., Sutt. 132 DC105
Avon Clo., Wat. 16 BW34
Avon Clo., Wor.Pk. 117 CU103
Avon Ct., Grnf. 72 CB70
Braund Ave.
Avon Ms., Pnr. 44 BZ53
Avon Path, S.Croy. 134 DQ107
Avon Pl. SE1 11 J5
Avon Rd. E17 65 ED55
Avon Rd. SE4 93 EA83
Avon Rd., Grnf. 72 CA70
Avon Rd., Sun. 99 BT94
Avon Way E18 66 EG55
Avondale Ave. N12 48 DB50
Avondale Ave. NW2 60 CS62
Avondale Ave., Barn. 48 DF46
Avondale Ave., Esher 115 CG104
Avondale Ave., Wor.Pk. 117 CT102
Avondale Clo., Loug. 53 EM45
Avondale Clo., Walt. 128 BW106
Pleasant Pl.
Avondale Ct. E11 66 EE60
Avondale Ct. E16 80 EE71
Avondale Rd.
Avondale Ct. E18 52 EH53
Avondale Cres., Enf. 37 DY41
Avondale Cres., Ilf. 66 EK57
Avondale Dr., Hayes 71 BU74
Avondale Dr., Loug. 53 EM45
Avondale Gdns., Houns. 100 BZ85
Avondale Ms., Brom. 108 EG93
Avondale Rd.
Avondale Pk. Gdns. W11 75 CY73
Avondale Pk. Rd. W11 75 CY73
Avondale Pavement SE1 92 DU78
Avondale Sq.
Avondale Ri. SE15 92 DT83
Avondale Rd. E16 80 EE71
Avondale Rd. E17 65 EA59
Avondale Rd. N3 48 DC53
Avondale Rd. N13 49 DN47
Avondale Rd. N15 63 DP57
Avondale Rd. SE9 108 EL89
Avondale Rd. SW14 88 CR83
Avondale Rd. SW19 104 DB92
Avondale Rd., Ashf. 98 BK90
Avondale Rd., Brom. 108 EE93

Avondale Rd., Har. 59 CF55
Avondale Rd., S.Croy. 134 DQ108
Avondale Rd., Well. 96 EW82
Avondale Sq. SE1 92 DU78
Avonley Rd. SE14 92 DW80
Avonmore Gdns. W14 89 CY77
Avonmore Rd.
Avonmore Pl. W14 89 CY77
Avonmore Rd.
Avonmore Rd. W14 89 CY77
Avonmouth St. SE1 11 H6
Avonmouth St. SE1 92 DQ76
Avonwick Rd., Houns. 86 CB82
Avril Way E4 51 EC50
Avro Way, Wall. 133 DL108
Avro Way, Wey. 126 BL111
Award Gdns., Orp. 137 EQ105
Awlfield Ave. N17 50 DR53
Awliscombe Rd., Well. 95 ET82
Axe St., Bark. 81 EQ67
Axholme Ave., Edg. 46 CN53
Axminster Cres., Well. 96 EW81
Axminster Rd. N7 63 DL62
Axtaine Rd., Orp. 124 EX101
Axwood, Epsom 144 CQ115
Aybrook St. W1 4 F7
Aybrook St. W1 76 DG71
Aycliffe Clo., Brom. 123 EM98
Aycliffe Rd. W12 75 CT74
Aycliffe Rd., Borwd. 32 CL39
Aylands Clo., Wem. 60 CL61
Preston Rd.
Aylands Rd., Enf. 37 DX36
Ayles Rd., Hayes 71 BV69
Aylesbury Clo. E7 80 EF65
Atherton Rd.
Aylesbury Est. SE17 92 DR78
Villa St.
Aylesbury Rd. SE17 92 DR78
Aylesbury Rd., Brom. 122 EG97
Aylesbury St. EC1 6 F5
Aylesbury St. EC1 77 DP70
Aylesbury St. NW10 60 CR62
Aylesford Ave., Beck. 121 DY99
Aylesford St. SW1 91 DK78
Aylesham Clo. NW7 47 CU52
Aylesham Rd., Orp. 123 ET101
Aylestone Ave. NW6 75 CX66
Aylett Rd. SE25 120 DV98
Belfast Rd.
Aylett Rd., Islw. 87 CE82
Ayley Cft., Enf. 36 DU43
Ayliffe Clo., Kings.T. 116 CN96
Cambridge Gdns.
Aylmer Clo., Stan. 45 CG49
Aylmer Dr., Stan. 45 CG49
Aylmer Par. N2 62 DF57
Aylmer Rd.
Aylmer Rd. E11 66 EF60
Aylmer Rd. N2 62 DE57
Aylmer Rd. W12 89 CT75
Aylmer Rd., Dag. 68 EY62
Ayloffe Rd., Dag. 82 EZ65
Aylsham Dr., Uxb. 57 BQ61
Aylton Est. SE16 92 DW75
Renforth St.
Aylward Rd. SE23 107 DX89
Aylward Rd. SW20 117 CZ96
Aylward St. E1 78 DW72
Aylwards Ri., Stan. 45 CG49
Aylwyn Est. SE1 11 N6
Aylwyn Est. SE1 92 DS76
Aynho St., Wat. 29 BV43
Aynhoe Rd. W14 89 CX77
Aynscombe Angle, Orp. 124 EU101
Aynscombe La. SW14 88 CQ83
Aynscombe Path SW14 88 CQ82
Thames Bank
Ayot Path, Borwd. 32 CN38
Walshford Way
Ayr Ct. W3 74 CN71
Monks Dr.
Ayr Grn., Rom. 55 FE52
Ayr Way, Rom. 55 FE52
Ayres Clo. E13 80 EG69
Ayres Cres. NW10 74 CR66
Ayres St. SE1 11 J4
Ayres St. SE1 92 DQ75
Ayrsome Rd. N16 64 DS62
Ayrton Rd. SW7 90 DD76
Wells Way
Aysgarth Rd. SE21 106 DS86
Aytoun Pl. SW9 91 DM82
Aytoun Rd. SW9 91 DM82
Azalea Clo. W7 73 CF74
Azalea Clo., Ilf. 67 EP64
Lavender Pl.
Azalea Ct., Wdf.Grn. 52 EE52
Bridle Path
Azalea Dr., Swan. 125 FD98
Azalea Wk., Pnr. 57 BV57
Azalea Wk., Sthl. 86 CC75
Navigator Dr.
Azenby Rd. SE15 92 DT82
Azile Everitt Ho. SE18 95 EQ78
Vicarage Pk.
Azof St. SE10 94 EE77

B

Baalbec Rd. N5 63 DP64
Babbacombe Clo., Chess. 129 CK106
Babbacombe Gdns., Ilf. 66 EL56
Babbacombe Rd., Brom. 122 EG95
Baber Dr., Felt. 100 BW86
Babington Ri., Wem. 74 CN65
Babington Rd. NW4 61 CV56
Babington Rd. SW16 105 DK92
Babington Rd., Dag. 68 EW64
Babington Rd., Horn. 69 FH60
Babmaes St. SW1 9 M2
Bacchus Wk. N1 7 M1
Bachelor's La., Wok. 140 BM124
Baches St. N1 7 L3
Baches St. N1 78 DR69
Back Ch. La. E1 78 DU73
Back Grn., Walt. 128 BW107
Back Hill EC1 6 D5
Back Hill EC1 77 DN70
Back La. N8 63 DL57
Back La. NW3 62 DC63
Heath St.
Back La., Bex. 110 FA87
Back La., Brent. 87 CK79
Back La., Edg. 46 CQ53
Back La., Rich. 101 CJ90
Back La., Rom. 68 EY59
St. Chad's Rd.
Back La. (Godden Grn.), Sev. 155 FN124
Back La. (Ide Hill), Sev. 154 FB128
Back La., Wat. 31 CE39
Back Rd., Sid. 110 EU91
Backhouse Pl. SE17 11 N9
Backley Gdns. SE25 120 DU100
Bacon Gro. SE1 11 P7
Bacon Gro. SE1 92 DT76
Bacon La. NW9 60 CP56
Bacon La., Edg. 46 CN53
Bacon Link, Rom. 55 FB51
Bacon St. E1 78 DT70
Bacon St. E2 78 DT70
Bacon Ter., Dag. 68 EV64
Fitzstephen Rd.
Bacons Dr. (Cuffley), Pot.B. 21 DL29
Bacons La. N6 62 DG60
Bacons Mead, Uxb. 56 BG61
Bacton NW5 62 DG64
Bacton St. E2 78 DW69
Roman Rd.
Badburgham Ct., Wal.Abb. 24 EF33
Baddow Clo., Dag. 82 FA67
Baddow Clo., Wdf.Grn. 52 EK51
Baden Clo., Stai. 98 BG94
Baden Pl. SE1 11 K4
Baden Powell Clo., Surb. 116 CM103
Baden Powell Rd., Sev. 154 FE122
Baden Rd. N8 63 DK56
Baden Rd., Ilf. 67 EP64
Bader Clo., Ken. 148 DR115
Bader Way, Rain. 83 FG65
Badger Clo., Felt. 99 BU90
Sycamore Clo.
Badger Clo., Houns. 86 BW83
Badger Clo., Ilf. 67 EQ59
Badgers Clo., Ashf. 98 BM92
Fordbridge Rd.
Badgers Clo., Borwd. 32 CM40
Kingsley Ave.
Badgers Clo., Enf. 35 DP41
Badgers Clo., Har. 59 CD58
Badgers Clo., Hayes 71 BS74
Badgers Copse, Orp. 123 ET103
Badgers Copse, Wor.Pk. 117 CT103
Badgers Cft. N20 47 CY46
Badgers Cft. SE9 109 EN90
Badgers Hole, Croy. 135 DX105
Badgers La., Warl. 148 DW119
Badgers Ri., Sev. 138 FA110
Badgers Rd., Sev. 139 FB110
Badgers Wk., N.Mal. 116 CS96
Badgers Wk., Pur. 133 DJ111
Badgers Wk., Whyt. 148 DT119
Badingham Dr., Lthd. 143 CE123
Badlis Rd. E17 51 EA54
Badlow Clo., Erith 97 FE80
Badminton Clo., Borwd. 32 CN40
Badminton Clo., Har. 59 CE56
Badminton Clo., Nthlt. 72 CA66
Badminton Ms. E16 80 EG74
Silvertown Way
Badminton Rd. SW12 104 DG86
Badsworth Rd. SE5 92 DQ81
Baffin Way E14 79 ED73
Prestons Rd.
Bagley Clo., West Dr. 84 BL75
Bagley's La. SW6 90 DB81
Bagleys Spring, Rom. 68 EY56
Bagot Clo., Ash. 144 CM116
Bagshot Ct. SE18 95 EN81
Prince Imperial Rd.
Bagshot Rd., Enf. 50 DT45
Bagshot St. SE17 92 DS78
Bahram Rd., Epsom 130 CR110
Baildon St. SE8 93 EA80
Watson's St.
Bailey Clo. E4 51 EC49
Bailey Pl. SE26 107 DX93
Baillie Clo., Rain. 83 FH70
Baillies Wk. W5 87 CK75
Liverpool Rd.
Bainbridge Rd., Dag. 68 EZ63
Bainbridge St. WC1 5 N8
Bainbridge St. WC1 77 DK72
Baird Ave., Sthl. 72 CB73
Baird Clo. NW9 60 CQ58
Baird Clo. (Bushey), Wat. 30 CB44
Ashfield Ave.
Baird Gdns. SE19 106 DS91
Baird Rd., Enf. 36 DV42
Baird St. EC1 7 J4
Bairstow Clo., Borwd. 32 CL39
Baizdon Rd. SE3 94 EE82
Baker Boy La., Croy. 135 DZ112
Baker La., Mitch. 118 DG96
Baker Pas. NW10 74 CS67
Acton La.
Baker Rd. NW10 74 CS67
Baker Rd. SE18 94 EL81
Baker St. NW1 4 E5
Baker St. NW1 76 DF70
Baker St. W1 4 E6
Baker St. W1 76 DF71
Baker St., Enf. 36 DR41
Baker St., Pot.B. 33 CY36
Baker St., Wey. 126 BN105
Bakers Ave. E17 65 EB58
Bakers Ct. SE25 120 DS97
Bakers End SW20 117 CY96
Bakers Fld. N7 63 DK63
Crayford Rd.
Bakers Gdns., Cars. 118 DE103
Bakers Hill E5 64 DV60
Bakers Hill, Barn. 34 DB40
Bakers La. N6 62 DF58
Bakers La., Epp. 25 ET30
Baker's Ms. W1 4 F8
Bakers Ms., Orp. 137 ET107
Bakers Pas. NW3 62 DC63
Heath St.
Baker's Rents E2 7 P3
Bakers Rd., Uxb. 70 BK66
Bakers Rd. (Cheshunt), Wal.Cr. 22 DV30
Bakers Row E15 80 EE68
Baker's Row EC1 6 D5
Baker's Row EC1 77 DN70
Baker's Yd. EC1 77 DN70
Baker's Row
Baker's Yd., Uxb. 70 BK66
Bakers Rd.
Bakery Clo. SW9 91 DM81
Bakery Path, Edg. 46 CP51
Station Rd.
Bakery Pl. SW11 90 DF84
Altenburg Gdns.
Bakewell Way, N.Mal. 116 CS96
Bala Gdn. NW9 60 CS58
Snowdon Dr.
Balaam St. E13 80 EG70
Balaams La. N14 49 DK47
Balaclava Rd. SE1 92 DT77
Balaclava Rd., Surb. 115 CJ101
Balben Path E9 79 DX66
Speldhurst Rd.
Balcaskie Rd. SE9 109 EM85
Balchen Rd. SE3 94 EK82
Balchier Rd. SE22 106 DV86
Balcombe Clo., Bexh. 96 EX84
Balcombe St. NW1 4 D4
Balcombe St. NW1 76 DF70
Balcon Way, Borwd. 32 CQ39
Balcorne St. E9 78 DW66
Balder Ri. SE12 108 EH89
Balderton St. W1 4 G9
Balderton St. W1 76 DG72
Baldock St. E3 79 EB68
Baldock Way, Borwd. 32 CM39
Baldocks Rd., Epp. 39 ES35
Baldry Gdns. SW16 105 DL93
Baldwin Cres. SE5 92 DQ81
Baldwin St. EC1 7 K3
Baldwin Ter. N1 78 DQ68
Baldwin's Gdns. EC1 6 D6
Baldwin's Gdns. EC1 77 DN71
Baldwins Hill, Loug. 39 EM40
Baldwins La., Rick. 28 BN42
Baldwyn Gdns. W3 74 CR73
Baldwyns Pk., Bex. 111 FD89
Baldwyns Rd., Bex. 111 FD89
Balfe St. N1 6 A1
Balfe St. N1 77 DL68
Balfern Gro. W4 88 CS78
Balfern St. SW11 90 DE82
Balfont Clo., S.Croy. 134 DU113
Balfour Ave. W7 73 CF74
Balfour Gro. N20 48 DF48
Balfour Ho. W10 75 CX71
St. Charles Sq.
Balfour Ms. N9 50 DU48
The Bdy.
Balfour Ms. W1 8 G2
Balfour Pl. SW15 89 CV84
Balfour Pl. W1 8 G1
Balfour Rd. N5 64 DQ63
Balfour Rd. SE25 120 DU99
Balfour Rd. SW19 104 DB94
Balfour Rd. W3 74 CQ71
Balfour Rd. W13 87 CG75
Balfour Rd., Brom. 122 EK99
Balfour Rd., Cars. 132 DF108
Balfour Rd., Har. 59 CD57
Balfour Rd., Houns. 86 CB83
Balfour Rd., Ilf. 67 EP61
Balfour Rd., Sthl. 86 BX76
Balfour Rd., Wey. 126 BN105
Balfour St. SE17 11 K8
Balfour St. SE17 92 DR77
Balgonie Rd. E4 51 ED46
Balgores Cres., Rom. 69 FH55
Balgores La., Rom. 69 FH55
Balgores Sq., Rom. 69 FH56
Balgowan Clo., N.Mal. 116 CS98
Balgowan Rd., Beck. 121 DY97
Balgowan St. SE18 95 ET77
Balham Continental Mkt. SW12 105 DH88
Balham Gro. SW12 104 DG87
Balham High Rd. SW12 104 DG90
Balham High Rd. SW17 104 DG90
Balham Hill SW12 105 DH87
Balham New Rd. SW12 105 DH87
Balham Pk. Rd. SW12 104 DF88
Balham Rd. N9 50 DU47
Balham Sta. Rd. SW12 105 DH88
Balkan Wk. E1 78 DV73
Pennington St.
Balladier Wk. E14 79 EB71
Morris Rd.
Ballamore Rd., Brom. 108 EG90
Ballance Rd. E9 79 DX65
Ballands N., The, Lthd. 143 CE122
Ballands S., The, Lthd. 143 CE123
Ballantine St. SW18 90 DC84
Ballantyne Dr., Tad. 145 CZ121
Ballard Clo., Kings.T. 102 CR94
Ballards Clo., Dag. 83 FB67
Ballards Fm. Rd., Croy. 134 DU107
Ballards Fm. Rd., S.Croy. 134 DU107
Ballards Grn., Tad. 145 CY119
Ballards La. N3 48 DA53
Ballards La. N12 48 DC51
Ballards Ms., Edg. 46 CN51
Ballards Ri., S.Croy. 134 DU107
Ballards Rd. NW2 61 CU61
Ballards Rd., Dag. 83 FB68
Ballards Way, Croy. 134 DV107
Ballards Way, S.Croy. 134 DU107
Ballast Quay SE10 93 ED78
Ballater Clo., Wat. 44 BW49
Ballater Rd. SW2 91 DL84
Ballater Rd., S.Croy. 134 DT106
Ballenger Ct., Wat. 29 BV41
Ballina St. SE23 107 DX87
Ballingdon Rd. SW11 104 DG86
Ballinger Pt. E3 79 EB69
Bromley High St.
Balliol Ave. E4 52 EE49
Balliol Rd. N17 50 DS53
Balliol Rd. W10 75 CX72
Balliol Rd., Well. 96 EV82
Balloch Rd. SE6 107 ED88
Ballogie Ave. NW10 60 CS63
Ballow Clo. SE5 92 DS80
Harris St.
Balls Pond Pl. N1 78 DR65
Balls Pond Rd.
Balls Pond Rd. N1 78 DR65
Balmain Clo. W5 73 CK74
Balmer Rd. E3 79 DZ68
Balmes Rd. N1 78 DR67
Balmoral Ave. N11 48 DG50
Balmoral Ave., Beck. 121 DY98
Balmoral Clo. SW15 103 CX86
Westleigh Ave.
Balmoral Cres., W.Mol. 114 CA97
Balmoral Dr., Borwd. 32 CR43
Balmoral Dr., Hayes 71 BS70
Balmoral Dr., Sthl. 72 BZ70
Balmoral Gdns. W13 87 CG76
Balmoral Gdns., Bex. 110 EZ87
Balmoral Gdns., Ilf. 67 ET60
Balmoral Gro. N7 77 DM65
Balmoral Ms. W12 89 CT76
Balmoral Rd. E7 66 EJ63
Balmoral Rd. E10 65 EB61
Balmoral Rd. NW2 75 CV65
Balmoral Rd., Abb.L. 15 BU32
Balmoral Rd., Enf. 37 DX36
Balmoral Rd., Har. 58 CA63
Balmoral Rd., Kings.T. 116 CM98
Balmoral Rd., Rom. 69 FH57
Balmoral Rd., Wat. 30 BW38
Balmoral Rd., Wor.Pk. 117 CV104
Balmoral Way, Sutt. 132 DA110
Balmore Cres., Barn. 34 DG43
Balmore St. N19 63 DH61
Balmuir Gdns. SW15 89 CW84
Balnacraig Ave. NW10 60 CS63
Balniel Gate SW1 9 N10
Balniel Gate SW1 91 DK78
Balquhain Clo., Ash. 143 CK117
Baltic Clo. SW19 104 DD94
Baltic Ct. SE16 93 DX75
Timber Pond Rd.
Baltic St. E. EC1 7 H5
Baltic St. E. EC1 78 DQ70
Baltic St. W. EC1 7 H5
Baltic St. W. EC1 78 DQ70
Baltimore Pl., Well. 95 ET82
Balvernie Gro. SW18 103 CZ87
Bamber Ho., Bark. 81 EQ67
St. Margarets
Bamborough Gdns. W12 89 CW75
Bamford Ave., Wem. 74 CM67
Bamford Ct. E15 65 EB64
Clays La.
Bamford Rd., Bark. 81 EQ65
Bamford Rd., Brom. 107 EC92
Bamford Way, Rom. 55 FB50
Bampfylde Clo., Wall. 119 DJ104
Bampton Rd. SE23 107 DX90
Banavie Gdns., Beck. 121 EC95
Banbury Clo., Enf. 35 DP39
Holtwhites Hill
Banbury Ct. WC2 5 P10
Banbury Ct., Sutt. 132 DA108
Banbury Enterprise Cen., Croy. 119 DP103
Factory La.
Banbury Rd. E9 79 DX66
Banbury Rd. E17 51 DY53
Banbury St. SW11 90 DE82
Banbury St., Wat. 29 BU43
Banbury Wk., Nthlt. 72 CA68
Brabazon Rd.
Banchory Rd. SE3 94 EH80
Bancroft Ave. N2 62 DE57
Bancroft Ave., Buck.H. 52 EG47
Bancroft Clo., Ashf. 98 BN92
Feltham Hill Rd.
Bancroft Ct., Nthlt. 72 BW67
Bancroft Gdns., Har. 44 CC53
Bancroft Gdns., Orp. 123 ET102
Bancroft Rd. E1 79 DX69
Bancroft Rd., Har. 44 CC53
Bandon Ri., Wall. 133 DK106
Bangalore St. SW15 89 CW83
Bangor Clo., Nthlt. 58 CB64
Banim St. W6 89 CV77
Banister Rd. W10 75 CX69
Bank, The N6 63 DH60
Cholmeley Pk.
Bank Ave., Mitch. 118 DD96
Bank End SE1 11 J2
Bank End SE1 78 DQ74
Bank La. SW15 102 CS85
Bank La., Kings.T. 102 CL94
Bank Ms., Sutt. 132 DA111
Sutton Ct. Rd.
Bank St., Sev. 155 FH125
Bankfoot Rd., Brom. 108 EE91
Bankhurst Rd. SE6 107 DZ87
Banks La., Bexh. 96 EZ84
Banks La., Epp. 26 EY33
Bank's La., Lthd. 141 BV122
Banks Rd., Borwd. 32 CQ40
Banksia Rd. N18 50 DW50
Banksian Wk., Islw. 87 CE81
The Gro.
Bankside SE1 11 H1
Bankside SE1 78 DQ73
Bankside, Enf. 35 DP39
Bankside, Sev. 154 FE121
Bankside, S.Croy. 134 DT107
Bankside, Sthl. 72 BX74
Bankside Ave., Nthlt. 71 BU68
Townson Ave.
Bankside Clo., Bex. 111 FD91
Bankside Clo., Cars. 132 DE107
Bankside Clo., Islw. 87 CF84
Bankside Clo., West. 150 EJ118
Bankside Dr., T.Ditt. 115 CH102
Bankside Way SE19 106 DS93
Lunham Rd.
Bankton Rd. SW2 91 DN84
Bankwell Rd. SE13 94 EE84
Banner St. EC1 7 J5
Banner St. EC1 78 DQ70
Bannerman Ho. SW8 91 DM79
Banning St. SE10 94 EE78
Bannister Clo. SW2 105 DN88
Ewen Cres.
Bannister Clo., Grnf. 59 CD64
Bannister Gdns., Orp. 124 EW97
Main Rd.
Bannister Ho. E9 65 DX64
Homerton High St.
Bannockburn Rd. SE18 95 ES77
Banstead Gdns. N9 50 DS48
Banstead Rd., Bans. 131 CX112
Banstead Rd., Cars. 132 DE107
Banstead Rd., Cat. 148 DR122
Banstead Rd., Epsom 131 CV110
Banstead Rd., Pur. 133 DN111
Banstead Rd. S., Sutt. 132 DC111
Banstead St. SE15 92 DW83
Banstead Way, Wall. 133 DL106
Banstock Rd., Edg. 46 CP51
Banting Dr. N21 35 DM43
Banton Clo., Enf. 36 DV40
Central Ave.
Bantry St. SE5 92 DR80
Banwell Rd., Bex. 110 EX86
Woodside La.
Banyard Rd. SE16 92 DV76
Southwark Pk. Rd.
Bapchild Pl., Orp. 124 EW98
Okemore Gdns.
Baptist Gdns. NW5 76 DG65
Queens Cres.
Barandon Wk. W11 75 CX73
Whitchurch Rd.
Barb Ms. W6 89 CW76
Barbara Brosnan Ct. NW8 76 DD68
Grove End Rd.
Barbara Clo., Shep. 113 BP99
Barbara Hucklesby Clo. N22 49 DP54
The Sandlings
Barbauld Rd. N16 64 DS62
Barbel Clo., Wal.Cr. 23 EA34
Barber Clo. N21 49 DN45
Barber's All. E13 80 EH69
Greengate St.
Barbers Rd. E15 79 EB68
Barbican, The EC2 7 H6
Barbican, The EC2 78 DQ71
Barbican Rd., Grnf. 72 CB72
Barbon Clo. WC1 6 A6
Barbot Clo. N9 50 DU48
Barchard St. SW18 104 DB85
Barchester Clo. W7 73 CF74
Barchester Clo., Uxb. 70 BJ70
Barchester Rd., Har. 45 CD54
Barchester St. E14 79 EB71
Barclay Clo. SW6 90 DA80
Barclay Clo., Lthd. 142 CB123
Barclay Clo., Wat. 29 BU44
Barclay Oval, Wdf.Grn. 52 EG49

Barclay Path E17 65 EC57
Grove Rd.
Barclay Rd. E11 66 EE60
Barclay Rd. E13 80 EJ70
Barclay Rd. E17 65 EC57
Barclay Rd. N18 50 DR51
Barclay Rd. SW6 90 DA80
Barclay Rd., Croy. 120 DR104
Barclay Way SE22 106 DU87
Lordship La.
Barcombe Ave. SW2 105 DL89
Barcombe Clo., Orp. 124 EU97
Bard Rd. W10 75 CX73
Barden Clo., Uxb. 42 BJ52
Barden St. SE18 95 ES80
Bardfield Ave., Rom. 68 EX55
Bardney Rd., Mord. 118 DB98
Bardolph Ave., Croy. 135 DY109
Bardolph Rd. N7 63 DL63
Bardolph Rd., Rich. 88 CM83
St. Georges Rd.
Bardsey Pl. E1 78 DW71
Bardsey Wk. N1 78 DQ65
Clephane Rd.
Bardsley Clo., Croy. 120 DT104
Bardsley La. SE10 93 EC79
Barfett St. W10 75 CZ70
Barfield Ave. N20 48 DF47
Barfield Rd. E11 66 EF60
Barfield Rd., Brom. 123 EN97
Barfields, Loug. 39 EN42
Barfields Gdns., Loug. 39 EN42
Barfields
Barfields Path, Loug. 39 EN42
Barford Clo. NW4 47 CU53
Barford St. N1 77 DN67
Barforth Rd. SE15 92 DV83
Barfreston Way SE20 120 DV95
Bargate Clo. SE18 95 ET78
Bargate Clo., N.Mal. 117 CU101
Barge Ho. Rd. E16 95 EP75
Barge Ho. St. SE1 10 E2
Barge Wk., E.Mol. 115 CD97
Barge Wk., Kings.T. 115 CK96
Barge Wk., Walt. 114 BW97
Bargery Rd. SE6 107 EB88
Bargrove Clo. SE20 106 DU94
Bargrove Cres. SE6 107 DZ89
Elm La.
Barham Ave., Borwd. 32 CM41
Barham Clo., Brom. 122 EL102
Barham Clo., Chis. 109 EP92
Barham Clo., Rom. 55 FB54
Barham Clo., Wem. 73 CH65
Barham Clo., Wey. 127 BQ105
Barham Rd. SW20 103 CU94
Barham Rd., Chis. 109 EP92
Barham Rd., S.Croy. 134 DQ105
Baring Clo. SE12 108 EG89
Baring Rd. SE12 108 EG87
Baring Rd., Barn. 34 DD42
Baring Rd., Croy. 120 DU102
Baring St. N1 78 DR67
Bark Hart Rd., Orp. 124 EV102
Bark Pl. W2 76 DB73
Barker Dr. NW1 77 DJ66
Barker Ms. SW4 91 DH84
Barker St. SW10 90 DC79
Barker Wk. SW16 105 DK90
Mount Ephraim Rd.
Barker Way SE22 106 DU88
Dulwich Common
Barkham Rd. N17 50 DR52
Barking Ind. Pk., Bark. 81 ET67
Barking Rd. E6 80 EK68
Barking Rd. E13 80 EG70
Barking Rd. E16 80 EE71
Barkis Way SE16 92 DV78
Egan Way
Barkston Gdns. SW5 90 DB77
Barkston Path, Borwd. 32 CN37
Walshford Way
Barkway Ct. N4 64 DQ62
Queens Dr.
Barkwood Clo., Rom. 69 FC57
Barkworth Rd. SE16 92 DV78
Credon Rd.
Barlborough St. SE14 93 DX80
Barlby Gdns. W10 75 CX70
Barlby Rd. W10 75 CW71
Barlee Cres., Uxb. 70 BJ71
Barley Clo. (Bushey), Wat. 30 CB43
Barley La., Ilf. 68 EU59
Barley La., Rom. 68 EV58
Barley Mow Pas. EC1 6 G7
Barley Mow Pas. W4 88 CR78
Heathfield Ter.
Barley Mow Way, Shep. 112 BN98
Barley Shotts Business Pk. W10 75 CZ71
St. Ervans Rd.
Barleycorn Way E14 79 DZ73
Barleyfields Clo., Rom. 68 EV58
Barlow Clo., Wall. 133 DL107
Cobham Clo.
Barlow Pl. W1 9 J1
Barlow Rd. NW6 75 CZ65
Barlow Rd. W3 74 CP74
Barlow Rd., Hmptn. 100 CA94
Barlow St. SE17 11 L9
Barlow Way, Rain. 83 FD71
Barmeston Rd. SE6 107 EB89
Barmor Clo., Har. 44 CB54
Barmouth Ave., Grnf. 73 CF68
Barmouth Rd. SW18 104 DC86
Barmouth Rd., Croy. 121 DX103
Barn Clo., Ashf. 99 BP92
Barn Clo., Bans. 146 DD115
Barn Clo., Epsom 144 CQ115
Barn Clo., Nthlt. 72 BW68
Barn Clo., Rad. 31 CG35
Barn Cres., Pur. 134 DR113
Barn Cres., Stan. 45 CJ51
Barn Elms Pk. SW15 89 CW82
Barn Hill, Wem. 60 CN60
Barn Lea, Rick. 42 BG46
Barn Mead, Epp. 39 ES36
Barn Mead, Ong. 27 FE29
Barn Meadow La., Lthd. 142 BZ124
Barn Ms., Har. 58 CA62
Barn Ri., Wem. 60 CN60
Barn St. N16 64 DS62
Stoke Newington Ch. St.
Barn Way, Wem. 60 CN60
Barnabas Ct. N21 35 DN43
Cheyne Wk.
Barnabas Rd. E9 65 DX64
Barnaby Clo., Har. 58 CC61
Barnaby Pl. SW7 90 DD77
Barnaby Way, Chig. 53 EN48
Barnacre Clo., Uxb. 70 BK72
New Peachey La.
Barnacres Rd., Hem.H. 14 BM25
Barnard Clo. SE18 95 EN76
Barnard Clo., Chis. 123 ER95
Barnard Clo., Sun. 99 BV94
Oak Gro.
Barnard Clo., Wall. 133 DK108
Barnard Gdns., Hayes 71 BV70
Barnard Gdns., N.Mal. 117 CU98
Barnard Gro. E15 80 EF66
Vicarage La.
Barnard Hill N10 49 DH53
Barnard Ms. SW11 90 DE84
Barnard Rd. SW11 90 DE84
Barnard Rd., Enf. 36 DV40
Barnard Rd., Mitch. 118 DG97
Barnard Rd., Warl. 149 EB119
Barnardo Dr., Ilf. 67 EQ56
Civic Way
Barnardo St. E1 79 DX72
Devonport St.
Barnard's Inn EC1 6 D8
Barnards Pl., S.Croy. 133 DP109
Barnato Clo., W.Byf. 126 BL112
Viscount Gdns.
Barnby Sq. E15 80 EE67
Barnby St.
Barnby St. E15 80 EE67
Barnby St. NW1 5 L2
Barnby St. NW1 77 DJ69
Barncroft Clo., Loug. 39 EM43
Barncroft Clo., Uxb. 71 BP71
Harlington Rd.
Barncroft Grn., Loug. 39 EN43
Barncroft Rd., Loug. 39 EN43
Barnehurst Ave., Bexh. 97 FC81
Barnehurst Ave., Erith 97 FC81
Barnehurst Clo., Erith 97 FC81
Barnehurst Rd., Bexh. 97 FC82
Barnes All., Hmptn. 114 CC96
Hampton Ct. Rd.
Barnes Ave. SW13 89 CU80
Barnes Ave., Sthl. 86 BZ77
Barnes Bri. SW13 88 CS82
Barnes Bri. W4 88 CS82
Barnes Clo. E12 66 EK63
Barnes Ct. E16 80 EJ71
Ridgwell Rd.
Barnes Ct., Wdf.Grn. 52 EK50
Barnes Cray Cotts., Dart. 111 FG85
Maiden La.
Barnes Cray Rd., Dart. 97 FG84
Barnes End, N.Mal. 117 CU99
Barnes High St. SW13 89 CT82
Barnes Ho., Bark. 81 ER67
St. Marys
Barnes La., Kings L. 14 BH27
Barnes Ri., Kings L. 14 BM27
Barnes Rd. N18 50 DW49
Barnes Rd., Ilf. 67 EQ64
Barnes St. E14 79 DY72
Barnes Ter. SE8 93 DZ78
Barnes Wallis Dr., Wey. 126 BL111
Barnesbury Ho. SW4 105 DK86
Barnesdale Cres., Orp. 124 EU100
Barnet Bypass, Barn. 32 CS39
Barnet Dr., Brom. 122 EL103
Barnet Gate La., Barn. 33 CT44
Barnet Gro. E2 78 DU69
Barnet Hill, Barn. 33 CZ42
Barnet Ho. N20 48 DC47
Barnet La. N20 47 CZ46
Barnet La., Barn. 34 DA44
Barnet La., Borwd. 31 CK44
Barnet Rd. (Arkley), Barn. 32 CR44
Barnet Rd., Pot.B. 20 DB34
Barnet Rd., St.Alb. 18 CL27
Barnet Trd. Est., Barn. 33 CZ41
Barnet Way NW7 46 CR48
Barnet Wd. Rd., Brom. 122 EH103
Barnett Clo., Erith 97 FF82
Barnett Clo., Lthd. 143 CH119
Barnett St. E1 78 DV72
Cannon St. Rd.
Barnett Wd. La., Ash. 143 CJ118
Barnett Wd. La., Lthd. 143 CH120
Barney Clo. SE7 94 EJ78
Barnfield, Bans. 132 DB114
Barnfield, Epp. 26 EU28
Barnfield, N.Mal. 116 CS100
Barnfield Ave., Croy. 120 DW103
Barnfield Ave., Kings.T. 102 CL92
Barnfield Ave., Mitch. 119 DH98
Barnfield Clo. N4 63 DL59
Crouch Hill
Barnfield Clo. SW17 104 DC90
Barnfield Clo., Couls. 148 DQ119
Barnfield Clo., Swan. 125 FC101
Barnfield Gdns. SE18 95 EP79
Plumstead Common Rd.
Barnfield Gdns., Kings.T. 102 CL92
Barnfield Pl. E14 93 EA77
Barnfield Rd. SE18 95 EP79
Barnfield Rd. W5 73 CJ70
Barnfield Rd., Belv. 96 EZ79
Barnfield Rd., Edg. 46 CQ53
Barnfield Rd., Orp. 124 EX97
Barnfield Rd., Sev. 154 FD123
Barnfield Rd., S.Croy. 134 DS109
Barnfield Rd., West. 150 EK120
Barnfield Wd. Clo., Beck. 121 ED100
Barnfield Wd. Rd., Beck. 121 ED100
Barnham Rd., Grnf. 72 CC69
Barnham St. SE1 11 N4
Barnham St. SE1 92 DS75
Barnhill, Pnr. 58 BW57
Barnhill Ave., Brom. 122 EF99
Barnhill La., Hayes 71 BV70
Barnhill Rd., Hayes 71 BV70
Barnhill Rd., Wem. 60 CQ62
Barnhurst Path, Wat. 44 BW50
Barningham Way NW9 60 CR58
Barnlea Clo., Felt. 100 BY89
Barnmead Gdns., Dag. 68 EZ64
Barnmead Rd., Beck. 121 DY95
Barnmead Rd., Dag. 68 EZ64
Barnsbury Clo., N.Mal. 116 CQ98
Barnsbury Cres., Surb. 116 CP102
Barnsbury Est. N1 77 DN67
Barnsbury Rd.
Barnsbury Gro. N7 77 DM65
Barnsbury La., Surb. 116 CP103
Barnsbury Pk. N1 77 DN66
Barnsbury Rd. N1 77 DN68
Barnsbury Sq. N1 77 DN66
Barnsbury St. N1 77 DN66
Barnsbury Ter. N1 77 DM66
Barnscroft SW20 117 CV97
Barnsdale Ave. E14 93 EB77
Barnsdale Clo., Borwd. 32 CM39
Barnsdale Rd. W9 75 CZ70
Barnsfield Pl., Uxb. 70 BJ67
Barnsley St. E1 78 DV70
Barnstaple Rd., Ruis. 58 BW62
Barnston Wk. N1 78 DQ67
Popham St.
Barnsway, Kings L. 14 BL28
Barnwell Rd. SW2 105 DN85
Barnwood Clo. W9 76 DB70
Barnwood Clo., Ruis. 57 BR61
Lysander Rd.
Barnwood Ct. E16 80 EG74
North Woolwich Rd.
Barnyard, The, Tad. 145 CU124
Baron Clo. N11 48 DG50
Balmoral Ave.
Baron Clo., Sutt. 132 DB110
Baron Gdns., Ilf. 67 EQ55
Baron Gro., Mitch. 118 DE98
Baron Rd., Dag. 68 EX60
Baron St. N1 6 D1
Baron St. N1 77 DN68
Baron Wk. E16 80 EF71
Baron Wk., Mitch. 118 DE98
Baroness Rd. E2 78 DT69
Diss St.
Baronet Gro. N17 50 DU53
St. Paul's Rd.
Baronet Rd. N17 50 DU53
Barons, The, Twick. 101 CH86
Barons Ct., Wall. 119 DK104
Whelan Way
Barons Ct. Rd. W14 89 CY78
Barons Gate, Barn. 34 DE44
Barons Hurst, Epsom 144 CQ116
Barons Keep W14 89 CY78
Barons Mead, Har. 59 CE56
Barons Pl. SE1 10 E5
Barons Pl. SE1 91 DN75
Barons Wk., Croy. 121 DY100
Baronsfield Rd., Twick. 101 CH86
Baronsmead Rd. SW13 89 CU81
Baronsmede W5 88 CM75
Baronsmere Rd. N2 62 DE56
Barque Ms. SE8 93 EA79
Watergate St.
Barr Rd., Pot.B. 20 DC33
Barra Hall Circ., Hayes 71 BS72
Barra Hall Rd., Hayes 71 BS73
Barrack Rd., Houns. 86 BX84
Barracks La., Barn. 33 CY41
High St.
Barratt Ave. N22 49 DM54
Barratt Ind. Pk., Sthl. 86 CA75
Barratt Way, Har. 59 CD55
Tudor Rd.
Barrenger Rd. N10 48 DF53
Barrett Clo., Rom. 55 FH52
Barrett Rd. E17 65 EC56
Barrett Rd., Lthd. 143 CD124
Barrett St. W1 4 G9
Barrett St. W1 76 DG72
Barretts Grn. Rd. NW10 74 CQ69
Barretts Gro. N16 64 DS64
Barretts Rd., Sev. 153 FD120
Barrhill Rd. SW2 105 DL89
Barrie Clo., Couls. 147 DJ115
Barrie Est. W2 76 DD73
Craven Ter.
Barrie Twr. W3 88 CQ75
Barriedale SE14 93 DY82
Barrier App. SE7 94 EK76
Barringer Sq. SW17 104 DG91
Barrington Clo. NW5 62 DG64
Grafton Rd.
Barrington Clo., Ilf. 53 EM53
Hurstleigh Gdns.
Barrington Clo., Loug. 39 EQ42
Barrington Rd.
Barrington Dr., Uxb. 42 BG52
Park La.
Barrington Grn., Loug. 39 EQ42
Barrington Lo., Wey. 127 BQ106
Barrington Rd. E12 81 EN65
Barrington Rd. N8 63 DK57
Barrington Rd. SW9 91 DP83
Barrington Rd., Bexh. 96 EX82
Barrington Rd., Loug. 39 EQ42
Barrington Rd., Pur. 133 DJ112
Barrington Rd., Sutt. 118 DA102
Barrington Vill. SE18 95 EN81
Barrow Ave., Cars. 132 DF108
Barrow Clo. N21 49 DP48
Barrow Hedges Clo., Cars. 132 DE108
Barrow Hedges Way, Cars. 132 DE108
Barrow Hill, Wor.Pk. 116 CS103
Barrow Hill Clo., Wor.Pk. 116 CS103
Barrow Hill
Barrow Hill Rd. NW8 4 B1
Barrow Hill Rd. NW8 76 DE68
Barrow La. (Cheshunt), Wal.Cr. 22 DT30
Barrow Pt. Ave., Pnr. 44 BY54
Barrow Pt. La., Pnr. 44 BY54
Barrow Rd. SW16 105 DK93
Barrow Rd., Croy. 133 DN106
Barrow Wk., Brent. 87 CJ78
Glenhurst Rd.
Barrow Way N7 63 DM62
Barrowdene Clo., Pnr. 44 BY54
Paines La.
Barrowell Grn. N21 49 DP47
Barrowfield Clo. N9 50 DV48
Barrowgate Rd. W4 88 CQ78
Barrowsfield, S.Croy. 134 DT112
Barrs Rd. NW10 74 CR66
Barry Ave. N15 64 DT58
Craven Pk. Rd.
Barry Ave., Bexh. 96 EY80
Barry Clo., Orp. 123 ES104
Barry Clo., St.Alb. 16 CB25
Barry Rd. E6 80 EL72
Barry Rd. NW10 74 CQ66
Barry Rd. SE22 106 DU86
Barset Rd. SE15 92 DW83
Barson Clo. SE20 106 DW94
Barston Rd. SE27 106 DQ89
Barstow Cres. SW2 105 DM88
Barter St. WC1 6 A7
Barter St. WC1 77 DL71
Barters Wk., Pnr. 58 BY55
High St.
Barth Rd. SE18 95 ES77
Bartholomew Clo. EC1 7 H7
Bartholomew Clo. EC1 78 DQ71
Bartholomew Clo. SW18 90 DC84
Bartholomew La. EC2 7 L9
Bartholomew Pl. EC1 7 H7
Bartholomew Rd. NW5 77 DJ65
Bartholomew Sq. E1 78 DV70
Coventry Rd.
Bartholomew Sq. EC1 7 J4
Bartholomew Sq. EC1 78 DQ70
Bartholomew St. SE1 11 L7
Bartholomew St. SE1 92 DR76
Bartholomew Vill. NW5 77 DJ65
Bartholomew Way, Swan. 125 FE97
Bartle Ave. E6 80 EL68
Bartle Rd. W11 75 CY72
Bartlett Clo. E14 79 EA72
Bartlett Ct. EC4 6 E8
Bartlett St., S.Croy. 134 DR106
Bartlow Gdns., Rom. 55 FD53
Barton, The, Cob. 128 BW112
Barton Ave., Rom. 69 FB60
Barton Clo. E6 81 EM72
Brandreth Rd.
Barton Clo. E9 64 DW64
Churchill Wk.
Barton Clo. SE15 92 DV83
Kirkwood Rd.
Barton Clo., Add. 126 BG107
Barton Clo., Bexh. 110 EY85
Barton Clo., Chig. 53 EQ47
Barton Clo., Shep. 113 BP100
Barton Grn., N.Mal. 116 CR96
Barton Meadows, Ilf. 67 EP56
Barton Rd. W14 89 CY78
Barton Rd., Horn. 69 FG60
Barton Rd., Sid. 110 EY93
Barton St. SW1 9 P6
Barton Way, Borwd. 32 CN40
Barton Way, Rick. 29 BP43
Bartons, The, Borwd. 31 CK44
Bartonway NW8 76 DD68
Queen's Ter.
Bartram Clo., Uxb. 71 BP70
Lees Rd.
Bartram Rd. SE4 107 DY85
Bartrams La., Barn. 34 DC38
Bartrop Clo., Wal.Cr. 22 DR28
Poppy Wk.
Barville Clo. SE4 93 DY84
St. Norbert Rd.
Barwell Trd. Est., Chess. 129 CK109
Barwick Rd. E7 66 EH63
Barwood Ave., W.Wick. 121 EB102
Basden Gro., Felt. 100 CA89
Basedale Rd., Dag. 82 EV66
Baseing Clo. E6 81 EN73
Bashley Rd. NW10 74 CR70
Basil Ave. E6 80 EL68
Basil Gdns., Croy. 121 DX102
Primrose La.
Basil St. SW3 8 D6
Basil St. SW3 90 DF76
Basildene Rd., Houns. 86 BX83
Basildon Ave., Ilf. 53 EN53
Basildon Clo., Sutt. 132 DB109
Basildon Rd. SE2 96 EU78
Basildon Rd., Bexh. 96 EY82
Basin S. E16 81 EP74
Basing Clo., T.Ditt. 115 CF101
Basing Ct. SE15 92 DT81
Basing Dr., Bex. 110 EZ86
Basing Hill NW11 61 CZ60
Basing Hill, Wem. 60 CM61
Basing Ho., Bark. 81 ER67
St. Margarets
Basing Ho. Yd. E2 7 N2
Basing Pl. E2 7 N2
Basing Rd., Bans. 131 CZ114
Basing St. W11 75 CZ72
Basing Way N3 62 DA55
Basing Way, T.Ditt. 115 CF101
Basingdon Way SE5 92 DR84
Basingfield Rd., T.Ditt. 115 CF101
Basinghall Ave. EC2 7 K7
Basinghall Ave. EC2 78 DR71
Basinghall Gdns., Sutt. 132 DB109
Basinghall St. EC2 7 K8
Basinghall St. EC2 78 DQ71
Basire St. N1 78 DQ67
Baskerville Rd. SW18 104 DE87
Basket Gdns. SE9 108 EL85
Baslow Clo., Har. 45 CD53
Baslow Wk. E5 65 DX63
Overbury St.
Basnett Rd. SW11 90 DG83
Basque Ct. SE16 93 DX75
Poolmans St.
Bassano St. SE22 106 DT85
Bassant Rd. SE18 95 ET79
Bassein Pk. Rd. W12 89 CT75
Basset Clo., Add. 126 BH110
Basset Ho., Dag. 82 EV67
Bassett Clo., Sutt. 132 DB109
Bassett Gdns., Epp. 27 FB26
Bassett Gdns., Islw. 86 CC80
Bassett Rd. W10 75 CX72
Bassett Rd., Uxb. 70 BJ66
New Windsor St.
Bassett St. NW5 76 DG65
Bassett Way, Grnf. 72 CB72
Bassetts Clo., Orp. 123 EP104
Bassetts Way, Orp. 137 EP105
Bassingham Rd. SW18 104 DC87
Bassingham Rd., Wem. 73 CK65
Bassishaw Highwalk EC2 78 DQ71
London Wall
Basswood Clo. SE15 92 DV83
Linden Gro.
Bastable Ave., Bark. 81 ES68
Bastion Highwalk EC2 78 DQ71
London Wall
Bastion Ho. EC2 78 DQ71
London Wall
Bastion Rd. SE2 96 EU78
Baston Manor Rd., Brom. 122 EH104
Baston Rd., Brom. 122 EH102
Bastwick St. EC1 7 H4
Bastwick St. EC1 78 DQ70
Basuto Rd. SW6 90 DA81
Bat & Ball Rd., Sev. 155 FJ121
Batavia Clo., Sun. 114 BW95
Batavia Ms. SE14 93 DY80
Goodwood Rd.
Batavia Rd. SE14 93 DY80
Batavia Rd., Sun. 113 BV95
Batchelor St. N1 77 DN68
Batchwood Grn., Orp. 124 EU97
Batchworth Heath Hill, Rick. 42 BN49
Batchworth Hill, Rick. 42 BM48
Batchworth La., Nthwd. 43 BP50
Batchworth Roundabout, Rick. 42 BK46
Bate St. E14 79 DZ73
Three Colt St.
Bateman Clo., Bark. 81 EQ65
Glenny Rd.
Bateman Ho. SE17 91 DP79
Otto St.
Bateman Rd. E4 51 EA51
Bateman Rd., Rick. 28 BN44
Bateman St. W1 5 M9
Bateman's Bldgs. W1 5 M9
Bateman's Row EC2 7 N4
Bateman's Row EC2 78 DS70
Bates Cres. SW16 105 DJ94
Bates Cres., Croy. 133 DN106
Bates Wk., Add. 126 BJ107
Bateson St. SE18 95 ES77
Gunning St.
Bath Clo. SE15 92 DV80
Asylum Rd.
Bath Ct. EC1 6 D5
Bath Ho. Rd., Croy. 119 DL102

Bedwell Rd., Belv. 96 FA78
Bedwin Way SE16 92 DV78
Catlin St.
Beeby Rd. E16 80 EH71
Beech Ave. N20 48 DE46
Beech Ave. W3 74 CS74
Beech Ave., Brent. 87 CH80
Beech Ave., Buck.H. 52 EH47
Beech Ave., Enf. 35 DN35
Beech Ave., Rad. 17 CG33
Beech Ave., Ruis. 57 BV60
Beech Ave., Sid. 110 EU87
Beech Ave., S.Croy. 134 DR111
Beech Ave., Swan. 125 FF98
Beech Ave., West. 150 EK119
Westmore Rd.
Beech Clo. N9 36 DU44
Beech Clo. SE8 93 DZ79
Clyde St.
Beech Clo. SW15 103 CU87
Beech Clo. SW19 103 CW93
Beech Clo., Ashf. 99 BR92
Beech Clo., Cars. 118 DF103
Beech Clo., Cob. 128 CA112
Beech Clo., Horn. 69 FH62
Beech Clo., Stai. 98 BK87
St. Marys Cres.
Beech Clo., Sun. 114 BX96
Harfield Rd.
Beech Clo., Walt. 128 BW105
Beech Clo., W.Byf. 126 BL112
Beech Clo., West Dr. 84 BN76
Beech Clo. Ct., Cob. 128 BZ111
Beech Copse, Brom. 123 EM96
Beech Copse, S.Croy. 134 DS106
Beech Ct. E17 65 ED55
Beech Ct. SE9 108 EL86
Beech Ct., Ilf. 67 EN62
Riverdene Rd.
Beech Dell, Kes. 137 EM105
Beech Dr. N2 48 DF54
Beech Dr., Borwd. 32 CM40
Beech Dr., Tad. 145 CZ122
Beech Dr., Wok. 140 BG124
Beech Fm. Rd., Warl. 149 EC120
Beech Gdns. EC2 78 DQ71
Aldersgate St.
Beech Gdns. W5 88 CL75
Beech Gdns., Dag. 83 FB66
Beech Gro., Add. 126 BH105
Beech Gro., Croy. 135 DY110
Beech Gro., Epsom 145 CV117
Beech Gro., Ilf. 53 ES51
Beech Gro., Mitch. 119 DK99
Beech Gro., N.Mal. 116 CR97
Beech Hall Cres. E4 51 ED52
Beech Hall Rd. E4 51 EC52
Beech Hill, Barn. 34 DD38
Beech Hill Ave., Barn. 34 DC39
Beech Hill Gdns., Wal.Abb. 38 EH37
Beech Holt, Lthd. 143 CJ122
Beech Ho., Croy. 135 EB107
Beech Ho. Rd., Croy. 120 DR104
Beech La., Buck.H. 52 EH47
Beech Lawns N12 48 DD50
Beech Pl., Epp. 25 ET31
Beech Rd. N11 49 DL51
Beech Rd. SW16 119 DL96
Beech Rd., Epsom 145 CT115
Beech Rd., Felt. 99 BS87
Beech Rd., Orp. 138 EU108
Beech Rd., Sev. 155 FH125
Victoria Rd.
Beech Rd., Wat. 29 BU37
Beech Rd., West. 150 EH118
Beech Rd., Wey. 127 BR105
Beech Row, Rich. 102 CL91
Beech St. EC2 7 H6
Beech St. EC2 78 DQ71
Beech St., Rom. 69 FC56
Beech Tree Glade E4 52 EF46
Forest Side
Beech Wk. NW7 46 CS51
Beech Wk., Dart. 97 FG84
Beech Wk., Epsom 131 CU111
Beech Way NW10 74 CR66
Beech Way, Epsom 145 CT115
Beech Way, S.Croy. 135 DX113
Beech Way, Twick. 100 CA90
Beechcroft, Ash. 144 CM119
Beechcroft, Chis. 109 EN94
Beechcroft Ave. NW11 61 CZ59
Beechcroft Ave., Bexh. 97 FD81
Beechcroft Ave., Har. 58 CA59
Beechcroft Ave., Ken. 148 DR115
Beechcroft Ave., N.Mal. 116 CQ95
Beechcroft Ave., Rick. 29 BQ44
Beechcroft Ave., Sthl. 72 BZ74
Beechcroft Clo., Houns. 86 BY80
Beechcroft Clo., Orp. 137 ER105
Beechcroft Gdns., Wem. 60 CM62
Beechcroft Manor, Wey. 113 BR104
Beechcroft Rd. E18 52 EH54
Beechcroft Rd. SW14 88 CQ83
Elm Rd.
Beechcroft Rd. SW17 104 DE89
Beechcroft Rd., Chess. 130 CM105
Beechcroft Rd., Orp. 137 ER105
Beechcroft Rd. (Bushey), Wat. 30 BY43
Beechdale N21 49 DM47
Beechdale Rd. SW2 105 DM86
Beechdene, Tad. 145 CV122
Beechen Cliff Way, Islw. 87 CF81
Henley Clo.
Beechen Gro., Pnr. 58 BZ55
Beechen Gro., Wat. 29 BV41
Beechenlea La., Swan. 125 FG98
Beeches, The, Bans. 146 DB116
Beeches, The, Houns. 86 CB81
Beeches, The, Lthd. 143 CE124
Beeches, The, St.Alb. 17 CD27
Beeches Ave., Cars. 132 DE108
Beeches Clo. SE20 120 DW95
Genoa Rd.
Beeches Clo., Tad. 146 DA123
Beeches Ct., Brom. 108 EG93
Avondale Rd.
Beeches Rd. SW17 104 DE90
Beeches Rd., Sutt. 117 CY102
Beeches Wk., Cars. 132 DD109
Beeches Wd., Tad. 146 DA122
Beechfield, Bans. 132 DB113
Beechfield, Kings L. 14 BM30
Beechfield Cotts., Brom. 122 EJ96
Widmore Rd.
Beechfield Gdns., Rom. 69 FC59
Beechfield Rd. N4 64 DQ58
Beechfield Rd. SE6 107 DZ88
Beechfield Rd., Brom. 122 EJ96
Beechfield Rd., Erith 97 FE80
Beechfield Wk., Wal.Abb. 37 ED35
Beechhill Rd. SE9 109 EN85
Beechmeads, Cob. 128 BX113
Beechmont Clo., Brom. 108 EE92
Beechmont Rd., Sev. 155 FH129
Beechmore Gdns., Sutt. 117 CX103
Beechmore Rd. SW11 90 DF81
Beechmount Ave. W7 73 CD71
Beecholm Ms., Wal.Cr. 23 DX28
Beecholme, Bans. 131 CY114
Beecholme Ave., Mitch. 119 DH95
Beecholme Est. E5 64 DV62
Prout Rd.
Beechpark Way, Wat. 29 BS37
Beechtree Clo., Stan. 45 CJ50
Beechtree Pl., Sutt. 132 DB106
St. Nicholas Way
Beechvale Clo. N12 48 DE50
Beechway, Bex. 110 EX86
Beechway, S.Croy. 135 DX113
Beechwood Ave. N3 61 CZ55
Beechwood Ave., Couls. 147 DH115
Beechwood Ave., Grnf. 72 CB69
Beechwood Ave., Har. 58 CB62
Beechwood Ave., Hayes 71 BR73
Beechwood Ave., Orp. 137 ES106
Beechwood Ave., Pot.B. 20 DB33
Beechwood Ave., Rich. 88 CN81
Beechwood Ave., Ruis. 57 BT61
Beechwood Ave., Stai. 98 BH93
Beechwood Ave., Sun. 99 BU93
Beechwood Ave., Tad. 146 DA121
Beechwood Ave., Th.Hth. 119 DP98
Beechwood Ave., Uxb. 70 BM72
Beechwood Ave., Wey. 127 BS105
Beechwood Clo. NW7 46 CR50
Beechwood Clo., Surb. 115 CK101
Beechwood Clo. (Cheshunt), Wal.Cr. 22 DS26
Beechwood Clo., Wey. 127 BS105
Beechwood Ct., Cars. 132 DF105
Beechwood Ct., Sun. 99 BU93
Beechwood Cres., Bexh. 96 EX83
Beechwood Dr., Cob. 128 CA111
Beechwood Dr., Kes. 136 EK105
Beechwood Dr., Wdf.Grn. 52 EF50
Beechwood Gdns. NW10 74 CM69
St. Annes Gdns.
Beechwood Gdns., Cat. 148 DU122
Beechwood Gdns., Har. 58 CB62
Beechwood Gdns., Ilf. 67 EM57
Beechwood Gdns., Rain. 83 FH71
Beechwood Gro. W3 74 CS73
East Acton La.
Beechwood Gro., Surb. 115 CJ101
Beechwood La., Warl. 149 DX119
Beechwood Manor, Wey. 127 BS105
Beechwood Ms. N9 50 DU47
Beechwood Pk. E18 66 EG55
Beechwood Pk., Lthd. 143 CJ123
Beechwood Ri., Chis. 109 EP91
Beechwood Ri., Wat. 29 BV36
Beechwood Rd. E8 78 DT65
Beechwood Rd. N8 63 DK56
Beechwood Rd., Cat. 148 DU122
Beechwood Rd., S.Croy. 134 DS110
Beechwoods Ct. SE19 106 DT92
Crystal Palace Par.
Beechworth Clo. NW3 62 DA61
Beecot La., Walt. 114 BW103
Beecroft Rd. SE4 107 DY85
Beehive Clo. E8 78 DT66
Beehive Clo., Borwd. 31 CK44
Beehive Clo., Uxb. 70 BM66
Honey Hill
Beehive La., Ilf. 67 EM57
Beehive Pas. EC3 7 M9
Beehive Pl. SW9 91 DN83
Beehive Rd. (Cheshunt), Wal.Cr. 21 DP28
Beeken Dene, Orp. 137 EQ105
Isabella Dr.
Beeleigh Rd., Mord. 118 DB98
Beeston Clo. E8 64 DU64
Ferncliff Rd.
Beeston Clo., Wat. 44 BX49
Beeston Dr., Wal.Cr. 23 DX27
Beeston Pl. SW1 9 J7
Beeston Pl. SW1 91 DH76
Beeston Rd., Barn. 34 DD44
Beeston Way, Felt. 100 BW86
Beethoven Rd., Borwd. 31 CJ44
Beethoven St. W10 75 CY69
Beeton Clo., Pnr. 44 CA52
Begbie Rd. SE3 94 EJ81
Beggars Bush La., Wat. 29 BR43
Beggars Hill, Epsom 130 CS107
Beggars Hollow, Enf. 36 DR37
Beggars Roost La., Sutt. 132 DA107
Begonia Clo. E6 80 EL71
Begonia Pl., Hmptn. 100 CA93
Gresham Rd.
Begonia Wk. W12 75 CT72
Du Cane Rd.
Beira St. SW12 105 DH87
Beken Ct., Wat. 30 BW35
Bekesbourne St. E14 79 DY72
Ratcliffe La.
Bekesbourne Twr., Orp. 124 EX102
Belcroft Clo., Brom. 108 EF94
Hope Pk.
Beldam Haw, Sev. 138 FA112
Beldham Gdns., W.Mol. 114 CB97
Belfairs Dr., Rom. 68 EW59
Belfairs Grn., Wat. 44 BX50
Heysham Dr.
Belfast Rd. N16 64 DT61
Belfast Rd. SE25 120 DV98
Belfield Rd., Epsom 130 CR109
Belfont Wk. N7 63 DL63
Belford Gro. SE18 95 EN77
Belford Rd., Borwd. 32 CM38
Belfort Rd. SE15 92 DW82
Belfry Ave., Uxb. 42 BG53
Belfry La., Rick. 42 BJ46
Belgrade Rd. N16 64 DS63
Belgrade Rd., Hmptn. 114 CB95
Belgrave Ave., Wat. 29 BT43
Belgrave Clo. N14 35 DJ43
Prince George Ave.
Belgrave Clo. W3 88 CQ75
Avenue Rd.
Belgrave Clo., Orp. 124 EW98
Belgrave Clo., Walt. 127 BV105
Belgrave Cres., Sun. 113 BV95
Belgrave Dr., Kings L. 15 BQ28
Belgrave Gdns. N14 35 DK43
Belgrave Gdns. NW8 76 DB67
Belgrave Gdns., Stan. 45 CJ50
Copley Rd.
Belgrave Ms., Uxb. 70 BK70
Belgrave Ms. N. SW1 8 F5
Belgrave Ms. N. SW1 90 DG76
Belgrave Ms. S. SW1 8 G6
Belgrave Ms. S. SW1 90 DG76
Belgrave Ms. W. SW1 8 F6
Belgrave Ms. W. SW1 90 DG76
Belgrave Pl. SW1 8 G6
Belgrave Pl. SW1 90 DG76
Belgrave Rd. E10 65 EC60
Belgrave Rd. E11 66 EG61
Belgrave Rd. E13 80 EJ69
Belgrave Rd. E17 65 EA57
Belgrave Rd. SE25 120 DU98
Belgrave Rd. SW1 9 K9
Belgrave Rd. SW1 91 DH77
Belgrave Rd. SW13 89 CT80
Belgrave Rd., Houns. 86 BZ83
Belgrave Rd., Ilf. 67 EM60
Belgrave Rd., Mitch. 118 DD97
Belgrave Rd., Sun. 113 BV95
Belgrave Sq. SW1 8 F6
Belgrave Sq. SW1 90 DG76
Belgrave St. E1 79 DX71
Belgrave Ter., Wdf.Grn. 52 EG48
Belgrave Wk., Mitch. 118 DD97
Belgrave Yd. SW1 9 H7
Belgravia Gdns., Brom. 108 EE93
Belgravia Ho. SW4 105 DK86
Belgravia Ms., Kings.T. 115 CK98
Belgrove St. WC1 6 A2
Belgrove St. WC1 77 DL69
Belham Rd., Kings L. 14 BM28
Belham Wk. SE5 92 DR81
D'Eynsford Rd.
Belhaven Ct., Borwd. 32 CM39
Belinda Rd. SW9 91 DP83
Belitha Vill. N1 77 DM66
Bell Ave., Rom. 55 FH53
Bell Ave., West Dr. 84 BM76
Bell Clo., Abb.L. 15 BT27
Bell Clo., Pnr. 44 BW54
Bell Clo., Ruis. 57 BT62
Bell Common, Epp. 25 ES32
Bell Ct., Surb. 116 CP103
Barnsbury La.
Bell Cres., Couls. 147 DH121
Maple Way
Bell Dr. SW18 103 CY87
Bell Fm. Ave., Dag. 69 FC62
Bell Gdns. E17 65 DZ57
Markhouse Rd.
Bell Gdns., Orp. 124 EW99
Bell Grn. SE26 107 DZ90
Bell Grn. La. SE26 107 DZ92
Bell Hill, Croy. 120 DQ104
Surrey St.
Bell Ho. Rd., Rom. 69 FC60
Bell Inn Yd. EC3 7 L9
Bell La. E1 7 P7
Bell La. E1 78 DT71
Bell La. E16 80 EG74
Bell La. NW4 61 CW56
Bell La., Abb.L. 15 BT27
Bell La., Enf. 37 DX38
Bell La., Hat. 20 DA25
Bell La., Lthd. 143 CD123
Bell La., St.Alb. 18 CL29
Bell La., Twick. 101 CG88
The Embk.
Bell La., Wem. 59 CK61
Magnet Rd.
Bell La. Clo., Lthd. 143 CD123
Bell Meadow SE19 106 DS91
Dulwich Wd. Ave.
Bell Rd., E.Mol. 115 CD99
Bell Rd., Enf. 36 DR39
Bell Rd., Houns. 86 CB83
Bell St. NW1 4 B6
Bell St. NW1 76 DE71
Bell Water Gate SE18 95 EN76
Bell Wf. La. EC4 7 J10
Bell Yd. WC2 6 D9
Bell Yd. WC2 77 DN72
Bellamy Clo. W14 89 CZ78
Aisgill Ave.
Bellamy Clo., Edg. 46 CQ48
Bellamy Clo., Uxb. 56 BN62
Bellamy Clo., Wat. 29 BU39
Bellamy Dr., Stan. 45 CH53
Bellamy Rd. E4 51 EB51
Bellamy Rd., Enf. 36 DR40
Bellamy Rd. (Cheshunt), Wal.Cr. 23 DY29
Bellamy St. SW12 105 DH87
Bellasis Ave. SW2 105 DL89
Bellclose Rd., West Dr. 84 BL75
Belle Staines Pleasaunce E4 51 EA47
Belle Vue, Grnf. 73 CD67
Belle Vue Clo., Stai. 112 BG95
Belle Vue Est. NW4 61 CW56
Bell La.
Belle Vue La. (Bushey), Wat. 45 CD46
Belle Vue Rd. E17 51 ED54
Belle Vue Rd. NW4 61 CW56
Bell La.
Belle Vue Rd., Orp. 137 EN110
Standard Rd.
Bellefield Rd., Orp. 124 EV99
Bellefields Rd. SW9 91 DM83
Bellegrove Clo., Well. 95 ET82
Bellegrove Rd., Well. 95 ES82
Bellenden Rd. SE15 92 DT83
Belleville Rd. SW11 104 DE85
Bellevue Ms. N11 48 DG50
Bellevue Rd.
Bellevue Par. SW17 104 DE88
Bellevue Rd.
Bellevue Pk., Th.Hth. 120 DQ97
Bellevue Pl. E1 78 DW70
Bellevue Rd. N11 48 DG49
Bellevue Rd. SW13 89 CU82
Bellevue Rd. SW17 104 DE88
Bellevue Rd. W13 73 CH70
Bellevue Rd., Bexh. 110 EZ85
Bellevue Rd., Kings.T. 116 CL97
Bellevue Rd., Rom. 55 FC51
Bellew St. SW17 104 DC90
Bellfield, Croy. 135 DZ108
Bellfield Ave., Har. 45 CD50
Bellflower Clo. E6 80 EL71
Sorrel Gdns.
Bellgate Ms. NW5 63 DH62
York Ri.
Bellingham Ct., Bark. 82 EV69
Renwick Rd.
Bellingham Grn. SE6 107 EA90
Bellingham Rd. SE6 107 EC90
Bellmarsh Rd., Add. 126 BH105
Bellmount Wd. Ave., Wat. 29 BS39
Bello Clo. SE24 105 DP87
Bellot Gdns. SE10 94 EE78
Bellot St. SE10 94 EE78
Bellring Clo., Belv. 96 FA79
Bells All. SW6 90 DA82
Bells Gdn. Est. SE15 92 DU80
Buller Clo.
Bells Hill, Barn. 33 CX43
Belltrees Gro. SW16 105 DM92
Bellwood Rd. SE15 93 DX84
Belmarsh Rd. SE28 95 ES75
Western Way
Belmont Ave. N9 50 DU46
Belmont Ave. N13 49 DL50
Belmont Ave. N17 64 DQ55
Belmont Ave., Barn. 34 DF43
Belmont Ave., N.Mal. 117 CU99
Belmont Ave., Sthl. 86 BY76
Belmont Ave., Well. 95 ES82
Belmont Ave., Wem. 74 CM67
Belmont Circle, Har. 45 CH54
Kenton La.
Belmont Clo. E4 51 ED50
Belmont Clo. N20 48 DB46
Belmont Clo. SW4 91 DJ83
Belmont Clo., Barn. 34 DF42
Belmont Clo., Uxb. 70 BK65
Belmont Clo., Wdf.Grn. 52 EH49
Belmont Ct. NW11 61 CZ57
Belmont Gro. SE13 93 ED83
Belmont Hall Ct. SE13 93 ED83
Belmont Gro.
Belmont Hill SE13 93 EC83
Belmont La., Chis. 109 ER92
Belmont La., Stan. 45 CJ52
Belmont Pk. SE13 93 ED84
Belmont Pk. Clo. SE13 93 ED84
Belmont Pk.
Belmont Pk. Rd. E10 65 EB58
Belmont Ri., Sutt. 131 CZ107
Belmont Rd. N15 64 DQ56
Belmont Rd. N17 64 DQ55
Belmont Rd. SE25 120 DV99
Belmont Rd. SW4 91 DJ83
Belmont Rd. W4 88 CR77
Belmont Rd., Beck. 121 DZ96
Belmont Rd., Chis. 109 EP92
Belmont Rd., Erith 96 FA80
Belmont Rd., Har. 59 CF55
Belmont Rd., Ilf. 67 EQ62
Belmont Rd., Lthd. 143 CG122
Belmont Rd., Sutt. 132 DA110
Belmont Rd., Twick. 101 CD89
Belmont Rd., Uxb. 70 BK66
Belmont Rd., Wall. 133 DH106
Belmont Rd. (Bushey), Wat. 30 BY43
Belmont St. NW1 76 DG66
Belmont Ter. W4 88 CR77
Belmont Rd.
Belmor, Borwd. 32 CN43
Belmore Ave., Hayes 71 BU72
Belmore La. N7 63 DK64
Belmore St. SW8 91 DK81
Beloe Clo. SW15 89 CU83
Belper Ct. E5 65 DX63
Pedro St.
Belsham St. E9 78 DW65
Belsize Ave. N13 49 DM51
Belsize Ave. NW3 76 DD65
Belsize Ave. W13 87 CH76
Belsize Cres. NW3 62 DD64
Belsize Gdns., Sutt. 132 DB105
Belsize Gro. NW3 76 DE65
Belsize La. NW3 76 DD65
Belsize Ms. NW3 76 DD65
Belsize La.
Belsize Pk. NW3 76 DD65
Belsize Pk. Gdns. NW3 76 DE65
Belsize Pk. Ms. NW3 76 DD65
Belsize La.
Belsize Pl. NW3 76 DD65
Belsize La.
Belsize Rd. NW6 76 DB67
Belsize Rd., Har. 45 CD52
Belsize Sq. NW3 76 DD65
Belsize Ter. NW3 76 DD65
Belson Rd. SE18 95 EM77
Beltane Dr. SW19 103 CX90
Belthorn Cres. SW12 105 DJ87
Belton Rd. E7 80 EH66
Belton Rd. E11 66 EE63
Belton Rd. N17 64 DS55
Belton Rd. NW2 75 CU65
Belton Rd., Sid. 110 EU91
Belton Way E3 79 EA71
Beltona Gdns. (Cheshunt), Wal.Cr. 23 DX27
Beltran Rd. SW6 90 DB82
Beltwood Rd., Belv. 97 FC77
Belvedere Ave. SW19 103 CY92
Belvedere Ave., Ilf. 53 EP54
Belvedere Bldgs. SE1 10 G5
Belvedere Clo., Esher 128 CB106
Belvedere Clo., Tedd. 101 CE92
Belvedere Clo., Wey. 126 BN106
Belvedere Ct. N2 62 DD57
Belvedere Dr. SW19 103 CY92
Belvedere Gdns., St.Alb. 16 CA27
Belvedere Gdns., W.Mol. 114 BZ99
Belvedere Gro. SW19 103 CY92
Belvedere Ho., Felt. 99 BU88
Belvedere Ind. Est., Belv. 97 FC76
Crabtree Manorway S.
Belvedere Ms. SE15 92 DW83
Belvedere Pl. SE1 10 G5
Belvedere Rd. E10 65 DY60
Belvedere Rd. SE1 10 C4
Belvedere Rd. SE1 91 DM75
Belvedere Rd. SE2 82 EX74
Belvedere Rd. SE19 106 DT94
Belvedere Rd. W7 87 CE76
Belvedere Rd., Bexh. 96 EZ83
Belvedere Rd., West. 151 EM118
Belvedere Sq. SW19 103 CY92
Belvedere Strand NW9 47 CT54
Belvedere Way, Har. 60 CL58
Belvoir Clo. SE9 108 EL90
Belvoir Rd. SE22 106 DU87
Belvue Clo., Nthlt. 72 CA66
Belvue Rd., Nthlt. 72 CA66
Bembridge Clo. NW6 75 CY66
Bembridge Gdns., Ruis. 57 BR61
Bemerton Est. N1 77 DL66
Bemerton St. N1 77 DM67
Bemish Rd. SW15 89 CX83
Bempton Dr., Ruis. 57 BV61
Bemsted Rd. E17 65 DZ55
Ben Hale Clo., Stan. 45 CH49
Ben Jonson Rd. E1 79 DX71
Ben Smith Way SE16 92 DU76
Jamaica Rd.
Ben Tillet Clo. E16 81 EM74
Newland St.
Ben Tillet Clo., Bark. 82 EU66
Benares Rd. SE18 95 ET77
Benbow Rd. W6 89 CV76
Benbow St. SE8 93 EA79
Benbow Waye, Uxb. 70 BJ71
Benbury Clo., Brom. 107 EC92
Bench Fld., S.Croy. 134 DT107
Bencombe Rd., Pur. 133 DN114
Bencroft (Cheshunt), Wal.Cr. 22 DU26
Bencroft Rd. SW16 105 DJ94
Bencurtis Pk., W.Wick. 121 ED104
Bendall Ms. NW1 4 C6
Bendemeer Rd. SW15 89 CX83
Bendish Rd. E6 80 EL66

Bendmore Ave. SE2 96 EU78
Bendon Valley SW18 104 DB87
Bendysh Rd. (Bushey), Wat. 30 BY41
Benedict Clo., Belv. 96 EY76
Tunstock Way
Benedict Clo., Orp. 123 ES104
Benedict Dr., Felt. 99 BR87
Benedict Rd. SW9 91 DM83
Benedict Rd., Mitch. 118 DD97
Benedict Way N2 62 DC55
Benedictine Gate, Wal.Cr. 23 DY27
Benenden Grn., Brom. 122 EF99
Benett Gdns. SW16 119 DL96
Benfleet Clo., Cob. 128 BY112
Benfleet Clo., Sutt. 118 DC104
Bengal Ct. EC3 78 DR72
Birchin La.
Bengal Rd., Ilf. 67 EP63
Bengarth Dr., Har. 45 CD54
Bengarth Rd., Nthlt. 72 BX67
Bengeworth Rd. SE5 92 DQ83
Bengeworth Rd., Har. 59 CG61
Benham Clo. SW11 90 DD83
Benham Clo., Chess. 129 CJ107
Merritt Gdns.
Benham Clo., Couls. 147 DP118
Benham Gdns., Houns. 86 BZ84
Benham Rd. W7 73 CE71
Benhams Pl. NW3 62 DC63
Holly Wk.
Benhill Ave., Sutt. 132 DB105
Benhill Rd. SE5 92 DR80
Benhill Rd., Sutt. 118 DC104
Benhill Wd. Rd., Sutt. 132 DC105
Benhilton Gdns., Sutt. 118 DB104
Benhurst Ave., Horn. 69 FH63
Benhurst Clo., S.Croy. 135 DX110
Benhurst Ct. SW16 105 DN92
Benhurst Gdns., S.Croy. 134 DW110
Benhurst La. SW16 105 DN92
Benin St. SE13 107 ED87
Benjafield Clo. N18 50 DV49
Brettenham Rd.
Benjamin Clo. E8 78 DU67
Benjamin Clo., Horn. 69 FG58
Benjamin St. EC1 6 F6
Benjamin St. EC1 77 DP71
Benledi St. E14 79 ED72
Benn St. E9 79 DY65
Bennerley Rd. SW11 104 DE85
Bennet's Hill EC4 6 G10
Bennetsfield Rd., Uxb. 71 BP74
Bennett Clo., Cob. 127 BU113
Bennett Clo., Kings.T. 115 CJ95
Bennett Clo., Nthwd. 43 BT52
Bennett Clo., Well. 96 EU82
Bennett Gro. SE13 93 EB81
Bennett Pk. SE3 94 EF83
Bennett Rd. E13 80 EJ70
Bennett Rd. N16 64 DS63
Bennett Rd., Rom. 68 EY58
Bennett St. SW1 9 K2
Bennett St. W4 88 CS79
Bennetts Ave., Croy. 121 DY103
Bennetts Ave., Grnf. 73 CE67
Bennetts Castle La., Dag. 68 EW63
Bennetts Clo. N17 50 DT51
Bennetts Clo., Mitch. 119 DH95
Bennetts Copse, Chis. 108 EL93
Bennetts Way, Croy. 121 DY103
Bennetts Yd. SW1 9 N7
Benningholme Rd., Edg. 46 CS51
Bennington Rd. N17 50 DS53
Bennington Rd., Wdf.Grn. 52 EE52
Benn's Wk., Rich. 88 CL84
Rosedale Rd.
Benrek Clo., Ilf. 53 EQ53
Bensbury Clo. SW15 103 CW87
Bensham Clo., Th.Hth. 120 DQ98
Bensham Gro., Th.Hth. 120 DQ96
Bensham La., Croy. 119 DP101
Bensham La., Th.Hth. 119 DP98
Bensham Manor Rd., Th.Hth. 120 DQ98
Bensington Ct., Felt. 99 BR86
Benskin Rd., Wat. 29 BU43
Bensley Clo. N11 48 DF50
Benson Ave. E6 80 EJ68
Benson Clo., Houns. 86 CA84
Benson Clo., Uxb. 70 BL71
Benson Quay E1 78 DW73
Garnet St.
Benson Rd. SE23 106 DW88
Benson Rd., Croy. 119 DN104
Bentfield Gdns. SE9 108 EJ90
Aldersgrove Ave.
Benthal Rd. N16 64 DU61
Benthall Gdns., Ken. 148 DQ116
Bentham Rd. E9 79 DX65
Bentham Rd. SE28 82 EV73
Bentham Wk. NW10 60 CQ64
Bentinck Ms. W1 4 G8
Bentinck Pl. NW8 4 B1
Bentinck Rd., West Dr. 70 BK74
Bentinck St. W1 4 G8
Bentinck St. W1 76 DG72
Bentley Dr., Ilf. 67 EQ58
Bentley Dr., Wey. 126 BN109
Bentley Heath La., Barn. 33 CZ35
Bentley Rd. N1 78 DS65
Tottenham Rd.
Bentley Way, Stan. 45 CG50
Bentley Way, Wdf.Grn. 52 EG48
Benton Rd., Ilf. 67 ER60
Benton Rd., Wat. 44 BX50
Bentons La. SE27 106 DQ91
Bentons Ri. SE27 106 DR92
Bentry Clo., Dag. 68 EY61
Bentry Rd., Dag. 68 EY61
Bentworth Rd. W12 75 CV72
Benwell Ct., Sun. 113 BU95
Benwell Rd. N7 63 DN63
Benwick Clo. SE16 92 DV77
Benworth St. E3 79 DZ69
Benyon Rd. N1 78 DR67
Southgate Rd.
Beomonds Row, Cher. 112 BG101
Berber Rd. SW11 104 DF85
Berberis Wk., West Dr. 84 BL77
Berceau Wk., Wat. 29 BS39
Bercta Rd. SE9 109 EQ89
Bere St. E1 79 DX73
Cranford St.
Berenger Wk. SW10 90 DD80
Blantyre St.
Berens Rd. NW10 75 CX69
Berens Rd., Orp. 124 EX99
Berens Way, Chis. 123 ET98
Beresford Ave. N20 48 DF47
Beresford Ave. W7 73 CD71
Beresford Ave., Surb. 116 CP102
Beresford Ave., Twick. 101 CJ86
Beresford Ave., Wem. 74 CM67
Beresford Dr., Brom. 122 EL97
Beresford Dr., Wdf.Grn. 52 EJ49
Beresford Gdns., Enf. 36 DS42
Beresford Gdns., Houns. 100 BZ85
Beresford Gdns., Rom. 68 EY57
Beresford Rd. E4 52 EE46
Beresford Rd. E17 51 EB53
Beresford Rd. N2 62 DE55
Beresford Rd. N5 64 DR64
Beresford Rd. N8 63 DN57
Beresford Rd., Har. 59 CD57
Beresford Rd., Kings.T. 116 CM95
Beresford Rd., N.Mal. 116 CQ98
Beresford Rd., Sthl. 72 BX74
Beresford Rd., Sutt. 131 CZ108
Beresford Sq. SE18 95 EP77
Beresford St. SE18 95 EP76
Beresford Ter. N5 64 DQ64
Berestede Rd. W6 89 CT78
Bergen Sq. SE16 93 DY76
Norway Gate
Berger Clo., Orp. 123 ER100
Berger Rd. E9 79 DX65
Berghem Ms. W14 89 CX76
Blythe Rd.
Bergholt Ave., Ilf. 66 EL57
Bergholt Cres. N16 64 DS59
Bergholt Ms. NW1 77 DJ66
Rossendale Way
Bering Wk. E16 80 EK72
Berisford Ms. SW18 104 DC86
Berkeley Ave., Bexh. 96 EX81
Berkeley Ave., Grnf. 73 CE65
Berkeley Ave., Houns. 85 BU81
Berkeley Ave., Ilf. 53 EN54
Berkeley Ave., Rom. 55 FC52
Berkeley Clo., Abb.L. 15 BT32
Berkeley Clo., Borwd. 32 CN43
Berkeley Clo., Kings.T. 102 CL94
Berkeley Clo., Orp. 123 ES101
Berkeley Clo., Pot.B. 19 CY32
Berkeley Clo., Ruis. 57 BU62
Berkeley Ct. N14 35 DJ44
Berkeley Ct., Wall. 119 DJ104
Berkeley Ct., Wey. 113 BR103
Berkeley Cres., Barn. 34 DD43
Berkeley Gdns. N21 50 DR45
Berkeley Gdns. W8 76 DA74
Brunswick Gdns.
Berkeley Gdns., Esher 129 CG107
Berkeley Gdns., Walt. 113 BT101
Berkeley Ho. E3 79 EA69
Wellington Way
Berkeley Ms. W1 4 E9
Berkeley Pl. SW19 103 CX93
Berkeley Pl., Epsom 144 CR115
Berkeley Rd. E12 66 EL64
Berkeley Rd. N8 63 DK57
Berkeley Rd. N15 64 DR58
Berkeley Rd. NW9 60 CN56
Berkeley Rd. SW13 89 CU81
Berkeley Rd., Uxb. 71 BQ66
Berkeley Sq. W1 9 J1
Berkeley Sq. W1 77 DH73
Berkeley St. W1 9 J2
Berkeley St. W1 77 DH74
Berkeley Wk. N7 63 DM61
Durham Rd.
Berkeley Waye, Houns. 86 BX80
Berkeleys, The, Lthd. 143 CE124
Berkhampstead Rd., Belv. 96 FA78
Berkhamsted Ave., Wem. 74 CM65
Berkley Ave., Wal.Cr. 23 DX34
Berkley Ct., Rick. 29 BR43
Mayfare
Berkley Dr., W.Mol. 114 BZ97
Berkley Gro. NW1 76 DF66
Berkley Rd.
Berkley Rd. NW1 76 DF66
Berkshire Clo., Cat. 148 DR122
Berkshire Gdns. N13 49 DN51
Berkshire Gdns. N18 50 DV50
Berkshire Rd. E9 79 DZ65
Berkshire Sq., Mitch. 119 DL98
Berkshire Way
Berkshire Way, Mitch. 119 DL98
Bermans Way NW10 60 CS63
Bermondsey Sq. SE1 11 N6
Bermondsey St. SE1 11 M3
Bermondsey St. SE1 92 DS75
Bermondsey Wall E. SE16 92 DU75
Bermondsey Wall W. SE16 92 DU75
Bernal Clo. SE28 82 EX73
Haldane Rd.
Bernard Ashley Dr. SE7 94 EH78
Bernard Ave. W13 87 CH76
Bernard Cassidy St. E16 80 EF71
Bernard Gdns. SW19 103 CZ92
Bernard Rd. N15 64 DT57
Bernard Rd., Rom. 69 FC59
Bernard Rd., Wall. 133 DH106
Bernard St. WC1 5 P5
Bernard St. WC1 77 DL70
Bernards Clo., Ilf. 53 EQ52
Bernato Clo., W.Byf. 126 BL112
Viscount Gdns.
Bernays Clo., Stan. 45 CJ51
Bernays Gro. SW9 91 DM84
Berne Rd., Th.Hth. 119 DP99
Bernel Dr., Croy. 121 DZ104
Berners Dr. W13 73 CG72
Berners Ms. W1 5 L7
Berners Ms. W1 77 DJ71
Berners Pl. W1 5 L8
Berners Pl. W1 77 DJ72
Berners Rd. N1 77 DN67
Berners Rd. N22 49 DN53
Berners St. W1 5 L7
Berners St. W1 77 DJ71
Bernersmede SE3 94 EG83
Blackheath Pk.
Berney Rd., Croy. 120 DR101
Bernville Way, Har. 60 CM57
Kenton Rd.
Bernwell Rd. E4 52 EE48
Berridge Grn., Edg. 46 CP52
Berridge Rd. SE19 106 DS92
Berriman Rd. N7 63 DM62
Berrington Dr., Lthd. 141 BT124
Berriton Rd., Har. 58 BZ60
Berry Ave., Wat. 29 BU36
Berry Clo. N21 49 DP46
Berry Clo. NW10 74 CS66
Berry Clo., Rick. 42 BH45
Berry Ct., Houns. 100 BZ85
Berry Gro. La. (Bushey), Wat. 30 BY38
Berry Hill, Stan. 45 CK49
Berry La. SE21 106 DR91
Berry La., Rick. 42 BH45
Berry Meade, Ash. 144 CM117
Berry Pl. EC1 6 G3
Berry St. EC1 6 G4
Berry St. EC1 77 DP70
Berry Wk., Ash. 144 CM119
Berry Way W5 88 CL76
Berry Way, Rick. 42 BH45
Berrybank Clo. E4 51 EC47
Greenbank Clo.
Berrydale Rd., Hayes 72 BY70
Berryfield Clo. E17 65 EB56
Berryfield Clo., Brom. 122 EL95
Berryfield Rd. SE17 10 G10
Berryfield Rd. SE17 91 DP78
Berryhill SE9 95 EP84
Berryhill Gdns. SE9 95 EP84
Berrylands SW20 117 CW97
Berrylands, Orp. 124 EW104
Berrylands, Surb. 116 CM100
Berrylands Rd., Surb. 116 CM100
Berryman Clo., Dag. 68 EW62
Bennetts Castle La.
Berrymans La. SE26 107 DX91
Berrymead Gdns. W3 88 CQ75
Berrymede Rd. W4 88 CR76
Berrys Grn. Rd., West. 151 EP115
Berrys Hill, West. 151 EP115
Berrys La., W.Byf. 126 BK111
Berryscroft Ct., Stai. 98 BJ94
Berryscroft Rd.
Berryscroft Rd., Stai. 98 BJ94
Bert Rd., Th.Hth. 120 DQ99
Bertal Rd. SW17 104 DD91
Berthon St. SE8 93 EA80
Bertie Rd. NW10 75 CU65
Bertie Rd. SE26 107 DX93
Bertram Cotts. SW19 104 DA94
Hartfield Rd.
Bertram Rd. NW4 61 CU58
Bertram Rd., Enf. 36 DU42
Bertram Rd., Kings.T. 102 CN94
Bertram St. N19 63 DH61
Bertram Way, Enf. 36 DT42
Bertrand St. SE13 93 EB83
Bertrand Way SE28 82 EV73
Berwick Ave., Hayes 72 BX72
Berwick Clo., Stan. 45 CF52
Gordon Ave.
Berwick Clo., Wal.Cr. 23 EA34
Berwick Cres., Sid. 109 ES86
Berwick La., Ong. 27 FE33
Berwick Rd. E16 80 EH72
Berwick Rd. N22 49 DP53
Berwick Rd., Borwd. 32 CL38
Berwick Rd., Well. 96 EV81
Berwick St. W1 5 L8
Berwick St. W1 77 DJ72
Berwick Way, Orp. 124 EU102
Berwick Way, Sev. 155 FH121
Berwyn Ave., Houns. 86 CB81
Berwyn Rd. SE24 105 DP88
Berwyn Rd., Rich. 88 CP84
Beryl Ave. E6 80 EL71
Beryl Rd. W6 89 CX78
Berystede, Kings.T. 102 CP94
Besant Ct. N1 64 DR64
Newington Grn. Rd.
Besant Rd. NW2 61 CY63
Besant Wk. N7 63 DM61
Newington Barrow Way
Besant Way NW10 60 CQ64
Besley St. SW16 105 DJ94
Bessant Dr., Rich. 88 CP81
Bessborough Gdns. SW1 9 N10
Bessborough Gdns. SW1 91 DK78
Bessborough Pl. SW1 9 M10
Bessborough Pl. SW1 91 DK78
Bessborough Rd. SW15 103 CU88
Bessborough Rd., Har. 59 CD60
Bessborough St. SW1 9 M10
Bessborough St. SW1 91 DK78
Bessels Grn. Rd., Sev. 154 FD123
Bessels Meadow, Sev. 154 FD124
Bessels Way, Sev. 154 FC124
Bessemer Rd. SE5 92 DQ82
Bessie Lansbury Clo. E6 81 EN72
Bessingby Rd., Ruis. 57 BV61
Bessingham Wk. SE4 93 DX84
Frendsbury Rd.
Besson St. SE14 92 DW81
Bessy St. E2 78 DW69
Roman Rd.
Bestwood St. SE8 93 DX77
Beswick Ms. NW6 76 DB65
Lymington Rd.
Betam Rd., Hayes 85 BR75
Betchworth Clo., Sutt. 132 DD106
Turnpike La.
Betchworth Rd., Ilf. 67 ES61
Betchworth Way, Croy. 135 EC109
Betenson Ave., Sev. 154 FF122
Betham Rd., Grnf. 73 CD69
Bethany Waye, Felt. 99 BS87
Bethecar Rd., Har. 59 CE57
Bethel Rd., Sev. 155 FJ123
Bethel Rd., Well. 96 EW83
Bethell Ave. E16 80 EF70
Bethell Ave., Ilf. 67 EN59
Bethersden Clo., Beck. 107 DZ94
Bethnal Grn. Rd. E1 7 P4
Bethnal Grn. Rd. E1 78 DT70
Bethnal Grn. Rd. E2 78 DT70
Bethune Ave. N11 48 DF49
Bethune Rd. N16 64 DR59
Bethune Rd. NW10 74 CR70
Bethwin Rd. SE5 91 DP80
Betjeman Clo., Couls. 147 DM117
Betjeman Clo., Pnr. 58 CA56
Betjeman Clo., Wal.Cr. 22 DU28
Rosedale Way
Betley Ct., Walt. 113 BV104
Betony Clo., Croy. 121 DX102
Primrose La.
Betoyne Ave. E4 52 EE49
Betsham Rd., Erith 97 FF80
Betstyle Rd. N11 49 DH49
Betterton Dr., Sid. 110 EY89
Betterton Rd., Rain. 83 FE69
Betterton St. WC2 5 P9
Betterton St. WC2 77 DL72
Bettles Clo., Uxb. 70 BJ68
Westcott Way
Bettons Pk. E15 80 EE67
Bettridge Rd. SW6 89 CZ82
Betts Clo., Beck. 121 DY96
Kendall Rd.
Betts Ms. E17 65 DZ58
Queen's Rd.
Betts Rd. E16 80 EH73
Victoria Dock Rd.
Betts St. E1 78 DV73
The Highway
Betts Way SE20 120 DV95
Betts Way, Surb. 115 CH102
Betula Clo., Ken. 148 DR115
Between Sts., Cob. 127 BU114
Beulah Ave., Th.Hth. 119 DM98
Beulah Rd.
Beulah Clo., Edg. 46 CP48
Beulah Cres., Th.Hth. 120 DQ96
Beulah Gro., Croy. 120 DQ100
Beulah Hill SE19 105 DP93
Beulah Path E17 65 EB57
Addison Rd.
Beulah Rd. E17 65 EB57
Beulah Rd. SW19 103 CZ94
Beulah Rd., Epp. 26 EU29
Beulah Rd., Sutt. 132 DA105
Beulah Rd., Th.Hth. 120 DQ97
Beulah Wk., Cat. 149 DY120
Beult Rd., Dart. 97 FG83
Bev Callender Clo. SW8 91 DH83
Daley Thompson Way
Bevan Ave., Bark. 82 EU66
Bevan Ct., Croy. 133 DN106
Bevan Pl., Swan. 125 FE98
Bevan Rd. SE2 96 EV78
Bevan Rd., Barn. 34 DF42
Bevan St. N1 78 DQ67
Bevenden St. N1 7 L2
Bevenden St. N1 78 DR69
Bevercote Wk., Belv. 96 EZ79
Osborne Rd.
Beveridge Rd. NW10 74 CS66
Curzon Cres.
Beverley NW8 4 B3
Beverley Ave. SW20 117 CT95
Beverley Ave., Houns. 86 BZ84
Beverley Ave., Sid. 109 ET87
Beverley Clo. N21 50 DQ46
Beverley Clo. SW11 90 DD84
Maysoule Rd.
Beverley Clo. SW13 89 CT82
Beverley Clo., Add. 126 BK106
Beverley Clo., Chess. 129 CJ105
Beverley Clo., Enf. 36 DS42
Beverley Clo., Epsom 131 CW111
Beverley Clo., Wey. 113 BS103
Beverley Cotts. SW15 102 CR91
Kingston Vale
Beverley Ct. N14 49 DJ45
Beverley Ct. SE4 93 DZ83
Beverley Cres., Wdf.Grn. 52 EH53
Beverley Dr., Edg. 60 CN55
Beverley Gdns. NW11 61 CY59
Beverley Gdns. SW13 89 CT83
Beverley Gdns., Stan. 45 CG53
Beverley Gdns. (Cheshunt), Wal.Cr. 22 DT30
Beverley Gdns., Wem. 60 CM60
Beverley Gdns., Wor.Pk. 117 CU102
Green La.
Beverley La. SW15 103 CT90
Beverley La., Kings.T. 102 CS94
Beverley Ms. E4 51 ED51
Beverley Rd.
Beverley Path SW13 89 CT82
Beverley Rd. E4 51 ED51
Beverley Rd. E6 80 EK69
Beverley Rd. SE20 120 DV96
Wadhurst Clo.
Beverley Rd. SW13 89 CT83
Beverley Rd. W4 89 CT78
Beverley Rd., Bexh. 97 FC82
Beverley Rd., Brom. 122 EL103
Beverley Rd., Dag. 68 EY63
Beverley Rd., Kings.T. 115 CJ95
Beverley Rd., Mitch. 119 DK98
Beverley Rd., N.Mal. 117 CU98
Beverley Rd., Ruis. 57 BU61
Beverley Rd., Sthl. 86 BY77
Beverley Rd., Sun. 113 BT95
Beverley Rd., Whyt. 148 DS116
Beverley Rd., Wor.Pk. 117 CW103
Beverley Way SW20 117 CT95
Beverley Way, N.Mal. 117 CT95
Beversbrook Rd. N19 63 DK62
Beverston Ms. W1 4 D7
Beverstone Rd. SW2 105 DM85
Beverstone Rd., Th.Hth. 119 DN98
Bevill Allen Clo. SW17 104 DF92
Bevill Clo. SE25 120 DU97
Bevin Clo. SE16 79 DY74
Bevin Ct. WC1 77 DN69
Holford St.
Bevin Rd., Hayes 71 BU69
Bevin Way WC1 6 D2
Bevington Rd. W10 75 CY71
Bevington Rd., Beck. 121 EB96
Bevington St. SE16 92 DU75
Bevis Marks EC3 7 N8
Bevis Marks EC3 78 DS72
Bewcastle Gdns., Enf. 35 DL42
Bewdley St. N1 77 DN66
Bewick St. SW8 91 DH82
Bewley Clo. (Cheshunt), Wal.Cr. 23 DX31
Bewley St. E1 78 DV73
Bewlys Rd. SE27 105 DP92
Bexhill Clo., Felt. 100 BY89
Bexhill Rd. N11 49 DK50
Bexhill Rd. SE4 107 DZ86
Bexhill Rd. SW14 88 CQ83
Bexhill Wk. E15 80 EE68
Mitre Rd.
Bexley Clo., Dart. 111 FE85
Bexley Gdns. N9 50 DR48
Bexley Gdns., Rom. 68 EV57
Bexley High St., Bex. 110 FA87
Bexley La., Dart. 111 FE85
Bexley La., Sid. 110 EW91
Bexley Rd. SE9 109 EP85
Bexley Rd., Erith 97 FC80
Beynon Rd., Cars. 132 DF106
Bianca Ho. N1 78 DS68
Crondall St.
Bianca Rd. SE15 92 DT79
Bibsworth Rd. N3 47 CZ54
Bibury Clo. SE15 92 DS79
Bicester Rd., Rich. 88 CN83
Bickenhall St. W1 4 E6
Bickenhall St. W1 76 DF71
Bickersteth Rd. SW17 104 DF93
Bickerton Rd. N19 63 DJ61
Bickley Cres., Brom. 122 EL98
Bickley Pk. Rd., Brom. 122 EL97
Bickley Rd. E10 65 EB59
Bickley Rd., Brom. 122 EK96
Bickley St. SW17 104 DE92
Bicknell Rd. SE5 92 DQ83
Bickney Way, Lthd. 142 CC122
Bicknoller Clo., Sutt. 132 DB110
Bicknoller Rd., Enf. 36 DS39
Bicknor Rd., Orp. 123 ES101
Bidborough Clo., Brom. 122 EF99
Bidborough St. WC1 5 P3
Bidborough St. WC1 77 DL69
Biddenden Way SE9 109 EN91
Biddenham Turn, Wat. 30 BW35
Bidder St. E16 80 EE71
Biddestone Rd. N7 63 DM63
Biddulph Rd. W9 76 DB69
Biddulph Rd., S.Croy. 134 DQ109
Bideford Ave., Grnf. 73 CH68
Bideford Clo., Edg. 46 CN53
Bideford Clo., Felt. 100 BZ90
Bideford Gdns., Enf. 50 DS45
Bideford Rd., Brom. 108 EF90
Bideford Rd., Enf. 37 DZ38

Blandford Clo. N2 62 DC57
Blandford Clo., Croy. 119 DL104
Blandford Clo., Rom. 69 FB56
Blandford Cres. E4 51 EC45
Blandford Rd. W4 88 CS76
Blandford Rd. W5 87 CK75
Blandford Rd., Beck. 120 DW96
Blandford Rd., Sthl. 86 CA77
Blandford Rd., Tedd. 101 CD92
Blandford Sq. NW1 4 C5
Blandford Sq. NW1 76 DE70
Blandford St. W1 4 E8
Blandford St. W1 76 DF72
Blandford Waye, Hayes 72 BW72
Blaney Cres. E6 81 EP69
Blanmerle Rd. SE9 109 EP88
Blann Clo. SE9 108 EK86
Blantyre St. SW10 90 DD80
Blantyre Wk. SW10 90 DD80
Blantyre St.
Blashford NW3 76 DF66
Blashford St. SE13 107 ED87
Blasker Wk. E14 93 EA78
Blattner Clo., Borwd. 32 CL42
Blawith Rd., Har. 59 CE56
Blaydon Clo. N17 50 DV52
Blaydon Clo., Ruis. 57 BS59
Blaydon Wk. N17 50 DV52
Bleak Hill La. SE18 95 ET79
Blean Gro. SE20 106 DW94
Bleasdale Ave., Grnf. 73 CG68
Blechynden St. W10 75 CX73
Bramley Rd.
Bleddyn Clo., Sid. 110 EW86
Bledlow Clo. SE28 82 EW73
Bledlow Ri., Grnf. 72 CC68
Bleeding Heart Yd. EC1 6 E7
Blegborough Rd. SW16 105 DJ93
Blendon Dr., Bex. 110 EX86
Blendon Path, Brom. 108 EF94
Hope Pk.
Blendon Rd., Bex. 110 EW86
Blendon Ter. SE18 95 EQ78
Blendworth Way SE15 92 DS80
Daniel Gdns.
Blenheim Ave., Ilf. 67 EN58
Blenheim Clo. N21 50 DQ46
Elm Pk. Rd.
Blenheim Clo. SW20 117 CW97
Blenheim Clo., Grnf. 73 CD68
Leaver Gdns.
Blenheim Clo., Rom. 69 FC56
Blenheim Clo., Wall. 133 DJ108
Blenheim Clo., Wat. 44 BX45
Blenheim Ct. N19 63 DL61
Marlborough Rd.
Blenheim Ct., Sid. 109 ER90
Blenheim Cres. W11 75 CY73
Blenheim Cres., Ruis. 57 BR61
Blenheim Cres., S.Croy. 134 DQ108
Blenheim Dr., Well. 95 ET81
Blenheim Gdns. NW2 75 CW65
Blenheim Gdns. SW2 105 DM86
Blenheim Gdns., Kings.T. 102 CP94
Blenheim Gdns., S.Croy. 134 DU112
Blenheim Gdns., Wall. 133 DJ107
Blenheim Gdns., Wem. 60 CL62
Blenheim Gro. SE15 92 DU82
Blenheim Pk. Rd., S.Croy. 134 DQ109
Blenheim Pas. NW8 76 DC68
Blenheim Ter.
Blenheim Ri. N15 64 DT56
Talbot Rd.
Blenheim Rd. E6 80 EK69
Blenheim Rd. E15 66 EE63
Blenheim Rd. E17 65 DX55
Blenheim Rd. NW8 76 DC68
Blenheim Rd. SE20 106 DW94
Maple Rd.
Blenheim Rd. SW20 117 CW97
Blenheim Rd. W4 88 CS76
Blenheim Rd., Abb.L. 15 BU32
Blenheim Rd., Barn. 33 CX41
Blenheim Rd., Brom. 122 EL98
Blenheim Rd., Epsom 130 CR111
Blenheim Rd., Har. 58 CB58
Blenheim Rd., Nthlt. 72 CB65
Blenheim Rd., Orp. 124 EW103
Blenheim Rd., Sid. 110 EW88
Blenheim Rd., Sutt. 118 DA104
Blenheim St. W1 5 H9
Blenheim Ter. NW8 76 DC68
Blenheim Way, Epp. 26 FA27
Blenheim Way, Islw. 87 CG81
Blenkarne Rd. SW11 104 DF86
Bleriot Rd., Houns. 86 BW80
Blessbury Rd., Edg. 46 CQ53
Blessing Way, Bark. 82 EW69
Blessington Clo. SE13 93 ED83
Blessington Rd. SE13 93 ED84
Bletchingley Clo., Th.Hth. 119 DP98
Bletchley Ct. N1 7 K1
Bletchley St. N1 7 J1
Bletchley St. N1 78 DQ68
Bletchmore Clo., Hayes 85 BR78
Bletsoe Wk. N1 78 DQ68
Cropley St.
Blighs Rd., Sev. 155 FH125
Blincoe Clo. SW19 103 CX89
Blind La., Bans. 146 DE115
Blind La., Loug. 38 EE40
Blind La., Wal.Abb. 24 EJ33
Blindman's La. (Cheshunt), Wal.Cr. 23 DX30
Bliss Cres. SE13 93 EB82
Coldbath St.
Blissett St. SE10 93 EC81
Blisworth Clo., Hayes 72 BY70
Braunston Dr.
Blithbury Rd., Dag. 82 EV65
Blithdale Rd. SE2 96 EU77
Blithfield St. W8 90 DB76
Blockley Rd., Wem. 59 CH61
Bloemfontein Ave. W12 75 CV74
Bloemfontein Rd. W12 75 CV73
Blomfield Rd. W9 76 DB71
Blomfield St. EC2 7 L7
Blomfield St. EC2 78 DR71
Blomfield Vill. W2 76 DB71
Blomville Rd., Dag. 68 EY62
Blondel St. SW11 90 DG82
Blondell Clo., West Dr. 84 BK79
Blondin Ave. W5 87 CJ77
Blondin St. E3 79 EA68
Bloom Gro. SE27 105 DP90
Bloom Pk. Rd. SW6 89 CZ80
Bloomburg St. SW1 9 L9
Bloomfield Cres., Ilf. 67 EP58
Bloomfield Pl. W1 5 J10
Bloomfield Rd. N6 62 DG58
Bloomfield Rd. SE18 95 EP78
Bloomfield Rd., Brom. 122 EK99
Bloomfield Rd., Kings.T. 116 CL98
Bloomfield Ter. SW1 8 G10
Bloomfield Ter. SW1 90 DG78
Bloomhall Rd. SE19 106 DR92
Bloomsbury Clo. W5 74 CM73
Bloomsbury Clo., Epsom 130 CR110
Bloomsbury Ct. WC1 6 A7
Bloomsbury Ct., Pnr. 58 BZ55
Bloomsbury Ho. SW4 105 DK86
Bloomsbury Pl. SW18 104 DC85
Fullerton Rd.
Bloomsbury Pl. WC1 6 A6
Bloomsbury Sq. WC1 6 A7
Bloomsbury Sq. WC1 77 DL71
Bloomsbury St. WC1 5 N7
Bloomsbury St. WC1 77 DK71
Bloomsbury Way WC1 5 P8
Bloomsbury Way WC1 77 DL71
Blore Clo. SW8 91 DK81
Thessaly Rd.
Blore Ct. W1 5 M10
Blossom Clo. W5 88 CL75
Almond Ave.
Blossom Clo., Dag. 82 EZ67
Blossom Clo., S.Croy. 134 DT106
Melville Ave.
Blossom La., Enf. 36 DQ39
Blossom St. E1 7 N5
Blossom St. E1 78 DS70
Blossom Way, Uxb. 70 BM66
Blossom Way, West Dr. 84 BN77
Blossom Waye, Houns. 86 BY80
Blount St. E14 79 DY71
Bloxam Gdns. SE9 108 EL85
Bloxhall Rd. E10 65 DZ60
Bloxham Cres., Hmptn. 100 BZ94
Bloxworth Clo., Wall. 119 DJ104
Blucher Rd. SE5 92 DQ80
Blue Anchor All., Rich. 88 CL84
Kew Rd.
Blue Anchor La. SE16 92 DU77
Blue Anchor Yd. E1 78 DU73
Blue Ball Yd. SW1 9 K3
Blue Barn La., Wey. 126 BN111
Blue Cedars, Bans. 131 CX114
Bluebell Ave. E12 66 EL64
Bluebell Clo. SE26 106 DT91
Bluebell Clo., Orp. 123 EQ103
Bluebell Clo., Wall. 119 DH102
Bluebell Dr., Abb.L. 15 BT27
Bluebell Dr., Wal.Cr. 22 DR28
St. James Rd.
Bluebell Way, Ilf. 81 EP65
Blueberry Gdns., Couls. 147 DM116
Blueberry La., Sev. 152 EW116
Bluebridge Ave., Hat. 19 CY27
Bluebridge Rd., Hat. 19 CY26
Bluefield Clo., Hmptn. 100 CA92
Bluegates, Epsom 131 CU108
Bluehouse Rd. E4 52 EE48
Bluett Rd., St.Alb. 17 CK27
Blundel La., Cob. 142 BZ116
Blundell Rd., Edg. 46 CR53
Blundell St. N7 77 DL66
Blunden Clo., Dag. 68 EW60
Blunesfield, Pot.B. 20 DD31
Blunt Rd., S.Croy. 134 DR106
Blunts Ave., West Dr. 84 BN80
Blunts La., St.Alb. 16 BW27
Blunts Rd. SE9 109 EN85
Blurton Rd. E5 64 DW63
Blyth Clo. E14 93 ED77
Manchester Rd.
Blyth Clo., Borwd. 32 CM39
Blyth Clo., Twick. 101 CF86
Grimwood Rd.
Blyth Rd. E17 65 DZ59
Blyth Rd. SE28 82 EW73
Blyth Rd., Brom. 122 EF95
Blyth Rd., Hayes 85 BS75
Blythe Clo. SE6 107 DZ87
Blythe Hill SE6 107 DZ87
Blythe Hill, Orp. 123 ET95
Blythe Hill La. SE6 107 DZ87
Blythe Rd. W14 89 CX76
Blythe St. E2 78 DV69
Blythe Vale SE6 107 DZ88
Blythswood Rd., Ilf. 68 EU60
Blythwood Rd. N4 63 DL59
Blythwood Rd., Pnr. 44 BX53
Boades Ms. NW3 62 DD63
New End
Boadicea St. N1 77 DM67
Copenhagen St.
Boakes Clo. NW9 60 CQ56
Roe Grn.
Boakes Meadow, Sev. 139 FF111
Boar Clo., Chig. 54 EU50
Boardman Ave. E4 37 EB43
Boardman Clo., Barn. 33 CY43
Boar's Head Yd., Brent. 87 CK80
Brent Way
Boat Lifter Way SE16 93 DY77
Sweden Gate
Boathouse Wk. SE15 92 DT80
Boathouse Wk., Rich. 87 CK81
Kew Rd.
Bob Anker Clo. E13 80 EG69
Chesterton Rd.
Bob Marley Way SE24 91 DN84
Mayall Rd.
Bobbin Clo. SW4 91 DJ83
Bobs La., Rom. 55 FF53
Bocketts La., Lthd. 143 CF124
Bockhampton Rd., Kings.T. 102 CM94
Bocking St. E8 78 DV67
Boddicott Clo. SW19 103 CY89
Bodiam Clo., Enf. 36 DR40
Bodiam Rd. SW16 105 DK94
Bodley Clo., Epp. 25 ET30
Bodley Clo., N.Mal. 116 CS99
Bodley Manor Way SW2 105 DN87
Papworth Way
Bodley Rd., N.Mal. 116 CR100
Bodmin Clo., Har. 58 BZ62
Bodmin Clo., Orp. 124 EW102
Bodmin Gro., Mord. 118 DB98
Bodmin St. SW18 104 DA88
Bodnant Gdns. SW20 117 CV97
Bodney Rd. E8 64 DV64
Boeing Way, Sthl. 85 BV76
Boevey Path, Belv. 96 EZ78
Orchard Ave.
Bogey La., Orp. 137 EM108
Bognor Gdns., Wat. 44 BW50
Bowring Grn.
Bognor Rd., Well. 96 EX81
Bohemia Pl. E8 78 DW65
Bohun Gro., Barn. 34 DE44
Boileau Par. W5 74 CM72
Boileau Rd.
Boileau Rd. SW13 89 CU80
Boileau Rd. W5 74 CM72
Bois Hall Rd., Add. 126 BK106
Bolden St. SE8 93 EB82
Bolderwood Way, W.Wick. 121 EB103
Boldmere Rd., Pnr. 58 BW59
Boleyn Ave., Enf. 36 DV39
Boleyn Ave., Epsom 131 CU110
Boleyn Clo. E17 65 EA56
Boleyn Clo., Loug. 38 EL44
Roding Gdns.
Boleyn Ct., Buck.H. 52 EG46
Boleyn Dr., Ruis. 58 BX61
Boleyn Dr., W.Mol. 114 BZ97
Boleyn Gdns., Dag. 83 FC66
Boleyn Gdns., W.Wick. 121 EB103
Boleyn Gro., W.Wick. 121 EC103
Boleyn Rd. E6 80 EK68
Boleyn Rd. E7 80 EG66
Boleyn Rd. N16 64 DS64
Boleyn Wk., Lthd. 143 CF120
Boleyn Way, Barn. 34 DC41
Boleyn Way, Ilf. 53 EQ51
Bolina Rd. SE16 92 DW78
Bolingbroke Gro. SW11 104 DF86
Bolingbroke Rd. W14 89 CX76
Bolingbroke Wk. SW11 90 DD81
Bolingbroke Way, Hayes 71 BR74
Bolliger Ct. NW10 74 CQ70
Park Royal Rd.
Bollo Bri. Rd. W3 88 CP76
Bollo La. W3 88 CP75
Bollo La. W4 88 CQ77
Bolney St. SW8 91 DM80
Bolney Way, Felt. 100 BY90
Bolsover St. W1 5 J5
Bolsover St. W1 77 DH70
Bolstead Rd., Mitch. 119 DH95
Bolt Cellar La., Epp. 25 ES30
Bolt Ct. EC4 6 E9
Bolters La., Bans. 131 CZ114
Boltmore Clo. NW4 61 CX55
Bolton Clo. SE20 120 DU96
Selby Rd.
Bolton Clo., Chess. 129 CK107
Bolton Cres. SE5 91 DP79
Bolton Gdns. NW10 75 CX68
Bolton Gdns. SW5 90 DB78
Bolton Gdns., Brom. 108 EF93
Bolton Gdns., Tedd. 101 CG93
Bolton Gdns. Ms. SW10 90 DB78
Bolton Rd. E15 80 EF65
Bolton Rd. N18 50 DT50
Bolton Rd. NW8 76 DB67
Bolton Rd. NW10 74 CS67
Bolton Rd. W4 88 CQ80
Bolton Rd., Chess. 129 CK107
Bolton Rd., Har. 58 CC56
Bolton St. W1 9 J2
Bolton St. W1 77 DH74
Bolton Wk. N7 63 DM61
Durham Rd.
Boltons, The SW10 90 DC78
Boltons, The, Wem. 59 CF63
Boltons, The, Wdf.Grn. 52 EG49
Boltons Clo., Wok. 140 BG116
Boltons La., Hayes 85 BQ81
Boltons La., Wok. 140 BG116
Boltons Pl. SW5 90 DC78
Bombay St. SE16 92 DV77
Bombers La., West. 151 ES120
Grays Rd.
Bomer Clo., West Dr. 84 BN80
Bomore Rd. W11 75 CY73
Bon Marche Ter. SE27 106 DS91
Gipsy Rd.
Bonar Pl., Chis. 108 EL94
Bonar Rd. SE15 92 DU80
Bonchester Clo., Chis. 109 EN94
Bonchurch Clo., Sutt. 132 DB108
Bonchurch Rd. W10 75 CY71
Bonchurch Rd. W13 73 CH74
Bond Clo., Sev. 152 EX115
Bond Clo., West Dr. 70 BM72
Bond Ct. EC4 7 K9
Bond Gdns., Wall. 133 DJ105
Bond Rd., Mitch. 118 DE96
Bond Rd., Surb. 116 CM102
Bond Rd., Warl. 149 DX118
Bond St. E15 66 EE64
Bond St. W4 88 CS77
Chiswick Common Rd.
Bond St. W5 73 CK73
Bondfield Rd. E6 80 EL71
Lovage App.
Bondfield Rd., Hayes 71 BU69
Bonding Yd. Wk. SE16 93 DY76
Finland St.
Bondway SW8 91 DL79
Boneta Rd. SE18 95 EM76
Bonfield Rd. SE13 93 EC84
Bonham Gdns., Dag. 68 EX61
Bonham Rd. SW2 105 DM85
Bonham Rd., Dag. 68 EX61
Bonheur Rd. W4 88 CR75
Bonhill St. EC2 7 L5
Bonhill St. EC2 78 DR70
Boniface Gdns., Har. 44 CB52
Boniface Rd., Uxb. 57 BP62
Boniface Wk., Har. 44 CB52
Bonner Hill Rd., Kings.T. 116 CM97
Bonner Rd. E2 78 DW68
Bonner St. E2 78 DW68
Bonnersfield Clo., Har. 59 CF58
Bonnersfield La., Har. 59 CF58
Bonneville Gdns. SW4 105 DJ86
Bonney Gro. (Cheshunt), Wal.Cr. 22 DU30
Bonney Way, Swan. 125 FE96
Bonnington Sq. SW8 91 DM79
Bonnington Twr., Brom. 122 EL100
Bonny St. NW1 77 DJ66
Bonser Rd., Twick. 101 CF89
Bonsor Dr., Tad. 145 CY122
Bonsor St. SE5 92 DS80
Bonville Gdns. NW4 61 CU56
Handowe Clo.
Bonville Rd., Brom. 108 EF92
Book Ms. WC2 5 N9
Booker Clo. E14 79 DZ71
Wallwood St.
Booker Rd. N18 50 DU50
Bookham Ct., Lthd. 142 BZ123
Church Rd.
Bookham Ind. Pk., Lthd. 142 BZ123
Bookham Rd., Cob. 142 BW119
Boone Ct. N9 50 DW48
Boone St. SE13 94 EE84
Boones Rd. SE13 94 EE84
Boord St. SE10 94 EE76
Boot St. N1 7 M3
Boot St. N1 78 DS69
Booth Clo. SE28 82 EV73
Booth Dr., Stai. 98 BK93
Booth Rd. NW9 46 CR54
Booth Rd., Croy. 119 DP103
Waddon New Rd.
Boothby Rd. N19 63 DK61
Booth's Pl. W1 5 L7
Bordars Rd. W7 73 CE71
Bordars Wk. W7 73 CE71
Borden Ave., Enf. 36 DR44
Border Cres. SE26 106 DV92
Border Gdns., Croy. 135 EB105
Border Rd. SE26 106 DV92
Bordergate, Mitch. 118 DF95
Borders La., Loug. 39 EN42
Bordesley Rd., Mord. 118 DB98
Bordon Wk. SW15 103 CU87
Boreas Wk. N1 6 G1
Boreham Ave. E16 80 EG72
Boreham Clo. E11 65 EC60
Hainault Rd.
Boreham Holt, Borwd. 32 CM42
Boreham Rd. N22 50 DQ54
Borehamwood Ind. Pk., Borwd. 32 CR40
Borer's Pas. E1 7 N8
Borgard Rd. SE18 95 EM77
Borkwood Pk., Orp. 137 ET105
Borkwood Way, Orp. 137 ES105
Borland Rd. SE15 92 DW84
Borland Rd., Tedd. 101 CH93
Bornedene, Pot.B. 19 CY31
Borneo St. SW15 89 CW83
Borough High St. SE1 11 J5
Borough High St. SE1 92 DQ75
Borough Hill, Croy. 119 DP104
Borough Rd. SE1 10 G6
Borough Rd. SE1 91 DP76
Borough Rd., Islw. 87 CE81
Borough Rd., Kings.T. 116 CN95
Borough Rd., Mitch. 118 DE96
Borough Rd., West. 150 EK121
Borough Sq. SE1 11 H5
Borough Way, Pot.B. 19 CY32
Borrett Clo. SE17 92 DQ78
Penrose St.
Borrodaile Rd. SW18 104 DB86
Borrowdale Ave., Har. 45 CG54
Borrowdale Clo., Ilf. 66 EL56
Borrowdale Clo., S.Croy. 134 DT113
Borrowdale Ct., Enf. 36 DQ39
Borrowdale Dr., S.Croy. 134 DT112
Borthwick Ms. E15 66 EE63
Borthwick Rd.
Borthwick Rd. E15 66 EE63
Borthwick Rd. NW9 61 CT58
West Hendon Bdy.
Borthwick St. SE8 93 EA78
Borwick Ave. E17 65 DZ55
Bosanquet Clo., Uxb. 70 BK70
Bosbury Rd. SE6 107 EC90
Boscastle Rd. NW5 63 DH62
Bosco Clo., Orp. 137 ET105
Strickland Way
Boscobel Pl. SW1 8 G8
Boscobel Pl. SW1 90 DG77
Boscobel St. NW8 4 A5
Boscobel St. NW8 76 DD70
Boscombe Ave. E10 65 ED59
Boscombe Clo. E5 65 DY64
Boscombe Gdns. SW16 105 DL93
Boscombe Rd. SW17 104 DG93
Boscombe Rd. SW19 118 DA95
Boscombe Rd. W12 75 CU74
Boscombe Rd., Wor.Pk. 117 CW102
Bosgrove E4 51 EC46
Boss St. SE1 11 P4
Bostal Row, Bexh. 96 EZ83
Harlington Rd.
Bostall Heath SE2 96 EV78
Bostall Hill SE2 96 EU78
Bostall La. SE2 96 EV78
Bostall Manorway SE2 96 EV77
Bostall Pk. Ave., Bexh. 96 EY80
Bostall Rd., Orp. 110 EV94
Boston Gdns. W4 88 CS79
Boston Gdns. W7 87 CG77
Boston Rd.
Boston Gdns., Brent. 87 CG77
Boston Gro., Ruis. 57 BQ58
Boston Manor Rd., Brent. 87 CH77
Boston Pk. Rd., Brent. 87 CJ78
Boston Pl. NW1 4 D5
Boston Pl. NW1 76 DF70
Boston Rd. E6 80 EL69
Boston Rd. E17 65 EA58
Boston Rd. W7 73 CE74
Boston Rd., Croy. 119 DM100
Boston Rd., Edg. 46 CQ52
Boston St. E2 78 DU68
Audrey St.
Boston Vale W7 87 CG77
Bostonthorpe Rd. W7 87 CE75
Bosville Ave., Sev. 154 FG123
Bosville Dr., Sev. 154 FG123
Bosville Rd., Sev. 154 FG123
Boswell Clo., Orp. 124 EW100
Killewarren Way
Boswell Ct. WC1 6 A6
Boswell Path, Hayes 85 BT77
Croyde Ave.
Boswell Rd., Th.Hth. 120 DQ98
Boswell St. WC1 6 A6
Boswell St. WC1 77 DL71
Bosworth Clo. E17 51 DZ53
Bosworth Rd. N11 49 DK51
Bosworth Rd. W10 75 CY70
Bosworth Rd., Barn. 34 DA41
Bosworth Rd., Dag. 68 FA62
Botany Bay La., Chis. 123 EQ96
Botany Clo., Barn. 34 DE42
Boteley Clo. E4 51 ED47
Botha Rd. E13 80 EH71
Botham Clo., Edg. 46 CQ52
Pavilion Way
Bothwell Clo. E16 80 EF71
Bothwell Rd., Croy. 135 EC110
Bothwell St. W6 89 CX79
Delorme St.
Botolph All. EC3 7 M10
Botolph La. EC3 7 M10
Botsford Rd. SW20 117 CY96
Bottom La., Kings L. 28 BH35
Botts Ms. W2 76 DA72
Chepstow Rd.
Botts Pas. W2 76 DA72
Chepstow Rd.
Botwell Common Rd., Hayes 71 BR73
Botwell Cres., Hayes 71 BS72
Botwell La., Hayes 71 BS73
Boucher Clo., Tedd. 101 CF92
Bouchier Wk., Rain. 83 FG65
Deere Ave.
Boughton Ave., Brom. 122 EF101
Boughton Rd. SE28 95 ES76
Boulcott St. E1 79 DX72
Boulevard, The SW17 104 DG89
Balham High Rd.
Boulevard, The, Pnr. 58 CA56
Pinner Rd.
Boulevard, The, Wat. 29 BR43
Boulmer Rd., Uxb. 70 BJ69
Boulogne Rd., Croy. 120 DQ100
Boulter Gdns., Rain. 83 FG65

Boulton Ho., Brent. 88 CL78
Green Dragon La.
Boulton Rd., Dag. 68 EY62
Boultwood Rd. E6 81 EM72
Bounce Hill (Navestock), Rom. 41 FH38
Mill La.
Bounces La. N9 50 DV47
Bounces Rd. N9 50 DV47
Boundaries Rd. SW12 104 DF89
Boundaries Rd., Felt. 100 BW88
Boundary Ave. E17 65 DZ59
Boundary Rd.
Boundary Clo. SE20 120 DU96
Haysleigh Gdns.
Boundary Clo., Ilf. 67 ES63
Loxford La.
Boundary Clo., Kings.T. 116 CP97
Boundary Clo., Sthl. 86 CA78
Boundary La. E13 80 EK69
Boundary La. SE17 92 DQ79
Boundary Par. N8 63 DL58
Boundary Pas. E2 7 P4
Boundary Rd. E13 80 EJ68
Boundary Rd. E17 65 DZ59
Boundary Rd. N9 36 DW44
Boundary Rd. N22 63 DP55
Boundary Rd. NW8 76 DC67
Boundary Rd. SW19 104 DD93
Boundary Rd., Ashf. 98 BJ92
Boundary Rd., Bark. 81 ER67
Boundary Rd., Cars. 132 DG108
Boundary Rd., Pnr. 58 BX59
Boundary Rd., Rom. 69 FG58
Boundary Rd., Sid. 109 ES85
Boundary Rd., Wall. 133 DH107
Boundary Rd., Wem. 60 CL62
Boundary Row SE1 10 F4
Boundary St. E2 7 P3
Boundary St. E2 78 DT70
Boundary St., Erith 97 FF80
Boundary Way, Croy. 135 EA106
Boundary Way, Wat. 15 BV32
Boundfield Rd. SE6 108 EE90
Bounds Grn. Rd. N11 49 DJ51
Bounds Grn. Rd. N22 49 DL52
Bourchier Clo., Sev. 155 FH126
Bourchier St. W1 5 M10
Bourdon Pl. W1 5 J10
Bourdon Rd. SE20 120 DW96
Bourdon St. W1 9 H1
Bourdon St. W1 77 DH73
Bourke Clo. NW10 74 CS65
Mayo Rd.
Bourke Clo. SW4 105 DL86
Bourke Hill, Couls. 146 DF118
Bourlet Clo. W1 5 K7
Bourn Ave. N15 64 DR56
Bourn Ave., Barn. 34 DD43
Bourn Ave., Uxb. 70 BN70
Bournbrook Rd. SE3 94 EK83
Bourne, The N14 49 DK46
Bourne Ave. N14 49 DL47
Bourne Ave., Cher. 112 BG97
Eastern Ave.
Bourne Ave., Hayes 85 BQ76
Bourne Ave., Ruis. 58 BW64
Bourne Bri. La., Rom. 54 EZ45
Bourne Clo., W.Byf. 126 BH113
Bourne Ct., Ruis. 57 BV64
Bourne Dr., Mitch. 118 DD96
Bourne End Rd., Nthwd. 43 BS49
Bourne Est. EC1 6 D6
Bourne Est. EC1 77 DN71
Bourne Gdns. E4 51 EB49
Bourne Gro., Ash. 143 CK119
Bourne Hill N13 49 DM47
Bourne Ind. Pk., Dart. 111 FE85
Bourne Rd.
Bourne La., Cat. 148 DR121
Bourne Mead, Bex. 111 FC85
Bourne Pk. Clo., Ken. 148 DS116
Bourne Pl. W4 88 CR78
Dukes Ave.
Bourne Rd. E7 66 EF62
Bourne Rd. N8 63 DL58
Bourne Rd., Bex. 111 FB87
Bourne Rd., Brom. 122 EK98
Bourne Rd., Dart. 111 FD85
Bourne Rd. (Bushey), Wat. 30 CA43
Bourne St. SW1 8 F9
Bourne St. SW1 90 DG77
Bourne St., Croy. 119 DP103
Waddon New Rd.
Bourne Ter. W2 76 DB71
Bourne Vale, Brom. 122 EF102
Bourne Vw., Grnf. 73 CF65
Bourne Vw., Ken. 148 DR115
Bourne Way, Add. 126 BJ106
Bourne Way, Brom. 122 EE103
Bourne Way, Epsom 130 CQ105
Bourne Way, Sutt. 131 CZ106
Bourne Way, Swan. 125 FC97
Bournefield Rd., Whyt. 148 DT118
Godstone Rd.
Bournehall Ave. (Bushey), Wat. 30 CA43
Bournehall La. (Bushey), Wat. 30 CA44
Bournehall Rd. (Bushey), Wat. 30 CA44
Bournemead Ave., Nthlt. 71 BU68
Bournemead Clo., Nthlt. 71 BU69
Bournemead Way, Nthlt. 71 BV68
Bournemouth Rd. SE15 92 DU82
Bournemouth Rd. SW19 118 DA95
Bourneside Cres. N14 49 DK46
Bourneside Gdns. SE6 107 EC92
Bourneside Rd., Add. 126 BK105
Bournevale Rd. SW16 105 DL91
Bournewood Rd. SE18 96 EU80
Bournewood Rd., Orp. 124 EV101
Bournville Rd. SE6 107 EA87
Bournwell Clo., Barn. 34 DF41
Bourton Clo., Hayes 71 BU74
Avondale Dr.
Bousfield Rd. SE14 93 DX82
Boutflower Rd. SW11 90 DE84
Bouverie Gdns., Har. 59 CK58
Bouverie Ms. N16 64 DS61
Bouverie Rd.
Bouverie Pl. W2 4 A8
Bouverie Pl. W2 76 DD72
Bouverie Rd. N16 64 DS60
Bouverie Rd., Couls. 146 DG118
Bouverie Rd., Har. 58 CC58
Bouverie St. EC4 6 E9
Bouverie St. EC4 77 DN72
Bouvier Rd., Enf. 36 DW38
Boveney Rd. SE23 107 DX87
Bovill Rd. SE23 107 DX87
Bovingdon Ave., Wem. 74 CN65
Bovingdon Clo. N19 63 DJ61
Junction Rd.
Bovingdon Cres., Wat. 16 BX34
Bovingdon La. NW9 46 CS53
Bovingdon Rd. SW6 90 DB81
Bovingdon Sq., Mitch. 119 DL98
Leicester Ave.
Bow Bri. Est. E3 79 EB68
Bow Chyd. EC4 7 J9
Bow Common La. E3 79 DY70
Bow Ind. Est. E15 79 EB66
Bow La. EC4 7 J9
Bow La. EC4 78 DQ72
Bow La. N12 48 DC52
Bow La., Mord. 117 CY100
Bow Rd. E3 79 DZ69
Bow St. E15 66 EE64
Bow St. WC2 6 A9
Bow St. WC2 77 DL72
Bowater Clo. NW9 60 CR57
Bowater Clo. SW2 105 DL86
Bowater Pl. SE3 94 EH80
Bowater Ridge, Wey. 127 BR110
Bowater Rd. SE18 94 EK76
Bowden Clo., Felt. 99 BS88
Bowden St. SE11 10 E10
Bowden St. SE11 91 DN78
Bowditch SE8 93 DZ78
Bowdon Rd. E17 65 EA59
Bowen Dr. SE21 106 DS90
Bowen Rd., Har. 58 CC59
Bowen St. E14 79 EB72
Bowens Wd., Croy. 135 DZ109
Bower Ave. SE10 94 EE81
Bower Clo., Nthlt. 72 BW68
Bower Clo., Rom. 55 FD52
Bower Ct., Epp. 26 EU32
Bower Fm. Rd. Rom. 55 FC48
(Havering-atte-Bower)
Bower Hill, Epp. 26 EU32
Bower Rd., Swan. 111 FG94
Bower St. E1 79 DX72
Bower Ter., Epp. 26 EU32
Bower Hill
Bower Vale, Epp. 26 EU32
Bowerdean St. SW6 90 DB81
Bowerman Ave. SE14 93 DY79
Bowers Rd., Sev. 139 FF111
Bowers Wk. E6 81 EM72
Northumberland Rd.
Bowes Clo., Sid. 110 EV86
Bowes Rd. N11 49 DH50
Bowes Rd. N13 49 DL50
Bowes Rd. W3 74 CS73
Bowes Rd., Dag. 68 EW63
Bowes Rd., Walt. 113 BV103
Bowfell Rd. W6 89 CW79
Bowford Ave., Bexh. 96 EY81
Bowhill Clo. SW9 91 DN80
Bowie Clo. SW4 105 DK87
Bowl Ct. EC2 7 N5
Bowl Ct. EC2 78 DS70
Bowland Rd. SW4 91 DK84
Bowland Rd., Wdf.Grn. 52 EJ51
Bowland Yd. SW1 8 E5
Bowles Grn., Enf. 36 DV36
Bowles Rd. SE1 92 DU79
Old Kent Rd.
Bowley Clo. SE19 106 DT93
Bowley La. SE19 106 DT92
Bowling Ct., Wat. 29 BU42
Bowling Grn. Clo. SW15 103 CV87
Bowling Grn. La. EC1 6 E4
Bowling Grn. La. EC1 77 DN70
Bowling Grn. Pl. SE1 11 K4
Bowling Grn. Pl. SE1 92 DR75
Bowling Grn. Row SE18 95 EM76
Samuel St.
Bowling Grn. St. SE11 91 DN79
Bowling Grn. Wk. N1 7 M2
Bowls, The, Chig. 53 ES48
Bowls Clo., Stan. 45 CH50
Bowman Ave. E16 80 EF73
Bowman Ms. SW18 103 CZ88
Bowmans Clo. W13 73 CH74
Bowmans Clo., Pot.B. 20 DD32
Bowmans Grn., Wat. 30 BX36
Bowmans Lea SE23 106 DW87
Bowmans Meadow, Wall. 119 DH104
Bowmans Ms. E1 78 DU72
Hooper St.
Bowmans Ms. N7 63 DL62
Seven Sisters Rd.
Bowmans Pl. N7 63 DL62
Holloway Rd.
Bowmans Rd., Dart. 111 FF87
Bowman's Trd. Est. NW9 60 CM55
Westmoreland Rd.
Bowmead SE9 109 EM89
Bowmore Wk. NW1 77 DK66
St. Paul's Cres.
Bowness Clo. E8 78 DT65
Beechwood Rd.
Bowness Cres. SW15 102 CS92
Bowness Dr., Houns. 86 BY84
Bowness Rd. SE6 107 EB87
Bowness Rd., Bexh. 97 FB82
Bowness Way, Horn. 69 FG64
Bowood Rd. SW11 104 DG85
Bowood Rd., Enf. 37 DX40
Bowring Grn., Wat. 44 BW50
Bowrons Ave., Wem. 73 CK66
Bowsprit, The, Cob. 142 BW115
Bowyer Clo. E6 81 EM71
Bowyer Pl. SE5 92 DQ80
Bowyer St. SE5 92 DQ80
Bowyers Clo., Ash. 144 CM118
Box La., Bark. 82 EV68
Box Ridge Ave., Pur. 133 DM112
Boxall Rd. SE21 106 DS86
Boxford Clo., S.Croy. 135 DX112
Boxgrove Rd. SE2 96 EV75
Boxley Rd., Mord. 118 DC98
Boxley St. E16 80 EH74
Boxmoor Rd., Har. 59 CH56
Boxmoor Rd., Rom. 55 FC50
Boxoll Rd., Dag. 68 EZ63
Boxted Clo., Buck.H. 52 EL46
Boxtree La., Har. 44 CC53
Boxtree Rd., Har. 45 CD52
Boxtree Wk., Orp. 124 EX102
Eldred Dr.
Boxwood Clo., West Dr. 84 BM75
Hawthorne Cres.
Boxwood Way, Warl. 149 DX117
Boxworth Clo. N12 48 DD50
Fenstanton Ave.
Boxworth Gro. N1 77 DM67
Richmond Ave.
Boyard Rd. SE18 95 EP78
Boyce Clo., Borwd. 32 CL39
Boyce St. SE1 10 B3
Boyce Way E13 80 EG70
Boycroft Ave. NW9 60 CQ58
Boyd Ave., Sthl. 72 BZ74
Boyd Clo., Kings.T. 102 CN94
Crescent Rd.
Boyd Rd. SW19 104 DD93
Boyd St. E1 78 DU72
Boydell Ct. NW8 76 DD66
St. John's Wd. Pk.
Boyfield St. SE1 10 G5
Boyfield St. SE1 91 DP75
Boyland Rd., Brom. 108 EF92
Boyle Ave., Stan. 45 CG51
Boyle Fm. Rd., T.Ditt. 115 CG100
Boyle St. W1 5 K10
Boyne Ave. NW4 61 CX56
Boyne Rd. SE13 93 EC83
Boyne Rd., Dag. 68 FA62
Boyne Ter. Ms. W11 75 CZ74
Boyseland Ct., Edg. 46 CQ47
Boyson Rd. SE17 92 DR79
Boythorn Way SE16 92 DV78
Credon Rd.
Boyton Clo. E1 79 DX70
Stayner's Rd.
Boyton Clo. N8 63 DL55
Boyton Rd. N8 63 DL55
Brabant Ct. EC3 7 M10
Brabant Rd. N22 49 DM54
Brabazon Ave., Wall. 133 DL108
Brabazon Rd., Houns. 86 BW80
Brabazon Rd., Nthlt. 72 CA68
Brabazon St. E14 79 EB72
Brabourn Gro. SE15 92 DW82
Brabourne Clo. SE19 106 DS92
Brabourne Cres., Bexh. 96 EZ79
Brabourne Heights NW7 46 CS48
Brabourne Ri., Beck. 121 EC99
Bracewell Ave., Grnf. 73 CG65
Bracewell Rd. W10 75 CW71
Bracewood Gdns., Croy. 120 DT104
Bracey Ms. N4 63 DL61
Bracey St.
Bracey St. N4 63 DL61
Bracken, The E4 51 EC47
Hortus Rd.
Bracken Ave. SW12 104 DG86
Bracken Ave., Croy. 121 EA104
Bracken Clo. E6 81 EM71
Bracken Clo., Borwd. 32 CN40
Hartforde Rd.
Bracken Clo., Lthd. 142 BZ124
Bracken Clo., Sun. 99 BT93
Cavendish Rd.
Bracken Clo., Twick. 100 CA87
Hedley Rd.
Bracken Dr., Chig. 53 EP51
Bracken End, Islw. 101 CD85
Bracken Gdns. SW13 89 CU82
Bracken Hill Clo., Brom. 122 EF95
Bracken Hill La.
Bracken Hill La., Brom. 122 EF95
Bracken Ind. Est., Ilf. 53 ET52
Bracken Ms. E4 51 EC47
Hortus Rd.
Bracken Ms., Rom. 69 FB58
Bracken Path, Epsom 130 CN113
Brackenbridge Dr., Ruis. 58 BX62
Brackenbury Gdns. W6 89 CV76
Brackenbury Rd. N2 62 DC55
Brackenbury Rd. W6 89 CV76
Brackendale N21 49 DM47
Brackendale, Pot.B. 20 DA33
Brackendale Clo., Houns. 86 CB81
Brackendene, Dart. 111 FE91
Brackendene, St.Alb. 16 BZ30
Brackenfield Clo. E5 64 DV63
Tiger Way
Brackenhill, Cob. 128 CA111
Brackens, The, Enf. 50 DS45
Brackens, The, Orp. 138 EU106
Brackenwood, Sun. 113 BU95
Brackley, Wey. 127 BR106
Brackley Clo., Wall. 133 DL108
Brackley Rd. W4 88 CS78
Brackley Rd., Beck. 107 DZ94
Brackley Sq., Wdf.Grn. 52 EK52
Brackley St. EC1 7 J6
Brackley Ter. W4 88 CS78
Bracklyn Clo. N1 78 DR68
Parr St.
Bracklyn Ct. N1 78 DR68
Wimbourne St.
Bracklyn St. N1 78 DR68
Bracknell Clo. N22 49 DN53
Bracknell Gdns. NW3 62 DB63
Bracknell Gate NW3 62 DB64
Bracknell Way NW3 62 DB63
Bracondale, Esher 128 CC107
Bracondale Rd. SE2 96 EU77
Brad St. SE1 10 E3
Bradbourne Pk. Rd., Sev. 154 FG123
Bradbourne Rd., Bex. 110 FA87
Bradbourne Rd., Sev. 155 FH122
Bradbourne St. SW6 90 DA82
Bradbourne Vale Rd., Sev. 154 FF122
Bradbury Clo., Borwd. 32 CP39
Bradbury Clo., Sthl. 86 BZ77
Bradbury Ms. N16 64 DS64
Bradbury St.
Bradbury St. N16 64 DS64
Braddock Clo., Islw. 87 CF83
Braddon Rd., Rich. 88 CM83
Braddyll St. SE10 94 EE78
Braden St. W9 76 DB70
Shirland Rd.
Bradenham Ave., Well. 96 EU84
Bradenham Clo. SE17 92 DR79
Bradenham Rd., Har. 59 CH56
Bradenham Rd., Hayes 71 BS69
Bradfield Dr., Bark. 68 EU64
Bradfield Rd. E16 94 EG75
Bradfield Rd., Ruis. 58 BY64
Bradford Clo. SE26 106 DV91
Coombe Rd.
Bradford Clo., Brom. 123 EM102
Bradford Dr., Epsom 131 CT107
Bradford Rd. W3 88 CS75
Warple Way
Bradford Rd., Ilf. 67 ER60
Bradgate (Cuffley), Pot.B. 21 DK27
Bradgate Clo. (Cuffley), Pot.B. 21 DK28
Bradgate Rd. SE6 107 EA86
Brading Cres. E11 66 EH61
Brading Rd. SW2 105 DM87
Brading Rd., Croy. 119 DM100
Bradiston Rd. W9 75 CZ69
Bradley Clo. N7 77 DM65
Sutterton St.
Bradley Clo., Sutt. 132 DA110
Station Rd.
Bradley Gdns. W13 73 CH72
Bradley Ms. SW17 104 DF88
Bellevue Rd.
Bradley Rd. N22 49 DM54
Bradley Rd. SE19 106 DQ93
Bradley Rd., Enf. 37 DY37
Bradley Stone Rd. E6 81 EM71
Bradley's Clo. N1 77 DN68
White Lion St.
Bradman Row, Edg. 46 CQ52
Pavilion Way
Bradmead SW8 91 DH80
Bradmore Grn., Couls. 147 DM118
Coulsdon Rd.
Bradmore Grn., Hat. 19 CY26
Bradmore Ho. E1 78 DW71
Jamaica St.
Bradmore La., Hat. 19 CW27
Bradmore Pk. Rd. W6 89 CV77
Bradmore Way, Couls. 147 DL117
Bradmore Way, Hat. 19 CY26
Bradshaw Clo. SW19 104 DA93
Bradshaw Rd., Wat. 30 BW39
Bradshawe Waye, Uxb. 70 BL71
Bradshaws Clo. SE25 120 DU97
Bradstock Rd. E9 79 DX65
Bradstock Rd., Epsom 131 CU106
Bradwell Ave., Dag. 68 FA61
Bradwell Clo. E18 66 EF56
Bradwell Clo., Horn. 83 FH65
Bradwell Ms. N18 50 DU49
Lyndhurst Rd.
Bradwell Rd., Buck.H. 52 EL46
Bradwell St. E1 79 DX69
Brady Ave., Loug. 39 EQ40
Brady St. E1 78 DV70
Bradymead E6 81 EP72
Warwall
Braemar Ave. N22 49 DL53
Braemar Ave. NW10 60 CR62
Braemar Ave. SW19 104 DA89
Braemar Ave., Bexh. 97 FC84
Braemar Ave., S.Croy. 134 DQ110
Braemar Ave., Th.Hth. 119 DN97
Braemar Ave., Wem. 73 CK66
Braemar Gdns. NW9 46 CR53
Braemar Gdns., Sid. 109 ER90
Braemar Gdns., W.Wick. 121 EC102
Braemar Rd. E13 80 EF70
Braemar Rd. N15 64 DS57
Braemar Rd., Brent. 87 CK79
Braemar Rd., Wor.Pk. 117 CV104
Braes St. N1 77 DP66
Braeside, Add. 126 BH111
Braeside, Beck. 107 EA92
Braeside Ave. SW19 117 CY95
Braeside Ave., Sev. 154 FF124
Braeside Clo., Pnr. 44 CA52
The Ave.
Braeside Clo., Sev. 154 FF123
Braeside Cres., Bexh. 97 FC84
Braeside Rd. SW16 105 DJ94
Braesyde Clo., Belv. 96 EZ77
Brafferton Rd., Croy. 134 DQ105
Braganza St. SE17 91 DP78
Braham St. E1 78 DT72
Braid Ave. W3 74 CS72
Braid Clo., Felt. 100 BZ89
Braidwood Rd. SE6 107 ED88
Braidwood St. SE1 11 M3
Brailsford Clo., Mitch. 104 DE94
Brailsford Rd. SW2 105 DN85
Brainton Ave., Felt. 99 BV87
Braintree Ave., Ilf. 66 EL56
Braintree Rd., Dag. 68 FA62
Braintree Rd., Ruis. 57 BV63
Braintree St. E2 78 DW70
Braithwaite Ave., Rom. 68 FA59
Braithwaite Gdns., Stan. 45 CJ53
Braithwaite Rd., Enf. 37 DZ41
Bramah Grn. SW9 91 DN81
Bramalea Clo. N6 62 DG58
Bramall Clo. E15 66 EF64
Idmiston Rd.
Bramber Ct., Brent. 88 CL77
Sterling Pl.
Bramber Rd. N12 48 DE50
Bramber Rd. W14 89 CZ79
Bramble Banks, Cars. 132 DG109
Bramble Clo., Cat. 148 DS122
Burntwood La.
Bramble Clo., Croy. 135 EA105
Bramble Clo., Shep. 113 BR98
Halliford Clo.
Bramble Clo., Stan. 45 CK52
Bramble Clo., Uxb. 70 BM71
Bramble Clo., Wat. 15 BU34
Bramble Cft., Erith 97 FC77
Bramble Gdns. W12 75 CT73
Wallflower St.
Bramble La., Hmptn. 100 BZ93
Bramble La., Sev. 155 FH128
Bramble Ri., Cob. 128 BW114
Bramble Wk., Epsom 130 CP114
Brambleacres Clo., Sutt. 132 DA108
Bramblebury Rd. SE18 95 EQ78
Brambledown, Stai. 112 BH95
Brambledown Clo., W.Wick. 122 EE99
Brambledown Rd., Cars. 132 DG108
Brambledown Rd., S.Croy. 134 DS108
Brambledown Rd., Wall. 133 DH108
Brambles, The, Chig. 53 EQ51
Brambles, The, Wal.Cr. 23 DX31
Brambles, The, West Dr. 84 BK77
Brambles Clo., Cat. 148 DS122
Brambles Clo., Islw. 87 CH80
Brambles Fm. Dr., Uxb. 70 BN69
Bramblewood Clo., Cars. 118 DF102
Brambling Clo., Wat. 30 BY42
Bramblings, The E4 51 ED49
Bramcote Ave., Mitch. 118 DF98
Bramcote Gro. SE16 92 DW78
Bramcote Rd. SW15 89 CV84
Bramdean Cres. SE12 108 EG88
Bramdean Gdns. SE12 108 EG88
Bramerton Rd., Beck. 121 DZ97
Bramerton St. SW3 90 DE79
Bramfield, Wat. 16 BY34
Garston La.
Bramfield Ct. N4 64 DQ61
Queens Dr.
Bramfield Rd. SW11 104 DE86
Bramford Ct. N14 49 DK47
Bramford Rd. SW18 90 DC84
Bramham Gdns. SW5 90 DB78
Bramham Gdns., Chess. 129 CK105
Bramhope La. SE7 94 EH79
Bramlands Clo. SW11 90 DE83
Bramleas, Wat. 29 BT42
Bramley Ave., Couls. 147 DJ115
Bramley Clo. E17 51 DY54
Bramley Clo. N14 35 DH43
Bramley Clo., Cher. 112 BH102
Bramley Clo., Hayes 71 BU73
Orchard Rd.
Bramley Clo., Orp. 123 EP102
Bramley Clo., S.Croy. 133 DP106
Bramley Clo., Stai. 98 BJ93
Bramley Clo., Swan. 125 FE98
Bramley Clo., Twick. 100 CC86
Bramley Ct., Wat. 15 BV31
Orchard Ave.
Bramley Ct., Well. 96 EV81
Bramley Cres. SW8 91 DK80
Pascal St.

Bramley Cres., Ilf. 67 EN58
Bramley Gdns., Wat. 44 BW50
Bramley Hill, S.Croy. 133 DP106
Bramley Pl., Dart. 97 FG84
Bramley Rd. N14 35 DH43
Bramley Rd. W5 87 CJ76
Bramley Rd. W10 75 CX73
Bramley Rd., Sutt. 132 DD106
Bramley Rd. (Cheam), Sutt. 131 CX109
Bramley Shaw, Wal.Abb. 24 EF33
Bramley Way, Ash. 144 CM117
Bramley Way, Houns. 100 BZ85
Bramley Way, W.Wick. 121 EB103
Brampton Clo. E5 64 DV61
Brampton Clo. (Cheshunt), Wal.Cr. 22 DU28
Brampton Gdns. N15 64 DQ57
Brampton Rd.
Brampton Gdns., Walt. 128 BW106
Brampton Gro. NW4 61 CV56
Brampton Gro., Har. 59 CG56
Brampton Gro., Wem. 60 CM60
Brampton La. NW4 61 CW56
Brampton Pk. Rd. N22 63 DN55
Brampton Rd. E6 80 EK70
Brampton Rd. N15 64 DQ57
Brampton Rd. NW9 60 CN56
Brampton Rd. SE2 96 EW79
Brampton Rd., Bexh. 96 EX83
Brampton Rd., Croy. 120 DT101
Brampton Rd., Uxb. 71 BP68
Brampton Rd., Wat. 43 BU48
Brampton Ter., Borwd. 32 CN38
Bramsham Gdns., Wat. 44 BX50
Bramshaw Ri., N.Mal. 116 CS100
Bramshaw Rd. E9 79 DX65
Bramshill Clo., Chig. 53 ES50
Tine Rd.
Bramshill Gdns. NW5 63 DH62
Bramshill Rd. NW10 74 CS68
Bramshot Ave. SE7 94 EG79
Bramshot Way, Wat. 43 BU47
Bramston Clo., Ilf. 53 ET51
Bramston Rd. NW10 75 CU68
Bramston Rd. SW17 104 DC90
Bramwell Clo., Sun. 114 BX96
Bramwell Ms. N1 77 DM67
Brancaster Dr. NW7 47 CU52
Brancaster La., Pur. 134 DQ110
Brancaster Pl., Loug. 39 EM41
Brancaster Rd. E12 67 EM63
Brancaster Rd. SW16 105 DL90
Brancaster Rd., Ilf. 67 ER58
Brancepeth Gdns., Buck.H. 52 EG47
Branch Hill NW3 62 DC62
Branch Pl. N1 78 DR67
Branch Rd. E14 79 DY73
Branch Rd., Ilf. 54 EV50
Branch Rd. (Park St.), St.Alb. 17 CD27
Branch St. SE15 92 DS80
Brancker Clo., Wall. 133 DL108
Brown Clo.
Brancker Rd., Har. 59 CK55
Brancroft Way, Enf. 37 DY39
Brand St. SE10 93 EC80
Brandlehow Rd. SW15 89 CZ84
Brandon Clo. (Cheshunt), Wal.Cr. 22 DS26
Brandon Est. SE17 91 DP79
Brandon Ms. EC2 78 DR71
Moor La.
Brandon Rd. E17 65 EC55
Brandon Rd. N7 77 DL66
Brandon Rd., Sthl. 86 BZ78
Brandon Rd., Sutt. 132 DB105
Brandon St. SE17 11 J9
Brandon St. SE17 92 DQ77
Brandram Rd. SE13 94 EE83
Brandreth Rd. E6 81 EM72
Brandreth Rd. SW17 105 DH89
Brandries, The, Wall. 119 DK104
Brandville Gdns., Ilf. 67 EP56
Brandville Rd., West Dr. 84 BL75
Brandy Way, Sutt. 132 DA108
Brangbourne Rd., Brom. 107 EC92
Brangton Rd. SE11 91 DM78
Brangwyn Cres. SW19 118 DC96
Branksea St. SW6 89 CY80
Branksome Ave. N18 50 DT51
Branksome Clo., Walt. 114 BX103
Branksome Rd. SW2 91 DL84
Branksome Rd. SW19 118 DA95
Branksome Way, Har. 60 CL58
Branksome Way, N.Mal. 116 CQ95
Bransby Rd., Chess. 130 CL108
Branscombe Gdns. N21 49 DN45
Branscombe St. SE13 93 EB83
Bransdale Clo. NW6 76 DB67
West End La.
Bransell Clo., Swan. 125 FC100
Bransgrove Rd., Edg. 46 CM53
Branston Cres., Orp. 123 ER102
Branstone Rd., Rich. 88 CM81
Brants Wk. W7 73 CE70
Brantwood Ave., Erith 97 FC80
Brantwood Ave., Islw. 87 CG84
Brantwood Clo. E17 65 EB55
Brantwood Gdns., Enf. 35 DL42
Brantwood Gdns., Ilf. 66 EL56
Brantwood Rd. N17 50 DT51
Brantwood Rd. SE24 106 DQ85
Brantwood Rd., Bexh. 97 FB82
Brantwood Rd., S.Croy. 134 DQ109
Brantwood Way, Orp. 124 EW97
Brasenose Dr. SW13 89 CV79
Trinity Ch. Rd.
Brasher Clo., Grnf. 59 CD64
Brass Tally All. SE16 93 DX75
Middleton Dr.
Brassey Clo., Felt. 99 BT88
Brassey Rd. NW6 75 CZ65
Brassey Sq. SW11 90 DG83
Brassie Ave. W3 74 CS72
Brasted Clo. SE26 106 DW91
Brasted Clo., Bexh. 110 EX85
Brasted Clo., Orp. 124 EU103
Brasted Clo., Sutt. 132 DA110
Brasted Hill, Sev. 152 EU120
Brasted Hill Rd., West. 152 EV121
Brasted La., Sev. 152 EU119
Brasted Rd., Erith 97 FF78
Brathway Rd. SW18 104 DA87
Bratley St. E1 78 DU70
Weaver St.
Brattle Wd., Sev. 155 FH129
Braund Ave., Grnf. 72 CB70
Braundton Ave., Sid. 109 ET88
Braunston Dr., Hayes 72 BY70
Bravington Clo., Shep. 112 BM99
Bravington Pl. W9 75 CZ70
Bravington Rd.
Bravington Rd. W9 75 CZ69
Brawne Ho. SE17 91 DP79
Hillingdon St.
Braxfield Rd. SE4 93 DY84
Braxted Pk. SW16 105 DM93
Bray NW3 76 DE66
Bray Clo., Borwd. 32 CQ39
Bray Cres. SE16 93 DX75
Marlow Way
Bray Dr. E16 80 EF73
Bray Pas. E16 80 EF73
Bowman Ave.
Bray Pl. SW3 8 D9
Bray Pl. SW3 90 DF77
Bray Rd. NW7 47 CX52
Bray Rd., Cob. 142 BY116
Brayards Rd. SE15 92 DV82
Brayards Rd. Est. SE15 92 DV82
Brayards Rd.
Braybourne Clo., Uxb. 70 BJ65
Braybourne Dr., Islw. 87 CF80
Braybrook St. W12 75 CT71
Braybrooke Gdns. SE19 106 DT94
Fox Hill
Brayburne Ave. SW4 91 DJ82
Braycourt Ave., Walt. 113 BV101
Braydon Rd. N16 64 DU59
Brayfield Ter. N1 77 DN66
Lofting Rd.
Brayford Sq. E1 79 DY72
Summercourt Rd.
Brayton Gdns., Enf. 35 DK42
Braywood Rd. SE9 95 ER84
Brazil Clo., Croy. 119 DL101
Breach La., Dag. 82 FA69
Bread St. EC4 7 J10
Bread St. EC4 78 DQ73
Breakfield, Couls. 147 DL116
Breakspear Ct., Abb.L. 15 BT30
The Cres.
Breakspear Rd., Ruis. 57 BP59
Breakspear Rd. N., Uxb. 42 BJ53
Breakspear Rd. S., Uxb. 56 BM62
Breakspeare Clo., Wat. 29 BV38
Breakspeare Rd., Abb.L. 15 BS31
Breakspears Dr., Orp. 124 EU95
Breakspears Ms. SE4 93 EA82
Breakspears Rd.
Breakspears Rd. SE4 93 DZ83
Bream Clo. N17 64 DV56
Bream Gdns. E6 81 EN69
Bream St. E3 79 EA66
Breamore Clo. SW15 103 CU88
Breamore Rd., Ilf. 67 ET61
Bream's Bldgs. EC4 6 D8
Bream's Bldgs. EC4 77 DN72
Breamwater Gdns., Rich. 101 CH90
Brearley Clo., Edg. 46 CQ52
Pavilion Way
Brearley Clo., Uxb. 70 BL65
Breasley Clo. SW15 89 CV84
Brechin Pl. SW7 90 DC77
Rosary Gdns.
Brecknock Rd. N7 63 DK64
Brecknock Rd. N19 63 DJ63
Brecknock Rd. Est. N7 63 DJ63
Brecon Clo., Mitch. 119 DL97
Brecon Clo., Wor.Pk. 117 CW103
Cotswold Way
Brecon Rd. W6 89 CY79
Brecon Rd., Enf. 36 DW42
Brede Clo. E6 81 EN69
Bredgar Rd. N19 63 DJ61
Bredhurst Clo. SE20 106 DW93
Bredon Rd. SE5 92 DQ83
Bredon Rd., Croy. 120 DT101
Bredune, Ken. 148 DR115
Church Rd.
Breech La., Tad. 145 CU124
Breer St. SW6 90 DB83
Breezers Hill E1 78 DU73
Pennington St.
Brember Rd., Har. 58 CC61
Bremer Ms. E17 65 EB56
Church La.
Bremer Rd., Stai. 98 BG90
Bremner Clo., Swan. 125 FG98
Bremner Rd. SW7 90 DC76
Queen's Gate
Brenchley Clo., Brom. 122 EF100
Brenchley Clo., Chis. 123 EN95
Brenchley Gdns. SE23 106 DW86
Brenchley Rd., Orp. 123 ES95
Brenda Rd. SW17 104 DF89
Brende Gdns., W.Mol. 114 CB98
Brendon Ave. NW10 60 CS63
Brendon Clo., Erith 97 FE81
Brendon Clo., Esher 128 CC107
Brendon Clo., Hayes 85 BQ80
Brendon Ct., Rad. 17 CH34
The Ave.
Brendon Dr., Esher 128 CC107
Brendon Gdns., Har. 58 CB63
Brendon Gdns., Ilf. 67 ES57
Brendon Gro. N2 48 DC54
Brendon Rd. SE9 109 ER89
Brendon Rd., Dag. 68 EZ60
Brendon St. W1 4 C8
Brendon St. W1 76 DE72
Brendon Way, Enf. 50 DS45
Brenley Clo., Mitch. 118 DG97
Brenley Gdns. SE9 94 EK84
Brent Clo., Bex. 110 EY88
Brent Cres. NW10 74 CM68
Brent Cross Gdns. NW4 61 CX58
Haley Rd.
Brent Cross Shop. Cen. NW4 61 CW59
Brent Grn. NW4 61 CW57
Brent Grn. Wk., Wem. 60 CQ62
Brent Lea, Brent. 87 CJ80
Brent Pk. NW10 60 CR64
Brent Pk. Rd. NW4 61 CV59
Brent Pk. Rd. NW9 61 CV59
Brent Pl., Barn. 34 DA43
Brent Rd. E16 80 EG71
Brent Rd. SE18 95 EP80
Brent Rd., Brent. 87 CJ79
Brent Rd., S.Croy. 134 DV109
Brent Rd., Sthl. 86 BW76
Brent St. NW4 61 CW56
Brent Ter. NW2 61 CW60
Brent Vw. Rd. NW9 61 CU58
Brent Way N3 48 DA51
Brent Way, Brent. 87 CK80
Brent Way, Wem. 74 CP65
Brentcot Clo. W13 73 CH70
Brentfield NW10 74 CP66
Brentfield Clo. NW10 74 CR65
Normans Mead
Brentfield Gdns. NW2 61 CX59
Hendon Way
Brentfield Rd. NW10 74 CR65
Brentford Business Cen., Brent. 87 CJ80
Brentford Clo., Hayes 72 BX70
Brentham Way W5 73 CK70
Brenthouse Rd. E9 78 DW65
Brenthurst Rd. NW10 75 CT65
Brentmead Clo. W7 73 CE73
Brentmead Gdns. NW10 74 CM68
Brentmead Pl. NW11 61 CX58
North Circular Rd.
Brenton St. E14 79 DY72
Brentside, Brent. 87 CJ79
Brentside Clo. W13 73 CG70
Brentside Executive Cen., Brent. 87 CH79
Brentvale Ave., Sthl. 73 CD74
Brentvale Ave., Wem. 74 CM67
Brentwick Gdns., Brent. 88 CL77
Brentwood Clo. SE9 109 EQ88
Brentwood Ct., Add. 126 BH105
Brentwood Ho. SE18 94 EK80
Shooter's Hill Rd.
Brentwood Rd., Rom. 69 FF58
Brereton Rd. N17 50 DT52
Bressenden Pl. SW1 9 J6
Bressenden Pl. SW1 91 DH76
Bressey Ave., Enf. 36 DU39
Bressey Gro. E18 52 EF54
Brett Clo. N16 64 DS61
Yoakley Rd.
Brett Clo., Nthlt. 72 BX69
Broomcroft Ave.
Brett Ct. N9 50 DW47
Brett Cres. NW10 74 CR66
Brett Gdns., Dag. 82 EY66
Brett Ho. Clo. SW15 103 CX86
Putney Heath La.
Brett Pas. E8 64 DV64
Kenmure Rd.
Brett Pl., Wat. 29 BU37
The Harebreaks
Brett Rd. E8 64 DV64
Brett Rd., Barn. 33 CW43
Brettell St. SE17 92 DR78
Merrow St.
Brettenham Ave. E17 51 EA53
Penrhyn Ave.
Brettenham Rd. E17 51 EA54
Brettenham Rd. N18 50 DU49
Brettgrave, Epsom 130 CQ111
Brewer St. W1 5 L10
Brewer St. W1 77 DJ73
Brewer's Grn. SW1 9 L6
Brewers Hall Gdns. EC2 7 J7
Brewers La., Rich. 101 CK85
George St.
Brewery Clo., Wem. 59 CG64
Brewery La., Sev. 155 FJ125
High St.
Brewery La., Twick. 101 CF87
Brewery La., W.Byf. 126 BL113
Brewery Rd. N7 77 DL66
Brewery Rd. SE18 95 ER78
Brewery Rd., Brom. 122 EL102
Brewery Sq. SE1 78 DT74
Horselydown La.
Brewhouse La. E1 78 DV74
Brewhouse Rd. SE18 95 EM77
Brewhouse St. SW15 89 CY83
Brewhouse Wk. SE16 79 DY74
Brewhouse Yd. EC1 6 F4
Brewood Rd., Dag. 82 EV65
Brewster Gdns. W10 75 CW71
Brewster Ho. E14 79 DZ73
Brewster Rd. E10 65 EB60
Breycaine Ind. Est., Wat. 30 BX37
Brian Ave., S.Croy. 134 DS112
Brian Clo., Horn. 69 FH63
Brian Rd., Rom. 68 EW57
Briane Rd., Epsom 130 CQ110
Briant St. SE14 93 DX81
Briants Clo., Pnr. 44 BZ54
Briar Ave. SW16 105 DM94
Briar Banks, Cars. 132 DG109
Briar Clo. N2 48 DB54
Briar Clo. N13 50 DQ48
Briar Clo., Buck.H. 52 EK47
Briar Clo., Hmptn. 100 BZ92
Briar Clo., Islw. 101 CF85
Briar Clo. (Cheshunt), Wal.Cr. 22 DW29
Briar Clo., W.Byf. 126 BH111
Briar Ct., Sutt. 131 CW105
Briar Cres., Nthlt. 72 CB65
Briar Gdns., Brom. 122 EF102
Briar Gro., S.Croy. 134 DU113
Briar Hill, Pur. 133 DL111
Briar La., Cars. 132 DG109
Briar La., Croy. 135 EB105
Briar Pas. SW16 119 DL97
Pollards Cres.
Briar Pl. SW16 119 DM97
Briar Rd.
Briar Rd. NW2 61 CW63
Briar Rd. SW16 119 DL97
Briar Rd., Bex. 111 FD90
Briar Rd., Har. 59 CJ57
Briar Rd., Shep. 112 BM99
Briar Rd., Twick. 101 CE88
Briar Rd., Wat. 15 BU34
Briar Wk. SW15 89 CV84
Briar Wk. W10 75 CY70
Droop St.
Briar Wk., Edg. 46 CQ52
Briar Wk., W.Byf. 126 BG112
Briar Way, West Dr. 84 BN75
Briarbank Rd. W13 73 CG72
Briardale Gdns. NW3 62 DA62
Briarfield Ave. N3 48 DB54
Briaris Clo. N17 50 DV52
Briars, The, Rick. 28 BH36
Briars, The (Cheshunt), Wal.Cr. 23 DY31
Briars, The (Bushey), Wat. 45 CE45
Briars Ct., Lthd. 129 CD114
Briarswood Way, Orp. 137 ET106
Briarwood Clo. NW9 60 CQ58
Briarwood Clo., Felt. 99 BS90
Briarwood Dr., Nthwd. 43 BU54
Briarwood Rd. SW4 105 DK85
Briarwood Rd., Epsom 131 CU107
Briary Clo. NW3 76 DE66
Fellows Rd.
Briary Ct., Sid. 110 EV92
Briary Gdns., Brom. 108 EH92
Briary Gro., Edg. 46 CP54
Briary La. N9 50 DT48
Brick Ct. EC4 6 D9
Brick Fm. Clo., Rich. 88 CP81
Brick Kiln Clo., Wat. 30 BY44
Brick La. E1 78 DT70
Brick La. E2 78 DT69
Brick La., Enf. 36 DV40
Brick La., Stan. 45 CK52
Honeypot La.
Brick St. W1 9 H3
Brick St. W1 77 DH74
Brickcroft, Brox. 23 DY26
Brickenden Ct., Wal.Abb. 24 EF33
Brickett Clo., Ruis. 57 BQ57
Brickfield Clo., Brent. 87 CJ80
Brickfield Cotts. SE18 95 ET79
Brickfield Fm. Gdns., Orp. 137 EQ105
Brickfield La., Barn. 33 CT44
Brickfield La., Hayes 85 BR79
Brickfield Rd. SW19 104 DB91
Brickfield Rd., Epp. 26 EX29
Brickfield Rd., Th.Hth. 119 DP95
Brickfields, Har. 59 CD61
Brickfields La., Epp. 26 EX29
Brickfield Rd.
Brickfields Way, West Dr. 84 BM76
Bricklayer's Arms SE1 11 N8
Brickwall La., Ruis. 57 BS60
Brickwood Clo. SE26 106 DV90
Brickwood Rd., Croy. 120 DS103
Bride Ct. EC4 6 F9
Bride La. EC4 6 F9
Bride St. N7 77 DM65
Brideale Clo. SE15 92 DT80
Colegrove Rd.
Bridewain St. SE1 11 P6
Bridewain St. SE1 92 DT76
Bridewell Pl. E1 78 DV74
Brewhouse La.
Bridewell Pl. EC4 6 F9
Bridford Ms. W1 5 J6
Bridge, The, Har. 59 CE55
Bridge App. NW1 76 DG66
Bridge Ave. W6 89 CV78
Bridge Ave. W7 73 CD71
Bridge Clo. W10 75 CX72
Kingsdown Clo.
Bridge Clo., Enf. 36 DV40
Bridge Clo., Rom. 69 FE58
Bridge Clo., Walt. 113 BT101
Bridge Clo., W.Byf. 126 BM112
Bridge Dr. N13 49 DM50
Bridge End E17 51 EC53
Bridge Gdns., Ashf. 99 BQ94
Bridge Gdns., E.Mol. 115 CD98
Bridge Gate N21 50 DQ45
Ridge Ave.
Bridge Hill, Epp. 25 ET33
Bridge Ho. Quay E14 79 EC74
Prestons Rd.
Bridge La. NW11 61 CY56
Bridge La. SW11 90 DE81
Bridge Meadows SE14 93 DX79
Bridge Pk. SW18 104 DA85
Bridge Pl. SW1 9 J8
Bridge Pl. SW1 91 DH77
Bridge Pl., Croy. 120 DR102
Bridge Pl., Wat. 30 BX43
Bridge Rd. E6 81 EM66
Bridge Rd. E15 79 ED67
Bridge Rd. E17 65 DZ59
Bridge Rd. N9 50 DU48
The Bdy.
Bridge Rd. N22 49 DL53
Bridge Rd. NW10 74 CS65
Bridge Rd., Beck. 107 DZ94
Bridge Rd., Bexh. 96 EY82
Bridge Rd., Cher. 112 BH101
Bridge Rd., Chess. 129 CK106
Bridge Rd., Croy. 120 DQ104
Duppas Hill Rd.
Bridge Rd., E.Mol. 115 CD99
Bridge Rd., Epsom 131 CT112
Bridge Rd., Erith 97 FF82
Bridge Rd., Houns. 87 CD83
Bridge Rd., Islw. 87 CD83
Bridge Rd., Kings L. 15 BQ33
Bridge Rd., Orp. 124 EV100
Bridge Rd., Rain. 83 FG70
Bridge Rd., Sthl. 86 BZ75
Bridge Rd., Sutt. 132 DB107
Bridge Rd., Twick. 101 CH86
Bridge Rd., Uxb. 70 BJ67
Bridge Rd., Wall. 133 DH106
Bridge Rd., Wem. 60 CN62
Bridge Rd., Wey. 126 BM105
Bridge Row, Croy. 120 DR102
Cross Rd.
Bridge St. SW1 9 P5
Bridge St. SW1 91 DL75
Bridge St. W4 88 CR77
Bridge St., Lthd. 143 CG122
Bridge St., Pnr. 58 BY55
Bridge St., Rich. 101 CK85
Bridge St., Walt. 113 BS102
Bridge Ter. E15 79 ED66
Bridge Vw. W6 89 CW78
Bridge Way N11 49 DJ48
Pymmes Grn. Rd.
Bridge Way NW11 61 CZ57
Bridge Way, Cob. 127 BT113
Bridge Way, Couls. 146 DE119
Bridge Way, Twick. 100 CC87
Bridge Way, Uxb. 57 BP64
Bridge Way, Wem. 74 CL66
Bridge Wf., Cher. 112 BJ102
Bridge Wf. Rd., Islw. 87 CH83
Church St.
Bridge Wks. Ind. Est., Uxb. 70 BJ70
Bridge Yd. SE1 11 L2
Bridgefield Clo., Bans. 145 CW115
Bridgefield Rd., Sutt. 132 DA107
Bridgefoot SE1 91 DL78
Bridgefoot La., Pot.B. 19 CX33
Bridgeham Clo., Wey. 126 BN106
Mayfield Rd.
Bridgeland Rd. E16 80 EG73
Bridgeman Rd. N1 77 DM66
Bridgeman Rd. W4 88 CQ76
Bridgeman Rd., Tedd. 101 CG93
Bridgeman St. NW8 4 B1
Bridgeman St. NW8 76 DE68
Bridgen Rd., Bex. 110 EY86
Bridgend Rd. SW18 90 DC84
Bridgend Rd., Enf. 36 DW35
Bridgenhall Rd., Enf. 36 DT39
Bridgeport Pl. E1 78 DU74
Kennet St.
Bridger Clo., Wat. 16 BX33
Bridges Ct. SW11 90 DD83
Bridges La., Croy. 133 DL105
Bridges Ms. SW19 104 DB93
Bridges Rd.
Bridges Pl. SW6 89 CZ81
Bridges Rd. SW19 104 DB93
Bridges Rd., Stan. 45 CF50
Bridges Rd. Ms. SW19 104 DB93
Bridges Rd.
Bridgetown Clo. SE19 106 DS92
St. Kitts Ter.
Bridgeview Ct., Ilf. 53 ER51
Bridgewater Clo., Chis. 123 ES97
Bridgewater Gdns., Edg. 46 CM54
Bridgewater Rd., Ruis. 57 BU63
Bridgewater Rd., Wem. 73 CJ65
Bridgewater Rd., Wey. 127 BR107
Bridgewater Sq. EC2 7 H6
Bridgewater St. EC2 7 H6
Bridgewater Way (Bushey), Wat. 30 CB44

Bridgeway, Bark. 81 ET66
Bridgeway St. NW1 5 L1
Bridgeway St. NW1 77 DJ68
Bridgewood Clo. SE20 106 DV94
Bridgewood Rd. SW16 105 DK94
Bridgewood Rd., Wor.Pk. 117 CU104
Bridgford St. SW18 104 DC90
Bridgwater Rd. E15 79 EC67
Bridle Clo., Enf. 37 DZ37
Bridle Clo., Epsom 130 CR106
Bridle Clo., Kings.T. 115 CK98
Bridle Clo., Sun. 113 BU97
Forge La.
Bridle End, Epsom 131 CT113
Bridle La. W1 5 L10
Bridle La., Cob. 142 CB115
Bridle La., Lthd. 142 CC115
Bridle La., Rick. 28 BJ41
Bridle La., Twick. 101 CH86
Crown Rd.
Bridle Path, Croy. 119 DL104
Bridle Path, Wat. 29 BV40
Station Rd.
Bridle Path, Wdf.Grn. 52 EE52
Bridle Path, The, Epsom 131 CV110
Bridle Rd., Croy. 121 EA104
Bridle Rd., Epsom 131 CT113
Bridle Rd., Esher 129 CH107
Bridle Rd., Pnr. 58 BW58
Bridle Rd., The, Pur. 133 DL110
Bridle Way, Croy. 135 EA106
Bridle Way, Orp. 137 EQ105
Bridle Way, The, Croy. 135 DY110
Bridle Way, The, Wall. 133 DJ105
Bridlepath Way, Felt. 99 BS87
Bridleway Clo., Epsom 131 CW110
Bridlington Clo., West. 150 EH119
Bridlington Rd. N9 50 DV45
Bridlington Rd., Wat. 44 BX48
Bridport Ave., Rom. 69 FB58
Bridport Pl. N1 78 DR67
Bridport Rd. N18 50 DS50
Bridport Rd., Grnf. 72 CB67
Bridport Rd., Th.Hth. 119 DN97
Bridport Ter. SW8 91 DK81
Wandsworth Rd.
Bridstow Pl. W2 76 DA72
Talbot Rd.
Brief St. SE5 91 DP81
Brier Rd., Tad. 145 CV119
Brierley, Croy. 135 EB107
Brierley Ave. N9 50 DW46
Brierley Clo. SE25 120 DU98
Brierley Rd. E11 65 ED63
Brierley Rd. SW12 105 DJ89
Brierly Gdns. E2 78 DW68
Royston St.
Briery Fld., Rick. 28 BG42
Brig Ms. SE8 93 EA79
Watergate St.
Brigade Clo., Har. 59 CD61
Brigade St. SE3 94 EF82
Royal Par.
Brigadier Ave., Enf. 36 DQ38
Brigadier Hill, Enf. 36 DQ38
Briggeford Clo. E5 64 DU61
Geldeston Rd.
Briggs Clo., Mitch. 119 DH95
Bright Clo., Belv. 96 EX77
Bright St. E14 79 EB72
Brightfield Rd. SE12 108 EF85
Brightling Rd. SE4 107 DZ86
Brightlingsea Pl. E14 79 DZ73
Brightman Rd. SW18 104 DD88
Brighton Ave. E17 65 DZ57
Brighton Clo., Add. 126 BJ106
Brighton Clo., Uxb. 71 BP66
Brighton Dr., Nthlt. 72 CA65
Brighton Gro. SE14 93 DY81
New Cross Rd.
Brighton Rd. E6 81 EN69
Brighton Rd. N2 48 DC54
Brighton Rd. N16 64 DS63
Brighton Rd., Add. 126 BJ105
Brighton Rd., Bans. 145 CZ116
Brighton Rd., Couls. 147 DH121
Brighton Rd., Pur. 133 DN111
Brighton Rd., S.Croy. 134 DQ106
Brighton Rd., Surb. 115 CJ100
Brighton Rd., Sutt. 132 DC108
Brighton Rd., Tad. 145 CY122
Brighton Rd., Wat. 29 BU38
Brighton Ter. SW9 91 DM84
Brights Ave., Rain. 83 FH70
Brightside, The, Enf. 37 DX39
Brightside Ave., Stai. 98 BJ94
Brightside Rd. SE13 107 ED86
Brightview Clo., St.Alb. 16 BY29
Brightwell Clo., Croy. 119 DN102
Sumner Rd.
Brightwell Cres. SW17 104 DF92
Brightwell Rd., Wat. 29 BU43
Brigstock Rd., Belv. 97 FB77
Brigstock Rd., Couls. 147 DH115
Brigstock Rd., Th.Hth. 119 DN99
Brill Pl. NW1 5 N1
Brill Pl. NW1 77 DK68
Brim Hill N2 62 DC56
Brimpsfield Clo. SE2 96 EV76
Brimsdown Ave., Enf. 37 DY40
Brimsdown Ind. Est., Enf. 37 DZ40
Brimstone Clo., Orp. 138 EW108
Brindle Gate, Sid. 109 ES88
Brindles, The, Bans. 145 CZ117
Brindley Clo., Bexh. 97 FB83
Brindley St. SE14 93 DZ81
Brindley Way, Brom. 108 EG92
Brindley Way, Sthl. 72 CB73
Brindwood Rd. E4 51 DZ48
Brinkburn Clo. SE2 96 EU77
Brinkburn Clo., Edg. 46 CP54
Brinkburn Gdns., Edg. 60 CN55
Brinkley Rd., Wor.Pk. 117 CV103
Brinklow Cres. SE18 95 EP80
Brinklow Ho. W2 76 DB71
Brinkworth Rd., Ilf. 66 EL55
Brinkworth Way E9 79 DZ65
Brinley Clo. (Cheshunt), Wal.Cr. 23 DX31
Brinsdale Rd. NW4 61 CX55
Brinsley Rd., Har. 45 CD54
Brinsley St. E1 78 DV72
Watney St.
Brinsmead (Park St.), St.Alb. 17 CD27
Brinsworth Clo., Twick. 101 CD88
Brinton Wk. SE1 10 F3
Brion Pl. E14 79 EC71
Brisbane Ave. SW19 118 DB95
Brisbane Ct. N10 49 DH52
Sydney Rd.
Brisbane Rd. E10 65 EB61
Brisbane Rd. W13 87 CG75
Brisbane Rd., Ilf. 67 EP59
Brisbane St. SE5 92 DR80
Briscoe Clo. E11 66 EF61
Briscoe Rd. SW19 104 DD93
Briset Rd. SE9 94 EK83
Briset St. EC1 6 F6
Briset Way N7 63 DM61
Brisson Clo., Esher 128 BZ107
Bristol Clo., Stai. 98 BL86
Bristol Gdns. W9 76 DB70
Bristol Ms. W9 76 DB70
Bristol Gdns.
Bristol Pk. Rd. E17 65 DY56
Hervey Pk. Rd.
Bristol Rd. E7 80 EJ65
Bristol Rd., Grnf. 72 CB67
Bristol Rd., Mord. 118 DC99
Briston Gro. N8 63 DL58
Briston Ms. NW7 47 CU52
Bristow Rd. SE19 106 DS92
Bristow Rd., Bexh. 96 EY81
Bristow Rd., Croy. 133 DL105
Bristow Rd., Houns. 86 CB83
Britannia Clo. SW4 91 DK84
Bowland Rd.
Britannia Clo., Nthlt. 72 BX69
Britannia Gate E16 80 EG74
Silvertown Way
Britannia La., Twick. 100 CC87
Britannia Rd. E14 93 EA77
Britannia Rd. N12 48 DC48
Britannia Rd. SW6 90 DB80
Britannia Rd., Ilf. 67 EP62
Britannia Rd., Surb. 116 CM101
Britannia Rd., Wal.Cr. 23 DZ34
Britannia Row N1 77 DP67
Britannia St. WC1 6 B2
Britannia St. WC1 77 DM69
Britannia Wk. N1 7 K2
Britannia Way NW10 74 CP70
Britannia Way SW6 90 DB81
Britannia Rd.
Britannia Way, Stai. 98 BK87
British Gro. W4 89 CT78
British Gro. Pas. W4 89 CT78
British Gro. S. W4 89 CT78
British Gro. Pas.
British Legion Rd. E4 52 EF47
British St. E3 79 DZ69
Briton Clo., S.Croy. 134 DS111
Briton Cres., S.Croy. 134 DS111
Briton Hill Rd., S.Croy. 134 DS110
Brittain Rd., Dag. 68 EY62
Brittain Rd., Walt. 128 BX106
Brittains La., Sev. 154 FF123
Britten Clo. NW11 62 DB60
Britten Clo., Borwd. 31 CK44
Rodgers Clo.
Britten Dr., Sthl. 72 CA72
Britten St. SW3 90 DE78
Brittenden Clo., Orp. 137 ES107
Britten's Ct. E1 78 DV73
The Highway
Britton Clo. SE6 107 ED87
Brownhill Rd.
Britton St. EC1 6 F5
Britton St. EC1 77 DP70
Brixham Cres., Ruis. 57 BU60
Brixham Gdns., Ilf. 67 ES64
Brixham Rd., Well. 96 EX81
Brixham St. E16 81 EM74
Brixton Est., Edg. 46 CP54
Brixton Hill SW2 105 DL87
Brixton Hill Pl. SW2 105 DL87
Brixton Hill
Brixton Oval SW2 91 DN84
Brixton Rd. SW9 91 DN83
Brixton Rd., Wat. 29 BV39
Brixton Sta. Rd. SW9 91 DN83
Brixton Water La. SW2 105 DN85
Broad Acre, St.Alb. 16 BY30
Broad Clo., Walt. 114 BX104
Broad Ct. WC2 6 A9
Broad Grn. Ave., Croy. 119 DP101
Broad Highway, Cob. 128 BX114
Broad La. EC2 7 M7
Broad La. EC2 78 DS71
Broad La. N8 63 DM57
Tottenham La.
Broad La. N15 64 DT56
Broad La., Dart. 111 FG89
Broad La., Hmptn. 100 BZ94
Broad Lawn SE9 109 EN89
Broad Mead, Ash. 144 CM117
Broad Oak, Wdf.Grn. 52 EH50
Broad Oak Clo. E4 51 EA50
Royston Ave.
Broad Oak Clo., Orp. 124 EU96
Broad Sanctuary SW1 9 N5
Broad Sanctuary SW1 91 DK75
Broad St., Dag. 82 FA66
Broad St., Tedd. 101 CF93
Broad St. Ave. EC2 7 M7
Broad St. Pl. EC2 7 L7
Broad Vw. NW9 60 CN58
Broad Wk. N21 49 DM47
Broad Wk. NW1 76 DG68
Broad Wk. SE3 94 EJ82
Broad Wk. W1 8 F2
Broad Wk. W1 76 DG74
Broad Wk., Cat. 148 DT122
Broad Wk., Couls. 146 DG123
Broad Wk., Epsom 144 CS117
Chalk La.
Broad Wk. (Burgh Heath), Epsom 145 CX119
Broad Wk., Houns. 86 BX81
Broad Wk., Orp. 124 EX104
Broad Wk., Rich. 88 CM80
Broad Wk., Sev. 155 FL128
Broad Wk., The W8 76 DC74
Broad Wk., The, E.Mol. 115 CF98
Broad Wk., The, Nthwd. 43 BQ54
Broad Wk. La. NW11 61 CZ59
Broad Water Cres., Wey. 113 BQ104
Churchill Dr.
Broad Yd. EC1 6 F5
Broadacre, Stai. 98 BG92
Broadacre Clo., Uxb. 57 BP62
Broadbent Clo. N6 63 DH60
Broadbent St. W1 5 H10
Broadberry Ct. N18 50 DV51
Alston Rd.
Broadbridge Clo. SE3 94 EG80
Broadcoombe, S.Croy. 134 DW108
Broadcroft Ave., Stan. 45 CK54
Broadcroft Rd., Orp. 123 ER101
Broadfield Clo. NW2 61 CW62
Broadfield Clo., Croy. 119 DM103
Progress Way
Broadfield Clo., Rom. 69 FF57
Broadfield Clo., Tad. 145 CW120
Broadfield Ct. (Bushey), Wat. 45 CE47
Broadfield La. NW1 77 DL66
Broadfield Rd. SE6 108 EE87
Broadfield Sq., Enf. 36 DV40
Broadfield Way, Buck.H. 52 EJ48
Broadfields, E.Mol. 115 CD100
Broadfields, Har. 44 CB53
Broadfields (Cheshunt), Wal.Cr. 21 DP29
Broadfields Ave. N21 49 DN45
Broadfields Ave., Edg. 46 CP49
Broadfields Heights, Edg. 46 CP49
Broadfields La., Wat. 43 BV46
Broadfields Way NW10 61 CT64
Broadgate E13 80 EJ68
Broadgate EC2 78 DS71
Liverpool St.
Broadgate, Wal.Abb. 24 EF33
Broadgate Circle EC2 7 M6
Broadgate Rd. E16 80 EK72
Fulmer Rd.
Broadgates Ave., Barn. 34 DB39
Broadgates Rd. SW18 104 DD88
Ellerton Rd.
Broadhead Strand NW9 47 CT53
Broadheath Dr., Chis. 109 EM92
Broadhinton Rd. SW4 91 DH83
Broadhurst, Ash. 144 CL116
Broadhurst Ave., Edg. 46 CP49
Broadhurst Ave., Ilf. 67 ET63
Broadhurst Clo. NW6 76 DC65
Broadhurst Gdns.
Broadhurst Clo., Rich. 102 CM85
Lower Gro. Rd.
Broadhurst Gdns. NW6 76 DB65
Broadhurst Gdns., Chig. 53 EQ49
Broadhurst Gdns., Ruis. 58 BW61
Broadhurst Wk., Rain. 83 FG65
Tuck Rd.
Broadlake Clo., St.Alb. 17 CK27
Broadlands, The, Felt. 100 BZ90
Broadlands Ave. SW16 105 DL89
Broadlands Ave., Enf. 36 DV41
Broadlands Ave., Shep. 113 BQ100
Broadlands Clo. N6 62 DG59
Broadlands Clo. SW16 105 DL89
Broadlands Clo., Enf. 36 DW41
Broadlands Clo., Wal.Cr. 23 DX34
Broadlands Dr., Warl. 148 DW119
Broadlands Rd. N6 62 DF59
Broadlands Rd., Brom. 108 EH91
Broadlands Way, N.Mal. 117 CT100
Broadlawns Ct., Har. 45 CF53
Broadley St. NW8 4 A6
Broadley St. NW8 76 DD71
Broadley Ter. NW1 4 C5
Broadley Ter. NW1 76 DE70
Broadmayne SE17 11 K10
Broadmead SE6 107 EA90
Broadmead Ave., Wor.Pk. 117 CU101
Broadmead Clo., Hmptn. 100 CA93
Broadmead Clo., Pnr. 44 BY52
Broadmead Est., Wdf.Grn. 52 EJ52
Broadmead Rd., Hayes 72 BY70
Broadmead Rd., Nthlt. 72 BY70
Broadmead Rd., Wdf.Grn. 52 EG51
Broadoak Ave., Enf. 37 DX35
Broadoak Rd., Erith 97 FD80
Broadoaks, Epp. 25 ET32
Broadoaks, Surb. 116 CP102
Broadoaks Cres., W.Byf. 126 BH113
Broadoaks Way, Brom. 122 EF99
Broadstone Pl. W1 4 F7
Broadstone Rd., Horn. 69 FG61
Broadstrood, Loug. 39 EN38
Broadview Est., Stai. 98 BN86
Broadview Rd. SW16 105 DK94
Broadwalk E18 66 EF55
Broadwalk, Croy. 135 DY111
Broadwalk, Har. 58 CA57
Broadwall SE1 10 E2
Broadwall SE1 77 DN74
Broadwater, Pot.B. 20 DB30
Broadwater Clo., Walt. 127 BU106
Broadwater Gdns., Orp. 137 EP105
Broadwater Gdns., Uxb. 56 BH56
Broadwater La., Uxb. 56 BH56
Broadwater Rd. N17 50 DS53
Broadwater Rd. SE28 95 EQ76
Broadwater Rd. SW17 104 DE91
Broadwater Rd. N., Walt. 127 BT106
Broadwater Rd. S., Walt. 127 BT106
Broadway E15 79 ED66
Broadway N20 48 DC47
Broadway SW1 9 M6
Broadway SW1 91 DK76
Broadway, Bark. 81 EQ66
Broadway, Bexh. 96 EY84
Broadway, Grnf. 72 CC70
Broadway, Rain. 83 FG70
Broadway, Rom. 55 FG54
Broadway, Stai. 98 BH92
Broadway, Surb. 116 CP102
Broadway, Swan. 125 FC100
Broadway, The E4 51 EC51
Broadway, The E13 80 EH68
Broadway, The N8 63 DL58
Broadway, The N9 50 DU48
Broadway, The N14 49 DK46
Winchmore Hill Rd.
Broadway, The N22 49 DN54
Broadway, The NW7 46 CS50
Broadway, The SW13 88 CS82
The Ter.
Broadway, The SW19 104 DA94
Broadway, The W5 73 CK73
Broadway, The W7 73 CE74
Broadway, The W13 73 CG74
Broadway, The, Add. 126 BG110
Broadway, The, Croy. 133 DL105
Croydon Rd.
Broadway, The, Dag. 68 EZ61
Whalebone La. S.
Broadway, The, Epsom 131 CU106
Broadway, The, Har. 45 CE54
Broadway, The, Horn. 69 FH63
Broadway, The, Loug. 39 EQ42
Broadway, The, Pnr. 44 BZ52
Broadway, The, Sthl. 72 BX73
Broadway, The, Stai. 112 BJ97
Broadway, The, Stan. 45 CJ50
Broadway, The, Sutt. 131 CY107
Broadway, The, T.Ditt. 115 CE102
Hampton Ct. Way
Broadway, The, Wat. 30 BW41
Broadway, The, Wem. 60 CL62
East La.
Broadway, The, Wdf.Grn. 52 EH51
Broadway Ave., Croy. 120 DR99
Broadway Ave., Twick. 101 CH86
Broadway Clo., S.Croy. 134 DV114
Broadway Clo., Wdf.Grn. 52 EH51
Broadway Ct. SW19 104 DA93
The Bdy.
Broadway E., Uxb. 56 BG59
Broadway Gdns., Mitch. 118 DE98
Broadway Mkt. E8 78 DV67
Broadway Mkt. Ms. E8 78 DU67
Brougham Rd.
Broadway Ms. E5 64 DT59
Broadway Ms. N13 49 DM50
Elmdale Rd.
Broadway Ms. N21 49 DP46
Compton Rd.
Broadway Par. N8 63 DL58
Broadway Pl. SW19 103 CZ93
Hartfield Rd.
Broadwick St. W1 5 L10
Broadwick St. W1 77 DJ72
Broadwood Ave., Ruis. 57 BS58
Brocas Clo. NW3 76 DE66
Fellows Rd.
Brock Pl. E3 79 EB70
Brock Rd. E13 80 EH71
Brock St. SE15 92 DW83
Evelina Rd.
Brockdish Ave., Bark. 67 ET64
Brockenhurst, W.Mol. 114 BZ100
Brockenhurst Ave., Wor.Pk. 116 CS102
Brockenhurst Gdns. NW7 46 CS51
Brockenhurst Gdns., Ilf. 67 EQ64
Brockenhurst Rd., Croy. 120 DV101
Brockenhurst Way SW16 119 DK96
Brocket Clo., Chig. 53 ET50
Burrow Rd.
Brocket Way, Chig. 53 ES50
Brockham Clo. SW19 103 CZ92
Brockham Cres., Croy. 135 ED108
Brockham Dr. SW2 105 DM87
Fairview Pl.
Brockham Dr., Ilf. 67 EP58
Brockham St. SE1 11 J6
Brockham St. SE1 92 DQ76
Brockhurst Clo., Stan. 45 CF51
Brockill Cres. SE4 93 DY84
Brocklebank Ct., Whyt. 148 DU118
Brocklebank Rd. SE7 94 EH77
Brocklebank Rd. SW18 104 DC87
Brocklehurst St. SE14 93 DX80
Brocklesbury Clo., Wat. 30 BW41
Brocklesby Rd. SE25 120 DV98
Brockley Ave., Stan. 46 CL48
Brockley Clo., Stan. 46 CL49
Brockley Combe, Wey. 127 BR105
Brockley Cres., Rom. 55 FC52
Brockley Cross SE4 93 DY83
Endwell Rd.
Brockley Footpath SE15 92 DW84
Brockley Gdns. SE4 93 DZ82
Brockley Gro. SE4 107 DZ85
Brockley Hall Rd. SE4 107 DY85
Brockley Hill, Stan. 45 CJ46
Brockley Ms. SE4 107 DY85
Brockley Pk. SE23 107 DY87
Brockley Ri. SE23 107 DY87
Brockley Rd. SE4 93 DZ83
Brockley Vw. SE23 107 DY87
Brockley Way SE4 107 DX85
Brockleyside, Stan. 46 CL49
Brockman Ri., Brom. 107 ED91
Brocks Dr., Sutt. 117 CY104
Brockshot Clo., Brent. 87 CK78
Brockton Clo., Rom. 69 FF56
Brockway Clo. E11 66 EE61
Brockwell Clo., Orp. 123 ET98
Brockwell Pk. Gdns. SE24 105 DN87
Brockworth Clo. SE15 92 DS79
Brodewater Rd., Borwd. 32 CP40
Brodia Rd. N16 64 DS62
Brodie Rd. E4 51 EC46
Brodie Rd., Enf. 36 DQ38
Brodie St. SE1 92 DT78
Coopers Rd.
Brodlove La. E1 79 DX73
Brodrick Gro. SE2 96 EV77
Brodrick Rd. SW17 104 DE89
Brograve Gdns., Beck. 121 EB96
Broke Fm. Dr., Orp. 138 EX109
Broke Wk. E8 78 DU67
Marlborough Ave.
Broken Wf. EC4 7 H10
Brokesley St. E3 79 DZ69
Bromar Rd. SE5 92 DS83
Bromborough Grn., Wat. 44 BW50
Brome Rd. SE9 95 EM83
Bromefield, Stan. 45 CJ53
Bromefield Ct., Wal.Abb. 24 EG33
Bromehead Rd. E1 78 DW72
Commercial Rd.
Bromell's Rd. SW4 91 DJ84
Bromet Clo., Wat. 29 BT38
Hempstead Rd.
Bromfelde Rd. SW4 91 DK83
Bromfelde Wk. SW4 91 DL82
Bromfield St. N1 77 DN68
Bromhall Rd., Dag. 82 EV65
Bromhedge SE9 109 EM90
Bromholm Rd. SE2 96 EV76
Bromleigh Clo. (Cheshunt), Wal.Cr. 23 DY28
Martins Dr.
Bromleigh Ct. SE23 106 DV89
Lapse Wd. Wk.
Bromley Ave., Brom. 108 EE94
Bromley Common, Brom. 122 EJ98
Bromley Cres., Brom. 122 EF97
Bromley Cres., Ruis. 57 BT63
Bromley Gdns., Brom. 122 EF97
Bromley Gro., Brom. 121 ED96
Bromley Hall Rd. E14 79 EC71
Bromley High St. E3 79 EB69
Bromley Hill, Brom. 108 EE93
Bromley La., Chis. 109 EQ94
Bromley Pl. W1 5 K6
Bromley Rd. E10 65 EB58
Bromley Rd. E17 51 EA54
Bromley Rd. N17 50 DT53
Bromley Rd. N18 50 DR48
Bromley Rd. SE6 107 EB89
Bromley Rd., Beck. 121 EB96
Bromley Rd., Brom. 121 EB96
Bromley Rd. (Downham), Brom. 107 ED91
Bromley Rd., Chis. 123 EP95
Bromley St. E1 79 DX71
Brompton Arc. SW3 8 D5
Brompton Clo. SE20 120 DU96
Selby Rd.
Brompton Clo., Houns. 100 BZ85
Brompton Dr., Erith 97 FH80
Brompton Gro. N2 62 DE56
Brompton Pk. Cres. SW6 90 DB79
Brompton Pl. SW3 8 C6
Brompton Pl. SW3 90 DE76
Brompton Rd. SW1 8 D5
Brompton Rd. SW1 90 DF75
Brompton Rd. SW3 8 B8
Brompton Rd. SW3 90 DE77
Brompton Rd. SW7 8 B7
Brompton Rd. SW7 90 DE76
Brompton Sq. SW3 8 B6
Brompton Sq. SW3 90 DE76
Brompton Ter. SE18 95 EN81
Prince Imperial Rd.

Bromwich Ave. N6 62 DG61
Bromyard Ave. W3 74 CS73
Bromyard Ho. SE15 92 DV80
Commercial Way
Brondesbury Ct. NW2 75 CX65
Brondesbury Ms. NW6 76 DA66
Willesden La.
Brondesbury Pk. NW2 75 CW66
Brondesbury Pk. NW6 75 CX66
Brondesbury Rd. NW6 75 CZ68
Brondesbury Vill. NW6 75 CZ68
Bronsart Rd. SW6 89 CY80
Bronson Rd. SW20 117 CX96
Bronte Clo. E7 66 EG63
Bective Rd.
Bronte Clo., Erith 97 FB81
Belmont Rd.
Bronte Clo., Ilf. 67 EN56
Bronte Ho. NW6 76 DA69
Bronti Clo. SE17 92 DQ78
Bronze Age Way, Belv. 97 FB75
Bronze Age Way, Erith 97 FB75
Bronze St. SE8 93 EA80
Brook Ave., Dag. 83 FB66
Brook Ave., Edg. 46 CP51
Brook Ave., Wem. 60 CN62
Brook Clo. NW7 47 CY52
Frith Ct.
Brook Clo. SW20 117 CV97
Brook Clo. W3 74 CN74
West Lo. Ave.
Brook Clo., Borwd. 32 CP41
Brook Clo., Chis. 123 EN95
Brook Clo., Rom. 55 FF53
Brook Clo., Ruis. 57 BS59
Brook Clo., Stai. 98 BM87
Brook Cres. E4 51 EA49
Brook Cres. N9 50 DV49
Brook Dr. SE11 10 E7
Brook Dr. SE11 91 DN76
Brook Dr., Har. 58 CC56
Brook Dr., Rad. 17 CF33
Brook Dr., Ruis. 57 BS58
Brook Dr., Sun. 99 BS92
Chertsey Rd.
Brook Fm. Rd., Cob. 142 BX115
Brook Gdns. E4 51 EB49
Brook Gdns. SW13 89 CT83
Brook Gdns., Kings.T. 116 CQ95
Brook Gate W1 8 E1
Brook Grn. W6 89 CW76
Brook Ind. Est., Hayes 72 BX74
Brook La. SE3 94 EH82
Brook La., Bex. 110 EX86
Brook La., Brom. 108 EG93
Brook La. N., Brent. 87 CK78
Brook Mead, Epsom 130 CS107
Brook Meadow N12 48 DB48
Brook Meadow Clo., Wdf.Grn. 52 EE51
Brook Ms. N. W2 76 DD73
Craven Ter.
Brook Par., Chig. 53 EP48
High Rd.
Brook Pk. Clo. N21 35 DP44
Brook Pl., Barn. 34 DA43
Brook Ri., Chig. 53 EN48
Brook Rd. N8 63 DL56
Brook Rd. N22 63 DM55
Brook Rd. NW2 61 CT61
Brook Rd., Borwd. 32 CN39
Brook Rd., Buck.H. 52 EG47
Brook Rd., Epp. 26 EU33
Brook Rd., Ilf. 67 ES58
Brook Rd., Loug. 38 EL42
Brook Rd., Rom. 55 FF53
Brook Rd., Surb. 116 CL103
Brook Rd., Swan. 125 FD97
Brook Rd., Th.Hth. 120 DQ98
Brook Rd., Twick. 101 CG86
Brook Rd., Wal.Cr. 23 DZ34
Brook Rd. S., Brent. 87 CK79
Brook St. N17 50 DT54
High Rd.
Brook St. W1 5 H10
Brook St. W1 76 DG73
Brook St. W2 4 A10
Brook St. W2 76 DD73
Brook St., Belv. 97 FB78
Brook St., Erith 97 FB79
Brook St., Kings.T. 116 CL96
Brook Wk. N2 48 DD53
Old Fm. Rd.
Brook Wk., Edg. 46 CR51
Brook Way, Chig. 53 EN48
Brook Way, Lthd. 143 CG118
Brook Way, Rain. 83 FH71
Brookbank Ave. W7 73 CD71
Brookbank Rd. SE13 93 EA83
Brookdale N11 49 DJ49
Brookdale Rd. E17 65 EA55
Brookdale Rd. SE6 107 EB86
Brookdale Rd., Bex. 110 EY86
Brookdene Ave., Wat. 43 BV45
Brookdene Dr., Nthwd. 43 BT52
Brookdene Rd. SE18 95 ET77
Brooke Ave., Har. 58 CC62
Brooke Clo. (Bushey), Wat. 44 CC45
Brooke Rd. E5 64 DU62
Brooke Rd. E17 65 EC56
Brooke Rd. N16 64 DT62
Brooke St. EC1 6 D7
Brooke St. EC1 77 DN71
Brooke Way (Bushey), Wat. 44 CC45
Richfield Rd.
Brookehowse Rd. SE6 107 EA89
Brookend Rd., Sid. 109 ES88
Brooker Rd., Wal.Abb. 23 EC34
Brookers Clo., Ash. 143 CJ117
Brooke's Ct. EC1 6 D6
Brookes Mkt. EC1 6 D6
Brookfield N6 62 DG62
Brookfield, Epp. 26 EW25
Brookfield Ave. E17 65 EC56
Brookfield Ave. NW7 47 CV51
Brookfield Ave. W5 73 CK70
Brookfield Ave., Sutt. 132 DE105
Brookfield Clo. NW7 47 CV51
Brookfield Ct., Grnf. 72 CC69
Brookfield Ct., Har. 59 CK57
Brookfield Cres. NW7 47 CV51
Brookfield Cres., Har. 60 CL57
Brookfield Gdns., Esher 129 CF107
Brookfield Gdns. (Cheshunt), Wal.Cr. 23 DX27
Brookfield La. (Cheshunt), Wal.Cr. 22 DV28
Brookfield Pk. NW5 63 DH62
Brookfield Path, Wdf.Grn. 52 EE51
Brookfield Rd. E9 79 DY65
Brookfield Rd. N9 50 DU48
Brookfield Rd. W4 88 CR75
Brookfields, Enf. 37 DX42
Brookfields Ave., Mitch. 118 DE99
Brookhill Clo. SE18 95 EP78
Brookhill Clo., Barn. 34 DE43
Brookhill Rd. SE18 95 EP77
Brookhill Rd., Barn. 34 DE43
Brookhouse Gdns. E4 52 EE49
Brookhurst Rd., Add. 126 BH107
Brooking Rd. E7 66 EG64
Brookland Clo. NW11 62 DB56
Brookland Garth NW11 62 DB56
Brookland Hill NW11 62 DB56
Brookland Ri. NW11 62 DA56
Brooklands App., Rom. 69 FD56
Brooklands Ave. SW19 104 DB89
Brooklands Ave., Sid. 109 ER89
Brooklands Clo., Cob. 142 BY115
Brooklands Clo., Rom. 69 FD56
Marshalls Rd.
Brooklands Clo., Sun. 113 BS95
Brooklands Ct., Add. 126 BK110
Brooklands Dr., Grnf. 73 CJ67
Brooklands Gdns., Pot.B. 19 CY32
Brooklands Ind. Est., Wey. 126 BL110
Brooklands La., Rom. 69 FD56
Brooklands La., Wey. 126 BM107
Brooklands Pk. SE3 94 EG83
Brooklands Rd., Rom. 69 FD56
Brooklands Rd., T.Ditt. 115 CF102
Brooklands Rd., Wey. 127 BP107
Brooklea Clo. NW9 46 CS53
Brooklyn Ave. SE25 120 DV98
Brooklyn Ave., Loug. 38 EL42
Brooklyn Clo., Cars. 118 DE103
Brooklyn Gro. SE25 120 DV98
Brooklyn Rd. SE25 120 DV98
Brooklyn Rd., Brom. 122 EK99
Brooklyn Way, West Dr. 84 BK76
Brookmans Ave., Hat. 19 CY26
Brookmarsh Ind. Est. SE10 93 EB80
Norman Rd.
Brookmead Ave., Brom. 123 EM99
Brookmead Clo., Orp. 124 EV101
Brookmead Rd., Croy. 119 DJ100
Brookmead Way, Orp. 124 EV100
Brookmeads Est., Mitch. 118 DE99
Brookmill Rd. SE8 93 EA81
Brooks Ave. E6 81 EM70
Brooks Clo. SE9 109 EN89
Brooks Clo., Wey. 126 BN110
Brooks Ct. E15 65 EB64
Clays La.
Brooks La. W4 88 CN79
Brook's Ms. W1 5 H10
Brook's Ms. W1 77 DH73
Brooks Rd. E13 80 EG67
Brooks Rd. W4 88 CN78
Brooks Way, Orp. 124 EW96
Brooksbank St. E9 78 DW65
Brooksby Ms. N1 77 DN66
Brooksby St.
Brooksby St. N1 77 DN66
Brooksby's Wk. E9 65 DX64
Brookscroft, Croy. 135 DZ110
Brookscroft Rd. E17 51 EB53
Brookshill, Har. 45 CD50
Brookshill Ave., Har. 45 CD50
Brookshill Dr., Har. 45 CD50
Brookside N21 35 DM44
Brookside, Barn. 34 DE44
Brookside, Cars. 132 DG106
Brookside, Ilf. 53 EQ51
Brookside, Orp. 123 ET101
Brookside, Pot.B. 19 CU32
Brookside, Uxb. 70 BM66
Brookside, Wal.Abb. 24 EE33
Broomstick Hall Rd.
Brookside Ave., Ashf. 98 BJ92
Brookside Clo., Barn. 33 CY44
Brookside Clo., Felt. 99 BU90
Sycamore Clo.
Brookside Clo., Har. 59 CK57
Brookside Clo. (Kenton), Har. 58 BY63
Brookside Cres. (Cuffley), Pot.B. 21 DL27
Brookside Cres., Wor.Pk. 117 CU102
Green La.
Brookside Gdns., Enf. 36 DW37
Brookside Rd. N9 50 DV49
Brookside Rd. N19 63 DJ61
Junction Rd.
Brookside Rd. NW11 61 CY58
Brookside Rd., Hayes 72 BW73
Brookside Rd., Wat. 43 BV45
Brookside S., Barn. 48 DG45
Brookside Wk. N3 61 CX55
Brookside Wk. N12 48 DA51
Brookside Wk. NW4 61 CY56
Brookside Wk. NW11 61 CY56
Brookside Way, Croy. 121 DX100
Brooksville Ave. NW6 75 CY67
Brookvale, Erith 97 FB81
Brookview Rd. SW16 105 DJ92
Brookville Rd. SW6 89 CZ80
Brookway SE3 94 EG83
Brookwood Ave. SW13 89 CT83
Brookwood Clo., Brom. 122 EF98
Brookwood Rd. SW18 103 CZ88
Brookwood Rd., Houns. 86 CB81
Broom Ave., Orp. 124 EV96
Broom Clo., Brom. 122 EL100
Broom Clo., Esher 128 CB106
Broom Clo., Tedd. 101 CK94
Broom Clo. (Cheshunt), Wal.Cr. 22 DU27
Broom Gdns., Croy. 121 EA104
Broom Gro., Wat. 29 BU38
Bay Tree Wk.
Broom Hall, Lthd. 128 CC114
Broom Lock, Tedd. 101 CJ93
Broom Mead, Bexh. 110 FA85
Broom Pk., Tedd. 101 CK94
Broom Rd., Croy. 121 EA104
Broom Rd., Tedd. 101 CH92
Broom Water, Tedd. 101 CJ93
Broom Water W., Tedd. 101 CJ92
Broom Way, Wey. 127 BS105
Broomcroft Ave., Nthlt. 72 BW69
Broome Rd., Hmptn. 100 BZ94
Broome Way SE5 92 DQ80
Broomer Pl., Wal.Cr. 22 DW29
Broomfield E17 65 DZ59
Broomfield, St.Alb. 16 CC27
Broomfield, Stai. 98 BG93
Broomfield, Sun. 113 BU95
Broomfield Ave. N13 49 DM50
Broomfield Ave., Brox. 23 DY26
Broomfield Ave., Loug. 39 EM44
Broomfield Clo., Rom. 55 FD52
Broomfield Ct., Wey. 127 BP107
Broomfield La. N13 49 DL49
Broomfield Pl. W13 73 CH74
Broomfield Rd.
Broomfield Ride, Lthd. 129 CD112
Broomfield Ri., Abb.L. 15 BR32
Broomfield Rd. N13 49 DL50
Broomfield Rd. W13 73 CH74
Broomfield Rd., Add. 126 BH111
Broomfield Rd., Beck. 121 DY98
Broomfield Rd., Bexh. 110 FA85
Broomfield Rd., Rich. 88 CM81
Broomfield Rd., Rom. 68 EX59
Broomfield Rd., Sev. 154 FF122
Broomfield Rd., Surb. 116 CM102
Broomfield Rd., Tedd. 101 CJ93
Melbourne Rd.
Broomfield St. E14 79 EA71
Broomfields, Esher 128 CC106
Broomgrove Gdns., Edg. 46 CN53
Broomgrove Rd. SW9 91 DM82
Broomhall Rd., S.Croy. 134 DR109
Broomhill Ri., Bexh. 110 FA85
Broomhill Rd. SW18 104 DA85
Broomhill Rd., Dart. 111 FH86
Broomhill Rd., Ilf. 68 EU61
Broomhill Rd., Orp. 124 EU101
Broomhill Rd., Wdf.Grn. 52 EG51
Broomhill Wk., Wdf.Grn. 52 EF52
Broomhouse La. SW6 90 DA82
Broomhouse Rd. SW6 90 DA82
Broomloan La., Sutt. 118 DA103
Broomsleigh St. NW6 61 CZ64
Broomstick Hall Rd., Wal.Abb. 23 ED33
Broomwood Clo., Croy. 121 DX99
Broomwood Rd. SW11 104 DF86
Broomwood Rd., Orp. 124 EV96
Broseley Gro. SE26 107 DY92
Broster Gdns. SE25 120 DT97
Brough Clo. SW8 91 DL80
Kenchester Clo.
Brough Clo., Kings.T. 101 CK92
Brougham Rd. E8 78 DU67
Brougham Rd. W3 74 CQ72
Brougham St. SW11 90 DF82
Reform St.
Broughinge Rd., Borwd. 32 CN40
Broughton Ave. N3 61 CY55
Broughton Ave., Rich. 101 CH90
Broughton Dr. SW9 91 DN84
Broughton Gdns. N6 63 DJ58
Broughton Rd. SW6 90 DB82
Broughton Rd. W13 73 CH73
Broughton Rd., Orp. 123 ER103
Broughton Rd., Sev. 153 FG116
Broughton Rd., Th.Hth. 119 DN100
Broughton Rd. App. SW6 90 DB82
Wandsworth Bri. Rd.
Broughton St. SW8 90 DG82
Broughton Way, Rick. 42 BG45
Brouncker Rd. W3 88 CQ75
Brow, The, Wat. 15 BV33
Brow Clo., Orp. 124 EX101
Brow Cres.
Brow Cres., Orp. 124 EW102
Browells La., Felt. 99 BV89
Brown Clo., Wall. 133 DL108
Brown Hart Gdns. W1 4 G10
Brown Hart Gdns. W1 76 DG73
Brown St. W1 4 D8
Brown St. W1 76 DF72
Browne Clo., Rom. 55 FB50
Bamford Way
Brownfield St. E14 79 EB72
Browngraves Rd., Hayes 85 BQ80
Brownhill Rd. SE6 107 EB87
Browning Ave. W7 73 CF72
Browning Ave., Sutt. 132 DE105
Browning Ave., Wor.Pk. 117 CV102
Browning Clo. E17 65 EC56
Greenacre Gdns.
Browning Clo. W9 76 DC70
Randolph Ave.
Browning Clo., Hmptn. 100 BZ91
Browning Clo., Rom. 54 EZ52
Browning Clo., Well. 95 ES81
Browning Est. SE17 11 J10
Browning Est. SE17 92 DQ78
Browning Ho. W12 75 CW72
Wood La.
Browning Ms. W1 4 G7
Browning Rd. E11 66 EF59
Browning Rd. E12 81 EM65
Browning Rd., Enf. 36 DR37
Browning St. SE17 11 J10
Browning St. SE17 92 DQ78
Browning Way, Houns. 86 BX81
Brownlea Gdns., Ilf. 68 EU61
Brownlow Ms. WC1 6 C5
Brownlow Ms. WC1 77 DM70
Brownlow Rd. E7 66 EH63
Woodford Rd.
Brownlow Rd. E8 78 DT67
Brownlow Rd. N3 48 DB52
Brownlow Rd. N11 49 DL51
Brownlow Rd. NW10 74 CS66
Brownlow Rd. W13 73 CG74
Brownlow Rd., Borwd. 32 CN42
Brownlow Rd., Croy. 134 DS105
Brownlow St. WC1 6 C7
Brownrigg Rd., Ashf. 98 BN91
Brown's Bldgs. EC3 7 N9
Browns La. NW5 63 DH64
Browns Rd. E17 65 EA55
Browns Rd., Surb. 116 CM101
Brownspring Dr. SE9 109 EP91
Brownswell Rd. N2 48 DD54
Brownswood Rd. N4 63 DP62
Broxash Rd. SW11 104 DG86
Broxbourne Ave. E18 66 EH56
Broxbourne Rd. E7 66 EG62
Broxbourne Rd., Orp. 123 ET102
Broxhill Rd. Rom. (Havering-atte-Bower) 55 FE48
Broxholm Rd. SE27 105 DN90
Broxted Rd. SE6 107 DZ89
Broxwood Way NW8 76 DE67
Bruce Ave., Shep. 113 BQ100
Bruce Castle Rd. N17 50 DT53
Bruce Clo. W10 75 CY71
Ladbroke Gro.
Bruce Clo., Well. 96 EV81
Bruce Clo., W.Byf. 126 BK113
Bruce Dr., S.Croy. 135 DX109
Bruce Gdns. N20 48 DF48
Balfour Gro.
Bruce Gro. N17 50 DS53
Bruce Gro., Orp. 124 EU101
Bruce Gro., Wat. 29 BV38
Bruce Hall Ms. SW17 104 DG91
Brudenell Rd.
Bruce Rd. E3 79 EB69
Bruce Rd. NW10 74 CR66
Bruce Rd. SE25 120 DR98
Bruce Rd., Barn. 33 CY41
St. Albans Rd.
Bruce Rd., Har. 45 CE54
Bruce Rd., Mitch. 104 DG94
Bruce Way, Wal.Cr. 23 DX33
Bruckner St. W10 75 CZ69
Brudenell Rd. SW17 104 DF90
Bruffs Meadow, Nthlt. 72 BY65
Bruges Pl. NW1 77 DJ66
Randolph St.
Brumana Clo., Wey. 127 BP106
Elgin Rd.
Brumfield Rd., Epsom 130 CQ106
Brummel Clo., Bexh. 97 FC83
Brundley Way, Brom. 108 EG92
Brune St. E1 7 P7
Brune St. E1 78 DT71
Brunel Clo. SE19 106 DT93
Brunel Clo., Houns. 85 BV80
Brunel Clo., Nthlt. 72 BZ69
Brunel Est. W2 76 DA71
Brunel Pl., Sthl. 72 CB72
Brunel Rd. E17 65 DY58
Brunel Rd. SE16 92 DW75
Brunel Rd. W3 74 CS71
Brunel Rd., Wdf.Grn. 53 EM50
Brunel St. E16 80 EF72
Victoria Dock Rd.
Brunel Wk. N15 64 DS56
Brunel Wk., Twick. 100 CA87
Stephenson Rd.
Brunner Clo. NW11 62 DB57
Brunner Rd. E17 65 DY57
Brunner Rd. W5 73 CK70
Bruno Pl. NW9 60 CQ61
Brunswick Ave. N11 48 DG48
Brunswick Cen. WC1 5 P4
Brunswick Clo., Bexh. 96 EX84
Brunswick Clo., Pnr. 58 BY58
Brunswick Clo., T.Ditt. 115 CF102
Brunswick Clo., Twick. 101 CD90
Brunswick Clo., Walt. 114 BW103
Brunswick Ct. EC1 77 DP69
Northampton Sq.
Brunswick Ct. SE1 11 N4
Brunswick Ct. SE1 92 DS75
Brunswick Ct., Barn. 34 DD43
Brunswick Cres. N11 48 DG48
Brunswick Gdns. W5 74 CL70
Brunswick Gdns. W8 76 DA74
Brunswick Gdns., Ilf. 53 EQ52
Brunswick Gro. N11 48 DG48
Brunswick Gro., Cob. 128 BW113
Brunswick Ind. Pk. N11 49 DH49
Brunswick Ms. SW16 105 DK93
Potters La.
Brunswick Ms. W1 4 E8
Brunswick Pk. SE5 92 DR81
Brunswick Pk. Gdns. N11 48 DG47
Brunswick Pk. Rd. N11 48 DG46
Brunswick Pl. N1 7 L3
Brunswick Pl. N1 78 DR69
Brunswick Pl. SE19 106 DU94
Brunswick Quay SE16 93 DX76
Brunswick Rd. E10 65 EC60
Brunswick Rd. E14 79 EC72
Blackwall Tunnel Northern App.
Brunswick Rd. N15 64 DS56
Brunswick Rd. W5 73 CK70
Brunswick Rd., Bexh. 96 EX84
Brunswick Rd., Kings.T. 116 CN95
Brunswick Rd., Sutt. 132 DB105
Brunswick Sq. N17 50 DT51
Brunswick Sq. WC1 6 A4
Brunswick Sq. WC1 77 DL70
Brunswick St. E17 65 EC57
Brunswick Vill. SE5 92 DS81
Brunswick Way N11 49 DH49
Brunton Pl. E14 79 DY72
Brushfield St. E1 7 N6
Brushfield St. E1 78 DS71
Brussels Rd. SW11 90 DD84
Bruton Clo., Chis. 109 EM94
Bruton La. W1 9 J1
Bruton La. W1 77 DH73
Bruton Pl. W1 9 J1
Bruton Pl. W1 77 DH73
Bruton Rd., Mord. 118 DC98
Bruton St. W1 9 J1
Bruton St. W1 77 DH73
Bruton Way W13 73 CG71
Bryan Ave. NW10 75 CV66
Bryan Clo., Sun. 99 BU94
Bryan Rd. SE16 93 DZ75
Bryan's All. SW6 90 DB82
Wandsworth Bri. Rd.
Bryanston Ave., Twick. 100 CB88
Bryanston Clo., Sthl. 86 BZ77
Bryanston Ms. E. W1 4 D7
Bryanston Ms. W. W1 4 D7
Bryanston Pl. W1 4 D7
Bryanston Pl. W1 76 DF71
Bryanston Sq. W1 4 D7
Bryanston Sq. W1 76 DF71
Bryanston St. W1 4 D9
Bryanston St. W1 76 DF72
Bryanstone Rd. N8 63 DK57
Bryanstone Rd., Wal.Cr. 23 DZ34
Bryant Clo., Barn. 33 CZ43
Bryant Ct. E2 78 DT68
Whiston Rd.
Bryant Rd., Nthlt. 72 BW69
Bryant St. E15 79 ED66
Bryantwood Rd. N7 63 DN64
Bryce Rd., Dag. 68 EW63
Brycedale Cres. N14 49 DJ49
Bryden Clo. SE26 107 DY92
Brydges Pl. WC2 9 P1
Brydges Rd. E15 65 ED64
Brydon Wk. N1 77 DL67
Outram Pl.
Bryer Ct. EC2 78 DQ71
Aldersgate St.
Bryett Rd. N7 63 DL62
Brymay Clo. E3 79 EA68
Bryn-y-Mawr Rd., Enf. 36 DT42
Brynmaer Rd. SW11 90 DF81
Bryony Clo., Loug. 39 EP42
Bryony Clo., Uxb. 70 BM71
Bryony Rd. W12 75 CU73
Bryony Way, Sun. 99 BT93
Bubblestone Rd., Sev. 153 FH116
Buchan Clo., Uxb. 70 BJ69
Buchan Rd. SE15 92 DW83
Buchanan Clo. N21 35 DM43
Buchanan Ct., Borwd. 32 CQ40
Buchanan Gdns. NW10 75 CV68
Bucharest Rd. SW18 104 DC87
Buck Hill Wk. W2 8 A1
Buck La. NW9 60 CR56
Buck St. NW1 77 DH66
Buck Wk. E17 65 ED56
Foresters Dr.
Buckden Clo. N2 62 DF56
Southern Rd.
Buckden Clo. SE12 108 EF86
Upwood Rd.
Buckettsland La., Borwd. 32 CR38
Buckfast Rd., Mord. 118 DB98
Buckfast St. E2 78 DU69
Buckhold Rd. SW18 104 DA86
Buckhurst Ave., Cars. 118 DE102
Buckhurst Ave., Sev. 155 FJ125
Buckhurst La., Sev. 155 FJ125

Buckhurst Rd., West. 151 EP121
Buckhurst St. E1 78 DV70
Buckhurst Way, Buck.H. 52 EK49
Buckingham Arc. WC2 10 A1
Buckingham Ave. N20 48 DC45
Buckingham Ave., Felt. 99 BV86
Buckingham Ave., Grnf. 73 CG67
Buckingham Ave., Th.Hth. 119 DN95
Buckingham Ave., Well. 95 ES84
Buckingham Ave., W.Mol. 114 CB97
Buckingham Clo. W5 73 CJ71
Buckingham Clo., Enf. 36 DS40
Buckingham Clo., Hmptn. 100 BZ92
Buckingham Clo., Orp. 123 ES101
Buckingham Ct. NW4 61 CU55
Buckingham Dr., Chis. 109 EP92
Buckingham Gdns., Edg. 46 CL52
Buckingham Gdns., Th.Hth. 119 DN96
Buckingham Gdns., W.Mol. 114 CB96
Buckingham Ave.
Buckingham Gate SW1 9 K5
Buckingham Gate SW1 91 DH76
Buckingham Gro., Uxb. 70 BN68
Buckingham La. SE23 107 DY87
Buckingham Ms. NW10 75 CT68
Buckingham Rd.
Buckingham Ms. SW1 9 K6
Buckingham Palace Rd. SW1 9 H9
Buckingham Palace Rd. SW1 91 DH77
Buckingham Pl. SW1 9 K6
Buckingham Rd. E10 65 EB62
Buckingham Rd. E11 66 EJ57
Buckingham Rd. E15 66 EF64
Buckingham Rd. E18 52 EF53
Buckingham Rd. N1 78 DS65
Buckingham Rd. N22 49 DL53
Buckingham Rd. NW10 75 CT68
Buckingham Rd., Borwd. 32 CR42
Buckingham Rd., Edg. 46 CM52
Buckingham Rd., Hmptn. 100 BZ91
Buckingham Rd., Har. 59 CD57
Buckingham Rd., Ilf. 67 ER61
Buckingham Rd., Kings.T. 116 CM98
Buckingham Rd., Mitch. 119 DL99
Buckingham Rd., Rich. 101 CK89
Buckingham Rd., Wat. 29 BV37
Buckingham St. WC2 10 A1
Buckingham Way, Wall. 133 DJ109
Buckland Cres. NW3 76 DD66
Buckland Ri., Pnr. 44 BW53
Buckland Rd. E10 65 EC61
Buckland Rd., Chess. 130 CM106
Buckland Rd., Orp. 137 ES105
Buckland Rd., Sutt. 131 CW110
Buckland St. N1 7 L1
Buckland St. N1 78 DR68
Buckland Wk., Mord. 118 DC98
Buckland Way, Wor.Pk. 117 CW102
Bucklands Rd., Tedd. 101 CJ93
Buckle St. E1 78 DT72
Leman St.
Buckleigh Ave. SW20 117 CY97
Buckleigh Rd. SW16 105 DK93
Buckleigh Way SE19 120 DT95
Buckler Gdns. SE9 109 EM90
Southold Ri.
Bucklers All. SW6 90 DA79
Haldane Rd.
Bucklers Way, Cars. 118 DF104
Bucklersbury EC4 7 K9
Bucklersbury EC4 78 DR72
Bucklersbury Pas. EC4 77 DP73
Queen Victoria St.
Buckles Ct., Belv. 96 EX76
Fendyke Rd.
Buckles Way, Bans. 145 CY116
Buckley Clo., Dart. 97 FF82
Buckley Rd. NW6 75 CZ66
Buckley St. SE1 10 B3
Buckmaster Rd. SW11 90 DE84
Bucknall St. WC2 5 N8
Bucknall St. WC2 76 DK72
Bucknalls Clo., Wat. 16 BY32
Bucknalls Dr., St.Alb. 16 BZ31
Bucknalls La., Wat. 16 BX32
Bucknell Clo. SW2 91 DM84
Buckner Rd. SW2 91 DM84
Bucknills Clo., Epsom 130 CQ114
Buckrell Rd. E4 51 ED47
Bucks Ave., Wat. 44 BY45
Bucks Clo., W.Byf. 126 BH114
Bucks Cross Rd., Orp. 138 EY106
Bucks Hill, Kings L. 14 BJ33
Buckstone Clo. SE23 106 DW86
Buckstone Rd. N18 50 DU50
Buckters Rents SE16 79 DY74
Buckthorne Ho., Chig. 54 EV49
Buckthorne Rd. SE4 107 DY86
Buckton Rd., Borwd. 32 CM38
Budd Clo. N12 48 DB49
Buddings Circle, Wem. 60 CQ62
Budd's All., Twick. 101 CJ85
Arlington Clo.
Budebury Rd., Stai. 98 BG92
Budge La., Mitch. 118 DF101
Budge Row EC4 7 K10
Budge's Wk. W2 76 DD73
Budgin's Hill, Orp. 138 EV112
Budich Ct., Ilf. 68 EU61
Budleigh Cres., Well. 96 EW81
Budoch Dr., Ilf. 68 EU61
Buer Rd. SW6 89 CY82
Buff Ave., Bans. 132 DB114
Bug Hill, Warl. 149 DX120
Bugsby's Way SE7 94 EG77
Bugsby's Way SE10 94 EF77
Bulganak Rd., Th.Hth. 120 DQ98
Bulinga St. SW1 9 P9
Bulinga St. SW1 91 DK77
Bull All., Well. 96 EV83
Welling High St.
Bull Hill, Lthd. 143 CG121
Bull Inn Ct. WC2 10 A1
Bull La. N18 50 DS50
Bull La., Chis. 109 ER94
Bull La., Dag. 69 FB62
Bull Rd. E15 80 EF68
Bull Wf. La. EC4 7 J10
Bull Yd. SE15 92 DU81
Peckham High St.
Bullace Row SE5 92 DQ81
Camberwell Rd.
Bullards Pl. E2 79 DX69
Bullbanks Rd., Belv. 97 FC77
Bullen St. SW11 90 DE82
Buller Clo. SE15 92 DU80
Buller Rd. N17 50 DU54
Buller Rd. N22 49 DN54
Buller Rd. NW10 75 CX69
Chamberlayne Rd.
Buller Rd., Bark. 81 ES66
Buller Rd., Th.Hth. 120 DR96
Bullers Clo., Sid. 110 EY92
Bullers Wd. Dr., Chis. 109 EM94
Bullescroft Rd., Edg. 46 CN48
Bullfinch Clo., Sev. 154 FD122
Bullfinch Dene, Sev. 154 FD122
Bullfinch La., Sev. 154 FD122
Bullfinch Rd., S.Croy. 135 DX110
Bullhead Rd., Borwd. 32 CQ40
Bullied Way SW1 9 J9
Bullivant St. E14 79 EC72
Bullrush Gro., Uxb. 70 BJ70
Bull's All. SW14 88 CR82
Bulls Bri. Ind. Est., Sthl. 85 BV76
Bulls Bri. Rd., Sthl. 85 BV76
Bulls Cross, Enf. 36 DU37
Bulls Cross Ride, Wal.Cr. 36 DU35
Bulls Gdns. SW3 8 C8
Bull's Head Pas. EC3 7 M9
Bullsbrook Rd., Hayes 72 BW74
Bullsmoor Clo., Wal.Cr. 36 DW35
Bullsmoor Gdns., Wal.Cr. 36 DV35
Bullsmoor La., Enf. 36 DW35
Bullsmoor La., Wal.Cr. 36 DU35
Bullsmoor Ride, Wal.Cr. 36 DW35
Bullsmoor Way, Wal.Cr. 36 DV35
Bullwell Cres. (Cheshunt), Wal.Cr. 23 DY29
Bulmer Gdns., Har. 59 CK59
Bulmer Ms. W11 76 DA73
Ladbroke Rd.
Bulmer Pl. W11 76 DA74
Bulow Est. SW6 90 DB82
Broughton Rd.
Bulstrode Ave., Houns. 86 BZ82
Bulstrode Gdns., Houns. 86 BZ83
Bulstrode La., Hem.H. 14 BG27
Bulstrode Pl. W1 4 G7
Bulstrode Rd., Houns. 86 CA83
Bulstrode St. W1 4 G8
Bulstrode St. W1 76 DG72
Bulwer Ct. Rd. E11 65 ED60
Bulwer Gdns., Barn. 34 DC42
Bulwer Rd.
Bulwer Rd. E11 65 ED59
Bulwer Rd. N18 50 DS49
Bulwer Rd., Barn. 34 DB42
Bulwer St. W12 75 CW74
Bumbles Grn. La., Wal.Abb. 24 EH25
Bunbury Way, Epsom 145 CV116
Bunce Dr., Cat. 148 DQ121
Coulsdon Rd.
Bunces La., Wdf.Grn. 52 EF52
Bungalow Rd. SE25 120 DS98
Bungalow Rd., Wok. 141 BQ124
Bungalows, The SW16 105 DH94
Bungalows, The, Wall. 133 DH106
Bunhill Row EC1 7 K4
Bunhill Row EC1 78 DR70
Bunhouse Pl. SW1 8 F10
Bunhouse Pl. SW1 90 DG78
Bunkers Hill NW11 62 DC59
Bunkers Hill, Belv. 96 FA77
Bunkers Hill, Sid. 110 EZ90
Bunkers La., Hem.H. 14 BN25
Bunning Way N7 77 DL66
Bunns La. NW7 46 CS51
Bunsen St. E3 79 DY68
Kenilworth Rd.
Bunting Clo. N9 51 DX46
Dunnock Clo.
Bunting Clo., Mitch. 118 DF99
Buntingbridge Rd., Ilf. 67 ER57
Bunton St. SE18 95 EN76
Creton St.
Bunyan Ct. EC2 78 DQ71
Beech St.
Bunyan Rd. E17 65 DY55
Buonaparte Ms. SW1 9 M10
Burbage Clo. SE1 11 K7
Burbage Clo. SE1 92 DR76
Burbage Clo. (Cheshunt), Wal.Cr. 23 DY31
Burbage Rd. SE21 106 DR87
Burbage Rd. SE24 106 DQ86
Burberry Clo., N.Mal. 116 CS96
Burbidge Rd., Shep. 112 BN98
Burbridge Way N17 50 DT54
Burcham St. E14 79 EB72
Burcharbro Rd. SE2 96 EX79
Burchell Ct. (Bushey), Wat. 44 CC45
Catsey La.
Burchell Rd. E10 65 EB60
Burchell Rd. SE15 92 DV81
Burchett Way, Rom. 68 EZ58
Burchetts Way, Shep. 113 BP100
Burchwall Clo., Rom. 55 FC52
Burcote, Wey. 127 BR107
Burcote Rd. SW18 104 DD87
Burcott Gdns., Add. 126 BJ107
Burcott Rd., Pur. 133 DN114
Burden Clo., Brent. 87 CJ78
Burden Way E11 66 EH61
Brading Cres.
Burdenshott Ave., Rich. 88 CP84
Burder Clo. N1 78 DS65
Burder Rd. N1 78 DS65
Balls Pond Rd.
Burdett Ave. SW20 117 CU95
Burdett Clo., Sid. 110 EY92
Burdett Ms. NW3 76 DD65
Belsize Cres.
Burdett Ms. W2 76 DB72
Hatherley Gro.
Burdett Rd. E3 79 DY70
Burdett Rd. E14 79 DZ71
Burdett Rd., Croy. 120 DR100
Burdett Rd., Rich. 88 CM82
Burdett St. SE1 10 D6
Burdetts Rd., Dag. 82 EZ67
Burdock Clo., Croy. 121 DX102
Burdock Rd. N17 64 DU55
Burdon La., Sutt. 131 CY108
Burdon Pk., Sutt. 131 CZ109
Burfield Clo. SW17 104 DD91
Burfield Dr., Warl. 148 DW119
Burford Clo., Dag. 68 EW62
Burford Clo., Ilf. 67 EQ56
Burford Clo., Uxb. 56 BL63
Burford Gdns. N13 49 DM48
Burford La., Epsom 131 CW111
Burford Rd. E6 80 EL69
Burford Rd. E15 79 ED66
Burford Rd. SE6 107 DZ89
Burford Rd., Brent. 88 CL78
Burford Rd., Brom. 122 EL98
Burford Rd., Sutt. 118 DA103
Burford Rd., Wor.Pk. 117 CT101
Burford Wk. SW6 90 DB80
Cambria St.
Burford Way, Croy. 135 EC107
Burgate Clo., Dart. 97 FF83
Burge St. SE1 11 L7
Burge St. SE1 92 DR76
Burges Ct. E6 81 EN66
Burges Gro. SW13 89 CV80
Burges Rd. E6 80 EL66
Burges Way, Stai. 98 BG92
Burgess Ave. NW9 60 CR58
Burgess Clo., Felt. 100 BY91
Burgess Ct., Borwd. 32 CM38
Belford Rd.
Burgess Hill NW2 62 DA63
Burgess Rd. E15 66 EE63
Burgess Rd., Sutt. 132 DB105
Burgess St. E14 79 EA71
Burgh Heath Rd., Epsom 130 CS114
Burgh Mt., Bans. 145 CZ115
Burgh St. N1 77 DP68
Burgh Wd., Bans. 145 CY115
Burghfield, Epsom 145 CT115
Burghill Rd. SE26 107 DY91
Burghley Ave., Borwd. 32 CQ43
Burghley Ave., N.Mal. 116 CR95
Burghley Pl., Mitch. 118 DF99
Burghley Rd. E11 66 EE60
Burghley Rd. N8 63 DN55
Burghley Rd. NW5 63 DH63
Burghley Rd. SW19 103 CX91
Burghley Twr. W3 75 CT73
Burgon St. EC4 6 G9
Burgos Gro. SE10 93 EB81
Burgoyne Rd. N4 63 DP58
Burgoyne Rd. SE25 120 DT98
Burgoyne Rd. SW9 91 DM83
Burgoyne Rd., Sun. 99 BS93
Burham Clo. SE20 106 DW94
Maple Rd.
Burhill Gro., Pnr. 44 BY54
Burhill Rd., Walt. 127 BV109
Burke Clo. SW15 88 CS84
Burke St. E16 80 EF72
Burket Clo., Sthl. 86 BZ77
Kingsbridge Rd.
Burland Rd. SW11 104 DF85
Burland Rd., Rom. 55 FC51
Burlea Clo., Walt. 127 BV106
Burleigh Ave., Sid. 109 ET85
Burleigh Ave., Wall. 118 DG104
Burleigh Clo., Add. 126 BH106
Burleigh Gdns. N14 49 DJ46
Burleigh Gdns., Ashf. 99 BQ92
Burleigh Ho. W10 75 CX71
St. Charles Sq.
Burleigh Pk., Cob. 128 BY112
Burleigh Pl. SW15 103 CX85
Burleigh Pl., Mitch. 118 DF99
Burleigh Rd., Add. 126 BH106
Burleigh Rd., Enf. 36 DS42
Burleigh Rd., Sutt. 117 CY102
Burleigh Rd., Uxb. 71 BP67
Burleigh Rd. (Cheshunt), Wal.Cr. 23 DY32
Burleigh St. WC2 6 A10
Burleigh Wk. SE6 107 EC88
Muirkirk Rd.
Burleigh Way, Enf. 36 DR41
Church St.
Burleigh Way (Cuffley), Pot.B. 21 DL30
Burley Clo. E4 51 EA50
Burley Clo. SW16 119 DK96
Burley Orchard, Cher. 112 BG100
Burley Rd. E16 80 EJ71
Burlings La., Sev. 151 ET118
Burlington Arc. W1 9 K1
Burlington Ave., Rich. 88 CN81
Burlington Ave., Rom. 69 FB58
Burlington Clo. E6 80 EL72
Northumberland Rd.
Burlington Clo. W9 75 CZ70
Burlington Clo., Felt. 99 BR87
Burlington Clo., Orp. 123 EP103
Burlington Clo., Pnr. 57 BV55
Tolcarne Dr.
Burlington Gdns. W1 9 K1
Burlington Gdns. W1 77 DJ73
Burlington Gdns. W3 74 CQ74
Burlington Gdns. W4 88 CQ78
Burlington Gdns., Rom. 68 EY59
Burlington La. W4 88 CS80
Burlington Ms. W3 74 CQ74
Burlington Pl. SW6 89 CY82
Burlington Rd.
Burlington Pl., Wdf.Grn. 52 EH48
Burlington Ri., Barn. 48 DE46
Burlington Rd. N10 48 DG54
Tetherdown
Burlington Rd. N17 50 DU53
Burlington Rd. SW6 89 CY82
Burlington Rd. W4 88 CQ78
Burlington Rd., Enf. 36 DR39
Burlington Rd., Islw. 87 CD81
Burlington Rd., N.Mal. 117 CT98
Burlington Rd., Th.Hth. 120 DQ96
Burma Rd. N16 64 DR63
Burmester Rd. SW17 104 DC90
Burn Clo., Add. 126 BK105
Burn Side N9 50 DW48
Burnaby Cres. W4 88 CQ79
Burnaby Gdns. W4 88 CP79
Burnaby St. SW10 90 DC80
Burnbrae Clo. N12 48 DB51
Burnbury Rd. SW12 105 DJ88
Burncroft Ave., Enf. 36 DW40
Burne Jones Ho. W14 89 CZ77
Burne St. NW1 4 B6
Burne St. NW1 76 DE71
Burnell Ave., Rich. 101 CJ92
Burnell Ave., Well. 96 EU82
Burnell Gdns., Stan. 45 CK53
Burnell Rd., Sutt. 132 DB105
Burnell Wk. SE1 92 DT78
Cadet Dr.
Burnels Ave. E6 81 EN69
Burness Clo. N7 77 DM65
Roman Way
Burness Clo., Uxb. 70 BK68
Whitehall Rd.
Burnet Gro., Epsom 130 CQ113
Burnett Clo. E9 64 DW64
Burney Ave., Surb. 116 CM99
Burney Dr., Loug. 39 EP40
Burney St. SE10 93 EC80
Burnfoot Ave. SW6 89 CY81
Burnfoot Ct. SE22 106 DV88
Burnham NW3 76 DE66
Burnham Ave., Uxb. 57 BQ63
Burnham Clo. NW7 47 CU52
Burnham Clo. SE1 92 DT77
Cadet Dr.
Burnham Clo., Enf. 36 DS38
Burnham Ct. NW4 61 CW56
Burnham Cres. E11 66 EJ56
Burnham Dr., Wor.Pk. 117 CX103
Burnham Gdns., Croy. 120 DT101
Burnham Gdns., Hayes 85 BR76
Burnham Gdns., Houns. 85 BV81
Burnham Rd. E4 51 DZ50
Burnham Rd., Dag. 82 EV66
Burnham Rd., Mord. 118 DB99
Burnham Rd., Rom. 69 FD55
Burnham Rd., Sid. 110 EY89
Burnham St. E2 78 DW69
Burnham St., Kings.T. 116 CN95
Burnham Way SE26 107 DZ92
Burnham Way W13 87 CH77
Burnhams Rd., Lthd. 142 BY124
Burnhill Rd., Beck. 121 EA96
Burnley Clo., Wat. 44 BW50
Burnley Rd. NW10 61 CT64
Burnley Rd. SW9 91 DM82
Burns Ave., Felt. 99 BU86
Burns Ave., Rom. 68 EW59
Burns Ave., Sid. 110 EU86
Burns Ave., Sthl. 72 CA73
Burns Clo. SW19 104 DD93
North Rd.
Burns Clo., Erith 97 FF81
Burns Clo., Hayes 71 BT71
Burns Clo., Well. 95 ET81
Burns Dr., Bans. 131 CY114
Burns Rd. NW10 75 CT67
Burns Rd. SW11 90 DF82
Burns Rd. W13 87 CH75
Burns Rd., Wem. 74 CL68
Burns Way, Houns. 86 BX82
Burnsall St. SW3 8 C10
Burnsall St. SW3 90 DE78
Burnside, Ash. 144 CM118
Burnside Ave. E4 51 DZ51
Burnside Clo. SE16 79 DX74
Burnside Clo., Barn. 34 DA41
Burnside Clo., Twick. 101 CG86
Burnside Cres., Wem. 73 CK67
Burnside Rd., Dag. 68 EW61
Burnt Ash Hill SE12 108 EF86
Burnt Ash La., Brom. 108 EG94
Burnt Ash Rd. SE12 108 EF85
Burnt Fm. Ride, Enf. 21 DP34
Burnt Fm. Ride, Wal.Cr. 21 DP31
Burnt Oak Bdy., Edg. 46 CP52
Burnt Oak Flds., Edg. 46 CQ53
Burnt Oak La., Sid. 110 EU89
Burnthwaite Rd. SW6 89 CZ80
Burntwood Clo. SW18 104 DD88
Burntwood Clo., Cat. 148 DU121
Burntwood Gra. Rd. SW18 104 DD88
Burntwood Gro., Sev. 155 FH127
Burntwood La. SW17 104 DC90
Burntwood La., Cat. 148 DS122
Burntwood Rd., Sev. 155 FH128
Burntwood Vw. SE19 106 DT92
Bowley La.
Buross St. E1 78 DV72
Commercial Rd.
Burr Clo. E1 78 DU74
Burr Clo., Bexh. 96 EZ83
Burr Clo., St.Alb. 18 CL27
Burr Rd. SW18 104 DA88
Burrage Gro. SE18 95 EQ77
Burrage Pl. SE18 95 EP78
Burrage Rd. SE18 95 EQ77
Burrard Rd. E16 80 EH72
Burrard Rd. NW6 62 DA64
Burrell Clo., Croy. 121 DY100
Burrell Clo., Edg. 46 CP47
Burrell Row, Beck. 121 EA96
High St.
Burrell St. SE1 10 F2
Burrell St. SE1 77 DP74
Burrell Twr. E10 65 EA59
Burrells Wf. Sq. E14 93 EB78
Burrfield Dr., Orp. 124 EX99
Burritt Rd., Kings.T. 116 CN96
Burroughs, The NW4 61 CV56
Burroughs Gdns. NW4 61 CV56
Burrow Clo., Chig. 53 ET50
Burrow Rd.
Burrow Grn., Chig. 53 ET50
Burrow Rd. SE22 92 DS84
Burrow Rd., Chig. 53 ET50
Burrow Wk. SE21 106 DQ87
Rosendale Rd.
Burrows Clo., Lthd. 142 BZ124
Burrows Hill Clo., Houns. 84 BJ84
Burrows Hill La., Houns. 84 BH84
Burrows Ms. SE1 10 F4
Burrows Rd. NW10 75 CW69
Bursdon Clo., Sid. 109 ET89
Bursland Rd., Enf. 37 DX42
Burslem Ave., Ilf. 54 EU51
Burslem St. E1 78 DU72
Burstead Clo., Cob. 128 BX112
Burstock Rd. SW15 89 CY84
Burston Dr., St.Alb. 16 CC28
Burston Rd. SW15 103 CX85
Burston Vill. SW15 103 CX85
St. John's Ave.
Burstow Rd. SW20 117 CY95
Burt Rd. E16 80 EJ74
Burtenshaw Rd., T.Ditt. 115 CG101
Burtley Clo. N4 64 DQ60
Burton Ave., Wat. 29 BU42
Burton Clo., Chess. 129 CK108
Burton Ct. SW3 90 DF78
Franklin's Row
Burton Gdns., Houns. 86 BZ81
Burton Gro. SE17 92 DR78
Portland St.
Burton La. SW9 91 DN82
Burton La. (Cheshunt), Wal.Cr. 22 DS29
Burton Ms. SW1 8 G9
Burton Pl. WC1 5 N3
Burton Rd. E18 66 EH55
Burton Rd. NW6 75 CZ66
Burton Rd. SW9 91 DP82
Burton Rd., Kings.T. 102 CL94
Burton Rd., Loug. 39 EQ42
Burton St. WC1 5 N3
Burton St. WC1 77 DK69
Burtonhole Clo. NW7 47 CX49
Burtonhole La. NW7 47 CW50
Burtons Rd., Hmptn. 100 CB91
Burtwell La. SE27 106 DR91
Burwash Ct., Orp. 124 EW99
Rookery Gdns.
Burwash Ho. SE1 11 L5
Burwash Rd. SE18 95 ER78
Burway Cres., Cher. 112 BG97
Burwell Ave., Grnf. 73 CE65
Burwell Clo. E1 78 DV72
Bigland St.
Burwell Rd. E10 65 DY60
Burwell Wk. E3 79 EA70
Burwood Ave., Brom. 122 EH103
Burwood Ave., Ken. 133 DP114
Burwood Ave., Pnr. 57 BV57
Burwood Clo., Surb. 116 CN102
Burwood Clo., Walt. 128 BW107
Burwood Gdns., Rain. 83 FF69
Burwood Pk. Rd., Walt. 127 BV105
Burwood Pl. W2 4 C8

Burwood Pl. W2 76 DE72
Burwood Rd., Walt. 127 BS108
Bury Ave., Hayes 71 BS68
Bury Ave., Ruis. 57 BQ58
Bury Clo. SE16 79 DX74
Rotherhithe St.
Bury Ct. EC3 7 N8
Bury Grn. Rd. (Cheshunt), Wal.Cr. 22 DU31
Bury Gro., Mord. 118 DB99
Bury La., Epp. 25 ER28
Bury La., Rick. 42 BK46
Bury Meadows, Rick. 42 BK46
Bury Pl. WC1 5 P7
Bury Pl. WC1 77 DL71
Bury Rd. E4 38 EE42
Bury Rd. N22 63 DN55
Bury Rd., Dag. 69 FB64
Bury Rd., Epp. 25 ES31
Bury St. EC3 7 N9
Bury St. EC3 78 DS72
Bury St. N9 50 DT45
Bury St. SW1 9 K2
Bury St. SW1 77 DJ74
Bury St., Ruis. 57 BQ57
Bury St. W. N9 50 DR45
Bury Wk. SW3 8 B9
Bury Wk. SW3 90 DE77
Burydell La., St.Alb. 17 CD27
Busbridge Ho. E14 79 EA71
Brabazon St.
Busby Ms. NW5 77 DK65
Busby Pl. NW5 77 DK65
Busby St. E2 78 DT70
Chilton St.
Bush Clo., Add. 126 BJ106
Bush Clo., Ilf. 67 ER57
Bush Cotts. SW18 104 DA85
Putney Bri. Rd.
Bush Ct. W12 89 CX75
Bush Elms Rd., Horn. 69 FG59
Bush Gro. NW9 60 CQ59
Bush Gro., Stan. 45 CK52
Bush Hill N21 50 DQ45
Bush Hill Rd. N21 36 DR44
Bush Hill Rd., Har. 60 CM58
Bush Ind. Est. NW10 74 CR70
Bush La. EC4 7 K10
Bush Rd. E8 78 DV67
Bush Rd. E11 66 EF59
Bush Rd. SE8 93 DX77
Bush Rd., Buck.H. 52 EK49
Bush Rd., Rich. 88 CM79
Bush Rd., Shep. 112 BM99
Bushbaby Clo. SE1 11 M7
Bushbarns (Cheshunt), Wal.Cr. 22 DU29
Bushberry Rd. E9 79 DY65
Bushell Clo. SW2 105 DM89
Bushell Grn. (Bushey), Wat. 45 CD47
Bushell St. E1 78 DU74
Hermitage Wall
Bushell Way, Chis. 109 EN92
Bushey Ave. E18 66 EF55
Bushey Ave., Orp. 123 ER101
Bushey Clo. E4 51 EC48
Bushey Clo., Ken. 148 DS116
Bushey Clo., Uxb. 56 BN61
Bushey Ct. SW20 117 CV97
Bushey Down SW12 105 DH89
Bedford Hill
Bushey Gro. Rd. (Bushey), Wat. 30 BX42
Bushey Hall Dr. (Bushey), Wat. 30 BY42
Bushey Hall Rd. (Bushey), Wat. 30 BX42
Bushey Hill Rd. SE5 92 DS81
Bushey La., Sutt. 118 DA104
Bushey Lees, Sid. 109 ET86
Fen Gro.
Bushey Mill Cres., Wat. 30 BW37
Bushey Mill La., Wat. 30 BW37
Bushey Mill La. (Bushey), Wat. 30 BY38
Bushey Rd. E13 80 EJ68
Bushey Rd. N15 64 DS58
Bushey Rd. SW20 117 CV97
Bushey Rd., Croy. 121 EA103
Bushey Rd., Hayes 85 BS77
Bushey Rd., Sutt. 132 DA105
Bushey Rd., Uxb. 56 BN61
Bushey Shaw, Ash. 143 CH117
Bushey Vw. Wk., Wat. 30 BW40
Raphael Dr.
Bushey Way, Beck. 121 ED100
Bushfield Clo., Edg. 46 CP47
Bushfield Cres., Edg. 46 CP47
Bushfields, Loug. 39 EN43
Bushgrove Rd., Dag. 68 EX63
Bushmead Clo. N15 64 DT56
Copperfield Dr.
Bushmoor Cres. SE18 95 EQ80
Bushnell Rd. SW17 105 DH89
Bushrise, Wat. 29 BU36
Bushway, Dag. 68 EX63
Bushwood E11 66 EF60
Bushwood Dr. SE1 92 DT77
Bushwood Rd., Rich. 88 CN79
Bushy Pk., Hmptn. 115 CF95
Bushy Pk., Tedd. 115 CF95
Bushy Pk. Gdns., Tedd. 101 CD92
Bushy Pk. Rd., Tedd. 101 CH94
Bushy Rd., Lthd. 142 CB122
Bushy Rd., Tedd. 101 CF93
Butcher Row E1 79 DX73
Butcher Row E14 79 DX73
Butchers Rd. E16 80 EG72
Bute Ave., Rich. 102 CL89
Bute Ct., Wall. 133 DJ106
Bute Rd.
Bute Gdns. W6 89 CX77
Bute Gdns., Wall. 133 DJ106
Bute Gdns. W., Wall. 133 DJ106
Bute Rd., Croy. 119 DN102
Bute Rd., Ilf. 67 EP57
Bute Rd., Wall. 133 DJ105
Bute St. SW7 90 DD77
Bute Wk. N1 78 DR65
Marquess Rd.
Butler Ave., Har. 59 CD59
Butler Pl. SW1 9 M6
Butler Rd. NW10 75 CT66
Curzon Cres.
Butler Rd., Dag. 68 EV63
Butler Rd., Har. 58 CC59
Butler St. E2 78 DW69
Knottisford St.
Butler St., Uxb. 71 BP70
Butlers Dene Rd., Cat. 149 DZ119
Butlers Dr. E4 37 EC38
Butlers Wf. SE1 92 DT75
Lafone St.
Butter Hill, Cars. 118 DG104
Butter Hill, Wall. 118 DG104
Buttercross La., Epp. 26 EU30
Buttercup Sq., Stai. 98 BK88
Diamedes Ave.
Butterfield Clo. SE16 92 DV75
Wilson Gro.
Butterfield Clo., Twick. 101 CF86
Rugby Rd.
Butterfield Sq. E6 81 EM72
Harper Rd.
Butterfields E17 65 EC57
Butterfly La. SE9 109 EP86
Butterfly La., Borwd. 31 CH41
Butterfly Wk. SE5 92 DR81
Denmark Hill
Butterfly Wk., Warl. 148 DW120
Butteridges Clo., Dag. 82 EZ67
Buttermere Clo. SE1 11 P9
Buttermere Clo., Felt. 99 BT88
Buttermere Clo., Mord. 117 CX100
Buttermere Dr. SW15 103 CY85
Buttermere Gdns., Pur. 134 DR113
Buttermere Rd., Orp. 124 EX98
Buttermere Wk. E8 78 DT65
Butterwick W6 89 CW77
Butterwick, Wat. 30 BY36
Butterworth Gdns., Wdf.Grn. 52 EG50
Harts Gro.
Buttesland St. N1 7 L2
Buttesland St. N1 78 DR69
Buttfield Clo., Dag. 83 FB65
Buttmarsh Clo. SE18 95 EP78
Butts, The, Brent. 87 CJ79
Butts, The, Sev. 153 FH116
Butts, The, Sun. 114 BW97
Elizabeth Gdns.
Butts Cotts., Felt. 100 BZ90
Butts Cres., Felt. 100 CA90
Butts Piece, Nthlt. 71 BV68
Longhook Gdns.
Butts Rd., Brom. 108 EE92
Buttsbury Rd., Ilf. 67 EQ64
Buttsmead, Nthwd. 43 BQ52
Buxted Rd. E8 78 DT66
Buxted Rd. N12 48 DE50
Buxted Rd. SE22 92 DS84
Buxton Ave., Cat. 148 DS121
Buxton Clo., Wdf.Grn. 52 EK51
Buxton Ct. N1 7 J2
Buxton Cres., Sutt. 131 CY105
Buxton Dr. E11 66 EE56
Buxton Dr., N.Mal. 116 CR96
Buxton Gdns. W3 74 CP73
Buxton La., Cat. 148 DR120
Buxton Path, Wat. 44 BW48
Buxton Rd. E4 51 ED45
Buxton Rd. E6 80 EL69
Buxton Rd. E15 66 EE64
Buxton Rd. E17 65 DY56
Buxton Rd. N19 63 DK60
Buxton Rd. NW2 75 CV65
Buxton Rd. SW14 88 CS83
Buxton Rd., Ashf. 98 BK92
Buxton Rd., Epp. 39 ES36
Buxton Rd., Erith 97 FD80
Buxton Rd., Ilf. 67 ES58
Buxton Rd., Th.Hth. 119 DP99
Buxton Rd., Wal.Abb. 24 EG33
Buxton St. E1 78 DT70
Buzzard Creek Ind. Est., Bark. 81 ET71
By the Wd., Wat. 44 BX47
Byam St. SW6 90 DC82
Byards Cft. SW16 119 DK95
Byatt Wk., Hmptn. 100 BY93
Victors Dr.
Bychurch End, Tedd. 101 CF92
Church Rd.
Bycroft Rd., Sthl. 72 CA70
Bycroft St. SE20 107 DX94
Parish La.
Bycullah Ave., Enf. 35 DP41
Bycullah Rd., Enf. 35 DP40
Bye, The W3 74 CS72
Bye Way, The, Har. 45 CF53
Bye Ways, Twick. 100 CB90
Byegrove Rd. SW19 104 DD93
Byers Clo., Pot.B. 20 DC34
Byeway, The SW14 88 CQ83
Byeway, The, Epsom 131 CT105
Byeway, The, Rick. 42 BL47
Byeways, The, Ash. 143 CK118
Skinners La.
Byeways, The, Surb. 116 CN99
Byfeld Gdns. SW13 89 CU81
Byfield Clo. SE16 93 DY75
Byfield Rd., Islw. 87 CG83
Byfleet Ind. Est., W.Byf. 126 BK111
Byfleet Rd., Add. 126 BK109
Byfleet Rd., Cob. 126 BN112
Byford Clo. E15 80 EE66
Bygrove, Croy. 135 EB107
Bygrove St. E14 79 EB72
Byland Clo. N21 49 DM45
Bylands Clo. SE2 96 EV76
Finchale Rd.
Bylands Clo. SE16 79 DX74
Rotherhithe St.
Byne Rd. SE26 106 DW93
Byne Rd., Cars. 118 DE103
Bynes Rd., S.Croy. 134 DR108
Byng Dr., Pot.B. 20 DA31
Byng Pl. WC1 5 M5
Byng Pl. WC1 77 DK70
Byng Rd., Barn. 33 CX41
Byng St. E14 93 EA75
Bynon Ave., Bexh. 96 EZ83
Byre, The N14 35 DH44
Farm La.
Byre Rd. N14 34 DG44
Farm La.
Byrne Rd. SW12 105 DH88
Byron Ave. E12 80 EL65
Byron Ave. E18 66 EF55
Byron Ave. NW9 60 CP56
Byron Ave., Borwd. 32 CN43
Byron Ave., Couls. 147 DL115
Byron Ave., Houns. 85 BU82
Byron Ave., N.Mal. 117 CU99
Byron Ave., Sutt. 132 DD105
Byron Ave., Wat. 30 BX39
Byron Ave. E., Sutt. 132 DD105
Byron Clo. E8 78 DU67
Byron Clo. SE26 107 DY91
Porthcawe Rd.
Byron Clo. SE28 82 EW74
Byron Clo., Hmptn. 100 BZ91
Byron Clo., Wal.Cr. 22 DT27
Allard Clo.
Byron Clo., Walt. 114 BY102
Byron Ct. W9 76 DA70
Lanhill Rd.
Byron Ct., Enf. 35 DP40
Bycullah Rd.
Byron Dr. N2 62 DD58
Byron Dr., Erith 97 FB81
Belmont Rd.
Byron Gdns., Sutt. 132 DD105
Byron Hill Rd., Har. 59 CD60
Byron Ho., Beck. 107 EB93
Byron Ms. NW3 62 DE63
Byron Ms. W9 76 DA70
Shirland Rd.
Byron Pl., Lthd. 143 CH122
Byron Rd. E10 65 EB60
Byron Rd. E17 65 EA55
Byron Rd. NW2 61 CV61
Byron Rd. NW7 47 CU50
Byron Rd. W5 74 CM74
Byron Rd., Add. 126 BK105
Byron Rd., Har. 59 CE58
Byron Rd. (Wealdstone), Har. 45 CF54
Byron Rd., S.Croy. 134 DV110
Byron Rd., Wem. 59 CJ61
Byron St. E14 79 EC72
St. Leonards Rd.
Byron Ter. N9 50 DW45
Byron Way, Hayes 71 BS70
Byron Way, Nthlt. 72 BY69
Byron Way, West Dr. 84 BM77
Bysouth Clo., Ilf. 53 EP53
Bythorn St. SW9 91 DM84
Byton Rd. SW17 104 DF93
Byward Ave., Felt. 100 BW86
Byward St. EC3 11 N1
Byward St. EC3 78 DS73
Bywater Pl. SE16 79 DY74
Bywater St. SW3 8 D10
Bywater St. SW3 90 DF78
Byway, The, Pot.B. 20 DA33
Byway, The, Sutt. 132 DD109
Bywell Pl. W1 5 K7
Bywood Ave., Croy. 120 DW100
Bywood Clo., Ken. 147 DP115
Byworth Wk. N19 63 DK60
Courtauld Rd.

C

C.I. Twr., N.Mal. 116 CS97
Cabbell Pl., Add. 126 BJ105
Cabbell St. NW1 4 B7
Cabbell St. NW1 76 DE71
Cabinet Way E4 51 DZ51
Cable Pl. SE10 93 EC81
Diamond Ter.
Cable St. E1 78 DU73
Cabot Sq. E14 79 EA74
Cabot Way E6 80 EK67
Parr Rd.
Cabul Rd. SW11 90 DE82
Cackets La., Sev. 151 ER115
Cactus Wk. W12 75 CT73
Du Cane Rd.
Cadbury Clo., Islw. 87 CG81
Cadbury Clo., Sun. 99 BS94
Cadbury Rd., Sun. 99 BS94
Cadbury Way SE16 92 DU76
Yalding Rd.
Caddington Clo., Barn. 34 DE43
Caddington Rd. NW2 61 CY62
Caddis Clo., Stan. 45 CF52
Daventer Dr.
Cade La., Sev. 155 FJ128
Cade Rd. SE10 93 ED81
Cadell Clo. E2 78 DT69
Shipton St.
Cader Rd. SW18 104 DC86
Cadet Dr. SE1 92 DT78
Cadet Pl. SE10 94 EE78
Cadiz Rd., Dag. 83 FC66
Cadiz St. SE17 92 DQ78
Cadley Ter. SE23 106 DW89
Cadlocks Hill, Sev. 138 EZ110
Cadmer Clo., N.Mal. 116 CS98
Cadmore La. (Cheshunt), Wal.Cr. 23 DX28
Cadmus Clo. SW4 91 DK83
Aristotle Rd.
Cadogan Clo., Beck. 121 ED95
Albemarle Rd.
Cadogan Clo., Har. 58 CB63
Cadogan Clo., Tedd. 101 CE92
Cadogan Ct., Sutt. 132 DB107
Cadogan Gdns. E18 66 EH55
Cadogan Gdns. N3 48 DB53
Cadogan Gdns. N21 35 DN43
Cadogan Gdns. SW3 8 E8
Cadogan Gdns. SW3 90 DF77
Cadogan Gate SW1 8 E8
Cadogan Gate SW1 90 DF77
Cadogan La. SW1 8 F7
Cadogan La. SW1 90 DG76
Cadogan Pl. SW1 8 E6
Cadogan Pl. SW1 90 DF76
Cadogan Rd., Surb. 115 CK99
Cadogan Sq. SW1 8 E7
Cadogan Sq. SW1 90 DF76
Cadogan St. SW3 8 D9
Cadogan St. SW3 90 DF77
Cadogan Ter. E9 79 DZ65
Cadoxton Ave. N15 64 DT58
Cadwallon Rd. SE9 109 EP89
Caedmon Rd. N7 63 DM63
Caen Wd. Rd., Ash. 143 CJ118
Caenshill Rd., Wey. 126 BN108
Caenwood Clo., Wey. 126 BN107
Caerleon Clo., Sid. 110 EW92
Caerleon Ter. SE2 96 EV77
Blithdale Rd.
Caernarvon Clo., Mitch. 119 DL97
Caernarvon Dr., Ilf. 53 EN53
Caesars Wk., Mitch. 118 DF99
Caesars Way, Shep. 113 BR100
Cage Pond Rd., Rad. 18 CM33
Cage Rd. E16 80 EE71
Malmesbury Rd.
Cahill St. EC1 7 J5
Cahir St. E14 93 EB77
Caillard Rd., W.Byf. 126 BL111
Cains La., Felt. 99 BR85
Caird St. W10 75 CY69
Cairn Ave. W5 73 CK74
Cairn Way, Stan. 45 CF51
Cairndale Clo., Brom. 108 EF94
Cairnfield Ave. NW2 60 CS62
Cairngorm Clo., Tedd. 101 CG92
Vicarage Rd.
Cairns Ave., Wdf.Grn. 52 EL51
Cairns Rd. SW11 104 DE85
Cairo New Rd., Croy. 119 DP103
Cairo Rd. E17 65 EA56
Caishowe Rd., Borwd. 32 CP39
Caistor Ms. SW12 105 DH87
Caistor Rd.
Caistor Pk. Rd. E15 80 EF67
Caistor Rd. SW12 105 DH87
Caithness Gdns., Sid. 109 ET86
Caithness Rd. W14 89 CX76
Caithness Rd., Mitch. 105 DH94
Calabria Rd. N5 77 DP65
Calais Gate SE5 91 DP81
Calais St.
Calais St. SE5 91 DP81
Calbourne Ave., Horn. 69 FH64
Calbourne Rd. SW12 104 DF87
Calcott Wk. SE9 108 EL91
Caldbeck, Wal.Abb. 23 ED34
Caldbeck Ave., Wor.Pk. 117 CU103
Caldecot Ave., Wal.Cr. 22 DT29
Caldecot Rd. SE5 92 DQ82
Caldecote Gdns. (Bushey), Wat. 31 CE44
Caldecote La. (Bushey), Wat. 45 CF45
Caldecott Way E5 65 DX62
Calder Ave., Grnf. 73 CF68
Calder Ave., Hat. 20 DA26
Calder Clo., Enf. 36 DS41
Calder Gdns., Edg. 60 CN55
Calder Rd., Mord. 118 DC99
Calderon Pl. W10 75 CW71
St. Quintin Gdns.
Calderon Rd. E11 65 EC63
Caldervale Rd. SW4 105 DK85
Calderwood St. SE18 95 EN77
Caldicot Grn. NW9 60 CS58
Snowdon Dr.
Caldwell Rd., Wat. 44 BX49
Caldwell St. SW9 91 DM80
Caldwell Yd. EC4 78 DQ73
Upper Thames St.
Caldy Rd., Belv. 97 FB76
Caldy Wk. N1 78 DQ65
Clephane Rd.
Cale St. SW3 8 B10
Cale St. SW3 90 DE78
Caleb St. SE1 11 H4
Caledon Rd. E6 80 EL67
Caledon Rd., St.Alb. 17 CJ26
Caledon Rd., Wall. 132 DG105
Caledonia Rd., Stai. 98 BL87
Caledonia St. N1 6 A1
Caledonia St. N1 77 DL68
Caledonian Clo., Ilf. 68 EV60
Caledonian Rd. N1 6 A1
Caledonian Rd. N1 77 DL68
Caledonian Rd. N7 63 DM63
Caledonian Wf. Rd. E14 93 ED77
Caletock Way SE10 94 EF78
Calico Row SW11 90 DC83
York Pl.
Calidore Clo. SW2 105 DM86
Endymion Rd.
California La. (Bushey), Wat. 45 CD46
California Rd., N.Mal. 116 CQ97
Callaby Ter. N1 78 DR65
Wakeham St.
Callaghan Clo. SE13 94 EE84
Glenton Rd.
Callander Rd. SE6 107 EB89
Callard Ave. N13 49 DP50
Callcott Rd. NW6 75 CZ66
Callcott St. W8 76 DA74
Hillgate Pl.
Callendar Rd. SW7 90 DD76
Calley Down Cres., Croy. 135 ED110
Callingham Clo. E14 79 DZ71
Wallwood St.
Callis Fm. Clo., Stai. 98 BL86
Bedfont Rd.
Callis Rd. E17 65 DZ58
Callow Fld., Pur. 133 DN113
Callow St. SW3 90 DD79
Callowland Clo., Wat. 29 BV38
Calmington Rd. SE5 92 DS78
Calmont Rd., Brom. 107 ED93
Calne Ave., Ilf. 53 EP53
Calonne Rd. SW19 103 CX91
Calshot Rd., Houns. 84 BN82
Calshot St. N1 77 DM68
Calshot Way, Enf. 35 DP41
Calthorpe Gdns., Edg. 46 CL50
Jesmond Way
Calthorpe Gdns., Sutt. 118 DC104
Calthorpe St. WC1 6 C4
Calthorpe St. WC1 77 DM70
Calton Ave. SE21 106 DS86
Calton Rd., Barn. 34 DC44
Calverley Clo., Beck. 107 EB93
Calverley Cres., Dag. 68 FA61
Calverley Gdns., Har. 59 CK59
Calverley Gro. N19 63 DK60
Calverley Rd., Epsom 131 CU107
Calvert Ave. E2 7 N3
Calvert Ave. E2 78 DS69
Calvert Clo., Belv. 96 FA77
Calvert Clo., Sid. 110 EY93
Calvert Rd. SE10 94 EF78
Calvert Rd., Barn. 33 CX40
Calvert St. NW1 76 DG67
Chalcot Rd.
Calverton SE5 92 DS79
Albany Rd.
Calverton Rd. E6 81 EN67
Calvert's Bldgs. SE1 11 K3
Calvin Clo., Orp. 124 EX97
Calvin St. E1 7 P5
Calvin St. E1 78 DT70
Calydon Rd. SE7 94 EH78
Calypso Way SE16 93 DZ77
Cam Rd. E15 79 ED67
Camac Rd., Twick. 101 CD88
Cambalt Rd. SW15 103 CX85
Camberley Ave. SW20 117 CV96
Camberley Ave., Enf. 36 DS42
Camberley Clo., Sutt. 117 CX104
Camberley Rd., Houns. 84 BN83
Cambert Way SE3 94 EH84
Camberwell Ch. St. SE5 92 DR81
Camberwell Glebe SE5 92 DS81
Camberwell Grn. SE5 92 DR81
Camberwell Gro. SE5 92 DR81
Camberwell New Rd. SE5 91 DN79
Camberwell Pas. SE5 92 DQ81
Camberwell Grn.
Camberwell Rd. SE5 92 DQ79
Camberwell Sta. Rd. SE5 92 DQ81
Cambeys Rd., Dag. 69 FB64
Camborne Ave. W13 87 CH75
Camborne Ms. W11 75 CY72
St. Marks Rd.
Camborne Rd. SW18 104 DA87
Camborne Rd., Croy. 120 DU101
Camborne Rd., Houns. 84 BN83
Camborne Rd., Mord. 117 CX99
Camborne Rd., Sid. 110 EW90
Camborne Rd., Sutt. 132 DA108
Camborne Rd., Well. 95 ET82
Camborne Way, Houns. 86 CA81
Cambourne Ave. N9 51 DX45
Cambray Rd. SW12 105 DJ88
Cambray Rd., Orp. 123 ET101
Cambria Clo., Houns. 86 CA84
Cambria Clo., Sid. 109 ER88

Cambria Ct., Felt. 99 BV87
Hounslow Rd.
Cambria Gdns., Stai. 98 BL87
Cambria Rd. SE5 92 DQ83
Cambria St. SW6 90 DB80
Cambrian Ave., Ilf. 67 ES57
Cambrian Clo. SE27 105 DP90
Cambrian Rd. E10 65 EA59
Cambrian Rd., Rich. 102 CM86
Cambridge Ave. NW6 76 DA68
Cambridge Ave., Grnf. 59 CF64
Cambridge Ave., N.Mal. 116 CS96
Cambridge Ave., Well. 95 ET84
Cambridge Barracks Rd. SE18 95 EM77
Cambridge Circ. WC2 5 N9
Cambridge Circ. WC2 77 DK72
Cambridge Clo. N22 49 DN53
Pellatt Gro.
Cambridge Clo. NW10 60 CQ62
Cambridge Clo. SW20 117 CV95
Cambridge Clo., Houns. 86 BY84
Cambridge Clo. (Cheshunt), Wal.Cr. 22 DW29
Cambridge Clo., West Dr. 84 BK79
Cambridge Cotts., Rich. 88 CN79
Cambridge Cres. E2 78 DV68
Cambridge Cres., Tedd. 101 CG92
Cambridge Dr. SE12 108 EG85
Cambridge Dr., Pot.B. 19 CX31
Cambridge Dr., Ruis. 58 BX61
Cambridge Gdns. N10 48 DG53
Cambridge Gdns. N13 49 DN50
Cambridge Gdns. N17 50 DR52
Great Cambridge Rd.
Cambridge Gdns. N21 50 DR45
Cambridge Gdns. NW6 76 DA68
Cambridge Gdns. W10 75 CX72
Cambridge Gdns., Enf. 36 DU40
Cambridge Gdns., Kings.T. 116 CN96
Cambridge Gate NW1 5 J4
Cambridge Gate Ms. NW1 5 J4
Cambridge Grn. SE9 109 EP88
Cambridge Gro. SE20 120 DV95
Cambridge Gro. W6 89 CV77
Cambridge Gro. Rd., Kings.T. 116 CN97
Cambridge Heath Rd. E1 78 DV70
Cambridge Heath Rd. E2 78 DW70
Cambridge Mans. SW11 90 DF81
Cambridge Rd.
Cambridge Par., Enf. 36 DU39
Great Cambridge Rd.
Cambridge Pk. E11 66 EG59
Cambridge Pk., Twick. 101 CJ86
Cambridge Pk. Rd. E11 66 EF59
Cambridge Pl. W8 90 DB75
Cambridge Rd. E4 51 ED46
Cambridge Rd. E11 66 EF58
Cambridge Rd. NW6 76 DA69
Cambridge Rd. SE20 120 DV97
Cambridge Rd. SW11 90 DF81
Cambridge Rd. SW13 89 CT82
Cambridge Rd. SW20 117 CV95
Cambridge Rd. W7 87 CF75
Cambridge Rd., Ashf. 99 BQ94
Cambridge Rd., Bark. 81 EQ66
Cambridge Rd., Brom. 108 EG94
Cambridge Rd., Cars. 132 DE107
Cambridge Rd., Hmptn. 100 BZ94
Cambridge Rd., Har. 58 CA57
Cambridge Rd., Houns. 86 BY84
Cambridge Rd., Ilf. 67 ES60
Cambridge Rd., Kings.T. 116 CN96
Cambridge Rd., Mitch. 119 DH97
Cambridge Rd., N.Mal. 116 CR98
Cambridge Rd., Rich. 88 CN80
Cambridge Rd., Sid. 109 ES91
Cambridge Rd., Sthl. 72 BZ74
Cambridge Rd., Tedd. 101 CF91
Cambridge Rd., Twick. 101 CK86
Cambridge Rd., Uxb. 70 BK65
Cambridge Rd., Walt. 113 BV100
Cambridge Rd., Wat. 30 BW42
Cambridge Rd., W.Mol. 114 BZ98
Cambridge Rd. Est., Kings.T. 116 CN96
Cambridge Rd. N. W4 88 CP78
Cambridge Rd. S. W4 88 CP78
Oxford Rd. S.
Cambridge Row SE18 95 EP78
Cambridge Sq. W2 4 B8
Cambridge Sq. W2 76 DE72
Cambridge St. SW1 9 J10
Cambridge St. SW1 91 DH77
Cambridge Ter. N13 49 DN50
Cambridge Ter. NW1 5 H3
Cambridge Ter. Ms. NW1 5 J3
Cambus Clo., Hayes 72 BY71
Cambus Rd. E16 80 EG71
Camdale Rd. SE18 95 ET80
Camden Ave., Felt. 100 BW89
Camden Ave., Hayes 72 BX73
Camden Clo., Chis. 123 EQ95
Camden Est. SE15 92 DT81
Camden Gdns. NW1 77 DH66
Kentish Town Rd.
Camden Gdns., Sutt. 132 DB106
Camden Gdns., Th.Hth. 119 DP97
Camden Gro., Chis. 109 EP93
Camden High St. NW1 77 DH67
Camden Hill Rd. SE19 106 DS93
Camden La. N7 77 DK65
Camden Lock Pl. NW1 77 DH66
Chalk Fm. Rd.
Camden Ms. NW1 77 DJ66
Camden Pk. Rd. NW1 77 DK65
Camden Pk. Rd., Chis. 109 EM94
Camden Pas. N1 77 DP67
Camden Rd. E11 66 EH58
Camden Rd. E17 65 DZ58
Camden Rd. N7 63 DL63
Camden Rd. NW1 77 DJ66
Camden Rd., Bex. 110 EY88
Camden Rd., Cars. 132 DF105
Camden Rd., Sev. 155 FH122
Camden Rd., Sutt. 132 DA106
Camden Row SE3 94 EE82
Camden Sq. NW1 77 DK65
Camden Sq. SE15 92 DT81
Exeter Rd.
Camden St. NW1 77 DJ66
Camden Ter. NW1 77 DK65
North Vill.
Camden Wk. N1 77 DP67
Camden Way, Chis. 109 EM94
Camden Way, Th.Hth. 119 DP97
Camdenhurst St. E14 79 DY72
Camel Gro., Kings.T. 101 CK92
Camel Rd. E16 80 EK74
Camelford Wk. W11 75 CY72
Lancaster Rd.
Camellia Ct., Wdf.Grn. 52 EE52
Bridle Path
Camellia Pl., Twick. 100 CB87
Camellia St. SW8 91 DL80
Camelot Clo. SE28 95 ER75
Camelot Clo. SW19 104 DA91
Camelot Clo., West. 150 EJ116
Camelot St. SE15 92 DV80
Bird in Bush Rd.
Camera Pl. SW10 90 DD79
Cameron Clo. N18 50 DV49
Cameron Clo. N20 48 DE47
Myddelton Pk.
Cameron Clo., Bex. 111 FD90
Cameron Dr., Wal.Cr. 23 DX34
Cameron Pl. E1 78 DV72
Varden St.
Cameron Rd. SE6 107 DZ89
Cameron Rd., Brom. 122 EG98
Cameron Rd., Croy. 119 DP100
Cameron Rd., Ilf. 67 ES60
Cameron Sq., Mitch. 118 DE95
Camerton Clo. E8 78 DT65
Buttermere Wk.
Camgate Est., Stai. 98 BM86
Camilla Clo., Sun. 99 BS93
Camilla Rd. SE16 92 DV77
Camille Clo. SE25 120 DU97
Camlan Rd., Brom. 108 EF91
Camlet St. E2 7 P4
Camlet St. E2 78 DT70
Camlet Way, Barn. 34 DA40
Camley St. NW1 77 DK66
Camm Gdns., Kings.T. 116 CM96
Church Rd.
Camm Gdns., T.Ditt. 115 CE101
Camomile Ave., Mitch. 118 DF95
Camomile St. EC3 7 M8
Camomile St. EC3 78 DS72
Camp End Rd., Wey. 127 BR110
Camp Rd. SW19 103 CV92
Camp Rd., Cat. 149 DY120
Camp Vw. SW19 103 CV92
Campana Rd. SW6 90 DA81
Campbell Ave., Ilf. 67 EP56
Campbell Clo. SE18 95 EN81
Moordown
Campbell Clo. SW16 105 DK92
Campbell Clo. Rom. (Havering-atte-Bower) 55 FE51
Campbell Clo., Ruis. 57 BU58
Campbell Clo., Twick. 101 CD89
Campbell Ct. N17 50 DT53
Campbell Cft., Edg. 46 CN50
Campbell Gordon Way NW2 61 CV63
Campbell Rd. E3 79 EA69
Campbell Rd. E6 80 EL67
Campbell Rd. E15 66 EF63
Trevelyan Rd.
Campbell Rd. E17 65 DZ56
Campbell Rd. N17 50 DT53
Campbell Rd. W7 73 CE73
Campbell Rd., Cat. 148 DR121
Campbell Rd., Croy. 119 DP101
Campbell Rd., E.Mol. 115 CF97
Hampton Ct. Rd.
Campbell Rd., Twick. 101 CD88
Campbell Rd., Wey. 126 BN108
Campbell Wk. N1 77 DL67
Outram Pl.
Campdale Rd. N7 63 DK62
Campden Cres., Dag. 68 EV63
Campden Cres., Wem. 59 CH62
Campden Gro. W8 90 DA75
Campden Hill W8 90 DA75
Campden Hill Gdns. W8 76 DA74
Campden Hill Gate W8 90 DA75
Duchess of Bedford's Wk.
Campden Hill Pl. W11 75 CZ74
Holland Pk. Ave.
Campden Hill Rd. W8 76 DA74
Campden Hill Sq. W8 75 CZ74
Campden Ho. Clo. W8 90 DA75
Hornton St.
Campden Rd., S.Croy. 134 DS106
Campden Rd., Uxb. 56 BM62
Campden St. W8 76 DA74
Campen Clo. SW19 103 CY89
Queensmere Rd.
Camperdown St. E1 78 DT72
Leman St.
Campfield Rd. SE9 108 EK87
Camphill Ct., W.Byf. 126 BG112
Camphill Ind. Est., W.Byf. 126 BH111
Camphill Rd., W.Byf. 126 BG113
Campine Clo. (Cheshunt), Wal.Cr. 23 DX28
Welsummer Way
Campion Clo. E6 81 EM73
Campion Clo., Croy. 134 DS105
Campion Clo., Har. 60 CM58
Campion Clo. (Denham), Uxb. 56 BG62
Lindsey Rd.
Campion Clo. (Hillingdon), Uxb. 70 BM71
Campion Clo., Wat. 15 BU33
Campion Dr., Tad. 145 CV120
Campion Gdns., Wdf.Grn. 52 EG50
Campion Pl. SE28 82 EV74
Campion Rd. SW15 89 CW84
Campion Rd., Islw. 87 CF81
Campion Ter. NW2 61 CX63
Campions, Epp. 26 EU28
Campions, Loug. 39 EN38
Campions, The, Borwd. 32 CM38
Campions Clo., Borwd. 32 CP37
Camplin Rd., Har. 60 CL57
Camplin St. SE14 93 DX80
Campsbourne, The N8 63 DL56
Rectory Gdns.
Campsbourne Rd. N8 63 DL55
Campsey Gdns., Dag. 82 EV66
Campsey Rd., Dag. 82 EV66
Campsfield Rd. N8 63 DL55
Campsbourne Rd.
Campshill Pl. SE13 107 EC85
Campshill Rd.
Campshill Rd. SE13 107 EC85
Campus Rd. E17 65 DZ58
Camrose Ave., Edg. 46 CM54
Camrose Ave., Erith 97 FB79
Camrose Ave., Felt. 99 BV91
Camrose Clo., Croy. 121 DY101
Camrose Clo., Mord. 118 DA98
Camrose St. SE2 96 EU78
Can Hatch, Tad. 145 CY118
Canada Ave. N18 50 DQ51
Canada Cres. W3 74 CQ70
Canada Est. SE16 92 DW76
Canada Gdns. SE13 107 EC85
Canada La., Brox. 23 DY25
Great Cambridge Rd.
Canada Rd. W3 74 CQ71
Canada Rd., Cob. 128 BW113
Canada Rd., Erith 97 FH80
Canada Rd., W.Byf. 126 BK111
Canada Sq. E14 79 EB74
Canada St. SE16 93 DX75
Canada Way W12 75 CV73
Canada Yd. S. SE16 93 DX76
Canadas, The, Brox. 23 DY25
Canadian Ave. SE6 107 EB88
Canal App. SE8 93 DY78
Canal Clo. E1 79 DY70
Canal Clo. W10 75 CX70
Canal Gro. SE15 92 DU79
Canal Head SE15 92 DU81
Peckham High St.
Canal Path E2 78 DT67
Canal Rd. E3 79 DY70
Canal St. SE5 92 DR79
Canal Wk. N1 78 DR67
Canal Wk. SE26 106 DW92
Canal Wk., Croy. 120 DS100
Canal Way NW1 76 DG67
Regents Pk. Rd.
Canal Way NW10 74 CR68
Canal Way W10 75 CX70
Canal Way, Wem. 74 CM67
Canal Way Wk. W10 75 CY70
Kensal Rd.
Canary Wf. E14 79 EA74
Canberra Clo. NW4 61 CU55
Canberra Clo., Dag. 83 FD66
Canberra Cres., Dag. 83 FD66
Canberra Dr., Hayes 72 BW69
Canberra Dr., Nthlt. 72 BW69
Canberra Rd. E6 81 EM67
Barking Rd.
Canberra Rd. SE7 94 EJ79
Canberra Rd. W13 73 CG74
Canberra Rd., Bexh. 96 EX79
Canberra Rd., Houns. 84 BN83
Canbury Ave., Kings.T. 116 CM95
Canbury Ms. SE26 106 DU90
Wells Pk. Rd.
Canbury Pk. Rd., Kings.T. 116 CL95
Canbury Pas., Kings.T. 115 CK95
Canbury Path, Orp. 124 EU97
Cancell Rd. SW9 91 DN81
Candahar Rd. SW11 90 DE82
Candler St. N15 64 DR58
Candover Clo., West Dr. 84 BK80
Candover Rd., Horn. 69 FH60
Candover St. W1 5 K7
Candy St. E3 79 DZ67
Cane Clo., Wall. 133 DL108
Kingsford Ave.
Caneland Ct., Wal.Abb. 24 EF34
Caney Ms. NW2 61 CX61
Claremont Rd.
Canfield Dr., Ruis. 57 BV64
Canfield Gdns. NW6 76 DB66
Canfield Pl. NW6 76 DC65
Canfield Gdns.
Canfield Rd., Rain. 83 FF67
Canfield Rd., Wdf.Grn. 52 EL52
Canford Ave., Nthlt. 72 BY67
Canford Clo., Enf. 35 DN40
Canford Dr., Add. 112 BH103
Canford Gdns., N.Mal. 116 CS100
Canford Pl., Tedd. 101 CH93
Canford Rd. SW11 104 DG85
Canham Rd. SE25 120 DS97
Canham Rd. W3 88 CS75
Canmore Gdns. SW16 105 DJ94
Cann Hall Rd. E11 66 EE63
Canning Cres. N22 49 DM53
Canning Cross SE5 92 DS82
Canning Pas. W8 90 DC75
Victoria Rd.
Canning Pl. W8 90 DC76
Canning Pl. Ms. W8 90 DC76
Canning Pl.
Canning Rd. E15 80 EE68
Canning Rd. E17 65 DY56
Canning Rd. N5 63 DP62
Canning Rd., Croy. 120 DT103
Canning Rd., Har. 59 CE55
Cannington Rd., Dag. 82 EW65
Cannizaro Rd. SW19 103 CW92
Cannon Clo. SW20 117 CW97
Cannon Clo., Hmptn. 100 CB93
Hanworth Rd.
Cannon Dr. E14 79 EA73
Cannon Gro., Lthd. 143 CE122
Cannon Hill N14 49 DK48
Cannon Hill NW6 62 DA64
Cannon Hill La. SW20 117 CY97
Cannon La. NW3 62 DD62
Cannon La., Pnr. 58 BY57
Cannon Ms., Wal.Abb. 23 EB33
Cannon Pl. NW3 62 DC62
Cannon Pl. SE7 94 EL78
Cannon Rd. N14 49 DL48
Cannon Rd., Bexh. 96 EY81
Cannon Rd., Wat. 30 BW43
Cannon St. EC4 7 H9
Cannon St. EC4 78 DQ72
Cannon St. Rd. E1 78 DV72
Cannon Way, Lthd. 143 CE121
Cannon Way, W.Mol. 114 CA98
Cannonbury Ave., Pnr. 58 BX58
Cannonside, Lthd. 143 CE122
Canon Ave., Rom. 68 EW57
Canon Beck Rd. SE16 92 DW75
Canon Hill, Couls. 147 DN118
Canon Mohan Clo. N14 35 DH44
Farm La.
Canon Rd., Brom. 122 EJ97
Canon Row SW1 9 P4
Canon Row SW1 91 DL75
Canon St. N1 78 DQ67
Canon Trd. Est., The, Wem. 60 CP63
Canonbie Rd. SE23 106 DW87
Canonbury Cres. N1 78 DQ66
Canonbury Gro. N1 78 DQ66
Canonbury La. N1 77 DP66
Canonbury Pk. N. N1 78 DQ65
Canonbury Pk. S. N1 78 DQ65
Canonbury Pl. N1 77 DP65
Canonbury Rd. N1 77 DP65
Canonbury Rd., Enf. 36 DS39
Canonbury Sq. N1 77 DP66
Canonbury St. N1 78 DQ66
Canonbury Vill. N1 77 DP66
Canonbury Yd. N1 78 DQ67
New N. Rd.
Canons Clo. N2 62 DD59
Canons Clo., Edg. 46 CM51
Canons Clo., Rad. 31 CH35
Canons Cor., Edg. 46 CL49
Canons Dr., Edg. 46 CL51
Canons Gate, Wal.Cr. 23 DZ26
Thomas Rochford Way
Canons Hatch, Tad. 145 CY118
Canon's Hill, Couls. 147 DN118
Canons La., Tad. 145 CY118
Canons Wk., Croy. 121 DX104
Canonsleigh Rd., Dag. 82 EV66
Canopus Way, Nthwd. 43 BU49
Canopus Way, Stai. 98 BL87
Canrobert St. E2 78 DV69
Cantelowes Rd. NW1 77 DK65
Canterbury Ave., Ilf. 66 EL59
Canterbury Ave., Sid. 110 EW89
Canterbury Clo. E6 81 EM72
Harper Rd.
Canterbury Clo., Beck. 121 EB95
Canterbury Clo., Chig. 53 ET48
Canterbury Clo., Grnf. 72 CB72
Canterbury Clo., Nthwd. 43 BT51
Canterbury Cres. SW9 91 DN83
Canterbury Gro. SE27 105 DN91
Canterbury Pl. SE17 10 G9
Canterbury Pl. SE17 91 DP77
Canterbury Rd. E10 65 EC59
Canterbury Rd. NW6 75 CZ68
Canterbury Rd., Borwd. 32 CN40
Canterbury Rd., Croy. 119 DN101
Canterbury Rd., Felt. 100 BY90
Canterbury Rd., Har. 58 CB57
Canterbury Rd., Mord. 118 DB101
Canterbury Rd., Wat. 29 BV40
Canterbury Ter. NW6 76 DA68
Canterbury Way, Rick. 29 BQ41
Cantley Gdns. SE19 120 DT95
Cantley Gdns., Ilf. 67 EQ58
Cantley Rd. W7 87 CG76
Canton St. E14 79 EA72
Cantrell Rd. E3 79 DZ70
Cantwell Rd. SE18 95 EP80
Canute Gdns. SE16 93 DX77
Canvey St. SE1 10 G2
Cape Clo., Bark. 81 EQ65
North St.
Cape Rd. N17 64 DU55
High Cross Rd.
Cape Yd. E1 78 DU74
Asher Way
Capel Ave., Wall. 133 DM106
Capel Clo. N20 48 DC48
Capel Clo., Brom. 123 EM102
Capel Ct. EC2 7 L9
Capel Ct. SE20 120 DW95
Melvin Rd.
Capel Gdns., Ilf. 67 ET63
Capel Gdns., Pnr. 58 BZ56
Capel Pt. E7 66 EH63
Capel Rd. E7 66 EH63
Capel Rd. E12 66 EJ63
Capel Rd., Barn. 34 DE44
Capel Rd., Enf. 36 DV36
Capel Rd., Wat. 30 BY44
Capel Vere Wk., Wat. 29 BS39
Capella Rd., Nthwd. 43 BT49
Capener's Clo. SW1 8 F5
Capern Rd. SW18 104 DC88
Cargill Rd.
Capital Business Cen., Wem. 73 CK67
Capital Interchange Way, Brent. 88 CN78
Capital Pl., Croy. 133 DM106
Stafford Rd.
Capitol Ind. Est. NW9 60 CQ55
Capitol Way NW9 60 CQ55
Capland St. NW8 4 A4
Capland St. NW8 76 DD70
Caple Rd. NW10 75 CT68
Capper St. WC1 5 L5
Capper St. WC1 77 DJ70
Caprea Clo., Hayes 72 BX71
Triandra Way
Capri Rd., Croy. 120 DT102
Capstan Clo., Rom. 68 EV58
Capstan Ride, Enf. 35 DN40
Crofton Way
Capstan Rd. SE8 93 DZ77
Capstan Sq. E14 93 EC75
Capstan Way SE16 79 DY74
Capstone Rd., Brom. 108 EF91
Capthorne Ave., Har. 58 BY60
Capuchin Clo., Stan. 45 CH51
Capulet Ms. E16 80 EG74
Silvertown Way
Capworth St. E10 65 EA60
Caractacus Cottage Vw., Wat. 43 BU45
Caractacus Grn., Wat. 29 BT44
Caradoc Clo. W2 76 DA72
Caradoc St. SE10 94 EE78
Caradon Clo. E11 66 EE61
Brockway Clo.
Caradon Way N15 64 DR56
Caravan La., Rick. 42 BL45
Caravel Clo. E14 93 EA76
Tiller Rd.
Caravel Ms. SE8 93 EA79
Watergate St.
Caravelle Gdns., Nthlt. 72 BX69
Javelin Way
Caraway Clo. E13 80 EH71
Caraway Pl., Wall. 119 DH104
Carberry Rd. SE19 106 DS93
Carbery Ave. W3 88 CM75
Carbis Clo. E4 51 ED46
Carbis Rd. E14 79 DZ72
Carbone Hill, Hert. 21 DJ27
Carbone Hill (Cuffley), Pot.B. 21 DJ27
Carbuncle Pas. Way N17 50 DU54
Carburton St. W1 5 J6
Carburton St. W1 77 DH71
Cardale St. E14 93 EC76
Plevna St.
Carden Rd. SE15 92 DV83
Cardiff Rd. W7 87 CG76
Cardiff Rd., Enf. 36 DV42
Cardiff Rd., Wat. 29 BV44
Cardiff St. SE18 95 ES80
Cardiff Way, Abb.L. 15 BU32
Cardigan Gdns., Ilf. 68 EU61
Cardigan Rd. E3 79 DZ68
Cardigan Rd. SW13 89 CU82
Cardigan Rd. SW19 104 DC93
Haydons Rd.
Cardigan Rd., Rich. 102 CL86
Cardigan St. SE11 10 D10
Cardigan St. SE11 91 DN78
Cardigan Wk. N1 78 DQ66
Ashby Gro.
Cardinal Ave., Borwd. 32 CP41
Cardinal Ave., Kings.T. 102 CL92
Cardinal Ave., Mord. 117 CY100
Cardinal Bourne St. SE1 11 L7
Cardinal Clo., Chis. 123 ER95
Cardinal Clo., Mord. 117 CY100
Cardinal Clo. (Cheshunt), Wal.Cr. 22 DT26
Adamsfield
Cardinal Clo., Wor.Pk. 131 CU105
Cardinal Cres., N.Mal. 116 CQ96
Cardinal Dr., Ilf. 53 EQ51
Cardinal Dr., Walt. 114 BX102
Cardinal Pl. SW15 89 CX84
Cardinal Rd., Felt. 99 BV88
Cardinal Rd., Ruis. 58 BX60

Cardinal Way, Har. 59 CE55
Wolseley Rd.
Cardinals Wk., Hmptn. 100 CC94
Cardinals Wk., Sun. 99 BS93
Cardinals Way N19 63 DK60
Cardine Ms. SE15 92 DV80
Cardington Sq., Houns. 86 BX84
Cardington St. NW1 5 L2
Cardington St. NW1 77 DJ69
Cardozo Rd. N7 63 DL64
Cardrew Ave. N12 48 DD50
Cardrew Clo. N12 48 DD50
Cardross St. W6 89 CV76
Cardwell Rd. N7 63 DL63
Cardwell Rd. SE18 95 EM77
Carew Clo. N7 63 DM61
Carew Clo., Couls. 147 DP119
Carew Rd. N17 50 DU54
Carew Rd. W13 87 CJ75
Carew Rd., Ashf. 99 BQ93
Carew Rd., Mitch. 118 DG96
Carew Rd., Nthwd. 43 BS51
Carew Rd., Th.Hth. 119 DP97
Carew Rd., Wall. 133 DJ107
Carew St. SE5 92 DQ82
Carey Ct., Bexh. 111 FB85
Carey Gdns. SW8 91 DJ81
Carey La. EC2 7 H8
Carey Pl. SW1 9 M9
Carey Rd., Dag. 68 EY63
Carey St. WC2 6 C9
Carey St. WC2 77 DM72
Carey Way, Wem. 60 CQ63
Fourth Way
Carfax Pl. SW4 91 DK84
Holwood Pl.
Carfax Rd., Hayes 85 BT78
Carfax Rd., Horn. 69 FF63
Carfree Clo. N1 77 DN66
Bewdley St.
Cargill Rd. SW18 104 DB88
Cargreen Pl. SE25 120 DT98
Cargreen Rd.
Cargreen Rd. SE25 120 DT98
Carholme Rd. SE23 107 DZ88
Carisbrook Ave., Wat. 30 BX39
Carisbrook Clo., Stan. 45 CK54
Carisbrook Rd., St.Alb. 16 CB26
Carisbrooke Ave., Bex. 110 EX88
Carisbrooke Clo., Enf. 36 DT39
Carisbrooke Gdns. SE15 92 DT80
Commercial Way
Carisbrooke Rd. E17 65 DY56
Carisbrooke Rd., Brom. 122 EJ98
Carisbrooke Rd., Mitch. 119 DK98
Carker's La. NW5 63 DH64
Carleton Ave., Wall. 133 DK108
Carleton Clo., Esher 115 CD102
Carleton Rd. N7 63 DK64
Carleton Rd. (Cheshunt), Wal.Cr. 23 DX27
Carleton Vill. NW5 63 DJ64
Leighton Gro.
Carlile Clo. E3 79 DZ68
Carlina Gdns., Wdf.Grn. 52 EH50
Carlingford Gdns., Mitch. 104 DF94
Carlingford Rd. N15 63 DP55
Carlingford Rd. NW3 62 DD63
Carlingford Rd., Mord. 117 CX100
Carlisle Ave. EC3 7 P9
Carlisle Ave. W3 74 CS72
Carlisle Clo., Kings.T. 116 CN95
Carlisle Gdns., Har. 59 CK59
Carlisle Gdns., Ilf. 66 EL58
Carlisle La. SE1 10 C7
Carlisle La. SE1 91 DM76
Carlisle Ms. NW8 4 A6
Carlisle Ms. NW8 76 DD71
Carlisle Pl. N11 49 DH49
Carlisle Pl. SW1 9 K7
Carlisle Pl. SW1 91 DJ76
Carlisle Rd. E10 65 EA60
Carlisle Rd. N4 63 DN59
Carlisle Rd. NW6 75 CY67
Carlisle Rd. NW9 60 CQ55
Carlisle Rd., Hmptn. 100 CB94
Carlisle Rd., Rom. 69 FF57
Carlisle Rd., Sutt. 131 CZ106
Carlisle St. W1 5 M9
Carlisle Wk. E8 78 DT65
Laurel St.
Carlisle Way SW17 104 DG92
Carlos Pl. W1 4 G10
Carlos Pl. W1 76 DG73
Carlow St. NW1 77 DJ68
Arlington Rd.
Carlton Ave. N14 35 DK43
Carlton Ave., Felt. 100 BW86
Carlton Ave., Har. 59 CH57
Carlton Ave., Hayes 85 BS77
Carlton Ave., S.Croy. 134 DS108
Carlton Ave. E., Wem. 59 CK61
Carlton Ave. W., Wem. 59 CH61
Carlton Clo. NW3 62 DA61
Carlton Clo., Borwd. 32 CR42
Carlton Clo., Chess. 129 CK107
Carlton Clo., Edg. 46 CN50
Carlton Ct. SW9 91 DP81
Carlton Ct., Ilf. 67 ER55
Carlton Ct., Uxb. 70 BK71
Carlton Cres., Sutt. 131 CY105
Carlton Dr. SW15 103 CX85
Carlton Dr., Ilf. 67 ER55
Carlton Gdns. SW1 9 M3
Carlton Gdns. SW1 77 DK74
Carlton Gdns. W5 73 CJ72
Carlton Gro. SE15 92 DV81
Carlton Hill NW8 76 DB68
Carlton Ho. Ter. SW1 9 M3
Carlton Ho. Ter. SW1 77 DK74
Carlton Par., Orp. 124 EV101
Carlton Par., Sev. 155 FJ122
St. John's Hill
Carlton Pk. Ave. SW20 117 CX96
Carlton Pl., Felt. 99 BT87
Carlton Pl., Nthwd. 43 BP50
Carlton Rd. E11 66 EF60
Carlton Rd. E12 66 EK63
Carlton Rd. E17 51 DY53
Carlton Rd. N4 63 DN59
Carlton Rd. N11 48 DG50
Carlton Rd. SW14 88 CQ83
Carlton Rd. W4 88 CR75
Carlton Rd. W5 73 CJ73
Carlton Rd., Erith 97 FB79
Carlton Rd., N.Mal. 116 CS96
Carlton Rd., Rom. 69 FF57
Carlton Rd., Sid. 109 ET92
Carlton Rd., S.Croy. 134 DR107
Carlton Rd., Sun. 99 BT94
Carlton Rd., Walt. 113 BV101
Carlton Rd., Well. 96 EV83
Carlton Sq. E1 79 DX70
Argyle Rd.
Carlton St. SW1 9 M1
Carlton Ter. E11 66 EH57
Carlton Ter. N18 50 DR48
Carlton Ter. SE26 106 DW90
Carlton Twr. Pl. SW1 8 E6
Carlton Twr. Pl. SW1 90 DF76
Carlton Vale NW6 76 DA68
Carlton Vill. SW15 103 CW85
St. John's Ave.
Carlwell St. SW17 104 DE92
Carlyle Ave., Brom. 122 EK97
Carlyle Ave., Sthl. 72 BZ73
Carlyle Clo. N2 62 DC58
Carlyle Clo. NW10 74 CR67
Carlyle Clo., W.Mol. 114 CB96
Carlyle Gdns., Sthl. 72 BZ73
Carlyle Pl. SW15 89 CX84
Carlyle Rd. E12 66 EL63
Carlyle Rd. SE28 82 EV73
Carlyle Rd. W5 87 CJ77
Carlyle Rd., Croy. 120 DU103
Carlyle Sq. SW3 90 DD78
Carlyon Ave., Har. 58 BZ63
Carlyon Clo., Wem. 74 CL67
Carlyon Rd., Hayes 72 BW71
Carlyon Rd., Wem. 74 CL68
Carmalt Gdns. SW15 89 CW84
Carmalt Gdns., Walt. 128 BW106
Carmarthen Gdn. NW9 60 CS58
Snowdon Dr.
Carmel Ct. W8 90 DB75
Holland St.
Carmel Ct., Wem. 60 CP61
Carmelite Clo., Har. 44 CC53
Carmelite Rd., Har. 44 CC53
Carmelite St. EC4 6 E10
Carmelite St. EC4 77 DN73
Carmelite Wk., Har. 44 CC53
Carmelite Way, Har. 44 CC54
Hampden Rd.
Carmen Ct., Borwd. 32 CM38
Belford Rd.
Carmen St. E14 79 EB72
Carmichael Clo. SW11 90 DD83
Darien Rd.
Carmichael Clo., Ruis. 57 BU63
Carmichael Ms. SW18 104 DD86
Heathfield Rd.
Carmichael Rd. SE25 120 DU98
Carminia Rd. SW17 105 DH89
Carnaby St. W1 5 K9
Carnaby St. W1 77 DJ72
Carnac St. SE27 106 DR91
Carnanton Rd. E17 51 ED53
Carnarvon Ave., Enf. 36 DT41
Carnarvon Dr., Hayes 85 BQ77
Carnarvon Rd. E10 65 EC58
Carnarvon Rd. E15 80 EF65
Carnarvon Rd. E18 52 EF54
Carnarvon Rd., Barn. 33 CY41
Carnation St. SE2 96 EV78
Carnbrook Rd. SE3 94 EK83
Carnecke Gdns. SE9 108 EL85
Carnegie Clo., Surb. 116 CM103
Fullers Ave.
Carnegie Pl. SW19 103 CX90
Carnegie St. N1 77 DM67
Carnforth Clo., Epsom 130 CP107
Carnforth Gdns., Horn. 69 FG64
Carnforth Rd. SW16 105 DK94
Carnie Lo. SW17 105 DH90
Manville Rd.
Carnoustie Dr. N1 77 DM66
Carnwath Rd. SW6 90 DA83
Carol St. NW1 77 DJ67
Carolina Clo. E15 66 EE64
Carolina Rd., Th.Hth. 119 DP96
Caroline Clo. N10 49 DH54
Alexandra Pk. Rd.
Caroline Clo. SW16 105 DM91
Caroline Clo. W2 76 DB73
Bayswater Rd.
Caroline Clo., Croy. 134 DS105
Brownlow Rd.
Caroline Clo., Islw. 87 CE80
Caroline Clo., West Dr. 84 BK75
Caroline Ct., Ashf. 99 BP93
Caroline Ct., Stan. 45 CG51
The Chase
Caroline Gdns. SE15 92 DV80
Caroline Pl. SW11 90 DG82
Caroline Pl. W2 76 DB73
Caroline Pl., Hayes 85 BS80
Caroline Pl., Wat. 30 BY44
Capel Rd.
Caroline Pl. Ms. W2 76 DB73
Orme La.
Caroline Rd. SW19 103 CZ94
Caroline St. E1 79 DX72
Caroline Ter. SW1 8 F9
Caroline Ter. SW1 90 DG77
Caroline Wk. W6 89 CY79
Laundry Rd.
Carolyn Dr., Orp. 124 EU104
Caroon Dr., Rick. 28 BH36
Carpenders Ave., Wat. 44 BY48
Carpenter Clo., Epsom 131 CT109
West St.
Carpenter Gdns. N21 49 DP47
Carpenter St. W1 9 H1
Carpenter Way, Pot.B. 20 DC33
Carpenters Arms La., Epp. 26 EV25
Carpenters Ct., Twick. 101 CE89
Carpenters Pl. SW4 91 DK84
Carpenters Rd. E15 79 EA65
Carpenters Rd., Enf. 36 DW36
Carr Gro. SE18 94 EL77
Carr Rd. E17 51 DZ54
Carr Rd., Nthlt. 72 CA65
Carr St. E14 79 DY71
Carrara Wk. SW9 91 DN84
Somerleyton Rd.
Carriage Dr. E. SW11 90 DG80
Carriage Dr. N. SW11 90 DF80
Carriage Dr. S. SW11 90 DF81
Carriage Dr. W. SW11 90 DF80
Carriageway, The, Sev. 152 EW124
Carrick Clo., Islw. 87 CG83
Carrick Dr., Ilf. 53 EQ53
Carrick Dr., Sev. 155 FH123
Carrick Gdns. N17 50 DS52
Flexmere Rd.
Carrick Gate, Esher 114 CC104
Carrick Ms. SE8 93 EA79
Watergate St.
Carrill Way, Belv. 96 EX77
Carrington Ave., Borwd. 32 CP43
Carrington Ave., Houns. 100 CB85
Carrington Clo., Barn. 33 CU43
Carrington Clo., Borwd. 32 CQ43
Carrington Clo., Croy. 121 DY101
Carrington Clo., Kings.T. 102 CQ92
Carrington Gdns. E7 66 EH63
Woodford Rd.
Carrington Pl., Esher 128 CB106
Carrington Rd., Rich. 88 CN84
Carrington Sq., Har. 44 CC52
Carrington St. W1 9 H3
Carrol Clo. NW5 63 DH63
Carroll Clo. E15 66 EF64
Carroll Hill, Loug. 39 EM41
Carron Clo. E14 79 EB72
Carronade Pl. SE28 95 EQ76
Carroun Rd. SW8 91 DM80
Carrow Rd., Dag. 82 EV66
Carrow Rd., Walt. 114 BX104
Kenilworth Dr.
Carroway La., Grnf. 73 CD69
Cowgate Rd.
Carrs La. N21 36 DQ43
Carshalton Gro., Sutt. 132 DD105
Carshalton Pk. Rd., Cars. 132 DF107
Carshalton Pl., Cars. 132 DG105
Carshalton Rd., Bans. 132 DF114
Carshalton Rd., Cars. 132 DC106
Carshalton Rd., Mitch. 118 DG98
Carshalton Rd., Sutt. 132 DC106
Carslake Rd. SW15 103 CW86
Carson Rd. E16 80 EG70
Carson Rd. SE21 106 DQ89
Carson Rd., Barn. 34 DF42
Carstairs Rd. SE6 107 EC90
Carston Clo. SE12 108 EF85
Carswell Clo., Ilf. 66 EK56
Roding La. S.
Carswell Rd. SE6 107 EC87
Cart La. E4 51 ED45
Cart Path, Wat. 16 BW33
Carter Clo., Rom. 55 FB52
Carter Clo., Wall. 133 DK108
Carter Ct. EC4 77 DP72
Carter La.
Carter Dr., Rom. 55 FB52
Carter La. EC4 6 G9
Carter La. EC4 77 DP72
Carter Pl. SE17 92 DQ78
Carter Rd. E13 80 EH67
Carter Rd. SW19 104 DD93
Carter St. SE17 92 DQ79
Carteret St. SW1 9 M5
Carteret St. SW1 91 DK75
Carteret Way SE8 93 DY77
Carterhatch La., Enf. 36 DT38
Carterhatch Rd., Enf. 36 DW39
Carters Clo., Wor.Pk. 117 CX103
Carters Hill, Sev. 155 FP127
Carters Hill Clo. SE9 108 EJ88
Carters La. SE23 107 DY89
Carters Rd., Epsom 145 CT115
Carters Yd. SW18 104 DA85
Wandsworth High St.
Cartersfield Rd., Wal.Abb. 23 EC34
Cartersfield Rd. Est., Wal.Abb. 23 EC34
Carthew Rd. W6 89 CV76
Carthew Vill. W6 89 CV76
Carthusian St. EC1 7 H6
Carthusian St. EC1 78 DQ71
Cartier Circle E14 79 EB74
Carting La. WC2 10 A1
Carting La. WC2 77 DL73
Cartmel Clo. N17 50 DV52
Heybourne Rd.
Cartmel Rd., Bexh. 96 FA81
Cartmell Gdns., Mord. 118 DC99
Carton St. W1 4 E8
Cartwright Gdns. WC1 5 P3
Cartwright Gdns. WC1 77 DL69
Cartwright Rd., Dag. 82 EY66
Cartwright St. E1 78 DT73
Cartwright Way SW13 89 CV80
Carver Rd. SE24 106 DQ86
Carville Cres., Brent. 88 CL77
Cary Rd. E11 66 EE63
Cary Wk., Rad. 17 CH34
Carysfort Rd. N8 63 DK57
Carysfort Rd. N16 64 DR62
Casband Ct., Abb.L. 15 BS31
Cascade Ave. N10 63 DJ56
Cascade Clo., Buck.H. 52 EK47
Cascade Rd.
Cascade Clo., Orp. 124 EW97
Cascade Rd., Buck.H. 52 EK47
Cascades, Croy. 135 DZ110
Caselden Clo., Add. 126 BJ106
Casella Rd. SE14 93 DX80
Casewick Rd. SE27 105 DN92
Casimir Rd. E5 64 DV62
Casino Ave. SE24 106 DR85
Caspian St. SE5 92 DR80
Caspian Wk. E16 80 EK72
King George Ave.
Caspian Wf. E3 79 EB71
Violet Rd.
Cassandra Clo., Nthlt. 59 CD63
Cassandra Gate, Wal.Cr. 23 DZ27
Casselden Rd. NW10 74 CR66
Cassidy Rd. SW6 90 DA80
Cassilda Rd. SE2 96 EU77
Cassilis Rd., Twick. 101 CH85
Cassio Rd., Wat. 29 BV41
Cassiobridge Rd., Wat. 29 BS42
Cassiobury Ave., Felt. 99 BT86
Cassiobury Ct., Wat. 29 BT40
Cassiobury Dr., Wat. 29 BS38
Cassiobury Pk. Ave., Wat. 29 BS41
Cassiobury Rd. E17 65 DX57
Cassis Ct., Loug. 39 EQ42
Cassland Rd. E9 79 DX66
Cassland Rd., Th.Hth. 120 DR98
Casslee Rd. SE6 107 DZ87
Cassocks Sq., Shep. 113 BR101
Casson St. E1 78 DU71
Casstine Clo., Swan. 111 FF94
Castalia Sq. E14 93 EC75
Roserton St.
Castalia St. E14 93 EC75
Plevna St.
Castano Ct., Abb.L. 15 BS31
Castell Rd., Loug. 39 EQ39
Castellain Rd. W9 76 DB70
Castellan Ave., Rom. 69 FH55
Castellane Clo., Stan. 45 CF52
Daventer Dr.
Castello Ave. SW15 103 CW85
Castelnau SW13 89 CU81
Castelnau Pl. SW13 89 CV79
Castelnau
Castelnau Row SW13 89 CV79
Lonsdale Rd.
Casterbridge NW6 76 DB67
Casterbridge Rd. SE3 94 EG83
Casterton St. E8 78 DV65
Wilton Way
Castile Rd. SE18 95 EN77
Castillon Rd. SE6 108 EE89
Castlands Rd. SE6 107 DZ89
Castle Ave. E4 51 ED50
Castle Ave., Epsom 131 CU109
Castle Ave., Rain. 83 FE66
Castle Ave., West Dr. 70 BL73
Castle Baynard St. EC4 6 G10
Castle Clo. E9 65 DY64
Swinnerton St.
Castle Clo. SW19 103 CX90
Castle Clo., Brom. 122 EE97
Castle Clo., Sun. 99 BS94
Mill Fm. Ave.
Castle Clo. (Bushey), Wat. 30 CB44
Castle Ct. EC3 7 L9
Castle Ct. SE26 107 DY91
Champion Rd.
Castle Dr., Ilf. 66 EL58
Castle Fm. Rd., Sev. 139 FF109
Castle Grn., Wey. 113 BS104
Castle Hill Ave., Croy. 135 EB109
Castle La. SW1 9 K6
Castle La. SW1 91 DJ76
Castle Ms. N12 48 DC50
Castle Rd.
Castle Ms. NW1 77 DH65
Castle Rd.
Castle Par., Epsom 131 CU108
Ewell Bypass
Castle Pl. NW1 77 DH65
Castle Rd.
Castle Pl. W4 88 CS77
Windmill Rd.
Castle Pt. E6 80 EJ68
Castle Rd. N12 48 DC50
Castle Rd. NW1 77 DH65
Castle Rd., Couls. 146 DE120
Castle Rd., Dag. 82 EV67
Castle Rd., Dart. 139 FH107
Castle Rd., Enf. 37 DY39
Castle Rd., Epsom 130 CP114
Castle Rd., Islw. 87 CF82
Castle Rd., Nthlt. 72 CB65
Castle Rd., Sev. 139 FG108
Castle Rd., Sthl. 86 BZ76
Castle Rd., Wey. 113 BR104
Castle St. E6 80 EJ68
Castle St., Kings.T. 116 CL96
Castle Vw., Epsom 130 CP114
Castle Vw. Rd., Wey. 127 BP105
Castle Wk., Sun. 114 BW97
Elizabeth Gdns.
Castle Way SW19 103 CX90
Castle Way, Epsom 131 CU109
Castle Ave.
Castle Way, Felt. 100 BW91
Castle Yd. N6 62 DG59
North Rd.
Castle Yd. SE1 10 G2
Castle Yd., Rich. 101 CK85
Hill St.
Castlebar Hill W5 73 CH71
Castlebar Ms. W5 73 CJ71
Castlebar Pk. W5 73 CH70
Castlebar Rd. W5 73 CJ72
Castlecombe Dr. SW19 103 CX87
Castlecombe Rd. SE9 108 EL91
Castledine Rd. SE20 106 DV94
Castleford Ave. SE9 109 EP88
Castlegate, Rich. 88 CM83
Castlehaven Rd. NW1 77 DH66
Castleleigh Ct., Enf. 36 DR43
Castlemaine Ave., Epsom 131 CV109
Castlemaine Ave., S.Croy. 134 DT106
Castlemaine Twr. SW11 90 DF82
Castlereagh St. W1 4 C8
Castleton Ave., Bexh. 97 FD81
Castleton Ave., Wem. 60 CL63
Castleton Clo., Bans. 146 DA115
Castleton Clo., Croy. 121 DY100
Castleton Dr., Bans. 146 DA115
Castleton Gdns., Wem. 60 CL62
Castleton Rd. E17 51 ED54
Castleton Rd. SE9 108 EK91
Castleton Rd., Ilf. 68 EU60
Castleton Rd., Mitch. 119 DK98
Castleton Rd., Ruis. 58 BX60
Castletown Rd. W14 89 CY78
Castleview Gdns., Ilf. 66 EL58
Castlewood Dr. SE9 95 EM82
Castlewood Rd. N15 64 DU58
Castlewood Rd. N16 64 DU59
Castlewood Rd., Barn. 34 DD41
Castor La. E14 79 EB73
Cat Hill, Barn. 34 DF43
Caterham Ave., Ilf. 53 EM54
Caterham Bypass, Cat. 148 DV120
Caterham Clo., Cat. 148 DS120
Caterham Ct., Wal.Abb. 24 EF34
Shernbroke Rd.
Caterham Dr., Couls. 147 DP118
Caterham Rd. SE13 93 EC83
Catesby St. SE17 11 L9
Catesby St. SE17 92 DR77
Catford Bdy. SE6 107 EB87
Catford Hill SE6 107 DZ88
Catford Ms. SE6 107 EB87
Holbeach Rd.
Catford Rd. SE6 107 EA87
Cathall Rd. E11 65 ED61
Cathay St. SE16 92 DV75
Cathay Wk., Nthlt. 72 CA68
Brabazon Rd.
Cathcart Dr., Orp. 123 ES103
Cathcart Hill N19 63 DJ62
Cathcart Rd. SW10 90 DB79
Cathcart St. NW5 77 DH65
Cathedral Pl. EC4 7 H8
Cathedral St. SE1 11 K2
Cathedral St. SE1 78 DR74
Catherall Rd. N5 64 DQ62
Catherine Clo. SE16 79 DX74
Rotherhithe St.
Catherine Clo., W.Byf. 126 BL114
Catherine Ct. N14 35 DJ43
Conisbee Ct.
Catherine Dr., Rich. 88 CL84
Catherine Dr., Sun. 99 BT93
Catherine Gdns., Houns. 87 CD84
Catherine Gdns., Loug. 39 EM44
Roding Gdns.
Catherine Griffiths Ct. EC1 6 E4
Catherine Gro. SE10 93 EB81
Catherine Howard Ct., Wey. 113 BP104
Old Palace Rd.
Catherine Pl. SW1 9 K6
Catherine Pl. SW1 91 DJ76
Catherine Rd., Enf. 37 DY36
Catherine Rd., Rom. 69 FH57
Catherine Rd., Surb. 115 CK99
Catherine St. WC2 6 B10
Catherine St. WC2 77 DM73
Catherine Wheel All. E1 7 N7
Catherine Wheel Rd., Brent. 87 CK80
Catherine Wheel Yd. SW1 9 K3
Catherine's Clo., West Dr. 84 BK76
Money La.
Cathles Rd. SW12 105 DH86
Cathnor Hill Ct. W12 89 CV76
Cathnor Rd. W12 89 CV75
Catisfield Rd., Enf. 37 DY37

Chambers St. SE16 92 DU75
Chambord St. E2 78 DT69
Champion Cres. SE26 107 DY91
Champion Gro. SE5 92 DR83
Champion Hill SE5 92 DR83
Champion Hill Est. SE5 92 DS83
Champion Pk. SE5 92 DR82
Champion Pk. Est. SE5 92 DR83
Denmark Hill
Champion Rd. SE26 107 DY91
Champness Clo. SE27 106 DR91
Rommany Rd.
Champneys Clo., Sutt. 131 CZ108
Chance St. E1 7 P4
Chance St. E1 78 DT70
Chance St. E2 7 P4
Chance St. E2 78 DT70
Chancel St. SE1 10 F3
Chancel St. SE1 77 DP74
Chancellor Gdns., S.Croy. 133 DP109
Chancellor Gro. SE21 106 DQ89
Chancellor Pas. E14 79 EA74
South Colonnade
Chancellor Pl. NW9 47 CT54
Chancellor Way, Sev. 154 FG122
Chancellors Rd. W6 89 CW78
Chancellors St. W6 89 CW78
Chancelot Rd. SE2 96 EV77
Chancery La. WC2 6 D8
Chancery La. WC2 77 DN72
Chancery La., Beck. 121 EB96
Chanctonbury Clo. SE9 109 EP90
Chanctonbury Gdns., Sutt. 132 DB108
Chanctonbury Way N12 48 DA49
Chandler Ave. E16 80 EG71
Chandler Clo., Hmptn. 114 CA95
Chandler Rd., Loug. 39 EP39
Chandler St. E1 78 DV74
Wapping La.
Chandler Way SE15 92 DT80
Chandlers Clo., Felt. 99 BT87
Chandlers Dr., Erith 97 FD77
West St.
Chandler's La., Rick. 28 BL36
Chandlers Ms. E14 93 EA75
Chandlers Way SW2 105 DN87
Chandlers Way, Rom. 69 FE57
Chandos Ave. E17 51 EA54
Chandos Ave. N14 49 DJ48
Chandos Ave. N20 48 DC46
Chandos Ave. W5 87 CK77
Chandos Clo., Buck.H. 52 EH47
Chandos Cres., Edg. 46 CM52
Chandos Par., Edg. 46 CM52
Chandos Pl. WC2 9 P1
Chandos Pl. WC2 77 DL73
Chandos Rd. E15 65 ED64
Chandos Rd. N2 48 DD54
Chandos Rd. N17 50 DS54
Chandos Rd. NW2 61 CW64
Chandos Rd. NW10 74 CS70
Chandos Rd., Borwd. 32 CM40
Chandos Rd., Har. 58 CC57
Chandos Rd., Pnr. 58 BX59
Chandos St. W1 5 J7
Chandos St. W1 77 DH71
Chandos Way NW11 62 DB60
Change All. EC3 7 L9
Channel Clo., Houns. 86 CA81
Channel Gate Rd. NW10 75 CT69
Old Oak La.
Channelsea Rd. E15 79 ED67
Chant Sq. E15 79 ED66
Chant St. E15 79 ED66
Chanton Dr., Sutt. 131 CW110
Chantress Clo., Dag. 83 FC67
Leys Ave.
Chantrey Clo., Ash. 143 CJ119
Chantrey Rd. SW9 91 DM83
Chantry, The, Uxb. 70 BM69
Chantry Clo., Enf. 36 DQ38
Bedale Rd.
Chantry Clo., Har. 60 CM57
Chantry Clo., Kings L. 14 BN29
Chantry Clo., Sid. 110 EY92
Ellenborough Rd.
Chantry Clo., West Dr. 70 BK73
Chantry Hurst, Epsom 144 CR115
Chantry La., Brom. 122 EK99
Bromley Common
Chantry La., St.Alb. 17 CK26
Chantry Pl., Har. 44 CB53
Chantry Pt. W9 75 CZ70
Chantry Rd., Cher. 112 BJ101
Chantry Rd., Chess. 130 CM106
Chantry Rd., Har. 44 CB53
Chantry St. N1 77 DP67
Chantry Way, Mitch. 118 DD97
Chantry Way, Rain. 83 FD68
Chapel Ave., Add. 126 BH105
Chapel Clo., Dart. 111 FE85
Chapel Clo., Hat. 20 DD27
Chapel Clo., Wat. 15 BT34
Chapel Ct. N2 62 DE55
Chapel Ct. SE1 11 K4
Chapel Cft., Kings L. 14 BG31
Chapel Fm. Rd. SE9 109 EM90
Chapel Gro., Add. 126 BH105
Chapel Gro., Epsom 145 CW119
Chapel Hill, Dart. 111 FE85
Chapel Ho. St. E14 93 EB78
Chapel La., Chig. 53 ET48
Chapel La., Pnr. 58 BX55
Chapel La., Rom. 68 EX59
Chapel La., Uxb. 70 BN72
Chapel Mkt. N1 77 DN68
Chapel Pk. Rd., Add. 126 BH105
Chapel Path E11 66 EH58
Chapel Pl. EC2 7 M3
Chapel Pl. N1 77 DN68
Chapel Mkt.
Chapel Pl. N17 50 DT52
White Hart La.
Chapel Pl. W1 5 H9
Chapel Pl. W1 77 DH72
Chapel Rd. SE27 105 DP91
Chapel Rd. W13 73 CH74
Chapel Rd., Bexh. 96 FA84
Chapel Rd., Epp. 25 ET30
Chapel Rd., Houns. 86 CB83
Chapel Rd., Ilf. 67 EN62
Chapel Rd., Tad. 145 CW123
Chapel Rd., Twick. 101 CH87
Orleans Rd.
Chapel Rd., Warl. 149 DX118
Chapel Row, Uxb. 42 BJ53
Chapel Side W2 76 DB73
Chapel Stones N17 50 DT53
King's Rd.
Chapel St. E15 79 ED66
Chapel St. NW1 4 B7
Chapel St. NW1 76 DE71
Chapel St. SW1 8 G5
Chapel St. SW1 90 DG76
Chapel St., Enf. 36 DR41
Chapel St., Uxb. 70 BJ67
Trumper Way
Chapel Ter., Loug. 38 EL42
Forest Rd.
Chapel Vw., S.Croy. 134 DW107
Chapel Wk. NW4 61 CV56
Chapel Wk., Croy. 120 DQ103
Wellesley Rd.
Chapel Way N7 63 DM62
Sussex Way
Chapel Way, Epsom 145 CW119
Chapel Yd. SW18 104 DA85
Wandsworth High St.
Chapelmount Rd., Wdf.Grn. 53 EM51
Chaplin Clo. SE1 10 E4
Chaplin Clo. SE1 91 DN75
Chaplin Cres., Sun. 99 BS93
Chaplin Rd. E15 80 EE67
Chaplin Rd. N17 64 DT55
Chaplin Rd. NW2 75 CU65
Chaplin Rd., Dag. 82 EY66
Chaplin Rd., Wem. 73 CJ65
Chaplin Sq. N12 48 DD52
Chapman Clo., West Dr. 84 BM76
Chapman Cres., Har. 60 CL57
Chapman Rd. E9 79 DZ65
Chapman Rd., Belv. 96 FA78
Chapman Rd., Croy. 119 DN102
Chapman St. E1 78 DV73
Chapman's La. SE2 96 EW77
Chapmans La., Belv. 96 EX77
Chapmans La., Orp. 124 EW96
Chapmans Pk. Ind. Est. NW10 75 CT65
Chapmans Rd., Sev. 152 EY124
Chapmans Yd., Wat. 30 BW42
New Rd.
Chapone Pl. W1 5 M9
Chapter Clo. W4 88 CQ76
Beaumont Rd.
Chapter Clo., Uxb. 70 BM66
Chapter Ho. Ct. EC4 6 G9
Chapter Rd. NW2 61 CU64
Chapter Rd. SE17 91 DP78
Chapter St. SW1 9 M9
Chapter St. SW1 91 DK77
Chapter Way, Hmptn. 100 CA91
Chara Pl. W4 88 CR79
Charcroft Gdns., Enf. 37 DX42
Chardin Rd. W4 88 CS77
Elliott Rd.
Chardmore Rd. N16 64 DU60
Chardwell Clo. E6 80 EL72
Northumberland Rd.
Charecroft Way W12 89 CX75
Charfield Ct. W9 76 DB70
Shirland Rd.
Charford Rd. E16 80 EG71
Chargate Clo., Walt. 127 BT107
Chargeable La. E13 80 EF70
Chargeable St. E16 80 EF70
Chargrove Clo. SE16 93 DX75
Marlow Way
Charing Clo., Orp. 137 ET105
Charing Cross SW1 9 P2
Charing Cross Rd. WC2 5 N9
Charing Cross Rd. WC2 77 DK72
Charlbert St. NW8 76 DE68
Charlbury Ave., Stan. 45 CK50
Charlbury Gdns., Ilf. 67 ET61
Charlbury Gro. W5 73 CJ72
Charlbury Rd., Uxb. 56 BM62
Charldane Rd. SE9 109 EP90
Charlecote Gro. SE26 106 DV90
Charlecote Rd., Dag. 68 EY62
Charlemont Rd. E6 81 EM69
Charles Barry Clo. SW4 91 DJ83
Charles Burton Ct. E5 65 DY64
Ashenden Rd.
Charles Clo., Sid. 110 EV91
Charles Coveney Rd. SE15 92 DT81
Southampton Way
Charles Cres., Har. 59 CD59
Charles Dickens Ho. E2 78 DV69
Charles Grinling Wk. SE18 95 EN77
Charles Ho. N17 50 DT52
Charles La. NW8 76 DD68
St. John's Wd. High St.
Charles Pl. NW1 5 L3
Charles Rd. E7 80 EJ66
Lens Rd.
Charles Rd. SW19 118 DA95
Charles Rd. W13 73 CG72
Charles Rd., Dag. 83 FD65
Charles Rd., Rom. 68 EX59
Charles Rd., Sev. 139 FB110
Charles Rd., Stai. 98 BK93
Charles II St. SW1 9 M2
Charles II St. SW1 77 DK74
Charles Sevright Dr. NW7 47 CX50
Charles Sq. N1 7 L3
Charles Sq. Est. N1 78 DR69
Pitfield St.
Charles St. E16 80 EK74
Charles St. SW13 88 CS82
Charles St. W1 9 H2
Charles St. W1 77 DH74
Charles St., Croy. 120 DQ104
Charles St., Enf. 36 DT43
Charles St., Epp. 26 EU32
Charles St., Houns. 86 BY82
Charles St., Uxb. 71 BP70
Charlesfield SE9 108 EJ90
Charleston Clo., Felt. 99 BU90
Charleston St. SE17 11 J9
Charleston St. SE17 92 DQ77
Charleville Circ. SE26 106 DU92
Charleville Rd. W14 89 CY78
Charlieville Rd., Erith 97 FC80
Northumberland Pk.
Charlmont Rd. SW17 104 DF93
Charlock Way, Wat. 29 BT44
Charlotte Clo., Bexh. 110 EY85
Charlotte Despard Ave. SW11 90 DG81
Charlotte Gdns., Rom. 55 FB51
Charlotte Ms. W1 5 L6
Charlotte Ms. W14 89 CY77
Munden St.
Charlotte Pl. NW9 60 CQ57
Uphill Dr.
Charlotte Pl. SW1 9 K9
Charlotte Pl. W1 5 L7
Charlotte Rd. EC2 7 M3
Charlotte Rd. EC2 78 DS70
Charlotte Rd. SW13 89 CT81
Charlotte Rd., Dag. 83 FB65
Charlotte Rd., Wall. 133 DJ107
Charlotte Row SW4 91 DJ83
North St.
Charlotte Sq., Rich. 102 CM86
Greville Rd.
Charlotte St. W1 5 L6
Charlotte St. W1 77 DJ71
Charlotte Ter. N1 77 DM67
Charlow Clo. SW6 90 DC82
Townmead Rd.
Charlton Ave., Walt. 127 BV105
Charlton Ch. La. SE7 94 EJ78
Charlton Clo., Uxb. 57 BP61
Charlton Cres., Bark. 81 ET68
Charlton Dene SE7 94 EJ80
Charlton Dr., West. 150 EK117
Charlton Gdns., Couls. 147 DJ118
Charlton Kings, Wey. 113 BS104
Charlton Kings Rd. NW5 63 DK64
Charlton La. SE7 94 EK78
Charlton La., Shep. 113 BQ97
Charlton Pk. La. SE7 94 EK80
Charlton Pk. Rd. SE7 94 EK79
Charlton Pl. N1 77 DP68
Charlton Rd. N9 51 DX46
Charlton Rd. NW10 74 CS67
Charlton Rd. SE3 94 EH80
Charlton Rd. SE7 94 EJ79
Charlton Rd., Har. 59 CK57
Charlton Rd., Shep. 113 BQ97
Charlton Rd., Wem. 60 CM60
Charlton Way SE3 94 EE81
Charlwood, Croy. 135 DZ109
Charlwood Clo., Har. 45 CE52
Kelvin Cres.
Charlwood Dr., Lthd. 143 CD115
Charlwood Pl. SW1 9 L9
Charlwood Pl. SW1 91 DJ77
Charlwood Rd. SW15 89 CX84
Charlwood Sq., Mitch. 118 DD97
Charlwood St. SW1 9 L10
Charlwood St. SW1 91 DJ78
Charlwood Ter. SW15 89 CX84
Cardinal Pl.
Charmian Ave., Stan. 59 CK55
Charminster Ave. SW19 118 DA96
Charminster Ct., Surb. 115 CK100
Charminster Rd. SE9 108 EK91
Charminster Rd., Wor.Pk. 117 CX102
Charmouth Rd., Well. 96 EV81
Charmwood La., Orp. 138 EV109
Charne, The, Sev. 153 FG117
Charnock, Swan. 125 FE98
Charnock Rd. E5 64 DV62
Charnwood Ave. SW19 118 DA96
Charnwood Clo., N.Mal. 116 CS98
Charnwood Dr. E18 66 EH55
Charnwood Gdns. E14 93 EA77
Charnwood Pl. N20 48 DC48
Charnwood Rd. SE25 120 DR99
Charnwood Rd., Enf. 36 DV36
Charnwood Rd., Uxb. 70 BN69
Charnwood St. E5 64 DV61
Charrington Rd., Croy. 119 DP103
Drayton Rd.
Charrington St. NW1 77 DK68
Charsley Rd. SE6 107 EB89
Chart Clo., Brom. 122 EE95
Chart Clo., Croy. 120 DW100
Stockbury Rd.
Chart St. N1 7 L2
Chart St. N1 78 DR69
Charter Ave., Ilf. 67 ER60
Charter Ct., N.Mal. 116 CS97
Charter Cres., Houns. 86 BY84
Charter Dr., Bex. 110 EY87
Charter Pl., Uxb. 70 BJ66
Charter Pl., Wat. 30 BW41
Beechen Gro.
Charter Rd., Kings.T. 116 CP97
Charter Rd., The, Wdf.Grn. 52 EE51
Charter Sq., Kings.T. 116 CP96
Charter Way N3 61 CZ56
Regents Pk. Rd.
Charter Way N14 35 DJ44
Charterhouse Ave., Wem. 59 CJ63
Charterhouse Bldgs. EC1 6 G5
Charterhouse Dr., Sev. 154 FG123
Charterhouse Ms. EC1 6 G6
Charterhouse Rd., Orp. 124 EU104
Charterhouse Sq. EC1 6 G6
Charterhouse Sq. EC1 77 DP71
Charterhouse St. EC1 6 F7
Charterhouse St. EC1 77 DN71
Charteris Rd. N4 63 DN60
Charteris Rd. NW6 75 CZ67
Charteris Rd., Wdf.Grn. 52 EH52
Charters Clo. SE19 106 DS92
Chartfield Ave. SW15 103 CV85
Chartfield Sq. SW15 103 CX85
Chartfield Ave.
Chartham Gro. SE27 105 DN90
Royal Circ.
Chartham Rd. SE25 120 DV97
Chartley Ave. NW2 60 CS62
Chartley Ave., Stan. 45 CF51
Charton Clo., Belv. 96 EZ79
Chartridge Clo., Barn. 33 CU43
Chartridge Clo. (Bushey), Wat. 30 CC44
Chartway, Sev. 155 FJ124
Chartwell Clo. SE9 109 EQ89
Chartwell Clo., Croy. 120 DR102
Tavistock Rd.
Chartwell Clo., Grnf. 72 CB67
Chartwell Clo., Wal.Abb. 24 EE33
Chartwell Dr., Orp. 137 ER106
Chartwell Gdns., Sutt. 131 CY105
Chartwell Pl., Epsom 130 CS114
Chartwell Pl., Har. 59 CD60
Chartwell Pl., Sutt. 117 CZ104
Chartwell Rd., Nthwd. 43 BT51
Chartwell Way SE20 120 DV95
Charville La., Hayes 71 BQ69
Charville La. W., Uxb. 71 BP69
Charwood SW16 105 DN91
Chase, The E12 66 EK63
Chase, The SW4 91 DH83
Chase, The SW16 105 DM94
Chase, The SW20 117 CY95
Chase, The, Ash. 143 CJ118
Chase, The, Bexh. 97 FB83
Chase, The, Brom. 122 EH97
Chase, The, Chig. 53 EQ49
Chase, The, Couls. 133 DJ114
Chase, The, Edg. 46 CP53
Chase, The, Horn. 69 FF62
Chase, The (Oxshott), Lthd. 142 CC115
Chase, The, Loug. 52 EJ45
Chase, The, Pnr. 58 BZ56
Chase, The (Eastcote), Pnr. 58 BW58
Chase, The, Rad. 31 CF35
Chase, The, Rom. 69 FE55
Chase, The (Chadwell Heath), Rom. 68 EY58
Chase, The (Rush Grn.), Rom. 69 FD62
Chase, The, Stan. 45 CG50
Chase, The, Sun. 113 BV95
Chase, The, Tad. 146 DA122
Chase, The, Uxb. 56 BN64
Chase, The, Wall. 133 DL106
Chase, The (Cheshunt), Wal.Cr. 21 DP28
Chase, The, Wat. 29 BS42
Chase Ct. Gdns., Enf. 36 DQ41
Chase Cross Rd., Rom. 55 FC52
Chase End, Epsom 130 CR112
Chase Gdns. E4 51 EA49
Chase Gdns., Twick. 101 CD86
Chase Grn., Enf. 36 DQ41
Chase Grn. Ave., Enf. 35 DP40
Chase Hill, Enf. 36 DQ41
Chase La., Chig. 53 ET48
Chase La., Ilf. 67 ER57
Chase Ridings, Enf. 35 DN40
Chase Rd. N14 35 DJ43
Chase Rd. NW10 74 CR70
Chase Rd. W3 74 CR70
Chase Rd., Epsom 130 CR112
Chase Side N14 34 DG43
Chase Side, Enf. 36 DQ41
Chase Side Ave. SW20 117 CY96
Chase Side Ave., Enf. 36 DQ40
Chase Side Cres., Enf. 36 DQ39
Chase Side Pl., Enf. 36 DQ41
Chase Side
Chase Way N14 49 DH47
Chasefield Rd. SW17 104 DF91
Chaseley Dr. W4 88 CP81
Wellesley Rd.
Chaseley Dr., S.Croy. 134 DR110
Chaseley St. E14 79 DY72
Chasemore Clo., Mitch. 118 DF101
Chasemore Gdns., Croy. 133 DP106
Thorneloe Gdns.
Chaseside Clo., Rom. 55 FE51
Chaseside Gdns., Cher. 112 BH101
Chaseville Pk. Rd. N21 35 DL43
Chasewood Ave., Enf. 35 DP40
Chastilian Rd., Dart. 111 FF87
Chatfield Ct., Cat. 148 DR122
York Gate
Chatfield Rd. SW11 90 DC83
Chatfield Rd., Croy. 119 DP102
Chatham Ave., Brom. 122 EF101
Chatham Clo. NW11 62 DA57
Chatham Clo., Sutt. 117 CZ101
Chatham Hill Rd., Sev. 155 FJ121
Chatham Pl. E9 78 DW65
Chatham Rd. E17 65 DY55
Chatham Rd. E18 52 EF54
Grove Hill
Chatham Rd. SW11 104 DF86
Chatham Rd., Kings.T. 116 CN96
Chatham Rd., Orp. 137 EQ106
Chatham St. SE17 11 K8
Chatham St. SE17 92 DR77
Chatsfield, Epsom 131 CU110
Chatsfield Pl. W5 74 CL72
Chatsworth Ave. NW4 47 CW54
Chatsworth Ave. SW20 117 CY95
Chatsworth Ave., Brom. 108 EH92
Chatsworth Ave., Sid. 110 EU88
Chatsworth Ave., Wem. 60 CM64
Chatsworth Clo. NW4 47 CW54
Chatsworth Clo., Borwd. 32 CN41
Chatsworth Clo., W.Wick. 122 EF103
Chatsworth Ct. W8 90 DA77
Pembroke Rd.
Chatsworth Cres., Houns. 87 CD84
Chatsworth Dr., Enf. 50 DU45
Chatsworth Est. E5 65 DX63
Elderfield Rd.
Chatsworth Gdns. W3 74 CP74
Chatsworth Gdns., Har. 58 CB60
Chatsworth Gdns., N.Mal. 117 CT99
Chatsworth Pl., Lthd. 129 CD113
Chatsworth Pl., Mitch. 118 DF97
Chatsworth Pl., Tedd. 101 CG91
Chatsworth Ri. W5 74 CM70
Chatsworth Rd. E5 64 DW62
Chatsworth Rd. E15 66 EF64
Chatsworth Rd. NW2 75 CX65
Chatsworth Rd. W4 88 CQ79
Chatsworth Rd. W5 74 CM70
Chatsworth Rd., Croy. 134 DR105
Chatsworth Rd., Hayes 71 BV70
Chatsworth Rd., Sutt. 131 CX106
Chatsworth Way SE27 105 DP90
Chattern Hill, Ashf. 99 BP91
Chattern Rd., Ashf. 99 BQ91
Chatterton Rd. N4 63 DP62
Chatterton Rd., Brom. 122 EK98
Chatto Rd. SW11 104 DF85
Chaucer Ave., Hayes 71 BU71
Chaucer Ave., Houns. 85 BV82
Chaucer Ave., Rich. 88 CN83
Chaucer Ave., Wey. 126 BN108
Chaucer Clo. N11 49 DJ50
Chaucer Clo., Bans. 131 CY114
Chaucer Ct. N16 64 DS63
Chaucer Dr. SE1 92 DT77
Chaucer Gdns., Sutt. 118 DA104
Chaucer Grn., Croy. 120 DW101
Chaucer Rd. E7 80 EG65
Chaucer Rd. E11 66 EG58
Chaucer Rd. E17 51 EC54
Chaucer Rd. SE24 105 DN85
Chaucer Rd. W3 74 CQ74
Chaucer Rd., Ashf. 98 BL91
Chaucer Rd., Rom. 55 FH52
Chaucer Rd., Sid. 110 EW88
Chaucer Rd., Sutt. 132 DA105
Chaucer Rd., Well. 95 ET81
Chaucer Way SW19 104 DD93
Chaucer Way, Add. 126 BG107
Chauncey Clo. N9 50 DU48
Chauncy Ave., Pot.B. 20 DC33
Chaundrye Clo. SE9 108 EL86
Chauntler Clo. E16 80 EH72
Chavecroft Ter., Epsom 145 CW119
Cheam Clo., Tad. 145 CV121
Waterfield
Cheam Common Rd., Wor.Pk. 117 CV103
Cheam Mans., Sutt. 131 CY108
Cheam Pk. Way, Sutt. 131 CY107
Cheam Rd., Epsom 131 CU110
Cheam Rd., Sutt. 131 CZ107
Cheam Rd. (East Ewell), Sutt. 131 CX110
Cheam St. SE15 92 DV83
Evelina Rd.
Cheapside EC2 7 H9
Cheapside EC2 78 DQ72
Cheddar Rd., Houns. 84 BN82
Cromer Rd.
Cheddar Waye, Hayes 71 BV72
Cheddington Rd. N18 50 DS48
Chedworth Clo. E16 80 EF72
Hallsville Rd.
Cheeseman Clo., Hmptn. 100 BY93
Cheesemans Ter. W14 89 CZ78
Chelford Rd., Brom. 107 ED92

Chicheley St. SE1 10 C4
Chicheley St. SE1 91 DM75
Chichester Ave., Ruis. 57 BR61
Chichester Clo. E6 80 EL72
Chichester Clo. SE3 94 EJ81
Chichester Clo., Hmptn. 100 BZ93
Maple Clo.
Chichester Ct., Epsom 131 CT109
Chichester Ct., Stan. 60 CL55
Chichester Dr., Pur. 133 DM112
Chichester Dr., Sev. 154 FF125
Chichester Gdns., Ilf. 66 EL59
Chichester Ms. SE27 105 DN91
Chichester Rents WC2 6 D8
Chichester Rd. E11 66 EE62
Chichester Rd. N9 50 DU47
Chichester Rd. NW6 76 DA68
Chichester Rd. W2 76 DB71
Chichester Rd., Croy. 120 DS104
Chichester St. SW1 91 DJ78
Chichester Way E14 93 ED77
Chichester Way, Felt. 100 BW87
Chichester Way, Wat. 16 BY33
Chicksand St. E1 78 DT71
Chiddingfold N12 48 DA48
Chiddingstone Ave., Bexh. 96 EZ80
Chiddingstone Clo., Sutt. 132 DA110
Chiddingstone St. SW6 90 DA82
Chieveley Rd., Bexh. 97 FB84
Chignell Pl. W13 73 CG74
The Bdy.
Chigwell Hill E1 78 DV73
Pennington St.
Chigwell Hurst Ct., Pnr. 44 BX54
Chigwell La., Loug. 39 EQ42
Chigwell Pk. Dr., Chig. 53 EN48
Chigwell Ri., Chig. 53 EN47
Chigwell Rd. E18 66 EH55
Chigwell Rd., Wdf.Grn. 52 EK52
Chigwell Vw., Rom. 54 FA51
Lodge La.
Chilbrook Rd., Cob. 141 BU118
Chilcot Clo. E14 79 EB72
Grundy St.
Chilcott Rd., Wat. 29 BS36
Childebert Rd. SW17 105 DH89
Childeric Rd. SE14 93 DY80
Childerley St. SW6 89 CX81
Fulham Palace Rd.
Childers, The, Wdf.Grn. 53 EM50
Childers St. SE8 93 DY79
Childs Ave., Uxb. 42 BJ54
Childs Hill Wk. NW2 61 CZ62
Church Wk.
Childs La. SE19 106 DS93
Westow St.
Child's Pl. SW5 90 DA77
Child's St. SW5 90 DA77
Child's Wk. SW5 90 DA77
Child's Pl.
Childs Way NW11 61 CZ57
Chilham Clo., Bex. 110 EZ87
Chilham Clo., Grnf. 73 CG68
Chilham Rd. SE9 108 EL91
Chilham Way, Brom. 122 EG101
Chillerton Rd. SW17 104 DG92
Chillingworth Gdns., Twick. 101 CF90
Tower Rd.
Chillingworth Rd. N7 63 DN64
Liverpool Rd.
Chilmark Gdns., N.Mal. 117 CT101
Chilmark Rd. SW16 119 DK96
Chiltern Ave., Twick. 100 CA88
Chiltern Ave. (Bushey), Wat. 30 CC44
Chiltern Clo., Bexh. 97 FE81
Cumbrian Ave.
Chiltern Clo., Borwd. 32 CM40
Chiltern Clo., Croy. 120 DS104
Chiltern Clo., Uxb. 56 BN61
Chiltern Clo. (Cheshunt), Wal.Cr. 21 DP27
Chiltern Clo. (Bushey), Wat. 30 CB44
Chiltern Clo., Wor.Pk. 117 CW103
Cotswold Way
Chiltern Dene, Enf. 35 DM42
Chiltern Dr., Surb. 116 CN100
Chiltern Gdns. NW2 61 CX62
Chiltern Gdns., Brom. 122 EF98
Chiltern Rd. E3 79 EA70
Knapp Rd.
Chiltern Rd., Ilf. 67 ES56
Chiltern Rd., Pnr. 58 BW57
Chiltern Rd., Sutt. 132 DB109
Chiltern St. W1 4 F6
Chiltern St. W1 76 DG71
Chiltern Vw. Rd., Uxb. 70 BJ68
Chiltern Way, Wdf.Grn. 52 EG48
Chilterns, The, Sutt. 132 DB109
Gatton Clo.
Chilthorne Clo. SE6 107 DZ87
Ravensbourne Pk. Cres.
Chilton Ave. W5 87 CK77
Chilton Ct., Walt. 127 BU105
Chilton Gro. SE8 93 DX77
Chilton Rd., Edg. 46 CN51
Manor Pk. Cres.
Chilton Rd., Rich. 88 CN83
Chilton St. E2 78 DT70
Chiltonian Ind. Est. SE12 108 EF86
Chiltons, The E18 52 EG54
Grove Hill
Chiltons Clo., Bans. 146 DB115
High St.
Chilver St. SE10 94 EF78
Chilwell Gdns., Wat. 44 BW49
Chilworth Ct. SW19 103 CX88
Chilworth Gdns., Sutt. 118 DC104
Chilworth Ms. W2 76 DD72
Chilworth St. W2 76 DC72
Chimes Ave. N13 49 DN50
Chinbrook Cres. SE12 108 EH90
Chinbrook Rd.
Chinbrook Est. SE9 108 EK90
Chinbrook Rd. SE12 108 EH90
Chinchilla Dr., Houns. 86 BW82
Chine, The N10 63 DJ56
Chine, The N21 35 DP44
Chine, The, Wem. 59 CH64
Ching Ct. WC2 5 P9
Ching Way E4 51 DZ51
Chingdale Rd. E4 52 EE48
Chingford Ave. E4 51 EA48
Chingford Hall Est. E4 51 DZ51
Chingford Ind. Est. E4 51 DY50
Chingford La., Wdf.Grn. 52 EE49
Chingford Mt. Rd. E4 51 EA49
Chingford Rd. E4 51 EA51
Chingford Rd. E17 51 EB53
Chingley Clo., Brom. 108 EE93
Chinnery Clo., Enf. 36 DT39
Garnault Rd.
Chinnor Cres., Grnf. 72 CB68
Chip St. SW4 91 DK84
Prescott Pl.
Chipka St. E14 93 EC75
Chipley St. SE14 93 DY79
Nynehead St.
Chipmunk Gro., Nthlt. 72 BY69
Argus Way
Chippendale All., Uxb. 70 BK66
Chippendale Waye
Chippendale St. E5 65 DX62
Chippendale Waye, Uxb. 70 BK66
Chippenham Ave., Wem. 60 CP64
Chippenham Clo., Pnr. 57 BT56
Chippenham Gdns. NW6 76 DA69
Chippenham Ms. W9 76 DA70
Chippenham Rd. W9 76 DA70
Chipperfield Rd., Kings L. 14 BJ30
Chipperfield Rd., Orp. 124 EU95
Chipping Clo., Barn. 33 CY41
St. Albans Rd.
Chipstead Ave., Th.Hth. 119 DP98
Chipstead Clo. SE19 106 DT94
Chipstead Clo., Couls. 146 DG116
Chipstead Clo., Sutt. 132 DB109
Chipstead Gdns. NW2 61 CV61
Chipstead Gate, Couls. 147 DJ119
Woodfield Clo.
Chipstead La., Couls. 146 DB124
Chipstead La., Sev. 154 FC122
Chipstead Pk., Sev. 154 FD122
Chipstead Pk. Clo., Sev. 154 FC122
Chipstead Pl. Gdns., Sev. 154 FC122
Chipstead Rd., Bans. 145 CZ117
Chipstead Rd., Erith 97 FE80
Chipstead Rd., Houns. 84 BN83
Chipstead Sta. Par., Couls. 146 DF118
Station App.
Chipstead St. SW6 90 DA81
Chipstead Valley Rd., Couls. 146 DG116
Chipstead Way, Bans. 146 DF115
Chirk Clo., Hayes 72 BY70
Braunston Dr.
Chisenhale Rd. E3 79 DY68
Chisholm Rd., Croy. 120 DS103
Chisholm Rd., Rich. 102 CM86
Chisledon Wk. E9 79 DZ65
Osborne Rd.
Chislehurst Ave. N12 48 DC52
Chislehurst Rd., Brom. 122 EK96
Chislehurst Rd., Chis. 122 EK96
Chislehurst Rd., Orp. 123 ES100
Chislehurst Rd., Rich. 102 CL85
Chislehurst Rd., Sid. 110 EU92
Chislet Clo., Beck. 107 EA94
Abbey La.
Chisley Rd. N15 64 DS58
Chiswell Ct., Wat. 30 BW38
Chiswell Grn. La., St.Alb. 16 BY25
Chiswell Sq. SE3 94 EH82
Brook La.
Chiswell St. EC1 7 K6
Chiswell St. EC1 78 DR71
Chiswick Bri. SW14 88 CQ82
Chiswick Bri. W4 88 CQ82
Chiswick Clo., Croy. 119 DM104
Chiswick Common Rd. W4 88 CR77
Chiswick Ct., Pnr. 58 BZ55
Chiswick Gdns. W4 88 CQ81
Hartington Rd.
Chiswick High Rd. W4 88 CN78
Chiswick High Rd., Brent. 88 CN78
Chiswick Ho. Grds. W4 88 CR79
Chiswick La. W4 88 CS78
Chiswick La. S. W4 89 CT78
Chiswick Mall W4 89 CT79
Chiswick Mall W6 89 CU78
Chiswick Quay W4 88 CQ81
Chiswick Rd. N9 50 DU47
Chiswick Rd. W4 88 CQ77
Chiswick Sq. W4 88 CS79
Hogarth Roundabout
Chiswick Staithe W4 88 CQ81
Chiswick Ter. W4 88 CQ77
Acton La.
Chiswick Village W4 88 CP79
Chiswick Wf. W4 89 CT79
Chittenden Cotts., Wok. 140 BL116
Chitterfield Gate, West Dr. 84 BN80
Chitty St. W1 5 L6
Chitty St. W1 77 DJ71
Chitty's La., Dag. 68 EX61
Chivalry Rd. SW11 104 DE85
Chivenor Gro., Kings.T. 101 CK92
Chivers Rd. E4 51 EB49
Choats Manor Way, Bark. 82 EV70
Renwick Rd.
Choats Rd., Bark. 82 EW68
Choats Rd., Dag. 82 EY69
Chobham Gdns. SW19 103 CX89
Chobham Rd. E15 65 ED64
Cholmeley Cres. N6 63 DH59
Cholmeley Pk. N6 63 DH60
Cholmley Gdns. NW6 62 DA64
Fortune Grn. Rd.
Cholmley Rd., T.Ditt. 115 CH100
Cholmondeley Ave. NW10 75 CU68
Cholmondeley Wk., Rich. 101 CJ85
Choppins Ct. E1 78 DV74
Wapping La.
Chopwell Clo. E15 79 ED66
Bryant St.
Chorleywood Clo., Rick. 42 BK45
Chorleywood Cres., Orp. 123 ET96
Chorleywood Rd., Rick. 28 BG42
Choumert Gro. SE15 92 DU82
Choumert Rd. SE15 92 DT83
Choumert Sq. SE15 92 DU82
Chow Sq. E8 64 DT64
Arcola St.
Chrislaine Clo. (Stanwell), Stai. 98 BK86
High St.
Chrisp St. E14 79 EB71
Christ Ch. Ave., Erith 97 FD79
Christ Ch. Pas. EC1 6 G8
Christ Ch. Rd. SW14 102 CP85
Christ Ch. Rd., Beck. 121 EA96
Fairfield Rd.
Christ Ch. Rd., Epsom 130 CL112
Christ Ch. Rd., Surb. 116 CM101
Christchurch Ave. N12 48 DC51
Christchurch Ave. NW6 75 CX67
Christchurch Ave., Har. 59 CF56
Christchurch Ave., Rain. 83 FF68
Christchurch Ave., Tedd. 101 CG92
Christchurch Ave., Wem. 74 CL65
Christchurch Clo. SW19 104 DD94
Christchurch Cres., Rad. 31 CG36
Christchurch Gdns., Epsom 130 CP111
Christchurch Gdns., Har. 59 CG56
Christchurch Grn., Wem. 74 CL65
Christchurch Hill NW3 62 DD62
Christchurch Ind. Cen., Har. 59 CF56
Christchurch La., Barn. 33 CY40
Christchurch Mt., Epsom 130 CP112
Christchurch Pk., Sutt. 132 DC108
Christchurch Pas. NW3 62 DD62
Christchurch Hill
Christchurch Pas., Barn. 33 CY41
Christchurch La.
Christchurch Rd. N8 63 DL58
Christchurch Rd. SW2 105 DM88
Christchurch Rd. SW19 118 DD95
Christchurch Rd., Houns. 84 BN82
Christchurch Rd., Ilf. 67 EP60
Christchurch Rd., Pur. 133 DP110
Christchurch Rd., Sid. 109 ET91
Christchurch Sq. E9 78 DW67
Victoria Pk. Rd.
Christchurch St. SW3 90 DF79
Christchurch Ter. SW3 90 DF79
Christchurch St.
Christchurch Way SE10 94 EE78
Christian Ct. SE16 79 DZ74
Christian Flds. SW16 105 DN94
Christian St. E1 78 DU72
Christie Dr., Croy. 120 DT100
Christie Gdns., Rom. 68 EV58
Christie Rd. E9 79 DY65
Christie Wk., Cat. 148 DQ121
Coulsdon Rd.
Christies Ave., Sev. 138 FA110
Christina Sq. N4 63 DP60
Adolphus Rd.
Christina St. EC2 7 M4
Christopher Ave. W7 87 CG76
Christopher Clo. SE16 93 DX75
Christopher Clo., Sid. 109 ET85
Christopher Clo., Tad. 145 CW123
High St.
Christopher Ct., Tad. 145 CW123
Christopher Gdns., Dag. 68 EX64
Wren Rd.
Christopher Pl. NW1 5 N3
Christopher Rd., Sthl. 85 BV77
Christopher St. EC2 7 L5
Christopher St. EC2 78 DR70
Christopher's Ms. W11 75 CY74
Penzance St.
Christy Rd., West. 150 EJ115
Chryssell Rd. SW9 91 DN80
Chubworthy St. SE14 93 DY79
Chucks La., Tad. 145 CV124
Chudleigh Cres., Ilf. 67 ES63
Chudleigh Gdns., Sutt. 118 DC104
Chudleigh Rd. NW6 75 CX66
Chudleigh Rd. SE4 107 DZ85
Chudleigh Rd., Twick. 101 CE86
Chudleigh St. E1 79 DX72
Chudleigh Way, Ruis. 57 BU60
Chulsa Rd. SE26 106 DV92
Chumleigh St. SE5 92 DS79
Chumleigh Wk., Surb. 116 CM98
Church All., Croy. 119 DP101
Handcroft Rd.
Church All., Wat. 30 CC38
Church App. SE21 106 DR90
Church App., Sev. 151 EQ115
Cudham La. S.
Church App., Stai. 98 BK86
Church Ave. E4 51 ED51
Church Ave. NW1 77 DH65
Kentish Town Rd.
Church Ave. SW14 88 CR83
Church Ave., Beck. 121 EA95
Church Ave., Nthlt. 72 BZ66
Church Ave., Pnr. 58 BY58
Church Ave., Ruis. 57 BR60
Church Ave., Sid. 110 EU92
Church Ave., Sthl. 86 BY76
Church Clo. N20 48 DE48
Church Clo. W8 90 DB75
Kensington Ch. St.
Church Clo., Add. 126 BH105
Church Clo., Edg. 46 CQ50
Church Clo., Hayes 71 BR71
Church Clo., Lthd. 143 CD124
Church Clo., Loug. 39 EM40
Church Clo., Nthwd. 43 BT52
Church Clo. (Cuffley), Pot.B. 21 DL29
Church Clo., Rad. 31 CG36
Church Clo., Stai. 112 BJ97
The Bdy.
Church Clo., Uxb. 70 BH68
Church Clo., West Dr. 84 BL76
Church Ct., Rich. 101 CK85
George St.
Church Cres. E9 79 DX66
Church Cres. N3 47 CZ53
Church Cres. N10 63 DH56
Church Cres. N20 48 DE48
Church Dr. NW9 60 CR60
Church Dr., Har. 58 BZ58
Church Dr., W.Wick. 122 EE104
Church Elm La., Dag. 82 FA65
Church End E17 65 EB56
Church End NW4 61 CV55
Church Entry EC4 77 DP72
Carter La.
Church Fm. Clo., Swan. 125 FC100
Church Fm. La., Sutt. 131 CY107
Church Fld., Epp. 26 EU29
Church Fld., Rad. 31 CG36
Church Fld., Sev. 154 FE122
Church Gdns. W5 87 CK75
Church Gdns., Wem. 59 CG63
Church Gate SW6 89 CY83
Church Grn., Hayes 71 BT72
Church Grn., Walt. 128 BW107
Church Gro. SE13 93 EB84
Church Gro., Kings.T. 115 CJ95
Church Hill E17 65 EA56
Church Hill N21 49 DM45
Church Hill SE18 95 EM76
Church Hill SW19 103 CZ92
Church Hill, Abb.L. 15 BT26
Church Hill, Cars. 132 DF106
Church Hill, Cat. 148 DT124
Church Hill (Crayford), Dart. 97 FE84
Church Hill, Epp. 26 EU30
Church Hill, Har. 59 CE60
Church Hill, Loug. 39 EM41
Church Hill, Orp. 124 EU101
Church Hill, Pur. 133 DL110
Church Hill, Sev. 151 EQ115
Church Hill, Uxb. 56 BJ55
Church Hill, West. 150 EK122
Church Hill Rd. E17 65 EB56
Church Hill Rd., Barn. 34 DE44
Church Hill Rd., Surb. 116 CL99
Church Hill Rd., Sutt. 131 CX105
Church Hill Wd., Orp. 124 EU99
Church Hyde SE18 95 ES79
Old Mill Rd.
Church La. E11 66 EE60
Church La. E17 65 EB56
Church La. N2 62 DC55
Church La. N8 63 DM56
Church La. N9 50 DU47
Church La. N17 50 DS53
Church La. NW9 60 CQ58
Church La. SW17 105 DH92
Church La. SW19 117 CZ95
Church La. W5 87 CJ75
Church La. (Nork), Bans. 145 CX117
Reigate Rd.
Church La., Brom. 122 EL102
Church La., Cat. 147 DN123
Church La., Chess. 130 CM107
Church La., Chis. 123 EQ95
Church La., Couls. 146 DG122
Church La., Dag. 83 FB65
Church La., Enf. 36 DR41
Church La., Epp. 27 FB27
Church La., Epsom 145 CX117
Reigate Rd.
Church La. (Headley), Epsom 144 CQ124
Church La., Har. 45 CF53
Church La., Kings L. 14 BN29
Church La., Loug. 39 EM41
Church La., Pnr. 58 BY55
Church La., Pot.B. 20 DG30
Church La., Rich. 102 CL88
Petersham Rd.
Church La. (Mill End), Rick. 42 BG46
Church La., Rom. 69 FE56
Church La. (Abridge), Rom. 40 EY40
Church La. (Stapleford Abbotts), Rom. 41 FC42
Church La., Tedd. 101 CF92
Church La., T.Ditt. 115 CF100
Church La., Twick. 101 CG88
Church La., Uxb. 70 BH68
Church La., Wall. 119 DK104
Church La. (Cheshunt), Wal.Cr. 22 DV29
Church La., Warl. 149 DX117
Church La. (Chelsham), Warl. 149 EB117
Church La., Wat. 30 CB38
Church La., West. 150 EK122
Church La. Ave., Couls. 147 DH122
Church La. Dr., Couls. 147 DH122
Church Manor Est. SW9 91 DN80
Vassall Rd.
Church Manorway SE2 96 EU78
Church Manorway, Erith 97 FD76
Church Meadow, Surb. 115 CJ103
Church Mt. N2 62 DD57
Church Pas. EC2 78 DQ72
Gresham St.
Church Pas., Barn. 33 CZ42
Wood St.
Church Pas., Surb. 116 CL99
Adelaide Rd.
Church Path E11 66 EG57
Church Path E17 65 EB56
St. Mary Rd.
Church Path N12 48 DC50
Church Path N17 50 DS52
White Hart La.
Church Path N20 48 DC49
Church Path NW10 74 CS66
Church Path SW14 88 CR83
North Worple Way
Church Path SW19 117 CZ96
Church Path W4 88 CQ76
Church Path W7 73 CE74
Station Rd.
Church Path, Cob. 127 BU114
Church Path, Couls. 147 DN118
Canon's Hill
Church Path, Croy. 120 DQ103
Keeley Rd.
Church Path, Mitch. 118 DE97
Church Path, Sthl. 86 BZ76
Church Pl. SW1 9 L1
Church Pl. W5 87 CK75
Church Pl., Mitch. 118 DE97
Church Pl., Twick. 101 CH88
Church St.
Church Pl., Uxb. 57 BQ62
Church Ri. SE23 107 DX89
Church Ri., Chess. 130 CM107
Church Rd. E10 65 EA60
Church Rd. E12 66 EL64
Church Rd. E17 51 DY54
Church Rd. N6 62 DG58
Church Rd. N17 50 DS53
Church Rd. NW4 61 CV56
Church Rd. NW10 74 CS66
Church Rd. SE19 120 DS95
Church Rd. SW13 89 CT82
Church Rd. (Wimbledon) SW19 103 CY92
Church Rd. W3 74 CQ74
Church Rd. W7 73 CD73
Church Rd., Add. 126 BG106
Church Rd., Ashf. 98 BM90
Church Rd., Ash. 143 CK117
Church Rd., Bark. 81 EQ65
Church Rd., Bexh. 96 EZ83
Church Rd., Brom. 122 EG96
Church Rd. (Shortlands), Brom. 122 EE97
Church Rd., Buck.H. 52 EH46
Church Rd., Cat. 148 DT123
Church Rd. (Woldingham), Cat. 149 DX122
Church Rd., Croy. 119 DP103
Church Rd., E.Mol. 115 CD98
Church Rd., Enf. 36 DW44
Church Rd., Epsom 130 CS112
Church Rd. (West Ewell), Epsom 130 CR108
Church Rd., Erith 97 FC78
Church Rd., Esher 129 CF107
Church Rd., Felt. 100 BX92
Church Rd., Hayes 71 BT74
Church Rd. (Cranford), Houns. 85 BV78
Church Rd. (Heston), Houns. 86 CA80
Church Rd., Ilf. 67 ES58
Church Rd., Islw. 87 CD81
Church Rd., Ken. 148 DR115
Church Rd., Kes. 136 EK108
Church Rd., Kings.T. 116 CM96
Church Rd., Lthd. 143 CH122
Church Rd. (Great Bookham), Lthd. 142 BZ123
Church Rd., Loug. 38 EG41
Church Rd., Mitch. 118 DD97
Church Rd., Nthlt. 72 BX68
Church Rd., Nthwd. 43 BT52
Church Rd. (Chelsfield), Orp. 138 EW108
Church Rd. (Farnborough), Orp. 137 EQ106

197

198

Courtney Rd., Houns. 84 BN83
Courtrai Rd. SE23 107 DY86
Courtside N8 63 DK58
Courtway, Wdf.Grn. 52 EJ50
Courtway, The, Wat. 44 BY47
Courtyard, The N1 77 DM66
Barnsbury Ter.
Cousin La. EC4 11 K1
Cousins Clo., West Dr. 70 BL73
Couthurst Rd. SE3 94 EH79
Coutts Ave., Chess. 130 CL106
Coutts Cres. NW5 62 DG62
Coval Gdns. SW14 88 CP84
Coval La. SW14 88 CP84
Coval Rd. SW14 88 CP84
Coveham Cres., Cob. 127 BU113
Covelees Wall E6 81 EN72
Covell Ct. SE8 93 EA80
Reginald Sq.
Covent Gdn. WC2 6 A10
Covent Gdn. WC2 77 DL73
Coventry Clo. E6 81 EM72
Harper Rd.
Coventry Clo. NW6 76 DA67
Kilburn High Rd.
Coventry Cross E3 79 EC70
Gillender St.
Coventry Rd. E1 78 DV70
Coventry Rd. E2 78 DV70
Coventry Rd. SE25 120 DU98
Coventry Rd., Ilf. 67 EP61
Coventry St. W1 9 M1
Coventry St. W1 77 DK73
Coverack Clo. N14 35 DJ44
Coverack Clo., Croy. 121 DY101
Coverdale Clo., Stan. 45 CH50
Coverdale Ct., Enf. 37 DY37
Raynton Rd.
Coverdale Gdns., Croy. 120 DT104
Park Hill Ri.
Coverdale Rd. NW2 75 CX66
Coverdale Rd. W12 89 CV75
Coverdales, The, Bark. 81 ER68
Coverley Clo. E1 78 DU71
Covert, The, Nthwd. 43 BQ52
Covert, The, Orp. 123 ES100
Covert Rd., Ilf. 53 ET51
Covert Way, Barn. 34 DC40
Coverton Rd. SW17 104 DE92
Coverts Rd., Esher 129 CF109
Covet Wd. Clo., Orp. 123 ET100
Lockesley Dr.
Covington Gdns. SW16 105 DP94
Covington Way SW16 105 DM93
Cow La., Grnf. 73 CD68
Oldfield La. S.
Cow La., Wat. 30 BW36
Cow Leaze E6 81 EN72
Cowan Clo. E6 80 EL71
Oliver Gdns.
Cowbridge La., Bark. 81 EP66
Cowbridge Rd., Har. 60 CM56
Cowcross St. EC1 6 F6
Cowcross St. EC1 77 DP71
Cowden Rd., Orp. 123 ET101
Cowden St. SE6 107 EA91
Cowdenbeath Path N1 77 DM67
Bingfield St.
Cowdray Rd., Uxb. 71 BQ67
Cowdray Way, Horn. 69 FF63
Cowdrey Clo., Enf. 36 DS40
Cowdrey Ct., Dart. 111 FH87
Cowdrey Rd. SW19 104 DB92
Cowdry Rd. E9 79 DY65
Wick Rd.
Cowen Ave., Har. 58 CC61
Cowgate Rd., Grnf. 73 CD68
Cowick Rd. SW17 104 DF91
Cowings Mead, Nthlt. 72 BY65
Cowland Ave., Enf. 36 DW42
Cowleaze Rd., Kings.T. 116 CL95
Cowles (Cheshunt), Wal.Cr. 22 DT27
Cowley Clo., S.Croy. 134 DW109
Cowley Cres., Uxb. 70 BJ71
Cowley Cres., Walt. 128 BW105
Cowley Hill, Borwd. 32 CP37
Cowley La. E11 66 EE62
Cathall Rd.
Cowley Mill Rd., Uxb. 70 BH68
Cowley Pl. NW4 61 CW57
Cowley Rd. E11 66 EH57
Cowley Rd. SW9 91 DN81
Cowley Rd. SW14 88 CS83
Cowley Rd. W3 75 CT74
Cowley Rd., Ilf. 67 EM59
Cowley Rd., Rom. 55 FH52
Cowley Rd., Uxb. 70 BJ67
Cowley St. SW1 9 P6
Cowling Clo. W11 75 CY74
Wilsham St.
Cowper Ave. E6 80 EL66
Cowper Ave., Sutt. 132 DD105
Cowper Clo., Brom. 122 EK98
Cowper Clo., Well. 110 EU85
Cowper Ct., Wat. 29 BU37
Cowper Gdns. N14 35 DH44
Cowper Gdns., Wall. 133 DJ107
Cowper Rd. N14 49 DH46
Cowper Rd. N16 64 DS64
Cowper Rd. N18 50 DU50
Cowper Rd. SW19 104 DC93
Cowper Rd. W3 74 CR74
Cowper Rd. W7 73 CF73
Cowper Rd., Belv. 96 FA77
Cowper Rd., Brom. 122 EK98
Cowper Rd., Kings.T. 102 CM92
Cowper Rd., Rain. 83 FG70
Cowper St. EC2 7 L4
Cowper St. EC2 78 DR70
Cowper Ter. W10 75 CX71
St. Marks Rd.
Cowslip Clo., Uxb. 70 BL66
Cowslip Rd. E18 52 EH54
Cowthorpe Rd. SW8 91 DK81
Cox Clo., Rad. 18 CM32
Cox La., Chess. 130 CL105
Cox La., Epsom 130 CP105
Coxdean, Epsom 145 CW119
Coxley Ri., Pur. 134 DQ113
Coxmount Rd. SE7 94 EK78
Cox's Wk. SE21 106 DU88
Coxson Pl. SE1 11 P5
Coxwell Rd. SE18 95 ER78
Coxwell Rd. SE19 106 DS94
Coxwold Path, Chess. 130 CL108
Garrison La.
Crab Hill, Beck. 107 ED94
Crab La., Wat. 30 CB35
Crabbs Cft. Clo., Orp. 137 EQ106
Ladycroft Way
Crabtree Ave., Rom. 68 EX56
Crabtree Ave., Wem. 74 CL68
Crabtree Clo. E2 78 DT68
Crabtree Clo. (Bushey), Wat. 30 CB43
Crabtree Ct. E15 65 EB64
Clays La.
Crabtree La. SW6 89 CX80
Crabtree Manorway N., Belv. 97 FC75
Crabtree Manorway S., Belv. 97 FC76
Crabtree Wk. SE15 92 DT81
Lisford St.
Crace St. NW1 5 M2
Craddock Rd., Enf. 36 DT41
Craddock St. NW5 76 DG65
Prince of Wales Rd.
Craddocks Ave., Ash. 144 CL117
Craddocks Par., Ash. 144 CL117
Cradley Rd. SE9 109 ER88
Cragg Ave., Rad. 31 CF36
Craig Dr., Uxb. 71 BP72
Craig Gdns. E18 52 EF54
Craig Mt., Rad. 31 CH35
Craig Pk. Rd. N18 50 DV50
Craig Rd., Rich. 101 CJ91
Craigdale Rd., Horn. 69 FF58
Craigen Ave., Croy. 120 DV102
Craigerne Rd. SE3 94 EH80
Craigholm SE18 95 EN82
Craigmuir Pk., Wem. 74 CM67
Craignair Rd. SW2 105 DN87
Craignish Ave. SW16 119 DM96
Craigs Ct. SW1 9 P2
Craigs Wk. (Cheshunt), Wal.Cr. 23 DX28
Davison Dr.
Craigton Rd. SE9 95 EM84
Craigweil Clo., Stan. 45 CK50
Craigweil Dr., Stan. 45 CK50
Craigwell Ave., Felt. 99 BU90
Craigwell Clo., Rad. 31 CH35
Craik Ct. NW6 75 CZ68
Carlton Vale
Crail Row SE17 11 L9
Cramer St. W1 4 G7
Crammerville Wk., Rain. 83 FH70
Baillie Clo.
Cramond Clo. W6 89 CY79
Cramond Ct., Felt. 99 BR88
Kilross Rd.
Crampshaw La., Ash. 144 CM119
Crampton Rd. SE20 106 DW93
Crampton St. SE17 11 H9
Crampton St. SE17 92 DQ77
Cramptons Rd., Sev. 153 FH120
Cranberry Clo., Nthlt. 72 BX68
Parkfield Ave.
Cranberry La. E16 80 EE70
Cranborne Ave., Sthl. 86 CA77
Cranborne Clo., Pot.B. 19 CY31
Cranborne Cres., Pot.B. 19 CY31
Cranborne Ind. Est., Pot.B. 19 CY30
Cranborne Rd., Bark. 81 ER67
Cranborne Rd., Pot.B. 19 CY31
Cranborne Rd. (Cheshunt), Wal.Cr. 23 DX32
Cranborne Waye, Hayes 71 BV72
Cranbourn All. WC2 5 N10
Cranbourn Pas. SE16 92 DV75
Marigold St.
Cranbourn St. WC2 5 N10
Cranbourn St. WC2 77 DK73
Cranbourne Ave. E11 66 EH56
Cranbourne Ave., Surb. 116 CN104
Cranbourne Clo. SW16 119 DL97
Cranbourne Dr., Pnr. 58 BX57
Cranbourne Gdns. NW11 61 CY57
Cranbourne Gdns., Ilf. 67 EQ55
Cranbourne Rd. E12 66 EL64
High St. N.
Cranbourne Rd. E15 65 EC63
Cranbourne Rd. N10 49 DH54
Cranbourne Rd., Nthwd. 57 BT55
Cranbrook Clo., Brom. 122 EG100
Cranbrook Dr., Esher 114 CC102
Cranbrook Dr., Rom. 69 FH56
Cranbrook Dr., Twick. 100 CB88
Cranbrook Est. E2 79 DX68
Cranbrook Ms. E17 65 DZ57
Cranbrook Pk. N22 49 DM53
Cranbrook Pt. E16 80 EG74
Cranbrook Ri., Ilf. 67 EM58
Cranbrook Rd. SE8 93 EA81
Cranbrook Rd. SW19 103 CY94
Cranbrook Rd. W4 88 CS78
Cranbrook Rd., Barn. 34 DD44
Cranbrook Rd., Bexh. 96 EZ81
Cranbrook Rd., Houns. 86 BZ84
Cranbrook Rd., Ilf. 67 EN57
Cranbrook Rd., Th.Hth. 120 DQ96
Cranbrook St. E2 79 DX68
Roman Rd.
Cranbury Rd. SW6 90 DB82
Crane Ave. W3 74 CQ73
Crane Ave., Islw. 101 CG85
Crane Clo., Dag. 82 FA65
Crane Clo., Har. 58 CC62
Crane Ct. EC4 6 E9
Crane Ct., Epsom 130 CQ105
Crane Gdns., Hayes 85 BT77
Crane Gro. N7 77 DN65
Crane Lo. Rd., Houns. 85 BV79
Crane Mead SE16 93 DX77
Crane Pk. Rd., Twick. 100 CB89
Crane Rd., Twick. 101 CE88
Crane St. SE10 93 ED78
Crane St. SE15 92 DT81
Southampton Way
Crane Way, Twick. 100 CC87
Cranebrook, Twick. 100 CC89
Manor Rd.
Craneford Clo., Twick. 101 CF87
Craneford Way, Twick. 101 CE87
Cranes Dr., Surb. 116 CL98
Cranes Pk., Surb. 116 CL98
Cranes Pk. Ave., Surb. 116 CL98
Cranes Pk. Cres., Surb. 116 CM98
Cranes Way, Borwd. 32 CQ43
Craneswater, Hayes 85 BT80
Craneswater Pk., Sthl. 86 BZ78
Cranfield Clo. SE27 106 DQ90
Dunelm Gro.
Cranfield Cres. (Cuffley), Pot.B. 21 DL29
Cranfield Dr. NW9 46 CS52
Cranfield Dr., Wat. 16 BY32
Cranfield Rd. SE4 93 DZ83
Cranfield Rd. E., Cars. 132 DG109
Cranfield Rd. W., Cars. 132 DF109
Cranfield Row SE1 10 E6
Cranford Ave. N13 49 DL50
Cranford Ave., Stai. 98 BL87
Cranford Clo. SW20 103 CV94
Cranford Clo., Pur. 134 DQ113
Cranford Clo., Stai. 98 BL87
Canopus Way
Cranford Cotts. E1 79 DX73
Cranford St.
Cranford Dr., Hayes 85 BT77
Cranford La., Hayes 85 BR79
Cranford La. (Cranford), Houns. 85 BT81
Cranford La. (Hatton Cross), Houns. 85 BT83
Cranford La. (Heston), Houns. 85 BV80
Cranford Pk. Rd., Hayes 85 BT77
Cranford Ri., Esher 128 CC106
Cranford St. E1 79 DX73
Cranford Way N8 63 DM57
Cranham Rd., Horn. 69 FH58
Cranhurst Rd. NW2 61 CW64
Cranleigh Clo. SE20 120 DV96
Cranleigh Clo., Bex. 111 FB86
Cranleigh Clo., Orp. 124 EU104
Cranleigh Clo., S.Croy. 134 DU112
Cranleigh Clo. (Cheshunt), Wal.Cr. 22 DU28
Cranleigh Dr., Swan. 125 FE99
Cranleigh Gdns. N21 35 DN43
Cranleigh Gdns. SE25 120 DS97
Cranleigh Gdns., Bark. 81 ER66
Cranleigh Gdns., Har. 60 CL57
Cranleigh Gdns., Kings.T. 102 CM93
Cranleigh Gdns., Loug. 39 EM44
Cranleigh Gdns., S.Croy. 134 DU112
Cranleigh Gdns., Sthl. 72 BZ72
Cranleigh Gdns., Sutt. 118 DB103
Cranleigh Ms. SW11 90 DE82
Cranleigh Rd. N15 64 DQ57
Cranleigh Rd. SW19 117 CZ97
Cranleigh Rd., Esher 114 CC102
Cranleigh Rd., Felt. 99 BT91
Cranleigh St. NW1 5 L1
Cranleigh St. NW1 77 DJ68
Cranley Dene Ct. N10 63 DH56
Cranley Dr., Ilf. 67 EQ59
Cranley Dr., Ruis. 57 BT61
Cranley Gdns. N10 63 DH56
Cranley Gdns. N13 49 DM48
Cranley Gdns. SW7 90 DC78
Cranley Gdns., Wall. 133 DJ108
Cranley Ms. SW7 90 DC78
Cranley Par. SE9 108 EL91
Beaconsfield Rd.
Cranley Pl. SW7 90 DD77
Cranley Rd. E13 80 EH71
Cranley Rd., Ilf. 67 EQ58
Cranley Rd., Walt. 127 BS106
Cranmer Ave. W13 87 CH76
Cranmer Clo., Mord. 117 CX100
Cranmer Clo., Pot.B. 20 DB30
Cranmer Clo., Ruis. 58 BX60
Cranmer Clo., Stan. 45 CJ52
Cranmer Clo., Warl. 149 DY117
Cranmer Clo., Wey. 127 BR108
Cranmer Ct. SW3 8 C9
Cranmer Ct. SW4 91 DK83
Cranmer Ct., Hmptn. 100 CB92
Cranmer Rd.
Cranmer Fm. Clo., Mitch. 118 DF98
Cranmer Gdns., Dag. 69 FC63
Cranmer Gdns., Warl. 149 DY117
Cranmer Rd. E7 66 EH63
Cranmer Rd. SW9 91 DN80
Cranmer Rd., Croy. 119 DP104
Cranmer Rd., Edg. 46 CP48
Cranmer Rd., Hmptn. 100 CB92
Cranmer Rd., Hayes 71 BR72
Cranmer Rd., Kings.T. 102 CL92
Cranmer Rd., Mitch. 118 DF98
Cranmer Rd., Sev. 154 FE123
Cranmer Ter. SW17 104 DD92
Cranmore Ave., Islw. 86 CC80
Cranmore Rd., Brom. 108 EF90
Cranmore Rd., Chis. 109 EM92
Cranmore Way N10 63 DJ56
Cranston Clo., Houns. 86 BY82
Cranston Clo., Uxb. 57 BR61
Cranston Est. N1 7 L1
Cranston Est. N1 78 DR68
Cranston Gdns. E4 51 EB50
Cranston Rd. SE23 107 DY88
Cranswick Rd. SE16 92 DV78
Crantock Rd. SE6 107 EB89
Cranwell Clo. E3 79 EB70
Cranwell Gro., Shep. 112 BM98
Cranwell Rd., Houns. 85 BP82
Cranwich Ave. N21 50 DR45
Cranwich Rd. N16 64 DR59
Cranwood St. EC1 7 L3
Cranwood St. EC1 78 DR69
Cranworth Cres. E4 51 ED46
Cranworth Gdns. SW9 91 DN81
Craster Rd. SW2 105 DM87
Crathie Rd. SE12 108 EH86
Crathorn St. SE13 93 EC83
Loampit Vale
Cravan Ave., Felt. 99 BU89
Craven Ave. W5 73 CJ73
Craven Ave., Sthl. 72 BZ71
Craven Clo., Hayes 71 BU72
Craven Gdns. SW19 104 DA92
Craven Gdns., Bark. 81 ES68
Craven Gdns., Ilf. 53 ER54
Craven Gdns. (Collier Row), Rom. 54 FA50
Craven Hill W2 76 DC73
Craven Hill Gdns. W2 76 DC73
Craven Hill Ms. W2 76 DC73
Craven Ms. SW11 90 DG83
Taybridge Rd.
Craven Pk. NW10 74 CS67
Craven Pk. Ms. NW10 74 CS67
Craven Pk. Rd. N15 64 DT58
Craven Pk. Rd. NW10 74 CS67
Craven Pas. WC2 9 P2
Craven Rd. NW10 74 CR67
Craven Rd. W2 76 DC72
Craven Rd. W5 73 CJ73
Craven Rd., Croy. 120 DV102
Craven Rd., Kings.T. 116 CM95
Craven Rd., Orp. 124 EX104
Craven St. WC2 9 P2
Craven St. WC2 77 DL74
Craven Ter. W2 76 DC73
Craven Wk. N16 64 DU59
Crawford Ave., Wem. 59 CK64
Crawford Clo., Islw. 87 CE82
Crawford Est. SE5 92 DQ82
Crawford Gdns. N13 49 DP48
Crawford Gdns., Nthlt. 72 BZ69
Crawford Ms. W1 4 D7
Crawford Pas. EC1 6 D5
Crawford Pl. W1 4 C8
Crawford Pl. W1 76 DE72
Crawford Rd. SE5 92 DQ81
Crawford St. W1 4 C7
Crawford St. W1 76 DF71
Crawfords, Swan. 111 FE94
Crawley Rd. E10 65 EB60
Crawley Rd. N22 50 DQ54
Crawley Rd., Enf. 50 DS45
Crawshaw Ct. SW9 91 DN81
Eythorne Rd.
Crawshay Clo., Sev. 154 FG123
Crawthew Gro. SE22 92 DT84
Cray Ave., Ash. 144 CL116
Cray Ave., Orp. 124 EV100
Cray Clo., Dart. 97 FG84
Cray Riverway, Dart. 111 FF85
Cray Rd., Belv. 96 FA79
Cray Rd., Sid. 110 EW94
Cray Rd., Swan. 125 FB100
Cray Valley Rd., Orp. 124 EU99
Craybrooke Rd., Sid. 110 EV91
Craybury End SE9 109 EQ89
Craydene Rd., Erith 97 FF81
Crayford Clo. E6 80 EL71
Neatscourt Rd.
Crayford High St., Dart. 111 FE85
Crayford Rd. N7 63 DK63
Crayford Rd., Dart. 111 FE85
Crayford Way, Dart. 111 FF85
Crayke Hill, Chess. 130 CL108
Craylands, Orp. 124 EW97
Craymill Sq., Dart. 97 FG83
Norris Way
Crayonne Clo., Sun. 113 BS95
Crayside Ind. Est., Dart. 97 FH84
Thames Rd.
Crealock Gro., Wdf.Grn. 52 EF50
Crealock St. SW18 104 DB86
Creasey Clo., Horn. 69 FH61
St. Leonards Way
Creasy Clo., Abb.L. 15 BT31
Creasy Est. SE1 11 M7
Crebor St. SE22 106 DU86
Credenhall Dr., Brom. 123 EM102
Credenhill St. SW16 105 DJ93
Crediton Hill NW6 62 DB64
Crediton Rd. E16 80 EG72
Pacific Rd.
Crediton Rd. NW10 75 CX67
Crediton Way, Esher 129 CG106
Credon Rd. E13 80 EJ68
Credon Rd. SE16 92 DV78
Cree Way, Rom. 55 FE52
Creechurch La. EC3 7 N9
Creechurch La. EC3 78 DS72
Creechurch Pl. EC3 7 N9
Creed Ct. EC4 77 DP72
Ludgate Hill
Creed La. EC4 6 G9
Creek, The, Sun. 113 BU99
Creek Rd. SE8 93 EA79
Creek Rd. SE10 93 EB79
Creek Rd., Bark. 81 ET69
Creek Rd., E.Mol. 115 CE98
Creekside SE8 93 EB80
Creekside, Rain. 83 FE70
Creeland Gro. SE6 107 DZ88
Catford Hill
Crefeld Clo. W6 89 CX79
Creffield Rd. W3 74 CM73
Creffield Rd. W5 74 CM73
Creighton Ave. E6 80 EK68
Creighton Ave. N2 62 DE55
Creighton Ave. N10 48 DF54
Creighton Clo. W12 75 CV73
Bloemfontein Rd.
Creighton Rd. N17 50 DS52
Creighton Rd. NW6 75 CX68
Creighton Rd. W5 87 CK76
Cremer St. E2 7 P1
Cremer St. E2 78 DT68
Cremorne Est. SW10 90 DD79
Milman's St.
Cremorne Gdns., Epsom 130 CR109
Cremorne Rd. SW10 90 DC80
Crescent, The E17 65 DY57
Crescent, The EC3 7 P10
Crescent, The N11 48 DG49
Crescent, The NW2 61 CV62
Crescent, The SW13 89 CT82
Crescent, The SW19 104 DA90
Crescent, The W3 74 CS72
Crescent, The, Abb.L. 15 BT30
Crescent, The, Ashf. 98 BM92
Crescent, The, Barn. 34 DB41
Crescent, The, Beck. 121 EA95
Crescent, The, Bex. 110 EW87
Crescent, The, Cat. 149 EA123
Crescent, The, Cher. 112 BG97
Western Ave.
Crescent, The, Croy. 120 DR99
Crescent, The, Epp. 25 ET32
Crescent, The, Epsom 130 CN114
Crescent, The, Har. 58 CC60
Crescent, The, Hayes 85 BQ80
Crescent, The, Ilf. 67 EN58
Crescent, The, Lthd. 143 CH122
Crescent, The, Loug. 38 EK43
Crescent, The, N.Mal. 116 CQ96
Crescent, The, Rick. 29 BP44
Crescent, The, St.Alb. 16 CA30
Crescent, The, Sev. 155 FK121
Crescent, The, Shep. 113 BT101
Crescent, The, Sid. 109 ET91
Crescent, The, Sthl. 86 BZ75
Crescent, The, Surb. 116 CL99
Crescent, The, Sutt. 132 DD106
Crescent, The (Belmont), Sutt. 132 DA111
Crescent, The, Wat. 30 BW42
Crescent, The (Aldenham), Wat. 44 CB47
Crescent, The, Wem. 59 CG61
Crescent, The, W.Mol. 114 CA98
Crescent, The, W.Wick. 122 EE100
Crescent, The, Wey. 112 BN104
Crescent Ave., Horn. 69 FF61
Crescent Cotts., Sev. 153 FE120
Crescent Dr., Orp. 123 EP100
Crescent E., Barn. 34 DC38
Crescent Gdns. SW19 104 DA90
Crescent Gdns., Ruis. 57 BV59
Crescent Gdns., Swan. 125 FC96
Crescent Gro. SW4 91 DJ84
Crescent Gro., Mitch. 118 DE98
Crescent La. SW4 91 DJ84
Crescent Pl. SW3 8 B8
Crescent Pl. SW3 90 DE77
Crescent Ri. N22 49 DK53
Crescent Ri., Barn. 34 DE43
Crescent Rd. E4 52 EE45
Crescent Rd. E6 80 EJ67
Crescent Rd. E10 65 EB61
Crescent Rd. E13 80 EG67
Crescent Rd. E18 52 EJ54
Crescent Rd. N3 47 CZ53
Crescent Rd. N8 63 DK58
Crescent Rd. N9 50 DU46
Crescent Rd. N11 48 DF49
Crescent Rd. N15 63 DP55
Carlingford Rd.
Crescent Rd. N22 49 DK53
Crescent Rd. SE18 95 EP78
Crescent Rd. SW20 117 CX95
Crescent Rd., Barn. 34 DD42
Crescent Rd., Beck. 121 EB96
Crescent Rd., Brom. 108 EG94

Crescent Rd., Cat. 148 DU124
Crescent Rd., Dag. 69 FB62
Crescent Rd., Enf. 35 DP42
Crescent Rd., Erith 97 FF79
Crescent Rd., Kings.T. 102 CN94
Crescent Rd., Shep. 113 BQ99
Crescent Rd., Sid. 109 ET90
Crescent Row EC1 7 H5
Crescent Stables SW15 89 CY84
Upper Richmond Rd.
Crescent St. N1 77 DM66
Crescent Vw., Loug. 38 EK43
Crescent Way N12 48 DE51
Crescent Way SE4 93 EA83
Crescent Way SW16 105 DM93
Crescent Way, Orp. 137 ES106
Crescent W., Barn. 34 DC39
Crescent Wd. Rd. SE26 106 DU90
Cresford Rd. SW6 90 DB81
Crespigny Rd. NW4 61 CV58
Cress End, Rick. 42 BG46
Springwell Ave.
Cressage Clo., Sthl. 72 CA70
Cressall Clo., Lthd. 143 CH120
Cresset Rd. E9 78 DW65
Cresset St. SW4 91 DK83
Cressfield Clo. NW5 62 DG64
Cressida Rd. N19 63 DJ60
Cressingham Gro., Sutt. 132 DC105
Cressingham Rd. SE13 93 EC83
Cressingham Rd., Edg. 46 CR51
Cressington Clo. N16 64 DS64
Wordsworth Rd.
Cresswell Gdns. SW5 90 DC78
Cresswell Pk. SE3 94 EF83
Cresswell Pl. SW10 90 DC78
Cresswell Rd. SE25 120 DU98
Cresswell Rd., Felt. 100 BY91
Cresswell Rd., Twick. 101 CK86
Cresswell Way N21 49 DN45
Cressy Ct. E1 78 DW71
Cressy Pl.
Cressy Ct. W6 89 CV76
Cressy Pl. E1 78 DW71
Cressy Rd. NW3 62 DF64
Crest, The N13 49 DN49
Crest, The NW4 61 CW57
Crest, The, Surb. 116 CN99
Crest, The (Cheshunt), Wal.Cr. 21 DP27
Orchard Way
Crest Clo., Sev. 139 FB111
Crest Dr., Enf. 36 DW38
Crest Gdns., Ruis. 58 BW62
Crest Rd. NW2 61 CT62
Crest Rd., Brom. 122 EF101
Crest Rd., S.Croy. 134 DV108
Crest Vw., Pnr. 58 BX56
Crest Vw. Dr., Orp. 123 EP99
Crestbrook Ave. N13 49 DP48
Crestfield St. WC1 6 A2
Crestfield St. WC1 77 DL69
Creston Way, Wor.Pk. 117 CX102
Crestway SW15 103 CU86
Crestwood Way, Houns. 100 BZ85
Creswick Rd. W3 74 CP73
Creswick Wk. E3 79 EA69
Malmesbury Rd.
Creswick Wk. NW11 61 CZ56
Creton St. SE18 95 EN76
Crewdson Rd. SW9 91 DN80
Crewe Pl. NW10 75 CT69
Crewe's Ave., Warl. 148 DW116
Crewe's Clo., Warl. 148 DW117
Crewe's La., Warl. 148 DW117
Crews St. E14 93 EA77
Crewys Rd. NW2 61 CZ61
Crewys Rd. SE15 92 DV82
Crichton Ave., Wall. 133 DK106
Crichton Rd., Cars. 132 DF108
Cricket Fld. Rd., Uxb. 70 BK67
Cricket Grn., Mitch. 118 DF97
Cricket Grd. Rd., Chis. 123 EP95
Cricket La., Beck. 107 DY92
Cricket Way, Wey. 113 BS103
Cricketers Arms Rd., Enf. 36 DQ40
Cricketers Clo. N14 49 DJ45
Cricketers Clo., Chess. 129 CK105
Cricketers Clo., Erith 97 FE78
Cricketers Ct. SE11 10 F9
Cricketers Ter., Cars. 118 DE104
Wrythe La.
Cricketfield Rd. E5 64 DV63
Cricketfield Rd., West Dr. 84 BJ77
Cricklade Ave. SW2 105 DL89
Cricklewood Bdy. NW2 61 CW62
Cricklewood La. NW2 61 CX63
Cricklewood Trd. Est. NW2 61 CY62
Cridland St. E15 80 EF67
Church St.
Crieff Ct., Tedd. 101 CJ94
Crieff Rd. SW18 104 DC86
Criffel Ave. SW2 105 DK89
Crimscott St. SE1 11 N7
Crimscott St. SE1 92 DS76
Crimsworth Rd. SW8 91 DK81
Crinan St. N1 77 DL68
Cringle St. SW8 91 DJ80
Cripplegate St. EC2 7 H6
Crisp Rd. W6 89 CW78
Crispe Ho., Bark. 81 ER68
Dovehouse Mead
Crispen Rd., Felt. 100 BY91
Crispian Clo. NW10 60 CS63
Crispin Clo., Ash. 144 CM118
Crispin Clo., Croy. 119 DL103
Harrington Clo.
Crispin Cres., Croy. 119 DK103
Crispin Rd., Edg. 46 CQ51
Crispin St. E1 7 P7
Crispin St. E1 78 DT71
Cristowe Rd. SW6 89 CZ82
Criterion Ms. N19 63 DK61
Crockenhill La., Swan. 125 FG101
Crockenhill Rd., Orp. 124 EX99
Crockenhill Rd., Swan. 124 EZ100
Crockerton Rd. SW17 104 DF89
Crockford Clo., Add. 126 BJ105
Crockford Pk. Rd., Add. 126 BJ106
Crockham Way SE9 109 EN91
Crocus Clo., Croy. 121 DX102
Cornflower La.
Crocus Fld., Barn. 33 CZ44
Croffets, Tad. 145 CX121
Croft, The NW10 75 CT68
Croft, The W5 74 CL71
Croft, The, Barn. 33 CY42
Croft, The, Houns. 86 BY79
Croft, The, Loug. 39 EN40
Croft, The, Pnr. 58 BZ59
Rayners La.
Croft, The, Ruis. 58 BW63
Croft, The, St.Alb. 16 CA25
Croft, The, Swan. 125 FC97
Croft, The, Wem. 59 CJ64
Croft Ave., W.Wick. 121 EC102
Croft Clo. NW7 46 CS48
Croft Clo., Belv. 96 EZ78
Croft Clo., Chis. 109 EM91
Croft Clo., Hayes 85 BQ80
Croft Clo., Kings L. 14 BG30
Croft Clo., Uxb. 70 BN66
Croft End Rd., Kings L. 14 BG30
Croft Fld., Kings L. 14 BG30
Croft Gdns. W7 87 CG75
Croft Gdns., Ruis. 57 BS60
Croft La., Kings L. 14 BG30
Croft Lo. Clo., Wdf.Grn. 52 EH51
Croft Meadow, Kings L. 14 BG30
Croft Ms. N12 48 DC48
Croft Rd. SW16 119 DN95
Croft Rd. SW19 104 DC94
Croft Rd., Brom. 108 EG93
Croft Rd., Cat. 149 DZ122
Croft Rd., Enf. 37 DY39
Croft Rd., Sutt. 132 DE106
Croft St. SE8 93 DY77
Croft Way NW3 62 DA63
Ferncroft Ave.
Croft Way, Sev. 154 FF125
Croft Way, Sid. 109 ES90
Croftdown Rd. NW5 62 DG62
Crofters Clo., Islw. 101 CD85
Ploughmans End
Crofters Ct. SE8 93 DY77
Crofters Mead, Croy. 135 DZ109
Crofters Rd., Nthwd. 43 BS49
Crofters Way NW1 77 DK67
Croftleigh Ave., Pur. 147 DP116
Crofton, Ash. 144 CL118
Crofton Ave. W4 88 CQ80
Crofton Ave., Bex. 110 EX87
Crofton Ave., Orp. 123 EQ103
Crofton Ave., Walt. 114 BW104
Crofton Gro. E4 51 ED49
Crofton La., Orp. 123 ER103
Crofton Pk. Rd. SE4 107 DZ86
Crofton Rd. E13 80 EH70
Crofton Rd. SE5 92 DS81
Crofton Rd., Orp. 123 EN104
Crofton Ter. E5 65 DY64
Studley Clo.
Crofton Ter., Rich. 88 CM84
Crofton Way, Barn. 34 DB44
Wycherley Cres.
Crofton Way, Enf. 35 DN40
Croftongate Way SE4 107 DY85
Crofts, The, Shep. 113 BS98
Crofts La. N22 49 DN52
Glendale Ave.
Crofts Rd., Har. 59 CG58
Crofts St. E1 78 DU73
Croftside SE25 120 DU97
Sunny Bank
Croftway NW3 62 DA63
Croftway, Rich. 101 CH90
Crogsland Rd. NW1 76 DG66
Croham Clo., S.Croy. 134 DS108
Croham Manor Rd., S.Croy. 134 DS108
Croham Mt., S.Croy. 134 DS108
Croham Pk. Ave., S.Croy. 134 DS106
Croham Rd., S.Croy. 134 DR106
Croham Valley Rd., S.Croy. 134 DT107
Croindene Rd. SW16 119 DL95
Cromartie Rd. N19 63 DK59
Cromarty Rd., Edg. 46 CP47
Crombie Clo., Ilf. 67 EM57
Crombie Rd., Sid. 109 ER88
Cromer Clo., Uxb. 71 BQ72
Dawley Ave.
Cromer Pl., Orp. 123 ER102
Andover Rd.
Cromer Rd. E10 65 ED58
James La.
Cromer Rd. N17 50 DU54
Cromer Rd. SE25 120 DV97
Cromer Rd. SW17 104 DG93
Cromer Rd., Barn. 34 DC42
Cromer Rd., Houns. 84 BN83
Cromer Rd., Rom. 69 FC58
Cromer Rd. (Chadwell Heath), Rom. 68 EY58
Cromer Rd., Wat. 30 BW38
Cromer Rd., Wdf.Grn. 52 EG49
Cromer Rd. W., Houns. 84 BN83
Cromer St. WC1 6 A3
Cromer St. WC1 77 DL69
Cromer Ter. E8 64 DU64
Ferncliff Rd.
Cromer Vill. Rd. SW18 103 CZ86
Cromford Clo., Orp. 123 ES104
Cromford Path E5 65 DX63
Overbury St.
Cromford Rd. SW18 104 DA85
Cromford Way, N.Mal. 116 CR95
Cromlix Clo., Chis. 123 EP96
Crompton St. W2 76 DD70
Cromwell Ave. N6 63 DH60
Cromwell Ave. W6 89 CV77
Cromwell Ave., Brom. 122 EH97
Cromwell Ave., N.Mal. 117 CT99
Cromwell Ave. (Cheshunt), Wal.Cr. 22 DU30
Cromwell Clo. E1 78 DU74
Vaughan Way
Cromwell Clo. N2 62 DD56
Cromwell Clo. W3 74 CQ74
High St.
Cromwell Clo., Brom. 122 EH98
Cromwell Clo., Walt. 113 BV102
Cromwell Cres. SW5 90 DA77
Cromwell Gdns. SW7 8 A7
Cromwell Gdns. SW7 90 DD76
Cromwell Gro. W6 89 CW76
Cromwell Gro., Cat. 148 DQ121
Cromwell Ind. Est. E10 65 DY60
Cromwell Ms. SW7 8 A8
Cromwell Ms. SW7 90 DD77
Cromwell Pl. N6 63 DH60
Cromwell Ave.
Cromwell Pl. SW7 8 A8
Cromwell Pl. SW7 90 DD77
Cromwell Pl. SW14 88 CQ83
Cromwell Pl. W3 74 CQ74
Grove Pl.
Cromwell Rd. E7 80 EJ66
Cromwell Rd. E17 65 EC57
Cromwell Rd. N3 48 DC54
Cromwell Rd. N10 48 DG52
Cromwell Rd. SW5 90 DB77
Cromwell Rd. SW7 90 DB77
Cromwell Rd. SW9 91 DP81
Cromwell Rd. SW19 104 DA92
Cromwell Rd., Beck. 121 DY96
Cromwell Rd., Borwd. 32 CL39
Cromwell Rd., Cat. 148 DQ121
Cromwell Rd., Croy. 120 DR101
Cromwell Rd., Felt. 99 BV88
Cromwell Rd., Hayes 71 BR72
Cromwell Rd., Houns. 86 CA84
Cromwell Rd., Kings.T. 116 CL95
Cromwell Rd., Tedd. 101 CG93
Cromwell Rd. (Cheshunt), Wal.Cr. 22 DV28
Cromwell Rd., Walt. 114 BW102
Cromwell Rd., Wem. 74 CL68
Cromwell Rd., Wor.Pk. 116 CR104
Cromwell St., Houns. 86 CA84
Cromwell Twr. EC2 78 DQ71
Whitecross St.
Cromwells Mere, Rom. 55 FD51
Havering Rd.
Crondace Rd. SW6 90 DA81
Crondall St. N1 7 M1
Crondall St. N1 78 DR68
Crook Log, Bexh. 96 EX83
Crooke Rd. SE8 93 DY78
Crooked Billet SW19 103 CW93
Woodhayes Rd.
Crooked Billet Roundabout E17 51 EA52
Crooked Billet Yd. E2 78 DS69
Kingsland Rd.
Crooked Mile, Wal.Abb. 23 EC33
Crooked Usage N3 61 CY55
Crookham Rd. SW6 89 CZ81
Crookston Rd. SE9 95 EN83
Croombs Rd. E16 80 EJ71
Crooms Hill SE10 93 EC80
Crooms Hill Gro. SE10 93 EC80
Cropley Ct. N1 78 DR68
Cropley St.
Cropley St. N1 78 DR68
Croppath Rd., Dag. 68 FA63
Cropthorne Ct. W9 76 DC69
Maida Vale
Crosby Clo., Felt. 100 BY91
Crosby Ct. SE1 11 K4
Crosby Rd. E7 80 EG65
Crosby Rd., Dag. 83 FB68
Crosby Row SE1 11 K4
Crosby Row SE1 92 DR75
Crosby Sq. EC3 7 M9
Crosby Wk. E8 78 DT65
Laurel St.
Crosby Wk. SW2 105 DN87
Crosier Rd., Uxb. 57 BQ63
Crosier Way, Ruis. 57 BS62
Crosland Pl. SW11 90 DG83
Taybridge Rd.
Cross Ave. SE10 93 ED79
Cross Deep, Twick. 101 CF90
Cross Deep Gdns., Twick. 101 CF89
Cross Keys Clo. W1 4 G7
Cross Keys Clo., Sev. 154 FG127
Brittains La.
Cross Keys Sq. EC1 7 H7
Cross Lances Rd., Houns. 86 CB84
Cross La. EC3 11 M1
Cross La. N8 63 DM55
Cross La., Bex. 110 EZ87
Cross Rd. E4 52 EE46
Cross Rd. N11 49 DH50
Cross Rd. N22 49 DN52
Cross Rd. SE5 92 DS82
Cross Rd. SW19 104 DA94
Cross Rd., Brom. 122 EL103
Cross Rd., Croy. 120 DR102
Cross Rd., Enf. 36 DT42
Cross Rd., Felt. 100 BY91
Cross Rd., Har. 59 CD56
Cross Rd. (South Harrow), Har. 58 CB62
Cross Rd. (Wealdstone), Har. 45 CG54
Cross Rd., Kings.T. 102 CM94
Cross Rd., Orp. 124 EV99
Cross Rd., Pur. 133 DP113
Cross Rd., Rom. 68 FA56
Cross Rd. (Chadwell Heath), Rom. 68 EW59
Cross Rd., Sid. 110 EV91
Sidcup Hill
Cross Rd., Sutt. 132 DD106
Cross Rd. (Belmont), Sutt. 132 DA110
Cross Rd., Tad. 145 CW122
Cross Rd., Uxb. 70 BJ66
New Windsor St.
Cross Rd., Wal.Cr. 23 DY33
Cross Rd., Wat. 30 BY44
Cross Rd., Wey. 113 BR104
Cross Rd., Wdf.Grn. 53 EM51
Cross Rds., Loug. 38 EH40
Cross St. N1 77 DP67
Cross St. SW13 88 CS82
Cross St., Erith 97 FE78
Bexley Rd.
Cross St., Hmptn. 100 CC92
Cross St., Uxb. 70 BJ66
Cross St., Wat. 30 BW41
Cross Way, Pnr. 43 BV54
Cross Way, The, Har. 45 CE54
Crossbow Rd., Chig. 53 ET50
Crossbrook Rd. SE3 94 EL82
Crossbrook St. (Cheshunt), Wal.Cr. 23 DX31
Crossfield Pl., Wey. 127 BP108
Crossfield Rd. N17 64 DQ55
Crossfield Rd. NW3 76 DD65
Crossfield St. SE8 93 EA80
Crossfields, Loug. 39 EP43
Crossford St. SW9 91 DL82
Crossgate, Edg. 46 CN48
Crossgate, Grnf. 73 CH65
Crossing Rd., Epp. 26 EU32
Crossland Rd., Th.Hth. 119 DP99
Crosslands Ave. W5 74 CM74
Crosslands Ave., Sthl. 86 BZ78
Crosslands Rd., Epsom 130 CR107
Crosslet St. SE17 11 L8
Crosslet Vale SE10 93 EB81
Blackheath Rd.
Crossley Clo., West. 150 EK115
Crossley St. N7 77 DN65
Crossmead SE9 109 EM88
Crossmead, Wat. 29 BV44
Crossmead Ave., Grnf. 72 CA69
Crossmount Ho. SE5 92 DQ80
Bowyer St.
Crossness La. SE28 82 EX73
Bayliss Ave.
Crossness Rd., Bark. 81 ET69
Crossoaks La., Borwd. 32 CR35
Crossoaks La. (South Mimms), Pot.B. 18 CS34
Crosspath, The, Rad. 31 CG35
Crossthwaite Ave. SE5 92 DR84
Crosswall EC3 7 P10
Crosswall EC3 78 DT73
Crossway N12 48 DD51
Crossway N16 64 DS64
Crossway N22 49 DP52
Crossway NW9 61 CT56
Crossway SE28 82 EW72
Crossway SW20 117 CW98
Crossway W13 73 CG70
Crossway, Dag. 68 EW62
Crossway, Enf. 50 DS45
Crossway, Hayes 71 BU74
Crossway, Orp. 123 ER98
Crossway, Ruis. 58 BW63
Crossway, Walt. 113 BV103
Crossway, Wdf.Grn. 52 EJ49
Crossway, The SE9 108 EK89
Crossway, The, Uxb. 70 BM68
Crossways N21 36 DQ44
Crossways, Rom. 69 FH55
Crossways, S.Croy. 135 DY108
Crossways, Sun. 99 BT94
Crossways, Sutt. 132 DD109
Crossways, West. 150 EJ120
Crossways, The, Couls. 147 DM119
Crossways, The, Houns. 86 BZ80
Crossways, The, Wem. 60 CN61
Crossways Rd., Beck. 121 EA98
Crossways Rd., Mitch. 119 DH97
Crosswell Clo., Shep. 113 BQ96
Croston St. E8 78 DU67
Crothall Clo. N13 49 DM48
Crouch Ave., Bark. 82 EV68
Crouch Clo., Beck. 107 EA93
Abbey La.
Crouch Cft. SE9 109 EN90
Crouch End Hill N8 63 DK59
Crouch Hall Rd. N8 63 DK58
Crouch Hill N4 63 DL59
Crouch Hill N8 63 DL58
Crouch La. (Cheshunt), Wal.Cr. 22 DQ28
Crouch Oak La., Add. 126 BJ105
Crouch Rd. NW10 74 CR66
Crouchman's Clo. SE26 106 DT90
Crow Clo., Warl. 149 DY118
Crow Dr., Sev. 153 FC115
Crow La., Rom. 68 EZ59
Crowborough Clo., Warl. 149 DY118
Crowborough Dr., Warl. 149 DY118
Crowborough Path, Wat. 44 BX49
Prestwick Rd.
Crowborough Rd. SW17 104 DG93
Crowden Way SE28 82 EW73
Crowder St. E1 78 DV73
Crowfoot Clo. E9 65 DZ64
Lee Conservancy Rd.
Crowhurst Clo. SW9 91 DN82
Crowhurst Way, Orp. 124 EW99
Crowland Ave., Hayes 85 BS77
Crowland Gdns. N14 49 DL45
Crowland Rd. N15 64 DT57
Crowland Rd., Th.Hth. 120 DR98
Crowland Ter. N1 78 DR66
Crowland Wk., Mord. 118 DB100
Crowlands Ave., Rom. 69 FB58
Crowley Cres., Croy. 133 DN106
Crowline Wk. N1 78 DR65
Clephane Rd.
Crowmarsh Gdns. SE23 106 DW87
Tyson Rd.
Crown Arc., Kings.T. 115 CK96
Union St.
Crown Ash Hill, West. 136 EH114
Crown Ash La., West. 150 EG116
Crown Clo. E3 79 EA67
Crown Clo. NW6 76 DB65
Crown Clo. NW7 47 CT47
Crown Clo., Hayes 85 BT75
Station Rd.
Crown Clo., Orp. 138 EU105
Crown Clo., Walt. 114 BW101
Crown Ct. EC2 7 J9
Crown Ct. SE12 108 EH86
Crown Ct. WC2 6 A9
Crown Ct., Brom. 122 EK99
Victoria Rd.
Crown Dale SE19 105 DP93
Crown Hill, Croy. 120 DQ103
Crown Hill, Epp. 25 EN34
Crown Hill, Wal.Abb. 24 EL33
Crown La. N14 49 DJ46
Crown La. SW16 105 DN92
Crown La., Brom. 122 EK99
Crown La., Chis. 123 EQ95
Crown La., Mord. 118 DA97
Crown La. Gdns. SW16 105 DN92
Crown La.
Crown La. Spur, Brom. 122 EK100
Crown Ms. E13 80 EJ67
Waghorn Rd.
Crown Ms. W6 89 CU77
Crown Office Row EC4 6 D10
Crown Par., Hayes 71 BT71
Crown Pas. SW1 9 L3
Crown Pas., Wat. 30 BW42
The Cres.
Crown Pl. NW5 77 DH65
Kentish Town Rd.
Crown Pt. Par. SE19 105 DP93
Beulah Hill
Crown Ri., Wat. 16 BW34
Crown Rd. N10 48 DG52
Crown Rd., Borwd. 32 CN39
Crown Rd., Enf. 36 DU41
Crown Rd., Ilf. 67 ER56
Crown Rd., Mord. 118 DA98
Crown Rd., N.Mal. 116 CQ95
Crown Rd., Orp. 138 EU106
Crown Rd., Ruis. 58 BX64
Crown Rd., Sev. 139 FF110
Crown Rd., Sutt. 132 DA105
Crown Rd., Twick. 101 CH86
Crown St. SE5 92 DQ80
Crown St. W3 74 CP74
Crown St., Dag. 83 FC65
Crown St., Har. 59 CD60
Crown Ter., Rich. 88 CM84
Crown Wk., Uxb. 70 BJ66
Oxford Rd.
Crown Wk., Wem. 60 CM62
Crown Way, West Dr. 70 BM74
Crown Wds. La. SE9 95 EQ82
Crown Wds. La. SE18 95 EP82
Crown Wds. Way SE9 109 ER85
Crown Yd., Houns. 86 CC83
High St.
Crowndale Rd. NW1 77 DJ68
Crownfield Ave., Ilf. 67 ES58
Crownfield Rd. E15 65 ED63
Crownfields, Sev. 155 FH125
Crownhill Rd. NW10 75 CT67
Crownhill Rd., Wdf.Grn. 52 EL52
Crownmead Way, Rom. 69 FB56
Crownstone Rd. SW2 105 DN85
Crowntree Clo., Islw. 87 CF79
Crows Rd. E15 79 ED69
Crows Rd., Epp. 25 ET30
Crowshott Ave., Stan. 45 CJ54
Crowther Ave., Brent. 88 CL77
Crowther Rd. SE25 120 DU98
Crowthorne Clo. SW18 103 CZ88
Crowthorne Rd. W10 75 CX72
Croxdale Rd., Borwd. 32 CM40
Croxden Clo., Edg. 60 CM55
Croxden Wk., Mord. 118 DC100

Dibden Row SE1 91 DN76
Gerridge St.
Dibden St. N1 78 DQ67
Dibdin Clo., Sutt. 118 DA104
Dibdin Rd., Sutt. 118 DA104
Diceland Rd., Bans. 145 CZ116
Dicey Ave. NW2 61 CW63
Dick Turpin Way, Felt. 85 BT84
Dickens Ave. N3 48 DC53
Dickens Ave., Uxb. 71 BP72
Dickens Clo., Erith 97 FB81
Belmont Rd.
Dickens Clo., Hayes 85 BS77
Croyde Ave.
Dickens Clo., Rich. 102 CL89
Dickens Clo., Wal.Cr. 22 DU26
Dickens Dr., Chis. 109 EQ93
Dickens Est. SE1 92 DT75
Dickens Est. SE16 92 DT75
Dickens La. N18 50 DS50
Dickens Ri., Chig. 53 EP48
Dickens Rd. E6 80 EK68
Dickens Sq. SE1 11 J6
Dickens Sq. SE1 92 DQ76
Dickens St. SW8 91 DH82
Dickenson Clo. N9 50 DU46
Croyland Rd.
Dickenson Rd. N8 63 DL59
Dickenson Rd., Felt. 100 BX92
Dickenson St. NW5 77 DH65
Dalby St.
Dickensons La. SE25 120 DU99
Dickensons Pl. SE25 120 DU100
Dickerage La., N.Mal. 116 CQ97
Dickerage Rd., Kings.T. 116 CQ95
Dickerage Rd., N.Mal. 116 CQ95
Dickinson Ave., Rick. 28 BN44
Dickinson Sq., Rick. 28 BN44
Dickson (Cheshunt), Wal.Cr. 22 DT27
Dickson Fold, Pnr. 58 BX56
Dickson Rd. SE9 94 EL83
Didsbury Clo. E6 81 EM67
Barking Rd.
Dig Dag Hill (Cheshunt), Wal.Cr. 22 DT27
Digby Cres. N4 64 DQ61
Digby Gdns., Dag. 82 FA67
Digby Pl., Croy. 120 DT104
Digby Rd. E9 65 DX64
Digby Rd., Bark. 81 ET66
Digby St. E2 78 DW69
Digby Way, W.Byf. 126 BM112
High Rd.
Digdens Ri., Epsom 144 CQ115
Dighton Ct. SE5 92 DQ79
Hillingdon St.
Dighton Rd. SW18 104 DC85
Digswell Clo., Borwd. 32 CN38
Digswell St. N7 77 DN65
Holloway Rd.
Dilhorne Clo. SE12 108 EH90
Dilke St. SW3 90 DF79
Dillwyn Clo. SE26 107 DY91
Dilston Clo., Nthlt. 72 BW69
Yeading La.
Dilston Gro. SE16 92 DW77
Abbeyfield Rd.
Dilston Rd., Lthd. 143 CG119
Dilton Gdns. SW15 103 CV88
Dimes Pl. W6 89 CV77
King St.
Dimmock Dr., Grnf. 59 CD64
Dimmocks La., Rick. 28 BH36
Dimond Clo. E7 66 EG63
Dimsdale Dr. NW9 60 CQ60
Dimsdale Dr., Enf. 36 DU44
Dimsdale Wk. E13 80 EG67
Stratford Rd.
Dimson Cres. E3 79 EA70
Wellington Way
Dingle, The, Uxb. 71 BP69
Dingle Clo., Barn. 33 CT44
Dingle Gdns. E14 79 EA73
Dingle Rd., Ashf. 99 BP92
Dingley La. SW16 105 DK89
Dingley Pl. EC1 7 J3
Dingley Pl. EC1 78 DQ69
Dingley Rd. EC1 7 H3
Dingley Rd. EC1 78 DQ69
Dingwall Ave., Croy. 120 DQ103
Dingwall Gdns. NW11 62 DA58
Dingwall Pl., Croy. 120 DR103
Dingwall Rd.
Dingwall Rd. SW18 104 DC87
Dingwall Rd., Cars. 132 DF109
Dingwall Rd., Croy. 120 DR102
Dinmont St. E2 78 DV68
Coate St.
Dinsdale Gdns. SE25 120 DS99
Dinsdale Gdns., Barn. 34 DB43
Dinsdale Rd. SE3 94 EF79
Dinsmore Rd. SW12 105 DH87
Dinton Rd. SW19 104 DD93
Dinton Rd., Kings.T. 102 CM94
Diploma Ave. N2 62 DE56
Dirdene Clo., Epsom 131 CT112
Dirdene Gdns., Epsom 131 CT112
Dirdene Gro., Epsom 131 CT112
Dirleton Rd. E15 80 EF67
Disbrowe Rd. W6 89 CY79
Discovery Wk. E1 78 DV74
Wapping La.
Dishforth La. NW9 46 CS53
Disney Ms. N4 63 DP57
Chesterfield Gdns.
Disney Pl. SE1 11 J4
Disney St. SE1 11 J4
Dison Clo., Enf. 37 DX39
Disraeli Clo. SE28 82 EW74
Disraeli Clo. W4 88 CR77
Acton La.
Disraeli Gdns. SW15 89 CZ84
Fawe Pk. Rd.
Disraeli Rd. E7 80 EG65
Disraeli Rd. NW10 74 CR68
Disraeli Rd. SW15 89 CY84
Disraeli Rd. W5 73 CK74
Diss St. E2 7 P2
Diss St. E2 78 DT69
Distaff La. EC4 7 H10
Distaff La. EC4 78 DQ73
Distillery La. W6 89 CW78
Fulham Palace Rd.
Distillery Rd. W6 89 CW78
Distillery Wk., Brent. 88 CL79
Pottery Rd.
Distin St. SE11 10 D9
District Rd., Wem. 59 CH64
Ditch All. SE10 93 EB81
Ditchburn St. E14 79 EC73
Ditches La., Couls. 147 DL120
Ditchfield Rd., Hayes 72 BY70
Dittisham Rd. SE9 108 EL91
Ditton Clo., T.Ditt. 115 CG101
Watts Rd.
Ditton Gra. Clo., Surb. 115 CK102
Ditton Gra. Dr., Surb. 115 CK102
Ditton Hill, Surb. 115 CJ102
Ditton Hill Rd., Surb. 115 CJ102
Ditton Lawn, T.Ditt. 115 CG102
Ditton Pl. SE20 120 DV95
Hartfield Gro.
Ditton Reach, T.Ditt. 115 CH100
Ditton Rd., Bexh. 110 EX85
Ditton Rd., Sthl. 86 BZ78
Ditton Rd., Surb. 115 CK103
Divis Way SW15 103 CV86
Dover Pk. Dr.
Dixon Clark Ct. N1 77 DP65
Canonbury Rd.
Dixon Clo. E6 81 EM72
Brandreth Rd.
Dixon Dr., Wey. 126 BM110
Dixon Pl., W.Wick. 121 EB102
Dixon Rd. SE14 93 DY81
Dixon Rd. SE25 120 DS97
Dixon's All. SE16 92 DV75
West La.
Dixons Hill Clo., Hat. 19 CV25
Dixons Hill Rd., Hat. 19 CU25
Dobbin Clo., Har. 45 CG54
Dobell Rd. SE9 109 EM85
Dobree Ave. NW10 75 CV66
Dobson Clo. NW6 76 DD66
Dock Hill Ave. SE16 93 DX75
Dock Rd. E16 80 EF73
Dock Rd., Brent. 87 CK80
Dock St. E1 78 DU73
Dockers Tanner Rd. E14 93 EA77
Dockett Eddy La., Shep. 112 BM102
Dockhead SE1 92 DT75
Dockland St. E16 81 EN74
Dockley Rd. SE16 92 DU76
Dockwell Clo., Felt. 85 BU84
Doctor Johnson Ave. SW17 105 DH90
Doctors Clo. SE26 106 DW92
Doctors La., Cat. 147 DN123
Docwra's Bldgs. N1 78 DS65
Dod St. E14 79 EA72
Dodbrooke Rd. SE27 105 DN90
Doddington Gro. SE17 91 DP79
Doddington Pl. SE17 91 DP79
Dodd's Cres., W.Byf. 126 BH114
Dodd's La., Wok. 126 BG114
Dodsley Pl. N9 50 DW48
Dodson St. SE1 10 E5
Dodson St. SE1 91 DN75
Doebury Wk. SE18 96 EU79
Prestwood Clo.
Doel Clo. SW19 104 DC94
Dog Kennel Hill SE22 92 DS83
Dog Kennel Hill Est. SE22 92 DS83
Dog La. NW10 60 CS63
Doggets Ct., Barn. 34 DE43
Doggett Rd. SE6 107 EA87
Doghurst Ave., Hayes 85 BP80
Doghurst Dr., West Dr. 85 BP80
Doghurst La., Couls. 146 DF120
Doherty Rd. E13 80 EG70
Dolben St. SE1 10 G3
Dolben St. SE1 77 DP74
Dolby Ct. EC4 78 DQ73
Garlick Hill
Dolby Rd. SW6 89 CZ82
Dolland St. SE11 91 DM78
Dollis Ave. N3 47 CZ53
Dollis Brook Wk., Barn. 33 CY44
Dollis Cres., Ruis. 58 BW60
Dollis Hill Ave. NW2 61 CV62
Dollis Hill Est. NW2 61 CU62
Dollis Hill La. NW2 61 CT63
Dollis Ms. N3 47 CZ53
Dollis Pk.
Dollis Pk. N3 47 CZ53
Dollis Rd. N3 47 CY53
Dollis Rd. NW7 47 CY52
Dollis Valley Grn. Wk. N20 48 DC47
Totteridge La.
Dollis Valley Grn. Wk., Barn. 33 CY44
Leeside
Dollis Valley Way, Barn. 33 CZ43
Dolman Clo. N3 48 DC54
Avondale Rd.
Dolman Rd. W4 88 CR77
Dolman St. SW4 91 DM84
Dolphin App., Rom. 69 FF56
Dolphin Clo. SE16 93 DX75
Kinburn St.
Dolphin Clo. SE28 82 EX72
Dolphin Clo., Surb. 115 CK100
Dolphin Ct. NW11 61 CY58
Dolphin Ct., Stai. 98 BG90
Bremer Rd.
Dolphin Ct. N., Stai. 98 BG90
Bremer Rd.
Dolphin Est., The, Sun. 113 BS95
Dolphin La. E14 79 EB73
Dolphin Rd., Nthlt. 72 BZ67
Dolphin Rd., Sun. 113 BS95
Dolphin Rd. N., Sun. 113 BS95
Dolphin Rd. S., Sun. 113 BR95
Dolphin Rd. W., Sun. 113 BS95
Dolphin Sq. SW1 91 DJ78
Dolphin Sq. W4 88 CS80
Dolphin St., Kings.T. 116 CL95
Dombey St. WC1 6 B6
Dombey St. WC1 77 DM71
Dome Hill Pk. SE26 106 DT91
Domett Clo. SE5 92 DR84
Domfe Pl. E5 64 DW63
Rushmore Rd.
Domingo St. EC1 7 H4
Dominion Dr., Rom. 55 FB51
Dominion Rd., Croy. 120 DT101
Dominion Rd., Sthl. 86 BY76
Dominion St. EC2 7 L6
Dominion Way, Rain. 83 FG69
Domonic Dr. SE9 109 EP91
Domville Clo. N20 48 DD47
Don Phelan Clo. SE5 92 DR81
Don Way, Rom. 55 FE52
Donald Dr., Rom. 68 EW57
Donald Rd. E13 80 EH67
Donald Rd., Croy. 119 DM100
Donald Wds. Gdns., Surb. 116 CP103
Donaldson Rd. NW6 75 CZ67
Donaldson Rd. SE18 95 EN81
Doncaster Dr., Nthlt. 58 BZ64
Doncaster Gdns. N4 64 DQ58
Stanhope Gdns.
Doncaster Gdns., Nthlt. 58 BZ64
Doncaster Grn., Wat. 44 BW50
Doncaster Rd. N9 50 DV45
Doncel Ct. E4 51 ED45
Donegal St. N1 6 C1
Donegal St. N1 77 DM68
Doneraile St. SW6 89 CX82
Dongola Rd. E13 80 EH69
Dongola Rd. N17 64 DS55
Dongola Rd. W. E13 80 EH69
Balaam St.
Donington Ave., Ilf. 67 EQ57
Donkey All. SE22 106 DU87
Donkey La., Enf. 36 DU40
Donne Ct. SE24 106 DQ86
Donne Pl. SW3 8 C8
Donne Pl. SW3 90 DE77
Donne Pl., Mitch. 119 DH98
Donne Rd., Dag. 68 EW61
Donnefield Ave., Edg. 46 CL52
Donnington Rd. NW10 75 CV66
Donnington Rd., Har. 59 CJ57
Donnington Rd., Sev. 153 FD120
Donnington Rd., Wor.Pk. 117 CU103
Donnybrook Rd. SW16 105 DJ94
Donovan Ave. N10 63 DH55
Donovan Clo., Epsom 130 CR110
Nimbus Rd.
Doon St. SE1 10 D2
Doone Clo., Tedd. 101 CG93
Dora Rd. SW19 104 DA92
Dora St. E14 79 DZ72
Dorado Gdns., Orp. 124 EX104
Doral Way, Cars. 132 DF106
Doran Gro. SE18 95 ES80
Doran Mans. N2 62 DF57
Great N. Rd.
Doran Wk. E15 79 EC66
Dorchester Ave. N13 50 DQ49
Dorchester Ave., Bex. 110 EX88
Dorchester Ave., Har. 58 CC58
Dorchester Clo., Nthlt. 58 CB64
Dorchester Clo., Orp. 110 EU94
Grovelands Rd.
Dorchester Ct. N14 49 DH45
Dorchester Ct. SE24 106 DQ85
Dorchester Ct., Rick. 29 BR43
Mayfare
Dorchester Dr. SE24 106 DQ85
Dorchester Dr., Felt. 99 BS86
Dorchester Gdns. E4 51 EA49
Dorchester Gdns. NW11 62 DA56
Dorchester Gro. W4 88 CS78
Dorchester Ms., N.Mal. 116 CR98
Elm Rd.
Dorchester Ms., Twick. 101 CJ87
Dorchester Rd., Mord. 118 DB101
Dorchester Rd., Nthlt. 58 CB64
Dorchester Rd., Wey. 113 BP104
Dorchester Rd., Wor.Pk. 117 CW102
Dorchester Way, Har. 60 CM58
Dorchester Waye, Hayes 71 BV72
Dorcis Ave., Bexh. 96 EY82
Dordrecht Rd. W3 74 CS74
Dore Ave. E12 67 EN64
Dore Gdns., Mord. 118 DB101
Doreen Ave. NW9 60 CR60
Dorell Clo., Sthl. 72 BZ71
Doria Rd. SW6 89 CZ82
Dorian Rd., Horn. 69 FG60
Doric Dr., Tad. 145 CZ120
Doric Way NW1 5 M2
Doric Way NW1 77 DK69
Dorien Rd. SW20 117 CX96
Doris Ave., Erith 97 FC81
Doris Rd. E7 80 EG66
Doris Rd., Ashf. 99 BR93
Dorking Clo. SE8 93 DZ79
Dorking Clo., Wor.Pk. 117 CX103
Dorking Rd., Epsom 144 CN116
Dorking Rd., Lthd. 143 CH122
Dorking Rd., Tad. 145 CX123
Dorlcote Rd. SW18 104 DE87
Dorling Dr., Epsom 131 CT112
Dorly Clo., Shep. 113 BS98
Dorma Trd. Est. E10 65 DX60
Dorman Pl. N9 50 DU47
Balham Rd.
Dorman Wk. NW10 60 CR64
Garden Way
Dorman Way NW8 76 DD67
Dormans Clo., Nthwd. 43 BR52
Dormay St. SW18 104 DB85
Dormer Clo. E15 80 EF65
Dormer Clo., Barn. 33 CX43
Dormers Ave., Sthl. 72 CA72
Dormers Ri., Sthl. 72 CB73
Dormers Wells La., Sthl. 72 CA72
Dormywood, Ruis. 57 BT57
Dornberg Clo. SE3 94 EG80
Dornberg Rd. SE3 94 EH80
Banchory Rd.
Dorncliffe Rd. SW6 89 CY82
Dorney NW3 76 DE66
Dorney Gro., Wey. 113 BP103
Dorney Ri., Orp. 123 ET98
Dorney Way, Houns. 100 BY85
Dornfell St. NW6 61 CZ64
Dornford Gdns., Couls. 148 DQ119
Dornton Rd. SW12 105 DH89
Dornton Rd., S.Croy. 134 DR106
Dorothy Ave., Wem. 74 CL66
Dorothy Evans Clo., Bexh. 97 FB84
Dorothy Gdns., Dag. 68 EV63
Dorothy Rd. SW11 90 DF83
Dorrell Pl. SW9 91 DN84
Brixton Rd.
Dorrien Wk. SW16 105 DK89
Dingley La.
Dorrington Ct. SE25 120 DS96
Dorrington Pt. E3 79 EB69
Bromley High St.
Dorrington St. EC1 6 D6
Dorrington St. EC1 77 DN71
Dorrit Ms. N18 50 DS50
Dorrit Way, Chis. 109 EQ93
Dorrofield Clo., Rick. 29 BQ43
Dors Clo. NW9 60 CR60
Dorset Ave., Hayes 71 BS69
Dorset Ave., Rom. 69 FD56
Dorset Ave., Sthl. 86 CA77
Dorset Ave., Well. 95 ET84
Dorset Bldgs. EC4 6 F9
Dorset Clo. NW1 4 D6
Dorset Clo., Hayes 71 BS69
Dorset Dr., Edg. 46 CM51
Dorset Est. E2 78 DT69
Dorset Gdns., Mitch. 119 DM98
Dorset Ms. N3 48 DA53
Dorset Ms. SW1 9 H6
Dorset Pl. E15 79 ED65
Dorset Pl. SW1 9 M10
Dorset Ri. EC4 6 F9
Dorset Ri. EC4 77 DP72
Dorset Rd. E7 80 EJ66
Dorset Rd. N15 64 DR56
Dorset Rd. N22 49 DL53
Dorset Rd. SE9 108 EL89
Dorset Rd. SW8 91 DL80
Dorset Rd. SW19 118 DA95
Dorset Rd. W5 87 CJ76
Dorset Rd., Ashf. 98 BK90
Dorset Rd., Beck. 121 DX97
Dorset Rd., Har. 58 CC58
Dorset Rd., Mitch. 118 DE96
Dorset Rd., Sutt. 132 DA110
Dorset Sq. NW1 4 D5
Dorset Sq. NW1 76 DF70
Dorset Sq., Epsom 130 CR110
Dorset St. W1 4 E7
Dorset St. W1 76 DF71
Dorset St., Sev. 155 FH125
High St.
Dorset Way, Twick. 101 CD88
Dorset Way, Uxb. 70 BM68
Dorset Way, W.Byf. 126 BK110
Dorset Waye, Houns. 86 BZ80
Dorton Dr., Sev. 155 FM122
Dorville Cres. W6 89 CV76
Dorville Rd. SE12 108 EF85
Dothill Rd. SE18 95 ER80
Douai Gro., Hmptn. 114 CC95
Doubleday Rd., Loug. 39 EQ41
Doughty Ms. WC1 6 B5
Doughty Ms. WC1 77 DM70
Doughty St. WC1 6 B4
Doughty St. WC1 77 DM70
Douglas Ave. E17 51 EA53
Douglas Ave., N.Mal. 117 CV98
Douglas Ave., Wat. 30 BX37
Douglas Ave., Wem. 74 CL66
Douglas Clo., Stan. 45 CG50
Douglas Clo., Wall. 133 DL107
Douglas Ct., Cat. 148 DQ122
Fairbourne La.
Douglas Ct., West. 150 EL117
Douglas Cres., Hayes 72 BW70
Douglas Dr., Croy. 121 EA104
Douglas Est. N1 78 DQ65
Douglas Ms. NW2 61 CY62
Douglas Pl. E14 93 EC78
Manchester Rd.
Douglas Rd. E4 52 EE45
Douglas Rd. E16 80 EG71
Douglas Rd. N1 78 DQ66
Douglas Rd. N22 49 DN53
Douglas Rd. NW6 75 CZ67
Douglas Rd., Add. 112 BH104
Douglas Rd., Esher 114 CB103
Douglas Rd., Horn. 69 FF58
Douglas Rd., Houns. 86 CB83
Douglas Rd., Ilf. 68 EU58
Douglas Rd., Kings.T. 116 CP96
Douglas Rd., Stai. 98 BK86
Douglas Rd., Surb. 116 CM103
Douglas Rd., Well. 96 EV81
Douglas Sq., Mord. 118 DA100
Douglas St. SW1 9 M9
Douglas St. SW1 91 DK77
Douglas Ter. E17 51 EA53
Douglas Ave.
Douglas Way SE8 93 DZ80
Doulton Ms. NW6 76 DB65
Lymington Rd.
Doultons, The, Stai. 98 BG94
Dounesforth Gdns. SW18 104 DB88
Douro Pl. W8 90 DB76
Douro St. E3 79 EA68
Douthwaite Sq. E1 78 DU74
Torrington Pl.
Dove App. E6 80 EL71
Dove Clo., Nthlt. 72 BX70
Wayfarer Rd.
Dove Clo., S.Croy. 135 DX111
Dove Ct. EC2 7 K9
Dove Ho. Gdns. E4 51 EA47
Dove La., Pot.B. 20 DB34
Dove Ms. SW5 90 DC77
Dove Pk., Pnr. 44 CA52
Dove Rd. N1 78 DR65
Dove Row E2 78 DU67
Dove Wk. SW1 8 F10
Dove Wk., Horn. 83 FH65
Heron Flight Ave.
Dovecot Clo., Pnr. 57 BV57
Dovecote Ave. N22 63 DN55
Dovecote Clo., Wey. 113 BP104
Dovecote Gdns. SW14 88 CR83
Avondale Rd.
Dovecott Gdns. SW14 88 CR83
North Worple Way
Dovedale Ave., Har. 59 CJ58
Dovedale Ave., Ilf. 53 EN54
Dovedale Clo., Uxb. 42 BJ54
Dovedale Clo., Well. 96 EU81
Dovedale Ri., Mitch. 104 DF94
Dovedale Rd. SE22 106 DV85
Dovedon Clo. N14 49 DL47
Dovehouse Grn., Wey. 127 BR105
Rosslyn Pk.
Dovehouse Mead, Bark. 81 ER68
Dovehouse St. SW3 8 B10
Dovehouse St. SW3 90 DD78
Doveney Clo., Orp. 124 EW97
Dover Clo. NW2 61 CX61
Brent Ter.
Dover Clo., Rom. 55 FC54
Dover Flats SE1 92 DS77
Old Kent Rd.
Dover Gdns., Cars. 118 DF104
Dover Ho. Rd. SW15 89 CU84
Dover Pk. Dr. SW15 103 CV86
Dover Rd. E12 66 EJ61
Dover Rd. N9 50 DW47
Dover Rd. SE19 106 DR93
Dover Rd., Rom. 68 EY58
Dover St. W1 9 J1
Dover St. W1 77 DH73
Dover Way, Rick. 29 BQ42
Dover Yd. W1 9 J2
Dovercourt Ave., Th.Hth. 119 DN99
Dovercourt Est. N1 78 DR65
Balls Pond Rd.
Dovercourt Gdns., Stan. 46 CL50
Dovercourt La., Sutt. 118 DC104
Dovercourt Rd. SE22 106 DS86
Doverfield, Wal.Cr. 22 DQ29
Doverfield Rd. SW2 105 DL86
Doveridge Gdns. N13 49 DP49
Doves Clo., Brom. 122 EL103
Doveton Rd., S.Croy. 134 DR106
Doveton St. E1 78 DW70
Malcolm Rd.
Dowanhill Rd. SE6 107 ED88
Dowdeswell Clo. SW15 88 CS84
Dowding Pl., Stan. 45 CG51
Dowding Rd., Uxb. 70 BM66
Dowding Rd., West. 150 EK115
Dowding Way, Horn. 83 FH66
Dower Ave., Wall. 133 DH109
Dowgate Hill EC4 7 K10
Dowgate Hill EC4 78 DR73
Dowland St. W10 75 CY69
Dowlas Est. SE5 92 DS80
Dowlas St.
Dowlas St. SE5 92 DS80
Dowlerville Rd., Orp. 137 ET107
Dowman Clo. SW19 118 DB95
Nelson Gro. Rd.
Down Clo., Nthlt. 71 BV68
Down Hall Rd., Kings.T. 115 CK95
Down Pl. W6 89 CV78

Down Rd., Tedd. 101 CH93
Down St. W1 9 H3
Down St. W1 77 DH74
Down St., W.Mol. 114 CA99
Down St. Ms. W1 9 H3
Down Way, Nthlt. 71 BV69
Downage NW4 61 CW55
Downalong (Bushey), Wat. 45 CD46
Downbank Ave., Bexh. 97 FD81
Downbarns Rd., Ruis. 58 BX62
Downbury Ms. SW18 104 DA86
Merton Rd.
Downderry Rd., Brom. 107 ED90
Downe Ave., Sev. 137 ER112
Downe Clo., Well. 96 EW80
Downe Rd., Kes. 136 EK109
Downe Rd., Mitch. 118 DF96
Downe Rd., Sev. 137 EQ114
Downend SE18 95 EP80
Moordown
Downer Dr., Rick. 28 BG36
Downers Cotts. SW4 91 DJ84
The Pavement
Downes Clo., Twick. 101 CH86
St. Margarets Rd.
Downes Ct. N21 49 DN46
Downfield, Wor.Pk. 117 CT102
Downfield Clo. W9 76 DB70
Downfield Rd. (Cheshunt), Wal.Cr. 23 DY31
Downham Clo., Rom. 54 FA52
Downham La., Brom. 107 ED92
Downham Way
Downham Rd. N1 78 DR66
Downham Way, Brom. 107 ED92
Downhills Ave. N17 64 DR55
Downhills Pk. Rd. N17 64 DQ55
Downhills Way N17 50 DQ54
Downhurst Ave. NW7 46 CR50
Downing Clo., Har. 58 CC55
Downing Dr., Grnf. 73 CD67
Downing Rd., Dag. 82 EZ67
Downing St. SW1 9 P4
Downing St. SW1 91 DL75
Downings E6 81 EN72
Downland Clo. N20 48 DC46
Downland Clo., Couls. 133 DH114
Downland Clo., Epsom 145 CV118
Downland Gdns., Epsom 145 CV118
Downland Way, Epsom 145 CV118
Downlands, Wal.Abb. 24 EE34
Downlands Rd., Pur. 133 DL114
Downleys Clo. SE9 108 EL89
Downman Rd. SE9 94 EL83
Downs, The SW20 103 CX94
Downs Ave., Chis. 109 EM92
Downs Ave., Epsom 130 CS114
Downs Ave., Pnr. 58 BZ58
Downs Bri. Rd., Beck. 121 ED95
Downs Ct. Rd., Pur. 133 DP112
Downs Hill, Beck. 107 ED94
Downs Hill Rd., Epsom 130 CS114
Downs Ho. Rd., Epsom 145 CT118
Downs La. E5 64 DV63
Downs Rd.
Downs La., Lthd. 143 CH123
Downs Pk. Rd. E5 64 DU64
Downs Pk. Rd. E8 64 DT64
Downs Rd. E5 64 DU63
Downs Rd., Beck. 121 EB96
Downs Rd., Couls. 147 DJ118
Downs Rd., Enf. 36 DS42
Downs Rd., Epsom 130 CS114
Downs Rd., Pur. 133 DP111
Downs Rd., Sutt. 132 DB110
Downs Rd., Th.Hth. 120 DQ95
Downs Side, Sutt. 131 CZ111
Downs Vw., Islw. 87 CF81
Downs Vw., Tad. 145 CV121
Downs Way, Epsom 145 CT116
Downs Way, Orp. 137 ES106
Southlands Ave.
Downs Way, Tad. 145 CV121
Downs Way Clo., Tad. 145 CU121
Downs Wd., Epsom 145 CV117
Downsbury Ms. SW18 104 DA85
Merton Rd.
Downsell Rd. E15 65 EC63
Downsfield Rd. E17 65 DY58
Downshall Ave., Ilf. 67 ES58
Downshire Hill NW3 62 DD63
Downside, Epsom 130 CS114
Downside, Sun. 113 BU95
Downside, Twick. 101 CF90
Downside Bri. Rd., Cob. 127 BV114
Downside Clo. SW19 104 DC93
Downside Common Rd., Cob. 141 BV118
Downside Cres. NW3 62 DE64
Downside Cres. W13 73 CG70
Downside Rd., Cob. 141 BV116
Downside Rd., Sutt. 132 DD107
Downside Wk., Nthlt. 72 BZ69
Invicta Gro.
Downsview Clo., Orp. 138 EW110
Downsview Clo., Swan. 125 FF97
Downsview Gdns. SE19 106 DQ94
Downsview Rd. SE19 106 DQ94
Downsview Rd., Sev. 154 FF125
Downsway, Orp. 137 ES106
Southlands Ave.
Downsway, S.Croy. 134 DS111
Downsway, Whyt. 148 DT116
Downsway, The, Sutt. 132 DC109
Downton Ave. SW2 105 DL89
Downtown Rd. SE16 93 DY75
Downview Clo., Cob. 141 BV119
Downway N12 48 DE52
Dowrey St. N1 77 DN67
Richmond Ave.
Dowry Wk., Wat. 29 BT38
Dowsett Rd. N17 50 DT54
Dowson Clo. SE5 92 DR84
Doyce St. SE1 11 H4
Doyle Clo., Erith 97 FE81
Doyle Gdns. NW10 75 CU67
Doyle Rd. SE25 120 DU98
D'Oyley St. SW1 8 F8
D'Oyley St. SW1 90 DG77
Doynton St. N19 63 DH61
Draco St. SE17 92 DQ79
Dragmire La., Mitch. 118 DD97
Benedict Rd.
Dragon La., Wey. 126 BN110
Dragonfly Clo. E13 80 EH69
Hollybush St.
Dragoon Rd. SE8 93 DZ78
Dragor Rd. NW10 74 CQ70
Drake Ave., Cat. 148 DQ122
Drake Clo. SE16 93 DX75
Middleton Dr.
Drake Ct. SE19 106 DT92
Drake Ct., Har. 58 BZ60
Drake Cres. SE28 82 EW72
Drake Ms., Horn. 83 FG66
Fulmar Rd.
Drake Rd. SE4 93 EA83
Drake Rd., Chess. 130 CN106
Drake Rd., Croy. 119 DM101
Drake Rd., Har. 58 BZ61
Drake Rd., Mitch. 118 DG100
Drake St. WC1 6 B7
Drake St., Enf. 36 DR39
Drakefell Rd. SE4 93 DY83
Drakefell Rd. SE14 93 DX82
Drakefield Rd. SW17 104 DG90
Drakeley Ct. N5 63 DP63
Highbury Hill
Drakes Clo., Esher 128 CA106
Drakes Clo. (Cheshunt), Wal.Cr. 23 DX28
Drakes Ctyd. NW6 75 CZ66
Drakes Dr., Nthwd. 43 BP53
Drakes Wk. E6 81 EN67
Talbot Rd.
Drakewood Rd. SW16 105 DK94
Draper Clo., Belv. 96 EZ77
Draper Pl. N1 77 DP67
Essex Rd.
Drapers Gdns. EC2 78 DR72
Copthall Ave.
Drapers Rd. E15 65 ED63
Drapers Rd. N17 64 DT55
Drapers Rd., Enf. 35 DP40
Drappers Way SE16 92 DU77
St. James's Rd.
Drawdock Rd. SE10 79 ED74
Drawell Clo. SE18 95 ES78
Drax Ave. SW20 103 CU94
Draxmont SW19 103 CY93
Dray Gdns. SW2 105 DM85
Draycot Rd. E11 66 EH58
Draycot Rd., Surb. 116 CN102
Draycott Ave. SW3 8 C8
Draycott Ave. SW3 90 DE77
Draycott Ave., Har. 59 CH58
Draycott Clo., Har. 59 CH58
Draycott Ms. SW6 89 CZ82
New Kings Rd.
Draycott Pl. SW3 8 D9
Draycott Pl. SW3 90 DF77
Draycott Ter. SW3 8 E9
Draycott Ter. SW3 90 DF77
Drayford Clo. W9 75 CZ70
Draymans Way, Islw. 87 CF83
Drayside Ms., Sthl. 86 BZ75
Kingston Rd.
Drayson Clo., Wal.Abb. 24 EE32
Drayson Ms. W8 90 DA75
Drayton Ave. W13 73 CG73
Drayton Ave., Loug. 39 EM44
Drayton Ave., Orp. 123 EP102
Drayton Ave., Pot.B. 19 CY32
Drayton Bri. Rd. W7 73 CF73
Drayton Bri. Rd. W13 73 CG72
Drayton Clo., Houns. 100 BZ85
Bramley Way
Drayton Clo., Ilf. 67 ER60
Drayton Clo., Lthd. 143 CE124
Drayton Gdns. N21 49 DP45
Drayton Gdns. SW10 90 DC78
Drayton Gdns. W13 73 CG73
Drayton Gdns., West Dr. 84 BK75
Drayton Grn. W13 73 CG73
Drayton Grn. Rd. W13 73 CH73
Drayton Gro. W13 73 CG73
Drayton Pk. N5 63 DN64
Drayton Pk. Ms. N5 63 DN64
Drayton Pk.
Drayton Rd. E11 65 ED60
Drayton Rd. N17 50 DS54
Drayton Rd. NW10 75 CT67
Drayton Rd. W13 73 CG73
Drayton Rd., Borwd. 32 CN42
Drayton Rd., Croy. 119 DP103
Drayton Waye, Har. 59 CH58
Dreadnought St. SE10 94 EE76
Drenon Sq., Hayes 71 BT73
Dresden Clo. NW6 76 DB65
Dresden Rd. N19 63 DJ60
Dresden Way, Wey. 127 BQ106
Dressington Ave. SE4 107 EA86
Drew Ave. NW7 47 CY51
Drew Gdns., Grnf. 73 CF65
Drew Pl., Cat. 148 DQ121
Coulsdon Rd.
Drew Rd. E16 80 EL74
Drewstead Rd. SW16 105 DK89
Driffield Rd. E3 79 DY68
Drift, The, Brom. 122 EK104
Drift Rd., Lthd. 141 BR124
Drift Way, Rich. 102 CM88
Driftway, The, Bans. 145 CW115
Driftway, The, Lthd. 143 CH123
Downs La.
Driftway, The, Mitch. 118 DG95
Driftwood Ave., St.Alb. 16 CA26
Driftwood Dr., Ken. 147 DP117
Drill Hall Rd., Cher. 112 BG101
Drinkwater Rd., Har. 58 CB61
Drive, The E4 51 ED45
Drive, The E17 65 EB55
Drive, The E18 66 EG56
Drive, The N3 48 DA52
Drive, The N6 62 DF57
Fordington Rd.
Drive, The N11 49 DJ51
Drive, The NW10 75 CT67
Longstone Ave.
Drive, The NW11 61 CY59
Drive, The SW6 89 CY82
Fulham Rd.
Drive, The SW16 119 DM97
Drive, The SW20 103 CW94
Drive, The W3 74 CQ72
Drive, The, Ashf. 99 BR94
Drive, The, Bans. 145 CY117
Drive, The, Bark. 81 ET66
Drive, The, Barn. 33 CY41
Drive, The (New Barnet), Barn. 34 DC44
Drive, The, Beck. 121 EA96
Drive, The, Bex. 110 EW86
Drive, The, Buck.H. 52 EJ45
Drive, The, Chis. 123 ET97
Drive, The, Cob. 128 BY114
Drive, The, Couls. 133 DL114
Drive, The, Edg. 46 CN50
Drive, The, Enf. 36 DR39
Drive, The, Epsom 131 CT107
Drive, The (Headley), Epsom 144 CP124
Drive, The, Erith 97 FB80
Drive, The, Esher 114 CC102
Drive, The, Felt. 100 BW87
Drive, The, Har. 58 CA59
Drive, The, Hat. 20 DA25
Drive, The, Houns. 86 CC82
Drive, The, Ilf. 66 EL58
Drive, The, Islw. 87 CD82
Drive, The, Kings.T. 102 CQ94
Drive, The, Lthd. 144 CL123
Drive, The (Fetcham), Lthd. 143 CE122
Drive, The, Loug. 38 EL41
Drive, The, Mord. 118 DC99
Drive, The, Nthwd. 43 BS54
Drive, The, Orp. 123 ET103
Drive, The, Pot.B. 19 CZ33
Drive, The, Rad. 17 CG34
Drive, The, Rick. 28 BH43
Drive, The, Rom. 55 FC53
Drive, The, St.Alb. 17 CG25
Drive, The, Sev. 155 FH124
Drive, The, Sid. 110 EV90
Drive, The, Surb. 116 CL101
Drive, The, Sutt. 131 CZ112
Drive, The, Th.Hth. 120 DR98
Drive, The, Uxb. 56 BL63
Drive, The, Wall. 133 DJ110
Drive, The (Cheshunt), Wal.Cr. 21 DP28
Drive, The, Wat. 29 BS37
Drive, The, Wem. 60 CQ61
Drive, The, W.Wick. 121 ED101
Drive Mead, Couls. 133 DL114
Drive Rd., Couls. 147 DM119
Drive Spur, Tad. 146 DA121
Driveway, The E17 65 EB58
Hoe St.
Driveway, The (Cuffley), Pot.B. 21 DL28
Droitwich Clo. SE26 106 DU90
Dromey Gdns., Har. 45 CF52
Dromore Rd. SW15 103 CY86
Dronfield Gdns., Dag. 68 EW64
Droop St. W10 75 CY70
Drop La., St.Alb. 16 CB30
Drove Way, Loug. 39 EP40
Drover La. SE15 92 DV80
Drovers Pl. SE15 92 DV80
Drovers Rd., S.Croy. 134 DR106
Druce Rd. SE21 106 DS86
Druid St. SE1 11 N4
Druid St. SE1 92 DS75
Druids Clo., Ash. 144 CM120
Druids Way, Brom. 121 ED98
Drum St. E1 78 DT72
Whitechapel High St.
Drumaline Ridge, Wor.Pk. 116 CS103
Drummond Ave., Rom. 69 FD56
Drummond Clo., Erith 97 FE81
Drummond Cres. NW1 5 M2
Drummond Cres. NW1 77 DK69
Drummond Dr., Stan. 45 CF52
Drummond Gate SW1 9 N10
Drummond Gate SW1 91 DK78
Drummond Pl., Rich. 88 CL84
Drummond Pl., Twick. 101 CH87
Drummond Rd. E11 66 EJ58
Drummond Rd. SE16 92 DV76
Drummond Rd., Croy. 120 DQ103
Drummond Rd., Rom. 69 FD56
Drummond St. NW1 5 K4
Drummond St. NW1 77 DJ70
Drummonds, The, Buck.H. 52 EH47
Drummonds, The, Epp. 26 EU30
Drury Cres., Croy. 119 DN103
Drury Ind. Est. NW10 60 CQ64
Drury La. WC2 6 A8
Drury La. WC2 77 DL72
Drury Rd., Har. 58 CC59
Drury Way NW10 60 CR64
Dryad St. SW15 89 CX83
Dryburgh Gdns. NW9 60 CN55
Dryburgh Rd. SW15 89 CV83
Dryden Ave. W7 73 CF72
Dryden Clo., Ilf. 53 ET51
Dryden Ct. SE11 10 E9
Dryden Rd. SW19 104 DC93
Dryden Rd., Enf. 36 DS44
Dryden Rd., Har. 59 CF63
Dryden Rd., Well. 95 ES81
Dryden St. WC2 6 A9
Dryden Twrs., Rom. 55 FH52
Dryden Way, Orp. 124 EU102
Lych Gate Rd.
Dryfield Clo. NW10 74 CQ65
Dryfield Rd., Edg. 46 CQ51
Dryfield Wk. SE8 93 EA79
New King St.
Dryhill La., Sev. 154 FB123
Dryhill Rd., Belv. 96 EZ79
Dryland Ave., Orp. 137 ET105
Drylands Rd. N8 63 DL58
Drynham Pk., Wey. 113 BS104
Drysdale Ave. E4 51 EB45
Drysdale Clo., Nthwd. 43 BS52
Northbrook Dr.
Drysdale Pl. N1 7 N2
Drysdale St. N1 7 N2
Drysdale St. N1 78 DS69
Du Burstow Ter. W7 87 CE75
Du Cane Clo. W12 75 CW72
Du Cane Rd.
Du Cane Ct. SW17 104 DG88
Du Cane Rd. W12 75 CT72
Du Cros Dr., Stan. 45 CK51
Du Cros Rd. W3 74 CS74
The Vale
Dublin Ave. E8 78 DU67
Ducal St. E2 78 DT69
Brick La.
Duchess Clo. N11 49 DH50
Duchess Gro., Buck.H. 52 EH47
Duchess Ms. W1 5 J7
Duchess of Bedford's Wk. W8 90 DA75
Duchess St. W1 5 J7
Duchess St. W1 77 DH71
Duchess Wk., Sev. 155 FK128
Duchy Rd., Barn. 34 DD38
Duchy St. SE1 10 E2
Duchy St. SE1 77 DN74
Ducie St. SW4 91 DM84
Duck La. W1 5 M9
Duck La., Epp. 26 EW26
Duck Lees La., Enf. 37 DY42
Duckett Ms. N4 63 DP58
Duckett Rd.
Duckett Rd. N4 63 DN58
Duckett St. E1 79 DX70
Ducketts Rd., Dart. 111 FF85
Ducking Stool Ct., Rom. 69 FE56
Ducks Hill, Nthwd. 42 BN54
Ducks Hill Rd., Nthwd. 43 BP54
Ducks Hill Rd., Ruis. 43 BP54
Ducks Wk., Twick. 101 CJ85
Dudden Hill La. NW10 61 CT63
Duddington Clo. SE9 108 EK91
Dudley Ave., Har. 59 CJ55
Dudley Ave., Wal.Cr. 23 DX32
Dudley Clo., Add. 112 BJ104
Dudley Ct. NW11 61 CZ56
Dudley Dr., Mord. 117 CY102
Dudley Dr., Ruis. 57 BV64
Dudley Gdns. W13 87 CH75
Dudley Gdns., Har. 59 CD60
Dudley Gro., Epsom 130 CQ114
Dudley Rd. E17 51 EA54
Dudley Rd. N3 48 DB54
Dudley Rd. NW6 75 CY68
Dudley Rd. SW19 104 DA93
Dudley Rd., Ashf. 98 BL92
Dudley Rd., Felt. 99 BQ88
Dudley Rd., Har. 58 CC61
Dudley Rd., Ilf. 67 EP63
Dudley Rd., Kings.T. 116 CM97
Dudley Rd., Rich. 88 CM82
Dudley Rd., Sthl. 86 BX75
Dudley Rd., Walt. 113 BU100
Dudley St. W2 76 DD71
Harrow Rd.
Dudlington Rd. E5 64 DW61
Dudmaston Ms. SW3 8 A10
Dudsbury Rd., Dart. 111 FG86
Dudsbury Rd., Sid. 110 EV93
Dudset La., Houns. 85 BU81
Duff St. E14 79 EB72
Dufferin Ave. EC1 7 K5
Dufferin St. EC1 7 J5
Dufferin St. EC1 78 DQ70
Duffield Clo., Har. 59 CF57
Duffield Dr. N15 64 DT56
Copperfield Dr.
Duffield Rd., Tad. 145 CV124
Dufour's Pl. W1 5 L9
Dugdale Hill La., Pot.B. 19 CY33
Dugdales, Rick. 28 BN42
Duke Gdns., Ilf. 67 ER56
Duke Rd.
Duke Hill Rd. SE1 10 F2
Duke Humphrey Rd. SE3 94 EE81
Duke of Cambridge Clo., Twick. 101 CD86
Duke of Edinburgh Rd., Sutt. 118 DD103
Duke of Wellington Pl. SW1 8 G4
Duke of Wellington Pl. SW1 90 DG75
Duke of York St. SW1 9 L2
Duke of York St. SW1 77 DJ74
Duke Rd. W4 88 CR78
Duke Rd., Ilf. 67 ER56
Duke Shore Pl. E14 79 DZ73
Narrow St.
Duke St. SW1 9 L2
Duke St. SW1 77 DJ74
Duke St. W1 4 G8
Duke St. W1 76 DG72
Duke St., Rich. 101 CK85
Duke St., Sutt. 132 DD105
Duke St., Wat. 30 BW41
Duke St. Hill SE1 11 L2
Dukes Ave. N3 48 DB53
Dukes Ave. N10 63 DJ55
Dukes Ave. W4 88 CR78
Dukes Ave., Edg. 46 CM51
Dukes Ave., Epp. 39 ES35
Dukes Ave., Har. 58 BZ58
Dukes Ave. (Wealdstone), Har. 59 CE56
Dukes Ave., Houns. 86 BY84
Dukes Ave., Kings.T. 101 CJ91
Dukes Ave., N.Mal. 117 CT97
Dukes Ave., Nthlt. 72 BY66
Dukes Ave., Rich. 101 CJ91
Dukes Clo., Ashf. 99 BQ91
Dukes Clo., Epp. 27 FB27
Dukes Clo., Hmptn. 100 BZ92
Dukes Clo., Kings.T. 101 CK91
Dukes Ct. E6 81 EN67
Dukes Grn. Ave., Felt. 99 BU85
Dukes Hill, Cat. 149 DY120
Dukes La. W8 90 DB75
Dukes Lo., Nthwd. 43 BS50
Eastbury Ave.
Duke's Meadows W4 88 CQ82
Great Chertsey Rd.
Dukes Ms. N10 63 DH55
Dukes Ave.
Duke's Ms. W1 4 G8
Dukes Orchard, Bex. 111 FC88
Duke's Pas. E17 65 EC55
Marlowe Rd.
Dukes Pl. EC3 7 N9
Dukes Pl. EC3 78 DS72
Dukes Ride, Uxb. 56 BL63
Dukes Rd. E6 81 EN67
Dukes Rd. W3 74 CN70
Duke's Rd. WC1 5 N3
Duke's Rd. WC1 77 DK69
Dukes Rd., Walt. 128 BX106
Dukes Way, W.Wick. 122 EE104
Duke's Yd. W1 4 G10
Dukesthorpe Rd. SE26 107 DX91
Dulas St. N4 63 DM60
Everleigh St.
Dulford St. W11 75 CY73
Dulka Rd. SW11 104 DF85
Dulverton Rd. SE9 109 EQ89
Dulverton Rd., Ruis. 57 BU60
Dulverton Rd., S.Croy. 134 DW110
Dulwich Common SE21 106 DS88
Dulwich Common SE22 106 DT88
Dulwich Lawn Clo. SE22 106 DT85
Melbourne Gro.
Dulwich Oaks, The SE21 106 DT90
Dulwich Rd. SE24 105 DN85
Dulwich Village SE21 106 DS86
Dulwich Way, Rick. 28 BN43
Dulwich Wd. Ave. SE19 106 DS91
Dulwich Wd. Pk. SE19 106 DS91
Dumbarton Ave., Wal.Cr. 23 DX34
Dumbarton Rd. SW2 105 DL86
Dumbleton Clo., Kings.T. 116 CP95
Gloucester Rd.
Dumbreck Rd. SE9 95 EM84
Dumfries Clo., Wat. 43 BT48
Dumont Rd. N16 64 DS62
Dumpton Pl. NW1 76 DG66
Gloucester Ave.
Dunally Pk., Shep. 113 BR101
Dunbar Ave. SW16 119 DN96
Dunbar Ave., Beck. 121 DY98
Dunbar Ave., Dag. 68 FA62
Dunbar Clo., Hayes 71 BU71
Dunbar Ct., Sutt. 132 DD106
Dunbar Ct., Walt. 113 BV103
Dunbar Gdns., Dag. 68 FA64
Dunbar Rd. E7 80 EG65
Dunbar Rd. N22 49 DN53
Dunbar Rd., N.Mal. 116 CQ98
Dunbar St. SE27 106 DQ90
Dunblane Clo., Edg. 46 CP47
Tayside Dr.
Dunblane Rd. SE9 94 EL82
Dunboe Pl., Shep. 113 BQ101
Dunboyne Rd. NW3 62 DF64
Dunbridge St. E2 78 DU70
Duncan Clo., Barn. 34 DC42

Duncan Gro. W3 74 CS72
Duncan Rd. E8 78 DV67
Duncan Rd., Rich. 88 CL84
Duncan Rd., Tad. 145 CY119
Duncan St. N1 77 DP68
Duncan Ter. N1 6 F1
Duncan Ter. N1 77 DP68
Duncan Way (Bushey), Wat. 30 BZ40
Duncannon St. WC2 9 P1
Duncannon St. WC2 77 DL73
Dunch St. E1 78 DV72
Watney St.
Duncombe Hill SE23 107 DY87
Duncombe Rd. N19 63 DK60
Duncrievie Rd. SE13 107 ED86
Duncroft SE18 95 ES80
Dundalk Rd. SE4 93 DY83
Dundas Gdns., W.Mol. 114 CB97
Dundas Rd. SE15 92 DW82
Dundee Rd. E13 80 EH68
Dundee Rd. SE25 120 DV99
Dundee St. E1 78 DV74
Dundela Gdns., Wor.Pk. 131 CV105
Dundonald Clo. E6 80 EL72
Northumberland Rd.
Dundonald Rd. NW10 75 CX67
Dundonald Rd. SW19 103 CY94
Dunedin Rd. E10 65 EB62
Dunedin Rd., Ilf. 67 EQ60
Dunedin Rd., Rain. 83 FE69
Dunedin Way, Hayes 72 BW70
Dunelm Gro. SE27 106 DQ91
Dunelm St. E1 79 DX72
Dunfee Way, W.Byf. 126 BL112
Dunfield Gdns. SE6 107 EB92
Dunfield Rd. SE6 107 EB92
Dunford Rd. N7 63 DM63
Dungarvan Ave. SW15 89 CU84
Dunheved Clo., Th.Hth. 119 DN100
Dunheved Rd. N., Th.Hth. 119 DN100
Dunheved Rd. S., Th.Hth. 119 DN100
Dunheved Rd. W., Th.Hth. 119 DN100
Dunholme Grn. N9 50 DT48
Dunholme La. N9 50 DT48
Dunholme Rd.
Dunholme Rd. N9 50 DT48
Dunkeld Rd. SE25 120 DR98
Dunkeld Rd., Dag. 68 EV61
Dunkery Rd. SE9 108 EK91
Dunkirk St. SE27 106 DQ91
Waring St.
Dunlace Rd. E5 64 DW63
Dunleary Clo., Houns. 100 BZ87
Dunley Dr., Croy. 135 EB108
Dunlin Ho. W13 73 CF70
Dunloe Ave. N17 64 DR55
Dunloe St. E2 78 DT68
Dunlop Pl. SE16 92 DT76
Spa Rd.
Dunlop Pt. E16 80 EG74
Dunmail Dr., Pur. 134 DS114
Dunmore Pt. E2 7 P3
Dunmore Rd. NW6 75 CY67
Dunmore Rd. SW20 117 CW95
Dunmow Clo., Felt. 100 BX91
Dunmow Clo., Loug. 38 EL44
Dunmow Clo., Rom. 68 EW57
Dunmow Dr., Rain. 83 FF67
Dunmow Ho., Dag. 82 EV67
Dunmow Rd. E15 65 ED63
Dunmow Wk. N1 78 DQ67
Popham St.
Dunn Mead NW9 47 CT52
Field Mead
Dunn St. E8 64 DT64
Dunnale Cres. SE16 93 DY77
Plough Way
Dunningford Clo., Horn. 69 FF64
Dunnock Clo. N9 51 DX46
Dunnock Clo., Borwd. 32 CN42
Dunnock Rd. E6 80 EL72
Dunns Pas. WC1 6 A8
Dunnymans Rd., Bans. 145 CZ115
Dunollie Pl. NW5 63 DJ64
Dunollie Rd.
Dunollie Rd. NW5 63 DJ64
Dunoon Rd. SE23 106 DW87
Dunraven Dr., Enf. 35 DN40
Dunraven Rd. W12 75 CU74
Dunraven St. W1 4 E10
Dunsany Rd. W14 89 CX76
Dunsborough Pk., Wok. 140 BJ120
Dunsbury Clo., Sutt. 132 DB109
Nettlecombe Clo.
Dunsfold Ri., Couls. 133 DK113
Dunsfold Way, Croy. 135 EB108
Dunsford Way SW15 103 CV86
Dover Pk. Dr.
Dunsmore Clo., Hayes 72 BY70
Kingsash Dr.
Dunsmore Clo. (Bushey), Wat. 31 CD44
Dunsmore Rd., Walt. 113 BV100
Dunsmore Way (Bushey), Wat. 31 CD44
Dunsmure Rd. N16 64 DS60
Dunspring La., Ilf. 53 EP54
Dunstable Ms. W1 4 G6
Dunstable Rd., Rich. 88 CL84
Dunstable Rd., W.Mol. 114 BZ98
Dunstall Rd. SW20 103 CV93
Dunstall Way, W.Mol. 114 CB97
Dunstan Clo. N2 62 DC55
Thomas More Way
Dunstan Rd. NW11 61 CZ60
Dunstan Rd., Couls. 147 DK117
Dunstans Gro. SE22 106 DV86
Dunstans Rd. SE22 106 DU87
Dunster Ave., Mord. 117 CX102
Dunster Clo., Barn. 33 CX42
Dunster Clo., Rom. 55 FC54
Dunster Clo., Uxb. 42 BH53
Dunster Ct. EC3 7 M10
Dunster Dr. NW9 60 CQ60
Dunster Gdns. NW6 75 CZ66
Dunster Way, Har. 58 BY62
Dunsterville Way SE1 11 L5
Dunston Rd. E8 78 DT67
Dunston Rd. SW11 90 DG83
Dunston St. E8 78 DT67
Dunton Clo., Surb. 116 CL102
Dunton Rd. E10 65 EB59
Dunton Rd. SE1 11 P9
Dunton Rd. SE1 92 DT77
Dunton Rd., Rom. 69 FE56
Duntshill Rd. SW18 104 DB88
Dunvegan Clo., W.Mol. 114 CB98
Dunvegan Rd. SE9 95 EM84
Dunwich Rd., Bexh. 96 EZ81
Dunworth Ms. W11 75 CZ72
Portobello Rd.
Duplex Ride SW1 8 E5
Dupont Rd. SW20 117 CX96
Dupont St. E14 79 DY71
Maroon St.
Duppas Ave., Croy. 133 DP105
Violet La.
Duppas Clo., Shep. 113 BR99
Green La.
Duppas Hill La., Croy. 133 DP105
Duppas Hill Rd.
Duppas Hill Rd., Croy. 133 DN105
Duppas Hill Ter., Croy. 119 DP104
Duppas Rd., Croy. 119 DN104
Dupree Rd. SE7 94 EH78
Dura Den Clo., Beck. 107 EB94
Durand Clo., Cars. 118 DF102
Durand Gdns. SW9 91 DM81
Durand Way NW10 74 CQ66
Durands Wk. SE16 93 DY75
Salter Rd.
Durant Rd., Swan. 111 FG93
Durant St. E2 78 DU69
Durants Pk. Ave., Enf. 37 DX42
Durants Rd., Enf. 36 DW42
Durban Gdns., Dag. 83 FC66
Durban Rd. E15 80 EE69
Durban Rd. E17 51 DZ53
Durban Rd. N17 50 DS51
Durban Rd. SE27 106 DQ91
Durban Rd., Beck. 121 DZ96
Durban Rd., Ilf. 67 ES60
Durban Rd. E., Wat. 29 BU42
Durban Rd. W., Wat. 29 BU42
Durbin Rd., Chess. 130 CL105
Durdans Rd., Sthl. 72 BZ72
Durell Gdns., Dag. 68 EX64
Durell Rd., Dag. 68 EX64
Durford Cres. SW15 103 CV88
Durham Ave., Brom. 122 EF98
Durham Ave., Houns. 86 BZ79
Durham Ave., Wdf.Grn. 52 EK50
Durham Clo. SW20 117 CV96
Durham Rd.
Durham Hill, Brom. 108 EF91
Durham Ho. St. WC2 10 A1
Durham Pl. SW3 90 DF78
Smith St.
Durham Pl., Ilf. 67 EQ63
Eton Rd.
Durham Ri. SE18 95 EQ78
Durham Rd. E12 66 EK63
Durham Rd. E16 80 EE70
Durham Rd. N2 62 DE55
Durham Rd. N7 63 DM61
Durham Rd. N9 50 DU47
Durham Rd. SW20 117 CV95
Durham Rd. W5 87 CK76
Durham Rd., Borwd. 32 CQ41
Durham Rd., Brom. 122 EF97
Durham Rd., Dag. 69 FC64
Durham Rd., Felt. 100 BW87
Durham Rd., Har. 58 CB57
Durham Rd., Sid. 110 EV92
Durham Row E1 79 DY71
Durham St. SE11 91 DM78
Durham Ter. W2 76 DB72
Durham Wf., Brent. 87 CJ80
High St.
Durham Yd. E2 78 DV69
Teesdale St.
Duriun Way, Erith 97 FH80
Durley Ave., Pnr. 58 BY59
Durley Gdns., Orp. 138 EV105
Durley Rd. N16 64 DS59
Durlston Rd. E5 64 DU61
Durlston Rd., Kings.T. 102 CL93
Durnell Way, Loug. 39 EN41
Durnford St. N15 64 DS57
Durnford St. SE10 93 EC79
Greenwich Ch. St.
Durning Rd. SE19 106 DR92
Durnsford Ave. SW19 104 DA89
Durnsford Rd. N11 49 DK53
Durnsford Rd. SW19 104 DA89
Durrant Way, Orp. 137 ER106
Durrants Dr., Rick. 29 BQ41
Durrell Rd. SW6 89 CZ81
Durrell Way, Shep. 113 BR100
Durrington Ave. SW20 117 CW95
Durrington Pk. Rd. SW20 117 CW95
Durrington Rd. E5 65 DY63
Dursley Clo. SE3 94 EJ82
Dursley Gdns. SE3 94 EK81
Dursley Rd. SE3 94 EJ82
Durward St. E1 78 DV71
Durweston Ms. W1 4 E6
Durweston St. W1 4 E7
Dury Rd., Barn. 33 CZ40
Dutch Barn Clo., Stai. 98 BK86
Dutch Gdns., Kings.T. 102 CP93
Windmill Ri.
Dutch Yd. SW18 104 DA85
Wandsworth High St.
Duthie St. E14 79 EC73
Prestons Rd.
Dutton St. SE10 93 EC81
Duxberry Clo., Brom. 122 EL99
Southborough La.
Duxford Clo., Horn. 83 FH65
Dwight Ct. SW6 89 CY82
Burlington Rd.
Dwight Rd., Wat. 43 BR45
Dye Ho. La. E3 79 EA67
Dyer's Bldgs. EC1 6 D7
Dyers Hall Rd. E11 66 EE61
Dyers La. SW15 89 CV84
Dyers Way, Rom. 55 FH52
Dyke Dr., Orp. 124 EW102
Dykes Way, Brom. 122 EF97
Dykewood Clo., Bex. 111 FE90
Dylan Clo., Borwd. 45 CK45
Coates Rd.
Dylan Rd. SE24 91 DP84
Dylan Rd., Belv. 96 FA76
Dylan Thomas Ho. N8 63 DM56
Dylways SE5 92 DR84
Dymchurch Clo., Ilf. 67 EN55
Dymchurch Clo., Orp. 137 ES105
Dymes Path SW19 103 CX89
Queensmere Rd.
Dymock St. SW6 90 DB83
Dymoke Rd., Horn. 69 FF59
Dymond Est. SW17 104 DE90
Glenburnie Rd.
Dyne Rd. NW6 75 CY66
Dyneley Rd. SE12 108 EJ91
Dynevor Rd. N16 64 DT62
Dynevor Rd., Rich. 102 CL85
Dynham Rd. NW6 76 DA66
Dyott St. WC1 5 N8
Dyott St. WC1 77 DK72
Dyrham La., Barn. 33 CU36
Dysart Ave., Kings.T. 101 CJ92
Dysart St. EC2 7 M5
Dyson Rd. E11 66 EE58
Dyson Rd. E15 80 EF65
Dysons Clo., Wal.Cr. 23 DX33
Dysons Rd. N18 50 DV50

E

Eade Rd. N4 64 DQ59
Eagans Clo. N2 62 DE55
Market Pl.
Eagle Ave., Rom. 68 EY58
Eagle Clo. SE16 92 DW78
Varcoe Rd.
Eagle Clo., Enf. 36 DW42
Eagle Clo., Horn. 83 FH65
Eagle Clo., Wall. 133 DL107
Eagle Clo., Wal.Abb. 24 EG34
Eagle Ct. EC1 6 F6
Eagle Ct. EC1 77 DP71
Eagle Dr. NW9 46 CS54
Eagle Hill SE19 106 DR93
Eagle La. E11 66 EG56
Eagle Ms. N1 78 DS65
Tottenham Rd.
Eagle Pl. SW1 9 L1
Eagle Pl. SW7 90 DC78
Old Brompton Rd.
Eagle Rd., Wem. 73 CK66
Eagle St. WC1 6 B7
Eagle St. WC1 77 DM71
Eagle Ter., Wdf.Grn. 52 EH52
Eagle Wf. E14 79 EB71
Broomfield St.
Eagle Wf. Rd. N1 78 DQ68
Eagles Dr., West. 150 EK118
Eaglesfield Rd. SE18 95 EP82
Ealdham Sq. SE9 94 EJ84
Ealing Clo., Borwd. 32 CR39
Ealing Downs Ct., Grnf. 73 CG69
Perivale La.
Ealing Grn. W5 73 CK74
Ealing Pk. Gdns. W5 87 CJ77
Ealing Rd., Brent. 87 CK77
Ealing Rd., Nthlt. 72 CA67
Ealing Rd., Wem. 74 CL65
Ealing Village W5 74 CL72
Eamont Clo., Ruis. 57 BP59
Allonby Dr.
Eamont St. NW8 76 DE68
Eardemont Clo., Dart. 97 FF84
Eardley Cres. SW5 90 DA78
Eardley Pt. SE18 95 EP77
Wilmount St.
Eardley Rd. SW16 105 DJ92
Eardley Rd., Belv. 96 FA78
Eardley Rd., Sev. 155 FH124
Earl Clo. N11 49 DH50
Earl Ri. SE18 95 ER77
Earl Rd. SE1 11 P10
Earl Rd. SE1 92 DT78
Earl Rd. SW14 88 CQ84
Elm Rd.
Earl St. EC2 7 L6
Earl St. EC2 78 DR71
Earl St., Wat. 30 BW41
Earldom Rd. SW15 89 CW84
Earle Gdns., Kings.T. 102 CL94
Earleswood, Cob. 128 BX112
Earlham Gro. E7 66 EF64
Earlham Gro. N22 49 DM52
Earlham St. WC2 5 N9
Earlham St. WC2 77 DK72
Earls Ct. Gdns. SW5 90 DB77
Earls Ct. Rd. SW5 90 DA77
Earls Ct. Rd. W8 90 DA77
Earls Ct. Sq. SW5 90 DB78
Earls Cres., Har. 59 CE56
Earls La., Pot.B. 18 CS32
Earl's Path, Loug. 38 EJ40
Earls Ter. W8 89 CZ76
Earls Wk. W8 90 DA76
Earls Wk., Dag. 68 EV63
Earls Way, Orp. 123 ET103
Station Rd.
Earlsdown Ho., Bark. 81 ER68
Wheelers Cross
Earlsferry Way N1 77 DM66
Earlsfield Rd. SW18 104 DC88
Earlshall Rd. SE9 95 EM84
Earlsmead, Har. 58 BZ63
Earlsmead Rd. N15 64 DT57
Earlsmead Rd. NW10 75 CW69
Earlsthorpe Ms. SW12 104 DG86
Earlsthorpe Rd. SE26 107 DX91
Earlstoke St. EC1 6 F2
Earlston Gro. E9 78 DV67
Earlswood Ave., Th.Hth. 119 DN99
Earlswood Clo. SE10 94 EE78
Earlswood St.
Earlswood Gdns., Ilf. 67 EN55
Earlswood St. SE10 94 EE78
Early Ms. NW1 77 DH67
Arlington Rd.
Earnshaw St. WC2 5 N8
Earnshaw St. WC2 77 DK72
Earsby St. W14 89 CY77
Easby Cres., Mord. 118 DB100
Easebourne Rd., Dag. 68 EW64
Easedale Dr., Horn. 69 FG64
Easedale Ho., Islw. 101 CF85
Easley's Ms. W1 4 G8
East Acton La. W3 74 CS73
East Arbour St. E1 79 DX72
East Ave. E12 80 EL66
East Ave. E17 65 EB56
East Ave., Hayes 85 BT75
East Ave., Sthl. 72 BZ73
East Ave., Wall. 133 DM106
East Ave., Walt. 127 BT110
Octagon Rd.
East Bank N16 64 DS59
East Barnet Rd., Barn. 34 DD42
East Churchfield Rd. W3 74 CR74
East Clo. W5 74 CN70
East Clo., Barn. 34 DG42
East Clo., Grnf. 72 CC68
East Clo., Rain. 83 FH70
East Clo., St.Alb. 16 CB25
East Ct., Wem. 59 CJ61
East Cres. N11 48 DF49
East Cres., Enf. 36 DS43
East Cross Route E3 79 DZ66
East Dr., Cars. 132 DE109
East Dr., Nthwd. 43 BS47
East Dr., Orp. 124 EV100
East Dr., Wat. 29 BV35
East Duck Lees La., Enf. 37 DY42
Duck Lees La.
East Dulwich Gro. SE22 106 DS85
East Dulwich Rd. SE15 92 DU84
East Dulwich Rd. SE22 92 DT84
East End Rd. N2 62 DB55
East End Rd. N3 47 CZ54
East End Way, Pnr. 58 BY55
East Entrance, Dag. 83 FB68
East Ferry Rd. E14 93 EB77
East Gdns. SW17 104 DE93
East Gorse, Croy. 135 DY112
East Grn., Hem.H. 14 BM25
East Hall Rd., Orp. 124 EY101
East Ham Ind. Est. E6 80 EK70
East Ham Manor Way E6 81 EN72
East Harding St. EC4 6 E8
East Heath Rd. NW3 62 DC62
East Hill SW18 104 DB85
East Hill, S.Croy. 134 DS110
East Hill, Wem. 60 CN61
East Hill, West. 150 EH118
East Holme, Erith 97 FD81
East Holme, Hayes 71 BU74
East India Dock Rd. E14 79 EA72
East India Dock Wall Rd. E14 79 ED73
East La. SE16 92 DU75
East La., Abb.L. 15 BT28
East La., Kings.T. 115 CK97
East La., Wem. 59 CH62
East Lo. La., Enf. 35 DK36
East Mascalls SE7 94 EJ79
Mascalls Rd.
East Mead, Ruis. 58 BX62
East Mt. St. E1 78 DV71
East Pk. Clo., Rom. 68 EX57
East Pas. EC1 7 H6
East Pier E1 78 DV74
Wapping High St.
East Pl. SE27 106 DQ91
Pilgrim Hill
East Poultry Ave. EC1 6 F7
East Ramp, Houns. 85 BP81
East Ridgeway (Cuffley), Pot.B. 21 DL28
East Rd. E15 80 EG67
East Rd. N1 7 L2
East Rd. N1 78 DR69
East Rd. SW19 104 DC93
East Rd., Barn. 48 DG46
East Rd., Edg. 46 CP53
East Rd., Enf. 36 DW38
East Rd., Felt. 99 BR87
East Rd., Kings.T. 116 CL95
East Rd. (Chadwell Heath), Rom. 68 EY57
East Rd. (Rush Grn.), Rom. 69 FD59
East Rd., Well. 96 EV82
East Rd., West Dr. 84 BM77
East Rd., Wey. 127 BR108
East Rochester Way SE9 95 ER84
East Rochester Way, Bex. 110 EX86
East Rochester Way, Sid. 95 ER84
East Row E11 66 EG58
East Row W10 75 CY70
East Sheen Ave. SW14 102 CR85
East Smithfield E1 78 DT73
East St. SE17 11 J10
East St. SE17 92 DQ78
East St., Bexh. 96 FA84
East St., Brent. 87 CJ80
East St., Brom. 122 EG96
East St., Cher. 112 BG101
East St., Epsom 130 CS113
East Surrey Gro. SE15 92 DT80
East Tenter St. E1 78 DT72
East Twrs., Pnr. 58 BX57
East Vw. E4 51 EC50
East Vw., Barn. 33 CZ40
East Wk. NW7 47 CU52
Northway
East Wk., Barn. 48 DG45
East Wk., Hayes 71 BU74
East Way E11 66 EH57
East Way, Brom. 122 EG101
East Way, Croy. 121 DY103
East Way, Hayes 71 BU74
East Way, Ruis. 57 BU60
East Woodside, Bex. 110 EY88
Maiden Erlegh Ave.
Eastbank Rd., Hmptn. 100 CC92
Eastbourne Ave. W3 74 CR72
Eastbourne Gdns. SW14 88 CQ83
Eastbourne Ms. W2 76 DC72
Eastbourne Rd. E6 81 EN69
Eastbourne Rd. E15 80 EE67
Eastbourne Rd. N15 64 DS58
Eastbourne Rd. SW17 104 DG93
Eastbourne Rd. W4 88 CQ79
Eastbourne Rd., Brent. 87 CK78
Eastbourne Rd., Felt. 100 BX89
Eastbourne Ter. W2 76 DC72
Eastbournia Ave. N9 50 DV48
Eastbrook Ave. N9 50 DW45
Eastbrook Ave., Dag. 69 FC63
Eastbrook Dr., Rom. 69 FE62
Eastbrook Rd. SE3 94 EH81
Eastbrook Rd., Wal.Abb. 24 EE33
Eastbury Ave., Bark. 81 ES67
Eastbury Ave., Enf. 36 DS39
Eastbury Ave., Nthwd. 43 BS50
Eastbury Clo., Nthwd. 43 BT50
Eastbury Ave.
Eastbury Ct., Bark. 81 ES67
Eastbury Gro. W4 88 CS78
Eastbury Ho., Bark. 81 ET67
Eastbury Pl., Nthwd. 43 BT50
Eastbury Ave.
Eastbury Rd. E6 81 EN70
Eastbury Rd., Kings.T. 102 CL94
Eastbury Rd., Nthwd. 43 BS50
Eastbury Rd., Orp. 123 ER100
Eastbury Rd., Rom. 69 FD58
Eastbury Rd., Wat. 43 BV45
Eastbury Sq., Bark. 81 ET67
Eastbury Ter. E1 79 DX70
Eastcastle St. W1 5 K8
Eastcastle St. W1 77 DJ72
Eastcheap EC3 7 L10
Eastcheap EC3 78 DR73
Eastchurch Rd., Houns. 85 BS82
Eastcombe Ave. SE7 94 EH79
Eastcote, Orp. 123 ET102
Eastcote Ave., Grnf. 73 CG65
Eastcote Ave., Har. 58 CB61
Eastcote Ave., W.Mol. 114 BZ99
Eastcote High Rd., Pnr. 57 BU58
Eastcote La., Har. 58 BY63
Eastcote La., Nthlt. 58 BZ64
Eastcote La. N., Nthlt. 72 BZ65
Eastcote Rd., Har. 58 CC62
Eastcote Rd., Pnr. 58 BX57
Eastcote Rd., Ruis. 57 BS59
Eastcote Rd., Well. 95 ER82
Eastcote St. SW9 91 DM82
Eastcote Vw., Pnr. 58 BW56
Eastcroft Rd., Epsom 130 CS108
Eastdean Ave., Epsom 130 CP113
Eastdown Pk. SE13 93 ED84
Eastern Ave. E11 66 EH58
Eastern Ave., Cher. 112 BG97
Eastern Ave., Ilf. 67 EP58
Eastern Ave., Pnr. 58 BX59
Eastern Ave., Rom. 68 EW56
Eastern Ave., Wal.Cr. 23 DY33
Eastern Ave. E., Rom. 69 FD55
Eastern Ave. W., Rom. 68 EY56
Eastern Ind. Est., Erith 96 EZ75

Eldon Gro. NW3 62 DD64
Eldon Pk. SE25 120 DV98
Eldon Rd. E17 65 DZ56
Eldon Rd. N9 50 DW47
Eldon Rd. N22 49 DP53
Eldon Rd. W8 90 DB76
Eldon Rd., Cat. 148 DR121
Eldon St. EC2 7 L7
Eldon St. EC2 78 DR71
Eldon Way NW10 74 CP68
Eldonwall Trd. Est. NW2 61 CU60
Eldred Dr., Orp. 124 EW102
Eldred Rd., Bark. 81 ES67
Eldrick Ct., Felt. 99 BR88
Kilross Rd.
Eldridge Clo., Felt. 99 BU88
Eleanor Ave., Epsom 130 CR110
Eleanor Clo. N15 64 DT55
Eleanor Clo. SE16 93 DX75
Eleanor Cres. NW7 47 CX49
Eleanor Cross Rd., Wal.Cr. 23 DY34
Eleanor Gdns., Barn. 33 CX43
Chesterfield Rd.
Eleanor Gdns., Dag. 68 EZ62
Nicholas Rd.
Eleanor Gro. SW13 88 CS83
Eleanor Gro., Uxb. 57 BP62
Eleanor Rd. E8 78 DV65
Eleanor Rd. E15 80 EF65
Eleanor Rd. N11 49 DL51
Eleanor Rd., Wal.Cr. 23 DY33
Eleanor St. E3 79 EA69
Eleanor Wk. SE18 95 EM77
Samuel St.
Eleanor Way, Wal.Cr. 23 DZ34
Electric Ave. SW9 91 DN84
Electric La. SW9 91 DN84
Electric Par., Surb. 115 CK100
Elephant & Castle SE1 10 G8
Elephant & Castle SE1 91 DP76
Elephant La. SE16 92 DW75
Elephant Rd. SE17 11 H8
Elephant Rd. SE17 92 DQ77
Elers Rd. W13 87 CJ75
Elers Rd., Hayes 85 BR77
Eleven Acre Ri., Loug. 39 EM41
Eley Est. N18 50 DW49
Eley Rd. N18 50 DW49
Elf Row E1 78 DW73
Elfin Gro., Tedd. 101 CF92
Broad St.
Elfindale Rd. SE24 106 DQ85
Elford Clo. SE3 94 EJ84
Elfort Rd. N5 63 DN63
Elfrida Cres. SE6 107 EA91
Elfrida Rd., Wat. 30 BW43
Elfwine Rd. W7 73 CE71
Elgal Clo., Orp. 137 EP106
Orchard Rd.
Elgar Ave. NW10 74 CR65
Mitchellbrook Way
Elgar Ave. SW16 119 DL97
Elgar Ave. W5 88 CL75
Elgar Ave., Surb. 116 CN102
Elgar Clo. E13 80 EJ68
Bushey Rd.
Elgar Clo. SE8 93 EA80
Comet St.
Elgar Clo., Borwd. 45 CJ45
Elgar Clo., Buck.H. 52 EK47
Elgar Clo., Uxb. 56 BN61
Elgar St. SE16 93 DY75
Elgin Ave. W9 76 DA70
Elgin Ave., Ashf. 99 BQ93
Elgin Ave., Har. 45 CH54
Elgin Cres. W11 75 CY73
Elgin Cres., Cat. 148 DU122
Elgin Cres., Houns. 85 BS82
Eastern Perimeter Rd.
Elgin Dr., Nthwd. 43 BS52
Elgin Est. W9 76 DA70
Elgin Ms. W11 75 CY72
Ladbroke Gro.
Elgin Ms. N. W9 76 DB69
Randolph Ave.
Elgin Ms. S. W9 76 DB69
Randolph Ave.
Elgin Rd. N22 49 DJ54
Elgin Rd., Croy. 120 DT103
Elgin Rd., Ilf. 67 ES60
Elgin Rd., Sutt. 118 DC104
Elgin Rd., Wall. 133 DJ107
Elgin Rd. (Cheshunt), Wal.Cr. 22 DW30
Elgin Rd., Wey. 126 BN106
Elgood Ave., Nthwd. 43 BT51
Elgood Clo. W11 75 CY73
Avondale Pk. Rd.
Elham Clo., Brom. 108 EK94
Elia Ms. N1 6 F1
Elia Ms. N1 77 DP68
Elia St. N1 6 F1
Elia St. N1 77 DP68
Elias Pl. SW8 91 DN79
Elibank Rd. SE9 95 EM84
Elim Est. SE1 11 M6
Elim Est. SE1 92 DR76
Elim Way E13 80 EF69
Eliot Bank SE23 106 DV89
Eliot Cotts. SE3 94 EE82
Eliot Pl.
Eliot Dr., Har. 58 CB61
Eliot Gdns. SW15 89 CU84
Eliot Hill SE13 93 EC82
Eliot Ms. NW8 76 DC68
Eliot Pk. SE13 93 EC82
Eliot Pl. SE3 94 EE82
Eliot Rd., Dag. 68 EX63
Eliot Vale SE3 93 ED82
Elizabeth Ave. N1 78 DQ66
Elizabeth Ave., Enf. 35 DP41
Elizabeth Ave., Ilf. 67 ER61
Elizabeth Ave., Stai. 98 BJ93
Elizabeth Blackwell Ho. N22 49 DN53
Progress Way
Elizabeth Bri. SW1 9 H9
Elizabeth Bri. SW1 91 DH77
Elizabeth Clo. E14 79 EB72
Grundy St.
Elizabeth Clo. W9 76 DC70
Randolph Ave.
Elizabeth Clo., Barn. 33 CX41
Elizabeth Clo., Rom. 55 FB53
Elizabeth Clo., Sutt. 131 CZ105
Sunningdale Rd.
Elizabeth Clyde Clo. N15 64 DS56
Elizabeth Cotts., Rich. 88 CM81
Elizabeth Ct. SW1 9 N7
Elizabeth Ct., Wat. 29 BT38
Elizabeth Dr., Epp. 39 ES36
Elizabeth Est. SE17 92 DR79
Elizabeth Fry Rd. E8 78 DV66
Lamb La.
Elizabeth Gdns. W3 75 CT74
Elizabeth Gdns., Stan. 45 CJ51
Elizabeth Gdns., Sun. 114 BW97
Elizabeth Ms. NW3 76 DF65
Elizabeth Pl. N15 64 DR56
Elizabeth Ride N9 50 DV45
Elizabeth Rd. E6 80 EK67
Elizabeth Rd. N15 64 DS57
Elizabeth Rd., Rain. 83 FH71
Elizabeth Sq. SE16 79 DY73
Rotherhithe St.
Elizabeth St. SW1 8 G8
Elizabeth St. SW1 90 DG77
Elizabeth Ter. SE9 109 EM86
Elizabeth Way SE19 106 DR94
Elizabeth Way, Felt. 100 BW91
Elizabeth Way, Orp. 124 EW99
Elizabethan Clo., Stai. 98 BK87
Elizabethan Way
Elizabethan Way, Stai. 98 BK87
Elkington Rd. E13 80 EH70
Elkins, The, Rom. 55 FE54
Elkstone Rd. W10 75 CZ71
Ella Rd. N8 63 DL59
Ellaline Rd. W6 89 CX79
Ellanby Cres. N18 50 DV49
Elland Rd. SE15 92 DW84
Elland Rd., Walt. 114 BX103
Ellement Clo., Pnr. 58 BX57
Ellen Clo., Brom. 122 EK97
Ellen Ct. N9 50 DW47
Densworth Gro.
Ellen St. E1 78 DU72
Ellen Webb Dr., Har. 59 CE55
Ellenborough Pl. SW15 89 CU84
Ellenborough Rd. N22 50 DQ53
Ellenborough Rd., Sid. 110 EX92
Ellenbridge Way, S.Croy. 134 DS109
Ellenbrook Clo., Wat. 29 BV39
Hatfield Rd.
Elleray Rd., Tedd. 101 CF93
Ellerby St. SW6 89 CX81
Ellerdale Clo. NW3 62 DC63
Ellerdale Rd.
Ellerdale Rd. NW3 62 DC64
Ellerdale St. SE13 93 EB84
Ellerdine Rd., Houns. 87 CD84
Ellerker Gdns., Rich. 102 CL85
Ellerman Ave., Twick. 100 BZ88
Ellerslie Gdns. NW10 75 CU67
Ellerslie Rd. W12 75 CV74
Ellerslie Sq. Ind. Est. SW2 91 DL84
Ellerton Gdns., Dag. 82 EW66
Ellerton Rd. SW13 89 CU81
Ellerton Rd. SW18 104 DD88
Ellerton Rd. SW20 103 CU94
Ellerton Rd., Dag. 82 EW66
Ellerton Rd., Surb. 116 CM103
Ellery Rd. SE19 106 DR94
Ellery St. SE15 92 DV82
Ellesborough Clo., Wat. 44 BW50
Ellesmere Ave. NW7 46 CR48
Ellesmere Ave., Beck. 121 EB96
Ellesmere Clo. E11 66 EF57
Ellesmere Clo., Ruis. 57 BQ59
Ellesmere Dr., S.Croy. 134 DV114
Ellesmere Gdns., Ilf. 66 EL57
Ellesmere Gro., Barn. 33 CZ43
Ellesmere Rd. E3 79 DY68
Ellesmere Rd. NW10 61 CU64
Ellesmere Rd. W4 88 CR79
Ellesmere Rd., Grnf. 72 CC70
Ellesmere Rd., Twick. 101 CJ86
Ellesmere Rd., Wey. 127 BS108
Ellesmere St. E14 79 EB72
Ellingfort Rd. E8 78 DV66
Ellingham Rd. E15 65 ED63
Ellingham Rd. W12 89 CU75
Ellingham Rd., Chess. 129 CK107
Ellington Rd. N10 63 DH56
Ellington Rd., Felt. 99 BT91
Ellington Rd., Houns. 86 CB82
Ellington St. N7 77 DN65
Ellington Way, Epsom 145 CV117
Elliot Clo. E15 80 EE66
Elliot Rd. NW4 61 CV58
Elliot Rd., Stan. 45 CG51
Elliott Ave., Ruis. 57 BV61
Elliott Clo., Wem. 60 CM62
Elliott Gdns., Rom. 55 FH53
Elliott Gdns., Shep. 112 BN98
Elliott Rd. SW9 91 DP80
Elliott Rd. W4 88 CS77
Elliott Rd., Brom. 122 EK98
Elliott Rd., Th.Hth. 119 DP98
Elliott Sq. NW3 76 DE66
Elliotts Clo., Uxb. 70 BJ71
Elliotts La., Sev. 152 EW124
Elliott's Pl. N1 77 DP67
St. Peters St.
Elliotts Row SE11 10 F8
Elliotts Row SE11 91 DP77
Ellis Ave., Rain. 83 FG71
Ellis Clo. SE9 109 EQ89
Ellis Clo., Couls. 147 DM120
Ellis Ct. W7 73 CF71
Ellis Ms. SE7 94 EJ79
Ellis Rd., Couls. 147 DM120
Ellis Rd., Mitch. 118 DF100
Ellis Rd., Sthl. 72 CC74
Ellis St. SW1 8 E8
Ellis St. SW1 90 DF77
Elliscombe Rd. SE7 94 EJ78
Ellisfield Dr. SW15 103 CT87
Ellison Gdns., Sthl. 86 BZ77
Ellison Rd. SW13 89 CT82
Ellison Rd. SW16 105 DK94
Ellison Rd., Sid. 109 ER88
Elliston Ho. SE18 95 EN77
Wellington St.
Ellmore Clo., Rom. 55 FH53
Ellora Rd. SW16 105 DK92
Ellsworth St. E2 78 DV69
Ellwood Ct. W9 76 DB70
Clearwell Dr.
Ellwood Gdns., Wat. 15 BV34
Elm Ave. W5 74 CL74
Elm Ave., Cars. 132 DF110
Elm Ave., Ruis. 57 BU60
Elm Ave., Wat. 44 BY45
Elm Bank N14 49 DL45
Elm Bank, Brom. 122 EK96
Elm Bank Gdns. SW13 88 CS82
Elm Clo. E11 66 EH58
Elm Clo. N19 63 DJ61
Hargrave Pk.
Elm Clo. NW4 61 CX57
Elm Clo. SW20 117 CW98
Grand Dr.
Elm Clo., Buck.H. 52 EK47
Elm Clo., Cars. 118 DF102
Elm Clo., Har. 58 CB58
Elm Clo., Hayes 71 BU72
Elm Clo., Lthd. 143 CH122
Elm Clo., Rom. 55 FB53
Elm Clo., S.Croy. 134 DS107
Elm Clo., Stai. 98 BK88
Elm Clo., Surb. 116 CQ101
Elm Clo., Twick. 100 CB89
Elm Clo., Wal.Abb. 23 ED34
Elm Clo., Warl. 149 DX117
Elm Clo. (Send Marsh), Wok. 140 BG124
Elm Ct. EC4 6 D10
Elm Ct., Mitch. 118 DF96
Armfield Cres.
Elm Ct., Sun. 99 BT94
Elm Cres. W5 74 CL74
Elm Cres., Kings.T. 116 CL95
Elm Cft., Sutt. 117 CX104
Elm Dr., Har. 58 CB58
Elm Dr., Lthd. 143 CH123
Elm Dr., Sun. 114 BW96
Elm Dr., Swan. 125 FD96
Elm Dr. (Cheshunt), Wal.Cr. 23 DY28
Elm Friars Wk. NW1 77 DK66
Maiden La.
Elm Gdns. N2 62 DC55
Elm Gdns., Enf. 36 DR38
Elm Gdns., Epp. 27 FB26
Elm Gdns., Epsom 145 CW119
Elm Gdns., Esher 129 CF107
Elm Gdns., Mitch. 119 DK98
Elm Grn. W3 74 CS72
Elm Gro. N8 63 DL58
Elm Gro. NW2 61 CX63
Elm Gro. SE15 92 DT82
Elm Gro. SW19 103 CY94
Elm Gro., Cat. 148 DS122
Elm Gro., Epsom 130 CQ114
Elm Gro., Erith 97 FD80
Elm Gro., Har. 58 CA59
Elm Gro., Kings.T. 116 CL95
Elm Gro., Orp. 123 ET102
Elm Gro., Sutt. 132 DB105
Elm Gro., Wat. 29 BU37
Elm Gro., West Dr. 70 BM73
Willow Ave.
Elm Gro., Wdf.Grn. 52 EF50
Elm Gro. Par., Wall. 118 DG104
Butter Hill
Elm Gro. Rd. SW13 89 CU82
Elm Gro. Rd. W5 88 CL75
Elm Gro. Rd., Cob. 142 BX116
Elm Hall Gdns. E11 66 EH58
Elm La. SE6 107 DZ89
Elm La., Wok. 140 BM118
Elm Lawn Clo., Uxb. 70 BL66
Park Rd.
Elm Ms., Rich. 102 CM86
Grove Rd.
Elm Pk. SW2 105 DM86
Elm Pk., Stan. 45 CH50
Elm Pk. Ave. N15 64 DT57
Elm Pk. Ave., Horn. 69 FG63
Elm Pk. Ct., Pnr. 58 BW55
Elm Pk. Gdns. NW4 61 CX57
Elm Pk. Gdns. SW10 90 DD78
Elm Pk. La. SW3 90 DD78
Elm Pk. Mans. SW10 90 DC79
Park Wk.
Elm Pk. Rd. E10 65 DY60
Elm Pk. Rd. N3 47 CZ52
Elm Pk. Rd. N21 50 DQ45
Elm Pk. Rd. SE25 120 DT97
Elm Pk. Rd. SW3 90 DD79
Elm Pk. Rd., Pnr. 44 BW54
Elm Pl. SW7 90 DD78
Elm Quay Ct. SW8 91 DK79
Elm Rd. E7 80 EF65
Elm Rd. E11 65 ED61
Elm Rd. E17 65 EC57
Elm Rd. N22 49 DP53
Granville Rd.
Elm Rd. SW14 88 CQ83
Elm Rd., Barn. 33 CZ42
Elm Rd., Beck. 121 DZ96
Elm Rd., Chess. 130 CL105
Elm Rd., Epsom 131 CT107
Elm Rd., Erith 97 FG81
Elm Rd., Esher 129 CF107
Elm Rd., Felt. 99 BR88
Elm Rd., Kings.T. 116 CM95
Elm Rd., Lthd. 143 CH122
Elm Rd., N.Mal. 116 CR97
Elm Rd., Orp. 138 EU108
Elm Rd., Pur. 133 DP113
Elm Rd., Rom. 55 FB54
Elm Rd., Sid. 110 EU91
Elm Rd., Th.Hth. 120 DR98
Elm Rd., Wall. 118 DG102
Elm Rd., Warl. 149 DX117
Elm Rd., Wem. 60 CL64
Elm Rd. W., Sutt. 117 CZ101
Elm Row NW3 62 DC62
Elm St. WC1 6 C5
Elm St. WC1 77 DM70
Elm Ter. NW2 62 DA62
Elm Ter. NW3 62 DE63
Constantine Rd.
Elm Ter. SE9 109 EN86
Elm Ter., Har. 45 CD53
Elm Tree Ave., Esher 115 CD101
Elm Tree Clo. NW8 76 DD69
Elm Tree Clo., Ashf. 99 BP92
Convent Rd.
Elm Tree Clo., Nthlt. 72 BZ68
Elm Tree Rd. NW8 76 DD69
Elm Wk. NW3 62 DA61
Elm Wk. SW20 117 CW98
Elm Wk., Orp. 123 EM104
Elm Wk., Rad. 31 CF36
Elm Wk., Rom. 69 FG55
Elm Way N11 48 DG51
Elm Way NW10 60 CS63
Elm Way, Epsom 130 CR106
Elm Way, Rick. 42 BH46
Elm Way, Wor.Pk. 117 CW104
Elmar Rd. N15 64 DR56
Elmbank Ave., Barn. 33 CW42
Elmbank Way W7 73 CD71
Elmbourne Dr., Belv. 97 FB77
Elmbourne Rd. SW17 104 DG90
Elmbridge Ave., Surb. 116 CP99
Elmbridge Clo., Ruis. 57 BU58
Elmbridge Dr., Ruis. 57 BT57
Elmbridge Rd., Ilf. 54 EU51
Elmbridge Wk. E8 78 DU66
Wilman Gro.
Elmbrook Clo., Sun. 113 BV95
Elmbrook Gdns. SE9 94 EL84
Elmbrook Rd., Sutt. 131 CZ105
Elmcote Way, Rick. 28 BM44
Elmcourt Rd. SE27 105 DP89
Elmcroft, Lthd. 142 CA124
Elmcroft Ave. E11 66 EH57
Elmcroft Ave. N9 36 DV44
Elmcroft Ave. NW11 61 CZ59
Elmcroft Ave., Sid. 109 ET87
Elmcroft Clo. E11 66 EH56
Elmcroft Clo. N8 63 DM57
Elmcroft Clo. W5 73 CK72
Elmcroft Clo., Chess. 116 CL104
Elmcroft Clo., Felt. 99 BT86
Elmcroft Cres. NW11 61 CX59
Elmcroft Cres., Har. 58 CA55
Elmcroft Dr., Ashf. 98 BN92
Elmcroft Dr., Chess. 116 CL104
Elmcroft Gdns. NW9 60 CN57
Elmcroft Rd., Orp. 124 EU101
Elmcroft St. E5 64 DW63
Elmdale Rd. N13 49 DM50
Elmdene, Surb. 116 CQ102
Elmdene Clo., Beck. 121 DZ99
Elmdene Rd. SE18 95 EP78
Elmdon Rd., Houns. 86 BX82
Elmdon Rd. (Hatton Cross), Houns. 85 BT83
Elmer Ave., Rom. (Havering-atte-Bower) 55 FE48
Elmer Clo., Enf. 35 DM41
Elmer Clo., Rain. 83 FG66
Elmer Cotts., Lthd. 143 CG123
Elmer Gdns., Edg. 46 CP52
Elmer Gdns., Islw. 87 CD83
Elmer Gdns., Rain. 83 FG66
Elmer Ms., Lthd. 143 CG122
Elmer Rd. SE6 107 EC87
Elmers Dr., Tedd. 101 CH93
Kingston Rd.
Elmers End Rd. SE20 120 DW96
Elmers End Rd., Beck. 120 DW96
Elmers Rd. SE25 120 DU101
Elmerside Rd., Beck. 121 DY98
Elmfield, Lthd. 142 CA123
Elmfield Ave. N8 63 DL57
Elmfield Ave., Mitch. 118 DG95
Elmfield Ave., Tedd. 101 CF92
Elmfield Clo., Har. 59 CE61
Elmfield Clo., Pot.B. 19 CY33
Elmfield Pk., Brom. 122 EG97
Elmfield Rd. E4 51 EC47
Elmfield Rd. E17 65 DX57
Elmfield Rd. N2 62 DD55
Elmfield Rd. SW17 104 DG89
Elmfield Rd., Brom. 122 EG97
Elmfield Rd., Pot.B. 19 CY32
Elmfield Rd., Sthl. 86 BY76
Elmfield Way W9 76 DA71
Elmfield Way, S.Croy. 134 DT109
Elmgate Ave., Felt. 99 BV90
Elmgate Gdns., Edg. 46 CR50
Elmgreen Clo. E15 80 EE67
Church St. N.
Elmgrove Cres., Har. 59 CF57
Elmgrove Gdns., Har. 59 CG57
Elmgrove Rd., Croy. 120 DV101
Elmgrove Rd., Har. 59 CF57
Elmgrove Rd., Wey. 126 BN105
Elmhurst, Belv. 96 EY79
Elmhurst Ave. N2 62 DD55
Elmhurst Ave., Mitch. 104 DG94
Elmhurst Dr. E18 52 EG54
Elmhurst Gdns. E18 52 EH53
Elmhurst Rd. E7 80 EH66
Elmhurst Rd. N17 50 DS54
Elmhurst Rd. SE9 108 EL89
Elmhurst Rd., Enf. 36 DW37
Elmhurst St. SW4 91 DK83
Elmhurst Way, Loug. 53 EM45
Elmington Clo., Bex. 111 FB86
Elmington Est. SE5 92 DR80
Elmington Rd. SE5 92 DR81
Elmira St. SE13 93 EB83
Elmlea Dr., Hayes 71 BS71
Grange Rd.
Elmlee Clo., Chis. 109 EM93
Elmley Clo. E6 80 EL71
Northumberland Rd.
Elmley St. SE18 95 ER77
Elmore Clo., Wem. 74 CL68
Elmore Rd. E11 65 EC62
Elmore Rd., Couls. 146 DF121
Elmore Rd., Enf. 37 DX38
Elmore St. N1 78 DR66
Elmores, Loug. 39 EN41
Elmpark Gdns., S.Croy. 134 DW110
Elmroyd Ave., Pot.B. 19 CZ33
Elmroyd Clo., Pot.B. 19 CZ33
Elms, The SW13 89 CT83
Elms Ave. N10 63 DH55
Elms Ave. NW4 61 CX57
Elms Ct., Wem. 59 CG63
Elms Cres. SW4 105 DJ86
Elms Gdns., Dag. 68 EZ63
Elms Gdns., Wem. 59 CG63
Elms La., Wem. 59 CG62
Elms Ms. W2 76 DD73
Elms Pk. Ave., Wem. 59 CG63
Elms Rd. SW4 105 DJ85
Elms Rd., Har. 45 CE52
Elms Wk. SE3 94 EF84
Elmscott Gdns. N21 36 DQ44
Elmscott Rd., Brom. 108 EE92
Elmscroft N8 63 DM57
Tottenham La.
Elmscroft Gdns., Pot.B. 19 CZ32
Elmsdale Rd. E17 65 DZ56
Elmshaw Rd. SW15 103 CU85
Elmshorn, Epsom 145 CW116
Elmshurst Cres. N2 62 DC56
Elmside, Croy. 135 EB107
Elmside Rd., Wem. 60 CN62
Elmsleigh Ave., Har. 59 CH56
Elmsleigh Rd., Twick. 101 CD89
Elmslie Clo., Epsom 130 CQ114
Elmslie Clo., Wdf.Grn. 53 EM51
Gwynne Pk. Ave.
Elmslie Pt. E3 79 DZ71
Ackroyd Dr.
Elmstead Ave., Chis. 109 EM92
Elmstead Ave., Wem. 60 CL60
Elmstead Clo. N20 48 DA47
Elmstead Clo., Epsom 130 CS106
Elmstead Clo., Sev. 154 FE122
Elmstead Cres., Well. 96 EW79
Elmstead Gdns., Wor.Pk. 117 CU104
Elmstead Glade, Chis. 109 EM93
Elmstead La., Chis. 108 EL94
Elmstead Rd., Erith 97 FE81
Elmstead Rd., Ilf. 67 ES61
Elmstead Rd., W.Byf. 126 BG113
Elmstone Rd. SW6 90 DA81
Elmsway, Ashf. 98 BM92
Elmswood, Lthd. 142 BZ124
Elmsworth Ave., Houns. 86 CB82
Elmton Way E5 64 DU62
Rendlesham Rd.
Elmtree Clo., W.Byf. 126 BL113
Elmtree Rd., Tedd. 101 CE91
Elmwood Ave. N13 49 DL50
Elmwood Ave., Borwd. 32 CP42
Elmwood Ave., Felt. 99 BU89
Elmwood Ave., Har. 59 CG57
Elmwood Clo., Ash. 143 CK117
Elmwood Clo., Epsom 131 CU108
Elmwood Clo., Wall. 118 DG103
Elmwood Ct., Ash. 143 CK117
Elmwood Clo.

Elmwood Ct., Wem. 59 CG62
Elmwood Cres. NW9 60 CQ56
Elmwood Dr., Bex. 110 EY87
Elmwood Dr., Epsom 131 CU107
Elmwood Gdns. W7 73 CE72
Elmwood Rd. SE24 106 DR85
Elmwood Rd. W4 88 CQ79
Elmwood Rd., Croy. 119 DP101
Elmwood Rd., Mitch. 118 DF97
Elmworth Gro. SE21 106 DR89
Elnathan Ms. W9 76 DB70
Shirland Rd.
Elphinstone Rd. E17 51 DZ54
Elphinstone St. N5 63 DP63
Avenell Rd.
Elrick Clo., Erith 97 FE79
Elrington Rd. E8 78 DU65
Elrington Rd., Wdf.Grn. 52 EG50
Elruge Clo., West Dr. 84 BK76
Elsa Rd., Well. 96 EV82
Elsa St. E1 79 DY71
Elsdale St. E9 78 DW65
Elsden Ms. E2 78 DW68
Old Ford Rd.
Elsden Rd. N17 50 DT53
Elsenham Rd. E12 67 EN64
Elsenham St. SW18 103 CZ88
Elsham Rd. E11 66 EE62
Elsham Rd. W14 89 CY75
Elsham Ter. W14 89 CY75
Elsie Rd. SE22 92 DT84
Elsiedene Rd. N21 50 DQ45
Elsiemaud Rd. SE4 107 DZ85
Elsinge Rd., Enf. 36 DV36
Elsinore Ave., Stai. 98 BL87
Elsinore Gdns. NW2 61 CY62
Elsinore Rd. SE23 107 DY88
Elsinore Way, Rich. 88 CP83
Lower Richmond Rd.
Elsley Rd. SW11 90 DF83
Elspeth Rd. SW11 90 DF84
Elspeth Rd., Wem. 60 CL64
Elsrick Ave., Mord. 118 DA99
Chalgrove Ave.
Elstan Way, Croy. 121 DY101
Elsted St. SE17 11 L9
Elsted St. SE17 92 DR77
Elston La., Sev. 153 FF117
Elstow Clo. SE9 109 EN85
Elstow Clo., Ruis. 58 BX59
Elstow Gdns., Dag. 82 EY67
Elstow Rd., Dag. 82 EY66
Elstree Gdns. N9 50 DV46
Elstree Gdns., Belv. 96 EY77
Elstree Gdns., Ilf. 67 EQ64
Elstree Hill, Brom. 108 EE94
Elstree Hill N., Borwd. 31 CK44
Elstree Hill S., Borwd. 45 CJ45
Elstree Rd., Borwd. 31 CH44
Elstree Rd. (Bushey), Wat. 45 CD45
Elstree Way, Borwd. 32 CP41
Elswick Rd. SE13 93 EB82
Elswick St. SW6 90 DC82
Elsworth Clo., Felt. 99 BS88
Elsworthy, T.Ditt. 115 CE100
Elsworthy Ri. NW3 76 DE66
Elsworthy Rd. NW3 76 DD67
Elsworthy Ter. NW3 76 DE66
Elsynge Rd. SW18 104 DD85
Eltham Grn. SE9 108 EJ85
Eltham Grn. Rd. SE9 94 EJ84
Eltham High St. SE9 109 EM86
Eltham Hill SE9 108 EK85
Eltham Palace Rd. SE9 108 EJ86
Eltham Pk. Gdns. SE9 95 EN84
Eltham Rd. SE9 108 EJ85
Eltham Rd. SE12 108 EG85
Elthiron Rd. SW6 90 DA81
Elthorne Ave. W7 87 CF75
Elthorne Ct., Felt. 100 BW88
Elthorne Pk. Rd. W7 87 CF75
Elthorne Rd. N19 63 DK61
Elthorne Rd. NW9 60 CR59
Elthorne Rd., Uxb. 70 BK68
Elthorne Way NW9 60 CR58
Elthruda Rd. SE13 107 ED86
Eltisley Rd., Ilf. 67 EP63
Elton Ave., Barn. 33 CZ43
Elton Ave., Grnf. 73 CE65
Elton Ave., Wem. 59 CH64
Elton Clo., Kings.T. 101 CJ94
Elton Ho. E3 79 DZ67
Elton Pk., Wat. 29 BV40
Elton Pl. N16 64 DS64
Elton Rd., Kings.T. 116 CM95
Elton Rd., Pur. 133 DJ112
Elton Way (Bushey), Wat. 30 CB40
Eltringham St. SW18 90 DC84
Elvaston Ms. SW7 90 DC76
Elvaston Pl. SW7 90 DC76
Elveden Clo., Wok. 140 BH117
Elveden Pl. NW10 74 CN68
Elveden Rd. NW10 74 CN68
Elvedon Rd., Cob. 127 BV111
Elvendon Rd. N13 49 DL51
Elver Gdns. E2 78 DU68
St. Peter's Clo.
Elverson Rd. SE8 93 EB82
Elverton St. SW1 9 M8
Elverton St. SW1 91 DK77
Elvington Grn., Brom. 122 EF99
Elvington La. NW9 46 CS53
Elvino Rd. SE26 107 DX92
Elvis Rd. NW2 75 CW65
Elwill Way, Beck. 121 EC98
Elwin St. E2 78 DU69
Elwood St. N5 63 DP62
Elwyn Gdns. SE12 108 EG87
Ely Clo., Erith 97 FF82
Ely Clo., N.Mal. 117 CT96
Ely Ct. EC1 6 E7
Ely Gdns., Borwd. 32 CR43
Ely Gdns., Dag. 69 FC62
Ely Gdns., Ilf. 66 EL59
Canterbury Ave.
Ely Pl. EC1 6 E7
Ely Pl., Wdf.Grn. 53 EN51
Ely Rd. E10 65 EC59
Ely Rd., Croy. 120 DR99
Ely Rd. (Heathrow Airport), Houns. 85 BT82
Eastern Perimeter Rd.
Ely Rd. (Hounslow W.), Houns. 86 BW83
Elyne Rd. N4 63 DN58
Elysian Ave., Orp. 123 ES100
Elysium Pl. SW6 89 CZ82
Fulham Pk. Gdns.
Elysium St. SW6 89 CZ82
Fulham Pk. Gdns.
Elystan Clo., Wall. 133 DH109
Elystan Pl. SW3 8 C10
Elystan Pl. SW3 90 DE78
Elystan St. SW3 8 B9
Elystan St. SW3 90 DE77
Elystan Wk. N1 77 DN67
Cloudesley Rd.
Emanuel Ave. W3 74 CQ72
Emanuel Dr., Hmptn. 100 BZ92
Emba St. SE16 92 DU75
Embankment SW15 89 CX82
Embankment, The, Twick. 101 CG88
Embankment Gdns. SW3 90 DF79
Embankment Pl. WC2 10 A2
Embankment Pl. WC2 77 DL74
Embassy Ct., Sid. 110 EV90
Embassy Ct., Well. 96 EV83
Ember Clo., Add. 126 BK106
Ember Clo., Orp. 123 EQ101
Ember Fm. Ave., E.Mol. 115 CD100
Ember Fm. Way, E.Mol. 115 CD100
Ember Gdns., T.Ditt. 115 CE101
Ember La., E.Mol. 115 CD100
Ember La., Esher 115 CD101
Embercourt Rd., T.Ditt. 115 CE100
Emberson Way, Epp. 27 FC26
Emberton SE5 92 DS79
Albany Rd.
Embleton Rd. SE13 93 EB84
Embleton Rd., Wat. 43 BU48
Embleton Wk., Hmptn. 100 BZ93
Fearnley Cres.
Embley Pt. E5 64 DV63
Tiger Way
Embry Clo., Stan. 45 CG49
Embry Dr., Stan. 45 CG51
Embry Way, Stan. 45 CG49
Emden Clo., West Dr. 84 BN75
Emden St. SW6 90 DB81
Emerald Clo. E16 80 EL72
Emerald Gdns., Dag. 68 FA60
Emerald St. WC1 6 B6
Emerald St. WC1 77 DM71
Emerson Gdns., Har. 60 CM58
Emerson Rd., Ilf. 67 EN59
Emerson St. SE1 11 H2
Emerson St. SE1 78 DQ74
Emersons Ave., Swan. 111 FF94
Emerton Clo., Bexh. 96 EY84
Emerton Rd., Lthd. 142 CC120
Emery Hill St. SW1 9 L7
Emery Hill St. SW1 91 DJ76
Emery St. SE1 10 E6
Emes Rd., Erith 97 FC80
Emily Jackson Clo., Sev. 155 FH124
Emily Pl. N7 63 DN63
Emley Rd., Add. 112 BG104
Emlyn Gdns. W12 88 CS75
Emlyn La., Lthd. 143 CG122
Emlyn Rd. W12 88 CS75
Emma Rd. E13 80 EF68
Emma St. E2 78 DV68
Emmanuel Clo., Nthwd. 43 BT52
Emmanuel Rd.
Emmanuel Lo., Wal.Cr. 22 DW30
College Rd.
Emmanuel Rd. SW12 105 DJ88
Emmanuel Rd., Nthwd. 43 BT52
Emmaus Way, Chig. 53 EN50
Emmott Ave., Ilf. 67 EQ57
Emmott Clo. E1 79 DY70
Emmott Clo. NW11 62 DC58
Emms Pas., Kings.T. 115 CK96
High St.
Emperor's Gate SW7 90 DB76
Empire Ave. N18 50 DQ50
Empire Cen., Wat. 30 BW39
Empire Ct., Wem. 60 CP62
Empire Rd., Grnf. 73 CH67
Empire Way, Wem. 60 CM63
Empire Wf. Rd. E14 93 ED77
Empire Yd. N7 63 DL62
Holloway Rd.
Empress Ave. E4 51 EB52
Empress Ave. E12 66 EJ61
Empress Ave., Ilf. 67 EM61
Empress Ave., Wdf.Grn. 52 EF52
Empress Dr., Chis. 109 EP93
Empress Pl. SW6 90 DA78
Empress St. SE17 92 DQ79
Empson St. E3 79 EB70
Emsworth Clo. N9 50 DW46
Emsworth Rd., Ilf. 53 EP54
Emsworth St. SW2 105 DL89
Emu Rd. SW8 91 DH82
Ena Rd. SW16 119 DL97
Enbrook St. W10 75 CY69
End Way, Surb. 116 CN101
Endale Clo., Cars. 118 DF103
Endeavour Rd. (Cheshunt), Wal.Cr. 23 DY27
Endeavour Way SW19 104 DB91
Endeavour Way, Bark. 82 EU68
Endeavour Way, Croy. 119 DK101
Endell St. WC2 5 P8
Endell St. WC2 77 DL72
Enderby St. SE10 94 EE78
Enderley Clo., Har. 45 CE53
Enderley Rd., Har. 45 CE53
Endersby Rd., Barn. 33 CW43
Endersleigh Gdns. NW4 61 CU56
Endlebury Rd. E4 51 EC47
Endlesham Rd. SW12 104 DG87
Endsleigh Clo., S.Croy. 134 DW110
Endsleigh Gdns. WC1 5 M4
Endsleigh Gdns. WC1 77 DK70
Endsleigh Gdns., Ilf. 67 EM61
Endsleigh Gdns., Surb. 115 CJ100
Endsleigh Gdns., Walt. 128 BW106
Endsleigh Pl. WC1 5 N4
Endsleigh Pl. WC1 77 DK70
Endsleigh Rd. W13 73 CG73
Endsleigh Rd., Sthl. 86 BY77
Endsleigh St. WC1 5 N4
Endsleigh St. WC1 77 DK70
Endwell Rd. SE4 93 DY82
Endymion Rd. N4 63 DN59
Endymion Rd. SW2 105 DM86
Enfield Clo., Uxb. 70 BK68
Villier St.
Enfield Retail Pk., Enf. 36 DU41
Crown Rd.
Enfield Rd. N1 78 DS66
Enfield Rd. W3 88 CP75
Enfield Rd., Brent. 87 CK78
Enfield Rd., Enf. 35 DL42
Enfield Rd., Houns. 85 BS82
Eastern Perimeter Rd.
Enfield Wk., Brent. 87 CK78
Enfield Rd.
Enford St. W1 4 D6
Enford St. W1 76 DF71
Engadine Clo., Croy. 120 DT104
Engadine St. SW18 103 CZ88
Engate St. SE13 93 EC84
Engel Pk. NW7 47 CW51
Engineer Clo. SE18 95 EN79
Engineers Way, Wem. 60 CN63
Englands La. NW3 76 DF65
Englands La., Loug. 39 EN40
Englefield Clo., Croy. 120 DQ100
Queen's Rd.
Englefield Clo., Enf. 35 DN40
Englefield Clo., Orp. 123 ET98
Englefield Cres., Orp. 123 ET98
Englefield Path, Orp. 124 EU98
Englefield Rd. N1 78 DR66
Englefield Rd., Orp. 124 EU98
Engleheart Dr., Felt. 99 BT86
Engleheart Rd. SE6 107 EB87
Englewood Rd. SW12 105 DH86
English Grds. SE1 11 M3
English St. E3 79 DZ70
Enid Clo., St.Alb. 16 BZ31
Enid St. SE16 92 DT76
Enmore Ave. SE25 120 DU99
Enmore Gdns. SW14 102 CR85
Enmore Rd. SE25 120 DU99
Enmore Rd. SW15 89 CW84
Enmore Rd., Sthl. 72 CA70
Ennerdale Ave., Horn. 69 FG64
Ennerdale Ave., Stan. 59 CJ55
Ennerdale Clo., Felt. 99 BT88
Ennerdale Clo. (Cheam), Sutt. 131 CZ105
Ennerdale Dr. NW9 60 CS57
Ennerdale Gdns., Wem. 59 CJ60
Ennerdale Ho. E3 79 DZ70
Ennerdale Rd., Bexh. 96 FA81
Ennerdale Rd., Rich. 88 CM82
Ennersdale Rd. SE13 107 ED85
Ennis Rd. N4 63 DN60
Ennis Rd. SE18 95 EQ79
Ennismore Ave. W4 89 CT77
Ennismore Ave., Grnf. 73 CE65
Ennismore Gdns. SW7 8 B6
Ennismore Gdns. SW7 90 DE75
Ennismore Gdns., T.Ditt. 115 CE100
Ennismore Gdns. Ms. SW7 8 B6
Ennismore Gdns. Ms. SW7 90 DE76
Ennismore Ms. SW7 8 B6
Ennismore Ms. SW7 90 DE76
Ennismore St. SW7 8 B6
Ennismore St. SW7 90 DE76
Ensign Clo., Pur. 133 DN110
Ensign Clo., Stai. 98 BL88
Ensign Dr. N13 50 DQ48
Ensign St. E1 78 DU73
Ensign Way, Stai. 98 BK88
Enslin Rd. SE9 109 EN87
Ensor Ms. SW7 90 DD78
Cranley Gdns.
Enstone Rd., Enf. 37 DY41
Enstone Rd., Uxb. 56 BM62
Enterprise Clo., Croy. 119 DN102
Enterprise Way NW10 75 CU69
Enterprise Way SW18 90 DA84
Enterprise Way, Tedd. 101 CF92
Enterprize Way SE8 93 DZ77
Epirus Ms. SW6 90 DA80
Epirus Rd.
Epirus Rd. SW6 89 CZ80
Epping Clo. E14 93 EA77
Epping Clo., Rom. 69 FB55
Epping Glade E4 37 EC44
Epping La., Rom. 40 EV40
Epping New Rd., Buck.H. 52 EG48
Epping New Rd., Loug. 38 EJ41
Epping Pl. N1 77 DN65
Liverpool Rd.
Epping Rd., Epp. 39 EM35
Epping Rd. (Epping Grn.), Epp. 25 ER26
Epping Rd., Epp. (North Weald Bassett) 26 EW28
Epping Rd. (Toot Hill), Ong. 27 FC30
Epping Way E4 37 EB44
Epple Rd. SW6 89 CZ81
Epsom Clo., Bexh. 97 FB83
Epsom Clo., Nthlt. 58 BZ64
Epsom Downs, Epsom 145 CT118
Epsom Gap, Lthd. 143 CH115
Kingston Rd.
Epsom La. N., Epsom 145 CV118
Epsom La. S., Tad. 145 CW121
Epsom Rd. E10 65 EC58
Epsom Rd., Ash. 144 CM118
Epsom Rd., Croy. 133 DN105
Epsom Rd., Epsom 131 CT111
Epsom Rd., Ilf. 67 ET58
Epsom Rd., Lthd. 143 CH121
Epsom Rd., Mord. 118 DA100
Epsom Rd., Sutt. 117 CZ101
Epsom Sq., Houns. 85 BT82
Eastern Perimeter Rd.
Epstein Rd. SE28 82 EU74
Epworth Rd., Islw. 87 CH81
Epworth St. EC2 7 L5
Epworth St. EC2 78 DR70
Equity Sq. E2 78 DT69
Shacklewell St.
Erasmus St. SW1 9 N9
Erasmus St. SW1 91 DK77
Erconwald St. W12 75 CT72
Eresby Dr., Beck. 121 EA102
Eresby Pl. NW6 76 DA66
Eric Clo. E7 66 EG63
Eric Rd. E7 66 EG63
Eric Rd. NW10 75 CT65
Church Rd.
Eric Rd., Rom. 68 EX59
Eric Steele Ho., St.Alb. 16 CB27
Eric St. E3 79 DZ70
Erica Ct., Swan. 125 FE98
Azalea Dr.
Erica Gdns., Croy. 121 EA104
Erica St. W12 75 CU73
Ericcson Clo. SW18 104 DA85
Eridge Grn. Clo., Orp. 124 EW102
Petten Gro.
Eridge Rd. W4 88 CR76
Erin Clo., Brom. 108 EE94
Erindale SE18 95 ER79
Erindale Ter. SE18 95 ER79
Eriswell Cres., Walt. 127 BS107
Eriswell Rd., Walt. 127 BT105
Erith Cres., Rom. 55 FC53
Erith High St., Erith 97 FE78
Erith Rd., Belv. 96 FA78
Erith Rd., Bexh. 97 FB84
Erith Rd., Erith 97 FC81
Erlanger Rd. SE14 93 DX81
Erlesmere Gdns. W13 87 CG76
Ermine Clo., Houns. 86 BW82
Ermine Clo. (Cheshunt), Wal.Cr. 22 DV31
Ermine Ho. N17 50 DT52
Ermine Rd. N15 64 DT58
Ermine Rd. SE13 93 EB84
Ermine Side, Enf. 36 DU43
Ermington Rd. SE9 109 EQ89
Ermyn Clo., Lthd. 143 CK121
Ermyn Way, Lthd. 143 CK121
Ernald Ave. E6 80 EL68
Erncroft Way, Twick. 101 CF86
Ernest Ave. SE27 105 DP91
Ernest Clo., Beck. 121 EA99
Ernest Gdns. W4 88 CP79
Ernest Gro., Beck. 121 DZ99
Ernest Rd., Kings.T. 116 CP96
Ernest Sq., Kings.T. 116 CP96
Ernest St. E1 79 DX70
Ernle Rd. SW20 103 CV94
Ernshaw Pl. SW15 103 CY85
Carlton Dr.
Erpingham Rd. SW15 89 CW83
Erridge Rd. SW19 118 DA96
Errington Rd. W9 75 CZ70
Errol Gdns., Hayes 71 BV70
Errol Gdns., N.Mal. 117 CU98
Errol St. EC1 7 J5
Errol St. EC1 78 DQ70
Erroll Rd., Rom. 69 FF56
Erskine Clo., Sutt. 118 DE104
Erskine Cres. N17 64 DV56
Erskine Hill NW11 62 DA57
Erskine Ms. NW3 76 DF66
Erskine Rd.
Erskine Rd. E17 65 DZ56
Erskine Rd. NW3 76 DF66
Erskine Rd., Sutt. 132 DD105
Erskine Rd., Wat. 44 BW48
Erwood Rd. SE7 94 EL78
Esam Way SW16 105 DN92
Escot Way, Barn. 33 CW43
Escott Gdns. SE9 108 EL91
Escreet Gro. SE18 95 EN77
Esher Ave., Rom. 69 FC58
Esher Ave., Sutt. 117 CX104
Esher Ave., Walt. 113 BU100
Esher Bypass, Chess. 129 CJ105
Esher Bypass, Cob. 127 BU112
Esher Bypass, Esher 129 CH108
Esher Clo., Bex. 110 EY88
Esher Clo., Esher 128 CB106
Esher Cres., Houns. 85 BS82
Eastern Perimeter Rd.
Esher Gdns. SW19 103 CX89
Esher Grn., Esher 128 CB105
Esher Ms., Mitch. 118 DF97
Esher Pk. Ave., Esher 128 CC105
Esher Pl. Ave., Esher 128 CA105
Esher Rd., E.Mol. 115 CD100
Esher Rd., Ilf. 67 ES62
Esher Rd., Walt. 128 BX106
Esk Rd. E13 80 EG70
Esk Way, Rom. 55 FD52
Eskdale, St.Alb. 18 CM27
Eskdale Ave., Nthlt. 72 BZ67
Eskdale Clo., Wem. 59 CK61
Eskdale Gdns., Pur. 134 DR114
Eskdale Rd., Bexh. 96 FA82
Eskdale Rd., Uxb. 70 BH68
Eskmont Ridge SE19 106 DS94
Esmar Cres. NW9 61 CU59
Esme Ho. SW15 89 CT84
Ludovick Wk.
Esmeralda Rd. SE1 92 DU77
Esmond Clo., Rain. 83 FH66
Dawson Dr.
Esmond Rd. NW6 75 CZ67
Esmond Rd. W4 88 CR77
Esmond St. SW15 89 CY84
Esparto St. SW18 104 DB87
Essenden Rd., Belv. 96 FA78
Essenden Rd., S.Croy. 134 DS108
Essendene Clo., Cat. 148 DS123
Essendene Rd., Cat. 148 DS123
Essendine Rd. W9 76 DA69
Essex Ave., Islw. 87 CE83
Essex Clo. E17 65 DY56
Essex Clo., Add. 126 BJ105
Essex Clo., Mord. 117 CX101
Essex Clo., Rom. 69 FB56
Essex Clo., Ruis. 58 BX60
Essex Ct. EC4 6 D9
Essex Ct. SW13 89 CT82
Essex Gdns. N4 63 DP58
Essex Gro. SE19 106 DR93
Essex Ho. E14 79 EB72
Giraud St.
Essex La., Kings L. 15 BR33
Essex Pk. N3 48 DB51
Essex Pk. Ms. W3 74 CS74
Essex Pl. W4 88 CQ77
Essex Rd. E4 52 EE46
Essex Rd. E10 65 EC58
Essex Rd. E12 66 EL64
Essex Rd. E17 65 DY58
Essex Rd. E18 52 EH54
Essex Rd. N1 77 DP67
Essex Rd. NW10 74 CS66
Essex Rd. W3 74 CQ73
Essex Rd. W4 88 CR77
Belmont Rd.
Essex Rd., Bark. 81 ER66
Essex Rd., Borwd. 32 CN41
Essex Rd., Dag. 69 FC64
Essex Rd., Enf. 36 DR42
Essex Rd., Rom. 68 FA56
Essex Rd. (Chadwell Heath), Rom. 68 EW59
Essex Rd., Wat. 29 BU40
Essex Rd. S. E11 65 ED59
Essex St. E7 66 EG64
Essex St. WC2 6 D10
Essex Twr. SE20 120 DV95
Essex Vill. W8 90 DA75
Essex Way, Epp. 26 EV32
Essex Way, Ong. 27 FF29
Essex Wf. E5 64 DW61
Essian St. E1 79 DY71
Essoldo Way, Edg. 60 CM55
Estate Way E10 65 DZ60
Estcourt Rd. SE25 120 DV100
Estcourt Rd. SW6 89 CZ80
Estcourt Rd., Wat. 30 BW41
Este Rd. SW11 90 DE83
Estella Ave., N.Mal. 117 CV98
Estelle Rd. NW3 62 DF63
Esterbrooke St. SW1 9 M9
Esterbrooke St. SW1 91 DK77
Esther Clo. N21 49 DN45
Esther Rd. E11 66 EE59
Estoria Clo. SW2 105 DM87
Upper Tulse Hill
Estreham Rd. SW16 105 DK93
Estridge Clo., Houns. 86 CA84
Estuary Clo., Bark. 82 EV69
Eswyn Rd. SW17 104 DF91
Etchingham Pk. Rd. N3 48 DB52
Etchingham Rd. E15 65 EC63
Eternit Wk. SW6 89 CW81
Etfield Gro., Sid. 110 EV92
Ethel Rd. E16 80 EH72
Ethel Rd., Ashf. 98 BL92
Ethel St. SE17 11 J9
Ethel Ter., Orp. 138 EW109
Ethelbert Clo., Brom. 122 EG97
Ethelbert Gdns., Ilf. 67 EM57
Ethelbert Rd. SW20 117 CX95

Ethelbert Rd., Brom. 122 EG97
Ethelbert Rd., Erith 97 FC80
Ethelbert Rd., Orp. 124 EX97
Ethelbert St. SW12 105 DH88
Fernlea Rd.
Ethelburga St. SW11 90 DE81
Ethelden Rd. W12 75 CV74
Etheldene Ave. N10 63 DJ56
Ethelwine Pl., Abb.L. 15 BT30
The Cres.
Etheridge Grn., Loug. 39 EQ41
Etheridge Rd.
Etheridge Rd. NW2 61 CW59
Etheridge Rd., Loug. 39 EP40
Etherley Rd. N15 64 DQ57
Etherow St. SE22 106 DU86
Etherstone Grn. SW16 105 DN91
Etherstone Rd.
Etherstone Rd. SW16 105 DN91
Ethnard Rd. SE15 92 DV79
Ethronvi Rd., Bexh. 96 EY83
Etloe Rd. E10 65 EA61
Eton Ave. N12 48 DC52
Eton Ave. NW3 76 DD66
Eton Ave., Barn. 34 DE44
Eton Ave., Houns. 86 BZ79
Eton Ave., N.Mal. 116 CR99
Eton Ave., Wem. 59 CH64
Eton College Rd. NW3 76 DF65
Eton Ct. NW3 76 DD66
Eton Ave.
Eton Ct., Wem. 59 CJ63
Eton Ave.
Eton Garages NW3 76 DE65
Lambolle Pl.
Eton Gro. NW9 60 CN55
Eton Gro. SE13 94 EE83
Eton Hall NW3 76 DF65
Eton College Rd.
Eton Pl. NW3 76 DG66
Haverstock Hill
Eton Ri. NW3 76 DF65
Eton College Rd.
Eton Rd. NW3 76 DF66
Eton Rd., Hayes 85 BT80
Eton Rd., Ilf. 67 EQ64
Eton Rd., Orp. 138 EV105
Eton St., Rich. 102 CL85
Eton Vill. NW3 76 DF65
Etta St. SE8 93 DY79
Ettrick St. E14 79 EC72
Etwell Pl., Surb. 116 CM100
Eugenia Rd. SE16 92 DW77
Eureka Rd., Kings.T. 116 CN96
Washington Rd.
Europa Pl. EC1 7 H3
Europe Rd. SE18 95 EM76
Eustace Rd. E6 80 EL69
Eustace Rd. SW6 90 DA80
Eustace Rd., Rom. 68 EX59
Euston Ave., Wat. 29 BT43
Euston Cen. NW1 5 K4
Euston Gro. NW1 5 M3
Euston Gro. NW1 77 DK69
Euston Rd. N1 77 DH70
Euston Rd. NW1 5 J5
Euston Rd. NW1 77 DH70
Euston Rd., Croy. 119 DN102
Euston Sq. NW1 5 M3
Euston Sq. NW1 77 DK69
Euston Sta. Colonnade NW1 5 M3
Euston St. NW1 5 L3
Euston St. NW1 77 DJ69
Eva Rd., Rom. 68 EW59
Evandale Rd. SW9 91 DN82
Evangelist Rd. NW5 63 DH63
Evans Ave., Wat. 29 BT35
Evans Clo. E8 78 DT65
Buttermere Wk.
Evans Clo., Rick. 28 BN43
New Rd.
Evans Gro., Felt. 100 CA89
Evans Rd. SE6 108 EE89
Evansdale, Rain. 83 FF69
New Zealand Way
Evanston Ave. E4 51 EC52
Evanston Gdns., Ilf. 66 EL58
Eve Rd. E11 66 EE63
Eve Rd. E15 80 EE68
Eve Rd. N17 64 DS55
Eve Rd., Islw. 87 CG84
Evelina Rd. SE15 92 DW83
Evelina Rd. SE20 107 DX94
Eveline Lowe Est. SE16 92 DU76
Eveline Rd., Mitch. 118 DF95
Evelyn Ave. NW9 60 CR55
Evelyn Ave., Ruis. 57 BT59
Evelyn Clo., Twick. 100 CB87
Evelyn Ct. N1 7 K1
Evelyn Cres., Sun. 113 BT95
Evelyn Denington Rd. E6 81 EM71
Evelyn Dr., Pnr. 44 BX52
Evelyn Fox Ct. W10 75 CW71
Evelyn Gdns. SW7 90 DD78
Evelyn Gdns., Rich. 88 CL84
Kew Rd.
Evelyn Gro. W5 74 CM74
Evelyn Gro., Sthl. 72 BZ72
Evelyn Rd. E16 80 EH74
Evelyn Rd. E17 65 EC56
Evelyn Rd. SW19 104 DB92
Evelyn Rd. W4 88 CR76
Evelyn Rd., Barn. 34 DF42
Evelyn Rd., Rich. 88 CL83
Evelyn Rd. (Ham), Rich. 101 CJ90
Evelyn St. SE8 93 DY78
Evelyn Ter., Rich. 88 CL83
Evelyn Wk. N1 7 K1
Evelyn Wk. N1 78 DR68
Evelyn Way, Cob. 142 BZ116
Evelyn Way, Sun. 113 BT95
Evelyn Way, Wall. 133 DK105
Evelyn Yd. W1 5 M8
Evelyns Clo., Uxb. 70 BN72
Evening Hill, Beck. 107 EC94
Evenwood Clo. SW15 103 CY85
Everard Ave., Brom. 122 EG102
Everard La., Cat. 148 DU122
Tillingdown Hill
Everard Way, Wem. 60 CL62
Everatt Clo. SW18 103 CZ86
Amerland Rd.
Everdon Rd. SW13 89 CU79
Everest Pl. E14 79 EC71
Everest Pl., Swan. 125 FD98
Everest Rd. SE9 109 EM85
Everest Rd., Stai. 98 BK87
Everett Clo., Pnr. 57 BT55
Everett Clo., Wat. 45 CE46
Everett Wk., Belv. 96 EZ78
Osborne Rd.
Everglade, West. 150 EK118
Everglade Strand NW9 47 CT53
Evergreen Ct., Stai. 98 BK87
Evergreen Way, Hayes 71 BT73
Evergreen Way, Stai. 98 BK87
Everilda St. N1 77 DM67
Evering Rd. E5 64 DU62
Evering Rd. N16 64 DU62
Everington Rd. N10 48 DF54
Everington St. W6 89 CX79
Everitt Rd. NW10 74 CR69
Everleigh St. N4 63 DM60
Eversfield Gdns. NW7 46 CS51
Eversfield Rd., Rich. 88 CM82
Evershed Wk. W4 88 CR76
Eversholt St. NW1 77 DJ68
Evershot Rd. N4 63 DM60
Eversleigh Rd. E6 80 EK67
Eversleigh Rd. N3 47 CZ52
Eversleigh Rd. SW11 90 DF83
Eversleigh Rd., Barn. 34 DC43
Eversley Ave., Bexh. 97 FD82
Eversley Ave., Wem. 60 CN61
Eversley Clo. N21 35 DM44
Eversley Cres. N21 35 DM44
Eversley Cres., Islw. 87 CD81
Eversley Cres., Ruis. 57 BS61
Eversley Cross, Bexh. 97 FE82
Eversley Mt. N21 35 DM44
Eversley Pk. SW19 103 CV92
Eversley Pk. Rd. N21 35 DM44
Eversley Rd. SE7 94 EH79
Eversley Rd. SE19 106 DR94
Eversley Rd., Surb. 116 CM98
Eversley Way, Croy. 135 EA105
Everthorpe Rd. SE15 92 DT83
Everton Bldgs. NW1 5 K3
Everton Dr., Stan. 60 CM55
Everton Rd., Croy. 120 DU102
Evesham Ave. E17 51 EA54
Evesham Clo., Grnf. 72 CB68
Evesham Clo., Sutt. 132 DA108
Evesham Grn., Mord. 118 DB100
Evesham Rd. E15 80 EF66
Evesham Rd. N11 49 DJ50
Evesham Rd., Felt. 100 BW87
Sparrow Fm. Dr.
Evesham Rd., Mord. 118 DB100
Evesham St. W11 75 CX73
Evesham Wk. SE5 92 DR82
Love Wk.
Evesham Wk. SW9 91 DN82
Evesham Way SW11 90 DG83
Evesham Way, Ilf. 67 EN55
Evry Rd., Sid. 110 EW93
Ewald Rd. SW6 89 CZ82
Ewanrigg Ter., Wdf.Grn. 52 EJ50
Ewart Gro. N22 49 DN53
Ewart Pl. E3 79 DZ68
Ewart Rd. SE23 107 DX87
Ewe Clo. N7 77 DL65
Ewell Bypass, Epsom 131 CU107
Ewell Ct. Ave., Epsom 130 CS106
Ewell Downs Rd., Epsom 131 CU111
Ewell Ho. Gro., Epsom 131 CT110
Ewell Pk. Way, Epsom 131 CU107
Ewell Rd., Surb. 116 CL96
Ewell Rd. (Long Ditton), Surb. 115 CH101
Ewell Rd., Sutt. 131 CX108
Ewellhurst Rd., Ilf. 52 EL54
Ewelme Rd. SE23 106 DW88
Ewen Cres. SW2 105 DN87
Ewer St. SE1 11 H3
Ewer St. SE1 78 DQ74
Ewhurst Ave., S.Croy. 134 DT109
Ewhurst Clo., Sutt. 131 CW109
Ewhurst Ho. E1 78 DW71
Jamaica St.
Ewhurst Rd. SE4 107 DZ86
Exbury Rd. SE6 107 EA89
Excel Ct. WC2 9 N1
Excelsior Clo., Kings.T. 116 CN96
Washington Rd.
Excelsior Gdns. SE13 93 EC82
Exchange Arc. EC2 7 N6
Exchange Arc. EC2 78 DS71
Exchange Bldgs. E1 78 DS72
Cutler St.
Exchange Ct. WC2 10 A1
Exchange Pl. EC2 7 M6
Exchange Pl. EC2 78 DS71
Exchange Rd., Wat. 29 BV41
Exchange Sq. EC2 7 M6
Exchange Sq. EC2 78 DS71
Exchange St., Rom. 69 FE57
Exeforde Ave., Ashf. 98 BN91
Exeter Clo. E6 81 EM72
Harper Rd.
Exeter Clo., Wat. 30 BW40
Exeter Gdns., Ilf. 66 EL60
Exeter Ho. SW15 103 CW86
Putney Heath
Exeter Ms. NW6 76 DB65
West Hampstead Ms.
Exeter Rd. E16 80 EG71
Exeter Rd. E17 65 EA57
Exeter Rd. N9 50 DW47
Exeter Rd. N14 49 DH46
Exeter Rd. NW2 61 CY64
Exeter Rd. SE15 92 DT81
Exeter Rd., Croy. 120 DS101
Exeter Rd., Dag. 83 FB65
Exeter Rd., Enf. 37 DX41
Exeter Rd., Felt. 100 BZ90
Exeter Rd., Har. 58 BY61
Exeter Rd., Well. 95 ET82
Exeter St. WC2 6 A10
Exeter St. WC2 77 DL73
Exeter Way SE14 93 DZ80
Exford Gdns. SE12 108 EH88
Exford Rd. SE12 108 EH89
Exhibition Clo. W12 75 CW73
Exhibition Rd. SW7 8 A6
Exhibition Rd. SW7 90 DD75
Exmoor Clo., Ilf. 53 EQ53
Exmoor St. W10 75 CX71
Exmouth Mkt. EC1 6 D4
Exmouth Mkt. EC1 77 DN70
Exmouth Ms. NW1 5 L3
Exmouth Pl. E8 78 DV66
Exmouth Rd. E17 65 DZ57
Exmouth Rd., Brom. 122 EH97
Exmouth Rd., Hayes 71 BS69
Exmouth Rd., Ruis. 58 BW62
Exmouth Rd., Well. 96 EW81
Exmouth St. E1 78 DW72
Commercial Rd.
Exning Rd. E16 80 EF70
Exon St. SE17 11 M9
Exon St. SE17 92 DS77
Explorer Ave., Stai. 98 BL87
Explorer Dr., Wat. 29 BT44
Express Dr., Ilf. 68 EV60
Exton Cres. NW10 74 CQ66
Exton Gdns., Dag. 68 EW64
Exton St. SE1 10 D3
Exton St. SE1 77 DN74
Eyebright Clo., Croy. 121 DX102
Primrose La.
Eyhurst Ave., Horn. 69 FG62
Eyhurst Clo. NW2 61 CU61
Eyhurst Clo., Tad. 145 CZ123
Eyhurst Spur, Tad. 145 CZ124
Eylewood Rd. SE27 106 DQ92
Eynella Rd. SE22 106 DT87
Eynham Rd. W12 75 CW72
Eynsford Clo., Orp. 123 EQ101
Eynsford Cres., Bex. 110 EW88
Eynsford Rd., Ilf. 67 ES61
Eynsford Rd., Sev. 139 FH110
Eynsford Rd., Swan. 125 FD100
Eynsham Dr. SE2 96 EU77
Eynswood Dr., Sid. 110 EV92
Eyot Gdns. W6 89 CT78
Eyot Grn. W4 89 CT79
Chiswick Mall
Eyre Clo., Rom. 69 FH56
Eyre Ct. NW8 76 DD68
Finchley Rd.
Eyre St. Hill EC1 6 D5
Eyston Dr., Wey. 126 BN110
Eythorne Rd. SW9 91 DN81
Ezra St. E2 78 DT69

F

Faber Gdns. NW4 61 CU57
Fabian Rd. SW6 89 CZ80
Fabian St. E6 81 EM70
Fackenden La., Sev. 139 FH113
Factory La. N17 50 DT54
Factory La., Croy. 119 DN102
Factory Pl. E14 93 EB78
Factory Rd. E16 80 EL74
Factory Sq. SW16 105 DL93
Factory Yd. W7 73 CE74
Uxbridge Rd.
Faesten Way, Bex. 111 FE90
Faggotts Clo., Rad. 31 CJ35
Faggs Rd., Felt. 99 BU85
Faints Clo., Wal.Cr. 22 DT29
Fair Acres, Brom. 122 EG99
Fair Clo. (Bushey), Wat. 44 CB45
Claybury
Fair St. SE1 11 N4
Fair St., Houns. 86 CC83
High St.
Fairacre, N.Mal. 116 CS97
Fairacres SW15 103 CU85
Fairacres, Cob. 128 BX112
Fairacres, Croy. 135 DZ109
Fairacres, Ruis. 57 BT59
Fairacres, Tad. 145 CW121
Fairacres Clo., Pot.B. 19 CZ33
Fairbairn Clo., Pur. 133 DN113
Fairbairn Grn. SW9 91 DN81
Fairbank Ave., Orp. 123 EP103
Fairbanks Rd. N17 64 DT55
Fairbourne, Cob. 128 BX113
Fairbourne La., Cat. 148 DQ122
Fairbourne Rd. N17 64 DS55
Fairbridge Rd. N19 63 DK61
Fairbrook Clo. N13 49 DN50
Fairbrook Rd. N13 49 DN51
Fairburn Clo., Borwd. 32 CN39
Fairburn Ct. SW15 103 CY85
Mercier Rd.
Fairby Rd. SE12 108 EH85
Fairchild Clo. SW11 90 DD82
Wye St.
Fairchild Pl. EC2 7 N5
Fairchild St. EC2 7 N5
Fairchildes Ave., Croy. 135 ED112
Fairchildes La., Warl. 135 ED114
Fairclough St. E1 78 DU72
Faircross Ave., Bark. 81 EQ65
Faircross Ave., Rom. 55 FD52
Fairdale Gdns. SW15 89 CV84
Fairdale Gdns., Hayes 85 BU75
Fairdene Rd., Couls. 147 DK118
Fairey Ave., Hayes 85 BT77
Fairfax Ave., Epsom 131 CV110
Fairfax Clo., Walt. 113 BV102
Fairfax Gdns. SE3 94 EJ81
Fairfax Pl. NW6 76 DC66
Fairfax Rd. N8 63 DN56
Fairfax Rd. NW6 76 DC66
Fairfax Rd. W4 88 CS76
Fairfax Rd., Tedd. 101 CG93
Fairfax Way N10 48 DG52
Cromwell Rd.
Fairfield Ave. NW4 61 CV58
Fairfield Ave., Edg. 46 CP51
Fairfield Ave., Ruis. 57 BQ59
Fairfield Ave., Twick. 100 CB88
Fairfield Ave., Wat. 44 BW48
Fairfield Clo. N12 48 DC49
Fairfield Clo., Enf. 37 DY42
Scotland Grn. Rd. N.
Fairfield Clo., Epsom 130 CS106
Fairfield Clo., Horn. 69 FG60
Fairfield Clo., Mitch. 104 DE94
Fairfield Clo., Nthwd. 43 BP50
Thirlmere Gdns.
Fairfield Clo., Rad. 31 CE37
Fairfield Clo., Sid. 109 ET86
Fairfield Ct. NW10 75 CU67
Fairfield Cres., Edg. 46 CP51
Fairfield Dr. SW18 104 DB85
Fairfield Dr., Grnf. 73 CJ67
Fairfield Dr., Har. 58 CC55
Fairfield E., Kings.T. 116 CL96
Fairfield Gdns. N8 63 DL57
Elder Ave.
Fairfield Gro. SE7 94 EK79
Fairfield Ind. Est., Kings.T. 116 CN97
Fairfield N., Kings.T. 116 CL96
Fairfield Pk., Cob. 128 BX114
Fairfield Path, Croy. 120 DR104
Fairfield Pl., Kings.T. 116 CL97
Fairfield Rd. E3 79 EA68
Fairfield Rd. E17 51 DY54
Fairfield Rd. N8 63 DL57
Fairfield Rd. N18 50 DU49
Fairfield Rd. W7 87 CG76
Southdown Ave.
Fairfield Rd., Beck. 121 EA96
Fairfield Rd., Bexh. 96 EZ82
Fairfield Rd., Brom. 108 EG94
Fairfield Rd., Croy. 120 DS104
Fairfield Rd., Epp. 26 EV29
Fairfield Rd., Ilf. 81 EP65
Fairfield Rd., Kings.T. 116 CL96
Fairfield Rd., Lthd. 143 CH121
Fairfield Rd., Orp. 123 ER100
Fairfield Rd., Sthl. 72 BZ72
Fairfield Rd., Uxb. 70 BK65
Fairfield Rd., West Dr. 70 BL73
Fairfield Rd., Wdf.Grn. 52 EG51
Fairfield S., Kings.T. 116 CL97
Fairfield St. SW18 104 DB85
Fairfield Wk., Lthd. 143 CH121
Fairfield Rd.
Fairfield Wk. (Cheshunt), Wal.Cr. 23 DY28
Martins Dr.
Fairfield Way, Barn. 34 DA43
Fairfield Way, Couls. 133 DK114
Fairfield Way, Epsom 130 CS106
Fairfield W., Kings.T. 116 CL96
Fairfields, Cher. 112 BG102
Fairfields Clo. NW9 60 CQ57
Fairfields Cres. NW9 60 CQ57
Fairfields Rd., Houns. 86 CC83
Fairfolds, Wat. 30 BY35
Fairfoot Rd. E3 79 EA70
Fairford Ave., Bexh. 97 FD81
Fairford Ave., Croy. 121 DX99
Fairford Clo., Croy. 121 DX99
Fairford Gdns., Wor.Pk. 117 CT103
Fairgreen, Barn. 34 DF41
Fairgreen E., Barn. 34 DF41
Fairgreen Rd., Th.Hth. 119 DP99
Fairhaven Ave., Croy. 121 DX100
Fairhaven Cres., Wat. 43 BU48
Fairhazel Gdns. NW6 76 DB65
Fairholme, Felt. 99 BR87
Fairholme Ave., Rom. 69 FG57
Fairholme Clo. N3 61 CY56
Fairholme Cres., Ash. 143 CJ117
Fairholme Cres., Hayes 71 BT70
Fairholme Gdns. N3 61 CY55
Fairholme Rd. W14 89 CY78
Fairholme Rd., Ashf. 98 BL92
Fairholme Rd., Croy. 119 DN101
Fairholme Rd., Har. 59 CF57
Fairholme Rd., Ilf. 67 EM59
Fairholme Rd., Sutt. 131 CZ107
Fairholt Clo. N16 64 DS60
Fairholt Rd. N16 64 DR60
Fairholt St. SW7 8 C6
Fairland Rd. E15 80 EF65
Fairlands Ave., Buck.H. 52 EG47
Fairlands Ave., Sutt. 118 DA103
Fairlands Ave., Th.Hth. 119 DM98
Fairlands Ct. SE9 109 EN86
North Pk.
Fairlawn SE7 94 EJ79
Fairlawn, Lthd. 142 BZ124
Fairlawn Ave. N2 62 DE56
Fairlawn Ave. W4 88 CQ77
Fairlawn Ave., Bexh. 96 EX82
Fairlawn Clo. N14 35 DJ44
Fairlawn Clo., Esher 129 CF107
Fairlawn Clo., Felt. 100 BZ91
Fairlawn Clo., Kings.T. 102 CQ93
Fairlawn Dr., Wdf.Grn. 52 EG52
Fairlawn Gdns., Sthl. 72 BZ73
Fairlawn Gro. W4 88 CQ77
Fairlawn Gro., Bans. 132 DD113
Fairlawn Pk. SE26 107 DY92
Fairlawn Rd. SW19 103 CZ94
Fairlawn Rd., Cars. 132 DC111
Fairlawns, Pnr. 44 BW54
Fairlawns, Sun. 113 BU97
Fairlawns, Twick. 101 CJ86
Fairlawns, Wat. 29 BT38
Langley Rd.
Fairlawns, Wey. 127 BS106
Fairlawns Clo., Stai. 98 BH93
Fairlea Pl. W5 73 CJ71
Fairley Way (Cheshunt), Wal.Cr. 22 DV28
Fairlie Gdns. SE23 106 DW87
Fairlight Ave. E4 51 ED47
Fairlight Ave. NW10 74 CS68
Fairlight Ave., Wdf.Grn. 52 EG51
Fairlight Clo. E4 51 ED47
Fairlight Clo., Wor.Pk. 131 CW105
Fairlight Dr., Uxb. 70 BK65
Fairlight Rd. SW17 104 DD91
Fairlop Clo., Horn. 83 FH65
Fairlop Gdns., Ilf. 53 EQ52
Fairlop Rd. E11 65 ED59
Fairlop Rd., Ilf. 53 EQ54
Fairmark Dr., Uxb. 70 BN65
Fairmead, Brom. 123 EM98
Fairmead, Surb. 116 CP102
Fairmead Clo., Brom. 123 EM98
Fairmead Clo., Houns. 86 BX80
Fairmead Clo., N.Mal. 116 CR97
Fairmead Cres., Edg. 46 CQ48
Fairmead Gdns., Ilf. 66 EL57
Fairmead Rd. N19 63 DK62
Fairmead Rd., Croy. 119 DM102
Fairmead Rd., Loug. 38 EH43
Fairmead Side, Loug. 38 EJ43
Fairmeads, Cob. 128 BZ113
Fairmeads, Loug. 39 EP40
Fairmile Ave. SW16 105 DK92
Fairmile Ave., Cob. 128 BY114
Fairmile La., Cob. 128 BX112
Fairmile Pk. Copse, Cob. 128 BZ112
Fairmile Pk. Rd., Cob. 128 BZ113
Fairmont Clo., Belv. 96 EZ78
Lullingstone Rd.
Fairmount Rd. SW2 105 DM86
Fairoak Clo., Ken. 147 DP115
Fairoak Clo., Lthd. 129 CD112
Fairoak Clo., Orp. 123 EP101
Fairoak Dr. SE9 109 ER85
Fairoak Gdns., Rom. 55 FE54
Fairoak La., Chess. 129 CH111
Fairoak La., Lthd. 128 CC113
Fairs Rd., Lthd. 143 CG119
Fairseat Clo. (Bushey), Wat. 45 CE47
Hive Rd.
Fairstead Wk. N1 78 DQ67
Popham Rd.
Fairthorn Rd. SE7 94 EG78
Fairtrough Rd., Orp. 138 EV113
Fairview, Epsom 131 CW111
Fairview, Erith 97 FF80
Guild Rd.
Fairview, Pot.B. 20 DB29
Hawkshead Rd.
Fairview Ave., Wem. 73 CK65
Fairview Clo. E17 51 DY53
Fairview Clo., Chig. 53 ES49
Fairview Ct., Ashf. 98 BN92
Fairview Cres., Har. 58 CA60
Fairview Dr., Chig. 53 ES49
Fairview Dr., Orp. 137 ER105
Fairview Dr., Shep. 112 BM99
Fairview Dr., Wat. 29 BS36
Fairview Gdns., Wdf.Grn. 52 EH53
Fairview Ind. Pk., Rain. 83 FD71
Fairview Pl. SW2 105 DM87
Fairview Rd. N15 64 DT57
Fairview Rd. SW16 119 DM95
Fairview Rd., Chig. 53 ES49
Fairview Rd., Enf. 35 DN39
Fairview Rd., Epsom 131 CT111
Fairview Rd., Sutt. 132 DD106
Fairview Way, Edg. 46 CN49
Fairwater Ave., Well. 96 EU84
Fairwater Dr., Add. 126 BK109
Fairway SW20 117 CW97

Fairway, Bexh. 110 EY85
Fairway, Cars. 132 DC111
Fairway, Cher. 112 BH102
Fairway, Orp. 123 ER99
Fairway, Wdf.Grn. 52 EJ50
Fairway, The N13 50 DQ48
Fairway, The N14 35 DH44
Fairway, The NW7 46 CR48
Fairway, The W3 74 CS72
Fairway, The, Abb.L. 15 BR32
Fairway, The, Barn. 34 DB44
Fairway, The, Brom. 123 EM99
Fairway, The, Lthd. 143 CG118
Fairway, The, N.Mal. 116 CR95
Fairway, The, Nthlt. 72 CC65
Fairway, The, Nthwd. 43 BS49
Fairway, The, Ruis. 58 BW63
Fairway, The, Uxb. 70 BM69
Fairway, The, Wem. 59 CH62
Fairway, The, W.Mol. 114 CB97
Fairway, The, Wey. 126 BN111
Fairway Ave. NW9 60 CP55
Fairway Ave., Borwd. 32 CP40
Fairway Ave., West Dr. 70 BJ74
Fairway Clo. NW11 62 DC59
Fairway Clo., Croy. 121 DY99
Fairway Clo., Epsom 130 CQ105
Fairway Clo., Houns. 100 BW85
Fairway Clo., St.Alb. 16 CC27
Fairway Clo., West Dr. 70 BK74
Fairway Ave.
Fairway Ct. NW7 46 CR48
The Fairway
Fairway Dr. SE28 82 EX72
Summerton Way
Fairway Dr., Grnf. 72 CB66
Fairway Est., Grnf. 72 CC66
Fairway Gdns., Beck. 121 ED100
Fairway Gdns., Ilf. 67 EQ64
Fairways, Ashf. 99 BP93
Fairways, Ken. 148 DQ117
Fairways, Stan. 46 CL54
Fairways, Tedd. 101 CK94
Fairways, Wal.Abb. 24 EE34
Fairways, Wal.Cr. 23 DX26
Fairweather Clo. N15 64 DS56
Fairweather Rd. N16 64 DU58
Fairwyn Rd. SE26 107 DY91
Fakenham Clo. NW7 47 CU52
Fakenham Clo., Nthlt. 72 CA65
Goodwood Dr.
Fakruddin St. E1 78 DU70
Falcon Ave., Brom. 122 EL98
Falcon Clo. SE1 10 G2
Falcon Clo. W4 88 CQ79
Sutton La. S.
Falcon Clo., Nthwd. 43 BS52
Falcon Clo., Wal.Abb. 24 EG34
Kestrel Rd.
Falcon Cres., Enf. 37 DX43
Falcon Dr., Stai. 98 BK86
Falcon Gro. SW11 90 DE83
Falcon Ho. W13 73 CF70
Falcon La. SW11 90 DE83
Falcon Rd. SW11 90 DE82
Falcon Rd., Enf. 37 DX43
Falcon Rd., Hmptn. 100 BZ94
Falcon St. E13 80 EF70
Falcon Ter. SW11 90 DE83
Falcon Trd. Est. NW10 60 CS63
Falcon Way E11 66 EG56
Falcon Way E14 93 EB77
Falcon Way NW9 46 CS54
Falcon Way, Felt. 99 BV85
Falcon Way, Har. 60 CL57
Falcon Way, Horn. 83 FG66
Falcon Way, Sun. 113 BS96
Falcon Way, Wat. 16 BY34
Falconberg Ct. W1 5 N8
Falconberg Ms. W1 5 M8
Falconer Rd., Ilf. 54 EV50
Falconer Rd. (Bushey), Wat. 30 BZ44
Falconer Wk. N7 63 DM61
Newington Barrow Way
Falconhurst, Lthd. 143 CD115
Falconwood, Lthd. 141 BT124
Falconwood Ave., Well. 95 ER82
Falconwood Par., Well. 95 ES84
Falconwood Rd., Croy. 135 DZ109
Falcourt Clo., Sutt. 132 DB106
Falkirk Gdns., Wat. 44 BX50
Blackford Rd.
Falkirk Ho. W9 76 DB69
Falkirk St. N1 7 N1
Falkirk St. N1 78 DS68
Falkland Ave. N3 48 DA52
Falkland Ave. N11 48 DG49
Falkland Pk. Ave. SE25 120 DS97
Falkland Pl. NW5 63 DJ64
Falkland Rd.
Falkland Rd. N8 63 DN56
Falkland Rd. NW5 63 DJ64
Falkland Rd., Barn. 33 CY40
Fallaize Ave., Ilf. 67 EP63
Riverdene Rd.
Falling La., West Dr. 70 BL73
Falloden Way NW11 62 DA56
Fallow Clo., Chig. 53 ET50
Fallow Ct. SE16 92 DU78
Argyle Way
Fallow Ct. Ave. N12 48 DC52
Fallow Flds., Loug. 38 EJ44
Fallowfield, Stan. 45 CG49
Fallowfield Clo., Uxb. 42 BJ53
Fallowfield Ct., Stan. 45 CG48
Stanmore Hill
Fallowfields Dr. N12 48 DE51
Fallows Clo. N2 48 DC54
Fallsbrook Rd. SW16 105 DH93
Falmer Rd. E17 65 EB55
Falmer Rd. N15 64 DQ57
Falmer Rd., Enf. 36 DS42
Falmouth Ave. E4 51 ED50
Falmouth Clo. N22 49 DM52
Truro Rd.
Falmouth Clo. SE12 108 EF85
Falmouth Gdns., Ilf. 66 EK56
Falmouth Rd. SE1 11 J7
Falmouth Rd. SE1 92 DQ76
Falmouth Rd., Walt. 128 BW105
Falmouth St. E15 65 ED64
Falstaff Ms., Hmptn. 101 CD92
Hampton Rd.
Fambridge Clo. SE26 107 DZ91
Fambridge Rd., Dag. 68 FA60
Famet Ave., Pur. 134 DQ113
Famet Clo., Pur. 134 DQ113
Famet Wk., Pur. 134 DQ113
Fane St. W14 89 CZ79
North End Rd.
Fann St. EC1 7 H5
Fann St. EC1 78 DQ70
Fann St. EC2 7 H5
Fann St. EC2 78 DQ70
Fanshaw St. N1 7 M2
Fanshaw St. N1 78 DS69
Fanshawe Ave., Bark. 81 EQ65
Fanshawe Cres., Dag. 68 EY64
Fanshawe Rd., Rich. 101 CJ91
Fanthorpe St. SW15 89 CW83
Faraday Ave., Sid. 110 EU89
Faraday Clo. N7 77 DM65
Bride St.
Faraday Clo., Wat. 29 BR44
Faraday Rd. E15 80 EF65
Faraday Rd. SW19 104 DA93
Faraday Rd. W3 74 CQ73
Faraday Rd. W10 75 CY71
Faraday Rd., Sthl. 72 CB73
Faraday Rd., Well. 96 EU83
Faraday Rd., W.Mol. 114 CA98
Faraday Way SE18 94 EK76
Faraday Way, Croy. 119 DM102
Ampere Way
Faraday Way, Orp. 124 EV98
Fareham Rd., Felt. 100 BW87
Fareham St. W1 5 M8
Farewell Pl., Mitch. 118 DE95
Faringdon Ave., Brom. 123 EN101
Faringford Clo., Pot.B. 20 DD31
Faringford Rd. E15 80 EE66
Farington Acres, Wey. 113 BR104
Farjeon Rd. SE3 94 EK81
Farleigh Ave., Brom. 122 EF100
Farleigh Border, Croy. 135 DX112
Farleigh Ct. Rd., Warl. 135 DZ114
Farleigh Dean Cres., Croy. 135 EB111
Farleigh Pl. N16 64 DT63
Farleigh Rd.
Farleigh Rd. N16 64 DT63
Farleigh Rd., Add. 126 BG111
Farleigh Rd., Warl. 149 DX118
Farley Dr., Ilf. 67 ES60
Farley Pl. SE25 120 DU98
Farley Rd. SE6 107 EC87
Farley Rd., S.Croy. 134 DU108
Farlington Pl. SW15 103 CV87
Roehampton La.
Farlow Rd. SW15 89 CW83
Farlton Rd. SW18 104 DB87
Farm Ave. NW2 61 CY62
Farm Ave. SW16 105 DL91
Farm Ave., Har. 58 BZ59
Farm Ave., Swan. 125 FC97
Farm Ave., Wem. 73 CJ65
Farm Clo., Barn. 33 CV43
Farm Clo., Borwd. 31 CK38
Farm Clo., Buck.H. 52 EJ48
Farm Clo., Couls. 146 DF120
Farm Clo., Dag. 83 FC66
Farm Clo. (Fetcham), Lthd. 143 CD124
Farm Clo. (Cuffley), Pot.B. 21 DK27
Farm Clo., Shep. 112 BN101
Farm Clo., Sthl. 72 CB73
Farm Clo., Sutt. 132 DD108
Farm Clo., Uxb. 57 BP61
Farm Clo., Wall. 133 DJ110
Farm Clo. (Cheshunt), Wal.Cr. 22 DW30
Farm Clo., W.Byf. 126 BM112
Farm Clo., W.Wick. 122 EE104
Farm Ct. NW4 61 CU55
Farm Dr., Croy. 121 DZ103
Farm Dr., Pur. 133 DK112
Farm End E4 38 EE43
Farm End, Nthwd. 43 BP53
Drakes Dr.
Farm Fld., Wat. 29 BS38
Farm Flds., S.Croy. 134 DS111
Farm Hill Rd., Wal.Abb. 23 ED33
Farm La. N14 34 DG44
Farm La. SW6 90 DA79
Farm La., Add. 126 BG107
Farm La., Ash. 144 CN116
Farm La., Cars. 132 DF110
Farm La., Croy. 121 DZ103
Farm La., Epsom 144 CP120
Farm La., Pur. 133 DJ110
Farm La., Rick. 28 BH41
Farm Pl. W8 76 DA74
Uxbridge St.
Farm Pl., Dart. 97 FG84
Farm Rd. N21 50 DQ46
Farm Rd., Edg. 46 CP51
Farm Rd., Esher 114 CB102
Farm Rd., Houns. 100 BY88
Farm Rd., Mord. 118 DB99
Farm Rd., Nthwd. 43 BQ50
Farm Rd., Sev. 155 FJ121
Farm Rd., Stai. 98 BH93
Farm Rd., Sutt. 132 DD108
Farm Rd., Warl. 149 DY119
Farm St. W1 9 H1
Farm St. W1 77 DH73
Farm Vale, Bex. 111 FB86
Farm Wk. NW11 61 CZ57
Farm Way, Buck.H. 52 EJ49
Farm Way, Horn. 69 FH63
Farm Way, Nthwd. 43 BS49
Farm Way (Bushey), Wat. 30 CB42
Farm Way, Wor.Pk. 117 CW104
Farman Gro., Nthlt. 72 BX69
Wayfarer Rd.
Farmborough Clo., Har. 59 CD59
Pool Rd.
Farmcote Rd. SE12 108 EG88
Farmdale Rd. SE10 94 EG78
Farmdale Rd., Cars. 132 DE108
Farmer Rd. E10 65 EB60
Farmer St. W8 76 DA74
Uxbridge St.
Farmers Clo., Wat. 15 BV33
Farmers Ct., Wal.Abb. 24 EG33
Winters Way
Farmers Rd. SE5 91 DP80
Farmfield Rd., Brom. 108 EE92
Farmhouse Clo., Brox. 23 DZ25
Farmhouse Rd. SW16 105 DJ94
Farmilo Rd. E17 65 DZ59
Farmington Ave., Sutt. 118 DD104
Farmland Wk., Chis. 109 EP92
Farmlands, Enf. 35 DN39
Farmlands, Pnr. 57 BU56
Farmlands, The, Nthlt. 72 CA65
Moat Fm. Rd.
Farmleigh N14 49 DJ45
Farmleigh Gro., Walt. 127 BS106
Farmstead Rd. SE6 107 EB91
Farmstead Rd., Har. 45 CD53
Farmview, Cob. 142 BX116
Farmway, Dag. 68 EW62
Farnaby Dr., Sev. 154 FF126
Farnaby Rd. SE9 94 EJ84
Farnaby Rd., Brom. 107 ED94
Farnan Ave. E17 51 EA54
Farnan Rd. SW16 105 DL92
Farnborough Ave. E17 65 DY55
Farnborough Ave., S.Croy. 135 DX108
Farnborough Clo., Wem. 60 CP61
Chalkhill Rd.
Farnborough Common, Orp. 123 EM104
Farnborough Cres., Brom. 122 EF102
Saville Row
Farnborough Cres., S.Croy. 135 DY109
Farnborough Hill, Orp. 137 ER106
Farnborough Way SE15 92 DS80
Daniel Gdns.
Farnborough Way, Orp. 137 EP106
Farncombe St. SE16 92 DU75
Farndale Ave. N13 49 DP48
Farndale Cres., Grnf. 72 CC69
Farnell Ms. SW5 90 DB78
Earls Ct. Sq.
Farnell Rd., Islw. 87 CD84
Farnell Rd., Stai. 98 BG90
Farnham Clo. N20 48 DC45
Farnham Gdns. SW20 117 CV96
Farnham Pl. SE1 10 G3
Farnham Rd., Ilf. 67 ET59
Farnham Rd., Well. 96 EW82
Farnham Royal SE11 91 DM78
Farningham Cres., Cat. 148 DU123
Commonwealth Rd.
Farningham Rd. N17 50 DU52
Farningham Rd., Cat. 148 DU123
Farnley Rd. E4 52 EE45
Farnley Rd. SE25 120 DR98
Faro Clo., Brom. 123 EN96
Faroe Rd. W14 89 CX76
Farorna Wk., Enf. 35 DN39
Farquhar Rd. SE19 106 DT92
Farquhar Rd. SW19 104 DA90
Farquharson Rd., Croy. 120 DQ102
Farr Ave., Bark. 82 EU68
Farr Rd., Enf. 36 DR39
Farraline Rd., Wat. 29 BV42
Farrance Rd., Rom. 68 EY58
Farrance St. E14 79 EA72
Farrans Ct., Har. 59 CH59
Farrant Ave. N22 49 DN54
Farrant Clo., Orp. 138 EU108
Farrant Way, Borwd. 32 CL39
Farrell Ho. E1 78 DW72
Devonport St.
Farren Rd. SE23 107 DY89
Farrer Ms. N8 63 DJ56
Farrer Rd.
Farrer Rd. N8 63 DJ56
Farrer Rd., Har. 60 CL57
Farrer's Pl., Croy. 135 DX105
Farrier Clo., Sun. 113 BU98
Farrier Rd., Nthlt. 72 CA68
Farrier St. NW1 77 DH66
Farrier Wk. SW10 90 DC79
Farriers Clo., Epsom 130 CS112
Farriers Ct., Wat. 15 BV32
Farriers End, Brox. 23 DZ26
Farriers Rd., Epsom 130 CS111
Farriers Way, Borwd. 32 CR43
Farringdon La. EC1 6 E5
Farringdon La. EC1 77 DN70
Farringdon Rd. EC1 6 D4
Farringdon Rd. EC1 77 DN70
Farringdon St. EC4 6 F8
Farringdon St. EC4 77 DP71
Farringford Clo., St.Alb. 16 CA26
Farrington Ave., Orp. 124 EV97
Farrington Pl., Chis. 109 ER94
Farrins Rents SE16 79 DY74
Farrow La. SE14 92 DW80
Farrow Pl. SE16 93 DY76
Ropemaker Rd.
Farthing All. SE1 92 DU75
Wolseley St.
Farthing Flds. E1 78 DV74
Raine St.
Farthing St., Orp. 137 EM108
Farthingale Ct., Wal.Abb. 24 EG34
Farthingale La., Wal.Abb. 24 EG34
Farthingale Wk. E15 79 ED66
Great Eastern Rd.
Farthings, The, Kings.T. 116 CN95
Brunswick Rd.
Farthings Clo. E4 52 EE48
Farthings Clo., Pnr. 57 BV58
Farwell Rd., Sid. 110 EV90
Farwig La., Brom. 122 EF95
Fashion St. E1 78 DT71
Fashoda Rd., Brom. 122 EJ98
Fassett Rd. E8 78 DU65
Fassett Rd., Kings.T. 116 CL98
Fassett Sq. E8 78 DU65
Fassnidge Way, Uxb. 70 BJ66
Oxford Rd.
Fauconberg Rd. W4 88 CQ79
Faulkner Clo., Dag. 68 EX59
Faulkner St. SE14 92 DW81
Faulkner's All. EC1 6 F6
Faulkners Rd., Walt. 128 BW106
Fauna Clo., Rom. 68 EW58
Faunce St. SE17 91 DP78
Harmsworth St.
Favart Rd. SW6 90 DA81
Faverolle Grn., Wal.Cr. 23 DX28
Faversham Ave. E4 52 EE46
Faversham Ave., Enf. 36 DR44
Faversham Clo., Chig. 54 EV47
Faversham Rd. SE6 107 DZ87
Faversham Rd., Beck. 121 DZ96
Faversham Rd., Mord. 118 DB100
Fawcett Clo. SW11 90 DD82
Fawcett Est. E5 64 DU60
Fawcett Rd. NW10 75 CT66
Fawcett Rd., Croy. 120 DQ104
Fawcett St. SW10 90 DB79
Fawcus Clo., Esher 129 CF107
Dalmore Ave.
Fawe Pk. Rd. SW15 89 CZ84
Fawe St. E14 79 EB71
Fawke Common Rd., Sev. 155 FN126
Fawley Rd. NW6 62 DB64
Fawn Rd. E13 80 EJ68
Fawn Rd., Chig. 53 ET50
Fawnbrake Ave. SE24 105 DP85
Fawns Manor Clo., Felt. 99 BQ88
Fawns Manor Rd., Felt. 99 BR88
Fawood Ave. NW10 74 CR66
Fay Grn., Abb.L. 15 BR33
Fayerfield, Pot.B. 20 DD31
Faygate Cres., Bexh. 110 FA85
Faygate Rd. SW2 105 DM89
Fayland Ave. SW16 105 DJ92
Fearney Mead, Rick. 42 BG46
Fearnley Cres., Hmptn. 100 BY92
Fearnley St., Wat. 29 BV42
Fearon St. SE10 94 EG78
Featherbed La., Abb.L. 15 BV26
Sergehill La.
Featherbed La., Croy. 135 DZ108
Featherbed La., Hem.H. 14 BG25
Featherbed La., Rom. 40 EX42
Featherbed La., Warl. 135 EB111
Feathers Pl. SE10 93 ED79
Featherstone Ave. SE23 106 DV89
Featherstone Clo., Pot.B. 20 DD32
Featherstone Gdns., Borwd. 32 CQ42
Featherstone Ind. Est., Sthl. 86 BY75
Featherstone Rd. NW7 47 CV51
Featherstone Rd., Sthl. 86 BY76
Featherstone St. EC1 7 K4
Featherstone St. EC1 78 DR70
Featherstone Ter., Sthl. 86 BY76
Featley Rd. SW9 91 DP83
Federal Rd., Grnf. 73 CJ68
Federal Way, Wat. 30 BW39
Federation Rd. SE2 96 EV77
Fee Fm. Rd., Esher 129 CF108
Felbridge Ave., Stan. 45 CG53
Felbridge Clo. SW16 105 DN91
Felbridge Clo., Sutt. 132 DB109
Felbrigge Rd., Ilf. 67 ET61
Felcott Clo., Walt. 114 BW104
Felcott Rd., Walt. 114 BW104
Felday Rd. SE13 107 EB86
Felden Clo., Pnr. 44 BY52
Felden Clo., Wat. 16 BX34
Felden St. SW6 89 CZ81
Feldman Clo. N16 64 DU60
Felgate Ms. W6 89 CV77
Felhampton Rd. SE9 109 EP89
Felhurst Cres., Dag. 69 FB63
Felix Ave. N8 63 DL58
Felix La., Shep. 113 BS100
Felix Rd. W13 73 CG73
Felix Rd., Walt. 113 BU100
Felix St. E2 78 DV68
Hackney Rd.
Felixstowe Rd. N9 50 DU48
Felixstowe Rd. N17 64 DT55
Felixstowe Rd. NW10 75 CV69
Felixstowe Rd. SE2 96 EV76
Fell Rd., Croy. 120 DQ104
Fell Wk., Edg. 46 CP53
East Rd.
Fellbrigg Rd. SE22 106 DT85
Fellbrigg St. E1 78 DV70
Headlam St.
Fellbrook, Rich. 101 CH90
Fellowes Clo., Hayes 72 BX70
Paddington Clo.
Fellowes Rd., Cars. 118 DE104
Fellows Ct. E2 7 P1
Fellows Rd. NW3 76 DD66
Felltram Way SE7 94 EG77
Felmersham Clo. SW4 91 DK84
Haselrigge Rd.
Felmingham Rd. SE20 120 DW96
Fels Clo., Dag. 69 FB62
Fels Fm. Ave., Dag. 69 FC62
Felsberg Rd. SW2 105 DL86
Felsham Rd. SW15 89 CX83
Felspar Clo. SE18 95 ET78
Felstead Ave., Ilf. 53 EN53
Felstead Gdns. E14 93 EC78
Ferry St.
Felstead Rd. E11 66 EG59
Felstead Rd., Epsom 130 CR111
Felstead Rd., Loug. 52 EL45
Felstead Rd., Orp. 124 EU103
Felstead Rd., Rom. 55 FC51
Felstead Rd., Wal.Cr. 23 DY32
Felstead St. E9 79 DZ65
Felsted Rd. E16 80 EK72
Feltham Ave., E.Mol. 115 CE98
Feltham Hill Rd., Ashf. 99 BP92
Feltham Hill Rd., Felt. 99 BU91
Feltham Rd., Ashf. 99 BP91
Feltham Rd., Mitch. 118 DF96
Felthambrook Ind. Est., Felt. 99 BV90
Felthambrook Way, Felt. 99 BV90
Felton Clo., Borwd. 32 CL38
Felton Clo., Brox. 23 DZ25
Felton Clo., Orp. 123 EP100
Felton Gdns., Bark. 81 ES67
Sutton Rd.
Felton Lea, Sid. 109 ET92
Felton Rd. W13 87 CJ75
Camborne Ave.
Felton Rd., Bark. 81 ES68
Sutton Rd.
Felton St. N1 78 DR67
Fen Ct. EC3 7 M10
Fen Gro., Sid. 109 ET86
Fen St. E16 80 EF73
Victoria Dock Rd.
Fencepiece Rd., Chig. 53 EQ50
Fencepiece Rd., Ilf. 53 EQ51
Fenchurch Ave. EC3 7 M9
Fenchurch Ave. EC3 78 DS72
Fenchurch Bldgs. EC3 7 N9
Fenchurch Pl. EC3 7 N10
Fenchurch St. EC3 7 M10
Fenchurch St. EC3 78 DS73
Fendall Rd., Epsom 130 CQ106
Fendall St. SE1 11 N7
Fendall St. SE1 92 DS76
Fendt Clo. E16 80 EF73
Bowman Ave.
Fendyke Rd., Belv. 96 EX76
Fenelon Pl. W14 89 CZ77
Fenham Rd. SE15 92 DU80
Fenman Ct. N17 50 DV53
Shelbourne Rd.
Fenman Gdns., Ilf. 68 EV60
Fenn Clo., Brom. 108 EG93
Fenn St. E9 64 DW64
Fennel Clo. E16 80 EE70
Cranberry La.
Fennel Clo., Croy. 121 DX102
Primrose La.
Fennel St. SE18 95 EN79
Fennells Mead, Epsom 131 CT109
Fenner Clo. SE16 92 DV77
Layard Rd.
Fenner Ho., Walt. 127 BU105
Fenner Sq. SW11 90 DD83
Thomas Baines Rd.
Fenning St. SE1 11 M4
Fens Way, Swan. 111 FG93
Fenstanton Ave. N12 48 DD51
Fenswood Clo., Bex. 110 FA86
Fentiman Rd. SW8 91 DL79
Fenton Ave., Stai. 98 BJ93
Fenton Clo. E8 78 DT65
Laurel St.
Fenton Clo. SW9 91 DM82
Fenton Clo., Chis. 109 EM92
Fenton Rd. N17 50 DQ52
Fentons Ave. E13 80 EH68
Fenwick Clo. SE18 95 EN79
Ritter St.
Fenwick Gro. SE15 92 DU83

Flamingo Gdns., Nthlt. 72 BY69
Jetstar Way
Flamingo Wk., Horn. 83 FG66
Flamstead End Rd. (Cheshunt), Wal.Cr. 22 DV28
Flamstead Gdns., Dag. 82 EW66
Flamstead Rd.
Flamstead Rd., Dag. 82 EW66
Flamsted Ave., Wem. 74 CN65
Flamsteed Rd. SE7 94 EL78
Flanchford Rd. W12 89 CT76
Flanders Cres. SW17 104 DF94
Flanders Rd. E6 81 EM68
Flanders Rd. W4 88 CS77
Flanders Way E9 79 DX65
Flank St. E1 78 DU73
Dock St.
Flash La., Enf. 35 DP37
Flask Cotts. NW3 62 DD63
New End Sq.
Flask Wk. NW3 62 DC63
Flavell Ms. SE10 94 EE78
Flaxen Clo. E4 51 EB48
Flaxen Rd.
Flaxen Rd. E4 51 EB48
Flaxley Rd., Mord. 118 DB100
Flaxman Ct. W1 5 M9
Flaxman Rd. SE5 91 DP83
Flaxman Ter. WC1 5 N3
Flaxman Ter. WC1 77 DK69
Flaxmore Pl., Beck. 121 ED100
Flaxton Rd. SE18 95 ER80
Flecker Clo., Stan. 45 CF50
Fleece Dr. N9 50 DU49
Fleece Rd., Surb. 115 CJ102
Fleece Wk. N7 77 DL65
Manger Rd.
Fleeming Clo. E17 51 DZ54
Pennant Ter.
Fleeming Rd. E17 51 DZ54
Fleet Clo., Ruis. 57 BQ58
Fleet Clo., W.Mol. 114 CA99
Fleet La., W.Mol. 114 BZ100
Fleet Pl. EC4 77 DN72
Farringdon St.
Fleet Rd. NW3 62 DE64
Fleet Sq. WC1 6 C3
Fleet St. EC4 6 E9
Fleet St. EC4 77 DN72
Fleet St. Hill E1 78 DU70
Weaver St.
Fleetside, W.Mol. 114 BZ99
Fleetway W. Business Pk., Grnf. 73 CH68
Fleetwood Clo. E16 80 EK71
Fleetwood Clo., Chess. 129 CK108
Fleetwood Clo., Croy. 120 DS104
Chepstow Ri.
Fleetwood Clo., Tad. 145 CX120
Fleetwood Ct. E6 81 EM71
Evelyn Denington Rd.
Fleetwood Ct., W.Byf. 126 BG113
Fleetwood Gro. W3 74 CS73
East Acton La.
Fleetwood Rd. NW10 61 CU64
Fleetwood Rd., Kings.T. 116 CP97
Fleetwood Sq., Kings.T. 116 CP97
Fleetwood St. N16 64 DS61
Stoke Newington Ch. St.
Fleetwood Way, Wat. 44 BW49
Fleming Ave., Ruis. 57 BV61
Fleming Clo. (Cheshunt), Wal.Cr. 22 DU26
Fleming Ct. W2 76 DD71
St. Marys Ter.
Fleming Ct., Croy. 133 DN106
Fleming Mead, Mitch. 104 DE94
Fleming Rd. SE17 91 DP79
Fleming Rd., Sthl. 72 CB72
Fleming Way SE28 82 EX73
Fleming Way, Islw. 87 CF83
Flemish Flds., Cher. 112 BG101
Flempton Rd. E10 65 DY60
Fletcher Clo. E6 81 EP72
Trader Rd.
Fletcher La. E10 65 EC59
Fletcher Path SE8 93 EA80
New Butt La.
Fletcher Rd. W4 88 CQ76
Fletcher Rd., Chig. 53 ET50
Fletcher St. E1 78 DU73
Fletchers Clo., Brom. 122 EH98
Fletching Rd. E5 64 DW62
Fletching Rd. SE7 94 EJ79
Fletton Rd. N11 49 DL52
Fleur de Lis St. E1 7 N5
Fleur de Lis St. E1 78 DS70
Fleur Gates SW19 103 CX87
Princes Way
Flexmere Gdns. N17 50 DR53
Flexmere Rd.
Flexmere Rd. N17 50 DR53
Flight App. NW9 47 CT54
Lanacre Ave.
Flimwell Clo., Brom. 108 EE92
Flint Clo., Sutt. 132 DB114
Flint Down Clo., Orp. 124 EU95
Flint St. SE17 11 L9
Flint St. SE17 92 DR77
Flintlock Clo., Stai. 84 BG84
Flintmill Cres. SE3 94 EL82
Flinton St. SE17 11 N10
Flinton St. SE17 92 DS78
Flitcroft St. WC2 5 N9
Flock Mill Pl. SW18 104 DB88
Flockton St. SE16 92 DU75
George Row
Flodden Rd. SE5 92 DQ81
Flood La., Twick. 101 CG88
Church La.
Flood Pas. SE18 95 EM77
Samuel St.
Flood St. SW3 90 DE78
Flood Wk. SW3 90 DE79
Flora Clo. E14 79 EB72
Flora Clo., Croy. 135 EC111
Flora Gdns. W6 89 CV77
Ravenscourt Rd.
Flora Gdns., Rom. 68 EW58
Flora St., Belv. 96 EZ78
Victoria St.
Floral Ct., Ash. 143 CJ118
Rosedale
Floral Dr., St.Alb. 17 CK26
Floral St. WC2 5 P10
Floral St. WC2 77 DL73
Florence Ave., Add. 126 BG111
Florence Ave., Enf. 36 DQ41
Florence Ave., Mord. 118 DC99
Florence Cantwell Wk. N19 63 DL59
Hillrise Rd.
Florence Clo., Walt. 113 BV101
Florence Rd.
Florence Clo., Wat. 29 BU35
Florence Dr., Enf. 36 DQ41
Florence Gdns. W4 88 CQ79
Florence Gdns., Stai. 98 BH94
Florence Nightingale Ho. N1 78 DR65
Clephane Rd.
Florence Rd. E6 80 EJ67
Florence Rd. E13 80 EF68
Florence Rd. N4 63 DN60
Florence Rd. SE2 96 EW76
Florence Rd. SE14 93 DZ81
Florence Rd. SW19 104 DB93
Florence Rd. W4 88 CR76
Florence Rd. W5 74 CL73
Florence Rd., Beck. 121 DY96
Florence Rd., Brom. 122 EG95
Florence Rd., Felt. 99 BV88
Florence Rd., Kings.T. 102 CM94
Florence Rd., S.Croy. 134 DR109
Florence Rd., Sthl. 86 BX77
Florence Rd., Walt. 113 BV101
Florence St. E16 80 EF70
Florence St. N1 77 DP66
Florence St. NW4 61 CW56
Florence Ter. SE14 93 DZ81
Florence Way SW12 104 DF88
Florfield Pas. E8 78 DV65
Reading La.
Florfield Rd. E8 78 DV65
Reading La.
Florian Ave., Sutt. 132 DD105
Florian Rd. SW15 89 CY84
Florida Clo. (Bushey), Wat. 45 CD47
Florida Rd., Th.Hth. 119 DP95
Florida St. E2 78 DU69
Floriston Ave., Uxb. 71 BQ66
Floriston Clo., Stan. 45 CH53
Floriston Gdns., Stan. 45 CH53
Floss St. SW15 89 CW82
Flower & Dean Wk. E1 78 DT71
Thrawl St.
Flower La. NW7 47 CT50
Flower Wk., The SW7 90 DC75
Flowerfield, Sev. 153 FF117
Flowers Ms. N19 63 DJ61
Tollhouse Way
Flowersmead SW17 104 DG89
Floyd Rd. SE7 94 EJ78
Floyds La., Wok. 140 BG116
Fludyer St. SE13 94 EE84
Folair Way SE16 92 DV78
Catlin St.
Foley Ms., Esher 129 CE107
Foley Rd., Esher 129 CE108
Foley Rd., West. 150 EK118
Foley St. W1 5 K7
Foley St. W1 77 DJ71
Folgate St. E1 7 N6
Folgate St. E1 78 DS71
Foliot St. W12 75 CT72
Folkestone Rd. E6 81 EN68
Folkestone Rd. E17 65 EB56
Folkestone Rd. N18 50 DU49
Folkingham La. NW9 46 CR53
Folkington Cor. N12 47 CZ50
Follet Dr., Abb.L. 15 BT31
Follett St. E14 79 EC72
Folly Clo., Rad. 31 CF36
Folly La. E4 51 DY53
Folly La. E17 51 DY53
Folly Ms. W11 75 CZ72
Portobello Rd.
Folly Pathway, Rad. 31 CF35
Folly Wall E14 93 EC75
Follyfield Rd., Bans. 132 DA114
Font Hills N2 48 DC54
Fontaine Rd. SW16 105 DM94
Fontarabia Rd. SW11 90 DG84
Fontayne Ave., Chig. 53 EQ49
Fontayne Ave., Rain. 83 FE66
Fontayne Ave., Rom. 69 FE55
Fontenoy Rd. SW12 105 DH89
Fonteyne Gdns., Wdf.Grn. 52 EK54
Lechmere Ave.
Fonthill Clo. SE20 120 DU96
Selby Rd.
Fonthill Ms. N4 63 DN61
Lennox Rd.
Fonthill Rd. N4 63 DM60
Fontley Way SW15 103 CU87
Fontmell Clo., Ashf. 98 BN92
Fontmell Pk., Ashf. 98 BM92
Fontwell Clo., Har. 45 CE52
Fontwell Clo., Nthlt. 72 CA65
Fontwell Dr., Brom. 123 EN99
Football La., Har. 59 CE60
Footbury Hill Rd., Orp. 124 EU101
Footpath, The SW15 103 CU85
Parkstead Rd.
Foots Cray High St., Sid. 110 EW93
Foots Cray La., Sid. 110 EW88
Footscray Rd. SE9 109 EN86
Footway, The SE9 109 EQ87
Forbench Clo., Wok. 140 BH122
Forbes Ave., Pot.B. 20 DD33
Forbes Clo. NW2 61 CU61
Forbes Clo., Horn. 69 FH60
St. Leonards Way
Forbes Ct. SE19 106 DS92
Forbes St. E1 78 DU72
Ellen St.
Forbes Way, Ruis. 57 BV61
Forburg Rd. N16 64 DU60
Force Grn. La., West. 151 ER124
Ford Clo. E3 79 DY68
Roman Rd.
Ford Clo., Ashf. 98 BL93
Ford Clo., Har. 59 CD59
Ford Clo., Rain. 83 FF66
Ford Clo., Shep. 112 BN98
Ford Clo., Th.Hth. 119 DP99
Ford Clo. (Bushey), Wat. 30 CC42
Ford End, Wdf.Grn. 52 EH51
Ford La., Iver 70 BG72
Ford La., Rain. 83 FF66
Ford Rd. E3 79 DY67
Ford Rd., Ashf. 98 BM91
Ford Rd., Cher. 112 BH102
Ford Rd., Dag. 82 EZ66
Ford Sq. E1 78 DV71
Ford St. E3 79 DY67
Ford St. E16 80 EF72
Fordbridge Clo., Cher. 112 BH102
Fordbridge Rd., Ashf. 98 BL93
Fordbridge Rd., Shep. 113 BS100
Fordbridge Rd., Sun. 113 BS100
Fordcroft Rd., Orp. 124 EV99
Forde Ave., Brom. 122 EJ97
Fordel Rd. SE6 107 ED88
Fordham Clo., Barn. 34 DE41
Fordham Rd., Barn. 34 DD41
Fordham St. E1 78 DU72
Fordhook Ave. W5 74 CM73
Fordingley Rd. W9 75 CZ69
Fordington Rd. N6 62 DF57
Fordmill Rd. SE6 107 EA89
Fords Gro. N21 50 DQ46
Fords Pk. Rd. E16 80 EG72
Fordwater Rd., Cher. 112 BH102
Fordwater Trd. Est., Cher. 112 BH102
Fordwich Clo., Orp. 123 ET101
Fordwych Rd. NW2 61 CY63
Fordyce Rd. SE13 107 EC86
Fordyke Rd., Dag. 68 EZ61
Fore St. EC2 7 J7
Fore St. EC2 78 DQ71
Fore St. N9 50 DU49
Fore St. N18 50 DT51
Fore St., Pnr. 57 BU57
Fore St. Ave. EC2 7 K7
Forefield, St.Alb. 16 CA27
Foreland Ct. NW4 47 CX53
Foreland St. SE18 95 ER77
Plumstead Rd.
Foreman Ct. W6 89 CW77
Hammersmith Bdy.
Foremark Clo., Ilf. 53 ET51
Foreshore SE8 93 DZ77
Forest, The E11 66 EE56
Forest App. E4 52 EE45
Forest App., Wdf.Grn. 52 EG52
Forest Ave. E4 52 EE45
Forest Ave., Chig. 53 EN50
Forest Business Pk. E17 65 DY59
Forest Clo. E11 66 EF57
Forest Clo., Chis. 123 EN95
Forest Clo., Wal.Abb. 38 EH37
Forest Clo., Wdf.Grn. 52 EH49
Forest Ct. E4 52 EF46
Forest Ct. E11 66 EE56
Forest Cres., Ash. 144 CN116
Forest Cft. SE23 106 DV89
Forest Dr. E12 66 EK62
Forest Dr., Epp. 39 ES36
Forest Dr., Kes. 136 EL105
Forest Dr., Sun. 99 BT94
Forest Dr., Tad. 145 CY121
Forest Dr., Wdf.Grn. 51 ED52
Forest Dr. E. E11 65 ED59
Forest Dr. W. E11 65 EC59
Forest Edge, Buck.H. 52 EJ49
Forest Gdns. N17 50 DT54
Forest Gate NW9 60 CS57
Forest Glade E4 52 EE49
Forest Glade E11 66 EE58
Forest Glade, Epp. 26 EY28
Forest Gro. E8 78 DT65
Forest Heights, Buck.H. 52 EG47
Forest Hill Rd. SE22 106 DV85
Forest Hill Rd. SE23 106 DW86
Forest Ind. Est., Ilf. 53 ES53
Forest La. E7 66 EG64
Forest La. E15 80 EE65
Forest La., Chig. 53 EN50
Forest La., Lthd. 141 BT124
Forest Mt. Rd., Wdf.Grn. 51 ED52
Forest Ridge, Beck. 121 EA97
Forest Ridge, Kes. 136 EL105
Forest Ri. E17 65 ED57
Forest Rd. E7 66 EG63
Forest Rd. E8 78 DT65
Forest Rd. E11 65 ED59
Forest Rd. E17 64 DW56
Forest Rd. N9 50 DV46
Forest Rd. N17 64 DW56
Forest Rd., Enf. 37 DY36
Forest Rd., Erith 97 FG81
Forest Rd., Felt. 100 BW89
Forest Rd., Ilf. 53 ES53
Forest Rd., Lthd. 141 BU123
Forest Rd., Loug. 38 EK41
Forest Rd., Rich. 88 CN80
Forest Rd., Rom. 69 FB55
Forest Rd., Sutt. 118 DA102
Forest Rd. (Cheshunt), Wal.Cr. 23 DX29
Forest Rd., Wat. 15 BV33
Forest Rd., Wdf.Grn. 52 EG48
Forest Side E4 52 EF45
Forest Side E7 66 EH63
Capel Rd.
Forest Side, Buck.H. 52 EH46
Forest Side, Epp. 25 ER33
Forest Side, Wal.Abb. 38 EJ36
Forest Side, Wor.Pk. 117 CT102
Forest St. E7 66 EG64
Forest Vw. E4 51 ED45
Forest Vw. E11 66 EF59
Forest Vw. Ave. E10 65 ED57
Forest Vw. Rd. E12 66 EL63
Forest Vw. Rd. E17 51 EC53
Forest Vw. Rd., Loug. 38 EK42
Forest Wk. (Bushey), Wat. 30 BZ39
Millbrook Rd.
Forest Way N19 63 DJ61
Hargrave Pk.
Forest Way, Ash. 144 CM117
Forest Way, Loug. 38 EL41
Forest Way, Orp. 123 ET99
Forest Way, Sid. 109 ER87
Forest Way, Wal.Abb. 24 EK33
Forest Way, Wdf.Grn. 52 EH49
Forestdale N14 49 DK49
Forester Rd. SE15 92 DV84
Foresters Clo., Wall. 133 DK108
Foresters Clo., Wal.Cr. 22 DS27
Foresters Cres., Bexh. 97 FB84
Foresters Dr. E17 65 ED56
Foresters Dr., Wall. 133 DK107
Forestholme Clo. SE23 106 DW89
Forfar Rd. N22 49 DP53
Forfar Rd. SW11 90 DG81
Forge Ave., Couls. 147 DN120
Forge Clo., Brom. 122 EG102
Forge Clo., Hayes 85 BR79
High St.
Forge Clo., Kings L. 14 BG31
Forge Cotts. W5 73 CK74
Ealing Grn.
Forge Dr., Esher 129 CG108
Forge End, St.Alb. 16 CA26
Forge La., Felt. 100 BY92
Forge La., Nthwd. 43 BS52
Forge La., Sun. 113 BU97
Forge La., Sutt. 131 CY108
Forge Pl. NW1 76 DG65
Malden Cres.
Forge Way, Sev. 139 FF111
Forgefield, West. 150 EK116
Main Rd.
Forman Pl. N16 64 DT63
Farleigh Rd.
Formby Ave., Stan. 59 CJ55
Formosa St. W9 76 DB70
Formunt Clo. E16 80 EF71
Vincent St.
Forres Gdns. NW11 62 DA58
Forrest Gdns. SW16 119 DM97
Forrester Path SE26 106 DW91
Forris Ave., Hayes 71 BT74
Forset St. W1 4 C8
Forset St. W1 76 DE72
Forstal Clo., Brom. 122 EG97
Ridley Rd.
Forster Rd. E17 65 DY58
Forster Rd. N17 64 DT55
Forster Rd. SW2 105 DL87
Forster Rd., Beck. 121 DY97
Forster Rd., Croy. 120 DQ101
Windmill Rd.
Forsters Clo., Rom. 68 EZ58
Forsters Way, Hayes 71 BV72
Forston St. N1 78 DR68
Cropley St.
Forsyte Cres. SE19 120 DS95
Forsyth Gdns. SE17 91 DP79
Forsyth Pl., Enf. 36 DS43
Forsythia Clo., Ilf. 67 EP64
Fort Rd. SE1 92 DT77
Fort Rd., Nthlt. 72 CA66
Fort Rd., Sev. 153 FC115
Fort St. E1 7 N7
Fort St. E1 78 DS71
Fort St. E16 80 EH74
Forterie Gdns., Ilf. 68 EU62
Fortescue Ave. E8 78 DV66
Mentmore Ter.
Fortescue Ave., Twick. 100 CC90
Fortescue Rd. SW19 104 DD94
Fortescue Rd., Edg. 46 CQ53
Fortescue Rd., Wey. 126 BM105
Fortess Gro. NW5 63 DH64
Fortess Rd.
Fortess Rd. NW5 63 DH64
Fortess Wk. NW5 63 DH64
Fortess Rd.
Forthbridge Rd. SW11 90 DG84
Fortis Clo. E16 80 EJ72
Fortis Grn. N2 62 DE56
Fortis Grn. N10 62 DG55
Fortis Grn. Ave. N2 62 DF55
Fortis Grn. Rd. N10 62 DG55
Fortismere Ave. N10 62 DG55
Fortnam Rd. N19 63 DK61
Fortnums Acre, Stan. 45 CF51
Fortrose Gdns. SW2 105 DK88
New Pk. Rd.
Fortuna Clo. N7 77 DM65
Vulcan Way
Fortune Gate Rd. NW10 74 CS67
Fortune Grn. Rd. NW6 62 DA63
Fortune La., Borwd. 31 CK44
Fortune St. EC1 7 J5
Fortune St. EC1 78 DQ70
Fortune Wk. SE28 95 ER76
Broadwater Rd.
Fortune Way NW10 75 CU69
Fortunes Mead, Nthlt. 72 BY65
Forty Acre La. E16 80 EG71
Forty Ave., Wem. 60 CM62
Forty Clo., Wem. 60 CM62
Forty Hill, Enf. 36 DS38
Forty La., Wem. 60 CP61
Fortyfoot Rd., Lthd. 143 CJ121
Forum, The, W.Mol. 114 CB98
Forum Way, Edg. 46 CN51
High St.
Forumside, Edg. 46 CN51
High St.
Forval Clo., Mitch. 118 DF99
Forward Dr., Har. 59 CF56
Fosbury Ms. W2 76 DB73
Inverness Ter.
Foscote Ms. W9 76 DA71
Amberley Rd.
Foscote Rd. NW4 61 CV57
Foskett Rd. SW6 89 CZ82
Foss Ave., Croy. 133 DN106
Foss Rd. SW17 104 DD91
Fossdene Rd. SE7 94 EH78
Fossdyke Clo., Hayes 72 BY71
Fosse Way W13 73 CG71
Fossil Rd. SE13 93 EA83
Fossington Rd., Belv. 96 EX77
Fossway, Dag. 68 EW61
Foster Clo. (Cheshunt), Wal.Cr. 23 DY30
Windmill La.
Foster La. EC2 7 H8
Foster La. EC2 78 DQ72
Foster Rd. E13 80 EG70
Foster Rd. W3 74 CS73
Foster Rd. W4 88 CR78
Foster St. NW4 61 CW56
Foster Wk. NW4 61 CW56
New Brent St.
Fosters Clo. E18 52 EH53
Fosters Clo., Chis. 109 EM92
Fothergill Clo. E13 80 EG68
Fothergill Dr. N21 35 DM43
Fotheringham Rd., Enf. 36 DT42
Foubert's Pl. W1 5 K9
Foubert's Pl. W1 77 DJ72
Foulden Rd. N16 64 DT63
Foulden Ter. N16 64 DT63
Foulden Rd.
Foulis Ter. SW7 8 A10
Foulis Ter. SW7 90 DD78
Foulser Rd. SW17 104 DF90
Foulsham Rd., Th.Hth. 120 DQ97
Founder Clo. E6 81 EP72
Trader Rd.
Founders Ct. EC2 7 K8
Founders Gdns. SE19 106 DQ94
Foundry Clo. SE16 79 DY74
Foundry Ms. NW1 5 L4
Fount St. SW8 91 DK80
Fountain Clo., Uxb. 71 BQ71
New Rd.
Fountain Ct. EC4 6 D10
Fountain Dr. SE19 106 DT91
Fountain Dr., Cars. 132 DF108
Fountain Grn. Sq. SE16 92 DU75
Bermondsey Wall E.
Fountain Ms. N5 64 DQ63
Kelross Rd.
Fountain Pl. SW9 91 DN81
Fountain Pl., Wal.Abb. 23 EC34
Fountain Rd. SW17 104 DD92
Fountain Rd., Th.Hth. 120 DQ96
Fountain Sq. SW1 9 H8
Fountain St. E2 78 DT69
Columbia Rd.
Fountains Ave., Felt. 100 BZ90
Fountains Clo., Felt. 100 BZ89
Fountains Cres. N14 49 DL45
Fountayne Rd. N15 64 DU56
Fountayne Rd. N16 64 DU61
Four Acres, Cob. 128 BY113
Four Seasons Cres., Sutt. 117 CZ103
Kimpton Rd.
Four Seasons Ind. Est., Sthl. 86 CB76
Four Tubs, The (Bushey), Wat. 45 CD45
Four Wents, Cob. 128 BW114
Four Wents, The E4 51 ED47
Kings Rd.

Fouracres SW12 105 DH89
Little Dimocks
Fouracres, Enf. 37 DY39
Fourland Wk., Edg. 46 CQ51
Fournier St. E1 78 DT71
Fourth Ave. E12 67 EM63
Fourth Ave. W10 75 CY69
Fourth Ave., Hayes 71 BT74
Fourth Ave., Rom. 69 FC60
Fourth Ave., Wat. 30 BX35
Fourth Cross Rd., Twick. 101 CD89
Fourth Dr., Couls. 147 DK116
Fourth Way, Wem. 60 CQ63
Fowey Ave., Ilf. 66 EK57
Fowey Clo. E1 78 DV74
Kennet St.
Fowler Clo. SW11 90 DD83
Fowler Rd. E7 66 EG63
Fowler Rd. N1 77 DP66
Halton Rd.
Fowler Rd., Ilf. 54 EV51
Fowler Rd., Mitch. 118 DG96
Fowlers Clo., Sid. 110 EY92
Thursland Rd.
Fowlers Wk. W5 73 CK70
Fowley Clo., Wal.Cr. 23 DZ34
Fowley Mead Caravan Pk., Wal.Cr. 23 EA34
Fownes St. SW11 90 DE83
Fox and Knot St. EC1 6 G6
Fox Clo. E1 78 DW70
Fox Clo. E16 80 EG71
Fox Clo., Borwd. 31 CK44
Rodgers Clo.
Fox Clo., Orp. 138 EU106
Fox Clo., Rom. 55 FB50
Fox Clo. (Bushey), Wat. 30 CB42
Fox Clo., Wey. 127 BR106
Fox Covert, Lthd. 143 CD124
Fox Hill SE19 106 DT94
Fox Hill, Kes. 136 EH106
Fox Hill Gdns. SE19 106 DT94
Fox Hollow Dr., Bexh. 96 EX83
Fox Ho. Rd., Belv. 97 FB77
Fox La. N13 49 DL47
Fox La. W5 74 CL70
Fox La., Cat. 147 DP121
Fox La., Kes. 136 EH106
Fox La., Lthd. 142 BY124
Fox Rd. E16 80 EF71
Foxacre, Cat. 148 DS122
Town End Clo.
Foxberry Rd. SE4 93 DY83
Foxborough Gdns. SE4 107 EA86
Foxbourne Rd. SW17 104 DG89
Foxburrow Rd., Chig. 54 EX49
Foxbury Ave., Chis. 109 ER93
Foxbury Clo., Brom. 108 EH93
Foxbury Clo., Orp. 138 EU106
Foxbury Dr.
Foxbury Dr., Orp. 138 EU107
Foxbury Rd., Brom. 108 EG93
Foxcombe, Croy. 135 EB107
Foxcombe Clo. E6 80 EK68
Boleyn Rd.
Foxcombe Rd. SW15 103 CU88
Alton Rd.
Foxcote SE5 92 DS78
Albany Rd.
Foxcroft Rd. SE18 95 EP81
Foxdell, Nthwd. 43 BR51
Foxearth Clo., West. 150 EL118
Foxearth Rd., S.Croy. 134 DV110
Foxearth Spur, S.Croy. 134 DW109
Foxes Dale SE3 94 EG83
Foxes Dale, Brom. 121 ED97
Foxes Dr., Wal.Cr. 22 DU29
Foxfield Clo., Nthwd. 43 BT51
Foxfield Rd., Orp. 123 ER103
Foxglove Clo., Sthl. 72 BY73
Foxglove Clo., Stai. 98 BK88
Foxglove Gdns. E11 66 EJ56
Foxglove Gdns., Pur. 133 DL111
Foxglove La., Chess. 130 CN105
Foxglove St. W12 75 CT73
Foxglove Way, Wall. 119 DH102
Foxgrove N14 49 DL48
Foxgrove Ave., Beck. 107 EB94
Foxgrove Path, Wat. 44 BX50
Foxgrove Rd., Beck. 107 EB94
Foxham Rd. N19 63 DK62
Foxhill, Wat. 29 BU36
Foxhole Rd. SE9 108 EL85
Foxholes, Wey. 127 BR106
Foxholt Gdns. NW10 74 CQ66
Foxhome Clo., Chis. 109 EN93
Foxlake Rd., W.Byf. 126 BM112
Foxlands Clo., Wat. 15 BU34
Foxlands Cres., Dag. 69 FC64
Foxlands La., Dag. 69 FD64
Rainham Rd. S.
Foxlands Rd., Dag. 69 FC64
Foxlees, Wem. 59 CG63
Foxley Clo. E8 64 DU64
Ferncliff Rd.
Foxley Clo., Loug. 39 EP40
Foxley Gdns., Pur. 133 DP113
Foxley Hill Rd., Pur. 133 DN112
Foxley La., Pur. 133 DJ111
Foxley Rd. SW9 91 DN80
Foxley Rd., Ken. 133 DP114
Foxley Rd., Th.Hth. 119 DP98
Foxley Sq. SW9 91 DP80
Cancell Rd.
Foxleys, Wat. 44 BY47
Foxmead Clo., Enf. 35 DM41
Foxmore St. SW11 90 DF81
Foxon Clo., Cat. 148 DS121
Foxon La., Cat. 148 DR121
Foxon La. Gdns., Cat. 148 DS121
Fox's Path, Mitch. 118 DE96
Foxton Gro., Mitch. 118 DD96
Foxwarren, Esher 129 CF109
Foxwell Clo. SE4 93 DY83
Foxwell St.
Foxwell Ms. SE4 93 DY83
Foxwell St.
Foxwell St. SE4 93 DY83
Foxwood Clo. NW7 46 CS49
Foxwood Clo., Felt. 99 BV90
Foxwood Grn. Clo., Enf. 36 DS44
Foxwood Gro., Orp. 138 EW110
Foxwood Rd. SE3 94 EF84
Foyle Rd. N17 50 DU53
Foyle Rd. SE3 94 EF79
Framfield Clo. N12 48 DA48
Framfield Ct., Enf. 36 DS44
Framfield Rd. N5 63 DP64
Framfield Rd. W7 73 CF72
Framfield Rd., Mitch. 104 DG94
Framlingham Clo. E5 64 DW61
Detmold Rd.
Framlingham Cres. SE9 108 EL91
Frampton Clo., Sutt. 132 DA108
Frampton Pk. Est. E9 78 DW66
Frampton Pk. Rd. E9 78 DW65
Frampton Rd., Epp. 26 EU28
Frampton Rd., Houns. 100 BY85
Frampton Rd., Pot.B. 20 DC30
Frampton St. NW8 4 A5
Frampton St. NW8 76 DD70
Francemary Rd. SE4 107 EA85
Frances Rd. E4 51 EA51
Frances St. SE18 95 EM77
Franche Ct. Rd. SW17 104 DC90
Francis Ave., Bexh. 96 FA82
Francis Ave., Felt. 99 BU90
Francis Ave., Ilf. 67 ER61
Francis Barber Clo. SW16 105 DM91
Well Clo.
Francis Chichester Way SW11 90 DG81
Francis Clo. E14 93 ED77
Saunders Ness Rd.
Francis Clo., Epsom 130 CR105
Francis Clo., Shep. 112 BN98
Francis Gro. SW19 103 CZ93
Francis Rd. E10 65 EC60
Francis Rd. N2 62 DF56
Lynmouth Rd.
Francis Rd., Cat. 148 DR122
Francis Rd., Croy. 119 DP101
Francis Rd., Grnf. 73 CH68
Francis Rd., Har. 59 CG57
Francis Rd., Houns. 86 BX82
Francis Rd., Ilf. 67 ER61
Francis Rd., Orp. 124 EX97
Francis Rd., Pnr. 58 BW57
Francis Rd., Wall. 133 DJ107
Francis Rd., Wat. 29 BV42
Francis St. E15 66 EE64
Francis St. SW1 9 K8
Francis St. SW1 91 DJ77
Francis St., Ilf. 67 ER61
Francis Ter. N19 63 DJ62
Junction Rd.
Francis Wk. N1 77 DM67
Bingfield St.
Franciscan Rd. SW17 104 DF92
Francklyn Gdns., Edg. 46 CN48
Francombe Gdns., Rom. 69 FG58
Franconia Rd. SW4 105 DK85
Frank Bailey Wk. E12 67 EN64
Gainsborough Ave.
Frank Burton Clo. SE7 94 EH78
Victoria Way
Frank Dixon Clo. SE21 106 DS88
Frank Dixon Way SE21 106 DS88
Frank Martin Ct., Wal.Cr. 22 DU30
Frank St. E13 80 EG70
Frank Towell Ct., Felt. 99 BU88
Frankfurt Rd. SE24 106 DQ85
Frankham St. SE8 93 EA80
Frankland Clo. SE16 92 DW77
Frankland Clo., Rick. 42 BN45
Frankland Clo., Wdf.Grn. 52 EJ50
Frankland Rd. E4 51 EA50
Frankland Rd. SW7 90 DD76
Frankland Rd., Rick. 29 BP44
Franklin Ave. (Cheshunt), Wal.Cr. 22 DU30
Franklin Clo. N20 48 DC45
Franklin Clo. SE13 93 EB81
Franklin Clo. SE27 105 DP90
Franklin Clo., Kings.T. 116 CN97
Franklin Cres., Mitch. 119 DJ98
Franklin Ho. NW9 61 CT59
Franklin Pas. SE9 94 EL83
Phineas Pett Rd.
Franklin Rd. SE20 106 DW94
Franklin Rd., Bexh. 96 EY81
Franklin Rd., Wat. 29 BV40
Franklin Sq. W14 89 CZ78
Marchbank Rd.
Franklin St. E3 79 EB69
St. Leonards St.
Franklin St. N15 64 DS58
Franklin Way, Croy. 119 DL102
Franklins Ms., Har. 58 CC61
Franklin's Row SW3 8 E10
Franklin's Row SW3 90 DF78
Franklyn Gdns., Ilf. 53 ER51
Franklyn Rd. NW10 75 CT66
Franklyn Rd., Walt. 113 BU100
Franks Ave., N.Mal. 116 CQ98
Frankswood Ave., Orp. 123 EP99
Frankswood Ave., West Dr. 70 BM72
Franlaw Cres. N13 50 DQ49
Franmil Rd., Horn. 69 FG60
Fransfield Gro. SE26 106 DV90
Frant Clo. SE20 106 DW94
Frant Rd., Th.Hth. 119 DP99
Franthorne Way SE6 107 EB89
Fraser Clo. E6 80 EL72
Linton Gdns.
Fraser Clo., Bex. 111 FC88
Dartford Rd.
Fraser Ho., Brent. 88 CM78
Green Dragon La.
Fraser Rd. E17 65 EB57
Fraser Rd. N9 50 DV48
Fraser Rd., Erith 97 FC78
Fraser Rd., Grnf. 73 CH67
Fraser Rd. (Cheshunt), Wal.Cr. 23 DY28
Fraser St. W4 88 CS78
Frating Cres., Wdf.Grn. 52 EH51
Frays Ave., West Dr. 84 BK75
Frays Clo., West Dr. 84 BK76
Frays Lea, Uxb. 70 BJ68
Frays Waye, Uxb. 70 BJ67
Frazer Ave., Ruis. 58 BW64
Frazer Clo., Rom. 69 FF59
Frazier St. SE1 10 D5
Frazier St. SE1 91 DN75
Frean St. SE16 92 DU76
Fred Wigg Twr. E11 66 EF61
Freda Corbett Clo. SE15 92 DU80
Bird in Bush Rd.
Frederic Ms. SW1 8 E5
Frederic St. E17 65 DY57
Frederica Rd. E4 51 ED45
Frederica St. N7 77 DM66
Caledonian Rd.
Frederick Clo. W2 4 C10
Frederick Clo. W2 76 DE73
Frederick Clo., Sutt. 131 CZ105
Frederick Ct. NW2 61 CY62
Douglas Ms.
Frederick Cres. SW9 91 DP80
Frederick Cres., Enf. 36 DW40
Frederick Gdns., Sutt. 131 CZ106
Frederick Pl. SE18 95 EP78
Frederick Rd. SE17 91 DP78
Chapter Rd.
Frederick Rd., Rain. 83 FD68
Frederick Rd., Sutt. 131 CZ106
Frederick Sq. SE16 79 DY73
Rotherhithe St.
Frederick St. WC1 6 B3
Frederick St. WC1 77 DM69
Frederick Ter. E8 78 DT67
Haggerston Rd.
Frederick's Pl. EC2 7 K9
Fredericks Pl. N12 48 DC49
Frederick's Row EC1 6 F2
Fredora Ave., Hayes 71 BT70
Free Prae Rd., Cher. 112 BG102
Freeborne Gdns., Rain. 83 FG65
Mungo Pk. Rd.
Freedom Clo. E17 65 DY56
Freedom Rd. N17 50 DR54
Freedom St. SW11 90 DF82
Freedown La., Sutt. 132 DB113
Freegrove Rd. N7 63 DL64
Freeland Pk. NW4 47 CY54
Freeland Rd. W5 74 CM73
Freeland Way, Erith 97 FG81
Slade Grn. Rd.
Freelands Ave., S.Croy. 135 DX109
Freelands Gro., Brom. 122 EH95
Freelands Rd., Brom. 122 EH95
Freelands Rd., Cob. 127 BV114
Freeling St. N1 77 DM66
Caledonian Rd.
Freeman Clo., Nthlt. 72 BY66
Freeman Dr., W.Mol. 114 BZ97
Freeman Rd., Mord. 118 DD99
Freemans Clo., Shep. 113 BS98
Freemans La., Hayes 71 BS73
Freemantle Ave., Enf. 37 DX43
Freemasons Rd. E16 80 EH71
Freemasons Rd., Croy. 120 DS102
Freesia Clo., Orp. 137 ET106
Briarswood Way
Freethorpe Clo. SE19 120 DS95
Freezeland Way, Uxb. 70 BN65
Western Ave.
Freke Rd. SW11 90 DG83
Fremantle Rd., Belv. 96 FA77
Fremantle Rd., Ilf. 53 EQ54
Fremantle St. SE17 11 M10
Fremantle St. SE17 92 DS78
Fremont St. E9 78 DW67
French Gdns., Cob. 128 BW114
French Ordinary Ct. EC3 78 DS73
Crutched Friars
French Pl. E1 7 N4
French St., Sun. 114 BW96
Frenchaye, Add. 126 BJ106
Frendsbury Rd. SE4 93 DY84
Frensham (Cheshunt), Wal.Cr. 22 DT27
Frensham Clo., Sthl. 72 BZ70
Frensham Ct., Mitch. 118 DD97
Phipps Bri. Rd.
Frensham Dr. SW15 103 CT90
Frensham Dr., Croy. 135 EC108
Frensham Rd. SE9 109 ER89
Frensham Rd., Ken. 133 DP114
Frensham St. SE15 92 DU79
Frensham Way, Epsom 145 CW116
Frere St. SW11 90 DE82
Fresh Wf. Rd., Bark. 81 EP67
Freshfield Ave. E8 78 DT66
Freshfield Clo. SE13 93 ED84
Marischal Rd.
Freshfield Dr. N14 49 DH45
Freshfields, Croy. 121 DZ101
Freshford St. SW18 104 DC90
Freshmount Gdns., Epsom 130 CP111
Freshwater Clo. SW17 104 DG93
Freshwater Rd. SW17 104 DG93
Freshwater Rd., Dag. 68 EX60
Freshwell Ave., Rom. 68 EW56
Freshwood Clo., Beck. 121 EB95
Freshwood Way, Wall. 133 DH109
Freston Gdns., Barn. 34 DF43
Freston Pk. N3 47 CZ54
Freston Rd. W10 75 CX73
Freston Rd. W11 75 CX73
Freta Rd., Bexh. 110 EZ85
Frewin Rd. SW18 104 DD88
Friar Ms. SE27 105 DP90
Prioress Rd.
Friar Rd., Hayes 72 BX70
Friar Rd., Orp. 124 EU99
Friar St. EC4 6 G9
Friars, The, Chig. 53 ES49
Friars Ave. N20 48 DE48
Friars Ave. SW15 103 CT90
Friars Clo. E4 51 EC48
Friars Clo. N2 62 DD56
Friars Clo., Nthlt. 72 BX69
Broomcroft Ave.
Friars Gdns. W3 74 CR72
St. Dunstans Ave.
Friars Gate Clo., Wdf.Grn. 52 EG49
Friars La., Rich. 101 CK85
Friars Mead E14 93 EC76
Friars Ms. SE9 109 EN85
Friars Orchard, Lthd. 143 CD121
Friars Pl. La. W3 74 CR73
Friars Rd. E6 80 EK67
Friars Stile Pl., Rich. 102 CL86
Friars Stile Rd.
Friars Stile Rd., Rich. 102 CL86
Friars Wk. N14 49 DH45
Friars Wk. SE2 96 EX78
Friars Way W3 74 CR72
Friars Way, Cher. 112 BG99
Friars Way, Kings L. 14 BN30
Friars Way (Bushey), Wat. 30 BZ39
Friars Wd., Croy. 135 DY109
Friary Clo. N12 48 DE50
Friary Ct. SW1 9 L3
Friary Est. SE15 92 DU79
Friary La., Wdf.Grn. 52 EG49
Friary Rd. N12 48 DD49
Friary Rd. SE15 92 DU80
Friary Rd. W3 74 CQ72
Friary Way N12 48 DE49
Friday Hill E4 52 EE47
Friday Hill E. E4 52 EE48
Friday Hill W. E4 52 EE47
Friday Rd., Erith 97 FD78
Friday Rd., Mitch. 104 DF94
Friday St. EC4 7 H9
Friday St. EC4 78 DQ73
Frideswide Pl. NW5 63 DJ64
Islip St.
Friend St. EC1 6 F2
Friend St. EC1 77 DP69
Friendly Pl. SE13 93 EB81
Lewisham Rd.
Friendly St. SE8 93 EA82
Friendly St. Ms. SE8 93 EA82
Friendly St.
Friends Ave., Wal.Cr. 23 DX31
Friends Rd., Croy. 120 DR104
Friends Rd., Pur. 133 DP112
Friends Wk., Uxb. 70 BK66
Bakers Rd.
Friendship Wk., Nthlt. 72 BX69
Wayfarer Rd.
Friern Barnet La. N11 48 DF49
Friern Barnet La. N20 48 DC47
Friern Barnet Rd. N11 48 DF50
Friern Ct. N20 48 DD48
Friern Mt. Dr. N20 48 DC45
Friern Pk. N12 48 DC50
Friern Rd. SE22 106 DU87
Friern Watch Ave. N12 48 DC49
Frigate Ms. SE8 93 EA79
Watergate St.
Frimley Ave., Wall. 133 DL106
Frimley Clo. SW19 103 CY89
Frimley Clo., Croy. 135 EC108
Frimley Ct., Sid. 110 EW92
Frimley Cres., Croy. 135 EC108
Frimley Gdns., Mitch. 118 DE97
Frimley Rd., Chess. 129 CK106
Frimley Rd., Ilf. 67 ES62
Frimley Way E1 79 DX70
Frimley Way, Wall. 133 DL106
Fringewood Clo., Nthwd. 43 BP53
Frinsted Clo., Orp. 124 EX98
Frinsted Rd., Erith 97 FD80
Frinton Clo., Wat. 43 BV47
Frinton Dr., Wdf.Grn. 51 ED52
Frinton Ms., Ilf. 67 EN58
Bramley Cres.
Frinton Rd. E6 80 EK69
Frinton Rd. N15 64 DS58
Frinton Rd. SW17 104 DG93
Frinton Rd., Rom. 54 EZ52
Frinton Rd., Sid. 110 EY89
Friston Path, Chig. 53 ES50
Manford Way
Friston St. SW6 90 DB82
Friswell Pl., Bexh. 96 FA84
Frith Ct. NW7 47 CY52
Frith Knowle, Walt. 127 BV106
Frith La. NW7 47 CY52
Frith Rd. E11 65 EC63
Frith Rd., Croy. 120 DQ103
Frith St. W1 5 M9
Frith St. W1 77 DK72
Fritham Clo., N.Mal. 116 CS100
Frithville Gdns. W12 75 CW74
Frithwood Ave., Nthwd. 43 BS51
Frizlands La., Dag. 69 FB63
Frobisher Clo., Ken. 148 DR117
Hayes La.
Frobisher Clo., Pnr. 58 BX59
Frobisher Cres., Stai. 98 BL87
Frobisher Gdns., Stai. 98 BL87
Frobisher Cres.
Frobisher Pas. E14 79 EA74
North Colonnade
Frobisher Rd. E6 81 EM72
Frobisher Rd. N8 63 DN56
Frobisher Rd., Erith 97 FF80
Frobisher St. SE10 94 EE79
Frog La., Rain. 83 FD71
Froghall La., Chig. 53 ER49
Frogley Rd. SE22 92 DT84
Frogmoor La., Rick. 42 BK47
Frogmore SW18 104 DA85
Frogmore, St.Alb. 17 CD27
Frogmore Ave., Hayes 71 BS70
Frogmore Clo., Sutt. 117 CX104
Frogmore Gdns., Hayes 71 BS70
Frogmore Gdns., Sutt. 131 CY105
Frogmore Mobile Home Pk., St.Alb. 17 CD27
Frognal NW3 62 DC64
Frognal Ave., Har. 59 CF56
Frognal Ave., Sid. 110 EU92
Frognal Clo. NW3 62 DC64
Frognal Ct. NW3 76 DC65
Frognal Gdns. NW3 62 DC63
Frognal La. NW3 62 DB64
Frognal Par. NW3 76 DC65
Frognal Ct.
Frognal Pl., Sid. 110 EU93
Frognal Ri. NW3 62 DC62
Frognal Way NW3 62 DC63
Froissart Rd. SE9 108 EK85
Frome Rd. N22 63 DP55
Westbury Ave.
Frome St. N1 78 DQ68
Fromondes Rd., Sutt. 131 CY106
Frostic Wk. E1 78 DU71
Chicksand St.
Froude St. SW8 91 DH82
Frowyke Cres., Pot.B. 19 CU32
Fruen Rd., Felt. 99 BT87
Fry Clo., Rom. 54 FA50
Fry Rd. E6 80 EK66
Fry Rd. NW10 75 CT67
Fryatt Rd. N17 50 DR52
Fryatt St. E14 80 EE72
Orchard Pl.
Fryent Clo. NW9 60 CN57
Fryent Cres. NW9 60 CS58
Fryent Flds. NW9 60 CS58
Fryent Gro. NW9 60 CS58
Fryent Way NW9 60 CN57
Fryern Wd., Cat. 148 DQ124
Frye's Bldgs. N1 77 DN68
Upper St.
Frying Pan All. E1 7 P7
Fryston Ave., Couls. 133 DH114
Fryston Ave., Croy. 120 DU103
Fuchsia St. SE2 96 EV78
Fulbeck Dr. NW9 46 CS53
Fulbeck Way, Har. 44 CC54
Fulbourne Rd. E17 51 EC53
Fulbourne St. E1 78 DV71
Durward St.
Fulbrook Ave., Add. 126 BG111
Fulbrook Ms. N19 63 DJ63
Junction Rd.
Fulbrook Rd. N19 63 DJ63
Junction Rd.
Fulbrooks Ave., Wor.Pk. 117 CT102
Fulford Gro., Wat. 43 BV47
Fulford Rd., Cat. 148 DR121
Fulford Rd., Epsom 130 CR108
Fulford St. SE16 92 DV75
Paradise St.
Fulham Bdy. SW6 90 DA80
Fulham Clo., Uxb. 71 BQ70
Uxbridge Rd.
Fulham Ct. SW6 90 DA80
Fulham Rd.
Fulham High St. SW6 89 CY82
Fulham Palace Rd. SW6 89 CX79
Fulham Palace Rd. W6 89 CW78
Fulham Pk. Gdns. SW6 89 CZ82
Fulham Pk. Rd. SW6 89 CZ82
Fulham Rd. SW3 90 DD78
Fulham Rd. SW6 89 CY82
Fulham Rd. SW10 90 DD78
Fuller Clo. E2 78 DU70
St. Matthew's Row
Fuller Clo., Orp. 137 ET106
Fuller Gdns., Wat. 29 BV37
Fuller Rd.
Fuller Rd., Dag. 68 EV62
Fuller Rd., Wat. 29 BV37
Fuller St. NW4 61 CW56

Fuller Ter., Ilf. 67 EQ64
Loxford La.
Fuller Way, Hayes 85 BT78
Fuller Way, Rick. 28 BN43
Fullers Ave., Surb. 116 CM103
Fullers Ave., Wdf.Grn. 52 EF52
Fullers Clo., Rom. 55 FC52
Fullers Clo., Wal.Abb. 24 EF33
Fullers La., Rom. 55 FC52
Fullers Rd. E18 52 EF53
Fullers Way N., Surb. 116 CM104
Fullers Way S., Chess. 130 CL105
Fullers Wd., Croy. 135 EA106
Fullerton Clo., W.Byf. 126 BM114
Fullerton Dr., W.Byf. 126 BL114
Fullerton Rd. SW18 104 DC85
Fullerton Rd., Cars. 132 DE109
Fullerton Rd., Croy. 120 DT101
Fullerton Rd., W.Byf. 126 BL114
Fullerton Way, W.Byf. 126 BL114
Fullwell Ave., Ilf. 53 EM53
Fullwoods Ms. N1 7 L2
Fulmar Ct., Surb. 116 CM100
Fulmar Rd., Horn. 83 FG66
Fulmead St. SW6 90 DB81
Fulmer Clo., Hmptn. 100 BY92
Fulmer Rd. E16 80 EK71
Fulmer Way W13 87 CH76
Fulready Rd. E10 65 ED57
Fulstone Clo., Houns. 86 BZ84
Fulthorp Rd. SE3 94 EF82
Fulton Ms. W2 76 DC73
Porchester Ter.
Fulton Rd., Wem. 60 CN62
Fulwell Cross Roundabout, Ilf. 53 ER54
Fencepiece Rd.
Fulwell Pk. Ave., Twick. 100 CB89
Fulwell Rd., Tedd. 101 CD91
Fulwood Ave., Wem. 74 CM68
Fulwood Clo., Hayes 71 BT72
Fulwood Gdns., Twick. 101 CF86
Fulwood Pl. WC1 6 C7
Fulwood Wk. SW19 103 CY88
Furber St. W6 89 CV76
Furham Feild, Pnr. 44 CA52
Furley Rd. SE15 92 DU80
Furlong Clo., Wall. 118 DG102
Furlong Rd. N7 77 DN65
Furmage St. SW18 104 DB87
Furmingers Rd., Orp. 139 FB106
Furneaux Ave. SE27 105 DP92
Furner Clo., Dart. 97 FF83
Furness Rd. NW10 75 CU68
Furness Rd. SW6 90 DB82
Furness Rd., Har. 58 CB59
Furness Rd., Mord. 118 DB101
Furness Way, Horn. 69 FG64
Furnival St. EC4 6 D8
Furnival St. EC4 77 DN72
Furrow La. E9 64 DW64
Furrows, The, Uxb. 56 BJ57
Furrows, The, Walt. 114 BW103
Furrows Pl., Cat. 148 DT123
Fursby Ave. N3 48 DA51
Further Acre NW9 47 CT54
Further Grn. Rd. SE6 108 EE87
Furtherfield, Abb.L. 15 BS32
Furtherfield Clo., Croy. 119 DN100
Furze Clo., Wat. 44 BW50
Furze Fm. Clo., Rom. 54 EY54
Furze Fld., Lthd. 129 CD113
Furze Gro., Tad. 145 CZ121
Furze Hill, Pur. 133 DL111
Furze Hill, Tad. 145 CZ120
Furze La., Pur. 133 DL111
Furze Rd., Th.Hth. 120 DQ97
Furze St. E3 79 EA71
Furzebushes La., St.Alb. 16 BY25
Furzedown Dr. SW17 105 DH92
Furzedown Rd. SW17 105 DH92
Furzedown Rd., Sutt. 132 DC111
Furzefield (Cheshunt), Wal.Cr. 22 DV28
Furzefield Clo., Chis. 109 EP93
Furzefield Rd. SE3 94 EH80
Furzeground Way, Uxb. 71 BQ74
Furzeham Rd., West Dr. 84 BL75
Furzehill Rd., Borwd. 32 CN41
Furzewood, Sun. 113 BU95
Fuschia Ct., Wdf.Grn. 52 EE52
Bridle Path
Fyfe Way, Brom. 122 EG96
Fyfield Clo., Brom. 121 ED98
Fyfield Ct. E7 80 EG65
Fyfield Rd. E17 65 ED55
Fyfield Rd. SW9 91 DN83
Fyfield Rd., Enf. 36 DS41
Fyfield Rd., Rain. 83 FF67
Fyfield Rd., Wdf.Grn. 52 EJ52
Fynes St. SW1 9 M8
Fynes St. SW1 91 DK77

G

Gable Clo. SE26 106 DV91
Lawrie Pk. Ave.
Gable Clo., Abb.L. 15 BS32
Gable Clo., Dart. 111 FG85
Gable Clo., Pnr. 44 CA52
Gable Ct. SE26 106 DV92
Lawrie Pk. Ave.
Gables, The, Bans. 145 CZ117
Gables, The, Lthd. 128 CC112
Gables, The, Wem. 60 CM63
Gables Ave., Ashf. 98 BM92
Gables Ave., Borwd. 32 CM41
Gables Clo. SE5 92 DS81
Gables Clo. SE12 108 EG88
Gabriel Clo., Felt. 100 BX91
Gabriel Clo., Rom. 55 FC52
Gabriel St. SE23 107 DX87
Gabrielle Clo., Wem. 60 CM62
Gabrielle Ct. NW3 76 DD65
Gad Clo. E13 80 EH69
Gaddesden Ave., Wem. 74 CM65
Gaddesden Cres., Wat. 16 BX34
Gade Ave., Wat. 29 BS42
Gade Bank, Rick. 29 BR42
Rousebarn La.
Gade Clo., Hayes 71 BV74
Gade Clo., Wat. 29 BS42
Gade Twr., Hem.H. 14 BN25
Gade Valley Clo., Kings L. 14 BN28
Gade Vw. Gdns., Kings L. 15 BQ32
Gadesden Rd., Epsom 130 CQ107
Gadsbury Clo. NW9 61 CT58
Gadswell Clo., Wat. 30 BX36
Gadwall Clo. E16 80 EH72
Freemasons Rd.
Gadwall Way SE28 95 ER75
Goldfinch Rd.
Gage Rd. E16 80 EE71
Malmesbury Rd.
Gage St. WC1 6 A6
Gainford St. N1 77 DN67
Richmond Ave.
Gainsborough Ave. E12 67 EN64
Gainsborough Clo., Beck. 107 EA94
Gainsborough Clo., Esher 115 CE102
Lime Tree Ave.
Gainsborough Ct. N12 48 DB50
Gainsborough Ct. W12 89 CW75
Lime Gro.
Gainsborough Ct., Walt. 127 BU105
Gainsborough Dr., S.Croy. 134 DU113
Gainsborough Gdns. NW3 62 DD62
Gainsborough Gdns. NW11 61 CZ59
Gainsborough Gdns., Edg. 46 CM54
Gainsborough Gdns., Grnf. 59 CE64
Gainsborough Gdns., Islw. 101 CD85
Gainsborough Ms. SE26 106 DV90
Panmure Rd.
Gainsborough Pl., Chig. 53 ET48
Gainsborough Rd. E11 66 EE59
Gainsborough Rd. E15 80 EE69
Gainsborough Rd. N12 48 DB50
Gainsborough Rd. W4 89 CT77
Gainsborough Rd., Dag. 68 EV63
Gainsborough Rd., Epsom 130 CQ110
Gainsborough Rd., Hayes 71 BQ68
Gainsborough Rd., N.Mal. 116 CR100
Gainsborough Rd., Rain. 83 FG67
Gainsborough Rd., Rich. 88 CM82
Gainsborough Rd., Wdf.Grn. 52 EL51
Gainsborough Sq., Bexh. 96 EX83
Regency Way
Gainsford Rd. E17 65 DZ56
Gainsford St. SE1 11 P4
Gainsford St. SE1 92 DT75
Gairloch Rd. SE5 92 DS82
Gaisford St. NW5 77 DJ65
Gaist Ave., Cat. 148 DV122
Gaitskell Rd. SE9 109 EQ88
Galahad Rd., Brom. 108 EG90
Galata Rd. SW13 89 CU80
Galatea Sq. SE15 92 DV83
Scylla Rd.
Galbraith St. E14 93 EC76
Galdana Ave., Barn. 34 DC41
Gale Clo., Hmptn. 100 BY93
Stewart Clo.
Gale Clo., Mitch. 118 DD97
Gale Cres., Bans. 146 DA117
Gale St. E3 79 EA71
Gale St., Dag. 68 EW64
Galeborough Ave., Wdf.Grn. 51 ED52
Galen Pl. WC1 6 A7
Galena Rd. W6 89 CV77
Gales Gdns. E2 78 DV69
Gales Way, Wdf.Grn. 52 EL52
Galesbury Rd. SW18 104 DC86
Galgate Clo. SW19 103 CY88
Gallants Fm. Rd., Barn. 48 DE45
Galleon Clo. SE16 93 DX75
Kinburn St.
Gallery Gdns., Nthlt. 72 BX68
Gallery Rd. SE21 106 DR88
Galley La., Barn. 33 CT38
Galleyhill Rd., Wal.Abb. 24 EE32
Galleywall Rd. SE16 92 DV77
Galleywood Cres., Rom. 55 FD51
Gallia Rd. N5 63 DP64
Galliard Clo. N9 36 DW44
Galliard Rd. N9 50 DU46
Gallions Clo., Bark. 82 EU69
Gallions Rd. E16 81 EP73
Gallions Rd. SE7 94 EH77
Gallions Roundabout E16 94 EK78
Royal Albert Way
Gallon Clo. SE7 94 EJ77
Gallop, The, S.Croy. 134 DV108
Gallop, The, Sutt. 132 DD110
Gallosson Rd. SE18 95 ES77
Galloway Clo., Brox. 23 DZ25
Galloway Path, Croy. 134 DR105
St. Peter's Rd.
Galloway Rd. W12 75 CU74
Gallows Hill, Kings L. 15 BQ31
Gallows Hill La., Abb.L. 15 BQ32
Gallus Clo. N21 35 DM44
Gallus Sq. SE3 94 EH83
Galpins Rd., Th.Hth. 119 DL99
Galsworthy Ave., Rom. 68 EV59
Galsworthy Clo. SE28 82 EV74
Galsworthy Cres. SE3 94 EJ81
Merriman Rd.
Galsworthy Rd. NW2 61 CY63
Galsworthy Rd., Cher. 112 BG101
Galsworthy Rd., Kings.T. 102 CP94
Galsworthy Ter. N16 64 DS62
Hawksley Rd.
Galton St. W10 75 CY69
Galva Clo., Barn. 34 DG42
Galvani Way, Croy. 119 DM102
Ampere Way
Galveston Rd. SW15 103 CZ85
Galway St. EC1 7 J3
Galway St. EC1 78 DQ69
Gambetta St. SW8 91 DH82
Gambia St. SE1 10 G3
Gambles La., Wok. 140 BJ124
Gambole Rd. SW17 104 DE91
Games Rd., Barn. 34 DF41
Gamlen Rd. SW15 89 CX84
Gammons Fm. Clo., Wat. 29 BT36
Gammons La., Brox. 22 DS25
Gammons La., Wat. 29 BS36
Gamuel Clo. E17 65 EA58
Gander Grn. La., Sutt. 117 CY103
Ganders Ash, Wat. 15 BU33
Gandhi Clo. E17 65 EA58
Gane Clo., Wall. 133 DL108
Kingsford Ave.
Gant Ct., Wal.Abb. 24 EF34
Ganton St. W1 5 K10
Ganton Wk., Wat. 44 BY49
Woodhall La.
Gantshill Cres., Ilf. 67 EN57
Gantshill Cross, Ilf. 67 EN58
Eastern Ave.
Gap Rd. SW19 104 DA92
Garage Rd. W3 74 CN72
Garbrand Wk., Epsom 131 CT109
Garbutt Pl. W1 4 G6
Gard St. EC1 6 G2
Garden Ave., Bexh. 96 FA83
Garden Ave., Mitch. 105 DH94
Garden City, Edg. 46 CN51
Garden Clo. E4 51 EA50
Garden Clo. SE12 108 EH90
Garden Clo. SW15 103 CV87
Garden Clo., Add. 126 BK105
Garden Clo., Ashf. 99 BQ93
Garden Clo., Bans. 146 DA115
Garden Clo., Barn. 33 CV42
Garden Clo., Hmptn. 100 BZ92
Garden Clo., Lthd. 143 CJ124
Garden Clo., Nthlt. 72 BY67
Garden Clo., Ruis. 57 BS61
Garden Clo., Wall. 133 DL106
Garden Clo., Wat. 29 BT40
Garden Cotts., Orp. 124 EW96
Main Rd.
Garden Ct. EC4 6 D10
Garden Ct. SE15 92 DT81
Sumner Est.
Garden Ct., Rich. 88 CM81
Lichfield Rd.
Garden Ct., W.Mol. 114 CB98
Avern Rd.
Garden La. SW2 105 DM88
Christchurch Rd.
Garden La., Brom. 108 EH93
Garden Ms. W2 76 DA73
Linden Gdns.
Garden Rd. NW8 76 DC69
Garden Rd. SE20 120 DW95
Garden Rd., Abb.L. 15 BS31
Garden Rd., Brom. 108 EH94
Garden Rd., Rich. 88 CN83
Garden Rd., Sev. 155 FK122
Garden Rd., Walt. 113 BV100
Garden Row SE1 10 F7
Garden Row SE1 91 DP76
Garden St. E1 79 DX71
Garden Ter. SW1 9 M10
Garden Wk. EC2 7 M3
Garden Wk., Beck. 121 DZ95
Hayne Rd.
Garden Wk., Couls. 147 DH123
Garden Way NW10 74 CQ65
Garden Way, Loug. 39 EN38
Gardeners Clo. N11 48 DG49
Gardeners Rd., Croy. 119 DP102
Gardenia Rd., Enf. 36 DS44
Gardenia Way, Wdf.Grn. 52 EH50
Harts Gro.
Gardens, The SE22 92 DU84
Gardens, The, Beck. 121 EC95
Gardens, The, Esher 128 CA105
Gardens, The, Felt. 99 BR86
Gardens, The, Har. 58 CC58
Gardens, The, Hat. 19 CY27
Gardens, The, Pnr. 58 BZ58
Gardens, The, Wat. 29 BT40
Gardiner Ave. NW2 61 CW64
Gardiner Clo., Dag. 68 EX63
Gardiner Clo., Orp. 124 EW96
Gardner Clo. E11 66 EH58
Gardner Gro., Felt. 100 BZ89
Gardner Rd. E13 80 EH70
Gardners La. EC4 7 H10
Gardnor Rd. NW3 62 DD63
Flask Wk.
Garendon Gdns., Mord. 118 DB101
Garendon Rd., Mord. 118 DA101
Gareth Clo., Wor.Pk. 117 CX103
Burnham Dr.
Gareth Gro., Brom. 108 EG91
Garfield Rd. E4 51 ED46
Garfield Rd. E13 80 EF70
Garfield Rd. SW11 90 DG83
Garfield Rd. SW19 104 DC92
Garfield Rd., Add. 126 BJ106
Garfield Rd., Enf. 36 DW42
Garfield Rd., Twick. 101 CG88
York St.
Garfield St., Wat. 29 BV38
Garford St. E14 79 EA73
Garganey Wk. SE28 82 EW73
Garibaldi St. SE18 95 ES77
Garland Clo., Wal.Cr. 23 DY31
Garland Rd. SE18 95 ER80
Garland Rd., Stan. 46 CL53
Garland Way, Cat. 148 DR122
Garlands Ct., Croy. 134 DR105
Chatsworth Rd.
Garlands Rd., Lthd. 143 CH121
Garlichill Rd., Epsom 145 CV117
Garlick Hill EC4 7 J10
Garlick Hill EC4 78 DQ73
Garlies Rd. SE23 107 DY90
Garlinge Rd. NW2 75 CZ65
Garman Clo. N18 50 DR50
Garman Rd. N17 50 DW52
Garnault Ms. EC1 6 E3
Garnault Pl. EC1 6 E3
Garnault Rd., Enf. 36 DT38
Garner Dr., Brox. 23 DY26
Garner Rd. E17 51 EC53
Garner St. E2 78 DU68
Coate St.
Garnet Rd. NW10 74 CS65
Garnet Rd., Th.Hth. 120 DQ98
Garnet St. E1 78 DW73
Garnet Wk. E6 80 EL71
Kingfisher St.
Garnett Clo. SE9 95 EM83
Garnett Clo., Wat. 30 BX37
Garnett Dr., St.Alb. 16 BZ29
Garnett Rd. NW3 62 DF64
Garnett Way E17 51 DY53
McEntee Ave.
Garnham Clo. N16 64 DT61
Garnham St.
Garnham St. N16 64 DT61
Garnies Clo. SE15 92 DT80
Daniel Gdns.
Garnon Mead, Epp. 26 EX28
Garrad's Rd. SW16 105 DK90
Garrard Clo., Bexh. 96 FA83
Garrard Clo., Chis. 109 EP92
Garrard Rd., Bans. 146 DA116
Garrard Wk. NW10 74 CS65
Garnet Rd.
Garratt Clo., Croy. 133 DL105
Garratt La. SW17 104 DD91
Garratt La. SW18 104 DB85
Garratt Rd., Edg. 46 CN52
Garratt Ter. SW17 104 DE91
Garratts La., Bans. 145 CZ116
Garratts Rd. (Bushey), Wat. 44 CC45
Garrett Clo. W3 74 CR71
Jenner Ave.
Garrett St. EC1 7 J4
Garrick Ave. NW11 61 CY58
Garrick Clo. SW18 90 DC84
Garrick Clo. W5 74 CL70
Garrick Clo., Rich. 101 CK85
The Grn.
Garrick Clo., Stai. 98 BG94
Garrick Clo., Walt. 127 BV105
Garrick Cres., Croy. 120 DS103
Garrick Dr. NW4 47 CW54
Garrick Dr. SE28 95 ER76
Broadwater Rd.
Garrick Gdns., W.Mol. 114 CA97
Garrick Pk. NW4 47 CX54
Garrick Rd. NW9 61 CT58
Garrick Rd., Grnf. 72 CB70
Garrick Rd., Rich. 88 CN82
Garrick St. WC2 5 P10
Garrick St. WC2 77 DL73
Garrick Way NW4 61 CX56
Garrison Clo. SE18 95 EN80
Red Lion La.
Garrison La., Chess. 129 CK108
Garrolds Clo., Swan. 125 FD96
Garry Clo., Rom. 55 FE52
Garry Way, Rom. 55 FE52
Garside Clo. SE28 95 ER76
Goosander Way
Garside Clo., Hmptn. 100 CB93
Garsington Ms. SE4 93 DZ83
Garsmouth Way, Wat. 30 BX36
Garson Mead, Esher 128 BZ106
Garson Rd., Esher 128 BZ107
Garston Cres., Wat. 16 BW34
Garston Dr., Wat. 16 BW34
Garston La., Ken. 134 DR114
Garston La., Wat. 16 BX34
Garston Pk. Par., Wat. 16 BX34
Garter Way SE16 93 DX75
Poolmans St.
Garth, The, Abb.L. 15 BR33
Garth, The, Cob. 128 BY113
Garth, The, Hmptn. 100 CB93
Uxbridge Rd.
Garth, The, Har. 60 CM58
Garth Clo. W4 88 CR78
Garth Clo., Kings.T. 102 CM92
Garth Clo., Mord. 117 CX101
Garth Clo., Ruis. 58 BX60
Garth Ct. W4 88 CR78
Garth Rd.
Garth Ms. W5 74 CL70
Greystoke Gdns.
Garth Rd. NW2 61 CZ61
Garth Rd. W4 88 CR79
Garth Rd., Kings.T. 102 CM92
Garth Rd., Mord. 117 CW100
Garth Rd., Sev. 155 FJ128
Garth Rd. Ind. Est., Mord. 117 CX101
Garthland Dr., Barn. 33 CV43
Garthorne Rd. SE23 107 DX87
Garthside, Rich. 102 CL92
Garthway N12 48 DE51
Gartlett Rd., Wat. 30 BW41
Gartmoor Gdns. SW19 103 CZ88
Gartmore Rd., Ilf. 67 ET61
Garton Pl. SW18 104 DC86
Gartons Clo., Enf. 36 DW42
Gartons Way SW11 90 DC83
Garvary Rd. E16 80 EH72
Garvock Dr., Sev. 154 FG126
Garway Rd. W2 76 DB72
Gascoigne Gdns., Wdf.Grn. 52 EE52
Gascoigne Pl. E2 7 P2
Gascoigne Pl. E2 78 DT69
Gascoigne Rd., Bark. 81 EQ67
Gascoigne Rd., Croy. 135 EC110
Gascoigne Rd., Wey. 113 BP104
Gascony Ave. NW6 76 DA66
Gascoyne Clo., Pot.B. 19 CU32
Gascoyne Dr., Dart. 97 FF82
Gascoyne Rd. E9 79 DX66
Gaselee St. E14 79 EC73
Gasholder Pl. SE11 91 DM78
Kennington La.
Gaskarth Rd. SW12 105 DH86
Gaskarth Rd., Edg. 46 CQ53
Gaskell Rd. N6 62 DF58
Gaskell St. SW4 91 DL82
Gaskin St. N1 77 DP67
Gaspar Clo. SW5 90 DB77
Courtfield Gdns.
Gaspar Ms. SW5 90 DB77
Courtfield Gdns.
Gassiot Rd. SW17 104 DF91
Gassiot Way, Sutt. 118 DD104
Gastein Rd. W6 89 CX79
Gaston Bell Clo., Rich. 88 CM83
Gaston Bri. Rd., Shep. 113 BR100
Gaston Rd., Mitch. 118 DG97
Gaston Way, Shep. 113 BQ99
Gataker St. SE16 92 DV76
Gatcombe Rd. E16 80 EG74
Silvertown Way
Gatcombe Rd. N19 63 DK62
Gatcombe Way, Barn. 34 DF41
Gate Clo., Borwd. 32 CQ39
Gate End, Nthwd. 43 BU52
Gate Ho. Sq. SE1 78 DQ74
Southwark Bri. Rd.
Gate Ms. SW7 8 C5
Gate Ms. SW7 90 DE75
Gate St. WC2 6 B8
Gateforth St. NW8 4 B5
Gateforth St. NW8 76 DE70
Gatehill Rd., Nthwd. 43 BT52
Gatehouse Clo., Kings.T. 102 CQ94
Gateley Rd. SW9 91 DM83
Gater Dr., Enf. 36 DR39
Gates Grn. Rd., Kes. 136 EH105
Gates Grn. Rd., W.Wick. 122 EF104
Gatesborough St. EC2 7 M4
Gatesden Rd., Lthd. 142 CC123
Gateshead Rd., Borwd. 32 CM40
Gateside Rd. SW17 104 DF90
Gatestone Rd. SE19 106 DS93
Gateway SE17 92 DQ79
Gateway, Wey. 113 BP104
Palace Dr.
Gateway Arc. N1 77 DP68
Islington High St.
Gateway Clo., Nthwd. 43 BQ51
Gateway Ind. Est. NW10 75 CT69
Gateway Ms. E8 64 DT64
Shacklewell La.
Gateways, The SW3 8 C9
Gateways, The, Wal.Cr. 22 DS28
Burton La.
Gatfield Gro., Felt. 100 CA89
Gathorne Rd. N22 49 DN54
Gathorne St. E2 79 DX68
Mace St.
Gatley Ave., Epsom 130 CP106
Gatliff Rd. SW1 91 DH78
Gatling Rd. SE2 96 EU78
Gatting Clo., Edg. 46 CQ52
Pavilion Way
Gatting Way, Uxb. 70 BL65
Gatton Clo., Sutt. 132 DB109
Gatton Rd. SW17 104 DE91
Gattons Way, Sid. 110 EZ91
Gatward Clo. N21 35 DP44
Gatward Grn. N9 50 DT47
Gatwick Rd. SW18 103 CZ87
Gauden Clo. SW4 91 DK83
Gauden Rd. SW4 91 DK82
Gaumont App., Wat. 29 BV41
Gaumont Ter. W12 89 CW75
Lime Gro.

Glebe Cotts., West. 152 EV123
Glebe Ct. W7 73 CD73
Glebe Ct., Mitch. 118 DF97
Glebe Ct., Stan. 45 CJ50
Glebe Rd.
Glebe Cres. NW4 61 CW56
Glebe Cres., Har. 60 CL55
Glebe Gdns., N.Mal. 116 CS101
Glebe Gdns., W.Byf. 126 BK114
Glebe Ho. Dr., Brom. 122 EH102
Glebe Hyrst SE19 106 DT91
Giles Coppice
Glebe Hyrst, S.Croy. 134 DT112
Glebe La., Barn. 33 CU43
Glebe La., Har. 60 CL56
Glebe La., Sev. 155 FH126
Glebe Path, Mitch. 118 DE97
Glebe Pl. SW3 90 DE79
Glebe Rd. E8 78 DT66
Middleton Rd.
Glebe Rd. N3 48 DC53
Glebe Rd. N8 63 DM56
Glebe Rd. NW10 75 CT65
Glebe Rd. SW13 89 CU82
Glebe Rd., Ash. 143 CK118
Glebe Rd., Brom. 122 EG95
Glebe Rd., Cars. 132 DF107
Glebe Rd., Dag. 83 FB65
Glebe Rd., Hayes 71 BT74
Glebe Rd., Rain. 83 FH69
Glebe Rd., Red. 147 DH124
Glebe Rd., Stai. 98 BH92
Glebe Rd., Stan. 45 CJ50
Glebe Rd., Sutt. 131 CY109
Glebe Rd., Uxb. 70 BJ68
Glebe Rd., Warl. 149 DX117
Glebe Side, Twick. 101 CF87
Glebe St. W4 88 CS78
Glebe Ter. E3 79 EA69
Bow Rd.
Glebe Way, Erith 97 FE79
Glebe Way, Felt. 100 CA90
Glebe Way, S.Croy. 134 DT112
Glebe Way, W.Wick. 121 EC103
Glebefield, The, Sev. 154 FF123
Glebeland Gdns., Shep. 113 BQ100
Glebelands, Chig. 54 EV48
Glebelands, Dart. 97 FF84
Glebelands, Esher 129 CF109
Glebelands, W.Mol. 114 CB99
Glebelands Ave. E18 52 EG54
Glebelands Ave., Ilf. 67 ER59
Glebelands Clo. SE5 92 DS83
Grove Hill Rd.
Glebelands Rd., Felt. 99 BU87
Glebeway, Wdf.Grn. 52 EJ50
Gledhow Gdns. SW5 90 DC77
Gledhow Wd., Tad. 146 DB121
Gledstanes Rd. W14 89 CY78
Gledwood Ave., Hayes 71 BT71
Gledwood Cres., Hayes 71 BT71
Gledwood Dr., Hayes 71 BT71
Gledwood Gdns., Hayes 71 BT71
Gleed Ave. (Bushey), Wat. 45 CD47
Gleeson Dr., Orp. 137 ET106
Glegg Pl. SW15 89 CX84
Glen, The, Brom. 122 EE96
Glen, The, Croy. 121 DX104
Glen, The, Enf. 35 DP42
Glen, The, Nthwd. 43 BR52
Glen, The, Orp. 123 EM104
Glen, The, Pnr. 58 BY59
Glen, The (Eastcote), Pnr. 57 BV57
Glen, The, Sthl. 86 BZ78
Glen, The, Wem. 59 CK63
Glen Albyn Rd. SW19 103 CX89
Glen Ave., Ashf. 98 BN91
Glen Clo., Shep. 112 BN98
Glen Clo., Tad. 145 CY123
Glen Cres., Wdf.Grn. 52 EH51
Glen Gdns., Croy. 119 DP104
Glen Ri., Wdf.Grn. 52 EH51
Glen Rd. E13 80 EJ70
Glen Rd. E17 65 DZ57
Glen Rd., Chess. 116 CL104
Glen Rd. End, Wall. 133 DH109
Glen Ter. E14 93 EC75
Manchester Rd.
Glen Wk., Islw. 101 CD85
Glen Way, Wat. 29 BS38
Glena Mt., Sutt. 132 DC105
Glenaffric Ave. E14 93 ED77
Glenalla Rd., Ruis. 57 BT59
Glenalmond Rd., Har. 60 CL56
Glenalvon Way SE18 94 EL77
Glenarm Rd. E5 64 DW64
Glenavon Clo., Esher 129 CG107
Glenavon Rd. E15 80 EE66
Glenbarr Clo. SE9 95 EP83
Dumbreck Rd.
Glenbow Rd., Brom. 108 EE93
Glenbrook N., Enf. 35 DM42
Glenbrook Rd. NW6 62 DA64
Glenbrook S., Enf. 35 DM42
Glenbuck Ct., Surb. 115 CK100
Glenbuck Rd.
Glenbuck Rd., Surb. 115 CK100
Glenburnie Rd. SW17 104 DE90
Glencairn Dr. W5 73 CJ70
Glencairn Rd. SW16 105 DL94
Glencairne Clo. E16 80 EK71
Glencoe Ave., Ilf. 67 ER59
Glencoe Dr., Dag. 68 FA63
Glencoe Rd., Hayes 72 BX70
Glencoe Rd. (Bushey), Wat. 30 CA44
Glencoe Rd., Wey. 112 BN104
Glencourse Grn., Wat. 44 BX49
Caldwell Rd.
Glendale, Swan. 125 FF99
Glendale Ave. N22 49 DN52
Glendale Ave., Edg. 46 CN49
Glendale Ave., Rom. 68 EW59
Glendale Clo. SE9 95 EN83
Dumbreck Rd.
Glendale Dr. SW19 103 CZ92
Glendale Gdns., Wem. 59 CK60
Glendale Ms., Beck. 121 EB95
Glendale Ri., Ken. 147 DP115
Glendale Rd., Erith 97 FC77
Glendale Wk. (Cheshunt), Wal.Cr. 23 DY30
Glendale Way SE28 82 EW73
Glendall St. SW9 91 DM84
Glendarvon St. SW15 89 CX83
Glendevon Clo., Edg. 46 CP48
Tayside Dr.
Glendish Rd. N17 50 DU53
Glendor Gdns. NW7 46 CR49
Glendower Cres., Orp. 124 EU100
Glendower Gdns. SW14 88 CR83
Glendower Rd.
Glendower Pl. SW7 90 DD77
Glendower Rd. E4 51 ED46
Glendower Rd. SW14 88 CR83
Glendown Rd. SE2 96 EU78
Glendun Rd. W3 74 CS73
Gleneagle Ms. SW16 105 DK92
Ambleside Ave.
Gleneagle Rd. SW16 105 DK93
Gleneagles, Stan. 45 CH51
Gleneagles Clo. SE16 92 DV78
Ryder Dr.
Gleneagles Clo., Orp. 123 ER102
Gleneagles Clo., Stai. 98 BK86
Gleneagles Clo., Stan. 45 CH51
Gleneagles Clo., Wat. 44 BX49
Gleneagles Grn., Orp. 123 ER102
Tandridge Dr.
Gleneagles Twr., Sthl. 72 CC72
Gleneldon Ms. SW16 105 DL91
Gleneldon Rd. SW16 105 DL91
Glenelg Rd. SW2 105 DL85
Glenesk Rd. SE9 95 EN83
Glenfarg Rd. SE6 107 ED88
Glenfield Cres., Ruis. 57 BR59
Glenfield Rd. SW12 105 DJ88
Glenfield Rd. W13 87 CH75
Glenfield Rd., Ashf. 99 BP93
Glenfield Rd., Bans. 146 DB115
Glenfield Ter. W13 73 CH74
Glenfinlas Way SE5 91 DP80
Glenforth St. SE10 94 EF78
Glengall Causeway E14 93 EA76
Glengall Gro. E14 93 EC76
Glengall Rd. NW6 75 CZ67
Glengall Rd. SE15 92 DT78
Glengall Rd., Bexh. 96 EY83
Glengall Rd., Edg. 46 CP48
Glengall Rd., Wdf.Grn. 52 EG51
Glengall Ter. SE15 92 DT79
Glengarnock Ave. E14 93 EC77
Glengarry Rd. SE22 106 DS85
Glenham Dr., Ilf. 67 EP57
Glenhaven Ave., Borwd. 32 CN41
Glenhead Clo. SE9 95 EP83
Dumbreck Rd.
Glenheadon Clo., Lthd. 143 CK123
Glenheadon Ri.
Glenheadon Ri., Lthd. 143 CK123
Glenhill Clo. N3 48 DA54
Glenhouse Rd. SE9 109 EN85
Glenhurst Ave. NW5 62 DG63
Glenhurst Ave., Bex. 110 EZ88
Glenhurst Ave., Ruis. 57 BQ59
Glenhurst Ct. SE19 106 DT92
Glenhurst Ri. SE19 106 DQ94
Glenhurst Rd. N12 48 DD50
Glenhurst Rd., Brent. 87 CJ79
Glenilla Rd. NW3 76 DE65
Glenister Ho., Hayes 71 BV74
Glenister Pk. Rd. SW16 105 DK94
Glenister Rd. SE10 94 EF78
Glenister St. E16 81 EN74
Glenlea Rd. SE9 109 EN85
Glenlion Ct., Wey. 113 BR104
Glenloch Rd. NW3 76 DE65
Glenloch Rd., Enf. 36 DW40
Glenluce Rd. SE3 94 EG79
Glenlyon Rd. SE9 109 EN85
Glenmere Ave. NW7 47 CU52
Glenmill, Hmptn. 100 BZ92
Glenmore Clo., Add. 112 BH104
Glenmore Gdns., Abb.L. 15 BU32
Stewart Clo.
Glenmore Rd. NW3 76 DE65
Glenmore Rd., Well. 95 ET80
Glenmore Way, Bark. 82 EU69
Glenmount Path SE18 95 EQ78
Raglan Rd.
Glenn Ave., Pur. 133 DP111
Glennie Rd. SE27 105 DN90
Glenny Rd., Bark. 81 EQ65
Glenorchy Clo., Hayes 72 BY71
Glenparke Rd. E7 80 EH65
Glenrosa St. SW6 90 DC82
Glenrose Ct., Sid. 110 EV92
Glenroy St. W12 75 CW72
Glensdale Rd. SE4 93 DZ83
Glenshee Clo., Nthwd. 43 BQ51
Merrows Clo.
Glenshiel Rd. SE9 109 EN85
Glenside, Chig. 53 EP51
Glentanner Way SW17 104 DD90
Aboyne Rd.
Glentham Gdns. SW13 89 CV79
Glentham Rd.
Glentham Rd. SW13 89 CU79
Glenthorne Ave., Croy. 120 DV102
Glenthorne Clo., Sutt. 118 DA102
Glenthorne Clo., Uxb. 70 BN69
Uxbridge Rd.
Glenthorne Gdns., Ilf. 67 EN55
Glenthorne Gdns., Sutt. 118 DA102
Glenthorne Ms. W6 89 CV77
Glenthorne Rd.
Glenthorne Rd. E17 65 DY57
Glenthorne Rd. N11 48 DF50
Glenthorne Rd. W6 89 CV77
Glenthorne Rd., Kings.T. 116 CM98
Glenthorpe Rd., Mord. 117 CX99
Glenton Clo., Rom. 55 FE51
Glenton Rd. SE13 94 EE84
Glenton Way, Rom. 55 FE52
Glentrammon Ave., Orp. 137 ET107
Glentrammon Clo., Orp. 137 ET106
Glentrammon Gdns., Orp. 137 ET107
Glentrammon Rd., Orp. 137 ET107
Glentworth St. NW1 4 E5
Glentworth St. NW1 76 DF70
Glenure Rd. SE9 109 EN85
Glenview SE2 96 EX79
Glenview Rd., Brom. 122 EK96
Glenville Ave., Enf. 36 DQ38
Glenville Gro. SE8 93 DZ80
Glenville Ms. SW18 104 DB87
Glenville Rd., Kings.T. 116 CN95
Glenwood Ave. NW9 60 CS60
Glenwood Ave., Rain. 83 FG70
Glenwood Clo., Har. 59 CF57
Glenwood Dr., Rom. 69 FG57
Glenwood Gdns., Ilf. 67 EN57
Glenwood Gro. NW9 60 CQ60
Glenwood Rd. N15 63 DP57
Glenwood Rd. NW7 46 CS48
Glenwood Rd. SE6 107 DZ88
Glenwood Rd., Epsom 131 CU107
Glenwood Rd., Houns. 87 CD83
Glenwood Way, Croy. 121 DX100
Glenworth Ave. E14 93 ED77
Gliddon Rd. W14 89 CY77
Glimpsing Grn., Erith 96 EY76
Glisson Rd., Uxb. 70 BN68
Gload Cres., Orp. 124 EX103
Global App. E3 79 EB68
Hancock Rd.
Globe Pond Rd. SE16 79 DY74
Globe Rd. E1 79 DX70
Globe Rd. E2 78 DW69
Globe Rd. E15 66 EF64
Globe Rd., Horn. 69 FG58
Globe Rd., Wdf.Grn. 52 EJ51
Globe Rope Wk. E14 93 EC77
Stebondale St.
Globe St. SE1 11 K5
Globe St. SE1 92 DR75
Globe Ter. E2 78 DW69
Globe Rd.
Globe Yd. W1 5 H9
Glossop Rd., S.Croy. 134 DR109
Gloster Rd., N.Mal. 116 CS98
Gloucester Ave. NW1 76 DG66
Gloucester Ave., Sid. 109 ES89
Gloucester Ave., Wal.Cr. 23 DY33
Gloucester Ave., Well. 95 ET84
Gloucester Circ. SE10 93 EC80
Gloucester Clo. NW10 74 CR66
Gloucester Clo., T.Ditt. 115 CG102
Gloucester Ct. EC3 11 N1
Gloucester Ct., Rich. 88 CN80
Gloucester Ct., Uxb. 56 BG58
Moorfield Rd.
Gloucester Cres. NW1 77 DH67
Gloucester Cres., Stai. 98 BK93
Gloucester Dr. N4 63 DP61
Gloucester Dr. NW11 62 DA56
Gloucester Gdns. NW11 61 CZ59
Gloucester Gdns. W2 76 DC72
Bishops Bri. Rd.
Gloucester Gdns., Barn. 34 DG42
Gloucester Gdns., Ilf. 66 EL59
Gloucester Gdns., Sutt. 118 DB103
Gloucester Gate NW1 77 DH68
Gloucester Gate Ms. NW1 77 DH68
Gloucester Gate
Gloucester Gro., Edg. 46 CR53
Gloucester Gro. Est. SE15 92 DS79
Gloucester Ho. N7 63 DL62
Gloucester Ho. NW6 76 DA68
Gloucester Ms. E10 65 EA59
Gloucester Rd.
Gloucester Ms. W2 76 DC72
Gloucester Ms. W. W2 76 DC72
Cleveland Ter.
Gloucester Par., Sid. 110 EU85
Gloucester Pl. NW1 4 D4
Gloucester Pl. NW1 76 DF70
Gloucester Pl. W1 4 E6
Gloucester Pl. W1 76 DF71
Gloucester Pl. Ms. W1 4 E7
Gloucester Rd. E10 65 EA59
Gloucester Rd. E11 66 EH57
Gloucester Rd. E12 67 EM62
Gloucester Rd. E17 51 DX54
Gloucester Rd. N17 64 DR55
Gloucester Rd. N18 50 DT50
Gloucester Rd. SW7 90 DC76
Gloucester Rd. W3 88 CQ75
Gloucester Rd. W5 87 CJ75
Gloucester Rd., Barn. 34 DB43
Gloucester Rd., Belv. 96 EZ78
Gloucester Rd., Croy. 120 DR102
Gloucester Rd., Dart. 111 FH87
Gloucester Rd., Enf. 36 DQ38
Gloucester Rd., Felt. 100 BW88
Gloucester Rd., Hmptn. 100 CB94
Gloucester Rd., Har. 58 CB57
Gloucester Rd., Houns. 86 BY84
Gloucester Rd., Kings.T. 116 CN96
Gloucester Rd., Rich. 88 CN80
Gloucester Rd., Rom. 69 FE58
Gloucester Rd., Tedd. 101 CE92
Gloucester Rd., Twick. 100 CC88
Gloucester Sq. E2 78 DU67
Whiston Rd.
Gloucester Sq. W2 4 A9
Gloucester Sq. W2 76 DD72
Gloucester St. SW1 91 DJ78
Gloucester Ter. W2 76 DB72
Gloucester Wk. W8 90 DA75
Gloucester Way EC1 6 E3
Gloucester Way EC1 77 DN69
Glover Clo. SE2 96 EW77
Glover Clo., Wal.Cr. 22 DT27
Allwood Rd.
Glover Dr. N18 50 DW51
Glover Rd., Pnr. 58 BX58
Glovers Gro., Ruis. 57 BP59
Gloxinia Wk., Hmptn. 100 CA93
The Ave.
Glycena Rd. SW11 90 DF83
Glyn Ave., Barn. 34 DD42
Glyn Clo. SE25 120 DS96
Glyn Clo., Epsom 131 CU109
Glyn Ct. SW16 105 DN90
Glyn Davies Clo., Sev. 153 FE120
Glyn Dr., Sid. 110 EV91
Glyn Rd. E5 65 DX64
Glyn Rd., Enf. 36 DW42
Glyn Rd., Wor.Pk. 117 CX103
Glyn St. SE11 91 DM78
Kennington La.
Glynde Ms. SW3 8 C7
Glynde Rd., Bexh. 96 EX83
Glynde St. SE4 107 DZ86
Glyndebourne Pk., Orp. 123 EP103
Glyndon Rd. SE18 95 EQ77
Glynfield Rd. NW10 74 CS66
Glynne Rd. N22 49 DN54
Glynwood Ct. SE23 106 DW90
Goat La., Enf. 36 DT38
Goat La., Surb. 115 CH103
Goat Rd., Mitch. 118 DF101
Goat St. SE1 11 P4
Goat Wf., Brent. 88 CL79
Goaters All. SW6 89 CZ80
Dawes Rd.
Goatsfield Rd., West. 150 EJ120
Goatswood La., Rom. 55 FH45
Gobions Ave., Rom. 55 FD52
Gobions Way, Pot.B. 20 DB28
Swanley Bar La.
Godalming Ave., Wall. 133 DL106
Godalming Rd. E14 79 EB71
Godbold Rd. E15 80 EE69
Goddard Clo., Shep. 112 BM97
Magdalene Rd.
Goddard Rd., Beck. 121 DX98
Goddards Way, Ilf. 67 ER60
Goddington Chase, Orp. 138 EV105
Goddington La., Orp. 124 EU104
Godfrey Ave., Nthlt. 72 BY67
Godfrey Ave., Twick. 101 CD87
Godfrey Hill SE18 94 EL77
Godfrey Rd. SE18 95 EM77
Godfrey St. E15 79 EC68
Godfrey St. SW3 8 C10
Godfrey St. SW3 90 DE78
Godfrey Way, Houns. 100 BZ87
Goding St. SE11 91 DL78
Godley Rd. SW18 104 DD88
Godley Rd., W.Byf. 126 BM114
Godliman St. EC4 7 H9
Godliman St. EC4 78 DQ72
Godman Rd. SE15 92 DV82
Godolphin Clo. N13 49 DP51
Godolphin Clo., Sutt. 131 CZ110
Godolphin Pl. W3 74 CR73
Vyner Rd.
Godolphin Rd. W12 75 CV74
Godolphin Rd., Wey. 127 BR107
Godric Cres., Croy. 135 ED110
Godson Rd., Croy. 119 DN104
Godson St. N1 77 DN68
White Lion St.
Godstone Rd., Cat. 148 DU124
Godstone Rd., Ken. 133 DN112
Godstone Rd., Pur. 133 DN112
Godstone Rd., Sutt. 132 DC105
Godstone Rd., Twick. 101 CG86
Godstone Rd., Whyt. 148 DT116
Godstow Rd. SE2 96 EV75
Godwin Clo. E4 37 EC38
Godwin Clo. N1 78 DQ68
Napier Gro.
Godwin Clo., Epsom 130 CQ107
Godwin Ct. NW1 77 DJ68
Crowndale Rd.
Godwin Rd. E7 66 EH63
Godwin Rd., Brom. 122 EJ97
Goffers Rd. SE3 94 EE82
Goffs Cres. (Cheshunt), Wal.Cr. 22 DQ29
Goffs La. (Cheshunt), Wal.Cr. 22 DR29
Goffs Oak Ave. (Cheshunt), Wal.Cr. 21 DP28
Goffs Rd., Ashf. 99 BR93
Goidel Clo., Wall. 133 DK105
Golborne Gdns. W10 75 CZ70
Golborne Rd.
Golborne Ms. W10 75 CY71
Portobello Rd.
Golborne Rd. W10 75 CY71
Gold Hill, Edg. 46 CR51
Gold La., Edg. 46 CR51
Golda Clo., Barn. 33 CX44
Goldbeaters Gro., Edg. 46 CS51
Goldcliff Clo., Mord. 118 DA101
Goldcrest Clo. E16 80 EK71
Sheerwater Rd.
Goldcrest Clo. SE28 82 EW73
Goldcrest Ms. W5 73 CK71
Montpelier Ave.
Goldcrest Way, Croy. 135 ED109
Goldcrest Way, Pur. 133 DK110
Goldcrest Way (Bushey), Wat. 44 CC46
Golden Ct., Rich. 101 CK85
George St.
Golden Cres., Hayes 71 BS74
Golden Cross Ms. W11 75 CZ72
Basing St.
Golden La. EC1 7 H5
Golden La. EC1 78 DQ70
Golden La. Est. EC1 7 H5
Golden Manor W7 73 CE73
Golden Plover Clo. E16 80 EH72
Maplin Rd.
Golden Sq. W1 5 L10
Golden Sq. W1 77 DJ73
Golden Yd. NW3 62 DC63
Heath St.
Golders Clo., Edg. 46 CP50
Golders Gdns. NW11 61 CY59
Golders Grn. Cres. NW11 61 CZ59
Golders Grn. Rd. NW11 61 CY58
Golders Manor Dr. NW11 61 CX58
Golders Pk. Clo. NW11 62 DA60
Golders Ri. NW4 61 CX57
Golders Way NW11 61 CZ59
Goldfinch Clo., Orp. 138 EU106
Goldfinch Rd. SE28 95 ER76
Goldfinch Rd., S.Croy. 135 DX110
Goldfinch Way, Borwd. 32 CN42
Siskin Clo.
Goldhawk Ms. W12 89 CV75
Devonport Rd.
Goldhawk Rd. W6 89 CT77
Goldhawk Rd. W12 89 CU76
Goldhaze Clo., Wdf.Grn. 52 EK52
Goldhurst Ter. NW6 76 DB66
Golding Clo., Chess. 129 CJ107
Coppard Gdns.
Golding Rd., Sev. 155 FJ122
Golding St. E1 78 DU72
Goldingham Ave., Loug. 39 EQ40
Goldings Hill, Loug. 39 EM37
Goldings Ri., Loug. 39 EN39
Goldings Rd., Loug. 39 EN39
Goldington Cres. NW1 77 DK68
Goldington Cres. Gdns. NW1 77 DK68
Goldington St. NW1 77 DK68
Goldman Clo. E2 78 DU70
Goldney Rd. W9 76 DA70
Goldrings Rd., Lthd. 128 CB113
Goldsborough Cres. E4 51 EB47
Goldsborough Rd. SW8 91 DK81
Goldsdown Clo., Enf. 37 DY40
Goldsdown Rd., Enf. 37 DX40
Goldsel Rd., Swan. 125 FD99
Goldsel Rd. Ind. Est., Swan. 125 FE98
Goldsmid St. SE18 95 ES78
Sladedale Rd.
Goldsmith Ave. E12 80 EL65
Goldsmith Ave. NW9 60 CS57
Goldsmith Ave. W3 74 CR73
Goldsmith Ave., Rom. 68 FA59
Goldsmith Clo. W3 74 CS74
East Acton La.
Goldsmith Clo., Har. 58 CB60
Goldsmith La. NW9 60 CP56
Goldsmith Rd. E10 65 EA60
Goldsmith Rd. E17 51 DX54
Goldsmith Rd. N11 48 DF50
Goldsmith Rd. SE15 92 DU81
Goldsmith Rd. W3 74 CR74
Goldsmith St. EC2 7 J8
Goldsmith's Row E2 78 DU68
Goldsmith's Sq. E2 78 DU68
Goldsworthy Gdns. SE16 92 DW77
Goldwell Rd., Th.Hth. 119 DM98
Goldwin Clo. SE14 92 DW81
Goldwing Clo. E16 80 EG72
Golf Clo., Stan. 45 CJ52
Golf Clo. (Bushey), Wat. 30 BX41
Golf Club Dr., Kings.T. 102 CR94
Golf Club Rd., Hat. 20 DA26
Golf Club Rd., Wey. 127 BP109
Golf Ride, Enf. 35 DN35
Golf Rd. W5 74 CM72
Boileau Rd.
Golf Rd., Brom. 123 EN97
Golf Rd., Ken. 148 DR118
Golf Side, Sutt. 131 CY111
Golf Side, Twick. 101 CD90
Golfe Rd., Ilf. 67 ER62
Golfside Clo. N20 48 DE48
Golfside Clo., N.Mal. 116 CS96
Goliath Clo., Wall. 133 DL108
Avro Way
Gollogly Ter. SE7 94 EJ78

Gomer Gdns., Tedd. 101 CG93
Gomer Pl., Tedd. 101 CG93
Gomm Rd. SE16 92 DW76
Gomshall Ave., Wall. 133 DL106
Gomshall Gdns., Ken. 148 DS115
Gomshall Rd., Sutt. 131 CW110
Gondar Gdns. NW6 61 CZ64
Gonson Pl. SE8 93 EA79
Gonson St. SE8 93 EB79
Gonston Clo. SW19 103 CY89
Boddicott Clo.
Gonville Ave., Rick. 29 BP44
Gonville Cres., Nthlt. 72 CB65
Gonville Rd., Th.Hth. 119 DM99
Gonville St. SW6 89 CY83
Putney Bri. App.
Goodall Rd. E11 65 EC62
Gooden Ct., Har. 59 CE62
Goodenough Clo., Couls. 147 DN120
Goodenough Rd. SW19 103 CZ94
Goodenough Way, Couls. 147 DM120
Goodge Pl. W1 5 L7
Goodge St. W1 5 L7
Goodge St. W1 77 DJ71
Goodhall St. NW10 74 CS69
Goodhart Pl. E14 79 DY73
Goodhart Way, W.Wick. 122 EE101
Goodhew Rd., Croy. 120 DU100
Gooding Clo., N.Mal. 116 CQ98
Goodinge Clo. N7 77 DL65
Goodman Cres. SW2 105 DK89
Goodman Rd. E10 65 EC59
Goodmans Ct., Wem. 59 CK63
Goodman's Flds. E1 78 DU72
Goodman's Stile
Goodman's Stile E1 78 DU72
Goodmans Yd. E1 7 P10
Goodmans Yd. E1 78 DT73
Goodmayes Ave., Ilf. 68 EU60
Goodmayes La., Ilf. 68 EU61
Goodmayes Rd., Ilf. 68 EU60
Goodmead Rd., Orp. 124 EU101
Goodrich Clo., Wat. 29 BU35
Goodrich Rd. SE22 106 DT86
Goods Way NW1 77 DL68
Goodson Rd. NW10 74 CS66
Goodway Gdns. E14 79 ED72
Goodwin Clo. SE16 92 DU76
Goodwin Clo., Mitch. 118 DD97
Goodwin Ct., Wal.Cr. 23 DY28
Goodwin Dr., Sid. 110 EX90
Goodwin Gdns., Croy. 133 DP107
Goodwin Rd. N9 50 DW46
Goodwin Rd. W12 89 CU75
Goodwin Rd., Croy. 133 DP106
Goodwin St. N4 63 DN61
Fonthill Rd.
Goodwins Ct. WC2 5 P10
Goodwood Ave., Enf. 36 DW37
Goodwood Ave., Wat. 29 BS35
Goodwood Clo., Mord. 118 DA98
Goodwood Clo., Stan. 45 CJ50
Goodwood Dr., Nthlt. 72 CA65
Goodwood Path, Borwd. 32 CN41
Stratfield Rd.
Goodwood Rd. SE14 93 DY80
Goodwyn Ave. NW7 46 CS50
Goodwyns Vale N10 48 DG53
Goodyers Ave., Rad. 17 CF33
Goodyers Gdns. NW4 61 CX57
Goosander Way SE28 95 ER76
Goose Grn., Cob. 141 BU119
Goose Grn. Clo., Orp. 124 EU96
Goose Sq. E6 81 EM72
Harper Rd.
Gooseacre La., Har. 59 CK57
Gooseley La. E6 81 EN69
Goossens Clo., Sutt. 132 DC106
Turnpike La.
Gophir La. EC4 7 K10
Gopsall St. N1 78 DR67
Goral Mead, Rick. 42 BK46
Gordon Ave. E4 52 EE51
Gordon Ave. SW14 88 CS84
Gordon Ave., Horn. 69 FF61
Gordon Ave., S.Croy. 134 DQ110
Gordon Ave., Stan. 45 CF52
Gordon Ave., Twick. 101 CG85
Gordon Clo. E17 65 EA58
Gordon Clo. N19 63 DJ60
Highgate Hill
Gordon Clo., Stai. 98 BH93
Gordon Ct. W12 75 CV72
Gordon Cres., Croy. 120 DS102
Gordon Cres., Hayes 85 BU76
Gordon Dr., Shep. 113 BR100
Gordon Gdns., Edg. 46 CP54
Gordon Gro. SE5 91 DP82
Gordon Hill, Enf. 36 DQ39
Gordon Ho. Rd. NW5 62 DG63
Gordon Pl. W8 90 DA75
Gordon Rd. E4 52 EE45
Gordon Rd. E11 66 EG58
Gordon Rd. E15 65 EC63
Gordon Rd. E18 52 EH53
Gordon Rd. N3 47 CZ52
Gordon Rd. N9 50 DV47
Gordon Rd. N11 49 DK52
Gordon Rd. SE15 92 DV82
Gordon Rd. W4 88 CP79
Gordon Rd. W5 73 CJ73
Gordon Rd. W13 73 CH73
Gordon Rd., Ashf. 98 BL90
Gordon Rd., Bark. 81 ES67
Gordon Rd., Beck. 121 DZ97
Gordon Rd., Belv. 97 FC77
Gordon Rd., Cars. 132 DF107
Gordon Rd., Cat. 148 DR121
Gordon Rd., Enf. 36 DR39
Gordon Rd., Esher 129 CE108
Gordon Rd., Har. 59 CE55
Gordon Rd., Houns. 86 CC84
Gordon Rd., Ilf. 67 ER62
Gordon Rd., Kings.T. 116 CM95
Gordon Rd., Rich. 88 CM82
Gordon Rd., Rom. 68 EZ58
Gordon Rd., Sev. 155 FH125
Gordon Rd., Shep. 113 BR100
Gordon Rd., Sid. 109 ES85
Gordon Rd., Sthl. 86 BY77
Gordon Rd., Surb. 116 CM101
Gordon Rd., Wal.Abb. 23 EA34
Gordon Rd., West Dr. 70 BL73
Gordon Sq. WC1 5 M4
Gordon Sq. WC1 77 DK70
Gordon St. E13 80 EG69
Grange Rd.
Gordon St. WC1 5 M4
Gordon St. WC1 77 DK70
Gordon Way, Barn. 33 CZ42
Gordon Way, Brom. 122 EG95
Gordonbrock Rd. SE4 107 EA85
Gordondale Rd. SW19 104 DA89
Gore Ct. NW9 60 CN57
Gore Rd. E9 78 DW67
Gore Rd. SW20 117 CW96
Gore St. SW7 90 DC76
Gorefield Pl. NW6 76 DA68
Goresbrook Rd., Dag. 82 EV67
Goresbrook Village, Dag. 82 EV67
Goresbrook Rd.
Gorham Pl. W11 75 CY73
Mary Pl.
Goring Clo., Rom. 55 FC53
Goring Gdns., Dag. 68 EW63
Goring Rd. N11 49 DL51
Goring Rd., Dag. 83 FD65
Goring St. EC3 7 N8
Goring St. EC3 78 DS72
Goring Way, Grnf. 72 CC68
Gorle Clo., Wat. 15 BU34
Gorleston Rd. N15 64 DR57
Gorleston St. W14 89 CY77
Gorman Rd. SE18 95 EM77
Gorringe Pk. Ave., Mitch. 104 DF94
Gorse Clo. E16 80 EG72
Gorse Clo., Tad. 145 CV120
Gorse Ri. SW17 104 DG92
Gorse Rd., Croy. 121 EA104
Gorse Rd., Orp. 124 EZ102
Gorse Wk., West Dr. 70 BL72
Gorselands Clo., W.Byf. 126 BJ111
Gorseway, Rom. 69 FD61
Gorst Rd. NW10 74 CQ70
Gorst Rd. SW11 104 DF86
Gorsuch Pl. E2 7 P2
Gorsuch St. E2 7 P2
Gorsuch St. E2 78 DT69
Gosberton Rd. SW12 104 DF88
Gosbury Hill, Chess. 130 CL105
Gosfield Rd., Dag. 68 FA61
Gosfield Rd., Epsom 130 CR112
Gosfield St. W1 5 K6
Gosfield St. W1 77 DJ71
Gosford Gdns., Ilf. 67 EM57
Gosforth La., Wat. 43 BU48
Gosforth Path, Wat. 43 BU48
Gosforth La.
Goshawk Gdns., Hayes 71 BS69
Goslett Yd. WC2 5 N9
Gosling Clo., Grnf. 72 CA69
Gosling Way SW9 91 DN81
Gospatrick Rd. N17 50 DQ52
Gospel Oak Est. NW5 62 DF64
Gosport Rd. E17 65 DZ57
Gosport Wk. N17 64 DV57
Yarmouth Cres.
Gosport Way SE15 92 DT80
Pentridge St.
Gossage Rd. SE18 95 ER78
Ancona Rd.
Gossage Rd., Uxb. 70 BM66
Gossamers, The, Wat. 30 BY35
Gosset St. E2 78 DT69
Gosshill Rd., Chis. 123 EN96
Gossington Clo., Chis. 109 EP91
Beechwood Ri.
Gosterwood St. SE8 93 DY79
Gostling Rd., Twick. 100 CA88
Goston Gdns., Th.Hth. 119 DN97
Goswell Rd. EC1 6 F1
Goswell Rd. EC1 77 DP68
Gothic Ct., Hayes 85 BR79
Sipson La.
Gothic Rd., Twick. 101 CD89
Gottfried Ms. NW5 63 DJ63
Fortess Rd.
Goudhurst Rd., Brom. 108 EE92
Gough Rd. E15 66 EF63
Gough Rd., Enf. 36 DV40
Gough Sq. EC4 6 E8
Gough St. WC1 6 C4
Gough St. WC1 77 DM70
Gough Wk. E14 79 EA72
Saracen St.
Gould Ct. SE19 106 DS92
Gould Rd., Felt. 99 BS87
Gould Rd., Twick. 101 CE88
Gould Ter. E8 64 DV64
Kenmure Rd.
Goulds Grn., Uxb. 71 BP72
Goulston St. E1 7 P8
Goulston St. E1 78 DT72
Goulton Rd. E5 64 DV63
Gourley Pl. N15 64 DS57
Gourley St.
Gourley St. N15 64 DS57
Gourock Rd. SE9 109 EN85
Govan St. E2 78 DU67
Whiston Rd.
Government Row, Enf. 37 EA38
Govett Ave., Shep. 113 BQ99
Govier Clo. E15 80 EE66
Gowan Ave. SW6 89 CY81
Gowan Rd. NW10 75 CV65
Gowar Fld., Pot.B. 19 CU32
Gower Clo. SW4 105 DJ86
Gower Ct. WC1 5 M4
Gower Ms. WC1 5 N7
Gower Ms. WC1 77 DK71
Gower Pl. WC1 5 L4
Gower Pl. WC1 77 DJ70
Gower Rd. E7 80 EG65
Gower Rd., Islw. 87 CF79
Gower Rd., Wey. 127 BR107
Gower St. WC1 5 M5
Gower St. WC1 77 DJ70
Gower's Wk. E1 78 DU72
Gowland Pl., Beck. 121 DZ96
Gowlett Rd. SE15 92 DU83
Gowrie Rd. SW11 90 DG83
Graburn Way, E.Mol. 115 CD97
Grace Ave., Bexh. 96 EZ82
Grace Clo. SE9 108 EK90
Grace Clo., Borwd. 32 CR39
Grace Clo., Edg. 46 CQ52
Pavilion Way
Grace Clo., Ilf. 53 ET51
Grace Jones Clo. E8 78 DU65
Parkholme Rd.
Grace Path SE26 106 DW91
Silverdale
Grace Rd., Croy. 120 DQ100
Grace St. E3 79 EB69
Gracechurch St. EC3 7 L10
Gracechurch St. EC3 78 DR73
Gracedale Rd. SW16 105 DH92
Gracefield Gdns. SW16 105 DL90
Grace's All. E1 78 DU73
Ensign St.
Graces Ms. SE5 92 DR82
Graces Rd. SE5 92 DS82
Gracious La., Sev. 154 FG130
Gracious La. End, Sev. 154 FF130
Gradient, The SE26 106 DU91
Graeme Rd., Enf. 36 DR40
Graemesdyke Ave. SW14 88 CP83
Grafton Clo. W13 73 CG72
Grafton Clo., Houns. 100 BY88
Grafton Clo., Wor.Pk. 116 CS104
Grafton Ct., Felt. 99 BR88
Loxwood Clo.
Grafton Cres. NW1 77 DH65
Grafton Gdns. N4 64 DQ58
Grafton Gdns., Dag. 68 EY61
Grafton Ho. E3 79 EA69
Wellington Way
Grafton Ms. W1 5 K5
Grafton Pk. Rd., Wor.Pk. 116 CS103
Grafton Pl. NW1 5 M3
Grafton Pl. NW1 77 DK69
Grafton Rd. NW5 62 DG64
Grafton Rd. W3 74 CQ73
Grafton Rd., Croy. 119 DN102
Grafton Rd., Dag. 68 EY60
Grafton Rd., Enf. 35 DM41
Grafton Rd., Har. 58 CC57
Grafton Rd., N.Mal. 116 CS97
Grafton Rd., Wor.Pk. 130 CR105
Grafton Sq. SW4 91 DJ83
Grafton St. W1 9 J1
Grafton St. W1 77 DH73
Grafton Ter. NW5 62 DF64
Grafton Way W1 5 K5
Grafton Way W1 77 DJ70
Grafton Way WC1 5 L5
Grafton Way WC1 77 DJ70
Grafton Way, W.Mol. 114 BZ98
Grafton Yd. NW5 77 DH65
Prince of Wales Rd.
Graftons, The NW2 62 DA62
Hermitage La.
Graham Ave. W13 87 CH75
Graham Ave., Mitch. 118 DG95
Graham Clo., Croy. 121 EA103
Graham Gdns., Surb. 116 CL102
Graham Rd. E8 78 DU65
Graham Rd. E13 80 EG69
Graham Rd. N15 63 DP55
Graham Rd. NW4 61 CV58
Graham Rd. SW19 103 CZ94
Graham Rd. W4 88 CR76
Graham Rd., Bexh. 96 FA84
Graham Rd., Hmptn. 100 CA91
Graham Rd., Har. 59 CE55
Graham Rd., Mitch. 118 DG95
Graham Rd., Pur. 133 DN113
Graham St. N1 6 G1
Graham St. N1 77 DP68
Graham Ter. SW1 8 F9
Graham Ter. SW1 90 DG77
Grahame Pk. Est. NW9 47 CT52
Grahame Pk. Way NW7 47 CT52
Grahame Pk. Way NW9 47 CT54
Grainger Clo., Nthlt. 58 CC64
Lancaster Rd.
Grainger Rd. N22 50 DQ53
Grainger Rd., Islw. 87 CF82
Grainge's Yd., Uxb. 70 BJ66
Cross St.
Gramer Clo. E11 65 ED61
Grampian Clo., Hayes 85 BR80
Grampian Clo., Orp. 123 ET100
Cotswold Ri.
Grampian Gdns. NW2 61 CY60
Granard Ave. SW15 103 CV85
Granard Rd. SW12 104 DF87
Granaries, The, Wal.Abb. 24 EE33
Granary Clo. N9 50 DW45
Turin Rd.
Granary Rd. E1 78 DV70
Granary St. NW1 77 DK67
Granby Bldgs. SE11 10 B9
Granby Pk. Rd. 22 DT28
(Cheshunt), Wal.Cr.
Granby Rd. SE9 95 EM82
Granby St. E2 78 DT70
Granby Ter. NW1 5 K1
Granby Ter. NW1 77 DJ68
Grand Ave. EC1 6 G6
Grand Ave. N10 62 DG56
Grand Ave., Surb. 116 CP99
Grand Ave., Wem. 60 CN64
Grand Ave. E., Wem. 74 CN65
Victoria Ave.
Grand Depot Rd. SE18 95 EN78
Grand Dr. SW20 117 CW96
Grand Dr., Sthl. 86 CC75
Grand Par. Ms. SW15 103 CY85
Upper Richmond Rd.
Grand Stand Rd., Epsom 145 CT117
Grand Union Cres. E8 78 DU67
Grand Union Ind. Est. 74 CP68
NW10
Grand Union Wk. NW1 77 DH66
Grand Vw. Ave., West. 150 EJ117
Grand Wk. E1 79 DY70
Solebay St.
Granden Rd. SW16 119 DL96
Grandfield Ave., Wat. 29 BT39
Grandis Cotts., Wok. 140 BH122
Grandison Rd. SW11 104 DF85
Grandison Rd., Wor.Pk. 117 CW103
Granfield St. SW11 90 DD81
Grange, The N2 48 DD54
Central Ave.
Grange, The N20 48 DC46
Grange, The SE1 11 P6
Grange, The SE1 92 DT76
Grange, The SW19 103 CX93
Grange, The, Croy. 121 DZ103
Grange, The, Walt. 113 BV103
Grange, The, Wem. 74 CN66
Grange, The, Wor.Pk. 116 CR104
Grange Ave. N12 48 DC50
Grange Ave. N20 47 CY45
Grange Ave. SE25 120 DS96
Grange Ave., Barn. 48 DE46
Grange Ave., Stan. 45 CH54
Grange Ave., Twick. 101 CE89
Grange Ave., Wdf.Grn. 52 EG51
Grange Clo., Edg. 46 CQ50
Grange Clo., Hayes 71 BS71
Grange Clo., Houns. 86 BZ79
Grange Clo., Lthd. 143 CK120
Grange Clo., Sid. 110 EU90
Grange Clo., W.Mol. 114 CB98
Grange Clo., Wdf.Grn. 52 EG52
Grange Ct. E8 78 DT66
Queensbridge Rd.
Grange Ct. WC2 6 C9
Grange Ct., Chig. 53 EQ47
Grange Ct., Loug. 38 EK43
Grange Ct., Nthlt. 72 BW68
Grange Ct., Stai. 98 BG92
Grange Ct., Wal.Abb. 23 EC34
Grange Ct., Walt. 113 BU103
Grange Cres. SE28 82 EW72
Grange Cres., Chig. 53 ER50
Grange Dr., Chis. 108 EL93
Grange Dr., Orp. 138 EW109
Rushmore Hill
Grange Fm. Clo., Har. 58 CC61
Grange Gdns. N14 49 DK46
Grange Gdns. NW3 62 DB62
Grange Gdns. SE25 120 DS96
Grange Gdns., Bans. 132 DB113
Grange Gdns., Pnr. 58 BY55
Grange Gro. N1 78 DQ65
Grange Hill SE25 120 DS96
Grange Hill, Edg. 46 CQ50
Grange Ho., Bark. 81 ER67
St. Margarets
Grange La. SE21 106 DT89
Grange La., Wat. 31 CD39
Grange Mans., Epsom 131 CT108
Grange Meadow, Bans. 132 DB113
Grange Ms. SE10 93 ED80
Crooms Hill
Grange Par., Hayes 71 BT71
Grange Pk. W5 74 CL74
Grange Pk. Ave. N21 36 DQ44
Grange Pk. Pl. SW20 103 CV94
Grange Pk. Rd. E10 65 EB60
Grange Pk. Rd., Th.Hth. 120 DR98
Grange Pl. NW6 76 DA66
Grange Pl., Stai. 112 BJ96
Grange Rd. E10 65 EA60
Grange Rd. E13 80 EF69
Grange Rd. E17 65 DY57
Grange Rd. N6 62 DG58
Grange Rd. N17 50 DU51
Grange Rd. N18 50 DU51
Grange Rd. NW10 75 CV65
Grange Rd. SE1 11 N7
Grange Rd. SE1 92 DS76
Grange Rd. SE19 120 DR96
Grange Rd. SE25 120 DR97
Grange Rd. SW13 89 CU81
Grange Rd. W4 88 CP78
Grange Rd. W5 73 CK74
Grange Rd., Add. 126 BG110
Grange Rd., Borwd. 32 CM43
Grange Rd., Chess. 116 CL104
Grange Rd., Edg. 46 CR51
Grange Rd., Har. 59 CG58
Grange Rd. 59 CD61
(South Harrow), Har.
Grange Rd., Hayes 71 BS72
Grange Rd., Ilf. 67 EP63
Grange Rd., Kings.T. 116 CL97
Grange Rd., Lthd. 143 CK120
Grange Rd., Orp. 123 EQ103
Grange Rd., Rom. 55 FH52
Grange Rd., Sev. 154 FG127
Grange Rd., S.Croy. 134 DQ110
Grange Rd., Sthl. 86 BY75
Grange Rd., Sutt. 132 DA108
Grange Rd., Th.Hth. 120 DR98
Grange Rd., Walt. 128 BY105
Grange Rd. (Bushey), 30 BY43
Wat.
Grange Rd., W.Mol. 114 CB98
Grange St. N1 78 DR68
Bridport Pl.
Grange Vale, Sutt. 132 DB108
Grange Wk. SE1 11 N6
Grange Wk. SE1 92 DS76
Grange Way N12 48 DB49
Grange Way, Erith 97 FH80
Grange Yd. SE1 11 P7
Grange Yd. SE1 92 DT76
Grangecliffe Gdns. SE25 120 DS96
Grangecourt Rd. N16 64 DS60
Grangedale Clo., Nthwd. 43 BS53
Grangehill Pl. SE9 95 EM83
Westmount Rd.
Grangehill Rd. SE9 95 EM84
Grangemill Rd. SE6 107 EA90
Grangemill Way SE6 107 EA89
Grangemount, Lthd. 143 CK120
Granger Way, Rom. 69 FG58
Grangeview Rd. N20 48 DC46
Grangeway NW6 76 DA66
Messina Ave.
Grangeway, Wdf.Grn. 52 EJ49
Grangeway, The N21 35 DP44
Grangeway Gdns., Ilf. 66 EL57
Grangewood, Bex. 110 EZ88
Hurst Rd.
Grangewood, Pot.B. 20 DB30
Grangewood Clo., Pnr. 57 BU57
Grangewood Dr., Sun. 99 BT94
Forest Dr.
Grangewood La., Beck. 107 DZ93
Grangewood St. E6 80 EK67
Granham Gdns. N9 50 DT47
Granite St. SE18 95 ET78
Granleigh Rd. E11 66 EE61
Gransden Ave. E8 78 DV66
Gransden Rd. W12 89 CT75
Wendell Rd.
Grant Clo. N14 49 DJ45
Grant Clo., Shep. 113 BP100
Grant Pl., Croy. 120 DT102
Grant Rd. SW11 90 DD84
Grant Rd., Croy. 120 DT102
Grant Rd., Har. 59 CE55
Grant St. E13 80 EG69
Grant St. N1 77 DN68
Chapel Mkt.
Grant Way, Islw. 87 CG80
Grantbridge St. N1 77 DP68
Grantchester Clo., Har. 59 CF62
Grantham Clo., Edg. 46 CL48
Grantham Gdns., Rom. 68 EZ58
Grantham Grn., Borwd. 32 CQ43
Grantham Pl. W1 9 H3
Grantham Rd. E12 67 EN63
Grantham Rd. SW9 91 DL83
Grantham Rd. W4 88 CS80
Grantley Rd., Houns. 86 BW82
Grantley St. E1 79 DX69
Grantock Rd. E17 51 ED53
Granton Rd. SW16 119 DJ95
Granton Rd., Ilf. 68 EU60
Granton Rd., Sid. 110 EW93
Grants Clo. NW7 47 CW52
Grantully Rd. W9 76 DB69
Granville Ave. N9 50 DW48
Granville Ave., Felt. 99 BU89
Granville Ave., Houns. 100 CA85
Granville Clo., Croy. 120 DS103
Granville Clo., W.Byf. 126 BM113
Church Rd.
Granville Clo., Wey. 127 BQ107
Granville Ct. N1 78 DR67
Granville Gdns. SW16 119 DM95
Granville Gdns. W5 74 CM74
Granville Gro. SE13 93 EC83
Granville Ms., Sid. 110 EU91
Granville Pk. SE13 93 EC83
Granville Pl. 48 DC52
(North Finchley) N12
High Rd.
Granville Pl. W1 4 F9
Granville Pl. W1 76 DG72
Granville Pl., Pnr. 44 BX54
Elm Pk. Rd.
Granville Rd. E17 65 EB58
Granville Rd. E18 52 EH54
Granville Rd. N4 63 DM58
Granville Rd. N12 48 DB51
Granville Rd. N13 49 DM51
Russell Rd.

Granville Rd. N22 49 DP53
Granville Rd. NW2 61 CZ61
Granville Rd. NW6 76 DA68
Granville Rd. SW18 103 CZ87
Granville Rd. SW19 104 DA94
Russell Rd.
Granville Rd., Barn. 33 CW42
Granville Rd., Epp. 26 EV29
Granville Rd., Hayes 85 BT77
Granville Rd., Ilf. 67 EP60
Granville Rd., Sev. 154 FG124
Granville Rd., Sid. 110 EU91
Granville Rd., Uxb. 71 BP65
Granville Rd., Wat. 30 BW42
Granville Rd., Well. 96 EW83
Granville Rd., Wey. 127 BQ108
Granville Sq. SE15 92 DS80
Blakes Rd.
Granville Sq. WC1 6 C3
Granville Sq. WC1 77 DM69
Granville St. WC1 6 C3
Granville St. WC1 77 DM69
Grape St. WC2 5 P8
Graphite Sq. SE11 10 B10
Grasdene Rd. SE18 96 EU80
Grasmere Ave. SW15 102 CR91
Grasmere Ave. SW19 118 DA97
Grasmere Ave. W3 74 CR73
Grasmere Ave., Houns. 100 CB86
Grasmere Ave., Orp. 123 EP104
Grasmere Ave., Ruis. 57 BQ59
Grasmere Ave., Wem. 59 CJ59
Grasmere Clo., Felt. 99 BT88
Grasmere Clo., Loug. 39 EM40
Grasmere Clo., Wat. 15 BV32
Grasmere Ct. N22 49 DM51
Palmerston Rd.
Grasmere Gdns., Har. 45 CG54
Grasmere Gdns., Ilf. 67 EM57
Grasmere Gdns., Orp. 123 EP104
Grasmere Rd. E13 80 EG68
Grasmere Rd. N10 49 DH53
Grasmere Rd. N17 50 DU51
Grasmere Rd. SE25 120 DV100
Grasmere Rd. SW16 105 DM92
Grasmere Rd., Bexh. 97 FC81
Grasmere Rd., Brom. 122 EF95
Grasmere Rd., Orp. 123 EP104
Grasmere Rd., Pur. 133 DP111
Grasmere Way, W.Byf. 126 BM112
Grass Pk. N3 47 CZ53
Grassfield Clo., Couls. 147 DJ119
Grassington Clo., St.Alb. 16 CA30
Grassington Rd., Sid. 110 EU91
Grassmount SE23 106 DV89
Grassmount, Pur. 133 DJ110
Grassway, Wall. 133 DJ105
Grassy La., Sev. 155 FH126
Grasvenor Ave., Barn. 34 DA44
Grately Way SE15 92 DT80
Daniel Gdns.
Gratton Rd. W14 89 CY76
Gratton Ter. NW2 61 CX62
Gravel Clo., Chig. 54 EU47
Gravel Hill N3 47 CZ54
Gravel Hill, Bexh. 111 FB85
Gravel Hill, Croy. 135 DX107
Gravel Hill, Lthd. 143 CH121
North St.
Gravel Hill, Loug. 38 EG38
Gravel Hill, Uxb. 56 BK64
Gravel Hill Clo., Bexh. 111 FB85
Gravel La. E1 7 P8
Gravel La., Chig. 39 ET42
Gravel Pit La. SE9 109 EQ85
Gravel Pit Way, Orp. 124 EU103
Gravel Rd., Brom. 122 EL104
Gravel Rd., Twick. 101 CE88
Graveley Ave., Borwd. 32 CQ42
Gravelly Ride SW19 103 CT91
Gravelwood Clo., Chis. 109 EQ90
Graveney Gro. SE20 106 DW94
Graveney Rd. SW17 104 DE91
Gravesend Rd. W12 75 CU73
Gray Ave., Dag. 68 EZ60
Gray Gdns., Rain. 69 FG64
Gray St. SE1 10 E5
Grayham Cres., N.Mal. 116 CR98
Grayham Rd., N.Mal. 116 CR98
Grayland Clo., Brom. 122 EK95
Graylands, Epp. 39 ER37
Grayling Clo. E16 80 EE70
Cranberry La.
Grayling Rd. N16 64 DR61
Grayling Sq. E2 78 DU69
Nelson Gdns.
Graylings, The, Abb.L. 15 BR33
Grays Fm. Rd., Orp. 124 EV95
Gray's Inn WC1 6 C6
Gray's Inn WC1 77 DM71
Gray's Inn Pl. WC1 6 C7
Gray's Inn Rd. WC1 6 A2
Gray's Inn Rd. WC1 77 DL69
Gray's Inn Sq. WC1 6 D6
Grays La., Ashf. 99 BP91
Gray's La., Ash. 144 CM119
Gray's La., Epsom 144 CP121
Shepherds' Wk.
Grays Rd., Uxb. 70 BL67
Grays Rd., West. 151 EP121
Gray's Yd. W1 4 G8
Grayscroft Rd. SW16 105 DK94
Grayshott Rd. SW11 90 DG82
Grayswood Gdns. SW20 117 CV96
Farnham Gdns.
Graywood Ct. N12 48 DC52
Grazebrook Rd. N16 64 DR61
Grazeley Clo., Bexh. 111 FC85
Grazeley Ct. SE19 106 DS91
Gipsy Hill
Great Acre Ct. SW4 91 DK84
St. Alphonsus Rd.
Great Bell All. EC2 7 K8
Great Benty, West Dr. 84 BL77
Great Brownings SE21 106 DT91
Great Bushey Dr. N20 48 DB46
Great Cambridge Rd. N9 50 DR48
Great Cambridge Rd. N17 50 DR52
Great Cambridge Rd. N18 50 DR49
Great Cambridge Rd., Brox. 23 DY26
Great Cambridge Rd., Enf. 36 DU41
Great Cambridge Rd. (Cheshunt), Wal.Cr. 22 DW32
Great Castle St. W1 5 J8
Great Castle St. W1 77 DH72
Great Cen. Ave., Ruis. 58 BW64
Great Cen. St. NW1 4 D6
Great Cen. St. NW1 76 DF71
Great Cen. Way NW10 60 CQ63
Great Cen. Way, Wem. 60 CQ63
Great Chapel St. W1 5 M8
Great Chapel St. W1 77 DK72
Great Chertsey Rd. W4 88 CQ82
Great Chertsey Rd., Felt. 100 CA90
Great Ch. La. W6 89 CX78
Great College St. SW1 9 P6
Great College St. SW1 91 DL76
Great Cross Ave. SE10 94 EE80
Great Cullings, Rom. 69 FE61
Great Cumberland Ms. W1 4 D9
Great Cumberland Pl. W1 4 E8
Great Cumberland Pl. W1 76 DF72
Great Dover St. SE1 11 K5
Great Dover St. SE1 92 DR75
Great Eastern Rd. E15 79 ED66
Great Eastern St. EC2 7 M3
Great Eastern St. EC2 78 DS69
Great Eastern Wk. EC2 7 M7
Great Ellshams, Bans. 146 DA116
Great Elms Rd., Brom. 122 EJ98
Great Fld. NW9 46 CS53
Great Fleete Way, Bark. 82 EW68
Great Galley Clo., Bark. 82 EV69
Great Gdns. Rd., Horn. 69 FH58
Great George St. SW1 9 N5
Great George St. SW1 91 DK75
Great Gregories La., Epp. 25 ES33
Great Gro. (Bushey), Wat. 30 CB42
Great Guildford St. SE1 11 H2
Great Guildford St. SE1 78 DQ74
Great Harry Dr. SE9 109 EN90
Great James St. WC1 6 B6
Great James St. WC1 77 DM71
Great Julians, Rick. 28 BN42
Grove Cres.
Great Marlborough St. W1 5 K9
Great Marlborough St. W1 77 DJ72
Great Maze Pond SE1 11 L4
Great Maze Pond SE1 78 DR74
Great New St. EC4 6 E8
Great Newport St. WC2 5 N10
Great N. Rd. N2 62 DE56
Great N. Rd. N6 62 DF57
Great N. Rd., Barn. 33 CZ40
Great N. Rd. (New Barnet), Barn. 34 DB43
Great N. Rd., Hat. 20 DB27
Great N. Rd., Pot.B. 20 DB27
Great N. Way NW4 47 CV53
Great Oaks, Chig. 53 EQ49
Great Ormond St. WC1 6 A6
Great Ormond St. WC1 77 DL71
Great Owl Rd., Chig. 53 EN48
Great Pk., Kings L. 14 BM30
Great Percy St. WC1 6 C2
Great Percy St. WC1 77 DM69
Great Peter St. SW1 9 M7
Great Peter St. SW1 91 DK76
Great Portland St. W1 5 J6
Great Portland St. W1 77 DH70
Great Pulteney St. W1 5 L10
Great Pulteney St. W1 77 DJ73
Great Queen St. WC2 6 A9
Great Queen St. WC2 77 DL72
Great Russell St. WC1 5 N8
Great Russell St. WC1 77 DK72
Great St. Helens EC3 7 M8
Great St. Thomas Apostle EC4 7 J10
Great Scotland Yd. SW1 9 P2
Great Scotland Yd. SW1 77 DL74
Great Slades, Pot.B. 19 CZ33
Great Smith St. SW1 9 N6
Great Smith St. SW1 91 DK76
Great South-West Rd., Felt. 99 BQ87
Great South-West Rd., Houns. 85 BV83
Great Spilmans SE22 106 DS85
Great Strand NW9 47 CT53
Great Suffolk St. SE1 10 G3
Great Suffolk St. SE1 77 DP74
Great Sutton St. EC1 6 G5
Great Sutton St. EC1 77 DP70
Great Swan All. EC2 7 K8
Great Tattenhams, Epsom 145 CV118
Great Thrift, Orp. 123 EQ98
Great Till Clo., Sev. 153 FE116
Great Titchfield St. W1 5 K6
Great Titchfield St. W1 77 DJ71
Great Twr. St. EC3 7 M10
Great Twr. St. EC3 78 DS73
Great Trinity La. EC4 7 J10
Great Turnstile WC1 6 C7
Great W. Rd. W4 88 CP78
Great W. Rd. W6 89 CU78
Great W. Rd., Brent. 88 CP78
Great W. Rd., Houns. 86 BY82
Great W. Rd., Islw. 87 CD80
Great Western Ind. Pk., Sthl. 86 CB75
Great Western Rd. W2 75 CZ71
Great Western Rd. W9 75 CZ71
Great Western Rd. W11 75 CZ71
Great Wf. Rd. E14 79 EB74
Churchill Pl.
Great Winchester St. EC2 7 L8
Great Winchester St. EC2 78 DR72
Great Windmill St. W1 5 M10
Great Windmill St. W1 77 DK73
Great Woodcote Dr., Pur. 133 DK110
Great Woodcote Pk., Pur. 133 DK110
Great Yd. SE1 11 N4
Greatdown Rd. W7 73 CF70
Greatfield Ave. E6 81 EM70
Greatfield Clo. N19 63 DJ63
Warrender Rd.
Greatfield Clo. SE4 93 EA84
Greatfields Dr., Uxb. 70 BN71
Greatfields Rd., Bark. 81 ER67
Greatham Rd. (Bushey), Wat. 30 BX41
Greatham Wk. SW15 103 CU88
Bessborough Rd.
Greathurst End, Lthd. 142 BZ124
Greatness La., Sev. 155 FJ121
Greatness Rd., Sev. 155 FJ121
Greatorex St. E1 78 DU71
Greatwood, Chis. 109 EN94
Greaves Clo., Bark. 81 ES66
Norfolk Rd.
Greaves Pl. SW17 104 DE91
Grebe Ave., Hayes 72 BX72
Cygnet Way
Grebe Clo. E7 66 EF64
Cormorant Rd.
Grebe Clo. E17 51 DY52
Grecian Cres. SE19 105 DP93
Gredo Ho., Bark. 82 EV69
Greek Ct. W1 5 N9
Greek St. W1 5 N9
Greek St. W1 77 DK72
Greek Yd. WC2 5 P10
Green, The E4 51 EC46
Green, The E11 66 EH58
Green, The E15 80 EE65
Green, The N9 50 DU47
Green, The N14 49 DK48
Green, The N21 49 DN45
Green, The SW14 88 CQ83
Green, The SW19 103 CX92
Green, The W3 74 CS72
Green, The W5 73 CK74
The Gro.
Green, The, Bexh. 96 FA81
Green, The, Brom. 122 EG101
Green, The, Cars. 132 DG105
Green, The, Cat. 149 EA123
Green, The, Croy. 135 DZ109
Green, The, Epp. 39 ES36
Green, The, Epsom 131 CU112
Green, The, Esher 129 CF107
Green, The, Felt. 99 BV89
Green, The, Hayes 71 BS72
Wood End
Green, The, Houns. 86 CA79
Heston Rd.
Green, The, Lthd. 143 CD124
Green, The, Mord. 117 CY98
Green, The, N.Mal. 116 CQ97
Green, The (Pratt's Bottom), Orp. 138 EW110
Rushmore Hill
Green, The (St. Paul's Cray), Orp. 110 EV94
The Ave.
Green, The, Rich. 101 CK85
Green, The (Croxley Grn.), Rick. 28 BM44
Green, The (Sarratt), Rick. 28 BG35
Green, The, Sev. 155 FK122
Green, The, Shep. 113 BS98
Green, The, Sid. 110 EU91
Green, The, Sthl. 86 BY76
Green, The, Sutt. 118 DB104
Green, The, Tad. 145 CY119
Green, The, Twick. 101 CE89
Green, The, Uxb. 57 BQ61
Green, The, Wal.Abb. 23 EC34
Sewardstone Rd.
Green, The (Cheshunt), Wal.Cr. 22 DW28
Green, The, Walt. 127 BS110
Octagon Rd.
Green, The, Warl. 149 DX117
Green, The, Wat. 31 CE39
Green, The, Well. 95 ES84
Green, The, Wem. 59 CG61
Green, The, West Dr. 84 BK76
Green, The, Wdf.Grn. 52 EG50
Green Acres, Croy. 120 DT104
Green Arbour Ct. EC1 6 F8
Green Ave. NW7 46 CR49
Green Ave. W13 87 CH76
Green Bank E1 78 DV74
Green Bank N12 48 DB49
Green Clo. NW9 60 CQ58
Green Clo. NW11 62 DC59
Green Clo., Brom. 122 EE97
Green Clo., Cars. 118 DF103
Green Clo., Felt. 100 BY92
Green Clo., Hat. 19 CY26
Station Rd.
Green Clo. (Cheshunt), Wal.Cr. 23 DY31
Green Ct. Rd., Swan. 125 FD100
Green Cft., Edg. 46 CQ50
Deans La.
Green Curve, Bans. 131 CZ114
Green Dale SE5 92 DR84
Wanley Rd.
Green Dale SE22 106 DS85
Green Dale Clo. SE22 106 DS85
Green Dale
Green Dragon Ct. SE1 11 K2
Green Dragon La. N21 35 DN43
Green Dragon La., Brent. 88 CL78
Green Dragon Yd. E1 78 DU71
Old Montague St.
Green Dr., Sthl. 72 CA74
Green End N21 49 DP47
Green End, Chess. 130 CL105
Green Gdns., Orp. 137 EQ106
Green Glade, Epp. 39 ES37
Green Hill, Buck.H. 52 EJ46
Green Hill, Orp. 137 EM112
Green Hill La., Warl. 149 DY117
Sunny Bank
Green Hill Ter. SE18 95 EM78
Green Hill Way, Croy. 135 DX112
Green Hundred Rd. SE15 92 DU79
Green La. E4 37 ED41
Green La. NW4 61 CX56
Green La. SE9 109 EP88
Green La. SE20 107 DX94
Green La. SW16 105 DM94
Green La. W7 87 CE75
Green La., Add. 112 BG104
Green La., Ash. 143 CJ117
Green La., Chess. 130 CL109
Green La., Chig. 53 EQ46
Green La., Chis. 109 EP90
Green La., Cob. 128 BY112
Green La., Dag. 68 EX61
Green La., Edg. 46 CM49
Green La., Felt. 100 BY92
Green La., Har. 59 CE62
Green La., Houns. 85 BV83
Green La., Ilf. 67 EQ61
Green La., Lthd. 143 CK121
Green La., Mord. 118 DA100
Green La., N.Mal. 116 CQ99
Green La., Nthwd. 43 BR52
Green La., Pur. 133 DJ111
Green La., Rick. 28 BM43
Green La., Shep. 113 BQ100
Green La., Stan. 45 CH49
Green La., Sun. 99 BT94
Green La., Th.Hth. 119 DP95
Green La., Uxb. 71 BQ71
Green La., Wal.Abb. 24 EJ34
Green La., Walt. 127 BV107
Green La., Warl. 149 DY116
Green La., Wat. 44 BW46
Green La., W.Byf. 126 BM112
Green La., W.Mol. 114 CB99
Green La. (Ockham), Wok. 141 BP124
Green La., Wor.Pk. 117 CU102
Green La. Ave., Walt. 128 BW106
Green La. Clo., W.Byf. 126 BM112
Green La. Gdns., Th.Hth. 119 DP96
Green Las. N4 63 DP59
Green Las. N8 63 DP55
Green Las. N13 49 DM51
Green Las. N15 63 DP55
Green Las. N16 64 DQ62
Green Las. N21 49 DP47
Green Las., Epsom 130 CS109
Green Lawns, Ruis. 58 BW60
Green Leaf Ave., Wall. 133 DK105
Ferrers Ave.
Green Leas, Sun. 99 BT94
Green Leas, Wal.Abb. 23 ED34
Roundhills
Green Leas Clo., Sun. 99 BT93
Green Leas
Green Man Gdns. W13 73 CG73
Green Man La. W13 73 CG73
Green Man La., Felt. 85 BU84
Green Mead, Esher 128 BZ107
Winterdown Gdns.
Green Meadow, Pot.B. 20 DA30
Green Moor Link N21 49 DP45
Green Pl., Dart. 111 FE85
Green Pt. E15 80 EE65
Green Pond Clo. E17 65 DY55
Green Pond Rd. E17 65 DY55
Green Ride, Epp. 39 EP35
Green Ride, Loug. 38 EG43
Green Rd. N14 35 DH44
Green Rd. N20 48 DC48
Green Shield Ind. Est. E16 80 EG74
Green St. E7 80 EH65
Green St. E13 80 EJ66
Green St. W1 4 E10
Green St. W1 76 DF73
Green St., Enf. 36 DW40
Green St., Rad. 18 CN34
Green St., Sun. 113 BU95
Green Vale W5 74 CM72
Green Vale, Bexh. 110 EX85
Green Verges, Stan. 45 CK52
Green Vw., Chess. 130 CM108
Green Wk. NW4 61 CX57
Green Wk. SE1 11 M7
Green Wk., Dart. 111 FF85
Green Wk., Hmptn. 100 BZ93
Orpwood Clo.
Green Wk., Ruis. 57 BT60
Green Wk., Sthl. 86 CA78
Green Wk., Wdf.Grn. 52 EL51
Green Wk., The E4 51 EC46
Green Way SE9 108 EK85
Green Way, Brom. 122 EL100
Green Way, Sun. 113 BU98
Green Wrythe Cres., Cars. 118 DE102
Green Wrythe La., Cars. 118 DD100
Greenacre Clo., Barn. 33 CZ38
Greenacre Clo., Swan. 125 FE98
Greenacre Gdns. E17 65 EC56
Greenacre Sq. SE16 93 DX75
Fishermans Dr.
Greenacre Wk. N14 49 DL48
Greenacres SE9 109 EN86
Greenacres, Epp. 25 ET28
Greenacres, Lthd. 142 CB124
Greenacres (Bushey), Wat. 45 CD47
Greenacres Ave., Uxb. 56 BM62
Greenacres Clo., Nthlt. 58 BZ64
Eastcote La.
Greenacres Clo., Orp. 137 EQ105
Greenacres Dr., Stan. 45 CH51
Greenall Clo. (Cheshunt), Wal.Cr. 23 DY30
Greenaway Gdns. NW3 62 DB63
Greenbank (Cheshunt), Wal.Cr. 22 DV28
Greenbank Ave., Wem. 59 CG64
Greenbank Clo. E4 51 EC47
Greenbank Cres. NW4 61 CY56
Greenbank Rd., Wat. 29 BR36
Greenbay Rd. SE7 94 EK80
Greenberry St. NW8 4 B1
Greenberry St. NW8 76 DE68
Greenbrook Ave., Barn. 34 DC39
Greencoat Pl. SW1 9 L8
Greencoat Pl. SW1 91 DJ77
Greencoat Row SW1 9 L7
Greencourt Ave., Croy. 120 DV103
Greencourt Ave., Edg. 46 CP53
Greencourt Gdns., Croy. 120 DV102
Greencourt Rd., Orp. 123 ER99
Greencrest Pl. NW2 61 CV62
Dollis Hill La.
Greencroft Ave., Ruis. 58 BW61
Greencroft Clo. E6 80 EL71
Neatscourt Rd.
Greencroft Gdns. NW6 76 DB66
Greencroft Gdns., Enf. 36 DS41
Greencroft Rd., Houns. 86 BZ81
Greene Fielde End, Stai. 98 BK94
Berryscroft Rd.
Greenend Rd. W4 88 CS75
Greenfarm Clo., Orp. 137 ET106
Greenfell St. SE10 94 EE76
Greenfield Ave., Surb. 116 CP101
Greenfield Ave., Wat. 44 BX47
Greenfield Gdns. NW2 61 CY61
Greenfield Gdns., Dag. 82 EX67
Greenfield Gdns., Orp. 123 ER101
Greenfield Link, Couls. 147 DL115
Greenfield Rd. E1 78 DU71
Greenfield Rd. N15 64 DS57
Greenfield Rd., Dag. 82 EW66
Greenfield Rd., Dart. 111 FD92
Greenfield St., Wal.Abb. 23 EC34
Greenfield Way, Har. 58 CB55
Greenfields, Loug. 39 EN42
Greenfields (Cuffley), Pot.B. 21 DL30
South Dr.
Greenfields Clo., Loug. 39 EN42
Greenford Ave. W7 73 CE70
Greenford Ave., Sthl. 72 BZ73
Greenford Gdns., Grnf. 72 CB69
Greenford Rd., Grnf. 72 CC72
Greenford Rd., Har. 59 CF63
Greenford Rd., Sthl. 72 CC72
Greenford Rd., Sutt. 132 DB105
Greengate, Grnf. 73 CH65
Greengate St. E13 80 EH68
Greenhalgh Wk. N2 62 DC56
Greenham Clo. SE1 10 D5
Greenham Clo. SE1 91 DN75
Greenham Cres. E4 51 DZ51
Greenham Rd. N10 48 DG54
Greenhayes Ave., Bans. 132 DA114
Greenhayes Gdns., Bans. 146 DA115
Greenheys Clo., Nthwd. 43 BS53
Greenheys Dr. E18 66 EF55
Greenhill NW3 62 DD63
Hampstead High St.
Greenhill SE18 95 EM78
Greenhill, Sutt. 118 DC103
Greenhill, Wem. 60 CP61
Greenhill Ave., Cat. 148 DV121
Greenhill Cres., Wat. 29 BS44
Greenhill Gdns., Nthlt. 72 BZ68
Greenhill Gro. E12 66 EL63
Greenhill Pk. NW10 74 CS67
Greenhill Pk., Barn. 34 DB43
Greenhill Rd. NW10 74 CS67
Greenhill Rd., Har. 59 CE58
Greenhill Ter., Nthlt. 72 BZ68
Greenhill Way, Har. 59 CE58
Greenhill Way, Wem. 60 CP61
Greenhills Clo., Rick. 28 BH43
Greenhill's Rents EC1 6 F6
Greenhills Ter. N1 78 DR65
Baxter Rd.

Grove Pl., Wey. 127 BQ106
Princes Rd.
Grove Rd. E3 79 DX67
Grove Rd. E4 51 EC49
Grove Rd. E11 66 EF59
Grove Rd. E17 65 EB58
Grove Rd. E18 52 EF54
Grove Rd. N11 49 DH50
Grove Rd. N12 48 DD50
Grove Rd. N15 64 DS57
Grove Rd. NW2 75 CW65
Grove Rd. SW13 89 CT82
Grove Rd. SW19 104 DC94
Grove Rd. W3 74 CQ74
Grove Rd. W5 73 CK73
Grove Rd., Ash. 144 CM118
Grove Rd., Barn. 34 DE41
Grove Rd., Belv. 96 EZ79
Grove Rd., Bexh. 97 FC84
Grove Rd., Borwd. 32 CN39
Grove Rd., Brent. 87 CJ78
Grove Rd., E.Mol. 115 CD98
Grove Rd., Edg. 46 CN51
Grove Rd., Epsom 130 CS113
Grove Rd., Houns. 86 CA84
Grove Rd., Islw. 87 CE81
Grove Rd., Mitch. 118 DG97
Grove Rd., Nthwd. 43 BR50
Grove Rd., Pnr. 58 BZ57
Grove Rd., Rich. 102 CM86
Grove Rd., Rick. 42 BG47
Grove Rd., Rom. 68 EV59
Grove Rd., Sev. 155 FJ121
Grove Rd. (Seal), Sev. 155 FN122
Grove Rd., Shep. 113 BQ100
Grove Rd., Surb. 115 CK99
Grove Rd., Sutt. 132 DA107
Grove Rd., Th.Hth. 119 DN98
Grove Rd., Twick. 101 CD90
Grove Rd., Uxb. 70 BK66
Grove Rd., West. 150 EJ120
Grove Rd. W., Enf. 36 DW37
Grove Shaw, Tad. 145 CY124
Grove St. N18 50 DT50
Grove St. SE8 93 DZ77
Grove Ter. NW5 63 DH62
Grove Ter., Tedd. 101 CG91
Grove Vale SE22 92 DS84
Grove Vale, Chis. 109 EN93
Grove Vill. E14 79 EB73
Grove Way, Esher 114 CC101
Grove Way, Uxb. 70 BK66
Grove Wd. Hill, Couls. 133 DJ114
Grovebarns, Stai. 98 BG93
Grovebury Clo., Erith 97 FD79
Grovebury Gdns., St.Alb. 16 CC27
Grovebury Rd. SE2 96 EV75
Grovedale Clo. (Cheshunt), Wal.Cr. 22 DT30
Grovedale Rd. N19 63 DK61
Grovehall Rd. (Bushey), Wat. 30 BY42
Groveland Ave. SW16 105 DM94
Groveland Ct. EC4 7 J9
Groveland Rd., Beck. 121 DZ97
Groveland Way, N.Mal. 116 CQ99
Grovelands, St.Alb. 16 CB27
Grovelands, W.Mol. 114 CA98
Grovelands Clo. SE5 92 DS82
Grovelands Clo., Har. 58 CB62
Grovelands Ct. N14 49 DK45
Grovelands Rd. N13 49 DM49
Grovelands Rd. N15 64 DU58
Grovelands Rd., Orp. 110 EU94
Grovelands Rd., Pur. 133 DL112
Groveley Rd., Sun. 99 BS92
Grover Rd., Wat. 30 BX44
Groveside Clo. W3 74 CP72
Groveside Clo., Cars. 118 DE103
Groveside Rd. E4 52 EE47
Grovestile Waye, Felt. 99 BR87
Groveway SW9 91 DM81
Groveway, Dag. 68 EX63
Groveway, Wem. 60 CQ64
Grovewood, Rich. 88 CN81
Sandycoombe Rd.
Grovewood Pl., Wdf.Grn. 53 EM51
Grummant Rd. SE15 92 DT81
Grundy St. E14 79 EB72
Gruneisen Rd. N3 48 DB52
Guardian Clo., Horn. 69 FH60
Gubyon Ave. SE24 105 DP85
Guerin Sq. E3 79 DZ69
Malmesbury Rd.
Guernsey Clo., Houns. 86 CA81
Guernsey Gro. SE24 106 DQ87
Guernsey Rd. E11 65 ED60
Guibal Rd. SE12 108 EH87
Guild Rd. SE7 94 EK78
Guild Rd., Erith 97 FF80
Guildersfield Rd. SW16 105 DL94
Guildford Ave., Felt. 99 BT89
Guildford Gro. SE10 93 EB81
Guildford Rd. E6 81 EM72
Guildford Rd. E17 51 EC53
Guildford Rd. SW8 91 DL81
Guildford Rd., Croy. 120 DR100
Guildford Rd., Ilf. 67 ES61
Guildford Rd., Lthd. 143 CF123
Guildford St., Stai. 98 BG93
Guildford Way, Wall. 133 DL106
Guildhall Bldgs. EC2 7 K8
Guildhall Yd. EC2 78 DR72
Gresham St.
Guildhouse St. SW1 9 K8
Guildhouse St. SW1 91 DJ77
Guildown Ave. N12 48 DB49
Guildsway E17 51 DZ53
Guileshill La., Wok. 140 BL123
Guilford Ave., Surb. 116 CM99
Guilford Pl. WC1 6 B5
Guilford Pl. WC1 77 DM70
Guilford St. WC1 6 A5
Guilford St. WC1 77 DL70
Guilford Vill., Surb. 116 CM100
Alpha Rd.
Guilsborough Clo. NW10 74 CS66
Guinevere Gdns., Wal.Cr. 23 DX31
Guinness Bldgs. SE1 11 M7
Guinness Bldgs. SE1 92 DS77
Guinness Clo. E9 79 DY66
Guinness Clo., Hayes 85 BR76
Guinness Sq. SE1 11 M8
Guinness Trust Bldgs. SE11 10 F10
Guinness Trust Bldgs. SE11 91 DP78
Guinness Trust Bldgs. SW3 8 D9
Guinness Trust Est. N16 64 DS60
Holmleigh Rd.
Guinness Trust Est. SW9 91 DP84
Guion Rd. SW6 89 CZ82
Gull Clo., Wall. 133 DL108
Gull Wk., Horn. 83 FH66
Heron Flight Ave.
Gulland Clo. (Bushey), Wat. 30 CC43
Gulland Wk. N1 78 DQ65
Clephane Rd.
Gullet Wd. Rd., Wat. 29 BU35
Gulliver Clo., Nthlt. 72 BZ67
Gulliver Rd., Sid. 109 ES89
Gulliver St. SE16 93 DZ76
Gulston Wk. SW3 8 E9
Gumleigh Rd. W5 87 CJ77
Gumley Gdns., Islw. 87 CG83
Gumping Rd., Orp. 123 EQ102
Gun St. E1 7 P7
Gun St. E1 78 DT71
Gundulph Rd., Brom. 122 EJ97
Gunmakers La. E3 79 DY67
Gunnell Clo. SE26 106 DU91
Gunnell Clo., Croy. 120 DU100
Gunner La. SE18 95 EN78
Gunners Gro. E4 51 EC48
Gunners Rd. SW18 104 DD89
Gunnersbury Ave. W3 74 CM74
Gunnersbury Ave. W4 74 CM74
Gunnersbury Ave. W5 74 CM74
Gunnersbury Clo. W4 88 CP78
Grange Rd.
Gunnersbury Ct. W3 88 CP75
Bollo La.
Gunnersbury Cres. W3 88 CN75
Gunnersbury Dr. W5 88 CM75
Gunnersbury Gdns. W3 88 CN75
Gunnersbury La. W3 88 CN76
Gunnersbury Ms. W4 88 CP78
Chiswick High Rd.
Gunnersbury Pk. W3 88 CM77
Gunnersbury Pk. W5 88 CM77
Gunning St. SE18 95 ES77
Gunpowder Sq. EC4 6 E8
Gunpowder Sq. EC4 77 DN72
Gunstor Rd. N16 64 DS63
Gunter Gro. SW10 90 DC79
Gunter Gro., Edg. 46 CR53
Gunterstone Rd. W14 89 CY77
Gunthorpe St. E1 78 DT71
Gunton Rd. E5 64 DV61
Gunton Rd. SW17 104 DG93
Gunwhale Clo. SE16 79 DX74
Gurdon Rd. SE7 94 EG78
Gurnard Clo., West Dr. 70 BK73
Trout Rd.
Gurnell Gro. W13 73 CF70
Gurney Clo. E15 66 EE64
Gurney Rd.
Gurney Clo. E17 51 DX53
Gurney Clo., Bark. 81 EP65
Gurney Cres., Croy. 119 DM102
Gurney Dr. N2 62 DC56
Gurney Rd. E15 66 EE64
Gurney Rd., Cars. 118 DG104
Gurney Rd., Nthlt. 71 BV69
Guthrie St. SW3 8 B10
Gutter La. EC2 7 J8
Gutter La. EC2 78 DQ72
Gutteridge La., Rom. 41 FC44
Guy Barnett Clo. SE3 94 EG83
Casterbridge Rd.
Guy Rd., Wall. 119 DK104
Guy St. SE1 11 L4
Guy St. SE1 92 DR75
Guyatt Gdns., Mitch. 118 DG96
Ormerod Gdns.
Guyscliff Rd. SE13 107 EC85
Guysfield Clo., Rain. 83 FG67
Guysfield Dr., Rain. 83 FG67
Gwalior Rd. SW15 89 CX83
Felsham Rd.
Gwendolen Ave. SW15 89 CX84
Gwendolen Clo. SW15 103 CX85
Gwendoline Ave. E13 80 EH67
Gwendwr Rd. W14 89 CY78
Gwent Clo., Wat. 16 BX34
Gwillim Clo., Sid. 110 EU85
Gwydor Rd., Beck. 121 DX98
Gwydyr Rd., Brom. 122 EF97
Gwyn Clo. SW6 90 DC80
Gwynne Ave., Croy. 121 DX101
Gwynne Clo. W4 89 CT79
Gwynne Pk. Ave., Wdf.Grn. 53 EM51
Gwynne Pl. WC1 6 C3
Gwynne Rd. SW11 90 DD82
Gwynne Rd., Cat. 148 DQ121
Coulsdon Rd.
Gyfford Wk., Wal.Cr. 22 DV31
Hawthorne Clo.
Gylcote Clo. SE5 92 DR84
Gyles Pk., Stan. 45 CJ52
Gyllyngdune Gdns., Ilf. 67 ET62
Gypsy La., Kings L. 15 BR33

H

Ha-Ha Rd. SE18 95 EM79
Haarlem Rd. W14 89 CX76
Haberdasher Pl. N1 7 L2
Haberdasher St. N1 7 L2
Haberdasher St. N1 78 DR69
Habgood Rd., Loug. 38 EL41
Haccombe Rd. SW19 104 DC93
Haydons Rd.
Hackbridge Grn., Wall. 118 DG103
Hackbridge Pk. Gdns., Cars. 118 DG103
Hackbridge Rd., Wall. 118 DG103
Hackford Rd. SW9 91 DM81
Hackforth Clo., Barn. 33 CV43
Hackington Cres., Beck. 107 EA93
Hackney Clo., Borwd. 32 CR43
Hackney Gro. E8 78 DV65
Reading La.
Hackney Rd. E2 7 P2
Hackney Rd. E2 78 DT69
Hadden Rd. SE28 95 ES76
Hadden Way, Grnf. 73 CD65
Haddington Rd., Brom. 107 ED91
Haddo St. SE10 93 EC79
Haddon Clo., Borwd. 32 CN40
Haddon Clo., Enf. 36 DU44
Haddon Clo., N.Mal. 117 CT99
Haddon Clo., Wey. 113 BR104
Haddon Gro., Sid. 109 ET87
Haddon Rd., Orp. 124 EW99
Haddon Rd., Sutt. 132 DB105
Haddonfield SE8 93 DX77
Hadfield Clo., Sthl. 72 BZ69
Adrienne Ave.
Hadfield Rd., Stai. 98 BK86
Hadleigh Clo. E1 78 DW70
Mantus Rd.
Hadleigh Clo. SW20 117 CZ96
Hadleigh Dr., Sutt. 132 DA109
Hadleigh Rd. N9 50 DV45
Hadleigh St. E2 78 DW69
Hadleigh Wk. E6 80 EL72
Kirkham Rd.
Hadley Clo. N21 35 DN44
Hadley Clo., Borwd. 32 CM43
Hadley Common, Barn. 34 DA40
Hadley Gdns. W4 88 CR78
Hadley Gdns., Sthl. 86 BZ78
Hadley Grn., Barn. 33 CZ40
Hadley Grn. Rd., Barn. 33 CZ40
Hadley Grn. W., Barn. 33 CY40
Hadley Gro., Barn. 33 CY40
Hadley Highstone, Barn. 33 CZ39
Hadley Pl., Wey. 126 BN108
Hadley Ridge, Barn. 33 CZ41
Hadley Rd. (Hadley Wd.), Barn. 34 DG38
Hadley Rd. (New Barnet), Barn. 34 DB41
Hadley Rd., Belv. 96 EZ77
Hadley Rd., Enf. 35 DL38
Hadley Rd., Mitch. 119 DK98
Hadley St. NW1 77 DH65
Hadley Way N21 35 DN44
Hadley Wd. Ri., Ken. 147 DP115
Hadlow Pl. SE19 106 DU94
Hadlow Rd., Sid. 110 EU91
Hadlow Rd., Well. 96 EW80
Hadrian Clo., Stai. 98 BL88
Hadrian Way
Hadrian Clo., Wall. 133 DL108
De Havilland Rd.
Hadrian Est. E2 78 DU68
Hackney Rd.
Hadrian St. SE10 94 EE78
Hadrian Way, Stai. 98 BK87
Hadrians Ride, Enf. 36 DT43
Hadyn Pk. Rd. W12 89 CU75
Hafer Rd. SW11 90 DF84
Hafton Rd. SE6 108 EE88
Hagden La., Wat. 29 BT43
Haggard Rd., Twick. 101 CG87
Haggerston Rd. E8 78 DT66
Haggerston Rd., Borwd. 32 CL38
Hague St. E2 78 DU69
Derbyshire St.
Haig Rd., Stan. 45 CJ50
Haig Rd., Uxb. 71 BP71
Haig Rd., West. 150 EL117
Haig Rd. E. E13 80 EJ69
Haig Rd. W. E13 80 EJ69
Haigville Gdns., Ilf. 67 EP56
Hailes Clo. SW19 104 DC93
North Rd.
Hailey Rd., Erith 96 FA75
Haileybury Ave., Enf. 36 DT44
Haileybury Rd., Orp. 138 EU105
Hailsham Ave. SW2 105 DM89
Hailsham Clo., Surb. 115 CK101
Hailsham Dr., Har. 59 CD55
Hailsham Rd. SW17 104 DG93
Hailsham Ter. N18 50 DQ50
Haimo Rd. SE9 108 EK85
Hainault Ct. E17 65 ED56
Hainault Gore, Rom. 68 EY57
Hainault Gro., Chig. 53 EQ49
Hainault Ind. Est., Ilf. 54 EW50
Hainault Rd. E11 65 EC60
Hainault Rd., Chig. 53 EP48
Hainault Rd., Rom. 55 FC54
Hainault Rd. (Chadwell Heath), Rom. 68 EZ58
Hainault Rd. (Hainault), Rom. 68 EV55
Hainault St. SE9 109 EP88
Hainault St., Ilf. 67 EQ61
Haines Ct., Wey. 127 BR106
St. George's Lo.
Haines Way, Wat. 15 BU34
Hainford Clo. SE4 93 DX84
Haining Clo. W4 88 CN78
Wellesley Rd.
Hainthorpe Rd. SE27 105 DP90
Hainton Clo. E1 78 DV72
Halberd Ms. E5 64 DV61
Knightland Rd.
Halbutt Gdns., Dag. 68 EZ62
Halbutt St., Dag. 68 EZ63
Halcomb St. N1 78 DS67
Halcot Ave., Bexh. 111 FB85
Halcrow St. E1 78 DV71
Newark St.
Haldan Rd. E4 51 EC51
Haldane Clo. N10 49 DH52
Haldane Pl. SW18 104 DB88
Haldane Rd. E6 80 EK69
Haldane Rd. SE28 82 EX73
Haldane Rd. SW6 89 CZ80
Haldane Rd., Sthl. 72 CC73
Haldon Clo., Chig. 53 ES50
Haldon Rd. SW18 103 CZ85
Hale, The E4 51 ED52
Hale, The N17 64 DU55
Hale Clo. E4 51 EC48
Hale Clo., Edg. 46 CQ50
Hale Clo., Orp. 137 EQ105
Hale Dr. NW7 46 CQ51
Hale End, Rom. 55 FH51
Hale End Clo., Ruis. 57 BU58
Hale End Rd. E4 51 ED51
Hale End Rd. E17 51 ED53
Hale End Rd., Wdf.Grn. 51 ED52
Hale Gdns. N17 64 DU55
Hale Gdns. W3 74 CN74
Hale Gro. Gdns. NW7 46 CR50
Hale La. NW7 46 CR50
Hale La., Edg. 46 CP50
Hale La., Sev. 153 FE117
Hale Path SE27 105 DP91
Hale Rd. E6 80 EL70
Hale Rd. N17 64 DU55
Hale St. E14 79 EB73
Hale Wk. W7 73 CE71
Benham Rd.
Halefield Rd. N17 50 DU53
Hales St. SE8 93 EA80
Deptford High St.
Halesowen Rd., Mord. 118 DB101
Haleswood, Cob. 127 BV114
Halesworth Clo. E5 64 DW61
Theydon Rd.
Halesworth Rd. SE13 93 EB83
Haley Rd. NW4 61 CW58
Half Acre, Brent. 87 CK79
Half Acre Rd. W7 73 CE74
Half Moon Ct. EC1 7 H7
Half Moon Cres. N1 77 DM68
Half Moon La. SE24 106 DQ86
Half Moon La., Epp. 25 ET31
Half Moon Pas. E1 78 DT72
Braham St.
Half Moon St. W1 9 J2
Half Moon St. W1 77 DH74
Halfhide La. (Cheshunt), Wal.Cr. 23 DX27
Halfhides, Wal.Abb. 23 ED33
Halford Rd. E10 65 ED57
Halford Rd. SW6 90 DA79
Halford Rd., Rich. 102 CL85
Halford Rd., Uxb. 56 BN64
Halfway Grn., Walt. 113 BV104
Halfway St., Sid. 109 ER87
Haliburton Rd., Twick. 101 CG85
Haliday Wk. N1 78 DR65
Balls Pond Rd.
Halidon Clo. E9 64 DW64
Urswick Rd.
Halifax Rd., Enf. 36 DQ40
Halifax Rd., Grnf. 72 CB67
Halifax St. SE26 106 DV91
Halifield Dr., Belv. 96 EY76
Haling Down Pas., S.Croy. 134 DQ109
Kingsdown Ave.
Haling Gro., S.Croy. 134 DQ108
Haling Pk., S.Croy. 134 DQ107
Haling Pk. Gdns., S.Croy. 133 DP107
Haling Pk. Rd., S.Croy. 133 DP107
Haling Rd., S.Croy. 134 DR107
Halkin Arc. SW1 8 F6
Halkin Ms. SW1 8 F6
Halkin Pl. SW1 8 F6
Halkin Pl. SW1 90 DG76
Halkin St. SW1 8 G5
Halkin St. SW1 90 DG75
Hall, The SE3 94 EG83
Hall Ave. N18 50 DR51
Weir Hall Ave.
Hall Clo. W5 74 CL71
Hall Clo., Rick. 42 BG46
Hall Ct., Tedd. 101 CF92
Teddington Pk.
Hall Dr. SE26 106 DW92
Hall Dr. W7 73 CE72
Hall Dr., Uxb. 42 BJ53
Hall Fm. Clo., Stan. 45 CH49
Hall Fm. Dr., Twick. 101 CD87
Hall Gdns. E4 51 DZ49
Hall Gate NW8 76 DC69
Hall Rd.
Hall Hill, Sev. 155 FP123
Hall La. E4 51 DY50
Hall La. NW4 47 CU53
Hall La., Hayes 85 BR80
Hall Oak Wk. NW6 75 CZ65
Maygrove Rd.
Hall Pl. W2 76 DD70
Hall Pl. Cres., Bex. 111 FC85
Hall Pl. Dr., Wey. 127 BS106
Hall Rd. E6 81 EM67
Hall Rd. E15 65 ED63
Hall Rd. NW8 76 DC69
Hall Rd., Islw. 101 CD85
Hall Rd., Rom. 68 EW58
Hall Rd. (Gidea Pk.), Rom. 69 FH55
Hall Rd., Wall. 133 DH109
Hall St. EC1 6 G2
Hall St. EC1 77 DP69
Hall St. N12 48 DC50
Hall Vw. SE9 108 EK89
Hall Way, Pur. 133 DP113
Downs Ct. Rd.
Hallam Clo., Chis. 109 EM92
Hallam Clo., Wat. 30 BW40
Hallam Gdns., Pnr. 44 BY52
Hallam Ms. W1 5 J6
Hallam Rd. N15 63 DP56
Hallam Rd. SW13 89 CV83
Hallam St. W1 5 J5
Hallam St. W1 77 DH71
Halland Way, Nthwd. 43 BR51
Halley Gdns. SE13 93 ED84
Halley Rd. E7 80 EJ65
Halley Rd. E12 80 EK65
Halley St. E14 79 DY71
Halleys Wk., Add. 126 BJ108
Hallfield Est. W2 76 DC72
Cleveland Ter.
Halliards, The, Walt. 113 BU100
Felix Rd.
Halliday Sq., Sthl. 73 CD74
Halliford Clo., Shep. 113 BR98
Halliford Rd., Shep. 113 BS99
Halliford Rd., Sun. 113 BT99
Halliford St. N1 78 DQ66
Hallingbury Ct. E17 65 EB55
Halliwell Rd. SW2 105 DM86
Halliwick Rd. N10 48 DG53
Hallmark Trd. Est. NW10 60 CQ63
Great Cen. Way
Hallmead Rd., Sutt. 118 DB104
Hallowell Ave., Croy. 133 DL105
Hallowell Clo., Mitch. 118 DG97
Hallowell Rd., Nthwd. 43 BS52
Hallowes Cres., Wat. 43 BU48
Hayling Rd.
Hallowfield Way, Mitch. 118 DD97
Hallside Rd., Enf. 36 DT38
Hallsville Rd. E16 80 EF72
Hallswelle Rd. NW11 61 CZ57
Hallywell Cres. E6 81 EM71
Halons Rd. SE9 109 EN87
Halpin Pl. SE17 11 L9
Halsbrook Rd. SE3 94 EJ83
Halsbury Clo., Stan. 45 CH49
Halsbury Rd. W12 75 CU74
Halsbury Rd. E., Nthlt. 58 CC63
Halsbury Rd. W., Nthlt. 58 CB64
Halsend, Hayes 71 BV74
Halsey Ms. SW3 8 D8
Halsey Pk., St.Alb. 18 CM27
Halsey Pl., Wat. 29 BV38
Halsey Rd., Wat. 29 BV41
Halsey St. SW3 8 D8
Halsey St. SW3 90 DF77
Halsham Cres., Bark. 81 ET65
Halsmere Rd. SE5 91 DP81
Halstead Clo., Croy. 120 DQ104
Charles St.
Halstead Ct. N1 7 L1
Halstead Gdns. N21 50 DR46
Halstead Hill (Cheshunt), Wal.Cr. 22 DS29
Halstead La., Sev. 138 EZ114
Halstead Rd. E11 66 EG57
Halstead Rd. N21 50 DR46
Halstead Rd., Enf. 36 DS42
Halstead Rd., Erith 97 FE81
Halston Clo. SW11 104 DF86
Halstow Rd. NW10 75 CX69
Halstow Rd. SE10 94 EG78
Halsway, Hayes 71 BU74
Halt Robin La., Belv. 97 FB77
Halt Robin Rd.
Halt Robin Rd., Belv. 96 FA77
Halter Clo., Borwd. 32 CR43
Clydesdale Clo.
Halton Cross St. N1 77 DP67
Halton Rd.
Halton Rd. N1 77 DP66
Ham, The, Brent. 87 CJ80
Ham Clo., Rich. 101 CJ90
Ham Common, Rich. 101 CK90
Ham Fm. Rd., Rich. 101 CK91
Ham Gate Ave., Rich. 102 CL91
Ham Pk. Rd. E7 80 EG66

Ham Pk. Rd. E15 80 EF66
Ham Ridings, Rich. 102 CM92
Ham St., Rich. 101 CH88
Ham Vw., Croy. 121 DY100
Ham Yd. W1 5 M10
Hambalt Rd. SW4 105 DJ85
Hamble Clo., Ruis. 57 BS61
Chichester Ave.
Hamble Ct., Kings.T. 101 CK94
Hamble St. SW6 90 DB83
Hamble Wk., Nthlt. 72 CA68
Brabazon Rd.
Hambledon Clo., Uxb. 71 BP71
Aldenham Dr.
Hambledon Gdns. SE25 120 DT97
Hambledon Hill, Epsom 144 CQ116
Hambledon Pl. SE21 106 DS88
Hambledon Rd. SW18 103 CZ87
Hambledon Rd., Cat. 148 DQ121
Coulsdon Rd.
Hambledon Vale, Epsom 144 CQ116
Hambledown Rd., Sid. 109 ER87
Hambleton Clo., Wor.Pk. 117 CW103
Cotswold Way
Hamblings Clo., Rad. 17 CK33
Hambridge Way SW2 105 DN87
Hambro Ave., Brom. 122 EG102
Hambro Rd. SW16 105 DK93
Hambrook Rd. SE25 120 DV97
Hambrough Rd., Sthl. 72 BY74
Hamburgh Ct., Wal.Cr. 23 DX28
Hamden Cres., Dag. 69 FB62
Hamel Clo., Har. 59 CK55
Hamelin St. E14 79 EC72
St. Leonards Rd.
Hameway E6 81 EN70
Hamfrith Rd. E15 80 EF65
Hamhaugh Island, Shep. 112 BN103
Hamilton Ave. N9 50 DU45
Hamilton Ave., Cob. 127 BU113
Hamilton Ave., Ilf. 67 EP56
Hamilton Ave., Rom. 55 FD54
Hamilton Ave., Surb. 116 CN103
Hamilton Ave., Sutt. 117 CY102
Hamilton Clo. N17 64 DT55
Hamilton Clo. NW8 76 DD69
Hamilton Clo. SE16 93 DY75
Somerford Way
Hamilton Clo., Barn. 34 DE42
Hamilton Clo., Epsom 130 CQ112
Hamilton Clo., Felt. 99 BT92
Hamilton Clo., Pot.B. 19 CU33
Hamilton Clo., Pur. 133 DP112
Hamilton Clo., St.Alb. 16 CA31
Hamilton Clo., Stan. 45 CF47
Hamilton Ct. W5 74 CM73
Hamilton Ct. W9 76 DC69
Maida Vale
Hamilton Cres. N13 49 DN49
Hamilton Cres., Har. 58 BZ62
Hamilton Cres., Houns. 100 CB85
Hamilton Gdns. NW8 76 DC69
Hamilton La. N5 63 DP63
Hamilton Pk.
Hamilton Ms. W1 9 H4
Hamilton Pk. N5 63 DP63
Hamilton Pk. W. N5 63 DP63
Hamilton Pl. W1 8 G3
Hamilton Pl. W1 76 DG74
Hamilton Pl., Sun. 99 BV94
Hamilton Pl., Tad. 145 CZ122
Hamilton Rd. E15 80 EE69
Hamilton Rd. E17 51 DY54
Hamilton Rd. N2 62 DC55
Hamilton Rd. N9 50 DU45
Hamilton Rd. NW10 61 CU64
Hamilton Rd. NW11 61 CX59
Hamilton Rd. SE27 106 DR91
Hamilton Rd. SW19 104 DB94
Hamilton Rd. W4 88 CS75
Hamilton Rd. W5 74 CL73
Hamilton Rd., Barn. 34 DE42
Hamilton Rd., Bexh. 96 EY82
Hamilton Rd., Brent. 87 CK79
Hamilton Rd., Felt. 99 BT91
Hamilton Rd., Har. 59 CE57
Hamilton Rd., Hayes 71 BV73
Hamilton Rd., Ilf. 67 EP63
Hamilton Rd., Kings L. 15 BQ33
Hamilton Rd., Rom. 69 FH57
Hamilton Rd., Sid. 110 EU91
Hamilton Rd., Sthl. 72 BZ74
Hamilton Rd., Th.Hth. 120 DR97
Hamilton Rd., Twick. 101 CE88
Hamilton Rd., Uxb. 70 BK70
Hamilton Rd., Wat. 43 BV48
Hamilton Sq. SE1 11 L4
Hamilton St. SE8 93 EA79
Deptford High St.
Hamilton St., Wat. 30 BW43
Hamilton Ter. NW8 76 DB68
Hamilton Wk., Erith 97 FF80
Frobisher Rd.
Hamilton Way N3 48 DA51
Hamilton Way N13 49 DP49
Hamilton Way, Wall. 133 DK109
Hamlea Clo. SE12 108 EG85
Hamlet, The SE5 92 DR83
Hamlet Clo. SE13 94 EE84
Old Rd.
Hamlet Clo., Rom. 54 FA52
Hamlet Gdns. W6 89 CU77
Hamlet Rd. SE19 106 DT94
Hamlet Rd., Rom. 54 FA52
Hamlet Sq. NW2 61 CY62
Cricklewood Trd. Est.
Hamlet Sq. NW11 61 CY62
The Vale
Hamlet Way SE1 11 L4
Hamlets Way E3 79 DZ70
Hamlin Cres., Pnr. 58 BW57
Hamlin Rd., Sev. 154 FE121
Hamlyn Clo., Edg. 46 CL48
Hamlyn Gdns. SE19 106 DS94
Hamm Ct., Wey. 112 BM104
Hamm Moor La., Add. 126 BL106
Hammelton Grn. SW9 91 DP81
Cromwell Rd.
Hammelton Rd., Brom. 122 EF95
Hammer Par., Wat. 15 BT33
Hammers Gate, St.Alb. 16 CA25
Hammers La. NW7 47 CU50
Hammersmith Bri. SW13 89 CV78
Hammersmith Bri. Rd. W6 89 CW78
Hammersmith Bdy. W6 89 CW77
Hammersmith Flyover W6 89 CW78
Hammersmith Gro. W6 89 CW75
Hammersmith Rd. W6 89 CX77
Hammersmith Rd. W14 89 CX77
Hammersmith Ter. W6 89 CU78
Hammet Clo., Hayes 72 BX71
Willow Tree La.
Hammett St. EC3 7 P10
Hammond Ave., Mitch. 119 DH96
Hammond Clo., Barn. 33 CY43
Hammond Clo., Grnf. 59 CD64
Lilian Board Way
Hammond Clo., Hmptn. 114 CA95
Hammond Clo. (Cheshunt), Wal.Cr. 22 DS26
Hammond Rd., Enf. 36 DV40
Hammond Rd., Sthl. 86 BY76
Hammond St. NW5 77 DJ65
Hammond Way SE28 82 EV73
Oriole Way
Hammonds Clo., Dag. 68 EW62
Hammondstreet Rd. (Cheshunt), Wal.Cr. 21 DP25
Hamond Clo., S.Croy. 133 DP109
Hamonde Clo., Edg. 46 CP47
Hampden Ave., Beck. 121 DY96
Hampden Clo. NW1 5 N1
Hampden Clo., Epp. 26 FA27
Hampden Cres. (Cheshunt), Wal.Cr. 22 DV31
Hampden Gurney St. W1 4 D9
Hampden La. N17 50 DT53
Hampden Pl., St.Alb. 17 CE29
Hampden Rd. N8 63 DN56
Hampden Rd. N10 48 DG52
Hampden Rd. N17 50 DU53
Hampden Rd. N19 63 DK61
Holloway Rd.
Hampden Rd., Beck. 121 DY96
Hampden Rd., Har. 44 CC53
Hampden Rd., Kings.T. 116 CN97
Hampden Rd., Rom. 55 FB52
Hampden Sq. N14 49 DH46
Osidge La.
Hampden Way N14 49 DH47
Hampden Way, Wat. 29 BS36
Hampermill La., Wat. 43 BT47
Hampshire Clo. N18 50 DV50
Hampshire Hog La. W6 89 CV77
King St.
Hampshire Rd. N22 49 DM52
Hampshire St. NW5 77 DK65
Torriano Ave.
Hampson Way SW8 91 DM81
Hampstead Clo. SE28 82 EV74
Hampstead Gdns. NW11 62 DA58
Hampstead Gdns., Rom. 68 EV57
Hampstead Grn. NW3 62 DE64
Hampstead Gro. NW3 62 DC62
Hampstead High St. NW3 62 DC63
Hampstead Hill Gdns. NW3 62 DD63
Hampstead La. N6 62 DD59
Hampstead La. NW3 62 DD60
Hampstead Rd. NW1 5 K1
Hampstead Rd. NW1 77 DJ68
Hampstead Sq. NW3 62 DC62
Hampstead Wk. E3 79 DZ67
Parnell Rd.
Hampstead Way NW11 61 CZ57
Hampton Clo. N11 49 DH50
Balmoral Ave.
Hampton Clo. NW6 76 DA69
Hampton Clo. SW20 103 CW94
Hampton Ct. N1 77 DP65
Upper St.
Hampton Ct. Ave., E.Mol. 115 CD99
Hampton Ct. Cres., E.Mol. 115 CD97
Hampton Ct. Palace, E.Mol. 115 CE97
Hampton Ct. Par., E.Mol. 115 CE98
Creek Rd.
Hampton Ct. Rd., E.Mol. 115 CF97
Hampton Ct. Rd., Hmptn. 114 CC96
Hampton Ct. Rd., Kings.T. 115 CJ96
Hampton Ct. Way, E.Mol. 115 CE100
Hampton Ct. Way, T.Ditt. 115 CE103
Hampton Fm. Ind. Est., Felt. 100 BY90
Hampton Gro., Epsom 131 CT111
Hampton La., Felt. 100 BY91
Hampton Mead, Loug. 39 EP41
Hampton Ri., Har. 60 CL58
Hampton Rd. E4 51 DZ50
Hampton Rd. E7 66 EH64
Hampton Rd. E11 65 ED60
Hampton Rd., Croy. 120 DQ100
Hampton Rd., Hmptn. 101 CD92
Hampton Rd., Ilf. 67 EP63
Hampton Rd., Tedd. 101 CD92
Hampton Rd., Twick. 101 CD90
Hampton Rd., Wor.Pk. 117 CU103
Hampton Rd. E., Felt. 100 BZ90
Hampton Rd. W., Felt. 100 BY89
Hampton St. SE1 10 G9
Hampton St. SE1 92 DQ77
Hampton St. SE17 10 G9
Hampton St. SE17 91 DP77
Hamsey Grn. Gdns., Warl. 148 DV116
Hamsey Way, S.Croy. 148 DV115
Hamshades Clo., Sid. 109 ET90
Hanah Ct. SW19 103 CX94
Hanameel St. E16 80 EH74
Hanbury Clo. (Cheshunt), Wal.Cr. 23 DX30
Hanbury Dr. N21 35 DM43
Hanbury Dr., West. 136 EH113
Hanbury Ms. N1 78 DQ67
Mary St.
Hanbury Rd. N17 50 DV54
Hanbury Rd. W3 88 CP75
Hanbury St. E1 78 DT71
Hanbury Wk., Bex. 111 FE90
Hancock Ct., Borwd. 32 CQ39
Hancock Rd. E3 79 EC69
Hancock Rd. SE19 106 DR93
Hand Ct. WC1 6 C7
Handa Wk. N1 78 DR65
Clephane Rd.
Handcroft Rd., Croy. 119 DP101
Handel Clo., Edg. 46 CM51
Handel Pl. NW10 74 CR65
Mitchellbrook Way
Handel St. WC1 5 P4
Handel St. WC1 77 DL70
Handel Way, Edg. 46 CN52
Handen Rd. SE12 108 EE85
Handforth Rd. SW9 91 DN80
Handforth Rd., Ilf. 67 EP62
Winston Way
Handley Rd. E9 78 DW67
Handowe Clo. NW4 61 CU56
Hands Wk. E16 80 EG72
Butchers Rd.
Handside Clo., Wor.Pk. 117 CX102
Carters Clo.
Handsworth Ave. E4 51 ED51
Handsworth Rd. N17 64 DR55
Handsworth Way, Wat. 43 BU48
Hayling Rd.
Handtrough Way, Bark. 81 EP68
Fresh Wf. Rd.
Hanford Clo. SW18 104 DA88
Hanford Row SW19 103 CW93
Hangar Ruding, Wat. 44 BZ48
Hanger Grn. W5 74 CN70
Hanger Hill, Wey. 127 BP107
Hanger La. W5 74 CL68
Hanger Vale La. W3 74 CM72
Hanger Vale La. W5 74 CM72
Hanger Vw. Way W3 74 CN72
Hangrove Hill, Orp. 137 EP113
Cudham Rd.
Hankey Pl. SE1 11 L5
Hankey Pl. SE1 92 DR75
Hankins La. NW7 46 CS47
Hanley Pl., Beck. 107 EA94
Hanley Rd. N4 63 DL60
Hanmer Wk. N7 63 DM62
Newington Barrow Way
Hannah Clo. NW10 60 CQ63
Hannah Clo., Beck. 121 EC97
Hannah Mary Way SE1 92 DU77
Simms Rd.
Hannah Ms., Wall. 133 DJ108
Hannards Way, Ilf. 54 EV50
Hannay La. N8 63 DK59
Hannay Wk. SW16 105 DK89
Dingley La.
Hannell Rd. SW6 89 CY80
Hannen Rd. SE27 105 DP90
Norwood High St.
Hannibal Rd. E1 78 DW71
Hannibal Rd., Stai. 98 BK87
Hannibal Way, Croy. 133 DM106
Hannington Rd. SW4 91 DH83
Hanover Ave. E16 80 EG74
Silvertown Way
Hanover Ave., Felt. 99 BU88
Hanover Circle, Hayes 71 BQ72
Hanover Clo., Rich. 88 CN80
Hanover Clo., Sutt. 131 CY105
Hanover Ct. W12 75 CU74
Uxbridge Rd.
Hanover Dr., Chis. 109 EQ91
Hanover Gdns. SE11 91 DN79
Hanover Gdns., Ilf. 53 EQ52
Hanover Gate NW1 4 C3
Hanover Gate NW1 76 DE69
Hanover Pk. SE15 92 DU81
Hanover Pl. WC2 6 A9
Hanover Rd. N15 64 DT56
Hanover Rd. NW10 75 CW66
Hanover Rd. SW19 104 DC94
Hanover Sq. W1 5 J9
Hanover Sq. W1 77 DH72
Hanover St. W1 5 J9
Hanover St. W1 77 DH72
Hanover St., Croy. 119 DP104
Abbey Rd.
Hanover Ter. NW1 4 C3
Hanover Ter. NW1 76 DE69
Hanover Ter., Islw. 87 CG81
Hanover Ter. Ms. NW1 4 C3
Hanover Wk., Wey. 113 BS104
Hanover Way, Bexh. 96 EX83
Hanover W. Ind. Est. NW10 74 CR69
Acton La.
Hanover Yd. N1 77 DP68
Noel Rd.
Hans Cres. SW1 8 D6
Hans Cres. SW1 90 DF76
Hans Pl. SW1 8 E6
Hans Pl. SW1 90 DF76
Hans Rd. SW3 8 D6
Hans Rd. SW3 90 DF76
Hans St. SW1 8 E7
Hansard Ms. W14 89 CX75
Holland Rd.
Hansart Way, Enf. 35 DN39
The Ridgeway
Hanselin Clo., Stan. 45 CF50
Chenduit Way
Hansen Dr. N21 35 DM43
Hansha Dr., Edg. 46 CR53
Hansler Gro., E.Mol. 115 CD99
Hansler Rd. SE22 106 DT85
Hansol Rd., Bexh. 110 EY85
Hanson Clo. SW12 105 DH87
Hanson Clo. SW14 88 CQ83
Hanson Clo., Beck. 107 EB93
Hanson Clo., Loug. 39 EQ40
Hanson Dr.
Hanson Clo., West Dr. 84 BM76
Hanson Dr., Loug. 39 EQ40
Hanson Gdns., Sthl. 86 BY75
Hanson Grn., Loug. 39 EQ40
Hanson Dr.
Hanson St. W1 5 K6
Hanson St. W1 77 DJ71
Hanway Pl. W1 5 M8
Hanway Rd. W7 73 CD72
Hanway St. W1 5 M8
Hanway St. W1 77 DK72
Hanworth Rd., Felt. 99 BV88
Hanworth Rd., Hmptn. 100 BZ91
Hanworth Rd., Houns. 100 BY88
Hanworth Rd., Sun. 99 BU94
Hanworth Ter., Houns. 86 CB84
Hanworth Trd. Est., Felt. 100 BY90
Hanyards End (Cuffley), Pot.B. 21 DL28
Hanyards La. (Cuffley), Pot.B. 21 DK28
Hapgood Clo., Grnf. 59 CD64
Harads Pl. E1 78 DU73
Ensign St.
Harben Rd. NW6 76 DC66
Harberson Rd. E15 80 EF67
Harberson Rd. SW12 105 DH88
Harberton Rd. N19 63 DJ60
Harbet Rd. E4 51 DX50
Harbet Rd. N18 51 DX50
Harbet Rd. W2 4 A7
Harbet Rd. W2 76 DD71
Harbex Clo., Bex. 111 FB87
Harbinger Rd. E14 93 EB77
Harbledown Pl., Orp. 124 EW98
Okemore Gdns.
Harbledown Rd. SW6 90 DA81
Harbledown Rd., S.Croy. 134 DU111
Harbord Clo. SE5 92 DR82
De Crespigny Pk.
Harbord St. SW6 89 CX81
Harborne Clo., Wat. 44 BW50
Harborough Ave., Sid. 109 ES87
Harborough Rd. SW16 105 DM91
Harbour Ave. SW10 90 DC81
Harbour Ex. Sq. E14 93 EB75
Harbour Rd. SE5 92 DQ83
Harbourer Clo., Ilf. 54 EV50
Harbourer Rd., Ilf. 54 EV50
Harbourfield Rd., Bans. 146 DB115
Harbridge Ave. SW15 103 CT87
Harbury Rd., Cars. 132 DE109
Harbut Rd. SW11 90 DD84
Harcombe Rd. N16 64 DS62
Harcourt Ave. E12 67 EM63
Harcourt Ave., Edg. 46 CQ48
Harcourt Ave., Sid. 110 EW86
Harcourt Ave., Wall. 133 DH105
Harcourt Clo., Islw. 87 CG83
Harcourt Fld., Wall. 133 DH105
Harcourt Rd. E15 80 EF68
Harcourt Rd. N22 49 DK53
Harcourt Rd. SE4 93 DY84
Harcourt Rd. SW19 104 DA94
Russell Rd.
Harcourt Rd., Bexh. 96 EY84
Harcourt Rd., Th.Hth. 119 DM100
Harcourt Rd., Wall. 133 DH105
Harcourt Rd. (Bushey), Wat. 30 CC43
Harcourt St. W1 4 C7
Harcourt St. W1 76 DE71
Harcourt Ter. SW10 90 DB78
Hardcastle Clo., Croy. 120 DT100
Hardcourts Clo., W.Wick. 121 EB104
Hardel Ri. SW2 105 DP88
Hardel Wk. SW2 105 DN87
Papworth Way
Hardens Manorway SE7 94 EK76
Harders Rd. SE15 92 DV82
Hardess St. SE24 92 DQ83
Herne Hill Rd.
Hardie Clo. NW10 60 CR64
Hardie Rd., Dag. 69 FC62
Harding Clo. SE17 92 DQ79
Hillingdon St.
Harding Clo., Wat. 16 BW33
Harding Ho., Hayes 71 BU72
Harding Rd., Bexh. 96 EZ82
Harding Rd., Epsom 144 CS119
Hardinge Clo., Uxb. 71 BP72
Dawley Ave.
Hardinge La. E1 78 DW72
Hardinge St.
Hardinge Rd. N18 50 DS50
Hardinge Rd. NW10 75 CV67
Hardinge St. E1 78 DW72
Hardings La. SE20 107 DX93
Hardman Rd. SE7 94 EH78
Hardman Rd., Kings.T. 116 CL96
Hardwick Clo., Lthd. 142 CC115
Hardwick Clo., Stan. 45 CJ50
Hardwick Grn. W13 73 CH71
Hardwick St. EC1 6 E3
Hardwick St. EC1 77 DN69
Hardwicke Ave., Houns. 86 CA81
Hardwicke Pl., St.Alb. 17 CK27
Hardwicke Rd. N13 49 DL51
Hardwicke Rd. W4 88 CQ77
Hardwicke Rd., Rich. 101 CJ91
Hardwicke St., Bark. 81 EQ67
Hardwicks Way SW18 104 DA85
Buckhold Rd.
Hardwidge St. SE1 11 M4
Hardy Ave. E16 80 EG74
Silvertown Way
Hardy Ave., Ruis. 57 BV64
Hardy Clo. SE16 93 DX75
Middleton Dr.
Hardy Clo., Barn. 33 CY43
Hardy Clo., Pnr. 58 BX59
Hardy Rd. E4 51 DZ51
Silver Birch Ave.
Hardy Rd. SE3 94 EF79
Hardy Rd. SW19 104 DB94
Hardy Way, Enf. 35 DN39
Hare & Billet Rd. SE3 93 ED81
Hare Ct. EC4 6 D9
Hare Cres., Wat. 15 BU32
Hare Hall La., Rom. 69 FH56
Hare Hill Clo., Wok. 140 BG115
Hare La., Esher 129 CD106
Hare Marsh E2 78 DU70
Cheshire St.
Hare Pl. EC4 6 E9
Hare Row E2 78 DV68
Hare St. SE18 95 EN76
Hare Wk. N1 7 N1
Hare Wk. N1 78 DS68
Harebell Dr. E6 81 EN71
Harebell Hill, Cob. 128 BX114
Harebreaks, The, Wat. 29 BU36
Harecastle Clo., Hayes 72 BY70
Braunston Dr.
Harecourt Rd. N1 78 DQ65
Harecroft, Lthd. 142 CB123
Haredale Rd. SE24 92 DQ84
Haredon Clo. SE23 106 DW87
Harefield, Esher 115 CE104
Harefield Ave., Sutt. 131 CY109
Harefield Clo., Enf. 35 DN39
Harefield Ms. SE4 93 DZ83
Harefield Rd. N8 63 DK57
Harefield Rd. SE4 93 DZ83
Harefield Rd. SW16 105 DM94
Harefield Rd., Rick. 42 BK47
Harefield Rd., Sid. 110 EX89
Harefield Rd., Uxb. 70 BJ66
Harendon, Tad. 145 CW121
Hares Bank, Croy. 135 ED110
Haresfield Rd., Dag. 82 FA65
Harestone Dr., Cat. 148 DT124
Harewood, Rick. 28 BH42
Harewood Ave. NW1 4 C5
Harewood Ave. NW1 76 DE70
Harewood Ave., Nthlt. 72 BY66
Harewood Clo., Nthlt. 72 BZ66
Harewood Dr., Ilf. 53 EM54
Harewood Gdns., S.Croy. 148 DV115
Harewood Hill, Epp. 39 ES35
Harewood Pl. W1 5 J9
Harewood Rd. SW19 104 DE93
Harewood Rd., Islw. 87 CF80
Harewood Rd., S.Croy. 134 DS107
Harewood Rd., Wat. 43 BV47
Harewood Row NW1 4 C6
Harewood Ter., Sthl. 86 BZ77
Harfield Gdns. SE5 92 DS83
Harfield Rd., Sun. 114 BX96
Harford Clo. E4 51 EB45
Harford Dr., Wat. 29 BS38
Harford Rd. E4 51 EB45
Harford St. E1 79 DY70
Harford Wk. N2 62 DD56
Harfst Way, Swan. 125 FC95
Hargood Clo., Har. 60 CL58
Hargood Rd. SE3 94 EJ81
Hargrave Pk. N19 63 DJ61
Hargrave Pl. N7 63 DK64
Brecknock Rd.
Hargrave Rd. N19 63 DJ61
Hargreaves Ave. (Cheshunt), Wal.Cr. 22 DV30
Hargreaves Clo. (Cheshunt), Wal.Cr. 22 DV31
Hargwyne St. SW9 91 DM83
Haringey Pk. N8 63 DL58
Haringey Pas. N4 63 DP57
Warham Rd.
Haringey Pas. N8 63 DP56
Haringey Rd. N8 63 DL56
Harington Ter. N9 50 DR48
Harington Ter. N18 50 DR48
Harkett Clo., Har. 45 CF54
Byron Rd.

Harkett Ct., Har. 45 CF54
Harkness (Cheshunt), Wal.Cr. 22 DV29
Harkness Clo., Epsom 145 CW116
Harland Ave., Croy. 120 DT104
Harland Ave., Sid. 109 ER90
Harland Clo. SW19 118 DB97
Harland Rd. SE12 108 EG88
Harlands Gro., Orp. 137 EP105
Pinecrest Gdns.
Harlech Gdns., Houns. 86 BW79
Harlech Rd. N14 49 DL48
Harlech Rd., Abb.L. 15 BU31
Harlech Twr. W3 88 CQ75
Harlequin Ave., Brent. 87 CG79
Harlequin Clo., Hayes 72 BX71
Cygnet Way
Harlequin Clo., Islw. 101 CE85
Harlequin Rd., Tedd. 101 CH94
Harlescott Rd. SE15 93 DX84
Harlesden Gdns. NW10 75 CT67
Harlesden La. NW10 75 CU67
Harlesden Rd. NW10 75 CU67
Harleston Clo. E5 64 DW61
Theydon Rd.
Harley Clo., Wem. 73 CK65
Harley Ct. E11 66 EG59
Blake Hall Rd.
Harley Cres., Har. 59 CD56
Harley Gdns. SW10 90 DC78
Harley Gdns., Orp. 137 ES105
Harley Gro. E3 79 DZ69
Harley Pl. W1 5 H7
Harley Pl. W1 77 DH71
Harley Rd. NW3 76 DD66
Harley Rd. NW10 74 CS68
Harley Rd., Har. 59 CD56
Harley St. W1 5 H5
Harley St. W1 77 DH71
Harleyford, Brom. 122 EJ95
Harleyford Rd. SE11 91 DM79
Harleyford St. SE11 91 DN79
Harlington Clo., Hayes 85 BQ80
New Rd.
Harlington Rd., Bexh. 96 EY83
Harlington Rd., Houns. 85 BT84
Harlington Rd., Uxb. 70 BN69
Harlington Rd. E., Felt. 99 BV87
Harlington Rd. W., Felt. 99 BV86
Harlow Gdns., Rom. 55 FC51
Harlow Rd. N13 50 DR48
Harlow Rd., Rain. 83 FF67
Harlton Ct., Wal.Abb. 24 EF34
Harlyn Dr., Pnr. 57 BV55
Harman Ave., Wdf.Grn. 52 EF51
Harman Clo. E4 51 ED49
Harman Clo. NW2 61 CY62
Harman Dr. NW2 61 CY62
Harman Dr., Sid. 109 ET86
Harman Pl., Pur. 133 DP111
Harman Rd., Enf. 36 DT43
Harmondsworth La., West Dr. 84 BL79
Harmondsworth Rd., West Dr. 84 BL78
Harmony Clo. NW11 61 CY57
Harmony Clo., Wall. 133 DK109
Harmony Way NW4 61 CW56
Harmood Gro. NW1 77 DH66
Clarence Way
Harmood Pl. NW1 77 DH66
Harmood St.
Harmood St. NW1 77 DH65
Harmsworth St. SE17 91 DP78
Harmsworth Way N20 47 CZ46
Harnage Rd., Brent. 87 CH80
Harness Rd. SE28 96 EU75
Harnetts Clo., Swan. 125 FD100
Harold Ave., Belv. 96 EZ78
Harold Ave., Hayes 85 BT76
Harold Cres., Wal.Abb. 23 EC32
Harold Est. SE1 11 N7
Harold Est. SE1 92 DS76
Harold Gibbons Ct. SE7 94 EJ79
Victoria Way
Harold Pl. SE11 91 DN78
Kennington La.
Harold Rd. E4 51 EC49
Harold Rd. E11 66 EE60
Harold Rd. E13 80 EH67
Harold Rd. N8 63 DM57
Harold Rd. N15 64 DT57
Harold Rd. NW10 74 CR69
Harold Rd. SE19 106 DR94
Harold Rd., Sutt. 132 DD105
Harold Rd., Wdf.Grn. 52 EG53
Haroldstone Rd. E17 65 DX57
Harp All. EC4 6 F8
Harp Island Clo. NW10 60 CR61
Harp La. EC3 11 M1
Harp Rd. W7 73 CE70
Harpenden Rd. E12 66 EJ61
Harpenden Rd. SE27 105 DP89
Harper Clo. N14 35 DJ43
Alexandra Ct.
Harper La., Rad. 17 CG32
Harper Rd. E6 81 EM72
Harper Rd. SE1 11 J6
Harper Rd. SE1 92 DQ76
Harpers Yd. N17 50 DT53
Ruskin Rd.
Harpley Sq. E1 78 DW69
Harpour Rd., Bark. 81 EQ65
Harpsden St. SW11 90 DG81
Harpur Ms. WC1 6 B6
Harpur St. WC1 6 B6
Harpur St. WC1 77 DM71
Harpurs, Tad. 145 CX122
Harraden Rd. SE3 94 EJ81
Harrap St. E14 79 EC73
Harrier Clo., Horn. 83 FH65
Harrier Ms. SE28 95 ER76
Harrier Rd. NW9 46 CS54
Harrier Way E6 81 EM71
Harrier Way, Wal.Abb. 24 EG34
Harriers Clo. W5 74 CL73
Harries Ct., Wal.Abb. 24 EG32
Harries Rd., Hayes 72 BW70
Harriet Clo. E8 78 DU67
Harriet Gdns., Croy. 120 DU103
Harriet St. SW1 8 E5
Harriet Tubman Clo. SW2 105 DM87
Upper Tulse Hill
Harriet Wk. SW1 8 E5
Harriet Wk. SW1 90 DF75
Harriet Way (Bushey), Wat. 45 CD45
Harringay Gdns. N8 63 DP56
Harringay Rd. N15 63 DP57
Harrington Clo. NW10 60 CR62
Harrington Clo., Croy. 119 DL103
Harrington Gdns. SW7 90 DC77
Harrington Hill E5 64 DV60
Harrington Rd. E11 66 EE60
Harrington Rd. SE25 120 DU98
Harrington Rd. SW7 8 A8
Harrington Rd. SW7 90 DD77
Harrington Sq. NW1 5 K1
Harrington Sq. NW1 77 DJ68
Harrington St. NW1 5 K1
Harrington St. NW1 77 DJ69
Harrington Way SE18 94 EK76
Harriott Clo. SE10 94 EF77
Harriotts Clo., Ash. 143 CJ120
Harriotts La.
Harriotts La., Ash. 143 CJ119
Harris Clo., Enf. 35 DP39
Harris Clo., Houns. 86 CA81
Harris La., Rad. 18 CN34
Harris Rd., Bexh. 96 EY81
Harris Rd., Dag. 68 EZ64
Harris Rd., Wat. 29 BU35
Harris St. E17 65 DZ59
Harris St. SE5 92 DR80
Harris Way, Sun. 113 BS95
Harrison Clo., Nthwd. 43 BQ51
Harrison Ct., Shep. 113 BP99
Greeno Cres.
Harrison Dr., Epp. 27 FB26
Harrison Rd., Dag. 83 FB65
Harrison St. WC1 6 A3
Harrison St. WC1 77 DL69
Harrison Wk. (Cheshunt), Wal.Cr. 23 DX30
Harrison Way, Sev. 154 FG122
Harrisons Ri., Croy. 119 DP104
Harrogate Rd., Wat. 44 BW48
Harrold Rd., Dag. 68 EV64
Harrow Ave., Enf. 36 DT44
Harrow Clo., Add. 112 BH103
Harrow Clo., Chess. 129 CK108
Harrow Cres., Rom. 55 FH52
Harrow Dr. N9 50 DT46
Harrow Dr., Horn. 69 FH58
Harrow Flds. Gdns., Har. 59 CE62
Harrow Gdns., Orp. 138 EV105
Harrow Gdns., Warl. 149 DZ116
Harrow Grn. E11 66 EE62
Harrow Rd.
Harrow La. E14 79 EC73
Harrow Manorway SE2 96 EW76
Harrow Pk., Har. 59 CE61
Harrow Pas., Kings.T. 115 CK96
Market Pl.
Harrow Pl. E1 7 N8
Harrow Pl. E1 78 DS72
Harrow Rd. E6 80 EL67
Harrow Rd. E11 66 EE62
Harrow Rd. NW10 75 CV69
Harrow Rd. W2 75 CX69
Harrow Rd. W9 75 CX69
Harrow Rd. W10 75 CX69
Harrow Rd., Bark. 81 ES67
Harrow Rd., Cars. 132 DE106
Harrow Rd., Felt. 98 BN88
Harrow Rd., Ilf. 67 EQ63
Harrow Rd., Sev. 152 EY115
Harrow Rd., Warl. 149 DZ115
Harrow Rd., Wem. 59 CF63
Harrow Rd. (Tokyngton), Wem. 60 CN64
Harrow Vw., Har. 44 CC53
Harrow Vw., Hayes 71 BU72
Harrow Vw., Uxb. 71 BQ69
Harrow Vw. Rd. W5 73 CH70
Harrow Way, Shep. 113 BQ96
Harrow Way, Wat. 44 BY48
Harrow Weald Pk., Har. 45 CD51
Harroway Rd. SW11 90 DD82
Harrowby St. W1 4 C8
Harrowby St. W1 76 DE72
Harrowdene Clo., Wem. 59 CK63
Harrowdene Gdns., Tedd. 101 CG93
Harrowdene Rd., Wem. 59 CK64
Harrowes Meade, Edg. 46 CN48
Harrowgate Rd. E9 79 DY65
Hart Cres., Chig. 53 ET50
Hart Dyke Cres., Swan. 125 FD97
Hart Dyke Rd.
Hart Dyke Rd., Orp. 124 EW102
Hart Dyke Rd., Swan. 125 FD96
Hart Gro. W5 74 CN74
Hart Gro., Sthl. 72 CA71
Hart Rd., W.Byf. 126 BL113
Hart St. EC3 7 N10
Harte Rd., Houns. 86 BZ82
Hartfield Ave., Borwd. 32 CN43
Hartfield Ave., Nthlt. 71 BV68
Hartfield Clo., Borwd. 32 CN43
Hartfield Cres. SW19 103 CZ94
Hartfield Cres., W.Wick. 122 EG104
Hartfield Gro. SE20 120 DW95
Hartfield Rd. SW19 103 CZ93
Hartfield Rd., Chess. 129 CK106
Hartfield Rd., W.Wick. 136 EG105
Hartfield Ter. E3 79 EA68
Hartford Ave., Har. 59 CG55
Hartford Rd., Bex. 110 FA86
Hartford Rd., Epsom 130 CN107
Hartforde Rd., Borwd. 32 CN40
Harthall La., Hem.H. 15 BP28
Hartham Clo. N7 63 DL64
Hartham Clo., Islw. 87 CG81
Hartham Rd. N7 63 DL64
Hartham Rd. N17 50 DT54
Hartham Rd., Islw. 87 CF81
Harting Rd. SE9 108 EL91
Hartington Clo., Har. 59 CE63
Hartington Ct. W4 88 CP80
Hartington Rd. E16 80 EH72
Hartington Rd. E17 65 DY58
Hartington Rd. SW8 91 DL81
Hartington Rd. W4 88 CP80
Hartington Rd. W13 73 CH73
Hartington Rd., Sthl. 86 BY76
Hartington Rd., Twick. 101 CH87
Hartismere Rd. SW6 89 CZ80
Hartlake Rd. E9 79 DX65
Hartland Clo. N21 36 DQ44
Elmscott Gdns.
Hartland Clo., Add. 126 BJ109
Hartland Clo., Edg. 46 CN47
Hartland Dr., Edg. 46 CN47
Hartland Dr., Ruis. 57 BV62
Hartland Rd. E15 80 EF66
Hartland Rd. N11 48 DF50
Hartland Rd. NW1 77 DH66
Hartland Rd. NW6 75 CZ68
Hartland Rd., Add. 126 BG108
Hartland Rd., Epp. 26 EU31
Hartland Rd., Hmptn. 100 CB91
Hartland Rd., Horn. 69 FG61
Hartland Rd., Islw. 87 CG83
Hartland Rd., Mord. 118 DA101
Hartland Rd. (Cheshunt), Wal.Cr. 23 DX30
Hartland Way, Croy. 121 DY103
Hartland Way, Mord. 117 CZ101
Hartlands Clo., Bex. 110 EZ86
Hartley Ave. E6 80 EL67
Hartley Ave. NW7 47 CT50
Hartley Clo. NW7 47 CT50
Hartley Clo., Brom. 123 EM96
Hartley Down, Pur. 147 DM115
Hartley Fm. Est., Pur. 147 DM115
Hartley Hill, Pur. 147 DM115
Hartley Old Rd., Pur. 147 DM115
Hartley Rd. E11 66 EF60
Hartley Rd., Croy. 119 DP101
Hartley Rd., Well. 96 EW80
Hartley St. E2 78 DW69
Hartley Way, Pur. 147 DM115
Hartmann Rd. E16 80 EK74
Hartmoor Ms., Enf. 37 DX37
Ordnance Rd.
Hartnoll St. N7 63 DM64
Eden Gro.
Harton Clo., Brom. 122 EK95
Harton Rd. N9 50 DV47
Harton St. SE8 93 EA81
Harts Clo. (Bushey), Wat. 30 CA39
Harts Gro., Wdf.Grn. 52 EG50
Harts Hill Clo., Uxb. 70 BN65
Harts La. SE14 93 DY80
Harts La., Bark. 81 EP65
Hartsbourne Ave. (Bushey), Wat. 44 CC47
Hartsbourne Clo. (Bushey), Wat. 45 CD47
Hartsbourne Rd. (Bushey), Wat. 45 CD47
Hartscroft, Croy. 135 DY109
Hartshorn All. EC3 7 N9
Hartshorn Gdns. E6 81 EN70
Hartslands Rd., Sev. 155 FJ123
Hartslock Dr. SE2 96 EX75
Hartsmead Rd. SE9 109 EM89
Hartsmoor Ms., Enf. 37 DX37
Hartspring Ind. Est., Wat. 30 CA40
Hartspring La. (Bushey), Wat. 30 CA40
Hartsway, Enf. 36 DW42
Hartswood Grn. (Bushey), Wat. 45 CD47
Hartswood Rd. W12 89 CT75
Hartsworth Clo. E13 80 EF68
Hartville Rd. SE18 95 ES77
Hartwell Dr. E4 51 EC51
Hartwell St. E8 78 DT65
Dalston La.
Harvard Hill W4 88 CP79
Harvard La. W4 88 CP78
Harvard Rd.
Harvard Rd. SE13 107 EC85
Harvard Rd. W4 88 CP78
Harvard Rd., Islw. 87 CE81
Harvard Wk., Horn. 69 FG63
Harvel Clo., Orp. 124 EU97
Harvel Cres. SE2 96 EX78
Harvest Bank Rd., W.Wick. 122 EF104
Harvest Ct., Shep. 112 BN98
Harvest End, Wat. 30 BX36
Harvest La., T.Ditt. 115 CG100
Harvest Rd., Felt. 99 BU91
Harvest Rd. (Bushey), Wat. 30 CB42
Harvest Way, Swan. 125 FD101
Harvester Rd., Epsom 130 CR110
Harvesters Clo., Islw. 101 CD85
Harvey Gdns. E11 66 EF60
Harvey Rd.
Harvey Gdns. SE7 94 EJ78
Harvey Gdns., Loug. 39 EP41
Harvey Ho., Brent. 88 CL78
Green Dragon La.
Harvey Pt. E16 80 EH71
Fife Rd.
Harvey Rd. E11 66 EE60
Harvey Rd. N8 63 DM57
Harvey Rd. SE5 92 DR81
Harvey Rd., Houns. 100 BZ87
Harvey Rd., Ilf. 67 EP64
Harvey Rd., Nthlt. 72 BW66
Harvey Rd., Rick. 28 BN44
Harvey Rd., St.Alb. 17 CJ26
Harvey Rd., Uxb. 70 BN68
Harvey Rd., Walt. 113 BU101
Harvey St. N1 78 DR67
Harveyfields, Wal.Abb. 23 EC34
Harveys La., Rom. 69 FD61
Harvil Rd. (Harefield), Uxb. 56 BJ56
Harvil Rd. (Ickenham), Uxb. 56 BL60
Harvill Rd., Sid. 110 EX92
Harvington Wk. E8 78 DU66
Wilman Gro.
Harvist Est. N7 63 DN63
Harvist Rd. NW6 75 CX68
Harwater Dr., Loug. 39 EM40
Harwell Clo., Ruis. 57 BR60
Harwell Pas. N2 62 DF56
Harwich La. EC2 7 N6
Harwich La. EC2 78 DS71
Harwood Ave., Brom. 122 EH96
Harwood Ave., Mitch. 118 DE97
Harwood Clo. N12 48 DE51
Summerfields Ave.
Harwood Clo., Wem. 59 CK63
Harrowdene Rd.
Harwood Dr., Uxb. 70 BM67
Harwood Rd. SW6 90 DA80
Harwood Ter. SW6 90 DB81
Harwoods Rd., Wat. 29 BU42
Harwoods Yd. N21 49 DN45
Wades Hill
Hascombe Ter. SE5 92 DR82
Haselbury Rd. N9 50 DS48
Haselbury Rd. N18 50 DS49
Haseldine Rd., St.Alb. 17 CK26
Haseley End SE23 106 DW87
Tyson Rd.
Haselrigge Rd. SW4 91 DK84
Haseltine Rd. SE26 107 DZ91
Haselwood Dr., Enf. 35 DP42
Haskard Rd., Dag. 68 EX63
Haskell Ho. NW10 74 CR67
Hasker St. SW3 8 C8
Hasker St. SW3 90 DE77
Haslam Ave., Sutt. 117 CY102
Haslam Clo. N1 77 DN66
Haslam Clo., Uxb. 57 BQ61
Haslemere Ave. NW4 61 CX58
Haslemere Ave. SW18 104 DB89
Haslemere Ave. W7 87 CG76
Haslemere Ave. W13 87 CG76
Haslemere Ave., Barn. 48 DF46
Haslemere Ave., Houns. 86 BW82
Haslemere Ave., Mitch. 118 DD96
Haslemere Clo., Hmptn. 100 BZ92
Haslemere Clo., Wall. 133 DL106
Stafford Rd.
Haslemere Gdns. N3 61 CZ55
Haslemere Heathrow Est., Houns. 85 BV82
Haslemere Rd. N8 63 DK59
Haslemere Rd. N21 49 DP47
Haslemere Rd., Bexh. 96 EZ82
Haslemere Rd., Ilf. 67 ET61
Haslemere Rd., Th.Hth. 119 DP99
Hasler Clo. SE28 82 EV73
Haslett Rd., Shep. 113 BS96
Hasluck Gdns., Barn. 34 DB44
Hassard St. E2 78 DT68
Hackney Rd.
Hassendean Rd. SE3 94 EH79
Hassett Rd. E9 79 DX65
Hassock Wd., Kes. 136 EK105
Hassocks Clo. SE26 106 DV90
Hassocks Rd. SW16 119 DJ95
Hassop Rd. NW2 61 CX63
Hassop Wk. SE9 108 EL91
Hasted Rd. SE7 94 EK78
Hastings Ave., Ilf. 67 EQ56
Hastings Clo. SE15 92 DU80
Hastings Clo., Barn. 34 DC42
Leicester Rd.
Hastings Dr., Surb. 115 CJ100
Hastings Ho. SE18 95 EM77
Cardwell Rd.
Hastings Rd. N11 49 DJ50
Hastings Rd. N17 64 DR55
Hastings Rd. W13 73 CH73
Hastings Rd., Brom. 122 EL102
Hastings Rd., Croy. 120 DT102
Hastings Rd., Rom. 69 FH57
Hastings St. WC1 5 P3
Hastings St. WC1 77 DL69
Hastings Way, Rick. 29 BQ42
Hastings Way (Bushey), Wat. 30 BY42
Hastoe Clo., Hayes 72 BY70
Kingsash Dr.
Hat and Mitre Ct. EC1 6 G5
Hatch, The, Enf. 37 DX39
Hatch Clo., Add. 112 BH104
Hatch Gdns., Tad. 145 CX120
Hatch Gro., Rom. 68 EY56
Hatch La. E4 51 ED49
Hatch La., Bans. 146 DF115
Rectory La.
Hatch La., Couls. 146 DG115
Hatch La., West Dr. 84 BK80
Hatch La., Wok. 141 BP120
Hatch Pl., Kings.T. 102 CM92
Hatch Rd. SW16 119 DL96
Hatch Side, Chig. 53 EN50
Hatcham Pk. Ms. SE14 93 DX81
Hatcham Pk. Rd.
Hatcham Pk. Rd. SE14 93 DX81
Hatcham Rd. SE15 92 DW79
Hatchard Rd. N19 63 DK61
Hatchcroft NW4 61 CV55
Hatchett Rd., Felt. 99 BQ88
Hatchwood Clo., Wdf.Grn. 52 EF49
Sunset Ave.
Hatcliffe Clo. SE3 94 EF83
Hatcliffe St. SE10 94 EF78
Woolwich Rd.
Hatfield Clo. SE14 93 DX80
Reaston St.
Hatfield Clo., Ilf. 67 EP55
Hatfield Clo., Mitch. 118 DD98
Hatfield Clo., Sutt. 132 DB109
Hatfield Clo., W.Byf. 126 BH112
Hatfield Mead, Mord. 118 DA99
Central Rd.
Hatfield Rd. E15 66 EE64
Hatfield Rd. W4 88 CR75
Hatfield Rd. W13 73 CG74
Hatfield Rd., Ash. 144 CM119
Hatfield Rd., Dag. 82 EY65
Hatfield Rd., Pot.B. 20 DC30
Hatfield Rd., Wat. 29 BV39
Hatfields SE1 10 E2
Hatfields SE1 77 DN74
Hatfields, Loug. 39 EP41
Hathaway Clo., Brom. 123 EM102
Hathaway Clo., Ruis. 57 BT63
Stafford Rd.
Hathaway Clo., Stan. 45 CG50
Hathaway Cres. E12 81 EM65
Hathaway Gdns. W13 73 CF71
Hathaway Gdns., Rom. 68 EX57
Hathaway Rd., Croy. 119 DP101
Hatherleigh Clo., Chess. 129 CK106
Hatherleigh Clo., Mord. 118 DA98
Hatherleigh Gdns., Pot.B. 20 DD31
Hatherleigh Rd., Ruis. 57 BU61
Hatherley Cres., Sid. 110 EU89
Hatherley Gdns. E6 80 EK68
Hatherley Gdns. N8 63 DL58
Hatherley Gro. W2 76 DB72
Hatherley Ms. E17 65 EA56
Hatherley Rd. E17 65 DZ56
Hatherley Rd., Rich. 88 CM81
Hatherley Rd., Sid. 110 EU91
Hatherley St. SW1 9 L9
Hathern Gdns. SE9 109 EN91
The Knole
Hatherop Rd., Hmptn. 100 BZ94
Hatherwood, Lthd. 143 CK121
Hathorne Clo. SE15 92 DV82
Hathway St. SE15 92 DW82
Gibbon Rd.
Hathway Ter. SE14 92 DW82
Gibbon Rd.
Hatley Ave., Ilf. 67 EQ56
Hatley Clo. N11 48 DF50
Hatley Rd. N4 63 DM61
Hatteraick St. SE16 92 DW75
Brunel Rd.
Hatters La., Wat. 29 BR44
Hattersfield Clo., Belv. 96 EZ77
Hatton Clo. SE18 95 ER80
Hatton Ct. E5 65 DY63
Gilpin Rd.
Hatton Gdn. EC1 6 E6
Hatton Gdn. EC1 77 DN70
Hatton Gdns., Mitch. 118 DF99
Hatton Grn., Felt. 85 BU84
Hatton Gro., West Dr. 84 BK75
Hatton Ho. E1 78 DU73
Wellclose Sq.
Hatton Pl. EC1 6 E6
Hatton Pl. EC1 77 DN70
Hatton Rd., Croy. 119 DN102
Hatton Rd., Felt. 99 BQ87
Hatton Rd. (Cheshunt), Wal.Cr. 23 DX29
Hatton Row NW8 4 A5
Hatton St. NW8 4 A5
Hatton Wall EC1 6 D6
Hatton Wall EC1 77 DN71
Haunch of Venison Yd. W1 5 H9
Havana Clo., Rom. 69 FE57
Havana Rd. SW19 104 DA89
Havannah St. E14 93 EA75
Havant Rd. E17 65 EC55
Havant Way SE15 92 DT80
Daniel Gdns.
Havelock Pl., Har. 59 CE58
Havelock Rd. N17 50 DU54
Havelock Rd. SW19 104 DC92

Havelock Rd., Belv. 96 EZ77
Havelock Rd., Brom. 122 EJ98
Havelock Rd., Croy. 120 DT103
Havelock Rd., Dart. 111 FH87
Havelock Rd., Har. 59 CE55
Havelock Rd., Kings L. 14 BM28
Havelock Rd., Sthl. 86 BY76
Havelock St. N1 77 DL67
Havelock St., Ilf. 67 EP61
Havelock Ter. SW8 91 DH80
Havelock Wk. SE23 106 DW88
Haven, The SE26 106 DV92
Springfield Rd.
Haven, The, Rich. 88 CN83
Haven Clo. SE9 109 EM90
Haven Clo. SW19 103 CX90
Haven Clo., Hayes 71 BS71
Haven Clo., Sid. 110 EW93
Haven Clo., Swan. 125 FF96
Haven Grn. W5 73 CK72
Haven Grn. Ct. W5 73 CK72
Haven La. W5 74 CL72
Haven Pl. W5 73 CK73
The Bdy.
Haven Rd., Ashf. 99 BP91
Haven St. NW1 77 DH66
Castlehaven Rd.
Haven Ter. W5 73 CK73
The Bdy.
Havenhurst Ri., Enf. 35 DN40
Havensfield, Kings L. 14 BH31
Nunfield
Havenwood, Wem. 60 CP62
Haverfield Gdns., Rich. 88 CN80
Haverfield Rd. E3 79 DY69
Haverford Way, Edg. 46 CM53
Haverhill Rd. E4 51 EC46
Haverhill Rd. SW12 105 DJ88
Havering Dr., Rom. 69 FE56
Havering Gdns., Rom. 68 EW57
Havering Rd., Rom. 69 FD55
Havering St. E1 79 DX72
Devonport St.
Havering Way, Bark. 82 EV69
Havers Ave., Walt. 128 BX106
Haversfield Est., Brent. 88 CL78
Haversham Clo., Twick. 101 CK86
Haversham Pl. N6 62 DF61
Haverstock Hill NW3 76 DF65
Haverstock Rd. NW5 62 DG64
Haverstock St. N1 6 G1
Haverstock St. N1 77 DP68
Haverthwaite Rd., Orp. 123 ER103
Havil St. SE5 92 DS80
Havisham Pl. SE19 105 DP93
Hawarden Gro. SE24 106 DQ87
Hawarden Hill NW2 61 CU62
Hawarden Rd. E17 65 DX56
Hawarden Rd., Cat. 148 DQ121
Hawbridge Rd. E11 65 ED60
Hawes Clo., Nthwd. 43 BT52
Hawes La. E4 37 EC38
Hawes La., W.Wick. 121 EC102
Hawes Rd. N18 50 DV51
Hawes Rd., Brom. 122 EH95
Hawes Rd., Tad. 145 CX120
Hatch Gdns.
Hawes St. N1 77 DP66
Haweswater Dr., Wat. 16 BW33
Haweswater Ho., Islw. 101 CF85
Hawfield Bank, Orp. 124 EX104
Hawfield Gdns., St.Alb. 17 CD26
Hawgood St. E3 79 EA71
Hawk Clo., Wal.Abb. 24 EG34
Hawkdene E4 37 EB44
Hawke Pk. Rd. N22 63 DP55
Hawke Pl. SE16 93 DX75
Middleton Dr.
Hawke Rd. SE19 106 DS93
Hawker Clo., Wall. 133 DL108
Kingsford Ave.
Hawke's Pl., Sev. 154 FG127
Hawkes Rd., Mitch. 118 DE95
Hawkesbury Rd. SW15 103 CV85
Hawkesfield Rd. SE23 107 DY89
Hawkesley Clo., Twick. 101 CG91
Hawkesworth Clo., Nthwd. 43 BS52
Hawkewood Rd., Sun. 113 BU97
Hawkhirst Rd., Ken. 148 DR115
Hawkhurst, Cob. 128 CA114
Hawkhurst Gdns., Chess. 130 CL105
Hawkhurst Gdns., Rom. 55 FD51
Hawkhurst Rd. SW16 119 DK95
Hawkhurst Way, N.Mal. 116 CR99
Hawkhurst Way, W.Wick. 121 EB103
Hawkinge Wk., Orp. 124 EV97
Farrington Ave.
Hawkins Clo. NW7 46 CR50
Hale La.
Hawkins Clo., Borwd. 32 CQ40
Banks Rd.
Hawkins Clo., Har. 59 CD59
Hawkins Rd., Tedd. 101 CH93
Hawkins Way SE6 107 EA91
Hawkley Gdns. SE27 105 DP89
Hawkridge Clo., Rom. 68 EW58
Hawks Hill, Lthd. 143 CF123
Guildford Rd.
Hawks Hill Clo., Lthd. 143 CF123
Hawks Ms. SE10 93 EC80
Luton Pl.
Hawks Rd., Kings.T. 116 CM96
Hawksbrook La., Beck. 121 EB100
Hawkshaw Clo. SW2 105 DL87
Tierney Rd.
Hawkshead Clo., Brom. 108 EE94
Hawkshead La., Hat. 19 CW28
Hawkshead Rd. NW10 75 CT66
Hawkshead Rd. W4 88 CS75
Hawkshead Rd., Pot.B. 19 CZ28
Hawkshill Clo., Esher 128 CA107
Hawkshill Way, Esher 128 BZ107
Hawkslade Rd. SE15 107 DX85
Hawksley Rd. N16 64 DR62
Hawksmead Clo., Enf. 37 DX35
Hawksmoor, Rad. 18 CN33
Hawksmoor Clo. E6 80 EL72
Allhallows Rd.
Hawksmoor Clo. SE18 95 ES78
Hawksmoor Ms. E1 78 DV73
Cable St.
Hawksmoor St. W6 89 CX79
Hawksmouth E4 51 EB45
Hawkstone Rd. SE16 92 DW77
Hawksview, Cob. 128 BZ113
Hawkwell Ct. E4 51 EC48
Colvin Gdns.
Hawkwell Wk. N1 78 DQ67
Basire St.
Hawkwood Cres. E4 37 EB44
Hawkwood La., Chis. 123 EQ95
Hawkwood Mt. E5 64 DV60
Hawlands Dr., Pnr. 58 BY59
Hawley Clo., Hmptn. 100 BZ93
Hawley Cres. NW1 77 DH66
Hawley Ms. NW1 77 DH66
Hawley St.
Hawley Rd. N18 51 DX50
Hawley Rd. NW1 77 DH66
Hawley St. NW1 77 DH66
Hawley Way, Ashf. 98 BN92
Haws La., Stai. 98 BG86
Hawstead La., Orp. 138 EZ106
Hawstead Rd. SE6 107 EB86
Hawsted, Buck.H. 52 EH45
Hawthorn Ave. N13 49 DL50
Hawthorn Ave., Cars. 132 DG108
Hawthorn Ave., Rain. 83 FH70
Hawthorn Ave., Rich. 88 CL82
Kew Rd.
Hawthorn Ave., Th.Hth. 119 DP95
Hawthorn Cen., Har. 59 CF56
Hawthorn Clo., Abb.L. 15 BU32
Magnolia Ave.
Hawthorn Clo., Bans. 131 CY114
Hawthorn Clo., Hmptn. 100 CA92
Hawthorn Clo., Houns. 85 BV80
Hawthorn Clo., Orp. 123 ER100
Hawthorn Clo., Wat. 29 BT38
Hawthorn Cotts., Well. 96 EU83
Hook La.
Hawthorn Ct., Rich. 88 CP81
West Hall Rd.
Hawthorn Cres. SW17 104 DG92
Hawthorn Dr., Har. 58 CA58
Hawthorn Dr., Uxb. 70 BJ65
Hawthorn Dr., W.Wick. 136 EE105
Hawthorn Gdns. W5 87 CK76
Hawthorn Gro. SE20 106 DV94
Hawthorn Gro., Barn. 33 CT44
Hawthorn Gro., Enf. 36 DR38
Hawthorn Hatch, Brent. 87 CH80
Hawthorn La., Sev. 154 FF122
Hawthorn Ms. NW7 47 CY53
Holders Hill Rd.
Hawthorn Pl., Erith 97 FC78
Hawthorn Pl., Hayes 71 BT73
Central Ave.
Hawthorn Rd. N8 63 DK55
Hawthorn Rd. N18 50 DT51
Hawthorn Rd. NW10 75 CU66
Hawthorn Rd., Bexh. 96 EZ84
Hawthorn Rd., Brent. 87 CH80
Hawthorn Rd., Buck.H. 52 EK49
Hawthorn Rd., Sutt. 132 DE106
Hawthorn Rd., Wall. 133 DH108
Hawthorn Wk. W10 75 CY70
Droop St.
Hawthorn Way N9 50 DS47
Hawthorn Way, Add. 126 BJ110
Hawthorn Way, Stai. 98 BK87
Hawthorndene Clo. N12 48 DE51
Fallowfields Dr.
Hawthorndene Clo., Brom. 122 EF103
Hawthorndene Rd., Brom. 122 EF103
Hawthorne Ave., Har. 59 CG58
Hawthorne Ave., Mitch. 118 DD96
Hawthorne Ave., Ruis. 57 BV59
Hawthorne Ave. (Cheshunt), Wal.Cr. 22 DV30
Hawthorne Ave., West. 150 EK115
Hawthorne Clo. N1 78 DS65
Hawthorne Clo., Brom. 123 EM97
Hawthorne Clo., Sutt. 118 DB103
Aultone Way
Hawthorne Clo. (Cheshunt), Wal.Cr. 22 DV31
Hawthorne Ct., Walt. 114 BX103
Ambleside Ave.
Hawthorne Cres., S.Croy. 134 DW111
Hawthorne Cres., West Dr. 84 BM75
Hawthorne Fm. Ave., Nthlt. 72 BY67
Hawthorne Gro. NW9 60 CQ59
Hawthorne Ms., Grnf. 72 CC72
Greenford Rd.
Hawthorne Pl., Epsom 130 CS112
Hawthorne Rd. E17 65 EA55
Hawthorne Rd., Brom. 123 EM97
Hawthorne Rd., Rad. 17 CG34
Hawthorne Way, Shep. 113 BR98
Hawthornes Cen., Har. 59 CF56
Hawthorns, Wdf.Grn. 52 EG48
Hawthorns, The, Epsom 131 CT107
Ewell Bypass
Hawthorns, The, Loug. 39 EN42
Hawtrees, Rad. 31 CF35
Hawtrey Ave., Nthlt. 72 BX68
Hawtrey Dr., Ruis. 57 BU59
Hawtrey Rd. NW3 76 DE66
Haxted Rd., Brom. 122 EH95
North Rd.
Hay Clo. E15 80 EE66
Hay Clo., Borwd. 32 CQ40
Hay Currie St. E14 79 EB72
Hay Hill W1 9 J1
Hay Hill W1 77 DH73
Hay La. NW9 60 CQ56
Hay St. E2 78 DU67
Hayburn Way, Horn. 69 FF60
Haycroft Clo., Couls. 147 DP118
Caterham Dr.
Haycroft Gdns. NW10 75 CU67
Haycroft Rd. SW2 105 DL85
Haycroft Rd., Surb. 115 CK104
Hayday Rd. E16 80 EG71
Hayden Ct., Add. 126 BH111
Hayden Way, Rom. 55 FC54
Haydens Clo., Orp. 124 EW100
Haydens Pl. W11 75 CZ72
Portobello Rd.
Haydn Ave., Pur. 133 DN114
Haydns Ms. W3 74 CQ72
Emanuel Ave.
Haydock Ave., Nthlt. 72 CA65
Haydock Grn., Nthlt. 72 CA65
Haydock Ave.
Haydon Clo. NW9 60 CQ56
Haydon Clo., Enf. 36 DS44
Mortimer Dr.
Haydon Dr., Pnr. 57 BV56
Haydon Pk. Rd. SW19 104 DA92
Haydon Rd., Dag. 68 EW61
Haydon Rd., Wat. 30 BY44
Haydon St. EC3 7 P10
Haydon Wk. E1 78 DT73
Mansell St.
Haydon Way SW11 90 DD84
St. John's Hill
Haydons Rd. SW19 104 DB92
Hayes, The, Epsom 144 CR119
Hayes Chase, W.Wick. 121 ED100
Hayes Clo., Brom. 122 EG103
Hayes Ct. SW2 105 DL88
Hayes Cres. NW11 61 CZ57
Hayes Cres., Sutt. 131 CX105
Hayes Dr., Rain. 83 FH66
Hayes End Clo., Hayes 71 BR70
Hayes End Dr., Hayes 71 BR70
Hayes End Rd., Hayes 71 BR70
Hayes Gdn., Brom. 122 EG103
Hayes Hill, Brom. 122 EE102
Hayes Hill Rd., Brom. 122 EF102
Hayes La., Beck. 121 EC97
Hayes La., Brom. 122 EG99
Hayes La., Ken. 147 DP116
Hayes Mead Rd., Brom. 122 EE102
Hayes Pk., Hayes 71 BS70
Hayes Pl. NW1 4 C5
Hayes Rd., Brom. 122 EG98
Hayes Rd., Sthl. 85 BV77
Hayes St., Brom. 122 EH102
Hayes Wk., Brox. 23 DZ25
Landau Way
Hayes Wk., Pot.B. 20 DB33
Hyde Ave.
Hayes Way, Beck. 121 EC98
Hayes Wd. Ave., Brom. 122 EH102
Hayesford Pk. Dr., Brom. 122 EF99
Hayfield Clo. (Bushey), Wat. 30 CB42
Hayfield Pas. E1 78 DW70
Stepney Grn.
Hayfield Rd., Orp. 124 EU99
Hayfield Yd. E1 78 DW70
Mile End Rd.
Haygarth Pl. SW19 103 CX92
Haygreen Clo., Kings.T. 102 CP93
Hayland Clo. NW9 60 CR56
Hayles St. SE11 10 F8
Hayles St. SE11 91 DP77
Haylett Gdns., Kings.T. 115 CK98
Anglesea Rd.
Hayling Ave., Felt. 99 BU90
Hayling Clo. N16 64 DS64
Pellerin Rd.
Hayling Rd., Wat. 43 BT48
Haymaker Clo., Uxb. 70 BM66
Honey Hill
Hayman Cres., Hayes 71 BR68
Hayman St. N1 77 DP66
Cross St.
Haymarket SW1 9 M1
Haymarket SW1 77 DK73
Haymarket Arc. SW1 9 M1
Haymeads Dr., Esher 128 CC107
Haymer Gdns., Wor.Pk. 117 CU104
Haymerle Rd. SE15 92 DU79
Haymill Clo., Grnf. 73 CF69
Hayne Rd., Beck. 121 DZ96
Hayne St. EC1 6 G6
Haynes Clo. N11 48 DG48
Haynes Clo. N17 50 DV52
Haynes Clo. SE3 94 EE83
Haynes Clo., Wok. 140 BH122
Haynes La. SE19 106 DS93
Haynes Rd., Wem. 74 CL66
Haynt Wk. SW20 117 CY97
Hay's La. SE1 11 M3
Hay's Ms. W1 9 H2
Hay's Ms. W1 77 DH74
Hays Wk., Sutt. 131 CX110
Haysleigh Gdns. SE20 120 DU96
Haysoms Clo., Rom. 69 FE56
Haystall Clo., Hayes 71 BS68
Hayter Rd. SW2 105 DL85
Hayton Clo. E8 78 DT65
Buttermere Wk.
Hayward Clo. SW19 104 DB94
Hayward Clo., Bex. 111 FD85
Hayward Clo., Dart. 111 FD85
Hayward Gdns. SW15 103 CW86
Hayward Rd. N20 48 DC47
Hayward's Pl. EC1 6 F5
Haywood Clo., Pnr. 44 BX54
Haywood Ct., Wal.Abb. 24 EF34
Haywood Ri., Orp. 137 ES105
Haywood Rd., Brom. 122 EK98
Hayworth Clo., Enf. 37 DY40
Green St.
Hazel Ave., West Dr. 84 BN76
Hazel Bank, Surb. 116 CQ102
Hazel Clo. N13 50 DR48
Hazel Clo. N19 63 DJ61
Hargrave Pk.
Hazel Clo. SE15 92 DU82
Copeland Rd.
Hazel Clo., Brent. 87 CH80
Hazel Clo., Croy. 121 DX101
Hazel Clo., Horn. 69 FH62
Hazel Clo., Mitch. 119 DK98
Hazel Clo., Twick. 100 CC87
Hazel Clo., Wal.Cr. 22 DS26
The Laurels
Hazel Dr., Erith 97 FG81
Hazel End, Swan. 125 FE99
Hazel Gdns., Edg. 46 CP49
Hazel Gro. SE26 107 DX91
Hazel Gro., Enf. 36 DU44
Dimsdale Dr.
Hazel Gro., Orp. 123 EP103
Hazel Gro., Rom. 68 EY55
Hazel Gro., Stai. 98 BH93
Hazel Gro., Wat. 29 BV35
Cedar Wd. Dr.
Hazel Gro., Wem. 74 CL67
Carlyon Rd.
Hazel Gro. Est. SE26 107 DX91
Hazel La., Rich. 102 CL89
Hazel Mead, Barn. 33 CV43
Hazel Mead, Epsom 131 CU110
Hazel Rd. E15 66 EE64
Wingfield Rd.
Hazel Rd. NW10 75 CV69
Hazel Rd., Erith 97 FG81
Hazel Rd., St.Alb. 16 CB28
Hazel Rd., W.Byf. 126 BG114
Hazel Tree Rd., Wat. 29 BV37
Hazel Wk., Brom. 123 EN100
Hazel Way E4 51 DZ51
Hazel Way SE1 11 P8
Hazel Way, Couls. 146 DF119
Hazel Way, Lthd. 142 CC122
Hazelbank Ct., Cher. 112 BJ102
Hazelbank Rd. SE6 107 ED89
Hazelbank Rd., Cher. 112 BJ101
Hazelbourne Rd. SW12 105 DH86
Hazelbrouck Gdns., Ilf. 53 ER52
Hazelbury Ave., Abb.L. 15 BQ32
Hazelbury Clo. SW19 118 DA96
Hazelbury Grn. N9 50 DS48
Hazelbury La. N9 50 DS48
Hazelcroft, Pnr. 44 CB51
Hazelcroft Clo., Uxb. 70 BM66
Hazeldean Rd. NW10 74 CR66
Hazeldene, Add. 126 BJ106
Hazeldene, Wal.Cr. 23 DY32
Hazeldene Ct., Ken. 148 DR115
Hazeldene Dr., Pnr. 58 BW55
Hazeldene Gdns., Uxb. 71 BQ67
Hazeldene Rd., Ilf. 68 EV61
Hazeldene Rd., Well. 96 EW82
Hazeldon Rd. SE4 107 DY85
Hazeleigh Gdns., Wdf.Grn. 52 EL50
Hazelgreen Clo. N21 49 DP46
Hazelhurst, Beck. 121 ED95
Hazelhurst Rd. SW17 104 DC91
Hazell Cres., Rom. 55 FB53
Hazellville Rd. N19 63 DK59
Hazelmere Clo., Felt. 99 BR86
Hazelmere Clo., Lthd. 143 CH119
Hazelmere Clo., Nthlt. 72 BZ68
Hazelmere Dr., Nthlt. 72 BZ68
Hazelmere Gdns., Horn. 69 FH57
Hazelmere Rd. NW6 75 CZ67
Hazelmere Rd., Nthlt. 72 BZ68
Hazelmere Rd., Orp. 123 EQ98
Hazelmere Wk., Nthlt. 72 BZ68
Hazelmere Way, Brom. 122 EG100
Hazeltree La., Nthlt. 72 BY69
Hazelwood, Loug. 38 EK43
Hazelwood Ave., Mord. 118 DB98
Hazelwood Clo. W5 88 CL75
Hazelwood Clo., Har. 58 CB56
Hazelwood Ct. NW10 60 CS62
Neasden La. N.
Hazelwood Cres. N13 49 DN49
Hazelwood Cft., Surb. 116 CL100
Hazelwood Dr., Pnr. 43 BV54
Hazelwood Gro., S.Croy. 134 DV113
Hazelwood La. N13 49 DN49
Hazelwood La., Abb.L. 15 BR31
Hazelwood La., Couls. 146 DE118
Hazelwood Pk. Clo., Chig. 53 ES50
Hazelwood Rd. E17 65 DY57
Hazelwood Rd., Enf. 36 DT44
Hazelwood Rd., Rick. 29 BQ44
Hazelwood Rd., Sev. 137 ER112
Hazlebury Rd. SW6 90 DB82
Hazledean Rd., Croy. 120 DR103
Hazledene Rd. W4 88 CQ79
Hazlemere Gdns., Wor.Pk. 117 CU102
Hazlewell Rd. SW15 103 CV85
Hazlewood Clo. E5 65 DY62
Mandeville St.
Hazlewood Cres. W10 75 CY70
Hazlitt Ms. W14 89 CY76
Hazlitt Rd.
Hazlitt Rd. W14 89 CY76
Hazon Way, Epsom 130 CQ112
Heacham Ave., Uxb. 57 BQ62
Head St. E1 79 DX72
Headcorn Pl., Th.Hth. 119 DM98
Headcorn Rd.
Headcorn Rd. N17 50 DT52
Headcorn Rd., Brom. 108 EG92
Headcorn Rd., Th.Hth. 119 DM98
Headfort Pl. SW1 8 G5
Headfort Pl. SW1 90 DG75
Headingley Clo., Ilf. 53 ET51
Headingley Clo., Rad. 18 CL32
Headingley Clo. (Cheshunt), Wal.Cr. 22 DT26
Headington Rd. SW18 104 DC89
Headlam Rd. SW4 105 DK86
Headlam St. E1 78 DV70
Headley App., Ilf. 67 EP57
Headley Ave., Wall. 133 DM106
Headley Clo., Epsom 130 CN107
Headley Ct. SE26 106 DW92
Headley Dr., Croy. 135 EB108
Headley Dr., Epsom 145 CV119
Headley Dr., Ilf. 67 EP58
Headley Gro., Tad. 145 CV120
Headley Rd. (Ashtead Pk.), Epsom 144 CP118
Headley Rd. (Tyrrell's Wd.), Epsom 144 CN122
Headley Rd., Lthd. 143 CJ122
Head's Ms. W11 76 DA72
Artesian Rd.
Headstone Dr., Har. 59 CD55
Headstone Gdns., Har. 58 CC56
Headstone La., Har. 44 CB52
Headstone Rd., Har. 59 CE57
Headway, The, Epsom 131 CT109
Headway Clo., Rich. 101 CJ91
Locksmeade Rd.
Heald St. SE14 93 DZ81
Healey Dr., Orp. 137 ET105
Healey Rd., Wat. 29 BT44
Healey St. NW1 77 DH65
Heanor Ct. E5 65 DX62
Pedro St.
Hearn Ri., Nthlt. 72 BX67
Hearn Rd., Rom. 69 FF58
Hearn St. EC2 7 N5
Hearn St. EC2 78 DS70
Hearne Rd. W4 88 CN79
Hearn's Bldgs. SE17 11 L9
Hearn's Ri., Orp. 124 EX98
Hearn's Rd., Orp. 124 EW98
Hearnville Rd. SW12 104 DG88
Heath, The W7 73 CE74
Lower Boston Rd.
Heath, The, Cat. 148 DQ124
Heath, The, Rad. 17 CG33
Heath Ave., Bexh. 96 EX79
Heath Brow NW3 62 DC62
North End Way
Heath Clo. NW11 62 DB59
Heath Clo. W5 74 CM70
Heath Clo., Bans. 132 DB114
Heath Clo., Hayes 85 BR80
Heath Clo., Orp. 124 EW100
Sussex Rd.
Heath Clo., Pot.B. 20 DB30
Heath Clo., Rom. 69 FG55
Heath Clo., Stai. 98 BJ86
Heath Cotts., Pot.B. 20 DB30
Heath Rd.
Heath Ct., Houns. 86 BZ84
Heath Ct., Uxb. 70 BL66
Heath Dr. NW3 62 DB63
Heath Dr. SW20 117 CW98
Heath Dr., Epp. 39 ES36
Heath Dr., Pot.B. 20 DA30
Heath Dr., Rom. 55 FG53
Heath Dr., Sutt. 132 DC109
Heath End Rd., Bex. 111 FE88
Heath Fm. Ct., Wat. 29 BR37
Grove Mill La.
Heath Gdns., Twick. 101 CF88
Heath Gro. SE20 106 DW94
Maple Rd.
Heath Gro., Sun. 99 BT94
Heath Hurst Rd. NW3 62 DE63
Heath La. SE3 93 ED82
Heath La., Dart. 111 FG89
Heath La. Upper, Dart. 111 FH88
Heath Mead SW19 103 CX90
Heath Pk. Ct., Rom. 69 FG57
Heath Pk. Rd.
Heath Pk. Dr., Brom. 122 EL97
Heath Pk. Rd., Rom. 69 FG57
Heath Ridge Grn., Cob. 128 CA113
Heath Ri. SW15 103 CX86
Heath Ri., Brom. 122 EF100
Heath Ri., Wok. 140 BH123
Heath Rd. SW8 91 DH82
Heath Rd., Bex. 111 FE86
Heath Rd., Cat. 148 DR123
Heath Rd., Dart. 111 FF86

Heath Rd., Har. 58 CC59
Heath Rd., Houns. 86 CB84
Heath Rd., Lthd. 128 CC112
Heath Rd., Pot.B. 20 DA30
Heath Rd., Rom. 68 EX59
Heath Rd., Th.Hth. 120 DQ97
Heath Rd., Twick. 101 CF88
Heath Rd., Uxb. 71 BQ70
Heath Rd., Wat. 44 BX45
Heath Rd., Wey. 126 BN105
Heath Side NW3 62 DD63
Heath Side, Orp. 123 EQ102
Heath St. NW3 62 DC62
Heath Vw. N2 62 DC56
Heath Vw. Clo. N2 62 DC56
Heath Vill. SE18 95 ET78
Heath Vill. SW18 104 DC88
Cargill Rd.
Heath Way, Erith 97 FC81
Heatham Pk., Twick. 101 CF87
Heathbourne Rd., Stan. 45 CE47
Heathbourne Rd. (Bushey), Wat. 45 CE46
Heathbridge, Wey. 126 BN108
Heathclose Ave., Dart. 111 FH87
Heathclose Rd., Dart. 111 FG88
Heathcock Ct. WC2 77 DL73
Strand
Heathcote, Tad. 145 CX121
Heathcote Ave., Ilf. 53 EM54
Heathcote Gro. E4 51 EC48
Heathcote Rd., Epsom 130 CR114
Heathcote Rd., Twick. 101 CH86
Heathcote St. WC1 6 B4
Heathcote St. WC1 77 DM70
Heathcote Way, West Dr. 70 BK74
Tavistock Rd.
Heathcroft NW11 62 DB60
Heathcroft W5 74 CM70
Heathcroft Ave., Sun. 99 BT94
Heathdale Ave., Houns. 86 BY83
Heathdene, Tad. 145 CY119
Canons La.
Heathdene Dr., Belv. 97 FB77
Heathdene Rd. SW16 105 DM94
Heathdene Rd., Wall. 132 DG108
Heathedge SE26 106 DV89
Heathend Rd., Bex. 111 FE88
Heather Ave., Rom. 55 FD54
Heather Clo. E6 81 EP72
Heather Clo. SE13 107 ED87
Heather Clo. SW8 91 DH83
Heather Clo., Abb.L. 15 BU32
Magnolia Ave.
Heather Clo., Add. 126 BH110
Heather Clo., Hmptn. 114 BZ95
Heather Clo., Islw. 101 CD85
Harvesters Clo.
Heather Clo., Rom. 55 FD53
Heather Clo., Tad. 145 CY122
Heather Clo., Uxb. 70 BM71
Violet Ave.
Heather Dr., Dart. 111 FG87
Heather Dr., Enf. 35 DP40
Chasewood Ave.
Heather Dr., Rom. 55 FD54
Heather End, Swan. 125 FD98
Heather Gdns. NW11 61 CY58
Heather Gdns., Rom. 55 FD54
Heather Gdns., Sutt. 132 DA107
Heather Glen, Rom. 55 FD54
Heather La., Wat. 29 BT35
Heather La., West Dr. 70 BL72
Heather Pk. Dr., Wem. 74 CN66
Heather Pl., Esher 128 CB105
Park Rd.
Heather Ri. (Bushey), Wat. 30 BZ40
Heather Rd. E4 51 DZ51
Silver Birch Ave.
Heather Rd. NW2 61 CT61
Heather Rd. SE12 108 EG89
Heather Wk. W10 75 CY70
Droop St.
Heather Wk., Edg. 46 CP50
Heather Wk., Twick. 100 CA87
Stephenson Rd.
Heather Wk., Walt. 127 BT110
Octagon Rd.
Heather Way, Pot.B. 19 CZ32
Heather Way, Rom. 55 FD54
Heather Way, S.Croy. 135 DX109
Heather Way, Stan. 45 CF51
Heatherbank SE9 95 EM82
Heatherbank, Chis. 123 EN96
Heatherbank Clo., Dart. 111 FE86
Heatherdale Clo., Kings.T. 102 CP94
Heatherdene Clo. N12 48 DC53
Bow La.
Heatherdene Clo., Mitch. 118 DE98
Heatherfields, Add. 126 BH110
Heatherlands, Sun. 99 BU93
Heatherley Dr., Ilf. 66 EL55
Heathers, The, Stai. 98 BM87
Heatherset Gdns. SW16 105 DM94
Heatherside Rd., Epsom 130 CR108
Heatherside Rd., Sid. 110 EX90
Wren Rd.
Heathervale Caravan Pk., Add. 126 BJ110
Heathervale Rd., Add. 126 BH110
Heatherwood Clo. E12 66 EJ61
Heatherwood Dr., Hayes 71 BR68
Charville La.
Heathfield E4 51 EC48
Heathfield, Chis. 109 EQ93
Heathfield, Cob. 128 CA114
Heathfield Ave. SW18 104 DD87
Heathfield Rd.
Heathfield Ave., S.Croy. 135 DY109
Heathfield Clo. E16 80 EK71
Heathfield Clo., Kes. 136 EJ106
Heathfield Clo., Pot.B. 20 DB30
Heathfield Dr., Mitch. 118 DE95
Heathfield Gdns. NW11 61 CX58
Heathfield Gdns. SW18 104 DD86
Heathfield Rd.
Heathfield Gdns. W4 88 CQ78
Heathfield Gdns., Croy. 134 DR105
Coombe Rd.
Heathfield La., Chis. 109 EP93
Heathfield N., Twick. 101 CF87
Heathfield Pk. NW2 75 CW65
Heathfield Pk. Dr., Rom. 68 EV57
Barley La.
Heathfield Ri., Ruis. 57 BQ59
Heathfield Rd. SW18 104 DC86
Heathfield Rd. W3 88 CP75
Heathfield Rd., Bexh. 96 EZ84
Heathfield Rd., Brom. 108 EF94
Heathfield Rd., Croy. 134 DR105
Heathfield Rd., Kes. 136 EJ106
Heathfield Rd., Sev. 154 FF122
Heathfield Rd., Walt. 128 BY105
Heathfield Rd. (Bushey), Wat. 30 BY42
Heathfield S., Twick. 101 CF87
Heathfield Sq. SW18 104 DD87
Heathfield St. W11 75 CY73
Portland Rd.
Heathfield Ter. SE18 95 ES79
Heathfield Ter. W4 88 CQ78
Heathfield Vale, S.Croy. 135 DX109
Heathfields Ct., Houns. 100 BY85
Frampton Rd.
Heathgate NW11 62 DB58
Heathland Rd. N16 64 DS60
Heathlands, Tad. 145 CX122
Heathlands Clo., Sun. 113 BT96
Heathlands Clo., Twick. 101 CF89
Heathlands Ri., Dart. 111 FH86
Heathlands Way, Houns. 100 BY85
Frampton Rd.
Heathlee Rd. SE3 94 EF84
Heathlee Rd., Dart. 111 FE86
Heathley End, Chis. 109 EQ93
Heathmans Rd. SW6 89 CZ81
Heathrow Clo., West Dr. 84 BH81
Heathrow International Trd. Est., Houns. 85 BV83
Heaths Clo., Enf. 36 DS40
Heathside, Esher 115 CE104
Heathside, Houns. 100 BZ87
Heathside, Wey. 127 BP106
Heathside Ave., Bexh. 96 EY82
Heathside Clo., Esher 115 CE104
Heathside Clo., Nthwd. 43 BR50
Heathside Ct., Tad. 145 CV123
Heathside Pl., Epsom 145 CX118
Heathside Rd., Nthwd. 43 BR49
Heathstan Rd. W12 75 CU72
Heathurst Rd., S.Croy. 134 DS109
Heathview Ave., Dart. 111 FE86
Heathview Ct. SW19 103 CX89
Heathview Cres., Dart. 111 FG87
Heathview Dr. SE2 96 EX79
Heathview Gdns. SW15 103 CW87
Heathview Rd., Th.Hth. 119 DN98
Heathville Rd. N19 63 DL59
Heathwall St. SW11 90 DF83
Heathway SE3 94 EG80
Heathway, Croy. 121 DZ104
Heathway, Dag. 68 EZ62
Heathway, Lthd. 141 BT124
Heathway, Wdf.Grn. 52 EJ49
Heathwood Gdns. SE7 94 EL77
Heathwood Gdns., Swan. 125 FC96
Heathwood Wk., Bex. 111 FE88
Heaton Ave., Rom. 55 FH52
Heaton Clo. E4 51 EC48
Friars Clo.
Heaton Ct., Wal.Cr. 23 DX29
Heaton Gra. Rd., Rom. 55 FF54
Heaton Rd. SE15 92 DU83
Heaton Rd., Mitch. 104 DG94
Heaver Rd. SW11 90 DD83
Wye St.
Heavitree Clo. SE18 95 ER78
Heavitree Rd. SE18 95 ER78
Hebden Ct. E2 78 DT67
Laburnum St.
Hebden Ter. N17 50 DS51
Commercial Rd.
Hebdon Rd. SW17 104 DE90
Heber Rd. NW2 61 CX64
Heber Rd. SE22 106 DT86
Hebron Rd. W6 89 CV76
Hecham Clo. E17 51 DY54
Heckfield Pl. SW6 90 DA80
Fulham Rd.
Heckford St. E1 79 DX73
The Highway
Hector St. SE18 95 ES77
Heddington Gro. N7 63 DM64
Heddon Clo., Islw. 87 CG84
Heddon Ct. Ave., Barn. 34 DF43
Heddon Rd., Barn. 34 DF43
Heddon St. W1 5 K10
Heddon St. W1 77 DJ73
Hedge Hill, Enf. 35 DP39
Hedge La. N13 49 DP48
Hedge Wk. SE6 107 EB92
Lushington Rd.
Hedgeley, Ilf. 67 EM56
Hedgemans Rd., Dag. 82 EX66
Hedgemans Way, Dag. 82 EY65
Hedgerley Gdns., Grnf. 72 CC68
Hedgerow Wk., Wal.Cr. 23 DX30
Hedgers Gro. E9 79 DY65
Hedgeside Rd., Nthwd. 43 BQ50
Hedgewood Gdns., Ilf. 67 EN56
Hedgley St. SE12 108 EF85
Hedingham Clo. N1 78 DQ66
Popham Rd.
Hedingham Rd., Dag. 68 EV64
Hedley Rd., Twick. 100 CA87
Hedley Row N5 64 DR64
Poets Rd.
Hedworth Ave., Wal.Cr. 23 DX33
Heenan Clo., Bark. 81 EQ65
Glenny Rd.
Heene Rd., Enf. 36 DR39
Heidegger Cres. SW13 89 CV79
Trinity Ch. Rd.
Heigham Rd. E6 80 EL66
Heighton Gdns., Croy. 133 DP106
Heights, The SE7 94 EJ78
Heights, The, Beck. 107 EC94
Heights, The, Loug. 39 EM40
Heights, The, Nthlt. 58 BZ64
Heights, The, Wal.Abb. 24 EH25
Heights, The, Wey. 126 BN110
Heights Clo. SW20 103 CV94
Heights Clo., Bans. 145 CY116
Heiron St. SE17 91 DP79
Helby Rd. SW4 105 DK86
Helder Gro. SE12 108 EF87
Helder St., S.Croy. 134 DR107
Heldmann Clo., Houns. 87 CD84
Helen Ave., Felt. 99 BV87
Helen Clo. N2 62 DC55
Thomas More Way
Helen Clo., Dart. 111 FH87
Helen Clo., W.Mol. 114 CB98
Helen St. SE18 95 EP77
Wilmount St.
Helena Clo., Barn. 34 DD38
Helena Clo., Wall. 133 DL108
Kingsford Ave.
Helena Pl. E9 78 DW67
Fremont St.
Helena Rd. E13 80 EF68
Helena Rd. E17 65 EA57
Helena Rd. NW10 61 CV64
Helena Rd. W5 73 CK71
Helena Sq. SE16 79 DY73
Rotherhithe St.
Helens Gate, Wal.Cr. 23 DZ26
Helen's Pl. E2 78 DW69
Roman Rd.
Helenslea Ave. NW11 61 CZ60
Helford Clo., Ruis. 57 BS61
Chichester Ave.
Helgiford Gdns., Sun. 99 BS94
Helix Gdns. SW2 105 DM86
Helix Rd.
Helix Rd. SW2 105 DM86
Hellings St. E1 78 DU74
Wapping High St.
Helme Clo. SW19 103 CZ92
Helmet Row EC1 7 J4
Helmet Row EC1 78 DQ70
Helmsdale Clo., Hayes 72 BY70
Berrydale Rd.
Helmsdale Clo., Rom. 55 FE52
Helmsdale Rd. SW16 119 DK95
Helmsdale Rd., Rom. 55 FE52
Helmsley Pl. E8 78 DV66
Helsinki Sq. SE16 93 DY76
Finland St.
Helston Clo., Pnr. 44 BZ52
Helston Pl., Abb.L. 15 BT32
Shirley Rd.
Helvetia St. SE6 107 DZ89
Hemans St. SW8 91 DK80
Hemberton Rd. SW9 91 DL83
Hemery Rd., Grnf. 59 CD64
Heming Rd., Edg. 46 CP52
Hemingford Clo. N12 48 DD50
Fenstanton Ave.
Hemingford Rd. N1 77 DM67
Hemingford Rd., Sutt. 131 CW105
Hemingford Rd., Wat. 29 BS36
Hemington Ave. N11 48 DF50
Hemlock Clo., Tad. 145 CY124
Warren Lo. Dr.
Hemlock Rd. W12 75 CT73
Hemmen La., Hayes 71 BT72
Hemming Clo., Hmptn. 114 CA95
Chandler Clo.
Hemming St. E1 78 DU70
Hemming Way, Wat. 29 BU35
Hemmings Clo., Sid. 110 EV89
Hemnall St., Epp. 25 ET31
Hemp Wk. SE17 11 L8
Hempshaw Ave., Bans. 146 DF116
Hempstead Clo., Buck.H. 52 EG47
Hempstead Rd. E17 51 ED54
Hempstead Rd., Kings L. 14 BM26
Hempstead Rd., Wat. 29 BR36
Hemsby Rd., Chess. 130 CM107
Hemstal Rd. NW6 76 DA66
Hemsted Rd., Erith 97 FE80
Hemswell Dr. NW9 46 CS53
Hemsworth Ct. N1 78 DS68
Hemsworth St.
Hemsworth St. N1 78 DS68
Hemus Pl. SW3 90 DE78
Chelsea Manor St.
Hen & Chicken Ct. EC4 77 DN72
Fleet St.
Henbit Clo., Tad. 145 CV119
Henbury Way, Wat. 44 BX48
Henchman St. W12 75 CT72
Hendale Ave. NW4 61 CU55
Henderson Clo. NW10 74 CQ65
Henderson Clo., Horn. 69 FH61
St. Leonards Way
Henderson Dr. NW8 76 DD70
Cunningham Pl.
Henderson Pl., Abb.L. 15 BT27
Henderson Rd. E7 80 EJ65
Henderson Rd. N9 50 DV46
Henderson Rd. SW18 104 DE87
Henderson Rd., Croy. 120 DR100
Henderson Rd., Hayes 71 BU69
Henderson Rd., West. 136 EJ112
Hendham Rd. SW17 104 DE89
Hendon Ave. N3 47 CY53
Hendon Gdns., Rom. 55 FC51
Hendon La. N3 61 CY55
Hendon Pk. Row NW11 61 CZ58
Hendon Rd. N9 50 DU47
Hendon Way NW2 61 CX59
Hendon Way NW4 61 CV58
Hendon Way, Stai. 98 BK86
Hendon Wd. La. NW7 47 CT45
Hendre Rd. SE1 11 N9
Hendren Clo., Grnf. 59 CD64
Dimmock Dr.
Hendrick Ave. SW12 104 DF87
Heneage Cres., Croy. 135 EC110
Heneage La. EC3 7 N9
Heneage St. E1 78 DT71
Henfield Clo. N19 63 DJ60
Henfield Clo., Bex. 110 FA86
Henfield Rd. SW19 117 CZ95
Hengelo Gdns., Mitch. 118 DD98
Hengist Rd. SE12 108 EH87
Hengist Rd., Erith 97 FB80
Hengist Way, Brom. 121 ED98
Hengrave Rd. SE23 106 DW87
Hengrove Ct., Bex. 110 EY88
Hurst Rd.
Hengrove Cres., Ashf. 98 BK90
Henley Ave., Sutt. 117 CY104
Henley Clo., Grnf. 72 CC68
Henley Clo., Islw. 87 CF81
Henley Ct. N14 49 DJ45
Henley Dr. SE1 92 DT77
Henley Dr., Kings.T. 103 CT94
Henley Gdns., Pnr. 57 BV55
Henley Gdns., Rom. 68 EY57
Henley Rd. E16 95 EM75
Henley Rd. N18 50 DS49
Henley Rd. NW10 75 CW67
Henley Rd., Ilf. 67 EQ63
Henley St. SW11 90 DG82
Henley Way, Felt. 100 BX92
Henlow Pl., Rich. 101 CK89
Sandpits Rd.
Hennel Clo. SE23 106 DW90
Henniker Gdns. E6 80 EK69
Henniker Ms. SW3 90 DD79
Callow St.
Henniker Pt. E15 66 EE64
Henniker Rd. E15 65 ED64
Henning St. SW11 90 DE81
Henningham Rd. N17 50 DR53
Henrietta Ms. WC1 6 A4
Henrietta Pl. W1 5 H8
Henrietta Pl. W1 77 DH72
Henrietta St. E15 65 EC64
Henrietta St. WC2 6 A10
Henrietta St. WC2 77 DL73
Henriques St. E1 78 DU72
Henry Clo., Enf. 36 DS38
Henry Cooper Way SE9 108 EK90
Henry Darlot Dr. NW7 47 CX50
Henry Dickens Ct. W11 75 CX73
Henry Jackson Rd. SW15 89 CX83
Henry Rd. E6 80 EL68
Henry Rd. N4 64 DQ60
Henry Rd., Barn. 34 DD43
Henry St., Brom. 122 EH95
Henry's Ave., Wdf.Grn. 52 EF50
Henry's Wk., Ilf. 53 ER52
Henryson Rd. SE4 107 EA85
Hensford Gdns. SE26 106 DV91
Wells Pk. Rd.
Henshall St. N1 78 DR65
Henshaw St. SE17 11 K8
Henshaw St. SE17 92 DR77
Henshawe Rd., Dag. 68 EX62
Henshill Pt. E3 79 EB69
Bromley High St.
Henslowe Rd. SE22 106 DU85
Henson Ave. NW2 61 CW64
Henson Clo., Orp. 123 EP103
Henson Path, Har. 59 CK55
Brancker Rd.
Henson Pl., Nthlt. 72 BW67
Henstridge Pl. NW8 76 DE68
Hensworth Rd., Ashf. 98 BK92
Henty Clo. SW11 90 DE80
Henty Wk. SW15 103 CV85
Henville Rd., Brom. 122 EJ95
Henwick Rd. SE9 94 EK83
Henwood Rd. SE16 92 DW76
Gomm Rd.
Henwood Side, Wdf.Grn. 53 EM51
Love La.
Hepburn Gdns., Brom. 122 EE102
Hepburn Ms. SW11 104 DF85
Webbs Rd.
Hepple Clo., Islw. 87 CH82
Hepplestone Clo. SW15 103 CV86
Dover Pk. Dr.
Hepscott Rd. E9 79 EA65
Hepworth Ct., Bark. 68 EU64
Hepworth Gdns., Bark. 68 EU64
Hepworth Rd. SW16 105 DL94
Hepworth Wk. NW3 62 DE64
Haverstock Hill
Hepworth Way, Walt. 113 BT102
Heracles Clo., Wall. 133 DL108
Gull Clo.
Herald Gdns., Wall. 119 DH104
Herald St. E2 78 DV70
Three Colts La.
Herald's Ct. SE11 10 F9
Herald's Pl. SE11 10 E8
Herbal Hill EC1 6 E5
Herbal Hill EC1 77 DN70
Herbert Cres. SW1 8 E6
Herbert Gdns. NW10 75 CV67
Herbert Gdns. W4 88 CP79
Magnolia Rd.
Herbert Gdns., Rom. 68 EX59
Herbert Pl. SE18 95 EP79
Plumstead Common Rd.
Herbert Rd. E12 66 EL63
Herbert Rd. E17 65 DZ59
Herbert Rd. N11 49 DL52
Herbert Rd. N15 64 DT57
Herbert Rd. NW9 61 CU58
Herbert Rd. SE18 95 EN80
Herbert Rd. SW19 103 CZ94
Herbert Rd., Bexh. 96 EY82
Herbert Rd., Brom. 122 EK99
Herbert Rd., Ilf. 67 ES61
Herbert Rd., Kings.T. 116 CM97
Herbert Rd., Sthl. 72 BZ74
Herbert Rd., Swan. 111 FH93
Herbert St. E13 80 EG68
Herbert St. NW5 76 DG65
Herbert Ter. SE18 95 EP79
Herbert Rd.
Herbrand St. WC1 5 P4
Herbrand St. WC1 77 DL70
Hercies Rd., Uxb. 70 BM66
Hercules Pl. N7 63 DL62
Hercules St.
Hercules Rd. SE1 10 C7
Hercules Rd. SE1 91 DM76
Hercules St. N7 63 DL62
Hercules Twr. SE14 93 DY79
Milton Ct. Rd.
Hereford Ave., Barn. 48 DF46
Hereford Clo., Epsom 130 CR113
Hereford Clo., Stai. 112 BH95
Hereford Gdns. SE13 108 EE85
Longhurst Rd.
Hereford Gdns., Ilf. 66 EL59
Hereford Gdns., Pnr. 58 BY57
Hereford Gdns., Twick. 100 CC88
Hereford Ho. NW6 76 DA68
Hereford Ms. W2 76 DA72
Hereford Rd.
Hereford Pl. SE14 93 DZ80
Hereford Retreat SE15 92 DU80
Bird in Bush Rd.
Hereford Rd. E11 66 EH57
Hereford Rd. W2 76 DA72
Hereford Rd. W3 74 CP73
Hereford Rd. W5 87 CJ76
Hereford Rd., Felt. 100 BW88
Hereford Sq. SW7 90 DC77
Hereford St. E2 78 DU70
Hereford Way, Chess. 129 CJ106
Herent Dr., Ilf. 66 EL56
Hereward Ave., Pur. 133 DN111
Hereward Clo., Wal.Abb. 23 EC32
Hereward Gdns. N13 49 DN50
Hereward Grn., Loug. 39 EQ39
Hereward Rd. SW17 104 DE91
Herga Ct., Har. 59 CE62
Herga Ct., Wat. 29 BU40
Herga Rd., Har. 59 CF56
Heriot Ave. E4 51 EA47
Heriot Rd. NW4 61 CW57
Heriot Rd., Cher. 112 BG101
Heriots Clo., Stan. 45 CG49
Heritage Clo., Uxb. 70 BJ70
Heritage Hill, Kes. 136 EJ106
Heritage Vw., Har. 59 CF62
Herkomer Clo. (Bushey), Wat. 30 CB44
Herkomer Rd. (Bushey), Wat. 30 CA43
Herlwyn Ave., Ruis. 57 BS61
Herlwyn Gdns. SW17 104 DF91
Hermes Pt. W9 76 DA70
Harrow Rd.
Hermes St. N1 6 D1
Hermes Wk., Nthlt. 72 CA68
Hotspur Rd.
Hermes Way, Wall. 133 DK108
Hermiston Ave. N8 63 DL57
Hermit Pl. NW6 76 DB67
Belsize Rd.
Hermit Rd. E16 80 EF70
Hermit St. EC1 6 F2
Hermit St. EC1 77 DP69
Hermitage, The SE23 106 DW88
Hermitage, The SW13 89 CT81
Hermitage, The, Felt. 99 BT90
Hermitage, The, Rich. 102 CL85
Hermitage, The, Uxb. 70 BK65
Hermitage Clo. E18 66 EF56
Hermitage Clo., Enf. 35 DP40
Hermitage Clo., Esher 129 CG107
Hermitage Clo., Shep. 112 BN98
Hermitage Ct. E18 66 EG56

Hermitage Ct. NW2 62 DA62
Hermitage La.
Hermitage Ct., Pot.B. 20 DC33
Southgate Rd.
Hermitage Gdns. NW2 62 DA62
Hermitage Gdns. SE19 106 DQ94
Hermitage La. N18 50 DR50
Hermitage La. NW2 62 DA62
Hermitage La. SE25 120 DU100
Hermitage La. SW16 105 DM94
Hermitage La., Croy. 120 DU100
Hermitage Path SW16 119 DL95
Hermitage Rd. N4 63 DP59
Hermitage Rd. N15 63 DP59
Hermitage Rd. SE19 106 DQ94
Hermitage Rd., Ken. 148 DQ116
Hermitage Row E8 64 DU64
Hermitage St. W2 76 DD71
Harrow Rd.
Hermitage Wk. E18 66 EF56
Hermitage Wall E1 78 DU74
Hermitage Way, Stan. 45 CG53
Hermon Gro., Hayes 71 BU74
Hermon Hill E11 66 EG57
Hermon Hill E18 66 EH55
Herndon Rd. SW18 104 DC85
Herne Clo. NW10 60 CR64
North Circular Rd.
Herne Hill SE24 106 DQ85
Herne Hill Rd. SE24 92 DQ83
Herne Ms. N18 50 DU49
Lyndhurst Rd.
Herne Pl. SE24 105 DP85
Herne Rd., Surb. 115 CK103
Herne Rd. (Bushey), Wat. 30 CB44
Heron Clo. E17 51 DZ54
Heron Clo. NW10 74 CS65
Heron Clo., Buck.H. 52 EG46
Heron Clo., Rick. 42 BK47
Heron Clo., Uxb. 70 BK65
Heron Ct., Brom. 122 EJ98
Heron Cres., Sid. 109 ES90
Heron Dale, Add. 126 BK106
Heron Flight Ave., Horn. 83 FH66
Heron Hill, Belv. 96 EZ78
Heron Ms., Ilf. 67 EP61
Balfour Rd.
Heron Pl. SE16 79 DY74
Heron Quay E14 79 EA74
Heron Rd. SE24 92 DQ84
Heron Rd., Croy. 120 DS103
Tunstall Rd.
Heron Rd., Twick. 87 CG84
Heron Sq., Rich. 101 CK85
Bridge St.
Heron Wk., Nthwd. 43 BS49
Herondale, S.Croy. 135 DX109
Herondale Ave. SW18 104 DD88
Heronfield, Pot.B. 20 DC30
Herongate Rd. E12 66 EJ61
Herongate Rd., Swan. 111 FE93
Herongate Rd. (Cheshunt), Wal.Cr. 23 DY27
Heronry, The, Walt. 127 BU107
Herons, The E11 66 EF58
Herons Cft., Wey. 127 BR107
Heron's Pl., Islw. 87 CH83
Herons Ri., Barn. 34 DE42
Heronsforde W13 73 CJ72
Heronsgate, Edg. 46 CN50
Heronslea, Wat. 30 BW36
Heronslea Dr., Stan. 46 CL50
Heronswood, Wal.Abb. 24 EE34
Roundhills
Heronway, Wdf.Grn. 52 EJ49
Herrick Rd. N5 64 DQ62
Herrick St. SW1 9 N9
Herrick St. SW1 91 DK77
Herries St. W10 75 CY68
Herringham Rd. SE7 94 EJ76
Herrings La., Cher. 112 BG100
Herrongate Clo., Enf. 36 DT40
Hersant Clo. NW10 75 CU67
Herschell Rd. SE23 107 DY87
Hersham Bypass, Walt. 127 BV106
Hersham Clo. SW15 103 CU87
Hersham Gdns., Walt. 128 BW105
Hersham Rd., Walt. 113 BU102
Hersham Trd. Est., Walt. 114 BY103
Hertford Ave. SW14 102 CR85
Hertford Clo., Barn. 34 DD41
Hertford Pl. W1 5 K5
Hertford Rd. N1 78 DS67
Hertford Rd. N2 62 DE55
Hertford Rd. N9 50 DU47
Hertford Rd., Bark. 81 EP66
Hertford Rd., Barn. 34 DC41
Hertford Rd., Enf. 36 DW40
Hertford Rd., Ilf. 67 ES58
Hertford Rd., Wal.Cr. 37 DY35
Hertford Sq., Mitch. 119 DL98
Hertford Way
Hertford St. W1 8 G3
Hertford St. W1 76 DG74
Hertford Wk., Belv. 96 FA78
Hoddesdon Rd.
Hertford Way, Mitch. 119 DL98
Hertslet Rd. N7 63 DM62
Hertsmere Rd. E14 79 EA73
Hervey Clo. N3 48 DA53
Hervey Pk. Rd. E17 65 DY56
Hervey Rd. SE3 94 EH81
Hesa Rd., Hayes 71 BU72
Hesiers Hill, Warl. 150 EE117
Hesiers Rd., Warl. 150 EE117
Hesketh Pl. W11 75 CY73
Hesketh Rd. E7 66 EG62
Heslop Rd. SW12 104 DF88
Hesper Ms. SW5 90 DB78
Hesperus Cres. E14 93 EB77
Hessel Rd. W13 87 CG75
Hessel St. E1 78 DV72
Hesselyn Dr., Rain. 83 FH66
Hessle Gro., Epsom 131 CT111
Hester Rd. N18 50 DU50
Hester Rd. SW11 90 DE80
Hester Ter., Rich. 88 CN83
Chilton Rd.
Hestercombe Ave. SW6 89 CY82
Hesterman Way, Croy. 119 DL102
Heston Ave., Houns. 86 BY79
Heston Gra. La., Houns. 86 BZ79
Heston Ind. Cen., Houns. 86 BW79
Heston Ind. Mall, Houns. 86 BZ80
Heston Rd., Houns. 86 CA79
Heston St. SE14 93 EA81
Heswell Grn., Wat. 43 BU48
Fairhaven Cres.
Hetherington Rd. SW4 91 DL84
Hetherington Rd., Shep. 113 BQ96
Hetherington Way, Uxb. 56 BL63
Hetley Gdns. SE19 106 DT94
Fox Hill
Hetley Rd. W12 75 CV74
Heton Gdns. NW4 61 CU56
Hevelius Clo. SE10 94 EF78
Hever Cft. SE9 109 EN91
Hever Gdns., Brom. 123 EN96
Heverham Rd. SE18 95 ES77
Heversham Rd., Bexh. 96 FA82
Hewens Rd., Hayes 71 BQ70
Hewens Rd., Uxb. 71 BQ70
Hewer St. W10 75 CX71
Hewers Way, Tad. 145 CV120
Hewett Clo., Stan. 45 CH49
Hewett Pl., Swan. 125 FD98
Hewett Rd., Dag. 68 EW64
Hewett St. EC2 7 N5
Hewins Clo., Wal.Abb. 24 EE33
Broomstick Hall Rd.
Hewish Rd. N18 50 DS49
Hewison St. E3 79 DZ68
Hewitt Ave. N22 49 DP54
Hewitt Clo., Croy. 121 EA104
Hewitt Rd. N8 63 DN57
Hewitts Rd., Orp. 138 EZ108
Hewlett Rd. E3 79 DY68
Hexagon, The N6 62 DF60
Hexal Rd. SE6 108 EE90
Hexham Gdns., Islw. 87 CG80
Hexham Rd. SE27 106 DQ89
Hexham Rd., Barn. 34 DB42
Hexham Rd., Mord. 118 DB102
Heybourne Rd. N17 50 DV52
Heybridge Ave. SW16 105 DL94
Heybridge Dr., Ilf. 53 ER54
Heybridge Way E10 65 DY59
Heyford Ave. SW8 91 DL80
Heyford Ave. SW20 117 CZ97
Heyford Rd., Mitch. 118 DE96
Heyford Rd., Rad. 31 CF37
Heygate St. SE17 11 H9
Heygate St. SE17 92 DQ77
Heylyn Sq. E3 79 DZ69
Malmesbury Rd.
Heymede, Lthd. 143 CJ123
Heynes Rd., Dag. 68 EW63
Heysham Dr., Wat. 44 BW50
Heysham La. NW3 62 DB62
Heysham Rd. N15 64 DR58
Heythorp St. SW18 103 CZ88
Heythrop Dr., Uxb. 56 BM63
Heywood Ave. NW9 46 CS53
Heyworth Rd. E5 64 DV63
Heyworth Rd. E15 66 EF63
Hibbert Ave., Wat. 30 BX38
Hibbert Rd. E17 65 DZ59
Hibbert Rd., Har. 45 CF54
Hibbert St. SW11 90 DC83
Hibbs Clo., Swan. 125 FD96
Hibernia Gdns., Houns. 86 CA84
Hibernia Rd., Houns. 86 CA84
Hichisson Rd. SE15 106 DW85
Hickin Clo. SE7 94 EK77
Hickin St. E14 93 EC76
Plevna St.
Hickling Rd., Ilf. 67 EP64
Hickman Ave. E4 51 EC51
Hickman Clo. E16 80 EK71
Hickman Rd., Rom. 68 EW59
Hickmore Wk. SW4 91 DJ83
Hickory Clo. N9 50 DU45
Hicks Ave., Grnf. 73 CD68
Hicks Clo. SW11 90 DE83
Hicks St. SE8 93 DY78
Hidcote Gdns. SW20 117 CV97
Hide E6 81 EN72
Downings
Hide Pl. SW1 9 M9
Hide Pl. SW1 91 DK77
Hide Rd., Har. 58 CC56
Hideaway, The, Abb.L. 15 BU31
Hides St. N7 77 DM65
Sheringham Rd.
Higgins Wk., Hmptn. 100 BY93
Abbott Clo.
High Acres, Abb.L. 15 BR32
High Beech, S.Croy. 134 DS108
High Beech Rd., Loug. 38 EL42
High Beeches, Bans. 131 CW114
High Beeches, Orp. 138 EU107
High Beeches, Sid. 110 EY92
High Beeches Clo., Pur. 133 DK110
High Bri. SE10 93 ED78
High Bri. Wf. SE10 93 ED78
High Bri.
High Broom Cres., W.Wick. 121 EB101
High Canons, Borwd. 32 CQ37
High Cedar Dr. SW20 103 CV94
High Clo., Rick. 28 BJ43
High Coombe Pl., Kings.T. 102 CR94
High Cross, Wat. 31 CD37
High Cross Cen. N15 64 DU56
High Cross Rd. N17 64 DU55
High Dr., Cat. 149 EA122
High Dr., Lthd. 129 CD114
High Dr., N.Mal. 116 CQ95
High Elms, Chig. 53 ES49
High Elms, Wdf.Grn. 52 EG50
High Elms Clo., Nthwd. 43 BR51
High Elms La., Wat. 15 BV31
High Elms Rd., Orp. 137 EN111
High Fld., Bans. 146 DE117
High Firs, Rad. 31 CF35
High Firs, Swan. 125 FE98
High Foleys, Esher 129 CH108
High Gables, Loug. 38 EK43
High Garth, Esher 128 CC107
High Gro. SE18 95 ER80
High Gro., Brom. 122 EJ95
High Hill Est. E5 64 DV60
Mount Pleasant La.
High Hill Ferry E5 64 DV60
High Hill Rd., Warl. 149 EC115
High Holborn WC1 5 P8
High Holborn WC1 77 DL72
High La. W7 73 CD71
High La., Cat. 149 DZ119
High La., Warl. 149 DZ118
High Lawns, Har. 59 CE62
High Level Dr. SE26 106 DU91
High Mead, Chig. 53 EQ47
High Mead, Har. 59 CE57
High Mead, W.Wick. 121 ED103
High Meadow Clo., Pnr. 57 BV56
Daymer Gdns.
High Meadow Cres. NW9 60 CR57
High Meadows, Chig. 53 ER50
High Meads Rd. E16 80 EK72
Fulmer Rd.
High Mt. NW4 61 CU58
High Oaks, Enf. 35 DM38
High Pk. Ave., Rich. 88 CN81
High Pk. Rd., Rich. 88 CN81
High Path SW19 118 DB95
High Pine Clo., Wey. 127 BQ106
High Pines, Warl. 148 DW119
High Pt. N6 62 DG59
High Pt. SE9 109 EP90
High Ridge (Cuffley), Pot.B. 21 DL27
High Ridge Clo., Hem.H. 14 BK25
High Ridge Rd., Hem.H. 14 BK25
High Rd. N2 48 DD53
High Rd. N11 49 DH50
High Rd. N12 48 DC49
High Rd. N15 64 DT58
High Rd. N17 64 DT55
High Rd. N20 48 DC47
High Rd. N22 49 DM51
High Rd. (Willesden) NW10 75 CT65
High Rd., Buck.H. 52 EH48
High Rd., Chig. 53 EN50
High Rd., Couls. 146 DE124
High Rd., Epp. 25 ER32
High Rd. (North Weald Bassett), Epp. 27 FB27
High Rd. (Thornwood), Epp. 26 EV28
High Rd. (Harrow Weald), Har. 45 CE52
High Rd., Ilf. 67 EQ61
High Rd. (Goodmayes), Ilf. 68 EU60
High Rd. (Seven Kings), Ilf. 67 ET60
High Rd., Loug. 38 EJ44
High Rd., Pnr. 57 BV57
High Rd. (Chadwell Heath), Rom. 68 EU60
High Rd., Uxb. 70 BJ71
High Rd. (Ickenham), Uxb. 57 BP62
High Rd. (Bushey), Wat. 45 CD46
High Rd. (Leavesden Grn.), Wat. 29 BT35
High Rd., Wem. 60 CL64
High Rd., W.Byf. 126 BK112
High Rd. Leyton E10 65 EB58
High Rd. Leyton E15 65 EC63
High Rd. Leytonstone E11 66 EE63
High Rd. Leytonstone E15 66 EE63
High Rd. Turnford, Brox. 23 DY25
High Rd. Woodford Grn. E18 52 EF53
High Rd. Woodford Grn., Wdf.Grn. 52 EF51
High Silver, Loug. 38 EK42
High St. E11 66 EG57
High St. E13 80 EG68
High St. E15 79 EC68
High St. E17 65 DY57
High St. N8 63 DL56
High St. N14 49 DK47
High St. NW7 47 CV50
High St. (Harlesden) NW10 75 CT68
High St. SE20 106 DW94
High St. (South Norwood) SE25 120 DT98
High St. SW6 89 CY83
High St. W3 74 CP74
High St. W5 73 CK73
High St., Abb.L. 15 BS31
High St. (Bedmond), Abb.L. 15 BT27
High St., Add. 126 BH105
High St., Bans. 146 DA115
High St., Barn. 33 CY41
High St., Beck. 121 EA96
High St. (Elstree), Borwd. 31 CK44
High St., Brent. 88 CL79
High St., Brom. 122 EG96
High St., Cars. 132 DF105
High St., Cat. 148 DS123
High St., Chis. 109 EP93
High St., Cob. 127 BV114
High St., Croy. 120 DQ104
High St., Edg. 46 CN51
High St. (Ponders End), Enf. 36 DW42
High St., Epp. 25 ET31
High St., Epsom 130 CR113
High St. (Ewell), Epsom 131 CT109
High St., Esher 128 CB105
High St. (Claygate), Esher 129 CF107
High St., Felt. 99 BT90
High St., Hmptn. 114 CB95
High St., Har. 59 CE60
High St. (Wealdstone), Har. 45 CE54
High St., Hayes 85 BR79
High St., Houns. 86 CB83
High St. (Cranford), Houns. 85 BU80
High St., Ilf. 67 EQ55
High St., Kings L. 14 BN29
High St., Kings.T. 115 CK97
High St. (Hampton Wick), Kings.T. 115 CJ95
High St., Lthd. 143 CH122
High St. (Oxshott), Lthd. 129 CD113
High St., N.Mal. 116 CS98
High St., Nthwd. 43 BT53
High St., Orp. 124 EU103
High St. (Downe), Orp. 137 EN111
High St. (Farnborough), Orp. 137 EP106
High St. (Green St. Grn.), Orp. 137 ET108
High St. (St. Mary Cray), Orp. 124 EW100
High St., Pnr. 58 BY55
High St., Pot.B. 20 DC33
High St., Pur. 133 DN111
High St., Rick. 42 BK46
High St., Rom. 69 FE57
High St., Ruis. 57 BS59
High St. (London Colney), St.Alb. 17 CJ25
High St., Sev. 155 FJ126
High St. (Chipstead), Sev. 154 FC122
High St. (Otford), Sev. 153 FF116
High St. (Seal), Sev. 155 FL121
High St. (Shoreham), Sev. 139 FF110
High St., Shep. 113 BP101
High St., Sthl. 72 BZ74
High St. (Stanwell), Stai. 98 BK86
High St., Sutt. 132 DB105
High St. (Cheam), Sutt. 131 CY107
High St., Swan. 125 FF97
High St., Tad. 145 CW123
High St., Tedd. 101 CF92
High St., T.Ditt. 115 CG101
High St., Th.Hth. 120 DQ98
High St. (Whitton), Twick. 100 CC87
High St., Uxb. 70 BJ66
High St. (Cowley), Uxb. 70 BJ69
High St. (Harefield), Uxb. 42 BJ54
High St., Wal.Cr. 23 DX33
High St. (Cheshunt), Wal.Cr. 23 DX29
High St., Walt. 113 BU102
High St., Wat. 29 BV41
High St. (Bushey), Wat. 30 BZ44
High St., Wem. 60 CM63
High St., West Dr. 84 BK79
High St. (Yiewsley), West Dr. 70 BK73
High St., W.Mol. 114 CA98
High St., W.Wick. 121 EB102
High St. (Brasted), West. 152 EV124
High St., Wey. 126 BN105
High St. (Ripley), Wok. 140 BH122
High St. Colliers Wd. SW19 104 DD94
High St. Ms. SW19 103 CY92
High St. N. E6 80 EL66
High St. N. E12 66 EL64
High St. S. E6 81 EM68
High St. Wimbledon SW19 103 CX92
High Timber St. EC4 7 H10
High Timber St. EC4 78 DQ73
High Tor Clo., Brom. 108 EH94
Babbacombe Rd.
High Tree Ct. W7 73 CE73
High Trees SW2 105 DN88
High Trees, Barn. 34 DE43
High Trees, Croy. 121 DY102
High Trees Clo., Cat. 148 DT123
High Vw., Pnr. 58 BW55
High Vw., Rick. 28 BG42
High Vw., Sutt. 131 CZ111
High Vw., Wat. 29 BT44
High Vw. Clo. SE19 120 DT96
High Vw. Clo., Loug. 38 EJ43
High Vw. Rd. E18 66 EF55
High Vw. Rd., Sid. 110 EV91
High Worple, Har. 58 BY59
Higham Hill Rd. E17 51 DY53
Higham Pl. E17 65 DY55
Higham Rd. N17 64 DR55
Higham Rd., Wdf.Grn. 52 EG51
Higham Sta. Ave. E4 51 EA51
Higham St. E17 65 DY55
Higham Vw., Epp. 27 FB26
Highams Lo. Business Cen. E17 65 DX55
Highams Pk. Ind. Est. E4 51 EC51
Highbank Way N8 63 DN58
Highbanks Clo., Well. 96 EV80
Highbanks Rd., Pnr. 44 CA51
Highbarns Rd., Hem.H. 14 BN25
Highbarrow Rd., Croy. 120 DU101
Highbridge SE10 93 ED78
Highbridge Rd., Bark. 81 EP67
Highbridge St., Wal.Abb. 23 EB33
Highbrook Rd. SE3 94 EK83
Highbury Ave., Th.Hth. 119 DN96
Highbury Clo., N.Mal. 116 CQ98
Highbury Clo., W.Wick. 121 EB103
Highbury Cor. N5 77 DP65
Highbury Cres. N5 63 DP64
Highbury Est. N5 64 DQ64
Highbury Gdns., Ilf. 67 ES61
Highbury Gra. N5 64 DQ63
Highbury Gro. N5 77 DP65
Highbury Hill N5 63 DN62
Highbury Ms. N7 77 DN65
Holloway Rd.
Highbury New Pk. N5 64 DQ64
Highbury Pk. N5 63 DP63
Highbury Pk. Ms. N5 64 DQ63
Highbury Gra.
Highbury Pl. N5 77 DP65
Highbury Quad. N5 64 DQ62
Highbury Rd. SW19 103 CY92
Highbury Sta. Rd. N1 77 DN65
Highbury Ter. N5 63 DP64
Highbury Ter. Ms. N5 63 DP64
Highclere Clo., Ken. 148 DQ115
Highclere Rd., N.Mal. 116 CR97
Highclere St. SE26 107 DY91
Highcliffe Dr. SW15 103 CT86
Highcliffe Gdns., Ilf. 66 EL57
Highcombe SE7 94 EH79
Highcombe Clo. SE9 108 EK88
Highcroft NW9 60 CS57
Highcroft Ave., Wem. 74 CN67
Highcroft Ct., Lthd. 142 CA123
Highcroft Gdns. NW11 61 CZ58
Highcroft Rd. N19 63 DL59
Highcroft Rd., Hem.H. 14 BG25
Highcross Way SW15 103 CU88
Highdaun Dr. SW16 119 DM98
Highdown, Wor.Pk. 116 CS103
Highdown La., Sutt. 132 DB111
Highdown Rd. SW15 103 CV86
Higher Dr., Bans. 131 CX112
Higher Dr., Pur. 133 DN113
Higher Grn., Epsom 131 CU113
Highfield, Felt. 99 BU88
Highfield, Kings L. 14 BL28
Highfield Ave. NW9 60 CQ57
Highfield Ave. NW11 61 CX59
Highfield Ave., Erith 97 FB79
Highfield Ave., Grnf. 59 CE64
Highfield Ave., Orp. 137 ET106
Highfield Ave., Pnr. 58 BZ57
Highfield Ave., Wem. 60 CL62
Highfield Clo. N22 49 DN53
Highfield Clo. NW9 60 CQ57
Highfield Clo. SE13 107 ED87
Highfield Clo., Lthd. 129 CD111
Highfield Clo., Nthwd. 43 BS53
Highfield Clo., Rom. 55 FC51
Highfield Clo., Surb. 115 CJ102
Highfield Clo., W.Byf. 126 BG113
Highfield Ct. N14 35 DJ44
Highfield Cres., Nthwd. 43 BS53
Highfield Dr., Brom. 122 EE98
Highfield Dr., Epsom 131 CT108
Highfield Dr., Uxb. 56 BL62
Highfield Dr., W.Wick. 121 EB103
Highfield Gdns. NW11 61 CY58
Highfield Grn., Epp. 25 ES31
Highfield Hill SE19 106 DR94
Highfield Link, Rom. 55 FD51
Highfield Pl., Epp. 25 ES31
Highfield Rd. N21 49 DP47
Highfield Rd. NW11 61 CY58
Highfield Rd. W3 74 CP71
Highfield Rd., Bexh. 110 EZ85
Highfield Rd., Brom. 123 EM98
Highfield Rd., Cat. 148 DU122
Highfield Rd., Cher. 112 BG102
Highfield Rd., Chis. 123 ET97
Highfield Rd., Felt. 99 BU88
Highfield Rd., Islw. 87 CF81
Highfield Rd., Nthwd. 43 BS53
Highfield Rd., Pur. 133 DM110
Highfield Rd., Rom. 55 FC52
Highfield Rd., Sun. 113 BT98
Highfield Rd., Surb. 116 CQ101
Highfield Rd., Sutt. 132 DE106
Highfield Rd. (Cheshunt), Wal.Cr. 22 DS26
Highfield Rd., Walt. 113 BU102
Highfield Rd. (Bushey), Wat. 30 BY43
Highfield Rd., W.Byf. 126 BG113

Highfield Rd., West. 150 EJ117
Highfield Rd., Wdf.Grn. 52 EL52
Highfield Twrs., Rom. 55 FD50
Highfield Way, Pot.B. 20 DB32
Highfield Way, Rick. 28 BG44
Highfields, Ash. 143 CK119
Highfields, Lthd. 143 CD124
Highfields (Cuffley), Pot.B. 21 DL28
Highfields, Rad. 31 CF35
Highfields Gro. N6 62 DF60
Highgate Ave. N6 63 DH59
Highgate Clo. N6 62 DG59
Highgate High St. N6 62 DG60
Highgate Hill N6 63 DH60
Highgate Hill N19 63 DH60
Highgate Rd. NW5 63 DH63
Highgate Wk. SE23 106 DW89
Highgate W. Hill N6 62 DG60
Highgrove Clo. N11 48 DG50
Balmoral Ave.
Highgrove Clo., Chis. 122 EL95
Highgrove Ct., Beck. 107 EA94
Park Rd.
Highgrove Ms., Cars. 118 DF104
Highgrove Rd., Dag. 68 EW64
Highgrove Way, Ruis. 57 BU58
Highland Ave. W7 73 CE72
Highland Ave., Dag. 69 FC62
Highland Ave., Loug. 38 EL44
Highland Cotts., Wall. 133 DH105
Highland Ct. E18 52 EH53
Highland Cft., Beck. 107 EB92
Highland Dr. (Bushey), Wat. 44 CC45
Highland Pk., Felt. 99 BT91
Highland Rd. SE19 106 DS93
Highland Rd., Bexh. 110 FA85
Highland Rd., Brom. 122 EF95
Highland Rd., Nthwd. 43 BT54
Highland Rd., Pur. 133 DN114
Highland Rd., Sev. 139 FB110
Highlands, Ash. 143 CJ119
Highlands, Wat. 44 BW46
Highlands, The, Edg. 46 CP54
Highlands, The, Pot.B. 20 DC30
Highlands, The, Rick. 42 BH45
Highlands Ave. N21 35 DM43
Worlds End La.
Highlands Ave. W3 74 CQ73
Highlands Ave., Lthd. 143 CJ122
Highlands Clo. N4 63 DL59
Mount Vw. Rd.
Highlands Clo., Houns. 86 CB81
Highlands Clo., Lthd. 143 CH122
Highlands Gdns., Ilf. 67 EM60
Highlands Heath SW15 103 CW87
Highlands Hill, Swan. 125 FG96
Highlands Pk., Lthd. 143 CK123
Highlands Pk., Sev. 155 FL121
Highlands Rd., Barn. 34 DA43
Highlands Rd., Lthd. 143 CH122
Highlands Rd., Orp. 124 EV101
Highlea Clo. NW9 46 CS53
Highlever Rd. W10 75 CW71
Highmead SE18 95 ET80
Highmead Cres., Wem. 74 CM66
Highmore Rd. SE3 94 EE80
Highpoint, Wey. 126 BN106
Highridge Clo., Epsom 144 CS115
Highshore Rd. SE15 92 DT82
Highstead Cres., Erith 97 FE80
Highstone Ave. E11 66 EG58
Highview, Cat. 148 DS124
Highview Ave., Edg. 46 CQ49
Highview Ave., Wall. 133 DM106
Highview Clo., Pot.B. 20 DC33
Highview Gdns.
Highview Gdns. N3 61 CY56
Highview Gdns. N11 49 DJ50
Highview Gdns., Edg. 46 CQ50
Highview Gdns., Pot.B. 20 DC33
Highview Ho., Rom. 68 EY56
Highview Rd. SE19 106 DR93
Highview Rd. W13 73 CG71
Highway, The E1 78 DU73
Highway, The E14 79 DX73
Highway, The, Orp. 138 EV106
Highway, The, Stan. 45 CF53
Highway, The, Sutt. 132 DC109
Highwold, Couls. 146 DG118
Highwood, Brom. 121 ED97
Highwood Ave. N12 48 DC49
Highwood Ave. (Bushey), Wat. 30 BZ39
Highwood Clo., Ken. 148 DQ117
Highwood Clo., Orp. 123 EQ103
Highwood Dr., Orp. 123 EQ103
Highwood Gdns., Ilf. 67 EM57
Highwood Gro. NW7 46 CR50
Highwood Hall La., Hem.H. 15 BQ25
Highwood Hill NW7 47 CT47
Highwood La., Loug. 39 EN43
Highwood Rd. N19 63 DL62
Highwoods, Lthd. 143 CJ121
Highworth Rd. N11 49 DK51
Hilary Ave., Mitch. 118 DG97
Hilary Clo. SW6 90 DB80
Hilary Clo., Erith 97 FB81
Hilary Rd. W12 75 CT72
Hilbert Rd., Sutt. 117 CX104
Hilborough Way, Orp. 137 ER106
Hilda May Ave., Swan. 125 FD97
Hilda Rd. E6 80 EK66
Hilda Rd. E16 80 EE70
Hilda Ter. SW9 91 DN82
Hilda Vale Clo., Orp. 137 EP105
Hilda Vale Rd., Orp. 137 EN105
Hilden Dr., Erith 97 FH80
Hildenborough Gdns., Brom. 108 EE93
Hildenlea Pl., Brom. 122 EE96
Hilders, The, Ash. 144 CP117
Hildreth St. SW12 105 DH88
Hildyard Rd. SW6 90 DA79
Hiley Rd. NW10 75 CW69
Hilfield La., Wat. 30 CB39
Hilfield La. S. (Bushey), Wat. 31 CF44
Hilgrove Rd. NW6 76 DC66
Hiliary Gdns., Stan. 45 CJ54
Hill, The, Cat. 148 DT124
Hill Barn, S.Croy. 134 DS111
Hill Brow, Brom. 122 EK95
Hill Brow, Dart. 111 FF86
Hill Brow Clo., Bex. 111 FD91
Hill Clo. NW2 61 CV62
Hill Clo. NW11 62 DA58
Hill Clo., Barn. 33 CW43
Hill Clo., Chis. 109 EP92
Hill Clo., Har. 59 CE62
Hill Clo., Pur. 134 DQ112
Hill Clo., Stan. 45 CH49
Hill Ct., Nthlt. 58 CA64
Hill Cres. N20 48 DB47
Hill Cres., Bex. 111 FC88
Hill Cres., Har. 59 CG57
Hill Cres., Surb. 116 CM99
Hill Cres., Wor.Pk. 117 CW103
Hill Crest, Pot.B. 20 DC34
Hill Crest, Sev. 154 FG122
Hill Crest, Sid. 110 EU87
Hill Crest Gdns. N3 61 CY56
Hill Dr. NW9 60 CQ60
Hill Dr. SW16 119 DM97
Hill End, Orp. 123 ET103
The App.
Hill End Rd., Uxb. 42 BJ52
Hill Fm. Ave., Wat. 15 BU33
Hill Fm. Clo., Wat. 15 BU33
Hill Fm. Rd. W10 75 CW71
Hill Gro., Rom. 69 FE55
Hill Ho. Ave., Stan. 45 CF52
Hill Ho. Clo. N21 49 DN45
Hill Ho. Dr., Wey. 126 BN111
Hill Ho. Rd. SW16 105 DM92
Hill La., Ruis. 57 BQ60
Hill La., Tad. 145 CY121
Hill Leys (Cuffley), Pot.B. 21 DL28
Hill Pk. Dr., Lthd. 143 CF119
Hill Path SW16 105 DM92
Valley Rd.
Hill Ri. N9 36 DV44
Hill Ri. NW11 62 DB56
Hill Ri. SE23 106 DV88
London Rd.
Hill Ri., Esher 115 CH103
Hill Ri., Grnf. 72 CC66
Hill Ri., Pot.B. 20 DC34
Hill Ri. (Cuffley), Pot.B. 21 DL28
Hill Ri., Rich. 101 CK85
Hill Ri., Rick. 42 BH45
Hill Ri., Ruis. 57 BQ60
Hill Ri., Walt. 113 BT101
Hill Rd. N10 48 DF53
Hill Rd. NW8 76 DC68
Hill Rd., Cars. 132 DE107
Hill Rd., Epp. 39 ES38
Hill Rd., Har. 59 CG57
Hill Rd., Lthd. 142 CB122
Hill Rd., Mitch. 119 DH95
Hill Rd., Nthwd. 43 BR51
Hill Rd., Pnr. 58 BY58
Hill Rd., Pur. 133 DM112
Hill Rd., Sutt. 132 DB106
Hill Rd., Wem. 59 CH62
Hill St. W1 8 G2
Hill St. W1 76 DG74
Hill St., Rich. 101 CK85
Hill Top NW11 62 DB56
Hill Top, Loug. 39 EN40
Hill Top, Mord. 118 DB100
Hill Top Clo., Loug. 39 EN41
Hill Top Pl., Loug. 39 EN41
Hill Top Vw., Wdf.Grn. 53 EM51
Hill Vw. Clo., Tad. 145 CW121
Shelvers Way
Hill Vw. Cres., Orp. 123 ET102
Hill Vw. Dr., Well. 95 ES82
Hill Vw. Gdns. NW9 60 CR57
Hill Vw. Rd., Esher 129 CG108
Hill Vw. Rd., Orp. 123 ET102
Hill Vw. Rd., Twick. 101 CG86
Hillars Heath Rd., Couls. 147 DL115
Hillary Cres., Walt. 114 BW102
Hillary Ri., Barn. 34 DA42
Hillary Rd., Sthl. 86 CA76
Hillbeck Clo. SE15 92 DW80
Hillbeck Way, Grnf. 73 CD67
Hillborne Clo., Hayes 85 BU78
Hillborough Ave., Sev. 155 FK122
Hillborough Clo. SW19 104 DC94
Hillbrook Gdns., Wey. 126 BN108
Hillbrook Rd. SW17 104 DF90
Hillbrow, N.Mal. 117 CT97
Hillbrow Rd., Brom. 108 EE94
Hillbrow Rd., Esher 128 CC105
Hillbury Ave., Har. 59 CH57
Hillbury Clo., Warl. 148 DW118
Hillbury Gdns., Warl. 148 DW118
Hillbury Rd. SW17 105 DH90
Hillbury Rd., Warl. 148 DU117
Hillbury Rd., Whyt. 148 DU117
Hillcote Ave. SW16 105 DN94
Hillcourt Ave. N12 48 DB51
Hillcourt Est. N16 64 DR60
Hillcourt Rd. SE22 106 DV86
Hillcrest N6 62 DG59
Hillcrest N21 49 DN45
Hillcrest, Wey. 127 BP105
Hillcrest Ave. NW11 61 CY57
Hillcrest Ave., Edg. 46 CP49
Hillcrest Ave., Pnr. 58 BX56
Hillcrest Clo. SE26 106 DU91
Hillcrest Clo., Beck. 121 DZ99
Hillcrest Clo., Epsom 145 CT115
Hillcrest Gdns. NW2 61 CU62
Hillcrest Gdns., Esher 115 CF104
Hillcrest Par., Couls. 133 DH114
Hillcrest Rd. E17 51 ED54
Hillcrest Rd. E18 52 EF54
Hillcrest Rd. W3 74 CN74
Hillcrest Rd. W5 74 CL71
Hillcrest Rd., Brom. 108 EG91
Hillcrest Rd., Dart. 111 FF87
Hillcrest Rd., Horn. 69 FG59
Hillcrest Rd., Loug. 38 EK44
Hillcrest Rd., Ong. 27 FE30
Hillcrest Rd., Orp. 124 EU103
Hillcrest Rd., Pur. 133 DM110
Hillcrest Rd., Rad. 18 CN33
Hillcrest Rd., West. 150 EK116
Hillcrest Rd., Whyt. 148 DT117
Hillcrest Vw., Beck. 121 DZ100
Hillcrest Way, Epp. 26 EU31
Hillcroft, Loug. 39 EN40
Hillcroft Ave., Pnr. 58 BZ58
Hillcroft Ave., Pur. 133 DJ113
Hillcroft Cres. W5 73 CK72
Hillcroft Cres., Ruis. 58 BX62
Hillcroft Cres., Wat. 43 BU46
Hillcroft Cres., Wem. 60 CM63
Hillcroft Rd. E6 81 EP71
Hillcroome Rd., Sutt. 132 DD107
Hillcross Ave., Mord. 117 CX100
Hilldale Rd., Sutt. 131 CZ105
Hilldeane Rd., Pur. 133 DN109
Hilldown Rd. SW16 105 DL94
Hilldown Rd., Brom. 122 EE102
Hilldrop Cres. N7 63 DK64
Hilldrop Est. N7 63 DK64
Hilldrop La. N7 63 DK64
Hilldrop Rd. N7 63 DK64
Hilldrop Rd., Brom. 108 EG93
Hillend SE18 95 EP81
Hillersdon Ave. SW13 89 CU82
Hillersdon Ave., Edg. 46 CM50
Hillery Clo. SE17 11 L9
Hilley Fld. La., Lthd. 142 CC122
Hillfield Ave. N8 63 DL57
Hillfield Ave. NW9 60 CS57
Hillfield Ave., Mord. 118 DE100
Hillfield Ave., Wem. 74 CL66
Hillfield Clo., Har. 58 CC56
Hillfield Ct. NW3 62 DE64
Hillfield Pk. N10 63 DH55
Hillfield Pk. N21 49 DN47
Hillfield Pk. Ms. N10 63 DH56
Hillfield Rd. NW6 61 CZ64
Hillfield Rd., Hmptn. 100 BZ94
Hillfield Rd., Sev. 153 FE120
Hillfoot Ave., Rom. 55 FC53
Hillfoot Rd., Rom. 55 FC53
Hillgate Pl. SW12 105 DH87
Hillgate Pl. W8 76 DA74
Hillgate St. W8 76 DA74
Hillhouse, Wal.Abb. 24 EF33
Hillhurst Gdns., Cat. 148 DS120
Hilliard Rd., Nthwd. 43 BT53
Hilliards Ct. E1 78 DV74
Wapping High St.
Hilliards Rd., Uxb. 70 BK72
Hilliards St. E1 78 DW74
Wapping High St.
Hillier Clo., Barn. 34 DB44
Hillier Gdns., Croy. 133 DN106
Crowley Cres.
Hillier Pl., Chess. 129 CJ107
Hillier Rd. SW11 104 DF86
Hilliers Ave., Uxb. 70 BN69
Harlington Rd.
Hilliers La., Croy. 119 DL104
Hillingdale, West. 150 EH118
Hillingdon Ave., Sev. 155 FJ121
Hillingdon Ave., Stai. 98 BL88
Hillingdon Hill, Uxb. 70 BL69
Hillingdon Ri., Sev. 155 FK122
Hillingdon Rd., Bexh. 97 FC82
Hillingdon Rd., Uxb. 70 BJ67
Hillingdon Rd., Wat. 15 BU34
Hillingdon St. SE5 91 DP79
Hillingdon St. SE17 91 DP79
Hillington Gdns., Wdf.Grn. 52 EK54
Hillman Clo., Uxb. 56 BL64
Hillman Dr. W10 75 CW70
Hillman St. E8 78 DV65
Hillmarton Rd. N7 63 DL64
Hillmead Dr. SW9 91 DP84
Hillmont Rd., Esher 115 CE104
Hillmore Gro. SE26 107 DX92
Hillreach SE18 95 EM78
Hillrise Ave., Wat. 30 BX38
Hillrise Rd. N19 63 DL59
Hillrise Rd., Rom. 55 FC51
Hills La., Nthwd. 43 BS53
Hills Ms. W5 74 CL73
Hills Pl. W1 5 K9
Hills Rd., Buck.H. 52 EH46
Hillsboro Rd. SE22 106 DS85
Hillsborough Grn., Wat. 43 BU48
Ashburnham Dr.
Hillsgrove Clo., Well. 96 EW80
Hillside NW9 60 CR56
Hillside NW10 74 CQ66
Hillside SW19 103 CX93
Hillside, Bans. 145 CY115
Hillside, Barn. 34 DC43
Hillside, Erith 97 FD77
Hillside, Uxb. 56 BJ57
Hillside, The, Orp. 138 EV109
Hillside Ave. N11 48 DF51
Hillside Ave., Borwd. 32 CP42
Hillside Ave., Pur. 133 DP113
Hillside Ave. (Cheshunt), Wal.Cr. 23 DX31
Hillside Ave., Wem. 60 CM63
Hillside Ave., Wdf.Grn. 52 EJ50
Hillside Clo. NW8 76 DB68
Hillside Clo., Abb.L. 15 BS32
Hillside Clo., Bans. 145 CY116
Hillside Clo., Mord. 117 CY98
Hillside Clo., Wdf.Grn. 52 EJ50
Hillside Ct., Swan. 125 FG98
Hillside Cres., Enf. 36 DR38
Hillside Cres., Har. 58 CC60
Hillside Cres., Nthwd. 43 BU53
Hillside Cres. (Cheshunt), Wal.Cr. 23 DX31
Hillside Cres., Wat. 30 BY44
Pinner Rd.
Hillside Dr., Edg. 46 CN51
Hillside Est. N15 64 DT58
Hillside Gdns. E17 65 ED55
Hillside Gdns. N6 62 DG58
Hillside Gdns. SW2 105 DN89
Hillside Gdns., Barn. 33 CY42
Hillside Gdns., Edg. 46 CM49
Hillside Gdns., Har. 60 CL59
Hillside Gdns., Nthwd. 43 BU52
Hillside Gdns., Wall. 133 DJ108
Hillside Gro. N14 49 DK45
Hillside Gro. NW7 47 CU52
Hillside La., Brom. 122 EG103
Hillside Pas. SW2 105 DM89
Hillside Ri., Nthwd. 43 BU52
Hillside Rd. N15 64 DS58
Hillside Rd. SW2 105 DM89
Hillside Rd. W5 74 CL71
Hillside Rd., Ash. 144 CM117
Hillside Rd., Brom. 122 EF97
Hillside Rd., Couls. 147 DL118
Hillside Rd., Croy. 133 DP106
Hillside Rd., Dart. 111 FG86
Hillside Rd., Epsom 131 CV110
Hillside Rd., Nthwd. 43 BU52
Hillside Rd., Pnr. 43 BV53
Hillside Rd., Rad. 31 CH35
Hillside Rd., Sev. 155 FK123
Hillside Rd., Sthl. 72 CA70
Hillside Rd., Surb. 116 CM98
Hillside Rd., Sutt. 131 CZ108
Hillside Rd. (Bushey), Wat. 30 BY43
Hillside Rd., West. 150 EL119
Hillside Rd., Whyt. 148 DU118
Hillsleigh Rd. W8 75 CZ74
Hillsmead Way, S.Croy. 134 DU113
Hillstowe St. E5 64 DW62
Hilltop, Sutt. 117 CZ101
Hilltop Clo., Lthd. 143 CJ123
Hilltop Clo. (Cheshunt), Wal.Cr. 22 DT26
Hilltop Gdns. NW4 47 CV53
Great N. Way
Hilltop Gdns., Orp. 123 ES103
Hilltop Rd. NW6 76 DA66
Hilltop Rd., Kings L. 15 BR27
Hilltop Rd., Whyt. 148 DS117
Hilltop Wk., Cat. 149 DY120
Hilltop Way, Stan. 45 CG48
Hillview SW20 103 CV94
Hillview, Mitch. 119 DL98
Hillview Ave., Har. 60 CL57
Hillview Clo., Pnr. 44 BZ51
Hillview Clo., Pur. 133 DP111
Hillview Cres., Ilf. 67 EM58
Hillview Gdns. NW4 61 CX56
Hillview Gdns., Har. 58 CA55
Hillview Gdns. (Cheshunt), Wal.Cr. 23 DX27
Hillview Rd. NW7 47 CX49
Hillview Rd., Chis. 109 EN92
Hillview Rd., Pnr. 44 BZ52
Hillview Rd., Sutt. 118 DC104
Hillway N6 62 DG60
Hillway NW9 60 CS59
Hillworth Rd. SW2 105 DN87
Hilly Flds. Cres. SE4 93 EA83
Hillyard Rd. W7 73 CE71
Hillyard St. SW9 91 DN81
Hillyfield E17 65 DY55
Hillyfields, Loug. 39 EN40
Hilsea St. E5 64 DW63
Hilton Ave. N12 48 DD50
Hilton Clo., Uxb. 70 BH68
Hilton Way, S.Croy. 148 DV115
Hilversum Cres. SE22 106 DS85
East Dulwich Gro.
Himalayan Way, Wat. 29 BT43
Himley Rd. SW17 104 DE92
Hinchcliffe Clo., Wall. 133 DM108
Roe Way
Hinchley Clo., Esher 115 CF104
Hinchley Dr., Esher 115 CF104
Hinchley Way, Esher 115 CG104
Hinckler Clo., Wall. 133 DL108
Kingsford Ave.
Hinckley Rd. SE15 92 DU84
Hind Clo., Chig. 53 ET50
Hind Ct. EC4 6 E9
Hind Cres., Erith 97 FD79
Hind Gro. E14 79 EA72
Hinde Ms. W1 76 DG72
Marylebone La.
Hinde St. W1 4 G8
Hinde St. W1 76 DG72
Hindes Rd., Har. 59 CD57
Hindhead Clo. N16 64 DS60
Hindhead Clo., Uxb. 71 BP71
Aldenham Dr.
Hindhead Gdns., Nthlt. 72 BY67
Hindhead Grn., Wat. 44 BW50
Hindhead Way, Wall. 133 DL106
Hindmans Rd. SE22 106 DU85
Hindmans Way, Dag. 82 EZ70
Hindmarsh Clo. E1 78 DU73
Cable St.
Hindrey Rd. E5 64 DV64
Hindsley's Pl. SE23 106 DW89
Hinkler Rd., Har. 59 CK55
Hinkley Clo., Uxb. 56 BJ56
Hinksey Path SE2 96 EX75
Hinstock Rd. SE18 95 EQ79
Hinton Ave., Houns. 86 BX84
Hinton Clo. SE9 108 EL88
Hinton Rd. N18 50 DS49
Hinton Rd. SE24 91 DP83
Hinton Rd., Uxb. 70 BJ67
Hinton Rd., Wall. 133 DJ107
Hippodrome Ms. W11 75 CY73
Portland Rd.
Hippodrome Pl. W11 75 CY73
Hiroshima Wk. SE7 94 EH76
Hiscocks Ho. NW10 74 CQ66
Hitcham Rd. E17 65 DZ59
Hitchcock Clo., Shep. 112 BM97
Hitchen Hatch La., Sev. 154 FG124
Hitchin Sq. E3 79 DY68
Hither Grn. La. SE13 107 EC85
Hitherbroom Rd., Hayes 71 BU74
Hitherfield Rd. SW16 105 DM89
Hitherfield Rd., Dag. 68 EY61
Hitherlands SW12 105 DH89
Hithermoor Rd., Stai. 98 BG86
Hitherwell Dr., Har. 45 CD53
Hitherwood Dr. SE19 106 DT91
Hive Clo. (Bushey), Wat. 45 CD47
Hive Rd. (Bushey), Wat. 45 CD47
Hoadly Rd. SW16 105 DK90
Hobart Clo. N20 48 DE47
Hobart Clo., Hayes 72 BX70
Hobart Dr., Hayes 72 BX70
Hobart Gdns., Th.Hth. 120 DR97
Hobart La., Hayes 72 BX70
Hobart Pl. SW1 9 H6
Hobart Pl. SW1 91 DH76
Hobart Pl., Rich. 102 CM86
Chisholm Rd.
Hobart Rd., Dag. 68 EX63
Hobart Rd., Hayes 72 BX70
Hobart Rd., Ilf. 53 EQ54
Hobart Rd., Wor.Pk. 117 CV104
Hobbayne Rd. W7 73 CD72
Hobbes Wk. SW15 103 CV85
Hobbs Clo. (Cheshunt), Wal.Cr. 23 DX29
Hobbs Clo., W.Byf. 126 BH113
Hobbs Cross Rd., Epp. 40 EW35
Hobbs Grn. N2 62 DC55
Hobbs Ms., Ilf. 67 ET61
Ripley Rd.
Hobbs Pl. Est. N1 78 DS67
Pitfield St.
Hobbs Rd. SE27 106 DQ91
Hobday St. E14 79 EB71
Hobill Wk., Surb. 116 CM100
Hoblands End, Chis. 109 ES93
Hobsons Pl. E1 78 DU71
Hanbury St.
Hobury St. SW10 90 DC79
Hockenden La., Swan. 124 FA97
Hocker St. E2 7 P3
Hockett Clo. SE8 93 DY77
Hockley Ave. E6 80 EL68
Hockley Dr., Rom. 55 FH54
Hocroft Ave. NW2 61 CZ62
Hocroft Rd. NW2 61 CZ63
Hocroft Wk. NW2 61 CZ62
Hodder Dr., Grnf. 73 CF68
Hoddesdon Rd., Belv. 96 FA78
Hoddesdon Rd., Brox. 23 DX26
Hodford Rd. NW11 61 CZ60
Hodges Way, Wat. 29 BU44
Hodgkin Clo. SE28 82 EX73
Fleming Way
Hodnet Gro. SE16 93 DX77
Hawkstone Rd.
Hodsoll Ct., Orp. 124 EX99
Hodson Clo., Har. 58 BZ62
Hodson Cres., Orp. 124 EX99
Hoe, The, Wat. 44 BX47
Hoe La., Enf. 36 DU38
Hoe La., Rom. 40 EV41
Hoe St. E17 65 EA57
Hofland Rd. W14 89 CX76
Hog Hill Rd., Rom. 54 EZ52
Hogan Ms. W2 76 DD71
Porteus Rd.
Hogan Way E5 64 DU61
Geldeston Rd.
Hogarth Ave., Ashf. 99 BQ93
Hogarth Clo. E16 80 EK71
Hogarth Clo. W5 74 CL71
Hogarth Ct. EC3 7 N10

Honeysuckle Gdns., Croy. 121 DX102
Primrose La.
Honeywell Rd. SW11 104 DE86
Honeywood Clo., Pot.B. 20 DD33
Honeywood Rd. NW10 75 CT68
Honeywood Rd., Islw. 87 CG84
Honeywood Wk., Cars. 132 DF105
Honister Clo., Stan. 45 CH53
Honister Gdns., Stan. 45 CH53
Honister Heights, Pur. 134 DR114
Honister Pl., Stan. 45 CH53
Honiton Rd. NW6 75 CZ68
Honiton Rd., Rom. 69 FD58
Honiton Rd., Well. 95 ET82
Honley Rd. SE6 107 EB87
Honnor Rd., Stai. 98 BK94
Honor Oak Pk. SE23 107 DX86
Honor Oak Ri. SE23 106 DW86
Honor Oak Rd. SE23 106 DW88
Hood Ave. N14 35 DH44
Hood Ave. SW14 102 CQ85
Hood Ave., Orp. 124 EV99
Hood Clo., Croy. 119 DP102
Parson's Mead
Hood Ct. EC4 6 E9
Hood Rd. SW20 103 CT94
Hood Rd., Rain. 83 FE68
Hood Wk., Rom. 55 FB53
Hoodcote Gdns. N21 49 DP45
Hook, The, Barn. 34 DD44
Hook Fm. Rd., Brom. 122 EK99
Hook Gate, Enf. 36 DV36
Hook Grn. La., Dart. 111 FF90
Hook Hill, S.Croy. 134 DS110
Hook La., Pot.B. 20 DF32
Hook La., Rom. 40 EZ44
Hook La., Well. 95 ET84
Hook Ri. N., Surb. 116 CN104
Hook Ri. S., Surb. 116 CN104
Hook Rd., Chess. 129 CK106
Hook Rd., Epsom 130 CQ108
Hook Rd., Surb. 116 CL104
Hook Wk., Edg. 46 CQ51
Hookers Rd. E17 65 DX55
Hookfield, Epsom 130 CQ113
Hooking Grn., Har. 58 CB57
Hooks Clo. SE15 92 DV81
Woods Rd.
Hooks Hall Dr., Dag. 69 FC62
Hooks Way SE22 106 DU88
Dulwich Common
Hookstone Way, Wdf.Grn. 52 EK52
Hookwood Rd., Orp. 138 EW111
Hoop La. NW11 61 CZ59
Hooper Rd. E16 80 EG72
Hooper Sq. E1 78 DU73
Hooper St.
Hooper St. E1 78 DU73
Hooper's Ct. SW3 8 D5
Hoopers Yd., Sev. 155 FJ126
Hop Gdns. WC2 77 DL73
St. Martin's La.
Hope Clo. N1 78 DQ65
Wallace Rd.
Hope Clo. SE12 108 EH90
Hope Clo., Sutt. 132 DC106
Hope Clo., Wdf.Grn. 52 EJ51
West Gro.
Hope Grn., Wat. 15 BU33
Hope Pk., Brom. 108 EF94
Hope St. SW11 90 DD83
Hopedale Rd. SE7 94 EH79
Hopefield Ave. NW6 75 CY68
Hopes Clo., Houns. 86 CA79
Old Cote Dr.
Hopetown St. E1 78 DT71
Brick La.
Hopewell St. SE5 92 DR80
Hopewell Yd. SE5 92 DR80
Hopewell St.
Hopfield Ave., W.Byf. 126 BL112
Hopgarden La., Sev. 154 FG128
Hopgood St. W12 75 CW74
Macfarlane Rd.
Hopkins Clo. N10 48 DG52
Cromwell Rd.
Hopkins Ms. E15 80 EF67
West Rd.
Hopkins St. W1 5 L9
Hopkinsons Pl. NW1 76 DG67
Fitzroy Rd.
Hoppers Rd. N13 49 DN47
Hoppers Rd. N21 49 DN47
Hoppett Rd. E4 52 EE47
Hoppety, The, Tad. 145 CX122
Hopping La. N1 77 DP65
St. Mary's Gro.
Hoppingwood Ave., N.Mal. 116 CS97
Hoppit Rd., Wal.Abb. 23 EB33
Hoppner Rd., Hayes 71 BQ68
Hopton Gdns. SE1 10 G2
Hopton Gdns., N.Mal. 117 CU100
Hopton Rd. SW16 105 DL92
Hopton St. SE1 10 G2
Hopton St. SE1 77 DP74
Hopwood Clo. SW17 104 DC90
Hopwood Rd. SE17 92 DR79
Hopwood Wk. E8 78 DU66
Wilman Gro.
Horace Ave., Rom. 69 FC60
Horace Rd. E7 66 EH63
Horace Rd., Ilf. 67 EQ55
Horace Rd., Kings.T. 116 CM97
Horatio Ct. SE16 78 DW74
Rotherhithe St.
Horatio Pl. E14 93 EC75
Cold Harbour
Horatio Pl. SW19 104 DA94
Kingston Rd.
Horatio St. E2 78 DU68
Horatius Way, Croy. 133 DM106
Horbury Cres. W11 76 DA73
Horbury Ms. W11 75 CZ73
Ladbroke Rd.
Horder Rd. SW6 89 CY81
Hordle Prom. E. SE15 92 DT80
Daniel Gdns.
Hordle Prom. N. SE15 92 DT80
Daniel Gdns.
Hordle Prom. S. SE15 92 DT80
Pentridge St.
Hordle Prom. W. SE15 92 DS80
Diamond St.
Horizon Way SE7 94 EH77
Horley Clo., Bexh. 110 FA85
Horley Rd. SE9 108 EL91
Hormead Rd. W9 75 CZ70
Horn La. SE10 94 EG77
Horn La. W3 74 CQ74
Horn La., Bexh. 97 FC82
Horn La., Wdf.Grn. 52 EG51
Horn Pk. Clo. SE12 108 EH85
Horn Pk. La. SE12 108 EH85
Hornbeam Clo. SE11 10 D8
Hornbeam Clo., Borwd. 32 CN39
Hornbeam Clo., Buck.H. 52 EK48
Hornbeam Rd.
Hornbeam Clo., Epp. 39 ER37
Hornbeam Clo., Nthlt. 58 BZ64
Hornbeam Cres., Brent. 87 CH80
Hornbeam Gro. E4 52 EE48
Hornbeam La. E4 38 EE43
Hornbeam La., Bexh. 97 FC82
Hornbeam Rd., Buck.H. 52 EK48
Hornbeam Rd., Epp. 39 ER37
Hornbeam Rd., Hayes 72 BW71
Hornbeam Ter., Cars. 118 DE102
Hornbeam Twr. E11 65 ED62
Hollydown Way
Hornbeam Wk., Rich. 102 CM89
Hornbeam Wk., Walt. 127 BT109
Octagon Rd.
Hornbeam Way, Brom. 123 EN100
Hornbeam Way, Wal.Cr. 22 DT29
Hornbeams, St.Alb. 16 BZ30
Hornbeams Ave., Enf. 36 DW35
Hornbeams Ri. N11 48 DG51
Hornbill Clo., Uxb. 70 BK72
Hornblower Clo. SE16 93 DY77
Greenland Quay
Hornbuckle Clo., Har. 59 CD61
Hornby Clo. NW3 76 DD66
Horncastle Clo. SE12 108 EG87
Horncastle Rd. SE12 108 EG87
Hornchurch Clo., Kings.T. 101 CK91
Hornchurch Hill, Whyt. 148 DT117
Hornchurch Rd., Horn. 69 FF60
Horndean Clo. SW15 103 CU88
Bessborough Rd.
Horndon Clo., Rom. 55 FC53
Horndon Grn., Rom. 55 FC53
Horndon Rd., Rom. 55 FC53
Horne Rd., Shep. 112 BM98
Horne Way SW15 89 CW82
Horner La., Mitch. 118 DD96
Hornets, The, Wat. 29 BV42
Hornfair Rd. SE7 94 EJ79
Hornford Way, Rom. 69 FE59
Horniman Dr. SE23 106 DV88
Horning Clo. SE9 108 EL91
Horns End, Pnr. 58 BW56
Horns Rd., Ilf. 67 EQ58
Hornsey La. N6 63 DH60
Hornsey La. N19 63 DH60
Hornsey La. Est. N19 63 DK59
Hornsey La.
Hornsey La. Gdns. N6 63 DJ59
Hornsey Pk. Rd. N8 63 DM55
Hornsey Ri. N19 63 DK59
Hornsey Ri. Gdns. N19 63 DK59
Hornsey Rd. N7 63 DM62
Hornsey Rd. N19 63 DL60
Hornsey St. N7 63 DM64
Hornshay St. SE15 92 DW79
Hornton Pl. W8 90 DA75
Hornton St.
Hornton St. W8 90 DA75
Horsa Clo., Wall. 133 DL108
Kingsford Ave.
Horsa Rd. SE12 108 EJ87
Horsa Rd., Erith 97 FB80
Horse and Dolphin Yd. W1 5 N10
Horse Fair, Kings.T. 115 CK96
Wood St.
Horse Guards Ave. SW1 9 P3
Horse Guards Ave. SW1 77 DL74
Horse Guards Rd. SW1 9 N3
Horse Guards Rd. SW1 77 DK74
Horse Leaze E6 81 EN72
Horse Ride SW1 9 M3
Horse Ride, Cars. 132 DF112
Horse Rd. E7 66 EH62
Centre Rd.
Horse Shoe Cres., Nthlt. 72 CA68
Horse Shoe Yd. W1 5 J10
Horse Yd. N1 77 DP67
Essex Rd.
Horsebridges Clo., Dag. 82 EY67
Horsecroft, Bans. 145 CZ117
Lyme Regis Rd.
Horsecroft Clo., Orp. 124 EV102
Horsecroft Rd., Edg. 46 CR52
Horseferry Pl. SE10 93 EC79
Horseferry Rd. E14 79 DX73
Horseferry Rd. SW1 9 M7
Horseferry Rd. SW1 91 DK77
Horsell Ct., Cher. 112 BH101
Stepgates
Horsell Rd. N5 63 DN64
Horsell Rd., Orp. 124 EV95
Horselydown La. SE1 11 P4
Horselydown La. SE1 92 DT75
Horseman Side, Brwd. 55 FH45
Horsemans Ride, St.Alb. 16 CA25
Horsenden Ave., Grnf. 59 CE64
Horsenden Cres., Grnf. 59 CF64
Horsenden La. N., Grnf. 73 CF65
Horsenden La. S., Grnf. 73 CG67
Horseshoe, The, Bans. 145 CZ115
Horseshoe, The, Couls. 133 DK113
Horseshoe Clo. E14 93 EC78
Ferry St.
Horseshoe Clo. NW2 61 CV61
Horseshoe Clo., Wal.Abb. 24 EG34
Horseshoe Grn., Sutt. 118 DB103
Aultone Way
Horseshoe Hill, Wal.Abb. 24 EH33
Horseshoe La. N20 47 CX46
Horseshoe La., Enf. 36 DQ41
Chase Side
Horseshoe La., Wat. 15 BV32
Horseshoe Ridge, Wey. 127 BQ111
Horsfeld Gdns. SE9 108 EL85
Horsfeld Rd. SE9 108 EK85
Horsford Rd. SW2 105 DM85
Horsham Ave. N12 48 DE50
Horsham Rd., Bexh. 110 FA86
Horsham Rd., Felt. 99 BQ86
Horsley Clo., Epsom 130 CR113
Horsley Dr., Croy. 135 EC108
Horsley Dr., Kings.T. 101 CK92
Horsley Rd. E4 51 EC47
Horsley Rd., Brom. 122 EH95
Palace Rd.
Horsley Rd., Cob. 141 BU122
Horsley St. SE17 92 DR79
Horsmonden Clo., Orp. 123 ET101
Horsmonden Rd. SE4 107 DZ85
Hortensia Rd. SW10 90 DC80
Horticultural Pl. W4 88 CR78
Heathfield Ter.
Horton Ave. NW2 61 CY63
Horton Bri. Rd., West Dr. 70 BM74
Horton Clo., West Dr. 70 BM74
Horton Gdns., Epsom 130 CQ111
Horton Hill
Horton Hill, Epsom 130 CQ111
Horton Ind. Pk., West Dr. 70 BM74
Horton La., Epsom 130 CP109
Horton Rd. E8 78 DV65
Horton Rd., Stai. 98 BG85
Horton Rd., West Dr. 70 BL74
Horton St. SE13 93 EB83
Horton Way, Croy. 121 DX99
Hortus Rd. E4 51 EC47
Hortus Rd., Sthl. 86 BZ75
Horvath Clo., Wey. 127 BR105
Horwood Ct., Wat. 30 BX37
Hosack Rd. SW17 104 DF88
Hoser Ave. SE12 108 EG89
Hosier La. EC1 6 F7
Hosier La. EC1 77 DP71
Hoskins Clo. E16 80 EJ72
Hoskins Clo., Hayes 85 BT78
Cranford Dr.
Hoskins St. SE10 93 ED78
Hospital Bri. Rd., Twick. 100 CB87
Hospital La., Islw. 101 CF85
Hospital Rd. E9 65 DX64
Homerton Row
Hospital Rd., Houns. 86 CA83
Hospital Rd., Sev. 155 FJ121
Hotham Clo., Swan. 125 FH95
Hotham Clo., W.Mol. 114 CA97
Garrick Gdns.
Hotham Rd. SW15 89 CW83
Hotham Rd. SW19 104 DC94
Hotham Rd. Ms. SW19 104 DC94
Haydons Rd.
Hotham St. E15 80 EE67
Hothfield Pl. SE16 92 DW76
Lower Rd.
Hotspur Rd., Nthlt. 72 CA68
Hotspur St. SE11 10 D10
Hotspur St. SE11 91 DN78
Houblon Rd., Rich. 102 CL85
Houblons Hill, Epp. 26 EW31
Houghton Clo. E8 78 DT65
Buttermere Wk.
Houghton Clo., Hmptn. 100 BY93
Houghton Rd. N15 64 DT57
West Grn. Rd.
Houghton St. WC2 6 C9
Houlder Cres., Croy. 133 DP107
Houndsden Rd. N21 35 DM44
Houndsditch EC3 7 N8
Houndsditch EC3 78 DS72
Houndsfield Rd. N9 50 DV45
Hounslow Ave., Houns. 100 CB85
Hounslow Gdns., Houns. 100 CB85
Hounslow Rd. (Feltham), Felt. 99 BV88
Hounslow Rd. (Hanworth), Felt. 100 BX91
Hounslow Rd., Twick. 100 CB86
Houseman Way SE5 92 DR80
Hopewell St.
Houston Pl., Esher 115 CE102
Lime Tree Ave.
Houston Rd. SE23 107 DY89
Hove Ave. E17 65 DZ57
Hove Gdns., Sutt. 118 DB102
Hoveden Rd. NW2 61 CY64
Hoveton Rd. SE28 82 EW72
How La., Couls. 146 DF119
How Wd., St.Alb. 16 CB28
Howard Ave., Bex. 110 EW88
Howard Ave., Epsom 131 CU110
Howard Business Pk., Wal.Abb. 23 ED33
Howard Clo.
Howard Clo. N11 48 DG47
Howard Clo. NW2 61 CY63
Howard Clo. W3 74 CP72
Howard Clo., Ash. 144 CM118
Howard Clo., Hmptn. 100 CC93
Howard Clo., Lthd. 143 CJ123
Windmill Dr.
Howard Clo., Loug. 38 EL44
Howard Clo., Sun. 99 BT93
Catherine Dr.
Howard Clo., Wal.Abb. 23 ED33
Howard Clo., Wat. 29 BU37
Howard Clo. (Bushey), Wat. 45 CE45
Howard Dr., Borwd. 32 CR42
Howard Ms. N5 63 DP63
Hamilton Pk.
Howard Pl. SW1 9 K7
Howard Rd. E6 81 EM68
Howard Rd. E11 66 EE62
Howard Rd. E17 65 EA55
Howard Rd. N15 64 DS58
Howard Rd. N16 64 DR63
Howard Rd. NW2 61 CX63
Howard Rd. SE20 120 DW95
Howard Rd. SE25 120 DU99
Howard Rd., Bark. 81 ER67
Howard Rd., Brom. 108 EG94
Howard Rd., Couls. 147 DJ115
Howard Rd., Ilf. 67 EP63
Howard Rd., Islw. 87 CF83
Howard Rd., Lthd. 141 BU122
Howard Rd., N.Mal. 116 CS97
Howard Rd., Sthl. 72 CB72
Howard Rd., Surb. 116 CM100
Howard St., T.Ditt. 115 CH101
Howard Wk. N2 62 DC56
Howard Way, Barn. 33 CX43
Howards Clo., Pnr. 43 BV54
Howards Crest Clo., Beck. 121 EC96
Howards La. SW15 103 CV85
Howards Rd. E13 80 EG69
Howarth Ct. E15 65 EC64
Taylor Ct.
Howarth Rd. SE2 96 EU78
Howberry Clo., Edg. 45 CK51
Howberry Rd., Edg. 45 CK51
Howberry Rd., Stan. 45 CK51
Howberry Rd., Th.Hth. 120 DR95
Howbury La., Erith 97 FG82
Howbury Rd. SE15 92 DW83
Howcroft Cres. N3 48 DA52
Howcroft La., Grnf. 73 CD69
Cowgate Rd.
Howden Clo. SE28 82 EX73
Howden Rd. SE25 120 DT96
Howden St. SE15 92 DU83
Howe Clo., Rad. 18 CL32
Howe Clo., Rom. 54 FA53
Howe Dr., Cat. 148 DR122
York Gate
Howell Clo., Rom. 68 EX57
Howell Hill Clo., Epsom 131 CW111
Howell Hill Gro., Epsom 131 CW110
Howell Wk. SE1 10 G9
Howes Clo. N3 62 DA55
Howgate Rd. SW14 88 CR83
Howick Pl. SW1 9 L7
Howick Pl. SW1 91 DJ76
Howie St. SW11 90 DE80
Howitt Rd. NW3 76 DE65
Howland Est. SE16 92 DW76
Lower Rd.
Howland Ms. E. W1 5 L6
Howland St. W1 5 K6
Howland St. W1 77 DJ71
Howland Way SE16 93 DY75
Howletts La., Ruis. 57 BQ57
Howletts Rd. SE24 106 DQ86
Howley Pl. W2 76 DC71
Howley Rd., Croy. 119 DP104
Hows Clo., Uxb. 70 BJ67
Hows Rd.
Hows Rd., Uxb. 70 BJ67
Hows St. E2 78 DT68
Howsman Rd. SW13 89 CU79
Howson Rd. SE4 93 DY84
Howson Ter., Rich. 102 CL86
Howton Pl. (Bushey), Wat. 45 CD46
Hoxton Mkt. N1 7 M3
Hoxton Sq. N1 7 M3
Hoxton Sq. N1 78 DS69
Hoxton St. N1 78 DS67
Hoy St. E16 80 EF72
Hoylake Cres., Uxb. 56 BN61
Hoylake Gdns., Mitch. 119 DJ97
Hoylake Gdns., Ruis. 57 BV60
Hoylake Gdns., Wat. 44 BX49
Hoylake Rd. W3 74 CS72
Hoyland Clo. SE15 92 DV80
Commercial Way
Hoyle Rd. SW17 104 DE92
Hubbard Dr., Chess. 129 CJ107
Hubbard Rd. SE27 106 DQ91
Hubbard St. E15 80 EE67
Hubbard's Hill, Sev. 155 FH130
Hubbinet Ind. Est., Rom. 69 FC55
Hubert Gro. SW9 91 DL83
Hubert Rd. E6 80 EK69
Hubert Rd., Rain. 83 FF69
Huddart St. E3 79 DZ71
Huddleston Clo. E2 78 DW68
Huddleston Rd. N7 63 DJ62
Huddlestone Rd. E7 66 EF63
Huddlestone Rd. NW2 75 CV65
Hudson Clo., Wat. 29 BT36
Hudson Ct. SW19 104 DB94
Hudson Gdns., Orp. 137 ET107
Superior Dr.
Hudson Pl. SE18 95 EQ78
Hudson Rd., Bexh. 96 EZ82
Hudson Rd., Hayes 85 BR79
Hudsons, Tad. 145 CX121
Hudson's Pl. SW1 9 K8
Huggin Ct. EC4 7 J10
Huggin Hill EC4 7 J10
Huggins Pl. SW2 105 DM88
Roupell Rd.
Hugh Dalton Ave. SW6 89 CZ79
Rylston Rd.
Hugh Gaitskell Clo. SW6 89 CZ79
Rylston Rd.
Hugh Ms. SW1 9 J9
Hugh Pl. SW1 9 M8
Hugh St. SW1 9 J9
Hugh St. SW1 91 DH77
Hughan Rd. E15 65 ED64
Hughenden Ave., Har. 59 CH57
Hughenden Gdns., Nthlt. 72 BW69
Hughenden Rd., Wor.Pk. 117 CU101
Hughendon Ter. E15 65 EC63
Westdown Rd.
Hughes Rd., Ashf. 99 BQ94
Hughes Rd., Hayes 71 BU73
Hughes Wk., Croy. 120 DQ101
St. Saviours Rd.
Hugo Gdns., Rain. 83 FF65
Hugo Rd. N19 63 DJ63
Hugon Rd. SW6 90 DB83
Huguenot Pl. E1 78 DT71
Huguenot Pl. SW18 104 DC85
Huguenot Sq. SE15 92 DV83
Scylla Rd.
Hull Clo. SE16 93 DX75
Hull Clo., Sutt. 132 DB110
Yardbridge Clo.
Hull St. EC1 7 H3
Hullbridge Ms. N1 78 DR67
Sherborne St.
Hulse Ave., Bark. 81 ER65
Hulse Ave., Rom. 55 FB53
Hulse Ter., Ilf. 67 EQ64
Loxford La.
Hulsewood Clo., Dart. 111 FH90
Hulton Clo., Lthd. 143 CJ123
Windmill Dr.
Hulverston Clo., Sutt. 132 DB110
Humber Dr. W10 75 CX70
Humber Rd. NW2 61 CV61
Humber Rd. SE3 94 EF79
Humberstone Rd. E13 80 EJ69
Humberton Clo. E9 65 DY64
Marsh Hill
Humbolt Rd. W6 89 CY79
Hume Ter. E16 80 EJ72
Prince Regent La.
Hume Way, Ruis. 57 BU58
Humes Ave. W7 87 CE76
Humphrey Clo., Ilf. 53 EM53
Humphrey Clo., Lthd. 142 CC122
Humphrey St. SE1 11 P10
Humphrey St. SE1 92 DT78
Humphries Clo., Dag. 68 EZ63
Hundred Acre NW9 47 CT54
Hungerdown E4 51 EC46
Hungerford Bri. SE1 10 B3
Hungerford Bri. SE1 77 DM74
Hungerford Bri. WC2 10 B3
Hungerford Bri. WC2 77 DM74
Hungerford La. WC2 10 A2
Hungerford Rd. N7 77 DK65
Hungerford Sq., Wey. 127 BR105
Rosslyn Pk.
Hungerford St. E1 78 DV72
Commercial Rd.
Hungry Hill, Wok. 140 BK124
Hungry Hill La.
Hungry Hill La., Wok. 140 BK124
Hunsdon Clo., Dag. 82 EY65
Hunsdon Dr., Sev. 155 FH123
Hunsdon Rd. SE14 93 DX80
Hunslett St. E2 78 DW68
Royston St.
Hunston Rd., Mord. 118 DB102
Hunt Rd., Sthl. 86 CA76
Hunt St. W11 75 CX74
Hunt Way SE22 106 DU88
Dulwich Common
Hunter Clo. SE1 11 L7
Hunter Clo. SW12 104 DG88
Balham Pk. Rd.
Hunter Clo., Borwd. 32 CQ43
Hunter Clo., Pot.B. 20 DB33
Hunter Ho., Felt. 99 BU88
Hunter Rd. SW20 117 CW95
Hunter Rd., Ilf. 67 EP64
Hunter Rd., Th.Hth. 120 DR97
Hunter St. WC1 6 A4
Hunter St. WC1 77 DL70
Hunter Wk. E13 80 EG67
Stratford Rd.

Hunter Wk., Borwd. 32 CQ43
Ashley Dr.
Huntercrombe Gdns., Wat. 44 BW50
Hunters, The, Beck. 121 EC95
Hunters Clo., Bex. 111 FE90
Hunters Clo., Epsom 130 CQ113
Marshalls Clo.
Hunters Ct., Rich. 101 CK85
Friars La.
Hunters Gro., Har. 59 CJ56
Hunters Gro., Hayes 71 BU74
Hunters Gro., Orp. 137 EP105
Hunters Gro., Rom. 55 FB50
Hunters Hall Rd., Dag. 68 FA63
Hunters Hill, Ruis. 58 BW62
Hunters La., Wat. 15 BT33
Hunters Meadow SE19 106 DS91
Dulwich Wd. Ave.
Hunters Reach, Wal.Cr. 22 DT29
Hunters Ride, St.Alb. 16 CA31
Hunters Rd., Chess. 116 CL104
Hunters Sq., Dag. 68 FA63
Hunters Wk., Sev. 138 EY114
Hunters Way, Croy. 134 DS105
Brownlow Rd.
Hunters Way, Enf. 35 DN39
Hunting Clo., Esher 128 CA105
Hunting Gate Clo., Enf. 35 DN41
Hunting Gate Dr., Chess. 130 CL108
Hunting Gate Ms., Sutt. 118 DB104
Hunting Gate Ms., Twick. 101 CE88
Colne Rd.
Huntingdon Clo., Mitch. 119 DL98
Huntingdon Gdns. W4 88 CQ80
Huntingdon Gdns., Wor.Pk. 117 CW104
Huntingdon Rd. N2 62 DE55
Huntingdon Rd. N9 50 DW46
Huntingdon St. E16 80 EF72
Huntingdon St. N1 77 DM66
Huntingfield, Croy. 135 DZ108
Huntingfield Rd. SW15 89 CU84
Huntings Rd., Dag. 82 FA65
Huntland Clo., Rain. 83 FH71
Huntley Dr. N3 48 DA51
Huntley St. WC1 5 L5
Huntley St. WC1 77 DJ70
Huntley Way SW20 117 CU96
Huntly Rd. SE25 120 DS98
Hunton Bri. Hill, Kings L. 15 BQ33
Hunton Bri. Ind. Est., Kings L. 15 BQ33
Hunton St. E1 78 DU71
Hunt's Clo. SE3 94 EG82
Hunt's Ct. WC2 9 N1
Hunts La. E15 79 EC68
Hunts Mead, Enf. 37 DX41
Hunts Mead Clo., Chis. 109 EM94
Hunts Slip Rd. SE21 106 DS90
Huntsman Clo., Warl. 148 DW119
Huntsman Rd., Ilf. 54 EU51
Huntsman St. SE17 11 L9
Huntsman St. SE17 92 DS77
Huntsmans Clo., Felt. 99 BV91
Huntsmans Clo., Lthd. 143 CD124
The Grn.
Huntsmoor Rd., Epsom 130 CR106
Huntspill St. SW17 104 DC90
Huntsworth Ms. NW1 4 D5
Hurley Clo., Walt. 113 BV103
Hurley Cres. SE16 93 DX75
Marlow Way
Hurley Rd., Grnf. 72 CB72
Hurlingham Ct. SW6 89 CZ83
Hurlingham Gdns. SW6 89 CZ83
Hurlingham Rd. SW6 89 CZ82
Hurlingham Rd., Bexh. 96 EZ80
Hurlingham Sq. SW6 90 DB83
Peterborough Rd.
Hurlock St. N5 63 DP62
Hurlstone Rd. SE25 120 DR99
Hurn Ct. Rd., Houns. 86 BX82
Renfrew Rd.
Hurnford Clo., S.Croy. 134 DS110
Huron Clo., Orp. 137 ET107
Winnipeg Dr.
Huron Rd. SW17 104 DG89
Hurren Clo. SE3 94 EE83
Hurricane Way, Abb.L. 15 BU32
Abbey Dr.
Hurricane Way, Epp. 26 FA27
Hurry Clo. E15 80 EE66
Hursley Rd., Chig. 53 ET50
Tufter Rd.
Hurst Ave. E4 51 EA49
Hurst Ave. N6 63 DJ58
Hurst Clo. E4 51 EA48
Hurst Clo. NW11 62 DB58
Hurst Clo., Brom. 122 EF102
Hurst Clo., Chess. 130 CN106
Hurst Clo., Nthlt. 72 BZ65
Hurst Dr., Wal.Cr. 23 DX34
Hurst Est. SE2 96 EX78
Hurst Gro., Walt. 113 BT102
Hurst La. SE2 96 EX78
Hurst La., E.Mol. 114 CC98
Hurst La., Epsom 144 CQ124
Hurst Pl., Nthwd. 43 BP53
Hurst Ri., Barn. 34 DA41
Hurst Rd. E17 65 EB55
Hurst Rd. N21 49 DN46
Hurst Rd., Bex. 110 EW88
Hurst Rd., Buck.H. 52 EK46
Hurst Rd., Croy. 134 DR106
Hurst Rd., E.Mol. 114 CA97
Hurst Rd., Epsom 130 CR111
Hurst Rd. (Headley), Epsom 144 CR123
Hurst Rd., Erith 97 FC81
Hurst Rd., Sid. 110 EU89
Hurst Rd., Tad. 145 CU123
Hurst Rd., Walt. 114 BW99
Hurst Rd., W.Mol. 114 CA97
Hurst Springs, Bex. 110 EY88
Hurst St. SE24 105 DP86
Hurst Vw. Rd., S.Croy. 134 DS108
Hurst Way, Sev. 155 FJ127
Hurst Way, S.Croy. 134 DS107
Hurstbourne, Esher 129 CF107
Hurstbourne Gdns., Bark. 81 ES65
Hurstbourne Rd. SE23 107 DY88
Hurstcourt Rd., Sutt. 118 DB102
Hurstdene Ave., Brom. 122 EF102
Hurstdene Ave., Stai. 98 BH93
Hurstdene Gdns. N15 64 DS59
Hurstfield, Brom. 122 EG99
Hurstfield Cres., Hayes 71 BS70
Hurstfield Rd., W.Mol. 114 CA97
Hurstleigh Gdns., Ilf. 53 EM53
Hurstmead Ct., Edg. 46 CP49
Hurstway Wk. W11 75 CX73
Whitchurch Rd.
Hurstwood Ave. E18 66 EH56
Hurstwood Ave., Bex. 110 EY88
Hurstwood Ave., Bexh. 97 FE81
Hurstwood Ave., Erith 97 FE81
Hurstwood Dr., Brom. 123 EM97
Hurstwood Rd. NW11 61 CY56
Hurtwood Rd., Walt. 114 BZ101
Huson Clo. NW3 76 DE66
Hussars Clo., Houns. 86 BY83
Husseywell Cres., Brom. 122 EG102
Hutchings St. E14 93 EA75
Hutchings Wk. NW11 62 DB56
Hutchingsons Rd., Croy. 135 EC111
Hutchins Clo. E15 79 EC66
Gibbins Rd.
Hutchinson Ter., Wem. 59 CK62
Hutton Clo., Grnf. 59 CD64
Mary Peters Dr.
Hutton Clo., Wdf.Grn. 52 EH51
Hutton Gdns., Har. 44 CC52
Hutton Wk.
Hutton Gro. N12 48 DB50
Hutton La., Har. 44 CC52
Hutton Row, Edg. 46 CQ52
Pavilion Way
Hutton St. EC4 6 E9
Hutton Wk., Har. 44 CC52
Huxbear St. SE4 107 DZ85
Huxley Clo., Nthlt. 72 BY67
Huxley Clo., Uxb. 70 BK70
Huxley Dr., Rom. 68 EV59
Huxley Gdns. NW10 74 CM69
Huxley Par. N18 50 DQ50
Huxley Pl. N13 49 DP48
Huxley Rd. E10 65 EC61
Huxley Rd. N18 50 DR49
Huxley Rd., Well. 95 ET83
Huxley Sayze N18 50 DQ50
Huxley St. W10 75 CY69
Hyacinth Clo., Hmptn. 100 CA93
Gresham Rd.
Hyacinth Ct., Pnr. 58 BW55
Tulip Ct.
Hyacinth Dr., Uxb. 70 BL66
Hyacinth Rd. SW15 103 CU88
Hyburn Clo., St.Alb. 16 BZ30
Hycliffe Gdns., Chig. 53 EQ49
Hyde, The NW9 60 CS56
Hyde Ave., Pot.B. 20 DB33
Hyde Clo. E13 80 EG68
Pelly Rd.
Hyde Clo., Ashf. 99 BS93
Hyde Ter.
Hyde Clo., Barn. 33 CZ41
Hyde Ct. N20 48 DD48
Hyde Cres. NW9 60 CS57
Hyde Dr., Orp. 124 EV98
Hyde Est. Rd. NW9 61 CT57
Hyde Ho. NW9 60 CS57
The Hyde
Hyde La. SW11 90 DE81
Battersea Bri. Rd.
Hyde La., Hem.H. 14 BN27
Hyde La., St.Alb. 17 CE28
Hyde La., Wok. 140 BN120
Hyde Pk. SW7 8 B2
Hyde Pk. SW7 76 DE74
Hyde Pk. W1 8 B2
Hyde Pk. W1 76 DE74
Hyde Pk. W2 8 B2
Hyde Pk. W2 76 DE74
Hyde Pk. Ave. N21 50 DQ47
Hyde Pk. Cor. W1 8 G4
Hyde Pk. Cor. W1 90 DG75
Hyde Pk. Cres. W2 4 B9
Hyde Pk. Cres. W2 76 DE72
Hyde Pk. Gdns. N21 50 DQ46
Hyde Pk. Gdns. W2 4 A10
Hyde Pk. Gdns. W2 76 DD73
Hyde Pk. Gdns. Ms. W2 4 A10
Hyde Pk. Gate SW7 90 DC75
Hyde Pk. Gate Ms. SW7 90 DC75
Hyde Pk. Gate
Hyde Pk. Pl. W2 4 C10
Hyde Pk. Sq. W2 4 B9
Hyde Pk. Sq. W2 76 DE72
Hyde Pk. Sq. Ms. W2 4 B9
Hyde Pk. St. W2 4 B9
Hyde Pk. St. W2 76 DE72
Hyde Rd. N1 78 DS67
Hyde Rd., Bexh. 96 EZ82
Hyde Rd., Rich. 102 CM85
Albert Rd.
Hyde Rd., S.Croy. 134 DR113
Hyde Rd., Wat. 29 BU40
Hyde St. SE8 93 EA79
Deptford High St.
Hyde Ter., Ashf. 99 BS93
Hyde Vale SE10 93 ED81
Hyde Wk., Mord. 118 DA101
Glastonbury Rd.
Hyde Way N9 50 DT47
Hyde Way, Hayes 85 BT77
Hydefield Clo. N21 50 DR46
Hydefield Ct. N9 50 DS47
Hyderabad Way E15 80 EE66
Hydes Pl. N1 77 DP66
Compton Ave.
Hydeside Gdns. N9 50 DT47
Hydethorpe Ave. N9 50 DT47
Hydethorpe Rd. SW12 105 DJ88
Hyland Clo., Horn. 69 FH59
Hyland Way, Horn. 69 FH59
Hylands Clo., Epsom 144 CQ115
Hylands Ms., Epsom 144 CQ115
Hylands Rd. E17 51 ED54
Hylands Rd., Epsom 144 CQ115
Hylton St. SE18 95 ET77
Hyndewood SE23 107 DX90
Hyndman St. SE15 92 DV79
Hynton Rd., Dag. 68 EW61
Hyperion Pl., Epsom 130 CR109
Hyrstdene, S.Croy. 133 DP105
Hyson Rd. SE16 92 DV77
Galleywall Rd.
Hythe Ave., Bexh. 96 EY80
Hythe Clo. N18 50 DU49
Hythe Clo., Orp. 124 EW98
Sandway Rd.
Hythe Path, Th.Hth. 120 DR97
Buller Rd.
Hythe Rd. NW10 75 CU70
Hythe Rd., Th.Hth. 120 DR96
Hyver Hill NW7 32 CR44

I

Ian Sq., Enf. 37 DX39
Lansbury Rd.
Ibbetson Path, Loug. 39 EP41
Ibbotson Ave. E16 80 EF72
Ibbott St. E1 78 DW70
Mantus Rd.
Iberian Ave., Wall. 133 DK105
Ibis La. W4 88 CQ81
Ibis Way, Hayes 72 BX72
Cygnet Way
Ibscott Clo., Dag. 83 FC65
Ibsley Gdns. SW15 103 CU88
Ibsley Way, Barn. 34 DE43
Iceland Rd. E3 79 EA67
Ickburgh Est. E5 64 DV62
Ickburgh Rd.
Ickburgh Rd. E5 64 DV62
Ickenham Clo., Ruis. 57 BR61
Ickenham Rd., Ruis. 57 BQ61
Ickenham Rd., Uxb. 57 BQ61
Ickleton Rd. SE9 108 EL91
Icklingham Gate, Cob. 128 BW112
Icklingham Rd.
Icklingham Rd., Cob. 128 BW112
Icknield Dr., Ilf. 67 EP57
Ickworth Pk. Rd. E17 65 DY56
Ida Rd. N15 64 DR57
Ida St. E14 79 EC72
Iden Clo., Brom. 122 EE97
Idlecombe Rd. SW17 104 DG93
Idmiston Rd. E15 66 EF64
Idmiston Rd. SE27 106 DQ90
Idmiston Rd., Wor.Pk. 117 CT101
Idmiston Sq., Wor.Pk. 117 CT102
Idol La. EC3 11 M1
Idonia St. SE8 93 EA80
Iffley Clo., Uxb. 70 BK66
Iffley Rd. W6 89 CV76
Ifield Rd. SW10 90 DB79
Ifor Evans Pl. E1 79 DX70
Mile End Rd.
Ightham Rd., Erith 96 FA80
Ikea Twr. NW10 60 CR64
Ikona Ct., Wey. 127 BQ106
Ilbert St. W10 75 CX69
Ilchester Gdns. W2 76 DB73
Ilchester Pl. W14 89 CZ76
Ilchester Rd., Dag. 68 EV64
Ildersly Gro. SE21 106 DR89
Ilderton Rd. SE15 92 DW80
Ilderton Rd. SE16 92 DV78
Ilex Clo., Sun. 114 BW96
Oakington Dr.
Ilex Ho. N4 63 DM59
Ilex Rd. NW10 75 CT65
Ilex Way SW16 105 DN92
Ilford Hill, Ilf. 67 EN62
Ilford La., Ilf. 67 EP62
Ilfracombe Gdns., Rom. 68 EV59
Ilfracombe Rd., Brom. 108 EF90
Iliffe St. SE17 10 G10
Iliffe St. SE17 91 DP78
Iliffe Yd. SE17 10 G10
Ilkeston Ct. E5 65 DX63
Overbury St.
Ilkley Clo. SE19 106 DR93
Ilkley Rd. E16 80 EJ71
Ilkley Rd., Wat. 44 BX50
Illingworth Clo., Mitch. 118 DD97
Illingworth Way, Enf. 36 DS42
Ilmington Rd., Har. 59 CK58
Ilminster Gdns. SW11 90 DE84
Imber Clo. N14 49 DJ45
Imber Clo., Esher 115 CD102
Ember La.
Imber Ct. Ind. Est., E.Mol. 115 CD100
Imber Gro., Esher 115 CD101
Imber Pk. Rd., Esher 115 CD102
Imber St. N1 78 DR67
Imer Pl., T.Ditt. 115 CF101
Imperial Ave. N16 64 DT62
Victorian Rd.
Imperial Clo., Har. 58 CA58
Imperial College Rd. SW7 90 DD76
Imperial Cres., Wey. 113 BQ104
Churchill Dr.
Imperial Dr., Har. 58 CA59
Imperial Gdns., Mitch. 119 DH97
Imperial Ms. E6 80 EJ68
Central Pk. Rd.
Imperial Rd. N22 49 DL53
Imperial Rd. SW6 90 DB81
Imperial Rd., Felt. 99 BS87
Imperial Sq. SW6 90 DB81
Imperial St. E3 79 EC69
Imperial Way, Chis. 109 EQ90
Imperial Way, Croy. 133 DN107
Imperial Way, Har. 60 CL58
Imperial Way, Wat. 30 BW39
Inca Dr. SE9 109 EP87
Ince Rd., Walt. 127 BS108
Inchmery Rd. SE6 107 EB89
Inchwood, Croy. 135 EB105
Independent Pl. E8 64 DT64
Downs Pk. Rd.
Independents Rd. SE3 94 EF83
Blackheath Village
Inderwick Rd. N8 63 DM57
Indescon Ct. E14 93 EA75
India Pl. WC2 6 B10
India St. EC3 7 P9
India Way W12 75 CV73
Indus Rd. SE7 94 EJ80
Industry Ter. SW9 91 DN83
Canterbury Cres.
Ingal Rd. E13 80 EG70
Ingate Pl. SW8 91 DH81
Ingatestone Rd. E12 66 EJ60
Ingatestone Rd. SE25 120 DV99
Ingatestone Rd., Wdf.Grn. 52 EH52
Ingelow Rd. SW8 91 DH82
Ingels Mead, Epp. 25 ET29
Ingersoll Rd. W12 75 CV74
Ingersoll Rd., Enf. 36 DW38
Ingestre Pl. W1 5 L9
Ingestre Rd. E7 66 EG63
Ingestre Rd. NW5 63 DH63
Ingham Clo., S.Croy. 135 DX109
Ingham Rd. NW6 62 DA63
Ingham Rd., S.Croy. 134 DW109
Ingle Clo., Pnr. 58 BZ55
Inglebert St. EC1 6 D2
Ingleboro Dr., Pur. 134 DQ113
Ingleborough St. SW9 91 DN82
Ingleby Clo., Dag. 83 FB65
Ingleby Dr., Har. 59 CD62
Ingleby Gdns., Chig. 54 EV48
Ingleby Rd. N7 63 DL62
Ingleby Rd., Dag. 83 FB65
Ingleby Rd., Ilf. 67 EP60
Ingleby Way, Chis. 109 EN92
Ingleby Way, Wall. 133 DJ109
Ingledew Rd. SE18 95 ER78
Inglefield, Pot.B. 20 DA30
Inglehurst, Add. 126 BH110
Inglehurst Gdns., Ilf. 67 EM57
Inglemere Rd. SE23 107 DX90
Inglemere Rd., Mitch. 104 DF94
Inglesham Wk. E9 79 DZ65
Beanacre Clo.
Ingleside Clo., Beck. 107 EA94
Ingleside Gro. SE3 94 EF79
Inglethorpe St. SW6 89 CX81
Ingleton Ave., Well. 110 EU85
Ingleton Rd. N18 50 DU51
Ingleton Rd., Cars. 132 DE109
Ingleton St. SW9 91 DN82
Ingleway N12 48 DD51
Inglewood, Croy. 135 DY109
Middlefields
Inglewood Clo. E14 93 EA77
Inglewood Clo., Ilf. 53 ET51
Inglewood Copse, Brom. 122 EL96
Inglewood Rd. NW6 62 DA64
Inglewood Rd., Bexh. 97 FD84
Inglis Barracks NW7 47 CY50
Inglis Rd. W5 74 CM73
Inglis Rd., Croy. 120 DT102
Inglis St. SE5 91 DP81
Ingram Ave. NW11 62 DC59
Ingram Clo. SE11 10 C8
Ingram Clo., Stan. 45 CJ50
Ingram Rd. N2 62 DE56
Ingram Rd., Th.Hth. 120 DQ95
Ingram Way, Grnf. 73 CD67
Ingrams Clo., Walt. 128 BW106
Ingrave Ho., Dag. 82 EV67
Ingrave Rd., Rom. 69 FD56
Ingrave St. SW11 90 DD83
Ingrebourne Rd., Rain. 83 FH70
Ingress St. W4 88 CS78
Devonshire Rd.
Inigo Jones Rd. SE7 94 EL80
Inigo Pl. WC2 5 P10
Inkerman Rd. NW5 77 DH65
Inks Grn. E4 51 EB50
Inman Rd. NW10 74 CS67
Inman Rd. SW18 104 DC87
Inmans Row, Wdf.Grn. 52 EG49
Inner Circle NW1 4 F3
Inner Circle NW1 76 DG69
Inner Pk. Rd. SW19 103 CX88
Inner Ring E., Houns. 85 BP83
Inner Ring W., Houns. 84 BN83
Inner Temple La. EC4 6 D9
Innes Clo. SW20 117 CY96
Innes Gdns. SW15 103 CV86
Innes Yd., Croy. 120 DQ104
High St.
Inniskilling Rd. E13 80 EJ68
Inskip Clo. E10 65 EB61
Inskip Rd., Dag. 68 EX60
Institute Pl. E8 64 DV64
Amhurst Rd.
Institute Rd., Epp. 26 EX29
Instone Clo., Wall. 133 DL108
De Havilland Rd.
Integer Gdns. E11 65 ED59
Forest Rd.
Interchange E. Ind. Est. E5 64 DW60
Theydon Rd.
International Ave., Houns. 86 BW78
International Trd. Est., Sthl. 85 BV76
Inver Clo. E5 64 DW61
Theydon Rd.
Inver Ct. W2 76 DB72
Inverness Ter.
Inveraray Pl. SE18 95 ER79
Old Mill Rd.
Inverclyde Gdns., Rom. 68 EX56
Inveresk Gdns., Wor.Pk. 117 CT104
Inverforth Clo. NW3 62 DC61
North End Way
Inverforth Rd. N11 49 DH50
Inverine Rd. SE7 94 EH78
Invermore Pl. SE18 95 EQ77
Inverness Ave., Enf. 36 DS39
Inverness Dr., Ilf. 53 ES51
Inverness Gdns. W8 76 DB74
Vicarage Gate
Inverness Ms. W2 76 DB73
Inverness Ter.
Inverness Pl. W2 76 DB73
Inverness Rd. N18 50 DV50
Aberdeen Rd.
Inverness Rd., Houns. 86 BZ84
Inverness Rd., Sthl. 86 BY77
Inverness Rd., Wor.Pk. 117 CX102
Inverness St. NW1 77 DH67
Inverness Ter. W2 76 DB72
Inverton Rd. SE15 93 DX84
Invicta Clo., Chis. 109 EN92
Invicta Gro., Nthlt. 72 BZ69
Invicta Plaza SE1 77 DP74
Southwark St.
Invicta Rd. SE3 94 EG80
Inville Rd. SE17 92 DR78
Inwen Ct. SE8 93 DY78
Inwood Ave., Couls. 147 DN120
Inwood Ave., Houns. 86 CC83
Inwood Clo., Croy. 121 DY103
Inwood Ct., Walt. 114 BW103
Inwood Rd., Houns. 86 CB84
Inworth St. SW11 90 DE82
Inworth Wk. N1 78 DQ67
Popham St.
Ion Sq. E2 78 DU68
Hackney Rd.
Iona Clo. SE6 107 EA87
Ipswich Rd. SW17 104 DG93
Ireland Clo. E6 81 EM71
Bradley Stone Rd.
Ireland Pl. N22 49 DL52
Whittington Rd.
Ireland Row E14 79 DZ72
Commercial Rd.
Ireland Yd. EC4 6 G9
Irene Rd. SW6 90 DA81
Irene Rd., Cob. 128 CB114
Irene Rd., Orp. 123 ET101
Ireton Ave., Walt. 113 BS103
Ireton Clo. N10 48 DG52
Cromwell Rd.
Ireton St. E3 79 EA70
Tidworth Rd.
Iris Ave., Bex. 110 EY86
Iris Clo. E6 80 EL71
Iris Clo., Croy. 121 DX102
Iris Clo., Surb. 116 CM101
Iris Ct., Pnr. 58 BW55
Iris Cres., Bexh. 96 EZ79
Iris Rd., Epsom 130 CP106
Iris Way E4 51 DZ51
Irkdale Ave., Enf. 36 DT39
Iron Bri. Clo. NW10 60 CS64
Iron Bri. Clo., Sthl. 72 CC74
Iron Bri. Rd., Uxb. 84 BN75
Iron Bri. Rd., West Dr. 84 BN75
Iron Mill La., Dart. 97 FE84
Iron Mill Pl. SW18 104 DB86
Garratt La.
Iron Mill Pl., Dart. 97 FF84
Iron Mill Rd. SW18 104 DB86
Ironmonger La. EC2 7 K9
Ironmonger Pas. EC1 7 J3
Ironmonger Row EC1 7 J3
Ironmonger Row EC1 78 DQ69
Ironmongers Pl. E14 93 EA77
Spindrift Ave.
Irons Way, Rom. 55 FC52
Ironside Clo. SE16 93 DX75
Kinburn St.

Irvine Ave., Har. 59 CG55
Irvine Clo. N20 48 DE47
Irvine Way, Orp. 123 ET101
Irving Ave., Nthlt. 72 BX67
Irving Gro. SW9 91 DM82
Irving Rd. W14 89 CX76
Irving St. WC2 9 N1
Irving St. WC2 77 DK73
Irving Way NW9 61 CT57
Irving Way, Swan. 125 FD96
Irwin Ave. SE18 95 ES80
Irwin Gdns. NW10 75 CV67
Isabel St. SW9 91 DM81
Isabella Clo. N14 49 DJ45
Isabella Dr., Orp. 137 EQ105
Isabella Rd. E9 64 DW64
Isabella St. SE1 10 F3
Isabella St. SE1 77 DP74
Isabelle Clo., Wal.Cr. 22 DQ29
Doverfield
Isambard Clo., Uxb. 70 BK70
Isambard Ms. E14 93 EC76
Isambard Pl. SE16 78 DW74
Rotherhithe St.
Isbell Gdns., Rom. 55 FE52
Isel Way SE22 106 DS85
East Dulwich Gro.
Isham Rd. SW16 119 DL96
Isis Clo. SW15 89 CW84
Isis Clo., Ruis. 57 BQ58
Isis St. SW18 104 DC89
Isla Rd. SE18 95 EQ79
Island Fm. Ave., W.Mol. 114 BZ99
Island Fm. Rd., W.Mol. 114 BZ99
Island Rd., Mitch. 104 DF94
Island Row E14 79 DY72
Commercial Rd.
Islay Gdns., Houns. 100 BX85
Islay Wk. N1 78 DQ66
Douglas Rd.
Isledon Rd. N7 63 DN62
Islehurst Clo., Chis. 123 EN95
Islington Grn. N1 77 DP67
Islington High St. N1 77 DN68
Islington Pk. Ms. N1 77 DN66
Islington Pk. St.
Islington Pk. St. N1 77 DN66
Islip Gdns., Edg. 46 CR52
Islip Gdns., Nthlt. 72 BY66
Islip Manor Rd., Nthlt. 72 BY66
Islip St. NW5 63 DJ64
Ismailia Rd. E7 80 EH66
Isom Clo. E13 80 EJ70
Belgrave Rd.
Ivanhoe Clo., Uxb. 70 BK71
Ivanhoe Dr., Har. 59 CG55
Ivanhoe Rd. SE5 92 DT83
Ivanhoe Rd., Houns. 86 BX83
Ivatt Pl. W14 89 CZ78
Ivatt Way N17 63 DP55
Ive Fm. Clo. E10 65 EA61
Ive Fm. La. E10 65 EA61
Iveagh Ave. NW10 74 CN68
Iveagh Clo. E9 79 DX67
Iveagh Clo. NW10 74 CN68
Iveagh Clo., Nthwd. 43 BP53
Iveagh Ter. NW10 74 CN68
Iveagh Ave.
Ivedon Rd., Well. 96 EW82
Iveley Rd. SW4 91 DJ82
Iver La., Iver 70 BG72
Iver La., Uxb. 70 BH70
Iver Rd., Iver 70 BG72
Ivere Dr., Barn. 34 DB44
Iverhurst Clo., Bexh. 110 EX85
Iverna Ct. W8 90 DA76
Iverna Gdns. W8 90 DA76
Iverna Gdns., Felt. 99 BR85
Ivers Way, Croy. 135 EB108
Iverson Rd. NW6 75 CZ65
Ives Gdns., Rom. 69 FF56
Sims Clo.
Ives Rd. E16 80 EE71
Ives St. SW3 8 C8
Ives St. SW3 90 DE77
Ivestor Ter. SE23 106 DW87
Ivimey St. E2 78 DU69
Ivinghoe Clo., Enf. 36 DS39
Ivinghoe Clo., Wat. 30 BX35
Ivinghoe Rd., Dag. 68 EV64
Ivinghoe Rd., Rick. 42 BG45
Ivinghoe Rd. (Bushey), Wat. 45 CD45
Ivor Gro. SE9 109 EP88
Ivor Pl. NW1 4 D5
Ivor Pl. NW1 76 DF70
Ivor St. NW1 77 DJ66
Ivory Sq. SW11 90 DC83
Gartons Way
Ivorydown, Brom. 108 EG91
Ivy Chimneys Rd., Epp. 25 ES32
Ivy Clo., Har. 58 BZ63
Ivy Clo., Pnr. 58 BW59
Ivy Clo., Sun. 114 BW96
Ivy Cotts. E14 79 EB73
Grove Vill.
Ivy Ct. SE16 92 DU78
Argyle Way
Ivy Cres. W4 88 CQ77
Ivy Gdns. N8 63 DL58
Ivy Gdns., Mitch. 119 DK97
Ivy Ho. La., Sev. 153 FD118
Ivy La., Houns. 86 BZ84
Ivy La., Sev. 152 EY116
Ivy Lea, Rick. 42 BG46
Springwell Ave.
Ivy Pl., Surb. 116 CM100
Alpha Rd.
Ivy Rd. E16 80 EG72
Pacific Rd.
Ivy Rd. E17 65 EA58
Ivy Rd. N14 49 DJ45
Ivy Rd. NW2 61 CW63
Ivy Rd. SE4 93 DZ84
Ivy Rd. SW17 104 DE92
Tooting High St.
Ivy Rd., Houns. 86 CB84
Ivy Rd., Surb. 116 CN103
Ivy St. N1 78 DS68
Ivy Wk., Dag. 82 EY65
Ivybridge Clo., Twick. 101 CG87
Ivybridge Clo., Uxb. 70 BL69
Ivybridge Est., Islw. 101 CF85
Ivybridge La. WC2 10 A1
Ivychurch Clo. SE20 106 DW94
Ivychurch La. SE17 11 N10
Ivydale Rd. SE15 93 DX83
Ivydale Rd., Cars. 118 DF103
Ivyday Gro. SW16 105 DM90
Ivydene, W.Mol. 114 BZ99
Ivydene Clo., Sutt. 132 DC105
Ivyhouse Rd., Dag. 82 EX65
Ivyhouse Rd., Uxb. 57 BP63
Ivymount Rd. SE27 105 DN90
Ixworth Pl. SW3 8 B10
Ixworth Pl. SW3 90 DE78
Izane Rd., Bexh. 96 EZ84

J

Jacaranda Clo., N.Mal. 116 CS97
Jack Barnett Way N22 49 DM54
Mayes Rd.
Jack Clow Rd. E15 80 EE68
Jack Cornwell St. E12 67 EN63
Jack Dash Way E6 80 EL70
Jack Walker Ct. N5 63 DP63
Jackass La., Kes. 136 EH106
Jackets La., Nthwd. 43 BP53
Jackets La., Uxb. 43 BP53
Jacketts Fld., Abb.L. 15 BT31
Jacklin Grn., Wdf.Grn. 52 EG49
Jackman Ms. NW10 60 CS62
Jackman St. E8 78 DV67
Jacks La., Uxb. 42 BG52
Jackson Clo., Epsom 130 CR114
Jackson Clo., Uxb. 70 BL66
Jackson Rd.
Jackson Rd. N7 63 DM63
Jackson Rd., Bark. 81 ER67
Jackson Rd., Barn. 34 DD44
Jackson Rd., Brom. 122 EL103
Jackson Rd., Uxb. 70 BL66
Jackson St. SE18 95 EN79
Jackson Way, Sthl. 86 CB75
Jacksons Dr., Wal.Cr. 22 DU28
Jacksons La. N6 62 DG59
Jacksons Pl., Croy. 120 DR102
Cross Rd.
Jacksons Way, Croy. 121 EA104
Jacob St. SE1 92 DT75
Jacobs Clo., Dag. 69 FB63
Jacobs Ho. E13 80 EJ69
Jacob's Well Ms. W1 4 G8
Jacqueline Clo., Nthlt. 72 BZ67
Canford Ave.
Jade Clo. E16 80 EK72
Jade Clo. NW2 61 CX59
Marble Dr.
Jade Clo., Dag. 68 EW60
Jaffe Rd., Ilf. 67 ER60
Jaffray Pl. SE27 105 DP91
Chapel Rd.
Jaffray Rd., Brom. 122 EK98
Jaggard Way SW12 104 DF87
Jago Clo. SE18 95 EQ79
Jago Wk. SE5 92 DR80
Lomond Gro.
Jail La. (Biggin Hill), West. 150 EK115
Jamaica Rd. SE1 92 DT75
Jamaica Rd. SE16 92 DU76
Jamaica Rd., Th.Hth. 119 DP100
Jamaica St. E1 78 DW71
James Ave. NW2 61 CW64
James Ave., Dag. 68 EZ60
James Bedford Clo., Pnr. 44 BW54
James Boswell Clo. SW16 105 DN91
Curtis Fld. Rd.
James Clo. E13 80 EG68
Richmond St.
James Clo. NW11 61 CY58
Woodlands
James Clo., Rom. 69 FG57
James Clo. (Bushey), Wat. 30 BY43
Aldenham Rd.
James Collins Clo. W9 75 CZ70
Fermoy Rd.
James Ct. N1 78 DQ66
Morton Rd.
James Dudson Ct. NW10 74 CQ66
James Gdns. N22 49 DP52
James Hammett Ho. E2 78 DT69
Ravenscroft St.
James Joyce Wk. SE24 91 DP84
Shakespeare Rd.
James La. E10 65 ED59
James La. E11 65 ED58
James Martin Clo., Uxb. 56 BG58
James Newman Ct. SE9 109 EN90
Great Harry Dr.
James Pl. N17 50 DT53
Ruskin Rd.
James Rd., Dart. 111 FF87
James Sinclair Pt. E13 80 EJ67
James St. W1 4 G8
James St. W1 76 DG72
James St. WC2 6 A10
James St., Bark. 81 EQ66
James St., Enf. 36 DT43
James St., Epp. 25 ET28
James St., Houns. 87 CD83
James Ter. SW14 88 CR83
Addington Ct.
James Yd. E4 51 ED51
Larkshall Rd.
Jameson Clo. W3 88 CQ75
Acton La.
Jameson St. W8 76 DA74
James's Cotts., Rich. 88 CN80
Kew Rd.
Jamestown Rd. NW1 77 DH67
Jamieson Ho., Houns. 100 BZ86
Jane St. E1 78 DV72
Commercial Rd.
Janet St. E14 93 EA76
Janeway Pl. SE16 92 DV75
Janeway St.
Janeway St. SE16 92 DU75
Janice Ms., Ilf. 67 EP62
Oakfield Rd.
Jansen Wk. SW11 90 DD84
Hope St.
Janson Clo. E15 66 EE64
Janson Rd.
Janson Clo. NW10 60 CS62
Janson Rd. E15 66 EE64
Jansons Rd. N15 64 DS55
Japan Cres. N4 63 DM59
Japan Rd., Rom. 68 EX58
Jardine Rd. E1 79 DX73
Jarrett Clo. SW2 105 DP88
Jarrow Clo., Mord. 118 DB99
Jarrow Rd. N17 64 DV56
Jarrow Rd. SE16 92 DW77
Jarrow Rd., Rom. 68 EW58
Jarrow Way E9 65 DZ64
Jarvis Cleys (Cheshunt), Wal.Cr. 22 DT26
Roundcroft
Jarvis Clo., Barn. 33 CX43
Jarvis Rd. SE22 92 DS84
Melbourne Gro.
Jarvis Rd., S.Croy. 134 DR107
Jasmin Clo., Nthwd. 43 BT53
Jasmin Rd., Epsom 130 CP107
Jasmine Clo., Ilf. 67 EP64
Jasmine Clo., Orp. 123 EP103
Jasmine Clo., Sthl. 72 BY73
Jasmine Gdns., Croy. 121 EA104
Jasmine Gdns., Har. 58 CA61
Jasmine Gro. SE20 120 DV95
Jasmine Ter., West Dr. 84 BN75
Jasmine Way, E.Mol. 115 CE98
Hampton Ct. Way
Jason Clo., Wey. 127 BQ106
Jason Ct. W1 76 DG72
Marylebone La.
Jason Wk. SE9 109 EN91
Jasper Clo., Enf. 36 DW38
Jasper Pas. SE19 106 DT93
Jasper Rd. E16 80 EK72
Jasper Rd. SE19 106 DT93
Jasper Wk. N1 7 K2
Javelin Way, Nthlt. 72 BX69
Jay Gdns., Chis. 109 EM91
Jay Ms. SW7 90 DC75
Jaycroft, Enf. 35 DN39
The Ridgeway
Jays Covert, Couls. 146 DG120
Jebb Ave. SW2 105 DL86
Jebb St. E3 79 EA68
Jedburgh Rd. E13 80 EJ69
Jedburgh St. SW11 90 DG84
Jeddo Rd. W12 89 CT75
Jefferies Ho. NW10 74 CR66
Jefferson Clo. W13 87 CH76
Jefferson Clo., Ilf. 67 EP57
Jefferson Wk. SE18 95 EN79
Kempt St.
Jeffreys Pl. NW1 77 DJ66
Jeffreys St.
Jeffreys Rd. SW4 91 DL82
Jeffreys Rd., Enf. 37 DZ41
Jeffreys St. NW1 77 DJ66
Jeffreys Wk. SW4 91 DL82
Jeffs Clo., Hmptn. 100 CB93
Uxbridge Rd.
Jeffs Rd., Sutt. 131 CZ105
Jeger Ave. E2 78 DT67
Jeken Rd. SE9 94 EJ84
Jelf Rd. SW2 105 DN85
Jellicoe Gdns., Stan. 45 CF51
Jellicoe Rd. E13 80 EG70
Jutland Rd.
Jellicoe Rd. N17 50 DR52
Jellicoe Rd., Wat. 29 BU44
Jengar Clo., Sutt. 132 DB105
Jenkins Ave., St.Alb. 16 BY30
Jenkins La. E6 81 EN68
Jenkins La., Bark. 81 EP68
Jenkins Rd. E13 80 EH70
Jenner Ave. W3 74 CR71
Jenner Ho. SE3 94 EE79
Jenner Pl. SW13 89 CV79
Jenner Rd. N16 64 DT62
Jennett Rd., Croy. 119 DN104
Jennifer Rd., Brom. 108 EF90
Jennings Clo., Add. 126 BJ109
Woodham La.
Jennings Rd. SE22 106 DT86
Jennings Way, Barn. 33 CW41
Jenningtree Rd., Erith 97 FH80
Jenningtree Way, Belv. 97 FC75
Jenny Hammond Clo. E11 66 EF62
Newcomen Rd.
Jenson Way SE19 106 DT94
Jenton Ave., Bexh. 96 EY81
Jephson Rd. E7 80 EJ66
Jephson St. SE5 92 DR81
Grove La.
Jephtha Rd. SW18 104 DA86
Jeppos La., Mitch. 118 DF98
Jerdan Pl. SW6 90 DA80
Fulham Bdy.
Jeremiah St. E14 79 EB72
Jeremys Grn. N18 50 DV49
Jermyn St. SW1 9 L2
Jermyn St. SW1 77 DJ74
Jerningham Ave., Ilf. 53 EP54
Jerningham Rd. SE14 93 DY82
Jerome Cres. NW8 4 B4
Jerome Cres. NW8 76 DE70
Jerome St. E1 7 P5
Jerrard St. N1 7 N1
Jerrard St. SE13 93 EB83
Jersey Ave., Stan. 45 CH54
Jersey Dr., Orp. 123 ER100
Jersey Par., Houns. 86 CB81
Jersey Rd. E11 65 ED60
Jersey Rd. E16 80 EJ72
Prince Regent La.
Jersey Rd. SW17 105 DH93
Jersey Rd. W7 87 CG75
Jersey Rd., Houns. 86 CB81
Jersey Rd., Ilf. 67 EP63
Jersey Rd., Islw. 87 CD80
Jersey Rd., Rain. 83 FG66
Jersey St. E2 78 DV69
Bethnal Grn. Rd.
Jerusalem Pas. EC1 6 F5
Jervis Ave., Enf. 37 DY36
Jervis Ct. W1 5 J9
Jerviston Gdns. SW16 105 DN92
Jesmond Ave., Wem. 74 CM65
Jesmond Clo., Mitch. 118 DG97
Jesmond Rd., Croy. 120 DT101
Jesmond Way, Stan. 46 CL50
Jessam Ave. E5 64 DV60
Jessamine Rd. W7 73 CE74
Jessamine Ter., Swan. 125 FC95
Birchwood Rd.
Jessamy Rd., Wey. 113 BP103
Jesse Rd. E10 65 EC60
Jessel Dr., Loug. 39 EQ39
Jessett Clo., Erith 97 FD77
West St.
Jessica Rd. SW18 104 DC86
Jessie Blythe La. N19 63 DL59
Hillrise Rd.
Jessiman Ter., Shep. 112 BN99
Jessop Ave., Sthl. 86 BZ77
Jessop Rd. SE24 91 DP84
Milkwood Rd.
Jessops Way, Croy. 119 DJ100
Jessup Clo. SE18 95 EQ77
Jetstar Way, Nthlt. 72 BY69
Jevington Way SE12 108 EH88
Jewel Rd. E17 65 EA55
Jewels Hill, West. 136 EG112
Jewry St. EC3 7 P9
Jewry St. EC3 78 DT72
Jew's Row SW18 90 DB84
Jews Wk. SE26 106 DV91
Jeymer Ave. NW2 61 CV64
Jeymer Dr., Grnf. 72 CC67
Jeypore Rd. SW18 104 DC87
Jillian Clo., Hmptn. 100 CA94
Jim Bradley Clo. SE18 95 EN77
John Wilson St.
Joan Cres. SE9 108 EK87
Joan Gdns., Dag. 68 EY61
Joan Rd., Dag. 68 EY60
Joan St. SE1 10 F3
Joan St. SE1 77 DP74
Jocelyn Rd., Rich. 88 CL83
Jocelyn St. SE15 92 DU81
Jockey's Flds. WC1 6 C6
Jockey's Flds. WC1 77 DM71
Jodane St. SE8 93 DZ77
Jodrell Clo., Islw. 87 CG81
Blenheim Way
Jodrell Rd. E3 79 DZ67
Joel St., Nthwd. 57 BU55
Joel St., Pnr. 57 BU55
Johanna St. SE1 10 D5
John Adam St. WC2 10 A1
John Adam St. WC2 77 DL73
John Aird Ct. W2 76 DC71
Howley Pl.
John Ashby Clo. SW2 105 DL86
John Barnes Wk. E15 80 EF65
Hamfrith Rd.
John Bradshaw Rd. N14 49 DK46
High St.
John Burns Dr., Bark. 81 ES66
John Campbell Rd. N16 64 DS64
John Carpenter St. EC4 6 E10
John Carpenter St. EC4 77 DP73
John Cobb Rd., Wey. 126 BN108
John Cornwall VC Ho. E12 67 EN63
John Deed Ind. Est., Mitch. 118 DF100
John Felton Rd. SE16 92 DU75
John Fisher St. E1 78 DU73
John Gooch Dr., Enf. 35 DP39
John Groom's Est., Edg. 46 CQ49
John Horner Ms. N1 78 DQ68
Frome St.
John Islip St. SW1 9 N10
John Islip St. SW1 91 DK78
John Keats Ho. N22 49 DM52
John Maurice Clo. SE17 11 K8
John Maurice Clo. SE17 92 DR77
John McKenna Wk. SE16 92 DU76
Tranton Rd.
John Newton Ct., Well. 96 EV83
Danson La.
John Parker Clo., Dag. 83 FB66
John Parker Sq. SW11 90 DD83
Thomas Baines Rd.
John Penn St. SE13 93 EB81
John Perrin Pl., Har. 60 CL59
John Princes St. W1 5 J8
John Princes St. W1 77 DH72
John Rennie Wk. E1 78 DV74
Wine Clo.
John Roll Way SE16 92 DU76
John Ruskin St. SE5 91 DP80
John Silkin La. SE8 93 DX78
John Smith Ave. SW6 89 CZ80
John Spencer Sq. N1 77 DP65
John St. E15 80 EF67
John St. SE25 120 DU98
John St. WC1 6 C5
John St. WC1 77 DM70
John St., Enf. 36 DT43
John St., Houns. 86 BY82
John Trundle Ct. EC2 78 DQ71
Beech St.
John Walsh Twr. E11 66 EF61
John Williams Clo. SE14 93 DX79
John Wilson St. SE18 95 EN76
John Woolley Clo. SE13 93 ED84
Johnby Clo., Enf. 37 DY37
Manly Dixon Dr.
Johns Ave. NW4 61 CW56
Johns Clo., Ashf. 99 BQ91
Johns La., Mord. 118 DC99
John's Ms. WC1 6 C5
John's Ms. WC1 77 DM70
John's Pl. E1 78 DV72
Damien St.
Johns Rd., West. 150 EK120
John's Ter., Croy. 120 DS102
Johns Wk., Whyt. 148 DU119
Johnson Clo. E8 78 DU67
Johnson Rd., Brom. 122 EK99
Johnson Rd., Croy. 120 DR101
Johnson Rd., Houns. 86 BW80
Johnson St. E1 78 DW73
Cable St.
Johnson St., Sthl. 86 BW76
Johnsons Ave., Sev. 139 FB110
Johnsons Clo., Cars. 118 DE104
Johnson's Ct. EC4 77 DN72
Fleet St.
Johnsons Ct., Sev. 155 FM121
School La.
Johnsons Dr., Hmptn. 114 CC95
Johnson's Pl. SW1 91 DJ78
Johnsons Way NW10 74 CP70
Johnsons Yd., Uxb. 70 BJ66
Redford Way
Johnston Clo. SW9 91 DM81
Hackford Rd.
Johnston Rd., Wdf.Grn. 52 EG50
Johnston Ter. NW2 61 CX62
Campion Ter.
Johnstone Rd. E6 81 EM69
Joiner St. SE1 11 L3
Joiner's Arms Yd. SE5 92 DR81
Denmark Hill
Joinville Pl., Add. 126 BK105
Jollys La., Har. 59 CD60
Lower Rd.
Jollys La., Hayes 72 BX71
Jonathan St. SE11 10 B10
Jonathan St. SE11 91 DM78
Jones Rd. E13 80 EH70
Holborn Rd.
Jones Rd. (Cheshunt), Wal.Cr. 21 DP30
Jones St. W1 9 H1
Jones Wk., Rich. 102 CM86
Pyrland Rd.
Jonquil Gdns., Hmptn. 100 BZ93
Partridge Rd.
Jonson Clo., Hayes 71 BU71
Jonson Clo., Mitch. 119 DH98
Joram Way SE16 92 DV78
Egan Way
Jordan Clo., Dag. 69 FB63
Muggeridge Rd.
Jordan Clo., Har. 58 BZ62
Hamilton Cres.
Jordan Clo., S.Croy. 134 DT111
Jordan Clo., Wat. 29 BT35
Jordan Rd., Grnf. 73 CH67
Jordans Clo., Islw. 87 CE81
Jordans Clo., Stai. 98 BJ87
Jordans Rd., Rick. 42 BG45
Jordans Way, St.Alb. 16 BZ30
Joseph Ave. W3 74 CR72
Joseph Locke Way, Esher 114 CA103
Mill Rd.
Joseph Powell Clo. SW12 105 DH86
Hazelbourne Rd.
Joseph Ray Rd. E11 66 EE61
High Rd. Leytonstone
Joseph St. E3 79 DZ70
Josephine Ave. SW2 105 DM85
Joshua St. E14 79 EC72
St. Leonards Rd.

Joubert St. SW11 90 DF82
Jowett St. SE15 92 DT80
Joyce Ave. N18 50 DT50
Joyce Ct., Wal.Abb. 23 ED34
Joyce Dawson Way SE28 82 EU73
Thamesmere Dr.
Joyce Page Clo. SE7 94 EK79
Lansdowne La.
Joyce Wk. SW2 105 DN86
Joydens Wd. Rd., Bex. 111 FD91
Joydon Dr., Rom. 68 EV58
Joyners Clo., Dag. 68 EZ63
Jubb Powell Ho. N15 64 DS58
Jubilee Ave. E4 51 EC51
Jubilee Ave., Rom. 69 FB57
Jubilee Ave., St.Alb. 17 CK26
Jubilee Ave., Twick. 100 CC87
Jubilee Clo. NW9 60 CR58
Jubilee Clo., Pnr. 44 BW54
Jubilee Clo., Rom. 69 FB57
Jubilee Clo., Stai. 98 BJ87
Jubilee Ct., Stai. 98 BG92
Leacroft
Jubilee Cres. E14 93 EC76
Jubilee Cres. N9 50 DU46
Jubilee Cres., Add. 126 BK106
Jubilee Dr., Ruis. 58 BX63
Jubilee Gdns., Sthl. 72 CA72
Jubilee Pl. SW3 8 C10
Jubilee Pl. SW3 90 DE78
Jubilee Ri., Sev. 155 FM121
Jubilee Rd., Grnf. 73 CH67
Jubilee Rd., Orp. 138 FA107
Jubilee Rd., Sutt. 131 CX108
Jubilee Rd., Wat. 29 BU38
Jubilee St. E1 78 DW72
Jubilee Wk., Wat. 43 BV49
Muirfield Rd.
Jubilee Way SW19 118 DB95
Jubilee Way, Chess. 130 CN105
Jubilee Way, Felt. 99 BT88
Jubilee Way, Sid. 110 EU89
Judd St. WC1 5 P3
Judd St. WC1 77 DL69
Jude St. E16 80 EF72
Judge Heath La., Hayes 71 BQ72
Judge Heath La., Uxb. 71 BQ72
Judge St., Wat. 29 BV38
Judge Wk., Esher 129 CE107
Judges Hill, Pot.B. 20 DE29
Judith Ave., Rom. 55 FB51
Juer St. SW11 90 DE80
Juglans Rd., Orp. 124 EU102
Julia Gdns., Bark. 82 EX68
Julia St. NW5 62 DG63
Oak Village
Julian Ave. W3 74 CP73
Julian Clo., Barn. 34 DB41
Julian Hill, Har. 59 CE61
Julian Hill, Wey. 126 BN108
Julian Pl. E14 93 EB78
Julian Rd., Orp. 138 EU107
Juliana Clo. N2 62 DB55
East End Rd.
Julians Clo., Sev. 154 FG127
Julians Way, Sev. 154 FG127
Julien Rd. W5 87 CJ77
Julien Rd., Couls. 147 DK115
Juliette Rd. E13 80 EF68
Junction App. SE13 93 EC83
Loampit Vale
Junction App. SW11 90 DE83
Junction Ave. W10 75 CW69
Harrow Rd.
Junction Ms. W2 4 B8
Junction Pl. W2 4 A8
Junction Rd. E13 80 EH68
Junction Rd. N9 50 DU46
Junction Rd. N17 64 DU55
Junction Rd. N19 63 DJ63
Junction Rd. W5 87 CK77
Junction Rd., Ashf. 99 BQ92
Junction Rd., Brent. 87 CK77
Junction Rd., Har. 59 CE58
Junction Rd., Rom. 69 FF56
Junction Rd., S.Croy. 134 DR106
Junction Rd. E., Rom. 68 EY59
Kenneth Rd.
Junction Rd. W., Rom. 68 EY59
Junction Wf. N1 7 H1
Junction Wf. N1 78 DQ68
June Clo., Couls. 133 DH114
Juniper Ave., St.Alb. 16 CA31
Juniper Clo., Barn. 33 CX43
Juniper Clo., Brox. 23 DZ25
Juniper Clo., Chess. 130 CM107
Juniper Clo., Rick. 42 BK48
Juniper Clo., Wem. 60 CN64
Juniper Clo., West. 150 EL117
Juniper Cres. NW1 76 DG66
Juniper Gdns. SW16 119 DJ95
Leonard Rd.
Juniper Gdns., Sun. 99 BT93
Juniper Gate, Rick. 42 BK47
Juniper Gro., Wat. 29 BU38
Bay Tree Wk.
Juniper La. E6 80 EL71
Juniper Rd., Ilf. 67 EP63
Juniper St. E1 78 DW73
Juniper Wk., Swan. 125 FD96
Pear Tree Clo.
Juniper Way, Hayes 71 BR73
Juno Way SE14 93 DX79
Jupiter Way N7 77 DM65
Jupp Rd. E15 79 ED66
Jupp Rd. W. E15 79 EC67
Justice Wk. SW3 90 DE79
Lawrence St.
Justin Clo., Brent. 87 CK80
Justin Rd. E4 51 DZ51
Jute La., Enf. 37 DY40
Jutland Clo. N19 63 DL60
Sussex Way
Jutland Gdns., Couls. 147 DL120
Goodenough Way
Jutland Rd. E13 80 EG70
Jutland Rd. SE6 107 EC87
Jutsums Ave., Rom. 69 FB58
Jutsums La., Rom. 69 FB58
Juxon Clo., Har. 44 CB53
Augustine Rd.
Juxon St. SE11 10 C8
Juxon St. SE11 91 DM77

K

Kaduna Clo., Pnr. 57 BV57
Kale Rd., Erith 96 EY75
Kambala Rd. SW11 90 DD83
Kangley Bri. Rd. SE26 107 DZ91
Kaplan Dr. N21 35 DL43
Pennington Dr.
Karen Clo., Rain. 83 FE68
Karen Ct. SE4 93 DZ82
Wickham Rd.
Karen Ct., Brom. 122 EF95
Blyth Rd.
Karen Ter. E11 66 EF61
Montague Rd.
Karoline Gdns., Grnf. 73 CD68
Oldfield La. N.
Kashgar Rd. SE18 95 ET77
Kashmir Clo., Add. 126 BK109
Kashmir Rd. SE7 94 EK80
Kassala Rd. SW11 90 DF81
Katella Trd. Est., Bark. 81 ES69
Kates Clo., Barn. 33 CU43
Katharine St., Croy. 120 DQ104
Katherine Clo., Add. 126 BG107
Katherine Gdns. SE9 94 EK84
Katherine Gdns., Ilf. 53 EQ52
Katherine Rd. E6 80 EK66
Katherine Rd. E7 80 EJ65
Katherine Rd., Twick. 101 CG88
London Rd.
Katherine Sq. W11 75 CY74
Wilsham St.
Kathleen Ave. W3 74 CQ71
Kathleen Ave., Wem. 74 CL66
Kathleen Rd. SW11 90 DF83
Kay Rd. SW9 91 DL82
Kay St. E2 78 DU68
Kay St. E15 79 ED66
Kay St., Well. 96 EV81
Kaye Don Way, Wey. 126 BN111
Kayemoor Rd., Sutt. 132 DE108
Kean St. WC2 6 B9
Kean St. WC2 77 DM72
Kearton Clo., Ken. 148 DQ117
Keatley Grn. E4 51 DZ51
Keats Ave., Rom. 55 FH52
Keats Clo. E11 66 EH57
Nightingale La.
Keats Clo. NW3 62 DE63
Keats Gro.
Keats Clo. SE1 11 P9
Keats Clo. SW19 104 DD93
North Rd.
Keats Clo., Chig. 53 EQ51
Keats Clo., Enf. 37 DX43
Keats Clo., Hayes 71 BU71
Keats Gro. NW3 62 DE63
Keats Ho., Beck. 107 EA93
Keats Pl. EC2 7 K7
Keats Rd., Belv. 97 FC76
Keats Rd., Well. 95 ES81
Keats Way, Croy. 120 DW100
Keats Way, Grnf. 72 CB71
Keats Way, West Dr. 84 BM77
Keble Clo., Nthlt. 58 CC64
Keble Clo., Wor.Pk. 117 CT102
Keble Pl. SW13 89 CV79
Trinity Ch. Rd.
Keble St. SW17 104 DC91
Keble Ter., Abb.L. 15 BT32
Kechill Gdns., Brom. 122 EG101
Kedelston Ct. E5 65 DX63
Redwald Rd.
Kedleston Dr., Orp. 123 ET100
Kedleston Wk. E2 78 DV69
Middleton St.
Keedonwood Rd., Brom. 108 EE92
Keel Clo. SE16 79 DX74
Keel Clo., Bark. 82 EY69
Choats Rd.
Keele Clo., Wat. 30 BW40
Keeley Rd., Croy. 120 DQ103
Keeley St. WC2 6 B9
Keeley St. WC2 77 DM72
Keeling Rd. SE9 108 EK85
Keely Clo., Barn. 34 DE43
Keemor Clo. SE18 95 EN80
Llanover Rd.
Keens Clo. SW16 105 DK92
Keens Rd., Croy. 134 DQ105
Keens Yd. N1 77 DP65
St. Paul's Rd.
Keep, The SE3 94 EG82
Keep, The, Kings.T. 102 CM93
Keep La. N11 48 DG49
Gardeners Clo.
Keepers Ms., Tedd. 101 CJ93
Keesey St. SE17 92 DR79
Keetons Rd. SE16 92 DV76
Keevil Dr. SW19 103 CX87
Keighley Clo. N7 63 DL64
Penn Rd.
Keightley Dr. SE9 109 EQ88
Keilder Clo., Uxb. 70 BN68
Charnwood Rd.
Keildon Rd. SW11 90 DF84
Keir, The SW19 103 CW92
West Side Common
Keir Hardie Est. E5 64 DV60
Springfield
Keir Hardie Ho. W6 89 CW79
Lochaline St.
Keir Hardie Way, Bark. 82 EU66
Keir Hardie Way, Hayes 71 BU69
Keith Connor Clo. SW8 91 DH83
Daley Thompson Way
Keith Gro. W12 89 CU75
Keith Pk. Cres., West. 136 EH113
Keith Pk. Rd., Uxb. 70 BM66
Keith Rd. E17 51 DZ53
Keith Rd., Bark. 81 ER68
Keith Rd., Hayes 85 BS76
Kelbrook Rd. SE3 94 EL82
Kelburn Way, Rain. 83 FG69
Dominion Way
Kelby Path SE9 109 EP90
Kelceda Clo. NW2 61 CU61
Kelf Gro., Hayes 71 BT72
Kelfield Gdns. W10 75 CW72
Kelfield Ms. W10 75 CX72
Kelfield Gdns.
Kell St. SE1 10 G6
Kelland Clo. N8 63 DK57
Palace Rd.
Kelland Rd. E13 80 EG70
Kellaway Rd. SE3 94 EJ82
Keller Cres. E12 66 EK63
Kellerton Rd. SE13 108 EE85
Kellett Rd. SW2 91 DN84
Kelling Gdns., Croy. 119 DP101
Kellino St. SW17 104 DF91
Kellner Rd. SE28 95 ET76
Kelly Clo., Shep. 113 BS96
Kelly Ct., Borwd. 32 CR40
Kelly Rd. NW7 47 CY51
Kelly St. NW1 77 DH65
Kelly Way, Rom. 68 EY57
Kelman Clo. SW4 91 DK82
Kelman Clo., Wal.Cr. 23 DX31
Kelmore Gro. SE22 92 DU84
Kelmscott Clo. E17 51 DZ54
Kelmscott Clo., Wat. 29 BU43
Kelmscott Cres., Wat. 29 BU43
Kelmscott Gdns. W12 89 CU76
Kelmscott Rd. SW11 104 DE85
Kelross Pas. N5 64 DQ63
Kelross Rd.
Kelross Rd. N5 64 DQ63
Kelsall Clo. SE3 94 EH82
Kelsey La., Beck. 121 EA97
Kelsey Pk. Ave., Beck. 121 EB96
Kelsey Pk. Rd., Beck. 121 EA96
Kelsey Rd., Orp. 124 EV96
Kelsey Sq., Beck. 121 EA96
High St.
Kelsey St. E2 78 DU70
Kelsey Way, Beck. 121 EA97
Kelshall, Wat. 30 BY36
Kelshall Ct. N4 64 DQ61
Brownswood Rd.
Kelsie Way, Ilf. 53 ES51
Kelso Pl. W8 90 DB76
Kelso Rd., Cars. 118 DC101
Kelson Ho. E14 93 EC76
Kelston Rd., Ilf. 53 EP54
Kelvedon Ave., Walt. 127 BS108
Kelvedon Clo., Kings.T. 102 CN93
Kelvedon Rd. SW6 89 CZ80
Kelvedon Wk., Rain. 83 FE67
Ongar Way
Kelvedon Way, Wdf.Grn. 53 EM51
Kelvin Ave. N13 49 DM51
Kelvin Ave., Lthd. 143 CF119
Kelvin Ave., Tedd. 101 CE93
Kelvin Clo., Epsom 130 CN107
Kelvin Cres., Har. 45 CE52
Kelvin Dr., Twick. 101 CH86
Kelvin Gdns., Croy. 119 DL101
Kelvin Gdns., Sthl. 72 CA72
Kelvin Gro. SE26 106 DV90
Kelvin Gro., Chess. 116 CL104
Kelvin Ind. Est., Grnf. 72 CB66
Kelvin Par., Orp. 123 ES102
Kelvin Rd. N5 63 DP63
Kelvin Rd., Well. 96 EU83
Kelvinbrook, W.Mol. 114 CB97
Kelvington Clo., Croy. 121 DY101
Kelvington Rd. SE15 107 DX85
Kember St. N1 77 DM66
Carnoustie Dr.
Kemble Clo., Pot.B. 20 DD33
Kemble Clo., Wey. 127 BR105
Kemble Cotts., Add. 112 BG104
Emley Rd.
Kemble Dr., Brom. 122 EL104
Kemble Par., Pot.B. 20 DC32
High St.
Kemble Rd. N17 50 DU53
Kemble Rd. SE23 107 DX88
Kemble Rd., Croy. 119 DN104
Kemble St. WC2 6 B9
Kemble St. WC2 77 DM72
Kembleside Rd., West. 150 EJ118
Kemerton Rd. SE5 92 DQ83
Kemerton Rd., Beck. 121 EB96
Kemerton Rd., Croy. 120 DT101
Kemeys St. E9 65 DY64
Kemnal Rd., Chis. 109 EQ94
Kemp Gdns., Croy. 120 DQ100
St. Saviours Rd.
Kemp Pl. (Bushey), Wat. 30 CA44
Kemp Rd., Dag. 68 EX60
Kempe Rd. NW6 75 CX68
Kempe Rd., Enf. 36 DV36
Kempis Way SE22 106 DS85
East Dulwich Gro.
Kemplay Rd. NW3 62 DD63
Kemprow, Wat. 31 CD36
Kemp's Ct. W1 5 L9
Kemps Dr. E14 79 EA73
Morant St.
Kemps Dr., Nthwd. 43 BT52
Kemps Gdns. SE13 107 EC85
Thornford Rd.
Kempsford Gdns. SW5 90 DA78
Kempsford Rd. SE11 10 F9
Kempsford Rd. SE11 91 DN77
Kempshott Rd. SW16 105 DK94
Kempson Rd. SW6 90 DA81
Kempt St. SE18 95 EN79
Kempthorne Rd. SE8 93 DY77
Kempton Ave., Nthlt. 72 CA65
Kempton Ave., Sun. 113 BV95
Kempton Clo., Erith 97 FC79
Kempton Clo., Uxb. 57 BQ63
Kempton Ct., Sun. 113 BV95
Kempton Rd. E6 81 EM67
Kempton Rd., Hmptn. 114 BZ96
Kempton Wk., Croy. 121 DY100
Kemsing Clo., Bex. 110 EY87
Kemsing Clo., Brom. 122 EF103
Bourne Way
Kemsing Clo., Th.Hth. 120 DQ98
Kemsing Rd. SE10 94 EG78
Kemsley Rd., West. 150 EK119
Ken Way, Wem. 60 CQ61
Kenbury Clo., Uxb. 56 BN62
Kenbury Gdns. SE5 92 DQ82
Kenbury St.
Kenbury St. SE5 92 DQ82
Kenchester Clo. SW8 91 DL80
Kencot Way, Erith 96 EZ75
Kendal Ave. N18 50 DR49
Kendal Ave. W3 74 CN70
Kendal Ave., Bark. 81 ES66
Kendal Ave., Epp. 26 EU30
Kendal Clo. SW9 91 DP80
Kendal Clo., Felt. 99 BT88
Ambleside Dr.
Kendal Clo., Hayes 71 BS68
Kendal Clo., Wdf.Grn. 52 EF47
Kendal Cft., Horn. 69 FG64
Kendal Gdns. N18 50 DR49
Kendal Gdns., Sutt. 118 DC103
Kendal Par. N18 50 DR49
Great Cambridge Rd.
Kendal Pl. SW15 103 CZ85
Upper Richmond Rd.
Kendal Rd. NW10 61 CU63
Kendal St. W2 4 C9
Kendal St. W2 76 DE72
Kendale Rd., Brom. 108 EE92
Kendall Ave., Beck. 121 DY96
Kendall Ave., S.Croy. 134 DR109
Kendall Ave. S., S.Croy. 134 DQ110
Kendall Ct. SW19 104 DD93
Byegrove Rd.
Kendall Pl. W1 4 F7
Kendall Rd., Beck. 121 DY96
Kendall Rd., Islw. 87 CG82
Kendalmere Clo. N10 49 DH53
Kendals Clo., Rad. 31 CE36
Kender St. SE14 92 DW81
Kendoa Rd. SW4 91 DK84
Kendon Clo. E11 66 EH57
The Ave.
Kendor Ave., Epsom 130 CQ111
Kendra Hall Rd., S.Croy. 133 DP108
Kendrey Gdns., Twick. 101 CE86
Kendrick Ms. SW7 90 DD77
Reece Ms.
Kendrick Pl. SW7 90 DD77
Kenelm Clo., Har. 59 CG62
Kenerne Dr., Barn. 33 CY43
Kenford Clo., Wat. 15 BV32
Kenilford Rd. SW12 105 DH87
Kenilworth Ave. E17 51 EA54
Kenilworth Ave. SW19 104 DA92
Kenilworth Ave., Cob. 128 CB114
Kenilworth Ave., Har. 58 BZ63
Kenilworth Clo., Bans. 146 DB116
Kenilworth Clo., Borwd. 32 CQ41
Kenilworth Ct. SW15 89 CX83
Kenilworth Ct., Wat. 29 BV39
Hempstead Rd.
Kenilworth Cres., Enf. 36 DS39
Kenilworth Dr., Borwd. 32 CQ41
Kenilworth Dr., Rick. 29 BP42
Kenilworth Dr., Walt. 114 BX104
Kenilworth Gdns. SE18 95 EP82
Kenilworth Gdns., Hayes 71 BT71
Kenilworth Gdns., Ilf. 67 ET61
Kenilworth Gdns., Loug. 39 EM44
Kenilworth Gdns., Sthl. 72 BZ69
Kenilworth Gdns., Stai. 98 BJ92
Kenilworth Gdns., Wat. 44 BW50
Kenilworth Rd. E3 79 DY68
Kenilworth Rd. NW6 75 CZ67
Kenilworth Rd. SE20 121 DX95
Kenilworth Rd. W5 74 CL74
Kenilworth Rd., Ashf. 98 BK90
Kenilworth Rd., Edg. 46 CQ48
Kenilworth Rd., Epsom 131 CU106
Kenilworth Rd., Orp. 123 EQ100
Kenley Ave. NW9 46 CS53
Kenley Clo., Bex. 110 FA87
Kenley Clo., Cat. 148 DR120
Kenley Clo., Chis. 123 ES97
Kenley Gdns., Th.Hth. 119 DP98
Kenley La., Ken. 134 DQ114
Kenley Rd. SW19 117 CZ96
Kenley Rd., Kings.T. 116 CP96
Kenley Rd., Twick. 101 CG86
Kenley Wk. W11 75 CY73
Princedale Rd.
Kenley Wk., Sutt. 131 CX105
Kenlor Rd. SW17 104 DD92
Kenmare Dr., Mitch. 104 DF94
Kenmare Gdns. N13 50 DQ49
Kenmare Rd., Th.Hth. 119 DN100
Kenmere Gdns., Wem. 74 CN67
Kenmere Rd., Well. 96 EW82
Kenmont Gdns. NW10 75 CV69
Kenmore Ave., Har. 59 CG56
Kenmore Clo., Rich. 88 CN80
Kent Rd.
Kenmore Cres., Hayes 71 BT69
Kenmore Gdns., Edg. 46 CP54
Kenmore Rd., Har. 59 CK55
Kenmore Rd., Ken. 133 DP114
Kenmure Rd. E8 64 DV64
Kenmure Yd. E8 64 DV64
Kenmure Rd.
Kennard Rd. E15 79 ED66
Kennard Rd. N11 48 DF50
Kennard St. E16 81 EM74
Kennard St. SW11 90 DG81
Kennedy Ave., Enf. 36 DW44
Kennedy Clo. E13 80 EG68
Kennedy Clo., Mitch. 118 DG95
Kennedy Clo., Orp. 123 ER102
Kennedy Clo., Pnr. 44 BZ51
Kennedy Clo. (Cheshunt), Wal.Cr. 23 DY28
Kennedy Gdns., Sev. 155 FJ123
Kennedy Path W7 73 CF70
Harp Rd.
Kennedy Rd. W7 73 CE71
Kennedy Rd., Bark. 81 ES67
Kennedy Wk. SE17 92 DR77
Flint St.
Kennel Clo., Lthd. 142 CC124
Kennel Hill SE22 92 DS83
Kennel La., Lthd. 142 CC122
Kennelwood Cres., Croy. 135 ED111
Kennet Clo. SW11 90 DD84
Maysoule Rd.
Kennet Rd. W9 75 CZ70
Kennet Rd., Dart. 97 FG83
Kennet Rd., Islw. 87 CF83
Kennet Sq., Mitch. 118 DE95
Kennet St. E1 78 DU74
Kennet Wf. La. EC4 7 J10
Kenneth Ave., Ilf. 67 EP63
Kenneth Cres. NW2 61 CV64
Kenneth Gdns., Stan. 45 CG51
Kenneth More Rd., Ilf. 67 EP62
Oakfield Rd.
Kenneth Rd., Bans. 146 DD115
Kenneth Rd., Rom. 68 EX59
Kenneth Robbins Ho. N17 50 DV52
Kennett Ct., Swan. 125 FE97
Kennett Dr., Hayes 72 BY71
Kenning St. SE16 92 DW75
Railway Ave.
Kenning Ter. N1 78 DS67
Kenninghall Rd. E5 64 DU62
Kenninghall Rd. N18 50 DW50
Kennings Way SE11 10 F10
Kennings Way SE11 91 DN78
Kennington Grn. SE11 91 DN78
Montford Pl.
Kennington Gro. SE11 91 DM79
Oval Way
Kennington La. SE11 91 DL78
Kennington Oval SE11 91 DM79
Kennington Pk. Est. SE11 91 DN79
Harleyford St.
Kennington Pk. Gdns. SE11 91 DN79
Montford Pl.
Kennington Pk. Pl. SE11 91 DN79
Kennington Pk. Rd. SE11 91 DN79
Kennington Rd. SE1 10 D6
Kennington Rd. SE1 91 DN76
Kennington Rd. SE11 10 D8
Kennington Rd. SE11 91 DN76
Kenny Rd. NW7 47 CY50
Kennylands Rd., Ilf. 54 EU52
Kenrick Pl. W1 4 F7
Kensal Rd. W10 75 CX70
Kensington Ave. E12 80 EL65
Kensington Ave., Th.Hth. 119 DN95
Kensington Ave., Wat. 29 BT42
Kensington Ch. Ct. W8 90 DB75
Kensington Ch. St. W8 76 DA74
Kensington Ch. Wk. W8 90 DB75
Kensington Clo. N11 48 DG51
Kensington Ct. W8 90 DB75
Kensington Ct. Gdns. W8 90 DB76
Kensington Ct. Pl.
Kensington Ct. Ms. W8 90 DB75
Kensington Ct. Pl.
Kensington Ct. Pl. W8 90 DB76
Kensington Dr., Wdf.Grn. 52 EK54
Kensington Gdns. W2 76 DB74
Kensington Gdns., Ilf. 67 EM60

Knightsbridge SW1 90 DF75
Knightsbridge SW7 8 C5
Knightsbridge SW7 90 DE75
Knightsbridge Cres., Stai. 98 BH93
Knightsbridge Gdns., Rom. 69 FD57
Knightsbridge Grn. SW1 8 D5
Knightsbridge Grn. SW1 90 DF75
Knightswood Clo., Edg. 46 CQ47
Knightwood Cres., N.Mal. 116 CS100
Knipp Hill, Cob. 128 BZ113
Knivet Rd. SW6 90 DA79
Knobs Hill Rd. E15 79 EB67
Knockholt Clo., Sutt. 132 DB110
Knockholt Main Rd., Sev. 152 EY115
Knockholt Rd. SE9 108 EK85
Knockholt Rd., Sev. 138 EZ113
Knole, The SE9 109 EN91
Knole Clo., Croy. 120 DW100
Stockbury Rd.
Knole Gate, Sid. 109 ES90
Woodside Cres.
Knole La., Sev. 155 FJ126
Knole Rd., Dart. 111 FG87
Knole Rd., Sev. 155 FK123
Knole Way, Sev. 155 FJ125
Knoll, The W13 73 CJ71
Knoll, The, Beck. 121 EB95
Knoll, The, Brom. 122 EG102
Knoll, The, Cob. 128 CA113
Knoll, The, Lthd. 143 CJ121
Knoll Ct. SE19 106 DT92
Knoll Cres., Nthwd. 43 BS54
Knoll Dr. N14 48 DG45
Knoll Ri., Orp. 123 ET102
Knoll Rd. SW18 104 DC85
Knoll Rd., Bex. 110 FA87
Knoll Rd., Sid. 110 EV92
Knollmead, Surb. 116 CQ102
Knolls, The, Epsom 145 CW116
Knolls Clo., Wor.Pk. 117 CV104
Knollys Clo. SW16 105 DN90
Knollys Rd. SW16 105 DM90
Knottisford St. E2 78 DW69
Knotts Grn. Ms. E10 65 EB58
Knotts Grn. Rd.
Knotts Grn. Rd. E10 65 EB58
Knotts Pl., Sev. 154 FG124
Knowl Pk., Borwd. 32 CL43
Knowl Way, Borwd. 32 CM43
Knowle, The, Tad. 145 CW121
Knowle Ave., Bexh. 96 EY80
Knowle Clo. SW9 91 DN83
Knowle Grn., Stai. 98 BG92
Knowle Pk., Cob. 142 BY115
Knowle Pk. Ave., Stai. 98 BH93
Knowle Rd., Brom. 122 EL103
Knowle Rd., Twick. 101 CE88
Knowles Clo., West Dr. 70 BL74
Knowles Hill Cres. SE13 107 ED85
Knowles Wk. SW4 91 DJ83
Knowlton Grn., Brom. 122 EF99
Knowsley Ave., Sthl. 72 CB74
Knowsley Rd. SW11 90 DF82
Knox Rd. E7 80 EF65
Knox St. W1 4 D6
Knox St. W1 76 DF71
Knoyle St. SE14 93 DY79
Chubworthy St.
Knutsford Ave., Wat. 30 BX38
Koh-i-noor Ave. 30 CA44
(Bushey), Wat.
Kohat Rd. SW19 104 DB92
Koonowla Clo., West. 150 EK115
Kooringa, Warl. 148 DV119
Korda Clo., Shep. 112 BM97
Kossuth St. SE10 94 EE78
Kotree Way SE1 92 DU77
Beatrice Rd.
Kramer Ms. SW5 90 DA78
Kempsford Gdns.
Kreedman Wk. E8 64 DU64
Kreisel Wk., Rich. 88 CM79
Kuala Gdns. SW16 119 DM95
Kuhn Way E7 66 EG64
Forest La.
Kydbrook Clo., Orp. 123 EQ101
Kylemore Clo. E6 80 EK68
Parr Rd.
Kylemore Rd. NW6 76 DA66
Kymberley Rd., Har. 59 CE58
Kyme Rd., Horn. 69 FF58
Kynance Gdns., Stan. 45 CJ53
Kynance Ms. SW7 90 DC76
Kynance Pl. SW7 90 DC76
Kynaston Ave. N16 64 DT62
Dynevor Rd.
Kynaston Ave., Th.Hth. 120 DQ99
Kynaston Clo., Har. 45 CD52
Kynaston Cres., Th.Hth. 120 DQ99
Kynaston Rd. N16 64 DS62
Kynaston Rd., Brom. 108 EG92
Kynaston Rd., Enf. 36 DR39
Kynaston Rd., Orp. 124 EV101
Kynaston Rd., Th.Hth. 120 DQ99
Kynaston Wd., Har. 45 CD52
Kynock Rd. N18 50 DW49
Kyrle Rd. SW11 104 DF86
Kytes Dr., Wat. 16 BX33
Kytes Est., Wat. 16 BX33
Kyverdale Rd. N16 64 DT59

L

La Tourne Gdns., Orp. 123 EQ104
Laburnham Ave., West Dr. 70 BM73
Laburnum Ave. N9 50 DS47
Laburnum Ave. N17 50 DR52
Laburnum Ave., Horn. 69 FF62
Laburnum Ave., Sutt. 118 DE104
Laburnum Ave., Swan. 125 FC97
Laburnum Clo. E4 51 DZ51
Laburnum Clo. N11 48 DG51
Laburnum Clo. SE15 92 DW80
Clifton Way
Laburnum Clo. 23 DX31
(Cheshunt), Wal.Cr.
Laburnum Ct. E2 78 DT67
Laburnum St.
Laburnum Ct., Stan. 45 CJ49
Laburnum Cres., Sun. 113 BV95
Batavia Rd.
Laburnum Gdns. N21 50 DQ47
Laburnum Gdns., Croy. 121 DX101
Laburnum Gro. N21 50 DQ47
Laburnum Gro. NW9 60 CQ59
Laburnum Gro., Houns. 86 BZ84
Laburnum Gro., N.Mal. 116 CR96
Laburnum Gro., Ruis. 57 BR58
Laburnum Gro., St.Alb. 16 CB25
Laburnum Gro., Sthl. 72 BZ70
Laburnum Ho., Dag. 68 FA61
Althorne Way
Laburnum Rd. SW19 104 DC94
Laburnum Rd., Cher. 112 BG102
Laburnum Rd., Epp. 26 EW29
Laburnum Rd., Epsom 130 CS113
Laburnum Rd., Hayes 85 BT77
Laburnum Rd., Mitch. 118 DG96
Laburnum St. E2 78 DT67
Laburnum Way, Brom. 123 EN101
Laburnum Way, Stai. 98 BM88
Laburnum Way 21 DP28
(Cheshunt), Wal.Cr.
Millcrest Rd.
Lacebark Clo., Sid. 109 ET87
Lacey Ave., Couls. 147 DN120
Lacey Clo. N9 50 DU47
Lacey Dr., Couls. 147 DN120
Lacey Dr., Dag. 68 EV63
Lacey Dr., Edg. 46 CL49
Lacey Dr., Hmptn. 114 BZ95
Lacey Grn., Couls. 147 DN120
Lacey Wk. E3 79 EA68
Lackford Rd., Couls. 146 DF118
Lackington St. EC2 7 L6
Lackington St. EC2 78 DR71
Lackmore Rd., Enf. 36 DW35
Lacock Clo. SW19 104 DC93
Lacon Rd. SE22 92 DU84
Lacy Rd. SW15 89 CX84
Ladas Rd. SE27 106 DQ91
Ladbroke Cres. W11 75 CY72
Ladbroke Gro.
Ladbroke Gdns. W11 75 CZ73
Ladbroke Gro. W10 75 CX70
Ladbroke Gro. W11 75 CY72
Ladbroke Ms. W11 75 CY74
Ladbroke Rd.
Ladbroke Rd. W11 75 CZ74
Ladbroke Rd., Enf. 36 DT44
Ladbroke Rd., Epsom 130 CR114
Ladbroke Sq. W11 75 CZ73
Ladbroke Ter. W11 75 CZ73
Ladbroke Wk. W11 75 CZ74
Ladbrook Clo., Pnr. 58 BZ57
Ladbrook Rd. SE25 120 DR97
Ladbrooke Clo., Pot.B. 20 DA32
Strafford Gate
Ladbrooke Cres., Sid. 110 EX90
Ladbrooke Dr., Pot.B. 20 DA32
Ladderstile Ride, Kings.T. 102 CQ92
Ladderswood Way N11 49 DJ50
Ladds Way, Swan. 125 FD98
Lady Booth Rd., Kings.T. 116 CL96
Lady Hay, Wor.Pk. 117 CT103
Lady Margaret Rd. N19 63 DJ63
Lady Margaret Rd. NW5 63 DJ64
Lady Margaret Rd., Sthl. 72 BZ71
Lady Somerset Rd. NW5 63 DH63
Ladybower Ct. E5 65 DY63
Gilpin Rd.
Ladycroft Gdns., Orp. 137 EQ106
Ladycroft Rd. SE13 93 EB83
Ladycroft Wk., Stan. 45 CK53
Ladycroft Way, Orp. 137 EQ106
Ladyfield Clo., Loug. 39 EP42
Ladyfields, Loug. 39 EP42
Ladygate La., Ruis. 57 BP58
Ladygrove, Croy. 135 DY109
Ladymeadow, Kings L. 14 BK27
Lady's Clo., Wat. 29 BV42
Ladysmith Ave. E6 80 EL68
Ladysmith Ave., Ilf. 67 ER59
Ladysmith Rd. E16 80 EF69
Ladysmith Rd. N17 50 DU54
Ladysmith Rd. N18 50 DV50
Ladysmith Rd. SE9 109 EN86
Ladysmith Rd., Enf. 36 DS41
Ladysmith Rd., Har. 45 CE54
Ladythorpe Clo., Add. 126 BH105
Church Rd.
Ladywell Clo. SE4 93 DZ84
Adelaide Ave.
Ladywell Heights SE4 107 DZ86
Ladywell Rd. SE13 107 EB85
Ladywell St. E15 80 EF67
Plaistow Gro.
Ladywood Ave., Orp. 123 ES99
Ladywood Clo., Rick. 28 BH41
Ladywood Rd., Surb. 116 CN103
Lafone Ave., Felt. 100 BW88
Alfred Rd.
Lafone St. SE1 11 P4
Lafone St. SE1 92 DT75
Lagado Ms. SE16 79 DX74
Lagonda Ave., Ilf. 53 ET51
Lagoon Rd., Orp. 124 EV99
Laing Clo., Ilf. 53 ER51
Laing Dean, Nthlt. 72 BW67
Laings Ave., Mitch. 118 DF96
Lainlock Pl., Houns. 86 CB81
Spring Gro. Rd.
Lainson St. SW18 104 DA87
Laird Ho. SE5 92 DQ80
Redcar St.
Lairdale Clo. SE21 106 DQ88
Lairs Clo. N7 77 DL65
Manger Rd.
Laitwood Rd. SW12 105 DH88
Lake, The (Bushey), Wat. 44 CC46
Lake Ave., Brom. 108 EG93
Lake Clo. SW19 103 CZ92
Lake Rd.
Lake Clo., W.Byf. 126 BK112
Lake Dr. (Bushey), Wat. 44 CC47
Lake Gdns., Dag. 68 FA64
Lake Gdns., Rich. 101 CH89
Lake Gdns., Wall. 119 DH104
Lake Ho. Rd. E11 66 EG62
Lake Ri., Rom. 55 FF54
Lake Rd. SW19 103 CZ92
Lake Rd., Croy. 121 DZ103
Lake Rd., Rom. 68 EX56
Lake Vw., Edg. 46 CM50
Lake Vw., Pot.B. 20 DC33
Lake Vw. Rd., Sev. 154 FG123
Lakedale Rd. SE18 95 ES78
Lakefield Rd. N22 49 DP54
Lakehall Gdns., Th.Hth. 119 DP99
Lakehall Rd., Th.Hth. 119 DP99
Lakehurst Rd., Epsom 130 CS106
Lakeland Clo., Chig. 54 EV49
Lakeland Clo., Har. 45 CD51
Lakenheath N14 35 DJ43
Laker Pl. SW15 103 CY86
Lakers Ri., Bans. 146 DE116
Lakes Rd., Kes. 136 EJ106
Lakeside N3 48 DB54
Lakeside W13 73 CJ72
Edgehill Rd.
Lakeside, Beck. 121 EB97
Lakeside, Enf. 35 DK42
Lakeside, Wall. 119 DH104
Derek Ave.
Lakeside, Wey. 113 BS103
Lakeside Ave. SE28 82 EU74
Lakeside Ave., Ilf. 66 EK56
Lakeside Clo. SE25 120 DU96
Lakeside Clo., Chig. 53 ET49
Lakeside Clo., Ruis. 57 BR56
Lakeside Clo., Sid. 110 EW85
Lakeside Ct. N4 63 DP61
Lakeside Ct., Borwd. 32 CN43
Cavendish Cres.
Lakeside Cres., Barn. 34 DF43
Lakeside Cres., Wey. 113 BQ104
Churchill Dr.
Lakeside Dr., Brom. 122 EL104
Lakeside Dr., Esher 128 CC107
Lakeside Pl., St.Alb. 17 CK27
Lakeside Rd. N13 49 DM49
Lakeside Rd. W14 89 CX76
Lakeside Rd. (Cheshunt), 22 DW28
Wal.Cr.
Lakeside Way, Wem. 60 CN63
Lakeswood Rd., Orp. 123 EP99
Lakeview Ct. SW19 103 CY89
Victoria Dr.
Lakeview Rd. SE27 105 DN92
Lakeview Rd., Well. 96 EV84
Lakis Clo. NW3 62 DC63
Flask Wk.
Laleham Ave. NW7 46 CR48
Laleham Pk., Stai. 112 BJ99
Laleham Reach, Cher. 112 BH96
Laleham Rd. SE6 107 EC87
Laleham Rd., Shep. 112 BL98
Lalor St. SW6 89 CY82
Lamb Clo., Wat. 16 BW34
Lamb La. E8 78 DV66
Lamb St. E1 7 P6
Lamb St. E1 78 DT71
Lamb Wk. SE1 11 M5
Lamb Yd., Wat. 30 BX43
Lambarde Ave. SE9 109 EN91
Lambarde Dr., Sev. 154 FG123
Lambarde Rd., Sev. 154 FG122
Lambardes Clo., Orp. 138 EW110
Lamberhurst Clo., Orp. 124 EX102
Lamberhurst Rd. SE27 105 DN91
Lamberhurst Rd., Dag. 68 EY60
Lambert Ave., Rich. 88 CN83
Lambert Clo., West. 150 EK116
Lambert Ct. (Bushey), 30 BX42
Wat.
Lambert Jones Ms. EC2 78 DQ71
Beech St.
Lambert Rd. E16 80 EH72
Lambert Rd. N12 48 DC50
Lambert Rd. SW2 105 DL85
Lambert Rd., Bans. 132 DA114
Lambert St. N1 77 DN66
Lambert Wk., Wem. 59 CK62
Clarendon Gdns.
Lambert Way N12 48 DC50
Woodhouse Rd.
Lamberts Pl., Croy. 120 DR102
Lamberts Rd., Surb. 116 CL99
Lambeth Bri. SE1 10 A8
Lambeth Bri. SE1 91 DL77
Lambeth Bri. SW1 10 A8
Lambeth Bri. SW1 91 DL77
Lambeth High St. SE1 10 B8
Lambeth High St. SE1 91 DM77
Lambeth Hill EC4 7 H10
Lambeth Hill EC4 78 DQ73
Lambeth Palace Rd. SE1 10 B7
Lambeth Palace Rd. SE1 91 DM76
Lambeth Rd. SE1 10 D7
Lambeth Rd. SE1 91 DM76
Lambeth Rd. SE11 91 DM76
Lambeth Rd., Croy. 119 DN101
Lambeth Wk. SE11 10 C8
Lambeth Wk. SE11 91 DM77
Lamble St. NW5 62 DG64
Lambley Rd., Dag. 82 EV65
Lambolle Pl. NW3 76 DE65
Lambolle Rd. NW3 76 DE65
Lambourn Chase, Rad. 31 CF36
Lambourn Clo. W7 87 CF75
Lambourn Rd. SW4 91 DH83
Lambourne Ave. SW19 103 CZ91
Lambourne Clo., Chig. 54 EV47
Lambourne Rd.
Lambourne Cres., Chig. 54 EV47
Lambourne Dr., Cob. 142 BX115
Lambourne Gdns. E4 51 EA47
Lambourne Gdns., Bark. 81 ET66
Lambourne Rd.
Lambourne Gdns., Enf. 36 DT40
Lambourne Gro., Kings.T. 116 CP96
Kenley Rd.
Lambourne Pl. SE3 94 EH81
Shooter's Hill Rd.
Lambourne Rd. E11 65 ED59
Lambourne Rd., Bark. 81 ES66
Lambourne Rd., Chig. 53 ET49
Lambourne Rd., Ilf. 67 ES61
Lambrook Ter. SW6 89 CY81
Lamb's Bldgs. EC1 7 K5
Lambs Clo. (Cuffley), 21 DM29
Pot.B.
Lambs Conduit Pas. WC1 6 B6
Lamb's Conduit St. WC1 6 B5
Lamb's Conduit St. WC1 77 DM70
Lambs La., Rain. 83 FH71
Lambs Meadow, 52 EK54
Wdf.Grn.
Lambs Ms. N1 77 DP67
Colebrooke Row
Lamb's Pas. EC1 7 K6
Lamb's Pas. EC1 78 DR71
Lambs Ter. N9 50 DR47
Lambs Wk., Enf. 36 DQ40
Lambscroft Ave. SE9 108 EJ90
Lambton Ave., Wal.Cr. 23 DX32
Lambton Pl. W11 75 CZ72
Westbourne Gro.
Lambton Rd. N19 63 DL60
Lambton Rd. SW20 117 CW95
Lamerock Rd., Brom. 108 EF91
Lamerton Rd., Ilf. 53 EP54
Lamerton St. SE8 93 EA79
Lamford Clo. N17 50 DR52
Lamington St. W6 89 CV77
Lamlash St. SE11 10 F8
Lammas Ave., Mitch. 118 DG96
Lammas Grn. SE26 106 DV90
Lammas La., Esher 128 CA106
Lammas Pk. W5 87 CJ75
Lammas Pk. Gdns. W5 73 CJ74
Lammas Pk. Rd. W5 73 CJ74
Lammas Rd. E9 79 DX66
Lammas Rd. E10 65 DY61
Lammas Rd., Rich. 101 CJ91
Lammas Rd., Wat. 30 BW43
Lammermoor Rd. SW12 105 DH87
Lamont Rd. SW10 90 DC79
Lamont Rd. Pas. SW10 90 DD79
Lamont Rd.
Lamorbey Clo., Sid. 109 ET88
Lamorna Clo. E17 51 EC54
Lamorna Clo., Orp. 124 EU101
Lamorna Clo., Rad. 17 CH34
Lamorna Gro., Stan. 45 CK53
Lampard Gro. N16 64 DT60
Lampern Sq. E2 78 DU69
Nelson Gdns.
Lampeter Sq. W6 89 CY79
Humbolt Rd.
Lamplighter Clo. E1 78 DW70
Cleveland Way
Lamplighters Clo., 24 EG34
Wal.Abb.
Lampmead Rd. SE12 108 EF85
Lamport Clo. SE18 95 EM77
Lampton Ave., Houns. 86 CB81
Lampton Ho. Clo. SW19 103 CX91
Lampton Pk. Rd., Houns. 86 CB82
Lampton Rd., Houns. 86 CB82
Lamson Rd., Rain. 83 FF70
Lanacre Ave. NW9 46 CR53
Lanark Clo. W5 73 CJ71
Lanark Pl. W9 76 DC70
Lanark Rd. W9 76 DB68
Lanark Sq. E14 93 EB76
Lanata Wk., Hayes 72 BX70
Ramulis Dr.
Lanbury Rd. SE15 93 DX84
Lancashire Ct. W1 5 J10
Lancaster Ave. E18 66 EH56
Lancaster Ave. SE27 105 DP89
Lancaster Ave. SW19 103 CX92
Lancaster Ave., Bark. 81 ES66
Lancaster Ave., Barn. 34 DC38
Lancaster Ave., Mitch. 119 DL99
Lancaster Clo. N1 78 DS66
Hertford Rd.
Lancaster Clo. N17 50 DU52
Park La.
Lancaster Clo. NW9 47 CT52
Corner Mead
Lancaster Clo., Brom. 122 EF98
Lancaster Clo., Kings.T. 101 CK92
Lancaster Cotts., Rich. 102 CL86
Lancaster Pk.
Lancaster Ct. SE27 105 DP89
Lancaster Ct. SW6 89 CZ80
Lancaster Ct. W2 76 DC73
Lancaster Gate
Lancaster Ct., Bans. 131 CZ114
Lancaster Ct., Walt. 113 BU101
Lancaster Dr. E14 79 EC74
Prestons Rd.
Lancaster Dr. NW3 76 DE65
Lancaster Dr., Horn. 69 FH64
Lancaster Dr., Loug. 38 EL44
Lancaster Gdns. SW19 103 CY92
Lancaster Gdns. W13 87 CH75
Lancaster Gdns., Kings.T. 101 CK92
Lancaster Gate W2 76 DC73
Lancaster Gro. NW3 76 DD65
Lancaster Ms. SW18 104 DB85
East Hill
Lancaster Ms. W2 76 DC73
Lancaster Ms., Rich. 102 CL86
Richmond Hill
Lancaster Pk., Rich. 102 CL85
Lancaster Pl. SW19 103 CX92
Lancaster Rd.
Lancaster Pl. WC2 6 B10
Lancaster Pl. WC2 77 DM73
Lancaster Pl., Houns. 86 BW82
Lancaster Pl., Ilf. 67 EQ64
Staines Rd.
Lancaster Pl., Twick. 101 CG86
Lancaster Rd. E7 80 EG66
Lancaster Rd. E11 66 EE61
Lancaster Rd. E17 51 DX54
Lancaster Rd. N4 63 DM59
Lancaster Rd. N11 49 DK51
Lancaster Rd. N18 50 DT50
Lancaster Rd. NW10 61 CU64
Lancaster Rd. SE25 120 DT96
Lancaster Rd. SW19 103 CX92
Lancaster Rd. W11 75 CY72
Lancaster Rd., Barn. 34 DD43
Lancaster Rd., Enf. 36 DR39
Lancaster Rd., Epp. 26 FA26
Lancaster Rd., Har. 58 CA57
Lancaster Rd., Nthlt. 72 CC65
Lancaster Rd., Sthl. 72 BY73
Lancaster Rd., Uxb. 70 BK65
Lancaster St. SE1 10 G5
Lancaster St. SE1 91 DP75
Lancaster Ter. W2 76 DD73
Lancaster Wk. W2 76 DD74
Lancaster Wk., Hayes 71 BQ72
Lancaster Way, Abb.L. 15 BT31
Lance Rd., Har. 58 CC59
Lancefield St. W10 75 CZ69
Lancell St. N16 64 DS61
Stoke Newington Ch. St.
Lancelot Ave., Wem. 59 CK63
Lancelot Cres., Wem. 59 CK63
Lancelot Gdns., Barn. 48 DG45
Lancelot Pl. SW7 8 D5
Lancelot Pl. SW7 90 DF75
Lancelot Rd., Ilf. 53 ES51
Lancelot Rd., Well. 96 EU84
Lancelot Rd., Wem. 59 CK63
Lancer Sq. W8 90 DB75
Old Ct. Pl.
Lancey Clo. SE7 94 EK77
Cleveley Clo.
Lanchester Rd. N6 62 DF57
Lancing Gdns. N9 50 DT46
Lancing Rd. W13 73 CH73
Drayton Grn. Rd.
Lancing Rd., Croy. 119 DM100
Lancing Rd., Felt. 99 BT89
Lancing Rd., Ilf. 67 ER58
Lancing Rd., Orp. 124 EU103
Lancing St. NW1 5 M3
Lancing Way, Rick. 29 BP43
Lancresse Clo., Uxb. 70 BK65
Lancresse Ct. N1 78 DS67
Landau Way, Brox. 23 DZ25
Landcroft Rd. SE22 106 DT85
Landells Rd. SE22 106 DT86
Landford Clo., Rick. 42 BL47
Landford Rd. SW15 89 CW83
Landgrove Rd. SW19 104 DA92
Landmann Way SE14 93 DX79
Landmead Rd. 23 DY29
(Cheshunt), Wal.Cr.
Landon Pl. SW1 8 D6
Landon Pl. SW1 90 DF76
Landon Wk. E14 79 EB73
Cottage St.
Landon Way, Ashf. 99 BP93
Courtfield Rd.
Landons Clo. E14 79 EC74
Landor Rd. SW9 91 DL83
Landor Wk. W12 89 CU75
Landport Way SE15 92 DT80
Daniel Gdns.
Landra Gdns. N21 35 DP44
Landridge Rd. SW6 89 CZ82
Landrock Rd. N8 63 DL58
Lands End, Borwd. 31 CK44
Landscape Pl., Warl. 148 DV119
Landscape Rd., Wdf.Grn. 52 EH52

Landseer Ave. E12	67	EN64	Langholme (Bushey),	44	CC46	Lansdown Clo., Walt.	114	BW102	Larcom St. SE17	92	DQ77
Landseer Clo. SW19	118	DC95	Wat.			St. Johns Dr.			Larcombe Clo., Croy.	134	DT105
Brangwyn Cres.			Langhorne Rd., Dag.	82	FA66	Lansdown Rd. E7	80	EJ66	Larden Rd. W3	74	CS74
Landseer Clo., Edg.	46	CN54	Langland Ct., Nthwd.	43	BQ52	Lansdown Rd., Sid.	110	EV90	Largewood Ave., Surb.	116	CM103
Landseer Clo., Horn.	69	FH60	Langland Cres., Stan.	45	CK54	Lansdowne Ave., Bexh.	96	EW80	Largo Wk., Erith	97	FE81
Landseer Rd. N19	.63	DL62	Langland Dr., Pnr.	44	BY52	Lansdowne Ave., Orp.	123	EP102	Selkirk Dr.		
Landseer Rd. N19	62	DB64	Langland Gdns. NW3	62	DB64	Lansdowne Clo. SW20	103	CX94	Larissa St. SE17	11	L10
Landseer Rd., Enf.	36	DU43	Langland Gdns., Croy.	121	DZ103	Lansdowne Clo., Surb.	116	CP103	Lark Row E2	78	DW67
Landseer Rd., N.Mal.	116	CR101	Langlands Ri., Epsom	130	CQ113	Kingston Rd.			Lark Way, Cars.	118	DE101
Landseer Rd., Sutt.	132	DA107	Burnet Gro.			Lansdowne Clo., Twick.	101	CF88	Larkbere Rd. SE26	107	DY91
Landstead Rd. SE18	95	ER80	Langler Rd. NW10	75	CW68	Lion Rd.			Larken Dr. (Bushey), Wat.	44	CC46
Landway, The, Orp.	124	EW97	Langley Ave., Ruis.	57	BV61	Lansdowne Clo., Wat.	30	BX35	Larkfield, Cob.	127	BU113
Lane, The NW8	76	DC68	Langley Ave., Surb.	115	CK102	Lansdowne Ct., Wor.Pk.	117	CU103	Larkfield Ave., Har.	59	CH55
Marlborough Pl.			Langley Ave., Wor.Pk.	117	CX102	Lansdowne Cres. W11	75	CZ73	Larkfield Clo., Brom.	122	EF103
Lane, The SE3	94	EG83	Langley Clo., Epsom	144	CR119	Lansdowne Dr. E8	78	DU65	Larkfield Rd., Rich.	88	CL84
Lane, The, Cher.	112	BG97	Langley Ct. SE9	109	EN86	Lansdowne Gdns. SW8	91	DL81	Larkfield Rd., Sev.	154	FC123
Lane App. NW7	47	CY50	Langley Ct. WC2	5	P10	Lansdowne Grn. SW8	91	DL81	Larkfield Rd., Sid.	109	ET90
Lane Clo. NW2	61	CV62	Langley Ct., Beck.	121	EB99	Hartington Rd.			Larkhall Clo., Walt.	128	BW107
Lane Clo., Add.	126	BH106	Langley Cres. E11	66	EH59	Lansdowne Gro. NW10	60	CS63	Larkhall Ct., Rom.	55	FC54
Lane End, Bexh.	97	FB83	Langley Cres., Dag.	82	EW66	Lansdowne Hill SE27	105	DP90	Larkhall La. SW4	91	DK82
Lane End, Epsom	130	CP114	Langley Cres., Edg.	46	CQ48	Lansdowne La. SE7	94	EK78	Larkhall Ri. SW4	91	DJ83
Lane Gdns. (Bushey),	45	CE45	Langley Cres., Hayes	85	BT80	Lansdowne Ms. SE7	94	EK78	Larkham Clo., Felt.	99	BS90
Wat.			Langley Cres., Kings L.	14	BN30	Lansdowne Ms. W11	75	CZ74	Larkhill Ter. SE18	95	EN80
Lane Ms. E12	67	EM62	Langley Dr. E11	66	EH59	Lansdowne Pl.			Larkin Clo., Couls.	147	DM117
Colchester Ave.			Langley Dr. W3	88	CP75	Lansdowne Pl. SE1	11	L6	Larks Gro., Bark.	81	ES66
Lanercost Clo. SW2	105	DN89	Langley Gdns., Brom.	122	EJ98	Lansdowne Pl. SE19	106	DT94	Larksfield Gro., Enf.	36	DV39
Lanercost Gdns. N14	49	DL45	Langley Gdns., Dag.	82	EX66	Lansdowne Ri. W11	75	CY73	Larkshall Cres. E4	51	EC49
Lanercost Rd. SW2	105	DN89	Langley Gdns., Orp.	123	EP100	Lansdowne Rd. E4	51	EA47	Larkshall Rd. E4	51	EC50
Lanesborough Pl. SW1	8	G4	Langley Gro., N.Mal.	116	CS96	Lansdowne Rd. E11	66	EF61	Larkspur Clo. E6	80	EL71
Laneside, Chis.	109	EP92	Langley Hill, Kings L.	14	BM29	Lansdowne Rd. E17	65	EA58	Larkspur Clo. N17	50	DR52
Laneside, Edg.	46	CQ50	Langley Hill Clo., Kings L.	14	BN29	Lansdowne Rd. E18	66	EG55	Fryatt Rd.		
Laneside Ave., Dag.	68	EZ59	Langley La. SW8	91	DL79	Lansdowne Rd. N3	47	CZ52	Larkspur Clo. NW9	60	CP57
Laneway SW15	103	CV85	Langley La., Abb.L.	15	BT31	Lansdowne Rd. N10	49	DJ54	Old Kenton La.		
Sunnymead Rd.			Langley Lo. La., Kings L.	14	BL31	Lansdowne Rd. N17	50	DU53	Larkspur Clo., Orp.	124	EW103
Lanfranc Rd. E3	79	DY68	Langley Meadow, Loug.	39	ER40	Lansdowne Rd. SW20	103	CW94	Larkspur Clo., Ruis.	57	BQ59
Lanfrey Pl. W14	89	CZ78	Langley Oaks Ave.,	134	DU110	Lansdowne Rd. W11	75	CY73	Glovers Gro.		
North End Rd.			S.Croy.			Lansdowne Rd., Brom.	108	EG94	Larkway Clo. NW9	60	CR56
Lang Clo., Lthd.	142	CB123	Langley Pk. NW7	46	CS51	Lansdowne Rd., Croy.	120	DQ103	Larmans Rd., Enf.	36	DW36
Lang St. E1	78	DW70	Langley Pk. Rd., Sutt.	132	DC106	Lansdowne Rd., Epsom	130	CQ108	Larnach Rd. W6	89	CX79
Langaller La., Lthd.	142	CB122	Langley Rd. SW19	117	CZ95	Lansdowne Rd., Har.	59	CE59	Larne Rd., Ruis.	57	BT59
Langbourne Ave. N6	62	DG61	Langley Rd., Abb.L.	15	BS31	Lansdowne Rd., Houns.	86	CB83	Larner Rd., Erith	97	FE80
Langbourne Way, Esher	129	CG107	Langley Rd., Beck.	121	DY98	Lansdowne Rd., Ilf.	67	ET60	Larpent Ave. SW15	103	CW85
Langbrook Rd. SE3	94	EK83	Langley Rd., Islw.	87	CF82	Lansdowne Rd., Pur.	133	DN112	Larsen Dr., Wal.Abb.	23	ED34
Langcroft Clo., Cars.	118	DF104	Langley Rd., Kings L.	14	BH30	Lansdowne Rd., Sev.	155	FK122	Larwood Clo., Grnf.	59	CD64
Langdale Ave., Mitch.	118	DF97	Langley Rd., S.Croy.	135	DX109	Lansdowne Rd., Stai.	98	BH94	Las Palmas Est., Shep.	113	BQ101
Langdale Clo. SE17	92	DQ79	Langley Rd., Surb.	116	CL101	Lansdowne Rd., Stan.	45	CJ51	Lascelles Ave., Har.	59	CD59
Langdale Clo. SW14	88	CP84	Langley Rd., Wat.	29	BT39	Lansdowne Rd., Uxb.	71	BP72	Lascelles Clo. E11	65	ED61
Clifford Ave.			Langley Rd., Well.	96	EW79	Lansdowne Row W1	9	J2	Lascotts Rd. N22	49	DM51
Langdale Cres., Bexh.	96	FA80	Langley Row, Barn.	33	CZ39	Lansdowne Ter. WC1	6	A5	Lassa Rd. SE9	108	EL85
Langdale Dr., Hayes	71	BS68	Langley St. WC2	5	P9	Lansdowne Wk. W11	75	CZ74	Lassell St. SE10	93	ED78
Langdale Gdns., Grnf.	73	CH69	Langley Vale Rd., Epsom	144	CP120	Lansdowne Way SW8	91	DK81	Lasseter Pl. SE3	94	EF79
Langdale Gdns., Horn.	69	FG64	Langley Way, Wat.	29	BS40	Lansdowne Wd. Clo. SE27	105	DP90	Vanbrugh Hill		
Langdale Gdns., Wal.Cr.	37	DX35	Langley Way, W.Wick.	121	ED102	Lansfield Ave. N18	50	DU49	Lasterton St. E8	78	DV65
Langdale Rd. SE10	93	EC80	Langleybury La., Kings L.	29	BP37	Lant St. SE1	11	H4	Wilton Way		
Langdale Rd., Th.Hth.	119	DN98	Langmead Dr. (Bushey),	45	CD45	Lant St. SE1	92	DQ75	Latchett Rd. E18	52	EH53
Langdale St. E1	78	DV72	Wat.			Lantern Clo. SW15	89	CU84	Latchford Pl., Chig.	54	EV49
Burslem St.			Langmead St. SE27	105	DP91	Lantern Clo., Wem.	59	CK64	Manford Way		
Langdon Ct. NW10	74	CS67	Beadman St.			Lanterns Ct. E14	93	EA75	Latchingdon Ct. E17	65	DX56
Langdon Cres. E6	81	EN68	Langmore Ct., Bexh.	96	EX83	Lanvanor Rd. SE15	92	DW82	Latchingdon Gdns.,	52	EL51
Langdon Dr. NW9	60	CQ60	Regency Way			Lapford Clo. W9	75	CZ70	Wdf.Grn.		
Langdon Pk. Rd. N6	63	DJ59	Langport Ct., Walt.	114	BW102	Lapponum Wk., Hayes	72	BX71	Latchmere Clo., Rich.	102	CL92
Langdon Pl. SW14	88	CQ83	Langridge Ms., Hmptn.	100	BZ93	Lochan Clo.			Latchmere La., Kings.T.	102	CM93
Rosemary La.			Oak Ave.			Lapse Wd. Wk. SE23	106	DV89	Latchmere Pas. SW11	90	DE82
Langdon Rd. E6	81	EN67	Langroyd Rd. SW17	104	DF89	Lapstone Gdns., Har.	59	CJ58	Cabul Rd.		
Langdon Rd., Brom.	122	EH97	Langside Ave. SW15	89	CU84	Lapwing Clo., Erith	97	FH80	Latchmere Rd. SW11	90	DF82
Langdon Rd., Mord.	118	DC99	Langside Cres. N14	49	DK48	Lapwing Clo., S.Croy.	135	DY110	Latchmere Rd., Kings.T.	102	CL94
Langdon Shaw, Sid.	109	ET92	Langston Hughes Clo.	91	DP84	Lapwing Ct., Surb.	116	CN104	Latchmere St. SW11	90	DF82
Langdon Wk., Mord.	118	DC99	SE24			Chaffinch Clo.			Lateward Rd., Brent.	87	CK79
Langdon Bd.			Shakespeare Rd.			Lapwing Way, Abb.L.	23	DX31	Latham Clo. E6	80	EL72
Langdon Way SE1	92	DU77	Langston Rd., Loug.	39	EQ43	College Rd.			Latham Clo., Twick.	101	CG87
Simms Rd.			Langthorn Ct. EC2	7	L8	Lapwing Way, Hayes	72	BX72	Latham Clo., West.	150	EJ116
Langford Clo. E8	64	DU64	Langthorne Rd. E11	65	EC62	Lapworth Clo., Orp.	124	EW103	Latham Ho. E1	79	DX72
Langford Clo. N15	64	DS58	Langthorne St. SW6	89	CX81	Lara Clo. SE13	107	EC86	Latham Rd., Bexh.	110	FA85
Langford Clo. NW8	76	DC68	Langton Ave. E6	81	EN69	Lara Clo., Chess.	130	CL108	Latham Rd., Twick.	101	CF87
Langford Pl.			Langton Ave. N20	48	DC45	Larbert Rd. SW16	105	DJ94	Lathams Way, Croy.	119	DM102
Langford Ct. NW8	76	DC68	Langton Ave., Epsom	131	CT111	Larby Pl., Epsom	130	CS110	Lathkill Clo., Enf.	50	DT45
Langford Pl.			Langton Clo. WC1	6	C4	Larch Ave. W3	74	CS74	Lathom Rd. E6	80	EL66
Langford Cres., Barn.	34	DF42	Langton Clo., Add.	112	BH104	Larch Ave., St.Alb.	16	BY30	Latimer SE17	92	DS78
Langford Grn. SE5	92	DS83	Langton Gro., Nthwd.	43	BQ50	Larch Clo. E13	80	EH70	Beaconsfield Rd.		
Langford Pl. NW8	76	DC68	Langton Ri. SE23	106	DV87	Larch Clo. N11	48	DG52	Latimer Ave. E6	81	EM67
Langford Pl., Sid.	110	EU90	Langton Rd. NW2	61	CW62	Larch Clo. N19	63	DJ61	Latimer Clo., Pnr.	44	BW53
Langford Rd. SW6	90	DB82	Langton Rd. SW9	91	DP80	Bredgar Rd.			Latimer Clo., Wat.	43	BS45
Gilstead Rd.			Langton Rd., Har.	44	CC52	Larch Clo. SE8	93	DZ79	Latimer Clo., Wor.Pk.	131	CV105
Langford Rd., Barn.	34	DE42	Langton Rd., W.Mol.	114	CC99	Clyde St.			Latimer Gdns., Pnr.	44	BW53
Langford Rd., Wdf.Grn.	52	EJ51	Langton St. SW10	90	DC79	Larch Clo. SW12	105	DH88	Latimer Pl. W10	75	CW72
Langfords, Buck.H.	52	EK47	Langton Way SE3	94	EF81	Larch Clo., Tad.	146	DC121	Latimer Rd. E7	66	EH63
Langfords Way, Croy.	135	DY111	Langton Way, Croy.	120	DS104	Larch Clo., Wal.Cr.	22	DS27	Latimer Rd. N15	64	DS58
Langham Clo. N15	63	DP55	Langtry Rd. NW8	76	DB67	The Firs			Latimer Rd. SW19	104	DB93
Langham Rd.			Langtry Rd., Nthlt.	72	BX68	Larch Clo., Warl.	149	DY119	Latimer Rd. W10	75	CW71
Langham Dene, Ken.	147	DP115	Langtry Wk. NW8	76	DC66	Larch Cres., Epsom	130	CP107	Latimer Rd., Barn.	34	DB41
Langham Dr., Rom.	68	EV58	Alexandra Pl.			Larch Cres., Hayes	72	BW70	Latimer Rd., Croy.	119	DP104
Langham Gdns. N21	35	DN43	Langwood Chase, Tedd.	101	CJ93	Larch Dr. W4	88	CN78	Abbey Rd.		
Langham Gdns. W13	73	CH73	Langwood Gdns., Wat.	29	BU39	Gunnersbury Ave.			Latimer Rd., Tedd.	101	CF92
Langham Gdns., Edg.	46	CQ52	Langworth Dr., Hayes	71	BU72	Larch Grn. NW9	46	CS53	Latimer Rd. E1	79	DX71
Langham Gdns., Rich.	101	CJ91	Lanhill Rd. W9	76	DA70	Larch Gro., Sid.	109	ET88	Stepney Way		
Langham Gdns., Wem.	59	CJ61	Lanier Rd. SE13	107	EC86	Larch Ms. N19	63	DJ61	Latona Rd. SE15	92	DU79
Langham Ho. Clo., Rich.	101	CK91	Lanigan Dr., Houns.	100	CB85	Bredgar Rd.			Lattimer Pl. W4	89	CT80
Langham Pl. N15	63	DP55	Lankaster Gdns. N2	48	DD53	Larch Rd. E10	65	EA61	Lattimore Rd., Esher	128	CB105
Langham Pl. W1	5	J7	Lankers Dr., Har.	58	BZ58	Walnut Rd.			Latton Clo., Esher	114	BY101
Langham Pl. W1	77	DH71	Lankton Clo., Beck.	121	EC95	Larch Rd. NW2	61	CW63	Latton Clo., Walt.	114	BY101
Langham Pl. W4	88	CS79	Lannock Rd., Hayes	71	BS74	Larch Tree Way, Croy.	121	EA104	Latymer Clo., Wey.	127	BQ105
Hogarth Roundabout			Lannoy Rd. SE9	109	EQ88	Larch Wk., Swan.	125	FD96	Latymer Ct. W6	89	CX77
Langham Rd. N15	63	DP55	Lanrick Rd. E14	79	ED72	Larchdene, Orp.	123	EN103	Latymer Rd. N9	50	DT47
Langham Rd. SW20	117	CW95	Lanridge Rd. SE2	96	EX76	Larches, The N13	50	DQ48	Latymer Way N9	50	DR47
Langham Rd., Edg.	46	CQ51	Lansbury Ave. N18	50	DR50	Larches, The, Nthwd.	43	BQ51	Laud St. SE11	10	B10
Langham Rd., Tedd.	101	CH92	Lansbury Ave., Bark.	82	EU66	Larches, The, Uxb.	71	BP68	Laud St., Croy.	120	DQ104
Langham St. W1	5	J7	Lansbury Ave., Felt.	99	BV86	Larches, The, Wat.	30	BY43	Lauder Clo., Nthlt.	72	BX68
Langham St. W1	77	DH71	Lansbury Ave., Rom.	68	EY57	Larches Ave. SW14	88	CR84	Lauderdale Dr., Rich.	101	CK90
Langhedge Clo. N18	50	DT51	Lansbury Dr., Hayes	71	BS68	Larches Ave., Enf.	36	DW35	Lauderdale Pl. EC2	78	DQ71
Langhedge La.			Lansbury Est. E14	79	EB72	Larchwood Ave., Rom.	55	FB51	Aldersgate St.		
Langhedge La. N18	50	DT51	Lansbury Gdns. E14	79	EC72	Larchwood Clo., Bans.	145	CY115	Lauderdale Rd. W9	76	DB69
Langhedge La. Ind. Est.	50	DT51	Lansbury Rd., Enf.	37	DX39	Larchwood Clo., Rom.	55	FC51	Lauderdale Rd., Kings L.	15	BQ33
N18			Lansbury Way N18	50	DS50	Larchwood Rd. SE9	109	EP89			
Langholm Clo. SW12	105	DK87	Lansbury Ave.			Larcom St. SE17	11	J9			
King's Ave.			Lansdell Rd., Mitch.	118	DG96						

Lauderdale Twr. EC2	78	DQ71	Laurel Pk., Har.	45	CF52
Beech St.			Laurel Rd. SW13	89	CU82
Laughton Ct., Borwd.	32	CR40	Laurel Rd. SW20	117	CV95
Banks Rd.			Laurel Rd., Hmptn.	101	CD92
Laughton Rd., Nthlt.	72	BX67	Laurel St. E8	78	DT65
Launcelot Rd., Brom.	108	EG91	Laurel Vw. N12	48	DB48
Launcelot St. SE1	10	D5	Laurel Way E18	66	EF56
Launceston Gdns., Grnf.	73	CJ67	Laurel Way N20	48	DA48
Launceston Pl. W8	90	DC76	Laurels, The, Bans.	145	CZ117
Launceston Rd., Grnf.	73	CJ67	Laurels, The, Cob.	142	BY115
Launch St. E14	93	EC76	Laurels, The, Wal.Cr.	22	DS27
Laundress La. N16	64	DU62	Laurels, The, Wey.	113	BR104
Laundry La. N1	78	DQ67	Laurence Ms. W12	89	CU75
Greenman St.			Askew Rd.		
Laundry La., Wal.Abb.	24	EE25	Laurence Pountney Hill	7	K10
Laundry Rd. W6	89	CY79	EC4		
Laura Clo. E11	66	EJ57	Laurence Pountney La.	7	K10
Laura Clo., Enf.	36	DS43	EC4		
Laura Dr., Swan.	111	FG94	Laurie Gro. SE14	93	DY81
Laura Pl. E5	64	DW63	Laurie Rd. W7	73	CE71
Lauradale Rd. N2	62	DF56	Laurie Wk., Rom.	69	FE56
Laurel Ave., Twick.	101	CF88	Laurier Rd. NW5	63	DH62
Laurel Bank Gdns. SW6	89	CZ82	Laurier Rd., Croy.	120	DT101
New Kings Rd.			Laurimel Clo., Stan.	45	CH51
Laurel Bank Rd., Enf.	36	DQ39	September Way		
Laurel Bank Vill. W7	73	CE74	Laurino Pl. (Bushey), Wat.	44	CC47
Lower Boston Rd.			Lauriston Rd. E9	79	DX67
Laurel Clo. N19	63	DJ61	Lauriston Rd. SW19	103	CX93
Hargrave Pk.			Lausanne Rd. N8	63	DN56
Laurel Clo. SW17	104	DE92	Lausanne Rd. SE15	92	DW81
Laurel Clo., Ilf.	53	EQ51	Lauser Rd., Stai.	98	BJ87
Laurel Clo., Sid.	110	EU90	Lavell St. N16	64	DR63
Laurel Cres., Croy.	121	EA104	Lavender Ave. NW9	60	CQ60
Laurel Cres., Rom.	69	FE60	Lavender Ave., Mitch.	118	DE95
Laurel Dr. N21	49	DN45	Lavender Ave., Wor.Pk.	117	CW104
Laurel Flds., Pot.B.	19	CZ31	Lavender Clo. SW3	90	DD79
Laurel Gdns. E4	51	EB45	Danvers St.		
Laurel Gdns. NW7	46	CR48	Lavender Clo., Brom.	122	EL100
Laurel Gdns. W7	73	CE74	Lavender Clo., Cars.	133	DH105
Laurel Gdns., Houns.	86	BY84	Lavender Clo., Couls.	147	DJ119
Laurel Gro. SE20	106	DW94	Lavender Clo.	22	DT27
Laurel Gro. SE26	107	DX91	(Cheshunt), Wal.Cr.		
Laurel La., West Dr.	84	BL77	Lavender Ct., W.Mol.	114	CB97
Laurel Lo. La., Barn.	33	CW36	Molesham Way		
Dancers La.			Lavender Gdns. SW11	90	DF84
Laurel Pk., Har.	45	CF52	Lavender Gdns., Enf.	35	DP39
Laurel Rd. SW13	89	CU82	Lavender Gdns., Har.	45	CE51
			Uxbridge Rd.		
			Lavender Gro. E8	78	DU66
			Lavender Gro., Mitch.	118	DE95
			Lavender Hill SW11	90	DF84
			Lavender Hill, Enf.	35	DN39
			Lavender Hill, Swan.	125	FD97
			Lavender Ms., Wall.	133	DL107
			Lavender Pk. Rd.,	126	BG112
			W.Byf.		
			Lavender Pl., Ilf.	67	EP64
			Lavender Ri., West Dr.	84	BN75
			Lavender Rd. SE16	79	DY74
			Lavender Rd. SW11	90	DD83
			Lavender Rd., Cars.	132	DG105
			Lavender Rd., Croy.	119	DM100
			Lavender Rd., Enf.	36	DR39
			Lavender Rd., Epsom	130	CP106
			Lavender Rd., Sutt.	132	DD105
			Lavender Rd., Uxb.	70	BM71
			Lavender Sq. E11	65	ED62
			Anglian Rd.		
			Lavender St. E15	80	EE65
			Manbey Gro.		
			Lavender Sweep SW11	90	DF84

Lavender Ter. SW11 90 DE83
Falcon Rd.
Lavender Vale, Wall. 133 DK107
Lavender Wk. SW11 90 DF84
Lavender Wk., Mitch. 118 DG97
Lavender Way, Croy. 121 DX100
Lavengro Rd. SE27 106 DQ89
Lavenham Rd. SW18 103 CZ89
Lavernock Rd., Bexh. 96 FA82
Lavers Rd. N16 64 DS62
Laverstoke Gdns. SW15 103 CT87
Laverton Ms. SW5 90 DB77
Laverton Pl.
Laverton Pl. SW5 90 DB77
Lavidge Rd. SE9 108 EL89
Lavina Gro. N1 77 DM68
Wharfdale Rd.
Lavington Rd. W13 73 CH74
Lavington Rd., Croy. 119 DM104
Lavington St. SE1 10 G3
Lavington St. SE1 77 DP74
Lavinia Ave., Wat. 16 BX34
Lavrock La., Rick. 42 BM45
Law Ho., Bark. 82 EU68
Law St. SE1 11 L6
Law St. SE1 92 DR76
Lawdons Gdns., Croy. 133 DP105
Lawford Clo., Wall. 133 DL109
Lawford Gdns., Ken. 148 DQ116
Lawford Rd. N1 78 DS66
Lawford Rd. NW5 77 DJ65
Lawford Rd. W4 88 CQ80
Lawless St. E14 79 EB73
Lawley Rd. N14 49 DH45
Lawley St. E5 64 DW63
Lawn, The, Sthl. 86 CA78
Lawn Ave., West Dr. 84 BJ75
Lawn Clo. N9 50 DT45
Lawn Clo., Brom. 108 EH93
Lawn Clo., N.Mal. 116 CS96
Lawn Clo., Ruis. 57 BT62
Lawn Clo., Swan. 125 FC96
Lawn Cres., Rich. 88 CN82
Lawn Fm. Gro., Rom. 68 EY56
Lawn Gdns. W7 73 CE74
Lawn Ho. Clo. E14 93 EC75
Lawn La. SW8 91 DL79
Lawn Pk., Sev. 155 FH127
Lawn Pl. SE15 92 DT81
Sumner Est.
Lawn Rd. NW3 62 DF64
Lawn Rd., Beck. 107 DZ94
Lawn Rd., Uxb. 70 BJ66
New Windsor St.
Lawn Ter. SE3 94 EE83
Lawn Vale, Pnr. 44 BY54
Lawnfield NW2 75 CX66
Coverdale Rd.
Lawns, The E4 51 EA50
Lawns, The SE3 94 EE83
Lee Ter.
Lawns, The SE19 120 DR95
Lawns, The, Pnr. 44 CB52
Lawns, The, Sid. 110 EV91
Lawns, The, Sutt. 131 CY108
Lawnside SE3 94 EF84
Lawnsway, Rom. 55 FC52
Lawrance Gdns. (Cheshunt), Wal.Cr. 23 DX28
Lawrence Ave. E12 67 EN63
Lawrence Ave. E17 51 DX53
Lawrence Ave. N13 49 DP49
Lawrence Ave. NW7 46 CS49
Lawrence Ave., N.Mal. 116 CR100
Lawrence Bldgs. N16 64 DT62
Lawrence Campe Clo. N20 48 DD48
Friern Barnet La.
Lawrence Clo. E3 79 EA69
Lawrence Clo. N15 64 DS55
Lawrence Rd.
Lawrence Ct. NW7 46 CS50
Lawrence Cres., Dag. 69 FB62
Lawrence Cres., Edg. 46 CN54
Lawrence Dr., Uxb. 57 BQ63
Lawrence Est., Houns. 86 BW84
Lawrence Gdns. NW7 47 CT48
Lawrence Hill E4 51 EA47
Lawrence La. EC2 7 J9
Lawrence Pl. N1 77 DL67
Outram Pl.
Lawrence Rd. E6 80 EL67
Lawrence Rd. E13 80 EH67
Lawrence Rd. N15 64 DS56
Lawrence Rd. N18 50 DV49
Lawrence Rd. SE25 120 DT98
Lawrence Rd. W5 87 CK77
Lawrence Rd., Erith 97 FB80
Sussex Rd.
Lawrence Rd., Hmptn. 100 BZ94
Lawrence Rd., Hayes 71 BQ68
Lawrence Rd., Houns. 86 BW84
Lawrence Rd., Pnr. 58 BX58
Lawrence Rd., Rich. 101 CJ91
Lawrence Rd., Rom. 69 FH57
Lawrence Rd., W.Wick. 136 EG105
Lawrence St. E16 80 EF71
Lawrence St. NW7 47 CT50
Lawrence St. SW3 90 DE79
Lawrence Way NW10 60 CQ63
Lawrence Weaver Clo., Mord. 118 DB100
Green La.
Lawrie Pk. Ave. SE26 106 DV92
Lawrie Pk. Cres. SE26 106 DV92
Lawrie Pk. Gdns. SE26 106 DV91
Lawrie Pk. Rd. SE26 106 DV93
Lawson Clo. E16 80 EJ71
Lawson Clo. SW19 103 CX90
Lawson Est. SE1 11 K7
Lawson Gdns., Pnr. 57 BV55
Lawson Rd., Enf. 36 DW39
Lawson Rd., Sthl. 72 BZ70
Lawton Rd. E3 79 DY69
Lawton Rd. E10 65 ED60
Lawton Rd., Barn. 34 DD41
Lawton Rd., Loug. 39 EP40
Laxcon Clo. NW10 60 CQ64
Laxey Rd., Orp. 137 ET107
Laxley Clo. SE5 91 DP80
Laxton Pl. NW1 5 J4
Layard Rd. SE16 92 DV77
Layard Rd., Enf. 36 DT39
Layard Rd., Th.Hth. 120 DR96
Layard Sq. SE16 92 DV77
Laycock St. N1 77 DN65
Layer Gdns. W3 74 CN73
Layfield Clo. NW4 61 CV59
Layfield Cres. NW4 61 CV59
Layfield Rd. NW4 61 CV59
Layhams Rd., Kes. 136 EF106
Layhams Rd., W.Wick. 121 ED104
Laymarsh Clo., Belv. 96 EZ76
Laymead Clo., Nthlt. 72 BY65
Laystall St. EC1 6 D5
Laystall St. EC1 77 DN70
Layton Ct., Wey. 127 BP105
Castle Vw. Rd.
Layton Cres., Croy. 133 DN106
Layton Rd. N1 77 DN68
Parkfield St.
Layton Rd., Brent. 87 CK78
Layton Rd., Houns. 86 CB84
Laytons Bldgs. SE1 11 K4
Laytons La., Sun. 113 BT96
Layzell Wk. SE9 108 EK88
Mottingham La.
Lazar Wk. N7 63 DM61
Briset Way
Le Corte Clo., Kings L. 14 BM29
Le May Ave. SE12 108 EH90
Le Personne Rd., Cat. 148 DR122
Lea Bri. Rd. E5 64 DV62
Lea Bri. Rd. E10 65 EA59
Lea Bri. Rd. E17 65 ED57
Lea Bushes, Wat. 30 CA35
Lea Clo. (Bushey), Wat. 30 CB43
Lea Cres., Ruis. 57 BT63
Lea Gdns., Wem. 60 CM63
Lea Hall Rd. E10 65 EA60
Lea Mt., Wal.Cr. 22 DS28
Lea Rd., Beck. 121 EA96
Fairfield Rd.
Lea Rd., Enf. 36 DR39
Lea Rd., Sev. 155 FJ127
Lea Rd., Sthl. 86 BY77
Lea Rd., Wal.Abb. 23 EA34
Lea Rd. Trd. Est., Wal.Abb. 23 EA34
Lea Side Ind. Est., Enf. 37 DZ41
Lea Vale, Dart. 97 FD84
Lea Valley Rd. E4 37 DX43
Lea Valley Rd., Enf. 37 DX43
Lea Valley Viaduct E4 51 DX50
Lea Valley Viaduct N18 51 DX50
Lea Vw. Hos. E5 64 DV60
Springfield
Leabank Clo., Har. 59 CE62
Leabank Sq. E9 79 EA65
Leabank Vw. N15 64 DU58
Leabourne Rd. N16 64 DU58
Leach Gro., Lthd. 143 CJ122
Leacroft, Stai. 98 BG92
Leacroft Ave. SW12 104 DF87
Leacroft Clo., Ken. 148 DQ116
Leacroft Clo., Stai. 98 BH91
Leacroft Clo., West Dr. 70 BL72
Leadale Ave. E4 51 DZ47
Leadale Rd. N15 64 DU58
Leadale Rd. N16 64 DU58
Leadbeaters Clo. N11 48 DF50
Goldsmith Rd.
Leadenhall Mkt. EC3 7 M9
Leadenhall Pl. EC3 7 M9
Leadenhall St. EC3 7 M9
Leadenhall St. EC3 78 DS72
Leader Ave. E12 67 EN64
Leadings, The, Wem. 60 CQ62
Leaf Clo., Nthwd. 43 BR52
Leaf Clo., T.Ditt. 115 CE99
Leaf Gro. SE27 105 DN92
Leafield Clo. SW16 105 DP93
Leafield La., Sid. 110 EZ91
Leafield Rd. SW20 117 CZ97
Leafield Rd., Sutt. 118 DA103
Leaford Cres., Wat. 29 BT37
Leaforis Rd., Wal.Cr. 22 DU28
Leafy Gro., Kes. 136 EJ106
Leafy Oak Rd. SE12 108 EJ91
Leafy Way, Croy. 120 DT103
Leagrave St. E5 64 DW62
Leaholme Way, Ruis. 57 BQ58
Leahurst Rd. SE13 107 ED85
Leake Ct. SE1 10 C4
Leake St. SE1 10 C4
Leake St. SE1 91 DM75
Lealand Rd. N15 64 DT58
Leamington Ave. E17 65 EA57
Leamington Ave., Brom. 108 EJ92
Leamington Ave., Mord. 117 CY98
Leamington Ave., Orp. 137 ES105
Leamington Clo. E12 67 EM64
Leamington Clo., Brom. 108 EJ91
Leamington Clo., Houns. 100 CC85
Leamington Cres., Har. 58 BY62
Leamington Gdns., Ilf. 67 ET61
Leamington Pk. W3 74 CR71
Leamington Pl., Hayes 71 BT70
Leamington Rd., Sthl. 86 BX77
Leamington Rd. Vill. W11 75 CZ71
Leamore St. W6 89 CV77
Leamouth Rd. E6 80 EL72
Leamouth Rd. E14 79 ED72
Leander Ct. SE8 93 EA81
Leander Gdns., Wat. 30 BY37
Leander Rd. SW2 105 DM87
Leander Rd., Nthlt. 72 CA68
Leander Rd., Th.Hth. 119 DM98
Learoyd Gdns. E6 81 EN73
Leas, The, Stai. 98 BG91
Leas, The (Bushey), Wat. 30 BZ39
Leas Clo., Chess. 130 CM108
Leas Dale SE9 109 EN90
Leas Grn., Chis. 109 ET93
Leas La., Warl. 149 DX118
Leas Rd., Warl. 149 DX118
Leaside, Lthd. 142 CA123
Leaside Ave. N10 62 DG55
Leaside Ct., Uxb. 71 BP69
The Larches
Leaside Rd. E5 64 DW60
Leasowes Rd. E10 65 EA60
Leathart Clo., Horn. 83 FH66
Dowding Way
Leather Bottle La., Belv. 96 EZ77
St. Augustine's Rd.
Leather Clo., Mitch. 118 DG96
Leather Gdns. E15 80 EE67
Abbey Rd.
Leather La. EC1 6 D6
Leather La. EC1 77 DN70
Leatherbottle Grn., Erith 96 EZ76
Leatherdale St. E1 78 DW70
Portelet Rd.
Leatherhead Bypass Rd., Lthd. 143 CH120
Leatherhead Clo. N16 64 DS60
Leatherhead Ind. Est., Lthd. 143 CG121
Station Rd.
Leatherhead Rd., Ash. 143 CK121
Leatherhead Rd., Chess. 129 CJ111
Leatherhead Rd. (Great Bookham), Lthd. 143 CK121
Leatherhead Rd. (Oxshott), Lthd. 129 CD114
Leathermarket Ct. SE1 92 DS75
Leathermarket St. SE1 11 M5
Leathermarket St. SE1 92 DS75
Leathersellers Clo., Barn. 33 CY42
The Ave.
Leathsail Rd., Har. 58 CB62
Leathwaite Rd. SW11 90 DF84
Leathwell Rd. SE8 93 EB82
Leaveland Clo., Beck. 121 EA98
Leaver Gdns., Grnf. 73 CD68
Leaves Grn. Cres., Kes. 136 EJ111
Leaves Grn. Rd., Kes. 136 EK111
Leavesden Rd., Stan. 45 CG51
Leavesden Rd., Wat. 29 BV38
Leavesden Rd., Wey. 127 BP106
Leaview, Wal.Abb. 23 EB33
Leaway E10 65 DX60
Leazes Ave., Cat. 147 DN124
Lebanon Ave., Felt. 100 BX92
Lebanon Clo., Wat. 29 BR36
Lebanon Ct., Twick. 101 CH87
Lebanon Dr., Cob. 128 CA113
Lebanon Gdns. SW18 104 DA85
Lebanon Gdns., West. 150 EK117
Lebanon Pk., Twick. 101 CH87
Lebanon Rd. SW18 104 DA85
Lebanon Rd., Croy. 120 DS102
Lebrun Sq. SE3 94 EH84
Lechmere App., Wdf.Grn. 52 EJ54
Lechmere Ave., Chig. 53 EQ49
Lechmere Ave., Wdf.Grn. 52 EK54
Lechmere Rd. NW2 75 CV65
Leckford Rd. SW18 104 DC89
Leckwith Ave., Bexh. 96 EY79
Lecky St. SW7 90 DD78
Leconfield Ave. SW13 89 CT83
Leconfield Rd. N5 64 DR63
Leda Ave., Enf. 37 DX38
Leda Rd. SE18 95 EM76
Ledbury Est. SE15 92 DV80
Ledbury Ms. N. W11 76 DA73
Ledbury Rd.
Ledbury Ms. W. W11 76 DA73
Ledbury Rd.
Ledbury Pl., Croy. 134 DQ105
Ledbury Rd.
Ledbury Rd. W11 75 CZ72
Ledbury Rd., Croy. 134 DQ105
Ledbury St. SE15 92 DU80
Ledgers Rd., Warl. 149 EB119
Ledrington Rd. SE19 106 DU93
Anerley Hill
Ledway Dr., Wem. 60 CM59
Lee Ave., Rom. 68 EY58
Lee Bri. SE13 93 EC83
Lee Ch. St. SE13 94 EE84
Lee Clo. E17 51 DX53
Lee Clo., Barn. 34 DC42
Lee Conservancy Rd. E9 65 DZ64
Lee Grn. SE12 108 EF85
Lee Grn., Orp. 124 EU99
Lee Grn. La., Epsom 144 CP124
Lee Gro., Chig. 53 EN47
Lee High Rd. SE12 94 EF84
Lee High Rd. SE13 93 ED84
Lee Pk. SE3 94 EF84
Lee Pk. Way N9 51 DY48
Lee Pk. Way N18 51 DX50
Lee Rd. NW7 47 CX52
Lee Rd. SE3 94 EF83
Lee Rd. SW19 118 DB95
Lee Rd., Enf. 36 DU44
Lee Rd., Grnf. 73 CJ67
Lee St. E8 78 DT67
Lee Ter. SE3 94 EE83
Lee Ter. SE13 94 EE83
Lee Valley Trd. Est. N18 51 DX50
Lee Vw., Enf. 35 DP39
Leechcroft Ave., Sid. 109 ET85
Leechcroft Ave., Swan. 125 FF97
Leechcroft Rd., Wall. 118 DG104
Leecroft Rd., Barn. 33 CY43
Leeds Clo., Orp. 124 EX103
Leeds Pl. N4 63 DM61
Tollington Pk.
Leeds Rd., Ilf. 67 ER60
Leeds St. N18 50 DU50
Leefe Way, Pot.B. 21 DK28
Leefern Rd. W12 89 CU75
Leegate SE12 108 EF85
Leeke St. WC1 6 B2
Leeke St. WC1 77 DM69
Leeland Rd. W13 73 CG74
Leeland Ter. W13 73 CG74
Leeland Way NW10 61 CT63
Leeming Rd., Borwd. 32 CM39
Leerdam Dr. E14 93 EC76
Lees, The, Croy. 121 DZ103
Lees Ave., Nthwd. 43 BT54
Lees Pl. W1 4 F10
Lees Pl. W1 76 DG73
Lees Rd., Uxb. 71 BP70
Leeside, Barn. 33 CY43
Leeside, Pot.B. 21 DD31
Wayside
Leeside Cres. NW11 61 CY58
Leeside Rd. N17 50 DV51
Leeson Rd. SE24 91 DN84
Leesons Hill, Chis. 123 ES97
Leesons Hill, Orp. 124 EU97
Leesons Way, Orp. 123 ET96
Leeward Gdns. SW19 103 CZ92
Leeway SE8 93 DZ78
Leeway Clo., Pnr. 44 BZ52
Leewood Clo. SE12 108 EF86
Upwood Rd.
Leewood Pl., Swan. 125 FD98
Lefevre Wk. E3 79 DZ67
Old Ford Rd.
Lefroy Rd. W12 89 CT75
Legard Rd. N5 63 DP62
Legatt Rd. SE9 108 EK85
Leggatt Rd. E15 79 EC68
Leggatts Clo., Wat. 29 BT36
Leggatts Ri., Wat. 29 BU35
Leggatts Way, Wat. 29 BT36
Leggatts Wd. Ave., Wat. 29 BV36
Legge St. SE13 107 EC85
Leghorn Rd. NW10 75 CT68
Leghorn Rd. SE18 95 ER78
Legion Clo. N1 77 DN66
Legion Ct., Mord. 118 DA100
Legion Rd., Grnf. 72 CC67
Legion Way N12 48 DE52
Downway
Legon Ave., Rom. 69 FC60
Legrace Ave., Houns. 86 BX82
Leicester Ave., Mitch. 119 DL98
Leicester Clo., Wor.Pk. 131 CW105
Leicester Ct. WC2 5 N10
Leicester Gdns., Ilf. 67 ES59
Leicester Pl. WC2 5 N10
Leicester Rd. E11 66 EH57
Leicester Rd. N2 62 DE55
Leicester Rd. NW10 74 CR66
Leicester Rd., Barn. 34 DB43
Leicester Rd., Croy. 120 DS101
Leicester Sq. WC2 9 N1
Leicester Sq. WC2 77 DK73
Leicester St. WC2 5 N10
Leigh Ave., Ilf. 66 EK56
Leigh Clo., N.Mal. 116 CR98
Leigh Cor., Cob. 128 BW114
Leigh Hill Rd.
Leigh Ct., Borwd. 32 CR40
Banks Rd.
Leigh Ct., Har. 59 CE60
Leigh Ct. Clo., Cob. 128 BW114
Leigh Cres., Croy. 135 EB108
Leigh Gdns. NW10 75 CW68
Leigh Hill Rd., Cob. 128 BW114
Leigh Hunt Dr. N14 49 DK46
Leigh Hunt St. SE1 11 H4
Leigh Orchard Clo. SW16 105 DM90
Leigh Pl. EC1 77 DN71
Baldwin's Gdns.
Leigh Pl., Cob. 128 BW114
Leigh Pl., Well. 96 EU82
Leigh Rd. E6 81 EN65
Leigh Rd. E10 65 EC59
Leigh Rd. N5 63 DP63
Leigh Rd., Cob. 127 BV113
Leigh Rd., Houns. 87 CD84
Leigh Rodd, Wat. 44 BZ48
Leigh St. WC1 5 P4
Leigh St. WC1 77 DL70
Leigh Ter., Orp. 124 EV97
Saxville Rd.
Leigham Ave. SW16 105 DL90
Leigham Ct. Rd. SW16 105 DL89
Leigham Dr., Islw. 87 CE80
Leigham Vale SW2 105 DN89
Leigham Vale SW16 105 DM90
Leighton Ave. E12 67 EN64
Leighton Ave., Pnr. 58 BY55
Leighton Clo., Edg. 46 CN54
Leighton Cres. NW5 63 DJ64
Leighton Gro.
Leighton Gdns. NW10 75 CV68
Leighton Gdns., S.Croy. 134 DV113
Leighton Gro. NW5 63 DJ64
Leighton Pl. NW5 63 DJ64
Leighton Rd. NW5 63 DJ64
Leighton Rd. W13 87 CG75
Leighton Rd., Enf. 36 DT43
Leighton Rd., Har. 45 CD54
Leighton St., Croy. 119 DP102
Leighton Way, Epsom 130 CR114
Leila Parnell Pl. SE7 94 EJ79
Leinster Ave. SW14 88 CQ83
Leinster Gdns. W2 76 DC72
Leinster Ms. W2 76 DC73
Leinster Pl. W2 76 DC72
Leinster Rd. N10 63 DH56
Leinster Rd. NW6 76 DA69
Stafford Rd.
Leinster Sq. W2 76 DA72
Leinster Ter. W2 76 DC73
Leisure La., W.Byf. 126 BH112
Leith Clo. NW9 60 CR60
Leith Hill, Orp. 124 EU95
Leith Hill Grn., Orp. 124 EU95
Leith Hill
Leith Rd. N22 49 DP53
Leith Rd., Epsom 130 CS112
Leith Yd. NW6 76 DA67
Quex Rd.
Leithcote Gdns. SW16 105 DM91
Leithcote Path SW16 105 DM90
Lela Ave., Houns. 86 BW82
Lelitia Clo. E8 78 DU67
Pownall Rd.
Leman St. E1 78 DT72
Lemark Clo., Stan. 45 CJ50
Lemmon Rd. SE10 94 EE79
Lemna Rd. E11 66 EE59
Lemonfield Dr., Wat. 16 BY33
Lemonwell Ct. SE9 109 EQ85
Lemonwell Dr.
Lemonwell Dr. SE9 109 EQ85
Lemsford Clo. N15 64 DU57
Lemsford Ct. N4 64 DQ61
Brownswood Rd.
Lemsford Ct., Borwd. 32 CQ42
Lemuel St. SW18 104 DB86
St. Ann's Hill
Len Freeman Pl. SW6 89 CZ80
John Smith Ave.
Lena Gdns. W6 89 CW76
Lena Kennedy Clo. E4 51 EC51
Lenanton Steps E14 93 EA75
Manilla St.
Lendal Ter. SW4 91 DK83
Lenelby Rd., Surb. 116 CN102
Lenham Rd. SE12 94 EF84
Lenham Rd., Bexh. 96 EZ79
Lenham Rd., Sutt. 132 DB105
Lenham Rd., Th.Hth. 120 DR96
Lennard Ave., W.Wick. 122 EE103
Lennard Clo., W.Wick. 122 EE103
Lennard Rd. SE20 107 DX93
Lennard Rd., Beck. 107 DY94
Lennard Rd., Brom. 123 EM102
Lennard Rd., Croy. 120 DQ102
Lennard Rd., Sev. 153 FE120
Lennon Rd. NW2 75 CW65
Lennox Clo., Rom. 69 FF58
Lennox Gdns. NW10 61 CT63
Lennox Gdns. SW1 8 D7
Lennox Gdns. SW1 90 DF76
Lennox Gdns., Croy. 133 DP105
Lennox Gdns., Ilf. 67 EM60
Lennox Gdns. Ms. SW1 8 D7
Lennox Gdns. Ms. SW1 90 DF76
Lennox Rd. E17 65 DZ58
Lennox Rd. N4 63 DM61
Lenor Clo., Bexh. 96 EY84
Lens Rd. E7 80 EJ66
Lensbury Clo. (Cheshunt), Wal.Cr. 23 DY28
Ashdown Cres.
Lensbury Way SE2 96 EW76
Lenthall Pl. SW7 90 DC77
Gloucester Rd.
Lenthall Rd. E8 78 DT66
Lenthall Rd., Loug. 39 ER42
Lenthorp Rd. SE10 94 EF77
Lentmead Rd., Brom. 108 EF90
Lenton Ri., Rich. 88 CL83
Evelyn Ter.
Lenton St. SE18 95 ER77
Lenville Way SE16 92 DU78
Catlin St.
Leo St. SE15 92 DV80
Leo Yd. EC1 6 G5
Leof Cres. SE6 107 EB92
Leominster Rd., Mord. 118 DC100
Leominster Wk., Mord. 118 DC100
Leonard Ave., Mord. 118 DC99
Leonard Ave., Rom. 69 FD60
Leonard Ave., Sev. 153 FH116
Leonard Rd. E4 51 EA51
Leonard Rd. E7 66 EG63
Leonard Rd. N9 50 DT48
Leonard Rd. SW16 119 DJ95
Leonard Rd., Sthl. 86 BX76
Leonard Robbins Path SE28 82 EV73
Tawney Rd.
Leonard St. E16 80 EL74
Leonard St. EC2 7 L4

Lowden Rd. SE24 92 DQ84
Lowden Rd., Sthl. 72 BY73
Lowe, The, Chig. 54 EU49
Lowe Ave. E16 80 EG71
Charford Rd.
Lowe Clo., Chig. 54 EU50
Lowell St. E14 79 DY72
Lowen Rd., Rain. 83 FD68
Lower Aberdeen Wf. E14 79 DZ74
Westferry Rd.
Lower Addiscombe Rd., Croy. 120 DS102
Lower Addison Gdns. W14 89 CY75
Lower Alderton Hall La., Loug. 39 EN43
Lower Barn Rd., Pur. 134 DR113
Lower Bedfords Rd., Rom. 55 FE51
Lower Belgrave St. SW1 9 H7
Lower Belgrave St. SW1 91 DH76
Lower Boston Rd. W7 73 CE74
Lower Broad St., Dag. 82 FA67
Lower Bury La., Epp. 25 ES31
Lower Camden, Chis. 109 EM94
Lower Ch. St., Croy. 119 DP103
Waddon New Rd.
Lower Clapton Rd. E5 64 DW64
Lower Clarendon Wk. W11 75 CY72
Lancaster Rd.
Lower Common S. SW15 89 CV83
Lower Coombe St., Croy. 134 DQ105
Lower Ct. Rd., Epsom 130 CQ111
Lower Cft., Swan. 125 FF98
Lower Downs Rd. SW20 117 CX95
Lower Drayton Pl., Croy. 119 DP103
Drayton Rd.
Lower Dunnymans, Bans. 131 CZ114
Basing Rd.
Lower Fm. Rd., Lthd. 141 BV124
Lower George St., Rich. 101 CK85
George St.
Lower Gravel Rd., Brom. 122 EL102
Lower Grn. Rd., Esher 114 CB103
Lower Grn. W., Mitch. 118 DE97
Lower Grosvenor Pl. SW1 9 H6
Lower Grosvenor Pl. SW1 91 DH76
Lower Gro. Rd., Rich. 102 CM86
Lower Hall La. E4 51 DY50
Lower Ham Rd., Kings.T. 101 CK93
Lower Hampton Rd., Sun. 114 BW97
Lower High St., Wat. 30 BW42
Lower Hill Rd., Epsom 130 CP112
Lower James St. W1 5 L10
Lower John St. W1 5 L10
Lower Kenwood Ave., Enf. 35 DK43
Lower Lea Crossing E14 80 EE73
Lower Maidstone Rd. N11 49 DJ51
Telford Rd.
Lower Mall W6 89 CV78
Lower Mardyke Ave., Rain. 83 FC68
Lower Marsh SE1 10 D5
Lower Marsh SE1 91 DM75
Lower Marsh La., Kings.T. 116 CM98
Lower Meadow, Wal.Cr. 23 DX27
Lower Merton Ri. NW3 76 DE66
Lower Morden La., Mord. 117 CX100
Lower Mortlake Rd., Rich. 88 CL84
Lower Northfield, Bans. 131 CZ114
Lower Paddock Rd., Wat. 30 BY44
Lower Pk. Rd. N11 49 DJ50
Lower Pk. Rd., Belv. 96 FA76
Lower Pk. Rd., Couls. 146 DE118
Lower Pk. Rd., Loug. 38 EK43
Lower Plantation, Rick. 28 BJ41
Lower Queens Rd., Buck.H. 52 EK47
Lower Richmond Rd. SW14 88 CP83
Lower Richmond Rd. SW15 89 CV83
Lower Richmond Rd., Rich. 88 CN83
Lower Rd. SE8 93 DX77
Lower Rd. SE16 92 DW76
Lower Rd., Belv. 97 FB76
Lower Rd., Erith 97 FD77
Lower Rd., Har. 59 CD60
Lower Rd., Hem.H. 14 BN25
Lower Rd., Ken. 133 DP113
Lower Rd., Lthd. 143 CD123
Lower Rd., Loug. 39 EN39
Lower Rd., Orp. 124 EV100
Lower Rd., Sutt. 132 DC105
Lower Rd., Swan. 111 FF94
Lower Robert St. WC2 10 A1
Lower Sawley Wd., Bans. 131 CZ114
Upper Sawley Wd.
Lower Shott (Cheshunt), Wal.Cr. 22 DT26
Lower Sloane St. SW1 8 F9
Lower Sloane St. SW1 90 DG77
Lower Sq., Islw. 87 CH83
Lower Sta. Rd. (Crayford), Dart. 111 FE86
Lower Strand NW9 47 CT54
Lower Sunbury Rd., Hmptn. 114 BZ96
Lower Swaines, Epp. 25 ES30
Lower Sydenham Ind. Est. SE26 107 DZ92
Lower Tail, Wat. 44 BY48
Lower Talbot Wk. W11 75 CY72
Lancaster Rd.
Lower Teddington Rd., Kings.T. 101 CK94
Lower Ter. NW3 62 DC62
Lower Thames St. EC3 11 L1
Lower Thames St. EC3 78 DR73
Lower Tub (Bushey), Wat. 45 CD45
Lower Wd. Rd., Esher 129 CG107
Lowestoft Clo. E5 64 DW61
Theydon Rd.
Lowestoft Rd., Wat. 29 BV39
Loweswater Clo., Wat. 16 BW33
Loweswater Clo., Wem. 59 CK61
Lowfield Rd. NW6 76 DA66
Lowfield Rd. W3 74 CQ72
Lowick Rd., Har. 59 CE56
Lowlands Dr., Stai. 98 BK85
Lowlands Gdns., Rom. 69 FB58
Lowlands Rd., Har. 59 CE58
Lowlands Rd., Pnr. 58 BW58
Lowman Rd. N7 63 DM63
Lowndes Clo. SW1 8 G7
Lowndes Clo. SW1 90 DG76
Lowndes Pl. SW1 8 F7
Lowndes Pl. SW1 90 DG76
Lowndes Sq. SW1 8 E5
Lowndes Sq. SW1 90 DF75
Lowndes St. SW1 8 E6
Lowndes St. SW1 90 DF76
Lowood Ct. SE19 106 DT92
Lowood St. E1 78 DV73
Dellow St.
Lowry Cres., Mitch. 118 DE96
Lowry Rd., Dag. 68 EV64
Lowshoe La., Rom. 54 FA53
Lowson Gro., Wat. 44 BY45
Lowswood Clo., Nthwd. 43 BQ53
Lowth Rd. SE5 92 DQ82
Lowther Clo., Borwd. 32 CM43
Lowther Dr., Enf. 35 DL42
Lowther Gdns. SW7 90 DD75
Prince Consort Rd.
Lowther Hill SE23 107 DY87
Lowther Rd. E17 51 DY54
Lowther Rd. N7 63 DN64
Mackenzie Rd.
Lowther Rd. SW13 89 CT81
Lowther Rd., Kings.T. 116 CM95
Lowther Rd., Stan. 60 CM55
Loxford Ave. E6 80 EK68
Loxford La., Ilf. 67 EQ64
Loxford Rd., Bark. 81 EP65
Loxham Rd. E4 51 EA52
Loxham St. WC1 6 A3
Loxley Clo. SE26 107 DX92
Loxley Rd. SW18 104 DD88
Loxley Rd., Hmptn. 100 BZ91
Loxton Rd. SE23 107 DX88
Loxwood Clo., Felt. 99 BR88
Loxwood Clo., Orp. 124 EX103
Loxwood Rd. N17 64 DS55
Lubbock Rd., Chis. 109 EM94
Lubbock St. SE14 92 DW80
Lucan Dr., Stai. 98 BK94
Lucan Pl. SW3 8 B9
Lucan Pl. SW3 90 DE77
Lucan Rd., Barn. 33 CY41
Lucas Ave. E13 80 EH67
Lucas Ave., Har. 58 CA61
Lucas Ct., Har. 58 CA60
Lucas Ct., Wal.Abb. 24 EF33
Lucas Rd. SE20 106 DW93
Lucas Sq. NW11 62 DA58
Hampstead Way
Lucas St. SE8 93 EA81
Lucerne Clo. N13 49 DL48
Lucerne Ct., Erith 96 EY76
Middle Way
Lucerne Gro. E17 65 ED56
Lucerne Ms. W8 76 DA74
Kensington Mall
Lucerne Rd. N5 63 DP63
Lucerne Rd., Orp. 123 ET102
Lucerne Rd., Th.Hth. 119 DP99
Lucey Rd. SE16 92 DU76
Lucey Way SE16 92 DU76
Linsey St.
Lucie Ave., Ashf. 99 BP93
Lucien Rd. SW17 104 DG91
Lucien Rd. SW19 104 DB89
Lucknow St. SE18 95 ES80
Lucorn Clo. SE12 108 EF86
Lucton Ms., Loug. 39 EP42
Luctons Ave., Buck.H. 52 EJ46
Lucy Cres. W3 74 CQ71
Lucy Gdns., Dag. 68 EY62
Grafton Rd.
Luddesdon Rd., Erith 96 FA79
Ludford Clo. NW9 46 CS54
Ludford Clo., Croy. 133 DP105
Warrington Rd.
Ludgate Bdy. EC4 6 F9
Ludgate Bdy. EC4 77 DP72
Ludgate Circ. EC4 6 F9
Ludgate Hill EC4 6 F9
Ludgate Hill EC4 77 DP72
Ludgate Sq. EC4 6 G9
Ludham Clo. SE28 82 EW72
Rollesby Way
Ludlow Clo., Brom. 122 EG97
Ludlow Clo., Har. 58 BZ63
Ludlow Mead, Wat. 43 BV48
Ludlow Rd. W5 73 CJ70
Ludlow Rd., Felt. 99 BU91
Ludlow St. EC1 7 H4
Ludlow Way N2 62 DC56
Ludlow Way, Rick. 29 BQ42
Ludovick Wk. SW15 88 CS84
Ludwick Ms. SE14 93 DY80
Luffield Rd. SE2 96 EV76
Luffman Rd. SE12 108 EH90
Lugard Rd. SE15 92 DV82
Lugg App. E12 67 EN62
Luke Ho. E1 78 DV72
Luke St. EC2 7 M4
Luke St. EC2 78 DS70
Lukin Cres. E4 51 ED48
Lukin St. E1 78 DW72
Lukintone Clo., Loug. 38 EL44
Lullarook Clo., West. 150 EJ116
Lullingstone Ave., Swan. 125 FF97
Lullingstone Clo., Orp. 110 EV94
Lullingstone Cres.
Lullingstone Cres., Orp. 110 EU94
Lullingstone La. SE13 107 ED86
Lullingstone Rd., Belv. 96 EZ79
Lullington Garth N12 47 CZ50
Lullington Garth, Borwd. 32 CP43
Lullington Garth, Brom. 108 EE94
Lullington Rd. SE20 106 DU94
Lullington Rd., Dag. 82 EY66
Lulot Gdns. N19 63 DH61
Dartmouth Pk. Hill
Lulworth SE17 11 K10
Lulworth Ave., Houns. 86 CB80
Lulworth Ave. (Cheshunt), Wal.Cr. 21 DP29
Lulworth Ave., Wem. 59 CJ59
Lulworth Clo., Har. 58 BZ62
Lulworth Cres., Mitch. 118 DE96
Lulworth Dr., Pnr. 58 BX59
Lulworth Dr., Rom. 55 FB50
Lulworth Gdns., Har. 58 BY61
Lulworth Rd. SE9 108 EL89
Lulworth Rd. SE15 92 DV82
Lulworth Rd., Well. 95 ET82
Lulworth Waye, Hayes 71 BV72
Lumen Rd., Wem. 59 CK61
Lumley Clo., Belv. 96 FA79
Lumley Ct. WC2 10 A1
Lumley Gdns., Sutt. 131 CY106
Lumley Rd., Sutt. 131 CY107
Lumley St. W1 4 G9
Lumley St. W1 76 DG72
Luna Rd., Th.Hth. 120 DQ97
Lunar Clo., West. 150 EK116
Lunar Ho., Croy. 120 DQ102
Lundin Wk., Wat. 44 BX49
Woodhall La.
Lundy Dr., Hayes 85 BS77
Lundy Wk. N1 78 DQ65
Clephane Rd.
Lunghurst Rd., Cat. 149 DZ120
Lunham Rd. SE19 106 DS93
Lupin Clo. SW2 105 DP89
Palace Rd.
Lupin Clo., Croy. 121 DX102
Primrose La.
Lupin Clo., West Dr. 84 BK78
Magnolia St.
Lupin Cres., Ilf. 67 EP62
Ilford La.
Lupton Clo. SE12 108 EH91
Lupton St. NW5 63 DJ63
Lupus St. SW1 91 DH78
Luralda Gdns. E14 93 EC78
Saunders Ness Rd.
Lurgan Ave. W6 89 CX79
Lurline Gdns. SW11 90 DG81
Luscombe Ct., Brom. 122 EE96
Luscombe Way SW8 91 DL80
Lushes Ct., Loug. 39 EP43
Lushes Rd.
Lushes Rd., Loug. 39 EP43
Lushington Dr., Cob. 127 BV114
Lushington Rd. NW10 75 CV68
Lushington Rd. SE6 107 EB92
Lushington Ter. E8 64 DU64
Wayland Ave.
Lusted Hall La., West. 150 EJ120
Lusted Rd., Sev. 153 FE120
Luther Clo., Edg. 46 CQ47
Luther King Clo. E17 65 DY58
Luther Rd., Tedd. 101 CF92
Luton Pl. SE10 93 EC80
Luton Rd. E17 65 DZ55
Luton Rd., Sid. 110 EW90
Luton St. NW8 4 A5
Luton St. NW8 76 DD70
Lutton Ter. NW3 62 DD63
Flask Wk.
Luttrell Ave. SW15 103 CV85
Lutwyche Rd. SE6 107 DZ89
Luxborough La., Chig. 52 EL48
Luxborough St. W1 4 F5
Luxborough St. W1 76 DG71
Luxemburg Gdns. W6 89 CX77
Luxfield Rd. SE9 108 EL88
Luxford St. SE16 93 DX77
Luxmore Gdns. SE4 93 DZ81
Luxmore St.
Luxmore St. SE4 93 DZ81
Luxor St. SE5 92 DQ83
Luxted Rd., Orp. 137 EN112
Lyal Rd. E3 79 DY68
Lyall Ave. SE21 106 DS90
Lyall Ms. SW1 8 F7
Lyall Ms. SW1 90 DG76
Lyall Ms. W. SW1 8 F7
Lyall St. SW1 8 F7
Lyall St. SW1 90 DG76
Lycett Pl. W12 89 CU75
Becklow Rd.
Lych Gate, Wat. 16 BX33
Lych Gate Rd., Orp. 124 EU102
Lych Gate Wk., Hayes 71 BT73
Lyconby Gdns., Croy. 121 DY101
Lydd Clo., Sid. 109 ES90
Lydd Rd., Bexh. 96 EZ80
Lydden Ct. SE9 109 ES86
Lydden Gro. SW18 104 DB87
Lydden Rd. SW18 104 DB87
Lydeard Rd. E6 81 EM66
Lydford Clo. N16 64 DS64
Pellerin Rd.
Lydford Rd. N15 64 DR57
Lydford Rd. NW2 75 CW65
Lydford Rd. W9 75 CZ70
Lydhurst Ave. SW2 105 DM89
Lydia Rd., Erith 97 FF79
Lydney Clo. SE15 92 DS80
Blakes Rd.
Lydney Clo. SW19 103 CY89
Princes Way
Lydon Rd. SW4 91 DJ83
Lydstep Rd., Chis. 109 EN91
Lye, The, Tad. 145 CW122
Lye La., St.Alb. 16 CA28
Lyfield, Lthd. 128 CB114
Lyford Rd. SW18 104 DD87
Lygon Pl. SW1 9 H7
Lyham Clo. SW2 105 DL86
Lyham Rd. SW2 105 DL85
Lyle Clo., Mitch. 118 DG101
Lyle Pk., Sev. 155 FH123
Lymbourne Clo., Sutt. 132 DA110
Lyme Fm. Rd. SE12 94 EG84
Lyme Gro. E9 78 DW66
St. Thomas's Sq.
Lyme Regis Rd., Bans. 145 CZ117
Lyme Rd., Well. 96 EV81
Lyme St. NW1 77 DJ66
Lyme Ter. NW1 77 DJ66
Royal College St.
Lymer Ave. SE19 106 DT92
Lymescote Gdns., Sutt. 118 DA103
Lyminge Clo., Sid. 109 ET91
Lyminge Gdns. SW18 104 DE88
Lymington Ave. N22 49 DN54
Lymington Clo. E6 81 EM71
Valiant Way
Lymington Clo. SW16 119 DK96
Lymington Dr., Ruis. 57 BR61
Lymington Gdns., Epsom 131 CT106
Lymington Rd. NW6 76 DB65
Lymington Rd., Dag. 68 EX60
Lympstone Gdns. SE15 92 DU80
Lyn Ms. E3 79 DZ69
Tredegar Sq.
Lynbridge Gdns. N13 49 DP49
Lynbrook Clo. SE15 92 DS80
Blakes Rd.
Lynbrook Clo., Rain. 83 FD68
Lynceley Gra., Epp. 26 EU29
Lynch, The, Uxb. 70 BJ67
New Windsor St.
Lynch Clo., Uxb. 70 BJ66
New Windsor St.
Lynch Wk. SE8 93 DZ79
Prince St.
Lynchen Clo., Houns. 85 BU81
The Ave.
Lyncott Cres. SW4 91 DH84
Lyncroft Ave., Pnr. 58 BY57
Lyncroft Gdns. NW6 62 DA64
Lyncroft Gdns. W13 87 CJ75
Lyncroft Gdns., Epsom 131 CT109
Lyncroft Gdns., Houns. 100 CC85
Lyndale NW2 61 CZ63
Lyndale Ave. NW2 61 CZ62
Lyndale Clo. SE3 94 EF79
Lyndale Ct., W.Byf. 126 BG113
Parvis Rd.
Lynden Way, Swan. 125 FC97
Lyndhurst Ave. N12 48 DF51
Lyndhurst Ave. NW7 46 CS51
Lyndhurst Ave. SW16 119 DK96
Lyndhurst Ave., Pnr. 43 BV53
Lyndhurst Ave., Sthl. 72 CB74
Lyndhurst Ave., Sun. 113 BU97
Lyndhurst Ave., Surb. 116 CP102
Lyndhurst Ave., Twick. 100 BZ88
Lyndhurst Clo. NW10 60 CR62
Lyndhurst Clo., Bexh. 97 FB83
Lyndhurst Clo., Croy. 120 DT104
Lyndhurst Clo., Orp. 137 EP105
Lyndhurst Dr. E10 65 EC59
Lyndhurst Dr., N.Mal. 116 CS100
Lyndhurst Dr., Sev. 154 FE124
Lyndhurst Gdns. N3 47 CY53
Lyndhurst Gdns. NW3 62 DD64
Lyndhurst Gdns., Bark. 81 ES65
Lyndhurst Gdns., Enf. 36 DS42
Lyndhurst Gdns., Ilf. 67 ER58
Lyndhurst Gdns., Pnr. 43 BV53
Lyndhurst Gro. SE15 92 DS82
Lyndhurst Ri., Chig. 53 EN49
Lyndhurst Rd. E4 51 EC52
Lyndhurst Rd. N18 50 DU49
Lyndhurst Rd. N22 49 DM51
Lyndhurst Rd. NW3 62 DD64
Lyndhurst Rd., Bexh. 97 FB83
Lyndhurst Rd., Couls. 146 DG116
Lyndhurst Rd., Grnf. 72 CB70
Lyndhurst Rd., Th.Hth. 119 DN98
Lyndhurst Sq. SE15 92 DT81
Lyndhurst Ter. NW3 62 DD64
Lyndhurst Way SE15 92 DT81
Lyndhurst Way, Sutt. 132 DA108
Lyndon Ave., Pnr. 44 BY51
Lyndon Ave., Sid. 109 ET85
Lyndon Ave., Wall. 118 DG104
Lyndon Rd., Belv. 96 FA77
Lyne Cres. E17 51 DZ53
Lynegrove Ave., Ashf. 99 BQ92
Lyneham Wk. E5 65 DY64
Ashenden Rd.
Lyneham Wk., Pnr. 57 BT55
Wiltshire La.
Lynett Rd., Dag. 68 EX61
Lynette Ave. SW4 105 DH86
Lynford Clo., Edg. 46 CQ53
Lynford Gdns., Edg. 46 CP48
Lynford Gdns., Ilf. 67 ET61
Lynhurst Cres., Uxb. 71 BQ66
Lynhurst Rd., Uxb. 71 BQ66
Lynmere Rd., Well. 96 EV82
Lynmouth Ave., Enf. 36 DT44
Lynmouth Ave., Mord. 117 CX101
Lynmouth Dr., Ruis. 57 BV61
Lynmouth Gdns., Grnf. 73 CH67
Lynmouth Gdns., Houns. 86 BX81
Lynmouth Ri., Orp. 124 EV98
Lynmouth Rd. E17 65 DY58
Lynmouth Rd. N2 62 DF56
Lynmouth Rd. N16 64 DT60
Lynmouth Rd., Grnf. 73 CH67
Lynn Clo., Ashf. 99 BR92
Goffs Rd.
Lynn Clo., Har. 45 CD54
Lynn Ms. E11 66 EE61
Lynn Rd.
Lynn Rd. E11 66 EE61
Lynn Rd. SW12 105 DH87
Lynn Rd., Ilf. 67 ER59
Lynn St., Enf. 36 DR39
Lynne Clo., Orp. 137 ET107
Lynne Clo., S.Croy. 134 DW111
Lynne Wk., Esher 128 CC106
Lynne Way NW10 74 CS65
Lynne Way, Nthlt. 72 BX68
Lynscott Way, S.Croy. 133 DP109
Lynsted Clo., Bexh. 111 FB85
Lynsted Clo., Brom. 122 EJ96
Lynsted Ct., Beck. 121 DY96
Churchfields Rd.
Lynsted Gdns. SE9 94 EK83
Lynton Ave. N12 48 DD49
Lynton Ave. NW9 61 CT56
Lynton Ave. W13 73 CG72
Lynton Ave., Orp. 124 EV98
Lynton Ave., Rom. 54 FA53
Lynton Clo. NW10 60 CS64
Lynton Clo., Chess. 130 CL105
Lynton Clo., Islw. 87 CF84
Lynton Cres., Ilf. 67 EP58
Lynton Crest, Pot.B. 20 DA32
Strafford Gate
Lynton Est. SE1 92 DU77
Lynton Rd.
Lynton Gdns. N11 49 DK51
Lynton Gdns., Enf. 50 DS45
Lynton Mead N20 48 DA48
Lynton Par., Wal.Cr. 23 DX30
Turners Hill
Lynton Rd. E4 51 EB50
Lynton Rd. N8 63 DK57
Lynton Rd. NW6 75 CZ67
Lynton Rd. SE1 92 DT77
Lynton Rd. W3 74 CN73
Lynton Rd., Croy. 119 DN100
Lynton Rd., Har. 58 BY61
Lynton Rd., N.Mal. 116 CR99
Lynton Wk., Hayes 71 BS69
Exmouth Rd.
Lynwood Ave., Couls. 147 DH115
Lynwood Ave., Epsom 131 CT114
Lynwood Clo. E18 52 EJ53
Gordon Rd.
Lynwood Clo., Har. 58 BY62
Lynwood Clo., Rom. 55 FB51
Lynwood Dr., Nthwd. 43 BS53
Lynwood Dr., Rom. 55 FB51
Lynwood Dr., Wor.Pk. 117 CU103
Lynwood Gdns., Croy. 133 DM105
Lynwood Gdns., Sthl. 72 BZ71
Lynwood Gro. N21 49 DN46
Lynwood Gro., Orp. 123 ES101
Lynwood Heights, Rick. 28 BH43
Lynwood Rd. SW17 104 DF90
Lynwood Rd. W5 74 CL70
Lynwood Rd., Epsom 131 CT114
Lynwood Rd., T.Ditt. 115 CF103
Lyon Business Pk., Bark. 81 ES68
Lyon Meade, Stan. 45 CJ53
Lyon Pk. Ave., Wem. 74 CL65
Lyon Rd. SW19 118 DC95
Lyon Rd., Har. 59 CF58
Lyon Rd., Rom. 69 FF59
Lyon Rd., Walt. 114 BY103
Lyon St. N1 77 DM66
Caledonian Rd.
Lyon Way, Grnf. 73 CE67
Lyons Pl. NW8 76 DD70
Lyons Wk. W14 89 CY77
Lyonsdown Ave., Barn. 34 DC44
Lyonsdown Rd., Barn. 34 DB44
Lyoth Rd., Orp. 123 EQ103
Lyric Dr., Grnf. 72 CB70
Lyric Rd. SW13 89 CT81
Lysander Gdns., Surb. 116 CM100
Ewell Rd.
Lysander Gro. N19 63 DK60
Lysander Rd., Croy. 133 DM107
Lysander Rd., Ruis. 57 BR61
Lysander Way, Abb.L. 15 BU32
Lysander Way, Orp. 123 EQ104
Lysia St. SW6 89 CX80
Lysias Rd. SW12 105 DH86

Lysons Wk. SW15 103 CU85
Swinburne Rd.
Lytchet Rd., Brom. 108 EH94
Lytchet Way, Enf. 36 DW39
Lytchgate Clo., S.Croy. 134 DS108
Lytcott Dr., W.Mol. 114 BZ97
Freeman Dr.
Lytcott Gro. SE22 106 DT85
Lyte St. E2 78 DW68
Bishops Way
Lytham Ave., Wat. 44 BX50
Lytham Gro. W5 74 CM69
Lytham St. SE17 92 DR78
Lyttelton Clo. NW3 76 DE66
Hawtrey Rd.
Lyttelton Rd. E10 65 EB62
Lyttelton Rd. N2 62 DC57
Lyttleton Rd. N8 63 DN55
Lytton Ave. N13 49 DN47
Lytton Ave., Enf. 37 DY38
Lytton Clo. N2 62 DC58
Lytton Clo., Loug. 39 ER41
Lytton Clo., Nthlt. 72 BZ66
Lytton Gdns., Wall. 133 DK105
Lytton Gro. SW15 103 CX85
Lytton Rd. E11 66 EE59
Lytton Rd., Barn. 34 DC42
Lytton Rd., Pnr. 44 BY52
Lytton Rd., Rom. 69 FH57
Lytton Strachey Path SE28 82 EV73
Titmuss Ave.
Lyveden Rd. SE3 94 EH80
Lyveden Rd. SW17 104 DE93
Lywood Clo., Tad. 145 CW122

M

Mabbotts, Tad. 145 CX121
Mabbutt Clo., St.Alb. 16 BY30
Mabel Rd., Swan. 111 FG93
Maberley Cres. SE19 106 DU94
Maberley Rd. SE19 120 DT95
Maberley Rd., Beck. 121 DX97
Mabledon Pl. WC1 5 N3
Mabledon Pl. WC1 77 DK69
Mablethorpe Rd. SW6 89 CY80
Mabley St. E9 65 DY64
Macaret Clo. N20 48 DC45
MacArthur Clo. E7 80 EG65
Macarthur Ter. SE7 94 EK79
Macaulay Ave., Esher 115 CE103
Macaulay Ct. SW4 91 DH83
Macaulay Rd. E6 80 EK68
Macaulay Rd. SW4 91 DH83
Macaulay Rd., Cat. 148 DS122
Macaulay Sq. SW4 91 DH84
Macaulay Way SE28 82 EV73
Booth Clo.
Macauley Ms. SE13 93 EC81
Macbean St. SE18 95 EP76
Macbeth St. W6 89 CV78
Macclesfield Bri. NW1 76 DE68
Macclesfield Rd. EC1 7 H2
Macclesfield Rd. EC1 78 DQ69
Macclesfield Rd. SE25 120 DV99
Macclesfield St. W1 5 N10
Macdonald Ave., Dag. 69 FB62
Macdonald Rd. E7 66 EG63
Macdonald Rd. E17 51 EC54
Macdonald Rd. N11 48 DF50
Macdonald Rd. N19 63 DJ61
Macdonnell Gdns., Wat. 29 BT35
High Rd.
Macduff Rd. SW11 90 DG81
Mace Clo. E1 78 DV74
Kennet St.
Mace La., Sev. 137 ER113
Mace St. E2 79 DX68
MacFarlane La., Islw. 87 CF79
Macfarlane Rd. W12 75 CW74
Macfarren Pl. NW1 4 G5
Macgregor Rd. E16 80 EJ71
Machell Rd. SE15 92 DW83
Macintosh Clo., Wal.Cr. 21 DP25
Hammondstreet Rd.
Mackay Rd. SW4 91 DH83
Mackennal St. NW8 76 DE68
Mackenzie Rd. N7 77 DM65
Mackenzie Rd., Beck. 120 DW96
Mackenzie Wk. E14 79 EA74
South Colonnade
Mackeson Rd. NW3 62 DF63
Mackie Rd. SW2 105 DN87
Mackintosh La. E9 65 DX64
Homerton High St.
Macklin St. WC2 6 A8
Macklin St. WC2 77 DL72
Mackrow Wk. E14 79 EC73
Robin Hood La.
Macks Rd. SE16 92 DU77
Mackworth St. NW1 5 K2
Mackworth St. NW1 77 DJ69
Maclaren Ms. SW15 89 CW84
Clarendon Dr.
Maclean Rd. SE23 107 DY86
Macleod Rd. N21 35 DL43
Macleod St. SE17 92 DQ78
Maclise Rd. W14 89 CY76
Macoma Rd. SE18 95 ER79
Macoma Ter. SE18 95 ER79
Maconochies Rd. E14 93 EB78
Macquarie Way E14 93 EB77
Macready Pl. N7 63 DL63
Warlters Rd.
Macroom Rd. W9 75 CZ69
Mada Rd., Orp. 123 EP103
Madans Wk., Epsom 144 CR115
Maddams St. E3 79 EB70
Maddison Clo., Tedd. 101 CF93
Maddock Way SE17 91 DP79
Cooks Rd.
Maddocks Clo., Sid. 110 EX92
Maddox La., Lthd. 142 BY123
Maddox Pk., Lthd. 142 BY123
Maddox St. W1 5 J10
Maddox St. W1 77 DH73
Madeira Ave., Brom. 108 EE94
Madeira Gro., Wdf.Grn. 52 EJ51
Madeira Rd. E11 65 ED60
Madeira Rd. N13 49 DP49
Madeira Rd. SW16 105 DL92
Madeira Rd., Mitch. 118 DF98
Madeley Rd. W5 74 CL72
Madeline Gro., Ilf. 67 ER64
Madeline Rd. SE20 106 DU94
Madells, Epp. 25 ET31
Madge Gill Way E6 80 EL67
Ron Leighton Way
Madinah Rd. E8 78 DU65
Madison Cres., Bexh. 96 EW80
Madison Gdns., Bexh. 96 EW80
Madison Gdns., Brom. 122 EF97
Madison Way, Sev. 154 FF123
Madras Pl. N7 77 DN65
Madras Rd., Ilf. 67 EP63
Madresfield Ct., Rad. 18 CL32
Russet Dr.
Madrid Rd. SW13 89 CU81
Madrigal La. SE5 91 DP80
Madron St. SE17 11 N10
Madron St. SE17 92 DS78
Maesmaur Rd., West. 150 EK121
Mafeking Ave. E6 80 EL68
Mafeking Ave., Brent. 88 CL79
Mafeking Ave., Ilf. 67 ER59
Mafeking Rd. E16 80 EF70
Mafeking Rd. N17 50 DU54
Mafeking Rd., Enf. 36 DT41
Magazine Pl., Lthd. 143 CH122
Magazine Rd., Cat. 147 DP122
Magdala Ave. N19 63 DH61
Magdala Rd., Islw. 87 CG83
Magdala Rd., S.Croy. 134 DR108
Napier Rd.
Magdalen Clo., W.Byf. 126 BL114
Magdalen Cres., W.Byf. 126 BL114
Magdalen Gro., Orp. 138 EV105
Magdalen Pas. E1 78 DT73
Prescot St.
Magdalen Rd. SW18 104 DC88
Magdalen St. SE1 11 M3
Magdalen St. SE1 78 DS74
Magdalene Clo. SE15 92 DV82
Heaton Rd.
Magdalene Gdns. E6 81 EN70
Magdalene Rd., Shep. 112 BM97
Magee St. SE11 91 DN79
Maggie Blake's Cause SE1 11 P3
Magnaville Rd. (Bushey), Wat. 45 CE45
Magnet Rd., Wem. 59 CK61
Magnin Clo. E8 78 DU67
Wilde Clo.
Magnolia Ave., Abb.L. 15 BU32
Magnolia Clo., Kings.T. 102 CP93
Magnolia Clo., St.Alb. 17 CD27
Magnolia Ct., Har. 60 CM59
Magnolia Ct., Rich. 88 CP81
West Hall Rd.
Magnolia Dr., West. 150 EK116
Magnolia Gdns. E10 65 EB61
Oliver Rd.
Magnolia Pl. SW4 105 DL85
Magnolia Pl. W5 74 CL71
Montpelier Rd.
Magnolia Rd. W4 88 CP79
Magnolia St., West Dr. 84 BK77
Magnolia Way, Epsom 130 CQ106
Magpie All. EC4 6 E9
Magpie Clo. E7 66 EF64
Magpie Clo. NW9 46 CS54
Eagle Dr.
Magpie Clo., Couls. 147 DJ118
Ashbourne Clo.
Magpie Clo., Enf. 36 DU39
Magpie Hall Clo., Brom. 122 EL100
Magpie Hall La., Brom. 122 EL101
Magpie Hall Rd. (Bushey), Wat. 45 CE47
Magpie Pl. SE14 93 DY79
Milton Ct. Rd.
Magri Wk. E1 78 DW71
Ashfield St.
Maguire Dr., Rich. 101 CJ91
Maguire St. SE1 92 DT75
Mahatma Gandhi Ho., Wem. 60 CM64
Mahlon Ave., Ruis. 57 BV64
Mahogany Clo. SE16 79 DY74
Mahon Clo., Enf. 36 DT39
Maida Ave. E4 51 EB45
Maida Ave. W2 76 DC71
Maida Rd., Belv. 96 FA76
Maida Vale W9 76 DB68
Maida Vale Rd., Dart. 111 FG85
Maida Way E4 51 EB45
Maiden Erlegh Ave., Bex. 110 EY88
Maiden La. NW1 77 DK66
Maiden La. SE1 11 J2
Maiden La. WC2 6 A10
Maiden La. WC2 77 DL73
Maiden La., Dart. 97 FG83
Maiden Rd. E15 80 EE66
Maidenshaw Rd., Epsom 130 CR112
Maidenstone Hill SE10 93 EC81
Maids of Honour Row, Rich. 101 CK85
The Grn.
Maidstone Ave., Rom. 55 FC54
Maidstone Bldgs. SE1 11 K3
Maidstone Ho. E14 79 EB72
Carmen St.
Maidstone Rd. N11 49 DJ51
Maidstone Rd., Sev. 154 FE122
Maidstone Rd. (Seal), Sev. 155 FN121
Maidstone Rd., Sid. 110 EX93
Maidstone Rd., Swan. 125 FC95
Maidstone St. E2 78 DU68
Audrey St.
Main Ave., Enf. 36 DT43
Main Ave., Nthwd. 43 BQ48
Main Dr., Wem. 59 CK62
Main Rd., Kes. 136 EJ112
Main Rd., Orp. 124 EW98
Main Rd., Rom. 69 FF56
Main Rd. (Knockholt), Sev. 151 ET119
Main Rd. (Sundridge), Sev. 152 EX124
Main Rd., Sid. 109 ES90
Main Rd., Swan. 111 FF94
Main Rd. (Crockenhill), Swan. 125 FC100
Main Rd., West. 136 EJ114
Main St., Felt. 100 BX92
Mainridge Rd., Chis. 109 EN91
Maisemore St. SE15 92 DU80
Peckham Pk. Rd.
Maisie Webster Clo., Stai. 98 BK87
Lauser Rd.
Maitland Clo. SE10 93 EB80
Maitland Clo., Houns. 86 BZ83
Maitland Clo., W.Byf. 126 BG113
Maitland Pk. Est. NW3 76 DF65
Maitland Pk. Rd. NW3 76 DF65
Maitland Pk. Vill. NW3 76 DF65
Maitland Pl. E5 64 DV63
Clarence Rd.
Maitland Rd. E15 80 EF65
Maitland Rd. SE26 107 DX93
Maize Row E14 79 DZ73
Commercial Rd.
Majendie Rd. SE18 95 ER78
Majestic Way, Mitch. 118 DF96
Major Rd. E15 65 ED64
Major Rd. SE16 92 DU76
Jamaica Rd.
Makepeace Ave. N6 62 DG61
Makepeace Rd. E11 66 EG56
Makepeace Rd., Nthlt. 72 BY67
Makins St. SW3 8 C9
Makins St. SW3 90 DE77
Malabar St. E14 93 EA75
Malam Gdns. E14 79 EB73
Wades Pl.
Malan Clo., West. 150 EL117
Malan Sq., Rain. 83 FH65
Malbrook Rd. SW15 89 CV84
Malcolm Ct., Stan. 45 CJ50
Malcolm Cres. NW4 61 CU58
Malcolm Dr., Surb. 115 CK102
Malcolm Pl. E2 78 DW70
Malcolm Rd. E1 78 DW70
Malcolm Rd. SE20 106 DW94
Malcolm Rd. SE25 120 DU100
Malcolm Rd. SW19 103 CY93
Malcolm Rd., Couls. 147 DK115
Malcolm Rd., Uxb. 56 BM63
Malcolm Way E11 66 EG57
Malcolms Way N14 35 DJ43
Malden Ave. SE25 120 DV97
Malden Ave., Grnf. 59 CE64
Malden Cres. NW1 76 DG65
Malden Grn. Ave., Wor.Pk. 117 CT102
Malden Hill, N.Mal. 117 CT97
Malden Hill Gdns., N.Mal. 117 CT97
Malden Pk., N.Mal. 117 CT100
Malden Pl. NW5 62 DG64
Grafton Ter.
Malden Rd. NW5 62 DF64
Malden Rd., Borwd. 32 CN41
Malden Rd., N.Mal. 116 CS99
Malden Rd., Sutt. 117 CW104
Malden Rd., Wat. 29 BU40
Malden Rd., Wor.Pk. 117 CT101
Malden Way, N.Mal. 116 CR100
Maldon Clo. E15 65 ED64
David St.
Maldon Clo. N1 78 DQ67
Maldon Clo. SE5 92 DS83
Maldon Rd. N9 50 DT48
Maldon Rd. W3 74 CQ73
Maldon Rd., Rom. 69 FC59
Maldon Rd., Wall. 133 DH106
Maldon Wk., Wdf.Grn. 52 EJ51
Malet Pl. WC1 5 M5
Malet Pl. WC1 77 DK70
Malet St. WC1 5 M5
Malet St. WC1 77 DK70
Maley Ave. SE27 105 DP89
Malford Ct. E18 52 EG54
Malford Gro. E18 66 EF56
Malfort Rd. SE5 92 DS83
Malham Rd. SE23 107 DX88
Malins Clo., Barn. 33 CV43
Mall, The E15 79 ED66
Broadway
Mall, The N14 49 DL48
Mall, The SW1 9 L4
Mall, The SW1 91 DJ75
Mall, The SW14 102 CQ85
Mall, The W5 74 CL73
Mall, The, Brom. 122 EG97
High St.
Mall, The, Croy. 120 DQ102
Poplar Wk.
Mall, The, Har. 60 CM58
Mall, The, Horn. 69 FH60
Mall, The, St.Alb. 16 CC27
Mall, The, Surb. 115 CK99
Mall Rd. W6 89 CV78
Mallams Ms. SW9 91 DP83
St. James's Cres.
Mallard Clo. E9 79 DZ65
Mallard Clo. W7 87 CE75
Mallard Clo., Barn. 34 DD44
The Hook
Mallard Clo., Twick. 100 CA87
Stephenson Rd.
Mallard Path SE28 95 ER76
Tom Cribb Rd.
Mallard Pl., Twick. 101 CH90
Mallard Rd., Abb.L. 15 BT31
College Rd.
Mallard Rd., S.Croy. 135 DX110
Mallard Wk. SE28 95 ER76
Goosander Way
Mallard Wk., Beck. 121 DX99
Mallard Wk., Sid. 110 EW93
Cray Rd.
Mallard Way NW9 60 CQ59
Mallard Way, Nthwd. 43 BQ52
Mallard Way, Wall. 133 DJ109
Mallard Way, Wat. 30 BY36
Mallards, The, Stai. 112 BH96
Thames Side
Mallards Reach, Wey. 113 BR103
Mallards Rd., Wdf.Grn. 52 EH52
Mallet Dr., Nthlt. 58 BZ64
Mallet Rd. SE13 107 ED86
Malling Clo., Croy. 120 DW100
Malling Gdns., Mord. 118 DC100
Malling Way, Brom. 122 EF101
Mallinson Rd. SW11 104 DE85
Mallinson Rd., Croy. 119 DK104
Mallion Ct., Wal.Abb. 24 EF33
Mallord St. SW3 90 DD79
Mallory Clo. SE4 93 DY84
Mallory Gdns., Barn. 48 DG45
Mallory St. NW8 4 B5
Mallory St. NW8 76 DE70
Mallow Clo., Croy. 121 DX102
Marigold Way
Mallow Clo., Tad. 145 CV119
Mallow Mead NW7 47 CY52
Mallow St. EC1 7 K4
Mallow Wk., Wal.Cr. 22 DR28
Mallows, The, Uxb. 57 BP62
Malm Clo., Rick. 42 BK47
Malmains Clo., Beck. 121 ED98
Malmains Way, Beck. 121 EC98
Malmesbury Clo., Pnr. 57 BT56
Malmesbury Rd. E3 79 DZ69
Malmesbury Rd. E16 80 EE71
Malmesbury Rd. E18 52 EF53
Malmesbury Rd., Mord. 118 DC101
Malmesbury Ter. E16 80 EF71
Malpas Dr., Pnr. 58 BX57
Malpas Rd. E8 78 DV65
Malpas Rd. SE4 93 DZ82
Malpas Rd., Dag. 82 EX65
Malt La., Rad. 31 CG35
Newlands Ave.
Malt St. SE1 92 DU79
Malta Rd. E10 65 EA60
Malta St. EC1 6 G4
Maltby Clo., Orp. 124 EU102
Vinson Clo.
Maltby Dr., Enf. 36 DV38
Maltby Rd., Chess. 130 CN107
Maltby St. SE1 11 P5
Maltby St. SE1 92 DT76
Malthouse Dr. W4 88 CS79
Malthouse Dr., Felt. 100 BX92
Malthouse Pas. SW13 88 CS82
The Ter.
Malthouse Pl., Rad. 17 CG34
Malthus Path SE28 82 EW74
Owen Clo.
Malting Ho. E14 79 DZ73
Oak La.
Malting Way, Islw. 87 CF83
Maltings, The, Kings L. 15 BQ33
Maltings, The, Orp. 123 ET102
Maltings, The, W.Byf. 126 BM113
Maltings Clo. SW13 88 CS82
Cleveland Gdns.
Maltings Dr., Epp. 26 EU29
Palmers Hill
Maltings La., Epp. 26 EU29
Maltings Ms., Sid. 110 EU90
Station Rd.
Maltings Pl. SW6 90 DB81
Malton Ms. SE18 95 ES79
Malton St.
Malton Ms. W10 75 CY72
Cambridge Gdns.
Malton Rd. W10 75 CY72
St. Marks Rd.
Malton St. SE18 95 ES79
Maltravers St. WC2 6 C10
Malva Clo. SW18 104 DB85
St. Ann's Hill
Malvern Ave. E4 51 ED52
Malvern Ave., Bexh. 96 EY80
Malvern Ave., Har. 58 BY62
Malvern Clo. SE20 120 DU96
Derwent Rd.
Malvern Clo. W10 75 CZ71
Malvern Clo., Mitch. 119 DJ97
Malvern Clo., Surb. 116 CL102
Malvern Clo., Uxb. 56 BN61
Malvern Ct. SE14 92 DW80
Avonley Rd.
Malvern Ct. SW7 8 A8
Malvern Ct. SW7 90 DD77
Malvern Dr., Felt. 100 BX92
Malvern Dr., Ilf. 67 ET63
Malvern Dr., Wdf.Grn. 52 EJ50
Malvern Gdns. NW2 61 CY61
Malvern Gdns. NW6 75 CZ68
Malvern Gdns., Har. 60 CL56
Malvern Gdns., Loug. 39 EM44
Malvern Ms. NW6 76 DA69
Malvern Rd.
Malvern Pl. NW6 75 CZ69
Malvern Rd. E6 80 EL67
Malvern Rd. E8 78 DU66
Malvern Rd. E11 66 EE61
Malvern Rd. N8 63 DM55
Malvern Rd. N17 64 DU55
Malvern Rd. NW6 76 DA69
Malvern Rd., Enf. 37 DY36
Malvern Rd., Hmptn. 100 CA94
Malvern Rd., Hayes 85 BS80
Malvern Rd., Horn. 69 FG58
Malvern Rd., Orp. 138 EV105
Malvern Rd., Surb. 116 CL103
Malvern Rd., Th.Hth. 119 DN98
Malvern Ter. N1 77 DN67
Malvern Ter. N9 50 DT46
Malvern Way W13 73 CH71
Templewood
Malvern Way, Rick. 29 BP43
Malwood Rd. SW12 105 DH86
Malyons, The, Shep. 113 BR100
Gordon Rd.
Malyons Rd. SE13 107 EB86
Malyons Rd., Swan. 111 FF94
Malyons Ter. SE13 107 EB85
Managers St. E14 79 EC74
Prestons Rd.
Manatee Pl., Wall. 119 DK104
Croydon Rd.
Manaton Clo. SE15 92 DV83
Manaton Cres., Sthl. 72 CA72
Manbey Gro. E15 80 EE65
Manbey Pk. Rd. E15 80 EE65
Manbey Rd. E15 80 EE65
Manbey St. E15 80 EE65
Manborough Ave. E6 81 EM69
Manbre Rd. W6 89 CW79
Manchester Dr. W10 75 CY70
Manchester Gro. E14 93 EC78
Manchester Ms. W1 4 F7
Manchester Rd. E14 93 EC78
Manchester Rd. N15 64 DR58
Manchester Rd., Th.Hth. 120 DQ97
Manchester Row, Dart. 111 FE85
Manchester Sq. W1 4 F8
Manchester Sq. W1 76 DG72
Manchester St. W1 4 F7
Manchester St. W1 76 DG71
Manchester Way, Dag. 69 FB63
Manchuria Rd. SW11 104 DG86
Manciple St. SE1 11 L5
Manciple St. SE1 92 DR75
Mandalay Rd. SW4 105 DJ85
Mandarin St. E14 79 EA73
Salter St.
Mandarin Way, Hayes 72 BX72
Mandela Clo. NW10 74 CQ66
Mandela Rd. E16 80 EG72
Mandela St. NW1 77 DJ67
Mandela St. SW9 91 DN80
Mandela Way SE1 11 N8
Mandela Way SE1 92 DS77
Mandeville Clo. SE3 94 EF80
Vanbrugh Pk.
Mandeville Clo. SW20 117 CY95
Mandeville Clo., Wat. 29 BT38
Mandeville Ct. E4 51 DY49
Mandeville Dr., Surb. 115 CK102
Mandeville Pl. W1 4 G8
Mandeville Pl. W1 76 DG72
Mandeville Rd. N14 49 DH47
Mandeville Rd., Enf. 37 DY36
Mandeville Rd., Islw. 87 CG82
Mandeville Rd., Nthlt. 72 BZ66
Mandeville Rd., Pot.B. 20 DC32
Mandeville Rd., Shep. 112 BN99
Mandeville St. E5 65 DY62
Mandrake Rd. SW17 104 DF89
Mandrake Way E15 80 EE66
Elliot Clo.
Mandrell Rd. SW2 105 DL85
Manette St. W1 5 N9
Manette St. W1 77 DK72
Manford Clo., Chig. 54 EU49
Manford Cross, Chig. 54 EU50
Manford Way, Chig. 53 ES49
Manfred Rd. SW15 103 CZ85
Manger Rd. N7 77 DL65
Mangold Way, Erith 96 EY76
Manhattan Ct., Nthlt. 72 BX69
Manhattan Wf. E16 94 EG75
Manilla St. E14 93 EA75
Manister Rd. SE2 96 EU76
Manitoba Ct. SE16 92 DW75
Renforth St.

Street	Page	Grid
Manitoba Gdns., Orp.	137	ET107
Superior Dr.		
Manley Ct. N16	64	DT62
Stoke Newington High St.		
Manley St. NW1	76	DG67
Manly Dixon Dr., Enf.	37	DY37
Mann Clo., Croy.	120	DQ104
Salem Pl.		
Mannamead, Epsom	144	CS119
Mannamead Clo., Epsom	144	CS119
Mannamead		
Mannin Rd., Rom.	68	EV59
Manning Gdns., Har.	59	CK59
Manning Pl., Rich.	102	CM86
Grove Rd.		
Manning Rd. E17	65	DY57
Southcote Rd.		
Manning Rd., Dag.	82	FA65
Manning Rd., Orp.	124	EX99
Manningtree Clo. EC1	**6**	**F2**
Manningtree Clo. SW19	103	CY88
Manningtree Rd., Ruis.	57	BV63
Manningtree St. E1	78	DU72
White Ch. La.		
Mannock Dr., Loug.	39	EQ40
Mannock Rd. N22	63	DP55
Manns Clo., Islw.	101	CF85
Manns Rd., Edg.	46	CN51
Manoel Rd., Twick.	100	CC89
Manor Ave. SE4	93	DZ82
Manor Ave., Cat.	148	DS124
Manor Ave., Houns.	86	BX83
Manor Ave., Nthlt.	72	BZ66
Manor Chase, Wey.	127	BP106
Manor Clo. E17	51	DY54
Manor Dr.		
Manor Clo. NW7	46	CR50
Manor Dr.		
Manor Clo. NW9	60	CP57
Manor Clo. SE28	82	EW73
Manor Clo., Barn.	33	CY42
Manor Clo., Dag.	83	FD65
Manor Clo. (Crayford), Dart.	97	FD84
Manor Clo. (Wilmington), Dart.	111	FG90
Manor Clo., Rom.	69	FG57
Manor Rd.		
Manor Clo., Ruis.	57	BT60
Manor Clo., Warl.	149	DY117
Manor Clo., Wor.Pk.	116	CS102
Manor Cotts., Nthwd.	43	BT53
Manor Cotts. App. N2	48	DC54
Manor Ct. E10	65	EB60
Grange Pk. Rd.		
Manor Ct. N2	62	DF57
Manor Ct. SW6	90	DB81
Bagley's La.		
Manor Ct., Enf.	36	DV36
Manor Rd.		
Manor Ct., Rad.	31	CF38
Manor Ct., Twick.	100	CC89
Manor Ct., Wem.	60	CL64
Manor Ct., Wey.	127	BP105
Manor Ct. Rd. W7	73	CE73
Manor Cres., Surb.	116	CN100
Manor Cres., W.Byf.	126	BM113
Manor Dr. N14	49	DH45
Manor Dr. N20	48	DE48
Manor Dr. NW7	46	CR50
Manor Dr., Add.	126	BG110
Manor Dr., Epsom	130	CS107
Manor Dr., Esher	115	CF104
Manor Dr., Felt.	100	BX92
Lebanon Ave.		
Manor Dr., St.Alb.	16	CA27
Manor Dr., Sun.	113	BU96
Manor Dr., Surb.	116	CM100
Manor Dr., Wem.	60	CM63
Manor Dr., The, Wor.Pk.	116	CS102
Manor Dr. N., N.Mal.	116	CR100
Manor Dr. N., Wor.Pk.	116	CS102
Manor Est. SE16	92	DV77
Manor Fm. Ave., Shep.	113	BP100
Manor Fm. Clo., Wor.Pk.	116	CS102
Manor Fm. Dr. E4	52	EE48
Manor Fm. Rd., Enf.	36	DV36
Manor Fm. Rd., Th.Hth.	119	DN96
Manor Fm. Rd., Wem.	73	CK67
Manor Flds. SW15	103	CX86
Manor Gdns. N7	63	DL62
Manor Gdns. SW20	117	CZ96
Manor Gdns. W3	88	CN77
Manor Gdns., Hmptn.	100	CB94
Manor Gdns., Rich.	88	CM84
Manor Gdns., Ruis.	58	BW64
Manor Gdns., S.Croy.	134	DT107
Manor Gdns., Sun.	113	BU95
Manor Gate, Nthlt.	72	BY66
Manor Grn. Rd., Epsom	130	CP113
Manor Gro. SE15	92	DW79
Manor Gro., Beck.	121	EB96
Manor Gro., Rich.	88	CN84
Manor Hall Ave. NW4	47	CW54
Manor Hall Dr. NW4	47	CX54
Manor Ho. Ct., Epsom	130	CQ113
Manor Ho. Ct., Shep.	113	BP101
Manor Ho. Dr. NW6	75	CX66
Manor Ho. Dr., Nthwd.	43	BP52
Manor Ho. Gdns., Abb.L.	15	BR31
Manor Ho. Way, Islw.	87	CH83
Manor La. SE12	108	EE86
Manor La. SE13	108	EE85
Manor La., Felt.	99	BU89
High St.		
Manor La., Hayes	85	BR79
Manor La., Sun.	113	BU96
Manor La., Sutt.	132	DC106
Manor La. Ter. SE13	94	EE84
Manor Ms. NW6	76	DA68
Cambridge Ave.		
Manor Ms. SE4	93	DZ82
Manor Mt. SE23	106	DW88
Manor Par. NW10	75	CT68
Station Rd.		
Manor Pk. SE13	107	ED85
Manor Pk., Chis.	123	ER96
Manor Pk., Rich.	88	CM84
Manor Pk. Clo., W.Wick.	121	EB102
Manor Pk. Cres., Edg.	46	CN51
Manor Pk. Dr., Har.	58	CB55
Manor Pk. Gdns., Edg.	46	CN50
Manor Pk. Par. SE13	93	ED84
Lee High Rd.		
Manor Pk. Rd. E12	66	EK63
Manor Pk. Rd. N2	62	DC55
Manor Pk. Rd. NW10	75	CT67
Manor Pk. Rd., Chis.	123	EQ95
Manor Pk. Rd., Sutt.	132	DC106
Manor Pk. Rd., W.Wick.	121	EB102
Manor Pl. SE17	**11**	**H10**
Manor Pl. SE17	91	DP78
Manor Pl., Chis.	123	ER96
Manor Pl., Felt.	99	BU88
Manor Pl., Mitch.	119	DJ97
Manor Pl., Stai.	98	BH92
Manor Pl., Sutt.	132	DB106
Manor Pl., Walt.	113	BT101
Manor Rd.		
Manor Rd. E10	65	EA59
Manor Rd. E15	80	EE68
Manor Rd. E16	80	EE70
Manor Rd. E17	51	DY54
Manor Rd. N16	64	DR61
Manor Rd. N17	50	DU53
Manor Rd. N22	49	DL51
Manor Rd. SE25	120	DU98
Manor Rd. SW20	117	CZ96
Manor Rd. W13	73	CG73
Manor Rd., Ashf.	98	BM92
Manor Rd., Bark.	81	ET65
Manor Rd., Barn.	33	CY43
Manor Rd., Beck.	121	EA96
Manor Rd., Bex.	111	FB88
Manor Rd., Chig.	53	EN51
Manor Rd., Dag.	83	FC65
Manor Rd., Dart.	97	FE84
Manor Rd., E.Mol.	115	CD98
Manor Rd., Enf.	36	DQ40
Manor Rd., Erith	97	FF79
Manor Rd., Har.	59	CG58
Manor Rd., Hayes	71	BU72
Manor Rd., Loug.	38	EH44
Manor Rd. (High Beach), Loug.	38	EH39
Manor Rd., Mitch.	119	DJ98
Manor Rd., Pot.B.	19	CZ31
Manor Rd., Rich.	88	CM83
Manor Rd., Rom.	69	FG57
Manor Rd. (Chadwell Heath), Rom.	68	EX58
Manor Rd. (Lambourne End), Rom.	54	EW47
Manor Rd., Ruis.	57	BR60
Manor Rd. (London Colney), St.Alb.	17	CJ26
Manor Rd., Sev.	152	EX124
Manor Rd., Sid.	110	EU90
Manor Rd., Sutt.	131	CZ108
Manor Rd., Tedd.	101	CG92
Manor Rd., Twick.	100	CC89
Manor Rd., Wall.	133	DH105
Manor Rd., Wal.Abb.	23	ED33
Manor Rd., Walt.	113	BT101
Manor Rd., Wat.	29	BU39
Manor Rd., W.Wick.	121	EB103
Manor Rd., West.	150	EL120
Manor Rd., Wdf.Grn.	53	EM51
Manor Rd. N., Esher	115	CF104
Manor Rd. N., T.Ditt.	115	CG103
Manor Rd. N., Wall.	133	DH105
Manor Rd. S., Esher	129	CE105
Manor Sq., Dag.	68	EW61
Manor Vale, Brent.	87	CJ78
Manor Vw. N3	48	DB54
Manor Way E4	51	ED49
Manor Way NW9	60	CS56
Manor Way SE3	94	EF84
Manor Way, Bans.	146	DF116
Manor Way, Beck.	121	EA96
Manor Way, Bex.	110	FA88
Manor Way, Bexh.	97	FD83
Manor Way, Borwd.	32	CQ40
Manor Way, Brom.	122	EL100
Manor Way, Har.	58	CB56
Manor Way, Lthd.	142	CC115
Manor Way, Mitch.	119	DJ97
Manor Way, Orp.	123	EQ99
Manor Way, Pot.B.	20	DA30
Manor Way, Pur.	133	DL112
Manor Way, Rain.	83	FE72
Manor Way, Rick.	28	BN42
Manor Way, Ruis.	57	BS59
Manor Way, S.Croy.	134	DS107
Manor Way, Sthl.	86	BX77
Manor Way (Cheshunt), Wal.Cr.	23	DY31
Russells Ride		
Manor Way, Wor.Pk.	116	CS102
Manor Way, The, Wall.	133	DH105
Manor Waye, Uxb.	70	BK67
Manor Wd. Rd., Pur.	133	DL113
Manorbrook SE3	94	EG84
Manordene Clo., T.Ditt.	115	CG102
Manordene Rd. SE28	82	EW72
Manorfield Clo. N19	63	DJ63
Tufnell Pk. Rd.		
Manorfields Clo., Chis.	123	ET97
Manorgate Rd., Kings.T.	116	CN95
Manorhall Gdns. E10	65	EA60
Manorside, Barn.	33	CY42
Manorside Clo. SE2	96	EW77
Manorway, Enf.	50	DS45
Manorway, Wdf.Grn.	52	EJ50
Manpreet Ct. E12	67	EM64
Morris Ave.		
Manresa Rd. SW3	90	DE78
Mansard Beeches SW17	104	DG92
Mansard Clo., Horn.	69	FG61
Mansard Clo., Pnr.	58	BX55
Manse Clo., Hayes	85	BR79
Manse Rd. N16	64	DT62
Manse Way, Swan.	125	FG98
Mansel Gro. E17	51	EA53
Mansel Rd. SW19	103	CY93
Mansell Rd. W3	88	CR75
Mansell Rd., Grnf.	72	CB71
Mansell St. E1	78	DT72
Mansell Way, Cat.	148	DR122
Manser Rd., Rain.	83	FE69
Mansergh Clo. SE18	94	EL80
Mansfield Ave. N15	64	DR56
Mansfield Ave., Barn.	34	DF44
Mansfield Ave., Ruis.	57	BV60
Mansfield Clo. N9	36	DU44
Mansfield Clo., Orp.	124	EX101
Mansfield Clo., Wey.	127	BP106
Mansfield Dr., Hayes	71	BS70
Mansfield Hill E4	51	EB46
Mansfield Ms. W1	**5**	**H7**
Mansfield Pl. NW3	62	DC63
New End		
Mansfield Rd. E11	66	EH58
Mansfield Rd. E17	65	DZ56
Mansfield Rd. NW3	62	DF64
Mansfield Rd. W3	74	CP70
Mansfield Rd., Chess.	129	CJ106
Mansfield Rd., Ilf.	67	EN61
Mansfield Rd., S.Croy.	134	DR107
Mansfield Rd., Swan.	111	FE93
Mansfield St. W1	**5**	**H7**
Mansfield St. W1	77	DH71
Mansford St. E2	78	DU68
Manship Rd., Mitch.	104	DG94
Mansion Gdns. NW3	62	DB62
Mansion Ho. EC4	**7**	**K9**
Mansion Ho. Pl. EC4	**7**	**K9**
Manson Ms. SW7	90	DC77
Manson Pl. SW7	90	DD77
Manstead Gdns., Rain.	83	FH72
Mansted Gdns., Rom.	68	EW59
Manston Ave., Sthl.	86	CA77
Manston Clo. SE20	120	DW95
Garden Rd.		
Manston Clo. (Cheshunt), Wal.Cr.	22	DW30
Manston Gro., Kings.T.	101	CK92
Manston Way, Horn.	83	FH65
Manstone Rd. NW2	61	CY64
Manthorp Rd. SE18	95	EQ78
Mantilla Rd. SW17	104	DG91
Mantle Rd. SE4	93	DY83
Mantle Way E15	80	EE66
Romford Rd.		
Mantlet Clo. SW16	105	DJ94
Manton Ave. W7	87	CF75
Manton Clo., Hayes	71	BS73
Manton Rd. SE2	96	EU77
Mantua St. SW11	90	DD83
Mantus Clo. E1	78	DW70
Mantus Rd.		
Mantus Rd. E1	78	DW70
Manus Way N20	48	DC47
Blakeney Clo.		
Manville Gdns. SW17	105	DH89
Manville Rd. SW17	104	DG89
Manwood Rd. SE4	107	DZ85
Manwood St. E16	81	EM74
Manygate La., Shep.	113	BQ101
Manygates SW12	105	DH89
Mape St. E2	78	DV70
Mapesbury Rd. NW2	75	CY66
Mapeshill Pl. NW2	75	CW65
Maple Ave. E4	51	DZ50
Maple Ave. W3	74	CS74
Maple Ave., Har.	58	CB61
Maple Ave., West Dr.	70	BL73
Maple Clo. N16	64	DU58
Maple Clo. SW4	105	DK86
Maple Clo., Buck.H.	52	EK48
Maple Clo., Epp.	39	ER37
Loughton La.		
Maple Clo., Hmptn.	100	BZ93
Maple Clo., Hayes	72	BX69
Maple Clo., Horn.	69	FH62
Maple Clo., Ilf.	53	ES50
Maple Clo., Mitch.	119	DH95
Maple Clo., Orp.	123	ER99
Maple Clo., Ruis.	57	BV58
Maple Clo., Swan.	125	FE96
Maple Clo. (Bushey), Wat.	30	BY40
Maple Clo., Whyt.	148	DT117
Maple Ct., N.Mal.	116	CR97
Maple Cres., Sid.	110	EU86
Maple Gdns., Edg.	46	CS52
Maple Gdns., Stai.	98	BL89
Maple Gate, Loug.	39	EN40
Maple Gro. NW9	60	CQ59
Maple Gro. W5	87	CJ76
Maple Gro., Brent.	87	CH80
Maple Gro., Sthl.	72	BZ71
Maple Gro., Wat.	29	BU39
Maple Ind. Est., Felt.	99	BU90
Maple Leaf Clo., Abb.L.	15	BU32
Magnolia Ave.		
Maple Leaf Clo., West.	150	EK116
Main Rd.		
Maple Leaf Dr., Sid.	109	ET88
Maple Leaf Sq. SE16	93	DX75
St. Elmos Rd.		
Maple Ms. NW6	76	DB68
Kilburn Pk. Rd.		
Maple Ms. SW16	105	DM92
Maple Pl. W1	**5**	**L5**
Maple Pl., Bans.	145	CX115
Maple Pl., West Dr.	70	BM73
Maple Ave.		
Maple Rd. E11	66	EE58
Maple Rd. SE20	120	DV95
Maple Rd., Ash.	143	CK119
Maple Rd., Hayes	72	BW69
Maple Rd., Surb.	115	CK100
Maple Rd., Whyt.	148	DT117
Maple Rd., Wok.	140	BG124
Maple Springs, Wal.Abb.	24	EG33
Maple St. W1	**5**	**K6**
Maple St. W1	77	DJ71
Maple St., Rom.	69	FC56
Maple Wk. W10	75	CX70
Droop St.		
Maple Wk., Sutt.	132	DB110
Maple Way, Couls.	147	DH121
Maple Way, Felt.	99	BU90
Maplecroft Clo. E6	80	EL72
Allhallows Rd.		
Mapledale Ave., Croy.	120	DU103
Mapledene, Chis.	109	EQ92
Kemnal Rd.		
Mapledene Rd. E8	78	DU66
Maplefield, St.Alb.	16	CB29
Maplehurst, Lthd.	143	CD123
Maplehurst Clo., Kings.T.	116	CL98
Mapleleafe Gdns., Ilf.	67	EP55
Maples, The, Bans.	132	DB114
Maples, The, Wal.Cr.	22	DS28
Burton La.		
Maples Pl. E1	78	DV71
Raven Row		
Maplestead Rd. SW2	105	DM87
Maplestead Rd., Dag.	82	EV67
Maplethorpe Rd., Th.Hth.	119	DN98
Mapleton Clo., Brom.	122	EG100
Mapleton Cres. SW18	104	DB86
Mapleton Cres., Enf.	36	DW38
Mapleton Rd. E4	51	EC48
Mapleton Rd. SW18	104	DA86
Mapleton Rd., Enf.	36	DV40
Maplin Clo. N21	35	DM44
Maplin Rd. E16	80	EG72
Maplin St. E3	79	DZ69
Mapperley Dr., Wdf.Grn.	52	EE52
Forest Dr.		
Maran Way, Erith	96	EX75
Marban Rd. W9	75	CZ69
Marble Arch W1	**4**	**D10**
Marble Arch W1	76	DF73
Marble Clo. W3	74	CP74
Marble Dr. NW2	61	CX60
Marble Hill Clo., Twick.	101	CH87
Marble Hill Gdns., Twick.	101	CH87
Marble Quay E1	78	DU74
Marbles Way, Tad.	145	CX119
Marbrook Ct. SE12	108	EJ90
Marcellina Way, Orp.	123	ES104
March Rd., Twick.	101	CG87
March Rd., Wey.	126	BN106
Marchant Rd. E11	65	ED61
Marchant St. SE14	93	DY79
Sanford St.		
Marchbank Rd. W14	89	CZ79
Marchmont Gdns., Rich.	102	CM85
Marchmont Rd.		
Marchmont Rd., Rich.	102	CM85
Marchmont Rd., Wall.	133	DJ108
Marchmont St. WC1	**5**	**P4**
Marchmont St. WC1	77	DL70
Marchside Clo., Houns.	86	BX81
Springwell Rd.		
Marchwood Clo. SE5	92	DS80
Marchwood Cres. W5	73	CJ72
Marcia Rd. SE1	**11**	**N9**
Marcia Rd. SE1	92	DS77
Marcilly Rd. SW18	104	DD85
Marco Rd. W6	89	CV76
Marcon Pl. E8	64	DV64
Marconi Way, Sthl.	72	CB72
Marcourt Lawns W5	74	CL70
Marcus Ct. E15	80	EE67
Marcus Garvey Way SE24	91	DN84
Marcus Rd., Dart.	111	FG87
Marcus St. E15	80	EE67
Marcus St. SW18	104	DB86
Marcus Ter. SW18	104	DB86
Marcuse Rd., Cat.	148	DQ121
Coulsdon Rd.		
Mardale Dr. NW9	60	CR57
Mardell Rd., Croy.	121	DX99
Marden Ave., Brom.	122	EF100
Marden Clo., Chig.	54	EV47
Marden Cres., Bex.	111	FC85
Marden Cres., Croy.	119	DM100
Marden Rd. N17	64	DS55
Marden Rd., Croy.	119	DM100
Marden Rd., Rom.	69	FE58
Kingsmead Ave.		
Marden Sq. SE16	92	DV76
Marder Rd. W13	87	CG75
Mardon St. E14	79	DY71
Mare St. E8	78	DV67
Marechal Niel Ave., Sid.	109	ER90
Mares Fld., Croy.	120	DS104
Maresfield Gdns. NW3	62	DC64
Marfleet Clo., Cars.	118	DE103
Margaret Ave. E4	37	EB44
Margaret Bondfield Ave., Bark.	82	EU66
Margaret Bldgs. N16	64	DT60
Margaret Rd.		
Margaret Clo., Abb.L.	15	BT32
Margaret Clo., Epp.	26	EU29
Margaret Clo., Pot.B.	20	DC33
Margaret Clo., Rom.	69	FH57
Margaret Rd.		
Margaret Clo., Stai.	98	BK93
Charles Rd.		
Margaret Clo., Wal.Abb.	23	EC33
Margaret Ct. W1	**5**	**K8**
Margaret Gardner Dr. SE9	109	EM89
Margaret Ingram Clo. SW6	89	CZ79
Rylston Rd.		
Margaret Rd. N16	64	DT60
Margaret Rd., Barn.	34	DD42
Margaret Rd., Bex.	110	EX86
Margaret Rd., Epp.	26	EU29
Margaret Rd., Rom.	69	FH57
Margaret Sq., Uxb.	70	BJ67
Margaret St. W1	**5**	**J8**
Margaret St. W1	77	DH72
Margaret Way, Couls.	147	DP118
Margaretta Ter. SW3	90	DE79
Margaretting Rd. E12	66	EJ60
Margate Rd. SW2	105	DL85
Margeholes, Wat.	44	BY47
Margery Pk. Rd. E7	80	EG65
Margery Rd., Dag.	68	EX62
Margery St. WC1	**6**	**D3**
Margery St. WC1	77	DN69
Margherita Pl., Wal.Abb.	24	EG34
Margherita Rd., Wal.Abb.	24	EG34
Margin Dr. SW19	103	CX92
Margravine Gdns. W6	89	CX78
Margravine Rd. W6	89	CX78
Marham Gdns. SW18	104	DE88
Marham Gdns., Mord.	118	DC100
Maria Clo. SE1	92	DU77
Beatrice Rd.		
Maria Ter. E1	79	DX70
Maria Theresa Clo., N.Mal.	116	CR99
Marian Clo., Hayes	72	BX70
Marian Ct., Sutt.	132	DB106
Marian Pl. E2	78	DV68
Marian Rd. SW16	119	DJ95
Marian Sq. E2	78	DU68
Pritchard's Rd.		
Marian St. E2	78	DV68
Hackney Rd.		
Marian Way NW10	75	CT66
Maricas Ave., Har.	45	CD52
Marie Lloyd Gdns. N19	63	DL59
Hornsey Ri. Gdns.		
Marie Lloyd Wk. E8	78	DU65
Forest Rd.		
Mariette Way, Wall.	133	DL109
Marigold All. SE1	**10**	**F1**
Marigold Clo., Sthl.	72	BY73
Lancaster Rd.		
Marigold Rd. N17	50	DW52
Marigold St. SE16	92	DV75
Marigold Way E4	51	DZ51
Silver Birch Ave.		
Marigold Way, Croy.	121	DX102
Marina App., Hayes	72	BY71
Marina Ave., N.Mal.	117	CV99
Marina Clo., Brom.	122	EG97
Marina Clo., Cher.	112	BH102
Marina Dr., Well.	95	ES82
Marina Gdns., Rom.	69	FB57
Marina Gdns. (Cheshunt), Wal.Cr.	22	DW30
Marina Way, Tedd.	101	CK94
Fairways		
Marine Dr. SE18	95	EM77
Marine St. SE16	92	DU76
Enid St.		
Marinefield Rd. SW6	90	DB82
Mariner Gdns., Rich.	101	CJ90
Mariner Rd. E12	67	EM63
Dersingham Ave.		
Mariners Ms. E14	93	ED77
Mariners Wk., Erith	97	FF79
Frobisher Rd.		
Marion Ave., Shep.	113	BP99
Marion Clo., Ilf.	53	ER52
Marion Clo. (Bushey), Wat.	30	BZ39
Marion Cres., Orp.	124	EU99
Marion Gro., Wdf.Grn.	52	EE50
Marion Rd. NW7	47	CU50
Marion Rd., Th.Hth.	120	DQ99
Marischal Rd. SE13	93	ED83
Maritime St. E3	79	DZ70
Marius Pas. SW17	104	DG89
Marius Rd.		
Marius Rd. SW17	104	DG89
Marjorams Ave., Loug.	39	EM40
Marjorie Gro. SW11	90	DF84
Marjorie Ms. E1	79	DX72
Arbour Sq.		
Mark Ave. E4	37	EB44
Mark Clo., Bexh.	96	EY81

Maud Gdns., Bark. 81 ET68
Maud Rd. E10 65 EC62
Maud Rd. E13 80 EF68
Maud St. E16 80 EF71
Maude Cres., Wat. 29 BV37
Maude Rd. E17 65 DY57
Maude Rd. SE5 92 DS81
Maude Rd., Swan. 111 FG93
Maude Ter. E17 65 DY56
Maudlin's Grn. E1 78 DU74
Marble Quay
Maudslay Rd. SE9 95 EM83
Maudsley Ho., Brent. 88 CL78
Green Dragon La.
Mauleverer Rd. SW2 105 DL85
Maundeby Wk. NW10 74 CS65
Neasden La.
Maunder Rd. W7 73 CE74
Maunsel St. SW1 9 M8
Maunsel St. SW1 91 DK77
Maurice Ave. N22 49 DP54
Maurice Ave., Cat. 148 DR122
Maurice Brown Clo. NW7 47 CX50
Maurice St. W12 75 CV72
Maurice Wk. NW11 62 DC56
Maurier Clo., Nthlt. 72 BW67
Mauritius Rd. SE10 94 EE77
Maury Rd. N16 64 DU61
Mavelstone Clo., Brom. 122 EL95
Mavelstone Rd., Brom. 122 EK95
Maverton Rd. E3 79 EA67
Mavis Ave., Epsom 130 CS106
Mavis Clo., Epsom 130 CS106
Mavis Wk. E6 80 EL71
Tollgate Rd.
Mawbey Est. SE1 92 DT78
Mawbey Pl. SE1 92 DT78
Mawbey Rd. SE1 92 DT78
Old Kent Rd.
Mawbey St. SW8 91 DL80
Mawney Clo., Rom. 55 FB54
Mawney Rd., Rom. 55 FB54
Mawson Clo. SW20 117 CY96
Mawson La. W4 89 CT79
Great W. Rd.
Maxey Gdns., Dag. 68 EY63
Maxey Rd. SE18 95 EQ77
Maxey Rd., Dag. 68 EY64
Maxfield Clo. N20 48 DC45
Maxilla Gdns. W10 75 CX72
Cambridge Gdns.
Maxilla Wk. W10 75 CX72
Kingsdown Clo.
Maxim Rd. N21 35 DN44
Maxim Rd., Dart. 111 FE85
Maxim Rd., Erith 97 FE77
Maximfeldt Rd., Erith 97 FE78
Maxted Pk., Har. 59 CE59
Maxted Rd. SE15 92 DT83
Maxwell Clo., Croy. 119 DL101
Maxwell Clo., Rick. 42 BG47
Maxwell Dr., W.Byf. 126 BJ111
Maxwell Gdns., Orp. 123 ET104
Maxwell Ri., Wat. 44 BY45
Maxwell Rd. SW6 90 DB80
Maxwell Rd., Ashf. 99 BQ93
Maxwell Rd., Borwd. 32 CP41
Maxwell Rd., Nthwd. 43 BR52
Maxwell Rd., Well. 96 EU83
Maxwell Rd., West Dr. 84 BM77
Maxwelton Ave. NW7 46 CR50
Maxwelton Clo. NW7 46 CR50
May Ave., Orp. 124 EV99
May Clo., Chess. 130 CM107
May Cotts., Wat. 30 BW43
Watford Fld. Rd.
May Ct. SW19 118 DB95
May Gdns., Wem. 73 CJ69
May Rd. E4 51 EA51
May Rd. E13 80 EG68
May Rd., Twick. 101 CE88
May St. W14 89 CZ78
North End Rd.
May Tree La., Stan. 45 CF52
May Wk. E13 80 EH68
Queens Rd. W.
Maya Rd. N2 62 DC56
Mayall Rd. SE24 105 DP85
Maybank Ave. E18 52 EH54
Maybank Ave., Wem. 59 CF64
Maybank Gdns., Pnr. 57 BU57
Maybank Rd. E18 52 EH53
Maybells Commercial Est., Bark. 82 EX68
Mayberry Pl., Surb. 116 CM101
Maybourne Clo. SE26 106 DV92
Maybrook Meadow Est., Bark. 68 EU64
Maybury Ave. (Cheshunt), Wal.Cr. 22 DV28
Maybury Clo., Loug. 39 EP42
Maybury Clo., Orp. 123 EP99
Maybury Clo., Tad. 145 CY119
Ballards Grn.
Maybury Gdns. NW10 75 CV65
Maybury Ms. N6 63 DJ59
Maybury Rd. E13 80 EJ70
Maybury Rd., Bark. 81 ET68
Maybury St. SW17 104 DE92
Maychurch Clo., Stan. 45 CK52
Maycock Gro., Nthwd. 43 BT51
Maycroft, Pnr. 43 BV54
Maycroft Rd. (Cheshunt), Wal.Cr. 22 DS26
Maycross Ave., Mord. 117 CZ97
Mayday Gdns. SE3 94 EL82
Mayday Rd., Th.Hth. 119 DP100
Maydwell Lo., Borwd. 32 CM40
Mayell Clo., Lthd. 143 CJ123
Mayerne Rd. SE9 108 EK85
Mayes Clo., Swan. 125 FG98
Mayes Clo., Warl. 149 DX118
Mayes Rd. N22 49 DM54
Mayesbrook Rd., Bark. 81 ET67
Mayesbrook Rd., Dag. 68 EV62
Mayesbrook Rd., Ilf. 68 EU62
Mayesford Rd., Rom. 68 EW59
Mayeswood Rd. SE12 108 EJ90
Mayfair Ave., Bexh. 96 EX81
Mayfair Ave., Ilf. 67 EM61
Mayfair Ave., Rom. 68 EX58
Mayfair Ave., Twick. 100 CC87
Mayfair Ave., Wor.Pk. 117 CT102
Mayfair Clo., Beck. 121 EB95
Mayfair Clo., Surb. 116 CL102
Mayfair Gdns. N17 50 DQ51
Mayfair Gdns., Wdf.Grn. 52 EG52
Mayfair Ms. NW1 76 DF66
Regents Pk. Rd.
Mayfair Pl. W1 9 J2
Mayfair Pl. W1 77 DH74
Mayfair Ter. N14 49 DK45
Mayfare, Rick. 29 BR43
Mayfield, Bexh. 96 EZ83
Mayfield, Wal.Abb. 23 ED34
Roundhills
Mayfield Ave. N12 48 DC49
Mayfield Ave. N14 49 DJ47
Mayfield Ave. W4 88 CS77
Mayfield Ave. W13 87 CH76
Mayfield Ave., Add. 126 BH110
Mayfield Ave., Har. 59 CH57
Mayfield Ave., Orp. 123 ET101
Mayfield Ave., Wdf.Grn. 52 EG51
Mayfield Clo. E8 78 DT65
Forest Rd.
Mayfield Clo. SW4 105 DK85
Mayfield Clo., Add. 126 BJ110
Mayfield Clo., Ashf. 99 BP93
Mayfield Clo., T.Ditt. 115 CH102
Mayfield Clo., Uxb. 71 BP69
Mayfield Clo., Walt. 127 BU105
Mayfield Cres. N9 36 DV44
Mayfield Cres., Th.Hth. 119 DM98
Mayfield Dr., Pnr. 58 BZ56
Mayfield Gdns. NW4 61 CX58
Mayfield Gdns. W7 73 CD72
Mayfield Gdns., Walt. 127 BU105
Mayfield Rd. E4 51 EC47
Mayfield Rd. E8 78 DT66
Mayfield Rd. E13 80 EF70
Mayfield Rd. E17 51 DY54
Mayfield Rd. N8 63 DM57
Mayfield Rd. SW19 117 CZ95
Mayfield Rd. W3 74 CP73
Mayfield Rd. W12 88 CS75
Mayfield Rd., Belv. 97 FC77
Mayfield Rd., Brom. 122 EL99
Mayfield Rd., Dag. 68 EW60
Mayfield Rd., Enf. 37 DX40
Mayfield Rd., S.Croy. 134 DR109
Mayfield Rd., Sutt. 132 DD107
Mayfield Rd., Th.Hth. 119 DM98
Mayfield Rd., Walt. 127 BU105
Mayfield Rd., Wey. 126 BM106
Mayfields, Wem. 60 CN61
Mayfields Clo., Wem. 60 CN61
Mayflower Clo. SE16 93 DX77
Greenland Quay
Mayflower Ct. SE16 92 DW75
St. Marychurch St.
Mayflower Rd. SW9 91 DL83
Mayflower Rd., St.Alb. 16 CB27
Mayflower St. SE16 92 DW75
Mayfly Clo., Orp. 124 EX98
Mayfly Clo., Pnr. 58 BW59
Mayfly Gdns., Nthlt. 72 BX69
Ruislip Rd.
Mayford Clo. SW12 104 DF87
Mayford Clo., Beck. 121 DX97
Mayford Rd. SW12 104 DF87
Maygood St. N1 77 DM68
Maygoods Clo., Uxb. 70 BK71
Maygoods Grn., Uxb. 70 BK71
Worcester Rd.
Maygoods La., Uxb. 70 BK71
Maygoods Vw., Uxb. 70 BJ71
Benbow Waye
Maygreen Cres., Horn. 69 FG59
Maygrove Rd. NW6 75 CZ65
Mayhew Clo. E4 51 EA48
Mayhill Rd. SE7 94 EH79
Mayhill Rd., Barn. 33 CY43
Maylands Ave., Horn. 69 FH63
Maylands Dr., Sid. 110 EX90
Maylands Dr., Uxb. 70 BK65
Maylands Rd., Wat. 44 BW49
Maynard Clo. N15 64 DS56
Brunswick Rd.
Maynard Clo. SW6 90 DB80
Cambria St.
Maynard Clo., Erith 97 FF80
Maynard Ct., Wal.Abb. 24 EF34
Maynard Path E17 65 EC57
Maynard Rd.
Maynard Pl., Pot.B. 21 DM29
Maynard Rd. E17 65 EC57
Maynards Quay E1 78 DW73
Garnet St.
Maynooth Gdns., Cars. 118 DF101
Middleton Rd.
Mayo Clo. (Cheshunt), Wal.Cr. 22 DV28
Mayo Rd. NW10 74 CS65
Mayo Rd., Croy. 120 DR99
Mayo Rd., Walt. 113 BT101
Mayola Rd. E5 64 DW63
Mayow Rd. SE23 107 DX90
Mayow Rd. SE26 107 DX91
Mayplace Ave., Dart. 97 FG84
Mayplace Clo., Bexh. 97 FB83
Mayplace La. SE18 95 EP80
Mayplace Rd. E., Bexh. 97 FB83
Mayplace Rd. E., Dart. 97 FE84
Mayplace Rd. W., Bexh. 96 FA84
Maypole Cres., Ilf. 53 ER52
Maypole Dr., Chig. 54 EU48
Maypole Rd., Orp. 138 EZ106
Mayroyd Ave., Surb. 116 CN103
Mays Clo., Wey. 126 BM110
Mays Ct. WC2 9 P1
Mays Hill Rd., Brom. 122 EE96
Mays La. E4 51 ED47
Mays La., Barn. 47 CU45
Mays Rd., Tedd. 101 CD92
Maysoule Rd. SW11 90 DD84
Mayswood Gdns., Dag. 83 FC65
Maythorne Clo., Wat. 29 BS42
Mayton St. N7 63 DM62
Maytree Clo., Edg. 46 CQ48
Maytree Clo., Rain. 83 FE68
Maytree Cres., Wat. 29 BT35
Maytree Gdns. W5 87 CK75
South Ealing Rd.
Maytree Wk. SW2 105 DN89
Kingsmead Rd.
Maytrees, Rad. 31 CG37
Mayville Est. N16 64 DS64
King Henry St.
Mayville Rd. E11 66 EE61
Mayville Rd., Ilf. 67 EP64
Maywater Clo., S.Croy. 134 DR111
Maywood Clo., Beck. 107 EB94
Maze Hill SE3 94 EE80
Maze Hill SE10 94 EE79
Maze Rd., Rich. 88 CN80
Mazenod Ave. NW6 76 DA66
McAdam Dr., Enf. 35 DP40
Rowantree Rd.
McAuley Clo. SE1 10 D6
McAuley Clo. SE1 91 DN76
McAuley Clo. SE9 109 EP85
McCall Clo. SW4 91 DL82
Jeffreys Rd.
McCall Cres. SE7 94 EL78
McCarthy Rd., Felt. 100 BX92
McCoid Way SE1 11 H5
McCrone Ms. NW3 76 DD65
Belsize La.
McCullum Rd. E3 79 DZ67
McDermott Clo. SW11 90 DE83
McDermott Rd. SE15 92 DU83
McDonough Clo., Chess. 130 CL105
McDowall Rd. SE5 92 DQ81
McDowell Clo. E16 80 EF71
McEntee Ave. E17 51 DY53
McEwan Way E15 79 ED67
McGrath Rd. E15 66 EF64
McGredy (Cheshunt), Wal.Cr. 22 DV29
McGregor Rd. W11 75 CZ71
McIntosh Clo., Rom. 69 FE55
McIntosh Clo., Wall. 133 DL108
McIntosh Rd., Rom. 69 FE55
McKay Rd. SW20 103 CV94
McKellar Clo. (Bushey), Wat. 44 CC47
McKerrell Rd. SE15 92 DU81
McLeod Rd. SE2 96 EU77
McLeod's Ms. SW7 90 DB77
McMillan St. SE8 93 EA79
McNeil Rd. SE5 92 DS82
McNicol Dr. NW10 74 CQ68
McRae La., Mitch. 118 DF101
Mead, The N2 48 DC54
Mead, The W13 73 CH71
Mead, The, Ash. 144 CL119
Mead, The, Beck. 121 EC95
Mead, The, Stan. 45 CJ53
Mead, The, Uxb. 56 BN61
Mead, The, Wall. 133 DK107
Mead, The (Cheshunt), Wal.Cr. 22 DW29
Mead, The, Wat. 44 BY48
Mead, The, W.Wick. 121 ED102
Mead Clo., Har. 45 CD53
Mead Clo., Loug. 39 EP40
Mead Clo., Rom. 55 FG54
Mead Clo., Swan. 125 FG99
Mead Clo., Uxb. 56 BG61
Mead Ct. NW9 60 CQ57
Mead Ct., Wal.Abb. 23 EB34
Mead Cres. E4 51 EC49
Mead Cres., Sutt. 132 DE105
Mead End, Ash. 144 CM117
Mead Gro., Rom. 68 EX55
Mead Ho. Rd., Hayes 71 BR70
Mead La., Cher. 112 BJ102
Mead La. Caravan Pk., Cher. 112 BJ102
Mead Path SW17 104 DC91
Mead Pl. E9 78 DW65
Mead Pl., Croy. 119 DP102
Mead Pl., Rick. 42 BH46
Mead Plat NW10 74 CQ65
Mead Rd., Cat. 148 DT123
Mead Rd., Chis. 109 EQ93
Mead Rd., Edg. 46 CN51
Mead Rd., Rad. 18 CN33
Mead Rd., Rich. 101 CJ90
Mead Rd., Uxb. 70 BK65
Mead Rd., Walt. 128 BY105
Mead Row SE1 10 D6
Mead Way, Brom. 122 EE100
Mead Way, Couls. 147 DL118
Mead Way, Croy. 121 DY103
Mead Way (Bushey), Wat. 30 BY40
Meadcroft Rd. SE11 91 DP79
Meade Clo. W4 88 CN79
Meade Ct., Tad. 145 CU124
Meades, The, Wey. 127 BR107
Meadfield, Edg. 46 CP47
Meadfield Grn., Edg. 46 CP47
Meadfoot Rd. SW16 105 DJ94
Meadgate Ave., Wdf.Grn. 52 EL50
Meadhurst Rd., Cher. 112 BH102
Meadlands Dr., Rich. 101 CK89
Meadow, The, Chis. 109 EQ93
Meadow Ave., Croy. 121 DX100
Meadow Bank N21 35 DM44
Meadow Clo. E4 51 EB46
Mount Echo Ave.
Meadow Clo. E9 65 DZ64
Meadow Clo. SE6 107 EA92
Meadow Clo. SW20 117 CW98
Meadow Clo., Barn. 33 CZ44
Meadow Clo., Bexh. 110 EZ85
Meadow Clo., Chis. 109 EP92
Meadow Clo., Enf. 37 DY38
Meadow Clo., Esher 115 CF104
Meadow Clo., Houns. 100 CA86
Meadow Clo., Nthlt. 72 CA68
Meadow Clo., Pur. 133 DK113
Meadow Clo., Rich. 102 CL88
Meadow Clo., Ruis. 57 BT58
Meadow Clo. (Bricket Wd.), St.Alb. 16 CA29
Meadow Clo. (London Colney), St.Alb. 17 CK27
Meadow Clo., Sev. 154 FG123
Meadow Clo., Sutt. 118 DB103
Aultone Way
Meadow Clo., Walt. 128 BZ105
Meadow Ct., Epsom 130 CQ113
Meadow Dr. N10 62 DG55
Meadow Dr. NW4 47 CW54
Meadow Gdns., Edg. 46 CP51
Meadow Garth NW10 74 CQ65
Meadow Hill, N.Mal. 116 CS100
Meadow Hill, Pur. 133 DJ113
Meadow La., Cars. 118 DE103
Meadow La., Lthd. 142 CC121
Meadow Ms. SW8 91 DM79
Meadow Pl. SW8 91 DL80
Meadow Pl. W4 88 CS80
Edensor Rd.
Meadow Ri., Couls. 133 DK113
Meadow Rd. SW8 91 DM80
Meadow Rd. SW19 104 DC94
Meadow Rd., Ashf. 99 BR92
Meadow Rd., Ash. 144 CL117
Meadow Rd., Bark. 81 ET66
Meadow Rd., Borwd. 32 CP40
Meadow Rd., Brom. 122 EE95
Meadow Rd., Dag. 82 EZ65
Meadow Rd., Epp. 25 ET29
Meadow Rd., Esher 129 CE106
Meadow Rd., Felt. 100 BY89
Meadow Rd., Loug. 38 EL43
Meadow Rd., Pnr. 58 BX56
Meadow Rd., Rom. 69 FC60
Meadow Rd., Sthl. 72 BZ73
Meadow Rd., Sutt. 132 DE106
Meadow Rd., Wat. 15 BU34
Meadow Rd. (Bushey), Wat. 30 CB43
Meadow Row SE1 11 H7
Meadow Row SE1 92 DQ76
Meadow Stile, Croy. 120 DQ104
High St.
Meadow Vw., Har. 59 CE60
Meadow Vw., Sid. 110 EV87
Meadow Vw. Rd., Hayes 71 BQ70
Meadow Vw. Rd., Th.Hth. 119 DP99
Meadow Wk. E18 66 EG56
Meadow Wk., Dag. 82 EZ65
Meadow Wk., Epsom 130 CS107
Meadow Wk., Tad. 145 CV124
Meadow Wk., Wall. 119 DH104
Meadow Way NW9 60 CR57
Meadow Way, Abb.L. 15 BT27
Meadow Way, Add. 126 BH105
Meadow Way, Chess. 130 CL106
Meadow Way, Chig. 53 EQ48
Meadow Way, Kings L. 14 BN30
Meadow Way (Great Bookham), Lthd. 142 CB123
Meadow Way, Orp. 123 EN104
Meadow Way, Pot.B. 20 DA34
Meadow Way, Rick. 42 BJ45
Meadow Way, Ruis. 57 BV58
Meadow Way, Tad. 145 CY117
Meadow Way, Wem. 59 CK63
Meadow Way, The, Har. 45 CE53
Meadow Waye, Houns. 86 BY79
Meadowbank NW3 76 DF66
Meadowbank SE3 94 EF83
Meadowbank, Kings L. 14 BN30
Meadowbank, Surb. 116 CM100
Meadowbank, Wat. 44 BW45
Meadowbank Clo. SW6 89 CW80
Meadowbank Clo., Barn. 33 CT43
Meadowbank Gdns., Houns. 85 BU81
Meadowbank Rd. NW9 60 CR59
Meadowbanks, Barn. 33 CU43
Barnet Rd.
Meadowcourt Rd. SE3 94 EF84
Meadowcroft, Brom. 123 EM97
Meadowcroft (Bushey), Wat. 30 CB44
Meadowcroft Rd. N13 49 DN47
Meadowcross, Wal.Abb. 24 EE34
Meadowlands, Cob. 127 BU113
Meadowlands Pk., Add. 112 BL104
Meadowlea Clo., West Dr. 84 BK79
Meadows, The, Orp. 138 EW107
Meadows, The, Sev. 138 EZ113
Meadows, The, Warl. 149 DX117
Meadows Clo. E10 65 EA61
Meadows End, Sun. 113 BU95
Meadows Leigh Clo., Wey. 113 BQ104
Meadowside SE9 94 EJ84
Meadowside, Lthd. 142 CA123
Meadowside, Walt. 114 BW103
Meadowside Rd., Sutt. 131 CY109
Meadowsweet Clo. E16 80 EK71
Monarch Dr.
Meadowview, Orp. 124 EW97
Meadowview Rd. SE6 107 EA91
Meadowview Rd., Bex. 110 EY86
Meadowview Rd., Epsom 130 CS109
Meads, The, Edg. 46 CR51
Meads, The, St.Alb. 16 BZ29
Meads, The, Sutt. 117 CY104
Meads, The, Uxb. 70 BL70
Meads La., Ilf. 67 ES59
Meads Rd. N22 49 DP54
Meads Rd., Enf. 37 DY39
Meadvale Rd. W5 73 CH70
Meadvale Rd., Croy. 120 DT101
Meadway N14 49 DK47
Meadway NW11 62 DB58
Meadway SW20 117 CW98
Meadway, Ashf. 98 BN91
Meadway, Barn. 33 CZ42
Meadway, Beck. 121 EC95
Meadway, Enf. 36 DW37
Meadway, Epsom 130 CQ113
Meadway, Esher 128 CB109
Meadway, Ilf. 67 ES63
Meadway (Oxshott), Lthd. 129 CD114
Meadway, Rom. 55 FG54
Meadway, Ruis. 57 BR58
Meadway, Sev. 138 EZ113
Meadway, Stai. 98 BG94
Meadway, Surb. 116 CQ102
Meadway, Twick. 101 CD88
Meadway, Warl. 148 DW116
Meadway, Wdf.Grn. 52 EJ50
Meadway, The SE3 93 ED82
Heath La.
Meadway, The, Buck.H. 52 EK46
Meadway, The, Loug. 39 EM44
Meadway, The, Orp. 138 EV106
Meadway, The (Cuffley), Pot.B. 21 DM28
Meadway, The, Sev. 154 FF122
Meadway Clo. NW11 62 DB58
Meadway Clo., Barn. 34 DA42
Meadway Clo., Pnr. 44 CB51
Highbanks Rd.
Meadway Ct. NW11 62 DB58
Meadway Dr., Add. 126 BJ108
Meadway Gdns., Ruis. 57 BR58
Meadway Gate NW11 62 DA58
Meaford Way SE20 106 DV94
Meakin Est. SE1 11 M6
Meakin Est. SE1 92 DS76
Meanley Rd. E12 66 EL63
Meard St. W1 5 M9
Meard St. W1 77 DK72
Meare Clo., Tad. 145 CW123
Meath Clo., Orp. 124 EV99
Meath Rd. E15 80 EF68
Meath Rd., Ilf. 67 EQ62
Meath St. SW11 91 DH81
Mechanics Path SE8 93 EA80
Deptford High St.
Mecklenburgh Pl. WC1 6 B4
Mecklenburgh Pl. WC1 77 DM70
Mecklenburgh Sq. WC1 6 B4
Mecklenburgh Sq. WC1 77 DM70
Mecklenburgh St. WC1 6 B4
Mecklenburgh St. WC1 77 DM69
Medburn St. NW1 77 DK68
Medcalf Rd., Enf. 37 DZ37
Medcroft Gdns. SW14 88 CQ84
Mede Fld., Lthd. 143 CD124
Medebourne Clo. SE3 94 EG83
Medesenge Way N13 49 DP51
Medfield St. SW15 103 CU87
Medhurst Clo. E3 79 DY68
Arbery Rd.
Medhurst Rd. E3 79 DY68
Arbery Rd.
Median Rd. E5 64 DW64
Medina Ave., Esher 115 CE104
Medina Gro. N7 63 DN62
Medina Rd.
Medina Rd. N7 63 DN62
Medland Clo., Wall. 118 DG102
Medlar Clo., Nthlt. 72 BY68
Parkfield Ave.
Medlar St. SE5 92 DQ81
Medley Rd. NW6 76 DA65
Medman Clo., Uxb. 70 BJ68
Chiltern Vw. Rd.
Medora Rd. SW2 105 DM87
Medora Rd., Rom. 69 FD56
Medow Mead, Rad. 17 CF33
Medusa Rd. SE6 107 EB86
Medway Bldgs. E3 79 DY68
Medway Rd.

Medway Clo., Croy. 120 DW100
Medway Clo., Ilf. 67 EQ64
Loxford La.
Medway Clo., Wat. 16 BW34
Medway Dr., Grnf. 73 CF68
Medway Gdns., Wem. 59 CG63
Medway Ms. E3 79 DY68
Medway Rd.
Medway Par., Grnf. 73 CF68
Medway Rd. E3 79 DY68
Medway Rd., Dart. 97 FG83
Medway St. SW1 9 N7
Medway St. SW1 91 DK76
Medwin St. SW4 91 DM84
Meerbrook Rd. SE3 94 EJ83
Meeson Rd. E15 80 EF67
Meeson St. E5 65 DY63
Meeting Flds. Path E9 78 DW65
Morning La.
Meeting Ho. La. SE15 92 DV81
Meetinghouse All. E1 78 DV74
Wapping La.
Megg La., Kings L. 14 BH29
Mehetabel Rd. E9 78 DW65
Meister Clo., Ilf. 67 ER60
Melancholy Wk., Rich. 101 CJ89
Melanda Clo., Chis. 109 EM92
Melanie Clo., Bexh. 96 EY81
Melba Way SE13 93 EB81
Melbourne Ave. N13 49 DM51
Melbourne Ave. W13 73 CG74
Melbourne Ave., Pnr. 58 CB55
Melbourne Clo., Orp. 123 ES101
Melbourne Clo., Uxb. 56 BN63
Melbourne Clo., Wall. 133 DJ106
Melbourne Rd.
Melbourne Ct. E5 65 DY63
Daubeney Rd.
Melbourne Ct. N10 49 DH52
Sydney Rd.
Melbourne Ct. SE20 106 DU94
Melbourne Gdns., Rom. 68 EY57
Melbourne Gro. SE22 92 DS84
Melbourne Ho., Hayes 72 BW70
Melbourne Ms. SE6 107 EC87
Melbourne Ms. SW9 91 DN81
Melbourne Pl. WC2 6 C9
Melbourne Pl. WC2 77 DM73
Melbourne Rd. E6 81 EM67
Melbourne Rd. E10 65 EB59
Melbourne Rd. E17 65 DY56
Melbourne Rd. SW19 118 DA95
Melbourne Rd., Ilf. 67 EP60
Melbourne Rd., Tedd. 101 CJ93
Melbourne Rd., Wall. 133 DH106
Melbourne Rd. (Bushey), Wat. 30 CB43
Melbourne Sq. SW9 91 DN81
Melbourne Ms.
Melbourne Ter. SW6 90 DB80
Waterford Rd.
Melbourne Way, Enf. 36 DT44
Melbury Ave., Sthl. 86 CB76
Melbury Clo., Cher. 112 BG101
Melbury Clo., Chis. 108 EL93
Melbury Clo., Esher 129 CH107
Melbury Clo., W.Byf. 126 BG114
Melbury Ct. W8 89 CZ76
Melbury Dr. SE5 92 DS80
Sedgmoor Pl.
Melbury Gdns. SW20 117 CV95
Melbury Rd. W14 89 CZ76
Melbury Rd., Har. 60 CM57
Melbury Ter. NW1 4 C5
Melbury Ter. NW1 76 DE70
Melcombe Gdns., Har. 60 CM58
Melcombe Pl. NW1 4 D6
Melcombe Pl. NW1 76 DF71
Melcombe St. NW1 4 E5
Melcombe St. NW1 76 DF70
Meldex Clo. NW7 47 CW51
Meldon Clo. SW6 90 DB81
Bagley's La.
Meldone Clo., Surb. 116 CP100
Meldrum Clo., Orp. 124 EW100
Killewarren Way
Meldrum Rd., Ilf. 68 EU61
Melfield Gdns. SE6 107 EB91
Melford Ave., Bark. 81 ES65
Melford Clo., Chess. 130 CM106
Melford Rd. E6 81 EM70
Melford Rd. E11 66 EE61
Melford Rd. E17 65 DY56
Melford Rd. SE22 106 DU87
Melford Rd., Ilf. 67 ER61
Melfort Ave., Th.Hth. 119 DP97
Melfort Rd., Th.Hth. 119 DP97
Melgund Rd. N5 63 DN64
Melina Clo., Hayes 71 BR71
Middleton Rd.
Melina Pl. NW8 76 DD69
Melina Rd. W12 89 CV75
Melior Pl. SE1 11 M4
Melior St. SE1 11 M4
Melior St. SE1 92 DR75
Meliot Rd. SE6 107 ED89
Mell St. SE10 94 EE78
Trafalgar Rd.
Meller Clo., Croy. 119 DL104
Melling Dr., Enf. 36 DU39
Melling St. SE18 95 ES79
Mellish Clo., Bark. 81 ET67
Mellish Gdns., Wdf.Grn. 52 EG50
Harts Gro.
Mellish St. E14 93 EA76
Mellison Rd. SW17 104 DE92
Mellitus St. W12 75 CT72
Mellor Clo., Walt. 114 BZ101
Mellow Clo., Bans. 132 DB114
Mellow La. E., Hayes 71 BQ69
Mellow La. W., Uxb. 71 BQ69
Mellows Rd., Ilf. 67 EM55
Mellows Rd., Wall. 133 DK106
Mells Cres. SE9 109 EM91
Melody La. N5 63 DP64
Highbury Gro.
Melody Rd. SW18 104 DC85
Melody Rd., West. 150 EJ118
Melon Pl. W8 90 DA75
Kensington Ch. St.
Melon Rd. E11 66 EE62
Melon Rd. SE15 92 DU81
Melrose Ave. N22 49 DP53
Melrose Ave. NW2 61 CV64
Melrose Ave. SW16 119 DM97
Melrose Ave. SW19 103 CZ89
Melrose Ave., Borwd. 32 CP43
Melrose Ave., Grnf. 72 CB68
Melrose Ave., Mitch. 105 DH94
Melrose Ave., Pot.B. 20 DB32
Melrose Ave., Twick. 100 CB87
Melrose Clo. SE12 108 EG88
Melrose Clo., Grnf. 72 CB68
Melrose Clo., Hayes 71 BU71
Melrose Cres., Orp. 137 ER105
Melrose Dr., Sthl. 72 CA74
Melrose Gdns. W6 89 CW76
Melrose Gdns., Edg. 46 CP54
Melrose Gdns., N.Mal. 116 CR97
Melrose Gdns., Walt. 128 BW106
Melrose Pl., Wat. 29 BT38
Wentworth Clo.
Melrose Rd. SW13 89 CT82
Melrose Rd. SW18 103 CZ86
Melrose Rd. SW19 118 DA96
Melrose Rd. W3 88 CQ76
Stanley Rd.
Melrose Rd., Couls. 147 DH115
Melrose Rd., Pnr. 58 BZ56
Melrose Rd., West. 150 EJ116
Melrose Rd., Wey. 126 BN106
Melrose Ter. W6 89 CW75
Melsa Rd., Mord. 118 DC100
Meltham Way SE16 92 DV78
Egan Way
Melthorne Dr., Ruis. 58 BW62
Melthorpe Gdns. SE3 94 EK81
Melton Clo., Ruis. 58 BW60
Melton Ct. SW7 8 A9
Melton Ct. SW7 90 DD77
Melton Flds., Epsom 130 CR109
Melton Gdns., Rom. 69 FF59
Melton Pl., Epsom 130 CR109
Melton St. NW1 5 L3
Melton St. NW1 77 DJ69
Melville Ave. SW20 103 CU94
Melville Ave., Grnf. 59 CF64
Melville Ave., S.Croy. 134 DT106
Melville Clo., Uxb. 57 BR62
Melville Gdns. N13 49 DN50
Melville Rd. E17 65 DZ55
Melville Rd. NW10 74 CR66
Melville Rd. SW13 89 CU81
Melville Rd., Rain. 83 FG70
Melville Rd., Rom. 55 FB52
Melville Rd., Sid. 110 EW89
Melville Vill. Rd. W3 74 CR74
High St.
Melvin Rd. SE20 120 DW95
Melvinshaw, Lthd. 143 CJ121
Melvyn Clo. (Cheshunt), Wal.Cr. 21 DP28
Melyn Clo. N7 63 DJ63
Anson Rd.
Memel Ct. EC1 7 H5
Memel St. EC1 7 H5
Memess Path SE18 95 EN79
Engineer Clo.
Memorial Ave. E15 80 EE69
Memorial Clo., Houns. 86 BZ79
Mendip Clo. SE26 106 DW91
Mendip Clo. SW19 103 CY89
Queensmere Rd.
Mendip Clo., Hayes 85 BR80
Mendip Clo., Wor.Pk. 117 CW103
Cotswold Way
Mendip Dr. NW2 61 CY61
Mendip Rd. SW11 90 DC83
Mendip Rd., Bexh. 97 FE81
Mendip Rd., Horn. 69 FG59
Mendip Rd., Ilf. 67 ES57
Mendip Rd. (Bushey), Wat. 30 CC44
Mendora Rd. SW6 89 CY80
Menelik Rd. NW2 61 CY63
Menlo Gdns. SE19 106 DR94
Menotti St. E2 78 DU70
Dunbridge St.
Mentmore Clo., Har. 59 CJ58
Mentmore Ter. E8 78 DV66
Meon Clo., Tad. 145 CV122
Meon Ct., Islw. 87 CE82
Meon Rd. W3 88 CQ75
Meopham Rd., Mitch. 119 DJ95
Mepham Cres., Har. 44 CC52
Mepham Gdns., Har. 44 CC52
Mepham St. SE1 10 D3
Mepham St. SE1 77 DM74
Mera Dr., Bexh. 96 FA84
Merantun Way SW19 118 DC95
Merbury Clo. SE13 107 ED85
Merbury Rd. SE28 95 ES75
Mercator Rd. SE13 93 ED84
Mercer Clo., T.Ditt. 115 CF101
Mercer Pl., Pnr. 44 BW54
Cross Way
Mercer St. WC2 5 P9
Mercer St. WC2 77 DL72
Mercer Wk., Uxb. 70 BJ66
High St.
Merceron St. E1 78 DV70
Mercers Clo. SE10 94 EF77
Mercers Pl. W6 89 CW77
Mercers Rd. N19 63 DK62
Merchant St. E3 79 DZ69
Merchiston Rd. SE6 107 ED89
Merchland Rd. SE9 109 EQ88
Mercia Gro. SE13 93 EC84
Mercier Rd. SW15 103 CY85
Mercury Cen. Ind. Est., Felt. 99 BU85
Mercury Gdns., Rom. 69 FE56
Mercury Way SE14 93 DX79
Mercy Ter. SE13 93 EB84
Mere Clo. SW15 103 CX87
Mere Clo., Orp. 123 EN103
Mere End, Croy. 121 DX101
Mere Rd., Shep. 113 BP100
Mere Rd., Tad. 145 CV124
Mere Rd., Wey. 113 BR104
Mere Side, Orp. 123 EN103
Merebank La., Croy. 133 DM106
Meredith Ave. NW2 61 CW64
Meredith Clo., Pnr. 44 BX52
Meredith St. E13 80 EG69
Meredith St. EC1 6 F3
Meredyth Rd. SW13 89 CU82
Merefield Gdns., Tad. 145 CX119
Meretone Clo. SE4 93 DY84
Merevale Cres., Mord. 118 DC100
Mereway Rd., Twick. 101 CD88
Merewood Clo., Brom. 123 EN96
Merewood Rd., Bexh. 97 FC82
Mereworth Clo., Brom. 122 EF99
Mereworth Dr. SE18 95 EP80
Merganser Gdns. SE28 95 ER76
Avocet Ms.
Meriden Clo., Brom. 108 EK94
Meriden Clo., Ilf. 53 EQ53
Meriden Way, Wat. 30 BY36
Meridian Gate E14 93 EC75
Meridian Rd. SE7 94 EK80
Meridian Trd. Est. SE7 94 EH77
Meridian Wk. N17 50 DS51
Commercial Rd.
Meridian Way N9 51 DX47
Meridian Way N18 50 DW51
Meridian Way, Enf. 37 DX44
Merifield Rd. SE9 94 EJ84
Merino Clo. E11 66 EJ56
Merino Pl., Sid. 110 EU86
Blackfen Rd.
Merivale Rd. SW15 89 CY84
Merivale Rd., Har. 58 CC59
Merland Clo., Tad. 145 CW120
Merland Grn., Tad. 145 CW120
Merland Ri.
Merland Ri., Epsom 145 CW119
Merland Ri., Tad. 145 CW120
Merle Ave., Uxb. 42 BH54
Merle Clo., Cat. 148 DR120
Merlewood, Sev. 155 FH123
Merlewood Clo., Cat. 148 DR120
Merlewood Dr., Chis. 123 EM95
Merley Ct. NW9 60 CQ60
Merlin Clo., Croy. 134 DS105
Minster Dr.
Merlin Clo., Ilf. 54 EW50
Merlin Clo., Mitch. 118 DE97
Merlin Clo., Nthlt. 72 BW69
Merlin Clo., Rom. 55 FD51
Merlin Clo., Wal.Abb. 24 EG34
Merlin Cres., Edg. 46 CM53
Merlin Gdns., Brom. 108 EG90
Merlin Gdns., Rom. 55 FD51
Merlin Gro., Beck. 121 DZ98
Merlin Gro., Ilf. 53 EP51
Merlin Rd. E12 66 EK61
Merlin Rd., Rom. 55 FD51
Merlin Rd., Well. 96 EU84
Merlin Rd. N., Well. 96 EU84
Merlin St. WC1 6 D3
Merlin Way, Epp. 26 FA25
Merling Clo., Chess. 129 CK106
Coppard Gdns.
Merlins Ave., Har. 58 BZ62
Mermagen Dr., Rain. 83 FH66
Mermaid Ct. SE1 11 K4
Mermaid Ct. SE1 92 DR75
Mermaid Ct. SE16 79 DZ74
Merredene St. SW2 105 DM86
Merriam Clo. E4 51 EC50
Merrick Rd., Sthl. 86 BZ75
Merrick Sq. SE1 11 K6
Merrick Sq. SE1 92 DQ76
Merridene N21 35 DP44
Merrielands Cres., Dag. 82 EZ67
Merrilands Rd., Wor.Pk. 117 CW102
Merrilees Rd., Sid. 109 ES88
Merrilyn Clo., Esher 129 CG107
Merriman Rd. SE3 94 EJ81
Merrington Rd. SW6 90 DA79
Merrion Ave., Stan. 45 CK50
Merrion Wk. SE17 92 DR78
Dawes St.
Merritt Gdns., Chess. 129 CJ107
Merritt Rd. SE4 107 DZ85
Merrivale N14 35 DK44
Merrivale Ave., Ilf. 66 EK56
Merrow Rd., Sutt. 131 CX109
Merrow St. SE17 92 DQ79
Merrow Wk. SE17 11 L10
Merrow Way, Croy. 135 EC107
Merrows Clo., Nthwd. 43 BQ51
Merry Hill Mt. (Bushey), Wat. 44 CB46
Merry Hill Rd. (Bushey), Wat. 30 BZ44
Merry Meet, Bans. 132 DF114
Merrydown Way, Chis. 122 EL95
Merryfield SE3 94 EF82
Merryfield Gdns., Stan. 45 CJ50
Merryfields, Uxb. 70 BL68
The Greenway
Merryfields Way SE6 107 EB87
Merryhill Clo. E4 51 EB45
Merryhills Clo., West. 150 EK116
Merryhills Ct. N14 35 DJ43
Merryhills Dr., Enf. 35 DK42
Merrylands Rd., Lthd. 142 BZ123
Mersea Ho., Bark. 81 EP65
Mersey Rd. E17 65 DZ55
Mersey Wk., Nthlt. 72 CA68
Brabazon Rd.
Mersham Dr. NW9 60 CN57
Mersham Pl. SE20 120 DV95
Jasmine Gro.
Mersham Rd., Th.Hth. 120 DR97
Merten Rd., Rom. 68 EY59
Merthyr Ter. SW13 89 CV79
Merton Ave. W4 89 CT77
Merton Ave., Nthlt. 58 CC64
Merton Ave., Uxb. 71 BP66
Merton Gdns., Orp. 123 EP99
Merton Gdns., Tad. 145 CX120
Marbles Way
Merton Hall Gdns. SW20 117 CY95
Merton Hall Rd. SW19 103 CY94
Merton High St. SW19 104 DC94
Merton Ind. Pk. SW19 118 DC95
Merton La. N6 62 DF61
Merton Mans. SW20 117 CX96
Merton Pk. Par. SW19 117 CZ95
Kingston Rd.
Merton Ri. NW3 76 DE66
Merton Rd. E17 65 EC57
Merton Rd. SE25 120 DU99
Merton Rd. SW18 104 DA85
Merton Rd. SW19 104 DB94
Merton Rd., Bark. 81 ET66
Merton Rd., Enf. 36 DR38
Merton Rd., Har. 58 CC60
Merton Rd., Ilf. 67 ET59
Merton Rd., Wat. 29 BV42
Merton Wk., Lthd. 143 CG118
Merton Way
Merton Way, Lthd. 143 CG118
Merton Way, Uxb. 71 BP66
Merton Way, W.Mol. 114 CB98
Merttins Rd. SE15 107 DX85
Meru Clo. NW5 62 DG63
Kiln Pl.
Mervan Rd. SW2 91 DN84
Mervyn Ave. SE9 109 EQ90
Mervyn Rd. W13 87 CG76
Mervyn Rd., Shep. 113 BQ101
Meryfield Clo., Borwd. 32 CM40
Mesne Way, Sev. 139 FF112
Messaline Ave. W3 74 CQ72
Messent Rd. SE9 108 EJ85
Messeter Pl. SE9 109 EN86
Messina Ave. NW6 76 DA66
Metcalf Rd., Ashf. 99 BP92
Metcalfe Wk., Felt. 100 BY91
Gabriel Clo.
Meteor St. SW11 90 DG84
Meteor Way, Wall. 133 DL108
Metheringham Way NW9 46 CS53
Methley St. SE11 91 DN78
Methuen Clo., Edg. 46 CN52
Methuen Pk. N10 49 DH54
Methuen Rd., Belv. 97 FB77
Methuen Rd., Bexh. 96 EZ84
Methuen Rd., Edg. 46 CN52
Methwold Rd. W10 75 CX71
Metro Ind. Cen., Islw. 87 CE82
Metropolitan Cen., The, Grnf. 72 CB67
Meux Clo. (Cheshunt), Wal.Cr. 22 DU31
Mews, The N1 78 DQ67
St. Paul St.
Mews, The, Ilf. 66 EK57
Mews, The, Rom. 69 FE56
Market Link
Mews, The, Sev. 154 FG123
Mews, The, Twick. 101 CH86
Bridge Rd.
Mews Deck E1 78 DV73
Sovereign Clo.
Mews End, West. 150 EK118
Mews Pl., Wdf.Grn. 52 EG49
Mews St. E1 78 DU74
Mexfield Rd. SW15 103 CZ85
Meyer Gro., Enf. 36 DU38
Meyer Rd., Erith 97 FC79
Meymott St. SE1 10 F3
Meymott St. SE1 77 DP74
Meynell Cres. E9 79 DX66
Meynell Gdns. E9 79 DX66
Meynell Rd. E9 79 DX66
Meynell Rd., Rom. 55 FH52
Meyrick Rd. NW10 75 CU65
Meyrick Rd. SW11 90 DD83
Mezen Clo., Nthwd. 43 BR50
Miah Ter. E1 78 DU74
Wapping High St.
Miall Wk. SE26 107 DY91
Micawber Ave., Uxb. 70 BN70
Micawber St. N1 7 J2
Micawber St. N1 78 DQ69
Michael Faraday Ho. SE17 92 DS78
Beaconsfield Rd.
Michael Gaynor Clo. W7 73 CF74
Michael Rd. E11 66 EE60
Michael Rd. SE25 120 DS97
Michael Rd. SW6 90 DB81
Michaelmas Clo. SW20 117 CW97
Michaels Clo. SE13 94 EE84
Micheldever Rd. SE12 108 EE86
Michelham Gdns., Tad. 145 CW121
Waterfield
Michelham Gdns., Twick. 101 CG90
Michels Row, Rich. 88 CL84
Kew Foot Rd.
Michigan Ave. E12 67 EM63
Michleham Down N12 47 CZ49
Micklefield Way, Borwd. 32 CL38
Mickleham Clo., Orp. 123 ET96
Mickleham Gdns., Sutt. 131 CY107
Mickleham Rd., Orp. 123 ET95
Mickleham Way, Croy. 135 ED108
Micklethwaite Rd. SW6 90 DA79
Midas Metropolitan Ind. Est., The, Mord. 117 CX102
Garth Rd.
Midcroft, Ruis. 57 BS60
Middle Boy, Rom. 40 EW41
Middle Clo., Couls. 147 DN120
Middle Clo., Epsom 130 CS112
Middle La.
Middle Dene NW7 46 CR48
Middle Fld. NW8 76 DD67
Middle Furlong (Bushey), Wat. 30 CB42
Middle Gorse, Croy. 135 DY112
Middle Grn., Stai. 98 BK94
Honnor Rd.
Middle Grn. Clo., Surb. 116 CM100
Alpha Rd.
Middle La. N8 63 DL57
Middle La., Epsom 130 CS112
Middle La., Sev. 155 FM121
Church Rd.
Middle La., Tedd. 101 CF93
Middle La. Ms. N8 63 DL57
Middle La.
Middle Ope, Wat. 29 BV37
The Thrums
Middle Pk. Ave. SE9 108 EK86
Middle Path, Har. 59 CD60
Middle Rd.
Middle Rd. E13 80 EG68
London Rd.
Middle Rd. SW16 119 DJ96
Middle Rd., Barn. 34 DE44
Middle Rd., Har. 59 CD61
Middle Rd., Lthd. 143 CH121
Middle Rd., Wal.Abb. 23 EB32
Middle Row W10 75 CY70
Middle St. EC1 7 H6
Middle St., Croy. 120 DQ104
Surrey St.
Middle Temple EC4 6 D10
Middle Temple La. EC4 6 D9
Middle Temple La. EC4 77 DN72
Middle Way SW16 119 DK96
Middle Way, Erith 96 EY76
Middle Way, Hayes 72 BX70
Douglas Cres.
Middle Way, Wat. 29 BV37
Middle Way, The, Har. 45 CF54
Middle Yd. SE1 11 M2
Middlefield Gdns., Ilf. 67 EP58
Middlefielde W13 73 CH71
Middlefields, Croy. 135 DY109
Middleham Gdns. N18 50 DU51
Middleham Rd. N18 50 DU51
Middlesborough Rd. N18 50 DU51
Middlesex Business Cen., The, Sthl. 86 BZ75
Middlesex Ct. W4 89 CT77
British Gro.
Middlesex Pas. EC1 6 G7
Middlesex Rd., Mitch. 119 DL98
Middlesex St. E1 7 N7
Middlesex St. E1 78 DS71
Middlesex Wf. E5 64 DW61
Middleton Ave. E4 51 DZ49
Middleton Ave., Grnf. 73 CD68
Middleton Ave., Sid. 110 EW93
Middleton Bldgs. W1 5 K7
Middleton Clo. E4 51 DZ48
Middleton Dr. SE16 93 DX75
Middleton Dr., Pnr. 57 BU55
Middleton Gdns., Ilf. 67 EP58
Middleton Gro. N7 63 DL64
Middleton Ms. N7 63 DL64
Middleton Gro.
Middleton Rd. E8 78 DT66
Middleton Rd. NW11 62 DA59
Middleton Rd., Cars. 118 DD101
Middleton Rd., Cob. 141 BV119
Middleton Rd., Epsom 130 CR110
Middleton Rd., Hayes 71 BR71
Middleton Rd., Mord. 118 DB100
Middleton Rd., Rick. 42 BG46
Middleton St. E2 78 DV69
Middleton Way SE13 93 ED84
Middleway NW11 62 DB57
Middlings, The, Sev. 154 FF125
Middlings Ri., Sev. 154 FF126
Middlings Wd., Sev. 154 FF125
Midfield Ave., Bexh. 97 FC83
Midfield Ave., Swan. 111 FG93

Midfield Way, Orp. 124 EU95
Midford Pl. W1 5 L5
Midgarth Clo., Lthd. 128 CC114
Midholm NW11 62 DB56
Midholm, Wem. 60 CN60
Midholm Clo. NW11 62 DB56
Midholm Rd., Croy. 121 DY103
Midhope St. WC1 6 A3
Midhurst Ave. N10 62 DG55
Midhurst Ave., Croy. 119 DN101
Midhurst Clo., Horn. 69 FG63
Midhurst Gdns., Uxb. 71 BQ66
Midhurst Hill, Bexh. 110 FA86
Midhurst Rd. W13 87 CG75
Midland Pl. E14 93 EC78
Ferry St.
Midland Rd. E10 65 EC59
Midland Rd. NW1 5 N1
Midland Rd. NW1 77 DK68
Midland Ter. NW2 61 CX62
Midland Ter. NW10 74 CS70
Shaftesbury Gdns.
Midleton Rd., N.Mal. 116 CQ96
Midlothian Rd. E3 79 DY71
Midmoor Rd. SW12 105 DJ88
Midmoor Rd. SW19 117 CX95
Midship Clo. SE16 79 DX74
Surrey Water Rd.
Midstrath Rd. NW10 60 CS63
Midsummer Ave., Houns. 86 BZ84
Midway, Sutt. 117 CZ101
Midway, Walt. 113 BV103
Midway Ave., Cher. 112 BG97
Eastern Ave.
Midwinter Clo., Well. 96 EU83
Hook La.
Midwood Clo. NW2 61 CV62
Miena Way, Ash. 143 CK117
Miers Clo. E6 81 EN67
Mighell Ave., Ilf. 66 EK57
Milborne Gro. SW10 90 DC78
Milborne St. E9 78 DW65
Milborough Cres. SE12 108 EE86
Milbourne La., Esher 128 CC107
Milbrook, Esher 128 CC107
Milburn Dr., West Dr. 70 BL73
Milburn Wk., Epsom 144 CS115
Milcote St. SE1 10 F5
Milcote St. SE1 91 DP75
Mildenhall Rd. E5 64 DW63
Mildmay Ave. N1 78 DR65
Mildmay Gro. N. N1 64 DR64
Mildmay Gro. S. N1 64 DR64
Mildmay Pk. N1 64 DR64
Mildmay Pl., Sev. 139 FF111
Mildmay Rd. N1 64 DR64
Mildmay Rd., Ilf. 67 EP62
Winston Way
Mildmay Rd., Rom. 69 FC57
Mildmay St. N1 78 DR65
Mildred Ave., Borwd. 32 CN42
Mildred Ave., Hayes 85 BR77
Mildred Ave., Nthlt. 58 CB64
Mildred Ave., Wat. 29 BT42
Mildred Rd., Erith 97 FE78
Mile Clo., Wal.Abb. 23 EC33
Mile End, The E17 51 DX53
Mile End Pl. E1 79 DX70
Mile End Rd. E1 78 DW71
Mile End Rd. E3 79 DY70
Mile Rd., Wall. 119 DH102
Miles La., Cob. 128 BY113
Miles Pl. NW1 4 B6
Miles Pl., Surb. 116 CM98
Villiers Ave.
Miles Rd. N8 63 DL55
Miles Rd., Epsom 130 CR112
Miles Rd., Mitch. 118 DD97
Miles St. SW8 91 DL79
Miles Way N20 48 DE47
Milespit Hill NW7 47 CV50
Milestone Clo. N9 50 DU47
Chichester Rd.
Milestone Clo., Sutt. 132 DD107
Milestone Clo., Wok. 140 BG122
Milestone Rd. SE19 106 DT93
Milfoil St. W12 75 CU73
Milford Clo. SE2 96 EY79
Milford Gdns., Croy. 121 DX99
Tannery Clo.
Milford Gdns., Edg. 46 CN52
Milford Gdns., Wem. 59 CK63
Milford Gro., Sutt. 132 DC105
Milford La. WC2 6 D10
Milford La. WC2 77 DM73
Milford Ms. SW16 105 DM90
Milford Rd. W13 73 CH74
Milford Rd., Sthl. 72 CA73
Milford Way SE15 92 DT81
Sumner Est.
Milk St. E16 81 EP74
Milk St. EC2 7 J8
Milk St., Brom. 108 EH93
Milk Yd. E1 78 DW73
Milking La., Kes. 136 EK112
Milking La., Orp. 136 EL112
Milkwell Gdns., Wdf.Grn. 52 EH52
Milkwell Yd. SE5 92 DQ81
Milkwood Rd. SE24 105 DP85
Mill Ave., Uxb. 70 BJ68
Mill Brook Rd., Orp. 124 EW98
Mill Clo., Cars. 118 DG103
Mill Clo., Hem.H. 14 BN25
Mill Clo., Lthd. 142 CA124
Mill Clo., West Dr. 84 BK76
Mill Cor., Barn. 33 CZ39
Mill Ct. E10 65 EC62
Mill Fm. Ave., Sun. 99 BS94
Mill Fm. Clo., Pnr. 44 BW54
Mill Fm. Cres., Houns. 100 BY88
Mill Gdns. SE26 106 DV91
Mill Grn., Mitch. 118 DG101
London Rd.
Mill Grn. Rd., Mitch. 118 DF101
Mill Hill SW13 89 CU82
Mill Hill Rd.
Mill Hill Circ. NW7 47 CT50
Watford Way
Mill Hill Gro. W3 74 CP74
Mill Hill Rd.
Mill Hill Rd. SW13 89 CU82
Mill Hill Rd. W3 88 CP75
Mill La. E4 37 EB41
Mill La. NW6 61 CY64
Mill La. SE18 95 EN78
Mill La., Cars. 132 DF105
Mill La., Croy. 119 DM104
Mill La., Epsom 131 CT109
Mill La., Kings L. 14 BN29
Mill La., Lthd. 143 CG122
Mill La. (Toot Hill), Ong. 27 FE29
Mill La. (Downe), Orp. 137 EN110
Mill La., Rick. 29 BQ44
Watford Rd.
Mill La. (Chadwell Heath), Rom. 68 EY58
Mill La. (Navestock), Rom. 41 FH38
Mill La., Sev. 155 FJ121
Mill La. (Shoreham), Sev. 139 FF110
Mill La., Wal.Cr. 23 DY28
Mill La., W.Byf. 126 BM113
Mill La., Wok. 140 BK119
Mill La., Wdf.Grn. 52 EF50
Mill Mead Ind. Cen. N17 50 DV54
Mill Mead Rd. N17 64 DV55
Mill Pl. E14 79 DZ72
East India Dock Rd.
Mill Pl., Chis. 123 EP95
Mill Pl., Dart. 97 FG84
Mill Pl., Kings.T. 116 CM97
Mill Plat, Islw. 87 CG82
Mill Plat Ave., Islw. 87 CG82
Mill Pond Clo., Sev. 155 FK121
Mill Ridge, Edg. 46 CM50
Mill Rd. E16 80 EH74
Mill Rd. SE13 93 EC83
Loampit Vale
Mill Rd. SW19 104 DC94
Mill Rd., Cob. 142 BW115
Mill Rd., Epsom 131 CT112
Mill Rd., Erith 97 FC80
Mill Rd., Esher 114 CA103
Mill Rd., Ilf. 67 EN62
Mill Rd., Sev. 154 FE121
Mill Rd., Tad. 145 CX123
Mill Rd., Twick. 100 CC89
Mill Rd., West Dr. 84 BJ76
Mill Row N1 78 DS67
Mill Shot Clo. SW6 89 CW81
Mill St. SE1 92 DT75
Mill St. W1 5 K10
Mill St. W1 77 DJ73
Mill St., Kings.T. 116 CL97
Mill Trd. Est., The NW10 74 CQ69
Mill Vale, Brom. 122 EF96
Mill Vw. Clo., Epsom 131 CT108
Mill Vw. Gdns., Croy. 121 DX104
Mill Way, Felt. 99 BV85
Mill Way, Lthd. 144 CM124
Mill Way (Bushey), Wat. 30 BY40
Mill Yd. E1 78 DU73
Cable St.
Millais Ave. E12 67 EN64
Millais Gdns., Edg. 46 CN54
Millais Rd. E11 65 EC63
Millais Rd., Enf. 36 DT43
Millais Rd., N.Mal. 116 CS101
Millais Way, Epsom 130 CQ105
Millan Clo., Add. 126 BH110
Milland Ct., Borwd. 32 CR39
Millard Clo. N16 64 DS64
Boleyn Rd.
Millard Ter., Dag. 82 FA65
Church Elm La.
Millbank SW1 9 P6
Millbank SW1 91 DL77
Millbank, Stai. 98 BH92
Millbank Twr. SW1 9 P9
Millbank Twr. SW1 91 DL77
Millbank Way SE12 108 EG85
Millbourne Rd., Felt. 100 BY91
Millbro, Swan. 111 FG94
Millbrook, Wey. 127 BS105
Millbrook Ave., Well. 95 ER84
Millbrook Gdns., Rom. 55 FE54
Millbrook Gdns. (Chadwell Heath), Rom. 68 EZ58
Millbrook Rd. N9 50 DV46
Millbrook Rd. SW9 91 DP83
Millbrook Rd. (Bushey), Wat. 30 BZ39
Millcrest Rd. (Cheshunt), Wal.Cr. 21 DP28
Millender Wk. SE16 92 DW77
Millennium Pl. E2 78 DV68
Millennium Sq. SE1 92 DT75
Tooley St.
Miller Clo., Mitch. 118 DF101
Miller Clo., Pnr. 44 BW54
Miller Rd. SW19 104 DD93
Miller Rd., Croy. 119 DM102
Miller St. NW1 77 DJ68
Miller Wk. SE1 10 E3
Miller Wk. SE1 77 DN74
Miller's Ave. E8 64 DT64
Millers Clo. NW7 47 CU49
Millers Clo., Chig. 54 EV46
Millers Clo., Stai. 98 BH92
Millers Copse, Epsom 144 CR119
Millers Ct. W4 89 CT78
Chiswick Mall
Millers Grn. Clo., Enf. 35 DP41
Miller's La., Chig. 54 EV46
Millers Meadow Clo. SE3 108 EF85
Meadowcourt Rd.
Miller's Ter. E8 64 DT64
Millers Way W6 89 CW75
Millet Rd., Grnf. 72 CB69
Millfield, Sun. 113 BR95
Millfield Ave. E17 51 DY53
Millfield La. N6 62 DF61
Millfield Pl. N6 62 DG61
Millfield Rd., Edg. 46 CQ54
Millfield Rd., Houns. 100 BY88
Millfields Clo., Orp. 124 EV98
Millfields Est. E5 65 DX62
Denton Way
Millfields Rd. E5 64 DW63
Millgrove St. SW11 90 DG81
Millharbour E14 93 EB76
Millhaven Clo., Rom. 68 EV58
Millhedge Clo., Cob. 142 BY116
Millhoo Ct., Wal.Abb. 24 EF34
Millhouse La., Abb.L. 15 BU27
Millhouse Pl. SE27 105 DP91
Millicent Rd. E10 65 DZ60
Milligan St. E14 79 DZ73
Milliners Ct., Loug. 39 EN40
The Cft.
Milling Rd., Edg. 46 CR52
Millington Rd., Hayes 85 BS76
Millman Ms. WC1 6 B5
Millman Ms. WC1 77 DM70
Millman Pl. WC1 6 B5
Millman St. WC1 6 B5
Millman St. WC1 77 DM70
Millmark Gro. SE14 93 DY82
Millmarsh La., Enf. 37 DY40
Millmead, W.Byf. 126 BM112
Millpond Ct., Add. 126 BL106
Millpond Est. SE16 92 DV75
West La.
Mills Clo., Uxb. 70 BN68
Mills Ct. EC2 7 M4
Mills Gro. E14 79 EC71
Dewberry St.
Mills Gro. NW4 61 CX55
Mills Rd., Walt. 128 BW106
Mills Row W4 88 CR77
Bridge St.
Millside, Cars. 118 DF103
Millside Pl., Islw. 87 CH82
Millsmead Way, Loug. 39 EM40
Millson Clo. N20 48 DD47
Millstead Clo., Tad. 145 CV122
Millstream Clo. N13 49 DN50
Millstream Rd. SE1 11 P5
Millstream Rd. SE1 92 DT75
Millthorn Clo., Rick. 28 BM43
Millwall Dock Rd. E14 93 EA76
Millway NW7 46 CS50
Millway Gdns., Nthlt. 72 BZ65
Millwell Cres., Chig. 53 ER50
Millwood Rd., Houns. 100 CC85
Millwood Rd., Orp. 124 EW97
Millwood St. W10 75 CY71
St. Charles Sq.
Milman Clo., Pnr. 58 BX55
Milman Rd. NW6 75 CX68
Milman's St. SW10 90 DD79
Milne Feild, Pnr. 44 CA52
Milne Gdns. SE9 108 EL85
Milne Pk. E., Croy. 135 ED111
Milne Pk. W., Croy. 135 ED111
Milne Way, Uxb. 42 BH53
Milner App., Cat. 148 DU121
Milner Clo., Cat. 148 DU121
Milner Clo., Wat. 15 BV34
Milner Ct. (Bushey), Wat. 30 CB44
Milner Dr., Cob. 128 BZ112
Milner Dr., Twick. 101 CD87
Milner Pl. N1 77 DN67
Milner Pl., Cars. 132 DG105
High St.
Milner Rd. E15 80 EE69
Milner Rd. SW19 118 DB95
Milner Rd., Cat. 148 DU122
Milner Rd., Dag. 68 EW61
Milner Rd., Kings.T. 115 CK97
Milner Rd., Mord. 118 DD99
Milner Rd., Th.Hth. 120 DR97
Milner Sq. N1 77 DP66
Milner St. SW3 8 D8
Milner St. SW3 90 DF77
Milnthorpe Rd. W4 88 CR79
Milo Rd. SE22 106 DT86
Milroy Wk. SE1 10 F2
Milson Rd. W14 89 CX76
Milton Ave. E6 80 EK66
Milton Ave. N6 63 DJ59
Milton Ave. NW9 60 CQ55
Milton Ave. NW10 74 CQ67
Milton Ave., Barn. 33 CZ43
Milton Ave., Croy. 120 DR101
Milton Ave., Horn. 69 FF61
Milton Ave., Sev. 139 FB110
Milton Ave., Sutt. 118 DD104
Milton Clo. N2 62 DC57
Milton Clo. SE1 11 P9
Milton Clo. SE1 92 DT77
Milton Clo., Hayes 71 BU72
Milton Clo., Sutt. 118 DD104
Milton Ct. EC2 7 K6
Milton Ct., Uxb. 57 BP62
Milton Ct., Wal.Abb. 23 EC34
Milton Ct. Rd. SE14 93 DY79
Milton Cres., Ilf. 67 EQ59
Milton Dr., Borwd. 32 CP43
Milton Dr., Shep. 112 BL98
Milton Gdn. Est. N16 64 DS63
Milton Gro.
Milton Gdns., Epsom 130 CS114
Milton Gdns., Stai. 98 BM88
Milton Gro. N11 49 DJ50
Milton Gro. N16 64 DR63
Milton Pk. N6 63 DJ59
Milton Pl. N7 63 DN64
George's Rd.
Milton Rd. E17 65 EA56
Milton Rd. N6 63 DJ59
Milton Rd. N15 63 DP56
Milton Rd. NW7 47 CU50
Milton Rd. NW9 61 CU59
West Hendon Bdy.
Milton Rd. SE24 105 DP86
Milton Rd. SW14 88 CR83
Milton Rd. SW19 104 DC93
Milton Rd. W3 74 CR74
Milton Rd. W7 73 CF73
Milton Rd., Add. 126 BG107
Milton Rd., Belv. 96 FA77
Milton Rd., Cat. 148 DR121
Milton Rd., Croy. 120 DR102
Milton Rd., Hmptn. 100 CA94
Milton Rd., Har. 59 CE56
Milton Rd., Mitch. 104 DG94
Milton Rd., Rom. 69 FG58
Milton Rd., Sev. 154 FE121
Milton Rd., Sutt. 118 DA104
Milton Rd., Uxb. 56 BN63
Milton Rd., Wall. 133 DJ107
Milton Rd., Walt. 114 BX104
Milton Rd., Well. 95 ET81
Milton St. EC2 7 K6
Milton St. EC2 78 DR71
Milton St., Wal.Abb. 23 EC34
Milton St., Wat. 29 BV38
Milton Way, West Dr. 84 BM77
Milverton Dr., Uxb. 57 BQ63
Milverton Gdns., Ilf. 67 ET61
Milverton Rd. NW6 75 CW66
Milverton St. SE11 91 DN78
Milverton Way SE9 109 EN91
Milward St. E1 78 DV71
Stepney Way
Milward Wk. SE18 95 EN79
Spearman St.
Mimms Hall Rd., Pot.B. 19 CX31
Mimms La., Pot.B. 18 CQ33
Mimms La., Rad. 18 CN33
Mimosa Clo., Orp. 124 EW104
Berrylands
Mimosa Rd., Hayes 72 BW71
Mimosa St. SW6 89 CZ81
Mina Rd. SE17 92 DS78
Mina Rd. SW19 118 DA95
Minard Rd. SE6 108 EE87
Minchenden Cres. N14 49 DJ48
Minchin Clo., Lthd. 143 CG122
Mincing La. EC3 7 M10
Mincing La. EC3 78 DS73
Minden Rd. SE20 120 DV95
Minden Rd., Sutt. 117 CZ103
Minehead Rd. SW16 105 DM92
Minehead Rd., Har. 58 CA62
Minera Ms. SW1 8 G8
Minera Ms. SW1 90 DG77
Mineral St. SE18 95 ES77
Minerva Clo. SW9 91 DN80
Minerva Clo., Sid. 109 ES90
Minerva Dr., Wat. 29 BS36
Minerva Rd. E4 51 EB52
Minerva Rd. NW10 74 CQ69
Minerva Rd., Kings.T. 116 CM96
Minerva St. E2 78 DV68
Minet Ave. NW10 74 CS68
Minet Dr., Hayes 71 BU74
Minet Gdns. NW10 74 CS68
Minet Gdns., Hayes 71 BU74
Minet Rd. SW9 91 DP82
Minford Gdns. W14 89 CX75
Ming St. E14 79 EA73
Mingard Wk. N7 63 DM61
Hornsey Rd.
Ministry Way SE9 109 EM89
Miniver Pl. EC4 78 DQ73
Garlick Hill
Mink Ct., Houns. 86 BW82
Minniedale, Surb. 116 CM99
Minnow St. SE17 92 DS77
East St.
Minnow Wk. SE17 11 N9
Minorca Rd., Wey. 126 BN105
Minories EC3 7 P9
Minories EC3 78 DT72
Minshull Pl., Beck. 107 EA94
Minshull St. SW8 91 DK81
Wandsworth Rd.
Minson Rd. E9 79 DX67
Minstead Gdns. SW15 103 CT87
Minstead Way, N.Mal. 116 CS100
Minster Ave., Sutt. 118 DA103
Leafield Rd.
Minster Ct. EC3 78 DR73
Mincing La.
Minster Dr., Croy. 134 DS105
Minster Gdns., W.Mol. 114 BZ99
Molesey Ave.
Minster Pavement EC3 78 DR73
Mincing La.
Minster Rd. NW2 61 CY64
Minster Rd., Brom. 108 EH94
Minster Wk. N8 63 DL56
Lightfoot Rd.
Minsterley Ave., Shep. 113 BS98
Minstrel Gdns., Surb. 116 CM99
Mint Clo., Uxb. 71 BP69
Mint Rd., Bans. 146 DC116
Mint Rd., Wall. 133 DH105
Mint St. SE1 11 H4
Mint Wk., Croy. 120 DQ104
High St.
Mint Wk., Warl. 149 DX117
Mintern Clo. N13 49 DP48
Mintern St. N1 78 DR68
Minterne Ave., Sthl. 86 CA77
Minterne Rd., Har. 60 CM57
Minterne Waye, Hayes 72 BW72
Minton Ms. NW6 76 DB65
Lymington Rd.
Mirabel Rd. SW6 89 CZ80
Miranda Clo. E1 78 DW71
Sidney St.
Miranda Ct. W3 74 CM72
Queens Dr.
Miranda Rd. N19 63 DJ60
Mirfield St. SE7 94 EK76
Miriam Rd. SE18 95 ES78
Mirror Path SE9 108 EJ90
Lambscroft Ave.
Misbourne Rd., Uxb. 70 BN67
Missenden Clo., Felt. 99 BT88
Missenden Gdns., Mord. 118 DC100
Mission Gro. E17 65 DY57
Mission Pl. SE15 92 DU81
Mission Sq., Brent. 88 CL79
Netley Rd.
Mistletoe Clo., Croy. 121 DX102
Marigold Way
Misty's Fld., Walt. 114 BW102
Mitali Pas. E1 78 DU72
Back Ch. La.
Mitcham Gdn. Village, Mitch. 118 DG99
Mitcham Ind. Est., Mitch. 118 DG95
Mitcham La. SW16 105 DH93
Mitcham Pk., Mitch. 118 DE98
Mitcham Rd. E6 80 EL69
Mitcham Rd. SW17 104 DF92
Mitcham Rd., Croy. 119 DL100
Mitcham Rd., Ilf. 67 ET59
Mitchell Clo. SE2 96 EW77
Mitchell Clo., Abb.L. 15 BU32
Mitchell Clo., Belv. 97 FC76
Mitchell Rd. N13 49 DP50
Mitchell Rd., Orp. 137 ET105
Mitchell St. EC1 7 H4
Mitchell St. EC1 78 DQ70
Mitchell Wk. E6 80 EL71
Oliver Gdns.
Mitchell Way NW10 74 CQ65
Mitchell Way, Brom. 122 EG95
Mitchellbrook Way NW10 74 CR65
Mitchison Rd. N1 78 DR65
Mitchley Ave., Pur. 134 DQ113
Mitchley Ave., S.Croy. 134 DS113
Mitchley Gro., S.Croy. 134 DU113
Mitchley Hill, S.Croy. 134 DS113
Mitchley Rd. N17 64 DU55
Mitchley Vw., S.Croy. 134 DU113
Mitford Clo., Chess. 129 CJ107
Merritt Gdns.
Mitford Rd. N19 63 DL61
Mitre, The E14 79 DZ73
Three Colt St.
Mitre Ave. E17 65 DZ55
Greenleaf Rd.
Mitre Clo., Brom. 122 EF96
Beckenham La.
Mitre Clo., Shep. 113 BR100
Gordon Dr.
Mitre Clo., Sutt. 132 DC108
Mitre Ct. EC2 7 J8
Mitre Ct. EC4 6 E9
Mitre Rd. E15 80 EE68
Mitre Rd. SE1 10 E4
Mitre Rd. SE1 91 DN75
Mitre Sq. EC3 7 N9
Mitre St. EC3 7 N9
Mitre St. EC3 78 DS72
Mitre Way W10 75 CV70
Mixbury Gro., Wey. 127 BR107
Mizen Clo., Cob. 128 BX114
Mizen Way, Cob. 142 BW115
Moat, The, N.Mal. 116 CS95
Moat, The, Ong. 27 FF29
Moat Clo., Orp. 137 ET107
Moat Clo., Sev. 154 FB123
Moat Clo. (Bushey), Wat. 30 CB43
Moat Ct., Ash. 144 CL117
Moat Cres. N3 62 DB55
Moat Cft., Well. 96 EW83
Moat Dr. E13 80 EJ68
Boundary Rd.
Moat Dr., Har. 58 CC56
Moat Dr., Ruis. 57 BS59
Moat Fm. Rd., Nthlt. 72 BZ65
Moat La., Erith 97 FG81
Moat Pl. SW9 91 DM83
Moat Pl. W3 74 CP72
Moat Pl., Uxb. 56 BH63
Moatfield Rd. (Bushey), Wat. 30 CB43

Morley Cres. W., Stan. 59 CJ55
Morley Hill, Enf. 36 DR38
Morley Rd. E10 65 EC60
Morley Rd. E15 80 EF68
Morley Rd. SE13 93 EC84
Morley Rd., Bark. 81 ER67
Morley Rd., Chis. 123 EQ95
Morley Rd., Rom. 68 EY57
Morley Rd., S.Croy. 134 DT110
Morley Rd., Sutt. 117 CZ102
Morley Rd., Twick. 101 CK86
Morley St. SE1 10 E6
Morley St. SE1 91 DN76
Morna Rd. SE5 92 DQ82
Morning La. E9 78 DW65
Morning Ri., Rick. 28 BK41
Morningside Rd., Wor.Pk. 117 CV103
Mornington Ave. W14 89 CZ77
Mornington Ave., Brom. 122 EJ97
Mornington Ave., Ilf. 67 EN59
Mornington Clo., West. 150 EK117
Mornington Clo., Wdf.Grn. 52 EG49
Mornington Ct., Bex. 111 FC88
Mornington Cres. NW1 77 DJ68
Mornington Cres., Houns. 85 BV81
Mornington Gro. E3 79 EA69
Mornington Ms. SE5 92 DQ81
Mornington Pl. NW1 77 DH68
Mornington Ter.
Mornington Rd. E4 51 ED45
Mornington Rd. E11 66 EF60
Mornington Rd. SE8 93 DZ80
Mornington Rd., Ashf. 99 BQ92
Mornington Rd., Grnf. 72 CB71
Mornington Rd., Loug. 39 EQ41
Mornington Rd., Rad. 17 CH34
Mornington Rd., Wdf.Grn. 52 EF49
Mornington St. NW1 77 DH68
Mornington Ter. NW1 77 DH68
Mornington Wk., Rich. 101 CJ91
Morocco St. SE1 11 M5
Morocco St. SE1 92 DS75
Morpeth Ave., Borwd. 32 CM38
Morpeth Gro. E9 79 DX67
Morpeth Rd. E9 78 DW67
Morpeth St. E2 79 DX69
Morpeth Ter. SW1 9 K7
Morpeth Ter. SW1 91 DJ76
Morpeth Wk. N17 50 DV52
West Rd.
Morrab Gdns., Ilf. 67 ET62
Morrell Clo., Barn. 34 DC41
Galdana Ave.
Morris Ave. E12 67 EM64
Morris Clo., Croy. 121 DY100
Morris Clo., Orp. 123 ES104
Morris Ct. E4 51 EB48
Flaxen Rd.
Morris Ct., Wal.Abb. 24 EF34
Morris Gdns. SW18 104 DA87
Morris Pl. N4 63 DN61
Morris Rd. E14 79 EB71
Morris Rd. E15 65 ED63
Morris Rd., Dag. 68 EZ61
Morris Rd., Islw. 87 CF83
Morris Rd., Rom. 55 FH52
Morris St. E1 78 DV72
Morris Way, St.Alb. 17 CK26
Morrish Rd. SW2 105 DL87
Morrison Ave. N17 64 DS55
Morrison Rd., Bark. 82 EY68
Morrison Rd., Hayes 71 BV69
Morrison St. SW11 90 DG83
Morriston Clo., Wat. 44 BW50
Morse Clo. E13 80 EG69
Morse Clo., Uxb. 42 BJ54
Morshead Rd. W9 76 DA69
Morson Rd., Enf. 37 DY44
Morston Clo., Tad. 145 CV120
Waterfield
Morston Gdns. SE9 109 EM91
Morten Clo. SW4 105 DK86
Morten Gdns., Uxb. 56 BG59
Morteyne Rd. N17 50 DR53
Mortgramit Sq. SE18 95 EN76
Powis St.
Mortham St. E15 80 EE67
Mortimer Clo. NW2 61 CZ62
Mortimer Clo. SW16 105 DK89
Mortimer Clo. (Bushey), Wat. 30 CB44
Mortimer Cres. NW6 76 DB67
Mortimer Cres., Wor.Pk. 116 CR104
Mortimer Dr., Enf. 36 DS43
Mortimer Est. NW6 76 DB67
Mortimer Gate, Wal.Cr. 23 DZ27
Mortimer Mkt. WC1 5 L5
Mortimer Pl. NW6 76 DB67
Mortimer Rd. E6 81 EM69
Mortimer Rd. N1 78 DS66
Mortimer Rd. NW10 75 CW69
Mortimer Rd. W13 73 CJ72
Mortimer Rd., Erith 97 FD79
Mortimer Rd., Mitch. 118 DF95
Mortimer Rd., Orp. 124 EU102
Mortimer Rd., West. 136 EJ112
Mortimer Sq. W11 75 CX73
St. Anns Rd.
Mortimer St. W1 5 K8
Mortimer St. W1 77 DJ72
Mortimer Ter. NW5 63 DH63
Gordon Ho. Rd.
Mortlake Clo., Croy. 119 DL104
Richmond Rd.
Mortlake Dr., Mitch. 118 DE95
Mortlake High St. SW14 88 CR83
Mortlake Rd. E16 80 EH72
Mortlake Rd., Ilf. 67 EQ63
Mortlake Rd., Rich. 88 CN80
Mortlake Ter., Rich. 88 CN80
Kew Rd.
Mortlock Clo. SE15 92 DV81
Cossall Wk.
Morton, Tad. 145 CX121
Morton Cres. N14 49 DK49
Morton Gdns., Wall. 133 DJ106
Morton Ms. SW5 90 DB77
Earls Ct. Gdns.
Morton Pl. SE1 10 D7
Morton Rd. E15 80 EF66
Morton Rd. N1 78 DQ66
Morton Rd., Mord. 118 DD99
Morton Way N14 49 DJ48
Morval Rd. SW2 105 DN85
Morvale Clo., Belv. 96 EZ77
Morven Clo., Pot.B. 20 DC31
Morven Rd. SW17 104 DF90
Morville St. E3 79 EA68
Morwell St. WC1 5 N7
Moscow Pl. W2 76 DB73
Moscow Rd.
Moscow Rd. W2 76 DB73
Moselle Ave. N22 49 DN54
Moselle Clo. N8 63 DM55
Miles Rd.
Moselle Ho. N17 50 DT52
Moselle Pl. N17 50 DT52
High Rd.
Moselle Rd., West. 150 EL118
Moselle St. N17 50 DT52
Mospey Cres., Epsom 145 CT115
Moss Clo. E1 78 DU71
Old Montague St.
Moss Clo., Pnr. 44 BZ54
Moss Clo., Rick. 42 BK47
Moss Gdns., Felt. 99 BU89
Rose Gdns.
Moss Gdns., S.Croy. 135 DX108
Warren Ave.
Moss Hall Cres. N12 48 DB51
Moss Hall Gro. N12 48 DB51
Moss La., Pnr. 44 BY53
Moss La., Rom. 69 FF58
Wheatsheaf Rd.
Moss Rd., Dag. 82 FA66
Moss Rd., Wat. 15 BV34
Moss Side, St.Alb. 16 BZ30
Mossborough Clo. N12 48 DB51
Mossbury Rd. SW11 90 DE83
Mossdown Clo., Belv. 96 FA77
Mossendew Clo., Uxb. 42 BK53
Mossfield, Cob. 127 BU113
Mossford Ct., Ilf. 67 EP55
Mossford Grn., Ilf. 67 EP55
Mossford La., Ilf. 53 EP54
Mossford St. E3 79 DZ70
Mossington Gdns. SE16 92 DW77
Abbeyfield Rd.
Mosslea Rd. SE20 106 DW93
Mosslea Rd., Brom. 122 EK99
Mosslea Rd., Orp. 123 EQ104
Mosslea Rd., Whyt. 148 DT116
Mossop St. SW3 8 C8
Mossop St. SW3 90 DE77
Mossville Gdns., Mord. 117 CZ97
Moston Clo., Hayes 85 BT78
Fuller Way
Mostyn Ave., Wem. 60 CM64
Mostyn Gdns. NW10 75 CX69
Mostyn Gro. E3 79 EA68
Mostyn Rd. SW9 91 DN81
Mostyn Rd. SW19 117 CZ95
Mostyn Rd., Edg. 46 CR52
Mostyn Rd. (Bushey), Wat. 30 CC43
Mosul Way, Brom. 122 EL100
Mosyer Dr., Orp. 124 EX103
Motcomb St. SW1 8 E6
Motcomb St. SW1 90 DG76
Mothers Sq., The E5 64 DV63
Motley Ave. EC2 78 DS70
Scrutton St.
Motley St. SW8 91 DJ82
St. Rule St.
Motspur Pk., N.Mal. 117 CT100
Mott St. E4 37 ED38
Mott St., Loug. 38 EE39
Mottingham Gdns. SE9 108 EK88
Mottingham La. SE9 108 EJ88
Mottingham La. SE12 108 EJ88
Mottingham Rd. N9 37 DX44
Mottingham Rd. SE9 108 EL89
Mottisfont Rd. SE2 96 EU76
Motts Hill La., Tad. 145 CU123
Mouchotte Clo., West. 136 EH112
Moulins Rd. E9 78 DW66
Moultain Hill, Swan. 125 FG98
Moulton Ave., Houns. 86 BY82
Mound, The SE9 109 EN90
Moundfield Rd. N16 64 DU58
Mount, The N20 48 DC47
Mount, The NW3 62 DC63
Heath St.
Mount, The, Couls. 146 DG115
Mount, The (Ewell), Epsom 131 CT110
Mount, The, Esher 128 CA107
Mount, The, Lthd. 143 CE123
Mount, The, N.Mal. 117 CT97
Mount, The, Pot.B. 20 DB30
Mount, The, Rick. 28 BJ44
Mount, The (Cheshunt), Wal.Cr. 22 DR26
Mount, The, Warl. 148 DU119
Mount, The, Wem. 60 CP61
Mount, The, Wey. 113 BS103
Mount, The, Wor.Pk. 131 CV105
Mount Adon Pk. SE22 106 DU87
Mount Angelus Rd. SW15 103 CT87
Laverstoke Gdns.
Mount Ararat Rd., Rich. 102 CL85
Mount Ash Rd. SE26 106 DV90
Mount Ave. E4 51 EA48
Mount Ave. W5 73 CJ71
Mount Ave., Cat. 148 DQ124
Mount Ave., Sthl. 72 CA72
Mount Clo. W5 73 CJ71
Mount Clo., Barn. 34 DG42
Mount Clo., Brom. 122 EL95
Mount Clo., Cars. 132 DG109
Mount Clo., Ken. 148 DR116
Mount Clo., Lthd. 143 CE123
Mount Clo., Sev. 154 FF123
Mount Cor., Felt. 100 BX89
Mount Ct. SW15 89 CY83
Weimar St.
Mount Ct., W.Wick. 122 EE103
Mount Culver Ave., Sid. 110 EX93
Mount Dr., Bexh. 110 EY85
Mount Dr., Har. 58 BZ57
Mount Dr., St.Alb. 17 CD25
Mount Dr., Wem. 60 CQ61
Mount Echo Ave. E4 51 EB47
Mount Echo Dr. E4 51 EB46
Mount Ephraim La. SW16 105 DK90
Mount Ephraim Rd. SW16 105 DK90
Mount Est., The E5 64 DV61
Mount Pleasant La.
Mount Felix, Walt. 113 BT102
Mount Gdns. SE26 106 DV90
Mount Grace Rd., Pot.B. 20 DA31
Mount Gro., Edg. 46 CQ48
Mount Harry Rd., Sev. 154 FG123
Mount Ms., Hmptn. 114 CB95
Mount Mills EC1 6 G3
Mount Nod Rd. SW16 105 DM90
Mount Pk., Cars. 132 DG109
Mount Pk. Ave., Har. 59 CD61
Mount Pk. Ave., S.Croy. 133 DP109
Mount Pk. Cres. W5 73 CK72
Mount Pk. Rd. W5 73 CK71
Mount Pk. Rd., Har. 59 CD62
Mount Pk. Rd., Pnr. 57 BU57
Mount Pleasant SE27 106 DQ92
Mount Pleasant WC1 6 D5
Mount Pleasant WC1 77 DN70
Mount Pleasant, Barn. 34 DE42
Mount Pleasant, Epsom 131 CT110
Mount Pleasant, Ruis. 58 BW61
Mount Pleasant, Uxb. 42 BG53
Mount Pleasant, Wem. 74 CL67
Mount Pleasant, West. 150 EK117
Mount Pleasant, Wey. 112 BN104
Mount Pleasant Cres. N4 63 DM59
Mount Pleasant Hill E5 64 DV61
Mount Pleasant La. E5 64 DV61
Mount Pleasant La., St.Alb. 16 BY30
Mount Pleasant Pl. SE18 95 ER77
Orchard Rd.
Mount Pleasant Rd. E17 51 DY54
Mount Pleasant Rd. N17 50 DS53
Mount Pleasant Rd. NW10 75 CW66
Mount Pleasant Rd. SE13 107 EC86
Mount Pleasant Rd. W5 73 CJ70
Mount Pleasant Rd., Cat. 148 DU123
Mount Pleasant Rd., Chig. 53 ER49
Mount Pleasant Rd., N.Mal. 116 CQ97
Mount Pleasant Rd., Rom. 55 FD51
Mount Pleasant Vill. N4 63 DM59
Mount Pleasant Wk., Bex. 111 FC85
Mount Rd. NW2 61 CV62
Mount Rd. NW4 61 CU58
Mount Rd. SE19 106 DR93
Mount Rd. SW19 104 DA89
Mount Rd., Barn. 34 DE43
Mount Rd., Bexh. 110 EX85
Mount Rd., Chess. 130 CM106
Mount Rd., Dag. 68 EZ60
Mount Rd., Dart. 111 FF86
Mount Rd., Epp. 26 EW32
Mount Rd., Felt. 100 BY90
Mount Rd., Hayes 85 BT75
Mount Rd., Ilf. 67 EP64
Mount Rd., Mitch. 118 DD96
Mount Rd., N.Mal. 116 CR97
Mount Row W1 9 H1
Mount Row W1 77 DH73
Mount Sq., The NW3 62 DC62
Heath St.
Mount Stewart Ave., Har. 59 CK58
Mount St. W1 8 F1
Mount St. W1 76 DG73
Mount Ter. E1 78 DV71
New Rd.
Mount Vernon NW3 62 DC63
Mount Vw. NW7 46 CR48
Mount Vw. W5 73 CK70
Mount Vw., Enf. 35 DM38
Mount Vw., Rick. 42 BH46
Mount Vw., St.Alb. 18 CL27
Mount Vw. Rd. E4 51 EC45
Mount Vw. Rd. N4 63 DL59
Mount Vw. Rd. NW9 60 CR57
Mount Vill. SE27 105 DP90
Mount Way, Cars. 132 DG109
Mountacre Clo. SE26 106 DT91
Mountague Pl. E14 79 EC73
Mountbatten Clo. SE18 95 ES79
Mountbatten Clo. SE19 106 DS92
Mountbatten Ct. SE16 78 DW74
Rotherhithe St.
Mountbatten Ct., Buck.H. 52 EK47
Mountbatten Gdns., Beck. 121 DY98
Balmoral Ave.
Mountbatten Ms. SW18 104 DC88
Inman Rd.
Mountbel Rd., Stan. 45 CG53
Mountcombe Clo., Surb. 116 CL101
Mountearl Gdns. SW16 105 DM90
Mountfield Clo. SE6 107 ED87
Mountfield Rd. E6 81 EN68
Mountfield Rd. N3 61 CZ55
Mountfield Rd. W5 73 CK72
Mountfield Way, Orp. 124 EW98
Mountford St. E1 78 DU72
Adler St.
Mountfort Cres. N1 77 DN66
Barnsbury Sq.
Mountfort Ter. N1 77 DN66
Barnsbury Sq.
Mountgrove Rd. N5 63 DP62
Mounthurst Rd., Brom. 122 EF101
Mountington Pk. Clo., Har. 59 CK58
Mountjoy Clo. SE2 96 EV75
Mountjoy Ho. EC2 78 DQ71
The Barbican
Mounts Pond Rd. SE3 93 ED82
Mountsfield Clo., Stai. 98 BG85
Mountsfield Ct. SE13 107 ED86
Mountside, Felt. 100 BY90
Mountside, Stan. 45 CF53
Mountview, Nthwd. 43 BT51
Mountview Ct. N8 63 DP56
Green Las.
Mountview Ct., Wat. 30 CB43
Mountview Rd., Esher 129 CH108
Mountview Rd., Orp. 124 EU101
Mountview Rd. (Cheshunt), Wal.Cr. 22 DS26
Mountway, Pot.B. 20 DA30
Mountwood, W.Mol. 114 CA97
Mountwood Clo., S.Croy. 134 DV110
Movers La., Bark. 81 ER67
Mowatt Clo. N19 63 DK60
Mowbray Ave., W.Byf. 126 BL113
Mowbray Rd. NW6 75 CY66
Mowbray Rd. SE19 120 DT95
Mowbray Rd., Barn. 34 DC42
Mowbray Rd., Edg. 46 CN49
Mowbray Rd., Rich. 101 CJ90
Mowbrays Clo., Rom. 55 FC53
Mowbrays Rd., Rom. 55 FC54
Mowbrey Gdns., Loug. 39 EQ39
Mowlem St. E2 78 DV68
Mowlem Trd. Est. N17 50 DW52
Mowll St. SW9 91 DN80
Moxom Ave. (Cheshunt), Wal.Cr. 23 DY30
Windmill La.
Moxon Clo. E13 80 EF68
Whitelegg Rd.
Moxon St. W1 4 F7
Moxon St. W1 76 DG71
Moxon St., Barn. 33 CZ41
Moye Clo. E2 78 DU67
Dove Row
Moyers Rd. E10 65 EC59
Moylan Rd. W6 89 CY79
Moyne Pl. NW10 74 CN68
Moynihan Dr. N21 35 DL43
Moys Clo., Croy. 119 DL100
Moyser Rd. SW16 105 DH92
Mozart St. W10 75 CZ69
Mozart Ter. SW1 8 G9
Muchelney Rd., Mord. 118 DC100
Mud La. W5 73 CK71
Mudlarks Way SE7 94 EH76
Mudlarks Way SE10 94 EF76
Muggeridge Rd., Dag. 69 FB63
Muir Rd. E5 64 DU63
Muir St. E16 81 EM74
Newland St.
Muirdown Ave. SW14 88 CR84
Muirfield W3 74 CS72
Muirfield Clo. SE16 92 DV78
Ryder Dr.
Muirfield Clo., Wat. 44 BW50
Muirfield Cres. E14 93 EB76
Millharbour
Muirfield Grn., Wat. 44 BW49
Muirfield Rd., Wat. 43 BV49
Muirkirk Rd. SE6 107 EC88
Mulberry Ave., Stai. 98 BL88
Mulberry Clo. E4 51 EA47
Mulberry Clo. N8 63 DL57
Mulberry Clo. NW3 62 DD63
Hampstead High St.
Mulberry Clo. NW4 61 CW55
Mulberry Clo. SE7 94 EK79
Mulberry Clo. SE22 106 DU86
Mulberry Clo. SW3 90 DD79
Beaufort St.
Mulberry Clo. SW16 105 DJ91
Mulberry Clo., Barn. 34 DD42
Mulberry Clo., Nthlt. 72 BY68
Parkfield Ave.
Mulberry Clo., Rom. 69 FH56
Mulberry Clo., St.Alb. 16 CB28
Mulberry Clo., Wey. 113 BP104
Mulberry Ct., Bark. 81 ET66
Westrow Dr.
Mulberry Cres., Brent. 87 CH80
Mulberry Cres., West Dr. 84 BN75
Mulberry La., Croy. 120 DT102
Mulberry Ms., Wall. 133 DJ107
Ross Rd.
Mulberry Par., West Dr. 84 BN76
Mulberry Pl. W6 89 CU78
Chiswick Mall
Mulberry Rd. E8 78 DT66
Mulberry St. E1 78 DU72
Adler St.
Mulberry Trees, Shep. 113 BR101
Mulberry Wk. SW3 90 DD79
Mulberry Way E18 52 EH54
Mulberry Way, Belv. 97 FC75
Mulberry Way, Ilf. 67 EQ56
Mulgrave Rd. NW10 61 CT63
Mulgrave Rd. SW6 89 CZ79
Mulgrave Rd. W5 73 CK70
Mulgrave Rd., Croy. 120 DR104
Mulgrave Rd., Har. 59 CG61
Mulgrave Rd., Sutt. 131 CZ108
Mulholland Clo., Mitch. 119 DH96
Mulkern Rd. N19 63 DK60
Mull Wk. N1 78 DQ65
Clephane Rd.
Mullards Clo., Mitch. 118 DF102
Muller Rd. SW4 105 DK86
Mullet Gdns. E2 78 DU68
St. Peter's Clo.
Mullins Path SW14 88 CR83
Mullion Clo., Har. 44 CB53
Mullion Wk., Wat. 44 BX49
Ormskirk Rd.
Mulready St. NW8 4 B5
Multi Way W3 88 CS75
Valetta Rd.
Multon Rd. SW18 104 DD87
Mulvaney Way SE1 11 L5
Mulvaney Way SE1 92 DR75
Mumford Ct. EC2 7 J8
Mumford Rd. SE24 105 DP85
Railton Rd.
Muncaster Clo., Ashf. 98 BN91
Muncaster Rd. SW11 104 DF85
Muncaster Rd., Ashf. 99 BP92
Muncies Ms. SE6 107 EC89
Mund St. W14 89 CZ78
Mundania Rd. SE22 106 DV86
Munday Rd. E16 80 EG72
Mundells, Wal.Cr. 22 DU27
Munden Dr., Wat. 30 BY37
Colne Way
Munden Gro., Wat. 30 BW38
Munden St. W14 89 CY77
Munden Vw., Wat. 30 BX36
Mundesley Clo., Wat. 44 BW49
Mundford Rd. E5 64 DW61
Mundon Gdns., Ilf. 67 ER60
Mundy St. N1 7 N2
Mundy St. N1 78 DS69
Mungo Pk. Clo. (Bushey), Wat. 44 CC47
Mungo Pk. Rd., Rain. 83 FG65
Mungo Pk. Way, Orp. 124 EW100
Munnery Way, Orp. 123 EN103
Munnings Gdns., Islw. 101 CD85
Munro Dr. N11 49 DJ51
Munro Ms. W10 75 CY71
Munro Rd. (Bushey), Wat. 30 CB43
Munro Ter. SW10 90 DD79
Munslow Gdns., Sutt. 132 DC105
Munster Ave., Houns. 86 BY84
Munster Ct., Tedd. 101 CJ93
Munster Gdns. N13 49 DP49
Munster Ms. SW6 89 CY80
Munster Rd.
Munster Rd. SW6 89 CY80
Munster Rd., Tedd. 101 CH93
Munster Sq. NW1 5 J3
Munster Sq. NW1 77 DH69
Munton Rd. SE17 11 J8
Munton Rd. SE17 92 DQ77
Murchison Ave., Bex. 110 EX88
Murchison Rd. E10 65 EC61
Murdoch Clo., Stai. 98 BG92
Murdock Clo. E16 80 EF72
Rogers Rd.
Murdock St. SE15 92 DV79
Murfett Clo. SW19 103 CY89
Muriel Ave., Wat. 30 BW43
Muriel St. N1 77 DM67
Murillo Rd. SE13 93 ED84
Murphy St. SE1 10 D5
Murphy St. SE1 91 DN75
Murray Ave., Brom. 122 EH97
Murray Ave., Houns. 100 CB85
Murray Cres., Pnr. 44 BX53
Murray Gro. N1 7 J1
Murray Gro. N1 78 DQ68
Murray Ms. NW1 77 DK66
Murray Rd. SW19 103 CX93
Murray Rd. W5 87 CK77
Murray Rd., Nthwd. 43 BS53
Murray Rd., Orp. 124 EV97
Murray Rd., Rich. 101 CH89
Murray Sq. E16 80 EG72
Murray St. NW1 77 DK66
Murray Ter. NW3 62 DD63
Flask Wk.
Murray Ter. W5 87 CK77
Murray Rd.
Murrays La., W.Byf. 126 BK114
Murrells Wk., Lthd. 142 CA123
Murreys, The, Ash. 143 CK118
Mursell Est. SW8 91 DM81
Murthering La., Rom. 55 FF45
Murtwell Dr., Chig. 53 EQ51
Musard Rd. W6 89 CY79
Musard Rd. W14 89 CY79

Musbury St. E1 78 DW72
Muscal W6 89 CY79
Muscatel Pl. SE5 92 DS81
Dalwood St.
Muschamp Rd. SE15 92 DT83
Muschamp Rd., Cars. 118 DE103
Muscovy St. EC3 11 N1
Museum La. SW7 8 A7
Museum Pas. E2 78 DV69
Victoria Pk. Sq.
Museum St. WC1 5 P7
Museum St. WC1 77 DL71
Musgrave Clo., Barn. 34 DC39
Musgrave Clo., Wal.Cr. 22 DT27
Allwood Rd.
Musgrave Cres. SW6 90 DA80
Musgrave Rd., Islw. 87 CF81
Musgrove Rd. SE14 93 DX81
Musjid Rd. SW11 90 DD82
Kambala Rd.
Muskalls Clo. (Cheshunt), Wal.Cr. 22 DU27
Musquash Way, Houns. 86 BW82
Muston Rd. E5 64 DV61
Mustow Pl. SW6 89 CZ82
Munster Rd.
Muswell Ave. N10 49 DH53
Muswell Hill N10 63 DH55
Muswell Hill Bdy. N10 63 DH55
Muswell Hill Pl. N10 63 DH56
Muswell Hill Rd. N6 62 DG58
Muswell Hill Rd. N10 62 DG58
Muswell Ms. N10 63 DH55
Muswell Rd.
Muswell Rd. N10 63 DH55
Mutchetts Clo., Wat. 16 BY33
Mutrix Rd. NW6 76 DA67
Mutton La., Pot.B. 19 CW31
Mutton Pl. NW1 77 DH65
Harmood St.
Muybridge Rd., N.Mal. 116 CQ96
Myatt Rd. SW9 91 DP81
Myatt's Flds. N. SW9 91 DN81
Eythorne Rd.
Myatt's Flds. S. SW9 91 DN82
Mycenae Rd. SE3 94 EG80
Myddelton Ave., Enf. 36 DS38
Myddelton Clo., Enf. 36 DT39
Myddelton Gdns. N21 49 DP45
Myddelton Pk. N20 48 DD48
Myddelton Pas. EC1 6 E2
Myddelton Rd. N8 63 DL56
Myddelton Sq. EC1 6 E2
Myddelton Sq. EC1 77 DN69
Myddelton St. EC1 6 E3
Myddelton St. EC1 77 DN69
Myddleton Ms. N22 49 DL52
Myddleton Path (Cheshunt), Wal.Cr. 22 DV31
Hawthorne Clo.
Myddleton Rd. N22 49 DL52
Myddleton Rd., Uxb. 70 BJ67
Myers La. SE14 93 DX79
Myles Ct., Wal.Cr. 22 DQ29
Mylis Clo. SE26 106 DV91
Mylius Clo. SE14 92 DW81
Kender St.
Mylne Clo., Wal.Cr. 22 DW27
Mylne St. EC1 6 D1
Mylne St. EC1 77 DN68
Mymms Dr., Hat. 20 DA26
Mynns Clo., Epsom 130 CP114
Myra St. SE2 96 EU77
Myrdle St. E1 78 DU71
Myrna Clo. SW19 104 DE94
Myron Pl. SE13 93 EC83
Myrtle Ave., Felt. 85 BS84
Myrtle Ave., Ruis. 57 BU59
Myrtle Clo., Barn. 48 DF46
Myrtle Clo., Erith 97 FE81
Myrtle Clo., Uxb. 70 BM71
Violet Ave.
Myrtle Clo., West Dr. 84 BM76
Myrtle Gdns. W7 73 CE74
Myrtle Gro., Enf. 36 DR38
Myrtle Gro., N.Mal. 116 CQ96
Myrtle Rd. E6 80 EL67
Myrtle Rd. E17 65 DY58
Myrtle Rd. N13 50 DQ48
Myrtle Rd. W3 74 CQ74
Myrtle Rd., Croy. 121 EA104
Myrtle Rd., Hmptn. 100 CC93
Myrtle Rd., Houns. 86 CC82
Myrtle Rd., Ilf. 67 EP61
Myrtle Rd., Sutt. 132 DC106
Myrtle Wk. N1 7 M1
Myrtle Wk. N1 78 DS68
Myrtleberry Clo. E8 78 DT65
Beechwood Rd.
Myrtledene Rd. SE2 96 EU78
Myrtleside Clo., Nthwd. 43 BR52
Mysore Rd. SW11 90 DF83
Myton Rd. SE21 106 DR90

N

Nadine St. SE7 94 EJ78
Nafferton Ri., Loug. 38 EK43
Nagasaki Wk. SE7 94 EJ76
Nagle Clo. E17 51 ED54
Nag's Head Ct. EC1 7 J5
Nags Head La., Well. 96 EV83
Nags Head Rd., Enf. 36 DW42
Nairn Grn., Wat. 43 BU48
Nairn Rd., Ruis. 72 BW65
Nairn St. E14 79 EC71
Nairne Gro. SE24 106 DR85
Naish Ct. N1 77 DL67
Nallhead Rd., Felt. 100 BW92
Namton Dr., Th.Hth. 119 DM98
Nan Clark's La. NW7 47 CT47
Nancy Downs, Wat. 44 BW45
Nankin St. E14 79 EA72
Nansen Rd. SW11 90 DG84
Nant Rd. NW2 61 CZ61
Nant St. E2 78 DV69
Cambridge Heath Rd.
Nantes Clo. SW18 90 DC84
Nantes Pas. E1 7 P6
Naoroji St. WC1 6 D3
Nap, The, Kings L. 14 BN29
Napier Ave. E14 93 EA78
Napier Ave. SW6 89 CZ83
Napier Clo. SE8 93 DZ80
Amersham Vale
Napier Clo. W14 89 CZ76
Napier Rd.
Napier Clo., Horn. 69 FH60
St. Leonards Way
Napier Clo., St.Alb. 17 CK25
Napier Clo., West Dr. 84 BM76
Napier Ct. SW6 89 CZ83
Ranelagh Gdns.
Napier Ct. (Cheshunt), Wal.Cr. 22 DV28
Flamstead End Rd.
Napier Dr. (Bushey), Wat. 30 BY42
Napier Gro. N1 78 DQ68
Napier Ho., Rain. 83 FF69
Napier Pl. W14 89 CZ76
Napier Rd. E6 81 EN67
Napier Rd. E11 66 EE63
Napier Rd. E15 80 EE68
Napier Rd. N17 64 DS55
Napier Rd. NW10 75 CV69
Napier Rd. SE25 120 DV98
Napier Rd. W14 89 CY76
Napier Rd., Ashf. 99 BR94
Napier Rd., Belv. 96 EZ77
Napier Rd., Brom. 122 EH98
Napier Rd., Enf. 37 DX43
Napier Rd., Houns. 84 BK81
Napier Rd., Islw. 87 CG84
Napier Rd., S.Croy. 134 DR108
Napier Rd., Wem. 59 CK64
Napier Ter. N1 77 DP65
Napoleon Rd. E5 64 DV62
Napoleon Rd., Twick. 101 CH87
Napsbury Ave., St.Alb. 17 CJ26
Napton Clo., Hayes 72 BY70
Kingsash Dr.
Narbonne Ave. SW4 105 DJ85
Narboro Ct., Rom. 69 FG57
Manor Rd.
Narborough Clo., Uxb. 57 BQ61
Aylsham Dr.
Narborough St. SW6 90 DB82
Narcissus Rd. NW6 62 DA64
Naresby Fold, Stan. 45 CJ51
Narford Rd. E5 64 DU62
Narrow La., Warl. 148 DV119
Narrow St. E14 79 DY73
Narrow Way, Brom. 122 EL100
Nascot Pl., Wat. 29 BV40
Stamford Rd.
Nascot Rd., Wat. 29 BV40
Nascot St. W12 75 CW72
Nascot St., Wat. 29 BV40
Nascot Wd. Rd., Wat. 29 BT37
Naseby Clo. NW6 76 DC66
Fairfax Rd.
Naseby Clo., Islw. 87 CE81
Naseby Ct., Walt. 114 BW103
Clements Rd.
Naseby Rd. SE19 106 DR93
Naseby Rd., Dag. 68 FA62
Naseby Rd., Ilf. 53 EM53
Nash Clo., Borwd. 32 CM42
Nash Grn., Brom. 108 EG93
Nash Grn., Hem.H. 14 BM25
Nash La., Kes. 136 EG108
Nash Pl. E14 79 EB74
South Colonnade
Nash Rd. N9 50 DW47
Nash Rd. SE4 93 DY84
Nash Rd., Rom. 68 EX56
Nash St. NW1 5 J2
Nash's Yd., Uxb. 70 BK66
Bakers Rd.
Nasmyth St. W6 89 CV76
Nassau Path SE28 82 EW74
Disraeli Clo.
Nassau Rd. SW13 89 CT81
Nassau St. W1 5 K7
Nassau St. W1 77 DJ71
Nassington Rd. NW3 62 DE63
Natal Rd. N11 49 DL51
Natal Rd. SW16 105 DK93
Natal Rd., Ilf. 67 EP63
Natal Rd., Th.Hth. 120 DR97
Natalie Clo., Felt. 99 BR87
Natalie Ms., Twick. 101 CD90
Sixth Cross Rd.
Nathan Way SE28 95 ES76
Nathaniel Clo. E1 78 DT71
Thrawl St.
Nathans Rd., Wem. 59 CJ60
Nation Way E4 51 EC46
Naval Row E14 79 EC73
Naval Wk., Brom. 122 EG97
High St.
Navarino Gro. E8 78 DU65
Navarino Rd. E8 78 DU65
Navarre Gdns., Rom. 55 FB50
Navarre Rd. E6 80 EL68
Navarre St. E2 7 P4
Navarre St. E2 78 DT70
Navenby Wk. E3 79 EA70
Rounton Rd.
Navestock Clo. E4 51 EC48
Mapleton Rd.
Navestock Cres., Wdf.Grn. 52 EJ53
Navestock Ho., Bark. 82 EV68
Navigator Dr., Sthl. 86 CC75
Navy St. SW4 91 DK83
Naylor Gro., Enf. 37 DX43
South St.
Naylor Rd. N20 48 DC47
Naylor Rd. SE15 92 DV80
Nazareth Gdns. SE15 92 DV82
Nazeing Wk., Rain. 83 FE67
Ongar Way
Nazrul St. E2 7 P2
Nazrul St. E2 78 DT69
Neagle Clo., Borwd. 32 CQ39
Balcon Way
Neal Ave., Sthl. 72 BZ69
Neal Clo., Nthwd. 43 BU53
Neal Ct., Wal.Abb. 24 EF33
Neal St. WC2 5 P9
Neal St. WC2 77 DL72
Neal St., Wat. 30 BW43
Nealden St. SW9 91 DM83
Neale Clo. N2 62 DC55
Neal's Yd. WC2 5 P9
Near Acre NW9 47 CT53
Neasden Clo. NW10 60 CS64
Neasden La. NW10 60 CS62
Neasden La. N. NW10 60 CR62
Neasden Underpass NW10 60 CR62
Neasham Rd., Dag. 68 EV64
Neate St. SE5 92 DS79
Neath Gdns., Mord. 118 DC100
Neathouse Pl. SW1 9 K8
Neats Acre, Ruis. 57 BR59
Neatscourt Rd. E6 80 EK71
Nebraska St. SE1 11 K5
Neckinger SE16 92 DT76
Neckinger Est. SE16 92 DT76
Neckinger St. SE1 92 DT75
Nectarine Way SE13 93 EB82
Needham Rd. W11 76 DA72
Westbourne Gro.
Needham Ter. NW2 61 CX62
Needleman St. SE16 93 DX75
Neela Clo., Uxb. 57 BP63
Neeld Cres. NW4 61 CV57
Neeld Cres., Wem. 60 CN64
Neil Clo., Ashf. 99 BQ92
Neil Wates Cres. SW2 105 DN88
Nelgarde Rd. SE6 107 EA87
Nell Gwynn Clo., Rad. 18 CL32
Nell Gwynne Ave., Shep. 113 BR100
Nella Rd. W6 89 CX79
Nelldale Rd. SE16 92 DW77
Nellgrove Rd., Uxb. 71 BP70
Nello James Gdns. SE27 106 DR91
Nelson Clo., Croy. 119 DP102
Nelson Clo., Felt. 99 BT88
Nelson Clo., Rom. 55 FB53
Nelson Clo., Uxb. 71 BP69
Nelson Clo., Walt. 113 BV102
Nelson Clo., West. 150 EL117
Nelson Ct. SE16 78 DW74
Brunel Rd.
Nelson Gdns. E2 78 DU69
Nelson Gdns., Houns. 100 CA86
Nelson Gro. Rd. SW19 118 DB95
Nelson La., Uxb. 71 BP69
Nelson Rd.
Nelson Mandela Clo. N10 48 DG54
Nelson Mandela Rd. SE3 94 EJ83
Nelson Pas. EC1 7 J3
Nelson Pas. EC1 78 DQ69
Nelson Pl. N1 6 G1
Nelson Pl. N1 77 DP68
Nelson Pl., Sid. 110 EU91
Nelson Rd. E4 51 EA51
Nelson Rd. E11 66 EG56
Nelson Rd. N8 63 DM57
Nelson Rd. N9 50 DV47
Nelson Rd. N15 64 DS56
Nelson Rd. SE10 93 EC79
Nelson Rd. SW19 104 DB94
Nelson Rd., Ashf. 98 BL92
Nelson Rd., Belv. 96 EZ78
Nelson Rd., Brom. 122 EJ98
Nelson Rd., Cat. 148 DR123
Nelson Rd., Enf. 37 DX44
Nelson Rd., Har. 59 CD60
Nelson Rd., Houns. 100 CA86
Nelson Rd. (Heathrow Airport), Houns. 84 BM81
Nelson Rd., N.Mal. 116 CR99
Nelson Rd., Rain. 83 FF68
Nelson Rd., Sid. 110 EU91
Nelson Rd., Stan. 45 CJ51
Nelson Rd., Twick. 100 CB87
Nelson Rd., Uxb. 71 BP69
Nelson Sq. SE1 10 F4
Nelson Sq. SE1 91 DP75
Nelson St. E1 78 DV72
Nelson St. E6 81 EM68
Nelson St. E16 80 EF73
Huntingdon St.
Nelson Ter. N1 6 G1
Nelson Ter. N1 77 DP68
Nelson Trd. Est. SW19 118 DB95
Nelson Wk. SE16 79 DY74
Rotherhithe St.
Nelson's Row SW4 91 DK84
Nelsons Yd. NW1 77 DJ68
Mornington Cres.
Nemoure Rd. W3 74 CQ73
Nene Gdns., Felt. 100 BZ89
Nene Rd., Houns. 85 BP81
Nepaul Rd. SW11 90 DE82
Afghan Rd.
Nepean St. SW15 103 CU86
Neptune Rd., Har. 59 CD58
Neptune Rd. (Heathrow Airport), Houns. 85 BR81
Neptune St. SE16 92 DW76
Nesbit Rd. SE9 94 EK84
Nesbitt Clo. SE3 94 EE83
Hurren Clo.
Nesbitt Sq. SE19 106 DS94
Coxwell Rd.
Nesbitts All., Barn. 33 CZ41
Bath Pl.
Nesham St. E1 78 DU74
Ness St. SE16 92 DU76
Spa Rd.
Nesta Rd., Wdf.Grn. 52 EE51
Nestles Ave., Hayes 85 BT76
Neston Rd., Wat. 30 BW37
Nestor Ave. N21 35 DP44
Nether Clo. N3 48 DA52
Nether St. N3 48 DA53
Nether St. N12 48 DB51
Netheravon Rd. W7 73 CF74
Netheravon Rd. N. W4 89 CT77
Netheravon Rd. S. W4 89 CT78
Netherbury Rd. W5 87 CK76
Netherby Gdns., Enf. 35 DL42
Netherby Pk., Wey. 127 BR106
Netherby Rd. SE23 106 DW87
Nethercourt Ave. N3 48 DA51
Netherfield Gdns., Bark. 81 ER65
Netherfield Rd. N12 48 DB50
Netherfield Rd. SW17 104 DG90
Netherford Rd. SW4 91 DJ82
Netherhall Gdns. NW3 76 DC65
Netherhall Way NW3 62 DC64
Netherhall Gdns.
Netherlands, The, Couls. 147 DJ119
Netherlands Rd., Barn. 34 DD44
Netherleigh Clo. N6 63 DH60
Nethern Ct. Rd., Cat. 149 EA123
Netherne La., Couls. 147 DJ123
Netherne La., Red. 147 DJ123
Netherpark Dr., Rom. 55 FF54
Netherton Gro. SW10 90 DC79
Netherton Rd. N15 64 DR58
Seven Sisters Rd.
Netherton Rd., Twick. 101 CG85
Netherwood N2 48 DD54
Netherwood Pl. W14 89 CX76
Netherwood Rd.
Netherwood Rd. W14 89 CX76
Netherwood St. NW6 75 CZ66
Netley Clo., Croy. 135 EC108
Netley Clo., Sutt. 131 CX106
Netley Dr., Walt. 114 BZ101
Netley Gdns., Mord. 118 DC101
Netley Rd. E17 65 DZ57
Netley Rd., Brent. 88 CL79
Netley Rd. (Heathrow Airport), Houns. 85 BR81
Netley Rd., Ilf. 67 ER57
Netley Rd., Mord. 118 DC101
Netley St. NW1 5 K3
Nettlecombe Clo., Sutt. 132 DB109
Nettleden Ave., Wem. 74 CN65
Nettlefold Pl. SE27 105 DP90
Nettlestead Clo., Beck. 107 DZ94
Copers Cope Rd.
Nettleton Rd. SE14 93 DX81
Nettleton Rd., Houns. 85 BP81
Nettleton Rd., Uxb. 56 BM63
Nettlewood Rd. SW16 105 DK94
Neuchatel Rd. SE6 107 DZ89
Nevada Clo., N.Mal. 116 CQ98
Georgia Rd.
Nevada St. SE10 93 EC79
Nevern Pl. SW5 90 DA77
Nevern Rd. SW5 90 DA77
Nevern Sq. SW5 90 DA77
Nevil Clo., Nthwd. 43 BR50
Nevill Clo. W3 88 CQ75
Acton La.
Nevill Gro., Wat. 29 BV39
Nevill Rd. N16 64 DS63
Nevill Way, Loug. 52 EL45
Valley Hill
Neville Ave., N.Mal. 116 CR95
Neville Clo. E11 66 EF62
Neville Clo. NW1 5 N1
Neville Clo. NW6 75 CZ68
Neville Clo. SE15 92 DU80
Neville Clo., Bans. 132 DB114
Neville Clo., Esher 128 BZ107
Neville Clo., Houns. 86 CB82
Neville Clo., Pot.B. 19 CZ31
Neville Clo., Sid. 109 ET91
Neville Dr. N2 62 DC58
Neville Gdns., Dag. 68 EX62
Neville Gill Clo. SW18 104 DB86
Neville Pl. N22 49 DM53
Neville Rd. E7 80 EG66
Neville Rd. NW6 75 CZ68
Neville Rd. W5 73 CK70
Neville Rd., Croy. 120 DR101
Neville Rd., Dag. 68 EX61
Neville Rd., Ilf. 53 EQ53
Neville Rd., Kings.T. 116 CN96
Neville Rd., Rich. 101 CJ89
Neville St. SW7 90 DD78
Neville Ter. SW7 90 DD78
Neville Wk., Cars. 118 DE101
Green Wrythe La.
Nevilles Ct. NW2 61 CU62
Nevin Dr. E4 51 EB46
Nevis Clo., Rom. 55 FE51
Nevis Rd. SW17 104 DG89
New Ash Clo. N2 62 DD55
Oakridge Dr.
New Barn La., Sev. 151 EQ116
New Barn La., West. 151 EQ118
New Barn La., Whyt. 148 DS116
New Barn Rd., Swan. 125 FE95
New Barn St. E13 80 EG70
New Barns Ave., Mitch. 119 DK98
New Barns Way, Chig. 53 EP48
New Berry La., Walt. 128 BX106
New Bond St. W1 5 H9
New Bond St. W1 77 DH72
New Brent St. NW4 61 CW57
New Bri. St. EC4 6 F9
New Bri. St. EC4 77 DP72
New Broad St. EC2 7 M7
New Bdy. W5 73 CJ73
New Bdy., Hmptn. 101 CD92
Hampton Rd.
New Burlington Ms. W1 5 K10
New Burlington Pl. W1 5 K10
New Burlington St. W1 5 K10
New Burlington St. W1 77 DJ73
New Butt La. SE8 93 EA80
New Butt La. N. SE8 93 EA80
Reginald Rd.
New Cavendish St. W1 4 G7
New Cavendish St. W1 76 DG71
New Change EC4 7 H9
New Change EC4 78 DQ72
New Chapel Sq., Felt. 99 BV88
New Charles St. EC1 6 G2
New Ch. Rd. SE5 92 DR80
New City Rd. E13 80 EJ69
New Clo. SW19 118 DC97
New Clo., Felt. 100 BY92
New College Ms. N1 77 DN66
Islington Pk. St.
New Compton St. WC2 5 N9
New Compton St. WC2 77 DK72
New Ct. EC4 6 D10
New Ct., Add. 112 BJ104
New Covent Gdn. Mkt. SW8 91 DK80
New Coventry St. W1 9 N1
New Crane Pl. E1 78 DW74
Garnet St.
New Cross Rd. SE14 92 DW80
New End NW3 62 DC63
New End Sq. NW3 62 DD63
New Era Est. N1 78 DS67
Phillipp St.
New Fm. Ave., Brom. 122 EG98
New Fm. Dr., Rom. 40 EW41
New Fm. La., Nthwd. 43 BS53
New Ferry App. SE18 95 EN76
New Fetter La. EC4 6 E8
New Fetter La. EC4 77 DN72
New Ford Rd., Wal.Cr. 23 DZ34
New Forest La., Chig. 53 EN51
New Gdn. Dr., West Dr. 84 BL75
Drayton Gdns.
New Globe Wk. SE1 11 H2
New Globe Wk. SE1 78 DQ74
New Goulston St. E1 7 P8
New Haw Rd., Add. 126 BJ106
New Heston Rd., Houns. 86 BZ80
New Horizon Ct., Brent. 87 CG79
Shield Dr.
New Ho. La., Epp. 27 FC25
New Inn Bdy. EC2 7 N4
New Inn Pas. WC2 6 C9
New Inn St. EC2 7 N4
New Inn Yd. EC2 7 N4
New Inn Yd. EC2 78 DS70
New James Ct. SE15 92 DV83
Nunhead La.
New Kent Rd. SE1 11 H7
New Kent Rd. SE1 92 DQ76
New King St. SE8 93 EA79
New Kings Rd. SW6 89 CZ82
New London St. EC3 7 N10
New Lydenburgh St. SE7 94 EJ76
New Mill Rd., Orp. 124 EW95
New Mt. St. E15 79 ED66
New N. Pl. EC2 7 M5
New N. Rd. N1 78 DQ66
New N. Rd., Ilf. 53 ER52
New N. St. WC1 6 B6
New N. St. WC1 77 DM71
New Oak Rd. N2 48 DC54
New Orleans Wk. N19 63 DK59
New Oxford St. WC1 5 N8
New Oxford St. WC1 77 DK72
New Par., Ashf. 98 BM91
Church Rd.
New Pk. Ave. N13 50 DQ48
New Pk. Clo., Nthlt. 72 BY65
New Pk. Ct. SW2 105 DL87
New Pk. Par. SW2 105 DL86
Doverfield Rd.
New Pk. Rd. SW2 105 DK88
New Pk. Rd., Ashf. 99 BQ92
New Pk. Rd., Uxb. 42 BJ53
New Peachey La., Uxb. 70 BK72
New Pl. Sq. SE16 92 DV76

Norwood Cres., Houns. 85 BQ81
Norwood Dr., Har. 58 BZ58
Norwood Fm. La., Cob. 127 BU111
Norwood Gdns., Hayes 72 BW70
Norwood Gdns., Sthl. 86 BZ77
Norwood Grn. Rd., Sthl. 86 CA77
Norwood High St. SE27 105 DP90
Norwood Pk. Rd. SE27 106 DQ92
Norwood Rd. SE24 105 DP88
Norwood Rd. SE27 105 DP89
Norwood Rd., Sthl. 86 BZ77
Norwood Rd. (Cheshunt), Wal.Cr. 23 DY30
Windmill La.
Norwood Ter., Sthl. 86 CB77
Tentelow La.
Nota Ms. N3 48 DA53
Station Rd.
Notley St. SE5 92 DR80
Notre Dame Est. SW4 91 DJ84
Notson Rd. SE25 120 DV98
Belfast Rd.
Notting Barn Rd. W10 75 CX70
Notting Hill Gate W11 76 DA74
Nottingdale Sq. W11 75 CY74
Wilsham St.
Nottingham Ave. E16 80 EJ71
Nottingham Clo., Wat. 15 BU33
Nottingham Ct. WC2 5 P9
Nottingham Pl. W1 4 F5
Nottingham Pl. W1 76 DG71
Nottingham Rd. E10 65 EC58
Nottingham Rd. SW17 104 DF88
Nottingham Rd., Islw. 87 CF82
Nottingham Rd., S.Croy. 134 DQ105
Nottingham St. W1 4 F6
Nottingham St. W1 76 DG71
Nottingham Ter. NW1 4 F5
Nova Ms., Sutt. 117 CY101
Nova Rd., Croy. 119 DP102
Novar Clo., Orp. 123 ET101
Novar Rd. SE9 109 EQ88
Novello St. SW6 90 DA81
Novello Way, Borwd. 32 CR39
Nowell Rd. SW13 89 CU79
Nower, The, Sev. 151 ET119
Nower Hill, Pnr. 58 BZ56
Noyna Rd. SW17 104 DF90
Nuding Clo. SE13 93 EA83
Nuffield Rd., Swan. 111 FG93
Nugent Rd. N19 63 DL60
Nugent Rd. SE25 120 DT97
Nugent Ter. NW8 76 DC68
Nugents Ct., Pnr. 44 BY53
St. Thomas' Dr.
Nugents Pk., Pnr. 44 BY53
Nun Ct. EC2 7 K8
Nuneaton Rd., Dag. 82 EX66
Nunfield, Kings L. 14 BH31
Nunhead Cres. SE15 92 DV83
Nunhead Est. SE15 92 DV84
Nunhead Grn. SE15 92 DV83
Nunhead Gro. SE15 92 DV83
Nunhead La. SE15 92 DV83
Nunhead Pas. SE15 92 DU83
Peckham Rye
Nunnington Clo. SE9 108 EL90
Nunns Rd., Enf. 36 DQ40
Nunsbury Dr., Brox. 23 DY25
Nupton Dr., Barn. 33 CW44
Nursery, The, Erith 97 FF80
Nursery Ave. N3 48 DC54
Nursery Ave., Bexh. 96 EZ83
Nursery Ave., Croy. 121 DX103
Nursery Clo. SE4 93 DZ82
Nursery Clo. SW15 89 CX84
Nursery Clo., Croy. 121 DX103
Nursery Clo., Enf. 37 DX39
Nursery Clo., Epsom 130 CS110
Nursery Clo., Felt. 99 BV87
Nursery Clo., Orp. 123 ET101
Nursery Clo., Rom. 68 EX58
Nursery Clo., Sev. 155 FJ122
Nursery Clo., Swan. 125 FC96
Nursery Clo., Wdf.Grn. 52 EH50
Nursery Ct. N17 50 DT52
Nursery St.
Nursery Gdns., Chis. 109 EP93
Nursery Gdns., Enf. 37 DX39
Nursery Gdns., Stai. 98 BH94
Nursery Gdns., Sun. 113 BT96
Nursery La. E2 78 DT67
Nursery La. E7 80 EG65
Nursery La. W10 75 CW71
Nursery Pl., Sev. 154 FD122
Nursery Rd. E9 78 DW65
Morning La.
Nursery Rd. N2 48 DD53
Nursery Rd. N14 49 DJ45
Nursery Rd. SW9 91 DM84
Nursery Rd., Brox. 23 DY25
Nursery Rd., Loug. 38 EJ43
Nursery Rd. (High Beach), Loug. 38 EH39
Nursery Rd., Pnr. 58 BW55
Nursery Rd., Sun. 113 BS96
Nursery Rd., Sutt. 132 DC105
Nursery Rd., Th.Hth. 120 DR98
Nursery Rd. Merton SW19 118 DB96
Nursery Rd. Mitcham, Mitch. 118 DE97
Nursery Rd. Wimbledon SW19 103 CY94
Worple Rd.
Nursery Row SE17 92 DR77
Orb St.
Nursery Row, Barn. 33 CY41
St. Albans Rd.
Nursery St. N17 50 DT52
Nursery Wk. NW4 61 CV55
Nursery Wk., Rom. 69 FD59
Nursery Waye, Uxb. 70 BK67
Nurserymans Rd. N11 48 DG49
Nurstead Rd., Erith 96 FA80
Nut Tree Clo., Orp. 124 EX104
Nutbourne St. W10 75 CY69
Nutbrook St. SE15 92 DU83
Nutbrowne Rd., Dag. 82 EZ67
Nutcroft Gro., Lthd. 143 CE121
Nutcroft Rd. SE15 92 DV80
Nutfield Clo. N18 50 DU51
Nutfield Clo., Cars. 118 DE104
Nutfield Gdns., Ilf. 67 ET61
Nutfield Gdns., Nthlt. 72 BW68
Nutfield Rd. E15 65 EC63
Nutfield Rd. NW2 61 CU61
Nutfield Rd. SE22 106 DT85
Nutfield Rd., Couls. 146 DG116
Nutfield Rd., Th.Hth. 119 DP98
Nutfield Way, Orp. 123 EN103
Nutford Pl. W1 4 C8
Nutford Pl. W1 76 DE72
Nuthatch Clo., Stai. 98 BM88
Nuthatch Gdns. SE28 95 ER75
Nuthurst Ave. SW2 105 DM89
Nutley Clo., Swan. 125 FF95
Nutley Ter. NW3 76 DC65
Nutmead Clo., Bex. 111 FC88
Nutmeg Clo. E16 80 EE70
Cranberry La.
Nutmeg La. E14 79 ED72
Nutt Gro., Edg. 45 CK47
Nutt St. SE15 92 DT80
Nuttall St. N1 78 DS68
Nutter La. E11 66 EJ58
Nuttfield Clo., Rick. 29 BP44
Nutty La., Shep. 113 BQ97
Nutwell St. SW17 104 DE92
Nuxley Rd., Belv. 96 EZ79
Nyanza St. SE18 95 ER79
Nye Bevan Est. E5 65 DX62
Nylands Ave., Rich. 88 CN81
Nymans Gdns. SW20 117 CV97
Hidcote Gdns.
Nynehead St. SE14 93 DY80
Nyon Gro. SE6 107 DZ89
Nyssa Clo., Wdf.Grn. 53 EM51
Gwynne Pk. Ave.
Nyton Clo. N19 63 DL60
Courtauld Rd.

O

Oak Apple Ct. SE12 108 EG89
Oak Ave. N8 63 DL56
Oak Ave. N10 49 DH52
Oak Ave. N17 50 DR52
Oak Ave., Croy. 121 EA102
Oak Ave., Enf. 35 DM39
Oak Ave., Hmptn. 100 BY92
Oak Ave., Houns. 86 BY80
Oak Ave., St.Alb. 16 CA30
Oak Ave., Sev. 155 FH128
Oak Ave., Uxb. 57 BP61
Oak Ave., West Dr. 84 BN76
Oak Bank, Croy. 135 EC107
Oak Clo. N14 49 DH45
Oak Clo., Dart. 97 FE84
Oak Clo., Sutt. 118 DC103
Oak Clo., Wal.Abb. 23 ED34
Oak Cottage Clo. SE6 108 EF88
Oak Cres. E16 80 EE71
Oak Dene W13 73 CH71
The Dene
Oak Gdns., Croy. 121 EA103
Oak Gdns., Edg. 46 CQ54
Oak Glade, Epp. 26 EX29
Coopersale Common
Oak Glade, Nthwd. 43 BP53
Oak Grn., Abb.L. 15 BS31
Oak Grn. Way, Abb.L. 15 BS32
Oak Grn.
Oak Gro. NW2 61 CX63
Oak Gro., Ruis. 57 BV59
Oak Gro., Sun. 99 BV94
Oak Gro., W.Wick. 121 EC103
Oak Gro. Rd. SE20 120 DW96
Oak Hill, Epsom 144 CR116
Oak Hill, Wdf.Grn. 51 ED52
Oak Hill Clo., Wdf.Grn. 51 ED52
Oak Hill Ct. SW19 103 CX94
Oak Hill Cres., Wdf.Grn. 51 ED52
Oak Hill Gdns., Wdf.Grn. 52 EE53
Oak Hill Pk. NW3 62 DB63
Oak Hill Pk. Ms. NW3 62 DC63
Oak Hill Rd., Rom. 55 FD45
Oak Hill Rd., Sev. 154 FG124
Oak Hill Way NW3 62 DC63
Oak La. E14 79 DZ73
Oak La. N2 48 DD54
Oak La. N11 49 DK51
Oak La., Islw. 87 CE84
Oak La. (Cuffley), Pot.B. 21 DM28
Oak La., Sev. 154 FF129
Oak La., Twick. 101 CG87
Oak La., Wdf.Grn. 52 EF49
Oak Leaf Clo., Epsom 130 CQ112
Oak Lo. Ave., Chig. 53 ER50
Oak Lo. Clo., Stan. 45 CJ50
Dennis La.
Oak Lo. Clo., Walt. 128 BW106
Oak Lo. Dr., W.Wick. 121 EB101
Oak Manor Dr., Wem. 60 CM64
Oakington Manor Dr.
Oak Pk. Gdns. SW19 103 CX87
Oak Path (Bushey), Wat. 30 CB44
Ashfield Ave.
Oak Piece, Epp. 27 FC25
Oak Pl. SW18 104 DB85
East Hill
Oak Ri., Buck.H. 52 EK48
Oak Rd. W5 73 CK73
The Bdy.
Oak Rd., Cat. 148 DS122
Oak Rd., Cob. 142 BX115
Oak Rd., Epp. 25 ET30
Oak Rd., Erith (Northumberland Heath) 97 FC80
Oak Rd. (Slade Grn.), Erith 97 FG81
Oak Rd., Lthd. 143 CG119
Oak Rd., N.Mal. 116 CR96
Oak Rd., Orp. 138 EU108
Oak Row SW16 119 DJ96
Oak Side, Uxb. 70 BH65
Oak St., Rom. 69 FC57
Oak Tree Clo. W5 73 CJ72
Pinewood Gro.
Oak Tree Clo., Abb.L. 15 BR32
Oak Tree Clo., Loug. 39 EQ39
Oak Tree Clo., Stan. 45 CH52
Oak Tree Ct., Borwd. 31 CK44
Barnet La.
Oak Tree Dell NW9 60 CQ57
Oak Tree Dr. N20 48 DB46
Oak Tree Gdns., Brom. 108 EH92
Oak Tree Rd. NW8 4 A3
Oak Tree Rd. NW8 76 DE69
Oak Village NW5 62 DG63
Oak Way N14 49 DH45
Oak Way W3 74 CS74
Oak Way, Ash. 144 CN116
Oak Way, Croy. 121 DX100
Oak Way, Felt. 99 BS88
Oakapple Clo., S.Croy. 134 DV114
Oakbank, Lthd. 142 CC123
Oakbank Ave., Walt. 114 BZ101
Oakbank Gro. SE24 92 DQ84
Oakbrook Clo., Brom. 108 EH91
Oakbury Rd. SW6 90 DB82
Oakcombe Clo., N.Mal. 116 CS95
Traps La.
Oakcroft Clo., Pnr. 43 BV54
Oakcroft Rd. SE13 93 ED82
Oakcroft Rd., Chess. 130 CM105
Oakcroft Vill., Chess. 130 CM105
Oakdale N14 49 DH46
Oakdale Ave., Har. 60 CL57
Oakdale Ave., Nthwd. 43 BU54
Oakdale Clo., Wat. 44 BW49
Oakdale Ct. E4 51 EC50
Oakdale Gdns. E4 51 EC50
Oakdale Rd. E7 80 EH66
Oakdale Rd. E11 65 ED61
Oakdale Rd. E18 52 EH54
Oakdale Rd. N4 64 DQ58
Oakdale Rd. SE15 92 DW83
Oakdale Rd. SW16 105 DL92
Oakdale Rd., Epsom 130 CR109
Oakdale Rd., Wat. 44 BW48
Oakdale Rd., Wey. 112 BN104
Oakdale Way, Mitch. 118 DG101
Wolseley Rd.
Oakden St. SE11 10 E8
Oakden St. SE11 91 DN77
Oakdene SE15 92 DV81
Carlton Gro.
Oakdene, Tad. 145 CY120
Oakdene (Cheshunt), Wal.Cr. 23 DY30
Oakdene Ave., Chis. 109 EN92
Oakdene Ave., Erith 97 FC79
Oakdene Ave., T.Ditt. 115 CG102
Oakdene Clo., Horn. 69 FH58
Oakdene Clo., Pnr. 44 BZ52
Oakdene Dr., Surb. 116 CQ101
Oakdene Ms., Sutt. 117 CZ102
Oakdene Pk. N3 47 CZ52
Oakdene Rd., Cob. 127 BV114
Oakdene Rd., Lthd. 142 BZ124
Oakdene Rd., Orp. 123 ET99
Oakdene Rd., Sev. 154 FG122
Oakdene Rd., Uxb. 71 BP68
Oakdene Rd., Wat. 29 BV36
Oake Ct. SW15 103 CY85
Oaken Coppice, Ash. 144 CN119
Oaken Dr., Esher 129 CF107
Oaken La., Esher 129 CE105
Oakenshaw Clo., Surb. 116 CL101
Oakes Clo. E6 81 EM72
Savage Gdns.
Oakeshott Ave. N6 62 DG61
Oakey La. SE1 10 D6
Oakfield E4 51 EB50
Oakfield Ave., Har. 59 CH55
Oakfield Clo., N.Mal. 117 CT99
Blakes La.
Oakfield Clo., Pot.B. 19 CZ31
Oakfield Clo., Ruis. 57 BT58
Evelyn Ave.
Oakfield Clo., Wey. 127 BQ105
Oakfield Ct. N8 63 DL59
Oakfield Ct. NW2 61 CX59
Hendon Way
Oakfield Gdns. N18 50 DS49
Oakfield Gdns. SE19 106 DT92
Oakfield Gdns., Beck. 121 EA99
Oakfield Gdns., Cars. 118 DE102
Oakfield Gdns., Grnf. 73 CD70
Oakfield Glade, Wey. 127 BQ105
Oakfield La., Bex. 111 FE89
Oakfield La., Dart. 111 FG89
Oakfield La., Kes. 136 EJ105
Oakfield Rd. E6 80 EL67
Oakfield Rd. E17 51 DY54
Oakfield Rd. N3 48 DB53
Oakfield Rd. N4 63 DN58
Oakfield Rd. N14 49 DL48
Oakfield Rd. SE20 120 DV95
Oakfield Rd. SW19 103 CX90
Oakfield Rd., Ashf. 99 BP91
Oakfield Rd., Ash. 143 CK117
Oakfield Rd., Cob. 127 BV113
Oakfield Rd., Croy. 120 DQ102
Oakfield Rd., Ilf. 67 EP61
Oakfield Rd., Orp. 124 EU101
Goodmead Rd.
Oakfield St. SW10 90 DC79
Oakfields, Sev. 155 FH126
Oakfields, Walt. 113 BU102
Oakfields, W.Byf. 126 BH114
Oakfields Rd. NW11 61 CY58
Oakford Rd. NW5 63 DJ63
Oakhall Ct. E11 66 EH58
Oakhall Dr., Sun. 99 BT92
Oakhall Rd. E11 66 EH58
Oakham Clo. SE6 107 DZ89
Rutland Wk.
Oakham Clo., Barn. 34 DG41
Oakham Dr., Brom. 122 EF98
Oakhampton Rd. NW7 47 CX52
Oakhill, Esher 129 CG107
Oakhill, Surb. 116 CL101
Oakhill Ave. NW3 62 DB63
Oakhill Ave., Pnr. 44 BY54
Oakhill Clo., Ash. 143 CJ118
Oakhill Ct. E11 66 EH58
Eastern Ave.
Oakhill Ct. SW19 103 CX94
Edge Hill
Oakhill Cres., Surb. 116 CL101
Oakhill Dr., Surb. 116 CL101
Oakhill Gdns., Wey. 113 BS103
Oatlands Dr.
Oakhill Gro., Surb. 116 CL100
Oakhill Path, Surb. 116 CL100
Glenbuck Rd.
Oakhill Pl. SW15 104 DA85
Oakhill Rd.
Oakhill Rd. SW15 103 CZ85
Oakhill Rd. SW16 119 DL95
Oakhill Rd., Ash. 143 CJ118
Oakhill Rd., Beck. 121 EC96
Oakhill Rd., Orp. 123 ET102
Oakhill Rd., Surb. 116 CL100
Oakhill Rd., Sutt. 118 DB104
Oakhouse Rd., Bexh. 110 FA85
Oakhurst Ave., Barn. 48 DE45
Oakhurst Ave., Bexh. 96 EY80
Oakhurst Clo. E17 66 EE56
Oakhurst Clo., Ilf. 53 EQ53
Oakhurst Clo., Tedd. 101 CE92
Oakhurst Gdns. E4 52 EF46
Oakhurst Gdns. E17 66 EE56
Oakhurst Gdns., Bexh. 96 EY80
Oakhurst Gro. SE22 92 DU84
Oakhurst Ri., Cars. 132 DE110
Oakhurst Rd., Enf. 37 DX36
Oakhurst Rd., Epsom 130 CQ107
Oakington Ave., Har. 58 CA59
Oakington Ave., Hayes 85 BR77
Oakington Ave., Wem. 60 CM62
Oakington Dr., Sun. 114 BW96
Oakington Manor Dr., Wem. 60 CN64
Oakington Rd. W9 76 DA70
Oakington Way N8 63 DL58
Oakland Pl., Buck.H. 52 EG47
Oakland Rd. E15 66 EE63
Crownfield Rd.
Oakland Way, Epsom 130 CR107
Oaklands N21 49 DM47
Oaklands, Ken. 134 DQ114
Oaklands, Lthd. 143 CD124
Oaklands, Twick. 100 CC87
Oaklands Ave. N9 36 DV44
Oaklands Ave., Esher 115 CD102
Oaklands Ave., Hat. 19 CY26
Oaklands Ave., Islw. 87 CF79
Oaklands Ave., Rom. 69 FE55
Oaklands Ave., Sid. 109 ET87
Oaklands Ave., Th.Hth. 119 DN98
Oaklands Ave., Wat. 43 BV46
Oaklands Ave., W.Wick. 121 EB104
Oaklands Clo., Bexh. 110 EZ85
Oaklands Clo., Chess. 129 CJ105
Oaklands Clo., Orp. 123 ES100
Oaklands Ct., Add. 112 BH104
Oaklands Ct., Wat. 29 BT39
Oaklands Ct., Wem. 59 CK64
Oaklands Est. SW4 105 DJ86
Oaklands Gdns., Ken. 134 DQ114
Oaklands Gate, Nthwd. 43 BS51
Green La.
Oaklands Gro. W12 75 CU74
Oaklands La., Barn. 33 CV42
Oaklands La., West. 136 EH113
Oaklands Pk. Ave., Ilf. 67 ER61
High Rd.
Oaklands Pl. SW4 91 DJ84
St. Alphonsus Rd.
Oaklands Rd. N20 47 CZ45
Oaklands Rd. NW2 61 CX63
Oaklands Rd. SW14 88 CR83
Oaklands Rd. W7 87 CF75
Oaklands Rd., Bexh. 96 EZ84
Oaklands Rd., Brom. 108 EE94
Oaklands Rd. (Cheshunt), Wal.Cr. 22 DS26
Oaklands Way, Tad. 145 CW122
Oaklands Way, Wall. 133 DK108
Oaklawn Rd., Lthd. 143 CE118
Oaklea Pas., Kings.T. 115 CK97
Oakleafe Gdns., Ilf. 67 EP55
Oakleigh Ave. N20 48 DD47
Oakleigh Ave., Edg. 46 CP54
Oakleigh Ave., Surb. 116 CN102
Oakleigh Clo. N20 48 DF48
Oakleigh Clo., Swan. 125 FE97
Oakleigh Ct., Barn. 34 DE44
Church Hill Rd.
Oakleigh Ct., Edg. 46 CQ54
Oakleigh Cres. N20 48 DE47
Oakleigh Dr., Rick. 29 BQ44
Oakleigh Gdns. N20 48 DC46
Oakleigh Gdns., Edg. 46 CM50
Oakleigh Gdns., Orp. 137 ES105
Oakleigh Ms. N20 48 DC47
Oakleigh Rd. N.
Oakleigh Pk. Ave., Chis. 123 EN96
Oakleigh Pk. N. N20 48 DD46
Oakleigh Pk. S. N20 48 DE45
Oakleigh Ri., Epp. 26 EU32
Bower Hill
Oakleigh Rd., Pnr. 44 BZ51
Oakleigh Rd., Uxb. 71 BQ66
Oakleigh Rd. N. N20 48 DE47
Oakleigh Rd. S. N11 48 DG48
Oakleigh Way, Mitch. 119 DH95
Oakleigh Way, Surb. 116 CN102
Oakley Ave. W5 74 CN73
Oakley Ave., Bark. 81 ET66
Oakley Ave., Croy. 133 DM105
Oakley Clo. E4 51 EC48
Mapleton Rd.
Oakley Clo. E6 80 EL72
Northumberland Rd.
Oakley Clo. W7 73 CE73
Oakley Clo., Add. 126 BK105
Oakley Clo., Islw. 87 CD81
Oakley Ct., Mitch. 118 DG102
London Rd.
Oakley Cres. EC1 6 G1
Oakley Dr. SE9 109 ER88
Oakley Dr. SE13 107 EC85
Hither Grn. La.
Oakley Dr., Brom. 122 EL104
Oakley Gdns. N8 63 DM57
Oakley Gdns. SW3 90 DE79
Oakley Gdns., Bans. 146 DB115
Oakley Pk., Bex. 110 EW87
Oakley Pl. SE1 92 DT78
Oakley Rd. N1 78 DR66
Oakley Rd. SE25 120 DV99
Oakley Rd., Brom. 122 EL104
Oakley Rd., Har. 59 CE58
Oakley Rd., Warl. 148 DU118
Oakley Sq. NW1 77 DJ68
Oakley St. SW3 90 DE79
Oakley Wk. W6 89 CX79
Greyhound Rd.
Oakley Yd. E2 78 DT70
Bacon St.
Oaklodge Way NW7 47 CT51
Oakmead Ave., Brom. 122 EG100
Oakmead Gdns., Edg. 46 CR49
Oakmead Grn., Epsom 144 CQ115
Oakmead Pl., Mitch. 118 DE95
Oakmead Rd. SW12 104 DG88
Oakmead Rd., Croy. 119 DK100
Oakmeade, Pnr. 44 CA51
Oakmere Ave., Pot.B. 20 DC33
Oakmere Clo., Pot.B. 20 DD31
Oakmere La., Pot.B. 20 DC32
Oakmere Rd. SE2 96 EU79
Oakmoor Way, Chig. 53 ES50
Oakmount Pl., Orp. 123 ER102
Oakridge, St.Alb. 16 BZ29
Oakridge Ave., Rad. 17 CF34
Oakridge Dr. N2 62 DD55
Oakridge La., Brom. 107 ED92
Downham Way
Oakridge La., Wat. 31 CD35
Oakridge Rd., Brom. 107 ED91
Oakroyd Ave., Pot.B. 19 CZ33
Oakroyd Clo., Pot.B. 19 CZ33
Oaks, The N12 48 DB49
Oaks, The SE18 95 EQ78
Oaks, The, Epsom 131 CT114
Oaks, The, Hayes 71 BQ68
Charville La.
Oaks, The, Ruis. 57 BS59
Oaks, The, Swan. 125 FE96
Oaks, The, Wat. 44 BW46
Oaks, The, W.Byf. 126 BG114
Oaks, The, Wdf.Grn. 52 EE52
Oaks Ave. SE19 106 DS92
Oaks Ave., Felt. 100 BY89
Oaks Ave., Rom. 55 FC54
Oaks Ave., Wor.Pk. 117 CV104
Oaks Clo., Lthd. 143 CG121
Oaks Clo., Rad. 31 CF35
Oaks Gro. E4 52 EE47
Oaks La., Croy. 120 DW104
Oaks La., Ilf. 67 ES57
Oaks Rd., Croy. 134 DV106
Oaks Rd., Ken 133 DP114
Oaks Rd., Stai. 98 BK86
Oaks Track, Cars. 132 DF111
Oaks Track, Wall. 133 DH110
Oaks Way, Cars. 132 DF108

Oaks Way, Epsom 145 CV119
Epsom La. N.
Oaks Way, Ken. 134 DQ114
Oaks Way, Surb. 115 CK103
Oaksford Ave. SE26 106 DV90
Oakshade Rd., Brom. 107 ED91
Oakshade Rd., Lthd. 128 CC114
Oakshaw Rd. SW18 104 DB87
Oakside, Uxb. 70 BH65
Oakthorpe Rd. N13 49 DN50
Oaktree Ave. N13 49 DP48
Oaktree Clo., Wal.Cr. 21 DP28
Oaktree Gro., Ilf. 67 ER64
Oakview Clo., Wal.Cr. 22 DV28
Oakview Gdns. N2 62 DD56
Oakview Gro., Croy. 121 DY102
Oakview Rd. SE6 107 EB92
Oakway SW20 117 CW98
Oakway, Brom. 121 ED96
Oakway Clo., Bex. 110 EY86
Oakways SE9 109 EP86
Oakwood, Wall. 133 DH109
Oakwood, Wal.Abb. 37 ED35
Roundhills
Oakwood Ave. N14 49 DK45
Oakwood Ave., Beck. 121 EC96
Oakwood Ave., Borwd. 32 CP42
Oakwood Ave., Brom. 122 EH97
Oakwood Ave., Mitch. 118 DD96
Oakwood Ave., Pur. 133 DP112
Oakwood Ave., Sthl. 72 CA73
Oakwood Clo. N14 35 DJ44
Oakwood Clo., Chis. 109 EM93
Oakwood Clo., Wdf.Grn. 52 EL51
Green Wk.
Oakwood Ct. W14 89 CZ76
Oakwood Cres. N21 35 DL44
Oakwood Cres., Grnf. 73 CG65
Oakwood Dr. SE19 106 DR93
Oakwood Dr., Bexh. 97 FD84
Oakwood Dr., Edg. 46 CQ51
Oakwood Dr., Sev. 155 FH123
Oakwood Gdns., Ilf. 67 ET61
Oakwood Gdns., Orp. 123 EQ103
Oakwood Gdns., Sutt. 118 DA103
Oakwood Hill, Loug. 39 EM44
Oakwood Hill Ind. Est., Loug. 39 EP43
Oakwood La. W14 89 CZ76
Oakwood Pk. Rd. N14 49 DK45
Oakwood Pl., Croy. 119 DN100
Oakwood Rd. NW11 62 DA56
Oakwood Rd. SW20 117 CU95
Oakwood Rd., Croy. 119 DN100
Oakwood Rd., Orp. 123 EQ103
Oakwood Rd., Pnr. 43 BV54
Oakwood Rd., St.Alb. 16 BY29
Oakwood Vw. N14 35 DK43
Oakworth Rd. W10 75 CW71
Oasthouse Way, Orp. 124 EV98
Oat La. EC2 7 J8
Oat La. EC2 78 DQ72
Oates Clo., Brom. 121 ED97
Oates Rd., Rom. 55 FB50
Oatfield Rd., Orp. 123 ET102
Oatfield Rd., Tad. 145 CV121
Oatland Ri. E17 51 DY54
Oatlands Ave., Wey. 127 BQ106
Oatlands Chase, Wey. 113 BS104
Oatlands Clo., Wey. 127 BQ105
Oatlands Dr., Wey. 113 BR104
Oatlands Grn., Wey. 113 BR104
Oatlands Dr.
Oatlands Mere, Wey. 113 BR104
Oatlands Rd., Enf. 36 DW39
Oatlands Rd., Tad. 145 CY119
Oban Clo. E13 80 EJ70
Oban Ho., Bark. 81 ER68
Wheelers Cross
Oban Rd. E13 80 EJ69
Oban Rd. SE25 120 DR98
Oban St. E14 79 ED72
Oberon Clo., Borwd. 32 CQ39
Oberon Way, Shep. 112 BL97
Oberstein Rd. SW11 90 DD84
Oborne Clo. SE24 105 DP85
Observatory Gdns. W8 90 DA75
Observatory Rd. SW14 88 CQ84
Occupation La. SE18 95 EP81
Occupation La. W5 87 CK77
Occupation Rd. SE17 11 H10
Occupation Rd. SE17 92 DQ78
Occupation Rd. W13 87 CH75
Occupation Rd., Wat. 29 BV43
Ocean Est. E1 79 DX70
Ocean St. E1 79 DX71
Ockendon Rd. N1 78 DR65
Ockham Dr., Lthd. 141 BR124
Ockham Dr., Orp. 110 EU94
Ockham La., Cob. 141 BR120
Ockham La., Wok. 140 BN121
Ockham Rd. N., Lthd. 141 BQ123
Ockham Rd. N., Wok. 140 BL120
Ockley Rd. SW16 105 DL91
Ockley Rd., Croy. 119 DM101
Octagon Arc. EC2 7 M7
Octagon Rd., Walt. 127 BS109
Octavia Clo., Mitch. 118 DE99
Octavia Rd., Islw. 87 CF83
Octavia St. SW11 90 DE81
Octavia Way SE28 82 EV73
Booth Clo.
Octavia Way, Stai. 98 BG93
Octavius St. SE8 93 EA80
Odard Rd., W.Mol. 114 CA98
Down St.
Oddesey Rd., Borwd. 32 CP39
Odessa Rd. E7 66 EF63
Odessa Rd. NW10 75 CU68
Odessa St. SE16 93 DZ75
Odger St. SW11 90 DF82
Odhams Wk. WC2 5 P9
Odyssey Business Pk., Ruis. 57 BV64
Offas Mead E9 65 DY63
Lindisfarne Way
Offenbach Ho. E2 79 DX68
Mace St.
Offenham Rd. SE9 109 EM91
Offerton Rd. SW4 91 DJ83
Offham Slope N12 47 CZ50
Offley Rd. SW9 91 DN80
Offord Clo. N17 50 DU52
Offord Rd. N1 77 DM66
Offord St. N1 77 DM66
Ogilby St. SE18 95 EM77
Oglander Rd. SE15 92 DT84
Ogle St. W1 5 K6
Ogle St. W1 77 DJ71
Oglethorpe Rd., Dag. 68 EZ62
Ohio Rd. E13 80 EF70
Oil Mill La. W6 89 CU78
Okeburn Rd. SW17 104 DG92
Okehampton Clo. N12 48 DD50
Okehampton Cres., Well. 96 EV81
Okehampton Rd. NW10 75 CW67
Okemore Gdns., Orp. 124 EW98
Olaf St. W11 75 CX73
Old Acre, Wok. 126 BG114
Old Ave., Wey. 127 BQ108
Old Bailey EC4 6 G9
Old Bailey EC4 77 DP72
Old Barn Clo., Sutt. 131 CY108
Old Barn La., Ken. 148 DT116
Old Barn La., Rick. 28 BM43
Old Barn Rd., Epsom 144 CQ117
Old Barn Way, Bexh. 97 FD83
Old Barrack Yd. SW1 8 F5
Old Barrowfield E15 80 EE67
New Plaistow Rd.
Old Bethnal Grn. Rd. E2 78 DU69
Old Bexley La., Bex. 111 FD89
Old Bexley La., Dart. 111 FF88
Old Bond St. W1 9 K1
Old Bond St. W1 77 DJ73
Old Brewers Yd. WC2 5 P9
Old Brewery Ms. NW3 62 DD63
Hampstead High St.
Old Bri. Clo., Nthlt. 72 CA68
Old Bri. St., Kings.T. 115 CK96
Old Broad St. EC2 7 L9
Old Broad St. EC2 78 DR72
Old Bromley Rd., Brom. 107 ED92
Old Brompton Rd. SW5 90 DB78
Old Brompton Rd. SW7 90 DB78
Old Bldgs. WC2 6 D8
Old Burlington St. W1 5 K10
Old Burlington St. W1 77 DJ73
Old Carriageway, The, Sev. 154 FC122
Old Castle St. E1 7 P8
Old Castle St. E1 78 DT72
Old Cavendish St. W1 5 H8
Old Cavendish St. W1 77 DH72
Old Change Ct. EC4 78 DQ72
Carter La.
Old Chapel Rd., Swan. 125 FC101
Old Charlton Rd., Shep. 113 BQ99
Old Chelsea Ms. SW3 90 DD79
Danvers St.
Old Chestnut Ave., Esher 128 CA107
Old Ch. La. NW9 60 CR61
Old Ch. La., Grnf. 73 CG69
Perivale La.
Old Ch. La., Stan. 45 CH50
Old Ch. Path, Esher 128 CB105
High St.
Old Ch. Rd. E1 79 DX72
Old Ch. Rd. E4 51 EA49
Old Ch. St. SW3 90 DD78
Old Claygate La., Esher 129 CG107
Old Clem Sq. SE18 95 EN79
Kempt St.
Old Common Rd., Cob. 127 BU112
Old Compton St. W1 5 M10
Old Compton St. W1 77 DK73
Old Cote Dr., Houns. 86 CA79
Old Ct., Ash. 144 CL119
Old Ct. Pl. W8 90 DB75
Old Deer Pk. Gdns., Rich. 88 CL83
Old Devonshire Rd. SW12 105 DH87
Old Dock Clo., Rich. 88 CN79
Watcombe Cotts.
Old Dover Rd. SE3 94 EG80
Old Esher Clo., Walt. 128 BX106
Old Esher Rd.
Old Esher Rd., Walt. 128 BX106
Old Farleigh Rd., S.Croy. 134 DW110
Old Farleigh Rd., Warl. 149 DY117
Old Fm. Ave. N14 49 DJ45
Old Fm. Ave., Sid. 109 ER88
Old Fm. Clo., Houns. 86 BZ84
Old Fm. Gdns., Swan. 125 FF97
Old Fm. Pas., Hmptn. 114 CC95
Old Fm. Rd. N2 48 DD53
Old Fm. Rd., Hmptn. 100 BZ93
Old Fm. Rd., West Dr. 84 BK75
Old Fm. Rd. E., Sid. 110 EU89
Old Fm. Rd. W., Sid. 109 ET89
Old Farmhouse Dr., Lthd. 143 CD115
Old Fish St. Hill EC4 7 H10
Old Fleet La. EC4 6 F8
Old Fold Clo., Barn. 33 CZ39
Old Fold La.
Old Fold La., Barn. 33 CZ39
Old Fold Vw., Barn. 33 CW41
Old Ford Rd. E2 78 DW68
Old Ford Rd. E3 79 DX68
Old Forge Clo., Stan. 45 CG49
Old Forge Clo., Wat. 15 BU33
Old Forge Cres., Shep. 113 BP100
Old Forge Ms. W12 89 CV75
Goodwin Rd.
Old Forge Rd., Enf. 36 DT38
Old Forge Way, Sid. 110 EV91
Old Fox Clo., Cat. 147 DP121
Old Fox Footpath, S.Croy. 134 DS108
Essenden Rd.
Old Gannon Clo., Nthwd. 43 BQ50
Old Gdn., The, Sev. 154 FD123
Old Gloucester St. WC1 6 A6
Old Gloucester St. WC1 77 DL71
Old Hall Clo., Pnr. 44 BY53
Old Hall Dr., Pnr. 44 BY53
Old Harrow La., West. 151 EQ119
Old Hatch Manor, Ruis. 57 BT59
Old Hill, Chis. 123 EN95
Old Hill, Orp. 137 ER107
Old Homesdale Rd., Brom. 122 EJ98
Old Hospital Clo. SW12 104 DF88
Old Ho. Clo. SW19 103 CY92
Old Ho. Clo., Epsom 131 CT110
Old Ho. Gdns., Twick. 101 CJ86
Old Ho. La., Kings L. 28 BL35
Old Howlett's La., Ruis. 57 BR58
Bury St.
Old Jamaica Rd. SE16 92 DU76
Old James St. SE15 92 DV83
Old Jewry EC2 7 K9
Old Jewry EC2 78 DR72
Old Kent Rd. SE1 11 M8
Old Kent Rd. SE1 92 DS77
Old Kent Rd. SE15 92 DV79
Old Kenton La. NW9 60 CP57
Old Kingston Rd., Wor.Pk. 116 CQ104
Old La., Cob. 141 BP117
Old La., West. 150 EK121
Old La. Gdns., Cob. 141 BT122
Old Lo. La., Ken. 147 DN116
Old Lo. La., Pur. 133 DM113
Old Lo. Pl., Twick. 101 CH86
St. Margarets Rd.
Old Lo. Way, Stan. 45 CG50
Old London Rd., Epsom 145 CU118
Old London Rd., Sev. 138 EY109
Old London Rd. (Knockholt Pound), Sev. 152 EY115
Old Maidstone Rd., Sid. 110 EZ94
Old Malden La., Wor.Pk. 116 CR104
Old Manor Dr., Islw. 100 CC86
Old Manor Ho. Ms., Shep. 112 BN97
Squires Bri. Rd.
Old Manor Way, Bexh. 97 FD82
Old Manor Way, Chis. 109 EM92
Old Manor Yd. SW5 90 DB77
Earls Ct. Rd.
Old Marylebone Rd. NW1 4 C7
Old Marylebone Rd. NW1 76 DE71
Old Ms., Har. 59 CE57
Hindes Rd.
Old Mill Ct. E18 66 EJ55
Old Mill La. W6 89 CU78
Old Mill La., Uxb. 70 BH71
Old Mill Pl., Rom. 69 FD58
Old Mill Rd. SE18 95 ER79
Old Mill Rd., Kings L. 15 BQ34
Old Mill Rd., Uxb. 56 BG62
Old Mitre Ct. EC4 77 DN72
Fleet St.
Old Montague St. E1 78 DU71
Old Nichol St. E2 7 P4
Old Nichol St. E2 78 DT70
Old N. St. WC1 6 B6
Old Oak Ave., Couls. 146 DE119
Old Oak Common La. NW10 74 CS70
Old Oak Common La. W3 74 CS71
Old Oak La. NW10 75 CT69
Old Oak Rd. W3 75 CT73
Old Oaks, Wal.Abb. 24 EE32
Old Orchard, St.Alb. 16 CC26
Old Orchard, Sun. 114 BW96
Old Orchard, W.Byf. 126 BM112
Old Orchard, The NW3 62 DF63
Nassington Rd.
Old Orchard Clo., Barn. 34 DD38
Old Orchard Clo., Uxb. 70 BN72
Old Otford Rd., Sev. 153 FH117
Old Palace La., Rich. 101 CJ85
Old Palace Rd., Croy. 119 DP104
Old Palace Rd., Wey. 113 BP104
Old Palace Ter., Rich. 101 CK85
King St.
Old Palace Yd. SW1 9 P6
Old Palace Yd. SW1 91 DL76
Old Palace Yd., Rich. 101 CK85
Old Paradise St. SE11 10 B8
Old Paradise St. SE11 91 DM77
Old Pk. Ave. SW12 104 DG86
Old Pk. Ave., Enf. 36 DQ42
Old Pk. Gro., Enf. 36 DQ42
Old Pk. La. W1 8 G3
Old Pk. La. W1 76 DG74
Old Pk. Ms., Houns. 86 BZ80
Old Pk. Ride, Wal.Cr. 21 DP31
Old Pk. Ridings N21 35 DP44
Old Pk. Rd. N13 49 DM49
Old Pk. Rd. SE2 96 EU78
Old Pk. Rd., Enf. 35 DP41
Old Pk. Rd. S., Enf. 35 DP42
Old Pk. Vw., Enf. 35 DN41
Old Parkbury La., St.Alb. 17 CF29
Old Parvis Rd., W.Byf. 126 BJ112
Old Perry St., Chis. 109 ES93
Old Polhill, Sev. 151 ET115
Old Pound Clo., Islw. 87 CG81
Old Pye St. SW1 9 M6
Old Pye St. SW1 91 DK76
Old Quebec St. W1 4 E9
Old Quebec St. W1 76 DF72
Old Queen St. SW1 9 N5
Old Queen St. SW1 91 DK75
Old Rectory Clo., Tad. 145 CU124
Old Rectory Gdns., Edg. 46 CN51
Old Rectory Rd., Ong. 27 FH34
Old Redding, Har. 44 CB50
Old Rd. SE13 94 EE84
Old Rd., Dart. 111 FD85
Old Rd., Enf. 36 DW39
Old Rope Wk., Sun. 113 BV97
The Ave.
Old Royal Free Pl. N1 77 DN67
Liverpool Rd.
Old Royal Free Sq. N1 77 DN67
Old Ruislip Rd., Nthlt. 72 BW68
Old Savill's Cotts., Chig. 53 EQ49
The Chase
Old Sch. Clo. SW19 118 DA96
Old Sch. Clo., Beck. 121 DX96
Old Sch. Ms., Wey. 127 BR105
Old Schools La., Epsom 131 CT109
Old Seacoal La. EC4 6 F9
Old Shire La., Wal.Abb. 38 EG35
Old S. Clo., Pnr. 44 BX53
Old S. Lambeth Rd. SW8 91 DL80
Old Sq. WC2 6 C8
Old Sq. WC2 77 DM72
Old Sta. App., Lthd. 143 CG121
Old Sta. Rd., Hayes 85 BT76
Old Sta. Rd., Loug. 38 EL43
Old Stockley Rd., West Dr. 85 BP75
Old St. E13 80 EH68
Old St. EC1 7 H5
Old St. EC1 78 DQ70
Old Swan Yd., Cars. 132 DF105
Old Town SW4 91 DJ83
Old Town, Croy. 119 DP104
Old Tram Yd. SE18 95 ES77
Lakedale Rd.
Old Tye Ave., West. 150 EL116
Old Wk., The, Sev. 153 FH117
Old Watford Rd., St.Alb. 16 BY30
Old Westhall Clo., Warl. 148 DW119
Old Woolwich Rd. SE10 93 ED78
Old York Rd. SW18 104 DB85
Oldacre Ms. SW12 105 DH87
Balham Gro.
Oldberry Rd., Edg. 46 CR51
Oldborough Rd., Wem. 59 CJ61
Oldbury Clo., Orp. 124 EX98
Oldbury Pl. W1 4 G6
Oldbury Pl. W1 76 DG71
Oldbury Rd., Enf. 36 DU40
Oldchurch Gdns., Rom. 69 FD59
Oldchurch Ri., Rom. 69 FD59
Oldchurch Rd., Rom. 69 FE58
Olden La., Pur. 133 DN112
Oldfield Circ., Nthlt. 72 CC65
The Fairway
Oldfield Clo., Brom. 123 EM98
Oldfield Clo., Grnf. 59 CE64
Oldfield Clo., Stan. 45 CG50
Oldfield Clo. (Cheshunt), Wal.Cr. 23 DY28
Oldfield Dr. (Cheshunt), Wal.Cr. 23 DY28
Oldfield Fm. Gdns., Grnf. 73 CD67
Oldfield Gdns., Ash. 143 CK119
Oldfield Gro. SE16 93 DX77
Oldfield La. N., Grnf. 73 CD68
Oldfield La. S., Grnf. 72 CC69
Oldfield Ms. N6 63 DJ59
Oldfield Rd. N16 64 DS62
Oldfield Rd. NW10 75 CT66
Oldfield Rd. SW19 103 CY93
Oldfield Rd. W3 89 CT75
Valetta Rd.
Oldfield Rd., Bexh. 96 EY82
Oldfield Rd., Brom. 122 EL98
Oldfield Rd., Hmptn. 114 BZ95
Oldfield Rd., St.Alb. 17 CK25
Oldfields Rd., Sutt. 117 CZ104
Oldham Ter. W3 74 CQ74
Oldhill St. N16 64 DU60
Oldridge Rd. SW12 104 DG87
Olds App., Wat. 43 BP46
Olds Clo., Wat. 43 BP46
Oldstead Rd., Brom. 107 ED91
Oleander Clo., Orp. 137 ER106
O'Leary Sq. E1 78 DW71
Oley Pl. E1 79 DX71
Redman's Rd.
Olinda Rd. N16 64 DT58
Oliphant St. W10 75 CX69
Olive Rd. E13 80 EJ69
Olive Rd. NW2 61 CW63
Olive Rd. SW19 104 DC94
Norman Rd.
Olive Rd. W5 87 CK76
Olive St., Rom. 69 FD57
Oliver Ave. SE25 120 DT97
Oliver Clo. W4 88 CP79
Oliver Clo., Add. 126 BG105
Oliver Clo., St.Alb. 17 CD27
Oliver Gdns. E6 80 EL72
Oliver Goldsmith Est. SE15 92 DU81
Goldsmith Rd.
Oliver Gro. SE25 120 DT98
Oliver Rd. E10 65 EB61
Oliver Rd. E17 65 EC57
Oliver Rd., N.Mal. 116 CQ96
Oliver Rd., Rain. 83 FF67
Oliver Rd., Sutt. 132 DD105
Oliver Rd., Swan. 125 FD97
Olivers Yd. EC1 7 L4
Olivette St. SW15 89 CX83
Felsham Rd.
Olivia Gdns., Uxb. 42 BJ53
Ollards Gro., Loug. 38 EK42
Ollerton Grn. E3 79 DZ67
Ollerton Rd. N11 49 DK50
Olley Clo., Wall. 133 DL107
Ollgar Clo. W12 75 CT74
Olliffe St. E14 93 EC76
Olmar St. SE1 92 DU79
Olney Rd. SE17 91 DP79
Olron Cres., Bexh. 110 EX85
Olven Rd. SE18 95 EQ79
Olveston Wk., Cars. 118 DD100
Olwen Ms., Pnr. 44 BX54
Olyffe Ave., Well. 96 EU81
Olyffe Dr., Beck. 121 EC95
Olympia Ms. W2 76 DB73
Queensway
Olympia Way W14 89 CY76
Olympic Way, Grnf. 72 CB67
Olympic Way, Wem. 60 CN62
Olympus Sq. E5 64 DU63
Nolan Way
Oman Ave. NW2 61 CV63
O'Meara St. SE1 11 J3
O'Meara St. SE1 78 DQ74
Omega Clo. E14 93 EB76
Tiller Rd.
Omega Pl. N1 6 A1
Omega St. SE14 93 EA81
Ommaney Rd. SE14 93 DX81
Omnibus Way E17 51 EA54
On The Hill, Wat. 44 BY47
Ondine Rd. SE15 92 DT84
One Tree Clo. SE23 106 DW86
Onega Gate SE16 93 DY76
O'Neill Path SE18 95 EN79
Kempt St.
Ongar Clo., Rom. 68 EW57
Ongar Pl., Add. 126 BG107
Ongar Rd. SW6 90 DA79
Ongar Rd., Add. 126 BG106
Ongar Rd., Rom. 40 EV41
Ongar Way, Rain. 83 FE67
Onra Rd. E17 65 EA59
Onslow Ave., Rich. 102 CL85
Onslow Ave., Sutt. 131 CZ110
Onslow Clo. E4 51 ED47
Onslow Clo., T.Ditt. 115 CE102
Onslow Cres., Chis. 123 EP95
Onslow Dr., Sid. 110 EX90
Onslow Gdns. E18 66 EH55
Onslow Gdns. N10 63 DH57
Onslow Gdns. N21 35 DN43
Onslow Gdns. SW7 90 DD78
Onslow Gdns., S.Croy. 134 DU112
Onslow Gdns., T.Ditt. 115 CE102
Onslow Gdns., Wall. 133 DJ107
Onslow Ms., Cher. 112 BG100
Onslow Ms. E. SW7 90 DD77
Cranley Pl.
Onslow Ms. W. SW7 90 DD77
Cranley Pl.
Onslow Rd., Croy. 119 DN102
Onslow Rd., N.Mal. 117 CU98
Onslow Rd., Rich. 102 CL85
Onslow Rd., Walt. 127 BT105
Onslow Sq. SW7 8 A9
Onslow Sq. SW7 90 DD77
Onslow St. EC1 6 E5
Onslow Way, T.Ditt. 115 CE102
Ontario St. SE1 10 G7
Ontario Way E14 79 EA73
Opal Clo. E16 80 EK72
Opal Ms. NW6 75 CZ67
Priory Pk. Rd.
Opal Ms., Ilf. 67 EP61
Ley St.
Opal St. SE11 10 F10
Opal St. SE11 91 DP77
Openshaw Rd. SE2 96 EV77
Openview SW18 104 DC88
Ophelia Gdns. NW2 61 CY62
The Vale
Ophir Ter. SE15 92 DU81
Opossum Way, Houns. 86 BW82
Oppenheim Rd. SE13 93 EC82
Oppidans Ms. NW3 76 DF66
Meadowbank
Oppidans Rd. NW3 76 DF66
Orange Ct. E1 78 DU74
Hermitage Wall
Orange Ct. La., Orp. 137 EM109
Orange Gro. E11 66 EE62
Orange Hill Rd., Edg. 46 CQ52
Orange Pl. SE16 92 DW76
Lower Rd.
Orange St. WC2 9 N1
Orange St. WC2 77 DK73
Orange Tree Hill, Rom. (Havering-atte-Bower) 55 FD50
Orange Yd. W1 5 N9
Orangery, The, Rich. 101 CJ89
Orangery La. SE9 109 EM85

Oratory La. SW3 8 A10
Orb St. SE17 11 K9
Orb St. SE17 92 DR77
Orbain Rd. SW6 89 CY80
Orbel St. SW11 90 DE81
Orbital Cres., Wat. 29 BT35
Orchard, The N14 35 DH43
Orchard, The N21 36 DR44
Orchard, The NW11 62 DA57
Orchard, The SE3 93 ED82
Orchard, The W4 88 CR77
Orchard, The W5 73 CK71
Orchard, The, Bans. 146 DA115
Orchard, The, Epsom 131 CT108
Orchard, The, Houns. 86 CC82
Orchard, The, Kings L. 14 BN29
Orchard, The, Rick. 28 BM43
Green La.
Orchard, The, Sev. 154 FE121
Orchard, The, Swan. 125 FD96
Orchard, The, Wey. 127 BP105
Orchard Ave. N3 62 DA55
Orchard Ave. N14 35 DJ44
Orchard Ave. N20 48 DD47
Orchard Ave., Ashf. 99 BQ93
Orchard Ave., Belv. 96 EY79
Orchard Ave., Croy. 121 DY103
Orchard Ave., Dart. 111 FH87
Orchard Ave., Felt. 99 BR85
Orchard Ave., Houns. 86 BY80
Orchard Ave., Mitch. 118 DG102
Orchard Ave., N.Mal. 116 CS96
Orchard Ave., Sthl. 72 BY74
Orchard Ave., T.Ditt. 115 CG102
Orchard Ave., Wat. 15 BV31
Orchard Clo. E4 51 EA49
Chingford Mt. Rd.
Orchard Clo. E11 66 EH56
Orchard Clo. N1 78 DQ66
Morton Rd.
Orchard Clo. NW2 61 CU62
Orchard Clo. SE23 106 DW86
Brenchley Gdns.
Orchard Clo. SW20 117 CW98
Grand Dr.
Orchard Clo. W10 75 CY71
Orchard Clo., Ashf. 99 BQ93
Orchard Clo., Bans. 132 DB114
Orchard Clo., Bexh. 96 EY81
Orchard Clo., Borwd. 32 CM42
Orchard Clo., Edg. 46 CL51
Orchard Clo., Epsom 130 CP107
Orchard Clo., Lthd. 143 CF119
Orchard Clo. (Effingham), Lthd. 141 BT124
Orchard Clo. (Fetcham), Lthd. 143 CD122
Orchard Clo., Nthlt. 58 CC64
Orchard Clo. (Cuffley), Pot.B. 21 DL28
Orchard Clo., Rad. 31 CE37
Orchard Clo., Ruis. 57 BQ59
Orchard Clo., Surb. 115 CH101
Orchard Clo., Uxb. 70 BH65
Orchard Clo., Walt. 113 BV101
Garden Rd.
Orchard Clo., Wat. 29 BT40
Orchard Clo. (Bushey), Wat. 45 CD46
Orchard Clo., Wem. 74 CL67
Orchard Ct., Islw. 87 CD81
Orchard Ct., Twick. 101 CD89
Orchard Ct., Wor.Pk. 117 CU102
Orchard Cres., Edg. 46 CQ50
Orchard Cres., Enf. 36 DT39
Orchard Dr. SE3 94 EE82
Orchard Dr., Ash. 143 CK120
Orchard Dr., Edg. 46 CM50
Orchard Dr., Epp. 39 ES36
Orchard Dr., St.Alb. 16 CB27
Orchard Dr., Uxb. 70 BK70
Orchard Dr., Wat. 29 BT39
Orchard End, Cat. 148 DS122
Orchard End, Lthd. 142 CC124
Orchard End, Wey. 113 BS103
Orchard Gdns., Chess. 130 CL105
Orchard Gdns., Epsom 130 CQ114
Orchard Gdns., Sutt. 132 DA106
Orchard Gdns., Wal.Abb. 23 EC34
Orchard Gate NW9 60 CS56
Orchard Gate, Esher 115 CD102
Orchard Gate, Grnf. 59 CH64
Orchard Grn., Orp. 123 ES103
Orchard Gro. SE20 106 DU94
Orchard Gro., Croy. 121 DY101
Orchard Gro., Edg. 46 CN53
Orchard Gro., Har. 60 CM57
Orchard Gro., Orp. 123 ET103
Orchard Hill SE13 93 EB82
Coldbath St.
Orchard Hill, Cars. 132 DF106
Orchard Hill, Dart. 111 FE85
Orchard La. SW20 117 CV95
Durham Rd.
Orchard La., E.Mol. 115 CD100
Orchard La., Wdf.Grn. 52 EJ49
Orchard Ms. N1 78 DR66
Southgate Gro.
Orchard Pl. E14 80 EE73
Orchard Pl. N17 50 DT52
Orchard Pl., Sev. 152 EY124
Orchard Ri., Croy. 121 DY102
Orchard Ri., Kings.T. 116 CQ95
Orchard Ri., Pnr. 57 BT55
Orchard Ri., Rich. 88 CP84
Orchard Ri. E., Sid. 109 ES85
Orchard Ri. W., Sid. 109 ES85
Orchard Rd. N6 63 DH59
Orchard Rd. SE3 94 EE82
Eliot Pl.
Orchard Rd. SE18 95 ER77
Orchard Rd., Barn. 33 CY42
Orchard Rd., Belv. 96 FA77
Orchard Rd., Brent. 87 CJ79
Orchard Rd., Brom. 122 EJ95
Orchard Rd., Chess. 130 CL105
Orchard Rd., Dag. 82 FA67
Orchard Rd., Enf. 36 DW43
Orchard Rd., Hmptn. 100 BZ94
Orchard Rd., Hayes 71 BT73
Orchard Rd., Houns. 100 BZ85
Orchard Rd., Kings.T. 116 CL96
Orchard Rd., Mitch. 118 DG102
Orchard Rd. (Farnborough), Orp. 137 EP106
Orchard Rd. (Pratt's Bottom), Orp. 138 EW110
Orchard Rd., Rich. 88 CN83
Orchard Rd., Rom. 55 FB54
Orchard Rd. (Otford), Sev. 153 FF116
Orchard Rd. (Riverhead), Sev. 154 FE122
Orchard Rd., Sid. 109 ES91
Orchard Rd., S.Croy. 134 DV114
Orchard Rd., Sun. 99 BV94
Hanworth Rd.
Orchard Rd., Sutt. 132 DA105
Orchard Rd., Twick. 101 CG85
Orchard Rd., Well. 96 EV83
Orchard Sq. W14 89 CZ78
Sun Rd.
Orchard St. E17 65 DY56
Orchard St. W1 4 F9
Orchard St. W1 76 DG72
Orchard Ter., Enf. 36 DU44
Great Cambridge Rd.
Orchard Vw., Uxb. 70 BK70
Orchard Way, Add. 126 BH106
Orchard Way, Ashf. 98 BM89
Orchard Way, Beck. 121 DY99
Orchard Way, Chig. 54 EU48
Orchard Way, Croy. 121 DY102
Orchard Way, Enf. 36 DS41
Orchard Way, Esher 128 CC107
Orchard Way, Pot.B. 20 DB28
Orchard Way, Rick. 42 BG45
Orchard Way, Sutt. 132 DD105
Orchard Way (Cheshunt), Wal.Cr. 21 DP27
Orchard Waye, Uxb. 70 BK68
Orchardleigh, Lthd. 143 CH122
Orchardleigh Ave., Enf. 36 DW40
Orchardmede N21 36 DR44
Orchards, The, Epp. 26 EU32
Orchardson St. NW8 76 DD70
Orchid Clo. E6 80 EL71
Orchid Clo., Rom. 40 EV41
Orchid Clo., Sthl. 72 BY72
Orchid Rd. N14 49 DJ45
Orchid St. W12 75 CU73
Orde Hall St. WC1 6 B6
Orde Hall St. WC1 77 DM71
Ordell Rd. E3 79 DZ68
Ordnance Clo., Felt. 99 BU90
Ordnance Cres. SE10 94 EE75
Ordnance Hill NW8 76 DD67
Ordnance Ms. NW8 76 DD68
St. Ann's Ter.
Ordnance Rd. E16 80 EF71
Ordnance Rd. SE18 95 EN79
Ordnance Rd., Enf. 37 DX37
Oregano Dr. E14 79 ED72
Oregon Ave. E12 67 EM63
Oregon Clo., N.Mal. 116 CQ98
Georgia Rd.
Oregon Sq., Orp. 123 ER102
Orestes Ms. NW6 62 DA64
Aldred Rd.
Orford Ct. SE27 105 DP89
Orford Gdns., Twick. 101 CF89
Orford Rd. E17 65 EA57
Orford Rd. E18 66 EH55
Orford Rd. SE6 107 EB90
Organ Hall Rd., Borwd. 31 CK39
Organ La. E4 51 EC47
Oriel Clo., Mitch. 119 DK98
Oriel Ct. NW3 62 DC63
Heath St.
Oriel Dr. SW13 89 CV79
Trinity Ch. Rd.
Oriel Gdns., Ilf. 67 EM55
Oriel Pl. NW3 62 DC63
Heath St.
Oriel Rd. E9 79 DX65
Oriel Way, Nthlt. 72 CB66
Orient Ind. Pk. E10 65 EA61
Orient St. SE11 10 F8
Orient Way E5 65 DX62
Oriental Rd. E16 80 EK74
Oriental St. E14 79 EA73
Morant St.
Oriole Clo., Abb.L. 23 DX31
College Rd.
Oriole Way SE28 82 EV73
Orion Way, Nthwd. 43 BT49
Orissa Rd. SE18 95 ES78
Orkney St. SW11 90 DG82
Orlando Gdns., Epsom 130 CR110
Orlando Rd. SW4 91 DJ83
Orleans Clo., Esher 115 CD103
Orleans Rd. SE19 106 DR93
Orleans Rd., Twick. 101 CH87
Orleston Ms. N7 77 DN65
Orleston Rd. N7 77 DN65
Orlestone Gdns., Orp. 138 EY106
Orley Fm. Rd., Har. 59 CE62
Orlop St. SE10 94 EE78
Ormanton Rd. SE26 106 DU91
Orme Ct. W2 76 DB73
Orme Ct. Ms. W2 76 DB73
Orme La.
Orme La. W2 76 DB73
Orme Rd., Kings.T. 116 CP96
Orme Sq. W2 76 DB73
Bayswater Rd.
Ormeley Rd. SW12 105 DH87
Ormerod Gdns., Mitch. 118 DG96
Ormesby Clo. SE28 82 EX73
Wroxham Rd.
Ormesby Dr., Pot.B. 19 CX32
Ormesby Way, Har. 60 CM58
Ormiston Gro. W12 75 CV74
Ormiston Rd. SE10 94 EG78
Ormond Ave., Hmptn. 114 CB95
Ormond Ave., Rich. 101 CK85
Ormond Rd.
Ormond Clo. WC1 6 A6
Ormond Cres., Hmptn. 114 CB95
Ormond Dr., Hmptn. 100 CB94
Ormond Ms. WC1 6 A5
Ormond Rd. N19 63 DL60
Ormond Rd., Rich. 101 CK85
Ormond Yd. SW1 9 L2
Ormonde Ave., Epsom 130 CR109
Ormonde Ave., Orp. 123 EQ103
Ormonde Gate SW3 90 DF78
Ormonde Pl. SW1 8 F9
Ormonde Ri., Buck.H. 52 EJ46
Ormonde Rd. SW14 88 CQ83
Ormonde Rd., Nthwd. 43 BR49
Ormonde Ter. NW8 76 DF67
Ormsby Gdns., Grnf. 72 CC68
Ormsby Pl. N16 64 DT62
Victorian Gro.
Ormsby Pt. SE18 95 EP77
Troy Ct.
Ormsby St. E2 7 P1
Ormsby St. E2 78 DT68
Ormside St. SE15 92 DW79
Ormskirk Rd., Wat. 44 BX49
Ornan Rd. NW3 62 DE64
Oronsay Wk. N1 78 DQ65
Clephane Rd.
Orpen Wk. N16 64 DS62
Orphanage Rd., Wat. 30 BW40
Orpheus St. SE5 92 DR81
Orpington Bypass, Orp. 138 EX106
Orpington Bypass, Sev. 138 EZ109
Orpington Gdns. N18 50 DS48
Orpington Rd. N21 49 DN46
Orpington Rd., Chis. 123 ES97
Orpwood Clo., Hmptn. 100 BZ93
Orsett St. SE11 10 C10
Orsett St. SE11 91 DM78
Orsett Ter. W2 76 DB72
Orsett Ter., Wdf.Grn. 52 EJ52
Orsman Rd. N1 78 DS67
Orton St. E1 78 DU74
Hermitage Wall
Orville Rd. SW11 90 DD82
Orwell Clo., Rain. 83 FD71
Orwell Ct. N5 64 DQ63
Orwell Rd. E13 80 EJ67
Osbaldeston Rd. N16 64 DU61
Osbert St. SW1 9 M9
Osberton Rd. SE12 108 EG85
Osborn Clo. E8 78 DU67
Osborn Gdns. NW7 47 CX52
Osborn La. SE23 107 DY87
Osborn St. E1 78 DT71
Osborn Ter. SE3 94 EF84
Lee Rd.
Osborne Ave., Stai. 98 BL87
Osborne Clo., Barn. 34 DG41
Osborne Clo., Beck. 121 DY98
Osborne Clo., Felt. 100 BX92
Osborne Clo., Horn. 69 FH58
Osborne Ct., Pot.B. 20 DB30
Osborne Rd.
Osborne Gdns., Pot.B. 20 DB30
Osborne Gdns., Th.Hth. 120 DQ96
Osborne Gro. E17 65 DZ56
Osborne Gro. N4 63 DN60
Osborne Ms. E17 65 DZ56
Osborne Gro.
Osborne Pl., Sutt. 132 DD106
Osborne Rd. E7 66 EH64
Osborne Rd. E9 79 DZ65
Osborne Rd. E10 65 EB62
Osborne Rd. N4 63 DN60
Osborne Rd. N13 49 DN48
Osborne Rd. NW2 75 CV65
Osborne Rd. W3 88 CP75
Osborne Rd., Belv. 96 EZ78
Osborne Rd., Buck.H. 52 EH46
Osborne Rd., Dag. 68 EZ64
Osborne Rd., Enf. 37 DY40
Osborne Rd., Horn. 69 FH58
Osborne Rd., Houns. 86 BZ83
Osborne Rd., Kings.T. 102 CL94
Osborne Rd., Pot.B. 20 DB30
Osborne Rd., Sthl. 72 CC72
Osborne Rd., Th.Hth. 120 DQ96
Osborne Rd., Uxb. 70 BJ66
Oxford Rd.
Osborne Rd., Wal.Cr. 23 DY27
Osborne Rd., Walt. 113 BU102
Osborne Rd., Wat. 30 BW38
Osborne Sq., Dag. 68 EZ63
Osborne Ter. SW17 104 DG92
Church La.
Osbourne Ave., Kings L. 14 BM28
Oscar St. SE8 93 EA81
Oseney Cres. NW5 77 DJ65
Osgood Ave., Orp. 137 ET106
Osgood Gdns., Orp. 137 ET106
O'Shea Gro. E3 79 DZ67
Osidge La. N14 48 DG46
Osier Ms. W4 89 CT79
Osier St. E1 78 DW70
Osier Way E10 65 EB62
Osier Way, Bans. 131 CY114
Osier Way, Mitch. 118 DE99
Osiers Rd. SW18 90 DA84
Oslac Rd. SE6 107 EB92
Oslo Ct. NW8 4 B1
Oslo Sq. SE16 93 DY76
Norway Gate
Osman Clo. N15 64 DR58
Tewkesbury Rd.
Osman Rd. N9 50 DU48
Osman Rd. W6 89 CW76
Batoum Gdns.
Osmond Clo., Har. 58 CC61
Osmond Gdns., Wall. 133 DJ106
Osmund St. W12 75 CT72
Braybrook St.
Osnaburgh St. NW1 5 J4
Osnaburgh St. NW1 77 DH70
Osnaburgh Ter. NW1 5 J4
Osney Wk., Cars. 118 DD100
Osprey Clo. E6 80 EL71
Dove App.
Osprey Clo. E11 66 EG56
Osprey Clo. E17 51 DY52
Osprey Clo., Wat. 16 BY34
Osprey Clo., West Dr. 84 BK75
Osprey Ct., Wal.Abb. 24 EG34
Osprey Gdns., S.Croy. 135 DX110
Osprey Ms., Enf. 36 DV43
Osprey Rd., Wal.Abb. 24 EG34
Ospringe Clo. SE20 106 DW94
Ospringe Ct. SE9 109 ER86
Ospringe Rd. NW5 63 DJ63
Osram Rd., Wem. 59 CK62
Osric Path N1 7 M1
Ossian Ms. N4 63 DM59
Ossian Rd. N4 63 DM59
Ossington Bldgs. W1 4 F6
Ossington Clo. W2 76 DB73
Ossington St.
Ossington St. W2 76 DB73
Ossory Rd. SE1 92 DU79
Ossulston St. NW1 5 M1
Ossulston St. NW1 77 DK68
Ossulton Pl. N2 62 DC55
East End Rd.
Ossulton Way N2 62 DC56
Ostade Rd. SW2 105 DM87
Osten Ms. SW7 90 DB76
McLeod's Ms.
Oster Ter. E17 65 DX57
Southcote Rd.
Osterley Ave., Islw. 87 CD80
Osterley Clo., Orp. 124 EU95
Leith Hill
Osterley Ct., Islw. 87 CD81
Osterley Cres., Islw. 87 CE81
Osterley Gdns., Th.Hth. 120 DQ96
Osterley Ho. E14 79 EB72
Giraud St.
Osterley La., Islw. 86 CC78
Osterley La., Sthl. 86 CA78
Osterley Pk., Islw. 87 CD78
Osterley Pk. Rd., Sthl. 86 BZ76
Osterley Pk. Vw. Rd. W7 87 CE75
Osterley Rd. N16 64 DS63
Osterley Rd., Islw. 87 CE80
Osterley Views, Sthl. 72 CC74
West Pk. Rd.
Ostliffe Rd. N13 49 DP50
Oswald Clo., Lthd. 142 CC122
Oswald Rd., Lthd. 142 CC122
Oswald Rd., Sthl. 72 BY74
Oswald St. E5 65 DX62
Oswald Ter. NW2 61 CW62
Temple Rd.
Oswalds Mead E9 65 DY63
Lindisfarne Way
Osward, Croy. 135 DZ109
Osward Pl. N9 50 DV47
Osward Rd. SW17 104 DF89
Oswell Ho. E1 78 DV74
Penang St.
Oswin St. SE11 10 G8
Oswin St. SE11 91 DP77
Oswyth Rd. SE5 92 DS82
Otford Clo. SE20 120 DW95
Otford Clo., Bex. 111 FB86
Southwold Rd.
Otford Clo., Brom. 123 EN97
Otford Cres. SE4 107 DZ86
Otford La., Sev. 138 EZ112
Otford Rd., Sev. 153 FH118
Othello Clo. SE11 10 F10
Otis St. E3 79 EC69
Otley App., Ilf. 67 EP58
Otley Dr., Ilf. 67 EP58
Otley Rd. E16 80 EJ72
Otley Ter. E5 65 DX62
Otley Way, Wat. 44 BW48
Otlinge Clo., Orp. 124 EX98
Ottawa Gdns., Dag. 83 FD66
Ottaway St. E5 64 DU62
Stellman Clo.
Ottenden Clo., Orp. 137 ES105
Southfleet Rd.
Otter Meadow, Lthd. 143 CF119
Otter Rd., Grnf. 72 CC70
Otterbourne Rd. E4 51 ED48
Otterbourne Rd., Croy. 119 DP103
Otterburn Gdns., Islw. 87 CG80
Otterburn Ho. SE5 92 DQ80
Sultan St.
Otterburn St. SW17 104 DF93
Otterden St. SE6 107 EA91
Otterfield Rd., West Dr. 70 BL73
Otters Clo., Orp. 124 EX98
Otterspool La., Wat. 30 BY38
Otterspool Service Rd., Wat. 30 BZ38
Otterspool Way, Wat. 30 BZ38
Otto Clo. SE26 106 DV90
Otto St. SE17 91 DP79
Ottoman Ter., Wat. 30 BW41
Ebury Rd.
Ottways Ave., Ash. 143 CK119
Ottways La., Ash. 143 CK120
Otway Gdns., Wat. 45 CE45
Otways Clo., Pot.B. 20 DB32
Oulton Clo. E5 64 DW61
Mundford Rd.
Oulton Clo. SE28 82 EW72
Rollesby Way
Oulton Cres., Bark. 81 ET65
Oulton Cres., Pot.B. 19 CX32
Oulton Rd. N15 64 DR57
Oulton Way, Wat. 44 BY49
Oundle Ave. (Bushey), Wat. 30 CC44
Ousden Clo. (Cheshunt), Wal.Cr. 23 DY30
Ousden Dr. (Cheshunt), Wal.Cr. 23 DY30
Ouseley Rd. SW12 104 DF88
Outer Circle NW1 4 F5
Outer Circle NW1 76 DG70
Outgate Rd. NW10 75 CT66
Outram Pl. N1 77 DL67
Outram Pl., Wey. 127 BQ106
Outram Rd. E6 80 EL67
Outram Rd. N22 49 DK53
Outram Rd., Croy. 120 DT103
Outwich St. EC3 7 N8
Outwich St. EC3 78 DS72
Outwood La., Couls. 146 DE120
Outwood La., Tad. 146 DB122
Oval, The E2 78 DV68
Oval, The, Bans. 132 DA114
Oval, The, Brox. 23 DY25
Oval, The, Sid. 110 EU87
Oval Pl. SW8 91 DM80
Oval Rd. NW1 77 DH67
Oval Rd., Croy. 120 DR103
Oval Rd. N., Dag. 83 FB67
Oval Rd. S., Dag. 83 FB68
Oval Way SE11 91 DM78
Ovenden Rd., Sev. 152 EX120
Overbrae, Beck. 107 EA93
Overbrook Wk., Edg. 46 CN52
Overbury Ave., Beck. 121 EB97
Overbury Cres., Croy. 135 EC110
Overbury Rd. N15 64 DR58
Overbury St. E5 65 DX63
Overcliff Rd. SE13 93 EA83
Overcourt Clo., Sid. 110 EV86
Overdale, Ash. 144 CL116
Overdale Ave., N.Mal. 116 CQ96
Overdale Rd. W5 87 CJ76
Overdown Rd. SE6 107 EA91
Overhill, Warl. 148 DW119
Overhill Rd. SE22 106 DU87
Overhill Rd., Pur. 133 DN109
Overhill Way, Beck. 121 EC99
Overlea Rd. E5 64 DU59
Overmead, Sid. 109 ER87
Overmead, Swan. 125 FE99
Oversley Ho. W2 76 DA71
Overstand Clo., Beck. 121 EA99
Overstone Gdns., Croy. 121 DZ101
Overstone Rd. W6 89 CW76
Overstream, Rick. 28 BH42
Overton Clo. NW10 74 CQ65
Overton Clo., Islw. 87 CF81
Avenue Rd.
Overton Ct. E11 66 EG59
Overton Dr. E11 66 EG59
Overton Dr., Rom. 68 EW59
Overton Rd. E10 65 DY60
Overton Rd. N14 35 DL43
Overton Rd. SE2 96 EW76
Overton Rd. SW9 91 DN82
Overton Rd., Sutt. 132 DA107
Overton Rd. E. SE2 96 EX76
Overtons Yd., Croy. 120 DQ104
Ovesdon Ave., Har. 58 BZ60
Ovett Clo. SE19 106 DS93
Ovex Clo. E14 93 EC75
Ovington Gdns. SW3 8 C7
Ovington Gdns. SW3 90 DE76
Ovington Ms. SW3 8 C7
Ovington Ms. SW3 90 DE76
Ovington Sq. SW3 8 C7
Ovington Sq. SW3 90 DE76
Ovington St. SW3 8 C7
Ovington St. SW3 90 DE77
Owen Clo. SE28 82 EW74
Owen Clo., Hayes 71 BV69
Owen Gdns., Wdf.Grn. 52 EL51
Owen Pl., Lthd. 143 CH122
Church Rd.
Owen Rd. N13 50 DQ49

Owen Rd., Hayes 71 BV69
Owen St. EC1 6 E1
Owen Wk. SE20 106 DU94
Sycamore Gro.
Owen Waters Ho., Ilf. 53 EN53
Owen Way NW10 60 CQ64
Owenite St. SE2 96 EV77
Owen's Ct. EC1 6 F2
Owen's Row EC1 6 F2
Owens Way SE23 107 DY87
Owens Way, Rick. 28 BN43
Owgan Clo. SE5 92 DR80
Benhill Rd.
Owl Clo., S.Croy. 135 DX110
Ownstead Gdns., S.Croy. 134 DT111
Ownsted Hill, Croy. 135 EC110
Ox La., Epsom 131 CU109
Church St.
Oxberry Ave. SW6 89 CY82
Oxdowne Clo., Cob. 128 CB114
Oxenden Wd. Rd., Orp. 138 EW108
Oxendon St. SW1 9 M1
Oxendon St. SW1 77 DK73
Oxenford St. SE15 92 DT83
Oxenholme NW1 5 L1
Oxenholme NW1 77 DJ68
Oxenpark Ave., Wem. 60 CL60
Oxestalls Rd. SE8 93 DY78
Oxford Ave. SW20 117 CY96
Oxford Ave., Hayes 85 BT80
Oxford Ave., Houns. 86 CA78
Oxford Circ. Ave. W1 5 K9
Oxford Clo. N9 50 DV47
Oxford Clo., Ashf. 99 BQ94
Oxford Clo., Mitch. 119 DJ97
Oxford Clo., Nthwd. 43 BQ49
Oxford Clo. (Cheshunt), Wal.Cr. 22 DW29
Oxford Ct. EC4 7 K10
Oxford Ct. W3 74 CN72
Queens Dr.
Oxford Ct., Felt. 100 BX91
Oxford Way
Oxford Cres., N.Mal. 116 CR100
Oxford Dr., Ruis. 58 BW61
Oxford Gdns. N20 48 DD46
Oxford Gdns. N21 50 DQ45
Oxford Gdns. W4 88 CN78
Oxford Gdns. W10 75 CX72
Oxford Gdns., Uxb. 56 BG62
Oxford Rd.
Oxford Gate W6 89 CX77
Oxford Ms., Bex. 110 FA87
Bexley High St.
Oxford Pl. NW10 60 CR62
Neasden La. N.
Oxford Rd. E15 79 ED65
Oxford Rd. N4 63 DN60
Oxford Rd. N9 50 DV47
Oxford Rd. NW6 76 DA68
Oxford Rd. SE19 106 DR93
Oxford Rd. SW15 89 CY84
Oxford Rd. W5 73 CK73
Oxford Rd., Cars. 132 DE107
Oxford Rd., Enf. 36 DV43
Oxford Rd., Har. 58 CC58
Oxford Rd. (Wealdstone), Har. 59 CF55
Oxford Rd., Ilf. 67 EQ64
Oxford Rd., Sid. 110 EV92
Oxford Rd., Tedd. 101 CD92
Oxford Rd., Uxb. 70 BJ65
Oxford Rd., Wall. 133 DJ106
Oxford Rd., Wdf.Grn. 52 EK50
Oxford Rd. N. W4 88 CP78
Oxford Rd. S. W4 88 CN78
Oxford Sq. W2 4 C9
Oxford Sq. W2 76 DE72
Oxford St. W1 4 F9
Oxford St. W1 76 DG72
Oxford St., Wat. 29 BV43
Oxford Wk., Sthl. 72 BZ74
Oxford Way, Felt. 100 BX91
Oxgate Gdns. NW2 61 CV62
Oxgate La. NW2 61 CV61
Oxhawth Cres., Brom. 123 EN99
Oxhey Ave., Wat. 44 BX45
Oxhey Dr., Nthwd. 43 BV49
Oxhey Dr., Wat. 44 BW48
Oxhey Dr. S., Nthwd. 43 BV50
Oxhey La., Har. 44 CA50
Oxhey La., Pnr. 44 CA50
Oxhey La., Wat. 44 BY46
Oxhey Ridge Clo., Nthwd. 43 BU50
Oxhey Rd., Wat. 30 BW44
Oxleas E6 81 EP72
Oxleas Clo., Well. 95 ER82
Oxleay Ct., Har. 58 CA60
Oxleay Rd., Har. 58 CA60
Oxleigh Clo., N.Mal. 116 CS99
Oxley Clo. SE1 92 DT78
Oxleys Rd. NW2 61 CV62
Oxleys Rd., Wal.Abb. 24 EG33
Oxlip Clo., Croy. 121 DX102
Marigold Way
Oxlow La., Dag. 68 EZ63
Oxonian St. SE22 92 DT84
Oxshott Ri., Cob. 128 BX113
Oxshott Rd., Lthd. 143 CE116
Oxshott Way, Cob. 142 BY115
Oxted Clo., Mitch. 118 DD97
Oxtoby Way SW16 119 DK95
Oyster Catchers Clo. E16 80 EH72
Freemasons Rd.
Oyster La., W.Byf. 126 BK110
Oyster Row E1 78 DW72
Lukin St.
Ozolins Way E16 80 EG72

P

Pablo Neruda Clo. SE24 91 DP84
Shakespeare Rd.
Pace Pl. E1 78 DV72
Bigland St.
Paceheath Clo., Rom. 55 FD51
Pachesham Dr., Lthd. 143 CF116
Oxshott Rd.
Pachesham Pk., Lthd. 143 CF117
Pacific Clo., Felt. 99 BT88
Pacific Rd. E16 80 EG72
Packet Boat La., Uxb. 70 BH72
Packham Clo., Orp. 124 EW104
Berrylands
Packhorse La., Borwd. 32 CS37
Buckettsland La.
Packhorse La., Pot.B. 18 CR32
Packhorse Rd., Sev. 154 FC123
Packington Rd. W3 88 CQ76
Packington Sq. N1 78 DQ67
Packington St. N1 77 DP67
Packmores Rd. SE9 109 ER85
Padbury SE17 92 DS78
Bagshot St.
Padbury Clo., Felt. 99 BR88
Padbury Ct. E2 78 DT69
Padcroft Rd., West Dr. 70 BK74
Paddenswick Rd. W6 89 CU76
Paddington Clo., Hayes 72 BX70
Paddington Grn. W2 4 A6
Paddington Grn. W2 76 DD71
Paddington St. W1 4 F6
Paddington St. W1 76 DG71
Paddock, The, Uxb. 57 BP63
Paddock Clo. SE3 94 EG83
Paddock Clo. SE26 107 DX91
Paddock Clo., Nthlt. 72 CA68
Paddock Clo., Orp. 137 EP105
State Fm. Ave.
Paddock Clo., Wor.Pk. 116 CS102
Paddock Gdns. SE19 106 DS93
Westow St.
Paddock Rd. NW2 61 CU62
Paddock Rd., Bexh. 96 EY84
Paddock Rd., Ruis. 58 BX62
Paddock Wk., Warl. 148 DV119
Paddock Way, Chis. 109 ER94
Paddocks, The, Add. 126 BH110
Paddocks, The, Barn. 34 DF41
Paddocks, The, Rom. 41 FF44
Paddocks, The, Sev. 155 FK124
Paddocks, The, Wem. 60 CP61
Paddocks, The, Wey. 113 BS104
Paddocks Clo., Ash. 144 CL118
Paddocks Clo., Cob. 128 BW114
Paddocks Clo., Har. 58 CB63
Paddocks Clo., Orp. 124 EX103
Paddocks Way, Ash. 144 CL118
Paddocks Way, Cher. 112 BH102
Padfield Rd. SE5 92 DQ83
Padnall Rd., Rom. 68 EX55
Padstow Rd., Enf. 35 DP40
Padstow Wk., Felt. 99 BT88
Padua Rd. SE20 120 DW95
Pagden St. SW8 91 DH81
Page Clo., Dag. 68 EY64
Page Clo., Hmptn. 100 BY93
Page Clo., Har. 60 CM58
Page Cres., Croy. 133 DN106
Page Cres., Erith 97 FF80
Page Grn. Rd. N15 64 DU57
Page Grn. Ter. N15 64 DT57
Page Heath La., Brom. 122 EK97
Page Heath Vill., Brom. 122 EK97
Page Meadow NW7 47 CU52
Page Rd., Felt. 99 BR86
Page St. NW7 47 CU51
Page St. SW1 9 N8
Page St. SW1 91 DK77
Pageant Ave. NW9 46 CR53
Pageant Wk., Croy. 120 DS104
Pageantmaster Ct. EC4 6 F9
Pagehurst Rd., Croy. 120 DV101
Pages Hill N10 48 DG54
Pages La. N10 48 DG54
Pages La., Uxb. 70 BJ65
Pages Wk. SE1 11 M8
Pages Wk. SE1 92 DS77
Pages Yd. W4 88 CS79
Church St.
Paget Ave., Sutt. 118 DD104
Paget Clo., Hmptn. 101 CD91
Paget Gdns., Chis. 123 EP95
Paget La., Islw. 87 CD83
Paget Pl., Kings.T. 102 CQ93
Paget Pl., T.Ditt. 115 CG102
Brooklands Rd.
Paget Ri. SE18 95 EN79
Paget Rd. N16 64 DR60
Paget Rd., Ilf. 67 EP63
Paget Rd., Uxb. 71 BQ70
Paget St. EC1 6 F2
Paget Ter. SE18 95 EN79
Pagitts Gro., Barn. 34 DB39
Pagnell St. SE14 93 DZ80
Pagoda Ave., Rich. 88 CM83
Pagoda Gdns. SE3 93 ED82
Paignton Rd. N15 64 DS58
Paignton Rd., Ruis. 57 BU62
Paines Clo., Pnr. 44 BY54
Paines La., Pnr. 44 BY53
Pains Clo., Mitch. 119 DH96
Painsthorpe Rd. N16 64 DS62
Oldfield Rd.
Painters La., Enf. 37 DY35
Painters Rd., Ilf. 67 ET55
Paisley Rd. N22 49 DP53
Paisley Rd., Cars. 118 DD102
Pakeman St. N7 63 DM62
Pakenham Clo. SW12 104 DG88
Balham Pk. Rd.
Pakenham St. WC1 6 C3
Pakenham St. WC1 77 DM69
Pakes Way, Epp. 39 ES37
Palace Ave. W8 76 DB74
Palace Clo., Kings L. 14 BM30
Palace Ct. NW3 62 DB64
Palace Ct. W2 76 DB73
Palace Ct., Brom. 122 EH95
Palace Gro.
Palace Ct., Har. 60 CL58
Palace Ct. Gdns. N10 63 DJ55
Palace Dr., Wey. 113 BP104
Palace Gdns., Buck.H. 52 EK46
Palace Gdns., Enf. 36 DR42
Sydney Rd.
Palace Gdns. Ms. W8 76 DA74
Palace Gdns. Ter. W8 76 DA74
Palace Gate W8 90 DC75
Palace Gates Rd. N22 49 DK54
Palace Grn. W8 90 DB75
Palace Grn., Croy. 135 DZ108
Palace Gro. SE19 106 DT94
Palace Gro., Brom. 122 EH95
Palace Ms. E17 65 DZ56
Palace Ms. SW1 8 G9
Palace Ms. SW6 89 CZ80
Hartismere Rd.
Palace Pl. SW1 9 K6
Palace Rd. N8 63 DK57
Palace Rd. N11 49 DK52
Palace Rd. SE19 106 DT94
Palace Rd. SW2 105 DM88
Palace Rd., Brom. 122 EH95
Palace Rd., E.Mol. 115 CD97
Palace Rd., Kings.T. 115 CK98
Palace Rd., Ruis. 58 BY63
Palace Rd., West. 151 EN121
Chestnut Ave.
Palace Rd. Est. SW2 105 DM88
Palace Sq. SE19 106 DT94
Palace St. SW1 9 K6
Palace St. SW1 91 DJ76
Palace Vw. SE12 108 EG89
Palace Vw., Brom. 122 EH97
Palace Vw., Croy. 135 DZ105
Palace Vw. Rd. E4 51 EB50
Palace Way, Wey. 113 BP104
Palace Dr.
Palamos Rd. E10 65 EA60
Palatine Ave. N16 64 DT63
Stoke Newington Rd.
Palatine Rd. N16 64 DS63
Palermo Rd. NW10 75 CU68
Palestine Gro. SW19 118 DD95
Palewell Clo., Orp. 124 EV96
Palewell Common Dr. SW14 102 CR85
Palewell Pk. SW14 102 CR85
Paley Gdns., Loug. 39 EP41
Palfrey Pl. SW8 91 DM80
Palgrave Ave., Sthl. 72 CA73
Palgrave Rd. W12 89 CT76
Palissy St. E2 7 P3
Pall Mall SW1 9 L3
Pall Mall SW1 77 DJ74
Pall Mall E. SW1 9 N2
Pall Mall E. SW1 77 DK74
Pall Mall Pl. SW1 9 L3
Pallant Way, Orp. 123 EN104
Pallet Way SE18 94 EL81
Palliser Dr., Rain. 83 FG71
Palliser Rd. W14 89 CY78
Palm Ave., Sid. 110 EX93
Palm Clo. E10 65 EB62
Palm Gro. W5 88 CL76
Palm Rd., Rom. 69 FC57
Palmar Cres., Bexh. 96 FA83
Palmar Rd., Bexh. 96 FA82
Palmarsh Clo., Orp. 124 EX98
Wotton Grn.
Palmeira Rd., Bexh. 96 EX83
Palmer Ave., Sutt. 131 CW105
Palmer Ave. (Bushey), Wat. 30 CB43
Palmer Clo., Houns. 86 CA81
Palmer Clo., W.Wick. 121 ED104
Palmer Cres., Kings.T. 116 CL97
Palmer Gdns., Barn. 33 CX43
Palmer Pl. N7 63 DN64
Palmer Rd. E13 80 EH70
Palmer Rd., Dag. 68 EX60
Palmer St. SW1 9 M6
Palmer St. SW1 91 DK76
Palmers Gro., W.Mol. 114 CA98
Palmers Hill, Epp. 26 EU29
Palmers La., Enf. 36 DW39
Palmers Moor La., Iver 70 BG70
Palmers Orchard, Sev. 139 FF111
Palmers Pas. SW14 88 CQ83
Palmers Rd.
Palmers Rd. E2 79 DX68
Palmers Rd. N11 49 DJ50
Palmers Rd. SW14 88 CQ83
Palmers Rd. SW16 119 DM96
Palmers Rd., Borwd. 32 CP39
Palmers Way (Cheshunt), Wal.Cr. 23 DY29
Palmersfield Rd., Bans. 132 DA114
Palmerston Cres. N13 49 DM50
Palmerston Cres. SE18 95 EQ79
Palmerston Gro. SW19 104 DA94
Palmerston Rd. E7 66 EH64
Palmerston Rd. E17 65 DZ55
Palmerston Rd. N22 49 DM52
Palmerston Rd. NW6 75 CZ66
Palmerston Rd. SW14 88 CQ84
Palmerston Rd. SW19 104 DA94
Palmerston Rd. W3 88 CQ76
Palmerston Rd., Buck.H. 52 EH47
Palmerston Rd., Cars. 132 DF105
Palmerston Rd., Croy. 120 DR99
Palmerston Rd., Har. 59 CE55
Palmerston Rd., Orp. 137 EQ105
Palmerston Rd., Sutt. 132 DC105
Vernon Rd.
Palmerston Rd., Twick. 101 CE86
Palmerston Way SW8 91 DH80
Bradmead
Pamela Gdns., Pnr. 57 BV57
Pamela Wk. E8 78 DU67
Marlborough Ave.
Pampisford Rd., Pur. 133 DN111
Pampisford Rd., S.Croy. 134 DQ107
Pams Way, Epsom 130 CR106
Pancras La. EC4 7 J9
Pancras Rd. NW1 5 P1
Pancras Rd. NW1 77 DK68
Pancroft, Rom. 40 EV41
Pandora Rd. NW6 76 DA65
Panfield Ms., Ilf. 67 EN58
Cranbrook Rd.
Panfield Rd. SE2 96 EU76
Pangbourne Ave. W10 75 CW71
Pangbourne Dr., Stan. 45 CK50
Pankhurst Clo. SE14 93 DX80
Briant St.
Pankhurst Clo., Islw. 87 CF83
Pankhurst Rd., Walt. 114 BW101
Panmuir Rd. SW20 117 CV95
Panmure Clo. N5 63 DP63
Panmure Rd. SE26 106 DV90
Pannard Pl., Sthl. 72 CB73
Pansy Gdns. W12 75 CU73
Panters, Swan. 111 FF94
Pantile Rd., Wey. 127 BR105
Pantile Wk., Uxb. 70 BJ66
High St.
Pantiles, The NW11 61 CZ57
Willifield Way
Pantiles, The, Bexh. 96 EZ80
Pantiles, The, Brom. 122 EL97
Pantiles, The (Bushey), Wat. 45 CD45
Pantiles Clo. N13 49 DP50
Princes Ave.
Panton St. SW1 9 M1
Panyer All. EC4 7 H8
Papermill Clo., Cars. 132 DG105
Papillons Wk. SE3 94 EG83
Papworth Gdns. N7 63 DM64
Liverpool Rd.
Papworth Way SW2 105 DN87
Parade, The SW11 90 DF80
Parade, The, Dart. 111 FF85
Crayford Way
Parade, The, Epsom 130 CR113
Parade, The, Esher 129 CE107
Parade, The, Sun. 99 BT94
Parade, The, Wat. 29 BV41
Parade, The (Carpenders Pk.), Wat. 44 BY48
Parade Ms. SE27 105 DP89
Norwood Rd.
Paradise Clo. (Cheshunt), Wal.Cr. 22 DV28
Paradise Pas. N7 77 DN65
Sheringham Rd.
Paradise Pl. SE18 94 EL77
Woodhill
Paradise Rd. SW4 91 DL82
Paradise Rd., Rich. 102 CL85
Paradise Rd., Wal.Abb. 23 EC34
Paradise Row E2 78 DV69
Bethnal Grn. Rd.
Paradise St. SE16 92 DV75
Paradise Wk. SW3 90 DF79
Paragon, The SE3 94 EF82
Paragon Clo. E16 80 EG72
Paragon Gro., Surb. 116 CM100
Paragon Ms. SE1 11 L8
Paragon Pl. SE3 94 EF82
Paragon Pl., Surb. 116 CM100
Berrylands Rd.
Paragon Rd. E9 78 DW65
Parbury Ri., Chess. 130 CL107
Parbury Rd. SE23 107 DY86
Parchmore Rd., Th.Hth. 119 DP96
Parchmore Way, Th.Hth. 119 DP96
Pardon St. EC1 6 G4
Pardoner St. SE1 11 L6
Pardoner St. SE1 92 DR76
Parfett St. E1 78 DU71
Parfitt Clo. NW3 62 DC61
North End
Parfour Dr., Ken. 148 DQ116
Parfrey St. W6 89 CW79
Parham Dr., Ilf. 67 EP58
Parham Way N10 49 DJ54
Paris Gdns. SE1 10 F2
Paris Gdns. SE1 77 DP74
Parish Clo., Horn. 69 FH61
St. Leonards Way
Parish Gate Dr., Sid. 109 ES86
Parish La. SE20 107 DX93
Parish Ms. SE20 107 DX94
Parish Wf. Pl. SE18 94 EL77
Woodhill
Park, The N6 62 DG58
Park, The NW11 62 DB60
Park, The SE19 106 DS94
Park, The SE23 106 DV88
Park Hill
Park, The W5 73 CK74
Park, The, Cars. 132 DF106
Park, The, Lthd. 142 CA123
Park, The, Sid. 110 EU91
Park App., Well. 96 EV84
Park Ave. E6 81 EN67
Park Ave. E15 80 EE65
Park Ave. N3 48 DB53
Park Ave. N13 49 DN48
Park Ave. N18 50 DU49
Park Ave. N22 49 DL54
Park Ave. NW2 75 CV65
Park Ave. NW10 74 CM68
Park Ave. NW11 62 DB60
Park Ave. SW14 88 CR84
Park Ave., Bark. 81 EQ65
Park Ave., Barn. 34 DC43
Park Ave., Brom. 108 EF94
Park Ave., Cars. 132 DG107
Park Ave., Cat. 148 DS124
Park Ave., Chis. 123 ES97
Park Ave., Enf. 36 DR43
Park Ave., Houns. 100 CB86
Park Ave., Ilf. 67 EN60
Park Ave., Mitch. 105 DH94
Park Ave., Orp. 124 EU103
Park Ave. (Farnborough), Orp. 123 EM104
Park Ave., Pot.B. 20 DC34
Park Ave., Rad. 17 CH34
Park Ave., Rick. 28 BG43
Park Ave., Ruis. 57 BR58
Park Ave., Sthl. 86 BZ75
Park Ave., Wat. 29 BU41
Park Ave. (Bushey), Wat. 30 BX41
Park Ave., W.Wick. 121 EC103
Park Ave., Wdf.Grn. 52 EH50
Park Ave. E., Epsom 131 CU107
Park Ave. Ms., Mitch. 105 DH94
Park Ave.
Park Ave. N. N8 63 DK55
Park Ave. N. NW10 61 CV64
Park Ave. Rd. N17 50 DV52
Park Ave. S. N8 63 DK56
Park Ave. W., Epsom 131 CU107
Park Boul., Rom. 55 FF53
Park Chase, Wem. 60 CM63
Park Clo. E9 78 DW67
Skipworth Rd.
Park Clo. NW2 61 CV62
Park Clo. NW10 74 CM69
Park Clo. SW1 8 D5
Park Clo. W4 88 CR78
Park Clo. W14 89 CZ76
Park Clo., Add. 126 BH110
Park Clo., Cars. 132 DF107
Park Clo., Epp. 26 FA27
Park Clo., Esher 128 BZ107
Park Clo., Hmptn. 114 CC95
Park Clo., Har. 45 CE53
Park Clo., Hat. 19 CZ26
Park Clo., Houns. 100 CC85
Park Clo., Kings.T. 116 CN95
Park Clo., Lthd. 143 CD124
Park Clo., Rick. 43 BP49
Park Clo., Walt. 113 BT103
Park Clo. (Bushey), Wat. 30 BX41
Park Ct. SE26 106 DV93
Park Ct., Kings.T. 115 CJ95
Park Ct., N.Mal. 116 CR98
Park Ct., Wem. 60 CL64
Park Ct., W.Byf. 126 BG113
Park Cres. N3 48 DB52
Park Cres. W1 5 H5
Park Cres. W1 77 DH70
Park Cres., Borwd. 32 CM41
Park Cres., Enf. 36 DR42
Park Cres., Erith 97 FC79
Park Cres., Har. 45 CE53
Park Cres., Horn. 69 FG59
Park Cres., Twick. 101 CD88
Park Cres. Ms. E. W1 5 J5
Park Cres. Ms. W. W1 5 H5
Park Cres. Rd., Erith 97 FD79
Park Cft., Edg. 46 CQ53
Park Dale N11 49 DK51
Bounds Grn. Rd.
Park Dr. N21 36 DQ44
Park Dr. NW11 62 DB60
Park Dr. SE7 94 EL79
Park Dr. SW14 88 CR84
Park Dr. W3 88 CN76
Park Dr., Dag. 69 FC62
Park Dr., Har. 58 CA59
Park Dr. (Harrow Weald), Har. 45 CE51
Park Dr., Pot.B. 20 DA31
Park Dr., Rom. 69 FD56
Park Dr., Wey. 127 BP106
Park Dr. Clo. SE7 94 EL78
Park End NW3 62 DE63
South Hill Pk.
Park End, Brom. 122 EF95
Park End Rd., Rom. 69 FE56
Park Fm. Clo. N2 62 DC55
Park Fm. Clo., Pnr. 57 BV57
Field End Rd.

Park Fm. Rd., Brom. 122 EK95
Park Fm. Rd., Kings.T. 102 CL94
Park Gdn. Pl. W2 4 A9
Park Gdns. NW9 60 CP55
Park Gdns., Erith 97 FD77
Valley Rd.
Park Gdns., Kings.T. 102 CM92
Park Gate N2 62 DD55
Park Gate N21 49 DM45
Park Gate W5 73 CK71
Mount Ave.
Park Gra. Gdns., Sev. 155 FJ127
Solefields Rd.
Park Grn., Lthd. 142 CA124
Park Gro. E15 80 EG67
Park Gro. N11 49 DK52
Park Gro., Bexh. 97 FC84
Park Gro., Brom. 122 EH95
Park Gro., Edg. 46 CM50
Park Gro. Rd. E11 66 EE61
Park Hall Rd. N2 62 DE56
Park Hall Rd. SE21 106 DR90
Park Hill SE23 106 DV89
Park Hill SW4 105 DK85
Park Hill W5 73 CK71
Park Hill, Brom. 122 EL98
Park Hill, Cars. 132 DE107
Park Hill, Loug. 38 EK43
Park Hill, Rich. 102 CM86
Park Hill Clo., Cars. 132 DE106
Park Hill Ct. SW17 104 DF90
Beeches Rd.
Park Hill Ri., Croy. 120 DS103
Park Hill Rd., Brom. 122 EE96
Park Hill Rd., Croy. 120 DS103
Park Hill Rd., Sid. 109 ES90
Park Hill Rd., Wall. 133 DH107
Park Ho. N21 49 DM45
Park Ho. Gdns., Twick. 101 CJ86
Park Ind. Est., St.Alb. 17 CE27
Park La. E15 79 ED67
High St.
Park La. N9 50 DS48
Park La. N17 50 DT52
Park La. N18 50 DS49
Sheldon Rd.
Park La. W1 4 E10
Park La. W1 76 DF73
Park La., Ash. 144 CM118
Park La., Bans. 146 DD118
Park La., Cars. 132 DG105
Park La., Couls. 147 DK121
Park La., Croy. 120 DR104
Park La., Har. 58 CB62
Park La., Hayes 71 BS71
Park La., Horn. 69 FF58
Park La. (Elm Pk.), Horn. 83 FH65
Park La., Houns. 85 BU80
Park La., Rich. 87 CK84
Park La. 68 EX58
(Chadwell Heath), Rom.
Park La., Sev. 155 FJ124
Park La. (Seal), Sev. 155 FN121
Park La., Stan. 45 CG48
Park La., Sutt. 131 CY107
Park La., Tedd. 101 CF93
Park La., Uxb. 42 BG53
Park La., Wall. 132 DG105
Park La., Wal.Cr. 22 DW33
Park La. (Cheshunt), 22 DU26
Wal.Cr.
Park La., Wem. 60 CL64
Park La. Clo. N17 50 DU52
Park La. Paradise 22 DU25
(Cheshunt), Wal.Cr.
Park Lawn Rd., Wey. 127 BQ105
Park Lawns, Wem. 60 CM63
Park Ley Rd., Cat. 149 DX120
Park Mead, Har. 58 CB62
Park Mead, Sid. 110 EV85
Park Ms. SE24 106 DQ86
Croxted Rd.
Park Ms., Chis. 109 EP93
Park Ms., E.Mol. 114 CC98
Park Ms., Hmptn. 100 CC92
Park Rd.
Park Nook Gdns., Enf. 36 DR37
Park Par. NW10 75 CT68
Park Pl. E14 79 EA74
Park Pl. SW1 9 K3
Park Pl. SW1 77 DJ74
Park Pl. W3 88 CN77
Park Pl. W5 73 CK74
Park Pl., Hmptn. 100 CC93
Park Pl., St.Alb. 17 CD27
Park Pl., Sev. 154 FD123
Park Pl., Wem. 60 CM63
Park Pl. Vill. W2 76 DC71
Park Ridings N8 63 DN55
Park Ri. SE23 107 DY88
Park Ri., Har. 45 CE53
Park Ri., Lthd. 143 CH121
Park Ri. Clo., Lthd. 143 CH121
Park Ri. Rd. SE23 107 DY88
Park Rd. E6 80 EJ67
Park Rd. E10 65 EA60
Park Rd. E12 66 EH60
Park Rd. E15 80 EG67
Park Rd. E17 65 DZ57
Park Rd. N2 62 DD55
Park Rd. N8 63 DJ56
Park Rd. N11 49 DK52
Park Rd. N14 49 DK45
Park Rd. N15 63 DP56
Park Rd. N18 50 DT49
Park Rd. NW1 4 D4
Park Rd. NW1 76 DF70
Park Rd. NW4 61 CU59
Park Rd. NW8 4 B2
Park Rd. NW8 76 DE69
Park Rd. NW9 60 CR59
Park Rd. NW10 74 CS67
Park Rd. SE25 120 DS98
Park Rd. SW19 104 DD94
Park Rd. W4 88 CQ80
Park Rd. W7 73 CF73
Park Rd., Ashf. 99 BP92
Park Rd., Ash. 144 CL118
Park Rd., Bans. 146 DB115
Park Rd., Barn. 33 CZ42
Park Rd. (New Barnet), 34 DD42
Barn.
Park Rd., Beck. 107 DZ94
Park Rd., Brom. 122 EH95
Park Rd., Cat. 148 DS123
Park Rd., Chis. 109 EP93
Park Rd., E.Mol. 114 CC98
Park Rd., Enf. 37 DY36
Park Rd., Esher 128 CB105
Park Rd., Felt. 100 BX91
Park Rd., Hmptn. 100 CB91
Park Rd., Hayes 71 BS71
Park Rd., Houns. 100 CB85
Park Rd., Ilf. 67 ER62
Park Rd., Islw. 87 CH81
Park Rd., Ken. 147 DP115
Park Rd., Kings.T. 102 CM92
Park Rd. (Hampton 115 CJ95
Wick), Kings.T.
Park Rd., N.Mal. 116 CR98
Park Rd., Orp. 124 EW99
Park Rd., Pot.B. 20 DG30
Park Rd., Rad. 31 CG35
Park Rd., Rich. 102 CM86
Park Rd., Rick. 42 BK45
Park Rd., Shep. 112 BN102
Park Rd., Stai. 98 BH86
Park Rd., Sun. 99 BV94
Park Rd., Surb. 116 CM100
Park Rd., Sutt. 131 CY107
Park Rd., Swan. 125 FF98
Park Rd., Tedd. 101 CF94
Park Rd., Twick. 101 CJ86
Park Rd., Uxb. 70 BL66
Park Rd., Wall. 133 DH106
Park Rd. (Hackbridge), 119 DH103
Wall.
Park Rd., Wal.Cr. 23 DX33
Park Rd., Warl. 136 EE114
Park Rd., Wat. 29 BV39
Park Rd. (Bushey), Wat. 30 CA44
Park Rd., Wem. 74 CL65
Park Rd. E. W3 88 CP75
Park Rd. E., Uxb. 70 BK68
Hillingdon Rd.
Park Rd. N. W3 88 CP75
Park Rd. N. W4 88 CR78
Park Rd. W., Kings.T. 115 CJ95
Park Row SE10 93 ED79
Park Royal Rd. NW10 74 CQ70
Park Royal Rd. W3 74 CQ70
Park Side, Add. 126 BH111
Park Side, Sutt. 131 CY107
Park Sq., Esher 128 CB105
Park Rd.
Park Sq. E. NW1 5 H4
Park Sq. E. NW1 77 DH70
Park Sq. Ms. NW1 5 H5
Park Sq. Ms. NW1 77 DH70
Park Sq. W. NW1 5 H4
Park Sq. W. NW1 77 DH70
Park St. SE1 11 H2
Park St. SE1 78 DQ74
Park St. W1 4 F10
Park St. W1 76 DG73
Park St., Croy. 120 DQ103
Park St., St.Alb. 17 CD26
Park St., Tedd. 101 CE93
Park St. La., St.Alb. 16 CB30
Park Ter. (Sundridge), 152 EX124
Sev.
Main Rd.
Park Ter., Wor.Pk. 117 CU102
Park Vw. N21 49 DM45
Park Vw. W3 74 CQ71
Park Vw., N.Mal. 117 CT97
Park Vw., Pnr. 44 BZ53
Park Vw., Pot.B. 20 DC33
Park Vw., Wem. 60 CP64
Park Vw. Ct., Ilf. 67 ES58
Brancaster Rd.
Park Vw. Cres. N11 49 DH49
Park Vw. Est. E2 79 DX68
Sewardstone Rd.
Park Vw. Gdns. NW4 61 CX58
Park Vw. Gdns., Bark. 81 ES68
River Rd.
Park Vw. Gdns., Ilf. 67 EM56
Woodford Ave.
Park Vw. Rd. N3 48 DB53
Park Vw. Rd. N17 64 DU55
Park Vw. Rd. NW10 61 CT63
Park Vw. Rd. W5 74 CL71
Park Vw. Rd., Cat. 149 DY122
Park Vw. Rd., Pnr. 43 BV52
Park Vw. Rd., Sthl. 72 CA74
Park Vw. Rd., Uxb. 70 BM72
Park Vw. Rd., Well. 96 EV83
Park Village E. NW1 77 DH68
Park Village W. NW1 77 DH68
Park Vill., Rom. 68 EX58
Park Vista SE10 93 ED79
Park Wk. N6 62 DG59
North Rd.
Park Wk. SW10 90 DC79
Park Wk., Ash. 144 CM119
Rectory La.
Park Way N20 48 DF49
Park Way NW11 61 CY57
Park Way, Bex. 111 FE90
Park Way, Edg. 46 CP53
Park Way, Enf. 35 DN40
Park Way, Felt. 99 BV87
Park Way, Ilf. 67 ET62
Park Way, Lthd. 142 CA123
Park Way, Rick. 42 BJ46
Park Way, Ruis. 57 BU60
Park Way, W.Mol. 114 CB97
Park W. W2 4 A9
Park W. Pl. W2 4 C8
Parkcroft Rd. SE12 108 EF87
Parkdale Cres., Wor.Pk. 116 CR104
Parkdale Rd. SE18 95 ES78
Parke Rd. SW13 89 CU81
Parke Rd., Sun. 113 BU98
Parker Clo. E16 80 EL74
Parker Ms. WC2 6 A8
Parker Rd., Croy. 134 DQ105
Parker St. E16 80 EL74
Parker St. WC2 6 A8
Parker St. WC2 77 DL72
Parker St., Wat. 29 BV39
Parkers Clo., Ash. 144 CL119
Parkers Hill, Ash. 144 CL119
Parkers La., Ash. 144 CL119
Parkers Row SE1 92 DT75
Jamaica Rd.
Parkes Rd., Chig. 53 ES50
Parkfield, Sev. 155 FM123
Parkfield Ave. SW14 88 CS84
Parkfield Ave., Felt. 99 BU90
Parkfield Ave., Har. 44 CC54
Parkfield Ave., Nthlt. 72 BX68
Parkfield Ave., Uxb. 71 BP69
Parkfield Clo., Edg. 46 CP51
Parkfield Clo., Nthlt. 72 BY68
Parkfield Cres., Felt. 99 BU90
Parkfield Cres., Har. 44 CC54
Parkfield Cres., Ruis. 58 BY62
Parkfield Dr., Nthlt. 72 BX68
Parkfield Gdns., Har. 58 CB55
Parkfield Rd. NW10 75 CU66
Parkfield Rd. SE14 93 DZ81
Parkfield Rd., Felt. 99 BU90
Parkfield Rd., Har. 58 CC62
Parkfield Rd., Nthlt. 72 BY68
Parkfield Rd., Uxb. 57 BP61
Parkfield St. N1 77 DN68
Parkfield Way, Brom. 123 EM100
Parkfields SW15 89 CW84
Parkfields, Croy. 121 DZ102
Parkfields, Lthd. 129 CD111
Parkfields Ave. NW9 60 CR60
Parkfields Ave. SW20 117 CV96
Parkfields Clo., Cars. 132 DG105
Devonshire Rd.
Parkfields Rd., Kings.T. 102 CM92
Parkgate SE3 94 EF83
Parkgate Ave., Barn. 34 DC39
Parkgate Clo., Kings.T. 102 CP93
Warboys App.
Parkgate Cres., Barn. 34 DC39
Parkgate Gdns. SW14 102 CR85
Parkgate Rd. SW11 90 DE80
Parkgate Rd., Orp. 139 FB105
Parkgate Rd., Wall. 132 DG106
Parkgate Rd., Wat. 30 BW37
Parkham Ct., Brom. 122 EE96
Parkham St. SW11 90 DD81
Parkhill Rd. E4 51 EC46
Parkhill Rd. NW3 62 DF64
Parkhill Rd., Bex. 110 EZ87
Parkhill Rd., Epsom 131 CT111
Parkhill Wk. NW3 62 DF64
Parkholme Rd. E8 78 DU65
Parkhouse St. SE5 92 DR80
Parkhurst, Epsom 130 CQ110
Parkhurst Gdns., Bex. 110 FA87
Parkhurst Rd. E12 67 EN63
Parkhurst Rd. E17 65 DY56
Parkhurst Rd. N7 63 DL63
Parkhurst Rd. N11 48 DG49
Parkhurst Rd. N17 50 DU54
Parkhurst Rd. N22 49 DM51
Parkhurst Rd., Bex. 110 FA87
Parkhurst Rd., Sutt. 132 DD105
Parkland Ave., Rom. 69 FE55
Parkland Clo., Chig. 53 EQ48
Parkland Clo., Sev. 155 FJ129
Parkland Gdns. SW19 103 CX88
Parkland Gro., Ashf. 98 BN91
Parkland Rd. N22 49 DM54
Parkland Rd., Ashf. 98 BN91
Parkland Rd., Wdf.Grn. 52 EG52
Parkland Wk. N4 63 DN59
Parkland Wk. N6 63 DJ59
Parkland Wk. N10 63 DH56
Parklands N6 63 DH59
Parklands, Add. 126 BJ106
Parklands, Chig. 53 EQ48
Parklands, Epp. 26 EX29
Parklands, Lthd. 142 CA123
Parklands, Surb. 116 CM99
Parklands, Wal.Abb. 23 EC33
Parklands Clo. SW14 102 CQ85
Parklands Clo., Barn. 34 DD38
Parklands Ct., Houns. 86 BX82
Parklands Dr. N3 61 CY55
Parklands Rd. SW16 105 DH92
Parklands Way, Wor.Pk. 116 CS103
Parklawn Ave., Epsom 130 CP113
Parklea Clo. NW9 46 CS53
Parkleigh Rd. SW19 118 DB96
Parkleys, Rich. 101 CK91
Parkmead SW15 103 CV86
Parkmead, Loug. 39 EN43
Parkmead Gdns. NW7 47 CT51
Parkmore Clo., Wdf.Grn. 52 EG49
Parkshot, Rich. 88 CL84
Parkside N3 48 DB53
Parkside NW2 61 CU62
Parkside NW7 47 CU51
Parkside SE3 94 EF80
Parkside SW19 103 CX91
Parkside, Buck.H. 52 EH47
Parkside, Hmptn. 101 CD92
Parkside, Pot.B. 20 DC32
High St.
Parkside, Sev. 138 EZ113
Parkside, Sid. 110 EV89
Parkside, Wal.Cr. 23 DY34
Parkside, Wat. 30 BW44
Parkside Ave. SW19 103 CX92
Parkside Ave., Bexh. 97 FD82
Parkside Ave., Brom. 122 EL98
Parkside Ave., Rom. 69 FD55
Parkside Clo. SE20 106 DW94
Parkside Ct., Wey. 126 BN105
Parkside Cres. N7 63 DN62
Parkside Cres., Surb. 116 CQ100
Parkside Cross, Bexh. 97 FE82
Parkside Dr., Edg. 46 CN48
Parkside Dr., Wat. 29 BS40
Parkside Est. E9 78 DW67
Rutland Rd.
Parkside Gdns. SW19 103 CX91
Parkside Gdns., Barn. 48 DF46
Parkside Gdns., Couls. 147 DH117
Parkside Ho., Dag. 69 FC62
Parkside Rd. SW11 90 DG81
Parkside Rd., Belv. 97 FB77
Parkside Rd., Houns. 100 CB85
Parkside Rd., Nthwd. 43 BT50
Parkside Ter. N18 50 DR49
Great Cambridge Rd.
Parkside Way, Har. 58 CB56
Parkstead Rd. SW15 103 CU85
Parkstone Ave. N18 50 DT50
Parkstone Rd. E17 65 EC55
Parkstone Rd. SE15 92 DU82
Rye La.
Parkthorne Clo., Har. 58 CB58
Parkthorne Dr., Har. 58 CA58
Parkthorne Rd. SW12 105 DK87
Parkview Ct. SW18 104 DA86
Broomhill Rd.
Parkview Dr., Mitch. 118 DD96
Parkview Rd. SE9 109 EP88
Parkview Rd., Croy. 120 DU102
Parkville Rd. SW6 89 CZ80
Parkway N14 49 DL47
Parkway NW1 77 DH67
Parkway SW20 117 CX98
Parkway, Croy. 135 EB109
Parkway, Erith 96 EY76
Parkway, Rain. 83 FG70
Upminster Rd. S.
Parkway, Rom. 55 FF54
Parkway, Uxb. 70 BN66
Parkway, Wey. 127 BR105
Parkway, Wdf.Grn. 52 EJ50
Parkway, The, Hayes 72 BW72
Parkway, The (Cranford), 85 BU79
Houns.
Parkway Ms., Mitch. 105 DH94
Park Ave.
Parkway Trd. Est., Houns. 86 BW79
Parkwood N20 48 DF48
Parkwood, Beck. 121 EA95
Parkwood Ave., Esher 114 CC102
Parkwood Clo., Bans. 145 CX115
Parkwood Gro., Sun. 113 BU97
Parkwood Ms. N6 63 DH58
Parkwood Rd. SW19 103 CZ92
Parkwood Rd., Bans. 145 CX115
Parkwood Rd., Bex. 110 EZ87
Parkwood Rd., Islw. 87 CF81
Parkwood Rd., West. 150 EL121
Parkwood Vw., Bans. 145 CW116
Parliament Ct. E1 78 DS71
Sandy's Row
Parliament Hill NW3 62 DE63
Parliament Ms. SW14 88 CQ82
Thames Bank
Parliament Sq. SW1 9 P5
Parliament Sq. SW1 91 DL75
Parliament St. SW1 9 P5
Parliament St. SW1 91 DL75
Parma Cres. SW11 90 DF84
Parmiter St. E2 78 DV68
Parnell Clo., Abb.L. 15 BT30
Parnell Clo., Edg. 46 CP49
Parnell Rd. E3 79 DZ67
Parnham St. E14 79 DY72
Blount St.
Parolles Rd. N19 63 DJ60
Paroma Rd., Belv. 96 FA76
Parr Ave., Epsom 131 CV109
Parr Clo. N9 50 DV49
Parr Clo. N18 50 DV49
Parr Clo., Lthd. 143 CF120
Parr Ct., Felt. 100 BW91
Parr Rd. E6 80 EK67
Parr Rd., Stan. 45 CK53
Parr St. N1 78 DR68
Parrotts Clo., Rick. 28 BN42
Parrs Clo., S.Croy. 134 DR109
Florence Rd.
Parrs Pl., Hmptn. 100 CA94
Parry Ave. E6 81 EM72
Parry Clo., Epsom 131 CU107
Parry Dr., Wey. 126 BN110
Parry Pl. SE18 95 EP77
Parry Rd. SE25 120 DS97
Parry Rd. W10 75 CY69
Parry St. SW8 91 DL79
Parsifal Rd. NW6 62 DA64
Parsley Gdns., Croy. 121 DX102
Primrose La.
Parsloes Ave., Dag. 68 EX63
Parson St. NW4 61 CW56
Parsonage Clo., Abb.L. 15 BS30
Parsonage Clo., Hayes 71 BT72
Parsonage Clo., Warl. 149 DY116
Parsonage Gdns., Enf. 36 DQ40
Parsonage La., Enf. 36 DR40
Parsonage La., Sid. 110 EZ91
Parsonage Manorway, 96 FA79
Belv.
Parsonage Rd., Rick. 42 BK45
Parsonage St. E14 93 EC77
Parsons Cres., Edg. 46 CN48
Parsons Grn. SW6 90 DA82
Parsons Grn. La. SW6 90 DA81
Parsons Gro., Edg. 46 CN48
Parsons Hill SE18 95 EN76
Powis St.
Parson's Ho. W2 76 DD70
Edgware Rd.
Parsons La., Dart. 111 FG90
Parson's Mead, Croy. 119 DP102
Parsons Mead, E.Mol. 114 CC97
Parsons Pightle, Couls. 147 DN120
Coulsdon Rd.
Parsons Rd. E13 80 EJ68
Old St.
Parsonsfield Clo., Bans. 145 CX115
Parsonsfield Rd., Bans. 145 CX115
Parthenia Rd. SW6 90 DA81
Parthia Clo., Tad. 145 CV119
Partingdale La. NW7 47 CX50
Partington Clo. N19 63 DK60
Partridge Clo. E16 80 EK71
Fulmer Rd.
Partridge Clo., Barn. 33 CW44
Partridge Clo. (Bushey), 44 CB46
Wat.
Partridge Ct. EC1 77 DP70
Percival St.
Partridge Dr., Orp. 123 EQ104
Partridge Grn. SE9 109 EN90
Partridge Knoll, Pur. 133 DP112
Partridge Mead, Bans. 145 CW116
Partridge Rd., Hmptn. 100 BZ93
Partridge Rd., Sid. 109 ES90
Partridge Sq. E6 80 EL71
Nightingale Way
Partridge Way N22 49 DL53
Parvills Rd., Wal.Abb. 23 ED32
Parvin St. SW8 91 DK81
Parvis Rd., W.Byf. 126 BG113
Pasadena Clo., Hayes 85 BU75
Pascal St. SW8 91 DK80
Pascoe Rd. SE13 107 ED85
Pasfield, Wal.Abb. 23 ED33
Pasley Clo. SE17 92 DQ78
Penrose St.
Pasquier Rd. E17 65 DY55
Passey Pl. SE9 109 EM86
Passfield Dr. E14 79 EB71
Uamvar St.
Passfield Path SE28 82 EV73
Booth Clo.
Passing All. EC1 6 F5
Passmore Gdns. N11 49 DK51
Passmore St. SW1 8 F9
Passmore St. SW1 90 DG78
Pasteur Clo. NW9 46 CS54
Pasteur Gdns. N18 49 DP50
Paston Clo. E5 65 DX62
Caldecott Way
Paston Cres. SE12 108 EH87
Pastor St. SE11 10 G8
Pastor St. SE11 91 DP77
Pasture Clo. (Bushey), 44 CC45
Wat.
Pasture Clo., Wem. 59 CH62
Pasture Rd. SE6 108 EE88
Pasture Rd., Dag. 68 EZ63
Pasture Rd., Wem. 59 CH61
Pastures, The N20 47 CZ46
Pastures, The, Wat. 44 BW45
Pastures Mead, Uxb. 70 BN65
Patch, The, Sev. 154 FE122
Patcham Ct., Sutt. 132 DC109
Patcham Ter. SW8 91 DH81
Pater St. W8 90 DA76
Paternoster Clo., 24 EF32
Wal.Abb.
Paternoster Hill, Wal.Abb. 24 EF32
Paternoster Row EC4 7 H9
Paternoster Sq. EC4 6 G8
Paterson Rd., Ashf. 98 BK92
Pates Manor Dr., Felt. 99 BR87
Path, The SW19 118 DB95
Pathfield Rd. SW16 105 DK93
Pathway, The, Rad. 31 CF36
Pathway, The, Wat. 44 BX46
Anthony Clo.
Patience Rd. SW11 90 DE82
Patio Clo. SW4 105 DK86
Patmore Est. SW8 91 DJ81
Patmore La., Walt. 127 BT107
Patmore Rd., Wal.Abb. 24 EE34
Patmore St. SW8 91 DJ81

Pentney Rd. SW19 117 CY95
Midmoor Rd.
Penton Dr. (Cheshunt), Wal.Cr. 23 DX29
Penton Gro. N1 6 D1
Penton Hall Dr., Stai. 112 BG95
Penton Hook Rd., Stai. 98 BG94
Penton Pk. Est., Cher. 112 BH97
Penton Pl. SE17 10 G10
Penton Pl. SE17 91 DP78
Penton Ri. WC1 6 C2
Penton Ri. WC1 77 DM69
Penton St. N1 6 D1
Penton St. N1 77 DN68
Pentonville Rd. N1 6 B1
Pentonville Rd. N1 77 DM68
Pentrich Ave., Enf. 36 DU38
Pentridge St. SE15 92 DT80
Pentyre Ave. N18 50 DR50
Penwerris Ave., Islw. 86 CC80
Penwith Rd. SW18 104 DA89
Penwortham Rd. SW16 105 DH93
Penwortham Rd., S.Croy. 134 DQ110
Penylan Pl., Edg. 46 CN52
Penywern Rd. SW5 90 DA78
Penzance Clo., Uxb. 42 BK53
Penzance Pl. W11 75 CY74
Penzance St. W11 75 CY74
Peony Ct., Wdf.Grn. 52 EE52
Bridle Path
Peony Gdns. W12 75 CU73
Peplins Clo., Hat. 19 CY26
Peplins Way, Hat. 19 CY25
Peploe Rd. NW6 75 CX68
Peplow Clo., West Dr. 70 BK74
Tavistock Rd.
Pepper All., Loug. 38 EF40
Pepper Clo. E6 81 EM71
Pepper St. E14 93 EB76
Pepper St. SE1 11 H4
Peppermead Sq. SE13 107 EA85
Peppermint Clo., Croy. 119 DL101
Peppermint Pl. E11 66 EE62
Birch Gro.
Peppie Clo. N16 64 DS61
Bouverie Rd.
Pepys Clo., Ash. 144 CN117
Pepys Clo., Uxb. 57 BP63
Pepys Cres. E16 80 EG74
Silvertown Way
Pepys Cres., Barn. 33 CW43
Pepys Ri., Orp. 123 ET102
Pepys Rd. SE14 93 DX81
Pepys Rd. SW20 117 CW96
Pepys St. EC3 7 N10
Pepys St. EC3 78 DS73
Perceval Ave. NW3 62 DE64
Perch St. E8 64 DT63
Percheron Clo., Islw. 87 CG83
Percheron Rd., Borwd. 32 CR44
Percival Ct. N17 50 DT52
High Rd.
Percival Ct., Nthlt. 58 CA64
Percival Gdns., Rom. 68 EW58
Percival Rd. SW14 88 CQ84
Percival Rd., Enf. 36 DT42
Percival Rd., Felt. 99 BT89
Percival Rd., Orp. 123 EP103
Percival St. EC1 6 F4
Percival St. EC1 77 DP70
Percival Way, Epsom 130 CQ105
Percy Ave., Ashf. 98 BN92
Percy Bryant Rd., Sun. 99 BS94
Percy Bush Rd., West Dr. 84 BM76
Percy Circ. WC1 6 C2
Percy Circ. WC1 77 DM69
Percy Gdns., Enf. 37 DX43
Percy Gdns., Hayes 71 BS69
Percy Gdns., Islw. 87 CG83
Percy Gdns., Wor.Pk. 116 CS102
Percy Ms. W1 5 M7
Percy Pas. W1 5 L7
Percy Rd. E11 66 EE59
Percy Rd. E16 80 EE71
Percy Rd. N12 48 DC50
Percy Rd. N21 50 DQ45
Percy Rd. NW6 76 DA69
Stafford Rd.
Percy Rd. SE20 121 DX95
Percy Rd. SE25 120 DU99
Percy Rd. W12 89 CU75
Percy Rd., Bexh. 96 EY82
Percy Rd., Hmptn. 100 CA94
Percy Rd., Ilf. 68 EU59
Percy Rd., Islw. 87 CG84
Percy Rd., Mitch. 118 DG101
Percy Rd., Rom. 69 FB55
Percy Rd., Twick. 100 CB88
Percy Rd., Wat. 29 BV42
Percy St. W1 5 M7
Percy St. W1 77 DK71
Percy Way, Twick. 100 CC88
Percy Yd. WC1 6 C2
Peregrin Rd., Wal.Abb. 24 EG34
Peregrine Clo. NW10 60 CR64
Peregrine Clo., Wat. 16 BY34
Peregrine Ct. SW16 105 DM91
Leithcote Gdns.
Peregrine Ct., Well. 95 ET81
Peregrine Gdns., Croy. 121 DY103
Peregrine Ho. EC1 6 G2
Peregrine Ho. EC1 77 DP69
Peregrine Rd., Ilf. 54 EV50
Peregrine Rd., Sun. 113 BT96
Peregrine Wk., Horn. 83 FH65
Heron Flight Ave.
Peregrine Way SW19 103 CW94
Perham Rd. W14 89 CY78
Perham Way, St.Alb. 17 CK26
Peridot St. E6 80 EL71
Perifield SE21 106 DQ88
Perimeade Rd., Grnf. 73 CJ68
Periton Rd. SE9 94 EK84
Perivale Gdns. W13 73 CH70
Bellevue Rd.
Perivale Gdns., Wat. 15 BV34
Perivale Gra., Grnf. 73 CG69
Perivale Ind. Pk., Grnf. 73 CG67
Perivale La., Grnf. 73 CG69
Perivale New Business Cen., Grnf. 73 CH68
Perkins Clo., Wem. 59 CH64
Perkins Ct., Ashf. 98 BM92
Perkin's Rents SW1 9 M6
Perkin's Rents SW1 91 DK76
Perkins Rd., Ilf. 67 ER57
Perkins Sq. SE1 11 J2
Perks Clo. SE3 94 EE83
Hurren Clo.
Perpins Rd. SE9 109 ER86
Perram Clo., Brox. 23 DY26
Perran Rd. SW2 105 DP89
Christchurch Rd.
Perran Wk., Brent. 88 CL78
Burford Rd.
Perren St. NW5 77 DH65
Ryland Rd.
Perrers Rd. W6 89 CV77
Perrin Clo., Ashf. 98 BM92
Fordbridge Rd.
Perrin Rd., Wem. 59 CG63
Perrins Ct. NW3 62 DC63
Hampstead High St.
Perrins La. NW3 62 DC63
Perrin's Wk. NW3 62 DC63
Perriors Clo. (Cheshunt), Wal.Cr. 22 DU27
Perrott St. SE18 95 EQ77
Perry Ave. W3 74 CR72
Perry Clo., Rain. 83 FD68
Lowen Rd.
Perry Clo., Uxb. 71 BQ72
Harlington Rd.
Perry Ct. N15 64 DS58
Albert Rd.
Perry Gdns. N9 50 DS48
Deansway
Perry Garth, Nthlt. 72 BW67
Perry Hall Clo., Orp. 124 EU101
Perry Hall Rd., Orp. 123 ET100
Perry Hill SE6 107 DZ90
Perry How, Wor.Pk. 117 CT102
Perry Mead, Enf. 35 DP40
Perry Mead (Bushey), Wat. 44 CB45
Perry Oaks Dr. (Heathrow Airport), Houns. 84 BH82
Perry Oaks Dr., West Dr. 84 BH82
Perry Ri. SE23 107 DY90
Perry Rd., Dag. 82 EZ70
Perry St., Chis. 109 ER93
Perry St., Dart. 97 FE84
Perry St. Gdns., Chis. 109 ES93
Old Perry St.
Perry Vale SE23 106 DW89
Perryfield Way NW9 61 CT58
Perryfield Way, Rich. 101 CH89
Perryman Ho., Bark. 81 EQ67
Perrymans Fm. Rd., Ilf. 67 ER58
Perrymead St. SW6 90 DA81
Perryn Rd. SE16 92 DV76
Drummond Rd.
Perryn Rd. W3 74 CR74
Perrys La., Sev. 138 EV113
Perrys Pl. W1 5 N8
Perrysfield Rd. (Cheshunt), Wal.Cr. 23 DY26
Persant Rd. SE6 108 EE90
Perseverance Pl. SW9 91 DN80
Perseverance Pl., Rich. 88 CL83
Shaftesbury Rd.
Persfield Clo., Epsom 131 CT110
Pershore Clo., Ilf. 67 EP57
Pershore Gro., Cars. 118 DD100
Pert Clo. N10 49 DH51
Perth Ave. NW9 60 CR59
Perth Ave., Hayes 72 BW70
Perth Clo. SW20 117 CU96
Perth Rd. E10 65 DY60
Perth Rd. E13 80 EH68
Perth Rd. N4 63 DN60
Perth Rd. N22 49 DP53
Perth Rd., Bark. 81 ER67
Perth Rd., Beck. 121 EC96
Perth Rd., Ilf. 67 EN59
Perth Ter., Ilf. 67 EQ59
Perwell Ave., Har. 58 BZ60
Perwell Ct., Har. 58 BZ60
Peter Ave. NW10 75 CV66
Peter St. W1 5 M10
Peter St. W1 77 DK73
Peterboat Clo. SE10 94 EE77
Tunnel Ave.
Peterborough Gdns., Ilf. 66 EL59
Peterborough Ms. SW6 90 DA82
Peterborough Rd. E10 65 EC57
Peterborough Rd. SW6 90 DA82
Peterborough Rd., Cars. 118 DE100
Peterborough Rd., Har. 59 CE60
Peterborough Vill. SW6 90 DB81
Peterchurch Ho. SE15 92 DV79
Commercial Way
Petergate SW11 90 DC84
Peters Ave., St.Alb. 17 CJ26
Peters Clo., Dag. 68 EX60
Peters Clo., Stan. 45 CK51
Peters Clo., Well. 95 ES82
Peters Hill EC4 7 H9
Peter's La. EC1 6 F6
Peters Path SE26 106 DV91
Petersfield Ave., Stai. 98 BJ92
Petersfield Clo. N18 50 DQ50
Petersfield Cres., Couls. 147 DL115
Petersfield Ri. SW15 103 CV88
Petersfield Rd. W3 88 CQ75
Petersfield Rd., Stai. 98 BJ92
Petersham Ave., W.Byf. 126 BL112
Petersham Clo., Rich. 101 CK89
Petersham Clo., Sutt. 131 CZ106
Petersham Clo., W.Byf. 126 BL112
Petersham Dr., Orp. 123 ET96
Petersham Gdns., Orp. 123 ET96
Petersham La. SW7 90 DC76
Petersham Ms. SW7 90 DC76
Petersham Pl. SW7 90 DC76
Petersham Rd., Rich. 101 CK86
Petersham Ter., Croy. 119 DL104
Richmond Grn.
Peterstone Rd. SE2 96 EV76
Peterstow Clo. SW19 103 CY89
Peterwood Way, Croy. 119 DM103
Petherton Rd. N5 64 DQ64
Petley Rd. W6 89 CW79
Peto Pl. NW1 5 J4
Peto Pl. NW1 77 DH70
Peto St. N. E16 80 EF73
Victoria Dock Rd.
Petrie Clo. NW2 75 CY65
Pett Clo., Horn. 69 FH61
St. Leonards Way
Pett St. SE18 94 EL77
Petten Clo., Orp. 124 EX102
Petten Gro., Orp. 124 EW102
Petters Rd., Ash. 144 CM116
Petticoat Sq. E1 7 P8
Pettits Boul., Rom. 55 FE53
Pettits Clo., Rom. 55 FE54
Pettits La., Rom. 55 FE54
Pettits La. N., Rom. 55 FD53
Pettits Pl., Dag. 68 FA64
Pettits Rd., Dag. 68 FA64
Pettiward Clo. SW15 89 CW84
Pettley Gdns., Rom. 69 FD57
Pettman Cres. SE28 95 ER76
Petts Hill, Nthlt. 58 CB64
Petts La., Shep. 112 BN98
Petts Wd. Rd., Orp. 123 EQ99
Pettsgrove Ave., Wem. 59 CJ64
Petty France SW1 9 L6
Petty France SW1 91 DJ76
Petworth Clo., Couls. 147 DJ119
Petworth Clo., Nthlt. 72 BZ66
Petworth Gdns. SW20 117 CV97
Hidcote Gdns.
Petworth Gdns., Uxb. 71 BQ67
Petworth Rd. N12 48 DE50
Petworth Rd., Bexh. 110 FA85
Petworth St. SW11 90 DE81
Petworth Way, Horn. 69 FF63
Petyt Pl. SW3 90 DE79
Old Ch. St.
Petyward SW3 8 C9
Petyward SW3 90 DE77
Pevel Ho., Dag. 68 FA61
Pevensey Ave. N11 49 DK50
Pevensey Ave., Enf. 36 DR40
Pevensey Clo., Islw. 86 CC80
Pevensey Rd. E7 66 EF63
Pevensey Rd. SW17 104 DD91
Pevensey Rd., Felt. 100 BY88
Peverel E6 81 EN72
Downings
Peveret Clo. N11 49 DH50
Woodland Rd.
Peveril Dr., Tedd. 101 CD92
Pewsey Clo. E4 51 EA50
Peyton Pl. SE10 93 EC80
Pharaoh Clo., Mitch. 118 DF101
Pharaoh's Island, Shep. 112 BM103
Pheasant Clo. E16 80 EG72
Maplin Rd.
Pheasant Clo., Pur. 133 DP113
Pheasants Way, Rick. 42 BH45
Phelp St. SE17 92 DR79
Phelps Way, Hayes 85 BT77
Phene St. SW3 90 DE79
Phil Brown Pl. SW8 91 DH82
Heath Rd.
Philan Way, Rom. 55 FD51
Philbeach Gdns. SW5 90 DA78
Philchurch Pl. E1 78 DU72
Ellen St.
Philip Ave., Rom. 69 FD60
Philip Ave., Swan. 125 FD98
Philip Clo., Rom. 69 FD60
Philip Ave.
Philip Gdns., Croy. 121 DZ103
Philip La. N15 64 DR56
Philip Rd. SE15 92 DU83
Peckham Rye
Philip Rd., Rain. 83 FE69
Philip Rd., Stai. 98 BK93
Philip St. E13 80 EG70
Philip Wk. SE15 92 DV83
Philipot Path SE9 109 EM86
Court Yd.
Philippa Gdns. SE9 108 EK85
Philips Clo., Cars. 118 DG102
Phillimore Gdns. NW10 75 CW67
Phillimore Gdns. W8 90 DA75
Phillimore Gdns. Clo. W8 90 DA76
Phillimore Gdns.
Phillimore Pl. W8 90 DA75
Phillimore Pl., Rad. 31 CE36
Phillimore Wk. W8 90 DA76
Phillipers, Wat. 30 BX36
Phillipp St. N1 78 DS67
Phillips Clo., Dart. 111 FH86
Philpot La. EC3 7 M10
Philpot Path, Ilf. 67 EQ62
Sunnyside Rd.
Philpot Sq. SW6 90 DB83
Peterborough Rd.
Philpot St. E1 78 DV72
Philpots Clo., West Dr. 70 BK73
Phineas Pett Rd. SE9 94 EL83
Phipp St. EC2 7 M4
Phipp St. EC2 78 DS70
Phipps Bri. Rd. SW19 118 DC96
Phipps Bri. Rd., Mitch. 118 DC96
Phipps Hatch La., Enf. 36 DQ38
Phipp's Ms. SW1 9 H7
Phoebeth Rd. SE4 107 EA85
Phoenix Clo. E8 78 DT67
Stean St.
Phoenix Clo., Nthwd. 43 BT49
Phoenix Clo., W.Wick. 121 ED103
Phoenix Dr., Kes. 122 EK104
Phoenix Pk., Brent. 87 CK78
Phoenix Pl. WC1 6 C4
Phoenix Pl. WC1 77 DM70
Phoenix Rd. NW1 77 DK69
Phoenix Rd. SE20 106 DW93
Phoenix St. WC2 5 N9
Phoenix Way, Houns. 86 BW79
Phoenix Wf. SE10 94 EF75
Phyllis Ave., N.Mal. 117 CV99
Physic Pl. SW3 90 DF79
Royal Hospital Rd.
Piazza, The WC2 77 DL73
Covent Gdn.
Picardy Manorway, Belv. 97 FB76
Picardy Rd., Belv. 96 FA78
Picardy St., Belv. 96 FA76
Piccadilly W1 9 J3
Piccadilly W1 77 DH74
Piccadilly Arc. SW1 9 K2
Piccadilly Circ. W1 9 M1
Piccadilly Circ. W1 77 DJ73
Piccadilly Pl. W1 9 L1
Pick Hill, Wal.Abb. 24 EF32
Pickard St. EC1 6 G2
Pickering Ave. E6 81 EN68
Pickering Gdns., Croy. 120 DT100
Pickering Ms. W2 76 DB72
Bishops Bri. Rd.
Pickering Pl. SW1 9 L3
Pickering St. N1 77 DP67
Essex Rd.
Pickets Clo. (Bushey), Wat. 45 CD46
Pickets St. SW12 105 DH87
Pickett Cft., Stan. 45 CK53
Picketts Lock La. N9 50 DW47
Pickford Clo., Bexh. 96 EY82
Pickford La., Bexh. 96 EY82
Pickford Rd., Bexh. 96 EY84
Pickford Wf. N1 7 H1
Pickford Wf. N1 78 DQ68
Pickhurst Grn., Brom. 122 EF101
Pickhurst La., Brom. 122 EF101
Pickhurst La., W.Wick. 122 EE99
Pickhurst Mead, Brom. 122 EF101
Pickhurst Pk., Brom. 122 EE99
Pickhurst Ri., W.Wick. 121 EC101
Pickle Herring St. SE1 78 DS74
Tooley St.
Pickmoss La., Sev. 153 FH116
Pickwick Clo., Houns. 100 BY85
Dorney Way
Pickwick Ct. SE9 108 EL88
West Pk.
Pickwick Ms. N18 50 DS50
Pickwick Pl., Har. 59 CE59
Pickwick Rd. SE21 106 DR87
Pickwick St. SE1 11 H5
Pickwick Way, Chis. 109 EQ93
Pickworth Clo. SW8 91 DL80
Kenchester Clo.
Picquets Way, Bans. 145 CZ117
Picton Pl. W1 4 G9
Picton St. SE5 92 DR80
Piedmont Rd. SE18 95 ER78
Pield Heath Ave., Uxb. 70 BN70
Pield Heath Rd., Uxb. 70 BL70
Pier Head E1 78 DV74
Wapping High St.
Pier Par. E16 95 EN75
Pier Rd.
Pier Rd. E16 95 EN75
Pier Rd., Erith 97 FE79
Pier Rd., Felt. 99 BV85
Pier St. E14 93 EC77
Pier Ter. SW18 90 DC84
Jew's Row
Pier Way SE28 95 ER76
Piercing Hill, Epp. 39 ER35
Piermont Grn. SE22 106 DV85
Piermont Pl., Brom. 122 EM96
Piermont Rd. SE22 106 DV85
Pierrepoint Arc. N1 77 DP68
Islington High St.
Pierrepoint Rd. W3 74 CP73
Pierrepoint Row N1 77 DP68
Islington High St.
Pigeon La., Hmptn. 100 CA91
Pigott St. E14 79 EA72
Pike Clo., Brom. 108 EH92
Pike Rd. NW7 46 CR49
Ellesmere Ave.
Pike Way, Epp. 26 FA27
Pikes End, Pnr. 57 BV56
Pikes Hill, Epsom 130 CS113
Pikestone Clo., Hayes 72 BY70
Berrydale Rd.
Pilgrim Clo., Mord. 118 DB101
Pilgrim Clo., St.Alb. 16 CC27
Pilgrim Hill SE27 106 DQ91
Pilgrim Hill, Orp. 124 EX96
Pilgrim St. EC4 6 F9
Pilgrim St. EC4 77 DP72
Pilgrimage St. SE1 11 K5
Pilgrimage St. SE1 92 DR75
Pilgrims Clo. N13 49 DM49
Pilgrims Clo., Nthlt. 58 CC64
Pilgrims Clo., Wat. 16 BX33
Kytes Dr.
Pilgrims Ct. SE3 94 EG81
Pilgrim's La. NW3 62 DD63
Pilgrims La., West. 150 EL123
Pilgrims Pl. NW3 62 DD63
Hampstead High St.
Pilgrims Ri., Barn. 34 DE43
Pilgrims Way E6 80 EL67
High St. N.
Pilgrims Way N19 63 DK60
Pilgrims Way (Sundridge), Sev. 152 EV121
Pilgrims Way, S.Croy. 134 DT107
Bench Fld.
Pilgrim's Way, Wem. 60 CP60
Pilgrims Way, West. 151 EM123
Pilgrims Way W., Sev. 153 FD116
Pilkington Rd. SE15 92 DV82
Pilkington Rd., Orp. 123 EQ103
Pilot Ind. Est. NW10 74 CR70
Pilsdon Clo. SW19 103 CX88
Inner Pk. Rd.
Piltdown Rd., Wat. 44 BX49
Pimento Ct. W5 87 CK76
Olive Rd.
Pimlico Rd. SW1 8 F10
Pimlico Rd. SW1 90 DG78
Pimlico Wk. N1 7 M2
Pinchbeck Rd., Orp. 137 ET107
Pinchin St. E1 78 DU73
Pincott Pl. SE4 93 DX83
Billingford Clo.
Pincott Rd. SW19 104 DC94
Pincott Rd., Bexh. 110 FA85
Pindar St. EC2 7 M6
Pindar St. EC2 78 DS71
Pindock Ms. W9 76 DB70
Warwick Ave.
Pine Ave. E15 65 ED64
Pine Ave., W.Wick. 121 EB102
Pine Clo. E10 65 EB61
Walnut Rd.
Pine Clo. N14 49 DJ45
Pine Clo. N19 63 DJ61
Hargrave Pk.
Pine Clo. SE20 106 DW94
Graveney Gro.
Pine Clo., Add. 126 BH111
Pine Clo., Ken. 148 DR117
Pine Clo., Stan. 45 CH49
Pine Clo., Swan. 125 FF98
Pine Clo. (Cheshunt), Wal.Cr. 23 DX28
Pine Coombe, Croy. 135 DX105
Pine Cres., Cars. 132 DD111
Pine Gdns., Ruis. 57 BV60
Pine Gdns., Surb. 116 CN100
Pine Glade, Orp. 137 EM105
Pine Gro. N4 63 DL61
Pine Gro. N20 47 CZ46
Pine Gro. SW19 103 CZ92
Pine Gro., Hat. 20 DB25
Pine Gro., St.Alb. 16 BZ30
Pine Gro. (Bushey), Wat. 30 BZ40
Pine Gro., Wey. 127 BP106
Pine Gro. Ms., Wey. 127 BQ106
Pine Hill, Epsom 144 CR115
Pine Pl., Bans. 131 CX114
Pine Pl., Hayes 71 BT70
Pine Ridge, Cars. 132 DG109
Pine Rd. N11 48 DG47
Pine Rd. NW2 61 CW63
Pine St. EC1 6 D4
Pine St. EC1 77 DN70
Pine Tree Clo., Houns. 85 BV81
Pine Trees Dr., Uxb. 56 BL63
Pine Vw. Manor, Epp. 26 EU30
Pine Wk., Bans. 146 DF117
Pine Wk., Cars. 132 DD110
Pine Wk., Cat. 148 DS122
Pine Wk., Cob. 128 BX114
Pine Wk., Surb. 116 CN100
Pine Wk. E., Cars. 132 DD111
Pine Wk. W., Cars. 132 DD111
Pine Wd., Sun. 113 BU95
Pineapple Ct. SW1 9 K6
Pinecrest Gdns., Orp. 137 EP105
Pinecroft Cres., Barn. 33 CY42
Hillside Gdns.
Pinedene SE15 92 DV81
Meeting Ho. La.
Pinefield Clo. E14 79 EA73
Pinehurst, Sev. 155 FL121
Pinehurst Clo., Abb.L. 15 BS32
Pinehurst Clo., Tad. 146 DA122
Pinehurst Wk., Orp. 123 ES102
Andover Rd.

Ridings, The, Chig. 54 EV49
Manford Way
Ridings, The, Cob. 128 CA112
Ridings, The, Epsom 144 CS115
Ridings, The (Ewell), Epsom 131 CT109
Ridings, The, Sun. 113 BU95
Ridings, The, Surb. 116 CN99
Ridings, The, Tad. 145 CZ120
Ridings, The, West. 150 EL117
Ridings, The, Wok. 140 BG123
Ridings Ave. N21 35 DP42
Ridings Clo. N6 63 DJ59
Hornsey La. Gdns.
Ridings La., Wok. 141 BP123
Ridler Rd., Enf. 36 DS38
Ridley Ave. W13 87 CH76
Ridley Clo., Rom. 55 FH53
Ridley Rd. E7 66 EJ63
Ridley Rd. E8 64 DT64
Ridley Rd. NW10 75 CU68
Ridley Rd. SW19 104 DB94
Ridley Rd., Brom. 122 EF97
Ridley Rd., Warl. 148 DW118
Ridley Rd., Well. 96 EV81
Ridley Several SE3 94 EH82
Blackheath Pk.
Ridsdale Rd. SE20 120 DV95
Riefield Rd. SE9 95 EQ84
Riesco Dr., Croy. 134 DW107
Riffel Rd. NW2 61 CW64
Rifle Butts All., Epsom 131 CT114
Rifle Pl. SE11 91 DN79
Stannary St.
Rifle Pl. W11 75 CX74
Rifle St. E14 79 EB71
Rigault Rd. SW6 89 CY82
Rigby Clo., Croy. 119 DN104
Rigby La., Hayes 85 BQ75
Rigby Ms., Ilf. 67 EP61
Cranbrook Rd.
Rigden St. E14 79 EB72
Rigeley Rd. NW10 75 CU69
Rigg App. E10 65 DX60
Rigge Pl. SW4 91 DK84
Rigger Row SW11 90 DC83
Cinnamon Row
Riggindale Rd. SW16 105 DK91
Riley Rd. SE1 11 P6
Riley Rd. SE1 92 DT76
Riley Rd., Enf. 36 DW38
Riley St. SW10 90 DD80
Rinaldo Rd. SW12 105 DH87
Ring, The W2 4 B10
Ring, The W2 76 DD73
Ring Clo., Brom. 108 EH94
Garden Rd.
Ring Rd. W12 75 CW73
Ringcroft St. N7 63 DN64
Ringers Rd., Brom. 122 EG97
Ringford Rd. SW18 103 CZ85
Ringlewell Clo., Enf. 36 DV40
Central Ave.
Ringmer Ave. SW6 89 CY81
Ringmer Gdns. N19 63 DL61
Sussex Way
Ringmer Pl. N21 36 DR43
Ringmer Way, Brom. 123 EM99
Ringmore Ri. SE23 106 DV87
Ringmore Rd., Walt. 114 BW104
Ringshall Rd., Orp. 124 EU97
Ringslade Rd. N22 49 DM54
Ringstead Rd. SE6 107 EB87
Ringstead Rd., Sutt. 132 DD105
Ringway N11 49 DJ51
Ringway, Sthl. 86 BX78
Ringway Rd., St.Alb. 16 CB27
Ringwold Clo., Beck. 107 DY94
Ringwood Ave. N2 48 DF54
Ringwood Ave., Croy. 119 DL101
Ringwood Ave., Orp. 138 EW110
Ringwood Clo., Pnr. 58 BW55
Ringwood Gdns. E14 93 EA77
Ringwood Gdns. SW15 103 CU89
Ringwood Rd. E17 65 DZ58
Ringwood Way N21 49 DP46
Ringwood Way, Hmptn. 100 CA91
Ripley Clo., Brom. 123 EM99
Ringmer Way
Ripley Clo., Croy. 135 EC107
Ripley Gdns. SW14 88 CR83
Ripley Gdns., Sutt. 132 DC105
Ripley La., Wok. 140 BL123
Ripley Ms. E11 66 EE59
Wadley Rd.
Ripley Rd. E16 80 EJ72
Ripley Rd., Belv. 96 FA77
Ripley Rd., Enf. 36 DQ39
Ripley Rd., Hmptn. 100 CA94
Ripley Rd., Ilf. 67 ET61
Ripley Vw., Loug. 39 EP38
Ripley Vill. W5 73 CJ72
Castlebar Rd.
Ripley Way (Cheshunt), Wal.Cr. 22 DV30
Riplington Ct. SW15 103 CU87
Longwood Dr.
Ripon Clo., Nthlt. 58 CA64
Ripon Gdns., Chess. 129 CK106
Ripon Gdns., Ilf. 66 EL59
Ripon Rd. N9 50 DV45
Ripon Rd. N17 64 DR55
Ripon Rd. SE18 95 EP79
Ripon Way, Borwd. 32 CQ43
Rippersley Rd., Well. 96 EU81
Ripple Rd., Bark. 81 ER67
Ripple Rd., Dag. 82 EX67
Rippleside Commercial Est., Bark. 82 EW68
Ripplevale Gro. N1 77 DM66
Rippolson Rd. SE18 95 ET78
Ripston Rd., Ashf. 99 BR92
Risborough Dr., Wor.Pk. 117 CU101
Risborough St. SE1 10 G4
Risdon St. SE16 92 DW75
Renforth St.
Rise, The E11 66 EG57
Rise, The N13 49 DN49
Rise, The NW7 47 CT51
Rise, The NW10 60 CR63
Rise, The, Bex. 110 EW87
Rise, The, Borwd. 32 CM43
Rise, The, Buck.H. 52 EK45
Rise, The, Dart. 97 FF84
Rise, The, Edg. 46 CP50
Rise, The, Epsom 131 CT110
Rise, The, Grnf. 59 CG64
Rise, The, St.Alb. 17 CD25
Rise, The, Sev. 155 FJ129
Rise, The, Sid. 110 EW87
Rise, The, S.Croy. 134 DW109
Rise, The, Tad. 145 CW121
Rise, The, Uxb. 70 BM68
Rise Pk. Boul., Rom. 55 FF53
Rise Pk. Par., Rom. 55 FE54
Pettits La. N.
Risebridge Chase, Rom. 55 FF52
Risebridge Rd., Rom. 55 FF54
Risedale Rd., Bexh. 97 FB83
Riseldine Rd. SE23 107 DY86
Rising Hill Clo., Nthwd. 43 BQ51
Ducks Hill Rd.
Rising Sun Ct. EC1 6 G7
Risinghill St. N1 77 DM68
Risingholme Clo., Har. 45 CE53
Risingholme Clo. (Bushey), Wat. 44 CB45
Risingholme Rd., Har. 45 CE54
Risings, The E17 65 ED56
Risley Ave. N17 50 DQ53
Rita Rd. SW8 91 DL79
Ritches Rd. N15 64 DQ57
Ritchie Rd., Croy. 120 DV100
Ritchie St. N1 77 DN68
Ritchings Ave. E17 65 DY56
Ritherdon Rd. SW17 104 DG89
Ritson Rd. E8 78 DU65
Ritter St. SE18 95 EN79
Ritz Ct., Pot.B. 20 DA31
Rivaz Pl. E9 78 DW65
Rivenhall Gdns. E18 66 EF56
River Ave. N13 49 DP48
River Ave., T.Ditt. 115 CG101
River Bank N21 50 DQ45
River Bank, E.Mol. 115 CE97
River Bank, T.Ditt. 115 CF99
River Bank, W.Mol. 114 BZ97
River Barge Clo. E14 93 EC75
Stewart St.
River Brent Business Pk. W7 87 CE76
River Clo. E11 66 EJ58
River Clo., Rain. 83 FH71
River Clo., Ruis. 57 BT58
River Clo., Surb. 115 CK99
Catherine Rd.
River Clo., Wal.Cr. 23 EA34
River Crane Wk., Felt. 100 BX88
River Crane Wk., Twick. 101 CG86
River Front, Enf. 36 DR41
River Gdns., Cars. 118 DG104
River Gdns., Felt. 85 BV84
River Gro. Pk., Beck. 121 DZ95
River Hill, Cob. 141 BV115
River Island Clo., Lthd. 143 CD121
River La., Lthd. 143 CD121
River La., Rich. 101 CK88
River Meads Ave., Twick. 100 CA90
River Pk. Gdns., Brom. 107 ED94
River Pk. Rd. N22 49 DM54
River Pl. N1 78 DQ66
River Reach, Tedd. 101 CJ92
River Rd., Bark. 81 ES68
River Rd., Buck.H. 52 EL46
River Rd. Business Pk., Bark. 81 ET69
River St. EC1 6 D2
River St. EC1 77 DN69
River Ter. W6 89 CW78
Crisp Rd.
River Vw., Enf. 36 DQ41
Chase Side
River Vw. Gdns., Twick. 101 CF89
River Wk., Uxb. 56 BJ64
River Wk., Walt. 113 BU100
River Way SE10 94 EF76
River Way, Epsom 130 CR107
River Way, Loug. 39 EM44
River Way, Twick. 100 CB89
Riverbank Way, Brent. 87 CJ79
Rivercourt Rd. W6 89 CV77
Riverdale SE13 93 EC83
Lewisham High St.
Riverdale Dr. SW18 104 DB88
Strathville Rd.
Riverdale Gdns., Twick. 101 CJ86
Riverdale Rd. SE18 95 ET78
Riverdale Rd., Bex. 110 EY87
Riverdale Rd., Erith 97 FB78
Riverdale Rd., Felt. 100 BZ91
Riverdale Rd., Twick. 101 CJ86
Riverdene, Edg. 46 CQ48
Riverdene Rd., Ilf. 67 EN62
Riverhead Clo. E17 51 DX54
Riverhead Dr., Sutt. 132 DB110
Riverhill, Sev. 155 FL130
Riverholme Dr., Epsom 130 CR109
Rivermead, E.Mol. 114 CC97
Rivermead, W.Byf. 126 BM113
Rivermead Clo., Add. 126 BJ108
Rivermead Clo., Tedd. 101 CH92
Rivermead Ct. SW6 89 CZ83
Rivermount, Walt. 113 BT101
Rivernook Clo., Walt. 114 BW99
Riversdale Rd. N5 63 DP62
Riversdale Rd., Rom. 55 FB52
Riversdale Rd., T.Ditt. 115 CG99
Riversfield Rd., Enf. 36 DS41
Riverside NW4 61 CV59
Riverside SE7 94 EH76
Anchor & Hope La.
Riverside, Cher. 112 BG97
Riverside, Twick. 101 CH88
Riverside, The, E.Mol. 115 CD97
Riverside Ave., E.Mol. 115 CD99
Riverside Clo. E5 64 DW60
Riverside Clo. W7 73 CE70
Riverside Clo., Kings L. 15 BP29
Riverside Clo., Kings.T. 115 CK98
Riverside Clo., Orp. 124 EW96
Riverside Clo., Wall. 119 DH104
Riverside Ct. E4 37 EB44
Chelwood Clo.
Riverside Ct. SW8 91 DK79
Riverside Dr. NW11 61 CY58
Riverside Dr. W4 88 CR80
Riverside Dr., Esher 128 CA105
Riverside Dr., Mitch. 118 DE99
Riverside Dr., Rich. 101 CH89
Riverside Dr., Rick. 42 BK46
Riverside Gdns. N3 61 CY55
Riverside Gdns. W6 89 CV78
Riverside Gdns., Enf. 36 DQ40
Riverside Gdns., Wem. 74 CL68
Riverside Ind. Est. SE10 94 EF76
Riverside Ind. Est., Bark. 82 EU69
Riverside Ind. Est., Enf. 37 DY44
Morson Rd.
Riverside Ms., Croy. 119 DL104
Wandle Rd.
Riverside Path (Cheshunt), Wal.Cr. 23 DY29
Church La.
Riverside Pl., Stai. 98 BK86
Riverside Rd. E15 79 EC68
Riverside Rd. N15 64 DU58
Riverside Rd. SW17 104 DB91
Riverside Rd., Sid. 110 EY90
Riverside Rd. (Stanwell), Stai. 98 BK85
Riverside Rd., Walt. 128 BX105
Riverside Rd., Wat. 29 BV44
Riverside Wk. SE1 10 C2
Riverside Wk. SE1 77 DN74
Riverside Wk., Bex. 110 EX87
Riverside Wk., Islw. 87 CE83
Riverside Wk., Kings.T. 115 CK96
High St.
Riverside Way, St.Alb. 17 CD31
Riverside Way, Uxb. 70 BH67
Riverton Clo. W9 75 CZ69
Riverview Gdns. SW13 89 CV79
Riverview Gro. W4 88 CP79
Riverview Pk. SE6 107 EA88
Riverview Rd. W4 88 CP79
Riverview Rd., Epsom 130 CR106
Riverway N13 49 DN49
Riverway, Stai. 112 BH95
Riverwood La., Chis. 123 ER95
Rivington Ave., Wdf.Grn. 52 EK54
Rivington Ct. NW10 75 CU67
Rivington Cres. NW7 47 CT52
Rivington Pl. EC2 7 N3
Rivington St. EC2 7 M3
Rivington St. EC2 78 DS69
Rivington Wk. E8 78 DU67
Wilde Clo.
Rivulet Rd. N17 50 DQ52
Rixon Ho. SE18 95 EP79
Barnfield Rd.
Rixon St. N7 63 DN62
Rixsen Rd. E12 66 EL64
Roach Rd. E3 79 EA66
Roads Pl. N19 63 DL61
Hornsey Rd.
Roakes Ave., Add. 112 BH103
Roan St. SE10 93 EB80
Robarts Clo., Pnr. 57 BV57
Field End Rd.
Robb Rd., Stan. 45 CG51
Robert Adam St. W1 4 F8
Robert Adam St. W1 76 DG72
Robert Clo. W9 76 DC70
Randolph Ave.
Robert Clo., Chig. 53 ET50
Robert Clo., Pot.B. 19 CY33
Robert Clo., Walt. 127 BV106
Robert Dashwood Way SE17 11 H9
Robert Dashwood Way SE17 92 DQ77
Robert Gentry Ho. W14 89 CY78
Comeragh Rd.
Robert Keen Clo. SE15 92 DU81
Cicely Rd.
Robert Lowe Clo. SE14 93 DX80
Robert Owen Ho. SW6 89 CX81
Robert St. E16 81 EP74
Robert St. NW1 5 J3
Robert St. NW1 77 DH69
Robert St. SE18 95 ER78
Robert St. WC2 10 A1
Robert St., Croy. 120 DQ104
High St.
Roberta St. E2 78 DU69
Roberton Dr., Brom. 122 EJ95
Roberts Clo. SE9 109 ER88
Roberts Clo., Orp. 124 EW99
Roberts Clo., Pnr. 57 BV57
Field End Rd.
Roberts Clo., Rom. 55 FH53
Roberts Clo., Stai. 98 BJ86
Roberts Clo., Sutt. 131 CX108
Roberts Clo. (Cheshunt), Wal.Cr. 23 DY30
Windmill La.
Roberts Clo., West Dr. 70 BL74
Roberts Ms. SW1 8 F7
Robert's Pl. EC1 6 E4
Roberts Rd. E17 51 EB53
Roberts Rd. NW7 47 CY51
Roberts Rd., Belv. 96 FA78
Roberts Rd., Wat. 30 BW43
Tucker St.
Robertsbridge Rd., Cars. 118 DC102
Robertson Clo., Brox. 23 DY26
Robertson Rd. E15 79 EC67
Robertson St. SW8 91 DH83
Robeson St. E3 79 DZ71
Ackroyd Dr.
Robeson Way, Borwd. 32 CQ39
Robin Clo. NW7 46 CS48
Robin Clo., Add. 126 BK106
Bois Hall Rd.
Robin Clo., Hmptn. 100 BY92
Robin Clo., Rom. 55 FD52
Robin Ct. SE16 92 DU77
Robin Cres. E6 80 EL71
Robin Gro. N6 62 DG61
Robin Gro., Brent. 87 CJ79
Robin Gro., Har. 60 CM58
Robin Hill Dr., Chis. 108 EL93
Robin Hood Dr., Har. 45 CF52
Robin Hood Dr. (Bushey), Wat. 30 BZ39
Robin Hood Grn., Orp. 124 EU99
Robin Hood La. E14 79 EC72
Robin Hood La. SW15 102 CS91
Robin Hood La., Bexh. 110 EY85
Robin Hood La., Sutt. 132 DA106
Robin Hood Rd. SW19 103 CV92
Robin Hood Way SW15 102 CS91
Robin Hood Way SW20 102 CS91
Robin Hood Way, Grnf. 73 CF65
Robin Way, Orp. 124 EV97
Robin Way (Cuffley), Pot.B. 21 DL28
Robina Clo., Bexh. 96 EX84
Robina Clo., Nthwd. 43 BT53
Robinhood Clo., Mitch. 119 DJ98
Robinhood La., Mitch. 119 DJ97
Robinia Clo., Ilf. 53 ES50
Robinia Cres. E10 65 EA61
Robins Clo., Uxb. 70 BJ71
Newcourt
Robins Ct. SE12 108 EJ90
Robins Gro., W.Wick. 122 EG104
Robins La., Epp. 39 EQ36
Robinscroft Ms. SE10 93 EB81
Sparta St.
Robinson Ave. (Cheshunt), Wal.Cr. 21 DP28
Robinson Clo., Horn. 83 FH66
Robinson Cres. (Bushey), Wat. 44 CC46
Robinson Rd. E2 78 DW68
Robinson Rd. SW17 104 DE93
Robinson Rd., Dag. 68 FA63
Robinson St. SW3 90 DF79
Christchurch St.
Robinsons Clo. W13 73 CG71
Robinsway, Wal.Abb. 24 EE34
Roundhills
Robinsway, Walt. 128 BW105
Robinwood Gro., Uxb. 70 BM70
Robinwood Pl. SW15 102 CR91
Robsart St. SW9 91 DM82
Robson Ave. NW10 75 CU67
Robson Clo. E6 80 EL72
Linton Gdns.
Robson Clo., Enf. 35 DP40
Robson Rd. SE27 105 DP90
Robsons Clo., Wal.Cr. 22 DW29
Robyns Way, Sev. 154 FF122
Roch Ave., Edg. 46 CM54
Rochdale Rd. E17 65 EA59
Rochdale Rd. SE2 96 EV78
Rochdale Way SE8 93 EA80
Idonia St.
Roche Rd. SW16 119 DL95
Roche Wk., Cars. 118 DD100
Rochelle Clo. SW11 90 DD84
Rochelle St. E2 7 P3
Rochemont Wk. E8 78 DT67
Pownall Rd.
Rochester Ave. E13 80 EJ67
Rochester Ave., Brom. 122 EH96
Rochester Ave., Felt. 99 BT89
Rochester Clo. SW16 105 DL94
Rochester Clo., Enf. 36 DS39
Rochester Clo., Sid. 110 EV86
Rochester Dr., Bex. 110 EZ86
Rochester Dr., Pnr. 58 BX57
Rochester Dr., Wat. 16 BW34
Rochester Gdns., Cat. 148 DS122
Rochester Gdns., Croy. 120 DS104
Rochester Gdns., Ilf. 67 EM59
Rochester Ms. NW1 77 DJ66
Rochester Pl. NW1 77 DJ65
Rochester Rd. NW1 77 DJ65
Rochester Rd., Cars. 132 DF105
Rochester Rd., Nthwd. 57 BT55
Rochester Row SW1 9 L8
Rochester Row SW1 91 DJ77
Rochester Sq. NW1 77 DJ66
Rochester St. SW1 9 M7
Rochester St. SW1 91 DK76
Rochester Ter. NW1 77 DJ65
Rochester Wk. SE1 11 K2
Rochester Way SE3 94 EJ82
Rochester Way SE9 95 EM83
Rochester Way, Dart. 111 FD87
Rochester Way, Rick. 29 BP42
Rochester Way Relief Rd. SE3 94 EH81
Rochester Way Relief Rd. SE9 94 EJ84
Rochford Ave., Loug. 39 EQ41
Rochford Ave., Rom. 68 EW57
Rochford Ave., Wal.Abb. 23 ED34
Rochford Clo. E6 80 EK68
Boleyn Rd.
Rochford Clo., Brox. 23 DY26
Rochford Clo., Horn. 83 FH65
Rochford Grn., Loug. 39 EQ41
Rochford St. NW5 62 DF64
Rochford Wk. E8 78 DU66
Wilman Gro.
Rochford Way, Croy. 119 DL100
Rock Ave. SW14 88 CR83
South Worple Way
Rock Gdns., Dag. 69 FB64
Rockwell Rd.
Rock Gro. Way SE16 92 DV77
Blue Anchor La.
Rock Hill SE26 106 DT91
Rock Hill, Orp. 138 FA107
Rock St. N4 63 DN61
Rockbourne Rd. SE23 107 DX88
Rockcliffe Ave., Kings L. 14 BN30
Rockdale Rd., Sev. 155 FH126
Rockells Pl. SE22 106 DV86
Rockford Ave., Grnf. 73 CG68
Rockhall Rd. NW2 61 CX63
Rockhampton Clo. SE27 105 DN91
Rockhampton Rd.
Rockhampton Rd. SE27 105 DN91
Rockhampton Rd., S.Croy. 134 DS107
Rockingham Ave., Horn. 69 FH58
Rockingham Clo. SW15 89 CT84
Rockingham Clo., Uxb. 70 BJ67
Rockingham Est. SE1 11 H7
Rockingham Est. SE1 92 DQ76
Rockingham Par., Uxb. 70 BJ66
Rockingham Rd., Uxb. 70 BH67
Rockingham St. SE1 11 H7
Rockingham St. SE1 92 DQ76
Rockland Rd. SW15 89 CY84
Rocklands Dr., Stan. 45 CH54
Rockley Rd. W14 89 CX75
Rockmount Rd. SE18 95 ET78
Rockmount Rd. SE19 106 DR93
Rocks La. SW13 89 CU83
Rockware Ave., Grnf. 73 CD67
Rockways, Barn. 33 CT44
Rockwell Gdns. SE19 106 DS91
Rockwell Rd., Dag. 69 FB64
Rockwood Pl. W12 89 CW75
Shepherds Bush Grn.
Rocliffe St. N1 6 G1
Rocmoale Way SE8 93 EA80
Octavius St.
Rocombe Cres. SE23 106 DW87
Rocque La. SE3 94 EF83
Rodborough Rd. NW11 62 DA60
Roden Ct. N6 63 DK59
Hornsey La.
Roden Gdns., Croy. 120 DS100
Roden St. N7 63 DM62
Roden St., Ilf. 67 EN62
Rodenhurst Rd. SW4 105 DJ86
Rodeo Clo., Erith 97 FH81
Hollywood Way
Roderick Rd. NW3 62 DF63
Rodgers Clo., Borwd. 31 CK44
Roding Ave., Wdf.Grn. 52 EL51
Roding Gdns., Loug. 38 EL44
Roding La., Buck.H. 52 EK46
Roding La., Chig. 53 EP47
Roding La. N., Wdf.Grn. 52 EL51
Roding La. S., Ilf. 66 EK56
Roding La. S., Wdf.Grn. 66 EK55
Roding Ms. E1 78 DU74
Kennet St.
Roding Rd. E5 65 DY63
Roding Rd. E6 81 EP71
Roding Rd., Loug. 38 EL43
Roding Trd. Est., Bark. 81 EP66
Roding Vw., Buck.H. 52 EK46
Rodings, The, Wdf.Grn. 52 EJ51
Rodings Row, Barn. 33 CY43
Leecroft Rd.
Rodmarton St. W1 4 E7
Rodmarton St. W1 76 DF71
Rodmell Clo., Hayes 72 BY70
Rodmell Slope N12 47 CZ50
Rodmere St. SE10 94 EE78
Trafalgar Rd.
Rodmill La. SW2 105 DL87
Rodney Clo., Croy. 119 DP102
Rodney Clo., N.Mal. 116 CS99
Rodney Clo., Pnr. 58 BY59
Rodney Clo., Walt. 114 BW102
Rodney Rd.

Rodney Ct. W9 76 DC70
Maida Vale
Rodney Gdns., Pnr. 57 BV57
Rodney Gdns., W.Wick. 136 EG105
Rodney Grn., Walt. 114 BW103
Rodney Pl. E17 51 DY54
Rodney Pl. SE17 11 J8
Rodney Pl. SE17 92 DQ77
Rodney Pl. SW19 118 DC95
Rodney Rd. E11 66 EH56
Rodney Rd. SE17 11 J8
Rodney Rd. SE17 92 DQ77
Rodney Rd., Mitch. 118 DE96
Rodney Rd., N.Mal. 116 CS99
Rodney Rd., Twick. 100 CA87
Rodney Rd., Walt. 114 BW103
Rodney St. N1 77 DM68
Rodney Way, Rom. 54 FA53
Rodona Rd., Wey. 127 BR111
Rodway Rd. SW15 103 CU87
Rodway Rd., Brom. 122 EH95
Rodwell Clo., Ruis. 58 BW60
Rodwell Ct., Add. 126 BJ105
Garfield Rd.
Rodwell Pl., Edg. 46 CN51
Whitchurch La.
Rodwell Rd. SE22 106 DT86
Roe End NW9 60 CQ56
Roe Grn. NW9 60 CQ57
Roe La. NW9 60 CP56
Roe Way, Wall. 133 DL108
Roebourne Way E16 95 EN75
Roebuck Clo., Ash. 144 CL120
Roebuck Clo., Felt. 99 BV91
Roebuck La. N17 50 DT51
High Rd.
Roebuck La., Buck.H. 52 EJ45
Roebuck Rd., Chess. 130 CN106
Roebuck Rd., Ilf. 54 EV50
Roedean Ave., Enf. 36 DW39
Roedean Clo., Enf. 36 DW39
Roedean Clo., Orp. 138 EV105
Roedean Cres. SW15 102 CS86
Roehampton Clo. SW15 89 CU84
Roehampton Dr., Chis. 109 EQ93
Roehampton Gate SW15 102 CS86
Roehampton High St. SW15 103 CU87
Roehampton La. SW15 89 CU84
Roehampton Vale SW15 103 CT90
Rofant Rd., Nthwd. 43 BS51
Roffes La., Cat. 148 DR124
Roffey Clo., Pur. 147 DP116
Roffey St. E14 93 EC75
Rogate Ho. E5 64 DU62
Muir Rd.
Roger St. WC1 6 C5
Roger St. WC1 77 DM70
Rogers Clo., Cat. 148 DV122
Tillingdown Hill
Rogers Clo., Couls. 147 DP118
Rogers Ct., Swan. 125 FG98
Rogers Gdns., Dag. 68 FA64
Rogers La., Warl. 149 DZ118
Rogers Rd. E16 80 EF72
Rogers Rd. SW17 104 DD91
Rogers Rd., Dag. 68 FA64
Rogers Ruff, Nthwd. 43 BQ53
Rogers Wk. N12 48 DB48
Brook Meadow
Rojack Rd. SE23 107 DX88
Roke Clo., Ken. 134 DQ114
Roke Lo. Rd., Ken. 133 DP113
Roke Rd., Ken. 148 DQ115
Rokeby Gdns., Wdf.Grn. 52 EG53
Rokeby Pl. SW20 103 CV94
Rokeby Rd. SE4 93 DZ82
Rokeby St. E15 79 ED67
Roker Pk. Ave., Uxb. 56 BL63
Rokesby Clo., Well. 95 ER82
Rokesby Pl., Wem. 59 CK64
Rokesly Ave. N8 63 DL57
Roland Gdns. SW7 90 DC78
Roland Gdns., Felt. 100 BZ90
Roland Ms. E1 79 DX71
Stepney Grn.
Roland Rd. E17 65 ED56
Roland Way SE17 92 DR78
Roland Way SW7 90 DC78
Roland Gdns.
Roland Way, Wor.Pk. 117 CT103
Roles Gro., Rom. 68 EX56
Rolfe Clo., Barn. 34 DE42
Rolinsden Way, Kes. 136 EK105
Roll Gdns., Ilf. 67 EN57
Rollesby Rd., Chess. 130 CN107
Rollesby Way SE28 82 EW73
Rolleston Ave., Orp. 123 EP100
Rolleston Clo., Orp. 123 EP101
Rolleston Rd., S.Croy. 134 DR108
Rollins St. SE15 92 DW79
Rollit Cres., Houns. 100 CA85
Rollit St. N7 63 DM64
Hornsey Rd.
Rollo Rd., Swan. 111 FF94
Rolls Bldgs. EC4 6 D8
Rolls Pk. Ave. E4 51 EA51
Rolls Pk. Rd. E4 51 EB50
Rolls Pas. EC4 6 D8
Rolls Rd. SE1 92 DT78
Rollscourt Ave. SE24 106 DQ85
Rolt St. SE8 93 DY79
Rolvenden Gdns., Brom. 108 EK94
Rolvenden Pl. N17 50 DU53
Manor Rd.
Rom Cres., Rom. 69 FF59
Rom Valley Way, Rom. 69 FE58
Roma Read Clo. SW15 103 CV87
Bessborough Rd.
Roma Rd. E17 65 DY55
Roman Clo. W3 88 CP75
Avenue Gdns.
Roman Clo., Felt. 100 BW85
Roman Clo., Rain. 83 FD68
Roman Clo., Uxb. 42 BG53
Roman Gdns., Kings L. 15 BP30
Roman Ri. SE19 106 DR93
Roman Rd. E2 78 DW69
Roman Rd. E3 79 DY68
Roman Rd. E6 80 EK70
Roman Rd. N10 49 DH52
Roman Rd. NW2 61 CW62
Roman Rd. SW2 105 DM87
Upper Tulse Hill
Roman Rd. W4 89 CT77
Roman Rd., Ilf. 81 EP65
Roman Sq. SE28 82 EU74
Roman Way N7 77 DM65
Roman Way SE15 92 DW80
Clifton Way
Roman Way, Croy. 119 DP103
Roman Way, Dart. 111 FE85
Roman Way, Enf. 36 DT43
Roman Way Ind. Est. N1 77 DM66
Offord St.
Romanhurst Ave., Brom. 122 EE98
Romanhurst Gdns., Brom. 122 EE98
Romans Way, Wok. 140 BG115
Romany Gdns. E17 51 DY53
McEntee Ave.
Romany Gdns., Sutt. 118 DA101
Romany Ri., Orp. 123 EQ102
Romberg Rd. SW17 104 DG90
Romborough Gdns. SE13 107 EC85
Romborough Way SE13 107 EC85
Romeland, Borwd. 31 CK44
Romeland, Wal.Abb. 23 EC33
Romero Clo. SW9 91 DM83
Stockwell Rd.
Romero Sq. SE3 94 EJ84
Romeyn Rd. SW16 105 DM90
Romford Rd. E7 66 EH64
Romford Rd. E12 66 EL63
Romford Rd. E15 80 EE65
Romford Rd., Chig. 54 EU48
Romford Rd., Rom. 54 EY52
Romford St. E1 78 DU71
Romilly Dr., Wat. 44 BY49
Romilly Rd. N4 63 DP61
Romilly St. W1 5 M10
Romilly St. W1 77 DK73
Rommany Rd. SE27 106 DR91
Romney Clo. N17 50 DV53
Romney Clo. NW11 62 DC60
Romney Clo. SE14 92 DW80
Kender St.
Romney Clo., Ashf. 99 BQ92
Romney Clo., Chess. 130 CL105
Romney Clo., Har. 58 CA59
Romney Dr., Brom. 108 EK94
Romney Dr., Har. 58 CA59
Romney Gdns., Bexh. 96 EZ81
Romney Ms. W1 4 F6
Romney Par., Hayes 71 BR68
Romney Rd.
Romney Rd. SE10 93 EC79
Romney Rd., Hayes 71 BR68
Romney Rd., N.Mal. 116 CR100
Romney Row NW2 61 CX61
Brent Ter.
Romney St. SW1 9 P7
Romney St. SW1 91 DL76
Romola Rd. SE24 105 DP88
Romsey Clo., Orp. 137 EP105
Romsey Gdns., Dag. 82 EX67
Romsey Rd. W13 73 CG73
Romsey Rd., Dag. 82 EX67
Ron Leighton Way E6 80 EL67
Rona Rd. NW3 62 DG63
Rona Wk. N1 78 DR65
Clephane Rd.
Ronald Ave. E15 80 EE69
Ronald Clo., Beck. 121 DZ98
Ronald St. E1 78 DW72
Devonport St.
Ronalds Rd. N5 63 DN64
Ronalds Rd., Brom. 122 EG95
Ronaldstone Rd., Sid. 109 ES86
Ronart St., Har. 59 CF55
Stuart Rd.
Rondu Rd. NW2 61 CY64
Ronelean Rd., Surb. 116 CM104
Roneo Cor., Horn. 69 FF60
Hornchurch Rd.
Roneo Link, Horn. 69 FF60
Ronfearn Ave., Orp. 124 EX99
Ronneby Clo., Wey. 113 BS104
Ronson Way, Lthd. 143 CG121
Randalls Rd.
Ronver Rd. SE12 108 EG88
Baring Rd.
Rood La. EC3 7 M10
Rood La. EC3 78 DS73
Rook Clo., Horn. 83 FG66
Rook La., Cat. 147 DM124
Rook Wk. E6 80 EL72
Allhallows Rd.
Rookdean, Sev. 154 FC122
Rooke Way SE10 94 EF78
Rookeries Clo., Felt. 99 BV90
Rookery Clo. NW9 61 CT57
Rookery Clo., Lthd. 143 CE124
Rookery Cres., Dag. 83 FB66
Rookery Dr., Chis. 123 EN95
Rookery Gdns., Orp. 124 EW99
Rookery Hill, Ash. 144 CN118
Rookery La., Brom. 122 EK100
Rookery Rd. SW4 91 DJ84
Rookery Rd., Orp. 137 EM110
Rookery Rd., Stai. 98 BH92
Rookery Way NW9 61 CT57
Rookesley Rd., Orp. 124 EX101
Rookfield Ave. N10 63 DJ56
Rookfield Clo. N10 63 DJ56
Cranmore Way
Rookley Clo., Sutt. 132 DB110
Rooks Hill, Rick. 28 BK42
Rooksmead Rd., Sun. 113 BT96
Rookstone Rd. SW17 104 DF92
Rookwood Ave., Loug. 39 EQ41
Rookwood Ave., N.Mal. 117 CU98
Rookwood Ave., Wall. 133 DK105
Rookwood Gdns. E4 52 EF46
Whitehall Rd.
Rookwood Gdns., Loug. 39 EQ41
Rookwood Ho., Bark. 81 ER68
St. Marys
Rookwood Rd. N16 64 DT59
Roosevelt Way, Dag. 83 FD65
Rootes Dr. W10 75 CX70
Rope St. SE16 93 DY76
Rope Wk., Sun. 114 BW97
Rope Wk. Gdns. E1 78 DU72
Commercial Rd.
Rope Yd. Rails SE18 95 EP76
Ropemaker Rd. SE16 93 DY75
Ropemaker St. EC2 7 K6
Ropemaker St. EC2 78 DR71
Ropemakers Flds. E14 79 DZ73
Narrow St.
Roper La. SE1 11 N5
Roper St. SE9 109 EM86
Roper Way, Mitch. 118 DG96
Ropers Ave. E4 51 EB50
Ropers Wk. SW2 105 DN87
Brockwell Pk. Gdns.
Ropery St. E3 79 DZ70
Ropley St. E2 78 DU68
Rosa Alba Ms. N5 64 DQ63
Kelross Rd.
Rosa Ave., Ashf. 98 BN91
Rosaline Rd. SW6 89 CY80
Rosamond St. SE26 106 DV90
Rosamund Clo., S.Croy. 134 DR105
Rosary Clo., Houns. 86 BY82
Rosary Ct., Pot.B. 20 DB30
Rosary Gdns. SW7 90 DC77
Rosary Gdns., Ashf. 99 BP91
Rosaville Rd. SW6 89 CZ80
Roscoe St. EC1 7 J5
Roscoff Clo., Edg. 46 CQ53
Rose All. SE1 11 J2
Rose All. SE1 78 DQ74
Rose & Crown Ct. EC2 7 H8
Rose & Crown Yd. SW1 9 L2
Rose Ave. E18 52 EH54
Rose Ave., Mitch. 118 DF95
Rose Ave., Mord. 118 DC99
Rose Bates Dr. NW9 60 CN56
Rose Bushes, Epsom 145 CV116
Rose Ct. E1 78 DS71
Sandy's Row
Rose Ct. SE26 106 DV89
Rose Ct., Pnr. 58 BW55
Nursery Rd.
Rose Ct., Wal.Cr. 22 DU27
Rose Dale, Orp. 123 EP103
Rose End, Wor.Pk. 117 CX102
Rose Gdn. Clo., Edg. 46 CL51
Rose Gdns. W5 87 CK76
Rose Gdns., Felt. 99 BU89
Rose Gdns., Sthl. 72 CA70
Rose Gdns., Stai. 98 BK87
Diamedes Ave.
Rose Gdns., Wat. 29 BU43
Rose Glen NW9 60 CR56
Rose Glen, Rom. 69 FE60
Rose Hill, Sutt. 118 DB104
Rose La., Rom. 68 EX55
Rose La., Wok. 140 BJ121
Rose Lawn (Bushey), Wat. 44 CC46
Rose St. WC2 5 P10
Rose Wk., Pur. 133 DK111
Rose Wk., Surb. 116 CP99
Rose Wk., W.Wick. 121 EC103
Rose Wk., The, Rad. 31 CH37
Rose Way SE12 108 EG85
Roseacre Clo. W13 73 CH71
Middlefielde
Roseacre Clo., Shep. 112 BN99
Roseacre Rd., Well. 96 EV83
Roseary Clo., West Dr. 84 BK77
Rosebank SE20 106 DV94
Rosebank, Epsom 130 CQ114
Rosebank, Wal.Abb. 24 EE33
Rosebank Ave., Wem. 59 CF63
Rosebank Clo. N12 48 DE50
Rosebank Clo., Tedd. 101 CG93
Rosebank Gdns. E3 79 DZ68
Rosebank Gro. E17 65 DZ55
Rosebank Rd. E17 65 EB58
Rosebank Rd. W7 87 CE75
Rosebank Vill. E17 65 EA56
Rosebank Wk. NW1 77 DK66
Maiden La.
Rosebank Wk. SE18 94 EL77
Woodhill
Rosebank Way W3 74 CR72
Roseberry Ct., Wat. 29 BU39
Grandfield Ave.
Roseberry Gdns. N4 63 DP58
Roseberry Gdns., Orp. 123 ES104
Roseberry Pl. E8 78 DT65
Roseberry St. SE16 92 DV77
Rosebery Ave. E12 80 EL65
Rosebery Ave. EC1 6 D4
Rosebery Ave. EC1 77 DN70
Rosebery Ave. N17 50 DU54
Rosebery Ave., Epsom 130 CS114
Rosebery Ave., Har. 58 BY63
Rosebery Ave., N.Mal. 117 CT96
Rosebery Ave., Sid. 109 ES87
Rosebery Ave., Th.Hth. 120 DQ96
Rosebery Clo., Mord. 117 CX100
Rosebery Ct. EC1 77 DN70
Rosebery Ave.
Rosebery Gdns. N8 63 DL57
Rosebery Gdns. W13 73 CG72
Rosebery Gdns., Sutt. 132 DB105
Rosebery Ms. N10 49 DJ54
Rosebery Ms. SW2 105 DL86
Rosebery Rd.
Rosebery Rd. N9 50 DU48
Rosebery Rd. N10 49 DJ54
Rosebery Rd. SW2 105 DL86
Rosebery Rd., Epsom 144 CR119
Rosebery Rd., Houns. 100 CC85
Rosebery Rd., Kings.T. 116 CP96
Rosebery Rd., Sutt. 131 CZ107
Rosebery Rd. (Bushey), Wat. 44 CB45
Rosebery Sq. EC1 6 D5
Rosebery Sq., Kings.T. 116 CP96
Rosebine Ave., Twick. 101 CD87
Rosebriar Clo., Wok. 140 BG116
Rosebriar Wk., Wat. 29 BT36
Rosebriars, Cat. 148 DS120
Salmons La. W.
Rosebriars, Esher 128 CC106
Rosebury Rd. SW6 90 DB82
Rosebury Vale, Ruis. 57 BU61
Rosecourt Rd., Croy. 119 DM100
Rosecroft Ave. NW3 62 DA62
Rosecroft Clo., Orp. 124 EW100
Rosecroft Clo., West. 151 EM118
Lotus Rd.
Rosecroft Dr., Wat. 29 BS36
Rosecroft Gdns. NW2 61 CU62
Rosecroft Gdns., Twick. 101 CD88
Rosecroft Rd., Sthl. 72 CA70
Rosecroft Wk., Pnr. 58 BX57
Rosecroft Wk., Wem. 59 CK64
Rosedale, Ash. 143 CJ118
Rosedale, Cat. 148 DS123
Rosedale Ave., Hayes 71 BR71
Rosedale Ave. (Cheshunt), Wal.Cr. 22 DT29
Rosedale Clo. SE2 96 EV76
Finchale Rd.
Rosedale Clo. W7 87 CF75
Boston Rd.
Rosedale Clo., St.Alb. 16 BY30
Rosedale Clo., Stan. 45 CH51
Rosedale Ct. N5 63 DP63
Panmure Clo.
Rosedale Gdns., Dag. 82 EV66
Rosedale Rd. E7 66 EJ64
Rosedale Rd., Dag. 82 EV66
Rosedale Rd., Epsom 131 CU106
Rosedale Rd., Rich. 88 CL84
Rosedale Rd., Rom. 55 FC54
Rosedale Ter. W6 89 CV76
Dalling Rd.
Rosedale Way (Cheshunt), Wal.Cr. 22 DU27
Rosedene NW6 75 CX67
Rosedene Ave. SW16 105 DM90
Rosedene Ave., Croy. 119 DL101
Rosedene Ave., Grnf. 72 CA69
Rosedene Ave., Mord. 118 DA99
Rosedene Ct., Ruis. 57 BS60
Rosedene Gdns., Ilf. 67 EN56
Rosedene Ter. E10 65 EB61
Rosedew Rd. W6 89 CX79
Rosefield, Sev. 154 FG124
Rosefield Clo., Cars. 132 DE106
Alma Rd.
Rosefield Gdns. E14 79 EA73
Rosefield Rd., Stai. 98 BG91
Roseford Ct. W12 89 CX75
Shepherds Bush Grn.
Rosehart Ms. W11 76 DA72
Westbourne Gro.
Rosehatch Ave., Rom. 68 EX55
Roseheath Rd., Houns. 100 BZ85
Rosehill, Esher 129 CG107
Rosehill, Hmptn. 114 CA95
Rosehill Ave., Sutt. 118 DC102
Rosehill Fm. Meadow, Bans. 146 DB115
The Tracery
Rosehill Gdns., Abb.L. 15 BQ32
Rosehill Gdns., Grnf. 59 CF64
Rosehill Gdns., Sutt. 118 DB103
Rosehill Pk. W., Sutt. 118 DB102
Rosehill Rd. SW18 104 DC86
Rosehill Rd., West. 150 EJ117
Roseland Clo. N17 50 DR52
Cavell Rd.
Roseleigh Ave. N5 63 DP63
Roseleigh Clo., Twick. 101 CK86
Rosemary Ave. N3 48 DB54
Rosemary Ave. N9 50 DV46
Rosemary Ave., Enf. 36 DR39
Rosemary Ave., Houns. 86 BX82
Rosemary Ave., Rom. 69 FF55
Rosemary Ave., W.Mol. 114 CA97
Rosemary Clo., Croy. 119 DL101
Rosemary Clo., Uxb. 70 BN71
Rosemary Dr. E14 79 ED72
Rosemary Dr., Ilf. 66 EK57
Rosemary Gdns. SW14 88 CQ83
Rosemary La.
Rosemary Gdns., Chess. 130 CL105
Rosemary Gdns., Dag. 68 EZ60
Rosemary La. SW14 88 CQ83
Rosemary Pl. N1 78 DR67
Shepperton Rd.
Rosemary Rd. SE15 92 DT80
Rosemary Rd. SW17 104 DC90
Rosemary Rd., Well. 95 ET81
Rosemary St. N1 78 DR67
Shepperton Rd.
Rosemead NW9 61 CT59
Rosemead, Cher. 112 BH101
Rosemead, Pot.B. 20 DC30
Rosemead Ave., Felt. 99 BT89
Rosemead Ave., Mitch. 119 DJ96
Rosemead Ave., Wem. 60 CL64
Rosemont Ave. N12 48 DC51
Rosemont Rd. NW3 76 DC65
Rosemont Rd. W3 74 CP73
Rosemont Rd., Kings.T. 116 CQ97
Rosemont Rd., N.Mal. 116 CQ97
Rosemont Rd., Rich. 102 CL86
Rosemont Rd., Wem. 74 CL67
Rosemoor St. SW3 8 D9
Rosemoor St. SW3 90 DF77
Rosemount Ave., W.Byf. 126 BG113
Rosemount Clo., Wdf.Grn. 53 EM51
Chapelmount Rd.
Rosemount Dr., Brom. 123 EM98
Rosemount Rd. W13 73 CG72
Rosenau Cres. SW11 90 DE81
Rosenau Rd. SW11 90 DE81
Rosendale Rd. SE21 106 DQ87
Rosendale Rd. SE24 106 DQ87
Roseneath Ave. N21 49 DP46
Roseneath Clo., Orp. 138 EW108
Roseneath Rd. SW11 104 DG86
Roseneath Wk., Enf. 36 DR42
Rosens Wk., Edg. 46 CP48
Rosenthal Rd. SE6 107 EB86
Rosenthorpe Rd. SE15 107 DX85
Roserton St. E14 93 EC75
Rosery, The, Croy. 121 DX100
Roses, The, Wdf.Grn. 52 EF52
Rosethorn Clo. SW12 105 DK87
Rosetta Clo. SW8 91 DL80
Kenchester Clo.
Rosetti Ter., Dag. 68 EV63
Marlborough Rd.
Roseveare Rd. SE12 108 EJ91
Roseville Ave., Houns. 100 CA85
Roseville Rd., Hayes 85 BU78
Rosevine Rd. SW20 117 CW95
Roseway SE21 106 DR86
Rosewell Clo. SE20 106 DV94
Rosewood, Dart. 111 FE91
Rosewood, Esher 115 CG103
Rosewood, Sutt. 132 DC110
Rosewood Ave., Grnf. 59 CG64
Rosewood Ave., Horn. 69 FG64
Rosewood Clo., Sid. 110 EW90
Rosewood Ct., Brom. 122 EJ95
Rosewood Ct., Rom. 68 EW57
Tendring Way
Rosewood Dr., Enf. 35 DN35
Rosewood Dr., Shep. 112 BM99
Rosewood Gdns. SE13 93 EC82
Lewisham Rd.
Rosewood Gro., Sutt. 118 DC103
Rosewood Sq. W12 75 CU72
Primula St.
Rosewood Ter. SE20 106 DW94
Laurel Gro.
Rosher Clo. E15 79 ED66
Rosina St. E9 65 DX64
Roskell Rd. SW15 89 CX83
Roslin Rd. W3 88 CP76
Roslin Way, Brom. 108 EG92
Roslyn Clo., Mitch. 118 DD96
Roslyn Gdns., Rom. 55 FE54
Roslyn Rd. N15 64 DR57
Rosmead Rd. W11 75 CY73
Rosoman Pl. EC1 6 E4
Rosoman St. EC1 6 E3
Rosoman St. EC1 77 DN69
Ross Ave. NW7 47 CY50
Ross Ave., Dag. 68 EZ61
Ross Clo., Har. 44 CC52
Ross Clo., Hayes 85 BR76
Ross Ct. SW15 103 CX87
Ross Cres., Wat. 29 BU35
Ross Par., Wall. 133 DH107
Ross Rd. SE25 120 DR97
Ross Rd., Cob. 128 BW113
Ross Rd., Dart. 111 FG86
Ross Rd., Twick. 100 CB88
Ross Rd., Wall. 133 DJ106
Ross Way SE9 94 EL83
Ross Way, Nthwd. 43 BT49
Rossall Clo., Horn. 69 FG58
Rossall Cres. NW10 74 CM69
Rossdale, Sutt. 132 DE106
Rossdale Dr. N9 36 DW44
Rossdale Dr. NW9 60 CQ60
Rossdale Rd. SW15 89 CW84
Rosse Ms. SE3 94 EH81
Rossendale St. E5 64 DV61
Rossendale Way NW1 77 DJ67

Rossetti Gdns., Couls. 147 DM118
Rossetti Rd. SE16 92 DV78
Rossignol Gdns., Cars. 118 DG103
Rossindel Rd., Houns. 100 CA85
Rossington Ave., Borwd. 32 CL38
Rossington St. E5 64 DU61
Rossiter Flds., Barn. 33 CY44
Rossiter Rd. SW12 105 DH88
Rossland Clo., Bexh. 111 FB85
Rosslyn Ave. E4 52 EF47
Rosslyn Ave. SW13 88 CS83
Rosslyn Ave., Barn. 34 DE44
Rosslyn Ave., Dag. 68 EZ59
Rosslyn Ave., Felt. 99 BU86
Rosslyn Clo., Hayes 71 BR71
Morgans La.
Rosslyn Clo., Sun. 99 BS93
Cadbury Rd.
Rosslyn Clo., W.Wick. 122 EF104
Rosslyn Cres., Har. 59 CF56
Rosslyn Cres., Wem. 60 CL63
Rosslyn Hill NW3 62 DD63
Rosslyn Ms. NW3 62 DD63
Rosslyn Hill
Rosslyn Pk., Wey. 127 BR105
Rosslyn Pk. Ms. NW3 62 DD64
Lyndhurst Rd.
Rosslyn Rd. E17 65 EC56
Rosslyn Rd., Bark. 81 ER66
Rosslyn Rd., Twick. 101 CJ86
Rosslyn Rd., Wat. 29 BV41
Rossmore Rd. NW1 4 C5
Rossmore Rd. NW1 76 DE70
Rossway Dr. (Bushey), Wat. 30 CC43
Rosswood Gdns., Wall. 133 DH107
Rostella Rd. SW17 104 DD91
Rostrevor Ave. N15 64 DT58
Rostrevor Gdns., Hayes 71 BS74
Rostrevor Gdns., Sthl. 86 BY78
Rostrevor Ms. SW6 89 CZ81
Rostrevor Rd.
Rostrevor Rd. SW6 89 CZ81
Rostrevor Rd. SW19 104 DA92
Roswell Clo. (Cheshunt), Wal.Cr. 23 DY30
Rotary St. SE1 10 F6
Roth Wk. N7 63 DM62
Durham Rd.
Rothbury Ave., Rain. 83 FH71
Rothbury Gdns., Islw. 87 CG80
Rothbury Rd. E9 79 DZ66
Rothbury Wk. N17 50 DU52
Northumberland Gro.
Rother Clo., Wat. 16 BW34
Rotherfield Rd., Cars. 132 DG105
Rotherfield Rd., Enf. 37 DX37
Rotherfield St. N1 78 DQ66
Rotherham Wk. SE1 10 F3
Rotherhill Ave. SW16 105 DK93
Rotherhithe New Rd. SE16 92 DV78
Rotherhithe Old Rd. SE16 93 DX77
Rotherhithe St. SE16 92 DW75
Rotherhithe Tunnel E1 79 DX74
Rotherhithe Tunnel App. E14 79 DY73
Rotherhithe Tunnel App. SE16 92 DW75
Rothermere Rd., Croy. 133 DM106
Rotherwick Hill W5 74 CM70
Rotherwick Rd. NW11 62 DA59
Rotherwood Clo. SW20 117 CY95
Rotherwood Rd. SW15 89 CX83
Rothery St. N1 77 DP67
Gaskin St.
Rothery Ter. SW9 91 DP80
Foxley Rd.
Rothesay Ave. SW20 117 CY96
Rothesay Ave., Grnf. 73 CD65
Rothesay Ave., Rich. 88 CP84
Rothesay Rd. SE25 120 DR98
Rothsay Rd. E7 80 EJ66
Rothsay St. SE1 11 M6
Rothsay St. SE1 92 DS76
Rothsay Wk. E14 93 EA77
Charnwood Gdns.
Rothschild Rd. W4 88 CQ76
Rothschild St. SE27 105 DP91
Rothwell Gdns., Dag. 82 EW66
Rothwell Rd., Dag. 82 EW67
Rothwell St. NW1 76 DF67
Rotten Row SW1 8 C4
Rotten Row SW7 8 C4
Rotten Row SW7 90 DE75
Rotterdam Dr. E14 93 EC76
Rouel Rd. SE16 92 DU76
Rougemont Ave., Mord. 118 DA100
Roughs, The, Nthwd. 43 BS48
Roughtallys, Epp. 26 EZ27
Roughwood Clo., Wat. 29 BS38
Round Gro., Croy. 121 DX101
Round Hill SE26 106 DW90
Round Oak Rd., Wey. 126 BM105
Roundacre SW19 103 CX89
Inner Pk. Rd.
Roundaway Rd., Ilf. 53 EM53
Roundcroft (Cheshunt), Wal.Cr. 22 DT26
Roundel Clo. SE4 93 DZ84
Adelaide Ave.
Roundhay Clo. SE23 107 DX89
Roundhedge Way, Enf. 35 DM38
Roundhill Dr., Enf. 35 DM42
Roundhill Way, Cob. 128 CB112
Roundhills, Wal.Abb. 23 ED34
Roundmead Ave., Loug. 39 EN40
Roundmead Clo., Loug. 39 EN41
Roundmoor Dr. (Cheshunt), Wal.Cr. 23 DX29
Roundtable Rd., Brom. 108 EF90
Roundtree Rd., Wem. 59 CH64
Roundway, West. 150 EK116
Norheads La.
Roundway, The N17 50 DQ53
Roundway, The, Esher 129 CF107
Roundway, The, Wat. 29 BT44
Roundways, The, Ruis. 57 BT62
Roundwood, Chis. 123 EP96
Roundwood, Kings L. 14 BL27
Roundwood Ave., Uxb. 71 BQ74
Roundwood Clo., Ruis. 57 BR59
Roundwood Rd. NW10 75 CT65
Roundwood Vw., Bans. 145 CX115
Roundwood Way, Bans. 145 CX115
Rounton Rd. E3 79 EA70
Rounton Rd., Wal.Abb. 24 EE33
Roupell Rd. SW2 105 DM88
Roupell St. SE1 10 E3
Roupell St. SE1 77 DN74
Rous Rd., Buck.H. 52 EL46
Rousden St. NW1 77 DJ66
Rouse Gdns. SE21 106 DS91
Rousebarn La., Rick. 28 BM38
Routemaster Clo. E13 80 EH69
Routh Ct., Felt. 99 BS88
Loxwood Clo.
Routh Rd. SW18 104 DE87
Routh St. E6 81 EM71
Routledge Clo. N19 63 DK60
Rover Ave., Ilf. 53 ET51
Rowallan Rd. SW6 89 CY80
Rowan Ave. E4 51 DZ51
Rowan Clo. SW16 119 DJ95
Rowan Clo. W5 88 CL75
Rowan Clo., N.Mal. 116 CS96
Rowan Clo. (Bricket Wd.), St.Alb. 16 CA31
Rowan Clo., Stan. 45 CF51
Woodlands Dr.
Rowan Clo., Wem. 59 CG62
Rowan Ct., Borwd. 32 CL39
Theobald St.
Rowan Cres. SW16 119 DJ95
Rowan Dr. NW9 61 CU55
Rowan Gdns., Croy. 120 DT104
Radcliffe Rd.
Rowan Grn., Couls. 147 DH121
Rowan Grn., Wey. 127 BR105
Rowan Gro., Couls. 147 DH121
Rowan Ind. Est., Croy. 120 DS101
Rowan Pl., Hayes 71 BT73
West Ave.
Rowan Rd. SW16 119 DJ96
Rowan Rd. W6 89 CX77
Rowan Rd., Bexh. 96 EY83
Rowan Rd., Brent. 87 CH80
Rowan Rd., Swan. 125 FD97
Rowan Rd., West Dr. 84 BK77
Rowan Ter. W6 89 CX77
Bute Gdns.
Rowan Wk. N2 62 DC57
Rowan Wk. N19 63 DJ61
Bredgar Rd.
Rowan Wk. W10 75 CY70
Droop St.
Rowan Wk., Brom. 123 EM104
Rowan Way, Rom. 68 EW55
Rowans, The N13 49 DP48
Rowans, The, Sun. 99 BT92
Rowans Way, Loug. 39 EM42
Rowantree Clo. N21 50 DR46
Rowantree Rd. N21 50 DR46
Rowantree Rd., Enf. 35 DP40
Rowanwood Ave., Sid. 110 EU88
Rowben Clo. N20 48 DB46
Rowberry Clo. SW6 89 CW80
Rowcross St. SE1 92 DT78
Rowdell Rd., Nthlt. 72 CA67
Rowden Pk. Gdns. E4 51 EA51
Rowden Rd.
Rowden Rd. E4 51 EA51
Rowden Rd., Beck. 121 DY95
Rowden Rd., Epsom 130 CP105
Rowditch La. SW11 90 DG82
Rowdon Ave. NW10 75 CV66
Rowdown Cres., Croy. 135 ED109
Rowdowns Rd., Dag. 82 EZ67
Rowe Gdns., Bark. 81 ET68
Rowe La. E9 64 DW64
Rowe Wk., Har. 58 CA62
Rowena Cres. SW11 90 DE82
Rowfant Rd. SW17 104 DG88
Rowhill Rd. E5 64 DV63
Rowhill Rd., Dart. 111 FF93
Rowhill Rd., Swan. 111 FF93
Rowhurst Ave., Add. 126 BH107
Rowhurst Ave., Lthd. 143 CF117
Rowington Clo. W2 76 DB71
Rowland Ave., Har. 59 CJ55
Rowland Ct. E16 80 EF70
Rowland Cres., Chig. 53 ES49
Rowland Gro. SE26 106 DV90
Dallas Rd.
Rowland Hill Ave. N17 50 DQ52
Rowland Hill St. NW3 62 DE64
Rowland Wk., Rom. (Havering-atte-Bower) 55 FE48
Rowland Way SW19 118 DB95
Hayward Clo.
Rowland Way, Ashf. 99 BQ94
Rowlands Ave., Pnr. 44 CA50
Rowlands Clo. N6 62 DG58
North Hill
Rowlands Clo. NW7 47 CU52
Rowlands Clo. (Cheshunt), Wal.Cr. 23 DX30
Rowlands Flds. (Cheshunt), Wal.Cr. 23 DX29
Rowlands Rd., Dag. 68 EZ61
Rowley Ave., Sid. 110 EV87
Rowley Clo., Wat. 30 BY44
Lower Paddock Rd.
Rowley Clo., Wem. 74 CM66
Rowley Clo., Wok. 140 BG116
Rowley Ct., Cat. 148 DR122
Fairbourne La.
Rowley Gdns. N4 64 DQ59
Rowley Gdns. (Cheshunt), Wal.Cr. 23 DX28
Warwick Dr.
Rowley Grn. Rd., Barn. 33 CT43
Rowley Ind. Est. W3 88 CP76
Rowley La., Barn. 32 CS42
Rowley La., Borwd. 32 CR39
Rowley Mead, Epp. 26 EW25
Rowley Rd. N15 64 DQ57
Rowley Way NW8 76 DB67
Rowlheys Pl., West Dr. 84 BL76
Rowlls Rd., Kings.T. 116 CM97
Rowney Gdns., Dag. 82 EW65
Rowney Rd., Dag. 82 EV65
Rowntree Clifford Clo. E13 80 EH69
Liddon Rd.
Rowntree Path SE28 82 EV73
Booth Clo.
Rowntree Rd., Twick. 101 CE88
Rowse Clo. E15 79 EC67
Rowsley Ave. NW4 61 CW55
Rowstock Gdns. N7 63 DK64
Rowton Rd. SE18 95 EQ80
Rowzill Rd., Swan. 111 FF93
Roxborough Ave., Har. 59 CE59
Roxborough Ave., Islw. 87 CF80
Roxborough Pk., Har. 59 CE59
Roxborough Rd., Har. 59 CD57
Roxbourne Clo., Nthlt. 72 BX65
Roxburgh Rd. SE27 105 DP92
Roxburn Way, Ruis. 57 BT62
Roxby Pl. SW6 90 DA79
Roxeth Ct., Ashf. 98 BN92
Roxeth Grn. Ave., Har. 58 CB62
Roxeth Gro., Har. 58 CB63
Roxeth Hill, Har. 59 CD61
Roxford Clo., Shep. 113 BS99
Roxley Rd. SE13 107 EB86
Roxton Gdns., Croy. 135 EA106
Roxwell Rd. W12 89 CU75
Roxwell Rd., Bark. 82 EU68
Roxwell Trd. Pk. E10 65 DY59
Roxwell Way, Wdf.Grn. 52 EJ52
Roxy Ave., Rom. 68 EW59
Roy Gdns., Ilf. 67 ES56
Roy Gro., Hmptn. 100 CB93
Roy Rd., Nthwd. 43 BT52
Roy Sq. E14 79 DY73
Narrow St.
Royal Albert Dock E16 80 EL73
Royal Albert Roundabout E16 94 EK75
Royal Albert Way
Royal Albert Way E16 80 EJ73
Royal Arc. W1 9 K1
Royal Ave. SW3 8 D10
Royal Ave. SW3 90 DF78
Royal Ave., Wal.Cr. 23 DY33
Royal Ave., Wor.Pk. 116 CS103
Royal Circ. SE27 105 DN90
Royal Clo. N16 64 DS60
Manor Rd.
Royal Clo., Ilf. 68 EU59
Royal Clo., Uxb. 70 BM72
Royal Clo., Wor.Pk. 116 CS103
Royal College St. NW1 77 DJ66
Royal Ct. EC3 78 DR72
Cornhill
Royal Ct. SE16 93 DZ76
Finland St.
Royal Cres. W11 75 CX74
Royal Cres., Ruis. 58 BY63
Royal Cres. Ms. W11 75 CX74
Queensdale Rd.
Royal Docks Rd. E6 81 EP72
Royal Docks Rd., Bark. 81 EP72
Royal Dr., Epsom 145 CV118
Royal Ex. EC3 7 L9
Royal Ex. EC3 78 DR72
Royal Ex. Ave. EC3 7 L9
Royal Ex. Bldgs. EC3 7 L9
Royal Ex. Steps EC3 78 DR72
Cornhill
Royal Hill SE10 93 EC80
Royal Hospital Rd. SW3 90 DF79
Royal La., Uxb. 70 BM71
Royal La., West Dr. 70 BM72
Royal London Est., The N17 50 DU51
Royal London Ind. Est. NW10 74 CR68
North Acton Rd.
Royal Mint Ct. EC3 78 DT73
Royal Mint Pl. E1 78 DT73
Blue Anchor Yd.
Royal Mint St. E1 78 DT73
Royal Mt. Ct., Twick. 101 CE90
Royal Naval Pl. SE14 93 DZ80
Royal Oak Ct. N1 78 DS69
Pitfield St.
Royal Oak Pl. SE22 106 DV86
Royal Oak Rd. E8 78 DV65
Royal Oak Rd., Bexh. 110 EZ85
Royal Opera Arc. SW1 9 M2
Royal Orchard Clo. SW18 103 CY87
Royal Par. SE3 94 EF82
Royal Par. SW6 89 CY80
Dawes Rd.
Royal Par. W5 74 CL69
Western Ave.
Royal Par., Chis. 109 EQ94
Royal Par. Ms. SE3 94 EF82
Royal Par.
Royal Par. Ms., Chis. 109 EQ94
Royal Pl. SE10 93 EC80
Royal Rd. E16 80 EJ72
Royal Rd. SE17 91 DP79
Royal Rd., Sid. 110 EX90
Royal Rd., Tedd. 101 CD92
Royal Route, Wem. 60 CN63
Royal St. SE1 10 C6
Royal St. SE1 91 DM76
Royal Victor Pl. E3 79 DX68
Royal Victoria Dock E16 80 EG73
Royal Wk., Wall. 119 DH104
Prince Charles Way
Royal Windsor Ct., Surb. 116 CN102
Royalty Ms. W1 5 M9
Roycraft Ave., Bark. 81 ET68
Roycraft Clo., Bark. 81 ET68
Roycroft Clo. E18 52 EH53
Roycroft Clo. SW2 105 DN88
Roydene Rd. SE18 95 ES79
Roydon Clo. SW11 91 DH81
Reform St.
Roydon Clo., Loug. 52 EL45
Roydon Ct., Walt. 127 BU105
Roydon St. SW11 91 DH81
Southolm St.
Royle Clo., Rom. 69 FH57
Royle Cres. W13 73 CG70
Royston Ave. E4 51 EA50
Royston Ave., Sutt. 118 DD104
Royston Ave., Wall. 133 DK105
Royston Ave., W.Byf. 126 BL112
Royston Clo., Houns. 85 BV81
Royston Clo., Walt. 113 BU102
Royston Ct. SE24 106 DQ86
Burbage Rd.
Royston Ct., Rich. 88 CM81
Lichfield Rd.
Royston Ct., Surb. 116 CN104
Hook Ri. N.
Royston Gdns., Ilf. 66 EK58
Royston Gro., Pnr. 44 CA51
Royston Par., Ilf. 66 EK58
Royston Pk. Rd., Pnr. 44 BZ51
Royston Rd. SE20 121 DX95
Royston Rd., Dart. 111 FF86
Royston Rd., Rich. 102 CL85
Royston Rd., W.Byf. 126 BL112
Royston St. E2 78 DW68
Roystons, The, Surb. 116 CP99
Rozel Ct. N1 78 DS67
Rozel Rd. SW4 91 DJ83
Rubastic Rd., Sthl. 86 BW76
Rubens Rd., Nthlt. 72 BW68
Rubens St. SE6 107 DZ89
Ruberoid Rd., Enf. 37 DZ41
Ruby Ms. E17 65 EA55
Ruby Rd.
Ruby Rd. E17 65 EA55
Ruby St. SE15 92 DV79
Ruby Triangle SE15 92 DV79
Sandgate St.
Ruckholt Clo. E10 65 EB62
Ruckholt Rd. E10 65 EB63
Rucklers La., Kings L. 14 BG28
Rucklidge Ave. NW10 75 CT68
Rudall Cres. NW3 62 DD63
Willoughby Rd.
Ruddington Clo. E5 65 DY63
Ruddstreet Clo. SE18 95 EP77
Ruddy Way NW7 47 CU51
Flower La.
Ruden Way, Epsom 145 CV116
Rudland Rd., Bexh. 97 FB83
Rudloe Rd. SW12 105 DJ87
Rudolf Pl. SW8 91 DL79
Miles St.
Rudolph Ct. SE22 106 DU87
Rudolph Rd. E13 80 EF68
Rudolph Rd. NW6 76 DA68
Rudolph Rd. (Bushey), Wat. 30 CA44
Rudyard Gro. NW7 46 CQ51
Rue de St. Lawrence, Wal.Abb. 23 EC34
Quaker La.
Ruffetts, The, S.Croy. 134 DV108
Ruffetts Clo., S.Croy. 134 DV108
Ruffetts Way, Tad. 145 CY118
Rufford Clo., Har. 59 CG58
Rufford St. N1 77 DL67
Rufford Twr. W3 74 CP74
Rufus Clo., Ruis. 58 BY62
Rufus St. N1 7 M3
Rugby Ave. N9 50 DT46
Rugby Ave., Grnf. 73 CD65
Rugby Ave., Wem. 59 CH64
Rugby Clo., Har. 59 CE56
Rugby Gdns., Dag. 82 EW65
Rugby La., Sutt. 131 CX109
Nonsuch Wk.
Rugby Rd. NW9 60 CN56
Rugby Rd. W4 88 CS75
Rugby Rd., Dag. 82 EV65
Rugby Rd., Islw. 101 CE85
Rugby Rd., Twick. 101 CE85
Rugby St. WC1 6 B5
Rugby St. WC1 77 DM70
Rugby Wk., Sutt. 131 CX109
Nonsuch Wk.
Rugby Way, Rick. 29 BP43
Rugg St. E14 79 EA73
Rugged La., Wal.Abb. 24 EK33
Ruggles-Brise Rd., Ashf. 98 BK92
Ruislip Clo., Grnf. 72 CB70
Ruislip Rd., Grnf. 72 CA69
Ruislip Rd., Nthlt. 72 BX69
Ruislip Rd., Sthl. 72 CA69
Ruislip Rd. E. W7 73 CD70
Ruislip Rd. E. W13 73 CF70
Ruislip Rd. E., Grnf. 73 CD70
Ruislip St. SW17 104 DF91
Rum Clo. E1 78 DW73
Rumbold Rd. SW6 90 DB80
Rumsey Clo., Hmptn. 100 BZ93
Rumsey Ms. N4 63 DP62
Monsell Rd.
Rumsey Rd. SW9 91 DM83
Rumsley, Wal.Cr. 22 DU27
Runbury Circle NW9 60 CR61
Runciman Clo., Orp. 138 EW110
Runcorn Clo. N17 64 DV56
Runcorn Pl. W11 75 CY73
Rundell Cres. NW4 61 CV57
Runes Clo., Mitch. 118 DD98
Runnel Fld., Har. 59 CE62
Running Horse Yd., Brent. 88 CL79
Pottery Rd.
Runnymede SW19 118 DC95
Runnymede Clo., Twick. 100 CB87
Runnymede Ct., Croy. 120 DT103
Runnymede Cres. SW16 119 DK95
Runnymede Gdns., Grnf. 73 CD68
Runnymede Gdns., Twick. 100 CB87
Runnymede Rd., Twick. 100 CB86
Runway, The, Ruis. 57 BV64
Rupack St. SE16 92 DW75
St. Marychurch St.
Rupert Ave., Wem. 60 CL64
Rupert Ct. W1 5 M10
Rupert Gdns. SW9 91 DP82
Rupert Rd. N19 63 DK62
Holloway Rd.
Rupert Rd. NW6 75 CZ68
Rupert Rd. W4 88 CS76
Rupert St. W1 5 M10
Rupert St. W1 77 DK73
Rural Clo., Horn. 69 FH60
Rural Way SW16 105 DH94
Ruscoe Rd. E16 80 EF72
Ruscombe Dr., St.Alb. 16 CB26
Ruscombe Way, Felt. 99 BT87
Rush, The SW19 117 CZ95
Kingston Rd.
Rush Grn. Gdns., Rom. 69 FC60
Rush Grn. Rd., Rom. 69 FC60
Rush Gro. St. SE18 95 EM77
Rush Hill Ms. SW11 90 DG83
Rush Hill Rd.
Rush Hill Rd. SW11 90 DG83
Rusham Rd. SW12 104 DF86
Rushbrook Cres. E17 51 DZ53
Rushbrook Rd. SE9 109 EQ89
Rushcroft Rd. E4 51 EA52
Rushcroft Rd. SW2 91 DN84
Rushden Clo. SE19 106 DR94
Rushden Gdns. NW7 47 CW51
Rushden Gdns., Ilf. 53 EN54
Rushdene SE2 96 EW76
Rushdene Ave., Barn. 48 DE45
Rushdene Clo., Nthlt. 72 BW68
Rushdene Cres., Nthlt. 72 BW68
Rushdene Rd., Pnr. 58 BX58
Rushdene Wk., West. 150 EK117
Rushdon Clo., Rom. 69 FG57
Rushen Wk., Cars. 118 DD102
Paisley Rd.
Rushes Mead, Uxb. 70 BJ67
Frays Waye
Rushet Rd., Orp. 124 EU96
Rushett Clo., T.Ditt. 115 CH102
Rushett La., Chess. 129 CJ111
Rushett La., Epsom 129 CJ111
Rushett Rd., T.Ditt. 115 CH101
Rushey Clo., N.Mal. 116 CR98
Rushey Grn. SE6 107 EB87
Rushey Hill, Enf. 35 DM42
Rushey Mead SE4 107 EA85
Rushfield, Pot.B. 19 CX32
Rushford Rd. SE4 107 DZ86
Rushgrove Ave. NW9 60 CS57
Rushleigh Ave. (Cheshunt), Wal.Cr. 23 DX31
Rushley Clo., Kes. 136 EK105
Rushmead E2 78 DV69
Florida St.
Rushmead, Rich. 101 CH90
Rushmead Clo., Croy. 134 DT105
Rushmere Ct., Wor.Pk. 117 CU103
The Ave.
Rushmere Pl. SW19 103 CX92
Rushmoor Clo., Pnr. 57 BV56
Rushmoor Clo., Rick. 42 BK47
Rushmore Clo., Brom. 122 EL97
Rushmore Cres. E5 65 DX63
Rushmore Rd.
Rushmore Hill, Orp. 138 EW109
Rushmore Hill, Sev. 138 EX112
Rushmore Rd. E5 64 DW63
Rusholme Ave., Dag. 68 FA62
Rusholme Gro. SE19 106 DS92
Rusholme Rd. SW15 103 CX86
Rushout Ave., Har. 59 CH58

Rushton Ave., Wat. 29 BU35
Rushton St. N1 78 DR68
Rushworth Ave. NW4 61 CU55
Rushworth Gdns.
Rushworth Gdns. NW4 61 CU55
Rushworth St. SE1 10 G4
Rushworth St. SE1 91 DP75
Rushy Meadow La., Cars. 118 DE103
Ruskin Ave. E12 80 EL65
Ruskin Ave., Felt. 99 BT86
Ruskin Ave., Rich. 88 CN80
Ruskin Ave., Wal.Abb. 24 EE34
Ruskin Ave., Well. 96 EU82
Ruskin Clo. NW11 62 DB58
Ruskin Clo. (Cheshunt), Wal.Cr. 22 DS26
Ruskin Dr., Orp. 123 ES104
Ruskin Dr., Well. 96 EU83
Ruskin Dr., Wor.Pk. 117 CV103
Ruskin Gdns. W5 73 CK70
Ruskin Gdns., Har. 60 CM56
Ruskin Gdns., Rom. 55 FH52
Ruskin Gro., Well. 96 EU82
Ruskin Pk. Ho. SE5 92 DR83
Ruskin Rd. N17 50 DT53
Ruskin Rd., Belv. 96 FA77
Ruskin Rd., Cars. 132 DF106
Ruskin Rd., Croy. 119 DP103
Ruskin Rd., Islw. 87 CF83
Ruskin Rd., Sthl. 72 BY73
Ruskin Wk. N9 50 DU47
Durham Rd.
Ruskin Wk. SE24 106 DQ85
Ruskin Wk., Brom. 122 EL100
Ruskin Way SW19 118 DD95
Rusland Ave., Orp. 123 ER104
Rusland Pk. Rd., Har. 59 CE56
Rusper Clo. NW2 61 CW62
Rusper Clo., Stan. 45 CJ49
Rusper Rd. N22 49 DP54
Rusper Rd., Dag. 82 EW65
Russell Ave. N22 49 DN54
Russell Clo. NW10 74 CQ66
Russell Clo. SE7 94 EJ80
Russell Clo. W4 89 CT79
Russell Clo., Beck. 121 EB97
Russell Clo., Bexh. 96 FA84
Russell Clo., Dart. 97 FG83
Russell Clo., Nthwd. 43 BQ50
Russell Clo., Ruis. 58 BW61
Russell Ct. SW1 9 L3
Russell Ct., Lthd. 143 CH122
Russell Ct., St.Alb. 16 CA30
Russell Cres., Wat. 29 BT35
High Rd.
Russell Dr., Stai. 98 BK86
Russell Gdns. N20 48 DE47
Russell Gdns. NW11 61 CY58
Russell Gdns. W14 89 CY76
Russell Gdns., Rich. 101 CJ89
Russell Gdns., West Dr. 84 BN78
Russell Gdns. Ms. W14 89 CY75
Russell Grn. Clo., Pur. 133 DN110
Russell Gro. NW7 46 CS50
Russell Gro. SW9 91 DN81
Russell Hill, Pur. 133 DM110
Russell Hill Pl., Pur. 133 DN111
Purley Way
Russell Hill Rd., Pur. 133 DN110
Russell Kerr Clo. W4 88 CQ80
Burlington La.
Russell La. N20 48 DE47
Russell La., Wat. 29 BR36
Russell Mead, Har. 45 CF52
Russell Pl. NW3 62 DE64
Aspern Gro.
Russell Pl. SE16 93 DY76
Onega Gate
Russell Rd. E4 51 DZ49
Russell Rd. E10 65 EB58
Russell Rd. E16 80 EG72
Russell Rd. E17 65 DZ55
Russell Rd. N8 63 DK58
Russell Rd. N13 49 DM51
Russell Rd. N15 64 DS57
Russell Rd. N20 48 DE47
Russell Rd. NW9 61 CT58
Russell Rd. SW19 104 DA94
Russell Rd. W14 89 CY76
Russell Rd., Buck.H. 52 EH46
Russell Rd., Enf. 36 DT38
Russell Rd., Mitch. 118 DE97
Russell Rd., Nthlt. 58 CC64
Russell Rd., Nthwd. 43 BQ48
Russell Rd., Shep. 113 BP101
Russell Rd., Twick. 101 CF86
Russell Rd., Walt. 113 BU100
Russell Sq. WC1 5 P5
Russell Sq. WC1 77 DL70
Russell St. WC2 6 A10
Russell St. WC2 77 DL73
Russell Wk., Rich. 102 CM86
Park Hill
Russell Way, Sutt. 132 DA106
Russell Way, Wat. 43 BV45
Russells, Tad. 145 CX122
Russell's Footpath SW16 105 DL92
Russells Ride (Cheshunt), Wal.Cr. 23 DY30
Russet Clo., Uxb. 71 BQ70
Uxbridge Rd.
Russet Clo., Walt. 114 BX104
Russet Cres. N7 63 DM64
Stock Orchard Cres.
Russet Dr., Croy. 121 DY102
Russet Dr., Rad. 18 CL32
Russets Clo. E4 51 ED49
Larkshall Rd.
Russett Clo., Orp. 138 EV106
Russett Clo., Wal.Cr. 22 DS26
Russett Way SE13 93 EB82
Conington Rd.
Russett Way, Swan. 125 FD96
Russia Ct. EC2 7 J9
Russia Dock Rd. SE16 79 DY74
Russia La. E2 78 DW68
Russia Row EC2 7 J9
Russia Wk. SE16 93 DX75
Archangel St.
Russington Rd., Shep. 113 BR100
Rust Sq. SE5 92 DR80
Rusthall Ave. W4 88 CR77
Rusthall Clo., Croy. 120 DW100
Rustic Ave. SW16 105 DH94
Rustic Pl., Wem. 59 CK63
Rustic Wk. E16 80 EH72
Lambert Rd.
Rustington Wk., Mord. 117 CZ101
Ruston Ave., Surb. 116 CP101
Ruston Gdns. N14 34 DG44
Farm La.
Ruston Ms. W11 75 CY72
St. Marks Rd.
Ruston St. E3 79 DZ67
Rutford Rd. SW16 105 DL92
Ruth Clo., Stan. 60 CM56
Ruthen Clo., Epsom 130 CP114
Rutherford Clo., Borwd. 32 CQ40
Rutherford Clo., Sutt. 132 DD107
Rutherford St. SW1 9 M8
Rutherford St. SW1 91 DK77
Rutherford Twr., Sthl. 72 CB72
Rutherford Way (Bushey), Wat. 45 CD46
Rutherford Way, Wem. 60 CN62
Rutherglen Rd. SE2 96 EU79
Rutherwick Ri., Couls. 147 DL117
Rutherwyke Clo., Epsom 131 CU107
Ruthin Clo. NW9 60 CS58
Ruthin Rd. SE3 94 EG79
Ruthven Ave., Wal.Cr. 23 DX33
Ruthven St. E9 79 DX67
Lauriston Rd.
Rutland Ave., Sid. 110 EU87
Rutland Clo. SW14 88 CP83
Rutland Clo. SW19 104 DE94
Rutland Rd.
Rutland Clo., Ash. 144 CL117
Rutland Clo., Bex. 110 EX88
Rutland Clo., Chess. 130 CM107
Rutland Clo., Epsom 130 CR110
Rutland Ct., Enf. 36 DV43
Rutland Dr., Mord. 117 CZ100
Rutland Dr., Rich. 101 CK88
Rutland Gdns. N4 63 DP58
Rutland Gdns. SW7 8 C5
Rutland Gdns. SW7 90 DE75
Rutland Gdns. W13 73 CG71
Rutland Gdns., Croy. 134 DS105
Rutland Gdns., Dag. 68 EW64
Rutland Gdns. Ms. SW7 8 C5
Rutland Gate SW7 8 C5
Rutland Gate SW7 90 DE75
Rutland Gate, Belv. 97 FB78
Rutland Gate, Brom. 122 EF98
Rutland Gate Ms. SW7 8 B5
Rutland Gro. W6 89 CV78
Rutland Ms. NW8 76 DB67
Boundary Rd.
Rutland Ms. E. SW7 8 B6
Rutland Ms. S. SW7 8 B6
Rutland Pk. NW2 75 CW65
Rutland Pk. SE6 107 DZ89
Rutland Pl. EC1 6 G6
Rutland Pl. (Bushey), Wat. 45 CD46
The Rutts
Rutland Rd. E7 80 EK66
Rutland Rd. E9 78 DW67
Rutland Rd. E11 66 EH57
Rutland Rd. E17 65 EA58
Rutland Rd. SW19 104 DE94
Rutland Rd., Har. 58 CC58
Rutland Rd., Hayes 85 BR77
Rutland Rd., Ilf. 67 EP63
Rutland Rd., Sthl. 72 CA70
Rutland Rd., Twick. 101 CD89
Rutland St. SW7 8 C6
Rutland St. SW7 90 DE76
Rutland Wk. SE6 107 DZ89
Rutland Way, Orp. 124 EW100
Rutley Clo. SE17 91 DP79
Royal Rd.
Rutlish Rd. SW19 118 DA95
Rutson Rd., W.Byf. 126 BM114
Rutter Gdns., Mitch. 118 DD98
Rutters Clo., West Dr. 84 BN75
Rutts, The (Bushey), Wat. 45 CD46
Rutts Ter. SE14 93 DX81
Ruvigny Gdns. SW15 89 CX83
Ruxley Clo., Epsom 130 CP106
Ruxley Clo., Sid. 110 EY93
Ruxley Cor. Ind. Est., Sid. 110 EX93
Ruxley Cres., Esher 129 CH107
Ruxley La., Epsom 130 CP107
Ruxley Ms., Epsom 130 CP106
Ruxley Ridge, Esher 129 CG108
Ruxton Clo., Swan. 125 FE97
Ryall Clo., St.Alb. 16 BY29
Ryalls Ct. N20 48 DF48
Ryan Clo. SE3 94 EJ84
Ryan Clo., Ruis. 57 BV60
Ryan Dr., Brent. 87 CG79
Ryan Way, Wat. 30 BW39
Ryarsh Cres., Orp. 137 ES105
Rycott Path SE22 106 DU87
Lordship La.
Rycroft La., Sev. 154 FE130
Rycroft Way N17 64 DT55
Ryculff Sq. SE3 94 EF82
Rydal Clo. NW4 47 CX53
Rydal Clo., Pur. 134 DR113
Rydal Ct., Wat. 15 BV32
Grasmere Clo.
Rydal Cres., Grnf. 73 CH69
Rydal Dr., Bexh. 96 EZ82
Rydal Dr., W.Wick. 122 EE103
Rydal Gdns. NW9 60 CS57
Rydal Gdns. SW15 102 CS92
Rydal Gdns., Houns. 100 CB86
Rydal Gdns., Wem. 59 CJ60
Rydal Rd. SW16 105 DK91
Rydal Way, Enf. 36 DW44
Rydal Way, Ruis. 58 BW63
Ryde, The, Stai. 112 BH95
Ryde Clo., Wok. 140 BJ121
Ryde Pl., Twick. 101 CJ86
Ryde Vale Rd. SW12 105 DH89
Rydens Ave., Walt. 113 BV103
Rydens Clo., Walt. 114 BW103
Rydens Gro., Walt. 128 BX105
Rydens Pk., Walt. 114 BX103
Rydens Rd.
Rydens Rd., Walt. 113 BV104
Ryder Clo., Brom. 108 EH92
Ryder Clo. (Bushey), Wat. 30 CB44
Ryder Ct. SW1 9 L2
Ryder Dr. SE16 92 DV78
Ryder Gdns., Rain. 83 FF65
Ryder Ms. E9 64 DW64
Homerton High St.
Ryder St. SW1 9 L2
Ryder St. SW1 77 DJ74
Ryder Yd. SW1 9 L2
Ryders Ter. NW8 76 DC68
Blenheim Ter.
Rydon St. N1 78 DQ67
St. Paul St.
Rydons Clo. SE9 94 EL83
Rydon's La., Couls. 148 DQ120
Rydons Pk., Walt. 113 BT102
Rydon's Wd. Clo., Couls. 148 DQ120
Rydston Clo. N7 77 DM66
Sutterton St.
Rye, The N14 49 DJ45
Rye Clo., Bex. 111 FB86
Rye Cres., Orp. 124 EW102
Rye Fld., Orp. 124 EX103
Rye Hill Est. SE15 92 DW84
Rye Hill Pk. SE15 92 DW84
Rye La. SE15 92 DU82
Rye La., Sev. 153 FE120
Rye Pas. SE15 92 DU83
Rye Rd. SE15 93 DX84
Rye Wk. SW15 103 CX85
Chartfield Ave.
Rye Way, Edg. 46 CM51
Canons Dr.
Ryebridge Clo., Lthd. 143 CG118
Ryebrook Rd., Lthd. 143 CG118
Ryecotes Mead SE21 106 DS88
Ryecroft Ave., Ilf. 53 EP54
Ryecroft Ave., Twick. 100 CB87
Ryecroft Cres., Barn. 33 CV43
Ryecroft Rd. SE13 107 EC85
Ryecroft Rd. SW16 105 DN93
Ryecroft Rd., Orp. 123 ER100
Ryecroft Rd., Sev. 153 FG116
Ryecroft St. SW6 90 DB81
Ryedale SE22 106 DV86
Ryefield Ave., Uxb. 71 BP66
Ryefield Path SW15 103 CU88
Ryefield Rd. SE19 106 DQ93
Ryeland Clo., West Dr. 70 BL72
Ryelands Clo., Cat. 148 DS121
Ryelands Ct., Lthd. 143 CG118
Ryelands Cres. SE12 108 EJ86
Ryelands Pl., Wey. 113 BS104
Ryfold Rd. SW19 104 DA90
Ryhope Rd. N11 49 DH49
Ryland Clo., Felt. 99 BT91
Ryland Ho., Croy. 120 DQ104
Ryland Rd. NW5 77 DH65
Rylandes Rd. NW2 61 CU62
Rylandes Rd., S.Croy. 134 DV109
Rylett Cres. W12 89 CT75
Rylett Rd. W12 89 CT76
Rylston Rd. N13 50 DR48
Rylston Rd. SW6 89 CZ79
Rymer Rd., Croy. 120 DS101
Rymer St. SE24 105 DP86
Rymill St. E16 81 EN74
Rysbrack St. SW3 8 D6
Rysbrack St. SW3 90 DF76
Rythe Ct., T.Ditt. 115 CG101
Rythe Rd., Esher 129 CD106

S

Sabah Ct., Ashf. 98 BN91
Sabbarton St. E16 80 EF72
Victoria Dock Rd.
Sabella Ct. E3 79 DZ68
Mostyn Gro.
Sabine Rd. SW11 90 DF83
Sable Clo., Houns. 86 BW83
Sable St. N1 77 DP66
Canonbury Rd.
Sach Rd. E5 64 DV61
Sackville Ave., Brom. 122 EG102
Sackville Clo., Har. 59 CD62
Sackville Clo., Sev. 155 FH122
Sackville Est. SW16 105 DL90
Sackville Gdns., Ilf. 67 EM60
Sackville Rd., Sutt. 132 DA108
Sackville St. W1 9 L1
Sackville St. W1 77 DJ73
Sackville Way SE22 106 DU88
Dulwich Common
Saddle Yd. W1 77 DH74
Hay's Ms.
Saddlebrook Pk., Sun. 99 BS94
Saddlers Clo., Borwd. 32 CR44
Farriers Way
Saddlers Clo., Pnr. 44 CA51
Saddlers Ms., Wem. 59 CF63
The Boltons
Saddlers Way, Epsom 144 CR119
Saddlescombe Way N12 48 DA50
Sadler Clo., Mitch. 118 DF96
Sadlers Ride, W.Mol. 114 CB97
Saffron Ave. E14 79 ED73
Saffron Clo. NW11 61 CZ57
Saffron Clo., Croy. 119 DL100
Saffron Ct., Felt. 99 BQ87
Staines Rd.
Saffron Hill EC1 6 E6
Saffron Hill EC1 77 DN70
Saffron Rd., Rom. 55 FC54
Saffron St. EC1 6 E6
Saffron Way, Surb. 115 CK102
Sage Clo. E6 81 EM71
Bradley Stone Rd.
Sage St. E1 78 DW73
Cable St.
Sage Way WC1 6 B3
Saigasso Clo. E16 80 EK72
Royal Rd.
Sail St. SE11 10 C8
Sail St. SE11 91 DM77
Sainfoin Rd. SW17 104 DG89
Sainsbury Rd. SE19 106 DS92
St. Agatha's Dr., Kings.T. 102 CM93
St. Agathas Gro., Cars. 118 DF102
St. Agnes Clo. E9 78 DW67
Gore Rd.
St. Agnes Pl. SE11 91 DP79
St. Agnes Well EC1 78 DR70
Old St.
St. Aidans Ct., Bark. 82 EV69
Choats Rd.
St. Aidan's Rd. SE22 106 DV86
St. Aidans Rd. W13 87 CH75
St. Albans Ave. E6 81 EM69
St. Alban's Ave. W4 88 CR76
St. Albans Ave., Felt. 100 BX92
St. Albans Ave., Wey. 112 BN104
St. Albans Clo. NW11 62 DA60
St. Albans Cres. N22 49 DN53
St. Alban's Cres., Wdf.Grn. 52 EG52
St. Alban's Gdns., Tedd. 101 CG92
St. Albans Gro. W8 90 DB76
St. Alban's Gro., Cars. 118 DE101
St. Albans La. NW11 62 DA60
West Heath Dr.
St. Albans La., Abb.L. 15 BT26
St. Albans Ms. W2 4 A6
St. Alban's Pl. N1 77 DP67
St. Albans Rd. NW5 62 DG62
St. Albans Rd. NW10 74 CS67
St. Albans Rd., Barn. 33 CW35
St. Albans Rd., Epp. 26 EX29
St. Albans Rd., Ilf. 67 ET60
St. Alban's Rd., Kings.T. 102 CL93
St. Albans Rd. (Dancers Hill), Pot.B. 33 CV35
St. Albans Rd. (South Mimms), Pot.B. 18 CS30
St. Albans Rd., Rad. 18 CN28
St. Albans Rd. (London Colney), St.Alb. 18 CN28
St. Alban's Rd., Sutt. 131 CZ105
St. Albans Rd., Wat. 29 BV40
St. Alban's Rd., Wdf.Grn. 52 EG52
St. Albans St. SW1 9 M1
St. Albans Ter. W6 89 CY79
Margravine Rd.
St. Albans Twr. E4 51 DZ51
St. Alfege Pas. SE10 93 EC79
St. Alfege Rd. SE7 94 EK79
St. Alphage Gdns. EC2 7 J7
St. Alphage Highwalk EC2 78 DR71
London Wall
St. Alphage Wk., Edg. 46 CQ54
St. Alphege Rd. N9 50 DW45
St. Alphonsus Rd. SW4 91 DK84
St. Amunds Clo. SE6 107 EA91
St. Andrew St. EC4 6 E7
St. Andrew St. EC4 77 DN71
St. Andrews Ave., Horn. 69 FF64
St. Andrews Ave., Wem. 59 CG63
St. Andrew's Clo. N12 48 DC49
Woodside Ave.
St. Andrews Clo. NW2 61 CV62
St. Andrews Clo. SE16 92 DV78
Ryder Dr.
St. Andrew's Clo., Islw. 87 CD81
St. Andrews Clo., Ruis. 58 BX61
St. Andrew's Clo., Shep. 113 BR98
St. Andrews Clo., Stan. 45 CJ54
St. Andrew's Ct. SW18 104 DC89
Waynflete St.
St. Andrews Ct., Wat. 29 BV39
St. Andrews Dr., Orp. 124 EV100
St. Andrews Dr., Stan. 45 CJ53
St. Andrews Gdns., Cob. 128 BW113
St. Andrew's Gro. N16 64 DR60
St. Andrew's Hill EC4 6 G10
St. Andrew's Hill EC4 77 DP73
St. Andrews Ms. N16 64 DS60
St. Andrews Ms. SE3 94 EG80
Mycenae Rd.
St. Andrews Pl. NW1 5 J4
St. Andrews Rd. E11 66 EE58
St. Andrews Rd. E13 80 EH69
St. Andrews Rd. E17 51 DX54
St. Andrews Rd. N9 50 DW45
St. Andrews Rd. NW9 60 CR60
St. Andrews Rd. NW10 75 CV65
St. Andrews Rd. NW11 61 CZ58
St. Andrews Rd. W3 74 CS72
St. Andrews Rd. W7 87 CE75
Church Rd.
St. Andrews Rd. W14 89 CY79
St. Andrews Rd., Cars. 118 DE104
St. Andrews Rd., Couls. 147 DH116
St. Andrews Rd., Croy. 134 DQ105
Lower Coombe St.
St. Andrews Rd., Enf. 36 DR41
St. Andrews Rd., Ilf. 67 EM59
St. Andrews Rd., Rom. 69 FD58
St. Andrews Rd., Sid. 110 EX90
St. Andrew's Rd., Surb. 115 CK100
St. Andrew's Rd., Uxb. 70 BL67
St. Andrew's Rd., Wat. 47 BX48
Bridlington Rd.
St. Andrews Sq. W11 75 CY72
St. Marks Rd.
St. Andrew's Sq., Surb. 115 CK100
St. Andrews Twr., Sthl. 72 CC73
St. Andrews Wk., Cob. 141 BV115
St. Andrews Way E3 79 EB70
St. Anna Rd., Barn. 33 CX43
Sampson Ave.
St. Annes Ave., Stai. 98 BK87
St. Anne's Clo. N6 62 DG62
Highgate W. Hill
St. Annes Clo. (Cheshunt), Wal.Cr. 22 DU28
St. Anne's Clo., Wat. 44 BW49
St. Anne's Ct. W1 5 M9
St. Annes Gdns. NW10 74 CM69
St. Anne's Ho. N16 64 DS60
St. Annes Pas. E14 79 DZ72
Newell St.
St. Annes Rd. E11 65 ED61
St. Annes Rd., St.Alb. 17 CK27
St. Anne's Rd., Uxb. 56 BJ55
St. Anne's Rd., Wem. 59 CK64
St. Anne's Row E14 79 DZ72
St. Anne's St. E14 79 DZ72
Commercial Rd.
St. Ann's, Bark. 81 EQ67
St. Ann's Cres. SW18 104 DB86
St. Ann's Gdns. NW5 76 DG65
Queens Cres.
St. Ann's Hill SW18 104 DB85
St. Ann's La. SW1 9 N6
St. Ann's Pk. Rd. SW18 104 DC86
St. Ann's Pas. SW13 88 CS83
Cross St.
St. Anns Rd. N9 50 DT47
St. Ann's Rd. N15 63 DP57
St. Ann's Rd. SW13 89 CT82
St. Anns Rd. W11 75 CX73
St. Ann's Rd., Bark. 81 EQ67
Axe St.
St. Ann's Rd., Har. 59 CE58
St. Ann's St. SW1 9 N6
St. Ann's St. SW1 91 DK76
St. Ann's Ter. NW8 76 DD68
St. Anns Vill. W11 75 CX74
St. Anns Way, S.Croy. 133 DP107
St. Anselm's Pl. W1 5 H9
St. Anselms Rd., Hayes 85 BT75
St. Anthonys Ave., Wdf.Grn. 52 EJ51
St. Anthonys Clo. E1 78 DU74
St. Anthonys Clo. SW17 104 DE89
College Gdns.
St. Anthony's Way, Felt. 85 BT84
St. Antony's Rd. E7 80 EH66
St. Arvans Clo., Croy. 120 DS104
St. Asaph Rd. SE4 93 DX83
St. Aubyn's Ave. SW19 103 CZ92
St. Aubyns Ave., Houns. 100 CA85
St. Aubyns Clo., Orp. 123 ET104
St. Aubyns Gdns., Orp. 123 ET103
St. Aubyn's Rd. SE19 106 DT93
St. Audrey Ave., Bexh. 96 FA82
St. Augustine's Ave. W5 74 CL68
St. Augustines Ave., Brom. 122 EL99
St. Augustine's Ave., S.Croy. 134 DQ107
St. Augustines Ave., Wem. 60 CL62
St. Augustine's Path N5 63 DP64
St. Augustines Rd. NW1 77 DK66
St. Augustine's Rd., Belv. 96 EZ77
St. Austell Clo., Edg. 46 CM54
St. Austell Rd. SE13 93 EC82
St. Awdry's Rd., Bark. 81 ER66
St. Awdry's Wk., Bark. 81 EQ66
Station Par.
St. Barnabas Clo., Beck. 121 EC96
St. Barnabas Ct., Har. 44 CC53
St. Barnabas Rd. E17 65 EA58
St. Barnabas Rd., Mitch. 104 DG94
St. Barnabas Rd., Sutt. 132 DD106
St. Barnabas Rd., Wdf.Grn. 52 EH53

St. Barnabas St. SW1 8 G10
St. Barnabas St. SW1 90 DG78
St. Barnabas Ter. E9 65 DX64
St. Barnabas Vill. SW8 91 DL81
St. Bartholomews Clo. SE26 106 DV91
St. Bartholomew's Rd. E6 81 EM68
St. Bejamins Dr., Orp. 138 EW109
St. Benedict's Clo. SW17 104 DG92
Church La.
St. Benet's Clo. SW17 104 DE89
College Gdns.
St. Benet's Gro., Cars. 118 DC101
St. Benet's Pl. EC3 7 L10
St. Bernards, Croy. 120 DS104
St. Bernard's Clo. SE27 106 DR91
St. Gothard Rd.
St. Bernard's Rd. E6 80 EK67
St. Blaise Ave., Brom. 122 EH96
St. Botolph Row EC3 7 P9
St. Botolph St. EC3 7 P8
St. Botolph St. EC3 78 DT72
St. Botolph's Ave., Sev. 154 FG124
St. Botolph's Rd., Sev. 154 FG124
St. Bride St. EC4 6 F8
St. Bride St. EC4 77 DP72
St. Bride's Ave. EC4 77 DP72
New Bri. St.
St. Brides Ave., Edg. 46 CM53
St. Brides Clo., Erith 96 EX75
St. Katherines Rd.
St. Bride's Pas. EC4 6 F9
St. Catherines Clo. SW17 104 DE89
College Gdns.
St. Catherines Dr. SE14 93 DX82
Kitto Rd.
St. Catherines Fm. Ct., Ruis. 57 BQ58
St. Catherine's Ms. SW3 8 D8
St. Catherines Rd. E4 51 EA47
St. Catherines Rd., Ruis. 57 BR57
St. Chads Clo., Surb. 115 CJ101
St. Chad's Gdns., Rom. 68 EY59
St. Chad's Pl. WC1 6 A2
St. Chad's Pl. WC1 77 DL69
St. Chad's Rd., Rom. 68 EY58
St. Chad's St. WC1 6 A2
St. Chad's St. WC1 77 DL69
St. Charles Ct., Wey. 126 BN106
St. Charles Pl. W10 75 CY71
Chesterton Rd.
St. Charles Pl., Wey. 126 BN106
St. Charles Sq. W10 75 CY71
St. Christopher Rd., Uxb. 70 BK71
St. Christopher's Clo., Islw. 87 CE81
St. Christopher's Dr., Hayes 71 BV73
St. Christophers Gdns., Th.Hth. 119 DN97
St. Christophers Ms., Wall. 133 DJ106
St. Christopher's Pl. W1 4 G8
St. Clair Dr., Wor.Pk. 117 CV104
St. Clair Rd. E13 80 EH68
St. Claire Clo., Ilf. 53 EM54
St. Clair's Rd., Croy. 120 DT103
St. Clare St. EC3 7 P9
St. Clement Clo., Uxb. 70 BK72
St. Clements Ct. EC4 78 DR73
Clements La.
St. Clements Ct. N7 77 DN65
Arundel Sq.
St. Clements Heights SE26 106 DU90
St. Clement's La. WC2 6 C9
St. Clements St. N1 77 DN65
St. Clements St. N7 77 DN65
St. Cloud Rd. SE27 106 DQ91
St. Crispins Clo. NW3 62 DE63
St. Crispins Clo., Sthl. 72 BZ72
St. Cross St. EC1 6 E6
St. Cross St. EC1 77 DN71
St. Cuthberts Gdns., Pnr. 44 BZ52
Westfield Pk.
St. Cuthberts Rd. N13 49 DN51
St. Cuthberts Rd. NW2 75 CZ65
St. Cyprian's St. SW17 104 DF91
St. David Clo., Uxb. 70 BK71
St. Davids, Couls. 147 DM117
St. Davids Clo., Wem. 60 CQ62
St. David's Clo., W.Wick. 121 EB101
St. David's Ct. E17 65 EC55
St. Davids Dr., Edg. 46 CM53
St. Davids Pl. NW4 61 CV59
St. Davids Rd., Swan. 111 FF93
St. Denis Rd. SE27 106 DR91
St. Dionis Rd. SW6 89 CZ82
St. Donatts Rd. SE14 93 DZ81
St. Dunstan's All. EC3 11 M1
St. Dunstans Ave. W3 74 CR73
St. Dunstans Clo., Hayes 85 BT77
St. Dunstan's Ct. EC4 77 DN72
Fleet St.
St. Dunstans Gdns. W3 74 CR73
St. Dunstans Ave.
St. Dunstan's Hill EC3 11 M1
St. Dunstan's Hill EC3 78 DS73
St. Dunstan's Hill, Sutt. 131 CY106
St. Dunstan's La. EC3 11 M1
St. Dunstan's La., Beck. 121 EC100
St. Dunstan's Rd. E7 80 EJ65
St. Dunstans Rd. SE25 120 DT98
St. Dunstans Rd. W6 89 CX78
St. Dunstans Rd. W7 87 CE75
St. Dunstan's Rd., Felt. 99 BT90
St. Dunstans Rd., Houns. 85 BV82
St. Edith Clo., Epsom 144 CN116
Dorking Rd.
St. Edmunds Ave., Ruis. 57 BR58
St. Edmunds Clo. NW8 76 DF67
St. Edmunds Ter.
St. Edmunds Clo. SW17 104 DE89
College Gdns.
St. Edmunds Clo., Erith 96 EX75
St. Katherines Rd.
St. Edmunds Dr., Stan. 45 CG53
St. Edmund's La., Twick. 100 CB87
St. Edmunds Rd. N9 50 DU45
St. Edmunds Rd., Ilf. 67 EM58
St. Edmunds Ter. NW8 76 DE68
St. Edwards Clo. NW11 62 DA58
St. Edwards Clo., Croy. 135 ED111
St. Edwards Way, Rom. 69 FD57
St. Egberts Way E4 51 EC46
St. Elizabeth Dr., Epsom 144 CN116
Dorking Rd.
St. Elmo Rd. W12 75 CT74
St. Elmos Rd. SE16 93 DX75
St. Erkenwald Ms., Bark. 81 ER67
St. Erkenwald Rd.
St. Erkenwald Rd., Bark. 81 ER67
St. Ermin's Hill SW1 9 M6
St. Ervans Rd. W10 75 CZ71
St. Fabian Twr. E4 51 DZ51
St. Faiths Clo., Enf. 36 DQ39
St. Faith's Rd. SE21 105 DP88
St. Fidelis Rd., Erith 97 FD77
St. Fillans Rd. SE6 107 EC88
St. Francis Clo., Orp. 123 ES100
St. Francis Clo., Pot.B. 20 DC33
St. Francis Clo., Wat. 43 BV46
St. Francis Rd. SE22 92 DS84
St. Francis Rd., Erith 97 FD77
West St.
St. Francis Twr. E4 51 DZ51
St. Gabriel's Clo. E11 66 EH60
St. Gabriels Rd. NW2 61 CX64
St. George St. W1 5 J10
St. George St. W1 77 DH73
St. Georges Ave. E7 80 EH66
St. Georges Ave. N7 63 DK63
St. Georges Ave. NW9 60 CQ56
St. George's Ave. W5 87 CK75
St. Georges Ave., Sthl. 72 BZ73
St. George's Ave., Wey. 127 BP107
St. Georges Circ. SE1 10 F6
St. Georges Circ. SE1 91 DP76
St. Georges Clo. NW11 61 CZ58
St. George's Clo. SW8 91 DJ81
Patmore Est.
St. Georges Clo., Wem. 59 CG62
St. George's Clo., Wey. 127 BQ106
St. Georges Ct. E6 81 EM70
St. Georges Ct. EC4 6 F8
St. Georges Ct. SW7 90 DC76
Gloucester Rd.
St. George's Dr. SW1 9 J9
St. George's Dr. SW1 91 DH77
St. Georges Dr., Uxb. 56 BM62
St. Georges Dr., Wat. 44 BY48
St. Georges Flds. W2 4 C9
St. Georges Flds. W2 76 DE72
St. Georges Gdns., Epsom 131 CT114
Lynwood Rd.
St. George's Gdns., Surb. 116 CP103
Hamilton Ave.
St. Georges Gro. SW17 104 DD90
St. Georges Gro. Est. SW17 104 DD90
St. Georges Ind. Est. N17 49 DP52
St. Georges La. EC3 7 L10
St. George's Lo., Wey. 127 BR106
St. Georges Ms. NW1 76 DF66
Regents Pk. Rd.
St. Georges Pl., Twick. 101 CG88
Church St.
St. Georges Rd. E7 80 EH65
St. Georges Rd. E10 65 EC62
St. Georges Rd. N9 50 DU48
St. Georges Rd. N13 49 DM48
St. Georges Rd. NW11 61 CZ58
St. Georges Rd. SE1 10 E6
St. Georges Rd. SE1 91 DN76
St. George's Rd. SW19 103 CZ94
St. Georges Rd. W4 88 CR75
St. Georges Rd. W7 73 CF74
St. Georges Rd., Add. 126 BJ105
St. George's Rd., Beck. 121 EB95
St. Georges Rd., Brom. 123 EM96
St. Georges Rd., Dag. 68 EY64
St. Georges Rd., Enf. 36 DT38
St. George's Rd., Felt. 100 BX91
St. Georges Rd., Ilf. 67 EM59
St. George's Rd., Kings.T. 102 CN94
St. George's Rd., Mitch. 119 DH97
St. Georges Rd., Orp. 123 ER100
St. Georges Rd., Rich. 88 CM83
St. George's Rd., Sev. 155 FH122
St. George's Rd., Sid. 110 EX93
St. Georges Rd., Swan. 125 FF98
St. Georges Rd., Twick. 101 CH85
St. Georges Rd., Wall. 133 DH106
St. Georges Rd., Wat. 29 BV38
St. George's Rd., Wey. 127 BR107
St. Georges Rd. W., Brom. 122 EL95
St. Georges Sq. E7 80 EH66
St. Georges Sq. E14 79 DY73
St. Georges Sq. SE8 93 DZ77
St. George's Sq. SW1 91 DK78
St. George's Sq., N.Mal. 116 CS97
High St.
St. George's Sq. Ms. SW1 91 DK78
St. Georges Ter. NW1 76 DF66
Regents Pk. Rd.
St. Georges Wk., Croy. 120 DQ104
St. Georges Way SE15 92 DS79
St. Gerards Clo. SW4 105 DJ85
St. German's Pl. SE3 94 EG81
St. Germans Rd. SE23 107 DY88
St. Giles Ave., Dag. 83 FB66
St. Giles Ave., Pot.B. 19 CV32
St. Giles Ave., Uxb. 57 BQ63
St. Giles Clo., Dag. 83 FB66
St. Giles Ave.
St. Giles Clo., Orp. 137 ER106
St. Giles High St. WC2 5 N8
St. Giles High St. WC2 77 DK72
St. Giles Pas. WC2 5 N9
St. Giles Rd. SE5 92 DS80
St. Gilles Ho. E2 79 DX68
Mace St.
St. Gothard Rd. SE27 106 DR91
St. Gregory Clo., Ruis. 58 BW63
St. Helena Rd. SE16 93 DX77
St. Helena St. WC1 6 D3
St. Helens Clo., Uxb. 70 BK71
St. Helens Ct., Epp. 26 EU30
Hemnall St.
St. Helens Ct., Rain. 83 FG70
St. Helens Cres. SW16 119 DM95
St. Helens Rd.
St. Helens Gdns. W10 75 CX71
St. Helens Pl. EC3 7 M8
St. Helens Rd. SW16 119 DM95
St. Helen's Rd. W13 73 CH74
Dane Rd.
St. Helens Rd., Erith 96 EX75
St. Helens Rd., Ilf. 67 EM58
St. Helier Ave., Mord. 118 DC101
St. Heliers Ave., Houns. 100 CA85
St. Heliers Rd. E10 65 EC58
St. Hildas Ave., Ashf. 98 BL92
St. Hildas Clo. NW6 75 CX67
St. Hildas Clo. SW17 104 DE89
St. Hilda's Rd. SW13 89 CV79
St. Hughe's Clo. SW17 104 DE89
College Gdns.
St. Hughs Rd. SE20 120 DV95
Ridsdale Rd.
St. Ivians Dr., Rom. 69 FG55
St. James Ave. E2 78 DW68
St. James Ave. N20 48 DE48
St. James Ave. W13 73 CG74
St. James Ave., Epsom 131 CT111
St. James Ave., Sutt. 132 DA106
St. James Clo. N20 48 DE48
St. James Clo. SE18 95 EQ78
Congleton Gro.
St. James Clo., Barn. 34 DD42
St. James Clo., Epsom 130 CS114
St. James Clo., N.Mal. 117 CT99
St. James Clo., Ruis. 58 BW61
St. James Gdns. W11 75 CY74
St. James Gdns., Wem. 73 CK66
St. James Gate NW1 77 DK66
St. Paul's Cres.
St. James Gro. SW11 90 DF82
Reform St.
St. James Ms. E14 93 EC76
St. James Ms., Wey. 127 BP105
St. James Rd. E15 66 EF64
St. James Rd. N9 50 DV47
Queens Rd.
St. James Rd., Cars. 118 DE104
St. James Rd., Kings.T. 115 CK96
St. James Rd., Mitch. 104 DG94
St. James Rd., Pur. 133 DP113
St. James Rd., Sev. 155 FH122
St. James Rd., Surb. 115 CK100
St. James Rd., Sutt. 132 DA106
St. James Rd. (Cheshunt), Wal.Cr. 22 DQ28
St. James Rd., Wat. 29 BV43
St. James St. W6 89 CW78
St. James Wk. EC1 6 F4
St. James Wk. SE15 92 DT80
Commercial Way
St. James Way, Sid. 110 EY92
St. James's SE14 93 DY81
St. James's Ave., Beck. 121 DY97
St. James's Ave., Hmptn. 100 CC92
St. James's Clo. SW17 104 DF89
St. James's Dr.
St. James's Cotts., Rich. 101 CK85
Paradise Rd.
St. James's Ct. SW1 9 L6
St. James's Ct. SW1 91 DJ76
St. James's Cres. SW9 91 DN83
St. James's Dr. SW12 104 DF88
St. James's Dr. SW17 104 DF88
St. James's La. N10 63 DH56
St. James's Mkt. SW1 9 M1
St. James's Ms. E17 65 DY57
St. James's St.
St. James's Palace SW1 9 L3
St. James's Palace SW1 77 DJ74
St. James's Pk. SW1 9 M6
St. James's Pk. SW1 91 DJ75
St. James's Pk., Croy. 120 DQ101
St. James's Pas. EC3 7 N9
St. James's Pl. SW1 9 K3
St. James's Pl. SW1 77 DJ74
St. James's Rd. SE1 92 DU78
St. James's Rd. SE16 92 DU76
St. James's Rd., Croy. 119 DP101
St. James's Rd., Hmptn. 100 CB92
St. James's Row EC1 6 F4
St. James's Sq. SW1 9 L2
St. James's Sq. SW1 77 DK74
St. James's St. E17 65 DY57
St. James's St. SW1 9 K2
St. James's St. SW1 77 DJ74
St. James's Ter. NW8 76 DF68
Prince Albert Rd.
St. James's Ter. Ms. NW8 76 DF67
St. Jeromes Gro., Hayes 71 BQ72
St. Joans Rd. N9 50 DT46
St. John Fisher Rd., Erith 96 EX76
St. John St. EC1 6 F2
St. John St. EC1 77 DN68
St. Johns Ave. N11 48 DF50
St. John's Ave. NW10 75 CT67
St. John's Ave. SW15 103 CX85
St. Johns Ave., Epsom 131 CT112
St. Johns Ave., Lthd. 143 CH121
St. John's Ch. Rd. E9 64 DW64
St. Johns Clo. N14 35 DJ44
Chase Rd.
St. John's Clo. SW6 90 DA80
Dawes Rd.
St. Johns Clo., Lthd. 143 CJ120
St. John's Clo., Pot.B. 20 DC33
St. Johns Clo., Rain. 83 FG66
St. John's Clo., Uxb. 70 BH67
St. John's Clo., Wem. 60 CL64
St. John's Cotts. SE20 106 DW94
Maple Rd.
St. Johns Cotts., Rich. 88 CL84
Kew Foot Rd.
St. Johns Ct., Buck.H. 52 EH46
St. John's Ct., Islw. 87 CF82
St. Johns Ct., Nthwd. 43 BS53
Murray Rd.
St. John's Cres. SW9 91 DN83
St. Johns Dr. SW18 104 DB88
St. Johns Dr., Walt. 114 BW102
St. John's Est. N1 7 L1
St. John's Est. N1 78 DR68
St. John's Est. SE1 11 P5
St. John's Gdns. W11 75 CY73
St. Johns Gro. N19 63 DJ61
St. Johns Gro. SW13 89 CT82
Terrace Gdns.
St. Johns Gro., Rich. 88 CL84
Kew Foot Rd.
St. John's Hill SW11 90 DD84
St. Johns Hill, Couls. 147 DN117
Canon's Hill
St. Johns Hill, Pur. 147 DN116
St. John's Hill, Sev. 155 FJ123
St. John's Hill Gro. SW11 90 DD84
St. John's La. EC1 6 F5
St. John's La. EC1 77 DP70
St. John's Ms. W11 76 DA72
Ledbury Rd.
St. Johns Par., Sid. 110 EU91
Church Rd.
St. John's Pk. SE3 94 EF80
St. Johns Pas. SE23 106 DW88
Davids Rd.
St. John's Pas. SW19 103 CY93
Ridgway Pl.
St. John's Path EC1 6 F5
St. Johns Pathway SE23 106 DW88
Devonshire Rd.
St. John's Pl. EC1 6 F5
St. John's Rd. E4 51 EB48
St. John's Rd. E6 80 EL67
Ron Leighton Way
St. Johns Rd. E16 80 EG72
St. John's Rd. E17 51 EB54
St. John's Rd. N15 64 DS58
St. Johns Rd. NW11 61 CZ58
St. John's Rd. SE20 106 DW94
St. John's Rd. SW11 90 DE84
St. Johns Rd. SW19 103 CY93
St. John's Rd., Bark. 81 ES67
St. John's Rd., Cars. 118 DE104
St. Johns Rd., Croy. 119 DP104
Sylverdale Rd.
St. Johns Rd., E.Mol. 115 CD98
St. John's Rd., Epp. 25 ET30
St. Johns Rd., Erith 97 FD78
St. John's Rd., Felt. 100 BY91
St. Johns Rd., Har. 59 CF58
St. Johns Rd., Ilf. 67 ER59
St. John's Rd., Islw. 87 CE82
St. Johns Rd., Kings.T. 115 CJ96
St. Johns Rd., Lthd. 143 CJ121
St. Johns Rd., Loug. 39 EM40
St. John's Rd., N.Mal. 116 CQ97
St. Johns Rd., Orp. 123 ER100
St. John's Rd., Rich. 88 CL84
St. Johns Rd., Rom. 55 FC50
St. John's Rd., Sev. 155 FH121
St. John's Rd., Sid. 110 EV91
St. Johns Rd., Sthl. 86 BY76
St. Johns Rd., Sutt. 118 DA103
St. Johns Rd., Uxb. 70 BH67
St. Johns Rd., Wat. 29 BV40
St. John's Rd., Well. 96 EV83
St. John's Rd., Wem. 60 CL64
St. John's Sq. EC1 6 F5
St. Johns Ter. E7 80 EH65
St. Johns Ter. SE18 95 EQ79
St. Johns Ter. SW15 102 CR91
Kingston Vale
St. Johns Ter. W10 75 CX70
Harrow Rd.
St. Johns Ter., Enf. 36 DR37
St. Johns Vale SE8 93 EA82
St. Johns Vill. N19 63 DK61
St. John's Vill. W8 90 DB76
St. Mary's Pl.
St. Johns Way N19 63 DJ61
St. John's Wd. Ct. NW8 4 A3
St. John's Wd. High St. NW8 4 A1
St. John's Wd. High St. NW8 76 DD68
St. John's Wd. Pk. NW8 76 DD67
St. John's Wd. Rd. NW8 76 DD70
St. John's Wd. Ter. NW8 76 DD68
St. Josephs Clo. W10 75 CY71
Bevington Rd.
St. Joseph's Clo., Orp. 137 ET105
St. Joseph's Ct. SE7 94 EH79
St. Josephs Dr., Sthl. 72 BY74
St. Joseph's Gro. NW4 61 CV56
St. Josephs Rd. N9 50 DV45
St. Joseph's Rd., Wal.Cr. 23 DY33
St. Joseph's Vale SE3 93 ED83
St. Jude St. N16 64 DS64
St. Jude's Rd. E2 78 DV68
St. Julians, Sev. 155 FL130
St. Julian's Clo. SW16 105 DN91
St. Julian's Fm. Rd. SE27 105 DN91
St. Julian's Rd. NW6 75 CZ66
St. Justin Clo., Orp. 124 EX97
St. Katharines Prec. NW1 77 DH68
Outer Circle
St. Katharine's Way E1 78 DU74
St. Katherines Rd., Erith 96 EX75
St. Katherine's Row EC3 7 N10
St. Keverne Rd. SE9 108 EL91
St. Kilda Rd. W13 73 CG74
St. Kilda Rd., Orp. 123 ET102
St. Kilda's Rd. N16 64 DR60
St. Kildas Rd., Har. 59 CE58
St. Kitts Ter. SE19 106 DS92
St. Laurence Clo. NW6 75 CX67
St. Laurence Clo., Orp. 124 EX97
Edmunds Ave.
St. Lawrence Clo., Abb.L. 15 BS30
St. Lawrence Clo., Edg. 46 CM52
St. Lawrence Clo., Uxb. 70 BJ71
St. Lawrence Dr., Pnr. 57 BV57
St. Lawrence St. E14 79 EC74
St. Lawrence Ter. W10 75 CY71
St. Lawrence Way SW9 91 DN82
St. Lawrence Way, Cat. 148 DQ121
Coulsdon Rd.
St. Lawrence Way, St.Alb. 16 BZ30
St. Leonards Ave. E4 51 ED51
St. Leonards Ave., Har. 59 CJ57
St. Leonards Clo. (Bushey), Wat. 30 BY42
St. Leonard's Clo., Well. 96 EU83
Hook La.
St. Leonards Ct. N1 7 L2
St. Leonard's Gdns., Houns. 86 BY81
St. Leonards Gdns., Ilf. 67 EQ64
St. Leonards Ri., Orp. 137 ES105
St. Leonards Rd. E14 79 EB71
St. Leonards Rd. NW10 74 CR70
St. Leonard's Rd. SW14 88 CP83
St. Leonards Rd. W13 73 CJ72
St. Leonards Rd., Croy. 119 DP104
St. Leonards Rd., Epsom 145 CW119
St. Leonards Rd., Esher 129 CF107
St. Leonard's Rd., Surb. 115 CK99
St. Leonards Rd., T.Ditt. 115 CG100
St. Leonards Rd., Wal.Abb. 24 EE25
St. Leonards Sq. NW5 76 DG65
St. Leonard's Sq., Surb. 115 CK99
St. Leonard's Rd.
St. Leonards St. E3 79 EB69
St. Leonard's Ter. SW3 90 DF78
St. Leonards Wk. SW16 105 DM94
St. Leonards Way, Horn. 69 FH61
St. Loo Ave. SW3 90 DE79
St. Louis Rd. SE27 106 DQ91
St. Loy's Rd. N17 50 DS54
St. Luke Clo., Uxb. 70 BK72
St. Luke's Ave. SW4 91 DK84
St. Lukes Ave., Enf. 36 DR38
St. Luke's Ave., Ilf. 67 EP64
St. Lukes Clo. EC1 78 DQ70
Old St.
St. Luke's Clo. SE25 120 DV100
St. Lukes Clo., Swan. 125 FD96
St. Luke's Est. EC1 7 K3
St. Luke's Est. EC1 78 DR69
St. Lukes Ms. W11 75 CZ72
Basing St.
St. Lukes Pas., Kings.T. 116 CM95
St. Lukes Rd. W11 75 CZ71
St. Lukes Rd., Uxb. 70 BL66
St. Lukes Rd., Whyt. 148 DT118
Whyteleafe Hill
St. Lukes Sq. E16 80 EF72
St. Luke's St. SW3 8 B10
St. Luke's St. SW3 90 DE78
St. Luke's Yd. W9 75 CZ69
St. Malo Ave. N9 50 DW48
St. Margaret Dr., Epsom 144 CN116
Dorking Rd.
St. Margarets, Bark. 81 EQ67
St. Margarets Ave. N15 63 DP56
St. Margarets Ave. N20 48 DC46
St. Margarets Ave., Ashf. 99 BP92
St. Margarets Ave., Har. 58 CC62
St. Margarets Ave., Sid. 109 ER90
St. Margaret's Ave., Sutt. 117 CY104
St. Margarets Ave., Uxb. 70 BN70
St. Margarets Clo., Orp. 138 EV105
St. Margaret's Ct. SE1 11 K3
St. Margarets Cres. SW15 103 CV85

St. Margaret's Dr., Twick. 101 CH85
St. Margaret's Gro. E11 66 EF62
St. Margaret's Gro. SE18 95 EQ79
St. Margarets Gro., Twick. 101 CG86
St. Margarets La. W8 90 DB76
St. Margarets Pas. SE13 94 EE83
Church Ter.
St. Margarets Rd. E12 66 EJ61
St. Margarets Rd. N17 64 DS55
St. Margaret's Rd. NW10 75 CW69
St. Margarets Rd. SE4 93 DZ84
St. Margarets Rd. W7 87 CE75
St. Margarets Rd., Couls. 147 DH121
St. Margarets Rd., Edg. 46 CP50
St. Margarets Rd., Islw. 87 CH84
St. Margarets Rd., Ruis. 57 BR58
St. Margarets Rd., Twick. 101 CH86
St. Margarets Sq. SE4 93 DZ84
Adelaide Ave.
St. Margaret's St. SW1 9 P5
St. Margaret's St. SW1 91 DL75
St. Margaret's Ter. SE18 95 EQ78
St. Mark St. E1 78 DT72
St. Marks Clo. SE10 93 EC80
Ashburnham Pl.
St. Marks Clo. W11 75 CY72
Lancaster Rd.
St. Mark's Clo., Barn. 34 DB41
St. Marks Cres. NW1 76 DG67
St. Marks Gate E9 79 DZ66
Cadogan Ter.
St. Mark's Gro. SW10 90 DB79
St. Mark's Hill, Surb. 116 CL100
St. Mark's Pl. SW19 103 CZ93
Wimbledon Hill Rd.
St. Marks Pl. W11 75 CY72
St. Marks Ri. E8 64 DT64
St. Marks Rd. SE25 120 DU98
Coventry Rd.
St. Mark's Rd. W5 74 CL74
The Common
St. Marks Rd. W7 87 CE75
St. Marks Rd. W10 75 CX71
St. Marks Rd. W11 75 CY72
St. Marks Rd., Brom. 122 EH97
St. Marks Rd., Enf. 36 DT43
St. Marks Rd., Epsom 145 CW118
St. Marks Rd., Mitch. 118 DF96
St. Mark's Rd., Tedd. 101 CH94
St. Marks Sq. NW1 76 DG67
Regents Pk. Rd.
St. Martin Clo., Uxb. 70 BK72
St. Martins App., Ruis. 57 BS59
St. Martins Ave. E6 80 EK68
St. Martins Ave., Epsom 130 CS114
St. Martin's Clo. NW1 77 DJ67
St. Martins Clo., Enf. 36 DV39
St. Martins Clo., Epsom 130 CS113
Church Rd.
St. Martins Clo., Erith 96 EX75
St. Helens Rd.
St. Martin's Clo., Wat. 44 BW49
Muirfield Rd.
St. Martin's Clo., West Dr. 84 BK76
St. Martin's Rd.
St. Martin's Ct. WC2 5 P10
St. Martin's Ct., Ashf. 98 BJ92
St. Martins Dr., Walt. 114 BW104
St. Martins Est. SW2 105 DN88
St. Martin's La. WC2 5 P10
St. Martin's La. WC2 77 DL73
St. Martins Meadow, West. 152 EW123
St. Martin's Pl. WC2 9 P1
St. Martin's Pl. WC2 77 DL73
St. Martins Rd. N9 50 DV47
St. Martin's Rd. SW9 91 DM82
St. Martin's Rd., West Dr. 84 BJ76
St. Martin's St. WC2 9 N1
St. Martins Way SW17 104 DC90
St. Martin's-le-Grand EC1 7 H8
St. Martin's-le-Grand EC1 78 DQ72
St. Mary Abbots Pl. W8 89 CZ76
St. Mary Abbots Ter. W14 89 CZ76
St. Mary at Hill EC3 11 M1
St. Mary at Hill EC3 78 DS73
St. Mary Ave., Wall. 118 DG104
St. Mary Axe EC3 7 M9
St. Mary Axe EC3 78 DS72
St. Mary Rd. E17 65 EA56
St. Mary St. SE18 95 EN77
St. Marychurch St. SE16 92 DW75
St. Marys, Bark. 81 ER67
St. Marys App. E12 67 EM64
St. Marys Ave. E11 66 EH58
St. Mary's Ave. N3 47 CY54
St. Mary's Ave., Brom. 122 EE97
St. Mary's Ave., Nthwd. 43 BS50
St. Mary's Ave., Sthl. 86 CA77
St. Mary's Ave., Stai. 98 BK87
St. Mary's Ave., Tedd. 101 CF93
St. Marys Clo. N17 50 DU53
Kemble Rd.
St. Marys Clo., Chess. 130 CM108
St. Marys Clo., Epsom 131 CU108
St. Mary's Clo., Lthd. 143 CD123
St. Marys Clo., Orp. 124 EV96
St. Mary's Clo., Stai. 98 BK87
St. Mary's Clo., Sun. 113 BU98
Green Way
St. Mary's Clo., Uxb. 56 BH55
St. Marys Clo., Wat. 29 BV42
St. Marys Ct. E6 81 EM70
St. Mary's Ct. SE7 94 EK80
St. Mary's Ct. W5 87 CK75
St. Mary's Rd.
St. Mary's Cres. NW4 61 CV55
St. Mary's Cres., Hayes 71 BT73
St. Marys Cres., Islw. 87 CD80
St. Marys Cres., Stai. 98 BK87
St. Marys Dr., Felt. 99 BQ87
St. Mary's Dr., Sev. 154 FE123
St. Mary's Gdns. SE11 10 E8
St. Mary's Gdns. SE11 91 DN77
St. Mary's Gate W8 90 DB76
St. Marys Grn. N2 62 DC55
Thomas More Way
St. Marys Grn., West. 150 EJ118
St. Mary's Gro. N1 77 DP65
St. Mary's Gro. SW13 89 CV83
St. Mary's Gro. W4 88 CP79
St. Mary's Gro., Rich. 88 CM84
St. Marys Gro., West. 150 EJ118
St. Marys Mans. W2 76 DD71
St. Mary's Ms. NW6 76 DB66
Priory Rd.
St. Mary's Ms., Rich. 101 CJ90
Back La.
St. Mary's Mt., Cat. 148 DT124
St. Marys Path N1 77 DP67
St. Mary's Pl. SE9 109 EN86
Eltham High St.
St. Mary's Pl. W5 87 CK75
St. Mary's Rd.
St. Mary's Pl. W8 90 DB76
St. Marys Rd. E10 65 EC62
St. Marys Rd. E13 80 EH68
St. Marys Rd. N8 63 DL56
High St.
St. Marys Rd. N9 50 DV46
St. Mary's Rd. NW10 74 CS67
St. Marys Rd. NW11 61 CY59
St. Mary's Rd. SE15 92 DW81
St. Mary's Rd. SE25 120 DS97
St. Mary's Rd. (Wimbledon) SW19 103 CY92
St. Mary's Rd. W5 87 CK75
St. Mary's Rd., Barn. 48 DF45
St. Marys Rd., Bex. 111 FC88
St. Marys Rd., E.Mol. 115 CD99
St. Mary's Rd., Hayes 71 BT73
St. Marys Rd., Ilf. 67 EQ61
St. Marys Rd., Lthd. 143 CH122
St. Marys Rd., S.Croy. 134 DR110
St. Marys Rd., Surb. 115 CK100
St. Marys Rd. (Long Ditton), Surb. 115 CJ101
St. Marys Rd., Swan. 125 FD98
St. Mary's Rd. (Harefield), Uxb. 56 BH56
St. Mary's Rd. (Cheshunt), Wal.Cr. 22 DW29
St. Marys Rd., Wat. 29 BV42
St. Marys Rd., Wey. 127 BR105
St. Mary's Rd., Wor.Pk. 116 CS103
St. Marys Sq. W2 76 DD71
St. Mary's Sq. W5 87 CK75
St. Mary's Rd.
St. Marys Ter. W2 76 DD71
St. Marys Vw., Har. 59 CJ57
St. Mary's Wk. SE11 10 E8
St. Mary's Wk. SE11 91 DN77
St. Mary's Wk., Hayes 71 BT73
St. Mary's Rd.
St. Mary's Way, Chig. 53 EN50
St. Matthew Clo., Uxb. 70 BK72
St. Matthew St. SW1 9 M7
St. Matthew's Ave., Surb. 116 CL102
St. Matthews Clo., Rain. 83 FG66
St. Matthews Clo., Wat. 30 BX44
St. Matthew's Dr., Brom. 123 EM97
St. Matthew's Rd. SW2 91 DM84
St. Matthews Rd. W5 74 CL74
The Common
St. Matthew's Row E2 78 DU69
St. Matthias Clo. NW9 61 CT57
St. Maur Rd. SW6 89 CZ81
St. Merryn Clo. SE18 95 ER80
St. Michael's All. EC3 7 L9
St. Michaels Ave. N9 50 DW45
St. Michael's Ave., Wem. 74 CN65
St. Michaels Clo. E16 80 EK71
Fulmer Rd.
St. Michael's Clo. N3 47 CZ54
St. Michaels Clo. N12 48 DE50
St. Michaels Clo., Brom. 122 EL97
St. Michaels Clo., Erith 96 EX75
St. Helens Rd.
St. Michaels Clo., Walt. 114 BW103
St. Michaels Clo., Wor.Pk. 117 CT103
St. Michaels Cres., Pnr. 58 BY58
St. Michaels Dr., Wat. 15 BV33
St. Michaels Gdns. W10 75 CY71
St. Lawrence Ter.
St. Michaels Rd. NW2 61 CW63
St. Michael's Rd. SW9 91 DM82
St. Michael's Rd., Ashf. 98 BN92
St. Michaels Rd., Cat. 148 DR122
St. Michaels Rd., Croy. 120 DQ102
St. Michaels Rd., Wall. 133 DJ107
St. Michaels Rd., Well. 96 EV83
St. Michaels St. W2 4 A8
St. Michaels St. W2 76 DD72
St. Michaels Ter. N22 49 DL54
St. Michaels Way, Pot.B. 20 DB30
St. Mildred's Ct. EC2 7 K9
St. Mildreds Rd. SE12 108 EF87
St. Monica's Rd., Tad. 145 CZ121
St. Neots Clo., Borwd. 32 CN38
St. Nicholas Ave., Horn. 69 FG62
St. Nicholas Clo., Borwd. 31 CK44
St. Nicholas Clo., Uxb. 70 BK72
St. Nicholas Dr., Sev. 155 FJ126
St. Nicholas Dr., Shep. 112 BN101
St. Nicholas Glebe SW17 104 DG92
St. Nicholas Hill, Lthd. 143 CH122
St. Nicholas Rd. SE18 95 ET78
St. Nicholas Rd., Sutt. 132 DB106
St. Nicholas Rd., T.Ditt. 115 CF100
St. Nicholas St. SE8 93 DZ81
Lucas St.
St. Nicholas Way, Sutt. 132 DB105
St. Nicolas La., Chis. 122 EL95
St. Ninian's Ct. N20 48 DF48
St. Norbert Grn. SE4 93 DY84
St. Norbert Rd. SE4 107 DX85
St. Normans Way, Epsom 131 CU110
St. Olaf's Rd. SW6 89 CY80
St. Olaves Ct. EC2 7 K9
St. Olave's Est. SE1 11 N4
St. Olaves Gdns. SE11 10 D8
St. Olaves Rd. E6 81 EN67
St. Olave's Wk. SW16 119 DJ96
St. Olav's Sq. SE16 92 DW75
Albion St.
St. Oswald's Pl. SE11 91 DM78
St. Oswald's Rd. SW16 119 DP95
St. Oswulf St. SW1 9 N9
St. Pancras Way NW1 77 DJ66
St. Patrick's Ct., Wdf.Grn. 52 EE52
St. Paul Clo., Uxb. 70 BK71
St. Paul St. N1 78 DQ67
St. Paul's All. EC4 77 DP72
St. Paul's Chyd.
St. Paul's Ave. NW2 75 CW65
St. Paul's Ave. SE16 79 DX74
St. Pauls Ave., Har. 60 CM57
St. Paul's Chyd. EC4 6 G9
St. Paul's Chyd. EC4 77 DP72
St. Paul's Clo. SE7 94 EK78
St. Paul's Clo. W5 88 CM75
St. Pauls Clo., Add. 126 BG106
St. Pauls Clo., Ashf. 99 BQ92
St. Paul's Clo., Cars. 118 DE102
St. Pauls Clo., Chess. 129 CK105
St. Pauls Clo., Hayes 85 BR78
St. Paul's Clo., Houns. 86 BY82
St. Paul's Ct. W14 89 CX77
Colet Gdns.
St. Pauls Ctyd. SE8 93 EA80
Deptford High St.
St. Pauls Cray Rd., Chis. 123 ER95
St. Paul's Cres. NW1 77 DK66
St. Pauls Dr. E15 65 ED64
St. Paul's Ms. NW1 77 DK66
St. Paul's Cres.
St. Paul's Pl. N1 78 DR65
St. Pauls Ri. N13 49 DP51
St. Paul's Rd. N1 77 DP65
St. Paul's Rd. N17 50 DU52
St. Paul's Rd., Bark. 81 EQ67
St. Paul's Rd., Brent. 87 CK79
St. Paul's Rd., Erith 97 FC80
St. Paul's Rd., Rich. 88 CM83
St. Paul's Rd., Th.Hth. 120 DQ97
St. Paul's Shrubbery N1 78 DR65
St. Pauls Sq., Brom. 122 EG96
St. Paul's Ter. SE17 91 DP79
Westcott Rd.
St. Pauls Twr. E10 65 EC59
St. Pauls Wk., Kings.T. 102 CN94
Alexandra Rd.
St. Paul's Way E3 79 DZ71
St. Paul's Way E14 79 DZ71
St. Paul's Way N3 48 DB52
St. Pauls Way, Wal.Abb. 23 ED33
Rochford Ave.
St. Pauls Way, Wat. 30 BW40
St. Pauls Wd. Hill, Orp. 123 ES96
St. Peter's All. EC3 7 L9
St. Peter's Ave. E2 78 DU68
St. Peter's Clo.
St. Peter's Ave. E17 66 EE56
St. Peters Ave. N18 50 DU49
St. Peter's Clo. E2 78 DU68
St. Peters Clo. SW17 104 DE89
College Gdns.
St. Peters Clo., Barn. 33 CV43
St. Peters Clo., Chis. 109 ER94
St. Peters Clo., Ilf. 67 ES56
St. Peters Clo., Rick. 42 BH46
St. Peters Clo., Ruis. 58 BX61
St. Peters Clo. (Bushey), Wat. 45 CD46
St. Peter's Ct. NW4 61 CW57
St. Peters Ct. SE3 94 EF84
Eltham Rd.
St. Peters Ct. SE4 93 DZ82
Wickham Rd.
St. Peters Ct., W.Mol. 114 CA98
St. Peter's Gdns. SE27 105 DN90
St. Peter's Gro. W6 89 CU77
St. Peters La., Orp. 124 EU96
St. Peter's Pl. W9 76 DB70
Shirland Rd.
St. Peters Rd. N9 50 DV46
St. Peter's Rd. W6 89 CU78
St. Peter's Rd., Croy. 134 DR105
St. Peters Rd., Kings.T. 116 CN96
St. Peters Rd., Sthl. 72 CA71
St. Peters Rd., Twick. 101 CH85
St. Peters Rd., Uxb. 70 BK71
St. Peter's Rd., W.Mol. 114 CA98
St. Peter's Sq. E2 78 DU68
St. Peter's Clo.
St. Peter's Sq. W6 89 CU78
St. Peters St. N1 77 DP67
St. Peter's St., S.Croy. 134 DR106
St. Peters Ter. SW6 89 CZ80
St. Peter's Vill. W6 89 CU77
St. Peter's Way N1 78 DS66
St. Peters Way W5 73 CK71
St. Peters Way, Hayes 85 BR78
St. Petersburgh Ms. W2 76 DB73
St. Petersburgh Pl. W2 76 DB73
St. Philip Sq. SW8 91 DH82
St. Philip St. SW8 91 DH82
St. Philip's Ave., Wor.Pk. 117 CV103
St. Philip's Rd. E8 78 DU65
St. Philips Rd., Surb. 115 CK100
St. Philip's Way N1 78 DQ67
Linton St.
St. Pinnock Ave., Stai. 112 BG95
St. Quentin Rd., Well. 95 ET83
St. Quintin Ave. W10 75 CW71
St. Quintin Gdns. W10 75 CW71
St. Quintin Rd. E13 80 EH68
St. Raphael's Way NW10 60 CQ64
St. Regis Clo. N10 49 DH54
St. Ronan's Clo., Barn. 34 DD38
St. Ronans Cres., Wdf.Grn. 52 EG52
St. Rule St. SW8 91 DJ82
St. Saviour's Est. SE1 11 P6
St. Saviour's Est. SE1 92 DT76
St. Saviour's Rd. SW2 105 DM85
St. Saviours Rd., Croy. 119 DP100
St. Silas Pl. NW5 76 DG65
St. Silas St. Est. NW5 76 DG65
St. Simon's Ave. SW15 103 CW85
St. Stephens Ave. E17 65 EC57
St. Stephens Ave. W12 89 CV75
St. Stephens Ave. W13 73 CH72
St. Stephen's Ave., Ash. 144 CL116
St. Stephens Clo. E17 65 EB57
St. Stephens Clo. NW8 76 DE67
St. Stephens Clo., Sthl. 72 CA71
St. Stephens Cres. W2 76 DA72
Talbot Rd.
St. Stephens Cres., Th.Hth. 119 DN97
St. Stephens Gdn. Est. W2 76 DA72
Shrewsbury Rd.
St. Stephens Gdns. SW15 103 CZ85
Manfred Rd.
St. Stephens Gdns. W2 76 DA72
St. Stephens Gdns., Twick. 101 CJ86
St. Stephens Gro. SE13 93 EC83
St. Stephens Ms. W2 76 DA71
Chepstow Rd.
St. Stephen's Par. E7 80 EJ66
Green St.
St. Stephen's Pas., Twick. 101 CJ86
Richmond Rd.
St. Stephen's Rd. E3 79 DY67
St. Stephens Rd. E6 80 EJ66
St. Stephen's Rd. E17 65 EB57
Grove Rd.
St. Stephens Rd. W13 73 CH72
St. Stephen's Rd., Barn. 33 CX43
St. Stephens Rd., Enf. 37 DX37
St. Stephens Rd., Houns. 100 CA86
St. Stephens Rd., West Dr. 70 BK74
St. Stephens Row EC4 7 K10
St. Stephens Ter. SW8 91 DM80
St. Stephen's Wk. SW7 90 DC77
Southwell Gdns.
St. Swithin's La. EC4 7 K10
St. Swithin's La. EC4 78 DR73
St. Swithun's Rd. SE13 107 ED85
St. Theresa Clo., Epsom 144 CN116
Dorking Rd.
St. Theresa's Rd., Felt. 85 BT84
St. Thomas' Clo., Surb. 116 CM102
St. Thomas Ct., Bex. 110 FA87
St. Thomas Dr., Orp. 123 EQ102
St. Thomas' Dr., Pnr. 44 BY53
St. Thomas Gdns., Ilf. 81 EQ65
St. Thomas Pl. NW1 77 DK66
Maiden La.
St. Thomas Rd. E16 80 EG72
St. Thomas Rd. N14 49 DK45
St. Thomas Rd., Belv. 97 FC75
St. Thomas St. SE1 11 L3
St. Thomas St. SE1 78 DR74
St. Thomas's Clo., Wal.Abb. 24 EH33
St. Thomas's Gdns. NW5 76 DG65
Queens Cres.
St. Thomas's Pl. E9 78 DW66
St. Thomas's Rd. N4 63 DN61
St. Thomas's Rd. NW10 74 CS67
St. Thomas's Rd. W4 88 CQ79
St. Thomas's Sq. E9 78 DW66
St. Thomas's Way SW6 89 CZ80
St. Timothy's Ms., Brom. 122 EH95
Wharton Rd.
St. Ursula Gro., Pnr. 58 BX57
St. Ursula Rd., Sthl. 72 CA72
St. Vincent Clo. SE27 105 DP92
St. Vincent Rd., Twick. 100 CC86
St. Vincent Rd., Walt. 113 BV104
St. Vincent St. W1 4 G7
St. Vincents Way, Pot.B. 20 DC33
St. Wilfrids Clo., Barn. 34 DD43
East Barnet Rd.
St. Wilfrids Rd., Barn. 34 DD43
East Barnet Rd.
St. Winefride's Ave. E12 67 EM64
St. Winifreds, Ken. 148 DQ115
St. Winifreds Clo., Chig. 53 EQ50
St. Winifreds Rd., Tedd. 101 CH93
St. Winifred's Rd., West. 151 EM118
Saints Clo. SE27 105 DP91
Wolfington Rd.
Saints Dr. E7 66 EK64
Saints La., Rick. 42 BN45
Salamanca Pl. SE1 10 B9
Salamanca St. SE1 10 B9
Salamanca St. SE1 91 DM77
Salamander Clo., Kings.T. 101 CJ92
Salamons Way, Rain. 83 FE72
Salcombe Dr., Mord. 117 CX102
Salcombe Dr., Rom. 68 EZ58
Salcombe Gdns. NW7 47 CW51
Salcombe Pk., Loug. 38 EK43
High Rd.
Salcombe Rd. E17 65 DZ59
Salcombe Rd. N16 64 DS64
Salcombe Rd., Ashf. 98 BL91
Salcombe Way, Hayes 71 BS69
Portland Rd.
Salcombe Way, Ruis. 57 BU61
Salcot Cres., Croy. 135 EC110
Salcott Rd. SW11 104 DE85
Salcott Rd., Croy. 119 DL104
Sale Pl. W2 4 B7
Sale Pl. W2 76 DE72
Sale St. E2 78 DU70
Salehurst Clo., Har. 60 CL57
Salehurst Rd. SE4 107 DZ86
Salem Pl., Croy. 120 DQ104
Salem Rd. W2 76 DB73
Salford Rd. SW2 105 DK88
Salhouse Clo. SE28 82 EW72
Rollesby Way
Salisbury Ave. N3 61 CZ55
Salisbury Ave., Bark. 81 ER66
Salisbury Ave., Sutt. 131 CZ107
Salisbury Ave., Swan. 125 FG98
Salisbury Clo. SE17 11 K8
Salisbury Clo., Pot.B. 20 DC32
Salisbury Clo., Wor.Pk. 117 CT104
Salisbury Ct. EC4 6 E9
Salisbury Ct. EC4 77 DP72
Salisbury Cres. (Cheshunt), Wal.Cr. 23 DX32
Salisbury Gdns. SW19 103 CY94
Salisbury Gdns., Buck.H. 52 EK47
Salisbury Hall Gdns. E4 51 EA51
Salisbury Ho. E14 79 EB72
Hobday St.
Salisbury Ms. SW6 89 CZ80
Dawes Rd.
Salisbury Pl. SW9 91 DP80
Salisbury Pl. W1 4 D6
Salisbury Pl. W1 76 DF71
Salisbury Pl., W.Byf. 126 BJ111
Salisbury Rd. E4 51 EA48
Salisbury Rd. E7 80 EG65
Salisbury Rd. E10 65 EC61
Salisbury Rd. E12 66 EK64
Salisbury Rd. E17 65 EC57
Salisbury Rd. N4 63 DP57
Salisbury Rd. N9 50 DU48
Salisbury Rd. N22 49 DP53
Salisbury Rd. SE25 120 DU100
Salisbury Rd. SW19 103 CY94
Salisbury Rd. W13 87 CG75
Salisbury Rd., Bans. 132 DB114
Salisbury Rd., Barn. 33 CY41
Salisbury Rd., Bex. 110 FA88
Salisbury Rd., Brom. 122 EL99
Salisbury Rd., Cars. 132 DF107
Salisbury Rd., Dag. 83 FB65
Salisbury Rd., Enf. 37 DZ37
Salisbury Rd., Felt. 100 BW88
Salisbury Rd., Har. 59 CD57
Salisbury Rd., Houns. 86 BW83
Salisbury Rd. (Heathrow Airport), Houns. 99 BQ85
Salisbury Rd., Ilf. 67 ES61
Salisbury Rd., N.Mal. 116 CR97
Salisbury Rd., Pnr. 57 BU56
Salisbury Rd., Rich. 88 CL84
Salisbury Rd., Rom. 69 FH57
Salisbury Rd., Sthl. 86 BY77
Salisbury Rd., Uxb. 70 BH68
Salisbury Rd., Wat. 29 BV38
Salisbury Rd., Wor.Pk. 130 CR105
Salisbury Sq. EC4 6 E9
Salisbury St. NW8 4 B5
Salisbury St. NW8 76 DE70
Salisbury St. W3 88 CQ75
Salisbury Ter. SE15 92 DW83
Salisbury Wk. N19 63 DJ61
Salix Clo., Sun. 99 BV94
Oak Gro.
Salliesfield, Twick. 101 CD86
Salmen Rd. E13 80 EF68
Salmon La. E14 79 DY72
Salmon Rd., Belv. 96 FA78
Salmon St. E14 79 DZ72
Salmon La.
Salmon St. NW9 60 CP60
Salmond Clo., Stan. 45 CG51
Robb Rd.
Salmons La., Cat. 148 DS120
Salmons La., Whyt. 148 DS120
Salmons La. W., Cat. 148 DS120
Salmons Rd. N9 50 DU46
Salmons Rd., Chess. 129 CK107
Salomons Rd. E13 80 EJ71
Chalk Rd.
Salop Rd. E17 65 DX58
Salt Box Hill, West. 136 EH113
Saltash Clo., Sutt. 131 CZ105
Saltash Rd., Ilf. 53 ER52
Saltash Rd., Well. 96 EW81

Saltcoats Rd. W4 88 CS75
Saltcroft Clo., Wem. 60 CP60
Salter Rd. SE16 79 DX74
Salter St. E14 79 EA73
Salter St. NW10 75 CU69
Salterford Rd. SW17 104 DG93
Salters Gdns., Wat. 29 BU39
Salters Hall Ct. EC4 7 K10
Salters Hill SE19 106 DR92
Salters Rd. E17 65 ED56
Salters Rd. W10 75 CX70
Salterton Rd. N7 63 DL62
Saltford Clo., Erith 97 FE78
Salthill Clo., Uxb. 56 BL64
Saltley Clo. E6 80 EL72
Dunnock Rd.
Saltoun Rd. SW2 91 DN84
Saltram Clo. N15 64 DT56
Saltram Cres. W9 75 CZ69
Saltwell St. E14 79 EA73
Saltwood Clo., Orp. 138 EW105
Saltwood Gro. SE17 92 DR78
Merrow St.
Salusbury Rd. NW6 75 CY67
Salvia Gdns., Grnf. 73 CG68
Selborne Gdns.
Salvin Rd. SW15 89 CX83
Salway Clo., Wdf.Grn. 52 EF52
Salway Pl. E15 80 EE65
Broadway
Salway Rd. E15 79 ED65
Sam Bartram Clo. SE7 94 EJ78
Samantha Clo. E17 65 DZ59
Samantha Ms., Rom. (Havering-atte-Bower) 55 FE48
Sambruck Ms. SE6 107 EB89
Inchmery Rd.
Samels Ct. W6 89 CU78
South Black Lion La.
Samford St. NW8 4 B5
Samford St. NW8 76 DE70
Samos Rd. SE20 120 DV96
Sampson Ave., Barn. 33 CX43
Sampson Clo., Belv. 96 EX76
Carrill Way
Sampson St. E1 78 DU74
Sampsons Ct., Shep. 113 BQ99
Linden Way
Samson St. E13 80 EJ68
Samuel Clo. E8 78 DT67
Pownall Rd.
Samuel Clo. SE14 93 DX79
Samuel Clo. SE18 94 EL77
Samuel Gray Gdns., Kings.T. 115 CK95
Skerne Rd.
Samuel Johnson Clo. SW16 105 DN91
Curtis Fld. Rd.
Samuel Lewis Trust Dws. E8 64 DU63
Amhurst Rd.
Samuel Lewis Trust Dws. N1 77 DN66
Liverpool Rd.
Samuel Lewis Trust Dws. SW3 8 B9
Samuel Lewis Trust Dws. SW6 90 DA80
Samuel St. SE18 95 EM77
Samuels Clo. W6 89 CU78
South Black Lion La.
Sancroft Clo. NW2 61 CV62
Sancroft Rd., Har. 45 CF54
Sancroft St. SE11 10 C10
Sancroft St. SE11 91 DM78
Sanctuary, The SW1 9 N6
Sanctuary, The, Bex. 110 EX86
Sanctuary, The, Mord. 118 DB100
Sanctuary Clo., Uxb. 42 BJ52
Sanctuary Rd., Houns. 98 BN86
Sanctuary St. SE1 11 J5
Sandal Rd. N18 50 DU50
Sandal Rd., N.Mal. 116 CR99
Sandal St. E15 80 EE67
Sandale Clo. N16 64 DR62
Stoke Newington Ch. St.
Sandall Clo. W5 74 CL70
Sandall Rd. NW5 77 DJ65
Sandall Rd. W5 74 CL70
Sandalwood Clo. E1 79 DY70
Solebay St.
Sandalwood Rd., Felt. 99 BV90
Sandbach Pl. SE18 95 EQ78
Sandbanks, Felt. 99 BS88
Sandbourne Ave. SW19 118 DB96
Sandbourne Rd. SE4 93 DY82
Sandbrook Clo. NW7 46 CR51
Sandbrook Rd. N16 64 DS62
Sandby Grn. SE9 94 EL83
Sandcliff Rd., Erith 97 FD77
Sandcroft Clo. N13 49 DP51
St. Pauls Ri.
Sandell St. SE1 10 D4
Sandells Ave., Ashf. 99 BQ91
Sanders Clo., Hmptn. 100 CC92
Sanders Clo., St.Alb. 17 CK27
Sanders La. NW7 47 CW52
Sanders Way N19 63 DK60
Sussex Way
Sandersfield Gdns., Bans. 146 DA115
Sandersfield Rd., Bans. 146 DB115
Sanderson Ave., Sev. 138 FA110
Sanderson Clo. NW5 63 DH63
Sanderson Rd., Uxb. 70 BJ65
Sanderstead Ave. NW2 61 CY61
Sanderstead Clo. SW12 105 DJ87
Atkins Rd.
Sanderstead Ct. Ave., S.Croy. 134 DU113
Sanderstead Hill, S.Croy. 134 DS111
Sanderstead Rd. E10 65 DY60
Sanderstead Rd., Orp. 124 EV100
Sanderstead Rd., S.Croy. 134 DR108
Sandes Pl., Lthd. 143 CG118
Sandfield Gdns., Th.Hth. 119 DP97
Sandfield Ind. Est., Hmptn. 114 BZ95
Sandfield Pas., Th.Hth. 120 DQ97
Sandfield Rd., Th.Hth. 119 DP97
Sandford Ave. N22 50 DQ53
Sandford Ave., Loug. 39 EP41
Sandford Clo. E6 81 EM70
Sandford Ct. N16 64 DS60
Sandford La. N16 64 DT61
Lawrence Bldgs.
Sandford Rd. E6 80 EL69
Sandford Rd., Bexh. 96 EY84
Sandford Rd., Brom. 122 EG97
Sandford St. SW6 90 DB80
King's Rd.
Sandgate Clo., Rom. 69 FC59
Sandgate La. SW18 104 DE88
Sandgate Rd., Well. 96 EW80
Sandgate St. SE15 92 DV79
Sandham Pt. SE18 95 EP77
Troy Ct.
Sandhills, Wall. 133 DK105
Sandhills Meadow, Shep. 113 BQ101
Sandhurst Ave., Har. 58 CB58
Sandhurst Ave., Surb. 116 CP101
Sandhurst Clo. NW9 60 CN55
Sandhurst Clo., S.Croy. 134 DS109
Sandhurst Dr., Ilf. 67 ET63
Sandhurst Rd. N9 36 DW44
Sandhurst Rd. NW9 60 CN55
Sandhurst Rd. SE6 107 ED88
Sandhurst Rd., Bex. 110 EX85
Sandhurst Rd., Orp. 124 EU104
Sandhurst Rd., Sid. 109 ET90
Sandhurst Way, S.Croy. 134 DS108
Sandiford Rd., Sutt. 117 CZ103
Sandiland Cres., Brom. 122 EF103
Sandilands, Croy. 120 DU103
Sandilands, Sev. 154 FD122
Sandilands Rd. SW6 90 DB81
Sandison St. SE15 92 DT83
Sandland St. WC1 6 C7
Sandland St. WC1 77 DM71
Sandlands Gro., Tad. 145 CU123
Sandlands Rd., Tad. 145 CU123
Sandling Ri. SE9 109 EN90
Sandlings, The N22 49 DN54
Sandmere Rd. SW4 91 DL84
Sandon Clo., Esher 115 CD101
Sandon Rd. (Cheshunt), Wal.Cr. 22 DW30
Sandow Cres., Hayes 85 BT76
Sandown Ave., Dag. 83 FC65
Sandown Ave., Esher 128 CC106
Sandown Clo., Houns. 85 BU81
Sandown Dr., Cars. 132 DG109
Sandown Gate, Esher 115 CD104
Sandown Ind. Pk., Esher 114 CA103
Sandown Rd. SE25 120 DV99
Sandown Rd., Couls. 146 DG116
Sandown Rd., Esher 128 CC105
Sandown Rd., Wat. 30 BW38
Sandown Way, Nthlt. 72 BY65
Sandpiper Clo. E17 51 DX53
Sandpiper Clo. SE16 93 DZ75
Sandpiper Dr., Erith 97 FH80
Wallhouse Rd.
Sandpiper Rd., S.Croy. 135 DX111
Sandpiper Way, Orp. 124 EX98
Sandpit Pl. SE7 94 EL78
Sandpit Rd., Brom. 108 EE92
Sandpits Rd., Croy. 135 DX105
Sandpits Rd., Rich. 101 CK89
Sandra Clo. N22 50 DQ53
New Rd.
Sandra Clo., Houns. 100 CB85
Sandridge Clo., Har. 59 CE56
Sandridge Ct. N4 64 DQ62
Queens Dr.
Sandridge St. N19 63 DJ61
Sandringham Ave. SW20 117 CY95
Sandringham Clo. SW19 103 CX88
Sandringham Clo., Enf. 36 DS40
Sandringham Clo., Ilf. 67 EQ55
Sandringham Gdns.
Sandringham Clo., Wok. 140 BG116
Sandringham Ct. W9 76 DC69
Maida Vale
Sandringham Cres., Har. 58 CA61
Sandringham Dr., Ashf. 98 BK91
Sandringham Dr., Well. 95 ES82
Sandringham Gdns. N8 63 DL58
Sandringham Gdns. N12 48 DC51
Sandringham Gdns., Houns. 85 BU81
Sandringham Gdns., Ilf. 67 EQ55
Sandringham Ms. W5 73 CK73
High St.
Sandringham Rd. E7 66 EJ64
Sandringham Rd. E8 64 DT64
Sandringham Rd. E10 65 ED58
Sandringham Rd. N22 64 DQ55
Sandringham Rd. NW2 75 CV65
Sandringham Rd. NW11 61 CY59
Sandringham Rd., Bark. 81 ET65
Sandringham Rd., Brom. 108 EG92
Sandringham Rd., Houns. 98 BK85
Sandringham Rd., Nthlt. 72 CA66
Sandringham Rd., Pot.B. 20 DB30
Sandringham Rd., Th.Hth. 120 DQ99
Sandringham Rd., Wat. 30 BW37
Sandringham Rd., Wor.Pk. 117 CU104
Sandringham Way, Wal.Cr. 22 DW34
Sandrock Pl., Croy. 135 DX105
Sandrock Rd. SE13 93 EA83
Sandroyd Way, Cob. 128 CA113
Sand's End La. SW6 90 DB81
Sands Way, Wdf.Grn. 53 EM51
Sandstone Pl. N19 63 DH61
Dartmouth Pk. Hill
Sandstone Rd. SE12 108 EH89
Sandtoft Rd. SE7 94 EH79
Sandway Path, Orp. 124 EW98
Okemore Gdns.
Sandway Rd., Orp. 124 EW98
Sandwell Cres. NW6 76 DA65
Sandwich St. WC1 5 P3
Sandwich St. WC1 77 DL69
Sandy Bury, Orp. 123 ER104
Sandy Dr., Cob. 128 CA111
Sandy Dr., Felt. 99 BS88
Sandy Hill Ave. SE18 95 EP78
Sandy Hill Rd. SE18 95 EP78
Sandy Hill Rd., Wall. 133 DJ109
Sandy La., Cob. 128 BZ112
Sandy La., Har. 60 CM58
Sandy La., Kings.T. 115 CH95
Sandy La., Lthd. 128 CB111
Sandy La., Mitch. 118 DG95
Sandy La., Nthwd. 43 BT47
Sandy La., Orp. 124 EU101
Sandy La. (St. Paul's Cray), Orp. 124 EW96
Sandy La., Rich. 101 CJ89
Sandy La., Sev. 155 FJ123
Sandy La., Sid. 110 EX94
Sandy La., Sutt. 131 CY108
Sandy La., Tad. 146 DA123
Sandy La., Tedd. 101 CG94
Sandy La., Walt. 113 BV100
Sandy La. (Bushey), Wat. 30 CC41
Sandy La. (Chobham), Wok. 140 BG116
Sandy La. Est., Rich. 101 CK89
Sandy La. N., Wall. 133 DK107
Sandy La. S., Wall. 133 DK107
Sandy Lo. La., Nthwd. 43 BR47
Sandy Lo. Rd., Rick. 43 BP47
Sandy Lo. Way, Nthwd. 43 BS50
Sandy Ridge, Chis. 109 EN93
Sandy Rd. NW3 62 DB61
Sandy Rd., Add. 126 BG107
Sandy Way, Cob. 128 CA112
Sandy Way, Croy. 121 DZ104
Sandy Way, Walt. 113 BT102
Sandycombe Rd., Felt. 99 BU88
Sandycombe Rd., Twick. 101 CJ86
Sandycoombe Rd., Rich. 88 CN83
Sandycroft SE2 96 EU79
Sandycroft, Epsom 131 CW110
Sandyhill Rd., Ilf. 67 EP63
Sandymount Ave., Stan. 45 CJ50
Sandy's Row E1 7 N7
Sandy's Row E1 78 DS71
Sanford La. N16 64 DT61
Stoke Newington High St.
Sanford St. SE14 93 DY79
Sanford Ter. N16 64 DT61
Sanford Wk. N16 64 DT61
Sanford Ter.
Sanford Wk. SE14 93 DY79
Cold Blow La.
Sanger Ave., Chess. 130 CL106
Sangley Rd. SE6 107 EB87
Sangley Rd. SE25 120 DS98
Sangora Rd. SW11 90 DD84
Sans Wk. EC1 6 E4
Sans Wk. EC1 77 DN70
Sansom Rd. E11 66 EF61
Sansom St. SE5 92 DR80
Santers La., Pot.B. 19 CY33
Santley St. SW4 91 DL84
Santos Rd. SW18 104 DA85
Santway, The, Stan. 45 CE50
Sanway Clo., W.Byf. 126 BL114
Sanway Rd., W.Byf. 126 BL114
Saphora Clo., Orp. 137 ER106
Oleander Clo.
Sapphire Clo. E6 81 EN72
Sapphire Clo., Dag. 68 EW60
Sapphire Rd. SE8 93 DY78
Sara Ct., Beck. 121 EB95
Albemarle Rd.
Saracen Clo., Croy. 120 DR100
Saracen St. E14 79 EA72
Saracen's Head Yd. EC3 7 P9
Sarah Ho. SW15 89 CT84
Arabella Dr.
Sarah St. N1 7 N2
Saratoga Rd. E5 64 DW63
Sardinia St. WC2 6 B9
Sargeant Clo., Uxb. 70 BK69
Ratcliffe Clo.
Sarita Clo., Har. 45 CD54
Sarjant Path SW19 103 CX89
Queensmere Rd.
Sark Clo., Houns. 86 CA80
Sark Wk. E16 80 EH72
Sarnesfield Ho. SE15 92 DV79
Pencraig Way
Sarnesfield Rd., Enf. 36 DR41
Church St.
Sarratt La., Rick. 28 BH40
Sarratt Rd., Rick. 28 BH37
Sarre Rd. NW2 61 CZ64
Sarre Rd., Orp. 124 EW99
Sarsen Ave., Houns. 86 BZ82
Sarsfeld Rd. SW12 104 DF89
Sarsfield Rd., Grnf. 73 CH68
Sartor Rd. SE15 93 DX84
Sarum Grn., Wey. 113 BS104
Satanita Clo. E16 80 EK72
Fulmer Rd.
Satchell Mead NW9 47 CT53
Satchwell Rd. E2 78 DU69
Satis Ct., Epsom 131 CT111
Windmill Ave.
Sauls Grn. E11 66 EE62
Napier Rd.
Saunders Clo. E14 79 DZ73
Limehouse Causeway
Saunders Clo., Wal.Cr. 23 DX27
Welsummer Way
Saunders Ness Rd. E14 93 EC78
Saunders Rd. SE18 95 ET78
Saunders Rd., Uxb. 70 BM66
Saunders St. SE11 10 D8
Saunders Way SE28 82 EV73
Oriole Way
Saunderton Rd., Wem. 59 CH64
Saunton Ave., Hayes 85 BT80
Saunton Rd., Horn. 69 FG60
Savage Gdns. E6 81 EM72
Savage Gdns. EC3 7 N10
Savay Clo., Uxb. 56 BG59
Savay La., Uxb. 56 BG58
Savernake Rd. N9 36 DU44
Savernake Rd. NW3 62 DF63
Savile Clo., N.Mal. 116 CS99
Savile Gdns., Croy. 120 DT103
Savile Row W1 5 K10
Savile Row W1 77 DJ73
Savill Gdns. SW20 117 CU97
Bodnant Gdns.
Savill Row, Wdf.Grn. 52 EF51
Saville Cres., Ashf. 99 BR93
Saville Rd. E16 80 EL74
Saville Rd. W4 88 CR76
Saville Rd., Rom. 68 EZ58
Saville Rd., Twick. 101 CF88
Saville Row, Brom. 122 EF102
Saville Row, Enf. 37 DX40
Green St.
Savona Clo. SW19 103 CY94
Savona Est. SW8 91 DJ80
Savona St. SW8 91 DJ80
Savoy Ave., Hayes 85 BS77
Savoy Bldgs. WC2 10 B1
Savoy Clo. E15 80 EE67
Arthingworth St.
Savoy Clo., Edg. 46 CN50
Savoy Clo., Uxb. 42 BK54
Savoy Ct. WC2 10 A1
Savoy Hill WC2 10 B1
Savoy Pl. WC2 10 A1
Savoy Pl. WC2 77 DL73
Savoy Row WC2 10 B1
Savoy Steps WC2 10 B1
Savoy St. WC2 10 B1
Savoy St. WC2 77 DM73
Savoy Way WC2 10 B1
Sawbill Clo., Hayes 72 BX71
Sawkins Clo. SW19 103 CY89
Sawley Rd. W12 75 CT74
Sawtry Clo., Cars. 118 DD101
Sawtry Way, Borwd. 32 CN38
Sawyer Clo. N9 50 DU47
Lion Rd.
Sawyer St. SE1 11 H4
Sawyer St. SE1 92 DQ75
Sawyers Chase, Rom. 40 EV41
Sawyers Clo., Dag. 83 FC65
Sawyer's Hill, Rich. 102 CM87
Sawyers La., Pot.B. 19 CX34
Sawyers Lawn W13 73 CF72
Saxby Rd. SW2 105 DL87
Saxham Rd., Bark. 81 ET68
Saxlingham Rd. E4 51 ED48
Saxon Ave., Felt. 100 BY89
Saxon Clo. E17 65 EA59
Saxon Clo., Sev. 153 FF117
Saxon Clo., Surb. 115 CK100
Saxon Clo., Uxb. 70 BL71
Saxon Ct., Borwd. 32 CL39
Saxon Dr. W3 74 CP72
Saxon Gdns., Sthl. 72 BY73
Saxon Rd.
Saxon Rd. E3 79 DZ68
Saxon Rd. E6 81 EM70
Saxon Rd. N22 49 DP53
Saxon Rd. SE25 120 DR99
Saxon Rd., Ashf. 99 BR93
Saxon Rd., Brom. 108 EF94
Saxon Rd., Ilf. 81 EP65
Saxon Rd., Sthl. 72 BY74
Saxon Rd., Walt. 114 BX104
Saxon Rd., Wem. 60 CQ62
Saxon Wk., Sid. 110 EW93
Cray Rd.
Saxon Way N14 35 DK44
Saxon Way, Wal.Abb. 23 EC33
Saxon Way, West Dr. 84 BJ79
Saxonbury Ave., Sun. 113 BV97
Saxonbury Clo., Mitch. 118 DD97
Saxonbury Gdns., Surb. 115 CJ102
Saxonfield Clo. SW2 105 DM87
Upper Tulse Hill
Saxons, Tad. 145 CX121
Saxony Par., Hayes 71 BQ71
Saxton Clo. SE13 93 ED83
Saxville Rd., Orp. 124 EV97
Sayers Clo., Lthd. 142 CC124
Sayers Wk., Rich. 102 CM87
Stafford Pl.
Sayes Ct. SE8 93 DZ78
Sayes Ct. St.
Sayes Ct., Add. 126 BJ106
Sayes Ct. Fm. Dr., Add. 126 BH106
Sayes Ct. Rd., Orp. 124 EU97
Sayes Ct. St. SE8 93 DZ79
Scads Hill Clo., Orp. 123 ET100
Scala St. W1 5 L6
Scala St. W1 77 DJ71
Scales Rd. N17 64 DT55
Scammel Way, Wat. 29 BT44
Scampston Ms. W10 75 CX72
Scandrett St. E1 78 DV74
Scarba Wk. N1 78 DR65
Marquess Rd.
Scarborough Clo., Sutt. 131 CZ111
Scarborough Clo., West. 150 EJ118
Scarborough Rd. E11 65 ED60
Scarborough Rd. N4 63 DN59
Scarborough Rd. N9 50 DW45
Scarborough St. E1 78 DT72
West Tenter St.
Scarbrook Rd., Croy. 120 DQ104
Scarle Rd., Wem. 73 CK65
Scarlet Clo., Orp. 124 EV98
Scarlet Rd. SE6 108 EE90
Scarlette Manor Way SW2 105 DN87
Papworth Way
Scarsbrook Rd. SE3 94 EK83
Scarsdale Pl. W8 90 DB76
Wrights La.
Scarsdale Rd., Har. 58 CC62
Scarsdale Vill. W8 90 DA76
Scarth Rd. SW13 89 CT83
Scawen Rd. SE8 93 DY78
Scawfell St. E2 78 DT68
Scaynes Link N12 48 DA50
Sceaux Est. SE5 92 DS81
Sceaux Gdns. SE5 92 DT81
Sceptre Rd. E2 78 DW69
Schofield Wk. SE3 94 EH80
Dornberg Clo.
Scholars Rd. E4 51 EC46
Scholars Rd. SW12 105 DJ88
Scholefield Rd. N19 63 DK61
School Cres., Dart. 97 FF84
School Grn. La., Epp. 27 FC25
School Ho. La., Tedd. 101 CH94
School La. SE23 106 DV89
School La., Add. 126 BG105
School La., Kings.T. 115 CJ95
School Rd.
School La., Lthd. 143 CD123
School La., Pnr. 58 BY56
School La., St.Alb. 16 BZ34
School La. (Seal), Sev. 155 FM121
School La., Shep. 113 BP100
High St.
School La., Surb. 116 CM102
School La., Swan. 125 FH95
School La. (Bushey), Wat. 44 CB45
School La., Well. 96 EV83
School La., Wok. 141 BP122
School Mead, Abb.L. 15 BS32
School Pas., Kings.T. 116 CM96
School Pas., Sthl. 72 BZ74
School Rd. E12 67 EM63
School Rd. NW10 74 CR70
School Rd., Ashf. 99 BP93
School Rd., Chis. 123 EQ95
School Rd., Dag. 82 FA67
School Rd., E.Mol. 115 CD98
School Rd., Hmptn. 100 CC93
School Rd., Houns. 86 CC83
School Rd., Kings.T. 115 CJ95
School Rd., Ong. 27 FF30
School Rd., Pot.B. 20 DC30
School Rd., West Dr. 84 BK79
School Rd. Ave., Hmptn. 100 CC93
School Wk., Sun. 113 BT98
School Way N12 48 DC49
High Rd.
Schoolbell Ms. E3 79 DY68
Arbery Rd.
Schoolhouse Gdns., Loug. 39 EP42
Schoolhouse La. E1 79 DX73
Schoolway N12 48 DD51
Schoolway, Dag. 68 EW62
Schooner Clo. SE16 93 DX75
Kinburn St.
Schubert Rd. SW15 103 CZ85
Schubert Rd., Borwd. 31 CK44
Sclater St. E1 7 P4
Sclater St. E1 78 DT70
Scoble Pl. N16 64 DT63
Amhurst Rd.
Scoles Cres. SW2 105 DN88
Scoresby St. SE1 10 F3
Scoresby St. SE1 77 DP74
Scorton Ave., Grnf. 73 CG68
Scot Gro., Pnr. 44 BX52
Scotch Common W13 73 CG71
Scoter Clo., Wdf.Grn. 52 EH52
Mallards Rd.
Scotia Rd. SW2 105 DM87
Upper Tulse Hill
Scotland Bri. Rd., Add. 126 BG111
Scotland Grn. N17 50 DT54

Shakespeare Sq., Ilf. 53 EQ51
Shakespeare St., Wat. 29 BV38
Shakespeare Twr. EC2 78 DQ71
Beech St.
Shakespeare Way, Felt. 100 BW91
Shakspeare Ms. N16 64 DS63
Shakspeare Wk.
Shakspeare Wk. N16 64 DS63
Shalcomb St. SW10 90 DC79
Shalcross Dr. (Cheshunt), Wal.Cr. 23 DZ30
Shaldon Dr., Mord. 117 CY99
Shaldon Dr., Ruis. 58 BW62
Shaldon Rd., Edg. 46 CM54
Shaldon Way, Walt. 114 BW104
Shalfleet Dr. W10 75 CX73
Shalford Clo., Orp. 137 EQ105
Shalimar Gdns. W3 74 CQ73
Shalimar Rd. W3 74 CQ73
Hereford Rd.
Shallons Rd. SE9 109 EP91
Shalston Vill., Surb. 116 CM100
Shalstone Rd. SW14 88 CP83
Shamrock Clo., Lthd. 143 CD121
Shamrock Rd., Croy. 119 DM100
Shamrock St. SW4 91 DK83
Shamrock Way N14 49 DH46
Shand St. SE1 11 N4
Shand St. SE1 92 DS75
Shandon Rd. SW4 105 DJ86
Shandy St. E1 79 DX71
Shanklin Clo., Wal.Cr. 22 DT29
Hornbeam Way
Shanklin Gdns., Wat. 44 BW49
Shanklin Rd. N8 63 DK57
Shanklin Rd. N15 64 DU56
Shanklin Way SE15 92 DT80
Pentridge St.
Shannon Clo. NW2 61 CX62
Shannon Clo., Sthl. 86 BX78
Shannon Gro. SW9 91 DM84
Shannon Pl. NW8 76 DE68
Allitsen Rd.
Shannon Way, Beck. 107 EB93
Shap Cres., Cars. 118 DF102
Shapland Way N13 49 DM50
Shardcroft Ave. SE24 105 DP85
Shardeloes Rd. SE14 93 DZ82
Sharland Clo., Th.Hth. 119 DN100
Sharman Ct., Sid. 110 EU91
Sharnbrooke Clo., Well. 96 EW83
Sharon Clo., Epsom 130 CQ113
Sharon Clo., Lthd. 142 CA124
Sharon Clo., Surb. 115 CJ102
Sharon Gdns. E9 78 DW67
Sharon Rd. W4 88 CR78
Sharon Rd., Enf. 37 DY40
Sharpe Clo. W7 73 CF71
Templeman Rd.
Sharpleshall St. NW1 76 DF66
Sharpness Clo., Hayes 72 BY71
Sharps La., Ruis. 57 BR60
Sharratt St. SE15 92 DW79
Sharsted St. SE17 91 DP78
Shavers Pl. SW1 9 M1
Shaw Ave., Bark. 82 EY68
Shaw Clo. SE28 82 EV74
Shaw Clo., Epsom 131 CT111
Shaw Clo., Horn. 69 FH60
Shaw Clo., S.Croy. 134 DT112
Shaw Clo. (Cheshunt), Wal.Cr. 22 DW28
Shaw Clo. (Bushey), Wat. 45 CE47
Shaw Cres., S.Croy. 134 DT112
Shaw Dr., Walt. 114 BW101
Shaw Gdns., Bark. 82 EY68
Shaw Rd. SE22 92 DS84
Shaw Rd., Brom. 108 EF90
Shaw Rd., Enf. 37 DX39
Shaw Rd., West. 150 EJ120
Shaw Sq. E17 51 DY53
Shaw Way, Wall. 133 DL108
Shawbrooke Rd. SE9 108 EJ85
Shawbury Rd. SE22 106 DT85
Shawfield Ct., West Dr. 84 BL76
Shawfield Pk., Brom. 122 EK96
Shawfield St. SW3 90 DE78
Shawford Ct. SW15 103 CU87
Shawford Rd., Epsom 130 CR107
Shawley Cres., Epsom 145 CW118
Shawley Way, Epsom 145 CV118
Shaws Cotts. SE23 107 DY90
Shaxton Cres., Croy. 135 EC109
Shearing Dr., Cars. 118 DC101
Stavordale Rd.
Shearling Way N7 77 DL65
Shearman Rd. SE3 94 EF84
Shearsmith Ho. E1 78 DU73
Cable St.
Shearwater Way, Hayes 72 BX72
Shearwood Cres., Dart. 97 FF83
Sheath's La., Lthd. 128 CB113
Sheaveshill Ave. NW9 60 CS56
Sheen Common Dr., Rich. 88 CN84
Sheen Ct., Rich. 88 CN84
Sheen Rd.
Sheen Ct. Rd., Rich. 88 CN84
Sheen Gate Gdns. SW14 88 CQ84
Sheen Gro. N1 77 DN67
Richmond Ave.
Sheen La. SW14 102 CQ85
Sheen Pk., Rich. 88 CL84
Sheen Rd., Orp. 123 ET98
Sheen Rd., Rich. 102 CL85
Sheen Way, Wall. 133 DM106
Sheen Wd. SW14 102 CQ85
Sheendale Rd., Rich. 88 CM84
Sheenewood SE26 106 DV92
Sheep La. E8 78 DV67
Sheep Wk., Epsom 144 CR122
Sheep Wk., Shep. 112 BM101
Sheep Wk. Ms. SW19 103 CY93
Sheepbarn La., Warl. 136 EF112
Sheepcot Dr., Wat. 16 BW34
Sheepcot La., Wat. 15 BU33
Sheepcote Clo., Houns. 85 BU80
Sheepcote Gdns., Uxb. 56 BG58
Sheepcote La. SW11 90 DF82
Sheepcote La., Orp. 124 EZ100
Sheepcote La., Swan. 124 FA98
Sheepcote Rd., Har. 59 CF58
Sheepcotes Rd., Rom. 68 EX56
Sheephouse Way, N.Mal. 116 CR102
Sheerwater Rd. E16 80 EK71
Sheffield Sq. E3 79 DZ69
Malmesbury Rd.
Sheffield St. WC2 6 B9
Sheffield Ter. W8 76 DA74
Shefton Ri., Nthwd. 43 BU52
Sheila Clo., Rom. 55 FB52
Sheila Rd., Rom. 55 FB52
Shelbourne Clo., Pnr. 58 BZ55
Shelbourne Rd. N17 50 DV54
Shelburne Rd. N7 63 DM63
Shelbury Clo., Sid. 110 EU90
Shelbury Rd. SE22 106 DV85
Sheldon Ave. N6 62 DE59
Sheldon Ave., Ilf. 53 EP54
Sheldon Clo. SE12 108 EH85
Sheldon Clo. SE20 120 DV95
Sheldon Clo. (Cheshunt), Wal.Cr. 22 DS26
Sheldon Rd. N18 50 DS49
Sheldon Rd. NW2 61 CX63
Sheldon Rd., Bexh. 96 EZ81
Sheldon Rd., Dag. 82 EY66
Sheldon St., Croy. 120 DQ104
Wandle Rd.
Sheldrake Clo. E16 81 EM74
Newland St.
Sheldrake Pl. W8 90 DA75
Sheldrick Clo. SW19 118 DD96
Shelduck Clo. E15 66 EF64
Sheldwich Ter., Brom. 122 EL100
Shelford Pl. N16 64 DR62
Stoke Newington Ch. St.
Shelford Ri. SE19 106 DT94
Shelford Rd., Barn. 33 CW44
Shelgate Rd. SW11 104 DE85
Shell Clo., Brom. 122 EL100
Shell Rd. SE13 93 EB83
Shellduck Clo. NW9 46 CS54
Swan Dr.
Shelley Ave. E12 80 EL65
Shelley Ave., Grnf. 73 CD69
Shelley Ave., Horn. 69 FF61
Shelley Clo., Bans. 145 CX115
Shelley Clo., Couls. 147 DM117
Shelley Clo., Edg. 46 CN49
Shelley Clo., Grnf. 73 CD69
Shelley Clo., Hayes 71 BU71
Shelley Clo., Nthwd. 43 BT50
Shelley Clo., Orp. 123 ES104
Shelley Cres., Houns. 86 BX81
Shelley Cres., Sthl. 72 BZ72
Shelley Dr., Well. 95 ES81
Shelley Gdns., Wem. 59 CJ61
Shelley Gro., Loug. 39 EM42
Shelley La., Uxb. 42 BG53
Shelley Way SW19 104 DD93
Shelleys La., Sev. 151 ET116
Shellfield Clo., Stai. 98 BG85
Shellgrove Est. N16 64 DS64
Shellness Rd. E5 64 DV64
Shellwood Rd. SW11 90 DF82
Shelmerdine Clo. E3 79 EA71
Shelson Ave., Felt. 99 BT90
Shelton Ave., Warl. 148 DW117
Shelton Clo., Warl. 148 DW117
Shelton Rd. SW19 118 DA95
Shelton St. WC2 5 P9
Shelton St. WC2 77 DL72
Shelvers Grn., Tad. 145 CW121
Shelvers Hill, Tad. 145 CW121
Ashurst Rd.
Shelvers Spur, Tad. 145 CW121
Shelvers Way, Tad. 145 CW121
Shenden Clo., Sev. 155 FJ128
Shenden Way, Sev. 155 FJ128
Shenfield Clo., Couls. 147 DJ119
Woodfield Clo.
Shenfield Ho. SE18 94 EK80
Shooter's Hill Rd.
Shenfield Rd., Wdf.Grn. 52 EH52
Shenfield St. N1 7 N1
Shenfield St. N1 78 DS68
Shenley Ave., Ruis. 57 BT61
Shenley Hill, Rad. 31 CG35
Shenley La., St.Alb. 17 CG25
Shenley Rd. SE5 92 DS81
Shenley Rd., Borwd. 32 CN42
Shenley Rd., Houns. 86 BY81
Shenley Rd., Rad. 17 CH34
Shenleybury, Rad. 17 CK30
Shenleybury Cotts., Rad. 18 CL31
Shenstone Clo., Dart. 97 FD84
Shepcot Ho. N14 35 DJ44
Shepherd Clo., Abb.L. 15 BT31
Jacketts Fld.
Shepherd Mkt. W1 9 H3
Shepherd St. W1 9 H3
Shepherdess Pl. N1 7 J2
Shepherdess Wk. N1 7 J1
Shepherdess Wk. N1 78 DQ68
Shepherds Bush Grn. W12 89 CW75
Shepherds Bush Mkt. W12 89 CW75
Uxbridge Rd.
Shepherds Bush Pl. W12 89 CX75
Shepherds Bush Rd. W6 89 CW77
Shepherds Clo. N6 63 DH58
Shepherds Clo., Lthd. 143 CK124
Shepherds Clo., Orp. 123 ET104
Stapleton Rd.
Shepherds Clo., Rom. 68 EX57
Shepherds Clo., Shep. 113 BP100
Shepherds Clo. (Cowley), Uxb. 70 BJ70
High St.
Shepherds Ct. W12 89 CX75
Shepherds Bush Grn.
Shepherds Grn., Chis. 109 ER94
Shepherds Hill N6 63 DH58
Shepherds La. E9 79 DX65
Shepherds La., Dart. 111 FG88
Shepherds Path, Nthlt. 72 BY65
Fortunes Mead
Shepherds Pl. W1 4 F10
Shepherds Rd., Wat. 29 BT41
Shepherds Wk. NW2 61 CU61
Shepherds Wk. NW3 62 DD63
Shepherds' Wk., Epsom 144 CP121
Shepherds Wk. (Bushey), Wat. 45 CD47
Shepherds Way, Hat. 20 DB27
Shepherds Way, Rick. 42 BH45
Shepherds Way, S.Croy. 135 DX108
Shepiston La., Hayes 85 BR78
Shepiston La., West Dr. 85 BP77
Shepley Clo., Cars. 118 DG104
Shepley Ms., Enf. 37 EA37
Sheppard Clo., Enf. 36 DV38
Sheppard Clo., Kings.T. 116 CL98
Beaufort Rd.
Sheppard Dr. SE16 92 DV78
Sheppard St. E16 80 EF70
Shepperton Business Pk., Shep. 113 BQ99
Shepperton Clo., Borwd. 32 CR39
Shepperton Ct. Dr., Shep. 113 BP99
Shepperton Rd. N1 78 DQ67
Shepperton Rd., Orp. 123 ER100
Shepperton Rd., Shep. 112 BL98
Shepperton Rd., Stai. 112 BJ97
Sheppey Clo., Erith 97 FH80
Sheppey Gdns., Dag. 82 EW66
Sheppey Rd.
Sheppey Rd., Dag. 82 EV66
Sheppey Wk. N1 78 DQ66
Clephane Rd.
Sheppeys La., Abb.L. 15 BS28
Sherard Rd. SE9 108 EL85
Sheraton Business Cen., Grnf. 73 CH68
Sheraton Clo., Borwd. 32 CM43
Sheraton Dr., Epsom 130 CQ113
Sheraton Ms., Wat. 29 BS42
Sheraton St. W1 5 M9
Sherborne Ave., Enf. 36 DW40
Sherborne Ave., Sthl. 86 CA77
Sherborne Clo., Epsom 145 CW117
Sherborne Clo., Hayes 72 BW72
Sherborne Cres., Cars. 118 DE101
Sherborne Gdns. NW9 60 CN55
Sherborne Gdns. W13 73 CH71
Sherborne Gdns., Rom. 54 FA50
Sherborne La. EC4 7 K10
Sherborne Rd., Chess. 130 CL106
Sherborne Rd., Felt. 99 BR87
Sherborne Rd., Orp. 123 ET98
Sherborne Rd., Sutt. 118 DA103
Sherborne St. N1 78 DR67
Sherborne Wk., Lthd. 143 CJ121
Windfield
Sherborne Way, Rick. 29 BP42
Sherboro Rd. N15 64 DT58
Ermine Rd.
Sherbourne Cotts., Wat. 30 BW43
Watford Fld. Rd.
Sherbourne Gdns., Shep. 113 BS101
Windmill Grn.
Sherbrook Gdns. N21 49 DP45
Sherbrooke Clo., Bexh. 96 FA84
Sherbrooke Rd. SW6 89 CY80
Shere Ave., Sutt. 131 CW110
Shere Clo., Chess. 129 CK106
Shere Rd., Ilf. 67 EN57
Sheredan Rd. E4 51 ED50
Sherfield Ave., Rick. 42 BK48
Sherfield Gdns. SW15 103 CT86
Sheridan Clo., Swan. 125 FF97
Willow Ave.
Sheridan Clo., Uxb. 71 BQ70
Alpha Rd.
Sheridan Ct., Houns. 100 BZ85
Vickers Way
Sheridan Cres., Chis. 123 EP96
Sheridan Gdns., Har. 59 CK58
Sheridan Ms. E11 66 EG58
Woodbine Pl.
Sheridan Pl. SW13 89 CT82
Brookwood Ave.
Sheridan Pl., Hmptn. 114 CB95
Sheridan Rd. E7 66 EF62
Sheridan Rd. E12 66 EL64
Sheridan Rd. SW19 117 CZ95
Sheridan Rd., Belv. 96 FA77
Sheridan Rd., Bexh. 96 EY83
Sheridan Rd., Rich. 101 CJ90
Sheridan Rd., Wat. 44 BX45
Sheridan St. E1 78 DV72
Watney St.
Sheridan Ter., Nthlt. 58 CB64
Whitton Ave. W.
Sheridan Wk. NW11 62 DA58
Sheridan Wk., Cars. 132 DF106
Carshalton Pk. Rd.
Sheridan Way, Beck. 121 DZ95
Turners Meadow Way
Sheriff Way, Wat. 15 BU33
Sheringham Ave. E12 67 EM63
Sheringham Ave. N14 35 DK43
Sheringham Ave., Felt. 99 BU90
Sheringham Ave., Rom. 69 FC58
Sheringham Ave., Twick. 100 BZ88
Sheringham Dr., Bark. 67 ET64
Sheringham Rd. N7 77 DM65
Sheringham Rd. SE20 120 DW97
Sheringham Twr., Sthl. 72 CB73
Sherington Ave., Pnr. 44 CA52
Sherington Rd. SE7 94 EH79
Sherland Rd., Twick. 101 CF87
Sherlies Ave., Orp. 123 ES103
Sherlock Ms. W1 4 F6
Sherman Rd., Brom. 122 EG95
Shermanbury Pl., Erith 97 FF80
Betsham Rd.
Shernbroke Rd., Wal.Abb. 24 EF34
Shernhall St. E17 65 EC55
Sherrard Rd. E7 80 EJ65
Sherrard Rd. E12 80 EK65
Sherrards Way, Barn. 34 DA43
Sherrick Grn. Rd. NW10 61 CV64
Sherriff Rd. NW6 76 DA65
Sherrin Rd. E10 65 EA63
Sherringham Ave. N17 50 DU54
Sherrock Gdns. NW4 61 CU56
Sherwin Rd. SE14 93 DX81
Sherwood Ave. E18 66 EH55
Sherwood Ave. SW16 105 DJ94
Sherwood Ave., Grnf. 73 CE65
Sherwood Ave., Hayes 71 BV70
Sherwood Ave., Pot.B. 19 CY32
Sherwood Ave., Ruis. 57 BS58
Sherwood Clo. SW13 89 CV83
Lower Common S.
Sherwood Clo. W13 73 CH74
Sherwood Clo., Bex. 110 EW86
Sherwood Clo., Lthd. 142 CC122
Sherwood Gdns. E14 93 EA77
Sherwood Gdns. SE16 92 DU78
Sherwood Gdns., Bark. 81 ER66
Sherwood Pk. Ave., Sid. 110 EU87
Sherwood Pk. Rd., Mitch. 119 DJ98
Sherwood Pk. Rd., Sutt. 132 DA106
Sherwood Rd. NW4 61 CW55
Sherwood Rd. SW19 103 CZ94
Sherwood Rd., Couls. 147 DJ116
Sherwood Rd., Croy. 120 DV101
Sherwood Rd., Hmptn. 100 CC92
Sherwood Rd., Har. 58 CC61
Sherwood Rd., Ilf. 67 ER56
Sherwood Rd., Well. 95 ES82
Sherwood St. N20 48 DD48
Sherwood St. W1 5 L10
Sherwood Ter. N20 48 DD48
Green Rd.
Sherwood Way, W.Wick. 121 EB103
Sherwoods Rd., Wat. 44 BY45
Shetland Clo., Borwd. 32 CR44
Percheron Rd.
Shetland Rd. E3 79 DZ68
Shewens Rd., Wey. 127 BR105
Shield Dr., Brent. 87 CG79
Shield Rd., Ashf. 99 BQ91
Shieldhall St. SE2 96 EW77
Shifford Path SE23 107 DX90
Shillibeer Pl. W1 4 C7
Shillibeer Wk., Chig. 53 ET48
Shillingford St. N1 77 DP66
Cross St.
Shillitoe Ave., Pot.B. 19 CX32
Shillitoe Rd. N13 49 DP50
Shinfield St. W12 75 CW72
Shingle Ct., Wal.Abb. 24 EG33
Shinglewell Rd., Erith 96 FA79
Shinners Clo. SE25 120 DU99
Stanger Rd.
Ship All. W4 88 CN79
Thames Rd.
Ship and Mermaid Row SE1 11 L4
Ship Hill, West. 150 EJ121
Ship La. SW14 88 CQ83
Ship St. SE8 93 EA81
Ship Tavern Pas. EC3 7 M10
Ship Yd. E14 93 EB78
Napier Ave.
Ship Yd., Wey. 127 BP105
High St.
Shipfield Clo., West. 150 EJ121
Shipka Rd. SW12 105 DH88
Shipman Rd. E16 80 EH72
Shipman Rd. SE23 107 DX89
Shipton Clo., Dag. 68 EX62
Shipton St. E2 78 DT68
Shipwright Rd. SE16 93 DY75
Shirburn Clo. SE23 106 DW87
Tyson Rd.
Shirbutt St. E14 79 EB73
Shire Clo., Brox. 23 DZ26
Groom Rd.
Shire Ct., Epsom 131 CT108
Shire Ct., Erith 96 EX76
St. John Fisher Rd.
Shire Horse Way, Islw. 87 CF83
Shire La., Kes. 136 EL109
Shire La., Orp. 136 EL109
Shire Pl. SW18 104 DC87
Whitehead Clo.
Shirebrook Rd. SE3 94 EK83
Shirehall Clo. NW4 61 CX58
Shirehall Gdns. NW4 61 CX58
Shirehall La. NW4 61 CX58
Shirehall Pk. NW4 61 CX58
Shiremeade, Borwd. 32 CM43
Shires, The, Rich. 102 CL91
Shires Clo., Ash. 143 CK119
Shires Ho., W.Byf. 126 BL113
Eden Gro. Rd.
Shirland Ms. W9 75 CZ69
Shirland Rd. W9 75 CZ69
Shirley Ave., Bex. 110 EX87
Shirley Ave., Couls. 147 DP119
Shirley Ave., Croy. 120 DW102
Shirley Ave., Sutt. 132 DD105
Shirley Ave. (Cheam), Sutt. 131 CZ109
Shirley Ch. Rd., Croy. 120 DW104
Shirley Clo. E17 65 EB57
Addison Rd.
Shirley Clo., Houns. 100 CC85
Shirley Clo. (Cheshunt), Wal.Cr. 22 DW29
Shirley Ct., Croy. 121 DX104
Shirley Cres., Beck. 121 DY98
Shirley Dr., Houns. 100 CC85
Shirley Gdns. W7 73 CF74
Shirley Gdns., Bark. 81 ES65
Shirley Gro. N9 50 DW45
Shirley Gro. SW11 90 DG83
Shirley Heights, Wall. 133 DJ109
Shirley Hills Rd., Croy. 135 DX106
Shirley Ho. Dr. SE7 94 EJ80
Shirley Oaks Rd., Croy. 121 DX102
Shirley Pk. Rd., Croy. 120 DV102
Shirley Rd. E15 80 EE66
Shirley Rd. W4 88 CR75
Shirley Rd., Abb.L. 15 BT32
Shirley Rd., Croy. 120 DV101
Shirley Rd., Enf. 36 DQ41
Shirley Rd., Sid. 109 ES90
Shirley Rd., Wall. 133 DJ109
Shirley St. E16 80 EF72
Shirley Way, Croy. 121 DY104
Shirlock Rd. NW3 62 DF63
Shobden Rd. N17 50 DR53
Shobroke Clo. NW2 61 CW62
Shoe La. EC4 6 E8
Shoe La. EC4 77 DN72
Shoebury Rd. E6 81 EM66
Sholden Gdns., Orp. 124 EW99
Sholto Rd., Houns. 98 BM85
Shonks Mill Rd., Rom. 41 FG37
Shoot Up Hill NW2 61 CY64
Shooters Ave., Har. 59 CJ56
Shooter's Hill SE18 95 EN81
Shooter's Hill, Well. 95 EQ82
Shooter's Hill Rd. SE3 94 EF81
Shooter's Hill Rd. SE10 93 ED81
Shooter's Hill Rd. SE18 94 EK81
Shooters Rd., Enf. 35 DP39
Shord Hill, Ken. 148 DR116
Shore Clo., Felt. 99 BU87
Shore Clo., Hmptn. 100 BY92
Stewart Clo.
Shore Gro., Felt. 100 CA89
Shore Pl. E9 78 DW66
Shore Rd. E9 78 DW66
Shorediche Clo., Uxb. 56 BM62
Shoreditch High St. E1 7 N5
Shoreditch High St. E1 78 DS70
Shoreham Clo. SW18 104 DB85
Ram St.
Shoreham Clo., Bex. 110 EX88
Stansted Cres.
Shoreham Clo., Croy. 120 DW99
Shoreham La., Orp. 138 FA107
Shoreham La., Sev. 154 FF122
Shoreham La. (Halstead), Sev. 138 EZ112
Shoreham Pl., Sev. 139 FG112
Shoreham Rd., Orp. 124 EV95
Shoreham Rd., Sev. 139 FH112
Shoreham Rd. E., Houns. 98 BL85
Shoreham Rd. W., Houns. 98 BL85
Shoreham Way, Brom. 122 EG100
Shorncliffe Rd. SE1 11 P10
Shorncliffe Rd. SE1 92 DT78
Shorndean St. SE6 107 EC88
Shorne Clo., Orp. 124 EX98
Shorne Clo., Sid. 110 EV86
Shornefield Clo., Brom. 123 EN97
Shornells Way SE2 96 EW78
Willrose Cres.
Shorrolds Rd. SW6 89 CZ80
Short Gate N12 47 CZ49
Short Hedges, Houns. 86 CA81
Lampton Ave.
Short Hill, Har. 59 CE60
High St.
Short La., St.Alb. 16 BZ29
Short La., Stai. 98 BM87
Short Path SE18 95 EP79
Westdale Rd.
Short Rd. E11 66 EE61
Short Rd. E15 79 ED67
Short Rd. W4 88 CS79
Short Rd., Houns. 98 BL86
Short St. NW4 61 CW56
New Brent St.
Short St. SE1 10 E4

Short Wall E15 79 ED69
Bisson Rd.
Short Way N12 48 DE51
Short Way SE9 94 EL83
Short Way, Twick. 100 CC87
Shortcroft Rd., Epsom 131 CT108
Shortcrofts Rd., Dag. 82 EZ65
Shorter St. E1 78 DT73
Shortlands W6 89 CX77
Shortlands, Hayes 85 BR79
Shortlands Clo. N18 50 DR48
Shortlands Clo., Belv. 96 EZ76
Shortlands Gdns., Brom. 122 EE96
Shortlands Gro., Brom. 121 ED97
Shortlands Rd. E10 65 EB59
Shortlands Rd., Brom. 121 ED97
Shortlands Rd., Kings.T. 102 CM94
Shortmead Dr. (Cheshunt), Wal.Cr. 23 DY31
Shorts Cft. NW9 60 CP56
Shorts Gdns. WC2 5 P9
Shorts Gdns. WC2 77 DL72
Shorts Rd., Cars. 132 DE105
Shortwood Ave., Stai. 98 BH90
Shortwood Common, Stai. 98 BH91
Shotfield, Wall. 133 DH107
Shott Clo., Sutt. 132 DC106
Turnpike La.
Shottendane Rd. SW6 90 DA81
Shottery Clo. SE9 108 EL90
Shottfield Ave. SW14 88 CS84
Shoulder of Mutton All. E14 79 DY73
Narrow St.
Shouldham St. W1 4 C7
Shouldham St. W1 76 DE71
Showers Way, Hayes 71 BU74
Shrapnel Clo. SE18 94 EL80
Shrapnel Rd. SE9 95 EM83
Shrewsbury Ave. SW14 88 CQ84
Shrewsbury Ave., Har. 60 CL56
Shrewsbury Clo., Surb. 116 CL103
Shrewsbury Ct. EC1 78 DQ70
Whitecross St.
Shrewsbury Cres. NW10 74 CR67
Shrewsbury La. SE18 95 EP81
Shrewsbury Ms. W2 76 DA71
Chepstow Rd.
Shrewsbury Rd. E7 66 EK64
Shrewsbury Rd. N11 49 DJ51
Shrewsbury Rd. W2 76 DA72
Shrewsbury Rd., Beck. 121 DY97
Shrewsbury Rd., Cars. 118 DE100
Shrewsbury St. W10 75 CW70
Shrewsbury Wk., Islw. 87 CG83
South St.
Shrewton Rd. SW17 104 DF94
Shroffold Rd., Brom. 108 EE91
Shropshire Clo., Mitch. 119 DL98
Shropshire Pl. WC1 5 L5
Shropshire Rd. N22 49 DM52
Shroton St. NW1 4 B6
Shroton St. NW1 76 DE71
Shrubberies, The E18 52 EG54
Shrubberies, The, Chig. 53 EQ50
Shrubbery Clo. N1 78 DQ67
St. Paul St.
Shrubbery Gdns. N21 49 DP45
Shrubbery Rd. N9 50 DU48
Shrubbery Rd. SW16 105 DL91
Shrubbery Rd., Sthl. 72 BZ74
Shrubland Gro., Wor.Pk. 117 CW104
Shrubland Rd. E8 78 DT67
Shrubland Rd. E10 65 EA59
Shrubland Rd. E17 65 EA57
Shrubland Rd., Bans. 145 CZ116
Shrublands, Hat. 20 DB26
Shrublands, The, Pot.B. 19 CY33
Shrublands Ave., Croy. 135 EA105
Shrublands Clo. N20 48 DD46
Shrublands Clo. SE26 106 DW90
Shrublands Clo., Chig. 53 EQ51
Shrubs Rd., Rick. 42 BM51
Shrubsall Clo. SE9 108 EL88
Shuna Wk. N1 78 DR65
St. Paul's Rd.
Shurland Ave., Barn. 34 DD44
Shurland Gdns. SE15 92 DT80
Rosemary Rd.
Shurlock Ave., Swan. 125 FD96
Shurlock Dr., Orp. 137 EQ105
Shuters Sq. W14 89 CZ78
Sun Rd.
Shuttle Clo., Sid. 109 ET87
Shuttle Rd., Dart. 97 FG83
Shuttle St. E1 78 DU70
Buxton St.
Shuttlemead, Bex. 110 EZ87
Shuttleworth Rd. SW11 90 DD82
Sibella Rd. SW4 91 DK82
Sibley Clo., Bexh. 110 EY85
Sibley Gro. E12 80 EL66
Sibthorpe Rd. SE12 108 EH86
Sibton Rd., Cars. 118 DE101
Sicilian Ave. WC1 6 A7
Sicklefield Clo. (Cheshunt), Wal.Cr. 22 DT26
Sidbury St. SW6 89 CY81
Sidcup Bypass, Chis. 109 ES91
Sidcup Bypass, Orp. 110 EV93
Sidcup Bypass, Sid. 109 ES91
Sidcup High St., Sid. 110 EU91
Sidcup Hill, Sid. 110 EV91
Sidcup Hill Gdns., Sid. 110 EW92
Sidcup Hill
Sidcup Pl., Sid. 110 EU92
Sidcup Rd. SE9 108 EJ86
Sidcup Rd. SE12 108 EH85
Sidcup Technology Cen., Sid. 110 EX92
Siddons La. NW1 4 E5
Siddons Rd. N17 50 DU53
Siddons Rd. SE23 107 DY89
Siddons Rd., Croy. 119 DN104
Side Rd. E17 65 DZ57
Sidewood Rd. SE9 109 ER88
Sidford Pl. SE1 10 C7
Sidings, The E11 65 EC60
Sidings, The, Loug. 38 EL44
Sidings, The, Stai. 98 BH91
Leacroft
Sidings Ms. N7 63 DN62
Sidmouth Ave., Islw. 87 CE82
Sidmouth Clo., Wat. 43 BV47
Sidmouth Dr., Ruis. 57 BU62
Sidmouth Par. NW2 75 CW66
Sidmouth Rd.
Sidmouth Rd. E10 65 EC62
Sidmouth Rd. NW2 75 CW66
Sidmouth Rd. SE15 92 DT81
Sidmouth Rd., Orp. 124 EV99
Sidmouth Rd., Well. 96 EW80
Sidmouth St. WC1 6 A3
Sidmouth St. WC1 77 DM69
Sidney Ave. N13 49 DM50
Sidney Elson Way E6 81 EN68
Edwin Ave.
Sidney Est. E1 78 DW72
Sidney Gdns., Brent. 87 CJ79
Sidney Gro. EC1 6 F1
Sidney Rd. E7 66 EG62
Sidney Rd. N22 49 DM52
Sidney Rd. SE25 120 DU99
Sidney Rd. SW9 91 DM82
Sidney Rd., Beck. 121 DY96
Sidney Rd., Epp. 39 ER36
Sidney Rd., Har. 58 CC55
Sidney Rd., Stai. 98 BG91
Sidney Rd., Twick. 101 CG86
Sidney Rd., Walt. 113 BU101
Sidney Sq. E1 78 DW71
Sidney St. E1 78 DW71
Sidworth St. E8 78 DV66
Siebert Rd. SE3 94 EG79
Siemens Rd. SE18 94 EK76
Sigdon Rd. E8 64 DU64
Sigers, The, Pnr. 57 BV58
Signmakers Yd. NW1 77 DH67
Delancey St.
Silbury Ave., Mitch. 118 DE95
Silbury St. N1 7 K2
Silchester Rd. W10 75 CX72
Silecroft Rd., Bexh. 96 FA81
Silesia Bldgs. E8 78 DV66
London La.
Silex St. SE1 10 G5
Silex St. SE1 91 DP75
Silk Clo. SE12 108 EG85
Silk Mill Rd., Wat. 43 BV45
Silk Mills Clo., Sev. 155 FJ121
Silk Mills Path SE13 93 EC82
Silk St. EC2 7 J6
Silk St. EC2 78 DQ71
Silkfield Rd. NW9 60 CS57
Silkin Ho., Wat. 44 BW48
Silkmills Sq. E9 79 DZ65
Silkstream Rd., Edg. 46 CQ53
Silsoe Rd. N22 49 DM54
Silver Birch Ave. E4 51 DZ51
Silver Birch Ave., Epp. 26 EY27
Silver Birch Clo. N11 48 DG51
Silver Birch Clo. SE28 82 EU74
Silver Birch Clo., Dart. 111 FE91
Silver Birch Gdns. E6 81 EM70
Silver Birch Ms., Ilf. 53 EQ51
Fencepiece Rd.
Silver Clo. SE14 93 DY80
Southerngate Way
Silver Clo., Har. 45 CD52
Silver Clo., Tad. 145 CY124
Silver Cres. W4 88 CP77
Silver Dell, Wat. 29 BT35
Silver Jubilee Way, Houns. 85 BV82
Silver La., Pur. 133 DK112
Silver La., W.Wick. 121 ED103
Silver Pl. W1 5 L10
Silver Rd. SE13 93 EB83
Elmira St.
Silver Rd. W12 75 CX73
Silver Spring Clo., Erith 97 FB79
Silver St. N18 50 DR49
Silver St., Enf. 36 DR41
Silver St., Rom. 40 EV41
Silver St., Wal.Abb. 23 EC33
Leverton Way
Silver St. (Cheshunt), Wal.Cr. 21 DP30
Silver Tree Clo., Walt. 127 BU105
Silver Trees, St.Alb. 16 BZ30
West Riding
Silver Wk. SE16 79 DZ74
Silver Way, Rom. 69 FB55
Silverbirch Clo., Uxb. 56 BL63
Silverbirch Wk. NW3 76 DG65
Queens Cres.
Silvercliffe Gdns., Barn. 34 DE42
Silverdale SE26 106 DW91
Silverdale, Enf. 35 DL42
Silverdale Ave., Ilf. 67 ES57
Silverdale Ave., Lthd. 128 CC114
Silverdale Ave., Walt. 113 BT104
Silverdale Clo. W7 73 CE74
Cherington Rd.
Silverdale Clo., Nthlt. 58 BZ64
Silverdale Clo., Sutt. 131 CZ105
Silverdale Ct., Stai. 98 BH92
Silverdale Dr. SE9 108 EL89
Silverdale Dr., Horn. 69 FH64
Silverdale Dr., Sun. 113 BV96
Silverdale Gdns., Hayes 85 BU75
Silverdale Rd. E4 51 ED51
Silverdale Rd., Bexh. 97 FB82
Silverdale Rd., Hayes 85 BT75
Silverdale Rd. (Petts Wd.), Orp. 123 EQ98
Silverdale Rd. (St. Paul's Cray), Orp. 124 EU97
Silverdale Rd. (Bushey), Wat. 30 BY43
Silverhall St., Islw. 87 CG83
Silverholme Clo., Har. 60 CL59
Silverland St. E16 81 EM74
Silverleigh Rd., Th.Hth. 119 DM98
Silvermere Ave., Rom. 55 FB51
Silvermere Rd. SE6 107 EB86
Silverst Clo., Nthlt. 72 CB65
Silverstead La., West. 151 ER121
Silverston Way, Stan. 45 CJ51
Silverthorn Gdns. E4 51 EA47
Silverthorne Rd. SW8 91 DH82
Silverton Rd. W6 89 CX79
Silvertown Way E16 80 EE72
Silvertree La., Grnf. 73 CD69
Cowgate Rd.
Silverwood Clo., Beck. 107 EA94
Silverwood Clo., Croy. 135 EA109
Silverwood Clo., Nthwd. 43 BQ53
Silvester Rd. SE22 106 DT85
Silvester St. SE1 11 K5
Silwood Est. SE16 92 DW77
Millender Wk.
Silwood St. SE16 92 DW77
Simla Clo. SE14 93 DY79
Chubworthy St.
Simla Ho. SE1 11 L5
Simmil Rd., Esher 129 CE106
Simmons Clo. N20 48 DE46
Simmons Clo., Chess. 129 CJ107
Merritt Gdns.
Simmons La. E4 51 ED47
Simmons Rd. SE18 95 EP78
Simmons Way N20 48 DE47
Simms Clo., Cars. 118 DE103
Simms Rd. SE1 92 DU77
Simnel Rd. SE12 108 EH87
Simon Clo. W11 75 CZ73
Portobello Rd.
Simonds Rd. E10 65 EA61
Simone Clo., Brom. 122 EK95
Simone Dr., Ken. 148 DQ116
Simons Wk. E15 65 ED64
Waddington St.
Simplemarsh Ct., Add. 126 BH105
Simplemarsh Rd.
Simplemarsh Rd., Add. 126 BG105
Simpson Clo. N21 35 DL43
Simpson Dr. W3 74 CR72
Simpson Rd., Houns. 100 BZ86
Simpson Rd., Rain. 83 FF65
Simpson Rd., Rich. 101 CJ91
Simpson St. SW11 90 DE82
Simpsons Rd. E14 79 EB73
Simpsons Rd., Brom. 122 EG97
Sims Clo., Rom. 69 FF56
Sims Wk. SE3 94 EF84
Lee Rd.
Sinclair Ct., Beck. 107 EA94
Sinclair Dr., Sutt. 132 DB109
Sinclair Gdns. W14 89 CX75
Sinclair Gro. NW11 61 CX58
Sinclair Rd. E4 51 DY50
Sinclair Rd. W14 89 CX75
Sinclare Clo., Enf. 36 DT39
Sinderby Clo., Borwd. 32 CL39
Singapore Rd. W13 73 CG74
Singer St. EC2 7 L3
Single St., West. 151 EP115
Singles Cross La., Sev. 138 EW114
Singleton Clo. SW17 104 DF94
Singleton Clo., Croy. 120 DQ101
St. Saviours Rd.
Singleton Clo., Horn. 69 FF63
Carfax Rd.
Singleton Rd., Dag. 68 EZ64
Singleton Scarp N12 48 DA50
Singret Pl. (Cowley), Uxb. 70 BJ70
High St.
Sinnott Rd. E17 51 DX53
Sion Rd., Twick. 101 CH87
Sipson Clo., West Dr. 84 BN79
Sipson La., Hayes 85 BQ79
Sipson La., West Dr. 84 BN79
Sipson Rd., West Dr. 84 BN78
Sipson Way, West Dr. 84 BN81
Sir Alexander Clo. W3 75 CT74
Sir Alexander Rd. W3 75 CT74
Sir Cyril Black Way SW19 104 DA94
Sir Thomas More Est. SW3 90 DD79
Beaufort St.
Sirdar Rd. N22 63 DP55
Sirdar Rd. W11 75 CX73
Sirdar Rd., Mitch. 104 DG93
Grenfell Rd.
Sirinham Pt. SW8 91 DM79
Sirus Rd., Nthwd. 43 BU50
Sise La. EC4 7 K9
Siskin Clo., Borwd. 32 CN42
Siskin Clo., Wat. 30 BY42
Sisley Rd., Bark. 81 ES67
Sispara Gdns. SW18 103 CZ86
Sissinghurst Rd., Croy. 120 DU101
Sister Mabel's Way SE15 92 DU80
Radnor Rd.
Sisters Ave. SW11 90 DF83
Sistova Rd. SW12 105 DH88
Sisulu Pl. SW9 91 DN83
Sittingbourne Ave., Enf. 36 DR44
Sitwell Gro., Stan. 45 CF50
Sivill Ho. E2 78 DT69
Siviter Way, Dag. 83 FB66
Siward Rd. N17 50 DR53
Siward Rd. SW17 104 DC90
Siward Rd., Brom. 122 EH97
Six Acres Est. N4 63 DN61
Six Bells La., Sev. 155 FJ126
Sixth Ave. E12 67 EM63
Sixth Ave. W10 75 CY69
Sixth Ave., Hayes 71 BT74
Sixth Ave., Wat. 30 BX35
Sixth Cross Rd., Twick. 100 CC90
Skardu Rd. NW2 61 CY64
Skarnings Ct., Wal.Abb. 24 EG33
Skeena Hill SW18 103 CY87
Skeet Hill La., Orp. 124 EX102
Skeffington Rd. E6 81 EM67
Skelbrook St. SW18 104 DB89
Skelgill Rd. SW15 89 CZ84
Skelley Rd. E15 80 EF66
Skelton Clo. E8 78 DT65
Buttermere Wk.
Skelton Rd. E7 80 EG65
Skeltons La. E10 65 EB59
Skelwith Rd. W6 89 CW79
Skenfrith Ho. SE15 92 DV79
Commercial Way
Skerne Rd., Kings.T. 115 CK95
Sketchley Gdns. SE16 93 DX78
Sketty Rd., Enf. 36 DS41
Skibbs La., Orp. 138 EY106
Skid Hill La., Warl. 136 EF113
Skidmore Way, Rick. 42 BL46
Skiers St. E15 80 EE67
Skiffington Clo. SW2 105 DN88
Skillet Hill, Wal.Abb. 38 EH35
Skinner Ct. E2 78 DV68
Parmiter St.
Skinner Pl. SW1 8 F9
Skinner St. EC1 6 E3
Skinner St. EC1 77 DN69
Skinners La. EC4 7 J10
Skinners La., Ash. 143 CK118
Skinners La., Houns. 86 CB81
Skinner's Row SE10 93 EB81
Blackheath Rd.
Skip La., Uxb. 56 BL60
Skipsey Ave. E6 81 EM69
Skipton Dr., Hayes 85 BQ76
Skipworth Rd. E9 78 DW67
Skomer Wk. N1 78 DQ65
Clephane Rd.
Sky Peals Rd., Wdf.Grn. 51 ED52
Skyport Dr., West Dr. 84 BK80
Slade, The SE18 95 ES79
Slade Ct., Rad. 31 CG35
Slade End, Epp. 39 ES36
Slade Gdns., Erith 97 FF81
Slade Grn. Rd., Erith 97 FG80
Slade Ho., Houns. 100 BZ86
Slade Twr. E10 65 EA61
Slade Wk. SE17 91 DP79
Heiron St.
Sladebrook Rd. SE3 94 EK83
Sladedale Rd. SE18 95 ES78
Slades Clo., Enf. 35 DN41
Slades Dr., Chis. 109 EQ90
Slades Gdns., Enf. 35 DN40
Slades Hill, Enf. 35 DN41
Slades Ri., Enf. 35 DN41
Slagrove Pl. SE13 107 EB85
Ladywell Rd.
Slaidburn St. SW10 90 DC79
Slaithwaite Rd. SE13 93 EC84
Slaney Pl. N7 63 DN64
Hornsey Rd.
Slaney Rd., Rom. 69 FE57
Slater Clo. SE18 95 EN78
Woolwich New Rd.
Slattery Rd., Felt. 100 BW88
Sleaford Grn., Wat. 44 BX48
Sleaford St. SW8 91 DJ80
Sledmore Ct., Felt. 99 BS88
Kilross Rd.
Slievemore Clo. SW4 91 DK83
Voltaire Rd.
Slines New Rd., Cat. 149 DX120
Slines Oak Rd., Cat. 149 EA123
Slines Oak Rd., Warl. 149 EA119
Slingsby Pl. WC2 5 P10
Slippers Pl. SE16 92 DV76
Sloane Ave. SW3 8 C9
Sloane Ave. SW3 90 DE77
Sloane Ct. E. SW3 8 F10
Sloane Ct. W. SW3 8 F10
Sloane Ct. W. SW3 90 DG78
Sloane Gdns. SW1 8 F9
Sloane Gdns. SW1 90 DG77
Sloane Gdns., Orp. 123 EQ104
Partridge Dr.
Sloane Sq. SW1 8 E9
Sloane Sq. SW1 90 DF77
Sloane St. SW1 8 E6
Sloane St. SW1 90 DF75
Sloane Ter. SW1 8 E8
Sloane Ter. SW1 90 DF77
Sloane Wk., Croy. 121 DZ100
Slocum Clo. SE28 82 EW73
Woodpecker Rd.
Slough La. NW9 60 CQ57
Sly St. E1 78 DV72
Cannon St. Rd.
Smallberry Ave., Islw. 87 CF82
Smallbrook Ms. W2 76 DD72
Craven Rd.
Smalley Clo. N16 64 DT62
Smalley Rd. Est. N16 64 DT62
Smalley Clo.
Smallholdings Rd., Epsom 131 CW114
Smallwood Rd. SW17 104 DD91
Smardale Rd. SW18 104 DC85
Alma Rd.
Smarden Clo., Belv. 96 FA78
Essenden Rd.
Smarden Gro. SE9 109 EM91
Smart Clo., Rom. 55 FH53
Smart St. E2 79 DX69
Smarts Grn. (Cheshunt), Wal.Cr. 22 DT26
Smarts La., Loug. 38 EK42
Smarts Pl. N18 50 DU50
Fore St.
Smart's Pl. WC2 6 A8
Smeaton Clo., Chess. 129 CK107
Merritt Gdns.
Smeaton Clo., Wal.Abb. 24 EE32
Smeaton Rd. SW18 104 DA87
Smeaton Rd., Wdf.Grn. 53 EM50
Smeaton St. E1 78 DV74
Smedley St. SW4 91 DK82
Smedley St. SW8 91 DK82
Smeed Rd. E3 79 EA66
Smiles Pl. SE13 93 EC82
Smith Clo. SE16 79 DX74
Smith Sq. SW1 9 P7
Smith Sq. SW1 91 DL76
Smith St. SW3 8 D10
Smith St. SW3 90 DF78
Smith St., Surb. 116 CM100
Smith St., Wat. 30 BW42
Smith Ter. SW3 90 DF78
Smitham Bottom La., Pur. 133 DJ111
Smitham Downs Rd., Pur. 133 DK113
Smithfield St. EC1 6 F7
Smithies Ct. E15 65 EC64
Clays La.
Smithies Rd. SE2 96 EV77
Smith's Ct. W1 5 L10
Smiths Fm. Est., Nthlt. 72 CA68
Smiths La. (Cheshunt), Wal.Cr. 22 DR26
Smiths Yd. SW18 104 DC89
Summerley St.
Smith's Yd., Croy. 120 DQ104
St. Georges Wk.
Smithson Rd. N17 50 DR53
Smithwood Clo. SW19 103 CY88
Smithy St. E1 78 DW71
Smock Wk., Croy. 120 DQ100
Smokehouse Yd. EC1 6 G6
Smokehouse Yd. EC1 77 DP71
Smug Oak Business Pk., St.Alb. 16 CB30
Smug Oak La., St.Alb. 16 CB30
Smugglers Way SW18 90 DB84
Smyrks Rd. SE17 92 DS78
Smyrna Rd. NW6 76 DA66
Smythe St. E14 79 EB73
Snag La., Sev. 137 ER112
Snakes La., Barn. 35 DJ41
Snakes La. E., Wdf.Grn. 52 EJ51
Snakes La. W., Wdf.Grn. 52 EG51
Snaresbrook Dr., Stan. 45 CK49
Snaresbrook Rd. E11 66 EE56
Snarsgate St. W10 75 CW71
Sneath Ave. NW11 61 CZ59
Snellings Rd., Walt. 128 BW106
Snells Pk. N18 50 DT51
Sneyd Rd. NW2 61 CW63
Snipe Clo., Erith 97 FH80
Snodland Clo., Orp. 137 EN110
Mill La.
Snow Hill EC1 6 F7
Snow Hill EC1 77 DP71
Snow Hill Ct. EC1 6 G8
Snowbury Rd. SW6 90 DB82
Snowden Ave., Uxb. 71 BP68
Snowden St. EC2 7 M5
Snowden St. EC2 78 DS70
Snowdon Cres., Hayes 85 BQ76
Snowdon Dr. NW9 60 CS58
Snowdown Clo. SE20 121 DX95
Snowdrop Clo., Hmptn. 100 CA93
Gresham Rd.
Snowman Ho. NW6 76 DB66
Snowsfields SE1 11 L4
Snowsfields SE1 92 DR75
Snowshill Rd. E12 66 EL64
Snowy Fielder Waye, Islw. 87 CH82
Soames St. SE15 92 DT83
Soames Wk., N.Mal. 116 CS95
Socket La., Brom. 122 EH100
Soham Rd., Enf. 37 DZ37
Soho Sq. W1 5 M8
Soho Sq. W1 77 DK72
Soho St. W1 5 M8
Sojourner Truth Clo. E8 78 DV65
Richmond Rd.

Stag Ride SW19 103 CT90
Stagbury Ave., Couls. 146 DE118
Stagbury Clo., Couls. 146 DE119
Stagg Hill, Barn. 34 DE36
Stagg Hill, Pot.B. 34 DD35
Staggart Grn., Chig. 54 EU51
Stags Way, Islw. 87 CF79
Stainash Cres., Stai. 98 BH92
Stainash Par., Stai. 98 BH92
Stainbank Rd., Mitch. 119 DH97
Stainby Clo., West Dr. 84 BL76
Stainby Rd. N15 64 DT56
Stainer Rd., Borwd. 31 CK39
Stainer St. SE1 11 L3
Stainer St. SE1 78 DR74
Staines Ave., Sutt. 117 CX103
Staines Bypass, Ashf. 98 BK92
Staines Rd., Felt. 99 BS87
Staines Rd., Houns. 100 BW85
Staines Rd., Ilf. 67 EQ63
Staines Rd., Stai. 98 BG94
Staines Rd., Twick. 100 CA90
Staines Rd. E., Sun. 99 BU94
Staines Rd. W., Ashf. 99 BP93
Staines Rd. W., Sun. 99 BT94
Staines Wk., Sid. 110 EW93
Evry Rd.
Stainford Clo., Ashf. 99 BR92
Stainforth Rd. E17 65 EA56
Stainforth Rd., Ilf. 67 ER59
Staining La. EC2 7 J8
Staining La. EC2 78 DQ72
Stainmore Clo., Chis. 123 ER95
Stains Clo. (Cheshunt), Wal.Cr. 23 DY28
Stainsbury St. E2 78 DW68
Royston St.
Stainsby Pl. E14 79 EA72
Stainsby Rd. E14 79 EA72
Stainton Rd. SE6 107 ED86
Stainton Rd., Enf. 36 DW39
Stairfoot La., Sev. 154 FC122
Staithes Way, Tad. 145 CV120
Stalbridge St. NW1 4 C6
Stalham St. SE16 92 DV76
Stalisfield Pl., Orp. 137 EN110
Mill La.
Stambourne Way SE19 106 DS94
Stambourne Way, W.Wick. 121 EC104
Stamford Brook Ave. W6 89 CT76
Stamford Brook Rd. W6 89 CT76
Stamford Clo. N15 64 DU56
Stamford Clo., Har. 45 CE52
Stamford Clo., Pot.B. 20 DD32
Stamford Clo., Sthl. 72 CA73
Stamford Cotts. SW10 90 DB80
Billing St.
Stamford Ct. W6 89 CT77
Goldhawk Rd.
Stamford Dr., Brom. 122 EF98
Stamford Gdns., Dag. 82 EW66
Stamford Grn. Rd., Epsom 130 CP113
Stamford Gro. E. N16 64 DU60
Oldhill St.
Stamford Gro. W. N16 64 DU60
Oldhill St.
Stamford Hill N16 64 DT61
Stamford Hill Est. N16 64 DT60
Stamford Rd. E6 80 EL67
Stamford Rd. N1 78 DS66
Stamford Rd. N15 64 DU56
Stamford Rd., Dag. 82 EV67
Stamford Rd., Walt. 114 BX104
Kenilworth Dr.
Stamford Rd., Wat. 29 BV40
Stamford St. SE1 10 D3
Stamford St. SE1 77 DN74
Stamp Pl. E2 7 P2
Stamp Pl. E2 78 DT69
Stanard Clo. N16 64 DS59
Stanborough Ave., Borwd. 32 CN37
Stanborough Clo., Borwd. 32 CN38
Stanborough Clo., Hmptn. 100 BZ93
Stanborough Pk., Wat. 29 BV35
Stanborough Pas. E8 78 DT65
Abbot St.
Stanborough Rd., Houns. 87 CD83
Stanbridge Pl. N21 49 DP47
Stanbridge Rd. SW15 89 CW83
Stanbrook Rd. SE2 96 EV75
Stanbury Ave., Wat. 29 BS37
Stanbury Rd. SE15 92 DV81
Stancroft NW9 60 CS57
Standale Gro., Ruis. 57 BQ57
Standard Ind. Est. E16 95 EM75
Standard Pl. EC2 7 N3
Standard Rd. NW10 74 CQ70
Standard Rd., Belv. 96 FA78
Standard Rd., Bexh. 96 EY84
Standard Rd., Enf. 37 DY37
Standard Rd., Houns. 86 BY83
Standard Rd., Orp. 137 EN110
Standen Rd. SW18 103 CZ87
Standfield, Abb.L. 15 BS31
Standfield Gdns., Dag. 82 FA65
Standfield Rd.
Standfield Rd., Dag. 68 FA64
Standish Rd. W6 89 CU77
Standlake Pt. SE23 107 DX90
Stane Clo. SW19 118 DB95
Hayward Clo.
Stane St., Lthd. 144 CM124
Reigate Rd.
Stane Way SE18 94 EL80
Stane Way, Epsom 131 CU110
Stanfield Rd. E3 79 DY68
Stanford Clo., Hmptn. 100 BZ93
Stanford Clo., Rom. 69 FB58
Stanford Clo., Ruis. 57 BQ58
Stanford Clo., Wdf.Grn. 52 EL50
Stanford Ct., Wal.Abb. 24 EG33
Stanford Ho., Bark. 82 EV68
Stanford Pl. SE17 11 M9
Stanford Rd. N11 48 DF50
Stanford Rd. SW16 119 DK96
Stanford Rd. W8 90 DB76
Stanford St. SW1 9 M9
Stanford Way SW16 119 DK96
Stangate Cres., Borwd. 32 CR43
Stangate Gdns., Stan. 45 CH49
Stanger Rd. SE25 120 DU98
Stanham Pl., Dart. 97 FG84
Crayford Way
Stanhope Ave. N3 61 CZ55
Stanhope Ave., Brom. 122 EF102
Stanhope Ave., Har. 45 CD53
Stanhope Clo. SE16 93 DX75
Middleton Dr.
Stanhope Gdns. N4 63 DP58
Stanhope Gdns. N6 63 DH58
Stanhope Gdns. NW7 47 CT50
Stanhope Gdns. SW7 90 DC77
Stanhope Gdns., Dag. 68 EZ62
Stanhope Rd.
Stanhope Gdns., Ilf. 67 EM60
Stanhope Gate W1 8 G2
Stanhope Gate W1 76 DG74
Stanhope Gro., Beck. 121 DZ99
Stanhope Heath, Stai. 98 BJ86
Stanhope Ms. E. SW7 90 DC77
Stanhope Ms. S. SW7 90 DC77
Gloucester Rd.
Stanhope Ms. W. SW7 90 DC77
Stanhope Par. NW1 5 K2
Stanhope Pk. Rd., Grnf. 72 CC70
Stanhope Pl. W2 4 D9
Stanhope Pl. W2 76 DF72
Stanhope Rd. E17 65 EB57
Stanhope Rd. N6 63 DJ58
Stanhope Rd. N12 48 DC50
Stanhope Rd., Barn. 33 CW43
Stanhope Rd., Bexh. 96 EY82
Stanhope Rd., Cars. 132 DG108
Stanhope Rd., Croy. 120 DS104
Stanhope Rd., Dag. 68 EZ61
Stanhope Rd., Grnf. 72 CC71
Stanhope Rd., Rain. 83 FG68
Stanhope Rd., Sid. 110 EU91
Stanhope Rd., Wal.Cr. 23 DY33
Stanhope Row W1 9 H3
Stanhope St. NW1 5 K2
Stanhope St. NW1 77 DJ69
Stanhope Ter. W2 4 A10
Stanhope Ter. W2 76 DD73
Stanhope Way, Sev. 154 FD122
Stanhope Way, Stai. 98 BJ86
Stanier Clo. W14 89 CZ78
Aisgill Ave.
Staniland Dr., Wey. 126 BM111
Stanlake Ms. W12 75 CW74
Stanlake Rd. W12 75 CW74
Stanlake Vill. W12 75 CW74
Stanley Ave., Bark. 81 ET68
Stanley Ave., Beck. 121 EC96
Stanley Ave., Dag. 68 EZ60
Stanley Ave., Grnf. 72 CC67
Stanley Ave., N.Mal. 117 CU99
Stanley Ave., Rom. 69 FG56
Stanley Ave., St.Alb. 16 CA25
Stanley Ave., Wem. 74 CL66
Stanley Clo. SW8 91 DM79
Stanley Clo., Couls. 147 DM117
Stanley Clo., Rom. 69 FG56
Stanley Clo., Uxb. 70 BK67
Stanley Clo., Wem. 74 CL66
Stanley Cres. W11 75 CZ73
Stanley Gdns. NW2 61 CW64
Stanley Gdns. W3 88 CS75
Stanley Gdns. W11 75 CZ73
Stanley Gdns., Borwd. 32 CL39
Stanley Gdns., Mitch. 104 DG93
Ashbourne Rd.
Stanley Gdns., S.Croy. 134 DU112
Stanley Gdns., Wall. 133 DJ107
Stanley Gdns., Walt. 128 BW107
Stanley Gdns. Ms. W11 75 CZ73
Stanley Cres.
Stanley Gdns. Rd., Tedd. 101 CE92
Stanley Gro. SW8 90 DG82
Stanley Gro., Croy. 119 DN100
Stanley Pk. Dr., Wem. 74 CM67
Stanley Pk. Rd., Cars. 132 DE108
Stanley Pk. Rd., Wall. 133 DH107
Stanley Pas. NW1 5 P1
Stanley Rd. E4 51 ED46
Stanley Rd. E10 65 EB58
Stanley Rd. E12 66 EL64
Stanley Rd. E15 79 ED67
Stanley Rd. E18 52 EF53
Stanley Rd. N2 62 DD55
Stanley Rd. N9 50 DT46
Stanley Rd. N10 49 DH52
Stanley Rd. N11 49 DK51
Stanley Rd. N15 63 DP56
Stanley Rd. NW9 61 CU59
West Hendon Bdy.
Stanley Rd. SW14 88 CP84
Stanley Rd. SW19 104 DA94
Stanley Rd. W3 88 CQ76
Stanley Rd., Ashf. 98 BL92
Stanley Rd., Brom. 122 EH98
Stanley Rd., Cars. 132 DG108
Stanley Rd., Croy. 119 DN101
Stanley Rd., Enf. 36 DS41
Stanley Rd., Har. 58 CC61
Stanley Rd., Houns. 86 CC84
Stanley Rd., Ilf. 67 ER61
Stanley Rd., Mitch. 104 DG94
Stanley Rd., Mord. 118 DA98
Stanley Rd., Nthwd. 43 BU53
Stanley Rd., Orp. 124 EU102
Stanley Rd., Sid. 110 EU90
Stanley Rd., Sthl. 72 BY73
Stanley Rd., Sutt. 132 DB107
Stanley Rd., Tedd. 101 CE91
Stanley Rd., Twick. 101 CD90
Stanley Rd., Wat. 30 BW41
Stanley Rd., Wem. 74 CM65
Stanley Rd. N., Rain. 83 FE67
Stanley Rd. S., Rain. 83 FF68
Stanley Sq., Cars. 132 DF109
Stanley St. SE8 93 DZ80
Stanley Ter. N19 63 DL61
Stanley Way, Orp. 124 EV99
Stanleycroft Clo., Islw. 87 CE81
Stanmer St. SW11 90 DE81
Stanmore Gdns., Rich. 88 CM83
Stanmore Gdns., Sutt. 118 DC104
Stanmore Hill, Stan. 45 CG48
Stanmore Pk., Stan. 45 CH51
Stanmore Pl. NW1 77 DH67
Arlington Rd.
Stanmore Rd. E11 66 EF60
Stanmore Rd. N15 63 DP56
Stanmore Rd., Belv. 97 FC77
Stanmore Rd., Rich. 88 CM83
Stanmore Rd., Wat. 29 BV39
Stanmore St. N1 77 DM67
Caledonian Rd.
Stanmore Ter., Beck. 121 EA96
Stanmore Way, Loug. 39 EN39
Stanmount Rd., St.Alb. 16 CA25
Stannard Ms. E8 78 DU65
Stannard Rd.
Stannard Rd. E8 78 DU65
Stannary Pl. SE11 91 DN78
Stannary St.
Stannary St. SE11 91 DN79
Stannet Way, Wall. 133 DJ105
Stannington Path, Borwd. 32 CN39
Warenford Way
Stansfeld Rd. E6 80 EK71
Stansfield Rd. SW9 91 DM83
Stansfield Rd., Houns. 85 BV82
Stansgate Rd., Dag. 68 FA61
Stanstead Clo., Brom. 122 EF99
Stanstead Gro. SE6 107 DZ88
Catford Hill
Stanstead Manor, Sutt. 132 DA107
Stanstead Rd. E11 66 EH57
Stanstead Rd. SE6 107 DZ88
Catford Hill
Stanstead Rd. SE23 107 DX88
Stanstead Rd., Houns. 98 BM86
Stansted Clo., Horn. 83 FH65
Stansted Cres., Bex. 110 EX88
Stanswood Gdns. SE5 92 DS80
Sedgmoor Pl.
Stanthorpe Clo. SW16 105 DL92
Stanthorpe Rd. SW16 105 DL92
Stanton Ave., Tedd. 101 CE92
Stanton Clo., Epsom 130 CP106
Stanton Clo., Orp. 124 EW101
Stanton Clo., Wor.Pk. 117 CX102
Stanton Rd. SE26 107 DZ91
Stanton Way
Stanton Rd. SW13 89 CT82
Stanton Rd. SW20 117 CX95
Stanton Rd., Croy. 120 DQ101
Stanton Sq. SE26 107 DZ91
Stanton Way
Stanton St. SE15 92 DU81
Stanton Way SE26 107 DZ91
Stanway Clo., Chig. 53 ES50
Stanway Ct. N1 78 DS68
Hoxton St.
Stanway Gdns. W3 74 CN74
Stanway Gdns., Edg. 46 CQ51
Stanway Rd., Wal.Abb. 24 EG33
Stanway St. N1 78 DS68
Stanwell Clo., Stai. 98 BK86
Stanwell Gdns., Stai. 98 BK86
Stanwell Moor Rd., Stai. 98 BH90
Stanwell Moor Rd., West Dr. 84 BH81
Stanwell New Rd., Stai. 98 BH90
Stanwell Rd., Ashf. 98 BL89
Stanwell Rd., Felt. 99 BQ87
Stanwick Rd. W14 89 CZ77
Stanworth St. SE1 11 P5
Stanworth St. SE1 92 DT75
Stanwyck Dr., Chig. 53 EQ50
Stanwyck Gdns., Rom. 55 FH50
Stapenhill Rd., Wem. 59 CH62
Staple Clo., Bex. 111 FD90
Staple Inn Bldgs. WC1 6 D7
Staple St. SE1 11 L5
Staple St. SE1 92 DR75
Staplefield Clo. SW2 105 DL88
Staplefield Clo., Pnr. 44 BY52
Stapleford Ave., Ilf. 67 ES57
Stapleford Clo. E4 51 EC48
Stapleford Clo. SW19 103 CY87
Stapleford Clo., Kings.T. 116 CN97
Stapleford Ct., Sev. 154 FF123
Stapleford Gdns., Rom. 54 FA51
Stapleford Rd., Rom. 41 FB43
Stapleford Rd., Wem. 73 CK66
Stapleford Tawney, Ong. 27 FC32
Stapleford Tawney, Rom. 41 FC35
Stapleford Way, Bark. 82 EV69
Staplehurst Rd. SE13 108 EE85
Staplehurst Rd., Cars. 132 DE108
Staples Clo. SE16 79 DY74
Staples Cor. NW2 61 CV60
Staples Cor. Business Pk. NW2 61 CU60
Staples Rd., Loug. 38 EK41
Stapleton Clo., Pot.B. 20 DE31
Stapleton Cres., Rain. 83 FG65
Stapleton Gdns., Croy. 133 DN106
Stapleton Hall Rd. N4 63 DM60
Stapleton Rd. SW17 104 DG90
Stapleton Rd., Bexh. 96 EZ80
Stapleton Rd., Borwd. 32 CN38
Stapleton Rd., Orp. 123 ET104
Stapley Rd., Belv. 96 FA78
Stapylton Rd., Barn. 33 CY41
Star & Garter Hill, Rich. 102 CL88
Star Hill, Dart. 111 FE85
Star Hill Rd., Sev. 152 EZ115
Star La. E16 80 EE70
Star La., Couls. 146 DG122
Star La., Epp. 26 EU30
Star La., Orp. 124 EW98
Star Path, Nthlt. 72 CA68
Brabazon Rd.
Star Pl. E1 78 DT73
Thomas More St.
Star Rd. W14 89 CZ79
Star Rd., Islw. 87 CD82
Star Rd., Uxb. 71 BP70
Star St. E16 80 EF71
Star St. W2 4 A8
Star St. W2 76 DE72
Star Yd. WC2 6 D8
Starboard Way E14 93 EA76
Starch Ho. La., Ilf. 53 ER54
Starcross St. NW1 5 L3
Starcross St. NW1 77 DJ69
Starfield Rd. W12 89 CU75
Starkleigh Way SE16 92 DV78
Egan Way
Starling Clo., Buck.H. 52 EG46
Starling Clo., Pnr. 58 BW55
Starling La. (Cuffley), Pot.B. 21 DM28
Starling Ms. SE28 95 ER75
Whinchat Rd.
Starling Wk., Hmptn. 100 BY93
Oak Ave.
Starlings, The, Lthd. 128 CC113
Starmans Clo., Dag. 82 EY67
Starrock La., Couls. 146 DF120
Starrock Rd., Couls. 147 DH119
Starts Clo., Orp. 123 EN104
Starts Hill Ave., Orp. 137 EP105
Starts Hill Rd., Orp. 123 EN104
Starveall Clo., West Dr. 84 BM76
Starwood Clo., W.Byf. 126 BJ111
State Fm. Ave., Orp. 137 EP105
Staten Gdns., Twick. 101 CF88
Lion Rd.
Statham Gro. N16 64 DQ63
Green Las.
Statham Gro. N18 50 DS50
Station App. E7 66 EH63
Woodford Rd.
Station App. (Snaresbrook) E11 66 EG57
High St.
Station App. N11 49 DH50
Friern Barnet Rd.
Station App. (Woodside Pk.) N12 48 DB49
Holden Rd.
Station App. (Stoke Newington) N16 64 DT61
Stamford Hill
Station App. NW10 75 CT69
Station Rd.
Station App. SE1 10 C5
Station App. SE3 94 EH83
Kidbrooke Pk. Rd.
Station App. (Mottingham) SE9 109 EM88
Station App. (Lower Sydenham) SE26 107 DZ92
Worsley Bri. Rd.
Station App. (Sydenham) SE26 106 DW91
Sydenham Rd.
Station App. SW6 89 CY83
Station App. SW16 105 DK92
Fore St.
Station App. W7 73 CE74
Station App., Ashf. 98 BM91
Station App., Bex. 110 FA87
Bexley High St.
Station App., Bexh. 96 EY82
Avenue Rd.
Station App. (Barnehurst), Bexh. 97 FC82
Station App., Brom. 122 EG102
Station App., Buck.H. 52 EK49
Cherry Tree Ri.
Station App., Chis. 123 EN95
Station App. (Elmstead Wds.), Chis. 108 EL93
Station App., Couls. 147 DK115
Station App. (Chipstead), Couls. 146 DF118
Station App. (Crayford), Dart. 111 FF86
Station App. (Theydon Bois), Epp. 39 ES36
Coppice Row
Station App., Epsom 130 CR113
Station App. (Ewell E.), Epsom 131 CV110
Station App. (Ewell W.), Epsom 131 CT109
Chessington Rd.
Station App. (Stoneleigh), Epsom 131 CT106
Station App. (Hinchley Wd.), Esher 115 CF104
Station App., Grnf. 73 CD66
Station App., Hmptn. 114 CA95
Milton Rd.
Station App., Har. 59 CE59
Station App., Hayes 85 BT75
Station App., Kings.T. 116 CN96
Station App., Lthd. 143 CG121
Station App. (Oxshott), Lthd. 128 CC113
Station App., Loug. 38 EL43
Station App. (Debden), Loug. 39 EQ42
Station App., Nthwd. 43 BS52
Station App., Orp. 123 ET103
Station App. (Chelsfield), Orp. 138 EV106
Station App. (St. Mary Cray), Orp. 124 EV98
Station App., Pnr. 58 BY56
Station App. (Hatch End), Pnr. 44 CA52
Uxbridge Rd.
Station App., Pot.B. 19 CZ32
Wyllyotts Pl.
Station App., Pur. 133 DN111
Whytecliffe Rd. S.
Station App., Rad. 31 CG35
Shenley Hill
Station App., Rich. 88 CN81
Station App., Ruis. 57 BV64
Station App., Shep. 113 BQ99
Station App., Sid. 110 EU89
Station App., S.Croy. 134 DR109
Sanderstead Rd.
Station App., Stai. 98 BG91
Station App., Sun. 113 BU95
Station App. (Belmont), Sutt. 132 DB110
Brighton Rd.
Station App. (Cheam), Sutt. 131 CY108
Station App., Swan. 125 FE98
Station App., Wal.Cr. 23 DY34
Station App. (Cheshunt), Wal.Cr. 23 DZ30
Station App., Wat. 29 BT41
Cassiobury Pk. Ave.
Station App. (Carpenders Pk.), Wat. 44 BX48
Prestwick Rd.
Station App., Well. 96 EU82
Station App., Wem. 73 CH65
Station App., W.Byf. 126 BG112
Station App., West Dr. 70 BL74
High St.
Station App., Wey. 126 BN107
Station App., Whyt. 148 DU118
Station App. Rd. W4 88 CQ80
Station App. Rd., Couls. 147 DK115
Station App. Rd., Tad. 145 CW122
Station Ave. SW9 91 DP83
Coldharbour La.
Station Ave., Cat. 148 DU124
Station Ave., Epsom 130 CS109
Station Ave., N.Mal. 116 CS97
Station Ave., Rich. 88 CN81
Station Ave., Walt. 127 BT105
Station Clo. N3 48 DA53
Station Clo., Hmptn. 114 CB95
Station Clo., Hat. 19 CY26
Station Rd.
Station Clo., Pot.B. 19 CZ31
Station Cres. N15 64 DR56
Station Cres. SE3 94 EG78
Station Cres., Ashf. 98 BK90
Station Cres., Wem. 73 CH65
Station Est., Beck. 121 DX98
Elmers End Rd.
Station Est. Rd., Felt. 99 BV88
Station Footpath, Kings L. 15 BP30
Station Gdns. W4 88 CQ80
Station Gro., Wem. 74 CL65
Station Hill, Brom. 122 EG103
Station Ho. Ms. N9 50 DU49
Fore St.
Station Par. E11 66 EG57
Station Par. N14 49 DK46
High St.
Station Par. NW2 75 CW65
Station Par. SW12 104 DG88
Balham High Rd.
Station Par. W3 74 CN72
Station Par., Bark. 81 EQ66
Station Par., Horn. 69 FH63
Rosewood Ave.
Station Par., Rich. 88 CN81
Station Ave.
Station Par., Sev. 154 FG124
London Rd.
Station Par., Uxb. 56 BG59
Station Pas. E18 52 EH54
Maybank Rd.
Station Pas. SE15 92 DW79
Asylum Rd.

Story St. N1 77 DM66
Carnoustie Dr.
Stothard Pl. EC2 78 DS71
Bishopsgate
Stothard St. E1 78 DW70
Colebert Ave.
Stoughton Ave., Sutt. 131 CX106
Stoughton Clo. SE11 10 C9
Stoughton Clo. SW15 103 CU88
Bessborough Rd.
Stour Ave., Sthl. 86 CA76
Stour Clo., Kes. 136 EJ105
Stour Rd. E3 79 EA66
Stour Rd., Dag. 68 FA61
Stour Rd., Dart. 97 FG83
Stourcliffe St. W1 4 D9
Stourcliffe St. W1 76 DF72
Stourhead Clo. SW19 103 CX87
Castlecombe Dr.
Stourhead Gdns. SW20 117 CU97
Stourton Ave., Felt. 100 BZ91
Stow Cres. E17 51 DY52
Stowage SE8 93 EA79
Stowe Cres., Ruis. 57 BP58
Stowe Gdns. N9 50 DT46
Latymer Rd.
Stowe Pl. N15 64 DS55
Stowe Rd. W12 89 CV75
Stowe Rd., Orp. 138 EV105
Stowell Ave., Croy. 135 ED109
Stowting Rd., Orp. 137 ES105
Stox Mead, Har. 45 CD53
Stracey Rd. E7 66 EG63
Stracey Rd. NW10 74 CR67
Strachan Pl. SW19 103 CW93
Woodhayes Rd.
Stradbroke Dr., Chig. 53 EN51
Stradbroke Gro., Buck.H. 52 EK46
Stradbroke Gro., Ilf. 66 EL55
Stradbroke Pk., Chig. 53 EP51
Stradbroke Rd. N5 64 DQ63
Stradella Rd. SE24 106 DQ86
Strafford Ave., Ilf. 53 EN54
Strafford Clo., Pot.B. 20 DA32
Strafford Gate
Strafford Gate, Pot.B. 20 DA32
Strafford Rd. W3 88 CQ75
Strafford Rd., Barn. 33 CY41
Strafford Rd., Houns. 86 BZ83
Strafford Rd., Twick. 101 CG87
Strafford St. E14 93 EA75
Strahan Rd. E3 79 DY69
Straight, The, Sthl. 86 BX75
Straight Rd., Rom. 55 FH50
Straightsmouth SE10 93 EC80
Strait Rd. E6 80 EL73
Straker's Rd. SE15 92 DV84
Strand WC2 9 P1
Strand WC2 77 DL73
Strand Clo., Epsom 144 CR119
Strand La. WC2 6 C10
Strand on the Grn. W4 88 CN79
Strand Pl. N18 50 DS49
Silver St.
Strand Sch. App. W4 88 CN79
Thames Rd.
Strandfield Clo. SE18 95 ES78
Strangeways, Wat. 29 BS36
Strangways Ter. W14 89 CZ76
Melbury Rd.
Stranraer Rd., Houns. 98 BL86
Stranraer Way N1 77 DL66
Strasburg Rd. SW11 91 DH81
Stratfield Pk. Clo. N21 49 DP45
Stratfield Rd., Borwd. 32 CM41
Stratford Ave. W8 90 DA76
Stratford Rd.
Stratford Ave., Uxb. 70 BM68
Stratford Cen., The E15 79 ED66
Broadway
Stratford Clo., Bark. 82 EU66
Stratford Clo., Dag. 83 FC66
Stratford Ct., N.Mal. 116 CR98
Kingston Rd.
Stratford Gro. SW15 89 CX84
Stratford Ho. Ave., Brom. 122 EL97
Stratford Mkt. E15 79 ED67
Bridge Rd.
Stratford Pl. W1 5 H9
Stratford Pl. W1 77 DH72
Stratford Rd. E13 80 EF67
Stratford Rd. W3 88 CQ75
Bollo Bri. Rd.
Stratford Rd. W8 90 DA76
Stratford Rd., Hayes 71 BV70
Stratford Rd., Houns. 99 BP86
Stratford Rd., Sthl. 86 BY77
Stratford Rd., Th.Hth. 119 DN98
Stratford Rd., Wat. 29 BU40
Stratford Vill. NW1 77 DJ66
Stratford Way, St.Alb. 16 BZ29
Stratford Way, Wat. 29 BT40
Strath Ter. SW11 90 DE84
Strathan Clo. SW18 103 CY86
Strathaven Rd. SE12 108 EH86
Strathblaine Rd. SW11 104 DD85
Strathbrook Rd. SW16 105 DM94
Strathcona Rd., Wem. 59 CK61
Strathdale SW16 105 DM92
Strathdon Dr. SW17 104 DD90
Strathearn Ave., Hayes 85 BT80
Strathearn Ave., Twick. 100 CB88
Strathearn Pl. W2 4 B10
Strathearn Pl. W2 76 DE73
Strathearn Rd. SW19 104 DA92
Strathearn Rd., Sutt. 132 DA106
Stratheden Par. SE3 94 EG80
Stratheden Rd.
Stratheden Rd. SE3 94 EG81
Strathfield Gdns., Bark. 81 ER65
Strathleven Rd. SW2 91 DL84
Strathmore Clo., Cat. 148 DS121
Strathmore Gdns. N3 48 DB53
Strathmore Gdns. W8 76 DA74
Palace Gdns. Ter.
Strathmore Gdns., Edg. 46 CP54
Strathmore Gdns., Horn. 69 FF60
Strathmore Rd. SW19 104 DA90
Strathmore Rd., Croy. 120 DQ101
Strathmore Rd., Tedd. 101 CE91
Strathnairn St. SE1 92 DU77
Strathray Gdns. NW3 76 DE65
Strathville Rd. SW18 104 DA89
Strathyre Ave. SW16 119 DN97
Stratton Ave., Enf. 36 DR37
Stratton Ave., Wall. 133 DK109
Stratton Clo. SW19 118 DA96
Stratton Clo., Bexh. 96 EY83
Stratton Clo., Edg. 46 CM51
Stratton Clo., Houns. 86 BZ81
Stratton Clo., Walt. 114 BW102
St. Johns Dr.
Stratton Dr., Bark. 67 ET64
Stratton Gdns., Sthl. 72 BZ72
Stratton Rd. SW19 118 DA96
Stratton Rd., Bexh. 96 EY83
Stratton Rd., Sun. 113 BT96
Stratton St. W1 9 J2
Stratton St. W1 77 DH74
Strattondale St. E14 93 EC76
Strauss Rd. W4 88 CR75
Straw Clo., Cat. 148 DQ121
Coulsdon Rd.
Strawberry Flds., Swan. 125 FE95
Strawberry Hill, Twick. 101 CF90
Strawberry Hill Clo., Twick. 101 CF91
Strawberry Hill Rd., Twick. 101 CF90
Strawberry La., Cars. 118 DF104
Strawberry Vale N2 48 DD53
Strawberry Vale, Twick. 101 CF90
Strayfield Rd., Enf. 35 DP37
Streakes Fld. Rd. NW2 61 CU61
Stream Clo., W.Byf. 126 BK112
Stream La., Edg. 46 CP50
Stream Way, Belv. 96 EZ79
Streamdale SE2 96 EU79
Streamside Clo. N9 50 DT46
Streamside Clo., Brom. 122 EG98
Streatfield Ave. E6 81 EM67
Streatfield Rd., Har. 60 CL55
Streatham Clo. SW16 105 DL90
Streatham Common N. SW16 105 DL92
Streatham Common S. SW16 105 DL93
Streatham Ct. SW16 105 DL90
Streatham High Rd. SW16 105 DL92
Streatham Hill SW2 105 DL89
Streatham Pl. SW2 105 DL87
Streatham Rd. SW16 118 DG95
Streatham Rd., Mitch. 118 DG95
Streatham St. WC1 5 P8
Streatham Vale SW16 119 DJ95
Streathbourne Rd. SW17 104 DG89
Streatley Pl. NW3 62 DC63
New End Sq.
Streatley Rd. NW6 75 CZ66
Street, The, Ash. 144 CM118
Street, The, Kings L. 14 BG31
Street, The, Lthd. 143 CD121
Streeters La., Wall. 119 DK104
Streetfield Ms. SE3 94 EG83
Streimer Rd. E15 79 EC68
Strelley Way W3 74 CS73
Stretton Rd., Croy. 120 DS101
Stretton Rd., Rich. 101 CJ89
Stretton Way, Borwd. 32 CL38
Strickland Rd., Belv. 96 FA77
Strickland Row SW18 104 DD87
Strickland St. SE8 93 EA81
Strickland Way, Orp. 137 ET105
Stride Rd. E13 80 EF68
Stripling Way, Wat. 29 BU44
Strode Clo. N10 48 DG52
Pembroke Rd.
Strode Rd. E7 66 EG63
Strode Rd. N17 50 DS54
Strode Rd. NW10 75 CU65
Strode Rd. SW6 89 CY80
Strodes Cres., Stai. 98 BJ92
Strone Rd. E7 80 EJ65
Strone Rd. E12 80 EK65
Strone Way, Hayes 72 BY70
Strongbow Cres. SE9 109 EM85
Strongbow Rd. SE9 109 EM85
Strongbridge Clo., Har. 58 CA60
Stronsa Rd. W12 89 CT75
Strood Ave., Rom. 69 FD60
Stroud Cres. SW15 103 CU90
Stroud Fld., Nthlt. 72 BY65
Stroud Gate, Har. 58 CB63
Stroud Grn. Gdns., Croy. 120 DW101
Stroud Grn. Rd. N4 63 DM60
Stroud Grn. Way, Croy. 120 DV101
Stroud Rd. SE25 120 DU100
Stroud Rd. SW19 104 DA90
Stroud Way, Ashf. 99 BP93
Courtfield Rd.
Stroudes Clo., Wor.Pk. 116 CS101
Stroudley Wk. E3 79 EB69
Stroudwater Pk., Wey. 127 BP107
Strouts Pl. E2 7 P2
Strutton Grd. SW1 9 M6
Strutton Grd. SW1 91 DK76
Strype St. E1 7 P7
Stuart Ave. NW9 61 CU59
Stuart Ave. W5 74 CM74
Stuart Ave., Brom. 122 EG102
Stuart Ave., Har. 58 BZ62
Stuart Ave., Walt. 113 BV102
Stuart Clo., Swan. 111 FF94
Stuart Clo., Uxb. 70 BN65
Stuart Ct. (Elstree), Borwd. 31 CK44
High St.
Stuart Cres. N22 49 DM53
Stuart Cres., Croy. 135 DZ105
Stuart Cres., Hayes 71 BQ72
Stuart Evans Clo., Well. 96 EW83
Stuart Gro., Tedd. 101 CE92
Stuart Mantle Way, Erith 97 FD80
Stuart Pl., Mitch. 118 DF95
Stuart Rd. NW6 76 DA69
Stuart Rd. SE15 92 DW84
Stuart Rd. SW19 104 DA90
Stuart Rd. W3 74 CQ74
Stuart Rd., Bark. 81 ET66
Stuart Rd., Barn. 48 DE45
Stuart Rd., Har. 59 CF55
Stuart Rd., Rich. 101 CH89
Stuart Rd., Th.Hth. 120 DQ98
Stuart Rd., Warl. 148 DV120
Stuart Rd., Well. 96 EV81
Stuart Twr. W9 76 DC69
Stuart Way, Stai. 98 BH93
Stuart Way (Cheshunt), Wal.Cr. 22 DV31
Stubbings Hall La., Wal.Abb. 23 EB28
Stubbs Dr. SE16 92 DV78
Stubbs Hill, Sev. 138 EW113
Stubbs Ms., Dag. 68 EV63
Marlborough Rd.
Stubbs Pt. E13 80 EG70
Stubbs Way SW19 118 DD95
Brangwyn Cres.
Stucley Pl. NW1 77 DH66
Hawley Cres.
Stucley Rd., Houns. 86 CC80
Stud Grn., Wat. 15 BV32
Studd St. N1 77 DP67
Studdridge St. SW6 90 DA82
Studholme Ct. NW3 62 DA63
Studholme St. SE15 92 DV80
Studio Ct., Borwd. 32 CQ40
Studio Pl. SW1 8 E5
Studio Way, Borwd. 32 CQ40
Studios, The (Bushey), Wat. 30 CA44
Studios Rd., Shep. 112 BM97
Studland SE17 11 K10
Studland Clo., Sid. 109 ET90
Studland Rd. SE26 107 DX92
Studland Rd. W7 73 CD72
Studland Rd., Kings.T. 102 CL93
Studland Rd., W.Byf. 126 BM113
Studland St. W6 89 CV77
Studley Ave. E4 51 ED52
Studley Clo. E5 65 DY64
Studley Ct., Sid. 110 EV92
Studley Dr., Ilf. 66 EK58
Studley Est. SW4 91 DL81
Studley Gra. Rd. W7 87 CE75
Studley Rd. E7 80 EH65
Studley Rd. SW4 91 DL81
Studley Rd., Dag. 82 EX66
Stukeley Rd. E7 80 EH66
Stukeley St. WC2 6 A8
Stukeley St. WC2 77 DL72
Stumps Hill La., Beck. 107 EA93
Stumps La., Whyt. 148 DS117
Sturdy Rd. SE15 92 DV82
Sturge Ave. E17 51 EB53
Sturge St. SE1 11 H4
Sturgeon Rd. SE17 91 DP78
Sturges Fld., Chis. 109 ER93
Sturgess Ave. NW4 61 CU59
Sturlas Way, Wal.Cr. 23 DX33
Sturmer Way N7 63 DM64
Stock Orchard Cres.
Sturminster Clo., Hayes 72 BW72
Sturrock Clo. N15 64 DR56
Sturry St. E14 79 EB72
Sturt St. N1 7 J1
Sturt St. N1 78 DQ68
Stutfield St. E1 78 DU72
Styles Gdns. SW9 91 DP83
Styles Way, Beck. 121 EC98
Succombs Hill, Warl. 148 DV120
Succombs Hill, Whyt. 148 DV120
Succombs Pl., Warl. 148 DV120
Sudbourne Rd. SW2 105 DL85
Sudbrook Gdns., Rich. 102 CL90
Sudbrook La., Rich. 102 CL88
Sudbrooke Rd. SW12 104 DF86
Sudbury E6 81 EN72
Newark Knok
Sudbury Ave., Wem. 59 CJ64
Sudbury Ct. E5 65 DY63
Sudbury Ct. Dr., Har. 59 CF62
Sudbury Ct. Rd., Har. 59 CF62
Sudbury Cres., Brom. 108 EG93
Sudbury Cres., Wem. 59 CH64
Sudbury Cft., Wem. 59 CF63
Sudbury Gdns., Croy. 134 DS105
Langton Way
Sudbury Heights Ave., Grnf. 59 CF64
Sudbury Hill, Har. 59 CE61
Sudbury Hill Clo., Wem. 59 CF63
Sudbury Rd., Bark. 67 ET64
Sudeley St. N1 6 G1
Sudeley St. N1 77 DP68
Sudicamps Ct., Wal.Abb. 24 EG33
Sudlow Rd. SW18 104 DA85
Sudrey St. SE1 11 H5
Suez Ave., Grnf. 73 CF68
Suez Rd., Enf. 37 DY42
Suffield Clo., S.Croy. 135 DX112
Suffield Rd. E4 51 EB48
Suffield Rd. N15 64 DT57
Suffield Rd. SE20 120 DW96
Suffolk Clo., Borwd. 32 CR43
Clydesdale Clo.
Suffolk Clo., St.Alb. 17 CJ25
Suffolk Ct. E10 65 EA59
Suffolk Ct., Ilf. 67 ES58
Suffolk La. EC4 7 K10
Suffolk Pk. Rd. E17 65 DY56
Suffolk Pl. SW1 9 N2
Suffolk Rd. E13 80 EG69
Suffolk Rd. N15 64 DR58
Suffolk Rd. NW10 74 CS66
Suffolk Rd. SE25 120 DT98
Suffolk Rd. SW13 89 CT80
Suffolk Rd., Bark. 81 ER66
Suffolk Rd., Dag. 69 FC64
Suffolk Rd., Enf. 36 DV43
Suffolk Rd., Har. 58 BZ58
Suffolk Rd., Ilf. 67 ES58
Suffolk Rd., Pot.B. 19 CY32
Suffolk Rd., Sid. 110 EW93
Suffolk Rd., Wor.Pk. 117 CT103
Suffolk St. E7 66 EG64
Suffolk St. SW1 9 N1
Suffolk Way, Sev. 155 FJ125
Sugar Bakers Ct. EC3 7 N9
Sugar Ho. La. E15 79 EC68
Sugar Loaf Wk. E2 78 DW69
Victoria Pk. Sq.
Sugar Quay Wk. EC3 78 DS73
Lower Thames St.
Sugden Rd. SW11 90 DG83
Sugden Rd., T.Ditt. 115 CH102
Sugden Way, Bark. 81 ET68
Sulgrave Gdns. W6 89 CW75
Sulgrave Rd.
Sulgrave Rd. W6 89 CW76
Sulina Rd. SW2 105 DL87
Sulivan Ct. SW6 90 DA82
Sulivan Rd. SW6 90 DA83
Sullivan Ave. E16 80 EK71
Sullivan Clo. SW11 90 DE83
Sullivan Clo., Dart. 111 FH86
Sullivan Clo., W.Mol. 114 CA97
Victoria Ave.
Sullivan Cres., Uxb. 42 BK54
Sullivan Rd. SE11 10 E8
Sullivan Rd. SE11 91 DN77
Sullivan Way, Borwd. 31 CJ44
Sullivans Reach, Walt. 113 BT101
Sultan Rd. E11 66 EH56
Sultan St. SE5 92 DQ80
Sultan St., Beck. 121 DX96
Sumatra Rd. NW6 62 DA64
Sumburgh Rd. SW12 104 DG86
Summer Ave., E.Mol. 115 CE99
Summer Clo., Lthd. 143 CD124
Summer Gdns., E.Mol. 115 CE99
Summer Gro., Borwd. 31 CK44
Summer Hill, Borwd. 32 CN43
Summer Hill, Chis. 123 EN96
Summer Hill Vill., Chis. 123 EN95
Summer Ho. Rd. N16 64 DS61
Stoke Newington Ch. St.
Summer Rd., E.Mol. 115 CE99
Summer Rd., T.Ditt. 115 CF99
Summer St. EC1 6 D5
Summer Trees, Sun. 113 BV95
The Ave.
Summercourt Rd. E1 78 DW72
Summerdene Clo. SW16 105 DJ94
Bates Cres.
Summerfield, Ash. 143 CK119
Summerfield Ave. NW6 75 CY68
Summerfield Clo., St.Alb. 17 CJ26
Summerfield La., Surb. 115 CK103
Summerfield Rd. W5 73 CH70
Summerfield Rd., Loug. 38 EK44
Summerfield Rd., Wat. 29 BU35
Summerfield St. SE12 108 EF87
Summerfields Ave. N12 48 DE51
Summerhays, Cob. 128 BX113
Summerhill Clo., Orp. 123 ES104
Summerhill Gro., Enf. 36 DS44
Summerhill Rd. N15 64 DR56
Summerhill Way, Mitch. 118 DG95
Summerhouse Ave., Houns. 86 BY81
Summerhouse Dr., Bex. 111 FD91
Summerhouse Dr., Dart. 111 FD92
Summerhouse La., Uxb. 42 BG52
Summerhouse La., Wat. 30 CC40
Summerhouse La., West Dr. 84 BK79
Summerhouse La. Ind. Est., Uxb. 42 BG51
Summerhouse Way, Abb.L. 15 BT30
Summerland Gdns. N10 63 DH55
Summerlands Ave. W3 74 CQ73
Summerlay Clo., Tad. 145 CY120
Summerlee Ave. N2 62 DF56
Summerlee Gdns. N2 62 DF56
Summerley St. SW18 104 DB89
Summers Clo., Sutt. 132 DA108
Overton Rd.
Summers Clo., Wem. 60 CP60
Summers Clo., Wey. 126 BN111
Summers La. N12 48 DD52
Summers Row N12 48 DE51
Summersby Rd. N6 63 DH58
Summerstown SW17 104 DC90
Summerswood Clo., Ken. 148 DR116
Longwood Rd.
Summerswood La., Borwd. 32 CS35
Summerton Way SE28 82 EX73
Summerville Gdns., Sutt. 131 CZ107
Summerwood Rd., Islw. 101 CF85
Summit, The, Loug. 39 EM39
Summit Ave. NW9 60 CR57
Summit Clo. N14 49 DJ47
Summit Clo. NW9 60 CR56
Summit Clo., Edg. 46 CN52
Summit Ct. NW2 61 CY64
Summit Dr., Wdf.Grn. 52 EK54
Summit Est. N16 64 DU59
Summit Pl., Wey. 126 BN108
Caenshill Rd.
Summit Rd. E17 65 EB56
Summit Rd., Nthlt. 72 CA66
Summit Rd., Pot.B. 19 CY30
Summit Way N14 49 DH47
Summit Way SE19 106 DS94
Sumner Ave. SE15 92 DT81
Sumner Rd.
Sumner Clo., Orp. 137 EQ105
Sumner Est. SE15 92 DT80
Sumner Gdns., Croy. 119 DN102
Sumner Pl. SW7 8 A9
Sumner Pl. SW7 90 DD77
Sumner Pl., Add. 126 BG106
Sumner Pl. Ms. SW7 8 A9
Sumner Rd. SE15 92 DT80
Sumner Rd., Croy. 119 DN102
Sumner Rd., Har. 58 CC59
Sumner Rd. S., Croy. 119 DN102
Sumner St. SE1 10 G2
Sumner St. SE1 77 DP74
Sumpter Clo. NW3 76 DC65
Sun Ct. EC3 7 L9
Sun Ct., Erith 97 FF82
Sun La. SE3 94 EH80
Sun Pas. SE16 92 DU76
Frean St.
Sun Rd. W14 89 CZ78
Sun St. EC2 7 L6
Sun St. EC2 78 DR71
Sun St., Wal.Abb. 23 EC33
Sun St. Pas. EC2 7 M7
Sun Wk. E1 78 DU74
Mews St.
Sunbeam Cres. W10 75 CW70
Sunbeam Rd. NW10 74 CR70
Sunbury Ave. NW7 46 CR50
Sunbury Ave. SW14 88 CR84
Sunbury Ct., Sun. 114 BX96
Sunbury Ct. Island, Sun. 114 BX96
Sunbury Ct. Ms., Sun. 114 BX96
Lower Hampton Rd.
Sunbury Ct. Rd., Sun. 114 BW96
Sunbury Cres., Felt. 99 BT91
Ryland Clo.
Sunbury Gdns. NW7 46 CR50
Sunbury La. SW11 90 DD81
Sunbury La., Walt. 113 BU100
Sunbury Rd., Felt. 99 BT90
Sunbury Rd., Sutt. 117 CX104
Sunbury St. SE18 95 EM76
Sunbury Way, Felt. 100 BW92
Suncroft Pl. SE26 106 DW90
Sundale Ave., S.Croy. 134 DW110
Sunderland Ct. SE22 106 DU87
Sunderland Mt. SE23 107 DX89
Sunderland Rd.
Sunderland Rd. SE23 107 DX88
Sunderland Rd. W5 87 CK76
Sunderland Ter. W2 76 DB72
Sunderland Way E12 66 EK61
Sundew Ave. W12 75 CU73
Sundial Ave. SE25 120 DT97
Sundorne Rd. SE7 94 EH78
Sundown Ave., S.Croy. 134 DT111
Sundown Rd., Ashf. 99 BQ92
Sundra Wk. E1 79 DX70
Beaumont Gro.
Sundridge Ave., Brom. 122 EK96
Sundridge Ave., Chis. 108 EL94
Sundridge Ave., Well. 95 ER82
Sundridge Ho., Brom. 108 EH92
Burnt Ash La.
Sundridge La., Sev. 152 EV117
Sundridge Pl., Croy. 120 DU102
Inglis Rd.
Sundridge Rd., Croy. 120 DT101
Sundridge Rd., Sev. 152 FA120
Sunfields Pl. SE3 94 EH80
Sunkist Way, Wall. 133 DL109
Sunland Ave., Bexh. 96 EY84
Sunleigh Rd., Wem. 74 CL67
Sunley Gdns., Grnf. 73 CG67
Sunmead Clo., Lthd. 143 CF122
Sunmead Rd., Sun. 113 BU97
Sunna Gdns., Sun. 113 BV96
Sunningdale N14 49 DK50
Wilmer Way
Sunningdale Ave. W3 74 CS73

Sunningdale Ave., Bark. 81 ER67
Sunningdale Ave., Felt. 100 BY89
Sunningdale Ave., Rain. 83 FH70
Sunningdale Ave., Ruis. 58 BW60
Sunningdale Clo. E6 81 EM69
Ascot Rd.
Sunningdale Clo. SE16 92 DV78
Ryder Dr.
Sunningdale Clo. SE28 82 EX72
Summerton Way
Sunningdale Clo., Stan. 45 CG52
Sunningdale Clo., Surb. 116 CL103
Culsac Rd.
Sunningdale Gdns. NW9 60 CQ57
Sunningdale Gdns. W8 90 DA76
Lexham Ms.
Sunningdale Rd., Brom. 122 EL98
Sunningdale Rd., Rain. 83 FG66
Sunningdale Rd., Sutt. 131 CZ105
Sunningfields Cres. NW4 47 CV54
Sunningfields Rd. NW4 61 CV55
Sunninghill Rd. SE13 93 EB82
Sunningvale Ave., West. 150 EJ115
Sunningvale Clo., West. 150 EK116
Sunny Bank SE25 120 DU97
Sunny Bank, Warl. 149 DY117
Sunny Cres. NW10 74 CQ66
Sunny Gdns. Par. NW4 47 CW54
Great N. Way
Sunny Gdns. Rd. NW4 47 CV54
Sunny Hill NW4 61 CV55
Sunny Nook Gdns., S.Croy. 134 DR107
Selsdon Rd.
Sunny Ri., Cat. 148 DR124
Sunny Rd., The, Enf. 37 DX39
Sunny Side, Walt. 114 BW99
Sunny Vw. NW9 60 CR57
Sunny Way N12 48 DE52
Sunnybank, Epsom 144 CQ116
Sunnybank Rd., Pot.B. 20 DA33
Sunnycroft Rd. SE25 120 DU97
Sunnycroft Rd., Houns. 86 CB82
Sunnycroft Rd., Sthl. 72 CA71
Sunnydale, Orp. 123 EN103
Sunnydale Gdns. NW7 46 CR51
Sunnydale Rd. SE12 108 EH85
Sunnydell, St.Alb. 16 CB26
Sunnydene Ave. E4 51 ED50
Sunnydene Ave., Ruis. 57 BU60
Sunnydene Gdns., Wem. 73 CJ65
Sunnydene Rd., Pur. 133 DP113
Sunnydene St. SE26 107 DY91
Sunnyfield NW7 47 CT49
Sunnyfield Rd., Chis. 124 EU97
Sunnyhill Clo. E5 65 DY63
Sunnyhill Rd. SW16 105 DL91
Sunnyhurst Clo., Sutt. 118 DA104
Sunnymead Ave., Mitch. 119 DJ97
Sunnymead Rd. NW9 60 CR59
Sunnymead Rd. SW15 103 CV85
Sunnymede, Chig. 54 EV47
Sunnymede Ave., Cars. 132 DD111
Sunnymede Ave., Epsom 130 CS109
Sunnymede Dr., Ilf. 67 EP57
Sunnyside NW2 61 CZ62
Sunnyside SW19 103 CY93
Sunnyside Dr. E4 51 EC45
Sunnyside Pas. SW19 103 CY93
Sunnyside Pl. SW19 103 CY93
Sunnyside
Sunnyside Rd. E10 65 EA60
Sunnyside Rd. N19 63 DK59
Sunnyside Rd. W5 73 CK74
Sunnyside Rd., Epp. 25 ET32
Sunnyside Rd., Ilf. 67 EQ62
Sunnyside Rd., Tedd. 101 CD91
Sunnyside Rd. E. N9 50 DU48
Sunnyside Rd. N. N9 50 DT48
Sunnyside Rd. S. N9 50 DT48
Sunray Ave. SE24 92 DR84
Sunray Ave., Brom. 122 EL100
Sunray Ave., Surb. 116 CP103
Sunray Ave., West Dr. 84 BK75
Sunrise Clo., Felt. 100 BZ90
Exeter Rd.
Sunset Ave. E4 51 EB46
Sunset Ave., Wdf.Grn. 52 EF49
Sunset Clo., Erith 97 FH80
Sunset Dr., Rom. (Havering-atte-Bower) 55 FH50
Sunset Gdns. SE25 120 DT96
Sunset Rd. SE5 92 DQ84
Sunset Rd. SE28 82 EU74
Sunset Vw., Barn. 33 CY40
Sunshine Way, Mitch. 118 DF96
Sunwell Clo. SE15 92 DV81
Cossall Wk.
Superior Dr., Orp. 137 ET107
Surbiton Ct., Surb. 115 CJ100
Surbiton Cres., Kings.T. 116 CL99
Surbiton Hall Clo., Kings.T. 116 CL98
Surbiton Hill Pk., Surb. 116 CM99
Surbiton Hill Rd., Surb. 116 CL98
Surbiton Par., Surb. 116 CL100
St. Mark's Hill
Surbiton Rd., Kings.T. 115 CK98
Surlingham Clo. SE28 82 EX73
Surma Clo. E1 78 DU70
Surr St. N7 63 DL64
Surrendale Pl. W9 76 DA70
Surrey Canal Rd. SE14 93 DX79
Surrey Canal Rd. SE15 92 DW79
Surrey Cres. W4 88 CN78
Surrey Gdns. N4 64 DQ58
Surrey Gdns., Lthd. 141 BU122
Surrey Gro. SE17 92 DS78
Surrey Sq.
Surrey Gro., Sutt. 118 DD104
Surrey La. SW11 90 DE81
Surrey La. Est. SW11 90 DE81
Surrey Lo. SE1 10 D7
Surrey Ms. SE27 106 DS91
Hamilton Rd.
Surrey Mt. SE23 106 DV88
Surrey Quays Rd. SE16 92 DW76
Surrey Rd. SE15 107 DX85
Surrey Rd., Bark. 81 ES66
Surrey Rd., Dag. 69 FB64
Surrey Rd., Har. 58 CC57
Surrey Rd., W.Wick. 121 EB102
Surrey Row SE1 10 F4
Surrey Row SE1 91 DP75
Surrey Sq. SE17 11 M10
Surrey Sq. SE17 92 DS78
Surrey St. E13 80 EH69
Surrey St. WC2 6 C10
Surrey St. WC2 77 DM73
Surrey St., Croy. 120 DQ103
Surrey Ter. SE17 11 N10
Surrey Ter. SE17 92 DS77
Surrey Water Rd. SE16 79 DX74
Surridge Gdns. SE19 106 DR93
Hancock Rd.
Susan Clo., Rom. 69 FC55
Susan Rd. SE3 94 EH82
Susan Wd., Chis. 123 EN95
Susannah St. E14 79 EB72
Sussex Ave., Islw. 87 CE83
Sussex Clo. N19 63 DL61
Cornwallis Rd.
Sussex Clo., Ilf. 67 EM58
Sussex Clo., N.Mal. 116 CS98
Sussex Clo., Twick. 101 CH86
Westmorland Clo.
Sussex Cres., Nthlt. 72 CA65
Sussex Gdns. N4 64 DQ57
Sussex Gdns. N6 62 DF57
Great N. Rd.
Sussex Gdns. W2 76 DD72
Sussex Gdns., Chess. 129 CK107
Sussex Ms. E. W2 4 A9
Sussex Ms. W. W2 4 A10
Sussex Pl. NW1 4 D3
Sussex Pl. NW1 76 DF70
Sussex Pl. W2 4 A9
Sussex Pl. W2 76 DD72
Sussex Pl. W6 89 CW78
Sussex Pl., Erith 97 FB80
Sussex Pl., N.Mal. 116 CS98
Sussex Ring N12 48 DA50
Sussex Rd. E6 81 EN67
Sussex Rd., Cars. 132 DF107
Sussex Rd., Erith 97 FB80
Sussex Rd., Har. 58 CC57
Sussex Rd., Mitch. 119 DL99
Lincoln Rd.
Sussex Rd., N.Mal. 116 CS98
Sussex Rd., Orp. 124 EW100
Sussex Rd., Sid. 110 EV92
Sussex Rd., S.Croy. 134 DR107
Sussex Rd., Sthl. 86 BX76
Sussex Rd., Uxb. 57 BQ63
Sussex Rd., Wat. 29 BU37
Sussex Rd., W.Wick. 121 EB102
Sussex Sq. W2 4 A10
Sussex Sq. W2 76 DD73
Sussex St. E13 80 EH69
Sussex St. SW1 91 DH78
Sussex Wk. SW9 91 DP84
Sussex Way N7 63 DL61
Sussex Way N19 63 DL60
Sussex Way, Barn. 35 DH43
Sutcliffe Clo. NW11 62 DB57
Sutcliffe Clo. (Bushey), Wat. 30 CC42
Sutcliffe Ho., Hayes 71 BU72
Sutcliffe Rd. SE18 95 ES79
Sutcliffe Rd., Well. 96 EW82
Sutherland Ave. W9 76 DA70
Sutherland Ave. W13 73 CH72
Sutherland Ave., Hayes 85 BU77
Sutherland Ave., Orp. 123 ET100
Sutherland Ave. (Cuffley), Pot.B. 21 DK28
Sutherland Ave., Sun. 113 BT96
Sutherland Ave., Well. 95 ES84
Sutherland Ave., West. 150 EK117
Sutherland Clo., Barn. 33 CY42
Sutherland Ct. NW9 60 CP56
Sutherland Dr. SW19 118 DD95
Willow Vw.
Sutherland Gdns. SW14 88 CS83
Sutherland Gdns., Sun. 113 BT96
Sutherland Ave.
Sutherland Gdns., Wor.Pk. 117 CV101
Sutherland Gro. SW18 103 CY86
Sutherland Gro., Tedd. 101 CE92
Sutherland Pl. W2 76 DA72
Sutherland Pt. E5 64 DV63
Tiger Way
Sutherland Rd. E17 51 DX54
Sutherland Rd. N9 50 DU46
Sutherland Rd. N17 50 DU52
Sutherland Rd. W4 88 CS79
Sutherland Rd. W13 73 CG72
Sutherland Rd., Belv. 96 FA76
Sutherland Rd., Croy. 119 DN101
Sutherland Rd., Enf. 37 DX43
Sutherland Rd., Sthl. 72 BZ72
Sutherland Rd. Path E17 65 DX55
Sutherland Row SW1 9 J10
Sutherland Row SW1 91 DH78
Sutherland Sq. SE17 92 DQ78
Sutherland St. SW1 9 H10
Sutherland St. SW1 91 DH78
Sutherland Wk. SE17 92 DQ78
Sutherland Way (Cuffley), Pot.B. 21 DK28
Sutlej Rd. SE7 94 EJ80
Sutterton St. N7 77 DM65
Sutton Clo., Beck. 121 EB95
Albemarle Rd.
Sutton Clo., Loug. 52 EL45
Sutton Clo., Pnr. 57 BU57
Sutton Common Rd., Sutt. 117 CZ101
Sutton Ct. W4 88 CQ79
Sutton Ct. Rd. E13 80 EJ69
Sutton Ct. Rd. W4 88 CQ80
Sutton Ct. Rd., Sutt. 132 DC107
Sutton Ct. Rd., Uxb. 71 BP67
Sutton Cres., Barn. 33 CX43
Sutton Dene, Houns. 86 CB81
Sutton Est. SW3 8 C10
Sutton Est. SW3 90 DE78
Sutton Est. W10 75 CW71
Sutton Est., The N1 77 DP66
Sutton Gdns., Bark. 81 ES67
Sutton Rd.
Sutton Gdns., Croy. 120 DT99
Sutton Grn., Bark. 81 ES67
Sutton Rd.
Sutton Gro., Sutt. 132 DD105
Sutton Hall Rd., Houns. 86 CA80
Sutton La., Bans. 146 DB115
Sutton La., Houns. 86 BZ83
Sutton La., Sutt. 132 DB111
Sutton La. N. W4 88 CQ78
Sutton La. S. W4 88 CQ79
Sutton Pk. Rd., Sutt. 132 DB107
Sutton Path, Borwd. 32 CN40
Stratfield Rd.
Sutton Pl. E9 64 DW64
Sutton Rd. E13 80 EF70
Sutton Rd. E17 51 DX53
Sutton Rd. N10 48 DG53
Sutton Rd., Bark. 81 ES68
Sutton Rd., Houns. 86 CA81
Sutton Rd., Wat. 30 BW41
Sutton Row W1 5 N8
Sutton Row W1 77 DK72
Sutton Sq. E9 64 DW64
Urswick Rd.
Sutton Sq., Houns. 86 BZ81
Sutton St. E1 78 DW73
Sutton Way W10 75 CW71
Sutton Way, Houns. 86 BZ81
Sutton's Way EC1 7 J5
Swaby Rd. SW18 104 DC88
Swaffham Way N22 49 DP52
White Hart La.
Swaffield Rd. SW18 104 DB87
Swaffield Rd., Sev. 155 FJ122
Swain Clo. SW16 105 DH93
Swain Rd., Th.Hth. 120 DQ99
Swains Clo., West Dr. 84 BL75
Swains La. N6 62 DG60
Swains Rd. SW17 104 DF94
Swainson Rd. W3 89 CT75
Swaisland Dr., Dart. 111 FF85
Swaisland Rd., Dart. 111 FH85
Swakeleys Dr., Uxb. 56 BM63
Swakeleys Rd., Uxb. 56 BL63
Swale Rd., Dart. 97 FG83
Swallands Rd. SE6 107 EA90
Swallow Clo. SE14 93 DX81
Swallow Clo., Erith 97 FE81
Swallow Clo., Rick. 42 BJ45
Swallow Clo. (Bushey), Wat. 44 CC46
Swallow Dr. NW10 74 CR65
Kingfisher Way
Swallow Dr., Nthlt. 72 CA68
Swallow Pas. W1 5 J9
Swallow Pl. W1 5 J9
Swallow St. E6 80 EL71
Swallow St. W1 9 L1
Swallow Wk., Horn. 83 FH65
Heron Flight Ave.
Swallowdale, S.Croy. 135 DX109
Swallowfield Rd. SE7 94 EH78
Swallowfield Way, Hayes 85 BR75
Swallows Oak, Abb.L. 15 BT31
Swallowtail Clo., Orp. 124 EX98
Swan & Pike Rd., Enf. 37 EA38
Swan App. E6 80 EL71
Swan Clo. E17 51 DY53
Swan Clo., Croy. 120 DS101
Swan Clo., Felt. 100 BY91
Swan Clo., Orp. 124 EU97
Swan Clo., Rick. 42 BK45
Parsonage Rd.
Swan Ct. SW3 90 DE78
Flood St.
Swan Dr. NW9 46 CS54
Swan La. EC4 11 K1
Swan La. N20 48 DC48
Swan La., Dart. 111 FF87
Swan La., Loug. 52 EJ45
Swan Mead SE1 11 M7
Swan Mead SE1 92 DS76
Swan Pas. E1 78 DT73
Cartwright St.
Swan Pl. SW13 89 CT82
Swan Rd. SE16 92 DW75
Swan Rd. SE18 94 EK76
Swan Rd., Felt. 100 BY92
Swan Rd., Sthl. 72 CB72
Swan Rd., West Dr. 84 BK75
Swan St. SE1 11 J6
Swan St. SE1 92 DQ76
Swan St., Islw. 87 CH83
Swan Wk. SW3 90 DF79
Swan Wk., Rom. 69 FE57
Swan Wk., Shep. 113 BS101
Swan Way, Enf. 37 DX40
Swan Yd. N1 77 DP65
Highbury Sta. Rd.
Swanage Rd. E4 51 EC52
Swanage Rd. SW18 104 DC86
Swanage Waye, Hayes 72 BW72
Swanbridge Rd., Bexh. 96 FA81
Swandon Way SW18 90 DB84
Swanfield Rd., Wal.Cr. 23 DY33
Swanfield St. E2 7 P3
Swanfield St. E2 78 DT69
Swanland Rd., Hat. 19 CV25
Swanland Rd., Pot.B. 19 CV33
Swanley Bar La., Pot.B. 20 DB28
Swanley Bypass, Sid. 125 FC96
Swanley Bypass, Swan. 125 FC96
Swanley Cres., Pot.B. 20 DB29
Swanley La., Swan. 125 FF97
Swanley Rd., Well. 96 EW81
Swanley Village Rd., Swan. 125 FH95
Swanscombe Rd. W4 88 CS78
Swanscombe Rd. W11 75 CX74
Swansea Rd., Enf. 36 DW42
Swanshope, Loug. 39 EP40
Swansland Gdns. E17 51 DY53
McEntee Ave.
Swanston Path, Wat. 44 BW48
Swanton Gdns. SW19 103 CX88
Swanton Rd., Erith 97 FB80
Swanwick Clo. SW15 103 CT87
Sward Rd., Orp. 124 EU100
Swaton Rd. E3 79 EA70
Swaylands Rd., Belv. 96 FA79
Swaythling Clo. N18 50 DV49
Sweden Gate SE16 93 DY76
Swedenborg Gdns. E1 78 DU73
Sweeney Cres. SE1 92 DT75
Sweeps Ditch Clo., Stai. 98 BG94
Sweeps La., Orp. 124 EX99
Sweet Briar Grn. N9 50 DT48
Sweet Briar Gro. N9 50 DT48
Sweet Briar La., Epsom 130 CR114
Madans Wk.
Sweet Briar Wk. N18 50 DT49
Sweetcroft La., Uxb. 70 BM66
Sweetmans Ave., Pnr. 58 BX55
Sweets Way N20 48 DD47
Swete St. E13 80 EG68
Swetenham Wk. SE18 95 EQ78
Sandbach Pl.
Sweyn Pl. SE3 94 EG82
Swievelands Rd., West. 150 EH119
Swift Clo. E17 51 DY53
Swift Clo., Har. 58 CB61
Swift Clo., Hayes 71 BT72
Church Rd.
Swift Rd., Felt. 100 BX91
Swift Rd., Sthl. 86 BZ76
Swift St. SW6 89 CZ81
Swiftsden Way, Brom. 108 EE93
Swinbrook Rd. W10 75 CY71
Swinburne Ct. SE5 92 DR84
Basingdon Way
Swinburne Cres., Croy. 120 DW100
Swinburne Rd. SW15 89 CU84
Swinderby Rd., Wem. 74 CL65
Swindon Clo., Ilf. 67 ES61
Salisbury Rd.
Swindon Rd., Houns. 99 BQ86
Southern Perimeter Rd.
Swindon St. W12 75 CV74
Swinfield Clo., Felt. 100 BY91
Swinford Gdns. SW9 91 DP83
Swingate La. SE18 95 ES80
Swinnerton St. E9 65 DY64
Swinton Clo., Wem. 60 CP60
Swinton Pl. WC1 6 B2
Swinton Pl. WC1 77 DM69
Swinton St. WC1 6 B2
Swinton St. WC1 77 DM69
Swires Shaw, Kes. 136 EK105
Swiss Ave., Wat. 29 BS42
Swiss Clo., Wat. 29 BS41
Swiss Ter. NW6 76 DD66
Swithland Gdns. SE9 109 EN91
Swyncombe Ave. W5 87 CH77
Swynford Gdns. NW4 61 CU56
Handowe Clo.
Sybil Ms. N4 63 DP58
Lothair Rd. N.
Sybil Phoenix Clo. SE8 93 DX78
Sybil Thorndike Ho. N1 78 DQ65
Clephane Rd.
Sybourn St. E17 65 DZ59
Sycamore App., Rick. 29 BQ43
Sycamore Ave. W5 87 CK76
Sycamore Ave., Hayes 71 BS73
Sycamore Ave., Sid. 109 ET86
Sycamore Clo. E16 80 EE70
Clarence Rd.
Sycamore Clo. N9 50 DU49
Pycroft Way
Sycamore Clo. SE9 108 EL89
Sycamore Clo. W3 74 CS74
Bromyard Ave.
Sycamore Clo., Barn. 34 DD44
Sycamore Clo., Cars. 132 DF105
Sycamore Clo., Felt. 99 BU90
Sycamore Clo., Lthd. 143 CE123
Sycamore Clo., Nthlt. 72 BY67
Sycamore Clo., Wal.Cr. 22 DS27
Sycamore Clo., Wat. 29 BV35
Sycamore Clo. (Bushey), Wat. 30 BY40
Sycamore Clo., West Dr. 70 BM73
Whitethorn Ave.
Sycamore Dr., St.Alb. 17 CD27
Sycamore Dr., Swan. 125 FE97
Sycamore Gdns. W6 89 CV75
Sycamore Gdns., Mitch. 118 DD96
Sycamore Gro. NW9 60 CQ59
Sycamore Gro. SE6 107 EC86
Sycamore Gro. SE20 106 DU94
Sycamore Gro., N.Mal. 116 CR97
Sycamore Hill N11 48 DG51
Sycamore Ms. SW4 91 DJ83
Sycamore Ri., Bans. 131 CX114
Sycamore Rd. SW19 103 CW93
Sycamore Rd., Rick. 29 BQ43
Sycamore St. EC1 7 H5
Sycamore Wk. W10 75 CY70
Fifth Ave.
Sycamore Wk., Ilf. 67 EQ56
Civic Way
Sycamore Way, Tedd. 101 CJ93
Sycamore Way, Th.Hth. 119 DN99
Grove Rd.
Sycamores, The, Rad. 17 CH34
Sydenham Ave. SE26 106 DV92
Sydenham Clo., Rom. 69 FF56
Sydenham Cotts. SE12 108 EJ89
Sydenham Hill SE23 106 DV88
Sydenham Hill SE26 106 DT91
Sydenham Hill Est. SE26 106 DU90
Sydenham Pk. SE26 106 DW90
Sydenham Pk. Rd. SE26 106 DW90
Sydenham Ri. SE23 106 DV89
Sydenham Rd. SE26 107 DX92
Sydenham Rd., Croy. 120 DQ102
Sydmons Ct. SE23 106 DW87
Sydner Ms. N16 64 DT63
Sydner Rd.
Sydner Rd. N16 64 DT63
Sydney Ave., Pur. 133 DM112
Sydney Clo. SW3 8 A9
Sydney Clo. SW3 90 DD77
Sydney Cres., Ashf. 99 BP93
Sydney Gro. NW4 61 CW57
Sydney Ms. SW3 8 A9
Sydney Pl. SW7 8 A9
Sydney Pl. SW7 90 DD77
Sydney Rd. E11 66 EH58
Mansfield Rd.
Sydney Rd. N8 63 DN56
Sydney Rd. N10 48 DG53
Sydney Rd. SE2 96 EW76
Sydney Rd. SW20 117 CX96
Sydney Rd. W13 73 CG74
Sydney Rd., Bexh. 96 EX84
Sydney Rd., Enf. 36 DR41
Sydney Rd., Felt. 99 BU88
Sydney Rd., Ilf. 53 EQ54
Sydney Rd., Rich. 88 CL84
Sydney Rd., Sid. 109 ES91
Sydney Rd., Sutt. 132 DA105
Sydney Rd., Tedd. 101 CF92
Sydney Rd., Wat. 29 BS43
Sydney Rd., Wdf.Grn. 52 EG49
Sydney St. SW3 8 B10
Sydney St. SW3 90 DE78
Sykes Dr., Stai. 98 BH92
Sylvan Ave. N3 48 DA54
Sylvan Ave. N22 49 DM52
Sylvan Ave. NW7 47 CT51
Sylvan Ave., Rom. 68 EZ58
Sylvan Clo., S.Croy. 134 DV110
Sylvan Est. SE19 120 DT95
Sylvan Gdns., Surb. 115 CK101
Sylvan Gro. NW2 61 CX63
Sylvan Gro. SE15 92 DV79
Sylvan Hill SE19 120 DS95
Sylvan Rd. E7 80 EG65
Sylvan Rd. E11 66 EG57
Sylvan Rd. E17 65 EA57
Sylvan Rd. SE19 120 DT95
Sylvan Rd., Ilf. 67 EQ61
Hainault St.
Sylvan Wk., Brom. 123 EM97
Sylvan Way, Chig. 54 EV48
Sylvan Way, Dag. 68 EV62
Sylvan Way, W.Wick. 136 EE105
Sylvana Clo., Uxb. 70 BM67
Sylverdale Rd., Croy. 119 DP104
Sylverdale Rd., Pur. 133 DP113
Sylvester Ave., Chis. 109 EM93
Sylvester Gdns., Ilf. 54 EV50
Sylvester Path E8 78 DV65
Sylvester Rd.
Sylvester Rd. E8 78 DV65
Sylvester Rd. E17 65 DZ59
Sylvester Rd. N2 48 DC54
Sylvester Rd., Wem. 59 CJ64
Sylvestres, Sev. 153 FD119
London Rd.
Sylvestrus Clo., Kings.T. 116 CN95
Sylvia Ave., Pnr. 44 BY51
Sylvia Gdns., Wem. 74 CP66
Symes Ms. NW1 77 DJ68
Camden High St.
Symons St. SW3 8 E9
Symons St. SW3 90 DF77
Syon Gate Way, Brent. 87 CG80
Syon La., Islw. 87 CF79
Syon Pk. Gdns., Islw. 87 CF80

Syon Vista, Rich. 87 CK81
Kew Rd.

T

Tabard Gdn. Est. SE1 11 L5
Tabard Gdn. Est. SE1 92 DR75
Tabard St. SE1 11 K5
Tabard St. SE1 92 DR75
Tabarin Way, Epsom 145 CW116
Tabernacle Ave. E13 80 EG70
Barking Rd.
Tabernacle St. EC2 7 L5
Tabernacle St. EC2 78 DR70
Tableer Ave. SW4 105 DJ85
Tabley Rd. N7 63 DL63
Tabor Gdns., Sutt. 131 CZ107
Tabor Gro. SW19 103 CY94
Tabor Rd. W6 89 CV76
Tachbrook Est. SW1 91 DK78
Tachbrook Ms. SW1 9 K8
Tachbrook Rd., Felt. 99 BT87
Tachbrook Rd., Sthl. 86 BX77
Tachbrook Rd., Uxb. 70 BJ68
Tachbrook St. SW1 9 L9
Tachbrook St. SW1 91 DJ77
Tack Ms. SE4 93 EA83
Tadema Rd. SW10 90 DC80
Tadmor Clo., Sun. 113 BT98
Tadmor St. W12 75 CX74
Tadorne Rd., Tad. 145 CW121
Tadworth Ave., N.Mal. 117 CT99
Tadworth Clo., Tad. 145 CX122
Tadworth Par., Horn. 69 FH63
Maylands Ave.
Tadworth Rd. NW2 61 CU61
Tadworth St., Tad. 145 CW123
Taeping St. E14 93 EB77
Taffy's How, Mitch. 118 DE97
Taft Way E3 79 EB69
St. Leonards St.
Tagg's Island, Hmptn. 115 CD96
Tailworth St. E1 78 DU71
Chicksand St.
Tait Rd., Croy. 120 DS101
Takeley Clo., Rom. 55 FD54
Takeley Clo., Wal.Abb. 23 ED33
Talacre Rd. NW5 76 DG65
Talbot Ave. N2 62 DD55
Talbot Ave., Wat. 44 BY45
Talbot Clo. N15 64 DT56
Talbot Ct. EC3 7 L10
Talbot Cres. NW4 61 CU57
Talbot Gdns., Ilf. 68 EU61
Talbot Ho. E14 79 EB72
Giraud St.
Talbot Pl. SE3 94 EE82
Talbot Rd. E6 81 EN68
Talbot Rd. E7 66 EG63
Talbot Rd. N6 62 DG58
Talbot Rd. N15 64 DT56
Talbot Rd. N22 49 DJ54
Talbot Rd. SE22 92 DS84
Talbot Rd. W2 76 DA72
Talbot Rd. W11 75 CZ72
Talbot Rd. W13 73 CG73
Talbot Rd., Ashf. 98 BK92
Talbot Rd., Brom. 122 EH98
Masons Hill
Talbot Rd., Cars. 132 DG106
Talbot Rd., Dag. 82 EZ65
Talbot Rd., Har. 45 CF54
Talbot Rd., Islw. 87 CG84
Talbot Rd., Rick. 42 BL46
Talbot Rd., Sthl. 86 BY77
Talbot Rd., Th.Hth. 120 DR98
Talbot Rd., Twick. 101 CE88
Talbot Rd., Wem. 59 CK64
Talbot Sq. W2 4 A9
Talbot Sq. W2 76 DD72
Talbot Wk. NW10 74 CS65
Garnet Rd.
Talbot Wk. W11 75 CY72
Lancaster Rd.
Talbot Yd. SE1 11 K3
Taleworth Clo., Ash. 143 CK120
Taleworth Pk., Ash. 143 CK120
Taleworth Rd., Ash. 143 CK119
Talfourd Pl. SE15 92 DT81
Talfourd Rd. SE15 92 DT81
Talgarth Rd. W6 89 CX78
Talgarth Rd. W14 89 CX78
Talgarth Wk. NW9 60 CS57
Talisman Clo., Ilf. 68 EV60
Talisman Sq. SE26 106 DU91
Talisman Way, Epsom 145 CW116
Talisman Way, Wem. 60 CM62
Forty Ave.
Tall Elms Clo., Brom. 122 EF99
Tall Trees SW16 119 DM97
Tallack Clo., Har. 45 CE52
College Hill Rd.
Tallack Rd. E10 65 DZ60
Tallis Clo. E16 80 EH72
Tallis Gro. SE7 94 EH79
Tallis St. EC4 6 E10
Tallis St. EC4 77 DN73
Tallis Vw. NW10 74 CR65
Mitchellbrook Way
Tallis Way, Borwd. 31 CK39
Tally Ho Cor. N12 48 DC50
Talma Gdns., Twick. 101 CE86
Talma Rd. SW2 91 DN84
Talmage Clo. SE23 106 DW87
Tyson Rd.
Talman Gro., Stan. 45 CK51
Talwin St. E3 79 EB69
Tamar Sq., Wdf.Grn. 52 EH51
Tamar St. SE7 94 EL76
Tamar Way N17 64 DT55
Tamarind Yd. E1 78 DU74
Asher Way
Tamarisk Sq. W12 75 CT73
Tamesis Gdns., Wor.Pk. 116 CS103
Tamian Est., Houns. 86 BW84
Tamian Way, Houns. 86 BW84
Tamworth Ave., Wdf.Grn. 52 EE51
Tamworth Gdns., Pnr. 43 BV54
Tamworth La., Mitch. 118 DG96
Tamworth Pk., Mitch. 119 DH98
Tamworth Pl., Croy. 120 DQ103
Tamworth Rd., Croy. 119 DP103
Tamworth St. SW6 90 DA79
Tancred Rd. N4 63 DP58
Tandridge Ct., Cat. 148 DU122
Tandridge Dr., Orp. 123 ER102
Tandridge Gdns., S.Croy. 134 DT113
Tandridge Pl., Orp. 123 ER101
Tandridge Dr.
Tandridge Rd., Warl. 149 DX119
Tanfield Ave. NW2 61 CT63
Tanfield Clo., Wal.Cr. 22 DV27
Spicersfield
Tanfield Rd., Croy. 134 DQ105
Tangier Rd., Rich. 88 CP84
Tangier Way, Tad. 145 CY117
Tangier Wd., Tad. 145 CY118
Tangle Tree Clo. N3 62 DB55
Tanglebury Clo., Brom. 122 EL98
Tangles Clo., Uxb. 70 BN69
Tanglewood Clo., Croy. 120 DW104
Tanglewood Clo., Stan. 45 CE47
Tanglewood Way, Felt. 99 BV90
Tangley Gro. SW15 103 CT87
Tangley Pk. Rd., Hmptn. 100 BZ92
Tanglyn Ave., Shep. 112 BN99
Tangmere Cres., Horn. 83 FH65
Tangmere Gdns., Nthlt. 72 BW68
Tangmere Gro., Kings.T. 101 CK92
Tangmere Way NW9 46 CS54
Tanhurst Wk. SE2 96 EX76
Alsike Rd.
Tankerton Rd., Surb. 116 CM103
Tankerton St. WC1 6 A3
Tankerville Rd. SW16 105 DK94
Tankridge Rd. NW2 61 CV61
Tanner St. SE1 11 N5
Tanner St. SE1 92 DS75
Tanner St., Bark. 81 EQ65
Tanners Clo., Walt. 113 BV100
Tanners Dean, Lthd. 143 CJ122
Tanners End La. N18 50 DS49
Tanners Hill SE8 93 DZ81
Tanners Hill, Abb.L. 15 BT31
Tanners La., Ilf. 67 EQ55
Tanners Wd. Clo., Abb.L. 15 BS32
Tanners Wd. La.
Tanners Wd. La., Abb.L. 15 BS32
Tannery Clo., Beck. 121 DX99
Tannery Clo., Dag. 69 FB62
Tannington Ter. N5 63 DN62
Tannsfeld Rd. SE26 107 DX92
Tansley Clo. N7 63 DK64
Hilldrop Rd.
Tanswell Est. SE1 10 E5
Tanswell St. SE1 10 D5
Tansy Clo. E6 81 EN72
Tant Ave. E16 80 EF72
Tantallon Rd. SW12 104 DG88
Tantony Gro., Rom. 68 EX55
Tanworth Clo., Nthwd. 43 BQ51
Tanyard La., Bex. 110 FA87
Bexley High St.
Tanza Rd. NW3 62 DF63
Tapestry Clo., Sutt. 132 DB108
Taplow NW3 76 DD66
Taplow SE17 92 DR78
Taplow Rd. N13 50 DQ49
Taplow St. N1 7 J1
Taplow St. N1 78 DQ68
Tapp St. E1 78 DV70
Tappesfield Rd. SE15 92 DW83
Tapster St., Barn. 33 CZ41
Tarbert Rd. SE22 106 DS85
Tarbert Wk. E1 78 DW73
Juniper St.
Target Clo., Felt. 99 BS86
Tariff Cres. SE8 93 DZ77
Enterprize Way
Tariff Rd. N17 50 DU51
Tarleton Gdns. SE23 106 DV88
Tarling Clo., Sid. 110 EV90
Tarling Rd. E16 80 EF72
Tarling Rd. N2 48 DC54
Tarling St. E1 78 DV72
Tarling St. Est. E1 78 DW72
Tarmac Way, West Dr. 84 BH80
Tarn St. SE1 11 H7
Tarnbank, Enf. 35 DL43
Tarnwood Pk. SE9 109 EM87
Tarpan Way, Brox. 23 DZ26
Tarquin Ho. SE26 106 DU91
Tarragon Clo. SE14 93 DY80
Tarragon Gdns. SE14 93 DY80
Southerngate Way
Tarragon Gro. SE26 107 DX93
Tarrant Pl. W1 4 D7
Tarrington Clo. SW16 105 DK90
Tarry La. SE8 93 DY77
Tartar Rd., Cob. 128 BW113
Tarver Rd. SE17 91 DP78
Tarves Way SE10 93 EB80
Tash Pl. N11 49 DH50
Woodland Rd.
Tasker Clo., Hayes 85 BQ80
Tasker Ho., Bark. 81 ER68
Dovehouse Mead
Tasker Rd. NW3 62 DF64
Tasman Rd. SW9 91 DL83
Tasman Wk. E16 80 EK72
Royal Rd.
Tasmania Ter. N18 50 DQ51
Tasso Rd. W6 89 CY79
Tatam Rd. NW10 74 CR66
Tate & Lyle Jetty E16 94 EL75
Tate Clo., Lthd. 143 CJ123
Windmill Dr.
Tate Rd. E16 81 EM74
Newland St.
Tate Rd., Sutt. 132 DA106
Tatnell Rd. SE23 107 DY86
Tatsfield App. Rd., West. 150 EH123
Tatsfield La., West. 150 EL121
Tattenham Cor. Rd., Epsom 144 CS117
Tattenham Cres., Epsom 145 CU118
Tattenham Gro., Epsom 145 CV118
Tattenham Way, Tad. 145 CX118
Tattersall Clo. SE9 108 EL85
Tatton Cres. N16 64 DT59
Clapton Common
Tatum St. SE17 11 L9
Tatum St. SE17 92 DR77
Tauber Clo., Borwd. 32 CM42
Taunton Ave. SW20 117 CV96
Taunton Ave., Cat. 148 DT123
Taunton Ave., Houns. 86 CC82
Taunton Clo., Bexh. 97 FD82
Taunton Clo., Ilf. 53 ET51
Taunton Clo., Sutt. 118 DA102
Taunton Ct. N17 50 DS52
Taunton Dr. N2 48 DC54
Taunton Dr., Enf. 35 DN41
Taunton La., Couls. 147 DN119
Taunton Ms. NW1 4 D5
Taunton Pl. NW1 4 D4
Taunton Pl. NW1 76 DF70
Taunton Rd. SE12 108 EE85
Taunton Rd., Grnf. 72 CB67
Taunton Way, Stan. 46 CL54
Tavern Clo., Cars. 118 DE101
Tavern La. SW9 91 DN82
Taverner Sq. N5 64 DQ63
Highbury Gra.
Taverners Clo. W11 75 CY74
Addison Ave.
Taverners Way E4 52 EE46
Douglas Rd.
Tavistock Ave. E17 65 DX55
Tavistock Ave., Grnf. 73 CG68
Tavistock Clo. N16 64 DS64
Crossway
Tavistock Clo., Pot.B. 20 DD31
Tavistock Clo., Stai. 98 BK94
Tavistock Cres. W11 75 CZ71
Tavistock Cres., Mitch. 119 DL98
Tavistock Gdns., Ilf. 67 ES63
Tavistock Gate, Croy. 120 DR102
Tavistock Gro., Croy. 120 DR101
Tavistock Ms. E18 66 EG56
Avon Way
Tavistock Ms. W11 75 CZ72
Lancaster Rd.
Tavistock Pl. E18 66 EG55
Avon Way
Tavistock Pl. N14 49 DH45
Chase Side
Tavistock Pl. WC1 5 P4
Tavistock Pl. WC1 77 DL70
Tavistock Rd. E7 66 EF63
Tavistock Rd. E15 80 EF65
Tavistock Rd. E18 66 EG55
Tavistock Rd. N4 64 DR58
Tavistock Rd. NW10 75 CT68
Tavistock Rd. W11 75 CZ72
Tavistock Rd., Brom. 122 EF98
Tavistock Rd., Cars. 118 DD102
Tavistock Rd., Croy. 120 DR102
Tavistock Rd., Edg. 46 CN53
Tavistock Rd., Uxb. 57 BQ64
Tavistock Rd., Wat. 30 BX39
Tavistock Rd., Well. 96 EW81
Tavistock Rd., West Dr. 70 BK74
Tavistock Sq. WC1 5 N4
Tavistock Sq. WC1 77 DK70
Tavistock St. WC2 6 A10
Tavistock St. WC2 77 DL73
Tavistock Ter. N19 63 DK62
Tavistock Wk., Cars. 118 DD102
Tavistock Rd.
Taviton St. WC1 5 M4
Taviton St. WC1 77 DK70
Tavy Bri. SE2 96 EW76
Tavy Clo. SE11 10 E10
Tawney Common, Epp. 26 FA32
Tawney Rd. SE28 82 EV73
Tawny Clo. W13 73 CH74
Tawny Clo., Felt. 99 BU90
Chervil Clo.
Tawny Way SE16 93 DX77
Tay Way, Rom. 55 FF53
Tayben Ave., Twick. 101 CE86
Taybridge Rd. SW11 90 DG83
Tayburn Clo. E14 79 EC72
Tayfield Clo., Uxb. 57 BQ62
Tayles Hill, Epsom 131 CT110
Taylor Ave., Rich. 88 CP82
Taylor Clo. N17 50 DU52
Taylor Clo., Hmptn. 100 CC92
Taylor Clo., Orp. 137 ET105
Taylor Clo., Rom. 54 FA52
Taylor Ct. E15 65 EC64
Taylor Rd., Ash. 143 CK117
Taylor Rd., Mitch. 104 DE94
Taylor Rd., Wall. 133 DH106
Taylors Bldgs. SE18 95 EP77
Spray St.
Taylors Clo., Sid. 109 ET91
Taylors Grn. W3 74 CS72
Long Dr.
Taylors La. NW10 74 CS66
Taylors La. SE26 106 DV91
Taylors La., Barn. 33 CZ39
Taymount Ri. SE23 106 DW89
Tayport Clo. N1 77 DL66
Tayside Dr., Edg. 46 CP48
Taywood Rd., Nthlt. 72 BZ69
Invicta Gro.
Teak Clo. SE16 79 DY74
Teal Ave., Orp. 124 EX98
Teal Clo. E16 80 EK71
Fulmer Rd.
Teal Clo., S.Croy. 135 DX111
Teal Dr., Nthwd. 43 BQ52
Teale St. E2 78 DU68
Tealing Dr., Epsom 130 CR105
Teardrop Ind. Est., Swan. 125 FH99
Teasel Clo., Croy. 121 DX102
Teasel Way E15 80 EE69
Teazle Wd. Hill, Lthd. 143 CE117
Oaklawn Rd.
Teazlewood Pk., Lthd. 143 CG117
Tebworth Rd. N17 50 DT52
Teck Clo., Islw. 87 CG82
Tedder Clo., Chess. 129 CJ107
Tedder Clo., Ruis. 57 BV64
West End Rd.
Tedder Clo., Uxb. 70 BM66
Tedder Rd., S.Croy. 134 DW108
Teddington Clo., Epsom 130 CR110
Teddington Lock, Tedd. 101 CG91
Teddington Pk., Tedd. 101 CF92
Teddington Pk. Rd., Tedd. 101 CF91
Tedworth Gdns. SW3 90 DF78
Tedworth Sq.
Tedworth Sq. SW3 90 DF78
Tee, The W3 74 CS72
Tees Ave., Grnf. 73 CE68
Teesdale Ave., Islw. 87 CG81
Teesdale Clo. E2 78 DU68
Teesdale Gdns. SE25 120 DS96
Grange Hill
Teesdale Gdns., Islw. 87 CG81
Teesdale Rd. E11 66 EF58
Teesdale St. E2 78 DV68
Teesdale Yd. E2 78 DV68
Teesdale St.
Teeswater Ct., Erith 96 EX76
Middle Way
Teevan Clo., Croy. 120 DU101
Teevan Rd., Croy. 120 DU102
Teignmouth Clo. SW4 91 DK84
Teignmouth Clo., Edg. 46 CM54
Teignmouth Gdns., Grnf. 73 CF68
Teignmouth Rd. NW2 61 CX64
Teignmouth Rd., Well. 96 EW82
Telcote Way, Ruis. 58 BW59
Woodlands Ave.
Telegraph Hill NW3 62 DB62
Telegraph La., Esher 129 CF107
Telegraph Ms., Ilf. 68 EU60
Telegraph Rd. SW15 103 CV87
Telegraph St. EC2 7 K8
Telegraph Track, Wall. 133 DH110
Telemann Sq. SE3 94 EH83
Telephone Pl. SW6 89 CZ79
Lillie Rd.
Telfer Clo. W3 88 CQ75
Church Rd.
Telferscot Rd. SW12 105 DK88
Telford Ave. SW2 105 DK88
Telford Clo. E17 65 DY59
Telford Clo. SE19 106 DT93
St. Aubyn's Rd.
Telford Clo. W3 88 CQ75
Church Rd.
Telford Clo., Wat. 30 BX35
Telford Dr., Walt. 114 BW101
Telford Rd. N11 49 DJ51
Telford Rd. NW9 61 CU58
West Hendon Bdy.
Telford Rd. SE9 109 ER89
Telford Rd. W10 75 CY71
Telford Rd., St.Alb. 17 CJ27
Telford Rd., Sthl. 72 CB73
Telford Rd., Twick. 100 CA87
Telford Ter. SW1 91 DJ79
Telford Way W3 74 CS71
Telford Way, Hayes 72 BY71
Telfords Yd. E1 78 DU73
The Highway
Telham Rd. E6 81 EN68
Tell Gro. SE22 92 DT84
Tellisford, Esher 128 CB105
Tellson Ave. SE18 94 EK81
Telscombe Clo., Orp. 123 ES103
Telston La., Sev. 153 FF117
Temeraire St. SE16 92 DW75
Albion St.
Temperley Rd. SW12 104 DG87
Tempest Ave., Pot.B. 20 DD32
Tempest Way, Rain. 83 FG65
Templar Dr. SE28 82 EX72
Templar Ho. NW2 75 CZ65
Shoot Up Hill
Templar Pl., Hmptn. 100 CA94
Templar St. SE5 91 DP82
Templars Ave. NW11 61 CZ58
Templars Cres. N3 48 DA54
Templars Dr., Har. 45 CD51
Temple EC4 6 D10
Temple EC4 77 DN73
Temple Ave. EC4 6 E10
Temple Ave. EC4 77 DN73
Temple Ave. N20 48 DD45
Temple Ave., Croy. 121 DZ103
Temple Ave., Dag. 68 FA60
Temple Clo. E11 66 EE59
Wadley Rd.
Temple Clo. N3 47 CZ54
Cyprus Rd.
Temple Clo. SE28 95 EQ76
Temple Clo. (Cheshunt), Wal.Cr. 22 DU31
Temple Clo., Wat. 29 BT40
Temple Ct., Pot.B. 19 CY31
Mimms Hall Rd.
Temple Fortune Hill NW11 62 DA57
Temple Fortune La. NW11 61 CZ57
Temple Gdns. N21 49 DP47
Barrowell Grn.
Temple Gdns. NW11 61 CZ58
Temple Gdns., Dag. 68 EX62
Temple Gdns., Rick. 43 BP49
Temple Gro. NW11 62 DA58
Temple Gro., Enf. 35 DP41
Temple La. EC4 6 E9
Temple Mead Clo., Stan. 45 CH51
Temple Mill La. E15 65 EA63
Temple Pk., Uxb. 70 BN69
Temple Pl. WC2 6 C10
Temple Pl. WC2 77 DM73
Temple Rd. E6 80 EL67
Temple Rd. N8 63 DM56
Temple Rd. NW2 61 CW63
Temple Rd. W4 88 CQ76
Temple Rd. W5 87 CK76
Temple Rd., Croy. 134 DR105
Temple Rd., Epsom 130 CR111
Temple Rd., Houns. 86 CB84
Temple Rd., Rich. 88 CM82
Temple Rd., West. 150 EK117
Temple Sheen SW14 88 CP84
Temple Sheen Rd. SW14 88 CP84
Temple St. E2 78 DV68
Temple Way, Sutt. 118 DD104
Temple W. Ms. SE11 10 F7
Temple W. Ms. SE11 91 DP76
Templecombe Rd. E9 78 DW67
Templecombe Way, Mord. 117 CY99
Templecroft, Ashf. 99 BR93
Templedene Ave., Stai. 98 BH94
Templefield Clo., Add. 126 BH107
Templehof Ave. NW2 61 CW59
Templeman Clo., Pur. 147 DP116
Croftleigh Ave.
Templeman Rd. W7 73 CF71
Templemead Clo. W3 74 CS72
Templemere, Wey. 113 BR104
Templepan La., Rick. 28 BL37
Templeton Ave. E4 51 EA49
Templeton Clo. N16 64 DS64
Truman's Rd.
Templeton Clo. SE19 120 DR95
Templeton Pl. SW5 90 DA77
Templeton Rd. N15 64 DR58
Templewood W13 73 CH71
Templewood Ave. NW3 62 DB62
Templewood Gdns. NW3 62 DB62
Tempsford Ave., Borwd. 32 CR42
Tempsford Clo., Enf. 36 DQ41
Gladbeck Way
Temsford Clo., Har. 44 CC54
Ten Acres, Lthd. 143 CD124
Ten Acres Clo., Lthd. 143 CD124
Tenbury Clo. E7 66 EK64
Romford Rd.
Tenbury Ct. SW2 105 DK88
Tenby Ave., Har. 45 CH54
Tenby Clo. N15 64 DT56
Hanover Rd.
Tenby Clo., Rom. 68 EY58
Tenby Gdns., Nthlt. 72 CA65
Tenby Rd. E17 65 DY57
Tenby Rd., Edg. 46 CM53
Tenby Rd., Enf. 36 DW41
Tenby Rd., Rom. 68 EY58
Tenby Rd., Well. 96 EX81
Tench St. E1 78 DV74
Tenda Rd. SE16 92 DV77
Roseberry St.
Tendring Way, Rom. 68 EW57
Tenham Ave. SW2 105 DK89
Tenison Ct. W1 5 K10
Tenison Way SE1 10 C3
Tenison Way SE1 77 DM74
Tennand Clo. (Cheshunt), Wal.Cr. 22 DT26
Tenniel Clo. W2 76 DC72
Porchester Gdns.
Tennis Ct. La., E.Mol. 115 CF97
Hampton Ct. Way
Tennis St. SE1 11 K4
Tennis St. SE1 92 DR75
Tennison Ave., Borwd. 32 CP43
Tennison Clo., Couls. 147 DP120
Tennison Rd. SE25 120 DT98
Tenniswood Rd., Enf. 36 DS39
Tennyson Ave. E11 66 EG59
Tennyson Ave. E12 80 EL66
Tennyson Ave. NW9 60 CQ55
Tennyson Ave., N.Mal. 117 CV99

Thurbarn Rd. SE6 107 EB92
Thurland Rd. SE16 92 DU76
Thurlby Clo., Har. 59 CG58
Gayton Rd.
Thurlby Clo., Wdf.Grn. 53 EM50
Thurlby Rd. SE27 105 DN91
Thurlby Rd., Wem. 73 CK65
Thurleigh Ave. SW12 104 DG86
Thurleigh Rd. SW12 104 DF87
Thurleston Ave., Mord. 117 CY99
Thurlestone Ave. N12 48 DF51
Thurlestone Ave., Ilf. 67 ET63
Thurlestone Clo., Shep. 113 BQ100
Thurlestone Rd. SE27 105 DN90
Thurloe Clo. SW7 8 B8
Thurloe Clo. SW7 90 DE77
Thurloe Gdns., Rom. 69 FF58
Thurloe Pl. SW7 8 A8
Thurloe Pl. SW7 90 DD77
Thurloe Pl. Ms. SW7 8 A8
Thurloe Sq. SW7 8 B8
Thurloe Sq. SW7 90 DE77
Thurloe St. SW7 8 A8
Thurloe St. SW7 90 DD77
Thurlow Clo. E4 51 EB51
Higham Sta. Ave.
Thurlow Gdns., Ilf. 53 ER51
Thurlow Gdns., Wem. 59 CK64
Thurlow Hill SE21 106 DQ88
Thurlow Pk. Rd. SE21 105 DP88
Thurlow Rd. NW3 62 DD64
Thurlow Rd. W7 87 CG75
Thurlow St. SE17 11 L10
Thurlow St. SE17 92 DR78
Thurlow Ter. NW5 62 DG64
Thurlston Rd., Ruis. 57 BU62
Thurnby Ct., Twick. 101 CE90
Thurnham Way, Tad. 145 CW120
Thursland Rd., Sid. 110 EY92
Thursley Cres., Croy. 135 EC108
Thursley Gdns. SW19 103 CX89
Thursley Rd. SE9 109 EM90
Thurso St. SW17 104 DD91
Thurstan Rd. SW20 103 CV94
Thurston Rd. SE13 93 EB82
Thurston Rd., Sthl. 72 BZ72
Thurtle Rd. E2 78 DT67
Thwaite Clo., Erith 97 FC79
Thyer Clo., Orp. 137 EQ105
Isabella Dr.
Thyra Gro. N12 48 DB51
Tibbatts Rd. E3 79 EB70
Tibbenham Wk. E13 80 EF68
Whitelegg Rd.
Tibberton Sq. N1 78 DQ66
Popham Rd.
Tibbets Clo. SW19 103 CX88
Tibbets Cor. SW19 103 CX87
Tibbet's Ride SW15 103 CX87
Tibbles Clo., Wat. 30 BY35
Tibbs Hill Rd., Abb.L. 15 BT30
Tiber Gdns. N1 77 DM67
Treaty St.
Ticehurst Clo., Orp. 110 EU94
Grovelands Rd.
Ticehurst Rd. SE23 107 DY89
Tichmarsh, Epsom 130 CQ110
Tickford Clo. SE2 96 EW75
Ampleforth Rd.
Tidal Basin Rd. E16 80 EF73
Tidenham Gdns., Croy. 120 DS104
Tideswell Rd. SW15 89 CW84
Tideswell Rd., Croy. 121 EA104
Tideway Clo., Rich. 101 CH91
Locksmeade Rd.
Tidey St. E3 79 EA71
Tidford Rd., Well. 95 ET82
Tidworth Rd. E3 79 EA70
Tidy's La., Epp. 26 EV29
Tiepigs La., Brom. 122 EF102
Tiepigs La., W.Wick. 122 EE103
Tierney Rd. SW2 105 DL87
Tiger La., Brom. 122 EH98
Tiger Way E5 64 DV63
Tilbrook Rd. SE3 94 EJ83
Tilbury Clo. SE15 92 DT80
Willowbrook Rd.
Tilbury Clo., Orp. 124 EV96
Tilbury Rd. E6 81 EM68
Tilbury Rd. E10 65 EC59
Tildesley Rd. SW15 103 CW86
Tile Fm. Rd., Orp. 123 ER104
Tile Kiln La. N6 63 DJ60
Winchester Rd.
Tile Kiln La. N13 50 DQ50
Tile Kiln La., Bex. 111 FC89
Tile Kiln La., Uxb. 57 BP59
Tile Yd. E14 79 DZ72
Commercial Rd.
Tilehouse Clo., Borwd. 32 CM41
Tilehurst Rd. SW18 104 DD88
Tilehurst Rd., Sutt. 131 CY106
Tilekiln Clo., Wal.Cr. 22 DT29
Tileyard Rd. N7 77 DL66
Tilford Ave., Croy. 135 EC108
Tilford Gdns. SW19 103 CX88
Tilia Rd. E5 64 DV63
Clarence Rd.
Tilia Wk. SW9 91 DP84
Moorland Rd.
Tiller Rd. E14 93 EA76
Tillett Clo. NW10 74 CQ65
Tillett Sq. SE16 93 DY75
Howland Way
Tillett Way E2 78 DU69
Gosset St.
Tilley La., Epsom 144 CQ123
Tilling Rd. NW2 61 CW60
Tilling Way, Wem. 59 CK63
Tillingbourne Gdns. N3 61 CZ55
Tillingbourne Grn., Orp. 123 ET98
Tillingbourne Way N3 61 CZ55
Tillingbourne Gdns.
Tillingdown Hill, Cat. 148 DU122
Tillingham Ct., Wal.Abb. 24 EG33
Tillingham Way N12 48 DA49
Tillman St. E1 78 DV72
Bigland St.
Tilloch St. N1 77 DM66
Carnoustie Dr.
Tillotson Rd. N9 50 DT47
Tillotson Rd., Har. 44 CB52
Tillotson Rd., Ilf. 67 EN59
Tilney Ct. EC1 7 J4
Tilney Dr., Buck.H. 52 EG47
Tilney Gdns. N1 78 DR65
Mitchison Rd.
Tilney Rd., Dag. 82 EZ65
Tilney Rd., Sthl. 86 BW77
Tilney St. W1 8 G2
Tilney St. W1 76 DG74
Tilson Gdns. SW2 105 DL87
Tilson Ho. SW2 105 DL87
Tilson Gdns.
Tilson Rd. N17 50 DU53
Tilt Clo., Cob. 142 BY116
Tilt Meadow, Cob. 142 BY116
Tilt Rd., Cob. 142 BW115
Tilt Yd. App. SE9 109 EM86
Tilton St. SW6 89 CY79
Tiltwood, The W3 74 CQ73
Acacia Rd.
Timber Clo., Chis. 123 EN96
Timber Hill Rd., Cat. 148 DU124
Timber La., Cat. 148 DU124
Timber Hill Rd.
Timber Mill Way SW4 91 DK83
Timber Pond Rd. SE16 79 DX74
Timber Ridge, Rick. 28 BJ42
Timber Slip Dr., Wall. 133 DK109
Timber St. EC1 7 H4
Timbercroft, Epsom 130 CS105
Timbercroft La. SE18 95 ES79
Timberdene NW4 47 CX54
Timberdene Ave., Ilf. 53 EQ53
Timberhill, Ash. 144 CL119
Ottways La.
Timberland Rd. E1 78 DV72
Timberling Gdns., S.Croy. 134 DR109
Sanderstead Rd.
Timbertop Rd., West. 150 EJ118
Timberwharf Rd. N16 64 DU58
Time Sq. E8 64 DT64
Times Sq., Sutt. 132 DB106
High St.
Timothy Clo. SW4 105 DJ85
Elms Rd.
Timothy Clo., Bexh. 110 EY85
Timothy Rd. E3 79 DZ71
Timsbury Wk. SW15 103 CU88
Tindal St. SW9 91 DP81
Tindale Clo., S.Croy. 134 DR111
Tinderbox All. SW14 88 CR83
Tine Rd., Chig. 53 ES50
Tinniswood Clo. N5 63 DN64
Drayton Pk.
Tinsley Rd. E1 78 DW71
Tintagel Clo., Epsom 131 CT114
Tintagel Cres. SE22 92 DT84
Tintagel Dr., Stan. 45 CK49
Tintagel Gdns. SE22 92 DT84
Oxonian St.
Tintagel Rd., Orp. 124 EW103
Tintern Ave. NW9 60 CP55
Tintern Clo. SW15 103 CY85
Tintern Clo. SW19 104 DC94
Tintern Gdns. N14 49 DL45
Tintern Path NW9 60 CS58
Ruthin Clo.
Tintern Rd. N22 50 DQ53
Tintern Rd., Cars. 118 DD102
Tintern St. SW4 91 DL84
Tintern Way, Har. 58 CB60
Tinto Rd. E16 80 EG70
Tinwell Ms., Borwd. 32 CQ43
Cranes Way
Tinworth St. SE11 10 A10
Tinworth St. SE11 91 DL78
Tippendell La., St.Alb. 16 CA25
Tippetts Clo., Enf. 36 DQ39
Tipthorpe Rd. SW11 90 DG83
Tipton Cotts., Add. 126 BG105
Oliver Clo.
Tipton Dr., Croy. 134 DS105
Tiptree Clo. E4 51 EC48
Tiptree Cres., Ilf. 67 EN55
Tiptree Dr., Enf. 36 DR42
Tiptree Est., Ilf. 67 EN55
Tiptree Rd., Ruis. 57 BV63
Tirlemont Rd., S.Croy. 134 DQ108
Tirrell Rd., Croy. 120 DQ100
Tisbury Ct. W1 5 M10
Tisbury Rd. SW16 119 DL96
Tisdall Pl. SE17 11 L9
Tisdall Pl. SE17 92 DR77
Titchborne Row W2 4 C9
Titchfield Rd. NW8 76 DF67
Titchfield Rd., Cars. 118 DD102
Titchfield Rd., Enf. 37 DY37
Titchfield Wk., Cars. 118 DD101
Titchfield Rd.
Titchwell Rd. SW18 104 DD87
Tite St. SW3 90 DF79
Tithe Barn Clo., Kings.T. 116 CM95
Tithe Barn Ct., Abb.L. 15 BT29
Tithe Barn Way, Nthlt. 71 BV68
Tithe Clo. NW7 47 CU53
Tithe Fm. Ave., Har. 58 CA62
Tithe Fm. Clo., Har. 58 CA62
Tithe Meadow, Wat. 29 BR44
Tithe Wk. NW7 47 CU53
Tithepit Shaw La., Warl. 148 DV117
Titian Ave. (Bushey), Wat. 45 CE45
Titley Clo. E4 51 EA50
Titmus Clo., Uxb. 71 BQ72
Titmuss Ave. SE28 82 EV73
Titmuss St. W12 89 CV75
Titsey Hill, Oxt. 150 EF123
Tiverton Ave., Ilf. 67 EN55
Tiverton Dr. SE9 109 EQ88
Tiverton Rd. N15 64 DR58
Tiverton Rd. N18 50 DS50
Tiverton Rd. NW10 75 CX67
Tiverton Rd., Edg. 46 CM54
Tiverton Rd., Houns. 86 CC82
Tiverton Rd., Pot.B. 20 DD31
Tiverton Rd., Ruis. 57 BU62
Tiverton Rd., Th.Hth. 119 DN99
Willett Rd.
Tiverton Rd., Wem. 74 CL68
Tiverton St. SE1 11 H7
Tiverton St. SE1 92 DQ76
Tiverton Way, Chess. 129 CJ106
Tivoli Ct. SE16 93 DZ75
Tivoli Gdns. SE18 94 EL77
Tivoli Rd. N8 63 DK57
Tivoli Rd. SE27 106 DQ92
Tivoli Rd., Houns. 86 BY84
Toad La., Houns. 86 BZ84
Tobacco Quay E1 78 DV73
Wapping La.
Tobago St. E14 93 EA75
Manilla St.
Tobin Clo. NW3 76 DE66
Toby La. E1 79 DY70
Toby Way, Surb. 116 CP103
Todds Wk. N7 63 DM61
Andover Rd.
Token Yd. SW15 89 CY84
Montserrat Rd.
Tokenhouse Yd. EC2 7 K8
Tokyngton Ave., Wem. 74 CN65
Toland Sq. SW15 103 CU85
Tolcarne Dr., Pnr. 43 BU54
Toley Ave., Wem. 60 CL59
Tollbridge Clo. W10 75 CY70
Kensal Rd.
Tollers La., Couls. 147 DM119
Tollesbury Gdns., Ilf. 67 ER55
Tollet St. E1 79 DX70
Tollgate Dr. SE21 106 DS89
Tollgate Gdns. NW6 76 DB68
Tollgate Rd. E6 80 EK71
Tollgate Rd. E16 80 EJ71
Tollgate Rd., Wal.Cr. 37 DX35
Tollhouse La., Wall. 133 DJ109
Tollhouse Way N19 63 DJ61
Tollington Pk. N4 63 DM61
Tollington Pl. N4 63 DM61
Tollington Rd. N7 63 DM63
Tollington Way N7 63 DL62
Tolmers Ave. (Cuffley), Pot.B. 21 DL28
Tolmers Gdns. (Cuffley), Pot.B. 21 DM29
Tolmers Ms., Hert. 21 DL25
Tolmers Pk., Hert. 21 DL25
Tolmers Rd. (Cuffley), Pot.B. 21 DK27
Tolmers Sq. NW1 5 L4
Tolpits Clo., Wat. 29 BT43
Tolpits La., Wat. 43 BQ46
Tolpuddle Ave. E13 80 EJ67
Rochester Ave.
Tolpuddle St. N1 77 DN68
Tolsford Rd. E5 64 DV64
Tolson Rd., Islw. 87 CG83
Tolverne Rd. SW20 117 CW95
Tolworth Clo., Surb. 116 CP102
Tolworth Gdns., Rom. 68 EX57
Tolworth Pk. Rd., Surb. 116 CM103
Tolworth Ri. N., Surb. 116 CQ101
Elmbridge Ave.
Tolworth Ri. S., Surb. 116 CQ102
Warren Dr. S.
Tolworth Rd., Surb. 116 CL103
Tom Coombs Clo. SE9 94 EL84
Well Hall Rd.
Tom Cribb Rd. SE28 95 EQ76
Tom Gros. Clo. E15 65 ED64
Maryland St.
Tom Hood Clo. E15 65 ED64
Maryland St.
Tom Mann Clo., Bark. 81 ES67
Tom Nolan Clo. E15 80 EE68
Tom Smith Clo. SE10 94 EE79
Maze Hill
Tom Thumbs Arch E3 79 EA68
Malmesbury Rd.
Tomahawk Gdns., Nthlt. 72 BX69
Javelin Way
Tomkins Clo., Borwd. 32 CL39
Tallis Way
Tomlin Clo., Epsom 130 CR111
Tomlins Gro. E3 79 EA69
Tomlins Orchard, Bark. 81 EQ67
Tomlins Ter. E14 79 DZ71
Rhodeswell Rd.
Tomlins Wk. N7 63 DM61
Briset Way
Tomlinson Clo. E2 78 DT69
Tomlinson Clo. W4 88 CP78
Oxford Rd. N.
Tompion St. EC1 6 F3
Toms Hill, Kings L. 14 BJ33
Bucks Hill
Toms La., Abb.L. 15 BS27
Toms La., Kings L. 15 BP29
Tomswood Ct., Ilf. 53 EQ53
Tomswood Hill, Ilf. 53 EP52
Tomswood Rd., Chig. 53 EN51
Tonbridge Clo., Bans. 132 DF114
Tonbridge Cres., Har. 60 CL56
Tonbridge Ho. SE25 120 DU97
Tonbridge Rd., Sev. 155 FJ126
Tonbridge Rd., W.Mol. 114 BY98
Tonbridge St. WC1 5 P2
Tonbridge St. WC1 77 DL69
Tonbridge Wk. WC1 5 P2
Tonfield Rd., Sutt. 117 CZ102
Tonge Clo., Beck. 121 EA99
Tonsley Hill SW18 104 DB85
Tonsley Pl. SW18 104 DB85
Tonsley Rd. SW18 104 DB85
Tonsley St. SW18 104 DB85
Tonstall Rd., Epsom 130 CR110
Tonstall Rd., Mitch. 118 DG96
Tony Cannell Ms. E3 79 DZ69
Maplin St.
Tooke Clo., Pnr. 44 BY53
Took's Ct. EC4 6 D8
Tooley St. SE1 11 L2
Tooley St. SE1 78 DS74
Toorack Rd., Har. 45 CD54
Toot Hill Rd., Ong. 27 FF30
Tooting Bec Gdns. SW16 105 DK91
Tooting Bec Rd. SW16 105 DH91
Tooting Bec Rd. SW17 104 DG90
Tooting Gro. SW17 104 DE92
Tooting High St. SW17 104 DE93
Tootswood Rd., Brom. 122 EE99
Tooveys Mill Clo., Kings L. 14 BN28
Top Dartford Rd., Swan. 111 FF94
Top Ho. Ri. E4 51 EC45
Parkhill Rd.
Top Pk., Beck. 122 EE99
Topaz Wk. NW2 61 CX59
Marble Dr.
Topcliffe Dr., Orp. 137 ER106
Topham Sq. N17 50 DQ53
Topham St. EC1 6 D4
Topiary, The, Ash. 144 CL121
Topiary Sq., Rich. 88 CM83
Topley St. SE9 94 EK84
Topp Wk. NW2 61 CW61
Topping La., Uxb. 70 BK69
Cleveland Rd.
Topsfield Clo. N8 63 DK57
Wolseley Rd.
Topsfield Par. N8 63 DL57
Tottenham La.
Topsfield Rd. N8 63 DL57
Topsham Rd. SW17 104 DF90
Tor Gdns. W8 90 DA75
Tor La., Wey. 127 BQ111
Tor Rd., Well. 96 EW81
Torbay Rd. NW6 75 CZ66
Torbay Rd., Har. 58 BY61
Torbay St. NW1 77 DH66
Hawley Rd.
Torbitt Way, Ilf. 67 ET57
Torbridge Clo., Edg. 46 CL52
Torbrook Clo., Bex. 110 EY86
Torcross Dr. SE23 106 DW89
Torcross Rd., Ruis. 57 BV62
Torland Dr., Lthd. 129 CD114
Tormead Clo., Sutt. 132 DA107
Tormount Rd. SE18 95 ES79
Toronto Ave. E12 67 EM63
Toronto Rd. E11 65 ED63
Toronto Rd., Ilf. 67 EP60
Torquay Gdns., Ilf. 66 EK56
Torquay St. W2 76 DB71
Harrow Rd.
Torr Rd. SE20 107 DX94
Torrance Clo., Horn. 69 FH60
Torre Wk., Cars. 118 DE102
Torrens Rd. E15 80 EF65
Torrens Rd. SW2 105 DM85
Torrens Sq. E15 80 EF65
Torrens St. EC1 6 E1
Torrens St. EC1 77 DN68
Torriano Ave. NW5 63 DK64
Torriano Cotts. NW5 63 DJ64
Torriano Ave.
Torriano Ms. NW5 63 DK64
Torriano Ave.
Torridge Gdns. SE15 92 DW84
Torridge Rd., Th.Hth. 119 DP99
Torridon Rd. SE6 107 ED87
Torridon Rd. SE13 108 EE87
Torrington Ave. N12 48 DD50
Torrington Clo. N12 48 DD49
Torrington Clo., Esher 129 CE107
Torrington Dr., Har. 58 CB63
Torrington Dr., Loug. 39 EQ42
Torrington Dr., Pot.B. 20 DD32
Torrington Gdns. N11 49 DJ51
Torrington Gdns., Grnf. 73 CJ67
Torrington Gdns., Loug. 39 EQ42
Torrington Gro. N12 48 DE50
Torrington Pk. N12 48 DC50
Torrington Pl. E1 78 DU74
Torrington Pl. WC1 5 L6
Torrington Pl. WC1 77 DK71
Torrington Rd. E18 66 EG55
Torrington Rd., Dag. 68 EZ60
Torrington Rd., Esher 129 CE107
Torrington Rd., Grnf. 73 CJ67
Torrington Rd., Ruis. 57 BT62
Torrington Sq. WC1 5 N5
Torrington Sq. WC1 77 DK70
Torrington Sq., Croy. 120 DR101
Tavistock Gro.
Torrington Way, Mord. 118 DA101
Torver Rd., Har. 59 CE56
Torver Way, Orp. 123 ER103
Torwood La., Whyt. 148 DT120
Torwood Rd. SW15 103 CU85
Torworth Rd., Borwd. 32 CM38
Tothill St. SW1 9 M5
Tothill St. SW1 91 DK75
Totnes Rd., Well. 96 EV80
Totnes Wk. N2 62 DD56
Tottan Ter. E1 79 DX72
Belgrave St.
Tottenhall Rd. N13 49 DN51
Tottenham Ct. Rd. W1 5 L5
Tottenham Ct. Rd. W1 77 DJ70
Tottenham Grn. E. N15 64 DT56
Tottenham La. N8 63 DL57
Tottenham Ms. W1 5 L6
Tottenham Rd. N1 78 DS65
Tottenham St. W1 5 L7
Tottenham St. W1 77 DJ71
Totterdown St. SW17 104 DF91
Totteridge Common N20 47 CU47
Totteridge Grn. N20 48 DA47
Totteridge La. N20 48 DA47
Totteridge Rd., Enf. 37 DX37
Totteridge Village N20 47 CY46
Totternhoe Clo., Har. 59 CJ57
Totton Rd., Th.Hth. 119 DN97
Toulmin St. SE1 11 H5
Toulmin St. SE1 92 DQ75
Toulon St. SE5 92 DQ80
Tournay Rd. SW6 89 CZ80
Toussaint Wk. SE16 92 DU76
John Roll Way
Tovey Clo., St.Alb. 17 CK26
Tovil Clo. SE20 120 DV96
Towcester Rd. E3 79 EB70
Tower Bri. E1 11 P3
Tower Bri. E1 78 DT74
Tower Bri. SE1 11 P3
Tower Bri. SE1 78 DT74
Tower Bri. App. E1 11 P2
Tower Bri. App. E1 78 DT74
Tower Bri. Piazza SE1 78 DT74
Horselydown La.
Tower Bri. Rd. SE1 11 M7
Tower Bri. Rd. SE1 92 DS76
Tower Clo. NW3 62 DD64
Lyndhurst Rd.
Tower Clo. SE20 106 DV94
Tower Clo., Ilf. 53 EP51
Tower Clo., Orp. 123 ET103
Tower Ct. WC2 5 P9
Tower Gdns. Rd. N17 50 DQ53
Tower Gro., Wey. 113 BS103
Tower Hamlets Rd. E7 66 EF63
Tower Hamlets Rd. E17 65 EA55
Tower Hill EC3 11 N1
Tower Hill EC3 78 DS73
Tower Hill Ter. EC3 78 DS73
Byward St.
Tower La., Wem. 59 CK62
Main Dr.
Tower Ms. E17 65 EA56
Tower Pier EC3 11 N2
Tower Pier EC3 78 DS73
Tower Pl. EC3 11 N1
Tower Pt., Enf. 36 DR42
Tower Ri., Rich. 88 CL83
Jocelyn Rd.
Tower Rd. NW10 75 CU66
Tower Rd., Belv. 97 FC77
Tower Rd., Bexh. 96 FA84
Tower Rd., Epp. 25 ES30
Tower Rd., Orp. 123 ET103
Tower Rd., Tad. 145 CW123
Tower Rd., Twick. 101 CF90
Tower Royal EC4 7 J10
Tower St. WC2 5 N9
Tower St. WC2 77 DK72
Tower Ter. N22 49 DM54
Mayes Rd.
Tower Vw., Croy. 121 DX101
Towers, The, Ken. 148 DQ115
Towers Ave., Uxb. 71 BQ69
Towers Pl., Rich. 102 CL85
Eton St.
Towers Rd., Pnr. 44 BY52
Towers Rd., Sthl. 72 CA70
Towers Wk., Wey. 127 BP107
Towfield Rd., Felt. 100 BZ89
Towing Path Wk. N1 77 DK67
York Way
Town, The, Enf. 36 DR41
Town Ct. Path N4 64 DQ60
Town End, Cat. 148 DS122
Town End Clo., Cat. 148 DS122
Town Fld. Way, Islw. 87 CG82
Town Hall App. N16 64 DS63
Milton Gro.
Town Hall App. Rd. N15 64 DT56
Town Hall Ave. W4 88 CR78
Town Hall Rd. SW11 90 DF83
Town La., Stai. 98 BK86
Town Meadow, Brent. 87 CK80
Town Quay, Bark. 81 EP67
Town Rd. N9 50 DV47

Town Sq., Erith 97 FE79
Pier Rd.
Town Tree Rd., Ashf. 98 BN92
Towncourt Cres., Orp. 123 EQ99
Towncourt La., Orp. 123 ER100
Towney Mead, Nthlt. 72 BZ68
Townfield, Rick. 42 BJ45
Townfield Rd., Hayes 71 BT74
Townfield Sq., Hayes 71 BT73
Towngate, Cob. 142 BY115
Townholm Cres. W7 87 CF76
Townley Ct. E15 80 EF65
Townley Rd. SE22 106 DS85
Townley Rd., Bexh. 110 EZ86
Townley St. SE17 11 K10
Townmead Rd. SW6 90 DB83
Townmead Rd., Rich. 88 CP82
Townmead Rd., Wal.Abb. 23 EC34
Townsend Ave. N14 49 DK49
Townsend Ind. Est. NW10 74 CQ68
Townsend La. NW9 60 CR59
Townsend Rd. N15 64 DT57
Townsend Rd., Ashf. 98 BL92
Townsend Rd., Sthl. 72 BY74
Townsend St. SE17 11 M8
Townsend St. SE17 92 DR77
Townsend Way, Nthwd. 43 BT52
Townsend Yd. N6 62 DG60
Townshend Clo., Sid. 110 EV93
Townshend Est. NW8 76 DE68
Townshend Rd. NW8 76 DE67
Townshend Rd., Chis. 109 EP92
Townshend Rd., Rich. 88 CM84
Townshend Ter., Rich. 88 CM84
Townslow La., Wok. 140 BK116
Townson Ave., Nthlt. 71 BU69
Townson Way, Nthlt. 71 BU68
Townson Ave.
Towpath, Shep. 112 BM102
Dockett Eddy La.
Towpath Way, Croy. 120 DT100
Towton Rd. SE27 106 DQ89
Toynbec Clo., Chis. 109 EP91
Beechwood Ri.
Toynbee Rd. SW20 117 CY95
Toynbee St. E1 7 P7
Toynbee St. E1 78 DT71
Toyne Way N6 62 DF58
Gaskell Rd.
Tracery, The, Bans. 146 DB115
Tracey Ave. NW2 61 CW64
Tracy Ct., Stan. 45 CJ52
Trade Clo. N13 49 DN49
Trader Rd. E6 81 EP72
Tradescant Rd. SW8 91 DL80
Trading Est. Rd. NW10 74 CQ70
Trafalgar Ave. N17 50 DS51
Trafalgar Ave. SE15 92 DT78
Trafalgar Ave., Wor.Pk. 117 CX102
Trafalgar Business Cen., Bark. 81 ET70
Trafalgar Clo. SE16 93 DY77
Greenland Quay
Trafalgar Ct., Cob. 127 BU113
Trafalgar Dr., Walt. 113 BU104
Trafalgar Gdns. E1 79 DX71
Trafalgar Gdns. W8 90 DB76
South End Row
Trafalgar Gro. SE10 93 ED79
Trafalgar Pl. E11 66 EG56
Trafalgar Pl. N18 50 DU50
Trafalgar Rd. SE10 93 ED79
Trafalgar Rd. SW19 104 DB94
Trafalgar Rd., Rain. 83 FF68
Trafalgar Rd., Twick. 101 CD89
Trafalgar Sq. SW1 9 N2
Trafalgar Sq. SW1 77 DK74
Trafalgar Sq. WC2 9 N2
Trafalgar Sq. WC2 77 DK74
Trafalgar St. SE17 11 K10
Trafalgar St. SE17 92 DR78
Trafalgar Ter., Har. 59 CE60
Nelson Rd.
Trafalgar Way E14 79 EC74
Trafalgar Way, Croy. 119 DM103
Trafford Clo. E15 65 EB64
Trafford Clo., Ilf. 53 ET51
Trafford Clo., Rad. 18 CL32
Trafford Rd., Th.Hth. 119 DM99
Tramway Ave. E15 80 EE66
Tramway Ave. N9 50 DV45
Tramway Path, Mitch. 118 DE98
London Rd.
Tranby Pl. E9 65 DX64
Homerton High St.
Tranley Ms. NW3 62 DE63
Fleet Rd.
Tranmere Rd. N9 50 DT45
Tranmere Rd. SW18 104 DC88
Tranmere Rd., Twick. 100 CB87
Tranquil Pas. SE3 94 EF82
Tranquil Vale
Tranquil Ri., Erith 97 FE78
West St.
Tranquil Vale SE3 94 EE82
Transay Wk. N1 78 DR65
Marquess Rd.
Transept St. NW1 4 C7
Transept St. NW1 76 DE71
Transmere Clo., Orp. 123 EQ100
Transmere Rd., Orp. 123 EQ100
Transom Clo. SE16 93 DY77
Plough Way
Transom Sq. E14 93 EB77
Transport Ave., Brent. 87 CG78
Tranton Rd. SE16 92 DU76
Traps Hill, Loug. 39 EM41
Traps La., N.Mal. 116 CS95
Travellers Way, Houns. 86 BW82
Travers Clo. E17 51 DX53
Travers Rd. N7 63 DN62
Treacy Clo. (Bushey), Wat. 44 CC47
Treadgold St. W11 75 CX73
Treadway St. E2 78 DV68
Treadwell Rd., Epsom 144 CS116
Treaty Rd., Houns. 86 CB83
Hanworth Rd.
Treaty St. N1 77 DM67
Trebeck St. W1 9 H2
Trebovir Rd. SW5 90 DA78
Treby St. E3 79 DZ70
Trecastle Way N7 63 DK63
Carleton Rd.
Tredegar Ms. E3 79 DZ69
Tredegar Ter.
Tredegar Rd. E3 79 DZ68
Tredegar Rd. N11 49 DK52
Tredegar Rd., Dart. 111 FG89
Tredegar Sq. E3 79 DZ69
Tredegar Ter. E3 79 DZ69
Trederwen Rd. E8 78 DU67
Tredown Rd. SE26 106 DW92
Tredwell Clo., Brom. 122 EL98
Tredwell Rd. SE27 105 DP91
Tree Clo., Rich. 101 CK88
Tree Rd. E16 80 EJ72
Treebourne Rd., West. 150 EJ117
Treen Ave. SW13 88 CS83
Treeside Clo., West Dr. 84 BK77
Treetops, Whyt. 148 DU118
Treetops Clo. SE2 96 EY78
Treetops Clo., Nthwd. 43 BR50
Treeview Clo. SE19 120 DS95
Treewall Gdns., Brom. 108 EH91
Trefgarne Rd., Dag. 68 FA61
Trefil Wk. N7 63 DL63
Trefoil Rd. SW18 104 DC85
Trefusis Wk., Wat. 29 BS39
Tregaron Ave. N8 63 DL58
Tregaron Gdns., N.Mal. 116 CS98
Avenue Rd.
Tregarthen Pl., Lthd. 143 CJ121
Tregarvon Rd. SW11 90 DG84
Tregenna Ave., Har. 58 BZ63
Tregenna Clo. N14 35 DJ43
Tregenna Ct., Har. 58 CA63
Trego Rd. E9 79 EA66
Tregothnan Rd. SW9 91 DL83
Tregunter Rd. SW10 90 DC79
Trehearn Rd., Ilf. 53 ES52
Trehern Rd. SW14 88 CR83
Treherne Ct. SW9 91 DN81
Eythorne Rd.
Treherne Ct. SW17 104 DG91
Trehurst St. E5 65 DY64
Trelawn Rd. E10 65 EC62
Trelawn Rd. SW2 105 DN85
Trelawney Clo. E17 65 EB56
Orford Rd.
Trelawney Est. E9 78 DW65
Trelawney Gro., Wey. 126 BN107
Trelawney Rd., Ilf. 53 ER52
Trellick Twr. W10 75 CZ70
Trellis Sq. E3 79 DZ69
Malmesbury Rd.
Treloar Gdns. SE19 106 DR93
Hancock Rd.
Tremadoc Rd. SW4 91 DK84
Tremaine Clo. SE4 93 EA82
Tremaine Rd. SE20 120 DV96
Trematon Pl., Tedd. 101 CJ94
Tremlett Gro. N19 63 DJ62
Tremlett Ms. N19 63 DJ62
Tremlett Gro.
Trenance Gdns., Ilf. 68 EU62
Trench Yd. Ct., Mord. 118 DB100
Green La.
Trenchard Ave., Ruis. 57 BV63
Trenchard Clo., Stan. 45 CG51
Trenchard Clo., Walt. 128 BW106
Trenchard Ct., Mord. 118 DB100
Trenchard St. SE10 93 ED78
Trenchold St. SW8 91 DL79
Trenham Dr., Warl. 148 DW116
Trenholme Clo. SE20 106 DV94
Trenholme Ct., Cat. 148 DU122
Trenholme Rd. SE20 106 DV94
Trenholme Ter. SE20 106 DV94
Trenmar Gdns. NW10 75 CV69
Trent Ave. W5 87 CJ76
Trent Clo., Rad. 18 CL32
Trent Gdns. N14 35 DH44
Trent Rd. SW2 105 DM85
Trent Rd., Buck.H. 52 EH46
Trent Way, Hayes 71 BS69
Trent Way, Wor.Pk. 117 CW104
Trentbridge Clo., Ilf. 53 ET51
Trentham Dr., Orp. 124 EU98
Trentham St. SW18 104 DA88
Trentwood Side, Enf. 35 DM41
Treport St. SW18 104 DB87
Tresco Clo., Brom. 108 EE93
Tresco Gdns., Ilf. 68 EU61
Tresco Rd. SE15 92 DV84
Trescoe Gdns., Har. 58 BY59
Trescoe Gdns., Rom. 55 FC50
Tresham Cres. NW8 4 B4
Tresham Cres. NW8 76 DE70
Tresham Rd., Bark. 81 ET66
Tresham Wk. E9 64 DW64
Churchill Wk.
Tresilian Ave. N21 35 DM43
Tressell Clo. N1 77 DP66
Sebbon St.
Tressillian Cres. SE4 93 EA83
Tressillian Rd. SE4 93 DZ84
Trestis Clo., Hayes 72 BY71
Jollys La.
Treswell Rd., Dag. 82 EY67
Tretawn Gdns. NW7 46 CS49
Tretawn Pk. NW7 46 CS49
Trevanion Rd. W14 89 CY77
Treve Ave., Har. 58 CC59
Trevellance Way, Wat. 16 BW33
Trevelyan Ave. E12 67 EM63
Trevelyan Cres., Har. 59 CK59
Trevelyan Gdns. NW10 75 CW67
Trevelyan Rd. E15 66 EF63
Trevelyan Rd. SW17 104 DE92
Treveris St. SE1 10 G3
Treverton St. W10 75 CY70
Treves Clo. N21 35 DM43
Worlds End La.
Treville St. SW15 103 CV87
Treviso Rd. SE23 107 DX89
Farren Rd.
Trevithick Clo., Felt. 99 BT88
Trevithick St. SE8 93 EA79
Trevone Gdns., Pnr. 58 BY58
Trevor Clo., Barn. 34 DD44
Trevor Clo., Brom. 122 EF101
Trevor Clo., Har. 45 CF52
Kenton La.
Trevor Clo., Islw. 101 CF85
Trevor Clo., Nthlt. 72 BW68
Trevor Cres., Ruis. 57 BT63
Trevor Gdns., Edg. 46 CR53
Trevor Gdns., Nthlt. 72 BW68
Trevor Gdns., Ruis. 57 BU63
Bedford Rd.
Trevor Pl. SW7 8 C5
Trevor Pl. SW7 90 DE75
Trevor Rd. SW19 103 CY94
Trevor Rd., Edg. 46 CR53
Trevor Rd., Hayes 85 BS75
Trevor Rd., Wdf.Grn. 52 EG52
Trevor Sq. SW7 8 D5
Trevor Sq. SW7 90 DE76
Trevor St. SW7 8 C5
Trevor St. SW7 90 DE75
Trevose Rd. E17 51 ED53
Trevose Way, Wat. 44 BW48
Trewenna Dr., Chess. 129 CK106
Trewenna Dr., Pot.B. 20 DD32
Trewince Rd. SW20 117 CW95
Trewint St. SW18 104 DC89
Trewsbury Rd. SE26 107 DX92
Triandra Way, Hayes 72 BX71
Triangle, The EC1 77 DP70
Goswell Rd.
Triangle, The N13 49 DN49
Lodge Dr.
Triangle, The, Bark. 81 EQ65
Tanner St.
Triangle, The, Hmptn. 114 CC95
High St.
Triangle, The, Kings.T. 116 CQ96
Kenley Rd.
Triangle Ct. E16 80 EK71
Tollgate Rd.
Triangle Pas., Barn. 34 DC42
Station Rd.
Triangle Pl. SW4 91 DK84
Triangle Rd. E8 78 DV67
Trident Gdns., Nthlt. 72 BX69
Jetstar Way
Trident Rd., Wat. 15 BT34
Trident St. SE16 93 DX77
Trident Wk. SE16 93 DX77
Greenland Quay
Trident Way, Sthl. 85 BV76
Trig La. EC4 7 H10
Trigo Ct., Epsom 130 CR111
Blakeney Clo.
Trigon Rd. SW8 91 DM80
Trilby Rd. SE23 107 DX89
Trim St. SE14 93 DZ79
Trimmer Wk., Brent. 88 CL79
Netley Rd.
Trinder Gdns. N19 63 DL60
Trinder Rd.
Trinder Rd. N19 63 DL60
Trinder Rd., Barn. 33 CW43
Tring Ave. W5 74 CM74
Tring Ave., Sthl. 72 BZ72
Tring Ave., Wem. 74 CN65
Tring Clo., Ilf. 67 ER57
Trinidad Gdns., Dag. 83 FD66
Trinidad St. E14 79 DZ73
Trinity Ave. N2 62 DD55
Trinity Ave., Enf. 36 DT44
Trinity Ch. Pas. SW13 89 CV79
Trinity Ch. Rd. SW13 89 CV79
Trinity Ch. Sq. SE1 11 J6
Trinity Ch. Sq. SE1 92 DQ76
Trinity Clo. E8 78 DT65
Trinity Clo. E11 66 EE61
Trinity Clo. NW3 62 DD63
Hampstead High St.
Trinity Clo. SE13 93 ED84
Wisteria Rd.
Trinity Clo., Brom. 122 EL102
Trinity Clo., Houns. 86 BY84
Trinity Clo., Nthwd. 43 BS51
Trinity Clo., S.Croy. 134 DS109
Trinity Clo., Stai. 98 BJ86
Trinity Cotts., Rich. 88 CM83
Trinity Rd.
Trinity Ct. N1 78 DS66
Downham Rd.
Trinity Ct. SE7 94 EK77
Charlton La.
Trinity Cres. SW17 104 DF89
Trinity Gdns. SW9 91 DM84
Trinity Gro. SE10 93 EC81
Trinity Hall Clo., Wat. 30 BW40
Trinity La., Wal.Cr. 23 DY32
Trinity Ms. SE20 120 DV95
Trinity Ms. W10 75 CX72
Cambridge Gdns.
Trinity Path SE26 106 DW90
Sydenham Pk.
Trinity Pl., Bexh. 96 EZ84
Trinity Ri. SW2 105 DN88
Trinity Rd. N2 62 DD55
Trinity Rd. N22 49 DL52
Whittington Rd.
Trinity Rd. SW17 104 DF89
Trinity Rd. SW18 104 DD85
Trinity Rd. SW19 104 DA93
Trinity Rd., Ilf. 67 EQ55
Trinity Rd., Rich. 88 CM83
Trinity Rd., Sthl. 72 BY74
Trinity Sq. EC3 11 N1
Trinity Sq. EC3 78 DS73
Trinity St. E16 80 EG71
Vincent St.
Trinity St. SE1 11 J5
Trinity St. SE1 92 DQ75
Trinity St., Enf. 36 DQ40
Trinity Wk. NW3 76 DC65
Trinity Way E4 51 DZ51
Trinity Way W3 74 CS73
Trio Pl. SE1 11 J5
Tristan Sq. SE3 94 EE83
Tristram Clo. E17 65 ED55
Tristram Rd., Brom. 108 EF91
Triton Sq. NW1 5 K4
Triton Sq. NW1 77 DJ70
Tritton Ave., Croy. 133 DL105
Tritton Rd. SE21 106 DR90
Trittons, Tad. 145 CW121
Triumph Clo., Hayes 85 BQ81
Triumph Ho., Bark. 82 EU69
Triumph Rd. E6 81 EM72
Trojan Ct. NW6 75 CY66
Willesden La.
Trojan Way, Croy. 119 DM104
Troon St. E1 79 DY72
White Horse Rd.
Trosley Rd., Belv. 96 FA79
Trossachs Rd. SE22 106 DS85
Trothy Rd. SE1 92 DU77
Monnow Rd.
Trott Rd. N10 48 DF52
Trott St. SW11 90 DD81
Trotters Bottom, Barn. 33 CU37
Trotwood, Chig. 53 ER51
Troughton Rd. SE7 94 EH78
Trout La., West Dr. 70 BH73
Trout Ri., Rick. 28 BH41
Trout Rd., West Dr. 70 BK74
Troutbeck Rd. SE14 93 DY81
Troutstream Way, Rick. 28 BH42
Trouville Rd. SW4 105 DJ86
Trowbridge Est. E9 79 DZ65
Osborne Rd.
Trowbridge Rd. E9 79 DZ65
Trowley Ri., Abb.L. 15 BS31
Trowlock Ave., Tedd. 101 CJ93
Trowlock Island, Tedd. 101 CJ92
Trowlock Way, Tedd. 101 CK93
Troy Clo., Tad. 145 CV120
Troy Ct. SE18 95 EP77
Troy Rd. SE19 106 DR93
Troy Town SE15 92 DU83
Truesdale Dr., Uxb. 56 BJ56
Truesdale Rd. E6 81 EM72
Trulock Ct. N17 50 DU52
Trulock Rd. N17 50 DU52
Truman Clo., Edg. 46 CP52
Pavilion Way
Truman's Rd. N16 64 DS64
Trump St. EC2 7 J9
Trumper Way, Uxb. 70 BJ67
Trumpers Way W7 87 CE75
Trumpington Rd. E7 66 EF63
Trundle St. SE1 11 H4
Trundlers Way (Bushey), Wat. 45 CE46
Trundleys Rd. SE8 93 DX78
Trundleys Ter. SE8 93 DX77
Trunks All., Swan. 125 FB96
Truro Gdns., Ilf. 66 EL59
Truro Rd. E17 65 DZ56
Truro Rd. N22 49 DL52
Truro St. NW5 76 DG65
Truro Way, Hayes 71 BS69
Portland Rd.
Truslove Rd. SE27 105 DN92
Trussley Rd. W6 89 CW76
Trust Rd., Wal.Cr. 23 DY34
Trust Wk. SE21 105 DP88
Peabody Hill
Trustons Gdns., Horn. 69 FG59
Tryfan Clo., Ilf. 66 EK57
Tryon St. SW3 8 D10
Tryon St. SW3 90 DF78
Trystings Clo., Esher 129 CG107
Tuam Rd. SE18 95 ER79
Tubbenden Clo., Orp. 123 ES103
Tubbenden Dr., Orp. 137 ER105
Tubbenden La., Orp. 137 ER105
Tubbenden La. S., Orp. 137 ER106
Tubbs Rd. NW10 75 CT68
Tubs Hill Par., Sev. 154 FG124
Tuck Rd., Rain. 83 FG65
Tucker St., Wat. 30 BW43
Tudor Ave., Hmptn. 100 CA93
Tudor Ave., Rom. 69 FG55
Tudor Ave. (Cheshunt), Wal.Cr. 22 DU31
Tudor Ave., Wat. 30 BX38
Tudor Ave., Wor.Pk. 117 CV104
Tudor Clo. N6 63 DJ59
Tudor Clo. NW3 62 DE64
Tudor Clo. NW7 47 CU51
Tudor Clo. NW9 60 CQ61
Tudor Clo. SW2 105 DM86
Elm Pk.
Tudor Clo., Ashf. 98 BL91
Tudor Clo., Bans. 145 CY115
Tudor Clo., Chess. 130 CL106
Tudor Clo., Chig. 53 EN49
Tudor Clo., Chis. 123 EM95
Tudor Clo., Cob. 128 BZ113
Tudor Clo., Couls. 147 DN118
Tudor Clo., Dart. 111 FH86
Tudor Clo., Lthd. 142 CA124
Tudor Clo., Pnr. 57 BU57
Tudor Clo., S.Croy. 148 DV115
Tudor Clo., Sutt. 131 CY107
Tudor Clo., Wall. 133 DJ108
Tudor Clo. (Cheshunt), Wal.Cr. 22 DV31
Tudor Clo., Wdf.Grn. 52 EH50
Tudor Ct. E17 65 DZ59
Tudor Ct., Borwd. 32 CL40
Tudor Ct., Felt. 100 BW91
Tudor Ct., Swan. 125 FC101
Tudor Ct. N., Wem. 60 CN64
Tudor Ct. S., Wem. 60 CN64
Tudor Cres., Enf. 36 DQ39
Tudor Cres., Ilf. 53 EP51
Tudor Dr., Kings.T. 101 CK92
Tudor Dr., Mord. 117 CX100
Tudor Dr., Rom. 69 FG56
Tudor Dr., Walt. 114 BX102
Tudor Dr., Wat. 30 BX38
Tudor Est. NW10 74 CP69
Tudor Gdns. NW9 60 CQ61
Tudor Gdns. SW13 88 CS83
Treen Ave.
Tudor Gdns. W3 74 CN71
Tudor Gdns., Rom. 69 FG56
Tudor Gdns., Twick. 101 CF88
Tudor Gdns., W.Wick. 121 EC104
Tudor Gro. E9 78 DW66
Tudor Gro. N20 48 DE48
Church Cres.
Tudor Manor Gdns., Wat. 16 BX32
Tudor Par., Rick. 42 BG45
Berry La.
Tudor Pl. W1 5 M8
Tudor Pl., Mitch. 104 DE94
Tudor Rd. E4 51 EB51
Tudor Rd. E6 80 EJ67
Tudor Rd. E9 78 DV67
Tudor Rd. N9 50 DV45
Tudor Rd. SE19 106 DT94
Tudor Rd. SE25 120 DV99
Tudor Rd., Ashf. 99 BR93
Tudor Rd., Bark. 81 ET67
Tudor Rd., Barn. 34 DA41
Tudor Rd., Beck. 121 EB97
Tudor Rd., Hmptn. 100 CA94
Tudor Rd., Har. 45 CD54
Tudor Rd., Hayes 71 BR72
Tudor Rd., Houns. 87 CD84
Tudor Rd., Kings.T. 102 CN94
Tudor Rd., Pnr. 44 BW54
Tudor Rd., Sthl. 72 BY73
Tudor Sq., Hayes 71 BR71
Tudor St. EC4 6 E10
Tudor St. EC4 77 DN73
Tudor Wk., Bex. 110 EY86
Tudor Wk., Lthd. 143 CF120
Tudor Wk., Wat. 30 BX37
Tudor Wk., Wey. 113 BP104
West Palace Gdns.
Tudor Way N14 49 DK46
Tudor Way W3 88 CN75
Tudor Way, Orp. 123 ER100
Tudor Way, Rick. 42 BG46
Tudor Way, Uxb. 70 BN65
Tudor Way, Wal.Abb. 23 ED33
Tudor Well Clo., Stan. 45 CH50
Tudway Rd. SE3 94 EH83
Tufnell Pk. Rd. N7 63 DK63
Tufnell Pk. Rd. N19 63 DJ63
Tufter Rd., Chig. 53 ET50
Tufton Gdns., W.Mol. 114 CB96
Tufton Rd. E4 51 EA49
Tufton St. SW1 9 P7
Tufton St. SW1 91 DK76
Tugboat St. SE28 95 ES75
Tugela Rd., Croy. 120 DR100
Tugela St. SE6 107 DZ89
Tugmutton Clo., Orp. 137 EP105
Acorn Way
Tuilerie St. E2 78 DU68
Hackney Rd.
Tulip Clo. E6 81 EM71
Bradley Stone Rd.
Tulip Clo., Croy. 121 DX102
Tulip Clo., Hmptn. 100 BZ93
Partridge Rd.
Tulip Clo., Sthl. 86 CC75
Chevy Rd.
Tulip Ct., Pnr. 58 BW55
Tulip Dr., Ilf. 67 EP64
Tulip Gdns., Ilf. 81 EP65

Upper Ter. NW3 62 DC62
Upper Thames St. EC4 6 G10
Upper Thames St. EC4 78 DQ73
Upper Tollington Pk. N4 63 DN59
Upper Tooting Pk. SW17 104 DF89
Upper Tooting Rd. SW17 104 DF91
Upper Town Rd., Grnf. 72 CB70
Upper Tulse Hill SW2 105 DM87
Upper Vernon Rd., Sutt. 132 DD106
Upper Walthamstow Rd. E17 65 ED56
Upper Wickham La., Well. 96 EV83
Upper Wimpole St. W1 4 G6
Upper Wimpole St. W1 76 DG71
Upper Woburn Pl. WC1 5 N3
Upper Woburn Pl. WC1 77 DK69
Upper Woodcote Village, Pur. 133 DK113
Upperton Rd., Sid. 109 ET92
Upperton Rd. E. E13 80 EJ69
Inniskilling Rd.
Upperton Rd. W. E13 80 EJ69
Uppingham Ave., Stan. 45 CH53
Upsdell Ave. N13 49 DN51
Upshire Rd., Wal.Abb. 24 EF32
Upstall St. SE5 91 DP81
Upton Ave. E7 80 EG66
Upton Clo., Bex. 110 EZ86
Upton Clo., St.Alb. 17 CD25
Upton Ct. SE20 106 DW94
Blean Gro.
Upton Dene, Sutt. 132 DB108
Upton Gdns., Har. 59 CH57
Upton La. E7 80 EH65
Upton Lo. Clo. (Bushey), Wat. 44 CC45
Upton Pk. Rd. E7 80 EH66
Upton Rd. N18 50 DU50
Upton Rd. SE18 95 EQ79
Upton Rd., Bex. 110 EZ86
Upton Rd., Bexh. 96 EY84
Upton Rd., Houns. 86 CA83
Upton Rd., Th.Hth. 120 DR96
Upton Rd., Wat. 29 BV42
Upton Rd. S., Bex. 110 EZ86
Upway N12 48 DE52
Upwood Rd. SE12 108 EG86
Upwood Rd. SW16 119 DL95
Urlwin St. SE5 92 DQ79
Urlwin Wk. SW9 91 DN81
Urmston Dr. SW19 103 CY88
Ursula Ms. N4 64 DQ60
Portland Ri.
Ursula St. SW11 90 DE81
Urswick Gdns., Dag. 82 EY66
Urswick Rd.
Urswick Rd. E9 64 DW64
Urswick Rd., Dag. 82 EX66
Usborne Ms. SW8 91 DM80
Usher Rd. E3 79 DZ68
Usk Rd. SW11 90 DC84
Usk St. E2 79 DX69
Utopia Village NW1 76 DG67
Chalcot Rd.
Uvedale Clo., Croy. 135 ED111
Uvedale Cres.
Uvedale Cres., Croy. 135 ED111
Uvedale Rd., Dag. 68 FA62
Uvedale Rd., Enf. 36 DR43
Uverdale Rd. SW10 90 DC80
Uxbridge Gdns., Felt. 100 BX89
Marlborough Rd.
Uxbridge Ind. Est., Uxb. 70 BH69
Uxbridge Rd. W3 74 CN74
Uxbridge Rd. W5 74 CM73
Uxbridge Rd. W7 73 CF74
Uxbridge Rd. W12 75 CU74
Uxbridge Rd. W13 73 CH74
Uxbridge Rd., Felt. 100 BW88
Uxbridge Rd., Hmptn. 100 CA91
Uxbridge Rd., Har. 45 CD52
Uxbridge Rd., Hayes 71 BT72
Uxbridge Rd., Kings.T. 115 CK98
Uxbridge Rd., Pnr. 44 BW54
Uxbridge Rd., Rick. 42 BG47
Uxbridge Rd., Sthl. 72 CA74
Uxbridge Rd., Stan. 45 CF51
Uxbridge Rd., Uxb. 71 BP69
Uxbridge St. W8 76 DA74
Uxendon Cres., Wem. 60 CL60
Uxendon Hill, Wem. 60 CM60

V

Vaillant Rd., Wey. 127 BQ105
Valan Leas, Brom. 122 EE97
Valance Ave. E4 52 EE46
Vale, The N10 48 DG53
Vale, The N14 49 DK45
Vale, The NW11 61 CX62
Vale, The SW3 90 DD79
Vale, The W3 74 CR74
Vale, The, Couls. 133 DK114
Vale, The, Croy. 121 DX103
Vale, The, Felt. 99 BV86
Vale, The, Houns. 86 BY79
Vale, The, Ruis. 58 BW63
Vale, The, Sun. 99 BU93
Ashridge Way
Vale, The, Wdf.Grn. 52 EG52
Vale Ave., Borwd. 32 CP43
Vale Border, Croy. 135 DX111
Vale Clo. N2 62 DF55
Church Vale
Vale Clo. W9 76 DC69
Maida Vale
Vale Clo., Orp. 137 EN105
Vale Clo., Wey. 113 BR104
Vale Cotts. SW15 102 CR91
Kingston Vale
Vale Ct. W9 76 DC69
Maida Vale
Vale Ct., Wey. 113 BR104
Vale Cres. SW15 102 CS90
Vale Cft., Esher 129 CE109
Vale Cft., Pnr. 58 BY57
Vale Dr., Barn. 33 CZ42
Vale End SE22 92 DS84
Grove Vale
Vale Gro. N4 64 DQ59
Vale Gro. W3 74 CR74
The Vale
Vale Ind. Pk., Wat. 43 BP46
Vale La. W3 74 CN71
Vale of Health NW3 62 DD62
East Heath Rd.
Vale Par. SW15 102 CR91
Kingston Vale
Vale Ri. NW11 61 CZ60
Vale Rd. E7 80 EH65
Vale Rd. N4 64 DQ59
Vale Rd., Brom. 123 EN96
Vale Rd., Dart. 111 FH88
Vale Rd., Epsom 131 CT105
Vale Rd., Esher 129 CE109
Vale Rd., Mitch. 119 DK97
Vale Rd., Sutt. 132 DB105
Vale Rd. (Bushey), Wat. 30 BY43
Vale Rd., Wey. 113 BR104
Vale Rd., Wor.Pk. 117 CT104
Vale Rd. N., Surb. 116 CL103
Vale Rd. S., Surb. 116 CL103
Vale Row N5 63 DP62
Gillespie Rd.
Vale Royal N7 77 DL66
Vale St. SE27 106 DR90
Vale Ter. N4 64 DQ58
Valence Ave., Dag. 68 EX60
Valence Circ., Dag. 68 EX62
Valence Dr. (Cheshunt), Wal.Cr. 22 DU28
Valence Rd., Erith 97 FD80
Valence Wd. Rd., Dag. 68 EX62
Valencia Rd., Stan. 45 CJ49
Valency Clo., Nthwd. 43 BT49
Valentia Pl. SW9 91 DN84
Brixton Sta. Rd.
Valentine Ave., Bex. 110 EY89
Valentine Ct. SE23 107 DX89
Valentine Pl. SE1 10 F4
Valentine Pl. SE1 91 DP75
Valentine Rd. E9 79 DX65
Valentine Rd., Har. 58 CC62
Valentine Row SE1 10 F5
Valentines Rd., Ilf. 67 EP60
Valentines Way, Rom. 69 FD61
Valentyne Clo., Croy. 136 EE111
Warbank Cres.
Valerian Way E15 80 EE69
Valerie Ct. (Bushey), Wat. 44 CC45
Valeswood Rd., Brom. 108 EF92
Valetta Gro. E13 80 EG68
Valetta Rd. W3 88 CS75
Valette St. E9 78 DV65
Valiant Clo., Nthlt. 72 BX69
Ruislip Rd.
Valiant Clo., Rom. 54 FA54
Valiant Ho. SE7 94 EJ78
Valiant Path NW9 46 CS52
Blundell Rd.
Valiant Way E6 81 EM71
Vallance Rd. E1 78 DU70
Vallance Rd. E2 78 DU69
Vallance Rd. N22 49 DJ54
Vallentin Rd. E17 65 EC56
Valley Ave. N12 48 DD49
Valley Clo., Dart. 111 FF86
Valley Clo., Loug. 39 EM44
Valley Clo., Pnr. 43 BV54
Alandale Dr.
Valley Clo., Wal.Abb. 23 EC32
Valley Ct., Ken. 134 DQ114
Hayes La.
Valley Dr. NW9 60 CN58
Valley Dr., Sev. 155 FH125
Valley Flds. Cres., Enf. 35 DN40
Valley Gdns. SW19 104 DD94
Valley Gdns., Wem. 74 CM66
Valley Gro. SE7 94 EJ78
Valley Hill, Loug. 52 EL45
Valley Link Ind. Est., Enf. 37 DY44
Valley Ms., Twick. 101 CG89
Cross Deep
Valley Ri., Wat. 15 BV33
Valley Rd. SW16 105 DM92
Valley Rd., Belv. 97 FB77
Valley Rd., Brom. 122 EE96
Valley Rd., Dart. 111 FF86
Valley Rd., Erith 97 FD77
Valley Rd., Ken. 134 DR114
Valley Rd., Orp. 124 EV95
Valley Rd., Rick. 28 BG43
Valley Rd., Uxb. 70 BL68
Valley Side E4 51 EA47
Valley Side Par. E4 51 EA47
Valley Side
Valley Vw., Barn. 33 CY44
Valley Vw. (Cheshunt), Wal.Cr. 22 DQ28
Valley Vw., West. 150 EJ118
Valley Vw. Gdns., Ken. 148 DS115
Godstone Rd.
Valley Wk., Croy. 120 DW103
Valley Wk., Rick. 29 BQ43
Valleyfield Rd. SW16 105 DM92
Valliere Rd. NW10 75 CU69
Valliers Wd. Rd., Sid. 109 ER88
Vallis Way W13 73 CG71
Vallis Way, Chess. 129 CK105
Valmar Rd. SE5 92 DQ81
Valnay St. SW17 104 DF92
Valognes Ave. E17 51 DY53
Valonia Gdns. SW18 103 CZ86
Vambery Rd. SE18 95 EQ79
Van Dyck Ave., N.Mal. 116 CR101
Vanbrough Cres., Nthlt. 72 BW67
Vanbrugh Clo. E16 80 EK71
Fulmer Rd.
Vanbrugh Dr., Walt. 114 BW101
Vanbrugh Flds. SE3 94 EF79
Vanbrugh Hill SE3 94 EF79
Vanbrugh Hill SE10 94 EF79
Vanbrugh Pk. SE3 94 EF80
Vanbrugh Pk. Rd. SE3 94 EF80
Vanbrugh Pk. Rd. W. SE3 94 EF80
Vanbrugh Rd. W4 88 CR76
Vanbrugh Ter. SE3 94 EF81
Vanburgh Clo., Orp. 123 ES102
Vancouver Clo., Epsom 130 CQ111
Vancouver Rd. SE23 107 DY89
Vancouver Rd., Edg. 46 CP53
Vancouver Rd., Hayes 71 BV70
Vancouver Rd., Rich. 101 CJ91
Vanderbilt Rd. SW18 104 DB88
Vandome Clo. E16 80 EH72
Vandon Pas. SW1 9 L6
Vandon St. SW1 9 L6
Vandon St. SW1 91 DJ76
Vandy St. EC2 7 M5
Vandyke Clo. SW15 103 CX86
Vandyke Cross SE9 108 EL85
Vane Clo. NW3 62 DD63
Vane Clo., Har. 60 CM58
Vane St. SW1 9 L8
Vanessa Clo., Belv. 96 FA78
Vanessa Way, Bex. 111 FD90
Vanguard Clo., Croy. 119 DP102
Vanguard Clo., Rom. 55 FB54
Vanguard St. SE8 93 EA81
Vanguard Way, Cat. 149 EB121
Slines Oak Rd.
Vanguard Way, Wall. 133 DL108
Vanguard Way, Warl. 149 EC120
Croydon Rd.
Vanners Par., W.Byf. 126 BL113
Brewery La.
Vanoc Gdns., Brom. 108 EG91
Vansittart Rd. E7 66 EF63
Vansittart St. SE14 93 DY80
Vanston Pl. SW6 90 DA80
Vant Rd. SW17 104 DF92
Vantage Ms. E14 79 EC74
Prestons Rd.
Varcoe Rd. SE16 92 DV78
Varden Clo. W3 74 CR72
Varden St. E1 78 DV72
Vardens Rd. SW11 90 DD84
Vardon Clo. N3 47 CY53
Claremont Pk.
Varley Par. NW9 60 CS56
Varley Rd. E16 80 EH72
Varley Way, Mitch. 118 DD96
Varna Rd. SW6 89 CY80
Varna Rd., Hmptn. 114 CB95
Varndell St. NW1 5 K2
Varndell St. NW1 77 DJ69
Varney Clo. (Cheshunt), Wal.Cr. 22 DU27
Varsity Dr., Twick. 101 CE85
Varsity Row SW14 88 CQ82
William's La.
Vartry Rd. N15 64 DR58
Vassall Rd. SW9 91 DN80
Vauban Est. SE16 92 DT76
Vauban St. SE16 92 DT76
Vaughan Ave. NW4 61 CU57
Vaughan Ave. W6 89 CT77
Vaughan Clo., Hmptn. 100 BY93
Oak Ave.
Vaughan Gdns., Ilf. 67 EM59
Vaughan Rd. E15 80 EF65
Vaughan Rd. SE5 92 DQ83
Vaughan Rd., Har. 58 CC59
Vaughan Rd., T.Ditt. 115 CH101
Vaughan Rd., Well. 95 ET82
Vaughan St. SE16 93 DZ75
Vaughan Way E1 78 DU73
Vaughan Williams Clo. SE8 93 EA80
Watson's St.
Vaux Cres., Walt. 127 BV107
Vauxhall Bri. SE1 91 DL78
Vauxhall Bri. SW1 91 DL78
Vauxhall Bri. Rd. SW1 9 L8
Vauxhall Bri. Rd. SW1 91 DJ76
Vauxhall Gdns., S.Croy. 134 DQ107
Vauxhall Gdns. Est. SE11 91 DM78
Vauxhall Gro. SW8 91 DM79
Vauxhall St. SE11 91 DM78
Vauxhall Wk. SE11 10 B10
Vauxhall Wk. SE11 91 DM78
Vawdrey Clo. E1 78 DW70
Veals Mead, Mitch. 118 DE95
Vectis Gdns. SW17 105 DH93
Vectis Rd.
Vectis Rd. SW17 105 DH93
Veda Rd. SE13 93 EA84
Vega Cres., Nthwd. 43 BT50
Vega Rd. (Bushey), Wat. 44 CC45
Velde Way SE22 106 DS85
East Dulwich Gro.
Velletri Ho. E2 79 DX68
Mace St.
Vellicoe Rd. E13 80 EG70
Jutland Rd.
Vellum Dr., Cars. 118 DG104
Venables Clo., Dag. 69 FB63
Venables St. NW8 4 A5
Venables St. NW8 76 DD70
Vencourt Pl. W6 89 CU77
Venetia Rd. N4 63 DP58
Venetia Rd. W5 87 CK75
Venetian Rd. SE5 92 DQ82
Venette Clo., Rain. 83 FH71
Venn St. SW4 91 DJ84
Venner Rd. SE26 106 DW93
Venners Clo., Bexh. 97 FE82
Ventnor Ave., Stan. 45 CH53
Ventnor Dr. N20 48 DB48
Ventnor Gdns., Bark. 81 ES65
Ventnor Rd. SE14 93 DX80
Ventnor Rd., Sutt. 132 DB108
Ventura Pk., St.Alb. 17 CF29
Venture Clo., Bex. 110 EY87
Venue St. E14 79 EC71
Venus Rd. SE18 95 EM76
Vera Ave. N21 35 DN43
Vera Ct., Wat. 44 BX45
Vera Lynn Clo. E7 66 EG63
Dames Rd.
Vera Rd. SW6 89 CY81
Verbena Clo. E16 80 EF70
Cranberry La.
Verbena Clo., West Dr. 84 BK78
Magnolia St.
Verbena Gdns. W6 89 CU78
Verdant La. SE6 108 EE88
Verdayne Ave., Croy. 121 DX102
Verdayne Gdns., Warl. 148 DW116
Verderers Rd., Chig. 54 EU50
Verdun Rd. SE18 96 EU79
Verdun Rd. SW13 89 CU79
Verdure Clo., Wat. 16 BY32
Vere Rd., Loug. 39 EQ42
Vere St. W1 5 H9
Vere St. W1 77 DH72
Vereker Dr., Sun. 113 BU97
Vereker Rd. W14 89 CY78
Verity Clo. W11 75 CY72
Vermont Clo., Enf. 35 DP42
Vermont Rd. SE19 106 DR93
Vermont Rd. SW18 104 DB86
Vermont Rd., Sutt. 118 DB104
Verney Gdns., Dag. 68 EY63
Verney Rd. SE16 92 DU79
Verney Rd., Dag. 68 EY63
Verney St. NW10 60 CR62
Verney Way SE16 92 DV78
Vernham Rd. SE18 95 EQ79
Vernon Ave. E12 67 EM63
Vernon Ave. SW20 117 CX96
Vernon Ave., Enf. 37 DY36
Vernon Ave., Wdf.Grn. 52 EH52
Vernon Clo., Epsom 130 CQ107
Vernon Clo., Orp. 124 EV97
Vernon Ct., Stan. 45 CH53
Vernon Dr.
Vernon Cres., Barn. 34 DG44
Vernon Dr., Stan. 45 CG53
Vernon Dr., Uxb. 42 BJ53
Vernon Ms. E17 65 DZ56
Vernon Rd.
Vernon Ms. W14 89 CY77
Vernon St.
Vernon Pl. WC1 6 A7
Vernon Pl. WC1 77 DL71
Vernon Ri. WC1 6 C2
Vernon Ri. WC1 77 DM69
Vernon Ri., Grnf. 59 CD64
Vernon Rd. E3 79 DZ68
Vernon Rd. E11 66 EE60
Vernon Rd. E15 80 EE66
Vernon Rd. E17 65 DZ56
Vernon Rd. N8 63 DN55
Vernon Rd. SW14 88 CR83
Vernon Rd., Felt. 99 BU90
Vernon Rd., Ilf. 67 ET60
Vernon Rd., Rom. 55 FC50
Vernon Rd., Sutt. 132 DC106
Vernon Rd. (Bushey), Wat. 30 BY43
Vernon Sq. WC1 6 C2
Vernon St. W14 89 CY77
Vernon Wk., Tad. 145 CX120
Vernon Way, Cat. 148 DQ122
Wellington Rd.
Vernon Yd. W11 75 CZ73
Portobello Rd.
Veroan Rd., Bexh. 96 EY82
Verona Clo., Uxb. 70 BJ71
Verona Dr., Surb. 116 CL103
Verona Rd. E7 80 EG66
Upton La.
Veronica Gdns. SW16 119 DJ95
Veronica Rd. SW17 105 DH90
Veronique Gdns., Ilf. 67 EQ57
Verran Rd. SW12 105 DH87
Balham Gro.
Versailles Rd. SE20 106 DU94
Verulam Ave. E17 65 DZ58
Verulam Ave., Pur. 133 DJ112
Verulam Bldgs. WC1 6 C6
Verulam Pas., Wat. 29 BV40
Station Rd.
Verulam Rd., Grnf. 72 CA70
Verulam St. WC1 6 D6
Verwood Dr., Barn. 34 DF41
Verwood Rd., Har. 44 CC54
Veryan Clo., Orp. 124 EW98
Vesey Path E14 79 EB72
East India Dock Rd.
Vespan Rd. W12 89 CU75
Vesta Rd. SE4 93 DY82
Vestris Rd. SE23 107 DX89
Vestry Ms. SE5 92 DS81
Vestry Rd. E17 65 EB56
Vestry Rd. SE5 92 DS81
Vestry St. N1 7 K2
Vestry St. N1 78 DR69
Vevey St. SE6 107 DZ89
Veysey Gdns., Dag. 68 FA62
Oglethorpe Rd.
Viaduct Pl. E2 78 DV69
Viaduct St.
Viaduct St. E2 78 DV69
Vian Ave., Enf. 37 DZ35
Vian St. SE13 93 EB83
Vibart Gdns. SW2 105 DM87
Vibart Wk. N1 77 DL67
Outram Pl.
Vicarage Ave. SE3 94 EG80
Vicarage Clo., Erith 97 FC79
Vicarage Clo., Nthlt. 72 BZ67
Vicarage Clo., Pot.B. 20 DG30
Vicarage Clo., Ruis. 57 BR59
Vicarage Clo., Tad. 145 CY124
Vicarage Ct. W8 90 DB75
Vicarage Gate
Vicarage Ct., Felt. 99 BQ87
Vicarage Cres. SW11 90 DD81
Vicarage Dr. SW14 102 CR85
Vicarage Dr., Bark. 81 EQ66
Vicarage Dr., Beck. 121 EA95
Vicarage Fm. Rd., Houns. 86 BY82
Vicarage Flds., Walt. 114 BW100
Vicarage Gdns. SW14 102 CQ85
Vicarage Rd.
Vicarage Gdns. W8 76 DA74
Vicarage Gate
Vicarage Gdns., Mitch. 118 DE97
Vicarage Gate W8 76 DB74
Vicarage Gate Ms., Tad. 145 CY124
Warren Lo. Dr.
Vicarage Gro. SE5 92 DR81
Vicarage La. E6 81 EM69
Vicarage La. E15 80 EE66
Vicarage La., Chig. 53 EQ47
Vicarage La., Epsom 131 CU109
Vicarage La., Ilf. 67 ER60
Vicarage La., Kings L. 14 BM29
Vicarage La., Lthd. 143 CH122
Vicarage La., Sev. 153 FD119
London Rd.
Vicarage La. (Laleham), Stai. 112 BH97
Vicarage Ms., Tad. 145 CY124
Vicarage Pk. SE18 95 EQ78
Vicarage Path N8 63 DL59
Oakfield Ct.
Vicarage Rd. E10 65 EA59
Vicarage Rd. E15 80 EF66
Vicarage Rd. N17 50 DU52
Vicarage Rd. NW4 61 CU58
Vicarage Rd. SE18 95 EQ78
Vicarage Rd. SW14 102 CR85
Vicarage Rd., Bex. 111 FB88
Vicarage Rd., Croy. 119 DN104
Vicarage Rd., Dag. 83 FB66
Vicarage Rd., Epp. 26 EW29
Vicarage Rd., Horn. 69 FG60
Vicarage Rd., Kings.T. 115 CK96
Vicarage Rd. (Hampton Wick), Kings.T. 115 CJ95
Vicarage Rd., Sun. 99 BT92
Vicarage Rd., Sutt. 132 DB105
Vicarage Rd., Tedd. 101 CG92
Vicarage Rd., Twick. 101 CE89
Vicarage Rd. (Whitton), Twick. 100 CC86
Vicarage Rd., Wat. 29 BU43
Vicarage Rd., Wdf.Grn. 52 EL52
Vicarage Way NW10 60 CR62
Vicarage Way, Har. 58 CA59
Vicars Bri. Clo., Wem. 74 CL68
Vicars Clo. E9 78 DW67
Victoria Pk. Rd.
Vicars Clo. E15 80 EG67
Vicars Clo., Enf. 36 DS40
Vicars Hill SE13 93 EB84
Vicars Moor La. N21 49 DN45
Vicars Oak Rd. SE19 106 DS93
Vicars Rd. NW5 62 DG64
Vicars Wk., Dag. 68 EV62
Viceroy Clo. N2 62 DE56
Market Pl.
Viceroy Ct. NW8 76 DE68
Prince Albert Rd.
Viceroy Par. N2 62 DE55
High Rd.
Viceroy Rd. SW8 91 DL81
Vickers Dr. N., Wey. 126 BL110
Vickers Dr. S., Wey. 126 BL111
Vickers Rd., Erith 97 FD78
Vickers Way, Houns. 100 BY85
Victor Ct., Rain. 83 FD68
Askwith Rd.
Victor Gro., Wem. 74 CL66
Victor Rd. NW10 75 CV68
Victor Rd. SE20 107 DX94
Victor Rd., Har. 58 CC55
Victor Rd., Tedd. 101 CE91

Waldo Rd. NW10 75 CU69
Waldo Rd., Brom. 122 EK97
Waldorf Clo., S.Croy. 133 DP109
Waldram Cres. SE23 106 DW88
Waldram Pk. Rd. SE23 107 DX88
Waldram Pl. SE23 106 DW88
Waldrist Way, Erith 96 EZ75
Waldron Gdns., Brom. 121 ED97
Waldron Ms. SW3 90 DD79
Old Ch. St.
Waldron Rd. SW18 104 DC90
Waldron Rd., Har. 59 CE60
Waldronhyrst, S.Croy. 133 DP105
Waldrons, The, Croy. 133 DP105
Waldrons Path, S.Croy. 134 DQ105
Bramley Hill
Waleran Clo., Stan. 45 CF51
Chenduit Way
Waleran Flats SE1 92 DS77
Old Kent Rd.
Walerand Rd. SE13 93 EC82
Wales Ave., Cars. 132 DE106
Wales Fm. Rd. W3 74 CR71
Waley St. E1 79 DY71
Walfield Ave. N20 48 DB45
Walford Rd. N16 64 DS63
Walford Rd., Uxb. 70 BK68
Walfrey Gdns., Dag. 82 EY66
Walham Gro. SW6 90 DA80
Walham Ri. SW19 103 CY93
Walham Yd. SW6 90 DA80
Walham Gro.
Walk, The, Pot.B. 20 DA32
Walk, The, Sun. 99 BT94
Walkden Rd., Chis. 109 EN92
Walker Clo. N11 49 DJ49
Walker Clo. SE18 95 EQ77
Walker Clo. W7 73 CE74
Walker Clo., Dart. 97 FF83
Walker Clo., Hmptn. 100 BZ93
Fearnley Cres.
Walkers Ct. E8 78 DU65
Wilton Way
Walkers Ct. W1 5 M10
Walkers Pl. SW15 89 CY83
Felsham Rd.
Walkerscroft Mead SE21 106 DQ88
Walkfield Dr., Epsom 145 CV117
Walkford Way SE15 92 DT80
Daniel Gdns.
Walkley Rd., Dart. 111 FH85
Walks, The N2 62 DD55
Wall End Rd. E6 81 EN66
Wall St. N1 78 DR65
Wallace Clo. SE28 82 EX73
Haldane Rd.
Wallace Clo., Shep. 113 BR98
Wallace Clo., Uxb. 70 BL68
Grays Rd.
Wallace Cres., Cars. 132 DF106
Wallace Flds., Epsom 131 CT112
Wallace Rd. N1 78 DQ65
Wallace Wk., Add. 126 BJ105
Wallace Way N19 63 DK61
Giesbach Rd.
Wallasey Cres., Uxb. 56 BN61
Wallbutton Rd. SE4 93 DY82
Wallcote Ave. NW2 61 CX60
Walled Gdn., The, Tad. 145 CX122
Heathcote
Wallenger Ave., Rom. 69 FH55
Waller Dr., Nthwd. 43 BU54
Waller La., Cat. 148 DT123
Waller Rd. SE14 93 DX81
Wallers Clo., Dag. 82 EY67
Wallers Clo., Wdf.Grn. 53 EM51
Waller's Hoppit, Loug. 38 EL40
Wallflower St. W12 75 CT73
Wallgrave Rd. SW5 90 DB77
Wallhouse Rd., Erith 97 FH80
Wallingford Ave. W10 75 CX71
Wallingford Rd., Uxb. 70 BH68
Wallington Clo., Ruis. 57 BQ58
Wallington Rd., Ilf. 67 ET59
Wallington Sq., Wall. 133 DH107
Woodcote Rd.
Wallis All. SE1 11 J5
Wallis Clo. SW11 90 DD83
Wallis Clo., Dart. 111 FG90
Wallis Clo., Horn. 69 FH60
Wallis Ms. N22 63 DN55
Brampton Pk. Rd.
Wallis Ms., Lthd. 143 CG122
Wallis Rd. E9 79 DZ65
Wallis Rd., Sthl. 72 CB72
Walliss Cotts. SW2 105 DL87
Wallorton Gdns. SW14 88 CR84
Wallside EC2 78 DQ71
Wood St.
Wallwood Rd. E11 65 ED60
Wallwood St. E14 79 DZ71
Walm La. NW2 75 CW65
Walmar Clo., Barn. 34 DD39
Walmer Clo. E4 51 EB47
Walmer Clo., Orp. 137 ER105
Tubbenden La. S.
Walmer Clo., Rom. 55 FB54
Walmer Gdns. W13 87 CG75
Walmer Ho. N9 50 DT46
Walmer Pl. W1 4 D6
Walmer Rd. W10 75 CW72
Latimer Rd.
Walmer Rd. W11 75 CY73
Walmer St. W1 4 D6
Walmer Ter. SE18 95 EQ77
Walmgate Rd., Grnf. 73 CH67
Walmington Fold N12 48 DA51
Walney Wk. N1 78 DQ65
St. Paul's Rd.
Walnut Ave., West Dr. 84 BN76
Walnut Clo. SE8 93 DZ79
Clyde St.
Walnut Clo., Cars. 132 DF106
Walnut Clo., Epsom 145 CT115
Walnut Clo., Hayes 71 BS73
Walnut Clo., Ilf. 67 EQ56
Civic Way
Walnut Clo., St.Alb. 16 CB27
Walnut Ct. W5 88 CL75
Walnut Dr., Tad. 145 CY124
Warren Lo. Dr.
Walnut Flds., Epsom 131 CT109
Walnut Gdns. E15 66 EE63
Burgess Rd.
Walnut Grn. (Bushey), Wat. 30 BZ40
Walnut Gro., Bans. 131 CX114
Walnut Gro., Enf. 36 DR43
Walnut Ms., Sutt. 132 DC108
Walnut Rd. E10 65 EA61
Walnut Tree Ave., Mitch. 118 DE97
Dearn Gdns.
Walnut Tree Clo. SW13 89 CT81
Walnut Tree Clo., Bans. 131 CY112
Walnut Tree Clo., Chis. 123 EQ95
Walnut Tree Clo. (Cheshunt), Wal.Cr. 23 DX31
Walnut Tree Cotts. SW19 103 CY91
Church Rd.
Walnut Tree La., W.Byf. 126 BK112
Walnut Tree Rd. SE10 94 EE78
Walnut Tree Rd., Brent. 88 CL79
Walnut Tree Rd., Dag. 68 EX61
Walnut Tree Rd., Erith 97 FE78
Walnut Tree Rd., Houns. 86 BZ79
Walnut Tree Rd., Shep. 113 BQ96
Walnut Tree Wk. SE11 10 D8
Walnut Tree Wk. SE11 91 DN77
Walnut Way, Buck.H. 52 EK48
Walnut Way, Ruis. 72 BW65
Walnut Way, Swan. 125 FD96
Walnuts, The, Orp. 124 EU102
High St.
Walnuts Rd., Orp. 124 EU102
Walpole Ave., Couls. 146 DF119
Walpole Ave., Rich. 88 CM82
Walpole Clo. W13 87 CJ75
Walpole Clo., Pnr. 44 CA51
Walpole Cres., Tedd. 101 CF92
Walpole Gdns. W4 88 CQ78
Walpole Gdns., Twick. 101 CE89
Walpole Ms. NW8 76 DD67
Queen's Gro.
Walpole Ms. SW19 104 DD93
Walpole Rd.
Walpole Pk. W5 73 CJ74
Walpole Pk., Wey. 126 BN108
Walpole Pl. SE18 95 EP77
Anglesea Rd.
Walpole Pl., Tedd. 101 CF92
Walpole Rd. E6 80 EJ66
Walpole Rd. E17 65 DY56
Walpole Rd. E18 52 EF53
Walpole Rd. (Downhills Way) N17 64 DQ55
Walpole Rd. (Lordship La.) N17 50 DQ54
Walpole Rd. SW19 104 DD93
Walpole Rd., Brom. 122 EK99
Walpole Rd., Croy. 120 DR103
Walpole Rd., Surb. 116 CL101
Walpole Rd., Tedd. 101 CF92
Walpole Rd., Twick. 101 CE89
Walpole St. SW3 8 D10
Walpole St. SW3 90 DF78
Walrond Ave., Wem. 60 CL64
Walsh Cres., Croy. 136 EE112
Walsham Clo. N16 64 DU59
Braydon Rd.
Walsham Clo. SE28 82 EX73
Walsham Rd. SE14 93 DX82
Walsham Rd., Felt. 99 BV87
Walshford Way, Borwd. 32 CN38
Walsingham Gdns., Epsom 130 CS105
Walsingham Pk., Chis. 123 ER96
Walsingham Pl. SW4 90 DF84
Clapham Common W. Side
Walsingham Rd. E5 64 DU62
Walsingham Rd. W13 73 CG74
Walsingham Rd., Croy. 135 EC110
Walsingham Rd., Enf. 36 DR42
Walsingham Rd., Mitch. 118 DF99
Walsingham Rd., Orp. 124 EV95
Walsingham Wk., Belv. 96 FA79
Walsingham Way, St.Alb. 17 CJ27
Walt Whitman Clo. SE24 91 DP84
Shakespeare Rd.
Walter Rodney Clo. E6 81 EM65
Stevenage Rd.
Walter St. E2 79 DX69
Walter St., Kings.T. 116 CL95
Sopwith Way
Walter Ter. E1 79 DX72
Walter Wk., Edg. 46 CQ51
Walters Ho. SE17 91 DP79
Otto St.
Walters Mead, Ash. 144 CL117
Walters Rd. SE25 120 DS98
Walters Rd., Enf. 36 DW43
Walters Way SE23 107 DX86
Walters Yd., Brom. 122 EG96
Walterton Rd. W9 75 CZ70
Waltham Ave. NW9 60 CN58
Waltham Ave., Hayes 85 BQ76
Waltham Clo., Dart. 111 FG86
Waltham Clo., Orp. 124 EX102
Waltham Dr., Edg. 46 CN54
Waltham Gdns., Enf. 36 DW36
Waltham Gate, Wal.Cr. 23 DZ26
Thomas Rochford Way
Waltham Pk. Way E17 51 EA53
Waltham Rd., Cars. 118 DD101
Waltham Rd., Cat. 148 DV122
Waltham Rd., Sthl. 86 BY76
Waltham Rd., Wal.Abb. 24 EE26
Waltham Rd., Wdf.Grn. 52 EL51
Waltham Way E4 51 DZ49
Walthamstow Ave. E4 51 DY50
Walthamstow Business Cen. E17 51 EC54
Waltheof Ave. N17 50 DR53
Waltheof Gdns. N17 50 DR53
Walton Ave., Har. 58 BZ64
Walton Ave., N.Mal. 117 CT98
Walton Ave., Sutt. 117 CY104
Walton Bri., Shep. 113 BS101
Walton Bri. Rd., Shep. 113 BR100
Walton Clo. E5 65 DX62
Orient Way
Walton Clo. NW2 61 CV61
Walton Clo. SW8 91 DL80
Walton Clo., Har. 59 CD56
Walton Cres., Har. 58 BZ63
Walton Dr. NW10 74 CR65
Mitchellbrook Way
Walton Dr., Har. 59 CD56
Walton Gdns. W3 74 CP71
Walton Gdns., Felt. 99 BT91
Walton Gdns., Wal.Abb. 23 EB33
Walton Gdns., Wem. 60 CL61
Walton Grn., Croy. 135 EB109
Walton La., Shep. 113 BR101
Walton La., Wey. 113 BP103
Walton Pk., Walt. 114 BX103
Walton Pk. La., Walt. 114 BX103
Walton Pl. SW3 8 D6
Walton Pl. SW3 90 DF76
Walton Rd. E12 67 EN63
Walton Rd. E13 80 EJ68
Walton Rd. N15 64 DT56
Walton Rd., E.Mol. 114 BY98
Walton Rd. (Epsom Downs), Epsom 145 CT117
Walton Rd. (Headley), Epsom 144 CQ121
Walton Rd., Har. 59 CD56
Walton Rd., Rom. 54 EZ52
Walton Rd., Sid. 110 EW89
Walton Rd., Walt. 114 BW99
Walton Rd. (Bushey), Wat. 30 BX42
Walton Rd., W.Mol. 114 BY98
Walton St. SW3 8 C8
Walton St. SW3 90 DE77
Walton St., Enf. 36 DR39
Walton St., Tad. 145 CU124
Walton Way W3 74 CP71
Walton Way, Mitch. 119 DJ98
Walverns Clo., Wat. 30 BW44
Walworth Pl. SE17 92 DQ78
Walworth Rd. SE1 11 H9
Walworth Rd. SE1 92 DQ77
Walworth Rd. SE17 11 H9
Walworth Rd. SE17 92 DQ77
Walwyn Ave., Brom. 122 EK97
Wanborough Dr. SW15 103 CV88
Wanderer Dr., Bark. 82 EV69
Wandle Bank SW19 104 DD94
Wandle Bank, Croy. 119 DL104
Wandle Ct., Epsom 130 CQ105
Wandle Ct. Gdns., Croy. 119 DL104
Wandle Rd. SW17 104 DE89
Wandle Rd., Croy. 120 DQ104
Wandle Rd. (Waddon), Croy. 119 DL104
Wandle Rd., Mord. 118 DC98
Wandle Rd., Wall. 119 DH103
Wandle Side, Croy. 119 DM104
Wandle Side, Wall. 119 DH104
Wandle Way SW18 104 DB88
Wandle Way, Mitch. 118 DF99
Wandon Rd. SW6 90 DB80
Wandsworth Bri. SW6 90 DB83
Wandsworth Bri. SW18 90 DB83
Wandsworth Bri. Rd. SW6 90 DB81
Wandsworth Business Cen., Grnf. 73 CJ68
Wandsworth Common SW12 104 DF87
St. James's Dr.
Wandsworth Common N. Side SW18 104 DC85
Wandsworth Common W. Side SW18 104 DC85
Wandsworth High St. SW18 104 DA85
Wandsworth Plain SW18 104 DA85
Wandsworth Rd. SW8 91 DH83
Wangey Rd., Rom. 68 EX59
Wanless Rd. SE24 92 DQ83
Wanley Rd. SE5 92 DR84
Wanlip Rd. E13 80 EH70
Wannock Gdns., Ilf. 53 EP52
Wansbeck Rd. E9 79 DZ66
Wansbury Way, Swan. 125 FG99
Wansdown Pl. SW6 90 DB80
Fulham Rd.
Wansey St. SE17 11 J9
Wansey St. SE17 92 DQ77
Wansford Pk., Borwd. 32 CR42
Wansford Rd., Wdf.Grn. 52 EJ53
Wanstead Clo., Brom. 122 EJ96
Wanstead La., Ilf. 66 EL58
Wanstead Pk. E11 66 EJ59
Wanstead Pk. Ave. E12 66 EK61
Wanstead Pk. Rd., Ilf. 66 EL58
Wanstead Pl. E11 66 EG58
Wanstead Rd., Brom. 122 EJ96
Wansunt Rd., Bex. 111 FC88
Wantage Rd. SE12 108 EF85
Wantz La., Rain. 83 FH70
Wantz Rd., Dag. 69 FB63
Waplings, The, Tad. 145 CV124
Deans La.
Wapping Dock St. E1 78 DV74
Cinnamon St.
Wapping High St. E1 78 DU74
Wapping La. E1 78 DV73
Wapping Wall E1 78 DW74
Warbank Clo., Croy. 136 EE110
Warbank Cres., Croy. 136 EE110
Warbank La., Kings.T. 103 CT94
Warbeck Rd. W12 89 CV75
Warberry Rd. N22 49 DM54
Warblers Grn., Cob. 128 BZ114
Warboys App., Kings.T. 102 CP93
Warboys Cres. E4 51 EC50
Warboys Rd., Kings.T. 102 CP93
Warburton Clo., Har. 45 CD51
Warburton Rd. E8 78 DV67
Warburton Rd., Twick. 100 CB88
Warburton St. E8 78 DV67
Warburton Rd.
Warburton Ter. E17 51 EB54
Ward Clo., Erith 97 FD79
Ward Clo., S.Croy. 134 DS106
Ward Clo. (Cheshunt), Wal.Cr. 22 DU27
Spicersfield
Ward La., Warl. 148 DW116
Ward Rd. E15 79 ED67
Ward Rd. N19 63 DJ62
Wardalls Gro. SE14 92 DW80
Wardell Clo. NW7 46 CS52
Wardell Fld. NW9 46 CS53
Warden Ave., Har. 58 BZ60
Warden Ave., Rom. 55 FC50
Warden Rd. NW5 76 DG65
Wardens Fld. Clo., Orp. 137 ES107
Wardens Gro. SE1 11 H3
Wardle St. E9 65 DX64
Wardley St. SW18 104 DB87
Garratt La.
Wardo Ave. SW6 89 CY81
Wardour Ms. W1 5 L9
Wardour St. W1 5 L8
Wardour St. W1 77 DJ72
Wardrobe Pl. EC4 6 G9
Wardrobe Ter. EC4 6 G10
Wards Rd., Ilf. 67 ER59
Wareham Clo., Houns. 86 CB84
Waremead Rd., Ilf. 67 EP57
Warenford Way, Borwd. 32 CN39
Warenne Rd., Lthd. 142 CC122
Warepoint Dr. SE28 95 ER75
Warfield Rd. NW10 75 CX69
Warfield Rd., Felt. 99 BS87
Warfield Rd., Hmptn. 114 CB95
Warfield Yd. NW10 75 CX69
Warfield Rd.
Wargrave Ave. N15 64 DT58
Wargrave Rd., Har. 58 CC62
Warham Rd. N4 63 DN57
Warham Rd., Har. 45 CF54
Warham Rd., Sev. 153 FH116
Warham Rd., S.Croy. 133 DP106
Warham St. SE5 91 DP80
Waring Clo., Orp. 137 ET107
Waring Dr., Orp. 137 ET107
Waring Rd., Sid. 110 EW93
Waring St. SE27 106 DQ91
Warkworth Gdns., Islw. 87 CG80
Warkworth Rd. N17 50 DR52
Warland Rd. SE18 95 ER80
Warley Ave., Dag. 68 EZ59
Warley Ave., Hayes 71 BU72
Warley Clo. E10 65 DZ60
Millicent Rd.
Warley Rd. N9 50 DW47
Warley Rd., Hayes 71 BU72
Warley Rd., Ilf. 53 EN53
Warley Rd., Wdf.Grn. 52 EH52
Warley St. E2 79 DX69
Warlingham Rd., Th.Hth. 119 DP98
Warlock Rd. W9 75 CZ70
Warlters Clo. N7 63 DL63
Warlters Rd.
Warlters Rd. N7 63 DL63
Warltersville Rd. N19 63 DL59
Warmington Clo. E5 65 DX62
Orient Way
Warmington Rd. SE24 106 DQ86
Warmington St. E13 80 EG70
Barking Rd.
Warminster Gdns. SE25 120 DU96
Warminster Rd. SE25 120 DU97
Warminster Sq. SE25 120 DU96
Warminster Rd.
Warminster Way, Mitch. 119 DH95
Warndon St. SE16 92 DW77
Warne Pl., Sid. 110 EV86
Westerham Dr.
Warneford Pl., Wat. 30 BY44
Warneford Rd., Har. 59 CK55
Warneford St. E9 78 DV67
Warner Ave., Sutt. 117 CY103
Warner Clo. E15 66 EE64
Warner Clo. NW9 61 CT59
Warner Clo., Hmptn. 100 BZ92
Tangley Pk. Rd.
Warner Clo., Hayes 85 BR80
Warner Par., Hayes 85 BR80
Warner Pl. E2 78 DU68
Warner Rd. E17 65 DY56
Warner Rd. N8 63 DK56
Warner Rd. SE5 92 DQ81
Warner Rd., Brom. 108 EF94
Warner St. EC1 6 D5
Warner St. EC1 77 DN70
Warner Yd. EC1 6 D5
Warners Clo., Wdf.Grn. 52 EG50
Warners La., Kings.T. 101 CK92
Warners Path, Wdf.Grn. 52 EG50
Warnford Ind. Est., Hayes 85 BS75
Warnford Rd., Orp. 137 ET106
Warnham Ct. Rd., Cars. 132 DF108
Warnham Rd. N12 48 DD50
Warple Ms. W3 88 CS75
Warple Way
Warple Way W3 88 CS75
Warren, The E12 66 EL63
Warren, The, Ash. 144 CL119
Warren, The, Cars. 132 DD109
Warren, The, Hayes 71 BU72
Warren, The, Houns. 86 BZ80
Warren, The, Lthd. 128 CC112
Warren, The, Rad. 17 CG33
Warren, The, Tad. 145 CY123
Warren, The, Wor.Pk. 130 CR105
Warren Ave. E10 65 EC62
Warren Ave., Brom. 108 EE94
Warren Ave., Orp. 137 ET106
Warren Ave., Rich. 88 CP84
Warren Ave., S.Croy. 135 DX108
Warren Ave., Sutt. 131 CZ110
Warren Clo. N9 51 DX45
Warren Clo. SE21 106 DQ87
Lairdale Clo.
Warren Clo., Bexh. 110 FA85
Pincott Rd.
Warren Clo., Esher 128 CB105
Warren Clo., Hayes 71 BV71
Warren Clo., Wem. 59 CK61
Warren Ct., Chig. 53 ER49
Warren Ct., Sev. 155 FJ125
Warren Ct., Wey. 126 BN106
Warren Cres. N9 50 DT45
Warren Cutting, Kings.T. 102 CR94
Warren Dr., Grnf. 72 CB70
Warren Dr., Horn. 69 FG63
Warren Dr., Orp. 138 EV106
Warren Dr., Ruis. 58 BX59
Warren Dr., Tad. 145 CZ122
Warren Dr., The E11 66 EJ59
Warren Dr. N., Surb. 116 CP102
Warren Dr. S., Surb. 116 CQ102
Warren Fld., Epp. 26 EU32
Warren Flds., Stan. 45 CJ49
Valencia Rd.
Warren Footpath, Twick. 101 CJ88
Warren Gdns. E15 65 ED64
Ashton Rd.
Warren Gdns., Orp. 138 EU106
Warren Gro., Borwd. 32 CR42
Warren Hill, Epsom 144 CR116
Warren Hill, Loug. 38 EJ43
Warren Ho. E3 79 EB69
Bromley High St.
Warren La. SE18 95 EP76
Warren La., Lthd. 128 CC111
Warren La., Stan. 45 CF48
Warren La., Wok. 140 BG118
Warren Lo. Dr., Tad. 145 CY124
Warren Mead, Bans. 145 CW115
Warren Ms. W1 5 K5
Warren Pk., Kings.T. 102 CQ93
Warren Pk., Warl. 149 DX118
Warren Pk. Rd., Sutt. 132 DD107
Warren Pl. E1 79 DX72
Pitsea St.
Warren Pond Rd. E4 52 EF46
Warren Ri., N.Mal. 116 CR95
Warren Rd. E4 51 EC47
Warren Rd. E10 65 EC62
Warren Rd. E11 66 EJ58
Warren Rd. NW2 61 CT61
Warren Rd. SW19 104 DE93
Warren Rd., Add. 126 BG110
Warren Rd., Ashf. 99 BS94
Warren Rd., Bans. 131 CW114
Warren Rd., Bexh. 110 FA85
Warren Rd., Brom. 122 EG103
Warren Rd., Croy. 120 DS102
Warren Rd., Ilf. 67 ER57
Warren Rd., Kings.T. 102 CQ93
Warren Rd., Orp. 137 ET106
Warren Rd., Pur. 133 DP112
Warren Rd., Sid. 110 EW90
Warren Rd., Twick. 100 CC86
Warren Rd., Uxb. 56 BL63
Warren Rd. (Bushey), Wat. 44 CC46
Warren St. W1 5 J5
Warren St. W1 77 DJ70
Warren Ter., Rom. 68 EX56
Warren Wk. SE7 94 EJ79
Warren Way NW7 47 CY51
Warren Way, Wey. 127 BQ106
Warren Wd. Clo., Brom. 122 EG103
Hillside La.
Warrender Rd. N19 63 DJ62
Warrender Way, Ruis. 57 BU59
Warreners La., Wey. 127 BR109

West St. E2 78 DV68
West St. E11 66 EE62
West St. E17 65 EB57
Grove Rd.
West St. WC2 5 N9
West St., Bexh. 96 EZ84
West St., Brent. 87 CJ79
West St., Brom. 122 EG95
West St., Cars. 118 DF104
West St., Croy. 134 DQ105
West St., Epsom 130 CQ113
West St. (Ewell), Epsom 130 CS110
West St., Erith 97 FD77
West St., Har. 59 CD60
West St., Sutt. 132 DB106
West St., Wat. 29 BV40
West St. La., Cars. 132 DF105
West Temple Sheen SW14 88 CP84
West Tenter St. E1 78 DT72
West Twrs., Pnr. 58 BX58
West Valley Rd., Hem.H. 14 BJ25
West Vw. NW4 61 CW56
West Vw., Felt. 99 BQ87
West Vw., Loug. 39 EM42
West Vw. Ave., Whyt. 148 DU118
Station Rd.
West Vw. Ct., Borwd. 31 CK44
High St.
West Vw. Gdns., Borwd. 31 CK44
High St.
West Vw. Rd., Swan. 125 FG98
West Vw. Rd. (Crockenhill), Swan. 125 FD100
West Wk. W5 74 CL71
West Wk., Barn. 48 DG45
West Wk., Hayes 71 BU74
West Warwick Pl. SW1 9 K9
West Warwick Pl. SW1 91 DJ77
West Way N18 50 DR49
West Way NW10 60 CR63
West Way, Cars. 132 DD110
West Way, Croy. 121 DY103
West Way, Edg. 46 CP51
West Way, Houns. 86 BZ80
West Way, Pnr. 58 BX56
West Way, Rick. 42 BH46
West Way, Ruis. 57 BT60
West Way, Shep. 113 BR100
West Way, W.Wick. 121 ED100
West Way Gdns., Croy. 121 DX103
West Woodside, Bex. 110 EY87
West World W5 74 CL69
Westacott, Hayes 71 BS71
Westacott Clo. N19 63 DK60
Westacres, Esher 128 BZ108
Westall Rd., Loug. 39 EP41
Westbank Rd., Hmptn. 100 CC93
Westbeech Rd. N22 63 DN55
Westbere Dr., Stan. 45 CK49
Westbere Rd. NW2 61 CY63
Westbourne Ave. W3 74 CR72
Westbourne Ave., Sutt. 117 CY103
Westbourne Bri. W2 76 DC71
Westbourne Clo., Hayes 71 BV70
Westbourne Cres. W2 76 DD73
Westbourne Cres. Ms. W2 76 DD73
Westbourne Cres.
Westbourne Dr. SE23 107 DX89
Westbourne Gdns. W2 76 DB72
Westbourne Gro. W2 76 DA72
Westbourne Gro. W11 75 CZ73
Westbourne Gro. Ms. W11 76 DA72
Westbourne Gro.
Westbourne Gro. Ter. W2 76 DB72
Westbourne Pk. Ms. W2 76 DB72
Westbourne Gdns.
Westbourne Pk. Pas. W2 76 DA71
Westbourne Pk. Rd. W2 76 DA71
Westbourne Pk. Rd. W11 75 CY72
Westbourne Pk. Vill. W2 76 DA71
Westbourne Pl. N9 50 DV48
Eastbournia Ave.
Westbourne Rd. N7 77 DM65
Westbourne Rd. SE26 107 DX93
Westbourne Rd., Bexh. 96 EX80
Westbourne Rd., Croy. 120 DT100
Westbourne Rd., Felt. 99 BT90
Westbourne Rd., Stai. 98 BH94
Westbourne Rd., Uxb. 71 BP70
Westbourne St. W2 76 DD73
Westbourne Ter. SE23 107 DX89
Westbourne Dr.
Westbourne Ter. W2 76 DC72
Westbourne Ter. Ms. W2 76 DC72
Westbourne Ter. Rd. W2 76 DC71
Westbridge Rd. SW11 90 DD81
Westbrook Ave., Hmptn. 100 BZ94
Westbrook Clo., Barn. 34 DD41
Westbrook Cres., Barn. 34 DD41
Westbrook Dr., Orp. 124 EW102
Westbrook Rd. SE3 94 EH81
Westbrook Rd., Houns. 86 BZ80
Westbrook Rd., Th.Hth. 120 DR95
Westbrook Sq., Barn. 34 DD41
Westbrooke Cres., Well. 96 EW83
Westbrooke Rd., Sid. 109 ER89
Westbrooke Rd., Well. 96 EV83
Westbury Ave. N22 63 DP55
Westbury Ave., Esher 129 CF107
Westbury Ave., Sthl. 72 CA70
Westbury Ave., Wem. 74 CL66
Westbury Clo., Ruis. 57 BU59
Westbury Clo., Shep. 113 BP100
Burchetts Way
Westbury Clo., Whyt. 148 DS116
Beverley Rd.
Westbury Gro. N12 48 DA51
Westbury La., Buck.H. 52 EJ47
Westbury Lo. Clo., Pnr. 58 BX55
Westbury Par. SW12 105 DH86
Balham Hill
Westbury Pl., Brent. 87 CK79
Westbury Rd. E7 66 EH64
Westbury Rd. E17 65 DZ56
Westbury Rd. N11 49 DL51
Westbury Rd. N12 48 DA51
Westbury Rd. SE20 121 DX95
Westbury Rd. W5 74 CL72
Westbury Rd., Bark. 81 ER67
Westbury Rd., Beck. 121 DY97
Westbury Rd., Brom. 122 EK95
Westbury Rd., Buck.H. 52 EJ47
Westbury Rd., Croy. 120 DR100
Westbury Rd., Felt. 100 BX88
Westbury Rd., Ilf. 67 EN61
Westbury Rd., N.Mal. 116 CR98
Westbury Rd., Nthwd. 43 BR49
Westbury Rd., Wat. 29 BV43
Westbury Rd., Wem. 74 CL66
Westbury St. SW8 91 DJ82
Westbury Ter. E7 80 EH65
Westcar La., Walt. 127 BV107
Westchester Dr. NW4 61 CX55
Westcombe Ave., Croy. 119 DL100
Westcombe Ct. SE3 94 EF80
Westcombe Pk. Rd.
Westcombe Dr., Barn. 34 DA43
Westcombe Hill SE3 94 EG79
Westcombe Hill SE10 94 EG78
Westcombe Lo. Dr., Hayes 71 BR71
Westcombe Pk. Rd. SE3 94 EE79
Westcoombe Ave. SW20 117 CT95
Westcote Ri., Ruis. 57 BQ59
Westcote Rd. SW16 105 DJ92
Westcott Clo. N15 64 DT58
Ermine Rd.
Westcott Clo., Brom. 122 EL99
Ringmer Way
Westcott Clo., Croy. 135 EB109
Castle Hill Ave.
Westcott Cres. W7 73 CE72
Westcott Rd. SE17 91 DP79
Westcott Way, Sutt. 131 CW110
Westcott Way, Uxb. 70 BJ68
Westcourt, Sun. 113 BV96
Westcroft Clo. NW2 61 CY63
Westcroft Clo., Enf. 36 DW38
Westcroft Gdns., Mord. 117 CZ97
Westcroft Rd., Cars. 132 DG105
Westcroft Rd., Wall. 132 DG105
Westcroft Sq. W6 89 CU77
Westcroft Way NW2 61 CY63
Westdale Pas. SE18 95 EP79
Westdale Rd.
Westdale Rd. SE18 95 EP79
Westdean Ave. SE12 108 EH88
Westdean Clo. SW18 104 DB85
Westdown Rd. E15 65 EC63
Westdown Rd. SE6 107 EA87
Wested La., Swan. 125 FG101
Westel Ho. W5 73 CJ73
Westerdale Rd. SE10 94 EG78
Westerfield Rd. N15 64 DT57
Westergate Rd. SE2 96 EY79
Westerham Ave. N9 50 DR48
Westerham Clo., Add. 126 BJ107
Westerham Clo., Sutt. 132 DA110
Westerham Dr., Sid. 110 EV86
Westerham Hill, West. 151 EN120
Westerham Rd. E10 65 EB58
Westerham Rd., Kes. 136 EK108
Westerham Rd., Sev. 154 FC123
Westerley Cres. SE26 107 DZ92
Westerly Ware, Rich. 88 CN79
Kew Grn.
Western Ave. NW11 61 CX58
Western Ave. W3 74 CN70
Western Ave. W5 74 CM70
Western Ave., Cher. 112 BG97
Western Ave., Dag. 83 FC65
Western Ave., Epp. 25 ET32
Western Ave., Grnf. 73 CE68
Western Ave., Nthlt. 72 BZ67
Western Ave., Ruis. 71 BQ65
Western Ave. (Denham), Uxb. 56 BJ63
Western Ave. (Ickenham), Uxb. 56 BK63
Western Clo., Cher. 112 BG97
Western Ave.
Western Ct. N3 48 DA51
Huntley Dr.
Western Dr., Shep. 113 BR100
Western Gdns. W5 74 CN73
Western Gateway E16 80 EG73
Western Ho. W5 74 CL69
Western La. SW12 104 DG87
Western Ms. W9 75 CZ70
Great Western Rd.
Western Perimeter Rd., Houns. 84 BH83
Western Pl. SE16 92 DW75
Canon Beck Rd.
Western Rd. E13 80 EJ67
Western Rd. E17 65 EC57
Western Rd. N2 62 DF56
Western Rd. N22 49 DM54
Western Rd. NW10 74 CQ70
Western Rd. SW9 91 DN83
Western Rd. SW19 118 DD95
Western Rd. W5 73 CK73
Western Rd., Epp. 25 ES32
Western Rd., Mitch. 118 DE95
Western Rd., Rom. 69 FE57
Western Rd., Sthl. 86 BW77
Western Rd., Sutt. 132 DA106
Western Ter. W6 89 CU78
Chiswick Mall
Western Trd. Est. NW10 74 CP70
Western Vw., Hayes 85 BT75
Station Rd.
Western Way SE28 95 ER76
Western Way, Barn. 34 DA44
Westernville Gdns., Ilf. 67 EQ59
Westferry Circ. E14 79 EA74
Westferry Rd. E14 93 EA75
Westfield, Ash. 144 CM118
Westfield, Loug. 38 EJ43
Westfield, Sev. 155 FJ122
Westfield Ave., S.Croy. 134 DR113
Westfield Ave., Wat. 30 BW37
Westfield Clo. NW9 60 CQ55
Westfield Clo. SW10 90 DC80
Westfield Clo., Enf. 37 DY41
Westfield Clo., Sutt. 131 CZ105
Westfield Clo., Wal.Cr. 23 DY31
Westfield Dr., Har. 59 CK56
Westfield Dr., Lthd. 142 CA122
Westfield Gdns., Har. 59 CK56
Westfield La., Har. 59 CK56
Westfield Par., Add. 126 BK110
Westfield Pk., Pnr. 44 BZ52
Westfield Rd. NW7 46 CR48
Westfield Rd. W13 73 CG74
Westfield Rd., Beck. 121 DZ96
Westfield Rd., Bexh. 97 FC82
Westfield Rd., Croy. 119 DP103
Westfield Rd., Dag. 68 EY63
Westfield Rd., Mitch. 118 DF96
Westfield Rd., Surb. 115 CK99
Westfield Rd., Sutt. 131 CZ105
Westfield Rd., Walt. 114 BY101
Westfield St. SE18 94 EK76
Westfield Wk., Wal.Cr. 23 DZ31
Westfield Clo.
Westfield Way E1 79 DY69
Westfield Way, Ruis. 57 BS62
Westfields SW13 89 CT83
Westfields Ave. SW13 88 CS83
Westfields Rd. W3 74 CP71
Westgate Clo., Epsom 144 CR115
Chalk La.
Westgate Ct., Wal.Cr. 37 DX35
Holmesdale
Westgate Rd. SE25 120 DV98
Westgate Rd., Beck. 121 EB96
Westgate St. E8 78 DV67
Westgate Ter. SW10 90 DB78
Westglade Ct., Har. 59 CK57
Westgrove La. SE10 93 EC81
Westhall Pk., Warl. 148 DW119
Westhall Rd., Warl. 148 DU118
Westhay Gdns. SW14 102 CP85
Westholm NW11 62 DB56
Westholme, Orp. 123 ES101
Westholme Gdns., Ruis. 57 BU60
Westhorne Ave. SE9 108 EK85
Westhorne Ave. SE12 108 EH86
Westhorpe Gdns. NW4 61 CW55
Westhorpe Rd. SW15 89 CW83
Westhurst Dr., Chis. 109 EP92
Westlake Clo. N13 49 DN48
Westlake Clo., Hayes 72 BY70
Lochan Clo.
Westlake Rd., Wem. 59 CK61
Westland Clo., Stai. 98 BL86
Westland Dr., Brom. 122 EF103
Westland Dr., Hat. 19 CY26
Westland Pl. N1 7 K2
Westland Rd., Wat. 29 BV40
Westlands Clo., Hayes 85 BU77
Granville Rd.
Westlands Ct., Epsom 144 CQ115
Westlands Est., Hayes 85 BS76
Westlands Ter. SW12 105 DJ86
Gaskarth Rd.
Westlea Ave., Wat. 30 BY36
Westlea Rd. W7 87 CG76
Westleigh Ave. SW15 103 CV85
Westleigh Ave., Couls. 146 DG116
Westleigh Dr., Brom. 122 EL95
Westleigh Gdns., Edg. 46 CN53
Westlinks, Wem. 73 CK69
Alperton La.
Westmacott Dr., Felt. 99 BT87
Westmead SW15 103 CV87
Westmead Cor., Cars. 132 DE105
Colston Ave.
Westmead Rd., Sutt. 132 DD105
Westmeade Clo. (Cheshunt), Wal.Cr. 22 DV29
Westmede, Chig. 53 EQ51
Westmere Dr. NW7 46 CR48
Westmill Ct. N4 64 DQ61
Brownswood Rd.
Westminster Ave., Th.Hth. 119 DP96
Westminster Bri. SE1 10 A5
Westminster Bri. SE1 91 DM75
Westminster Bri. SW1 10 A5
Westminster Bri. SW1 91 DL75
Westminster Bri. Rd. SE1 10 C5
Westminster Bri. Rd. SE1 91 DM75
Westminster Cathedral Piazza SW1 9 K7
Westminster Clo., Felt. 99 BU88
Westminster Clo., Ilf. 53 ER54
Westminster Clo., Tedd. 101 CG92
Westminster Dr. N13 49 DL50
Westminster Gdns. E4 52 EE46
Westminster Gdns., Bark. 81 ES68
Westminster Gdns., Ilf. 53 EQ54
Westminster Rd. N9 50 DV46
Westminster Rd. W7 73 CE74
Westminster Rd., Sutt. 118 DD103
Westmoat Clo., Beck. 107 EC94
Westmont Rd., Esher 115 CE103
Westmoor Gdns., Enf. 37 DX40
Westmoor Rd., Enf. 37 DX40
Westmoor St. SE7 94 EK76
Westmore Grn., West. 150 EJ121
Westmore Rd., West. 150 EJ121
Westmoreland Ave., Well. 95 ES83
Westmoreland Bldgs. EC1 78 DQ71
Bartholomew Clo.
Westmoreland Dr., Sutt. 132 DB109
Westmoreland Pl. SW1 91 DH78
Westmoreland Pl. W5 73 CK71
Mount Ave.
Westmoreland Rd. NW9 60 CM55
Westmoreland Rd. SE17 92 DR79
Westmoreland Rd. SW13 89 CT81
Westmoreland Rd., Brom. 122 EE99
Westmoreland St. W1 4 G7
Westmoreland St. W1 76 DG71
Westmoreland Ter. SW1 91 DH78
Westmoreland Wk. SE17 92 DR79
Westmoreland Rd.
Westmorland Clo. E12 66 EK61
Westmorland Clo., Epsom 130 CS110
Westmorland Clo., Twick. 101 CH86
Westmorland Rd. E17 65 EA58
Westmorland Rd., Har. 58 CB57
Westmorland Ter. SE20 106 DV94
Hawthorn Gro.
Westmorland Way, Mitch. 119 DK98
Westmount Rd. SE9 95 EM82
Westoe Rd. N9 50 DV47
Weston Ave., Add. 126 BG105
Weston Ave., T.Ditt. 115 CE101
Weston Ave., W.Mol. 114 BY97
Weston Clo., Couls. 147 DM120
Weston Clo., Pot.B. 19 CZ32
Weston Ct. N4 64 DQ62
Queens Dr.
Weston Dr., Stan. 45 CH53
Weston Gdns., Islw. 87 CD81
Weston Grn., Dag. 68 EZ63
Weston Grn., T.Ditt. 115 CE102
Weston Grn. Rd., Esher 115 CD102
Weston Grn. Rd., T.Ditt. 115 CE102
Weston Gro., Brom. 108 EF94
Weston Pk. N8 63 DL58
Weston Pk., Kings.T. 116 CL96
Fairfield W.
Weston Pk., T.Ditt. 115 CE102
Weston Pk. Clo., T.Ditt. 115 CE102
Weston Pk.
Weston Ri. WC1 6 C1
Weston Ri. WC1 77 DM69
Weston Rd. W4 88 CQ76
Weston Rd., Brom. 108 EF94
Weston Rd., Dag. 68 EY63
Weston Rd., Enf. 36 DR39
Weston Rd., Epsom 130 CS111
Weston Rd., T.Ditt. 115 CE102
Weston St. SE1 11 L4
Weston St. SE1 92 DR75
Weston Wk. E8 78 DV66
Mare St.
Westover Clo., Sutt. 132 DB109
Westover Hill NW3 62 DA61
Westover Rd. SW18 104 DC87
Westow Hill SE19 106 DS93
Westow St. SE19 106 DS93
Westpoint Trd. Est. W3 74 CN70
Westpole Ave., Barn. 34 DG42
Westport Rd. E13 80 EH70
Westport St. E1 79 DX72
Westrow SW15 103 CW86
Westrow Dr., Bark. 81 ET65
Westrow Gdns., Ilf. 67 ET61
Westside NW4 47 CV54
Westvale Ms. W3 88 CS75
Westview Clo. NW10 61 CT64
Westview Clo. W7 73 CE72
Westview Clo. W10 75 CW72
Westview Cres. N9 50 DS45
Westview Dr., Wdf.Grn. 52 EK54
Westview Rd., Warl. 148 DV119
Westville Rd. W12 89 CU75
Westville Rd., T.Ditt. 115 CG102
Westward Rd. E4 51 DY50
Westward Way, Har. 60 CL58
Westway NW7 47 CU52
Westway SW20 117 CV97
Westway W2 76 DA71
Westway W9 76 DA71
Westway W10 75 CY72
Westway W12 75 CT73
Westway, Cat. 148 DR122
Westway, Orp. 123 ER99
Westway Clo. SW20 117 CV97
Westways, Epsom 131 CT105
Westwell Clo., Orp. 124 EX102
Westwell Rd. SW16 105 DL93
Westwell Rd. App. SW16 105 DL93
Westwell Rd.
Westwick Gdns. W14 89 CX75
Westwick Gdns., Houns. 85 BV82
Westwick Pl., Wat. 16 BW34
Westwood Ave. SE19 120 DQ95
Westwood Ave., Har. 58 CB63
Westwood Clo., Brom. 122 EK97
Westwood Clo., Esher 114 CC104
Westwood Clo., Pot.B. 20 DA30
Westwood Clo., Ruis. 57 BP58
Westwood Gdns. SW13 89 CT83
Westwood Hill SE26 106 DU92
Westwood La., Sid. 110 EU85
Westwood La., Well. 95 ET83
Westwood Pk. SE23 106 DV87
Westwood Rd. E16 80 EH74
Westwood Rd. SW13 89 CT83
Westwood Rd., Couls. 147 DK118
Westwood Rd., Ilf. 67 ET60
Westwood Way, Sev. 154 FF122
Wetheral Dr., Stan. 45 CJ53
Wetherby Clo., Nthlt. 72 CB65
Wetherby Gdns. SW5 90 DC77
Wetherby Ms. SW5 90 DB78
Bolton Gdns.
Wetherby Pl. SW7 90 DC77
Wetherby Rd., Borwd. 32 CL39
Wetherby Rd., Enf. 36 DQ39
Wetherby Way, Chess. 130 CL108
Wetherden St. E17 65 DZ59
Wetherell Rd. E9 79 DX67
Wetherill Rd. N10 48 DG53
Wettern Clo., S.Croy. 134 DS110
Purley Oaks Rd.
Wexfenne Gdns., Wok. 140 BH116
Wexford Rd. SW12 104 DF87
Wey Ave., Cher. 112 BG97
Wey Clo., W.Byf. 126 BH113
Broadoaks Cres.
Wey Ct., Add. 126 BK109
Wey Ct., Epsom 130 CQ105
Wey Manor Rd., Add. 126 BK109
Wey Meadows, Wey. 126 BL106
Wey Rd., Wey. 112 BM104
Weybank, Wok. 140 BL116
Weybarton, W.Byf. 126 BM113
Weybourne Pl., S.Croy. 134 DR110
Weybourne St. SW18 104 DC89
Weybridge Business Pk., Add. 126 BL105
Weybridge Ct. SE16 92 DU78
Argyle Way
Weybridge Pk., Wey. 126 BN106
Weybridge Pt. SW11 90 DF82
Weybridge Rd., Add. 112 BK104
Weybridge Rd., Th.Hth. 119 DN98
Weybridge Rd., Wey. 112 BK104
Weydown Clo. SW19 103 CY88
Weyhill Rd. E1 78 DU72
Commercial Rd.
Weylands Clo., Walt. 114 BZ102
Weylands Pk., Wey. 127 BS107
Ellesmere Rd.
Weylond Rd., Dag. 68 EY62
Weyman Rd. SE3 94 EJ81
Weymead Clo., Cher. 112 BJ102
Weymede, W.Byf. 126 BM112
Weymouth Ave. NW7 46 CS50
Weymouth Ave. W5 87 CJ76
Weymouth Clo. E6 81 EP72
Covelees Wall
Weymouth Ct., Sutt. 132 DA108
Weymouth Ms. W1 5 H6
Weymouth Ms. W1 77 DH71
Weymouth Rd., Hayes 71 BS69
Weymouth St. W1 4 G7
Weymouth St. W1 76 DG71
Weymouth Ter. E2 78 DT68
Weymouth Wk., Stan. 45 CG51
Weyside Clo., W.Byf. 126 BM112
Weystone Rd., Add. 126 BM105
Weybridge Rd.
Whadcote St. N4 63 DN61
Seven Sisters Rd.
Whalebone Ave., Rom. 68 EZ58
Whalebone Ct. EC2 7 L8
Whalebone Gro., Rom. 68 EZ58
Whalebone La. E15 80 EE66
West Ham La.
Whalebone La. N., Rom. 54 EY54
Whalebone La. S., Dag. 68 EZ59
Whalebone La. S., Rom. 68 EZ58
Whaley Rd., Pot.B. 20 DC33
Wharf La., Rick. 42 BL46
Wharf La., Twick. 101 CG88
Wharf La. (Ripley), Wok. 140 BK119
Mill La.
Wharf Pl. E2 78 DU67
Wharf Rd. E15 79 ED67
Wharf Rd. N1 7 H1
Wharf Rd. N1 78 DQ68
Wharf Rd., Enf. 37 DY44
Wharf Rd. Ind. Est., Enf. 37 DY44
Wharf St. E16 80 EE71
Wharfdale Ct. E5 65 DX63
Rushmore Rd.
Wharfdale Rd. N1 77 DL68
Wharfedale Gdns., Th.Hth. 119 DM98
Wharfedale St. SW10 90 DB78
Coleherne Rd.
Wharfside Rd. E16 80 EE71
Wharncliffe Dr., Sthl. 73 CD74
Wharncliffe Gdns. SE25 120 DS96
Wharncliffe Rd. SE25 120 DS96
Wharton Clo. NW10 74 CS65
Wharton Rd., Brom. 122 EH95
Wharton St. WC1 6 C3
Wharton St. WC1 77 DM69
Whateley Rd. SE20 107 DX94
Whateley Rd. SE22 106 DT85
Whatley Ave. SW20 117 CX97

Windmill La. (Cheshunt), Wal.Cr. 23 DY30
Windmill La. (Bushey), Wat. 45 CD46
Windmill Ms. W4 88 CS77
Chiswick Common Rd.
Windmill Pas. W4 88 CS77
Chiswick Common Rd.
Windmill Ri., Kings.T. 102 CP94
Windmill Rd. N18 50 DR49
Windmill Rd. SW18 104 DD86
Windmill Rd. SW19 103 CW90
Windmill Rd. W4 88 CS77
Windmill Rd. W5 87 CJ77
Windmill Rd., Brent. 87 CK78
Windmill Rd., Croy. 120 DQ101
Windmill Rd., Hmptn. 100 CB92
Windmill Rd., Mitch. 119 DJ99
Windmill Rd., Sev. 155 FH130
Windmill Rd., Sun. 113 BS95
Windmill Rd. W., Sun. 113 BS96
Windmill Row SE11 91 DN78
Windmill St. W1 5 M7
Windmill St. W1 77 DK71
Windmill St. (Bushey), Wat. 45 CE46
Windmill Wk. SE1 10 E3
Windmill Wk. SE1 77 DN74
Windmill Way, Ruis. 57 BT60
Windmore Ave., Pot.B. 19 CW31
Windover Ave. NW9 60 CR56
Windrose Clo. SE16 93 DX75
Windrush Clo. SW11 90 DD84
Maysoule Rd.
Windrush Clo. W4 88 CQ81
Windrush Clo., Uxb. 56 BM63
Windrush La. SE23 107 DX90
Windsock Clo. SE16 93 DZ76
Windsor Ave. E17 51 DY54
Windsor Ave. SW19 118 DC95
Windsor Ave., Edg. 46 CP49
Windsor Ave., N.Mal. 116 CQ99
Windsor Ave., Sutt. 117 CY104
Windsor Ave., Uxb. 71 BP67
Windsor Ave., W.Mol. 114 CA97
Windsor Cen., The SE27 106 DQ91
Advance Rd.
Windsor Clo. N3 47 CY54
Windsor Clo. SE27 106 DQ91
Windsor Clo., Borwd. 32 CN39
Warenford Way
Windsor Clo., Brent. 87 CH79
Windsor Clo., Chis. 109 EP92
Windsor Clo., Har. 58 CA62
Windsor Clo., Nthwd. 43 BU54
Windsor Clo. (Cheshunt), Wal.Cr. 22 DU30
Windsor Ct. N14 49 DJ45
Windsor Ct., Sun. 99 BU93
Windsor Rd.
Windsor Cres., Har. 58 CA62
Windsor Cres., Wem. 60 CP62
Windsor Dr., Ashf. 98 BK91
Windsor Dr., Barn. 34 DF44
Windsor Dr., Dart. 111 FG86
Windsor Dr., Orp. 138 EU107
Windsor Gdns. W9 76 DA71
Windsor Gdns., Croy. 119 DL104
Richmond Rd.
Windsor Gdns., Hayes 85 BR76
Windsor Gro. SE27 106 DQ91
Windsor Pk. Rd., Hayes 85 BT80
Windsor Pl. SW1 9 L7
Windsor Pl., Cher. 112 BG100
Windsor St.
Windsor Rd. E4 51 EB49
Chivers Rd.
Windsor Rd. E7 66 EH64
Windsor Rd. E10 65 EB61
Windsor Rd. E11 66 EG60
Windsor Rd. N3 47 CY54
Windsor Rd. N7 63 DL62
Windsor Rd. N13 49 DN48
Windsor Rd. N17 50 DU54
Windsor Rd. NW2 75 CV65
Windsor Rd. W5 74 CL73
Windsor Rd., Barn. 33 CX44
Windsor Rd., Bexh. 96 EY84
Windsor Rd., Dag. 68 EY62
Windsor Rd., Enf. 37 DX36
Windsor Rd., Har. 45 CD53
Windsor Rd., Houns. 85 BV82
Windsor Rd., Ilf. 67 EP63
Windsor Rd., Kings.T. 102 CL94
Windsor Rd., Rich. 88 CM82
Windsor Rd., Sthl. 86 BZ76
Windsor Rd., Sun. 99 BU93
Windsor Rd., Tedd. 101 CD92
Windsor Rd., Th.Hth. 119 DP96
Windsor Rd., Wat. 30 BW38
Windsor Rd., Wor.Pk. 117 CU103
Windsor St. N1 77 DP67
Windsor St., Cher. 112 BG100
Windsor St., Uxb. 70 BJ66
Windsor Ter. N1 7 J2
Windsor Ter. N1 78 DQ69
Windsor Wk. SE5 92 DR82
Windsor Wk., Walt. 114 BX102
King George Ave.
Windsor Wk., Wey. 127 BP106
Windsor Way W14 89 CX77
Windsor Way, Rick. 42 BG46
Windsor Wf. E9 65 DZ64
Windsor Wd., Wal.Abb. 24 EE33
Monkswood Ave.
Windsors, The, Buck.H. 52 EL47
Windspoint Dr. SE15 92 DV79
Ethnard Rd.
Windus Rd. N16 64 DT60
Windus Wk. N16 64 DT60
Alkham Rd.
Windward Clo., Enf. 37 DX35
Windy Ridge, Brom. 122 EL95
Windycroft Clo., Pur. 133 DK113
Windyridge Clo. SW19 103 CX92
Wine Clo. E1 78 DW73
Wine Office Ct. EC4 6 E9
Winern Glebe, W.Byf. 126 BK113
Winery La., Kings.T. 116 CM97
Winford Ho. E3 79 DZ66
Jodrell Rd.
Winforton St. SE10 93 EC81
Winfrith Rd. SW18 104 DC87
Wingate Cres., Croy. 119 DK100
Wingate Rd. W6 89 CV76
Wingate Rd., Ilf. 67 EP64
Wingate Rd., Sid. 110 EW93
Wingate Trd. Est. N17 50 DT52
Wingfield Clo., Add. 126 BH110
Wingfield Ms. SE15 92 DU83
Wingfield St.
Wingfield Rd. E15 66 EE63
Wingfield Rd. E17 65 EB57
Wingfield Rd., Kings.T. 102 CN93
Wingfield St. SE15 92 DU83
Wingfield Way, Ruis. 71 BV65
Wingford Rd. SW2 105 DL86
Wingmore Rd. SE24 92 DQ83
Wingrave Rd. W6 89 CW79
Wingrove Rd. SE6 108 EE89
Wings Clo., Sutt. 132 DA105
Winifred Gro. SW11 90 DF84
Winifred Rd. SW19 118 DA95
Winifred Rd., Couls. 146 DG116
Winifred Rd., Dag. 68 EY61
Winifred Rd., Dart. 111 FH85
Winifred Rd., Erith 97 FE78
Winifred Rd., Hmptn. 100 CA91
Winifred St. E16 81 EM74
Winifred Ter. E13 80 EG68
Victoria Rd.
Winifred Ter., Enf. 50 DT45
Great Cambridge Rd.
Winkfield Rd. E13 80 EH68
Winkfield Rd. N22 49 DN53
Winkley St. E2 78 DV68
Winkworth Pl., Bans. 131 CZ114
Bolters La.
Winkworth Rd., Bans. 132 DA114
Winlaton Rd., Brom. 107 ED91
Winmill Rd., Dag. 68 EZ62
Winn Common Rd. SE18 95 ES79
Winn Rd. SE12 108 EH88
Winnett St. W1 5 M10
Winnings Wk., Nthlt. 72 BY65
Arnold Rd.
Winnington Clo. N2 62 DD58
Winnington Rd. N2 62 DD60
Winnington Rd., Enf. 36 DW38
Winnipeg Dr., Orp. 137 ET107
Winnock Rd., West Dr. 70 BK74
Winns Ave. E17 65 DY55
Winns Ms. N15 64 DS56
Grove Pk. Rd.
Winns Ter. E17 51 EA54
Winsbeach E17 51 ED54
Winscombe Cres. W5 73 CK70
Winscombe St. N19 63 DH61
Winscombe Way, Stan. 45 CG50
Winsford Rd. SE6 107 DZ90
Winsford Ter. N18 50 DR50
Winsham Gro. SW11 104 DG85
Winslade Rd. SW2 105 DL85
Winslade Way SE6 107 EB87
Rushey Grn.
Winsland Ms. W2 76 DD72
London St.
Winsland St. W2 76 DD72
Winsley St. W1 5 K8
Winsley St. W1 77 DJ72
Winslow SE17 92 DS78
Kinglake St.
Winslow Clo. NW10 60 CS62
Neasden La. N.
Winslow Clo., Pnr. 57 BV58
Winslow Gro. E4 52 EE47
Winslow Rd. W6 89 CW79
Winslow Way, Felt. 100 BX90
Winslow Way, Walt. 114 BW104
Winsor Ter. E6 81 EN71
Winstanley Clo., Cob. 127 BV114
Winstanley Est. SW11 90 DD83
Winstanley Rd. SW11 90 DD83
Winstead Gdns., Dag. 69 FC64
Winston Ave. NW9 60 CS59
Winston Clo., Har. 45 CF51
Winston Clo., Rom. 69 FB56
Winston Ct., Har. 44 CB52
Winston Dr., Cob. 142 BY116
Winston Rd. N16 64 DR63
Winston Wk. W4 88 CR77
Acton La.
Winston Way, Ilf. 67 EP62
Winston Way, Pot.B. 20 DA33
Winstre Rd., Borwd. 32 CN39
Winter Ave. E6 80 EL67
Winter Box Wk., Rich. 88 CM84
Winterborne Ave., Orp. 123 ER104
Winterbourne Gro., Wey. 127 BQ107
Winterbourne Rd. SE6 107 DZ88
Winterbourne Rd., Dag. 68 EW61
Winterbourne Rd., Th.Hth. 119 DN98
Winterbrook Rd. SE24 106 DQ86
Winterdown Gdns., Esher 128 BZ107
Winterdown Rd., Esher 128 BZ107
Winterfold Clo. SW19 103 CY89
Wintergreen Clo. E6 80 EL71
Yarrow Cres.
Winters Rd., T.Ditt. 115 CH101
Winters Way, Wal.Abb. 24 EG33
Wintersells Rd., W.Byf. 126 BK110
Winterstoke Gdns. NW7 47 CU50
Winterstoke Rd. SE6 107 DZ88
Winterton Ho. E1 78 DV72
Winterton Pl. SW10 90 DC79
Park Wk.
Winterwell Rd. SW2 105 DL85
Winthorpe Rd. SW15 89 CY84
Winthrop St. E1 78 DV71
Brady St.
Winthrop Wk., Wem. 60 CL62
Everard Way
Winton App., Rick. 29 BQ43
Winton Ave. N11 49 DJ52
Winton Clo. N9 51 DX45
Winton Cres., Rick. 29 BP43
Winton Dr., Rick. 29 BP44
Winton Dr. (Cheshunt), Wal.Cr. 23 DY29
Winton Gdns., Edg. 46 CM52
Winton Rd., Orp. 137 EP105
Winton Way SW16 105 DN92
Wireless Rd., West. 150 EK115
Wisbeach Rd., Croy. 120 DR99
Wisborough Rd., S.Croy. 134 DT109
Wisdons Clo., Dag. 69 FB60
Wise La. NW7 47 CU50
Wise La., West Dr. 84 BK76
Wise Rd. E15 79 ED67
Wiseman Ct. SE19 106 DT92
Wiseman Rd. E10 65 EA61
Wise's La., Hat. 19 CW27
Wiseton Rd. SW17 104 DE88
Wishart Rd. SE3 94 EK82
Wishford Ct., Ash. 144 CM118
The Marld
Wisley Common, Wok. 140 BM117
Wisley La., Wok. 140 BJ116
Wisley Rd. SW11 104 DG85
Wisley Rd., Orp. 110 EU94
Wisteria Clo. NW7 47 CT51
Wisteria Clo., Ilf. 67 EP64
Wisteria Clo., Orp. 123 EP103
Wisteria Gdns., Swan. 125 FD96
Wisteria Rd. SE13 93 ED84
Witan St. E2 78 DV69
Witches La., Sev. 154 FD123
Witham Clo., Loug. 38 EL44
Witham Rd. SE20 120 DW97
Witham Rd. W13 73 CG74
Witham Rd., Dag. 68 FA64
Witham Rd., Islw. 87 CD81
Witham Rd., Rom. 69 FH57
Withens Clo., Orp. 124 EW98
Witherby Clo., Croy. 134 DS106
Witherfield Way SE16 92 DV78
Egan Way
Witherington Rd. N5 63 DN64
Withers Clo., Chess. 129 CJ107
Coppard Gdns.
Withers Mead NW9 47 CT53
Witherston Way SE9 109 EN89
Witheygate Ave., Stai. 98 BH93
Withies, The, Lthd. 143 CH121
Withy La., Ruis. 57 BQ57
Withy Mead E4 51 ED48
Withy Pl., St.Alb. 16 CC28
Withybed Cor., Tad. 145 CV123
Withycombe Rd. SW19 103 CX87
Witley Cres., Croy. 135 EC107
Witley Gdns., Sthl. 86 BZ77
Witley Rd. N19 63 DJ61
Holloway Rd.
Witney Clo., Pnr. 44 BZ51
Witney Clo., Uxb. 56 BM63
Witney Path SE23 107 DX90
Inglemere Rd.
Wittenham Way E4 51 ED48
Wittering Clo., Kings.T. 101 CK92
Wittersham Rd., Brom. 108 EF92
Wivenhoe Clo. SE15 92 DV83
Wivenhoe Ct., Houns. 86 BZ84
Wivenhoe Rd., Bark. 82 EU68
Wiverton Rd. SE26 106 DW93
Wix Rd., Dag. 82 EX67
Wixs La. SW4 91 DH83
Woburn Ave., Epp. 39 ES37
Woburn Ave., Horn. 69 FG63
Woburn Ave., Pur. 133 DN111
High St.
Woburn Clo. SE28 82 EX72
Summerton Way
Woburn Clo. SW19 104 DC93
Tintern Clo.
Woburn Clo. (Bushey), Wat. 30 CC43
Woburn Hill, Add. 112 BJ103
Woburn Pl. WC1 5 N4
Woburn Pl. WC1 77 DK70
Woburn Rd., Cars. 118 DE102
Woburn Rd., Croy. 120 DQ102
Woburn Sq. WC1 5 N5
Woburn Sq. WC1 77 DK70
Woburn Wk. WC1 5 N3
Woffington Clo., Kings.T. 115 CJ95
Woking Clo. SW15 89 CT84
Wold, The, Cat. 149 EA122
Woldham Pl., Brom. 122 EJ98
Woldham Rd., Brom. 122 EJ98
Woldingham Rd., Cat. 148 DV120
Wolds Dr., Orp. 137 EN105
Wolfe Clo., Brom. 122 EG100
Wolfe Clo., Hayes 71 BV69
Ayles Rd.
Wolfe Cres. SE7 94 EK78
Wolfe Cres. SE16 93 DX75
Wolferton Rd. E12 67 EM63
Wolffe Gdns. E15 80 EF65
Wolffram Clo. SE13 108 EE85
Wolfington Rd. SE27 105 DP91
Wolftencroft Clo. SW11 90 DD83
Wollaston Clo. SE1 11 H8
Wolmer Clo., Edg. 46 CP49
Wolmer Gdns., Edg. 46 CN48
Wolseley Ave. SW19 104 DA89
Wolseley Gdns. W4 88 CP79
Wolseley Rd. E7 80 EH66
Wolseley Rd. N8 63 DK58
Wolseley Rd. N22 49 DM53
Wolseley Rd. W4 88 CQ77
Wolseley Rd., Har. 59 CE55
Wolseley Rd., Mitch. 118 DG101
Wolseley Rd., Rom. 69 FD59
Wolseley St. SE1 92 DU75
Wolsey Ave. E6 81 EN69
Wolsey Ave. E17 65 DZ55
Wolsey Ave., T.Ditt. 115 CF99
Aragon Ave.
Wolsey Ave. (Cheshunt), Wal.Cr. 22 DT29
Wolsey Clo. SW20 103 CV94
Wolsey Clo., Houns. 86 CC84
Wolsey Clo., Kings.T. 116 CP95
Wolsey Clo., Sthl. 86 CC76
Wolsey Clo., Wor.Pk. 131 CU105
Wolsey Cres., Croy. 135 EC109
Wolsey Cres., Mord. 117 CY101
Wolsey Dr., Kings.T. 102 CL92
Wolsey Dr., Walt. 114 BX102
Wolsey Gdns., Ilf. 53 EP51
Wolsey Gro., Edg. 46 CR52
Wolsey Gro., Esher 128 CB105
Wolsey Ms. NW5 77 DJ65
Wolsey Ms., Orp. 137 ET106
Osgood Ave.
Wolsey Pk., Wat. 43 BR45
Wolsey Rd. N1 64 DR64
Wolsey Rd., Ashf. 98 BL91
Wolsey Rd., E.Mol. 115 CD98
Wolsey Rd., Enf. 36 DV40
Wolsey Rd., Esher 128 CB105
Wolsey Rd., Hmptn. 100 CB93
Wolsey Rd., Nthwd. 43 BQ47
Wolsey Rd., Sun. 99 BT94
Wolsey St. E1 78 DW71
Sidney St.
Wolsey Way, Chess. 130 CN106
Wolsley Clo., Dart. 111 FE85
Wolstan Clo., Uxb. 56 BG62
Lindsey Rd.
Wolstonbury N12 48 DA50
Wolvercote Rd. SE2 96 EX75
Wolverley St. E2 78 DV69
Bethnal Grn. Rd.
Wolverton SE17 11 M10
Wolverton Ave., Kings.T. 116 CN95
Wolverton Gdns. W5 74 CM73
Wolverton Gdns. W6 89 CX77
Wolverton Rd., Stan. 45 CH51
Wolverton Way N14 35 DJ43
Wolves La. N13 49 DN51
Wolves La. N22 49 DN52
Womersley Rd. N8 63 DM58
Wonersh Way, Sutt. 131 CX109
Wonford Clo., Kings.T. 116 CS95
Wontford Rd., Pur. 147 DN115
Wontner Clo. N1 78 DQ66
Greenman St.
Wontner Rd. SW17 104 DF89
Wood Clo. E2 78 DU70
Wood Clo. NW9 60 CR59
Wood Clo., Bex. 111 FE90
Wood Clo., Har. 59 CD59
Wood Dr., Chis. 108 EL93
Wood Dr., Sev. 154 FF126
Wood End, Hayes 71 BS72
Wood End, St.Alb. 16 CC28
Wood End Ave., Har. 58 CB63
Wood End Clo., Nthlt. 59 CD64
Wood End Gdns., Nthlt. 58 CC64
Wood End Grn. Rd., Hayes 71 BR71
Wood End La., Nthlt. 72 CB65
Wood End Rd., Har. 59 CD63
Wood End Way, Nthlt. 58 CC64
Wood Grn. Way (Cheshunt), Wal.Cr. 23 DY31
Holme Clo.
Wood La. N6 63 DH58
Wood La. NW9 60 CR59
Wood La. W12 75 CW72
Wood La., Cat. 148 DR124
Wood La., Dag. 68 EW63
Wood La., Horn. 69 FG64
Wood La., Islw. 87 CE79
Wood La., Ruis. 57 BR60
Wood La., Stan. 45 CG48
Wood La., Tad. 145 CZ117
Brighton Rd.
Wood La., Wey. 127 BQ109
Wood La., Wdf.Grn. 52 EF49
Wood Lo. Gdns., Brom. 108 EL94
Wood Lo. La., W.Wick. 121 EC104
Wood Meads, Epp. 26 EU29
Wood Pt. E16 80 EG71
Fife Rd.
Wood Retreat SE18 95 ER80
Clothworkers Rd.
Wood Ride, Barn. 34 DD39
Wood Ride, Orp. 123 ER98
Wood Rd., Shep. 112 BN98
Wood Rd., West. 150 EJ118
Wood St. E16 80 EH73
Ethel Rd.
Wood St. E17 65 EC55
Wood St. EC2 7 J9
Wood St. EC2 78 DQ72
Wood St. W4 88 CS78
Wood St., Barn. 33 CW42
Wood St., Kings.T. 116 CL95
Wood St., Mitch. 118 DG101
Wood Vale N10 63 DJ57
Wood Vale SE23 106 DV88
Wood Vale Est. SE23 106 DW86
Wood Vw. (Cuffley), Pot.B. 21 DL27
Wood Way, Orp. 123 EN103
Wood Wf. SE10 93 EB79
Thames St.
Woodall Clo. E14 79 EB73
Lawless St.
Woodall Rd., Enf. 37 DX44
Woodbank Rd., Brom. 108 EF90
Woodbastwick Rd. SE26 107 DX92
Woodberry Ave. N21 49 DN47
Woodberry Ave., Har. 58 CB56
Woodberry Clo., Sun. 99 BU93
Ashridge Way
Woodberry Cres. N10 63 DH55
Woodberry Down N4 64 DQ59
Woodberry Down, Epp. 26 EU29
Woodberry Down Est. N4 64 DQ59
Woodberry Gdns. N12 48 DC51
Woodberry Gro. N4 64 DQ59
Woodberry Gro. N12 48 DC51
Woodberry Gro., Bex. 111 FD90
Woodberry Way E4 51 EC46
Woodberry Way N12 48 DC51
Woodbine Clo., Twick. 101 CD89
Woodbine Clo., Wal.Abb. 38 EJ35
Woodbine Gro. SE20 106 DV94
Woodbine Gro., Enf. 36 DR38
Woodbine La., Wor.Pk. 117 CV104
Woodbine Pl. E11 66 EG58
Woodbine Rd., Sid. 109 ES88
Woodbine Ter. E9 78 DW65
Morning La.
Woodbines Ave., Kings.T. 115 CK97
Woodborough Rd. SW15 89 CV84
Woodbourne Ave. SW16 105 DK90
Woodbourne Clo. SW16 105 DL90
Woodbourne Ave.
Woodbourne Dr., Esher 129 CF107
Woodbourne Gdns., Wall. 133 DH108
Woodbridge Ave., Lthd. 143 CG118
Woodbridge Clo. N7 63 DM61
Woodbridge Clo. NW2 61 CU62
Woodbridge Ct., Wdf.Grn. 52 EL52
Woodbridge Gro., Lthd. 143 CG118
Woodbridge Rd., Bark. 67 ET64
Woodbridge St. EC1 6 F4
Woodbridge St. EC1 77 DP70
Woodbrook Gdns., Wal.Abb. 24 EE33
Woodbrook Rd. SE2 96 EU79
Woodburn Clo. NW4 61 CX57
Woodburn Clo., Uxb. 71 BP70
Aldenham Dr.
Woodbury Clo. E11 66 EH56
Woodbury Clo., Croy. 120 DT103
Woodbury Clo., West. 151 EM118
Woodbury Dr., Sutt. 132 DC110
Woodbury Hill, Loug. 38 EL41
Woodbury Hollow, Loug. 38 EL40
Woodbury Pk. Rd. W13 73 CH70
Woodbury Rd. E17 65 EB56
Woodbury Rd., West. 151 EM118
Woodbury St. SW17 104 DE92
Woodchester Sq. W2 76 DB71
Woodchurch Clo., Sid. 109 ER90
Woodchurch Dr., Brom. 108 EK94
Woodchurch Rd. NW6 76 DA66
Woodclyffe Dr., Chis. 123 EN96
Woodcock Ct., Har. 60 CL59
Woodcock Dell Ave., Har. 59 CK59
Woodcock Hill, Har. 59 CJ57
Woodcock Hill, Rick. 42 BL50
Woodcock Hill Trd. Est., Rick. 42 BL49
Woodcocks E16 80 EJ71
Woodcombe Cres. SE23 106 DW88
Woodcote Ave. NW7 47 CW51
Woodcote Ave., Horn. 69 FG63
Woodcote Ave., Th.Hth. 119 DP98
Woodcote Ave., Wall. 133 DH109
Woodcote Clo., Enf. 36 DW44
Woodcote Clo., Epsom 130 CR114
Woodcote Clo., Kings.T. 102 CM92
Woodcote Clo. (Cheshunt), Wal.Cr. 22 DW30
Woodcote Dr., Orp. 123 ER102
Woodcote Dr., Pur. 133 DK110
Woodcote End, Epsom 144 CR115
Woodcote Grn., Wall. 133 DJ109
Woodcote Grn. Rd., Epsom 144 CQ116
Woodcote Gro., Couls. 133 DH112
Woodcote Gro. Rd., Couls. 147 DK115
Woodcote Hurst, Epsom 144 CQ116
Woodcote La., Pur. 133 DK111

The following is a comprehensive listing of all named places which appear in this atlas. Bold references can be found within the Central London enlarged scale section (pages 4-11). Postal information is in either London postal district or non-London post town form. For an explanation of post town abbreviations please consult page 170.

Dormer's Wells, Sthl.	72	CB73	Gidea Park, Rom.	69	FG55	Hillingdon, Uxb.	70	BM69
Downe, Orp.	137	EM111	Goathurst Common, Sev.	154	FB130	Hinchley Wood, Esher	115	CF104
Downham, Brom.	108	EF91	Godden Green, Sev.	155	FN125	Hither Green SE13	108	EE86
Downside, Cob.	141	BV118	Goddington, Orp.	124	EW104	**Holborn WC2**	**6**	**B8**
Ducks Island, Barn.	33	CX44	Goffs Oak, Wal.Cr.	22	DQ29	Holdbrook, Wal.Cr.	23	EA34
Dulwich SE21	106	DS87	Golders Green NW11	62	DA59	Holders Hill NW4	47	CX54
Dunton Green, Sev.	153	FC119	Goodmayes, Ilf.	68	EV61	Holloway N7	63	DL63
Ealing W5	73	CJ73	Gospel Oak NW5	62	DG63	Holyfield, Wal.Abb.	23	ED28
Earls Court SW5	89	CZ78	Grange Hill, Chig.	53	ER51	Holywell, Wat.	29	BS44
Earlsfield SW18	104	DC88	Grange Park N21	35	DP43	Homerton E9	65	DY64
East Acton W3	74	CS73	Green Street, Borwd.	32	CP37	Honor Oak SE23	106	DW86
East Barnet, Barn.	34	DE44	Green Street Green, Orp.	137	ES107	Honor Oak Park SE4	107	DZ86
East Bedfont, Felt.	99	BS88	Greenford, Grnf.	72	CB69	Hook Green, Dart.	111	FG91
East Dulwich SE22	106	DU86	Greensted Green, Ong.	27	FH28	Hooley, Couls.	146	DG122
East Ewell, Sutt.	131	CX110	Greenwich SE10	93	ED79	Horns Green, Sev.	151	ES117
East Finchley N2	62	DD56	Grove Park SE12	108	EG89	Hornsey N8	63	DM55
East Ham E6	80	EL68	Grove Park W4	88	CQ80	Horton, Epsom	130	CP110
East Molesey, E.Mol.	115	CD97	Gunnersbury W4	88	CP77	Hounslow, Houns.	86	BZ84
East Sheen SW14	88	CR84	Hackbridge, Wall.	119	DH103	Hounslow West, Houns.	86	BX83
East Wickham, Well.	96	EU80	Hackney E8	78	DV65	How Wood, St.Alb.	16	CB27
Eastbury, Nthwd.	43	BS49	Hackney Wick E9	65	DZ64	**Hoxton N1**	**7**	**M1**
Eastcote, Pnr.	58	BW58	Hadley, Barn.	33	CZ40	Hulberry, Swan.	125	FG103
Eastcote Village, Pnr.	57	BV57	Hadley Wood, Barn.	34	DD38	Hunton Bridge, Kings L.	15	BP33
Eden Park, Beck.	121	EA99	Haggerston E2	78	DT68	Hyde, The NW9	61	CT57
Edgware, Edg.	46	CP50	Hainault, Ilf.	53	ET52	Ickenham, Uxb.	57	BQ62
Edmonton N9	50	DU49	Hale End E4	51	ED51	Ilford, Ilf.	67	EQ62
Elm Corner, Wok.	140	BN119	Halstead, Sev.	138	EZ113	Isleworth, Islw.	87	CF83
Elm Park, Horn.	69	FH64	Ham, Rich.	101	CJ90	Islington N1	77	DN67
Elmers End, Beck.	121	DX97	Hammersmith W6	89	CW78	Ivy Chimneys, Epp.	25	ES32
Elmstead, Chis.	108	EK92	Hammond Street, Wal.Cr.	22	DR26	Joydens Wood, Bex.	111	FC92
Elstree, Borwd.	31	CK44	Hampstead NW3	62	DD63	Kenley, Ken.	148	DQ116
Eltham SE9	108	EK86	Hampstead Garden Suburb N2	62	DC57	Kennington SE11	91	DN79
Enfield, Enf.	36	DT41				Kensal Green NW10	75	CW69
Enfield Highway, Enf.	36	DW40	Hampton, Hmptn.	114	CB95	Kensal Rise NW6	75	CX68
Enfield Lock, Enf.	37	DZ37	Hampton Hill, Hmptn.	101	CD93	Kensal Town W10	75	CX70
Enfield Town, Enf.	36	DR40	Hampton Wick, Kings.T.	115	CH95	Kensington W8	75	CZ74
Enfield Wash, Enf.	37	DX38	Hamsey Green, Warl.	148	DW116	Kentish Town NW5	77	DJ65
Epping, Epp.	25	ET32	Hanwell W7	73	CF74	Kenton, Har.	59	CH57
Epsom, Epsom	130	CQ114	Hanworth, Felt.	100	BX91	Keston, Brom.	136	EH106
Erith, Erith	97	FD79	Harefield, Uxb.	42	BL53	Kew, Rich.	88	CN79
Esher, Esher	128	CC105	Harlesden NW10	74	CS68	Kidbrooke SE3	94	EJ82
Ewell, Epsom	131	CU110	Harlington, Hayes	85	BQ79	Kilburn NW6	75	CZ68
Fairmile, Cob.	128	BZ112	Harmondsworth, West Dr.	84	BK79	King's Cross N1	77	DK67
Falconwood, Well.	95	ER83	Harringay N8	63	DN57	Kings Langley, Kings L.	14	BM30
Farleigh, Warl.	135	DZ114	Harrow, Har.	59	CD59	Kingsbury NW9	60	CP58
Farnborough, Orp.	137	EP106	Harrow on the Hill, Har.	59	CE60	Kingston upon Thames, Kings.T.	116	CL96
Feltham, Felt.	99	BU89	Harrow Weald, Har.	45	CE53			
Felthamhill, Felt.	99	BT92	Hatch End, Pnr.	44	BY52	Kingston Vale SW15	102	CS91
Fetcham, Lthd.	143	CD123	Hatton, Felt.	85	BT84	Kingswood, Tad.	145	CZ123
Fiddlers Hamlet, Epp.	26	EW32	Havering Park, Rom.	54	FA50	Kingswood, Wat.	15	BV34
Finchley N3	48	DB53	Havering-atte-Bower, Rom.	55	FE48	Kippington, Sev.	154	FG126
Finsbury EC1	**6**	**E2**	Hayes, Brom.	122	EH101	Kitt's End, Barn.	33	CY37
Finsbury Park N4	63	DN60	Hayes, Hayes	71	BS72	Knockholt, Sev.	152	EU116
Flamstead End, Wal.Cr.	22	DU28	Hayes End, Hayes	71	BQ71	Knockholt Pound, Sev.	152	EY116
Foots Cray, Sid.	110	EV93	Hayes Town, Hayes	85	BS75	Ladywell SE13	107	EA85
Forest Gate E7	66	EG64	Headstone, Har.	58	CC56	Laleham, Stai.	112	BJ97
Forest Hill SE23	107	DX88	Hendon NW4	61	CV56	**Lambeth SE1**	**10**	**C6**
Forestdale, Croy.	135	DZ109	Herne Hill SE24	106	DQ85	Lambourne End, Rom.	40	EX44
Forty Hill, Enf.	36	DS37	Hersham, Walt.	128	BX107	Lamorbey, Sid.	109	ET88
Freezy Water, Wal.Cr.	37	DY35	Heston, Houns.	86	BZ80	Lampton, Houns.	86	CB81
Friday Hill E4	51	ED47	Hextable, Swan.	111	FG94	Langley Vale, Epsom	144	CR119
Friern Barnet N11	48	DE49	High Barnet, Barn.	33	CX40	Lea Bridge E5	65	DX62
Frogmore, St.Alb.	17	CE28	High Beach, Loug.	38	EG39	Leatherhead, Lthd.	143	CF121
Fulham SW6	89	CX81	Higham Hill E17	51	DY54	Leatherhead Common, Lthd.	143	CF119
Fullwell Cross, Ilf.	53	ER53	Highams Park E4	51	ED50	Leavesden Green, Wat.	15	BT34
Furzedown SW17	104	DG92	Highbury N5	63	DP64	Lee SE12	108	EF86
Gants Hill, Ilf.	67	EN57	Highgate N6	63	DH59	Lessness Heath, Belv.	97	FB78
Ganwick Corner, Barn.	34	DB35	Highwood Hill NW7	47	CU47	Letchmore Heath, Wat.	31	CD38
Garston, Wat.	30	BW35	Hill End, Uxb.	42	BJ51	Lewisham SE13	93	EB83

Place	Page	Grid
Somers Town NW1	**5**	**N1**
South Acton W3	88	CP76
South Beddington, Wall.	133	DK107
South Chingford E4	51	DZ50
South Croydon, S.Croy.	134	DQ107
South Hackney E9	78	DW67
South Hampstead NW6	76	DB66
South Harefield, Uxb.	56	BJ56
South Harrow, Har.	58	CB62
South Hornchurch, Rain.	83	FE67
South Kensington SW7	90	DB76
South Lambeth SW8	91	DL81
South Mimms, Pot.B.	19	CT32
South Norwood SE25	120	DT97
South Oxhey, Wat.	44	BW48
South Ruislip, Ruis.	58	BW63
South Street, West.	151	EM119
South Tottenham N15	64	DS57
South Wimbledon SW19	104	DA94
South Woodford E18	52	EF54
Southall, Sthl.	72	BX74
Southborough, Brom.	123	EM100
Southend SE6	107	EC91
Southfields SW18	104	DA88
Southgate N14	49	DJ47
Southwark SE1	**10**	**G3**
Spring Grove, Islw.	87	CE81
Staines, Stai.	98	BG93
Stamford Hill N16	64	DS60
Stanmore, Stan.	45	CG50
Stanwell, Stai.	98	BL87
Stanwell Moor, Stai.	98	BG85
Stapleford Abbotts, Rom.	41	FC43
Stapleford Tawney, Rom.	41	FC37
Stepney E1	78	DW71
Stockwell SW9	91	DK83
Stoke D'Abernon, Cob.	142	BZ116
Stoke Newington N16	64	DS61
Stonebridge NW10	74	CP67
Stoneleigh, Epsom	131	CU106
Strand WC2	**5**	**P10**
Stratford E15	79	EC65
Strawberry Hill, Twick.	101	CE90
Streatham SW16	105	DL91
Streatham Hill SW2	105	DM88
Streatham Park SW16	105	DJ91
Streatham Vale SW16	105	DK94
Stroud Green N4	63	DM58
Sudbury, Wem.	59	CG64
Summerstown SW17	104	DB91
Sunbury, Sun.	113	BV97
Sundridge, Brom.	108	EJ93
Sundridge, Sev.	152	EZ124
Surbiton, Surb.	116	CL101
Sutton, Sutt.	132	DA107
Swanley, Swan.	125	FE98
Swanley Village, Swan.	125	FH95
Sydenham SE26	106	DV92
Tadworth, Tad.	145	CV122
Tatsfield, West.	150	EL120
Tattenham Corner, Epsom	145	CV118
Teddington, Tedd.	101	CG93
Thames Ditton, T.Ditt.	115	CF100
Thamesmead SE28	82	EU74
Thamesmead North SE28	82	EX72
Thamesmead West SE18	95	EQ76
Theydon Bois, Epp.	39	ET37
Theydon Garnon, Epp.	40	EW36
Theydon Mount, Epp.	26	FA34
Thorney, Iver	84	BH76
Thornton Heath, Th.Hth.	119	DP98
Thornwood, Epp.	26	EW25
Tokyngton, Wem.	74	CP65
Tolworth, Surb.	116	CN103
Toot Hill, Ong.	27	FF30
Tooting Graveney SW17	104	DE93
Tottenham N17	50	DS53
Tottenham Hale N17	64	DU55
Totteridge N20	47	CY46
Tufnell Park N7	63	DK63
Tulse Hill SE21	106	DQ88
Turnford, Brox.	23	DZ26
Twickenham, Twick.	101	CG89
Twitton, Sev.	153	FE116
Tyrrell's Wood, Lthd.	144	CM123
Underhill, Barn.	34	DA43
Underriver, Sev.	155	FN130
Upper Clapton E5	64	DV60
Upper Edmonton N18	50	DU50
Upper Elmers End, Beck.	121	DZ99
Upper Halliford, Shep.	113	BS97
Upper Holloway N19	63	DJ62
Upper Norwood SE19	106	DR94
Upper Sydenham SE26	106	DU91
Upper Tooting SW17	104	DE90
Upper Walthamstow E17	65	EC56
Upshire, Wal.Abb.	24	EJ32
Upton E7	80	EH66
Upton Park E6	80	EJ67
Uxbridge, Uxb.	70	BK66
Uxbridge Moor, Iver	70	BG67
Uxbridge Moor, Uxb.	70	BG67
Vauxhall SW8	91	DK79
Waddon, Croy.	119	DN103
Walham Green SW6	90	DB80
Wallington, Wall.	133	DJ106
Waltham Abbey, Wal.Abb.	38	EF35
Waltham Cross, Wal.Cr.	23	DZ33
Walthamstow E17	51	EB54
Walton-on-Thames, Walt.	113	BT103
Walworth SE17	**11**	**H10**
Wandsworth SW18	103	CZ85
Wanstead E11	66	EG59
Wapping E1	78	DU74
Warlingham, Warl.	149	DX118
Water End, Hat.	19	CV26
Watford, Wat.	29	BU41
Watford Heath, Wat.	44	BX46
Wealdstone, Har.	59	CF55
Well End, Borwd.	32	CR38
Well Hill, Orp.	139	FB107
Welling, Well.	96	EU83
Wembley, Wem.	60	CL64
Wembley Park, Wem.	60	CM61
West Acton W3	74	CN72
West Barnes, N.Mal.	117	CV98
West Brompton SW10	90	DA79
West Byfleet, W.Byf.	126	BH113
West Drayton, West Dr.	84	BK76
West Dulwich SE21	106	DR90
West End, Esher	128	BZ107
West Ewell, Epsom	130	CS108
West Green N15	64	DQ56
West Ham E15	80	EF66
West Hampstead NW6	62	DB64
West Harrow, Har.	58	CC59
West Heath SE2	96	EX79
West Hendon NW9	60	CS59
West Kilburn W9	75	CZ69
West Molesey, W.Mol.	114	BZ98
West Norwood SE27	106	DQ90
West Watford, Wat.	29	BU42
West Wickham, W.Wick.	121	EC103
Westbourne Green W2	76	DA71
Westminster SW1	**9**	**K6**
Weston Green, T.Ditt.	115	CF102
Weybridge, Wey.	126	BN105
Whetstone N20	48	DB47
Whitechapel E1	78	DU72
Whiteley Village, Walt.	127	BS110
Whitton, Twick.	100	CB87
Whyteleafe, Cat.	148	DS118
Widmore, Brom.	122	EJ97
Wildernesse, Sev.	155	FL122
Willesden NW10	75	CT65
Willesden Green NW10	75	CV66
Wimbledon SW19	103	CY93
Wimbledon Park SW19	103	CZ90
Winchmore Hill N21	49	DM45
Wisley, Wok.	140	BL116
Woldingham, Cat.	149	EB122
Woldingham Garden Village, Cat.	149	DY121
Wood Green N22	49	DL53
Woodcote, Epsom	144	CQ116
Woodcote, Pur.	133	DK111
Woodford, Wdf.Grn.	52	EH51
Woodford Bridge, Wdf.Grn.	53	EM52
Woodford Green, Wdf.Grn.	52	EG50
Woodford Wells, Wdf.Grn.	52	EH48
Woodlands, Islw.	87	CE82
Woodmansterne, Bans.	146	DE115
Woodside, Croy.	120	DT100
Woodside, Wat.	15	BU33
Woolwich SE18	95	EM78
Worcester Park, Wor.Pk.	117	CT103
World's End, Enf.	35	DN41
Wrythe, The, Cars.	118	DE103
Yeading, Hayes	71	BV69
Yiewsley, West Dr.	70	BL74

The following is a comprehensive listing of the places of interest which appear in this atlas. Bold references can be found within the Central London enlarged scale section (pages 4–11).

AYLESBURY VALE

DACORUM

ST. ALBANS

WELWYN

HATFIELD

CHILTERN

WYCOMBE

THREE RIVERS

WATFORD

HERTSMERE

BARNET

HARROW

HAR

SOUTH BUCKS

HILLINGDON

BRENT

CAMDEN

ISL

SLOUGH

EALING

WESTMINSTER

KENSINGTON & CHELSEA

HAMMERSMITH & FULHAM

WINDSOR & MAIDENHEAD

HOUNSLOW

WANDSWORTH

RICHMOND UPON THAMES

WOKINGHAM

SPELTHORNE

KINGSTON UPON THAMES

MERTON

BRACKNELL FOREST

RUNNYMEDE

ELMBRIDGE

SUTTON

EPSOM & EWELL

SURREY HEATH

WOKING

HART

RUSHMOOR

REIGATE & BANSTEAD

GUILDFORD

MOLE VALLEY

EAST HANTS

WAVERLEY

CRAWLEY

EAS

14 15 16 17 18 19 20 2

28 29 30 31 32 33 34 35

42 43 44 45 46 47 48 49

56 57 58 59 60 61 62 63

70 71 72 73 74 75 76 7

84 85 86 87 88 89 90 9

98 99 100 101 102 103 104 10

112 113 114 115 116 117 118 11

126 127 128 129 130 131 132 13

140 141 142 143 144 145 146 14

ERTFORDSHIRE

UTTLESFORD

BRAINTREE

HARLOW

MALDON

CHELMSFORD

ROXBOURNE

22   23   24   25   26   27

EPPING

FOREST

ELD

36   37   38   39   40   41

BRENTWOOD

ROCHFORD

50   51   52   53   54   55

BASILDON

WALTHAM FOREST

REDBRIDGE

SOUTHEND ON-SEA

HACKNEY

64   65   66   67   68   69

HAVERING

CASTLE POINT

BARKING & DAGENHAM

NEWHAM

78   79   80   81   82   83

Y

TOWER HAMLETS

THURROCK

RIVER THAMES

92   93   94   95   96   97

GREENWICH

BEXLEY

ARK

MEDWAY

LEWISHAM

106 107 108 109 110 111

DARTFORD

GRAVESHAM

120 121 122 123 124 125

BROMLEY

ROYDON

SWALE

134 135 136 137 138 139

S
E
V
E
N
O
A
K
S

148 149 150 151 152 153

154 155

TONBRIDGE & MALLING

MAIDSTONE

ANDRIDGE

MID SUSSEX

EAST SUSSEX

TUNBRIDGE WELLS

ASHFORD